D0769148

INTERNATIONAL CRIMINAL LAW

Second Edition

Volume II

PROCEDURAL AND ENFORCEMENT MECHANISMS

Edited
by

M. Cherif Bassiouni

Transnational Publsihers, Inc.
Ardsley, New York

Library of Congress Cataloging-in-Publication Data

International criminal law / edited by M. Cherif Bassiouni.—2nd ed.
p. cm.
Includes bibliographical references.
Contents: v. 1. Crimes—v. 2. Procedural and enforcement mechanisms—v. 3. Enforcement.
ISBN 1-57105-018-3
1. International offenses. I. Bassiouni, M. Cherif, 1937–
K5165.I58 1998
341.7'7—dc21 98–45093
CIP

Manufactured in the United States

Table of Contents

List of Contributors to Volumes I, II and III

Mohamed Abdul-Aziz [Volume II]
Social Affairs Officer; Crime Prevention and Criminal Justice Division, United Nations; Vienna, Austria (Libya)

Christopher Amerasinghe [Volume III]
Senior Trial Attorney; Former Deputy Head, Office of War Crimes Prosecution, Department of Justice; Toronto, Ontario (Canada)

M. Cherif Bassiouni [Volumes I, II, III]
Professor of Law, DePaul University College of Law; President, International Association of Penal Law; President, International Institute of Higher Studies in Criminal Sciences; Former Vice-Chairman, UN Preparatory Committee on the Establishment of a Permanent International Criminal Court; Former Chairman and Rapporteur on the Gathering and Analysis of the Facts, Commission of Experts established pursuant to Security Council Resolution 780 (1992) to investigate violations of international humanitarian law in the Former Yugoslavia; Chicago, Illinois (USA/Egypt)

Douglas J. Besharov [Volume I]
Professor for School of Public Affairs, University of Maryland; Resident Scholar, American Enterprise Institute for Public Policy Research, Washington, DC (USA)

Remigus Bierzaneck [Volume III]
Professor of International Law (Ret.), University of Warsaw; Warsaw (Poland)

Christopher L. Blakesley [Volume II]
J.Y. Sanders Professor of Law, Louisiana State University Law Center; Baton Rouge, Louisiana (USA)

Graham T. Blewitt [Volume III]
Deputy Prosecutor, International Criminal Tribunal for the Former Yugoslavia; Former Head of War Crimes Prosecution Unit, Office of the Attorney General of Australia; The Hague, The Netherlands (Australia)

Bartram Brown [Volume III]
Assistant Professor, Chicago-Kent College of Law, Illinois Institute of Technology; Chicago, Illinois (USA)

Roger S. Clark [Volume I]
Distinguished Professor of Law, Rutgers University, School of Law; Camden, New Jersey (USA/New Zealand)

Anthony D'Amato [Volume III]
Judd & Mary Morris Leighton Professor of Law, Northwestern University School of Law; Chicago, Illinois (USA)

Daniel H. Derby [Volume I]
Professor of Law, Touro Law School; Huntington, New York (USA)

John Dugard [Volume I]
Member, International Law Commission; Professor of International Law, Witwatersraand University (South Africa)

Alan Ellis [Volume II]
Attorney-at-Law; Washington, D.C. (USA)

Helmut Epp [Volume II]
Judge; Parliamentary Secretary, Austrian National Parliament; Vienna (Austria)

John T. Evrard [Volume I]
Attorney-at-Law; Chicago, Illinois (USA)

Benjamin B. Ferencz [Volume I]
Adjunct Professor of Law, Pace University; Former Assistant Prosecutor, USA Military Trials (Subsequent Proceedings, Nuremberg); White Plains, New York (USA)

Robert A. Friedlander* [Volume I]
Professor of Law, Ohio Northern University College of Law; Former Minority Council Senate Judiciary Committee (USA)

Kenneth S. Gallant [Volume III]
Professor of Law, University of Idaho (USA)

Jane Garwood-Cutler [Volume III]
Member, Illinois State Bar (USA)

B. James George, Jr. [Volume II]
Professor of Law (Ret.), New York Law School; New York, New York (USA)

Bohunka Goldstein [Volume I]
Attorney-at-Law, Bratislava (Slovakia)

Leslie C. Green [Volume I]
Professor Emeritus of International Law, Law of Armed Conflict, and Human Rights, Department of Politic Science, University of Alberta, Saskatchewan (Canada)

David Gualtieri [Volume II]
Attorney-at-Law, Chicago, Illinois (USA)

Paul Gully-Hart [Volume II]
Attorney-at-Law; Geneva (Switzerland)

Malvina Halberstam [Volume I]
Professor of Law, Yeshiva University, Benjamin N. Cardozo School of Law: New York, New York (USA)

Larry Johnson [Volume III]
Legal Adviser, International Atomic Energy Agency, United Nations, Vienna (USA)

Christopher C. Joyner [Volume I]
Professor of International Law, Department of Government, Georgetown University, Washington, DC (USA)

Barry Kellman [Volume I]
Professor of Law, DePaul University College of Law; Chicago, Illinois (USA)

Howard S. Levie [Volume I]
Professor Emeritus, University of St. Louis College of Law; Former Director, Office of International Affairs, Judge Advocate General Corp., U.S. Army; Newport, Rhode Island (USA)

Matthew Lippman [Volume I]
Professor of Criminal Justice, Department of Criminal Justice, University of Illinois at Chicago; Chicago, Illinois (USA)

Daniel Mac Sweeney [Volume III]
Attorney-at-Law, Cork (Ireland)

Farhad Malekian [Volume I]
Director, Institute of International Law; Stockholm (Sweden/Iran)

Stephen C. McCaffrey [Volume I]
Former Member, International Law Commission; Professor of Law, University of the Pacific, McGeorge School of Law; Sacramento, California (USA)

Madeline H. Morris [Volume III]
Professor of Law, Duke University School of Law; Former Advisor on Justice to the President of Rwanda; Durham, North Carolina (USA)

Virginia Morris [Volume III]
Associate Legal Officer, Office of Legal Affairs, United Nations, New York, New York (USA)

Ekkehart Muller-Rappard [Volume II]
Head of Department, Responsible for Cooperation Programmes with Central and Eastern European Countries in the Field of Local Democracy, Council of Europe; Strasbourg (France/Germany)

Gerhard O.W. Mueller [Volume I]
Former Director, United Nations Crime Prevention and Criminal Justice Branch; Distinguished Professor of Criminal Justice, Administration of Criminal Justice Program, Rutgers University; Newark, New Jersey (USA)

James A.R. Nafziger [Volume I]
Thomas B. Stoel Professor of Law, Willamette University College of Law; Salem, Oregon (USA)

Dietrich Oehler* [Volume II]
Professor of Criminal Law, The University of Cologne Faculty of Law, Köln (Germany)

Jordan Paust [Volume I]
Professor of Law, University of Houston Law Center; Houston, Texas (USA)

Robert L. Pisani [Volume II]
Attorney-at-Law; Philadelphia, Pennsylvania (USA)

Dominique Poncet [Volume II]
Professor of Criminal Law and Procedure (Ret.), University of Geneva; Attorney-at-Law; Geneva (Switzerland)

R. John Pritchard [Volume III]
Inter-Faculty Research Fellow, St. Antony's College, Oxford University (United Kingdom)

Yves Sandoz [Volume I]
Director, Legal Affairs, International Committee of the Red Cross; Geneva (Switzerland)

William A. Schabas [Volume III]
Professor of Criminology; Director, Department of Law, University of Quebec in Montreal; Montreal, Quebec (Canada)

Michael Scharf [Volume III]
Professor of Law, New England School of Law; Former Attorney Advisor, Department of State; Boston, Massachusetts (USA)

Julian Schutte [Volume II]
Legal Advisor, Council of the European Union; Former Legal Advisor, Ministry of Justice of the Netherlands; Brussels, Belgium (The Netherlands)

Dionysios Spinellis [Volume II]
Professor of Criminal Law, The University of Athens; Athens (Greece)

Jacob W.F. Sundberg [Volume I]
Professor of Jurisprudence (Ret.), University of Stockholm; Stockholm (Sweden)

Bert Swart [Volume II]
Judge, Court of Appeals; Professor of International Criminal Law, University of Utrecht; Utrecht (The Netherlands)

Jean François Thony [Volume I]
Senior Legal Advisor, United Nations Drug Control Programme, Vienna (Austria)

Christine Van den Wyngaert [Volume III]
Professor of Criminal Law and Criminal Procedure; Vice Dean, Faculty of Law, University of Antwerp; Antwerp (Belgium)

Michel Veuthey [Volume I]
Legal Adviser, Assistant to the President, International Committee of the Red Cross; Geneva (Switzerland)

Leila Sadat Wexler [Volume III]
Professor of Law, Washington University; St. Louis, Missouri (USA)

Peter Wilkitzki [Volume II]
Agent of the Government of the Federal Republic of Germany to the Council of Europe; Former Director, Division of International Affairs, Ministry of Justice; Bonn (Germany)

Edward M. Wise [Volume I, II]
Professor of Law; Director, Comparative Criminal Law Project, Wayne State University Law School; Detroit, Michigan (USA)

Herman F. Woltring [Volume II]
Executive Director, United Nations Inter-Regional Criminal Research Institute (UNICRI); Former Prosecuting Attorney, Office of the Attorney General of Australia (Australia)

Barbara Yarnold [Volume I]
Associate Professor, Department of Public Administration, Florida International University; North Miami, Florida (USA)

Bruce Zagaris [Volume II]
Attorney-at-Law; Adjunct Professor, American University, College of Law; Former Assistant Attorney General, State of Idaho; Washington, DC (USA)

Mark S. Zaid [Volume III]
Attorney, Washington, D.C. (USA)

Preface

When I started my academic work in international criminal law three decades ago, the subject was largely regarded as esoteric. For many years I was the only one in U.S. legal education teaching a regular course or seminar on the subject, and for that freedom I am grateful to DePaul University.[1] Today, some 35 law schools offer a course or seminar on the subject, and this is a great source of gratification.[2]

By 1968, I had already recognized that international criminal law needed a theory that could be accepted by academics and experts throughout the world. More efforts were needed in the United States and elsewhere to make the subject and its contents better known to a wider audience. However, I was too young an academic to venture into the articulation of a theoretical and doctrinal framework for a new legal discipline. Between 1970-72, I found within three successive academic opportunities the necessary standing and opportunity to be heard in the international scholarly community. In 1970, I was invited to teach a course on international criminal law as a Fulbright Professor at the world renowned Max-Planck Institute for International and Comparative Criminal Law.[3] In 1971, I was fortunate to be invited to join the faculty of NYU Law School as a visiting professor of law, and to take the interim direction of its Criminal Justice Center.[4] Lastly, in 1972 I was named Guest Scholar at the prestigious Woodrow Wilson Center for Scholars in Washington, where I continued to focus on international criminal law. With the exposure and experience gained in these three years, the support of my many friends and colleagues all over the world, I continued to develop and express my views. In time, these views became well accepted. Indeed, I cannot sufficiently express my gratitude to the many who have given credence to my views and acceptance to my writings. Without them, my achievements would have been minimal.

International criminal law consists of several components which, though not a perfect fit, constitute blocks that combine to form a complementary whole. This new discipline, in consisting of parts of multiple legal sources whose methods and techniques are distinct, is characterized by inherent incongruities which are difficult to reconcile. A pragmatic approach to this problem is reflected in the first two volume series on international criminal law, published in 1973, which I co-edited with my dear friend and distinguished colleague, Professor Ved P. Nanda of the University of Denver. These two volumes are divided into sections on substance and procedure. The very organization of the material presented an unarticulated legal theory, one which would face its initial test in the academic community's response. Their tacit acceptance encouraged me to pursue the pragmatic approach to shaping a theoretical framework for ICL.

I published my first book on the codification of international criminal law in 1980 and updated and expanded this text in 1987. By then I had also produced, in 1985, two volumes

---

1 An earlier pioneer was my dear friend and distinguished colleague, Professor Gerhard O.W. Mueller, who occasionally taught a seminar on international criminal law at New York University Law School. He and Edward M. Wise co-edited, in 1965, the first ontology on international criminal law published in the United States.

2 In the last two years, many schools have adopted the case book INTERNATIONAL CRIMINAL LAW: CASES AND MATERIALS co-authored by Professor Jordan Paust, myself and other colleagues.

3 I am grateful to Professor Hans-Heinrich Jescheck, then Director of the Max-Planck Institute and one of the world's leading experts on international and comparative criminal law, for having given me the opportunity to go to Freiburg and to team-teach a course with him.

4 My gratitude goes to Professor Gerhard O.W. Mueller who recommended me for that post as a substitute for him, and also for his friendship and guidance during my formative years.

containing a compilation of international criminal law conventions.[5] No one heretofore had developed a methodology for identifying international crimes, or had classified these crimes and compiled the relevant international instruments to support those propositions. Upon this foundation I constructed, in 1987, a comprehensive codification of the general part, special part, procedural part and enforcement part as a model international criminal code and statute for an international criminal court.[6] The latter work became useful to the International Law Commission and other U.N. bodies and experts working on the establishment of *ad hoc* international tribunals[7] and the prospective ICC.[8] Clearly, these works in 1980, 1985, and 1987 made disparate and hard-to-find information easily accessible and understandable to researchers, experts and students of the subject.

In 1986, I expanded upon the approach developed in the 1973 ICL text and edited the three volumes, of which this series is the second revised edition. The three volumes of the first edition (1986) were divided into substance, procedure and enforcement, though the distinction between procedure and enforcement is not a true difference. The PROCEDURE volume represented what I had earlier called the "indirect enforcement system," which is a form of enforcement based on national legal systems. The ENFORCEMENT volume dealt with the "direct enforcement system," *i.e.* international (as opposed to national) enforcement. The terms used in 1973 and 1986 were convenient sub-titles, not indicative of a doctrinal difference between procedure and enforcement; they both referred to enforcement techniques, though the "indirect enforcement system" arose out of what most authors since the 1920s refer to as procedural ICL.

In 1973 and in 1986, and now with this second edition, I went the way of editing a collection of articles by others in order to bring the writings of the world's better known experts within the covers of a single publication. This has been done in accordance with the methodology which I have developed. The editorial work on these articles, many of which are by authors whose native language is not English and who are not conversant with the American system of citations, was arduous and time consuming. However, the benefit of such collective expertise to the new discipline was of great importance, and has far outweighed the work and effort that was put into these editorial projects. In addition, I have contributed 20 articles to this new series.

The first edition of this three-volume series was quite popular and used extensively throughout the world, as evidenced by its frequent citation. I believe that this second edition

---

5 In 1997, a one volume book was published containing a new version of the 274 conventions falling in the 25 categories of international crimes which I identified on the basis of a new methodology. *See* M. CHERIF BASSIOUNI , INTERNATIONAL CRIMINAL LAW CONVENTIONS AND THEIR PENAL PROVISIONS (1997).

6 M. CHERIF BASSIOUNI, A DRAFT INTERNATIONAL CRIMINAL CODE AND DRAFT STATUTE FOR AN INTERNATIONAL CRIMINAL TRIBUNAL (1987). This work was translated into French, Spanish, Chinese, and Hungarian.

7 As Chairman of the U.N. Commission of Experts which investigated violations of international humanitarian law in the former Yugoslavia, I contributed to the drafting of the Statute of the International Criminal Tribunal for the Former Yugoslavia. That Tribunal was established pursuant to a recommendation of the Commission of Experts. *See* Final Report of the Commission of Experts Established Pursuant to Security Council Resolution 780 (1992), U.N. SCOR, 4th Sess., Annex, U.N. Doc. S/1994/674 (1994); Annexes to the Final Report, U.N. SCOR, 47th Sess., U.N. Doc. S/1994/674 Add. 2 (1994). *See also*, M. Cherif Bassiouni, *The Commission of Experts Established Pursuant to Security Resolution* 780: *Investigating Violations of International Humanitarian in the Former Yugoslavia,* 5 CRIM. L. FOR. *279 (1994).*

8 I served in 1995 as Vice-Chairman of the U.N.'s *Ad Hoc* Committee on the Establishment of an International Criminal Court and then again in 1996, 1997 as vice-chairman of the Preparatory Committee on the International Criminal Court.

with its many improvements will prove to be even more useful to those interested in the field. The principal reason is that the contributors to this series, most of whom contributed to the earlier one, are among the world's leading experts on the subjects about which they have written. Thus, the method and approach which I advocate are supported not only by my own academic writings, but also those of so many others.

In the last ten years, I have had the opportunity to test many of my ideas and the benefit of feedback from colleagues and experts throughout the world. The positive reinforcement received from so many and intellectual maturity reached over years of study and reflection have enabled me to develop a doctrinal framework, included in Volume I of this new series. It is titled *The Sources and Content of International Criminal Law: A Doctrinal Framework.* I was tempted to expand the text of this contribution and develop it as a separate book, but came to the conclusion that it served a better didactic purpose as an introductory article in Volume I. In time, I hope to complete a separate book on the doctrine of international criminal law.

Academic pursuit is not, however, my only goal in the development of international criminal law. I am driven by the fact that international crime has been on the increase in the past 50 years. There is greater mobility of peoples and goods as means of transportation become faster, more diverse and more accessible to a larger population. Communications are heard instantaneous. Opportunities for national crime to become internationalized have increased with the presence of a global economy and a global financial network. Contemporaneously, international crimes like aggression, genocide, crimes against humanity, war crimes and torture have also increased dramatically, as have human rights depredations.

There have been 250 conflicts since World War II—in which an estimated 170 million people have been killed. Most of these deaths have been the result of international crimes. Yet, most of the perpetrators have escaped accountability. Very few responsible leaders or executors of these crimes have been held accountable.[9] Tragically, the converse has been true. Crimes decried by the international community and elevated to the level of *jus cogens*, including aggression, genocide, crimes against humanity, war crimes and torture have been committed on a widespread scale, producing significant victimization. The leaders and senior executors of these crimes have almost always benefitted from *de jure* or *de facto* impunity. International criminal law provides the means to prevent such crimes and to punish its perpetrators. But its norms defining prohibited conduct must be clearly articulated, and its proscriptions must be enforced effectively and fairly, and that is still lacking.

In the spectrum of legal continuum of norms, ICL is the ultimate normative stage in the protection of human rights, and that is one of the principal goals of ICL. It is also one of my principal goals in the development of this discipline.

Academics hold no power to affect justice outcomes, save the power of persuasion. Thus, the academic must be an activist in order to be truly relevant to the social order. Just as Gandhi, a lawyer, utilized civil disobedience to uphold moral values and effectuate social change, so must we impact the minds of others, employing both moral and physical courage

---

9 See M. Cherif Bassiouni, *Accountability for International Crimes*, 594 LAW AND CONTEMPORARY PROBLEMS 6 (1997).

to oppose the commission of major international crimes.[10] We must continue to resist the temptation of *realpolitik* solutions which grant impunity to the perpetrators in exchange for political settlements.

The 170 million victims that I referred to above individually and collectively cry out for truth and justice, and their survivors cry out for redress. We owe it to them, as well as to greater humanity, to do just that. Only then will we be able to reinforce prevention and strengthen deterrence, and thereby minimize future victimization. If we are unable to do so, then we are condemned as a civilization to keep repeating our mistakes and, in the final analysis, to find ourselves benefitting from scientific and technological advances, but suffering from humanistic decline.

Civilizations are not judged by their scientific and technological advances, or by the wealth and might of nations alone, but by the quality of humanism that they reflect and by their respect for the rule of law. That is our global challenge as human beings. More directly, however, as jurists we have a more particular task with regard to the shaping, making and enforcing of the law. International criminal law is an important means through which to carry out that task. If there is to be a new world order, justice must be one of its important components.

Hopefully, this three volume series and other works on international criminal law will stimulate an increased interest in the subject and advance the humanistic and policy goals stated above.

As others will follow to take the baton and continue the relay, they will add their advances to that of their predecessors, much as I did, in the hope that our collective efforts will contribute to the ultimate attainment of a better humanity.

---

10 During the two and a half years (1993-1994) of my work on documenting violations of international humanitarian law in the former Yugoslavia while that conflict was ongoing, I tried to the best of my ability, and at the risk of my life, to measure up to these expectations. *See supra* note 6.

Introduction

This three volume series is a second, updated and revised edition of the 1986 series. Each volume covers a separate area of international criminal law (ICL) and is to that extent both dependent and independent of the others. Together they form the most comprehensive collection of writings and documents ever to be published in an integrated series. Volume I contains 31 contributions by 26 authors and 18 appendices. Volume II contains 21 contributions by 19 authors and 19 appendices. Volume III contains 21 contributions by 18 authors and 18 appendices.

The series is intended to provide the scholar, researcher, practitioner, and student of ICL with the necessary basis of understanding this important subject. Admittedly, every topic contained in these volumes is not exhaustively covered for obvious reasons of space limitations. Nevertheless, the size of these three volumes, which exceed 3,000 pages, reveals the increasingly overall coverage given to this new discipline

International criminal law is becoming increasingly relevant to our contemporary world, and it will surely continue to become an even more important legal discipline. In the United States alone, 35 law schools offer courses on the subject.

Present and future generations of researchers and students of law and allied fields, such as political science and criminology, will need to learn more about this subject that deals with the problems of international and transnational crimes which are constantly increasing in number, intensity, and threat to the peace and stability of the world order and the security and safety of individuals all over the world. These dangers come from states, individuals, and groups from every corner of the globe, irrespective of ideology, belief, purpose or other distinguishing factor.

As these crimes increase more efforts will be needed in such areas as: codification of international and transnational crimes, international cooperation in penal matters (as one of the means of enforcement), and the eventual establishment of international machinery and of an international criminal jurisdiction to directly enforce certain types of violations and to protect and preserve fundamental rights against all forms of threat and violations from whatever source, be it public or private. The next stage of LCL's developments is in the area of sanctions to be meted out by international criminal jurisdictions.

Furthermore, as new forms and manifestations of international and transnational criminality appear, new proscriptions will have to be developed and new enforcement techniques will have to be devised. One has only to consider the future potential of computer, financial, economic, and environmental crimes to see what the future holds in terms of needs for new and imaginative forms of regulation and control. This is also true of such crimes that fall into the category of terrorism and organized crime.

In a different vein the ever growing need to protect individual and collective human rights from a variety of state and state-sponsored violations is another area of increasing concern. All of that means that international criminal law with its human rights component is a discipline that commands the attention of scholars, legal educators, government and international organizations officials, and future generations of jurists.

Regrettably international and transnational criminal activity is a growth industry and a growing business that the international community will have to deal with more effectively in the years to come.

In 1973 this writer and Professor V.P. Nanda co-edited two volumes titled A TREATISE ON INTERNATIONAL CRIMINAL LAW. Along with the single volume, INTERNATIONAL CRIMINAL LAW, edited by Professors G.O.W. Mueller and E.M. Wise in 1965, they constituted the only books on the subject to be published in the United States since the publication of this three volumes series. But while there have been no other general texts on the subject, there are many specialized books on specific topics, such as: aggression, the regulation of armed conflicts, *apartheid*, terrorism, international traffic in drugs, the creation of an international court, and extradition. The number of law review articles on international criminal law topics has also increased significantly, particularly in the last ten years. Nevertheless, a large number of the topics covered in these three volumes have not yet benefitted from the particular attention of scholars and writers. Among these are the formulation of a theory for international criminal law, a doctrinal basis for the discipline, a rationale and framework for international crimes, a policy for international criminalization and the technical and formal requirements for codifying international crimes, and the procedural and enforcement aspects thereof. One reason for these and other *lacunae* is simply the fact that all aspects of international criminal law have developed in an *ad hoc* manner, without doctrine, framework or policy. The result has been inconsistency, lack of predictability, uncertainty, conflicting and inconsistent use of legal concepts and terminology, and with respect to international conventions many drafting deficiencies. While these three volumes do not necessarily provide solutions to all these problems and concerns, they do however answer many of them. In particular Volume I, part 1, which describes, discusses and analyzes the theory, history, scope, content, and policy of international criminal law, provides a rather unique conceptual, doctrinal and policy analysis of the discipline. It formulates the theoretical basis of the discipline, sets forth its values, defines the parameters of its application, by identifying its scope and content and formulates the criteria of its policy application. As such it becomes the basis and foundation for the other areas of the discipline, and more particularly for that aspect which in national criminal codes would be called the Special Part, namely the crimes, in this case the international crimes. The General Part is limited to issues of command responsibility and the defense of obedience to superior orders because they are the only two issues that customary international law deals with.

Part II of Volume I deals with international crimes. Having established in Part I what they are and why, Part II proceeds with a crime by crime discussion. Like a national criminal code, this Special Part proceeds from the most seriously perceived violations to the lesser ones. It is based on a value judgment that is predicated on certain criteria, namely: the seriousness of the threat and harm to humanity that could result from the prohibited conduct.

This Special Part covers 16 of the 25 international crimes, namely: genocide, crimes against humanity, aggression, war crimes, unlawful use of weapons, slavery and slavery-related crimes, torture, unlawful human experimentation, piracy, aircraft hijacking, threat and use of force against internationally protected persons, taking of civilian hostages, drug offenses, theft and/or destruction of national treasures, and environmental protection. It does not cover: crimes against U.N. personnel, international traffic in obscene publications, theft of nuclear materials, unlawful use of the mails, interference with submarine cables, falsification and counterfeiting, and bribery of foreign public officials.

Important as all these omitted crimes may be, the choice was dictated by the need to keep this volume within a reasonable size. Considering, however, what has been included and what has been excluded, the editor's judgment is not likely to be challenged by knowledgeable experts. Furthermore, considerations of size also required a judgment as to the degree of in-depth treatment of each of these crimes. Thus some crimes like aggression, war crimes, and genocide received slightly more coverage than others. Here, too, the editor's decision was based on the degree of seriousness of these crimes and the threat they pose to humankind.

The purpose of this volume is not to provide an in-depth treatment of each crime but a basic understanding and eventually a starting point for further specialized study and research. Many of these crimes have been discussed in numerous books and articles, and no single volume could cover all aspects and facets of these subjects.

Each crime is treated in a separate chapter by a specialist in that subject, and almost every study is followed by appendices containing important original documents. The contributors who are among the world's leading authorities have provided a unique insight into this area.

The reader will undoubtedly appreciate the fact that the origins, development and growth of any one of these crimes has been on an *ad hoc* basis with little identifiable juridical reason for the processes which brought about their existence, and which shaped and determined their development and growth. These considerations may have been discussed contextually in the descriptive aspects of each crime, but they are also found in greater detail in the doctrinal and policy expositions in part I of that volume, thus further interrelating these two parts of Volume I.

As the title of Volume II implies, it deals with the procedural aspects of international criminal law. These aspects, however, apply to international crimes, transnational crimes, and purely national crimes which require, for their prosecution or enforcement, the same international cooperation as do international transnational crimes. The procedural aspects discussed in Volume II are those which, with respect to the enforcement of international criminal law, have been formerly named by this writer as the "indirect enforcement method." That method implies that enforcement of international crimes is, by virtue of the Conventions establishing them, entrusted to the state parties to these Conventions. Under such a method a state that becomes a party to an international convention assumes the duty to prohibit the proscribed conduct in its national law, prosecute and cooperate with other state parties seeking to prosecute or punish the alleged and convicted offender. Not all conventions require all such undertakings by the state parties, however, most require one or more, with the most common combination being to prosecute or extradite and to provide judicial assistance and cooperation to state parties seeking extradition and assistance in order to prosecute and execute a penalty resulting from a prior criminal conviction. This formula was originally reflected in a maxim by Hugo Grotius in his book, DE JURE BELLI AC PACIS (1624) as *aut dedere aut punire*. It was rephrased by this author in 1973 as *aut dedere aut judicare* for the reason that the object of penal legislation is to prosecute alleged wrongdoers and not simply to punish them. Punishment is one of the consequences of a conviction and not a corollary of the alleged act prior to its adjudication. That concept reflects the now well established presumption of innocence which is recognized in all legal systems of civilized nations. To carry out the maxim *aut dedere aut judicare* requires a variety of legal modalities which are procedural in nature though they constitute the essence of ICL enforcement.

Volume II describes, discusses and analyzes the six modalities of inter-state cooperation in penal matters. Jurisdiction is the first subject discussed, followed by exceptions thereto, and thereafter by the subjects of: extradition, judicial assistance and mutual cooperation, transfer of prisoners, recognition of foreign penal judgements, transfer of criminal proceedings, freezing and seizure of assets, and international and regional developments. The logic of the order of presentation is self-evident.

Because the Western European experience, under the impetus of the Council of Europe, is in several of these areas so well developed, it is described, discussed and analyzed in greater detail. In fact, no other books published in the United States give such detailed coverage to the European law and practice.

Volume II thus logically follows Volume I which by analogy to national criminal codes contains the general and special parts and the procedural part.

Volume III - Enforcement, refers to what this writer has also previously called the "direct enforcement system." As stated above, the modalities of the "indirect enforcement system" discussed in Volume II also apply to the "direct enforcement system."

The historical precedents of international prosecution for violations of international criminal law and the various United Nations efforts at establishing international criminal tribunals are described, discussed and analyzed in Volume III. A number of relevant documents give the reader an opportunity to study the most significant texts in modern history. By analogy to national legal systems, this volume deals with the international judicial system, as it developed since World War I.

In keeping with the analogy to national criminal codes it would have followed that a fourth volume should have been devoted to sanctions. But none have so far developed in international criminal law save for the penalties applied in the post-World War I Leipzig trials, and the post-World War II Nuremberg and Tokyo War Crimes Trials and the International Criminal Tribunal for the former Yugoslavia (ICTY) and International Criminal Tribunal for Rwanda (ICTR) which are discussed in Volume III. No international Convention so far contains any specific penal sanctions for the violation of its prohibitions. Some, however, contain guidelines as to penalties, such as the Geneva Convention of 12 August 1899 which distinguishes between "breaches" and "grave breaches" as a means for identifying violations punishable respectively by administrative sanctions and penal ones. Other Conventions like the 1961 Single Convention on Narcotic Drugs and its 1972 Amending Proposal, and the 1971 Convention on Psychotropic Substances, require penalties adequate to the seriousness of the violations. This is also the case for example with the 1971 Montreal Convention on Aircraft Hijacking and Sabotage. The statutes of the ICTY and ICTR provide for penalties by analogies to certain national systems.

It should be noted, however, that a growing body of international norms presently exists as means of protecting the individual human rights in the context of criminal justice processes. These norms prohibit *inter alia*: arbitrary arrest and detention, incommunicado detention, torture (now an international crime discussed in Volume I), cruel, inhuman, and degrading treatment or punishment. "Codes of conduct" have been developed for law enforcement officials and personnel in the medical field. Also, the United Nations Standard Minimum Rules for the Treatment of Offenders contains detailed rules on conditions of imprisonment and treatment of detainees. But all of the above and other international efforts are in the area of individual human rights protection. The advent of the ICTY and ICTR and the prospects of an international criminal court (ICC) have also brought about a new interest in norms and standards of procedure and evidence applicable to international judicial bodies. This is a new area for ICL which is covered in Volume III with reference to the ICC.

The prospects for an ICC which now seems likely in the next few years will be a historical breakthrough for ICL.

To give the three volumes a broadly based intellectual and international dimension 58 distinguished scholars in the field of international criminal law from 19 countries of the world have contributed their valuable views. Cumulatively there are 72 contributions.

Lastly, it should be mentioned that the three volumes contain 52 appendices of primary documents, which are contextually integrated. They provide the reader with important basic documentation enriching the contributions on the various subjects and facilitating research.

At the risk of sounding presumptuous, these three volumes constitute another milestone in the legal literature on international criminal law. Hopefully they will serve a useful purpose by contributing to this important discipline.

Acknowledgment

The administrative and technical work needed to produce such a three volume series containing 73 contributions by 60 authors from 20 countries totaling 3,000 pages was enormous. All of the work was done by Tabita Sherfinski to whom I wish to express my appreciation for her hard work, diligence and patience.

A number of student assistants have worked on different articles over a period of almost two years. Their task was essentially to cite check and conform footnotes to the format followed in U.S. legal publications. Those who worked on this volume's articles are: Kristen Burns, Robert Krug, Douglas Ramsey, Andrew Schwaba, and Robert Woolson.

I also want to express my appreciation to Heike Fenton, President of Transnational Publishers, for publishing this second revised edition and for her support of international criminal law publications over the last decade.

My appreciation also goes to DePaul University for giving me a semester's leave and a lighter class load for one semester during 1997-1998 so that I could finish these three volumes.

Table of Abbreviations

AKRON L. REV.	AKRON LAW REVIEW
A.J.I.L.	AMERICAN JOURNAL OF INTERNATIONAL LAW
ALBERTA L. REV.	ALBERTA LAW REVIEW
AIDP	Association Internationale de Droit Penal
AM. DEC.	AMERICAN DECISIONS
AM. J. COMP. L.	AMERICAN JOURNAL OF COMPARATIVE LAW
AM. CRIM. L.Q.	AMERICAN CRIMINAL LAW QUATERLY
AM. J. INT'L L.	AMERICAN JOURNAL OF INTERNATIONAL LAW
AM. SOC'Y INT'L	AMERICAN SOCIETY OF INTERNATIONAL LAW
AM. U. J. INT'L L. & POL'Y	AMERICAN UNIVERSITY JOURNAL OF INTERNATIONAL LAW AND POLICY
AM. U. L. REV.	AMERICAN UNIVERSITY LAW REVIEW
ARIZ. L.R.	ARIZONA LAW REVIEW
Apartheid Conv.	International Convention on the Suppression and Punishment of Apartheid
Austrian ARHG.	Über die Auslieferung und die Rechtshilfe
AUST. Y.B. INT'L L.	AUSTRALIAN YEARBOOK ON INTERNATIONAL LAW
BASSIOUNI, EXTRADITION	M. CHERIF BASSIOUNI, INTERNATIONAL EXTRADITION: U.S. LAW AND PRACTICE (3rd rev. ed. 1996)
BASSIOUNI, YUGOSLAVIA TRIBUNAL	M. CHERIF BASSIOUNI (WITH THE COLLABORATION OF PETER MANIKAS) THE LAW OF THE INTERNATIONAL CRIMINAL TRIBUNAL FOR THE FORMER YUGOSLAVIA (1996)
BEMIS, JAY'S TREATY	SAMUEL F. BEMIS, JAY'S TREATY: A STUDY IN COMMERCE AND DIPLOMACY (2d ed. 1965)
BERKELEY WOMEN'S L. J.	BERKELEY WOMEN'S LAW JOURNAL
BRIT. Y.B. INT'L L.	BRITISH YEARBOOK OF INTERNATIONAL LAW
BUFFALO L. REV.	BUFFALO LAW REVIEW

B.U. L. REV.	BOSTON UNIVERSITY LAW REVIEW
CAL. L. REV.	CALIFORNIA LAW REVIEW
CAL. L. W. INT'L L.J.	CALIFORNIA WEST INTERNATIONAL LAW JOURNAL
CAMBRIDGE L.J.	CAMBRIDGE LAW JOURNAL
Canadian Treaty	Treaty on the Execution of Penal Sentences, Mar. 2, 1977, U.S.-Can., 30 U.S.T. 6263.
CAN. Y.B. INT'L L.	CANADIAN YEARBOOK OF INTERNATIONAL LAW
CASE W. RES. J.INT'L L.	CASE WESTERN RESERVE JOURNAL OF INTERNATIONAL LAW
CHI. TRIB.	CHICAGO TRIBUNE
CHITTY'S L.J.	CHITTY'S LAW JOURNAL
C. Pr. Pén	Code de Procédure Pénal
C. Pén.	Code Pénal
COLO. L.R.	COLORADO LAW REVIEW
COLUM. J. TRANSNAT'L L.	COLUMBIA JOURNAL OF TRANSNATIONAL LAW
COLUM. L. REV.	COLUMBIA LAW REVIEW
Comm'n	Commission
COMMON MKT. L. REV.	COMMON MARKET LAW REVIEW
CONG. REC.	CONGRESSIONAL RECORD
CONN. L. REV.	CONNECTICUT LAW REVIEW
Conv. Against Taking of Hostages	International Convention Against the Taking of Hostages, Dec. 17, 1979, T.I.A.S. No. 11, 081, 1315 U.N.T.S. 205.
Conv. On the High Seas	Convention on the High Seas, Apr. 28, 1958, 13 U.S.T. 2312, 450 U.N.T.S. 82
Conv. Protection of Nuclear Material	1980 Convention on the Protection of Nuclear Material
CORNELL INT'L L.J.	CORNELL INTERNATIONAL LAW JOURNAL
THE CQ RESEARCHER	THE CONGRESSIONAL QUARTERLY RESEARCHER

CRIM. L.F.	CRIMINAL LAW FORUM
CURRENT LEGAL PROBS.	CURRENT LEGAL PROBLEMS
DALHOUSIE L.J.	DALHOUSIE LAW JOURNAL
DEPAUL L. REV.	DEPAUL LAW REVIEW
DICK. J. INT'L L.	DICKINSON JOURNAL OF INTERNATIONAL LAW
DIG. U.S. PREC. INT'L L.	DIGEST OF UNITED STATES PRACTICES IN INTERNATIONAL LAW
DUKE J. COMP. & INT'L L.	DUKE JOURNAL OF COMPARATIVE AND INTERNATIONAL LAW
EC	European Community
EC Directive	The Council Directive on Prevention of the Use of the Financial System for the Purpose of Money Laundering, Council Directive No. 91/308, 1991 O.J. (L 166) 77 (June 10, 1991).
ECHR	European Convention on Human Rights
EHRR	European Human Rights Report
EMORY INT'L L. REV.	EMORY INTERNATIONAL LAW REVIEW
EMORY J. INT'L L.	EMORY JOURNAL OF INTERNATIONAL LAW
ENCYCLOPEDIA OF PUB. INT'L L	ENCYCLOPEDIA OF PUBLIC INTERNATIONAL LAW
EU	European Union
Euro. Conv. Add. Prot. Extradition	Additional Protocol to the European Convention on Extradition of 1975 Europ. T.S. No. 86 (1975)
Euro. Conv. Add. Prot. Infor.	Additional Protocol to the European Convention For. Law Convention on Information on Foreign Law of 1978, Europ. T.S. No. 97 (1978)
Euro. Conv. Add. Prot. Mutual Assistance	Additional Protocol to the European Convention on Mutual Assistance in Criminal Matters of 1978, Europ. T.S. No. 99 (1978) .
Euro. Conv. Cultural Prop.	European Convention on Offences relating to Cultural Property of 1985, Europ. T.S. No. 119 (1985).
Euro. Conv. Int'l Val. Crim. Judg.	European Convention on the International Validity of Criminal Judgments of 1970, Europ. T.S. No. 70.

Euro. Conv. Money Laundering	The 1990 Council of Europe Convention on Laundering, Search, Seizure and Confiscation of the Proceeds from Crime, contains even more detailed and precise provisions governing the seizure and forfeiture of assets. Europ. T.S. No. 141, Nov. 8, 1990, *reprinted in* 30 I.L.M. 148
Euro. Conv. 2d Add. Prot. Extradition	Second Additional Protocol to the European Convention on Extradition of 1978, Europ. T.S. No. 98 (1978)
Euro. Conv. Trans. Sent. Per	Convention on the Transfer of Sentenced Persons of 1983, Europ. T. S. No. 112.
Euro. Ct. Hum. Rts.	European Court of Human Rights
Euro. Driving Conv.	European Convention on the International Drive Convention of Deprivation of the Right to Drive a Motor Vehicle of 1976, Europ. T.S. No. 88 (1976).
Euro. Extradition Conv.	European Convention on Extradition, Europ. T.S. No. 24 (1957).
Euro. Firearms Conv.	European Convention on the Control of the Acquisition and Possession of Firearms by Individuals of 1978, Europ. T.S. No. 101 (1978).
EURO. J. CRIME.	EUROPEAN JOURNAL OF CRIMINAL LAW
EUROPEAN J. INT'L L.	EUROPEAN JOURNAL OF INTERNATIONAL LAW
Euro. Minors Conv.	European Convention on the Repatriation of Minors of 1970 Europ. T.S. No. 71 (1979)
Euro. Mutual Assistance Conv.	European Convention on Mutual Assistance in Criminal Matters of 1959, Europ. T.S. No. 30 (1959)
Euro. Non-app. of Stat. Limit. Conv.	European Convention on the Non-applicability of Statutory Limitations to Crimes against Humanity and War Crimes of 1974, Europ. T.S. No. 82 (1974)
Euro. Road Traffic Conv.	European Convention on the Punishment of Road Traffic Offences of 1964 Europ. T.S. No. 52 (1964)
Euro. Supervision Convention	European Convention on the Supervision of Conditionally Sentenced or Conditionally Released Offenders of 1964 Europ. T.S. No. 51 (1964)
Euro. Trans. of Proc. Conv.	European Convention on the Transfer of Proceedings Prosecution Convention in Criminal Matters of 1972, Europ. T.S. No. 73 (1972).

Euro. Terrorism Conv.	European Convention on the Suppression of Terrorism, *opened for signature* Jan. 27, 1977, E.T.S. No. 90, 25 EUR. Y. B. 289 *reprinted in* 15 I.L.M. 1272-76 (1976).
Euro. Victims Conv.	European Convention on the Compensation of Victims of Violent Crimes of 1983, Europ. T.S. No. 116 (1983)
EUR. Y.B.	EUROPEAN YEARBOOK
FATF	Financial Action Task Force
Fed. R. Civ. P.	Federal Rules of Civil Procedure
FORDHAM INT'L L.J.	FORDHAM INTERNATIONAL LAW JOURNAL
FOREIGN AFF.	FOREIGN AFFAIRS
FOREIGN POL'Y	FOREIGN POLICY
GA	(UN) General Assembly
GAOR	(UN) General Assembly Official Records
GA. J. INT'L & COMP. L.	GEORGIA JOURNAL OF INTERNATIONAL AND COMPARATIVE LAW
1949 Geneva Conventions	The four Geneva Conventions of 12 August 1949 for the Protection of War Victims, 12 Aug. 1949, 75 U.N.T.S. 2, 6 U.S.T. 3114.
Geneva Convention I	Geneva Convention for the Amelioration of the Condition of the Wounded and Sick in Armed Forces in the Field, 12 Aug. 1949, 75 U.N.T.S. 31, 6 U.S.T. 3114.
Geneva Convention II	Geneva Convention for the Amelioration of the Condition of the Wounded, Sick and Shipwrecked Members of Armed Forces at Sea, 12 Aug. 1949, 75 U.N.T.S. 85, 6 U.S.T. 3217
Geneva Convention III	Geneva Convention Relative to the Treatment of Prisoners of War, 12 Aug. 1949, 75 U.N.T.S. 135, 6 U.S.T. 3316.
Geneva Convention IV	Geneva Convention Relative to the Protection of Civilian Persons in Time of War, 12 Aug. 1949, 6 U.S.T. 3516, 75 U.N.T.S. 287.

Geneva High Seas Conv.	Geneva Convention on the High Seas, Apr. 28, 1958, art. 19, on the High Seas 13 U.S.T. 2312, T.I.A.S. No. 5200, 450 U.N.T.S. 82.
Genocide Convention	Convention on the Prevention and Punishment of the Crime of Genocide, Dec. 9, 1978 U.N.T.S. 277.
GEO. WASH. L. REV.	GEORGE WASHINGTON LAW REVIEW
German IRG	Gesetz óber die Internationale Rechtshilfe in Strafsachen vom Dec. 23, 1982, *reprinted in* Shomburg, Gesetz Óber Die Internationale Reschtshilfe in Strafsachen (1983)
Greek CCP	Greek Code of Penal Procedure
GG	Government Gazette
Hague Highjacking Convention	Convention for Suppression of Unlawful Seizure of Aircraft, Dec. 16, 1970. 22 U.S.T. 1641, T.I.A.S. No. 7192, 860 U.N.T.S. 105 (entered into force in U.S. Oct. 14, 1971) , *reprinted in* 65 AM. J. INT'L L. 440 (1971)
HARV. INT'L J. H.R.	HARVARD INTERNATIONAL JOURNAL HUMAN RIGHTS
HARV. INT'L L.J.	HARVARD INTERNATIONAL LAW JOURNAL
HARV. L. REV.	HARVARD LAW REVIEW
Harvard Research	Harvard Research in International Law, *Draft Convention on Jurisdiction with Respect to Crime,* 29 AM. J. INT'L L. 435, 445 (Supp. 1935)(part of an effort by the American Society of International Law to codify international law)
HASTINGS L. J.	HASTINGS LAW JOURNAL
HASTINGS WOMEN'S L.J.	HASTINGS WOMEN'S LAW JOURNAL
HUM. RTS. J.	HUMAN RIGHTS JOURNAL
IAEA	International Atomic Energy Agency
ICJ	International Court of Justice
ICJ Rep.	International Court of Justice Reporter

ICL CONVENTIONS	M. CHERIF BASSIOUNI, INTERNATIONAL CRIMINAL LAW CONVENTIONS AND THEIR PENAL PROVISIONS (1997)
ICL CRIMES	INTERNATIONAL CRIMINAL LAW, CRIMES (M. Cherif Bassiouni, ed. 1987)
ICL PROCEDURE	INTERNATIONAL CRIMINAL LAW, PROCEDURE (M. Cherif Bassiouni, ed. 1987)
ICRC	International Committee of the Red Cross
ICTFY	International Tribunal for the Former Yugoslavia
ILC	International Law Commission
I.L.M.	INTERNATIONAL LEGAL MATERIALS
IMAC	International Mutual Assistance Code
IMO Convention	Convention for the Suppression of Unlawful Acts Against the Safety of Maritime Navigation, Mar. 10, 1988, 27 I.L.M. 668
IMO Protocol	Protocol for the Suppression of Unlawful Acts Against the Safety of Fixed Platforms Located on the Continental Shelf, Feb. 24, 1988, 27 I.L.M.
IMT	International Military Tribunal at Nuremberg
IMTFE	International Military Tribunal for the Far East
IND. INT'L & COMP. L. REV.	INDIANA INTERNATIONAL AND COMPARATIVE LAW REVIEW
INT'L AFF.	INTERNATIONAL AFFAIRS
INT'L COMM'N. JURISTS REV.	INTERNATIONAL COMMISSION OF JURISTS REVIEW
INT'L & COMP. L.Q.	INTERNATIONAL AND COMPARATIVE LAW QUARTERLY
INT'L CRIM. POLICE REV.	INTERNATIONAL CRIMINAL POLICE REVIEW
INT'L L. & ECON.	INTERNATIONAL LAW AND ECONOMICS
INT'L L. COMM'N YB	INTERNATIONAL LAW COMMISSION YEAR BOOK
THE INTERNATIONAL LEGAL SYSTEM	THE INTERNATIONAL LEGAL SYSTEM: CASES & MATERIALS (4th ed. 1995)

Int' Protected Persons Conv.	Convention on the Prevention and Punishment of Crimes Against Internationally Protected Persons, including Diplomatic Agents, Dec. 14, 1973, 28 U.S.T. 1975, 1035 U.N.T.S. 167
INT'L REV. RED CROSS	INTERNATIONAL REVIEW OF THE RED CROSS
IOWA L. REV.	IOWA LAW REVIEW
ISISC	International Institute of Higher Studies in Criminal Sciences
ISR. L. REV	ISRAEL LAW REVIEW
ISR. Y.B. HUM. RTS.	ISRAEL YEARBOOK ON HUMAN RIGHTS
Italian Report	Mutual Legal Assistance Treat with Italy, S. Exec. Rep. No. 35, 98th Cong., 2nd Sess (1984)
Italian CPP	Codice di Procedura Penale (Italian Code of Penal Procedure)
J. CRIM. L. & CRIMINOLOGY	JOURNAL OF CRIMINAL LAW AND CRIMINOLOGY
L.N.T.S.	League of Nations Treaty Series
L.Q.	LAW QUARTERLY
L.Q. REV.	LAW QUARTERLY REVIEW
MD. J. INT'L L. & TRADE	MARYLAND JOURNAL OF INTERNATIONAL LAW AND TRADE
MD. L. REV.	MARYLAND LAW REVIEW
MICH. J. INT'L L.	MICHIGAN JOURNAL OF INTERNATIONAL LAW
MICH Y.B. INT'L L.	MICHIGAN YEAR BOOK OF INTERNATIONAL LAW
MIL. L. REV.	MILITARY LAW REVIEW
MILLENNIUM J. OF INT'L STUD.	MILLENNIUM JOURNAL OF INTERNATIONAL STUDIES
MLAT	Mutual Legal Assistance Treaty
Money Laundering Task Force Report	European Committee on Crime Problems, Recommendations by the Financial Action Task Force on Money Laundering (done at Strasbourg Feb. 7, 1990)

Montreal Convention	Convention for the Suppression of Unlawful Acts Against the Safety of Civil Aviation, Sept. 23, 1971, 2 U.S.T. 564, 974
MOORE, EXTRADITION	JOHN B. MOORE, A TREATISE ON EXTRADITION AND INTER-STATE RENDITION (2 vols. 1891)
Model U.N. Extradition Treaty	G.A. Res. 45/117 (1990), *reprinted in* Eighth United Nations Congress on Crime Prevention and the Treatment of Offenders (Havana, Cuba, Aug.-Sept. 1990), A/Conf.144/28/Rev. 1, at 77-89
Moroccan Report	Convention on Mutual Legal Assistance with the Republic of Morocco, S. Exec. Rep. No. 98-35, 98th Cong., 2nd Sess. (1981)
NATO/SOFA	Agreement Between the Parties to the North Atlantic Treaty Regarding the Status of Their Forces, June 19, 1951, 4 U.S.T. 1792, 199 U.N.T.S. 67,(entered into force with respect to the United States Aug. 23, 1953)
NAVAL WAR COL. REV.	NAVAL WAR COLLEGE REVIEW
Netherlands Report	Treaty on Mutual Legal Assistance With the Kingdom of the Netherlands, S. EXEC. REP. No. 97-36, 97th Cong., 1st Sess., at 2 (1981)
NGO	Non-Governmental Organization
NORDIC J. INT'L L.	NORDIC JOURNAL OF INTERNATIONAL LAW
NOVA L. REV.	NOVA LAW REVIEW
Nuclear Material Convention	Convention on the Physical Protection of Nuclear Material, Oct. 26, 1979, T.I.A.S. No. 11, 080, 18 I.L.M. 1419
NW. J. CRIM L. & CRIMINOLOGY	NORTHWESTERN JOURNAL OF CRIMINAL LAW AND CRIMINOLOGY
N.W.U.L. REV.	NORTHWESTERN UNIVERSITY LAW REVIEW
N.Y. INT'L L. POL.	NEW YORK INT'L LAW AND POLITICS
N.Y. L. F.	NEW YORK LAW FORUM
N.Y. SCH. J. INT'L & COMP. L.	NEW YORK LAW SCHOOL JOURNAL OF INTERNATIONAL AND COMPARATIVE LAW
N.Y. TIMES	NEW YORK TIMES

N.Y.U. J. INT'L L. & POL.	NEW YORK UNIVERSITY JOURNAL OF INTERNATIONAL LAW AND POLITICS
N.Y.U. REV. L. & SOC. CHANGE	NEW YORK UNIVERSITY REVIEW OF LAW AND SOCIAL CHANGE
OAS	Organization of American States
OAS Money Laundering Report	Inter-American Drug Abuse Control Commission, *Final Report of the Group of Experts to Prepare Model Regulations Concerning Laundering Offenses Connected to Illicit Drug Trafficking and Related Offenses*, OEA/Ser.L/XIV.2.11/CICAD/doc.391/92 (Mar. 9, 1992) at 1
OAS Sentence Convention	Inter-American Convention on Serving Criminal Sentence Abroad, Jan. 10, 1995, S. Treaty Doc. No. 104-35, 104th Cong., 2d Sess. (1996).
OAS Terrorist Conv.	Convention to Prevent and Punish the Acts of Terrorism Taking the Form of Crimes Against Persons and Related Extortion that are of International Significance, Feb. 2, 1971, O.A.S. Doc. A6/doc. 88, rev. 1 corr. 1, 27 U.S.T. 3949, T.I.A.S. No. 8431
OEJZ	OSTERREICHSCHE JURISTEN-ZEITUNG
OLA	United Nations Office of Legal Affairs
PACE INT'L L. REV.	PACE INTERNATIONAL LAW REVIEW
PCIJ	Permanent Court of International Justice
Protocol I	1977 Protocol Additional to the Geneva Conventions of 12 Aug. 1949, and Relating to the Protection of Victims of International Armed Conflicts, U.N. Doc. A/32/144, 15 Aug. 1977, Annexes I, II referenced in 16 ILM 1391
Protocol II	1977 Protocol Additional to the Geneva Conventions of 12 Aug. 1949, and Relating to the Protection of Victims of Non-International Armed Conflicts, UN Doc. A/32/144, 15 Aug. 1977, Annexes I, II referenced in 16 ILM 1391
Protocol to the Montreal Convention	Protocol for the Suppression of Unlawful Acts of Violence at Airports serving International Civil Aviation, Supplementary to the Convention for the Suppression of Unlawful Acts Against the Safety of Civil Aviation, Sept. 23, 1971, 24 U.S.T. 564, 974 U.N.T.S.

RAPPARD & BASSIOUNI, EURO. COOPERATION	EKKEHARD MÜLLER RAPPARD AND M. CHERIF BASSIOUNI, EUROPEAN INTER-STATE COOPERATION IN CRIMINAL MATTERS (LA COOPÉRATION INTER-ETATIQUE EUROPÉENNEEN MATIÈRE PÉNALE) (2 ed. 2 vols. 1991)
RECUEIL DES COURS	RECUEIL DES COURS D'ACADEMIE DE DROIT INTERNATIONAL
RES or Res	(UN) Resolution
RESTATEMENT (FIRST)	RESTATEMENT (FIRST) OF THE FOREIGN RELATIONS LAW OF THE UNITED STATES
RESTATEMENT (SECOND)	RESTATEMENT (SECOND) OF THE FOREIGN RELATIONS LAW OF THE UNITED STATES
RESTATEMENT (THIRD)	RESTATEMENT (THIRD) OF THE FOREIGN RELATIONS LAW OF THE UNITED STATES (1987)
Rev. Sci. Crim. et Dr. Pén Comp.	Revue de Science Criminalle et de droit Pénal comparé (p. 67
Rev. Stat.	Revised Statute
Rev. Stat. Ann.	Revised Statute Annotated
RICO	Racketeer-Influenced and Corrupt Organization Act
RUT. CAM. L.J.	RUTGERS-CAMDEN LAW JOURNAL
Rwanda Statute	S.C. Res. 955, *Establishing the International Tribunal for Rwanda* (and Annex, which contains the Statute) (Nov. 8, 1994), Statute, art. 1 (Competence of the Tribunal), 33 I.L.M. 1598 (1994)
SC	(UN) Security Council
SCOR	(UN) Security Council Official Records
Secretary-General's Report on Yugo. Tribunal	Report of the Secretary-General Pursuant to ¶ 2 of Security Council Resolution 808 (1993, UN Doc. S/25704 (3 May 1993))
SLAVIC REV.	SLAVIC REVIEW
STAN. L. REV.	STANFORD LAW REVIEW
Stat.	United States Statutes at Large
STUDENTS INT'L L.J.	STUDENTS INTERNATIONAL LAW JOURNAL

Supp.	Supplement
Swiss Report	Treaty with the Swiss Confederation on Mutual Assistance in Criminal Matters, S. Exec. Rep. No. 29, 49th Cong. 2d Sess. (1976)
Swiss IMAC	Swiss Bundesgestetz ober Internationale Rechtshilfe in Strafsachen of Mar. 20, 1981
SW. U. L. REV.	SOUTHWESTERN UNIVERSITY LAW REVIEW
SYRACUSE J. INT'L L. & COM	SYRACUSE JOURNAL OF INTERNATIONAL LAW AND COMMERCE
SYRACUSE L. REV.	SYRACUSE LAW REVIEW
TERRORISM: DOCUMENTS	1 ROBERT A. FRIEDLANDER, TERRORISM: DOCUMENTS 253 (1979)
TERRORISM, DRUGS	CHRISTOPHER L. BLAKESLEY, TERRORISM, DRUGS, INTERNATIONAL LAW AND THE PROTECTION OF HUMAN LIBERTY (1992)
TEXAS L. REV.	TEXAS LAW REVIEW
TEXAS INT'L L. REV.	TEXAS INTERNATIONAL LAW REVIEW
T.I.A.S.	Treaties and other International Acts Series
TREATIES IN FORCE	UNITED STATES DEPARTMENT OF STATE, TREATIES IN FORCE: A LIST OF TREATIES AND OTHER INTERNATIONAL AGREEMENTS OF THE UNITED STATES IN FORCE ON JANUARY 1, 1996 345-46 (1996)
Tokyo Convention	Convention on Offences and Certain Other Acts Committed on Board Aircraft, Sept. 14, 1963 20 U.S.T. 2941, 704 U.N.T.S. 219
U. CHI. L.REV.	UNIVERSITY OF CHICAGO LAW REVIEW
UCLA L.REV.	UNIVERSITY OF CALIFORNIA, LOS ANGLES, LAW REVIEW
UCLA WOMEN'S L.J.	UNIVERSITY OF CALIFORNIA, LOS ANGLES, WOMEN'S LAW JOURNAL
U. ILL. L. REV.	UNIVERSITY OF ILLINOIS LAW REVIEW
U.K. Extradition Act 1973	United Kingdom Extradition Act of 1870

U.K. Evidence Act of 1975	United Kingdom Evidence Proceedings in Other Jurisdictions
U.K. Criminal Justice Act 1990	United Kingdom Criminal Justice (International Cooperation) Act of 1990.
U.N.	United Nations
U.N. Compendium	Seventh United Nations Congress on the Prevention of Crime and the Treatment of Offenders, Milan, Aug. 26-Sept. 6, 1985, Report prepared by the Secretariat, U.N. Doc. A/CONF./121/22/Rev.1, 53 (1986), and Compendium of United Nations Standards and Norms in Crime Prevention and Criminal Justice, U.N. Sales No. E.92.IV. at 105.
U.N. Doc.	United Nations Document
U.N. Drug Convention	United Nations Convention Against Illicit Traffic in Narcotic Drugs and Psychotropic Substances, *opened for signature* Dec. 20, 1988, U.N. Doc. E/Conf.82/15 Corr. 1 and Corr. 2, 28 I.L.M. 493 (1989) (*entered into force* Nov. 1990)
U.N. GUIDING PRINCIPLES ON CRIME PREVENTION	UNITED NATIONS CONGRESS ON THE PREVENTION OF CRIME FROM THE SEVENTH AND THE TREATMENT OF OFFENDERS, GUIDING PRINCIPLES UNITED NATIONS FOR CRIME PREVENTION AND CRIMINAL JUSTICE IN THE CONGRESS ON CONTEXT OF DEVELOPMENT AND A NEW INTERNATIONAL CRIME PREVENTION ECONOMIC ORDER, adopted by the Seventh United Nations Congress on the Prevention of Crime and the Treatment of Prisoners, A/Conf.121/22/Rev/1
U.N. Headquarters Agreement	Agreement Between the United Nations and the United States of America Regarding the Headquarters of the United Nations, 61 Stat. 3416, T.I.A.S. No. 1676 § 9 (June 26, 1947) (entered into force with respect to the United States Nov. 27, 1947)
UNICEF	United Nations International Children's Emergency Fund
U.N. Model Agr. Tran. For. Pris.	United Nations Model Agreement for the Transfer of Foreign Prisoners and the Recommendation on the Treatment of Foreign Prisoners, Seventh United Nations Congress on the Prevention of Crime and the Treatment of Offenders, U.N. Doc. A/CONF.121/22/Rev.1 (1985)

U.N. Model MLAT	United Nations Treaty on Mutual Assistance in Criminal Matters and its Optional Protocol, G.A. Res. 45/117 (14 Dec. 1990).
U.N. Money Laundering Report	*Money Laundering and Associated Issues: The Need for International Cooperation*, U.N. Doc. No. E/CN.15/1992/4/Add.5 , ¶ 63.
U.N. Privileges Conv.	Convention on Privileges and Immunities of the United Nations, Feb. 13, 1946, 21 U.S.T. 1418, 1 U.N.T.S. 16 (entered into force with respect to the United States Apr. 29, 1970).
UNPROFOR	United Nations Protective Force
U.N. Sea Traffic Conv.	Agreement on Illicit Traffic by Sea, implementing Article 17 of the [1995] United Nations Convention against Illicit Traffic in Narcotic Drugs and Psychotropic Substances, of 1995, Europ. T.S. No. 156 (1995)
U.N.T.S.	United Nations Treaty Service
U. PA. L. REV.	UNIVERSITY OF PENNSYLVANIA LAW REVIEW
U. PITTS L. REV.	UNIVERSITY OF PITTSBURGH LAW REVIEW
U. RICH. L. REV.	UNIVERSITY OF RICHMOND LAW REVIEW
U.S.	United States [case decision reporter]
U.S.-Bolvia Sentence Treaty	Treaty on the Execution of Penal Sentences, Feb. 10, 1978, U.S.-Bolvia, 30 U.S.T. 796
USC	Unites States Code
U.S. Code Cong. Admin News	United States Code of Congressional and Administrative news
U.S. Const.	United States Constitution
U.S.-Canada Sentence Treaty	Treaty on the Execution of Penal Sentences, Mar. 2, 1977, U.S.-Canada, 30 U.S.T. 6263
U.S.-Cayman Islands MLTA	Treaty Between the United States and the United Kingdom of Great Britain and Northern Ireland Concerning the Cayman Islands Relating to Mutual Legal Assistance in Criminal Matters, July 3, 1986, S. TREATY DOC. NO. 8, 100th Cong., 2d Sess. (1987), 26 I.L.M. 536 (entered into force Mar. 19, 1990).

U.S. DEA	United States Drug Enforcement Agency
U.S.-France Transfer Treaty	Convention on the Transfer of Sentenced Persons, Jan. 25, 1983, U.S.-France, 35 U.S.T. 2847
U.S.-Italian MLAT	Treaty on Mutual Assistance in Criminal Matters, Nov. 9, 1982, U.S.-Italy, S. TREATY DOC. NO. 25, 98th Cong., 2d Sess. (1984), 24 I.L.M. 1536 (entered into force Nov. 13, 1985).
U.S.-Korea Trenasfer POW Treaty	Memorandum of Agreement on the Transfer of Prisoner of War/Civil Internees, Feb. 12, 1982, U.S.-Korea, 34 U.S.T. 1173
U.S.-Mexico Sentence Treaty	Treaty on the Execution of Penal Sentences, Nov. 25, 1976, U.S.-Mex., 28 U.S.T. 7399
U.S.-Netherlands MLAT	Treaty on Mutual Legal Assistance in Criminal Matters, June 12, 1981, U.S.-Neth., T.I.A.S. No. 10734, 21 I.L.M. 48 (entered into force Sept. 15, 1983).
U.S.-Peru Sentence Treaty	Treaty on the Execution of Penal Sentences, July 6, 1979, U.S.-Peru, 32 U.S.T. 1471
U.S.-Panama Sentence Treaty	Treaty on the Execution of Penal Sentences, Jan. 11, 1979, U.S.-Panama, 32 U.S.T. 1565
U.S-Swiss MLAT	Treaty on Mutual Assistance in Criminal Matters, May 25, 1973, U.S.-Switz., 27 U.S.T. 2019, 12 I.L.M. 916 (entered into force Jan. 23, 1977).
U.S.T.	United States Treaty Series
U.S.-Thailand Sentence Treaty	Treaty on the Execution of Penal Sentences, Oct. 29, 1982, U.S.-Thailand, Hein's No. KAV 1942
U.S.-Turkey Sentence Treaty	Treaty on the Execution of Penal Sentences, June 7, 1979, U.S.-Turkey, 32 U.S.T. 3187
UTAH L. REV.	UTAH LAW REVIEW
VA. J. INT'L L.	VIRGINIA JOURNAL OF INTERNATIONAL LAW
VAND. J. TRANSNAT'L L.	VANDERBILT JOURNAL OF TRANSNATIONAL LAW
Vanderbilt Note	Note, *The Law of the Flag, the Law of Extradition, the NATO Status of Forces Agreement and Their Application to Members of the United States Army National Guard*, 15 VAND. J. TRANSNAT'L L. 179, 185-91 (1982)

Vienna Consular	Vienna Convention on Consular Relations art. 1(k), Relations Convention Apr. 24, 1963, 21 U.S.T. 77, 596 U.N.T.S. 261 (entered into force with respect to the United States Dec. 24, 1969)
Vienna Treaties Conv.	Vienna Convention on the Law of Treaties, *opened for signature*, May 23, 1969, U.N. Doc. A/CHEF. 39/27 (1969), *reprinted in* 8 I.L.M. 679 (1969) *and in* 63 AM. J. INT'L. L. 875 (1969)
Vienna Diplomatic Conv.	Vienna Convention on Diplomatic Relations, April 18, 1961, Relations Convention preamble para. 5, 23 U.S.T. 3227, 500 U.N.T.S. 95 (entered into force with respect to the United States Dec. 13, 1972)
WALL ST. J.	WALL STREET JOURNAL
WASH. POST	WASHINGTON POST
WASH. TIMES	WASHINGTON TIMES
WHITEMAN DIGEST	6 MARJORIE WHITEMAN, DIGEST OF INTERNATIONAL LAW (1963)
WHITTIER L. REV.	WHITTIER LAW REVIEW
Working Group Report	*Report of the Chairman of the Working Group to Study the Draft Inter-American Convention on Mutual Assistance in Criminal Matters*, OEA/Ser.G/CP/CAJP.860/92
YALE J. INT'L L.	YALE JOURNAL OF INTERNATIONAL LAW
Y.B. EUR. L.	YEAR BOOK OF THE INTERNATIONAL LAW COMMISSION
Y.B. INT'L L. COM.	YEAR BOOM OF THE INTERNATIONAL LAW COMMISSION
Y.B. EUR. CONV. ON H.R.	YEAR BOOK OF THE EUROPEAN CONVENTION ON HUMAN RIGHTS

Table of Authorities

BOOKS:

MICHAEL ABBELL & BRUNO A. RISTAU, 3 INTERNATIONAL JUDICIAL ASSISTANCE — CRIMINAL OBTAINING EVIDENCE (1990).

THE ALLEGED TRANSNATIONAL CRIMINAL (Richard D. Atkins ed., 1995)

ARGOMENTI DI PROCEDURA PENALE INTERNAZIONALE (Oreste Doniniani ed., 1982)

THE BASES OF INTERNATIONAL ORDER (Alan James ed., 1973)

M. CHERIF BASSIOUNI, A DRAFT INTERNATIONAL CRIMINAL CODE AND DRAFT STATUTE FOR AN INTERNATIONAL CRIMINAL TRIBUNAL (1987)

M. CHERIF BASSIOUNI, CRIMES AGAINST HUMANITY IN INTERNATIONAL CRIMINAL LAW (1992)

M. CHERIF BASSIOUNI, EUROPEAN INTER-STATE CO-OPERATION IN CRIMINAL MATTERS: THE COUNCIL OF EUROPE'S LEGAL INSTRUMENTS (Ekkehart Muller-Rappard & M. Cherif Bassiouni eds., 2d rev. ed. 1993).

M. CHERIF BASSIOUNI, INTERNATIONAL CRIMINAL LAW: A DRAFT INTERNATIONAL CRIMINAL CODE (1980)

M. CHERIF BASSIOUNI, INTERNATIONAL CRIME: DIGEST/INDEX OF INTERNATIONAL INSTRUMENTS 1815-1985 (2 vols. 1987)

M. CHERIF BASSIOUNI, INTERNATIONAL EXTRADITION AND WORLD PUBLIC ORDER (1974)

M. CHERIF BASSIOUNI, INTERNATIONAL EXTRADITION: UNITED STATES LAW AND PRACTICE (3d rev. ed. 1995)

M. CHERIF BASSIOUNI (IN COOPERATION WITH PETER MANIKAS), THE LAW OF THE INTERNATIONAL CRIMINAL TRIBUNAL FOR THE FORMER YUGOSLAVIA (1996)

M. CHERIF BASSIOUNI & EDWARD M. WISE, AUT DEDERE AUT JUDICARE: THE OBLIGATION TO EXTRADITE OR PROSECUTE IN INTERNATIONAL LAW (1995)

CHARLES R. BEITZ, POLITICAL THEORY AND INTERNATIONAL RELATIONS (1979)

PAOLO BERNASCONI, NEW JUDICIAL INSTRUMENTS AGAINST INTERNATIONAL BUSINESS CRIMES (1995)

ALBERT BILLOT, TRAITÉ DE L'EXTRADITION (1874)

WILLIAM BISHOP, INTERNATIONAL LAW CASES & MATERIALS (3d ed. 1971)

BLACK'S LAW DICTIONARY (rev. 4th ed. 1968)

WILLIAM BLACKSTONE, COMMENTARIES ON THE LAWS OF ENGLAND 1776

CHRISTOPHER L. BLAKESLEY, LE DEVELOPPEMENT DU DROIT PÉNAL AUX ETATS-UNIS (1991)

CHRISTOPHER L. BLAKESLEY, TERRORISM, DRUGS, INTERNATIONAL LAW AND THE PROTECTION OF HUMAN LIBERTY (1992)

LOUIS M. BLOOMFIELD & GERALD F. FITZGERALD, CRIMES AGAINST INTERNATIONALLY PROTECTED PERSONS, PREVENTION AND PUNISHMENT: AN ANALYSIS OF THE UN CONVENTION (1975)

HARTLEY BOOTH, BRITISH EXTRADITION LAW AND PROCEDURE (1980)

HAFID ALOSUI BOUKHRISS, LA COOPÉRATION PÉNALE INTERNATIONALE PAR VOIE D'EXTRADITION AU MAROC (1986)

PIERRE BOUZAT & JEAN PINATEL, TRAITÉ DE DROIT PÉNAL (2d ed. 1970)

LEA BRILMAYER, JUSTIFYING INTERNATIONAL ACTS (1989)

IAN BROWNLIE, INTERNATIONAL LAW AND THE USE OF FORCE BY STATES (1963)

IAN BROWNLIE, PRINCIPLES OF PUBLIC INTERNATIONAL LAW (4th ed. 1990)

HEDLEY BULL, THE ANARCHICAL SOCIETY: A STUDY OF ORDER IN WORLD POLITICS (1977)

JACOB BURCKHARDT, UBER DAS STUDIUM DER GESCHICHTE

HEINER BUSCH, GRENZENLOSE POLIZEI? NEUE GRENZEN UND POLIZEILICHE ZUSAMMENARBEIT IN EUROPA (1995)

ALBERT CAMUS, NEITHER VICTIMS NOR EXECUTIONERS (Dwight MacDonald trans., 1972)

ALBERT CAMUS, RESISTANCE, REBELLION AND DEATH (J. O'Brien trans., 1961)

ANTHONY CARTY, THE DECAY OF INTERNATIONAL LAW: A REAPPRAISAL OF THE LIMITS OF LEGAL IMAGINATION IN INTERNATIONAL AFFAIRS (1986)

ANTONIO CASSESE, INTERNATIONAL LAW IN A DIVIDED WORLD (1986)

GIULIO CATELANI & DANIELE STRIANI, L'ESTRADIZIONE (1983)

CHANGES IN SOCIETY, CRIME AND CRIMINAL JUSTICE IN EUROPE: CHALLENGE FOR A CRIMINOLOGICAL EDUCATION AND RESEARCH: 2 INTERNATIONAL ORGANIZED AND CORPORATE CRIME (Cyrille Fejnaut, et al. eds., 1996)

ROGER S. CLARK, THE UNITED NATIONS CRIME PREVENTION AND CRIMINAL JUSTICE PROGRAM: FORMULATION OF STANDARDS AND EFFORTS AT THEIR IMPLEMENTATION (1994)

ROBIN GEORGE COLLINGWOOD, THE NEW LEVIATHAN, ON MA, SOCIETY, CIVILIZATIO, AND BARBARISM (rev. ed. 1992)

JEAN-LUC COLOMBINI, LA PRISE EN CONSIDÉRATION DU DROIT ÉTRANGER DANS LE JUGEMENT PÉNAL (1983)

THE COMMONWEALTH REVIEW OF EXTRADITION ARRANGEMENTS (1982)

THE COMMUNITY OF STATES (James Mayall ed., 1982)

CONTEMPORARY PROBLEMS OF INTERNATIONAL LAW: ESSAYS IN HONOUR OF GEORG SCHWARZENBERGER (Bin Cheng & E.D. Brown eds., 1988).

CONTROL OF TERRORISM: INTERNATIONAL DOCUMENTS (Yonah Alexander et. al., eds., 1979)

FRED COPLESTON, A HISTORY OF PHILOSOPHY (1946)

COUNCIL OF EUROPE PUBLICATIONS: ASPECTS JURIDIQUES DE L'EXTRADITION ENTRE ETATS EUROPÉENS (1970)

LA CONVENZIONE EUROPA DI ASSISTENZA GIUDIZIARIA IN MATERIA PENALE (Paolo Laszloczky ed. 1984)

CRIMINAL POLICY DEPARTMENT., THE REPATRIATION OF PRISONERS, REPORT OF THE INTERDEPARTMENTAL WORKING PARTY (Feb. 1980)

JACQUES DALLOZ, CODE DE PROCEDURE PENAL ET CODE DE JUSTICE MILITAIRE (1992-1993)

JACQUES DALLOZ, ENCYCLOPEDIE JURIDIQUE, RIPERTOIRE DE DROIT INTERNATIONAL (1968)

GENNADII MIKHAILOVICH M. DANILENKO, LAW-MAKING IN THE INTERNATIONAL COMMUNITY (1993)

DECISIONS AND REPORTS OF THE EUROPEAN COMMISSION OF HUMAN RIGHTS (1985)

DE LA CONSTITUTION, ETUDES EN L'HONNEUR DE JEAN-FRANÇOIS (Aubert et al., eds., 1996)

EMERICH DE VATTEL, THE LAW OF NATIONS; OR, PRINCIPLES OF THE LAW OF NATURE, APPLIED TO THE CONDUCT AND AFFAIRS OF NATIONS AND SOVEREIGNS (Pomroy trans., 1805)

CHARLES DE VISSCHER, THEORY AND REALITY IN PUBLIC INTERNATIONAL LAW (P. E. Corbett trans., rev. ed. 1957)

YORAM DINSTEIN & MALA TABORY, WAR CRIMES IN INTERNATIONAL LAW (1996)

DIPLOMATIC INVESTIGATIONS (Sir Herbert Butterfield & Martin Wight eds., 1966)

DOING BUSINESS ABROAD: IDENTIFYING AND AVOIDING CRIMINAL RISKS (1992)

HENRI DONNEDIEU DE VABRES, ANNUAIRE DE L'INSTITUT DE DROIT INTERNATIONAL (1950)

HENRI DONNEDIEU DE VABRES, LES PRINCIPES MODÈRNE DU DROIT PÉNAL INTERNATIONAL (1928)

HENRI DONNEDIEU DE VABRES, TRAITÉ ELÉMENTAIRE DE DROIT CRIMINEL ET DE LÉGISLATION PÉNALE COMPARÉE (2d ed. 1943)

DOUBLE CRIMINALITY, STUDIES IN INTERNATIONAL CRIMINAL LAW (Nils Jareborg ed., 1989)

DURKHEIM AND THE LAW (Steven Lukes & Andrew Scull eds., 1983)

EMILE DURKHEIM, DE LA DIVISION DU TRAVAIL SOCIAL (7TH ED. 1960)

EMILE DURKHEIM, ON THE DIVISION OF LABOR IN SOCIETY (GEORGE SIMPSON TRANS., 1947)

ESSAYS IN CRIMINAL SCIENCE (Gerhard O. W. Mueller ed., 1961)

EUROPEAN COMMITTEE ON CRIME PROBLEMS, COUNCIL OF EUROPE, PROBLEMS ARISING FROM THE PRACTICAL APPLICATION OF THE EUROPEAN CONVENTION ON MUTUAL ASSISTANCE IN CRIMINAL MATTERS (1971)

EUROPEAN COMMITTEE ON CRIME PROBLEMS, COUNCIL OF EUROPE, LEGAL ASPECTS OF EXTRADITION AMONG EUROPEAN STATES (1970)

2 EUROPEAN INTER-STATE CO-OPERATION IN CRIMINAL MATTERS: THE COUNCIL OF EUROPE'S LEGAL INSTRUMENTS 1405 (Ekkehart Müller-Rappard & M. Cherif Bassiouni eds., rev'd 2d ed. 1993)

RICHARD FALK, REVITALIZING INTERNATIONAL LAW (1989)

RICHARD A. FALK, REVOLUTIONARIES & FUNCTIONARIES: THE DUAL FACE OF TERRORISM (1988)

BENJAMIN FERENCZ, AN INTERNATIONAL CRIMINAL COURT — A STEP TOWARD WORLD PEACE (1980)

FESTSCHRIFT FUR BOCKELMANN (1979)

JOHN FINNIS, NATURAL LAW AND NATURAL RIGHTS (1980)

FREE MOVEMENT OF PERSONS IN EUROPE (Henry G. Schermers et al. eds., 1993)

ROBERT A. FRIEDLANDER, TERROR-VIOLENCE: ASPECTS OF SOCIAL CONTROL (1983)

ROBERT A. FRIEDLANDER, TERRORISM: DOCUMENTS of International And Local Control (4 vols. 1978)

OTTO GIERKE, NATIONAL LAW AND THE THEORY OF SOCIETY 1500 TO 1800 (Ernest Barker trans., (1934)

GEOFF GILBERT, ASPECTS OF EXTRADITION LAW (1991)

WILLIAM C. GILMORE, DIRTY MONEY: THE EVOLUTION OF MONEY LAUNDERING COUNTER-MEASURES (1995)

STEFAN GLASER, LE DROIT PÉNAL INTERNATIONAL CONVENTION (2 vols. 1977-79)

JOHANN GOETHE, FAUST, (1800)

BERNHARD GROSSFELD, THE STRENGTH AND WEAKNESS OF COMPARATIVE LAW (1990)

GROTIAN SOCIETY PAPERS (Charles Henry Alexandrowicz ed., 1972)

HUGO GROTIUS, 2 DE BELLI AC PACIS LIBRIS TRES (Francis W. Kelsey trans., 1925)

HUGO GROTIUS AND INTERNATIONAL RELATIONS (Hedley Bull, etd eds., 1990)

HUGO GROTIUS, TREATING OF THE RIGHTS OF WAR AND PEACE INCLUDING THE LAW OF NATURE AND OF NATION (William Evats trans., 1945)

HEINRICH GRUTZNER, INTERNATIONALER RECHTSHILFEVERKEHR IN STRAFSACHEN (1967)

GREEN HAYWOOD HACKWORTH, DIGEST OF INTERNATIONAL LAW (1940)

WILLIAM KEITH HANCOCK, FOUR STUDIES OF WAR AND PEACE IN THIS CENTURY (1961)

CHRISTOPHER HARDING, EUROPEAN INVESTIGATIONS AND SANCTIONS (1993)

V. E. HARTLEY-BOOTH, BRITISH EXTRADITION LAW AND PRACTICE (2 vols. 1980)

BILL HEBENTON & TERRY THOMAS, POLICING EUROPE: COOPERATION, CONFLICT AND CONTROL (1995)

LOUIS HENKIN, FOREIGN AFFAIRS AND THE CONSTITUTION (1972)

LOUIS HENKIN, HOW NATIONS BEHAVE: LAW AND FOREIGN POLICY (1979)

LOUIS HENKIN, ET AL., INTERNATIONAL LAW: CASES AND MATERIALS (3d ed. 1993)

FRANCIS HARRY HINSLEY, SOVEREIGNTY (1966)

THOMAS HOBBES, LEVIATHAN (Michael Joseph Oakeshott ed., 1957)

HOLMES POLLOCK LETTERS (Mark de Wolfe Howe ed., 1941)

MANLEY O. HUDSON, INTERNATIONAL LEGISLATION (1931)

CHARLES HYDE, INTERNATIONAL LAW CHIEFLY AS INTERPRETED BY THE UNITED STATES (2d ed. 1922)

PROCEEDINGS OF THE INTERNATIONAL CONGRESS OF PENAL LAW, STRUCTURES AND METHODS OF INTERNATIONAL COOPERATION, Cairo (Nov. 1984)

INTERNATIONAL CRIMES OF STATE: A CRITICAL ANALYSIS OF THE ILC'S DRAFT ARTICLE 19 ON STATE RESPONSIBILITY (Joseph H.H. Weiler et al. eds., 1989)

INTERNATIONAL CRIMINAL LAW (Gerhard O.W. Mueller & Edward M. Wise eds., 1965)

INTERNATIONAL CRIMINAL LAW: A GUIDE TO U.S. PRACTICE AND PROCEDURE (Ved P. Nanda and M. Cherif Bassiouni eds., 1987)

INTERNATIONAL CRIMINAL LAW: PROCEDURE (M. Cherif Bassiouni ed., 1987)

INTERNATIONAL EFFORTS TO COMBAT MONEY LAUNDERING (William C. Gilmore ed., 1992)

INTERNATIONAL EXCHANGE OF TAX INFORMATION RECENT DEVELOPMENTS (Richard A Gordon & Bruce Zagaris eds., 1985)

INTERNATIONAL LAW: ACHIEVEMENTS AND PROSPECTS (Mohammed Bedjaoui ed., 1991)

INTERNATIONAL LAW: A CONTEMPORARY PERSPECTIVE (Richard A. Falk, 1985)

INTERNATIONAL LAW ASSOCIATION, REPORT OF THE SIXTY-FIRST CONFERENCE (Paris 1984)

INTERNATIONAL MILITARY TRIBUNAL, TRIAL OF THE MAJOR WAR CRIMINALS BEFORE THE INTERNATIONAL MILITARY TRIBUNAL (1947)

INTERNATIONAL PROTECTIONS OF VICTIMS, 7 NOUVELLES ETUDE PÉNALES (M. Cherif Bassiouni ed., 1988)

INTERNATIONAL RELATIONS: A HANDBOOK OF CURRENT THEORY (Margot Light & A.J.R. Groom eds., 1985)

INTERNATIONAL TERRORISM AND POLITICAL CRIMES (M. Cherif Bassiouni ed., 1975)

INTERNATIONAL TERRORISM: U.S. PROCEDURAL ASPECTS (M. Cherif Bassiouni ed., 1987)

THE INTERNATIONALIZATION OF POLICE COOPERATION IN WESTERN EUROPE (Cyrille Fijnaut ed., 1993)

INTRODUCTION TO THE LAW OF THE UNITED STATES (1991)

ALUN JONES, JONES ON EXTRADITION (1995)

BARRY KELLMAN ET AL.,IMPLEMENTING OF THE CHEMICAL WEAPONS CONVENTION: LEGAL ISSUES (1994)

G.V. LA FOREST, EXTRADITION TO AND FROM CANADA (1977)

OTTO LAGODNY, DIE RECHTESSTELLUNG DES AUSZULIEFERNDEN IN DER BUNDESREPUBLIK DEUTSCHLAND (1987)

JOSEPH J. LAMBERT, TERRORISM AND HOSTAGES IN INTERNATIONAL LAW (1990)

SIR HERSCH LAUTERPACHT, INTERNATIONAL LAW AND HUMAN RIGHTS (1950)

SIR HERSH. LAUTERPACHT, INTERNATIONAL LAW,: COLLECTED PAPERS of Sir Hersh Lauterpacht (Elihu Lauterpacht ed., 1970)

THE LAWS OF WAR: A COMPREHENSIVE COLLECTION OF PRIMARY DOCUMENTS ON INTERNATIONAL LAWS GOVERNING ARMED CONFLICT (W. MICHAEL REISMAN & CHRIS ANTONIOU eds., 1994)

LEGAL RESPONSES TO INTERNATIONAL TERRORISM: U.S. PROCEDURAL ASPECTS (M. Cherif Bassiouni ed., 1987)

KARINE LESCURE, LE TRIBUNAL PÉNAL INTERNATIONAL POUR L'EX-YOUGOSLAVIE (1994)

HAIDONG LI, DIE PRINZIPIEN DES INTERNATIONALEN STRAFRECHTS (1991)

ROBERT LINKE, GRUNDRISS DES AUSLIEFERUNGSRECHTS (1983)

ROBERT LINKE ET AL., INTERNATIONALES STRAFRECHT, COMMENTARY ON THE AUSTRIAN LAW ON INTERNATIONAL MUTUAL ASSISTANCE IN CRIMINAL MATTERS OF 4TH DECEMBER 1979 (1981)

CLAUDE LOMBOIS, DROIT PÉNAL INTERNATIONAL (2d. ed. 1979)

THE LOW COUNTRIES IN EARLY MODERN TIMES (Herbert H. Rowen ed., 1972)

TIZIANA TREVISSON LUPACCHINI, L'ESTRADIZIONE DALL' ESTERO PER L'ITALIA (1989)

LUIGI MAGISTRO, RICICLAGGIO DEI CAPITALI ILLECITI (1991)

FARHAD MALEKIAN, INTERNATIONAL CRIMINAL LAW (2 vols. 1991)

MANUAL OF PUBLIC INTERNATIONAL LAW (Max Sorensen ed., 1968)

MASS RAPE: THE WAR AGAINST WOMEN IN BOSNIA-HERZEGOVINA (Alexandra Stiglmayer ed., 1994)

LORD MCNAIR, THE LAW OF TREATIES (1961)

H. MEIJERS ET AL., SCHENGEN: INTERNATIONALIZATION OF CENTRAL CHAPTERS OF THE LAW ON ALIENS, REFUGEES, SECURITY AND THE POLICE (1991)

MELANGES OFFERTS À GEORGES LEVASSEUR:Droit Penal, Droit Eeuropen (1992)

ROGER MERLE & ANDRE VITU, TRAITÉ DE DROIT CRIMINEL (4th ed. 1989)

THEODOR MERON, HUMAN RIGHTS AND HUMANITARIAN NORMS AS CUSTOMARY LAW (1989)

THOMAS MERTON, THE LITERARY ESSAYS OF THOMAS MERTON (Brother Patrick Hart ed., 1981)

DAVID MCCLEAN, INTERNATIONAL JUDICIAL ASSISTANCE (1992)

JAMES W. MOORE ET. AL., MOORE'S FEDERAL PRACTICE (1994)

JOHN B. MOORE, INTERNATIONAL LAW DIGEST (1906)

JOHN B. MOORE, A TREATISE ON EXTRADITION AND INTERSTATE RENDITION (2 VOLS. 1891)

VIRGINIA MORRIS & MICHAEL SCHARF, AN INSIDER'S GUIDE TO THE INTERNATIONAL CRIMINAL TRIBUNAL FOR THE FORMER YUGOSLAVIA (1995)

FRANCO MOSCONI & MARIO PISANI, LE CONVENZIONI DI ASSISTENZA GIUDIZIARIA (1984)

EKKEHART MÜLLER-RAPPARD & M. CHERIF BASSIOUNI, EUROPEAN INTER-STATE CO-OPERATION IN CRIMINAL MATTERS (2d ed. 1991)

JOHN F. MURPHY, LEGAL ASPECTS OF INTERNATIONAL TERRORISM: SUMMARY REPORT OF AN INTERNATIONAL CONFERENCE (American Society of International Law Studies in Transnational Legal Policy No. 19, 1980)

JOHN F. MURPHY, PUNISHING INTERNATIONAL TERRORISTS (1985)

MUTUAL ASSISTANCE IN CRIMINAL AND BUSINESS REGULATORY MATTERS (William C. Gilmore ed., 1995)

ETHAN A. NADELMANN, COPS ACROSS BORDERS (1993)

KARL-FRIEDRICH NAGEL, BEWEISAUFNAHME IM AUSLAND (1988)

TERRY NARDIN, LAW, MORALITY, AND THE RELATION OF STATES (1983)

NEDERLANDS TIJDSCHRIFT VOOR INTERNATIONAAL RECHT (1967)

EBERHAND NORDMANN, DIE BESCHAFFUNG VON BEWEISMITTELN AUS DEM AUSLAND DURCH STAATLICHE STELLEN (1979)

THE NUREMBERG TRIAL AND INTERNATIONAL LAW (George Ginsburgs & Vladimir Nickolaevich Kudraiavstev eds., 1990)

ARTHUR NUSSBAUM, A CONCISE HISTORY OF THE LAW OF NATIONS (2d ed. 1954)

JOSEPH S. NYE, JR., NUCLEAR ETHICS (1986)

DEITRICH OEHLER, INTERNATIONALES STRAFRECHT (2d ed. 1983)

LASSA OPPENHEIM, 1 INTERNATIONAL LAW (3d ed. 1920)

OPPENHEIM'S INTERNATIONAL LAW (Robert Y. Jennings & Sir Arthur Watts eds., 9th ed. 1992)

ORDER AND VIOLENCE: HEDLEY BULL AND INTERNATIONAL RELATIONS (J. D. B. Miller & R. J. Vincent eds., 1990)

EDITH PALMER, THE AUSTRIAN LAW ON EXTRADITION AND MUTUAL ASSISTANCE IN CRIMINAL MATTERS (Library of Congress trans., 1983)

NICOLETTA PARISI, ESTRADIZIONE E DIRITTI DELL' UOMO (1983)

CLIVE PARRY, THE SOURCES AND EVIDENCES OF INTERNATIONAL LAW (1965)

BLANCA PASTOR, ASPECTOS PRCESALES DE LA EXTRADICIÓN EN DERECHO ESPAÑOL (1984)

VESPASIAN V. PELLA, LA CODIFICATION DU DROIT PÉNAL INTERNATIONAL (1922)

THE PENAL CODE OF SWEDEN (G.O.W. Mueller ed., T. Sellin trans., 1972)

ROLLIN PERKINS & RONALD BOYCE, CRIMINAL LAW (3d ed. 1982)

MARIO PISANI & FRANCO MOSCONI, CODICE DELLE CONVENZIONI DI ESTRADIZIONE E DI ASSISTENZA GIUDIZIARIA IN MATERIA PENALE (2d ed. 1993)

DOMINIQUE PONCET & PHILIPPE NEYROUD, L'EXTRADITION ET L'ASILE POLITIQUE EN SUISSE (1976)

PRACTICING LAW INSTITUTE, EXTRATERRITORIAL DISCOVERY IN INTERNATIONAL LITIGATION (1984)

PRINCIPLES AND PROCEDURES FOR A NEW TRANSNATIONAL CRIMINAL LAW, REPORTS AND MATERIALS FROM THE MAX PLANCK INSTITUTE (Albin Eser & Otto Lagodny eds., 1991)

HENRI DONNEDIEU DE VABRES, LES PRINCIPES MODERNES DE DROIT PÉNAL INTERNATIONAL (1928)

PROSECUTING INTERNATIONAL CRIMES (Roger Clark & Madeline Sann, eds. 1996)

PROTECTION OF WAR VICTIMS: PROTOCOL I TO THE GENEVA CONVENTION (Howard Levie ed., 1979)

ANTONIO QUINTANO-RIPPOLLES, TRATADO DE DERECHO PENAL INTERNACIONAL E INTERNACIONAL PENAL (2 vols. 1955-57)

THE REASON OF STATES (Michael Donelan ed., 1978)

RESPONDING TO MONEY LAUNDERING (Ernesto U. Savona ed. 1997)

MARIA RICCARDA- MARCHETTI, INSTITUZIONI EUROPEE E LOTTA AL TERRORISMO (1986)

JEFFREY ROBINSON, THE LAUNDRYMEN (1996)

HOLGER ROMANDER, OM ÖVERFÖRING AV ÅTAL INOM NORDEN (1984)

CLAUS ROXIN, STRAFVERFAHRENSRECHT (20th ed., 1987)

ALFRED P. RUBIN, THE LAW OF PIRACY (1988)

SCANDINAVIAN CRIMINAL POLICY AND CRIMINOLOGY 1986-1990 (Norman Bishop ed., 1990)

WILLIAM SCHABAS, THE ABOLITION OF THE DEATH PENALTY IN INTERNATIONAL LAW (1993)

OSCAR SCHACHTER, INTERNATIONAL LAW IN THEORY AND PRACTICE (1991)

SCHENGEN, INTERNATIONALIZATION OF CENTRAL CHAPTERS OF THE LAW ON ALIENS, REFUGEES, PRIVACY, SECURITY AND THE POLICE (Henri Meijers ed., 1991)

WALTER SCHIFFER, THE LEGAL COMMUNITY OF MANKIND (1954)

FRIEDRICH SCHILLER, DILETTANT IN TABULAE VOTIVAE, I WERKE (1952)

Swiss Bank Corp., BANKING SECRECY AND MUTUAL ASSISTANCE IN CRIMINAL MATTERS (1983)

HANS SCHULTZ, SCHWEIZERISCHES AUSLIEFERUNGSRECHT (1953)

KLAUS SCHWAIGHOFER, AUS LIEFERUNG UND INTERNATIONALES STRAFRECHT (1988)

GEORG SCHWARZENBERGER, THE DYNAMICS OF INTERNATIONAL LAW (1976)

GEORG SCHWARZENBERGER, POWER POLITICS (2d ed. 1951)

SECRETARIA DE RELACIONES EXTERIORES, LIMITS TO NATIONAL JURISDICTION (1993)

LA SEMAINE JURIDIQUE, EDITION GENERALE (1997)

IAN SHEARER, EXTRADITION IN INTERNATIONAL LAW (1971)

STRUPP-SCHLOCHAUER, WORRTERBUCH DES VOLKERRECHTS (1962)

A.H.J. SWART, NEDERLANDS UITLEVERINGSRECHT (1986)

TELFORD TAYLOR, NUREMBERG AND VIETNAM: AN AMERICAN TRAGEDY (1970)

TERTULLIAN, APOLOGY (Loeb Classical Library, 1931)

THE THIRD PILLAR OF THE EUROPEAN UNION (Jeorg Monar & Robert Morgan eds., 1994)

FRANCOISE THOMAS, DE EUROPESE RECHTSHULPVERDRAGEN IN STRAFZAKEN (1980)

KATARINA TOMAŠEVSKI, FOREIGNERS IN PRISON (1994)

TRANSFER OF PRISONERS UNDER INTERNATIONAL INSTRUMENTS AND DOMESTIC LEGISLATION (1993)

TRANSNATIONAL LITIGATION: PRACTICAL APPROACHES TO CONFLICTS AND ACCOMMODATIONS (1984)

TRANSNATIONAL TERRORISM: CONVENTIONS & COMMENTARY (Richard Lillich ed., 1982)

TREATISE ON INTERNATIONAL CRIMINAL LAW (2 vols. M. Cherif Bassiouni & Ved P. Nanda eds., 1973)

OTTO TRIFFTERER, DOGMATISCHE UNTERSUCHENGEN ZUR ENTWICKLUNG DES MATERIELLEN VOLKRESTRAFRECHT SEIT NURNBERG (1966)

SIGMAR UHLIG & WOLFGANG SHOMBURG, GESETZ OBER DIE INTERNATIONALE RECHTSHILFE IN STRAFSACHEN (1983)

CHRISTINE VAN DEN WYNGAERT, THE POLITICAL OFFENSE EXCEPTION TO EXTRADITION (1980)

JOHN A.E. VERVAELE, FRAUD AGAINST THE COMMUNITY (1992)

THEO VOGLER, AUSLIEFERUNGRECHT UND GUNDGESETZ (1970)

THEO VOGLER & PETER WILKITZKI, GESETZ UBER DIE INTERNATIONALE RECHTSHILFE IN STRAFSACHEN (IRG): Kommentar (1992)

GAETANO ARANGIO-RUIZ, THE UNITED NATIONS DECLARATION ON FRIENDLY RELATIONS AND THE SYSTEM OF THE SOURCES OF INTERNATIONAL LAW (1979)

U.S. DEPT. JUSTICE, BUREAU OF NARCOTICS & DANGEROUS DRUGS, A STUDY OF INTERNATIONAL CONTROL OF NARCOTICS & DANGEROUS DRUGS (1972)

UNIVERSIDAD NACIONAL AUTÓNOMA DE MÉXICO, COOPERACIÓN INTERAMERICANO EN LOS PROCEDIMIENTOS PENALES (1983)

MANUEL ADOLFO VIEIRA, L'EVOLUTION RÉCENTE DE L'EXTRADITION DANS LE CONTINENT AMÉRICAIN

OTTO VON GIERKE, DAS DEUTSCHE GENOSSENSCHAFTSRECHT (1954 reprint)(1913)

WAR CRIMES: A SYNTHESIS OF INTERNATIONAL AND NATIONAL APPROACHES (1997)

EMIL WEZEL, SPRACHE UND GEIST IV (1935)

FRANCIS WHARTON, WHARTON'S CRIMINAL LAW (12th ed. 1932)

MARJORIE M. WHITEMAN, DIGEST OF INTERNATIONAL LAW (1968)

MARTIN WIGHT, INTERNATIONAL THEORY: THE THREE TRADITIONS (Gabriele. Wight & Brian. Porter eds., 1991)

MARTIN WIGHT, POWER POLITICS (Hedley. Bull & Carsten. Hobraad eds., 1978)

MARTIN WIGHT, SYSTEMS OF STATES (Hedley. Bull ed., 1977)

GARRY WILLS, INVENTING AMERICA, JEFFERSON'S DECLARATION OF INDEPENDENCE (1978)

LUDWIG WITTGENSTEIN, TRACTATUS LOGICO-PHILOSOPHICUS (1933)

CHRISTIAN WOLFF, JUS GENTIUM METHODO SCIENTIFICA PERTRACTATUM (Joseph H. Drake trans., 1934)

BARBARA YARNOLD, INTERNATIONAL FUGITIVES (1991)

ZISSIADIS, PENAL PROCEDURE (1975)

ARTICLES:

Michael Abbell, *International Assistance in Criminal Investigations and Prosecutions*, *in,* PRACTICING LAW INSTITUTE, EXTRATERRITORIAL DISCOVERY IN INTERNATIONAL LITIGATION (1984)

Michael Abbell, *Obtaining Evidence in the U.S. in Criminal Cases Through the Use of Compulsory Process*, *in* THE ALLEGED TRANSNATIONAL CRIMINAL (R. Atkins ed., 1995)

Albin Eser, *Common Goals and Different Ways in International Criminal Law: Reflections from a European Perspective*, 31 HARV. INT'L L.J. 117 (1990)

Abraham Abramovsky, *Extraterritorial Jurisdiction: The United States' Unwarranted Attempt to Alter International Law in* United States v. Yunis, 15 YALE J. INT'L L. 121 (1990)

George H. Aldrich, Commentary, *Progressive Development of the Laws of War: A Reply to Criticisms of the 1977 Geneva Protocol I*, 26 VA.J. INT'L L. (1986)

Duncan E. Alford, *Anti-Money Laundering Regulations: A Burden on Financial Institutions*, 19 N.C.J. INT'L L. & COM. REG. 437 (1994)

Serge April and Johnathan T. Fried, *Compelling Discovery and Disclosure in Transnational Litigation: A Canadian View*, 16 N.Y. U. J. INTL' L. & POL. 961 (1984)

Gaetano Arangio-Ruiz, *The Concept of International Law and the Theory of International Organization, in* THE UNITED NATIONS DECLARATION ON FRIENDLY RELATIONS AND THE SYSTEM OF THE SOURCES OF INTERNATIONAL LAW (1979)

Evelyn Mary Aswad, *Torture By Means of Rape*, 84 GEO. L.J. 1913 (1996)

Jean-Luc Aubert, *Quelques Aspects de la Portee du Secret Bancaire au Droit Penal Interne dans l' Entraide Judiciaire Internationale*, 1984 REVUE PENALE SUISSE 173

Budimir Babovic, *Interpol and Human Rights*, INT'L CRIM. POLICE REV. 4 (July-Aug. 1990)

Hans-Jürgen Bartsch, *Council of Europe-Legal Cooperation in 1982, Repatriation of Foreign Prisoners*, Y.B. EUR. L. 306 (1982)

Hans-Jürgen Bartsch, *Strafvollstreckung im Heimatstaat*, NJW 513 (1984)

M.Cherif Bassiouni, *Characteristics of International Criminal Law Conventions, in* 1 INTERNATIONAL CRIMINAL LAW: CRIMES (M. Cherif Bassiouni ed., 1986)

M. Cherif Bassiouni, *The Commission of Experts Established pursuant to Security Council Resolution 780: Investigation of Violations of International Humanitarian Law in the Former Yugoslavia,* 5 CRIM. L.F. 279-340 (1994)

M.Cherif Bassiouni, *A Comprehensive Strategic Approach on International Cooperation for the Prevention, Control and Suppression of International and Transnational Criminality*, 15 NOVA L. REV. 354 (1991)

M. Cherif Bassiouni, *Critical Reflections on International and National Control of Drugs*, 18 DENV. J. INT'L L. & POL'Y 311, 321 (1990).

M. Cherif Bassiouni, *Draft Statute: International Criminal Tribunal*, 15 NOVA L. REV. 373 (1991)

M. Cherif Bassiouni, *Effective National and International Action Against Organized Crime and Terrorist Criminal Activities* 4 EMORY INT'L L. REV. 9 (1990)

M. Cherif Bassiouni, *Extradition Reform Legislation in the United States: 1981-1983*, 17 AKRON L.REV. (1984)

M. Cherif Bassiouni, *A Functional Approach to 'General Principles of International Law,'* 11 MICH. J. INT'L L. (1990)

M. Cherif Bassiouni, *General Report on the Juridical Status of the Requested State Denying Extradition, in* PROCEEDINGS OF THE ELEVENTH INTERNATIONAL CONGRESS OF COMPARATIVE LAW *reprinted in* 30 AM. J. COMP. L. (1982)

M. Cherif Bassiouni, *Ideologically Motivated Offences and the Political Offence Exception in Extradition: A proposed juridical standard for an unruly problem*, 19 DEPAUL L. REV. 217 (1969)

M. Cherif Bassiouni, *The International Narcotics Control Scheme* in 1 INTERNATIONAL CRIMINAL LAW (M. Cherif Bassiouni ed., 1986)

M. Cherif Bassiouni, *Methodological Options for International Control of Terrorism, in* INTERNATIONAL TERRORISM AND POLITICAL CRIMES (M. Cherif. Bassiouni ed., 1975)

M. Cherif Bassiouni, *The Penal Characteristics of Conventional International Criminal Law,* 15 CASE W. RES. J. INT'L L. (1983)

M. Cherif Bassiouni, *Perspectives on the Transfer of Prisoners Between the United States and Mexico and the United States and Canada*, 11 VAND. J. TRANSNAT'L L. 249 (1978)

M. Cherif Bassiouni, *Policy Considerations on Inter-State Cooperation in Criminal Matters, in* PRINCIPLES AND PROCEDURES FOR A NEW TRANSNATIONAL CRIMINAL LAW (Albin Eser & Otto Lagodny eds., 1992)

M. Cherif Bassiouni, *Protections of Diplomats under Islamic Law*, 74 AM. J. INT'L L. 609 (1980)

M. Cherif Bassiouni, *Organized Crime and Terrorism*, 4 EMORY J. INT'L L. 90 (1990)

M. Cherif Bassiouni, *Sexual Violence: An Invisible Weapon of War in the Former Yugoslavia,* An Occasional Paper, DePaul International Human Rights Law Institute (1996)

M. Cherif Bassiouni, *Terrorism, Law Enforcement, and the Mass Media: Perspectives, Problems, Proposals,* 72 J. CRIM. L. & CRIMINOLOGY (1981)

M. Cherif Bassiouni, *The Time Has Come for an International Criminal Court*, 1 IND. INT'L AND COMP. L. REV. 1 (1991)

M. Cherif Bassiouni, *The United Nations Commission of Experts Established pursuant to Security Council Resolution 780 (1992),* 66 REVUE INTERNATIONALE DE DROIT PENAL, Nos. 1-2 (1995)

M. Cherif Bassiouni, *World Public Order and Extradition, in* AKTUELLE PROBLEME DES INTERNATIONALEN STRAFRECHT (Oehler & Potz eds., 1970)

Suzanne Bastid, *Les problomes territoriaux dans la jurisprudence de la Cour Internationale de Justice, in* III RECUEIL DES COURS, ACADIMIE DE DROIT INTERNATIONAL (1963)

Cheryl Benard, *Rape as Terror: The Case of Bosnia,* 6 TERRORISM & POL. VIOLENCE 29 (1994)

Christopher L. Blakesley, *Atrocity and Its Prosecution, in* WAR CRIMES: A SYNTHESIS OF INTERNATIONAL AND NATIONAL APPROACHES (1997)

Christopher L. Blakesley, *A Conceptual Framework for Extradition and Jurisdiction Over Extraterritorial Crime,* UTAH L.REV. (1984)

Christopher L. Blakesley, *Book Review,* 90 A.J.I.L. (1996)

Christopher L. Blakesley, *Comparing the Ad Hoc Tribunal for Crimes Against Humanitarian Law in the Former Yugoslavia and the Project for an International Criminal Court prepared by the International Law Commission,* 67 REVUE INTERNATIONALE DE DROIT PÉNAL (1996)

Christopher L. Blakesley, *Comparing the I.L.C. and Bosnia Tribunals,* 66 REVUE INTERNATIONALE DE DROIT PÉNAL (1995)

Christopher L. Blakesley, *A Conceptual Framework for Extradition and Jurisdiction over Extraterritorial Crimes*, 1984 UTAH L. REV. 685 (1984)

Christopher L. Blakesley, *Criminal Procedure*, *in* INTRODUCTION TO THE LAW OF THE UNITED STATES (1991)

Christopher L. Blakesley, *Criminal Procedure for Foreign Lawyers*, *in* INTRODUCTION TO THE LAW OF THE UNITED STATES (1992)

Christopher L. Blakesley, *Evisceration of the Political Offense Exception to Extradition,* 15 DEN.J.INT'L L & POL'Y 109, (1986)

Christopher L. Blakesley & Otto Lagodny, *Finding Harmony Amidst Disagreement Over Extradition, Jurisdiction, the Role of Human Rights*, 24 VAND .J. TRANSNAT'L L. (1991)

Christopher L. Blakesley, *International Extradition For Business Crimes*, *in* DOING BUSINESS ABROAD: IDENTIFYING AND AVOIDING CRIMINAL RISKS (1992)

Christopher L. Blakesley, *The Regionalization of International Criminal Law & the Protection of Human Rights in International Cooperation in Criminal Proceedings,* 65 REV. INT'L DE DROIT PÉNAL (1994)

Christopher L. Blakesley, *Report for the International Law Association, on Jurisdiction, Offenses, and Triggering Mechanisms for the War Crimes Tribunals*, 25 DEN.J.INT'L L. & POL'Y. (1997)

Christopher L. Blakesley, *Review Essay,* 62 REVUE INTERNATIONALE DE DROIT PÉNAL (1996)

Christopher L. Blakesley, *Review Essay: Comparative Law: Its Purposes & Possibilities,* 27 TEX. INT'L L.J. (1991)

Christopher L. Blakesley, *Terrorism: Problems Relating to and Conflicts of Jurisdiction, in* INTERNATIONAL TERRORISM: U.S. PROCEDURAL ASPECTS (M. Cherif Bassiouni ed., 1987)

Christopher L. Blakesley, *United States Jurisdiction Over Extraterritorial Crime,* 73 J.CRIM. L. & CRIMINOLOGY (1982)

James H. Bloem, *Treaty on Mutual Assistance in Criminal Matters between the United States and Switzerland,* 7 VAND. J. TRANSNAT'L L. 469 (1974)

David Boling, *Mass Rape, Enforced Prostitution, and the Japanese Imperial Army: Japan Eschews International Legal Responsibility?* 32 COLUM.J.TRANSNAT'L L. 533 (1995)

James E. Bond, *Application of the Law of War to Civil Conflicts*, 3 GA. J. INT'L & COMP. L. (1973)

Antonio Brancaccio, *Metodi di Cooperazione e Assistenza Giudiziaria, in* DIRITTO PENALE INTERNAZIONALE (1979)

Walter F. Brown, *Criminal Jurisdiction Over Visiting Naval Forces Under International Law*, 24 WASH. & LEE L. REV. 9 (1967)

Rupert Bruce, *Offshore Financial Centers Move to Shake the Stigma of Shadiness*, INT'L HERALD TRIB.,(Feb. 11, 1995)

Margaret Buckley, *Origins of Diplomatic Immunity in England,* 21 U. MIAMI L. REV (1966)

H. Buhler, Die Bedeutung auslandischer schweizerischem Recht, Diss. Koln 1 (1966).

Hedley Bull, *The Importance of Grotius in the Study of International Relations, in* HUGO GROTIUS AND INTERNATIONAL RELATIONS (Hedley. Bull,etal eds.., 1990)

Hedley Bull, *Martin Wight and the Theory of International Relations,* 2 BRIT. J. INT'L STUD. (1976)

Colm Campbell, *Extradition to Northern Ireland: Prospects and Problems*, 52 MOD. L. REV (1989)

Charles M. Carberry & Stuart E. Abrams, *The Money Laundering Laws — Civil and Criminal Ramifications*, CORPORATE COUNSEL'S QUARTERLY, Apr. 1990, at 88 (1990)

Scott Carlson & Bruce Zagaris, *International Cooperation in Criminal Matters: Western Europe's International Approach to International Crime*, 15 NOVA L. REV. 551 (1991)

Will H. Carroll, *Official Duty Cases Under Status of Forces Agreements: Modest Guidelines Toward a Definition,* 12 JAG L. REV. 284 (1970)

Larry Chamblee, *International Legal Assistance in Criminal Cases, in* 1 TRANSNATIONAL LITIGATION: PRACTICAL APPROACHES TO CONFLICTS AND ACCOMMODATIONS 188 (1984)

Bin Cheng, *Aviation, Criminal Jurisdiction and Terrorism: The Hague/Extradition Prosecution Formula and Attacks at Airports, in* CONTEMPORARY PROBLEMS OF INTERNATIONAL LAW: ESSAYS IN HONOUR OF GEORG SCHWARZENBERGER, (1988)

Roger Clark, *Crimes Against Humanity, in* THE NUREMBERG TRIAL AND INTERNATIONAL LAW (Georget Ginsburgs & Vladimir K. Kudraiavstev eds., 1990)

Roger S. Clark, *Crime: The UN Agenda on International Cooperation in the Criminal Process*, 15 NOVA L. REV. 475 (1991)

Comment, *The Right to Financial Privacy Versus Computerized Law Enforcement: A New Fight in an Old Battle*, 86 Nw. U.L. Rev. 1169 (1992)

G. Costa-Lascoux, *De Schengen à Maastricht: Libertés et contrôles dans l'Europe des citoyens, in* MÉLANGES OFFERTS À GEORGES LEVASSEUR 1992 (1992)

Declan Costello, *International Terrorism and the Development of the Principle aut dedere aut judicare*, 10, .J. INT'L L. & ECON. (1975)

William A. Crawford, *The Air Force Local Liaison Authority for Criminal Offenses in Germany*, 9 JAG L. REV. 11 (1967)

Anthony A. D'Amato, *Is International Law Really "Law"?* 79 NW. U.L. REV. 1293 (1984-85)

Anthony A. D'Amato, *Public International Law as a Career,* 1 AM. U.J. INT'L L. & POL'Y (1986)

Anthony A. D'Amato, *War Crimes and Vietnam: The "Nuremberg Defense" and the Military Service Register,* 57 CAL. L. REV. (1969)

Meir Dan-Cohen, *Decision Rules and Conduct Rules: On Acoustic Separation in Criminal Law,* 97 HARV. L. REV. 625 (1984)

L. Davis, *House Subcommittee Holds Hearings on Telemarketing Fraud and International Enforcement Efforts to Combat It*, 6 INT'L ENFORCEMENT L. REP. 336 (1990)

Werner De Capitani, *Internationale Rechtshilfe: Eine Standortbestimmung*, 100 REVUE DE DROIT SUISSE, II, 391 (1981)

Rene de Gouttes, *Variations sur L'Espace Judiciare Pénal Européen,* 33 RECEUIL DALLOZ SIREY 245 (1990)

Rene de Gouttes, *Vers un Espace Judiciare Pénal Pan Européen?*, 22 RECEUIL DALLOZ SIREY 154 (1991)

Georges R. Delaume, *Jurisdiction Over Crimes Committed Abroad: French and American Law,* 21 GEO. WASH. L. REV. (1952-53)

Brian DeSchutter, *International Criminal Cooperation the Benelux Example*, *in* A TREATISE ON INTERNATIONAL CRIMINAL LAW (M. Cherif Bassiouni & Ved P. Nanda eds., 1973)

Brian de Schutter, *International Criminal Law in Evolution: Mutual Assistance between the Benelux Countries,* 14 NEDERLANDS TIJDSCHRIFT VOOR INTERNATIONAAL RECHT (1967)

Brian DeSchutter, *Problems of Jurisdiction in the International Control and Repression of Terrorism, in* INTERNATIONAL TERRORISM AND POLITICAL CRIMES (M. Cherif. Bassiouni ed., 1975)

Deutsch, *Judicial Assistance: Obtaining Evidence in the United States under 28 U.S.C. § 1782, for Use in a Foreign or International Tribunal*, 5 B.C. INT'L & COMP. L. REV. 175, (1982)

Edwin D. Dickinson, *Is the Crime of Piracy Obsolete*?, 38 HARV.L.REV. (1925)

Janet Dine, *European Community Criminal Law?* CRIMINAL L. REV. 246 (1993)

Yoram Dinstein, *International Criminal Law*, 55 ISR. Y.B. HUMAN RIGHTS (1975)

Yoram Dinstein, *International Criminal Law*, 20 ISR. L. REV. (1985)

G.I.A.D. Draper, *The Modern Pattern of War Criminality*, ISR. Y.B. HUMAN .RIGHTS. 9 (1976)

Joseph J. Duffy & John A. Hedges, *United States Money Laundering Statutes: The Business Executive's Conundrum, in* INTERNATIONAL TRADE: AVOIDING CRIMINAL RISKS 14-1 (1991)

Dussaix, *Some problems arising from the practical application from the judicial point of view of the European Convention on Mutual Assistance in Criminal Matters, in* EUROPEAN COMMITTEE ON CRIME PROBLEMS, COUNCIL OF EUROPE, PROBLEMS ARISING FROM THE PRACTICAL APPLICATION OF THE EUROPEAN CONVENTION ON MUTUAL ASSISTANCE IN CRIMINAL MATTERS (1971)

Alan Ellis & Robert L. Pisani, *The United States Treaties on Mutual Legal Assistance in Criminal Matters, in* 2 INTERNATIONAL CRIMINAL LAW: PROCEDURE (M. Cherif Bassiouni ed., 1986)

William Empson, *The Application of Criminal Law to Acts Committed Outside the Jurisdiction,* 6 AM. CRIM. L. Q. (1967)

Helmut Epp, *Der Auslander im Strafvollzug unter besonderer Berücksichtigung der Übertragung der Strafvollstreckung*, 37 OSTERREICHISCHE JURISTEN-ZEITUNG 119 (1982)

Helmut Epp, *Der Frundsatz der identen Normen und die beiderseitige Strafbarkeit*, 36 OEJZ 197 (1981)

Valerie Epps, *The Political Offense Exception in the U.S. Extradition, in* LEGAL RESPONSES TO INTERNATIONAL TERRORISM (M. Cherif Bassiouni ed., 1987)

Albin Eser, *Common Goals and Different Ways in International Criminal Law, Reflections from a European Perspective*, 31 HARV. INT'L L.J. 125 (1990)

Tony Evans & Peter Wilson, *Regime Theory and the English School of International Relations: A Comparison,* 21 MILLENNIUM: J. OF INT'L STUD. (1992)

Richard Falk, *The Interplay of Westphalia and Charter Conceptions of International Legal Order, in* INTERNATIONAL LAW: A CONTEMPORARY PERSPECTIVE (Richard. Falk, eds., 1985)

Richard Falk, *A New Paradigm for International Legal Studies: Prospects and Proposals, in* INTERNATIONAL LAW: A CONTEMPORARY PERSPECTIVE (Richard. Falk, eds., 1985)

Fayard, *La localisation international de l'infraction,* 1968 REV.SCI.CRIM. ET DR.PÉN.COMP.

Shaul Z. Feller, *Jurisdiction Over Offenses With a Foreign Element, in* 2 A TREATISE ON INTERNATIONAL CRIMINAL LAW (M. Cherif Bassiouni & Ved P. Nanda, eds., 1973)

J.G. Fennessy, *The 1975 Vienna Convention on the Representation of States in Their Relations With International Organizations of a Universal Character*; 70 AM. J. INT'L L. 62(1976)

Cyrille Fijnaut, *The Schengen Treaties and European Police Cooperation*, EUR. J. CRIME, CRIM. L. & CRIM. JUST. 37 (1993)

Jean F. Flauss, *Le Principe "ne bis idem" dans le cadre de la convention européenne des droits de l'homme, bilan et perspectives, in* LE DROIT PÉNAL ET SES LIENS AVEC LES AUTRES BRANCHES DU DROIT, MÉLANGE EN L'HONNEUR DU PROFESSEUR JEAN GAUTHIER, REVUE PÉNALE SUISSE (1996)

James D. Harmon, *United States Money Laundering Laws: International Implications*, 9 N.Y.L. SCH. J. INT'L & COMP. L. 1, 25 (1988)

Henning Fode, *Cooperation on Law Enforcement, Criminal Justice and Legislation in Europe, Nordic Experience, in* FREE MOVEMENT OF PERSONS IN EUROPE (Henry G. Schermers et al. eds., 1993)

Lionel Frei, *Das neue Bundesgesetz uber Internationale Rechtshilfe in Strafsachen - Neue Losungen und neue Probleme*, 96 SCHW ZSTRR 57 (1983)

Lionel Frei & Stefan Trechsel, *Origins and Application of the U.S. - Switzerland Treaty on Mutual Assistance in Criminal Matters*, 31 HARV. INT' L L. J. 84 (1990)

Robert A. Friedlander, *The Enforcement of International Criminal Law: Fact or Fiction?,* 17 CASE W. RES. J. INT'L L. (1985)

Robert A. Friedlander, *The Origins of International Terrorism: A Micro Legal-Historical Perspective,* 6 ISR. Y.B. HUMAN RIGHTS. (1976)

Robert A. Friedlander, *Terrorism and National Liberation Movements: Can Rights Derive From Wrongs?,* 13 CASE W. RES. J. INT'L L.

Novella Galantini, *La Cooperazione Internazionale per la ricerca e l' acquisizione della prova, in* ARGOMENTI DI PROCEDURA PENALE INTERNAZIONALE 41, 66 (O. Doniniani ed., 1982)

Manuel R. Garcia-Mora, *Criminal Jurisdiction Over Foreigners for Treason and Offenses Against the Safety of the State Committed Upon Foreign Territory,* 19 U. PITT. L. REV. (1958)

Albert H. Garretson, *The Immunity of Representatives of Foreign States,* 41 N.Y.U. L. REV. 67 (1966)

Jean J. Gauthier, *La nouvelle legislation suisse sur l'entraide internationale in matiere penale*, 97 SCHWAZSTR 51 (1984)

Y. Gautier, *Accords de Schengen, in* EDITIONS DU JURIS-CLASSEUR 1996, EUROPE FASCICULE 140, DROIT INTERNATIONAL FASCICULE 408

Geck, *Hoheitsakte auf fremdem Staatsgebiet, in* 3 STRUPP-SCHLOCHAUER, WÖRTERBUCH DES VÖLKERRECHTS 795 (1962)

B.J. George, *Criminal Law Aspects of Legislation on the Prevention, Control and Suppression of Terrorism, International Terrorism, in* LEGAL RESPONSES TO INTERNATIONAL TERRORISM, (M. Cherif. Bassiouni ed., 1975)

B.J. George, *Extraterritorial Application of Penal Legislation,* 64 MICH. L. REV. (1966)

B.J. George, *Jurisdictional Bases for Criminal Legislation and Its Enforcement,* 1983 MICH. Y.B. INT'L L. 3,

B.J. George, *The United States in the Ryukyus: The Insular Cases Revised,* 39 N.Y.U.L.R 785, (1964)

William C. Gilmore, *International Responses to Money Laundering: A General Overview,* Conference Paper: The Money Laundering Conference, M.L 92(10) (Strasbourg, Sept. 28-30, 1992)

Riccardo Gori-Montanelli and David A. Botwinik. *International Judicial Assistance, Italy,* 9 INT'L LAW. 722 (1975)

Leslie C. Green, *An International Criminal Code Now?* 3 DALHOUSIE L.J. 560 (1976)

Leslie C. Green, *Trends in the Law Concerning Diplomats*, 1981 CAN. Y.B. INT'L L. 132, (1981).

Nicholas Greenwood Onuf, *Civitas Maxima: Wolff, Vattel and the Fate of Republicanism,* 88 AM. J. INT'L L. 280 (1994)

Leo Gross, *The Case Concerning United States Diplomatic and Consular Staff in Tehran: Phase of Provisional Measures*, 74 AM. J. INT'L L. 395 (1980)

Heinrich Grutzner, *International Judicial Assistance and Cooperation in Criminal Matters, in* 2 A TREATISE ON INTERNATIONAL CRIMINAL LAW (M. Cherif Bassiouni & Ved P. Nanda eds. 1973)

Heinrich Grutzner, *Die zwischenstaatliche Anerkennung europaischer Strafurteile*, 22 NJW 345 (1969)

Perry Gulbrandsen, *Humanitarian Law of Armed Conflicts*, *in* 1 A TREATISE ON INTERNATIONAL CRIMINAL LAW (M. Cherif Bassiouni and Ved. P. Nanda eds., 1973)

Paul Gully-Hart, *Loss of Time through Formal and Procedural Requirements in International Cooperation, in* 33 PRINCIPLES AND PROCEDURES FOR A NEW TRANSNATIONAL CRIMINAL LAW, REPORTS AND MATERIALS FROM THE MAX PLANCK INSTITUTE 257-58 (Albin Eser & Otto Lagodny eds., 1991)

Paul Gully-Hart, *Obtaining Evidence in the Civil Law System, in* THE ALLEGED TRANSNATIONAL CRIMINAL(Richard D. Atkins ed., 1995)

James D. Harmon, *United States Money Laundering Laws: International Implications*, 9 N.Y.L. SCH. J. INT'L & COMP. L. 1 (1988)

Erik Harremoes, *Une nouvelle Convention du Conseil de l'Europe: le transferement des personnes condamnees*, 1983 REVUE DE SCIENCE CRIMINELLE ET DROIT PÉNAL COMPARÉ 235 (1983)

Stratton Health, *Status of forces Agreements as a Basis for United States Custody of an Accused,* 49 MIL. L. REV. 45(1970)

Philip B. Heymann & Ian H. Gershengorn, *Pursuing Justice, Respecting the Law,* 3 CRIM.L.F. (1991)

Rosalyn Higgins, *Recent Development in the Law of Sovereign Immunity in the United Kingdom,* 71 AM. J. INT'L L. 423 (1977)

Mark J. Hoffman, *Normative Approaches, in* INTERNATIONAL RELATIONS: A HANDBOOK OF CURRENT THEORY (M. Light & A.J.R. Groom eds., 1985)

Adolph Homberger, *Enforcement of Foreign Judgments,* 18 AM. J. COMP. L. (1970)

Manley O. Hudson, *The Sixth year of the Permanent Court of International Justice*, 22 AM. J. INT'L L. (1928).

Robert Y. Jennings, *Treaties as 'Legislation,' in* JUS ET SOCIETAS: ESSAYS IN TRIBUTE TO WOLFGANG FRIEDMANN (G. M. Wilner ed., 1979)

Robert Y. Jennings, *Extraterritorial Jurisdiction and the United States Antitrust Laws,* 33 BRIT. Y.B. INT'L (1957)

Robert Y. Jennings, *Treaties, in* INTERNATIONAL LAW: ACHIEVEMENTS AND PROSPECTS (Mohammed Bedjaoui ed., 1991)

Hans-Heinrich Jescheck, *Rapport general provisoire*, 34 REVUE INTERNATIONAL DE DROIT PÉNAL 209 (1963).

Larry D. Johnson, *The International Tribunal for Rwanda,* 67 REVUE INTERNATIONALE DE DROIT PÉNAL (1996)

Paul W. Johnson, *Judicial Assistance, Criminal Procedure, Treaty With Switzerland Affects Banking Secrecy Law, Provisions Against Organized Crime Set New Precedent*, 15 HARV. J. INT'L L. 360 (1974)

Henry L. Jones, *International Judicial Assistance: Procedural Chaos and a Program for Reform,* 62 YALE L.J. 520 (1953)

Barry Kellman & David S. Gualtieri, *Barricading the Nuclear Window: A Legal Regime to Curtail Nuclear Smuggling,* 3 U. ILL. L. REV. 667 (1996)

William S. Kenney, *Structures and Methods of International and Regional Cooperation in Penal Matters*, 29 N.Y. L. SCH. L. REV. 65 (1984)

Archibald King, *Further Developments Concerning Jurisdiction Over Friendly Foreign Armed Forces*, 40 AM. J. INT'L L. 257 (1946)

Archibald King, *Jurisdiction Over Friendly Foreign Armed Forces*, 36 AM. J. INT'L L. 539 (1942)

James K. Knapp, *Mutual Assistance Treaties as a Way to Pierce Bank Secrecy,* 20 CASE W. RES. J. INT'L L. 413 (1988)

Krómpelman, *Bericht óber ein Kolloquium anlδsslich der konstituierenden Sitzung des Kuratoriums des Max-Planck-Instituts fór auslδndisches und internationales Strafrecht*, 79 ZEITSCHRIFT F'OR DIE GESAMTE STRAFRECHTSWISSENSCHAFT 390 (1967)

Mario Kronauer, *Information Given for Tax Purposes From Switzerland to Foreign Countries Especially to the United States for the Prevention of Fraud and the Like in Relation to Certain American Taxes*, 30 TAX L. REV. 47 (1974)

Luis Kutner, *A Legal Note on the Nixon Pardon: Equal Justice vis-B-vis Due Process,* 9 AKRON L. REV. 243 (1975)

Otto Lagodny, *The European Convention on the Suppression of Terrorism: A Substantial Step to Combat Terrorism?* 60 U.COLO. L. REV. (1989)

Otto Lagodny, *Grundkonstellationen des Internationalen Strafrechtes*, 101 ZEITSCHIFT FÜR DIE GESAMTE STRAFRECHTSWISSENSCHAFT 987 (1989)

Raimo Lahti, *Sub-regional Criminal Policy: The Experience of the Nordic Countries, in* SCANDINAVIAN CRIMINAL POLICY AND CRIMINOLOGY 1986-1990, 93-99 (Norman Bishop ed., 1990)

Steven J. Lepper, *The Legal Status of Military Personnel in United Nations Peace Operation: One Delegate's Analysis*, 18 HOUS. J. INT'L L 359, (1996)

Richard B. Lillich & John M. Paxman, *State Responsibility for Injuries to Aliens Occasioned by Terrorist Activities,* 26 AM. U.L.REV. (1977)

Robert Linke, *Aktuelle Fragen der Rechtshilfe in Strafsachen, in* NEUE ZEITSCHRIFT F'OR STRAFRECHT (1982)

Robert Linke, *Leitende Grundsatze der Reform des Auslieferungs und Rechtshilferechts*, 52 OEJZ 365 (1980)

Robert Linke, *Wechselseitige Anerkennung und Vollstreckung europascher Strafurteile*, 26 OEJZ 29 (1971)

Oliver Lissitzyn, *In Flight Crime and the United States Legislation,* 67 A.J.I.L. (1973)

Steven Lubet & Jan Stern Reed, *Extradition of Nazis from the US to Israel: A Survey of Issues in Transnational Criminal Law,* 22 STAN.J.INT'L L. (1986)

Luther, *Zum Verbrauch der Strafklage im Internationalen Recht*, 1969 NJW 1027.

Curt Markees, *The Difference in Concept Between Civil and Common Law Countries as to Judicial Assistance and Cooperation in Criminal Matters*, *in* 2 A TREATISE ON INTERNATIONAL CRIMINAL LAW (M. Cherif Bassiouni & Ved P. Nanda eds., 1973)

G. Marston, *Crimes on Board Foreign Merchant Ships at Sea: Some Aspects of English Practice,* 88 L.Q.REV. (1972)

Howard E. Martin, *International Judicial Assistance, Letters Rogatory, Federal Courts Are to Grant Assistance Only To Those Foreign Bodies That Qualify As Tribunals Under 28 USC §1782*, 9 TEX. INT'L L. J. 108 (1974)

David McClean, *Mutual assistance in criminal matters: the Commonwealth initiative*, 14 COMMONWEALTH L. BULL. 841 (1988)

Jeffrey Allan McCredie, *Contemporary Uses of Force Against Terrorism: The U.S. Response to Achille Lauro —Questions of Jurisdiction and Its Exercise,* 16 GA. J. INT'L & COMP. L. (1986)

Walter Meier, *Banking Secrecy in Swiss and International Taxation*, 7 INT'L LAW. 19 (1973)

Theodor Meron, *Nonextradition of Israeli National and Extraterritorial Jurisdiction Reflections on Bill No. 1306,* 13 ISR. L. REV. (1978)

Theodor Meron, *War Crimes in Yugoslavia and the Development of International Law*, 88 AM. J. INT'L L. (1994)

Thomas Merton, *The Plague of Albert Camus: A Commentary and Introduction*, (originally in pamphlet, Seabury Press, 1968), *reprinted in* THOMAS MERTON, THE LITERARY ESSAYS OF THOMAS MERTON (Brother Patrick Hart ed., 1981)

Jurgen Meyer, *German Criminal Law Relating to International Terrorism*, 60 U. COLO .L .REV. (1989)

John Bassett Moore, *Report on Extraterritorial Crime and the Cutting Case*, 1887 FOR. REL.

Thomas O. Moore, *Judicial Cooperation in the Taking of Evidence Abroad*, 8 TEX. INT'L L.J. 57 (1973)

Gerhard O. W. Mueller, *Enforcement Models of International Criminal Law, in* NEW HORIZONS IN INTERNATIONAL CRIMINAL LAW (1985).

Gerhard O. W. Mueller, *International Criminal Law: Civitas Maxima -- An Overview,* 15 CASE W. RES. J. INT'L L. (1983)

Gerhard O. W. Mueller, *International Judicial Assistance in Criminal Matters, in* INTERNATIONAL CRIMINAL LAW (Gerhard O.W. Mueller & Edward M. Wise eds., 1965)

Gerhard O.W. Mueller, *International Judicial Assistance in Criminal Matters*, 7 VILL. L. REV. 196 (1962).

Ekkehart Müller-Rappard, *The European Response to International Terrorism, in* LEGAL RESPONSES TO INTERNATIONAL TERRORISM: U.S. PROCEDURAL ASPECTS 409 (M. Cherif Bassiouni ed., 1988)

Ekkehart Müller-Rappard, *The European System, in* 2 INTERNATIONAL CRIMINAL LAW: PROCEDURE (M. Cherif Bassiouni ed. 1986)

John F. Murphy, *Legal Controls and the Deterrence of Terrorism: Performance and Prospects*, 13 RUTGERS L. J. 465 (1982)

Ethan A. Nadelmann, *Negotiations in Criminal Law Assistance Treaties*, 33 AM. J. INT'L. L. 467 (1985)

Newcomb, *United States Litigation and Foreign Bank Secrecy: The Origins of Conflict*, 9 N.Y.L. SCH. J. INT'L. & COMP. L. 47 (1988)

Hans G. Nilsson, *The Council of Europe Laundering Convention: A Recent Example of a Developing International Criminal Law*, 2 CRIM. L. F. 419 (1991)

Note, *The International Attack on Money Laundering: European Initiatives*, 1991 DUKE J. COMP. & INT'L L. 213 (1991)

Note, *Political Legitimacy in the Law of Political Asylum*, 99 HARV. L. REV. 450 (1985)

Note, *Putting Starch in European Efforts to Combat Money Laundering*, 60 FORDHAM L. REV. 429, (1992)

Note, *Recordkeeping and Reporting in an Attempt to Stop the Money Laundering Cycle: Why Blanket Recording and Reporting of Wire and Electronic Funds Transfers is Not the Answer*, 66 NOTRE DAME L. REV. 863 (1990)

Pietro Nuvolone, *Die Kollisionsnormen auf dem Gebiet des Strafrechts in Europa*, 66 ZEITSCHRIFT FÜR DIE GESAMTE STRAFRECHTSWISSENSCHAFT 567 (1954).

Dietrich Oehler, *The European System, in* 2 INTERNATIONAL CRIMINAL LAW: PROCEDURE (M. Cherif Bassiouni ed. 1986)

Dietrich Oehler, *Recognition of Foreign Penal Judgments and Their Enforcement, in* 2 A TREATISE ON INTERNATIONAL CRIMINAL LAW (M. Cherif Bassiouni & Ved P. Nanda eds., 1973)

Patrick J. O'Keefe, *Privileges and Immunities of the Diplomatic Family,* 25 INT'L & COMP. L. Q. 329 (1976)

David O'Keeffe, *The Schengen Convention: A Suitable Model for European Integration?,* 11 Y.B. EUR. L., 185 (1991)

Didier Opertti, *Juridical Mutual Cooperation in Criminal Matters: The Latest Trends in the Inter-American System and the Bilateral Treaties Between the United States and Latin-American Countries*, 39 NETHERLANDS INT'L L. REV. 89 (1992)

Krishna Patel, *Recognizing the Rape of Bosnian Women as Gender-Based Persecution*, 60 BROOK. L. REV. 929 (1994)

Jordan Paust, *Aggression Against Authority: The Crime of Oppression, Politicize and Other Crimes Against Human Rights,* 18 CASE W. RES. J. INT'L L. (1986)

Jordan Paust, *Applicability of International Criminal Laws to Events in the Former Yugoslavia*, 9 AM.U.J. INT'L L.& POL. 499, (1994)

Jordan Paust, *Customary International Law: Its Nature, Sources and Status of Law of the United States,* 12 MICH. J. INT'L L. 59 (1990)

Jordan Paust, *Congress and Genocide: They're Not Going to Get Away With It*, 11 MICH.J.INT'L L. (1989)

Jordan Paust, *Federal Jurisdiction over Extraterritorial Acts of Terrorism and Nonimmunity for Foreign Violators of International Law Under the FSIA and the Act of State Doctrine,* 23 VA. J. INT'L L. (1983)

Rollin M. Perkins, *The Territorial Principle in Criminal Law*, 22 HASTINGS L.J. (1971)

Rachael Pine, *Pregnancy as Evidence of a Crime*, 94 NAT'L L.J. 15.1 (Jan. 24, 1994)

Mario Pisani, *Italia-Stati Uniti d'America: Appunti sul nuovo Trattato di Estradizione* 18 L'INDICE PENALE 398 (1984)

Michal Plachta, *Foreign Offenders in Prison: A Social and Legal Problem*, *in* TRANSFER OF PRISONERS UNDER INTERNATIONAL INSTRUMENTS AND DOMESTIC LEGISLATION (1993)

Michal Plachta, *Sentencing Policy Towards Foreigners*, *in* TRANSFER OF PRISONERS UNDER INTERNATIONAL INSTRUMENTS AND DOMESTIC LEGISLATION (1993)

Dominique Poncet & Paul Gully-Hart, *Le principe de la spécialité en matière d'extradition, in* INTERNATIONAL REVIEW OF PENAL LAW (EXTRADITION), (1991)

Brian Porter, *Patterns of Thought and Practice: Martin Wight's 'International Theory.' in* THE REASON OF STATES (M. Donelan ed., 1978)

Theodore R. Posner, *Alien Tort Claims Act — Genocide — War Crimes — Violations of International Law by Non-State Actors: Kadic v. Karadzic, 70 F.2d 232 (2d Cir.1996), cert. denied 64 U.S.L.W. 3832 (June 18, 1996)*, 90 A.J.I.L. 658 (1996)

Vladimir S. Pozdniakov, *The Legal Status of Soviet Trade Representations Abroad*, 5 DENV. J. INT'L L. & POL'Y. 261 (1975)

A. Kenneth Pye, *Recognition of Foreign Criminal Judgments*, *in* INTERNATIONAL CRIMINAL LAW, (Gerhard O.W. Mueller & Edward M. Wise eds., 1965)

Christopher Pyle, *The November Treaty Approved, in* LEGAL RESPONSES TO INTERNATIONAL TERRORISM (M. Cherif Bassiouni ed., 1987)

Amir Rafat, *The Iran Hostage Crisis and the International Court of Justice: Aspects of the Case Concerning United States Diplomatic and Consular Staff in Tehran*, 10 DENV. J. INT'L L. & POL'Y. 425 (1981)

Kenneth C. Randall, *Universal Jurisdiction Under International Law*, 66 TEXAS L. REV. (1988)

Lene Ravn, *Er det nordiske samarbejdsmodel forældet (Is the Nordic model of cooperation outdated)? in* KRIMINALISTIK INSTITUTS ÅRBORG(1994)

Willis L. M. Reese, *Limitations on Extraterritorial Application of Law,* 4 DALHOUSIE L.J. (1978)

Francesco D. Riccioli, *L' accordo fra Italia e Stati Uniti etc., in* LA RIVISTA DI DIRITTO INTERNAZIONALE (1977)

D. Richard, *Une contribution européenne aux tendances actuelles du droit extraditionnel: la Convention du 27 septembre 1996, in* LA SEMAINE JURIDIQUE, 3988, ÉDITION GÉNÉRALE N 1, (1997)

Bruno K. Ristau, *International Cooperation in Penal Matters: The Lockheed Agreements, in* MICH. Y.B. INT'L LEGAL STUD. 91-93

Guy B. Roberts, *The New Rules for Waging War: The Case Against Ratification of Additional Protocol I,* 26 VA.J.INT'L L. (1986)

Mark Rosenthal, *Jurisdictional Conflicts Between Sovereign Nations,* 19 INT'L L. (1985)

C. Rouiller, *L'évolution du concept de délit politique en droit de l'entraide internationale en matière pénale*, REVUE PÉNALE SUISSE 40-41 (1986)

C. Rouiller, *L'extradition du condamné par défaut: illustration des rapports entre l'ordre constitutionel et autonome le "Jus cogens" et le droit des traités, in* DE LA CONSTITUTION, ETUDES EN L'HONNEUR DE JEAN-FRANÇOIS (Aubert et al., eds., 1996)

Arthur W. Rovine, *The Contemporary International Legal Attack on Terrorism,* 3 ISR. Y.B.HUMAN RIGHTS. (1973)

Alfred P. Rubin, *Can the United States Police the World?*, 13 THE FLETCH. F. (1989)

Alfred P. Rubin, *International Law and the Use of Force by National Liberation Movements*, 13 THE FLETCH. F. (1989)

Michael H. Ryan, *The Status of Agents on Special Mission in Customary International Law*, 1978 CAN.Y.B. INT'L L. 157

Sahovic & Bishop, *The Authority of the State: Its Range with Respect to Persons and Places, in* MANUAL OF PUBLIC INTERNATIONAL LAW (Max Sorensen ed., 1968)

Ernesto Savona, *Mafia Money Laundering Versus Italian Legislation*, EUR. J. CRIM. POL'Y & RES. (June 1993).

L. Sbolci, *Il Principio di specialità dell' estradizione nel diritto internazionale, in* RIVISTA DI DIRITTO INTERNAZIONALE (1980)

Dominique Schouwey, *Nouvelles perspectives pur les ressortissants suisses condamnes a Petranger*, 3 REVUE INTERNATIONALE DE CRIMINOLOGIE ET DE POLICE TECHNIQUE 342 (1985)

Peter Schroth, *Bank Confidentiality and the War on Money Laundering in the United States*, 42 AM. J. COMP. L. 369, (1994)

Hans Schultz, *Bemerkungen zum Verhältnis von Völkerrecht und Landesrecht im Strafrecht*, 19 ANNUAIRE SUISSE DE DROIT INT'L 9, (1962).

Hans Schultz, *The Classic Law of Extradition and Contemporary Needs, in* 2 TREATISE ON INTERNATIONAL CRIMINAL LAW (M. Cherif. Bassiouni & Veel Nanda eds., 1973)

Hans Schultz, *Les principes du droit d'extradition traditionnel, in* COUNCIL OF EUROPE PUBLICATIONS: ASPECTS JURIDIQUES DE L'EXTRADITION ENTRE ETATS EUROPÉENS (1970)

Julian J. Schutte, *The European Market of 1993: Test for a Regional Model of Supranational Criminal Justice or of Interregional Cooperation in Criminal Law*, 3 CRIM. L.F. 77 (1991)

Julian J.E. Schutte, *Expanding the Scope of Extradition and Judicial Assistance and Cooperation in Penal Matters, in* NEW HORIZONS IN INTERNATIONAL CRIMINAL LAW (1985).

Julian J.E. Schutte, *Judicial Cooperation Under the Union Treaty, in* THE THIRD PILLAR OF THE EUROPEAN UNION (Jeorg Monar & Robert Morgan eds., 1994).

Julian J.E. Schutte, *Schengen: Its Meaning for the Free Movement of Persons in Europe,* 28 COMMON MKT. L. REV. 549 (1991)

Georg Schwarzenberger, *Civitas Maxima?, reprinted in* GEORG SCHWARZENBERGER, THE DYNAMICS OF INTERNATIONAL LAW (1976)

Edmund H. Schwenk, *Jurisdiction of the Receiving State Over Forces of the Sending State Under the NATO Status of Forces Agreement*, 6 INT'L LAW 525 (1972)

Hanna G. Sevenster, *Criminal Law and EEC Law*, 29 COMMON MKT. L. REV. 24 (1992)

Helen Silving, *In re Eichmann: A Dilemma of Law and Morality,* 55 AM. J. INT'L L. (1961)

David Simonetti & Bruce Zagaris, *International Terrorism: Italian Investigation into International Terrorism,* 2 INT'L ENFORCEMENT L.REP. (1986)

Hans Smit, *International Litigation under the United States Code*, 65 COLUM. L. REV. 1015 (1965)

William J. Snider, *Developments in Criminal Law and Criminal Justice: International Cooperation in the Forfeiture of Illicit Drug Proceeds*, 6 CRIM. L. F. 377(1995)

Felix Soh, *Cleaning Up Dirty Money,* THE STRAITS TIMES (Singapore),(Jan. 8, 1995)

J. G. Starke, *The Influence of Grotius upon the Development of International Law in the Eighteenth Century, in* GROTIAN SOCIETY PAPERS (C.H. Alexandrowicz ed., 1972)

David P. Stewart, *Internationalizing The War on Drugs: The U.N. Convention Against Illicit Traffic in Narcotic Drugs and Psychotropic Substances,* 18 DENV. J. INT'L L. & POL'Y 387 (1990)

A.H.J. Swart, *Human Rights and the Abolition of Traditional Principles, in* 33 PRINCIPLES AND PROCEDURES FOR A NEW TRANSNATIONAL CRIMINAL LAW, REPORTS AND MATERIALS FROM THE MAX PLANCK INSTITUTE (Albin Eser & Otto Lagodny eds., (1991)

A.H.J. Swart, *Police and Security in the Schengen Agreement and the Schengen Convention, in* SCHENGEN, INTERNATIONALIZATION OF CENTRAL CHAPTERS OF THE LAW ON ALIENS, REFUGEES, PRIVACY, SECURITY AND THE POLICE (Henri Meijers ed., 1991)

Paul W. Tappan, *Pre-Classical Penology, in* ESSAYS IN CRIMINAL SCIENCE (GerhardO.W. Mueller ed., 1961)

Klaus Tiedemann, *Privatdienstliche Amtshandlungen im Ausland - strafprozessuales Verwertungsverbot?, in* FESTSCHRIFT FÜR BOCKELMANN (1979)

Michael E. Tigar & Austin J. Doyle Jr., *International Exchange of Information in Criminal Cases,* 1983 MICH. Y.B. INT'L LEGAL STUD. 62

Katarina Tomaševski, *Data on foreigners, in* FOREIGNERS IN PRISON (1994)

Katarina Tomaševski, *Gaps in the legal protection of foreigners, in* FOREIGNERS IN PRISON (1994)

Katarina Tomaševski, *Guidance for prison administrations, in* FOREIGNERS IN PRISON (1994)

Katarina Tomaševski, *Protection against ill-treatment, in* FOREIGNERS IN PRISON (1994)

Ole Träskman, *Should we take the Condition of Double Criminality Seriously? in* DOUBLE CRIMINALITY, STUDIES IN INTERNATIONAL CRIMINAL LAW (Nils Jareborg ed., 1989)

Christine Van Den Wyngaert, *La Belgique et l'exception politique en matière d'extradition,* in 59 REVUE DE DROIT PÉNAL ET DE CRIMINOLOGIE, 833 (1970)

Christine Van den Wyngaert, *Criminal Law and the European Communities: Defining Issues, in* TRANSNATIONAL ASPECTS OF CRIMINAL PROCEDURE (1983).

Christine Van den Wyngaert, *L'Espace Judiciare Européen Face a L'Euro-Terrorisme et la Sauvegarde des Droits Fondamentaux,* 3 REVUE INTERNATIONALE DE CRIMINOLOGIE ET LA POLICE TECHNIQUE 289 (1980)

Christine Van den Wyngaert, *L'Espace Judiciare Europeen: Vers une Fissure au Sein du Conseil de L'Europe?* 61 REV. DROIT PÉNAL ET DE CRIM. 511 (1981)

Christine Van den Wyngaert & G. Stessens, *Mutual Legal Assistance in Criminal Matters in the European Union, in* CHANGES IN SOCIETY, CRIME AND CRIMINAL JUSTICE IN EUROPE: CHALLENGE FOR A CRIMINOLOGICAL EDUCATION AND RESEARCH: 2 INTERNATIONAL ORGANIZED AND CORPORATE CRIME 137-76 (Cyrille Fejnaut, Johan Goethals et al. eds., 1996)

Christine Van den Wyngaert, *The Political Offense Exception to Extradition: How to Plug the Terrorist's Loophole Without Departing from Fundamental Human Rights, in* 62 REVUE INTERNATIONALE DE DROIT PÉNAL (Nos. 1-2. 1991).

Christine Van den Wyngaert, *Rethinking the Law of International Criminal Cooperation: the Restrictive Function of International Human Rights through Individual-oriented Bars, in* 33 PRINCIPLES AND PROCEDURES FOR A NEW TRANSNATIONAL CRIMINAL LAW, REPORTS AND MATERIALS FROM THE MAX PLANCK INSTITUTE 496 (A. Eser & O. Lagodny eds., 1991)

Gerard Wyrsch, *Treasury Regulation of International Wire Transfer and Money Laundering: A Case for a Permanent Moratorium*, 20 DENV. J. INT'L L. & POL'Y 515 (1992).

Eduardo Vetere, *The Role of the United Nations Working for More Effective International Cooperation in* PRINCIPLES AND PROCEDURES FOR A NEW TRANSNATIONAL CRIMINAL LAW (Albin Eser & Otto Lagodny eds., 1992)

John K. Villa, *A Critical View of Bank Secrecy Act Enforcement and the Money Laundering Statutes*, 37 CATH. U. L. REV. 489 (1988).

R. J. Vincent, *Order in International Politics, in* ORDER AND VIOLENCE: HEDLEY BULL AND INTERNATIONAL RELATIONS (J. D. B. Miller & R. J. Vincent eds., 1990)

Theo Vogler, *Das neue Gesetz über die internationale Rechtshilfe in Strafsachen*, 36 NJW 2114 (1983)

Theo Vogler, *The Expanding Scope of International Judicial Assistance and Cooperation in Legal Matters*, DIE FRIEDENS WARTE BAND 66, Heft 3-4, 287 (1986)

Theo Vogler, *Perspectives on Extradition and Terrorism, in* INTERNATIONAL TERRORISM AND POLITICAL CRIMES (M. Cherif. Bassiouni ed., 1975)

Colin Warbrick, *The Criminal Justice Act 1988 (1) The New Law on Extradition*, 4 CRIM. L. REV. 14 (1989)

Ruth Wedgwood, *War Crimes in the Former Yugoslavia: Comments on the International War Crimes Tribunal,* 34 VA. J. INT'L L. (1994)

Prosper Weil, *Towards Normative Relativity in International Law?* 77 AM.J.INT'L L. (1983)

Nicholas J. Wheeler, *Pluralist or Solidarist Conceptions of International Society: Bull and Vincent on Humanitarian Intervention,* 21 MILLENNIUM: J. OF INT'L STUD. (1992)

Martin Wight, *An Anatomy of International Thought*, 13 REV. INT'L STUD. (1987)

Martin Wight, *The Balance of Power and International Order, in* THE BASES OF INTERNATIONAL ORDER (A. James ed., 1973)

D.S. Wijewardane, *Criminal Jurisdiction Over Visiting Forces With Special Reference to International Forces*, 1965 BRIT. Y.B. INT'L LAW 122

Peter Wilkitzki, *Defences, Exceptions and Exemptions in the Extradition Law and Practice in the Criminal Policy of the Federal Republic of Germany, in* INTERNATIONAL REVIEW OF PENAL LAW (EXTRADITION) (1991)

Peter Wilkitzki, *Rechtshilfe durch Vollstreckung*, 37 (N.S.) JR 227 (1983)

M. D. Wims, *Reexamining the Traditional Exceptions to Extradition, in* INTERNATIONAL REVIEW OF PENAL LAW (EXTRADITION) (1991)

Edward M. Wise, Book Review, 30 AM. J. COMP. L. 362 (1982)

Edward M. Wise, *Extradition: The Hypothesis of a Civitas Maxima and the Maxim Aut Dedere Aut Judicare* 109, in 62 REVUE INTERNATIONALE DE DROIT PÉNAL (NOS. 1-2. 1991)

Edward M. Wise, *International Crimes and Domestic Criminal Law,* 38 DEPAUL L. REV. (1989)

Edward M. Wise, *Prolegomenon to the Principles of International Criminal Law*, 16 N.Y.L.F. 562 (1970)

Edward M. Wise, *Some Problems of Extradition*, 15 WAYNE L. REV. 709 (1969)

Edward M. Wise, *Terrorism and the Problems of an International Criminal Law*, 19 CONN. L. REV. (1987)

Ellen Yearwood, *Data Bank Control, in* LEGAL RESPONSES TO INTERNATIONAL TERRORISM, U.S. PROCEDURAL ASPECTS (M. Cherif Bassiouni ed., 1988)

Bruce Zagaris & Castilla, *Constructing an International Financial Enforcement Subregime: The Implementation of Anti-Money-Laundering Policy*, 19 BROOKLYN J. INT'L L. 872 (1993).

Bruce Zagaris, *Developments in International Judicial Assistance and Related Matters*, 18 DENV. J. INT'L L. & POL'Y 339 (1990)

Bruce Zagaris, *Dollar Diplomacy: International Enforcement of Money Movement and Related Matters - A United States Perspective*, 22 GEO. WASH. J. INT'L. LAW & ECON. 465, (1989)

Bruce Zagaris, *Exchange of information Outside Tax Agreements*, *in* INTERNATIONAL EXCHANGE OF TAX INFORMATION RECENT DEVELOPMENTS 63, 94-98 (R. Gordon & Bruce Zagaris eds., 1985)

Bruce Zagaris & Razdan, *Florida Bankers Are Concerned about Judicial Assistance to Law Enforcement Officials in the Absence of a Treaty and a Court Request*, 4 INT'L ENFORCEMENT L. REP. 366 (Nov., 1988)

Bruce Zagaris, *International Tax and Related Crimes: Gathering Evidence, Comparative Ethics, and Related Matters* in THE ALLEGED TRANSNATIONAL CRIMINAL 364 (R. Atkins ed., 1995)

Bruce Zagaris, *International Enforcement Matters-Money Movement and Related Matters*, *in* 1 FIFTH ANNUAL INTERNATIONAL INSTITUTE ON INTERNATIONAL TAXATION (Fla. Bar Jan. 15-16, 1987)

Bruce Zagaris & David Simonetti, *Judicial Assistance Under Bilateral Treaties to Combat International Terrorism, in* LEGAL RESPONSES TO INTERNATIONAL TERRORISM: U.S. PROCEDURAL ASPECTS (M. Cherif Bassiouni ed., 1987)

Bruce Zagaris, *Mark Rich Caves In*, 46 TAXES INT'L, 55(Aug. 1983)

Bruce Zagaris, *Mark Rich and Similar Cases Prompt Other Countries to Assert Their Sovereignty*, 48 TAXES INT'L,(Oct. 1983)

Bruce Zagaris & Scott B. MacDonald, *Money Laundering, Financial Fraud, and Technology: The Perils of an Instantaneous Economy*, 26 GEO.WASH. J. INT'L L. & ECON. 62 (1992).

Bruce Zagaris, *Protecting the Rule of Law from Assault in the War Against Drugs and Narco-Terrorism*, 15 NOVA L. REV. 703 (1991)

Bruce Zagaris, *U.N. Drug Convention Signed*, 5 INT'L ENF.L.REP. (Mar. 1989)

Bruce Zagaris & S. Gardner, *U.S. Circuit Court Considers Letters Rogatory from Scotland Yard*, 5 INT'L ENFORCEMENT L. REP. 12 (Jan. 1989)

Bruce Zagaris & Jay Rosenthal, *United States Jurisdictional Considerations in International Criminal Law,* 15 CAL. W. INT'L L.J. (1985)

Bruce Zagaris et. al., *The U.S. and U.K. Lock Horns Over a U.S. Transfer-Pricing Criminal Investigation,* 44 TAXES INT'L, 11 (June 1983)

Section I

Modalities

Policy Considerations on Inter-State Cooperation in Criminal Matters[*]

M. Cherif Bassiouni

Introduction

The same modalities and techniques of inter-state cooperation in penal matters are relied upon to enforce international, transnational, and domestic crimes. These modalities, which are independent of one another, are: extradition, mutual legal assistance in penal matters, transfer of prisoners, seizure and forfeiture of illicit proceeds of crime, recognition of foreign penal judgements, and transfer of penal proceedings. The order of their listing reflects the ranking of their level of recognition and application in states' practice. These modalities are independent of one another, and relied upon separately in the practice of states, which reduces their cumulative effect. As discussed below, they are rarely part of an integrated or unified text, either as convention or as part of national legislation. This lack of an integrated approach reduces the effectiveness of these modalities which can be best used as complementary to one another in order to avoid the gaps created by resorting to them singularly. Multilateral conventions on substantive ICL refer to them, but mostly in general terms. Specialized regional conventions developed mostly by the Council of Europe and the organizations of American States deal with these modalities in detail. They are also the object of bilateral treaties and national legislation.

Cumulatively, these modalities of inter-state cooperation are the foundation of ICL enforcement. Without them, international, transnational, and national crimes would be deprived of effective inter-state enforcement means.

International criminal law enforcement essentially relies on the "indirect enforcement scheme,"[1] whereby states carrying out their enforcement duties resort to these modalities. Multilateral conventions contain provisions on one or more of these modalities, but seldom do they provide detailed prescriptions for their application. Of all ICL Conventions, the 1988 Convention Against Illicit Traffic in Narcotic Drugs and Psychotropic Substances contains detailed provisions delineating a state's enforcement obligations.[2]

---

[*] This article was first published in Germany as part of the proceedings of an international workshop on "Principles and Procedures for a New Transnational Criminal Law," held at the Max-Planck Institute for Foreign and International Criminal Law, Freiburg, Germany, May 21-25 [1991].

[1] The "indirect enforcement scheme" derives from the notion that states obligate themselves, through various regional and international instruments, to carry out the enforcement of international criminal law. The "direct enforcement scheme," on the other hand, presupposes the existence of an international criminal code, an international criminal court, and the existence of international enforcement machinery. For a thorough discussion of both schemes and the Draft International Criminal Code and the Draft Statute for an International Criminal Tribunal, *see* M. CHERIF BASSIOUNI, A DRAFT INTERNATIONAL CRIMINAL CODE AND DRAFT STATUTE FOR AN INTERNATIONAL CRIMINAL TRIBUNAL (1987).

[2] The seizure and forfeiture of the illicit proceeds of crime has been an element of inter-state penal cooperation since the 1988 United Nations Convention Against Illicit Traffic in Narcotic Drugs and Psychotropic Substances, U.N. Doc. E/Conf./82/15 (1988), *reprinted in* 28 I.L.M. 493-526 (1989)[hereinafter U.N. Drug Convention] which contained such a provision. *See* U.N. Drug Convention, art. 5:

Each Party shall adopt such measures as may be necessary to enable confiscation of . . . proceeds

ICL instruments do not, however, deal with international law enforcement cooperation except through Interpol. But in recent times, inter-governmental groups have been established to coordinate inter-state law enforcement activities. Among these are the Council of Europe's "Pompidou Group"[3] whose subject matter is drugs, and the "Trevi Group"[4] which operates at the Cabinet and sub-Cabinet level of representation for purposes of enhancing cooperation against terrorism. That group consists of some European States, the U.S., Canada, and Japan. Lastly, another group is the "Financial Action Task Force"[5] which deals with money laundering.

The work done by police and intelligence agencies is crucial to the prevention, control and suppression of international, transnational and national criminality. It should be encouraged, but legally regulated. Absent such regulation, preferably by international conventions, there are dangers inherent in unstructured and legally uncontrolled law enforcement cooperation which are likely to produce: human rights abuses,[6] violations of privacy rights[7] and, at times, breaches of national sovereignty.[8]

> derived from . . . narcotic drugs and psychotropic substances, materials and equipment or other instrumentalities used in [the manufacture or distribution of narcotic drugs].
>
> Each Party shall also adopt such measures as may be necessary to enable its competent authorities to identify, trace, and freeze or seize proceeds, property, instrumentalities or any other things [used in or derived from narcotics manufacture or distribution].
>
> . . .
>
> Following a request made . . . by another Party . . . the Party in whose territory [the things requested] are situated shall . . . submit the request to its competent authorities . . .

Id.

The 1990 Council of Europe Convention on Laundering, Search, Seizure and Confiscation of the Proceeds from Crime, contains even more detailed and precise provisions governing the seizure and forfeiture of assets. Europ. T.S. No. 141, Nov. 8, 1990, *reprinted in* 30 I.L.M. 148 [hereinafter Eur. Conv. Money Laundering].

3 In response to terrorism and international criminality, the European Economic Community, via the "Trevi Group" and "Pompidou Group," has engaged in the interstate sharing of intelligence and police technology, exchange of police staff and information, and cooperation in public security. Like Interpol, both groups operate on the basis of operational police cooperation. Thus, neither group established a legal basis or an institutional structure for inter-state police cooperation. Ekkehart Müller-Rappard, *The European Response to International Terrorism, in* LEGAL RESPONSES TO INTERNATIONAL TERRORISM: U.S. PROCEDURAL ASPECTS 409-10 (M. Cherif Bassiouni ed., 1988).

4 *Id.*

5 *See* in this volume, M. Cherif Bassiouni and David Gualtieri, *International and National Responses to the Globalization of Money Laundering.*

6 Of particular concern in the realm of human rights are incidences of torture and kidnaping. For a discussion of the role of human rights in international police cooperation, and in relation to Interpol in particular, *see* Budimir Babovic, *Interpol and Human Rights*, INT'L CRIM. POLICE REV. 4 (July-Aug. 1990).

7 The use by national police agencies of computer databases to compile data on offenders rise to personal privacy concerns and the need to protect personal data privacy. For an analysis of government use of computer databases in the battle against terrorism, *see* Ellen Yearwood, *Data Bank Control, in* LEGAL RESPONSES TO INTERNATIONAL TERRORISM, U.S. PROCEDURAL ASPECTS 249-76 (M. Cherif Bassiouni ed., 1988) and Budimir Babovic, *Interpol and Human Rights*, INT'L CRIM. POLICE REV. 4 (July-Aug. 1990), discussing computerization and the protection of personal privacy and individual rights.

8 An example of this problem, which also implicates human rights and privacy concerns, is the cooperation between states in arranging the kidnaping or abduction of relators across national borders as an alternative to extradition. *See* M. CHERIF BASSIOUNI, INTERNATIONAL EXTRADITION: U.S. LAW AND PRACTICE, ch. IV (3d rev. ed., 1996)[hereinafter BASSIOUNI, EXTRADITION].

It should be noted that in the "Direct Enforcement Scheme" which now exists with the International Criminal Tribunal for the Former Yugoslavia (ICTY)[9] and International Criminal Tribunal for Rwanda (ICTR),[10] some of these modalities are relied upon. They are: extradition, referred to as surrender,[11] and mutual legal assistance. By implication, the judgements of the ICTFY and ICTR are to be enforced by all states because these bodies are subsidiary organs of the Security Council whose decisions are under Chapter VII of the United Nations Charter and binding on Member-States. Eventually, a permanent international criminal court would also rely on these same modalities.[12]

Enforcement Assumptions and Policies

As stated above, substantive ICL so far relies on the "indirect enforcement scheme" by which international duties are incumbent upon states who have voluntarily accepted them by virtue of treaty obligations and who enforce these obligations through their domestic criminal justice processes.

The maxim *aut dedere aut judicare*: to prosecute or extradite,[13] which some see as alternative and others as cumulative,[14] provide states with a choice. But so far it is not clearly established that such a duty exists for anything but certain international crimes of a *jus cogens* character. Some, like this writer, maintain that the duty is a *civitas maxima* which obligates all states under general international law to prosecute or extradite for all 25 categories of crimes. But that is a progressive view. The problem with the *aut dedere aut judicare* principle is that it does not provide content. Presumably the two-prong duty is predicated on an unarticulated premise, namely that the prosecution is to be effective and fair, and that the extradition be to a state whose prosecution will also be effective and fair. But nowhere do we find a clear statement as to these premises, nor are there guidelines for the resolution of conflicts between states in case of disagreement as to the effective execution of the dual obligation to prosecute or extradite. Lastly, the general treaty

---

[9] *See* M. CHERIF BASSIOUNI (WITH THE COLLABORATION OF PETER MANIKAS), THE LAW OF THE INTERNATIONAL CRIMINAL TRIBUNAL FOR THE FORMER YUGOSLAVIA 775-793 (1996) [hereinafter BASSIOUNI, YUGOSLAVIA TRIBUNAL], and VIRGINIA MORRIS & MICHAEL SCHARF, AN INSIDER'S GUIDE TO THE INTERNATIONAL CRIMINAL TRIBUNAL FOR THE FORMER YUGOSLAVIA (1995).

[10] *See* Larry Johnson, *The International Tribunal for Rwanda* 67 REVUE INTERNATIONALE DE DROIT PÉNAL 211 (1996), reprinted in Volume 3.

[11] *See* M. Cherif Bassiouni, *The United Nations Commission of Experts Established pursuant to Security Council Resolution 780 (1992),* 66 REVUE INTERNATIONALE DE DROIT PÉNAL, Nos. 1-2 (1995), and M. Cherif Bassiouni, *The Commission of Experts Established pursuant to Security Council Resolution 780: Investigation of Violations of International Humanitarian Law in the Former Yugoslavia,* 5 CRIM. L.F. 279-340 (1994).

[12] *See* Report of the Preparatory Committee on the Establishment of an International Criminal Court, Proceedings of the Preparatory Committee during March-April and August 1996), Volume I, GAOR., Supp. No. 22 (A/51/22), and Volume II, Compilation of proposals, GAOR, No. 22A (A/51/22).

[13] *See* BASSIOUNI, EXTRADITION, *supra* note 8, at § 2-3 (2d., 1987). *See also* Declan Costello, *International Terrorism and the Development of the Principle aut dedere aut judicare*, 10 J. INT'L L. & ECON. 483 (1975); Edward M. Wise, *Some Problems of Extradition*, 15 WAYNE L. REV. 709, 720-23 (1969); Edward M. Wise, *Prolegomenon to the Principles of International Criminal Law*, 16 N.Y.L.F. 562, 575 (1970).

[14] *See* CHRISTINE VAN DEN WYNGAERT, THE POLITICAL OFFENSE EXCEPTION TO EXTRADITION: THE DELICATE PROBLEM OF BALANCING THE RIGHTS OF THE INDIVIDUAL AND THE INTERNATIONAL WORLD PUBLIC ORDER 8, 158-62 (1980). *See* also Edward M. Wise, Book Review, 30 AM. J. COMP. L. 362, 370 n. 64 (1982). The issue was also discussed at the Eleventh International Congress on Comparative Law. *See generally* M. Cherif Bassiouni, *General Report on the Juridical Status of the Requested State Denying Extradition, in* PROCEEDINGS OF THE ELEVENTH INTERNATIONAL CONGRESS OF COMPARATIVE LAW *reprinted in* 30 AM. J. COMP. L. (1982).

obligation of "general faith" applies to states who are bound by treaty provisions concerning the duties of prosecution, extradition and mutual legal assistance. Thus, the implementation of these obligations remains imperfect for lack of norms.

To effectively carry out these obligations, states rely on international criminal procedural law, which relies, in turn, on modalities and techniques of inter-state penal cooperation. Any obligations, however, are limited to the extent and the manner in which these modalities are embodied in a state's respective domestic legislation. The very obligation to prosecute or extradite is, therefore, dependent upon what a state's national criminal justice system permits and is capable of executing.

ICL, however, has other international implementation mechanisms which include non-penal modalities that do not necessarily rely on domestic criminal justice processes. But these non-penal modalities are compliance-inducement mechanisms, whereas enforcement modalities rely on the coercive techniques of the domestic criminal justice processes of states and cooperating inter-governmental bodies like Interpol.

Integrating the Modalities of Inter-State Cooperation for the Prevention, Control and Suppression of International, Transnational and Domestic Criminality

The six modalities of inter-state cooperation arise under diverse law-making processes, namely: international, regional, and national ones. However, even within the context of these three law-making processes, the resulting product differs in scope and legal technique while lacking consistency and systematization. What is needed is the integration of these modalities into a comprehensive codification that would permit the cumulative and alternative utilization of these modalities to ensure their enhanced effectiveness. In this respect the national legislative approach adopted by Austria,[15] Germany[16] and Switzerland,[17] which integrates all of these modalities of inter-state penal cooperation, is a valuable model. Hungary, Czechoslovakia and other countries are also considering the integrated approach in their codification reforms. Under this approach, the modalities of inter-state cooperation operate like multiple gears in a single gear-box, allowing states to shift from one modality to the next instead of being limited to only one gear at a time. This same approach is needed at the regional and international levels. While a number of regional and sub-regional multilateral agreements have been developed, their elaboration has been piecemeal. None

---

[15] Austrian Law on Mutual Assistance in Criminal Matters, Bundesgesetz vom 4 Dezember 1979 über die Auslieferung und die Rechtshilfe in Strafsachen (Auslieferungs - und Rechtshilfegesetz -ARHG), BGBI, Nr. 529/1979. *See also* KLAUS SCHWAIGHOFER, AUSLIEFERUNG UND INTERNATIONALES STRAFRECHT (1988); ROBERT LINKE, ET AL., INTERNATIONALES STRAFRECHT (1981).

[16] Germany (Act Concerning International Mutual Assistance in Criminal Matters) "Gesetz über die Internationale Rechtsthilfe im Strafrecht" of Dec. 31, 1982, (entered into force Jan. 7, 1983), Bundesgeszetzblatt 1982, Teil I, No. 2071, (FEDERAL OFFICIAL GAZETTE 1982, part I, at 2071). The act replaced the German Extradition Act of 1929 and provides for comprehensive measures of extradition and other forms of mutual assistance in penal matters, including execution of foreign sentences. *See* OTTO LAGODNY, DIE RECHTSSTELLUNG DES AUSZULIEFERNDEN IN DER BUNDESREPUBLIK DEUTSCHLAND (1987); THEO VOGLER, AUSLIEFERUNGSRECHT UND GRUNDGESETZ (1970); Theo Vogler, *The Expanding Scope of International Judicial Assistance and Cooperation in Legal Matters*, DIE FRIEDENS WARTE BAND 66, Heft 3-4, 287 (1986).

[17] *See* Swiss Federal Law on International Mutual Assistance in Criminal Matters, ENTRAIDE INTERNATIONALE EN MATIÈRE PÉNALE of 20 Mar. 1981.

of these agreements integrate the various modalities into a comprehensive, codified form of inter-state penal cooperation.[18]

At the regional level, the Council of Europe has been considering such an integrated approach since 1987 on the basis of a project developed by an *ad hoc* Committee of Experts. This committee convened twice at the International Institute of Higher Studies in Criminal Sciences in Siracusa, Italy. There, the Committee of Experts determined that the Council of Europe should integrate all of the European Conventions into a single, integrated code of inter-state penal cooperation. This conclusion was supported by a Resolution of the Council of Ministers of Justice in 1987. In addition, the Council of Arab Ministers of Justice developed such a model code in 1988. Regrettably, it has not received attention by the Arab governments, as those states have not yet made international penal cooperation a priority.

The integrated approach has been accepted at a relatively slow pace within international and regional organizations. This hesitation stems from the familiarity and comfort which government representatives feel toward the bilateral approach and with the process of gradually strengthening modalities in a piecemeal fashion. Efforts by a few scholars and government experts to spur the multinational integrated approach have been met with some reluctance in international conferences because some government representatives feel that such an approach may not be politically acceptable to their superiors.

Due, in part, to diplomatic timidity, regional and international organizations have not advanced beyond the fragmented or uncoordinated use of the modalities discussed above. This situation persists even though the resort to these modalities on a singular and unintegrated basis has not worked effectively and has been inadequate in coping with increased international, transnational and national criminality, particularly with respect to organized crime, drug traffic, and terrorism.[19] Consequently, international, transnational, and national criminal phenomena are not controlled as they could be due to this weakness.

It must be admitted, however, that this state of affairs is mainly due to the fact that government officials, whether in ministries of foreign affairs or justice, are not sufficiently knowledgeable in the field of international criminal law to envision better and more effective means of international cooperation. Instead, they persist in traditional ways, with their concomitant weaknesses, or they seek to develop less than lawful methods of accomplishing that which they can not seem to accomplish lawfully. These practices pose very serious problems in the field of international penal cooperation.

Furthermore, the administrative and bureaucratic divisions, which exist among the national organs of law enforcement and prosecution, impair the effectiveness of inter-state penal enforcement. National criminal justice systems consist of different sub-systems. The most common divisions are among law enforcement, prosecution, judiciary and corrections.

---

[18] *See* Rec. No. R/87/1 of the Committee of Ministers of Justice to the Member States on Inter-State Cooperation in Penal Matters among Member States, (adopted by Committee of Ministers of Justice, Council of Europe 19/1/87); 3 EKKEHARD MÜLLER-RAPPARD & M. CHERIF BASSIOUNI, EUROPEAN INTER-STATE COOPERATION IN CRIMINAL MATTERS, app., at 1-30 in English and at 1-32 in French (2d rev. ed. 1991) [hereinafter RAPPARD & BASSIOUNI, EUROP. COOPERATION]. A special Committee of Experts has since been established to work on this project.

[19] *See* M. Cherif Bassiouni, *Organized Crime and Terrorism*, 4 EMORY J. INT'L L. 90 (1990) adopted from the author's report to the Eighth United Nations Congress on the Prevention of Crime and the Treatment of Offenders (Havana, Aug-Sept. 1990) A/CONF.144/NGO 1. *See also*, effective national and international action against: (a) organized crime; (b) terrorist criminal activities A/CONF.144/15. Report of the Interregional preparatory meeting . . . on topic I: Crime Prevention and Criminal Justice in the Context of Development: Realities and Perspectives of International Cooperation, A/CONF.144/IPM.1.

In addition, within each sub-system, there are separate bureaucratic and administrative units. All too frequently, each of these sub-systems is a self-contained entity with its own peculiar bureaucratic and administrative exigencies with each having a life of its own.

As a result, each sub-system defends its respective turf and supports its own methods, goals and purposes; all of which leads to difficulties of integration, and ultimately, to the fragmentation of the criminal justice system. Conversely, criminal organizations and individual offenders are not similarly hindered by the inefficiencies of bureaucratic and administrative divisions.

The international response to criminal phenomena which does not stop at national boundaries is piecemeal, divided, and ineffective. More significantly, few states make the effort to use all the existing modalities of inter-state cooperation and even fewer states seek to develop new modalities of cooperation in other fields. Such new modalities could include the following:

i. sharing law enforcement intelligence;
ii. increasing teamwork in inter-state law enforcement cooperation;
iii. tracing international financial transactions;
iv. developing effective national financial controls to trace proceeds of illicit activities; and
v. developing regional "judicial spaces."[20]

None of the above, however, should be construed or applied in a manner that violates international and regional human rights norms and standards.[21]

A multilateral or regional integrated approach is an eminently desirable course of conduct, and both the Council of Europe and the United Nations could significantly contribute to the field of international criminal justice by developing such a model. Any such model should also include new approaches to the problems of criminal jurisdiction.

The United Nations General Assembly adopted a set of measures approved by the Eighth United Congress on the Prevention of Crime and Treatment of Offenders (Havana, August-September, 1990) which included the following: measures for international

---

[20] This latter idea was floated within the Council of Europe by France in the late 1970's but was discarded within that regional context. It has survived in discussions during 1989 among certain countries within that region, namely the Benelux countries and Germany. In the Andean Region, a parliamentary Commission is considering that option and is also working on the elaboration of an integrated code of interregional cooperation which would include the traditional modalities described above. *Supra* note 3. *See* Rene de Gouttes, *Variations sur L'Espace Judiciare Pénal Européen,* 33 RECUEIL DALLOZ SIREY 245 (1990); Rene de Gouttes, *Vers un Espace Judiciare Pénal Pan Européen?*, 22 RECUEIL DALLOZ SIREY 154 (1991); Council of Europe, *International Cooperation in the Prosecution and Punishment of Acts of Terrorism: Recommendation No. R(82)1*, adopted by the Committee of Ministers of the Council of Europe on 15 Jan. 1982 and explanatory memorandum (Strasbourg 1983); MARIA RICCARDA-MARCHETTI, INSTITUZIONI EUROPEE E LOTTA AL TERRORISMO (1986); Franco Mosconi, *L'Accordo Di Dublino Del 4/12/1979, Le Communita Europee e la Repressione Del Terrorismo*, LA LEGISLAZIONE PENALE, 543 (No. 3, 1986) (referring to the European Judicial Space); Christine Van den Wyngaert, *L'Espace Judiciare Européen Face a L'Euro-Terrorisme et la Sauvegarde des Droits Fondamentaux*, 3 REVUE INTERNATIONALE DE CRIMINOLOGIE ET LA POLICE TECHNIQUE 289 (1980); Christine Van den Wyngaert, *L'Espace Judiciare Europeen: Vers une Fissure au Sein du Conseil de L'Europe?*, 61 REVUE DROIT PÉNAL ET DE CRIMINOLOGIE 511 (1981). *See also* CONSIGLIO SUPERIOR DELLA MAGISTRATURA, ESTRADIZIONE E SPAZIO GIURIDICO EUROPEO (1979); SCHENGEN, INTERNATIONALIZATION OF CENTRAL CHAPTERS OF THE LAW ON ALIENS, REFUGEES, SECURITY AND THE POLICE (H. Meijers et al. eds., 1991).

[21] *See* 49 REVUE INTERNATIONALE DE DROIT PÉNAL (No. 3 1978) and in particular the General Report of Professor Stefan Trechsel *id.*, at 541.

cooperation for crime prevention and criminal justice;[22] a model treaty on extradition;[23] a model treaty on mutual assistance in criminal matters;[24] and a model treaty on the transfer of proceedings in criminal matters. These model treaties are expected to provide a useful framework for states interested in negotiating bilateral arrangements in these areas; however, they are too general and are not integrated.[25]

The Organization of American States has, in the last few years, followed in the footsteps of the Council of Europe and developed, *inter alia*: 1) the American Convention on Human Rights; 2) the Convention to Prevent and Punish the Acts of Terrorism Taking the Form of Crimes Against Persons and Related Extortion that are of International Significance; 3) various instruments concerning extradition, asylum and international penal law; and 4) the establishment of the Inter-American Drug Abuse Control Commission via the Inter-American Program of Action of Rio de Janeiro Against the Illicit Use and Production of Narcotic Drugs and Psychotropic Substances and Traffic Therein. Qualitatively, the European Conventions on Inter-State Cooperation[26] are moving into the stage of second generation, whereas the OAS and U.N. are still at the stage of first generation. However, we are now at a time when we need a third generation of international instruments.

Principles and Policies for the Increase in Effectiveness of the "Indirect Enforcement Scheme"[27]

In order to render the international system of prevention, control and suppression of domestic, transnational and international criminality more effective, the following recommendations are offered:

1. Recognition of the rule *aut dedere aut judicare* as a *civitas maxima*[28] and development of international minimum standards of compliance, including standards for effective, good faith prosecution and extradition;
2. Recognition of a ranking of criminal jurisdiction in this order: territoriality, nationality, passive personality, protected interest, and universality and development of rules

---

22 G.A. Res. 45/107, U.N. GAOR (1990).

23 G.A. Res. 45/116, U.N. GAOR (1990).

24 G.A. Res. 45/117, U.N. GAOR (1990).

25 For a discussion of the differences in approach and effectiveness between the United Nations and regional bodies, like the Council of Europe, *see supra* note 12. Despite these institutional differences, and in recognition of the fact that the United Nations has not adopted an integrated approach, this writer has propounded such an approach in a report submitted to a Committee of Experts Meeting at ISISC (Siracusa) June 1990 and presented to the Eighth United Nations Congress on Crime Prevention and the Treatment of Offenders (Havana, Cuba, Aug.-Sept. 1990) A/CONF.144/NGO5, 31 July 1990, *reprinted in* 15 NOVA L. REV. 354 (1991).

26 *See* RAPPARD & BASSIOUNI, EUROP. COOPERATION, *supra* note 18.

27 The author submitted a report on this topic to a Committee of Experts Meeting at ISISC (Siracusa) June 1990 and to the Eighth United Nations Congress on Crime Prevention and the Treatment of Offenders (Havana, Cuba, Aug.-Sept. 1990) A/Conf.144/NGO5, 31 July 1990, *reprinted in* 15 NOVA L. REV. 354 (1991). The International Law Commission has subsequently reported favorably on this position. *See Report of the International Law Commission on the Work of its Forty-Third Session*, 29 Apr.-19 July 1991, U.N. GAOR 46th Sess., Supp. No. 10, U.N. Doc. A/46/10 (1991).

28 BASSIOUNI, EXTRADITION, *supra* note 8, at § 2-3 (2d rev. ed. 1987); Gerhard Müeller, *International Criminal Law: Civitas Maxima*, 15 CASE W. RES. J. INT'L L. 1 (1982).

and mechanisms for conflict resolution, including compulsory adjudication before an International Criminal Court, the International Court of Justice or regional tribunals;[29]

3. Granting individual victims the right to initiate prosecution as *partie civile*, including countries other than that of their nationality;[30]

4. Codification of international and transnational crimes and their inclusion in the national legislation of all countries;[31]

5. Developing means by which to detect abuses of power by those public officials who may commit international offences or who, by purposeful omission, are derelict of their duties to enforce international criminal law;[32]

6. Integrating modalities for inter-state penal cooperation in a codified fashion. This should be done in specialized international and regional instruments and in national

---

[29] *See* Christopher L. Blakesley, *Extraterritorial Jurisdiction, in* 2 INTERNATIONAL CRIMINAL LAW: PROCEDURE 3 (M. Cherif Bassiouni ed., 2d ed. 1998) [hereinafter ICL PROCEDURE]; HAIDONG LI, DIE PRINZIPIEN DES INTERNATIONALEN STRAFRECHTS (1991).

[30] This idea was accepted by the United Nations Committee on Crime Prevention and Control on the basis of a proposal made by a Committee of Experts meeting at ISISC (Siracusa) for the implementation of the United Nations Declaration on Basic Principles of Justice for Victims of Crime and Abuse of Power G.A. Res. 40/34, U.N. GAOR, 40th Sess., Supp. No. 53, at 213, U.N. Doc. A/40/53 (1985). *See* INTERNATIONAL PROTECTIONS OF VICTIMS, 7 NOUVELLES ETUDE PÉNALES (M. Cherif Bassiouni ed., 2d ed. 1998).

[31] *See* 60 REVUE INTERNATIONALE DE DROIT PÉNAL (No. 1-2, 1989) (in particular the General Reports of Professors Otto Triffterer at 29 and Lech Gardocki at 89). The Fifteenth International Penal Law Congress, held in Vienna, Oct. 1989, adopted a resolution to that effect. *See* Proceedings of the Fifteenth International Penal Law Congress (1991).

The Association Internationale de Droit Pénal (AIDP) has been a leader in this effort since 1926. *See* 6 REVUE INTERNATIONALE DE DROIT PÉNAL 275 (1928). The Association's former president made contributions to this effort prior to 1926 in his work VESPASIAN V. PELLA, LA CODIFICATION DU DROIT PÉNAL INTERNATIONAL (1922). Subsequently the AIDP sponsored a project directed by the author, then its Secretary-General, which was presented to the Sixth United Nations Congress on Crime Prevention and The Treatment of Offenders (Caracas, Venezuela, Aug.-Sept.1980) and published as M. CHERIF BASSIOUNI, INTERNATIONAL CRIMINAL LAW: A DRAFT INTERNATIONAL CRIMINAL COURT (1980), translated into French by Christine Van den Wyngaert as *Projet de Code Pénal International*, 51 REVUE INTERNATIONALE DE DROIT PÉNAL (vols. 1-2, 1980), which was followed by a symposium issue of commentaries, 51 REVUE INTERNATIONALE DE DROIT PÉNAL (vols. 3-4, 1980); the Draft Code was translated into Spanish by Professor José Luis de la Cuesta and was published as DERECHO PENAL INTERNACIONAL PROJECTO DE CODIGO PENAL INTERNATIONAL (1983); and it was translated into Hungarian by the Hungarian Ministry of Justice in 1984. A revised edition was published in 1987 as M. CHERIF BASSIOUNI, A DRAFT INTERNATIONAL CRIMINAL CODE AND A DRAFT STATUTE FOR AN INTERNATIONAL CRIMINAL TRIBUNAL (1987).

In 1947, the United Nations began working on the codification of certain international crimes and produced in 1954 a Draft Code of Offences Against the Peace and Security of Mankind, 9 U.N. GAOR Supp. No. 9 at 9, U.N. Doc. A/2693 (1954), *reprinted in* 1954 Y.B. INT'L L. COM. 112-22; since 1982, *see* the annual reports of the International Law Commission each reprinted in the Yearbook. For a recent assessment, *see* Hans-Heinrich Jescheck, *Developments and Future Prospects, in* 1 INTERNATIONAL CRIMINAL LAW: CRIMES 83 (M. Cherif Bassiouni ed. 1986)[hereinafter ICL CRIMES]; Sharon A. Williams, *The Draft Code of Offences Against the Peace and Security of Mankind, id.*, at 109; Edward M. Wise, *Perspectives and Approaches, id.*, at 101. *See also* STEFAN GLASER, LE DROIT PÉNAL INTERNATIONAL CONVENTION (2 vols. 1977-79); CLAUDE LOMBOIS, DROIT PÉNAL INTERNATIONAL (2d. ed. 1919); FARHAD MALEKIAN, INTERNATIONAL CRIMINAL LAW (2 vols. 1991); DIETRICH OEHLER, INTERNATIONALES STRAFRECHT (2d. ed. 1983); ANTONIO QUINTANO-RIPPOLLES, TRATADO DE DERECHO PENAL INTERNACIONAL E INTERNACIONAL PENAL (2 vols. 1955-57); OTTO TRIFFTERER, DOGMATISCHE UNTERSUCHUNGEN ZUR ENTWICKLUNG DES MATERIELLEN VÖLKERSTRAFRECHT SEIT NÜRNBERG (1966); Yoram Dinstein, *International Criminal Law*, 1975 ISR. Y.B. HUM. RTS. 55; Leslie C. Green, *An International Criminal Code Now?* 3 DALHOUSIE L.J. 560 (1976); Edward M. Wise, *International Crimes and Domestic Criminal Law*, 38 DEPAUL L. REV. 923 (1989).

[32] *See infra* note 54.

legislation for application to international and transnational crimes, as well as to domestic crimes requiring inter-state cooperation;[33]

7. Development of a convention on inter-state cooperation between law enforcement agencies setting forth the means, methods and limitations of such cooperation, including the protection of fundamental human rights and the right to privacy. This systematized approach should be included in an integrated code of inter-state penal cooperation;

8. The consistent and specific inclusion of the integrated modalities of enforcement in all substantive international criminal law conventions;

9. Development of new modalities of inter-state cooperation and enforcement mechanisms similar to those outlined above;

10. Development of education and training programs in international criminal law at the level of legal education as well as within public agencies[34] and specialization programs for judges, prosecutors and law enforcement officials in international criminal law aspects of their work. A specialized cadre of legal technicians should be developed in each government and within international, regional and inter-governmental organizations to draft instruments and provisions on international criminal law;

11. International, regional, inter-governmental and non-governmental organizations and academic institutions should develop educational, training, professional and practical materials in international criminal law which can be widely used by all professional categories;[35]

12. Development of networks of information and criminal justice data-sharing within states and as between states;[36]

13. Providing and requiring increased technical assistance to states;[37] and

14. Development of regional centers for the accumulation of specialized library materials, documents, and research with the capacity to provide technical legal advice to government and public agencies and to academic and scientific organizations. All of the above recommendations must be applied in conformity with international, regional and national human rights norms and standards. This caveat is particularly important in light of some law enforcement branches. In this respect, it should be stated that the observance of human rights norms and standards does not reduce the efficiency or effectiveness of the criminal justice system. The inefficiency of criminal justice derives from a variety of other factors.

Suffice it to observe that if any successful industrial or commercial enterprise, in today's world of modern management techniques, was administered like many of the criminal justice systems, that enterprise would cease to be successful and would eventually become bankrupt. The symptoms of the bankruptcy of our criminal justice systems are all too evident, from law enforcement to corrections, as almost every aspect needs reform.

---

33 *See infra* notes 32 through 35.

34 *See* UNITED NATIONS CONGRESS ON THE PREVENTION OF CRIME AND THE TREATMENT OF OFFENDERS, GUIDING PRINCIPLES FOR CRIME PREVENTION AND CRIMINAL JUSTICE IN THE CONTEXT OF DEVELOPMENT AND A NEW INTERNATIONAL ECONOMIC ORDER, adopted by the Seventh United Nations Congress on the Prevention of Crime and the Treatment of Offenders [hereinafter U.N. GUIDING PRINCIPLES ON CRIME PREVENTION] (Milano, Italy, 26 Aug.-6 Sept. 1985) A/Conf.121/22/Rev./1. For a Commentary on the "Guiding Principles," *see* 6 NOUVELLES ETUDES PÉNALES 121 (1985).

35 *Id.*

36 *Id.*

37 *Id.*

Conclusion

Since the end of World War II, international, transnational, and national incidents of crime and the number of offenders have consistently increased. The distinction between the increase in the incidents of crime and the number of offenders is critical because any system of criminal justice is based on substantial compliance with the law. Thus, the system is only equipped to deal with a particular, limited number of offenders. As the number of offenders increases, the criminal justice system's resources become strained. Eventually, the system becomes unable to handle the increased volume of offenders and ultimately breaks down.[38]

At the inter-state level, other factors which have enhanced this phenomenon are the extraordinary ease of inter-state movement of persons and goods and the free flow of financial transactions in a worldwide banking system that provides maximum flexibility and anonymity. National criminal justice systems, which are no longer capable of meeting their domestic challenges, must face the added difficulties of pursuing offenders, and seeking evidence in multiple states. However, the lack of expert personnel and the limited resources allocated by governments to such endeavors and to inter-state penal cooperation render these processes slow and ineffective.

Governments believe that the problems in extradition and other forms of international cooperation stem from approaches which tend to elevate the procedural rights of the requested person to the detriment of the process. The argument is not entirely without merit, but it is limited to occasional effects and ignores endemic and operational causes. One of these causes is the limited number of experts among judges, prosecutors, and administrative officials working in this field. They face a large volume of cases with limited resources and personnel.

Probably the most serious of all problems is bureaucratic divisions which burden the administration of criminal justice and sometimes paralyze the system. Even those law enforcement agencies which have exhibited increased capacity for inter-state cooperation have become less concerned with the proper application of the law. As some of these public officials engage in questionable or unlawful practices such as abduction, they compel greater procedural rigidity and tighter judicial controls. The cumulative effect of these and other systematic and operational deficiencies reduces the speed and effectiveness of the processes of inter-state penal cooperation.

Operational problems, though more visible, are not, however, the most serious causes of the systemic problems in interstate penal cooperation. Many states still favor bilateral treaties and make extradition and other forms of cooperation a consequence of, and contingent upon, their political relations. Thus, governments reduce procedural barriers to extradition and other forms of cooperation with friendly nations and increase these barriers with less friendly ones. Extradition and other forms of cooperation are therefore still a

---

[38] In fact, the increased number of offenders has caused many states to decriminalize certain activities in a variety of categories. These categories of offenses are, instead, treated in the administrative law rather than in the criminal law context. Such treatment has extended to the development of alternative modalities designed to ease the added strain on the criminal justice system such as restitution, victim compensation, and arbitration in crimes which involve patrimonial and personal injury matters. For example, the Council of Europe's Committee of Ministers recently adopted a directive concerning the establishment of arbitral tribunals for claims arising out of Eur. Conv. Money Laundering, *supra* note 2.

process of political accommodation. They should be a judicial process based on an international *civitas maxima* free from political considerations.[39]

A new approach is needed whereby modalities of inter-state cooperation are regarded as an objective and politically neutral international judicial process which preserves international standards of legality and human rights protections in its judicial and administrative workings. It is particularly important to understand that the protection of individual human rights is not and should not be placed in a confrontational relationship with the effectiveness of the process.

Multilateralism should replace the archaic, inefficient and politicized bilateralism, and all modalities of inter-state penal cooperation should be integrated. Thus, multilateral treaties and national legislations should integrate the following modalities: extradition; legal assistance; transfer of criminal proceedings; transfer of prisoners; transfer of sentences; recognition of foreign penal judgements; tracing, freezing and seizing of assets derived from criminal activity; and, law-enforcement and prosecutorial cooperation. Only then will these complementary processes work to the benefit of ensuring efficiency without sacrificing proper legal procedures and violating individual human rights. Lastly, we must not forget the need to establish an International Criminal Court.[40]

Without the intellectual and technical contribution of scholars and experts and without the leadership of international and regional organizations, states will probably continue to pursue familiar courses charted by years of practice, even though that practice has proven unsatisfactory. Instead, states should explore new courses in the hopes of discovering the best route to a brave new world of effective inter-state penal cooperation.

---

[39] *See* Edward M. Wise, *Extradition: The Hypothesis of a Civitas Maxima and the Maxim Aut Dedere Aut Judicare* 109, Christine Van den Wyngaert, *The Political Offense Exception to Extradition: How to Plug the Terrorist's Loophole Without Departing from Fundamental Human Rights, in* 62 REVUE INTERNATIONALE DE DROIT PÉNAL (Nos. 1-2. 1991).

[40] *See* M. Cherif Bassiouni, *The Time Has Come for an International Criminal Court*, 1 IND. INT'L & COMP. L. REV. 1 (1991). *See also* a report submitted to a Committee of Experts Meeting at ISISC (Siracusa) June 1990 and presented to the Eighth United Nations Congress on Crime Prevention and the Treatment of Offenders (Havana, Cuba, Aug.-Sept. 1990) A/Conf.144/NGO5, 31 July 1990) *reprinted in* 15 NOVA L. REV. 354 (1991) and M. Cherif Bassiouni, *Draft Statute: International Criminal Tribunal*, 15 NOVA L. REV. 373 (1991).

Aut Dedere Aut Judicare: The Duty to Prosecute or Extradite*

Edward M. Wise

Introduction

International law traditionally has been the law of a society made up almost exclusively of sovereign states. It is becoming the law of a planetary community of which all human beings are members. The transition to an inclusive world community is taking place, however, by fits and starts, and not without retrograde movements. The international system still contains the large pockets of anarchy that are bound to exist in any social system that regards its constituent units as "sovereign."

Development of the sense that the world constitutes a single community has been accompanied by growth of a true body of international criminal law concerned not only with mutual cooperation between law enforcement authorities of different states, but also with the repression of conduct perceived to be harmful to interests of the international community as a whole. That these developments have occurred in tandem should hardly occasion surprise. Criminal law is concerned, after all, with harms to "the whole community, considered as a community, in its social aggregate capacity."[1] The notion of crime, of public wrong, depends on the existence of at least a rudimentary sense of community, while conversely, as Durkheim particularly emphasized, a basic function of the criminal law is to affirm and strengthen this feeling of communal solidarity. Punishment of criminals, he said:

> does not serve, or serves only incidentally, to correct the offender or to intimidate possible imitators. Its effectiveness in these respects can rightly be doubted and is, in any case, mediocre. Its real function is to maintain intact the cohesion of society by sustaining in all its vigor the communal consciousness. Where that consciousness has been so clearly thwarted, it would necessarily lose some of its power if an emotional reaction from the community were not forthcoming to compensate for the loss, and the result would be a weakening of social solidarity. That consciousness must therefore emphatically reaffirm itself the moment it meets with opposition. The sole means of doing so is to express the universal aversion the crime continues to evoke, by an official act which can only consist in suffering inflicted on the wrongdoer.[2]

---

* This chapter is an abridged version, prepared by Edward Wise, of material contained in the Preface and Part I of M. CHERIF BASSIOUNI & EDWARD M. WISE, AUT DEDERE AUT JUDICARE: THE OBLIGATION TO EXTRADITE OR PROSECUTE IN INTERNATIONAL LAW (Martinus Nijhoff Publishers 1995).

[1] 4 WILLIAM BLACKSTONE, COMMENTARIES ON THE LAWS OF ENGLAND 5 (3rd ed. 1762).

[2] EMILE DURKHEIM, DE LA DIVISION DU TRAVAIL SOCIAL 76-77 (7TH ED. 1960). The translation in the text is a pastiche based in part on EMILE DURKHEIM, ON THE DIVISION OF LABOR IN SOCIETY 108 (G. Simpson trans., 1933), and in part on the translation by W.D. Hall, *in* DURKHEIM AND THE LAW 68-69 (S. Lukes & A. Scull eds., 1983).

The growth of international criminal law has been retarded by a system of "indirect enforcement" which relies almost entirely on national authorities to prosecute international wrongdoers.[3] (The Nuremberg tribunal was an exception, as are the *ad hoc* tribunals established to try crimes committed in former Yugoslavia and Rwanda.) Indirect enforcement is not necessarily incompatible with the existence of a genuine international criminal law. In a system of indirect enforcement, the relevant norms take the form of treaty provisions requiring participating states to criminalize certain conduct rather than the form of rules addressed directly to prospective offenders. But even in developed domestic systems, rules of criminal law likewise can be represented as directions to officials about how to proceed rather than as commands issued to the public at large.[4] The stumbling block is not the form of the relevant rules, but indifference or worse on the part of national authorities regarding the need to bring to justice malefactors who have committed crimes in or against other countries.

So long as the world is divided into nations possessed of exclusive authority to enforce the law against people within their own territories, bringing an offender to trial will necessarily depend on the willingness of the state where an offender is found either to undertake prosecution itself or to hand the offender over for trial elsewhere. The efficacy of any system of international criminal law thus requires that states accept an obligation to try international offenders before their own courts or else surrender them for trial before a foreign (or international) court. To the extent that states accept and act on this obligation, the idea of an international community comes closer to reality; to the extent they do not, efforts to realize that idea suffer a setback.

An obligation to prosecute or extradite appears in various forms in a number of multilateral conventions dealing with the suppression of international offenses. These treaties reflect widespread (and increasing) recognition of the principle that states are bound to act, either through prosecution or through extradition, to ensure that individuals who perpetrate harms inimical to fundamental interests of the international community are brought to justice. It might even be argued that the obligation to extradite or prosecute has solidified as an obligation imposed not only by treaty, but by customary or general international law.

The argument for saying that the obligation to extradite or prosecute is a rule of general international law depends on cutting loose from positivistic learning about the "sources" of international law. It involves viewing the various occasions on which an obligation to prosecute or extradite has been given concrete form in international agreements as so many partial and incomplete expressions of an underlying principle essential for constitution of an "international community" in the true sense of the term. In "classical" international law, the fundamental norms according to which states enjoy autonomy, independence, and equality are not so much a product of state practice or explicit agreement as they are postulates implicit in the very concept of a pluralistic society of states. They are axiomatic in character and "authoritative by virtue of the inherent necessities of a pluralist society."[5]

---

[3] On the distinction between the "indirect" and "direct" enforcement of international criminal law, see M. Cherif Bassiouni, *The Penal Characteristics of Conventional International Criminal Law,* 15 CASE W. RES. J. INT'L L. 27, 29-30, 32-34 (1983).

[4] *See* M. Dan-Cohen, *Decision Rules and Conduct Rules: On Acoustic Separation in Criminal Law,* 87 HARV. L. REV. 625, 625-36 (1984).

[5] OSCAR SCHACHTER, INTERNATIONAL LAW IN THEORY AND PRACTICE 30 (1991); *See also* LOUIS HENKIN, ET AL., INTERNATIONAL LAW: CASES AND MATERIALS 93 (3d ed. 1993).

Similarly, it might be said, an obligation on the part of state officials to cooperate in assuring repression of offenses harmful to the international community is a basic postulate inherent in the concept of a world community. This argument assumes, however, that the transition from a loose society of independent states to an inclusive world community has in fact progressed to a point where it is permissible to derive rules of international law from the inherent necessities of communal life. It is the object of the following remarks to highlight the connection between the argument for saying that the obligation to extradite or prosecute is a rule of general international law and the particular vision of the nature of international order which that argument presupposes.

The Principle *Aut Dedere Aut Judicare* in International Conventions

The expression *aut dedere aut judicare* is a modern adaptation of a phrase used by Grotius: *aut dedere aut punire* (extradite or punish).[6] It is nowadays used to refer to the obligation to extradite or prosecute contained in a number of multilateral treaties aimed at securing international cooperation in the suppression of certain kinds of criminal conduct.[7] The obligation is phrased in different ways in different treaties, but basically it requires a state which has hold of someone who has committed a crime of international concern either to extradite the offender to another state which is prepared to try him, or else to take steps to have him prosecuted before its own courts.[8]

The first treaty imposing such an obligation was the Convention for the Suppression of Counterfeiting of 1929.[9] In the Counterfeiting Convention, a distinction is drawn depending on whether the case involves a national or non-national of the state which is requested to extradite someone who committed an offense abroad. A state which refuses to extradite its

---

[6] See M. Cherif Bassiouni, *Introduction, in* 1 INTERNATIONAL CRIMINAL LAW: CRIMES xviii (M. Cherif Bassiouni ed., 1986) [hereinafter ICL, CRIMES]; M. CHERIF BASSIOUNI, INTERNATIONAL EXTRADITION AND WORLD PUBLIC ORDER 7 (1974). The expression *aut dedere aut judicare* does not seem to have been widely used much before 1974. It figures in the Final Document: Conclusions and Recommendations of the Conference on Terrorism and Political Crimes held at Siracusa in June 1973, which is printed in INTERNATIONAL TERRORISM AND POLITICAL CRIMES xi, xix (M. Cherif Bassiouni ed., 1975), and in several other papers in that volume: DeSchutter, *Problems of Jurisdiction in the International Control and Repression of Terrorism, id.* at 377, 386; Vogler, *Perspectives on Extradition and Terrorism, id.* 391, 396; Bassiouni, *Methodological Options for International Control of Terrorism, id.* at 485, 490; and in the Greek submission to the United Nations Ad Hoc Committee on International Terrorism, *reprinted in id.* at Appendix S, 564-5. It appears even earlier in the comments of the International Law Commission on its draft of what became the New York Convention on the Prevention and Punishment of Crimes Against Internationally Protected Persons, Including Diplomatic Agents, of 1973, *in* 1972 INT'L L. COMM'N Y.B. 219, 318. *See also* LOUIS M. BLOOMFIELD & GERALD F. FITZGERALD, CRIMES AGAINST INTERNATIONALLY PROTECTED PERSONS 96, 102 (1975); Declan Costello, *International Terrorism and the Development of the Principle aut dedere aut judicare*, 10.J. INT'L L. & ECON. 483 (1975).

[7] For this use of the expression, *see, e.g.*, 1 OPPENHEIM'S INTERNATIONAL LAW 953, 971 (R. Jennings & A. Watts eds., 9th ed. 1992). A nearly complete list of the treaties containing this kind of obligation appears in *id.* at 953-54. The list includes, however, the Genocide Convention of 1948 and the Tokyo Convention on Offenses and Certain Other Acts Committed on Board Aircraft of 1963, neither of which explicitly imposes such an obligation; and it omits the 1971 OAS Terrorism Convention (note 25 *infra*) and 1980 Convention on the Physical Protection of Nuclear Material (note 21 *infra*), both of which do.

[8] A state subject to this obligation is bound to adopt one of two possible courses of action: it must extradite if it does not prosecute, and prosecute if it does not extradite. Whether one or the other of these alternative courses of action should be entitled to preference, at least under certain circumstances, is an entirely separate question; it is one of the questions involved in the *Lockerbie* case, now before the International Court of Justice.

[9] International Convention for the Suppression of Counterfeiting Currency, Apr. 20, 1929, 112 L.N.T.S. 371.

own nationals is expected to prosecute them at home; but, in cases involving non-nationals, a state which refuses extradition is expected to prosecute only if its "internal legislation recognizes as a general rule the principle of prosecution of offenses committed abroad." This distinction recurs in a series of subsequent agreements likewise imposing obligations to extradite or prosecute: the Convention on Illicit Traffic in Dangerous Drugs of 1936,[10] the abortive Convention on Terrorism of 1937,[11] the Convention on Traffic in Persons (White Slavery) of 1950,[12] the Single Convention on Narcotic Drugs of 1961,[13] the Convention on Psychotropic Substances of 1971[14] and, to some extent, the Vienna Convention on Traffic in Narcotics Drugs of 1988.[15]

A stronger version of the obligation to prosecute or extradite appears in the common article of the four Geneva Conventions of 1949 by which each contracting party is required to "search for" persons alleged to have committed acts constituting "grave breaches" of the those Conventions, and to "bring such persons, regardless of their nationality, before its courts"; or else, "if it prefers, and in accordance with the provisions of its own legislation, hand such persons over for trial to another High Contracting Party concerned, provided such High Contracting Party has made out a *prima facie* case.[16]

A somewhat different formulation is contained in Article 7 of the 1970 Hague Convention for the Suppression of Unlawful Seizure of Aircraft.[17] This formulation requires the state in which an alleged offender is found to extradite him to a state (such as the state of registry of a hijacked aircraft) which has jurisdiction over the offense; or, if it does not extradite, "to submit the case to its competent authorities for the purpose of prosecution." This formula is also used in the Montreal Convention on Unlawful Acts Against the Safety of Civil Aviation of 1971,[18] the New York Convention on Crimes Against Internationally

---

[10] Convention for the Suppression of Illicit Traffic in Dangerous Drugs, June 26, 1936, arts. 7 & 8, 198 L.N.T.S. 299.

[11] Convention for the Prevention and Punishment of Terrorism, Nov. 16, 1937, arts. 9 & 10, 19 LEAGUE OF NATIONS O.J. 23 (1938).

[12] Convention for the Suppression of Traffic in Persons and the Exploitation of the Prostitution of Others, Mar. 21, 1950, art. 9, 96 U.N.T.S. 271.

[13] Single Convention on Narcotic Drugs, Mar. 30, 1961, 18 U.S.T. 1407, 520 U.N.T.S. 151.

[14] Convention of Psychotropic Substances, Feb. 21, 1971, art. 22(2)(a)(iv), T.I.A.S. No. 9725, 1019 U.N.T.S. 175.

[15] United Nations Convention Against Illicit Traffic in Narcotic Drugs and Psychotropic Substances, Dec. 19, 1988, 28 U.N.T.S. 493.

[16] Convention for the Amelioration of the Condition of the Wounded and Sick in the Armed Forces in the Field, Aug. 12, 1949, art. 49, 6 U.S.T. 3114, 75 U.N.T.S. 31; Convention for the Amelioration of the Condition of the Wounded, Sick, and Shipwrecked Members of the Armed Forces at Sea, Aug. 12, 1949, art. 50, 6 U.S.T. 3217, 75 U.N.T.S. 85; Convention Relative to the Treatment of Prisoners of War, Aug. 12, 1949, art. 129, 6 U.S.T. 3316, 75 U.N.T.S. 135, 236; Convention Relative to the Protection of Civilian Persons in Time of War, Aug. 12, 1949, 6 U.S.T. 3516, 75 U.N.T.S. 287. Further, Protocol I Additional to the Geneva Conventions of 12 August 1949, and Relating to to Protection of Victims of International Armed Conflict, June 10, 1977, art. 85, UN. Doc. A/32/144 Annex I, *reprinted in* 16 I.L.M. 1391 (1977), provides that the provisions of the Geneva Conventions "relating to the repressions of breaches and grave breaches" also "shall apply to the repression of breaches and grave breaches of this Protocol."

[17] Convention for the Suppression of Unlawful Seizure of Aircraft, Dec. 16, 1970, 22 U.S.T. 1641, 860 U.N.T.S. 105.

[18] Convention for the Suppression of Unlawful Acts Against the Safety of Civil Aviation, Sept. 23, 1971, 24 U.S.T. 564, 974 U.N.T.S. 177.

Protected Persons of 1973,[19] the Hostages Convention of 1979,[20] the Convention on the Physical Protection of Nuclear Material of 1980,[21] the Torture Convention of 1984,[22] the Rome Convention on the Safety of Maritime Navigation of 1988,[23] and the Mercenaries Convention of 1989.[24] Variants appear in the OAS Terrorism Convention of 1971,[25] the European Terrorism Convention of 1977,[26] and the OAS Torture Convention of 1985.[27] With the exception of the Apartheid Convention of 1973,[28] a version of the 1970 Hague formula appears in practically every subsequent general multilateral treaty requiring the repression of an international offense.

The Irish Attorney General, Mr. Costello, remarked as early as 1975 that, of all possible methods for ensuring that international offenders are brought to trial, the obligation to extradite or prosecute seemed to be "the one which the international community favors."[29] The evidence for that conclusion is even stronger today, giving rise to the question of whether the obligation to extradite or prosecute is so sufficiently favored as to have become a rule of customary international law.

The Case for Customary Status

Assertions about the customary status of the principle *aut dedere aut judicare* can take different forms. It may be asserted that the principle has become a customary rule with respect to the particular offense defined in a particular treaty; or it may be asserted, more broadly, that the principle is a customary rule with respect to a whole class of international law offenses, or with respect to international offenses as a whole. The suggestion that the principle applies to all international offenses has been put forward on several occasions by

---

[19] Convention on the Prevention and Punishment of Crimes Against Internationally Protected Persons, Including Diplomatic Agents, Dec. 14, 1973, 28 U.S.T. 1975, 1035 U.N.T.S. 167.

[20] International Convention Against the Taking of Hostages, Dec. 17, 1979, G.A. Res. 34/146, U.N. GAOR Supp. (No. 46), at 245, U.N. Doc. A/34/46 (1980), 18 I.L.M. 1456 (1979).

[21] International Atomic Energy Agency Convention on the Physical Protection of Nuclear Material, Mar. 3, 1980, I.A.E.A. Legal Series No. 12 (1982), 18 I.L.M. 1419 (1979).

[22] Convention Against Torture and Other Cruel, Inhuman or Degrading Treatment or Punishment, Dec. 17, 1984, G.A. Res. 39/46, 39 GAOR Supp. (No. 51) at 197, U.N. Doc. A/39/51 (1984), 23 I.L.M. 1027 (1984).

[23] International Maritime Organization Convention for the Suppression of Unlawful Acts Against the Safety of Maritime Navigation, Mar. 10, 1988, I.M.O. Doc. SUA/CON/15, 27 I.L.M. 672 (1988).

[24] International Convention Against the Recruitment, Use, Financing and Training of Mercenaries, G.A. Res. 44/34, adopted Dec. 4, 1989, U.N. Doc. A/Res/44/34 (Dec. 11, 1989), 29 I.L.M. 89 (1990).

[25] Organization of American States Convention to Prevent and Punish the Acts of Terrorism Taking the Form of Crimes Against Persons and Related Extortion that are of International Significance, Feb. 2, 1971, art. 5, 27 U.S.T. 3949, T.I.A.S. No. 8413, 10 I.L.M. 255 (1971). This has been largely superseded by the Convention on Crimes Against Internationally Protected Persons, *supra* note 19.

[26] European Convention on the Suppression of Terrorism, Jan. 27, 1977, art. 7, Eur. T.S. No. 90, 15 I.L.M. 1272.

[27] Inter-American Convention to Prevent and Punish Torture, Dec. 9, 1985, art. 14, O.A.S. T.S. No. 67, O.A.S. Doc. OEA/Ser. P, AG/Doc. 2023/85 rev. 1, Mar. 12, 1986.

[28] International Convention on the Suppression and Punishment of the Crime of Apartheid, Nov. 30, 1973, G.A. Res. 28/3068, 28 U.N. GAOR Supp. (No. 30) at 75, U.N. Doc. A/9030 (1973). For parallel cite, *see* 1015 U.N.T.S. 243, 13 I.L.M. 50 (1974).

[29] Costello, *supra* note 6, at 490.

Cherif Bassiouni,[30] and appears to have been endorsed by Judge Weeramantry in his opinion dissenting from the order denying provisional measures in the *Lockerbie* case:

> The principle *aut dedere aut judicare* is an important facet of a State's sovereignty over its nationals and the well-established nature of this principle in customary international is evident from the following description: "The widespread use of the formula 'prosecute or extradite' either specifically stated, explicitly stated in a duty to extradite, or implicit in the duty to prosecute or criminalize, and the number of signatories to these numerous conventions, attests to the existing general *jus cogens* principle." [31]

The argument in favor of saying that the principle represents a rule of customary international law runs essentially as follows:

(1) While with ordinary offenses there is no obligation to extradite in the absence of a treaty prescribing such an obligation,[32] international offenses may well constitute an exception to this rule. It has sometimes been asserted that an obligation to extradite (or prosecute) exists, as a matter of general international law, with respect to certain kinds of international offenses, such as war crimes, crimes against humanity, and acts of international terrorism.[33] In principle, this should be the case with respect to all international offenses. These are offenses reprehended by the international community as a whole. They are offenses against world public order. They are of concern to all states, and all states ought therefore to cooperate in bringing those who commit such offenses to justice. Absent a system of direct enforcement through prosecution before an international criminal court, reliance has to be placed on individual states to prosecute international offenders before their own courts. The whole effort to bring such offenders to justice will be frustrated if states do not accept a duty to prosecute or else extradite them to a state which is prepared to prosecute.[34]

---

[30] M. CHERIF BASSIOUNI, CRIMES AGAINST HUMANITY IN INTERNATIONAL CRIMINAL LAW 499-508 (1992); M. CHERIF BASSIOUNI, INTERNATIONAL EXTRADITION: UNITED STATES LAW AND PRACTICE 22-24 (2d ed. 1987) [hereinafter BASSIOUNI, EXTRADITION]; M. Cherif Bassiouni, *Characteristics of International Criminal Law Conventions, in* 1 ICL, CRIMES, *supra* note 6, at 1, 7-8; Bassiouni, *supra* note 3, at 34-36.

[31] Case concerning Questions and Interpretation and Application of the 1971 United Kingdom, Provisional Measures Order of 14 Apr. 1991, 1992 I.C.J. Reports 3, 69 (Weeramantry J., Dissenting); Case Concerning Questions of Interpretation and Apllication of the 1971 Montreal Convention Arising from the Aerial Incident at Lockerbie (Libya v. U.S.), Provisional Measures, Order of 14 Apr. 1992, 1992 I.C.J. Reports 114, 179 (Weeramantry J., dissenting); BASSIOUNI, EXTRADITION, *supra* note 30, at 22.

[32] *See, e.g.,* 1 OPPENHEIM'S INTERNATIONAL LAW, *supra* note 7, at 901, 950; IAN SHEARER, EXTRADITION IN INTERNATIONAL LAW 24-27 (1971); IAN BROWNLIE, PRINCIPLES OF PUBLIC INTERNATIONAL LAW 315 (4th ed. 1990); Hans Schultz, *The Classic Law of Extradition and Contemporary Needs, in* 2 TREATISE ON INTERNATIONAL CRIMINAL LAW 309, 310 (M. Cherif Bassiouni & Ved Nanda eds., 1973).

[33] With respect to war crimes and crimes against humanity, *see, e.g.,* BROWNLIE, *supra* note 32, at 315. It likewise has been argued that there is a general obligation to extradite (or prosecute) those who commit acts of international terrorism, on the ground that these acts as well so evoke the execration of the entire "international community" that all states are bound to cooperate in ensuring that their perpetrators are brought to justice. *See, e.g., "Statement of the Rules of International Law Applicable to International Terrorism," in* INTERNATIONAL LAW ASSOCIATION, REPORT OF THE SIXTY-FIRST CONFERENCE 6-7 (Paris 1984).

[34] A system of direct enforcement before an international criminal court is also likely to be ineffective unless states are obliged to surrender offenders for prosecution before that court (or, alternatively, to prosecute them before national courts).

(2) Whatever may be the case with respect to ordinary crimes, a duty to extradite or prosecute therefore follows from the common interest which all states have in the suppression of international offenses. It is a duty owing to the international community as a whole, the *civitas maxima*. Nonetheless, it still must be regarded, in naturalist terms, as an "imperfect obligation" unless accepted either explicitly in an international agreement or tacitly as a matter of state practice. In fact, this duty has been accepted as a definite legal obligation in an increasing number of multilateral treaties defining international offenses. Moreover, consistent reaffirmation in these treaties of the duty to extradite or prosecute may be taken to confirm that, at least so far as international offenses are concerned, the principle *aut dedere aut judicare* has been accepted as a positive norm of general international law.

(3) The principle is more than an ordinary norm of international law. It is a condition for the effective repression of offenses which are universally condemned. In large part, the rules prohibiting these offenses constitute *jus cogens* norms: they are rules of paramount importance for world public order, and cannot be set aside or modified in a subsequent treaty. States, by treaty, could not validly agree, for instance, to permit piracy against the merchant ships of another state, or to wage war by methods that violate the rules of war, such as the duty to give quarter.[35] They could not validly agree to acquiesce in genocide or other crimes against humanity. Thus, in so far as it constitutes a rule of general international law, the principle *aut dedere aut judicare* is also a *jus cogens* principle.

Evidence of Customary Status

As traditionally defined, customary international law is composed of the rules of conduct generally observed by states in their mutual relations and regarded by them as legally binding.[36] There must be a general practice, and it must be accepted as law.[37] Both elements are essential. A rule that states do not generally follow would not normally qualify as a rule of customary law. If the question is whether state practice in this sense supports the assertion that the principle *aut dedere aut judicare* has become a customary norm, the answer may well be no. Contemporary practice furnishes "far from consistent evidence" of the "actual existence" of a general obligation to extradite or prosecute with respect to international offenses.[38] It is questionable, for instance, how far the obligation to extradite or prosecute imposed by anti-terrorism treaties can be regarded as a customary rule binding on states apart from the special arrangements prescribed in those treaties, and very questionable how

---

[35] LORD MCNAIR, THE LAW OF TREATIES 215 (1961). *Cf.* Robert Y. Jennings, *Treaties in,* INTERNATIONAL LAW: ACHIEVEMENTS AND PROSPECTS 135, 154 (Mohammed Bedjaoui ed., 1991)("It is unthinkable that an agreement between two States to dismember a third State could be regarded as valid and enforceable by an international court; or, an agreement contrary to the law against the slave trade, or piracy or genocide.").

[36] *See, e.g.,* CLIVE PARRY, THE SOURCES AND EVIDENCES OF INTERNATIONAL LAW 62-67 (1965).

[37] G. M. DANILENKO, LAW-MAKING IN THE INTERNATIONAL COMMUNITY 81 (1993)("Although many aspects of custom formation in international law remain controversial, there is almost unanimous agreement that a legitimate customary law-making process requires the presence of two basic elements: practice and acceptance of this practice as law.").

[38] BASSIOUNI, EXTRADITION, *supra* note 30, at 22. *See also* JOSEPH J. LAMBERT, TERRORISM AND HOSTAGES IN INTERNATIONAL LAW 190 (1990); Kenneth C. Randall, *Universal Jurisdiction Under International Law*, 66 TEXAS L. REV. 785, 832-834 (1988).

far that obligation applies to forms of terrorism not covered by treaty.[39] Even with respect to the paradigmatic case of war crimes, the picture is cloudy.[40]

The claim that the obligation to extradite or prosecute represents a rule of customary international law does not entirely rest, however, on the actual behavior of states. Contemporary views about the formation of general international law downplay the importance of actual state practice. The focus instead is on normative utterances. One manifestation of this development is the ascription of quasi-legislative effect to resolutions of the United Nations General Assembly;[41] another is the tendency to speak as if multilateral treaties "could in some way legislate for states generally, without their cooperation."[42] Especially in connection with humanitarian norms and human rights, expressions of principles deemed deserving of recognition as the positive law of the "international community" are assumed to have become law even in the face of inconclusive or contrary practice.[43] The idea that reiteration of the "extradite or prosecute" formula in numerous conventions might elevate it to the status of a general duty under customary international law is very much in line with these developments.

This is a realm of acute controversy. For present purposes, however, we need only note that we are not dealing with a claim that the particular rule laid down in a particular treaty has become a rule of general international law binding independently of the treaty and therefore on states which are not parties to it. The assertion that the principle *aut dedere aut judicare* is a customary norm applicable to all (or to a large class of) international offenses involves more than treating the principle stated with respect to a particular offense in a particular treaty as binding on states which are not parties to treaty. It further involves abstracting the principle from the various guises in which it appears in one mass of treaty provisions and projecting it into circumstances dealt with in other treaties in which the principle is not so clearly stated or simply not stated at all. It is not as if there were a single document expressing the general view of the organized "international community" that the principle *aut dedere aut judicare* applies to all (or to a particular class) of international offenses. The conclusion that it does involves extrapolation from specific rules applicable to particular offenses to the general conclusion that the same rules must apply to every other offense falling within the same class. The underlying assumption seems to be that whatever holds some international offenses must hold for all. This looks very much like the fallacy of the undistributed middle. But it derives plausibility in this instance from a background

---

[39] *See* JOHN F. MURPHY, PUNISHING INTERNATIONAL TERRORISTS 36, 62, 131 (1985); Bin Cheng, *Aviation, Criminal Jurisdiction and Terrorism: The Hague/Extradition Prosecution Formula and Attacks at Airports, in* CONTEMPORARY PROBLEMS OF INTERNATIONAL LAW: ESSAYS IN HONOUR OF GEORG SCHWARZENBERGER 25, 41; Richard B. Lillich & John M. Paxman, *State Responsibility for Injuries to Aliens Occasioned by Terrorist Activities,* 26 AM. U.L. REV. 217, 276-307 (1977); and Lillich's remarks in, JOHN F. MURPHY, LEGAL ASPECTS OF INTERNATIONAL TERRORISM: SUMMARY REPORT OF AN INTERNATIONAL CONFERENCE 26-27 (American Society of International Law Studies in Transnational Legal Policy No. 19, 1980).

[40] *See generally* Christine van den Wyngaert, *War Crimes, Crimes Against Humanity, and Statutory Limitations, in* 3 INTERNATIONAL CRIMINAL LAW: ENFORCEMENT 89, 90-94 (M. Cherif Bassiouni ed., 1987) [hereinafter ICL, ENFORCEMENT].

[41] On the controversy concerning the legal effect of General Assembly resolutions, *see, e.g.,* SCHACHTER, *supra* note 5, at 85-94.

[42] Robert Y. Jennings, *Treaties as 'Legislation,' in* JUS ET SOCIETAS: ESSAYS IN TRIBUTE TO WOLFGANG FRIEDMANN 159, 168 (G. M. Wilner ed., 1979).

[43] *See* THEODOR MERON, HUMAN RIGHTS AND HUMANITARIAN NORMS AS CUSTOMARY LAW 41, 113-14, 131-32 (1989).

theory which postulates that international offenses must have certain attributes—that certain principles must be applicable to any offense which states are obliged by treaty to penalize. The symmetry and coherence of an international *Straftatsystem* require it.[44]

Underlying this line of thought is a combination of some or all of the following points:

(1) Certain conduct is so reprehended by the entire international community that it can be considered to amount to an international crime.

(2) An authentic guide to the kind of conduct that amounts to an international crime is a multilateral treaty requiring its repression.

(3) Conduct condemned in a widely ratified multilateral treaty also can be regarded as a violation of customary international law.

(4) International law directly imposes liability on individuals who commit international crimes.

(5) In prosecuting offenders who commit international crimes, states act to enforce international law.

(6) These crimes are the concern of all states.

(7) All states therefore have power to prosecute those who commit them.

(8) For the same reason, all states are bound to assist in bringing those who commit such crimes to justice—which implies an obligation either to prosecute or to extradite alleged offenders.

In this respect, the assertion that the principle *aut dedere aut judicare* constitutes a rule of customary law generally applicable to international offenses is based not so much on induction from the existing materials of international law as on spinning out certain possibilities implicit in the use in an international context of the terms "crime" and "community" and then weaving them into a coherent pattern.

The Hypothesis of a *Civitas Maxima*

This line of argument presupposes the existence of a world community, of a social or moral order common to all states or all humanity, such that certain types of crimes committed in one country are the legitimate concern of people in every other country.

The idea of the world as a single community, a "community of mankind," goes back to the Stoics.[45] Although sometimes associated with the idea of world government, it does not necessarily depend on accepting the desirability of a world state.[46] It primarily expresses a sense of human solidarity; it postulates certain universal objects and moral imperatives that are believed to limit the action of states and impel them to cooperate for the common good of a community of which everyone in the world is ultimately a member.

Various names have been used to refer to this hypothetical international community. That popularized by Christian Wolff in the eighteenth century speaks of a *civitas maxima*, a

---

[44] This kind of theory underlies, for instance, the masterful survey provided in Yoram Dinstein, *International Criminal Law*, 20 ISR. L. REV. 206 (1985).

[45] On the history of this idea, *see* WALTER SCHIFFER, THE LEGAL COMMUNITY OF MANKIND (1954).

[46] *See* CHARLES R. BEITZ, POLITICAL THEORY AND INTERNATIONAL RELATIONS 182-83 (1979).

supreme state or body politic.[47] Wolff was reviving an old expression.[48] To a greater or lesser extent, it is belief in the ultimate reality of this *civitas maxima* that underlies assertions about a common interest in repressing crime wherever it occurs and assertions about the existence of a genuine body of international criminal law.[49]

There are elements in international relations that lend plausibility to the hypothesis of a *civitas maxima* and to the cluster of ideas about international relations that it encapsulates. But there also are elements that lend plausibility to two other competing and very different images or pictures of what relations between states really are like, two alternative constellations of thought about the nature of international relations.[50]

One is the school of thought that sees the international system as essentially anarchial (*i.e.*, not subject to rule), a field of perennial conflict and power politics. States are depicted as existing in a Hobbesian "state of nature." Politics among nations is ultimately a war of all against all. Each state pursues its own interests, defines its own purposes, limited only by

---

[47] Wolff's expression is often translated as "supreme state." This is the convention adopted in the translation in the Classics of International Law series: 2 C. WOLFF, JUS GENTIUM METHODO SCIENTIFICA PERTRACTATUM (J. Drake trans., 1934). *See also, e.g.,* 6 (pt. 2) F. COPLESTON, A HISTORY OF PHILOSOPHY 134 (Image Books ed., 1960); SCHIFFER, *supra* note 45, at 69, 73; J. G. Starke, *The Influence of Grotius upon the Development of International Law in the Eighteenth Century, in* GROTIAN SOCIETY PAPERS 162, 170 (C.H. Alexandrowicz ed., 1972). But, for criticism of this usage, *see* Nicholas Greenwood Onuf, *Civitas Maxima: Wolff, Vattel and the Fate of Republicanism,* 88 AM. J. INT'L L. 280, 287-96 (1994).

[48] For Wolff himself, the civitas maxima was a formal concept, a fiction, a "postulate of reasoning," with "no constitutional or political content." W.K. HANCOCK, FOUR STUDIES OF WAR AND PEACE IN THIS CENTURY 94 (1961). Wolff was quite satisfied with the existing states-system. *See* ARTHUR NUSSBAUM, A CONCISE HISTORY OF THE LAW OF NATIONS 153-4 (2d ed. 1954); *See also* Onuf, *supra* note 47. On the other hand, he does make the presumed existence and "will" of the international community a basis of international law. Thus, Hersch Lauterpacht linked the expression to the assertion that international law ultimately is based on the "will of the international community," not the "will of the States." 2 H. LAUTERPACHT, INTERNATIONAL LAW: COLLECTED PAPERS 15-6 (E. Lauterpacht ed., 1975). For recurrent references to the concept by Lauterpacht, see indexes to vols. 2 and 3 of his *Collected Papers, s.v. "civitas maxima." See also* H. LAUTERPACHT, INTERNATIONAL LAW AND HUMAN RIGHTS 463 (1950)("recognition and protection of human rights may in itself become a significant contributory factor in the consummation of the organized *civitas maxima,* with the individual human being in the very centre of the constitution of the world.").

[49] *See* Edward M. Wise, *Terrorism and the Problems of an International Criminal Law,* 19 CONN. L. REV. 799 (1987); *cf.* G.O.W. Mueller, *International Criminal Law: Civitas Maxima—An Overview,* 15 CASE W. RES. J. INT'L L. 1 (1983).

[50] The following discussion is a reworking of the three "traditions" or categories of thought about international relations identified by Martin Wight in his lectures on "International Theory" at the London School of Economics in the 1950s. *See* MARTIN WIGHT, INTERNATIONAL THEORY: THE THREE TRADITIONS (G. Wight & B. Porter eds., 1991); *See also* Martin Wight, *An Anatomy of International Thought,* 13 REV. INT'L STUD. 221 (1987). These lectures have only recently been published and for a long while were known mainly through second-hand accounts, such as Hedley Bull, *Martin Wight and the Theory of International Relations,* 2 BRIT. J. INT'L STUD. 101 (1976); and Brian Porter, *Patterns of Thought and Practice: Martin Wight's 'International Theory,' in* THE REASON OF STATES 64 (M. Donelan ed., 1978). The three categories are only implicit in Wight's other published work. *See* MARTIN WIGHT, POWER POLITICS (H. Bull & C. Hobraad eds., 1979); MARTIN WIGHT, SYSTEMS OF STATES (H. Bull ed., 1977); Martin Wight, *The Balance of Power and International Order, in* THE BASES OF INTERNATIONAL ORDER 85 (A. James ed., 1973); and his essays in DIPLOMATIC INVESTIGATIONS (H. Butterfield & M. Wight ed., 1968). Nonetheless, Wight's categories had a considerable influence on academic writing about international relations in Britain. *See, e.g.,* HEDLEY BULL, THE ANARCHICAL SOCIETY 24-27 (1977); and the papers collected in DIPLOMATIC INVESTIGATIONS, *supra*; THE REASON OF STATES, *supra*; and THE COMMUNITY OF STATES (J. Mayall ed., 1982). A comparable three-part distinction now seems to be "fairly standard" in categorizing normative thinking about international relations. LEA BRILMAYER, JUSTIFYING INTERNATIONAL ACTS 29 (1989). *Cf.* JOSEPH S. NYE, JR., NUCLEAR ETHICS 27-41 (1986); Mark J. Hoffman, *Normative Approaches, in* INTERNATIONAL RELATIONS: A HANDBOOK OF CURRENT THEORY 27 (M. Light & A.J.R. Groom eds., 1985).

considerations of expediency and prudence. Force, mitigated so far as may be by such considerations, is the *ultima ratio*. No moral rules restrain states in their relations with one another. Nor are they bound by legal rules. Such rules are only valid in the context of a "civil society." There is no international society. The international system is a moral and legal vacuum (or, as in the Hegelian version, the morality of states lies in self-assertion). There must be some minimum ground rules to govern interactions between states, as every game requires rules; but these are not necessarily rules of law. The rules governing relations between states do not have the quality of law in the same sense that rules governing relations between individuals in civil society do; they are considerably more fragile, open to interpretation by those subject to them, and likely to give way as soon as countervailing considerations of self interest appear. The disjunctive forces in international life so far predominate as to make it implausible to take seriously the idea of "international law" actually restraining states in their mutual relations. There certainly is no international "community," and therefore there can be no universal concept of crime:[51] even "the sacredness of human life is a purely municipal idea of no validity outside the jurisdiction."[52]

There is a third main pattern of thought about international relations in which the international system is seen neither as a "state of nature" nor as the inclusive moral community implicit in the hypothesis of a *civitas maxima*, but rather as a "society of states." States, not individuals, are the chief members of this society. Rules of international law represent customary or agreed restraints on the conduct of its members. States, for the most part, pursue purposes which they set for themselves. They are constrained, however, by prescriptions regarding toleration and accommodation that make it possible for them to continue to coexist as a society. In this international society, there is no "common superior." There is no universal "common good" requiring states to pursue particular substantive aims.[53] There is not the degree of cohesion normally associated with the idea of a "community."[54] But neither is there such complete anarchy as to render the idea of "international law" implausible.

These three competing views of the nature of international relations are paradigms, analytical categories and ideal-types. No actual thinker fits exactly within any one of them. Rather, elements of each appear in the thinking of us all. Each can be divided into sub-categories defined in terms of qualifications and involutions suggested by the others. For instance, one can come up with more or less "realistic," "idealistic" or "cosmopolitan"

---

[51] THOMAS HOBBES, LEVIATHAN 190 (M. Oakeshott ed., 1957)(1651)("Where no civil society is, there is no crime.") .

[52] *Letter from O. W. Holmes to Frederick Pollock (Feb. 1, 1920), in* 2 HOLMES POLLOCK LETTERS 36 (M. Howe ed., 1941).

[53] This is the central argument of TERRY NARDIN, LAW, MORALITY, AND THE RELATION OF STATES (1983).

[54] The terms "community" and "society" are said to have "slightly different ranges and flavours in ordinary usage" and no completely "settled resonance or connotation."JOHN FINNIS, NATURAL LAW AND NATURAL RIGHTS 135, 156-57 (1980). They are used here to indicate, like Tönnies' distinction between *Gemeinschaft* and *Gesellschaft*, two polar forms of human association: "community" implies the higher, "society" a lesser degree of cohesion or solidarity. *See also* GEORG SCHWARZENBERGER, POWER POLITICS 12-13 (2d ed. 1951); Schwarzenberger, *Civitas Maxima?*, 1975 Y.B. WORLD AFFAIRS 337, *reprinted in* GEORG SCHWARZENBERGER, THE DYNAMICS OF INTERNATIONAL LAW 107-134 (1976). But, for a different usage of the two terms, *cf.* R.G. COLLINGWOOD, THE NEW LEVIATHAN 138-47 (rev. ed. 1992)(1942), where "community" is treated as the looser form of association (almost equivalent to "class"), while "society"" is defined as a community whose members share a "social consciousness."

versions of a "society of states;"[55] and more or less "progressive" and "humanitarian," more or less backward-looking and vicious versions of what the idea of an "international community" implies.[56]

Further, international relations cannot be adequately described entirely in terms of any one of these three patterns. None provides a completely accurate account of what the international system actually is like. None catches exactly the whole reality of international relations. Each points to important features, but gets others out of focus. It is not a matter of deciding which one is true. None are. All are. Only their complementary adequacies and inadequacies supply anything like a whole truth about international relations—although at different times, for different purposes, one or the other may seem to come closer than the others to describing the actual conduct of states.

Each of these paradigms imports elements of prescribing and describing a view of how international relations ought to be conducted. Readiness to accept one or another as an accurate description turns, to some extent, on beliefs about what international relations should be like. Yet each embodies an influential and durable set of ideals. The principles implicit in each, such as national self-assertion, non-intervention, and universal respect for human rights, represent important but ultimately incompatible aspirations. Thus, in their prescriptive aspect, these paradigms are a way of expressing the implications and the incommensurability of the ends that shape the conduct of international relations.

The pattern of thought which represents the international system as a "society of states" incorporates many of the premises of traditional international law. The two are closely connected. From its beginnings, what we know as international law has been largely based on the idea of a "society of states." It has been predicated on a rejection both of the idea that states exist in a Hobbesian "state of nature" and of the medieval view that Europe in some sense formed a single community. Gierke's account of natural law thinking draws a distinction between three views of the nature of international relations prevalent in early modern Europe that coincides with the three paradigms discussed above: (1) the tendency (sustained by the lingering medieval idea of a universal empire) for the concept of an international society to harden into that of a world-state, with a real group authority attributed to the international legal community; (2) the view of Bodin and Hobbes, which rejected *in toto* the idea of a natural community uniting states together; and (3) the idea of an international society involving a system of rights and duties mutually binding on states in their

---

[55] Wight's term for the paradigm that postulates a "society of states" was the "Rationalist" or "Grotian tradition." Within this tradition, Grotius himself stands toward the "cosmopolitan" pole. The notion of a "Grotian conception" has sometimes been used more narrowly to refer to the cosmopolitan or solidarist pole of the wider "Grotian tradition." *See, e.g.*, Hedley Bull, *The Grotian Conception of International Society, in* DIPLOMATIC INVESTIGATIONS, *supra* note 50, at 51; Hedley Bull, *The Importance of Grotius in the Study of International Relations, in* HUGO GROTIUS AND INTERNATIONAL RELATIONS 65 (H. Bull, B. Kingsbury & A. Roberts eds., 1990). This is a rife source of confusion. On these two senses of "the Grotian conception," *see* Tony Evans & Peter Wilson, *Regime Theory and the English School of International Relations: A Comparison,* 21 MILLENNIUM: J. OF INT'L STUD. 329, 224 (1992); Nicholas J. Wheeler, *Pluralist or Solidarist Conceptions of International Society: Bull and Vincent on Humanitarian Intervention,* 21 MILLENNIUM: J. OF INT'L STUD. 463 (1992); R. J. Vincent, *Order in International Politics, in* ORDER AND VIOLENCE: HEDLEY BULL AND INTERNATIONAL RELATIONS 38, 40-41 (J.D.B. Miller & R. J. Vincent eds., 1990).

[56] Wight termed his third paradigm "Revolutionist;" it is exemplified in ideologies of the Reformation and French Revolution, and also in ideologies of Counter-Reformation and Counter-Revolution—in all ideologies that preach the imperative of human solidarity. *See* H. Bull, *Martin Wight and the Theory of International Relations, supra* note 50, at 105.

relations with each other, but not the authority of the whole over its parts.[57] It was the third view which ultimately predominated and shaped the development of modern international law. Grotius, although inspired, to a large extent, by ideas of human solidarity and Christian unity, is a significant precursor primarily because he tried to strike a middle ground between thinking of Latin Christendom as a single community or super-state and the temptation to conclude that otherwise there could be no moral or legal bonds between separate sovereigns.[58] But each of these three views corresponds to persistent elements in international relations; each has continuing validity as a partial description of important features of the international system. While one may be dominant at a given moment, a full picture requires taking all three into account.

Like the paradigm of a "society of states," the concepts of traditional international law present a partial and fragmented view of what the world is really like.[59] They have come to seem inadequate precisely because they exclude significant developments that make our world seem more than ever like a genuine community, and also more like a jungle. The contemporary world seems to be undergoing a long-term process of transition from an international system in which the dominant element is the nation-state to one more nearly predicated on the common good of the global community. In certain respects, this movement toward global integration is a reversal of the break-up of Latin Christendom associated with the Peace of Westphalia (1648), which marked the beginning of the modern states-system. Richard Falk, among others, has referred to a movement from a system order based on "the Westphalian tradition" of territorial sovereignty to a more cohesive form of international order.[60] Contemporary international law thus embodies two intersecting systems, one superseding the other.[61] Indeed, we sometimes argue as if a global community were actually in being.[62] But reality is far more complicated. No one coherent pattern of thought captures it all. In many respects, the global community is, at best, an order *in posse*. To treat it as a fully existing reality is to "take as proven precisely what requires proof: namely the existence of a sense of community and the willingness of particular collectivities to keep their conduct

---

57 OTTO GIERKE, NATIONAL LAW AND THE THEORY OF SOCIETY 1500 TO 1800 85-86, 195-98 (Ernest Barker trans., Beacon Press reprint 1957)(1934). This is a translation of 4 OTTO VON GIERKE, DAS DEUTSCHE GENOSSENSCHAFTSRECHT 361-63, 535-41 (1954 reprint)(1913).

58 *See* F.H. HINSLEY, SOVEREIGNTY 186-192 (1966); *cf.* Bull, *The Importance of Grotius, supra* note 55, at 71-72.

59 *Cf.* ANTHONY CARTY, THE DECAY OF INTERNATIONAL LAW (1986).

60 *See, e.g.*, RICHARD FALK, REVITALIZING INTERNATIONAL LAW (1989); Richard Falk, *A New Paradigm for International Legal Studies: Prospects and Proposals, in* INTERNATIONAL LAW: A CONTEMPORARY PERSPECTIVE 651-702 (R. Falk, F. Kratochwil & S. Mendlovitz eds., 1985); Richard Falk, *The Interplay of Westphalia and Charter Conceptions of International Legal Order, in id.* at 116-142.

61 An idea worked out in ANTONIO CASSESE, INTERNATIONAL LAW IN A DIVIDED WORLD (1986).

62 The picture is sometimes confused, moreover, by a tendency to use the expression "international community" as if it were synonymous with what we have been calling a "society of states." Thus, writers who dismiss the idea of "a planetary community of individuals" as unrealistic, and who admit that the primary actors in the international system are still states, and that the continued insistence on state sovereignty prevents "far-reaching integration and community actions in many areas," nonetheless insist that there can be "no serious doubts about the existence of the international community" because states are prepared to recognize, if not common substantive rules, at least certain procedural rules governing the processes by which international law is made. *See, e.g.*, DANILENKO, *supra* note 37, at 11-15 (1993). In the sense in which we have been using these terms, this proves the existence of an "international society," but not an "international community."

in conformity with the higher good of a universal community."[63] This is not without its dangers.[64] A shift of the center of gravity of international law away from states and towards the international community would be a decisive advance if it corresponded to a real transformation in the behavior of states. But, in the present state of international relations, to speak as if an "international community" actually were in being runs the risk of exciting expectations that are bound to be disappointed and, worse yet, of encouraging use of the rhetoric of universality as a cloak for hegemonic objectives.[65]

The Principle as a Rule of *Jus Cogens*

A final word should be said about the suggestion that the principle *aut dedere aut judicare* represents not only a rule of customary international law, but also a rule of *jus cogens*, since this further illustrates how the argument for the customary status of that principle hinges on a particular vision of the nature of the international system as comprising a genuine community.

The term *jus cogens* refers to a body of overriding or "peremptory" norms of such paramount importance that they cannot be set aside by acquiescence or agreement of the parties to a treaty;[66] rather, a treaty will be void if it conflicts with a peremptory norm "from which no derogation is permitted."[67] The concept of *jus cogens* is one of a cluster of related ideas that emphasize the primacy of the interests of the "international community" as a whole. Cognate ideas include the notion of "obligations *erga omnes*" adumbrated by the International Court of Justice in the *Barcelona Traction* case,[68] and the distinction between "international crimes" and "international delicts" set out in Article 19 of the International Law Commission's Draft Articles on State Responsibility.[69]

All of these concepts involve an effort to differentiate between norms of international law, to establish degrees of international legal obligation, reflecting a sense that certain

---

63 CHARLES DE VISSCHER, THEORY AND REALITY IN PUBLIC INTERNATIONAL LAW 89 (P. E. Corbett trans., rev. ed. 1968).

64 *See,* especially, Prosper Weil, *Towards Normative Relativity in International Law?*, 77 AM.J.INT'L L. 413, 441-42 (1983); *See also* Gaetano Arangio-Ruiz, *The Concept of International Law and the Theory of International Organization, in* THE UNITED NATIONS DECLARATION ON FRIENDLY RELATIONS AND THE SYSTEM OF THE SOURCES OF INTERNATIONAL LAW app. 199-301 (1979).

65 To cite only historical examples, the misappropriation of cosmopolitan ideals to serve the ends of power or ideology appears, for instance, in the appeals to solidarity by which the Holy Alliance sought to guarantee the existing order against revolution, and in the recurrent tendency to refer to opponents as *hostis humani generis* (enemies of all mankind), the expression typically applied to pirates. TERTULLIAN, APOLOGY xxxvii, 8, 170 (Loeb Classical Library 1931) indicates that the expression was applied to early Christians as well. William the Silent was assassinated in 1584 pursuant to a decree in which Philip II likewise condemned him as "an enemy of the human race." *See The Proscription of William the Silent, in* THE LOW COUNTRIES IN EARLY MODERN TIMES 71, 79 (Herbert H. Rowen ed., 1972).

66 *See* CRIMES AGAINST HUMANITY, *supra* note 30, at 489-99; M. Cherif Bassiouni, *A Functional Approach to 'General Principles of International Law,'* 11 MICH. J. INT'L L. 768, 801-09 (1990).

67 Vienna Convention on the Law of Treaties, May 23, 1969, art. 53, 1155 U.N.T.S. 331, 344.

68 Case Concerning the Barcelona Traction, Light & Power Co. Ltd. (Belg. v. Spain), 1970 I.C.J. Reports 3, 32 (Judgement of Feb. 5).

69 *Report of the International Law Commission to the General Assembly, U.N. Doc. A/31/10 (1976), in* 1976 INT'L L. COMM'N Y.B. 73, 75. For further discussion of the Commission's concept of an "international crime," *see* Edward M. Wise, *International Crimes and Domestic Criminal Law,* 38 DEPAUL L. REV. 923, 928-931 (1989), and the various papers and bibliography in INTERNATIONAL CRIMES OF STATE: A CRITICAL ANALYSIS OF THE ILC'S DRAFT ARTICLE 19 ON STATE RESPONSIBILITY (Joseph H.H. Weiler et al. eds., 1989).

norms have a special importance because associated with the fundamental interests or common good of the entire "international community." The immediate implication of characterizing such norms as *jus cogens* is that they cannot then be abrogated by agreement among a particular set of states any more than they could be set aside unilaterally by action of a single state.

A number of the rules prohibiting international offenses (such as aggression, genocide, and serious breaches of international humanitarian law) are widely believed to constitute rules of *jus cogens*: these prohibitions are supposed to be of paramount importance for the maintenance of the public order of the "international community" and therefore are not susceptible of being set aside by agreement. In so far as it constitutes a rule of customary international law with respect to these offenses, the same might be said of the principle *aut dedere aut judicare*.

Arguments in favor of the customary status of the obligation to extradite or prosecute, at least in cases involving international offenses, do not primarily rely on evidence that the practice of states is to do one or the other in such cases; these arguments turn rather on postulating the existence of a genuine international community which has, in effect, legislated through multilateral conventions to create a genuine body of criminal law which all states are bound to enforce, either by prosecuting offenders themselves or extraditing them to a state which is prepared to prosecute.

If one accepts that the obligation to extradite or prosecute international offenders is an obligation imposed by customary international law, it is perhaps only a short step to regarding it as a rule of *jus cogens*—a rule of paramount importance for world public order whose states are not free to contract out of whenever they please.

The assertion that the principle *aut dedere aut judicare* represents a *jus cogens* norm may look like gilding the lily. But it is meant to underscore the crucial importance of the principle for the effective repression of international offenses. In an international system that is still largely decentralized, prohibitions of international offenses will be meaningful only in so far as states are regarded as having an overriding obligation to bring those who perpetrate such offenses to justice. This is not or should not be an obligation that can be contracted away. In so far as the prohibition of a particular offense is regarded as being of paramount importance for the maintenance of international public order, states should not be entitled to acquiesce in violations. Any state having hold of an individual who has committed such an offense must take steps to bring the malefactor to justice (either by prosecution or by extradition); if it does not do one or the other, then it has, in effect, by its inaction impermissibly acquiesced in the violation of a peremptory norm. The very notion of a peremptory norm, however, presupposes the existence of a larger community whose interests trump those of its individual members.

Section II

Jurisdiction

Extraterritorial Jurisdiction

Christopher L. Blakesley[1]

Introduction: Brief Overview of the Traditional Bases of Jurisdiction over Extraterritorial Crime

This chapter studies prescriptive jurisdiction. We will consider the legal bases upon which jurisdiction over extraterritorial crime may be founded. We will analyze and compare the law of several prototypical nations as well as international law on jurisdiction. We will try to determine what the proper bases of jurisdiction are and whether there is any hierarchy among them when concurrent jurisdiction exists. We will pay special attention to the crimes of terrorism (in their various forms), crimes against humanity, and narcotics trafficking, because these crimes seem prototypical. We will also analyze the jurisdictional rules of the Ad Hoc Tribunals for the former Yugoslavia and Rwanda and in the potential permanent international criminal court. We will analyze jurisdictional properties of legislation[2] and international conventions.[3]

---

[1] J.Y. Sanders Professor of Law, Louisiana State University Law Center. Portions of this chapter are adapted from the following works by the author: Covey T. Oliver et al., *in* THE INTERNATIONAL LEGAL SYSTEM: CASES & MATERIALS (4th ed. 1995) [hereinafter THE INTERNATIONAL LEGAL SYSTEM]; CHRISTOPHER L. BLAKESLEY, TERRORISM, DRUGS, INTERNATIONAL LAW AND THE PROTECTION OF HUMAN LIBERTY (1992) [hereinafter TERRORISM, DRUGS].

[2] For example, 18 U.S.C. §§ 2331-2334 (1996 Supp.). Also, the Italian government has been working to prevent the use of Italy as a base for terrorist acts and has developed information in conjunction with its investigation and prosecution of 14 persons involved in the *Achille Lauro* hijacking. *See* David Simonetti & Bruce Zagaris, *International Terrorism: Italian Investigation into International Terrorism,* 2 INT'L ENFORCEMENT L. REP. 228 (1986). In Germany, one finds the *Antiterrorismus-Gesetz* (Antiterrorism Law) of 1976, § 129a StGB; §§ 112.3, 148.2 StPO (1976); the *Kontaktsperre-Gesetz* (Law Banning Contacts), §§ 31-38 EGGVG(1977), § 34a (1985) (German Judicial Code); the *Gezetz zur Änderung der Strafprozessordnung* (Law on the Reform of the Code of Criminal Procedure), §§ 111, 148.2, at 3 StPO (1978); *Gesetz zur Änderung der Strafprozessordnung,* § 163d StPO (1986); the *Gezetz zur Bekämpfung des Terrorismus* (Law on the Suppression of Terrorism), §§ 129a, 130a StGB (1986) (reviving the old prohibition of "propagandizing violence by distributing writings or providing instructional guidance for the commission of a violent act at a meeting) (cited and discussed in Jürgen Meyer, *German Criminal Law Relating to International Terrorism,* 60 U. COLO. L. REV. 571, 576-78 (1989)). *See also, e.g.,* Philip B. Heymann & Ian H. Gershengorn, *Pursuing Justice, Respecting the Law,* 3 CRIM. L.F. 1 (1991); *See also Tokyo Summit Agrees on Methods to Fight International Terrorism,* 2 INT'L ENFORCEMENT L. REP. 138 (1986); Bruce Zagaris & David Simonetti, *Judicial Assistance Under Bilateral Treaties to Combat International Terrorism, in* LEGAL RESPONSES TO INTERNATIONAL TERRORISM: U.S. PROCEDURAL ASPECTS (M. Cherif Bassiouni ed., 1987).

[3] *E.g.,* Convention and Protocol From the International Conference on the Suppression of Unlawful Acts Against the Safety of Maritime Navigation, *opened for signature* Mar. 10, 1988, IMO Doc. SUA/CON/15 (1988) and IMO Doc. SUA/CON/16/Rev. 1 (1988), *reprinted in* 27 I.L.M. 668 (1988); *Recent Developments,* 30 HARV. INT'L L.J. 226 (1989); Malvina Halberstam, *Terrorism on the High Seas: The Achille Lauro & the IMO Convention on Maritime Safety,* 82 A.J.I.L. 269 (1988). This convention provides that assertion of jurisdiction in the flagship state is mandatory when an offense is committed against a flagship of a state by a national of the state or in the territory of the state (art. 6). A state is permitted to assert jurisdiction when a resident of that state has committed an offense, or when a resident has committed one of the offenses, when a national is seized, threatened, injured or killed during the commission of one of the listed offenses, or when conduct is aimed at coercing a state to act in a certain way. *Recent Development, supra* this note, at 230-31. The offenses covered by the treaty are: hijacking a ship; violence against a person on board a ship, if the violence is likely to endanger the safe navigation of the

It is necessary that we clearly define the bases of jurisdiction conceptually and comparatively. This will be done to determine the extent of expansion. This chapter first defines the traditional theoretical bases of extraterritorial jurisdiction, applying treaties, legislation and jurisprudence. Jurisdictional theory will be applied to various offenses, such as terrorism and thwarted extraterritorial narcotics conspiracies. We will compare U.S. law with that of some continental countries and their interaction with international law. We will also discuss the relationship between jurisdiction, extradition and other mutual assistance measures.

International law is the language by which nations attempt to resolve competing legal interests. As with any other language, if the definitions or essential concepts become muddled, it is difficult to communicate. The traditional bases of jurisdiction over extraterritorial crime are essential concepts in the language of international law. The decision to grant or deny extradition, or to perform any other form of mutual assistance in criminal matters, for example, often depends on whether the interested nation recognizes the basis of jurisdiction asserted by another. Confusion over the traditional bases of jurisdiction therefore often leads to disagreement, diplomatic protest, or refusal to cooperate.

A discussion of language and culture may take on metaphysical qualities. For example, consider Noam Chomsky's thesis that people are born with a deep linguistic structure, a "proto-human-grammar" embedded into them, from which all human grammars flow.[4] One may wonder whether there is some deeply embedded notion of legal grammar of law in each of us and each nation.[5] Kipling notes that language is the "mightiest drug" of humankind and that this drug has legal side effects. He discusses language as a creative force, focusing on the *Bible*, *The Odyssey*, Wagner, Goethe's *Faust*, and the beliefs of the Bambara, in West Africa, in all of which, creation, even of ourselves, occurs with the "word."[6] Undoubtedly, language forms us and our perceptions. Learning a language gives us a new personality. It is through language, our own and any others that we take the time and effort to learn, that we become who we are. Is Goethe's reference to "the law innate in us" pertinent to a study of jurisdiction in international criminal law?

> Laws are transmitted, like some dread disease,
> Father to son, and spread from place to place.
> Reason turns to folly, boon becomes a bane
> To later generations. Yet the law
> Innate in us is meanwhile quite ignored.[7]

---

ship; sabotage of a ship or of maritime navigational facilities; communication of false information regarding navigation; and injuring or killing any person in connection with other offenses. *Id.*

4 BERNHARD GROSSFELD, THE STRENGTH AND WEAKNESS OF COMPARATIVE LAW (1990); Christopher L. Blakesley, *Review Essay: Comparative Law: Its Purposes & Possibilities,* 27 TEXAS INT'L L.J. 315 (1991) (citing NOAM CHOMSKY, LANGUAGE AND MIND 76 (2d ed. 1972)).

5 GROSSFELD, *supra* note 4, at 103-05.

6 *Id.* at 88-91.

7 *Id.* at 104 (citing JOHANN GOETHE, FAUST, Part One, The Student Scene (1800). Grossfeld asks us to compare this with Thomas Jefferson's view that "[t]here should be a revolution every twenty years." *Id.* (citing GARRY WILLS, INVENTING AMERICA, JEFFERSON'S DECLARATION OF INDEPENDENCE 124 (1978)).

Wittgenstein's notion that "the limits of language (the language I understand) mean the limits of my world,"[8] reminds us that "[w]hen we learn another language we unconsciously adopt its speakers' world of thought: '[L]anguage thinks in us.'"[9] The poet Schiller wrote: "[a] developed language . . . composes and thinks for you."[10] Language is certainly a world picture, given form.[11] Similarly, "[m]an [sic] has as many hearts as he has languages."[12]

Thus, as law is language, it is necessary to develop it well and in a principled way. Law is language and that the "constitutive and cognitive power of language is especially significant for law, for only in language do the concepts of positive law have any being at all."[13] Different languages represent different "world-views."[14] The term "verdict" in its Latin derivative, for example, means telling the truth (*verum dicere*). In this regard it is interesting to compare the philology and focus of the continental, formerly inquisitorial, systems of criminal justice with those of Common Law derivation. I have discussed elsewhere the implications of evolution in these two systems, which today seem to be converging.[15] The goal of the continental investigation and trial was and still is to "find the objective truth." Anciently and in the Middle Ages, it was so important that there were formulary tortures to be applied to "find the truth."[16] The term "verdict" came to mean something different in the U.S. constitutional system, although the current Supreme Court seems to be moving us toward the continental model. The Bill of Rights and its evolution via judicial interpretation represented the "don't tread on me" vision of the relationship between the state and the people held by revolutionaries such as Thomas Paine and Patrick Henry. Barriers were established to prevent government from having so much power to "find the truth" that it could also establish a police state.[17] Truth finding, while important, was secondary to that.

Thus, language etymology tells us a great deal of each other's legal culture and this lets us understand how each other thinks. We take our own world-view for granted as the product of our natural sane common sense, but in reality it is provided by our mother tongue. *Vox populi, vox dei.*[18] This feeling may be a weakness, which may be overcome by comparative analysis. Another example of this comes to mind. The term "to represent" in English is the same in French. Yet the conceptual meaning and mental picture created by the word in the mind of an United States attorney and his or her French counterpart is startlingly different. In a case in which the United States sought the extradition of one Willie Holder,

---

8 *Id.* at 92 (quoting LUDWIG WITTGENSTEIN, TRACTATUS LOGICO-PHILOSOPHICUS 62 (1933)).

9 *Id.* at 96 (quoting EMIL WEZEL, SPRACHE UND GEIST IV (1935)).

10 FRIEDRICH SCHILLER, DILETTANT IN TABULAE VOTIVAE, I WERKE 319 (1952).

11 GROSSFELD, *supra* note 4 (referring to GOTTFRIED BENN, WORTE: "Alone: really alone—just you and words.").

12 *Id.* at 95-96 (citing JACOB BURCKHARDT, ÜBER DAS STUDIUM DER GESCHICHTE 276 (E. Ganz, Munich 1982)). Also, didn't Victor Hugo say that a person has as many personalities as he or she has languages?

13 *Id.* at 92.

14 *Id.* at 96.

15 *See* TERRORISM, DRUGS, *supra* note 1; Christopher L. Blakesley, *Criminal Procedure, in* INTRODUCTION TO THE LAW OF THE UNITED STATES (1991); CHRISTOPHER L. BLAKESLEY, LE DEVELOPPEMENT DU DROIT PÉNAL AUX ETATS-UNIS (1991).

16 TERRORISM, DRUGS, *supra* note 1, at Ch. 1.

17 *See* discussion in TERRORISM, DRUGS, *supra* note 1; Blakesley, *supra* note 15; BLAKESLEY & CURTIS, *supra* note 15; Christopher L. Blakesley & Otto Lagodny, *Finding Harmony Amidst Disagreement Over Extradition, Jurisdiction, the Role of Human Rights*, 24 VAND. J. TRANSNAT'L L. 1, 65-68 (1991).

18 GROSSFELD, *supra* note 4, at 97.

who was charged with hijacking an American airliner,[19] the French Avocat General, who "represents" the United States Government before the French courts in extradition matters, presented the evidence against Holder and then proceeded to recommend to the French court that Holder not be extradited, because the Avocat General felt that the crime was one of a political character. The United States Government was outraged that the person "representing" the United States in France would simply present the evidence and then argue against the United States position. The American vision of "represent" conjured up the aggressive adversarial paradigm. On the other hand, the French Avocat General was functioning under the French concept of the term "*representé*," which requires him to present all the papers and to speak to the court as his perception of justice would require. Thus, he must present exculpatory evidence and arguments if he feels that they are appropriate. Both sides in this controversy were right, based on their own notion of "representation." Notwithstanding the use of the same term, misunderstanding arose due to different visions of criminal justice raised by the term.[20] Obviously, the practitioner needs to become familiar with the legal culture behind the legal language.

Perhaps it is true that "our basic feeling for play, rhythm, and proportion [plus the sense of right and wrong?] is inborn" in language and in law.[21] Law, if it is really law, Grossfeld says, causes an appropriate response in all peoples' "spiritual wave-length." Comparative law and comparative thinking help us address difficult issues. It is absolutely necessary in the international arena.

Jurisdiction in General[22]

Jurisdiction is the means of making law functional. Neither international law nor domestic law can have any immediate impact on a criminal, unless legislative, adjudicatory, and enforcement jurisdiction obtain.[23] Moreover, any international legal definition of crime and any action against it make no practical sense, except in relation to jurisdiction, the only practical means for translating law to reality. The term jurisdiction may be defined as the authority to effect legal interests—to prescribe rules of law, to adjudicate legal questions and to compel, to induce compliance or to take any other enforcement action. Adjudicative and enforcement jurisdiction are dependent on prescriptive or legislative jurisdiction.

U.S. and other national courts recently have expanded the traditional bases of jurisdiction over extraterritorial crime. The major impetus behind the expansion is a

---

19 *In re Holder, reprinted in* 1975 DIG. U.S. PRAC. INT'L L. 168-75.

20 *Ce sont des faux amis.*

21 GROSSFELD, *supra* note 4, at 104.

22 For full authority and discussion of these jurisdictional issues, *see* TERRORISM, DRUGS, *supra* note 1, at Chs. 3, 4; THE INTERNATIONAL LEGAL SYSTEM: *supra* note 1, at Ch. 3, especially pages 1-10; *see also, generally,* Jordan J. Paust *et al,* INTERNATIONAL CRIMINAL LAW: CASES & MATERIALS Ch. 3 (1996); Christopher L. Blakesley, *International Extradition For Business Crimes, in* DOING BUSINESS ABROAD: IDENTIFYING AND AVOIDING CRIMINAL RISKS (1992); Christopher L. Blakesley, *Criminal Procedure for Foreign Lawyers, in* INTRODUCTION TO THE LAW OF THE UNITED STATES (1992); Christopher L. Blakesley, *The Regionalization of International Criminal Law & the Protection of Human Rights in International Cooperation in Criminal Proceedings,* 65 REVUE INTERNATIONALE DE DROIT PÉNAL 493 (1994); Christopher L. Blakesley, *Review Essay, Comparative Law: Its Purposes and Possibilities, thoughts prompted by* Grossfeld's COMPARATIVE LAW, *supra* note 4.

23 THE INTERNATIONAL LEGAL SYSTEM, *supra* note 1, at Ch. 3; RESTATEMENT (THIRD) OF THE FOREIGN RELATIONS LAW OF THE UNITED STATES § 401 (1987) [hereinafter RESTATEMENT (THIRD)].

perceived burgeoning of transnational and international crime. Cooperation among governments in investigation and extradition is of paramount importance to combating international crime. Hence, a state requesting assistance in criminal matters must live up to any and all limitations and requirements made by the requested state.[24] Any disparagement of a nation's sovereignty, treaty formulations, or agreements to extradite or otherwise cooperate will ultimately be detrimental to the effectiveness of international crime prevention. The U.S. Congress and courts in their "war on drugs," for example, have sought prophylactically to discourage narcotics importation by asserting jurisdiction over even thwarted extraterritorial conspiracies[25] and have asserted jurisdiction over alleged terrorists who have committed their violence outside U.S. territory.[26] Although expansion of jurisdiction might help by broadening enforcement, it sometimes comes at a cost; expediency occasionally prevails over the rule of law or coherent strategy.[27] Courts have tugged and stretched the traditional bases of jurisdiction in order to obtain jurisdiction over sometimes anomalous cases such as extraterritorial narcotics conspiracies which have been thwarted before fruition. In so doing, courts have sometimes muddled the language of international and domestic law and created the risk that cooperation will be hampered. Expediency and a tendency to seek immediate, spectacular symbolism for domestic consumption must not be allowed to overcome the rule of law and prudence. Thus, one may question whether the invasion of Panama and the seizure of Manuel Noriega or the abduction of *Alvarez-Machain* promote or detract from the rule of law and the battle against international crime.

The definition, nature, and scope of jurisdiction vary depending on the context in which jurisdiction is to be asserted. United States domestic law, for example, defines and applies notions of jurisdiction pursuant to the constitutional provisions relating to the separation of powers, federalism, and due process. Also, jurisdictional issues are made more difficult and more like the international system, because of the variegated federal and state systems. Conflicts of jurisdiction are resolved by reference to the Full Faith and Credit Clause, U.S. Constitution, art. IV. § 1, which provides: "full faith and credit shall be given in each state to the Public Acts, Records and judicial proceedings of every other state," and other constitutional principles.[28] The international setting gives rise to definitions and applications of jurisdiction. International law has failed to develop jurisdictional rules that are as comprehensive or precise as the domestic jurisdictional laws of individual nations.[29]

The set of rules relating to legislative, judicial, and enforcement jurisdiction in the international criminal setting is not as well developed as the parallel domestic laws of the

---

24 *E.g.*, U.S. v. Saccoccia, 58 F.3d 754, 766 (1st Cir. 1995).

25 *E.g.*, U.S. v. DeWeese, 532 F.2d 1267 (5th Cir. 1980), *cert. denied*, 451 U.S. 902 (1981).

26 *See, e.g.*, U.S. v. Yunis, 681 F. Supp. 896 (D.D.C. 1988), *rev'd* 859 F.2d 953 (D.C. Cir. 1988); Abraham Abramovsky, *Extraterritorial Jurisdiction: The United States' Unwarranted Attempt to Alter International Law in United States v. Yunis*, 15 YALE J. INT'L L. 201 (1990); Note, *U.S. Legislation Prosecute Terrorists: Antiterrorism or Legalized Kidnapping?*, 18 VAND. J. TRANSNAT'L L. 915, 916 n.2 (1985).

27 *See* TERRORISM, DRUGS, *supra* note 1, at Chs. 1, 2.

28 *See generally* Zschernig v. Miller, 389 U.S. 429, 440-41 (1968) (states are precluded from infringing on the exclusive federal authority in matters of foreign affairs); Hines v. Davidowitz, 312 U.S. 52, 62-65 (1941) (states' jurisdiction to prescribe law is limited by the supremacy clause, U.S. CONST. art. VI, § 2, as well as by federal law, international custom and treaties); U.S. v. Curtiss-Wright Export Corp., 299 U.S. 304, 318 (1936) (identifying federal authority based on "foreign affairs power" incident to sovereignty).

29 *See* LOUIS HENKIN, INTERNATIONAL LAW: CASES AND MATERIALS 421 (3d ed. 1993).

various nations.[30] Domestic constitutional law and international law may limit a state's authority to apply domestic law to events occurring outside that state's territory.[31] Domestic law obviously limits jurisdiction[32] and may preclude prosecution or enforcement of a judgment rendered by the state assuming jurisdiction or seeking extradition.[33]

The U.S. Omnibus Antiterrorism Act of 1986, with portions amended since 1992, is an example of expanding jurisdiction.[34] The law provides jurisdiction to extradite or prosecute perpetrators of certain terroristic violence. The Act allows domestic prosecution of those who commit terror-violence against American citizens abroad if the offense is "intended to coerce, intimidate, or retaliate against a government or a civilian population."[35] Thus,

---

30 *See generally* Bruce Zagaris & Jay Rosenthal, *United States Jurisdictional Considerations in International Criminal Law,* 15 CAL. W. INT'L L.J. 303, 314 (1985) [hereinafter *Jurisdictional Considerations*].

31 *See, e.g., Cutting* case, 1887 FOR. REL. 751 (1888) (sanction for violating international law on jurisdiction may be an unfavorable diplomatic protest); The *S.S. "Lotus"* case (France v. Turkey), 1927 P.C.I.J. (ser. A) No. 9 (judgement of Sept. 7, 1927) (although international law is permissive, sanction for violation may be an unfavorable judgement in the Int'l Court of Justice). *See generally* TERRORISM, DRUGS, *supra* note 1, at Ch. 3; Christopher L. Blakesley, *United States Jurisdiction Over Extraterritorial Crime,* 73 J. CRIM. L. & CRIMINOLOGY 1109 (1982) [hereinafter *U.S. Jurisdiction*]; Christopher L. Blakesley, *A Conceptual Framework for Extradition and Jurisdiction Over Extraterritorial Crime,* 1984 UTAH L.REV. 685 [hereinafter *Conceptual Framework*].

32 *See* Willis L. M. Reese, *Limitations on Extraterritorial Application of Law,* 4 DALHOUSIE L.J. 589 (1978).

33 *See* Adolph Homberger, *Enforcement of Foreign Judgments,* 18 AM. J. COMP. L. 367, 375 n.55 (1970). For discussion of the dual or double criminality condition and the rule of speciality, see TERRORISM, DRUGS, *supra* note 1, at Ch. 4.

34 18 U.S.C. § 2331 (Supp. 1996); The Anti-Terrorism & Effective Death Penalty Act of 1996, Pub.L. No. 104-132, 104th Cong., 2d Sess., 110 Stat. 1214. *See* Ahmad v. Wigen, 726 F. Supp 389, 399 (E.D.N.Y. 1989) ("The United States recognizes nationality of the victim as a basis for criminal jurisdiction.") (citing 18 U.S.C. § 2331).

35 18 U.S.C. § 2332 (Supp. 1996). The Act provides for fines and imprisonment for those who commit murder or manslaughter against American nationals abroad, or for those who attempt or conspire to do so. The legislative history makes it clear that the Act does not "reach nonterrorist violence inflicted upon American victims. Simple barroom brawls or normal street crime, for example, are not intended to be covered by this provision . . ." Omnibus Diplomatic Security and Antiterrorism Act of 1986, H.R. Rep. No. 494, 99th Cong., 2d Sess., at 87 (1986). Earlier draft bills applied a broad passive-personality principle theory of jurisdiction, so as to include all common criminal violence against American nationals. *See* Antiterrorism Act of 1986: Hearing on H.R. 4292 Before the Subcomm. on Crime of the House Comm. on the Judiciary, 99th Cong., 2d Sess. 57-62 (1986) (Blakesley). Representative Wyden proposed the adoption of his Terrorist Prosecution Act of 1986, H.R. 4288, designed to extend 18 U.S.C. §§ 1114, 1116, which protect our diplomats and other internationally protected persons, to all U.S. citizens. *Id.* at 18-21. H.R. 4288 tracked the language of the Terrorist Prosecution Act of 1985, S.1429, as amended: "the purpose of this chapter is to provide for the prosecution and punishment of persons who, in furtherance of terrorist activities *or because of the nationality of the victims, commit violent acts upon an American outside the United States* or conspire outside the United States to murder Americans within the U.S." (emphasis added). This language does pose a problem, however. If it is not intended to allow jurisdiction to be asserted for non-terroristic type violence against Americans, *i.e.*, not to robbery-killing of an American abroad, where the perpetrator acted because he believed that an American would have more cash, or simply because he hated Americans, or to a bar fight that ends in homicide when the violence was directed towards an American, the definition of the crime needs clearly to be tied to some definition of terrorism. *See* Christopher L. Blakesley, *Terrorism: Problems Relating to and Conflicts of Jurisdiction, in* INTERNATIONAL TERRORISM: U.S. PROCEDURAL ASPECTS (Bassiouni ed., 1987) and concomitant chapters of this current edition. The Act apparently is designed to extend to all United States citizens, regardless of status, the protections of 18 U.S.C. §§ 1114-1116. The domestic charges levied against the *Achille Lauro* hijackers appear to have been based on an earlier version of yet another relevant Congressional act, the 1984 Act for the Prevention and Punishment of the Crime of Hostage Taking, 18 U.S.C. § 1203 (Supp. 1996). Today, § 1203 reads: ". . . whoever, *whether inside or outside the United States,* seizes or detains or threatens to kill, to injure, or to continue to detain another person in order to compel a

Congress has allowed jurisdiction over certain specific extraterritorial crimes. The legislation generally does not articulate the theoretical underpinnings of its jurisdiction, but these may be inferred.

In 1935, Harvard research in international law described five traditional bases of jurisdiction over transnational crime:[36] territorial; protective; nationality; universal; and

---

third person or a governmental organization to do or abstain from doing any act as an explicit or implicit condition for the release . . . or attempts to do so, shall be punished. . . . It is not an offense under this section if the conduct . . . occurred outside [the U.S.] unless — . . . the offender or person seized or detained is a national of the United States; . . . the offender is found in the United States; or the governmental organization sought to be compelled is the Government of the United States. . . ." The Hostage Act provides that: "(a) . . . [W]hoever, whether inside or outside the United States, seizes or detains and threatens to kill, to injure, or to continue to detain another person in order to compel a third person or governmental organization to do or abstain from doing any act as an explicit or implicit condition for the release of the person detained, or attempts to do so, shall be punished by imprisonment for any term of years or for life. (b)(1) It is not an offense under this section if the conduct required for the offense occurred outside the United States unless—(A) the offender or the person seized or detained is a national of the United States; (B) the offender is found in the United States; or (C) the governmental organization sought to be compelled is the Government of the United States. . . ." 18 U.S.C. § 1203(a) & (b); U.S. v. Yunis, 681 F. Supp. 896 (D.D.C. 1988) (jurisdiction asserted pursuant to 18 U.S.C. §1203). *See also* Terrorist Death Penalty Act, S. 1508, 99th Cong., 1st Sess., 131 CONG. REC. S10, 180 (1985) (proposal to amend 18 U.S.C. § 1203, to include the death penalty). Other relevant legislation includes 10 U.S.C. §§ 818, 821 (1976) (providing for war crimes prosecutions); 10 U.S.C. §§ 918-19 (1976) (the murder and manslaughter provisions of the Uniform Code of Military Justice); 18 U.S.C. § 7(7) (1982) (creating a special maritime jurisdiction, under which certain acts may be punished if they occur at "any place outside the jurisdiction of any nation with respect to an offense by or a against a U.S. national"); *see also* Special maritime or territorial jurisdiction specifically for Terrorism Act, *in* 18 U.S.C. § 2334(b) (Supp. 1996); *see also* 18 U.S.C. § 1651 (1982) (piracy); 49 U.S.C. § 1472(i) (proscribing air hijacking). *See generally* Jordan Paust, *U.S. Military Law, in* LEGAL RESPONSES TO INTERNATIONAL TERRORISM, *supra* note 2; Jordan Paust, *Aggression Against Authority: The Crime of Oppression, Politicize and Other Crimes Against Human Rights,* 18 CASE W. RES. J. INT'L L. 283 (1986) [hereinafter *Aggression Against Authority*]; Jordan Paust, *Federal Jurisdiction over Extraterritorial Acts of Terrorism and Nonimmunity for Foreign Violators of International Law Under the FSIA and the Act of State Doctrine,* 23 VA. J. INT'L L. 191 (1983) [hereinafter *Federal Jurisdiction*]. In addition to the aforementioned congressional acts the U.S. government is a party to the Convention on the Prevention and Punishment of Crimes Against Internationally Protected Persons, Including Diplomatic Agents, done at New York, 14 Dec. 1973, G.A. Res. 3166 (XXVIII), 28 U.N. GAOR Supp. (No. 30) at 146, U.N. Doc. A/9030, 28 U.S.T. 1975, T.I.A.S. No. 8532 (Feb. 20, 1977).

[36] Harvard Research in International Law, *Draft Convention on Jurisdiction with Respect to Crime,* 29 AM. J. INT'L L. 435, 445 (Supp. 1935) [hereinafter Harvard Research] (part of an effort by the American Society of International Law to codify international law). Pertinent U.S. judicial decisions on international law, as well as most international law casebooks and treatises have adopted the Harvard Research designations. *See, e.g.,* Rivard v. U.S., 375 F.2d 882, 885 (5th Cir. 1967); Rocha v. U.S., 288 F.2d 545, 549 (9th Cir. 1961); U.S. v. Rodriguez, 182 F. Supp. 479, 487 (S.D. Cal. 1960); WILLIAM BISHOP, INTERNATIONAL LAW CASES & MATERIALS 531, 551, 552 (3d ed. 1971). *See also* HENKIN, *supra* note 29, at 420-51; THE INTERNATIONAL LEGAL SYSTEM, *supra* note 1, at Chs. 3, 4, especially at pp. 285-97, and authority discussed therein. Some other areas of extraterritorial jurisdiction include, for example, the following: *Jurisdiction over crimes committed aboard sea-going vessels: discussed in* U.S. v. Aikins, 923 F.2d 650 (9th Cir.1991); 18 U.S.C. § 7 (*Special Maritime & Territorial Jurisdiction of the United States*) — crimes proscribed and competence provided in §§ 113 (assault), 114 (maiming), 661 (theft), 662 (receiving stolen property) 1111 (murder), 1112 (manslaughter), 1113 (attempt to commit murder or manslaughter), 2031 (rape), 2032 (statutory rape), 2111 (robbery); *see also* 49 U.S.C. § 1472(k) for these same offenses committed in the *special aircraft jurisdiction of the U.S.*. *See also* G. Marston, *Crimes on Board Foreign Merchant Ships at Sea: Some Aspects of English Practice,* 88 L.Q.REV. 357 (1972); *The People v. Robert J. Thomas,* 22 I.L.R. 295 (Eire, 1958); *In re Bianchi,* 24 I.L.R. 173 (Argentina, 1961). *Jurisdiction over crime committed aboard aircraft: See also* THE INTERNATIONAL LEGAL SYSTEM, *supra* note 1, at Ch. 5, pp. 385-402, and authority discussed therein; Chumney v. Nixon, 615 F.2d 389 (6th Cir. 1980); *See also* Oliver Lissitzyn, *In Flight Crime and the United States Legislation,* 67 AM. J. INT'L L. 306 (1973). *Jurisdiction over crime committed in outer space: See also* THE INTERNATIONAL LEGAL SYSTEM, *supra* note 1, at Ch. 5, pp. 402-16, and authority discussed therein; Treaty on Principles Governing the Activities of States in the Exploration and Use of

passive-personality.[37] They provide the foundation upon which a state may assert jurisdiction over extraterritorial criminal conduct. The "territorial theory" allows for jurisdiction over conduct, an element or the effect of which takes place within the territorial boundaries of the state. Subjective territoriality applies when a material element of an offense occurs within the territory. Objective territoriality applies when a significant effect of an offense impacts on the asserting state's territory. The nationality theory (*personalité actif*) bases jurisdiction on the allegiance or nationality of the perpetrator.[38] The protective principle is applicable whenever the criminal conduct has an impact on or threatens the asserting state's sovereignty, security, or some important governmental function.[39] The passive-personality theory applies simply on the basis of the victim's nationality.[40] This latter basis of jurisdiction is not widely accepted and has been roundly rejected in the United States,[41] except perhaps in relation to terrorism against U.S. nationals.[42] Because of the paramount nature of the territorial principle in U.S. criminal law, extradition has traditionally been refused when the sole basis of jurisdiction is the victim's nationality. The universality theory allows any forum to assert jurisdiction over particular universally condemned acts, when no other state has a prior interest in asserting jurisdiction.[43] Generally, nations have an obligation either to prosecute or to extradite perpetrators of these crimes.[44] A brief analysis of the parameters of the traditional theories of extraterritorial jurisdiction follows, providing a foundation for criticism of recent developments in extraterritorial jurisdiction theory.

The Restatement (Third) adopts the traditional basis of jurisdiction over extraterritorial crime[45] and posits the rule of reasonableness as a means of limiting the assertion of jurisdiction in the international context.[46] The "rule of reasonableness" requires that even

---

Outer Space, including the Moon and other Celestial Bodies, Jan. 27, 1967, art. IV, 18 U.S.T. 2410, 610 U.N.T.S. 205; S. Gorove, *Criminal Jurisdiction in Outer Space,* 6 INT'L L. 313 (1972).

37 For now, the "protective principle" or "injured-forum theory" emphasizes the effect or possible effect of the offense and provides for jurisdiction over conduct deemed harmful to specific national interests of the forum state. *E.g.*, U.S. v. Pizzarusso, 388 F.2d 8, 9 (2d Cir. 1968) (recognizing and describing protective principle). The "passive-personality principle" extends jurisdiction over offenses where the victims are nationals of the forum state, *e.g.*, French Law of July 11, 1975, No. 75-624, modifying C. PR. PÉN. art. 689 to read: "Any foreigner who, beyond the territory of the Republic, is guilty of a crime, either as author or accomplice, may be prosecuted and convicted in accordance with the disposition of French law, when the victim of the crime is a French national." C.PR.PÉN. art. 689 § 1 (author's translation). The "universality theory" allows jurisdiction in any forum that obtains jurisdiction over the person of the perpetrator of certain offenses considered particularly heinous or harmful to human kind generally. *E.g., The Marianna Flora*, 24 U.S. (11 Wheat.) 1, 40 (1826) ("pirates may, without doubt, be lawfully captured on the ocean by the public or private ships of every nation: for they are in truth common enemies of all mankind, and, as such are liable to the extreme rights of war"). *See also* Convention on the Law of the Sea (Montego Bay Convention), U.N. Doc. A/CONF. 62/122, 21 I.L.M. 1261 (1982), arts. 100-111; M. CHERIF BASSIOUNI, INTERNATIONAL CRIME: DIGEST/INDEX OF INTERNATIONAL INSTRUMENTS 1815-1925 (2 vols. 1987).

38 *E.g.*, Rose v. Himely, 8 U.S. (4 Cranch) 241, 279 (1808) (dictum) (recognizing the existence of the power to punish offenses perpetrated extraterritorially by U.S. nationals); 21 U.S.C. § 955a(b), makes it unlawful for any citizen of the United States on board any vessel intentionally to possess a controlled substance with intent to distribute.

39 *See* section on the Protective Principle, *infra.*

40 *See* section on Passive-Personality, *infra.*

41 *Id.*

42 *See* Omnibus Diplomatic Security and Anti-Terrorism Act of 1986, *supra* note 35.

43 *See* discussion on the Universality Principle, *infra.*

44 M. CHERIF BASSIOUNI & EDWARD M. WISE, AUT DEDERE AUT JUDICARE (1995).

45 RESTATEMENT (THIRD), *supra* note 23, § 402.

46 *Id.* § 403.

when an appropriate traditional basis for jurisdiction exists, exorbitant or unreasonable assertion will not be proper. Assertion of jurisdiction is exorbitant if another state has a more significant interest. Using the terminology of private international or conflicts of law, the rule of reasonableness is an attempt to determine the proper forum when two or more states have a traditional basis for asserting jurisdiction. We will see that, while the Restatement (Third) and United States case law ostensibly adheres to the traditional theories of jurisdiction as the essential and sole bases of jurisdiction over extraterritorial crime, the expansion of the objective territoriality theory and its limitation by the "rule of reasonableness" appears to suggest that the rule of reasonableness has become the actual basis, with the traditional theories being factors relating to reasonableness.

No assertion of jurisdiction is proper without the existence of one or more of the bases. But even if such a basis exists, an exorbitant or unreasonable assertion of jurisdiction may be blocked by operation of the so-called "rule of reasonableness."[47] The rule of reasonableness poses some difficulty internationally because, although the rule of reasonableness has become a term of art in Anglo-American jurisprudence,[48] non-Anglo-American jurists have no historical or theoretical background or frame of reference from which to understand the term. Moreover, American decisions applying the rule of reasonableness have been criticized as arbitrary and discriminatory to foreign nations.[49] In developing a theoretical concept of jurisdiction over terrorism, and in determining the priorities for assertion of that jurisdiction, this chapter also attempts to bring new meaning to the rule of reasonableness. We will determine, therefore, whether the assertion of jurisdiction over thwarted extraterritorial conspiracies and acts of terrorism is properly based on any one of the traditional theories.

Expansive assertion of jurisdiction presents serious problems. For example, Fawaz Yunis was convicted of hijacking a Jordanian airliner with either two or four Americans aboard (released unharmed). The hijacking appeared to have been an Amal militia action

---

[47] *Id.* § 403(1) ("[a]lthough one of the bases for jurisdiction under § 402 is present, a state may not apply law to the conduct, relations, status, or interest . . . if the exercise of such jurisdiction is unreasonable. . . ."). *See also id.* § 403, Comment (a); *U.S. Jurisdiction, supra* note 31, at nn.156-88 and accompanying text.

[48] The concept of reasonableness is pervasive in Anglo-American case law. It has become a term of art that requires a balancing or weighing of competing interests. *See* U.S. v. Carroll Towing Co., 159 F.2d 169 (2d Cir. 1947) (applying the notion in the tort setting).

[49] European and other commentators have criticized U.S. expansion of jurisdiction and the application of the rule of reasonableness. *See generally* THE INTERNATIONAL LEGAL SYSTEM, *supra* note 1, at Ch.3. Reidweg, *The Extra-Territorial Application of Restriction Trade Legislation—Jurisdiction—Jurisdiction and International Law,* Int'l Ass'n Report of the 51st Conference 357, 372-73 (1965); R. Y. Jennings, *Extraterritorial Jurisdiction and the United States Antitrust Laws,* 33 BRIT. Y.B. INT'L 146, 159 (1957). Even some American courts have found the notion difficult: "[w]hen one state exercises its jurisdiction and another, in protection of its interest, attempts to squash the first exercise of jurisdiction 'it is simply impossible to judicially "balance" these totally contradictory and mutually negating actions.'" Laker Airways, Ltd. v. Sabena, Belg. World Airlines, 731 F.2d 909 (D.C. Cir. 1984). *See also* recent decision out of the European Court of Justice which applied the *subjective and objective territoriality theories* to anticompetitive behavior of wood pulp producers: ". . . constituent elements of the offense, and more especially its effects" occurred within national territory, "providing jurisdiction as a matter of both [European] Community and public international law." Wood Pulp Judgement, joining cases 89, 104, 114, 116-17 and 125-29/85, European Court of Justice, Sept. 27, 1988["pratiques concertées entre entreprises établies dans des pays tiers portant sur les prix de vente à des acheteurs établis dans la Communauté"] (discussed in Recent Developments, *European Community Law: The Territorial Scope of Application of EEC Antitrust Law—The Wood Pulp Judgement,* 30 HARV. INT'L L.J. 195 (1989)).

aimed at Jordan, the PLO, and Lebanon.[50] Hijacking is certainly an international crime which creates an obligation to extradite or prosecute, but the issue of which of those options predominates is problematic. In the *Yunis* case, FBI agents arrested the defendant aboard a Cypriot vessel on the high seas, where the flag state generally has exclusive enforcement jurisdiction. Notwithstanding statements by the U.S. Attorney General at the time, the FBI violates international law and the law of the flag state when, without permission, it makes arrests or takes enforcement action within the jurisdiction of another state.[51] There is also a serious question about the wisdom and the legality of prescriptive jurisdiction in those circumstances. Why extend U.S. jurisdiction over conduct by a Lebanese national against a Jordanian aircraft in the Middle East?[52] Like other extensions of jurisdiction to be discussed herein, such vigorous assertions of jurisdiction ultimately erode cooperation. Terrorists and drug traffickers ought to be apprehended and prosecuted, but to establish a precedent that domestic policy allows assertion of jurisdiction so expansively over conduct committed abroad by a foreign national could prove damaging to both domestic and international interests.

This chapter will focus on these problems and will criticize aspects of some current conceptualization of the recent expansion of the theoretical bases of jurisdiction to prescribe. Thwarted extraterritorial narcotics conspiracies will be a primary example and focus of this criticism. The offense comes close to fitting into several of the traditional theoretical bases of extraterritorial jurisdiction, but actually fits none. The U.S. judicially expanded the objective territoriality theory as the means of covering these offenses. The theory behind the expansion is invalid. When a conspiracy is thwarted, it never actually causes an effect. To

---

[50] U.S. v. Yunis, 681 F. Supp. 896 (D.D.C. 1988), *rev'd* 859 F.2d 953 (D.C. Cir. 1988); Abramovsky, *supra* note 26, at 201. Alfred P. Rubin, *Can the United States Police the World?*, 13 THE FLETCH. F. 371 (1989).

[51] The Schooner Exch. v. McFaddon, 11 U.S. (7 Cranch) 116, 136 (1812) (makes the violation clear); Rubin, *supra* note 50; Abramovsky, *supra* note 26. Inserting ourselves in a quarrel between Cyprus and Jordan involving international Lebanese politics insulted all of the parties. *Id.* at 372. *Cf.*, U.S. v. Alvarez-Machain, 504 U.S. 655 (1992). The U.S. Congress and courts have stridently expanded jurisdiction over extraterritorial crime and other conduct. For example, particularly in the past decade, the U.S. Government has sought, successfully, to hold foreign nationals criminally liable under federal laws for conduct committed entirely beyond the territorial limits of the United States that nevertheless has effects in this country. *See, e.g.*, 18 U.S.C.§32(b) (violence against an individual aboard or destruction of any "civil aircraft registered in a country other than the United States while such aircraft is in flight"); §111 (assaulting, resisting, or impeding certain officers or employees); §115 (influencing, impeding, or retaliating against a federal official by threatening or injuring a family member); §§1114, 1117 (murder, attempted murder, and conspiracy to murder certain federal officers and employees); §1201(a)(5) (kidnaping of federal officers and employees listed in §1114); §1201(e) (kidnaping of "an internationally protected person," if the alleged offender is found in the United States, "irrespective of the place where the offense was committed or the nationality of the victim or the alleged offender"); §1203 (hostage taking outside the United States, if the offender or the person seized is a United States national, if the offender is found in the United States, or if "the governmental organization sought to be compelled is the Government of the United States"); §1546 (fraud and misuse of visas, permits, and other immigration documents); §2331 (terrorist acts abroad against United States nationals); 49 U.S.C. App. §1472(n) (1982 ed. and Supp. V) (aircraft piracy outside the special aircraft jurisdiction of the United States, if the offender is found in the United States). Foreign nationals may also be criminally liable for numerous federal crimes falling within the "special maritime and territorial jurisdiction of the United States," which includes "any place outside the jurisdiction of any nation with respect to an offense by or against a national of the United States." 18 U.S.C. §7(7). Finally, broad construction of federal conspiracy statutes may permit prosecution of foreign nationals who have had no direct contact with anyone or anything in the United States.

[52] Rubin, *supra* note 50, at 372 (citing U.S. v. Palmer, 16 U.S. (3 Wheat.) 610 (1818); ALFRED P. RUBIN, THE LAW OF PIRACY 418 (1988) ("[n]o general words of a statute ought to be construed to embrace [offenses] committed by foreigners against a foreign government"); *see also The Antelope*, 23 U.S. (10 Wheat.) 66, 123 (1825).

claim that the "effects" theory provides jurisdiction obviously is spurious. Its application obliterates the theory's meaning. Other theories should apply. This chapter will consider which are apt. The chapter's purpose is to develop a proper theoretical vehicle to understand jurisdiction over international crime.

The Territorial Principle

The territorial principle is the primary basis of jurisdiction over crime. Criminal law may be said to be rooted in the conception of law enforcement as a means of keeping peace within the territory.[53] The "king's peace" at the inception of the nation-state and "modern" international law was the ideological tool used to promote the consolidation of power against "private justice:"

> [W]e observe the evolution among the Germanic people, and especially among the Franks, from blood-revenge, essentially anti-legal in character [but nevertheless, in reaction to acts considered common crimes today] to a system in which rules of public law and procedure were developed and penalties prescribed and designed primarily to keep the peace. The retaliatory element gave way in large measure to public defense, but the elimination of the dangerous offender, whether by exile, death, or slavery, continued to be a primary means of protection. The objectives of general deterrence and individual prevention inhered in the establishment of the king's peace. . . .[54]

The territorial theory is most basic in a system where nation-states are subjects. Nation-states by definition are competent to prescribe laws and to prosecute all offenses committed, in whole or in part, within their territory. Complexities of a transient world, however, cause nations to expand jurisdiction by applying fictions and exceptions that transfuse actions taken abroad into their notions of jurisdiction. Generally, statutory authority is required to authorize extension of jurisdiction beyond territory. Courts of most states have been adept at interpreting statutory authority to authorize the extension of jurisdiction to cover offenses committed beyond their territorial limits.[55] Harvard Research describes the territorial principle as follows: "[A] crime is committed 'in whole' within the territory when every essential constituent element is consummated within the territory; it is committed 'in part within the territory' when any essential constituent element is consummated there. If it is committed either 'in whole or in part' within the territory, there is territorial jurisdiction."[56]

---

53 Rollin M. Perkins, *The Territorial Principle in Criminal Law*, 22 HASTINGS L.J. 1155 (1971).

54 Paul W. Tappan, *Pre-Classical Penology*, *in* ESSAYS IN CRIMINAL SCIENCE 33, 45 (G.O.W. Mueller ed., 1961).

55 *See* Georges R. Delaume, *Jurisdiction Over Crimes Committed Abroad: French and American Law*, 21 GEO. WASH. L. REV. 173, 181 (1952-53). Professor Delaume explains: "[O]nce a statute is promulgated, it is irrelevant whether its scope is limited to the punishment of national or to that of foreigner, or rather whether it combines the idea of jurisdiction based on allegiance with that of the punishment of only certain types of offenses." It is also irrelevant that such is not express, provided there cannot be any doubt as to the legislative intent. *Id.* (footnotes omitted). For example, in U.S. v. Bowman, 260 U.S. 94 (1922), the U.S. Supreme Court interpreted a statute to allow jurisdiction over an offense committed on the high seas and in a foreign port, although the statute did not expressly provide for such jurisdiction. *Id.* at 98-99.

56 Harvard Research, *supra* note 36, at 495; *see, e.g.*, State v. Willoughby, 862 P.2d 1319, 1328, 1329-31 (Ariz. 1995) (subjective territorial jurisdiction obtained for Arizona over a murder committed in Mexico, where

Sovereignty requires that the state govern its own territory. It must promulgate, adjudicate, and enforce its laws on that territory; any state that does not maintain such jurisdiction within its territory is not sovereign. In 1892, the U.S. Supreme Court stated that, "[l]aws have no force of themselves beyond the [territorial] jurisdiction of the State which enacts them, and can have extraterritorial effect only by the comity of other States."[57] Earlier, in 1812, Chief Justice Marshall expressed what has become the traditional U.S. vision of sovereignty:

> The jurisdiction of the nation, within its own territory, is necessarily exclusive and absolute; it is susceptible of no limitation not imposed by itself. Any restriction upon it, derived validity from an external source, would imply a diminution of its sovereignty, to the extent of the restriction . . . in that power which could impose such restriction. All exceptions, therefore, to the full and complete power of a nation, within its own territories, must be traced up to the consent of the nation itself.[58]

Thirteen years later, Chief Justice Marshall noted the relationship between sovereignty and territorial jurisdiction over crime, declaring that "[the] courts of no country execute the penal laws of another."[59]

The territorial principle of jurisdiction historically has been applied very strictly. It has had negative as well as positive application. For example, in reference to a case in which a French citizen was suspected of murdering an American citizen in China, the Secretary of State said that the U.S. Government would "not exercise jurisdiction over crimes committed beyond the territorial limits of this country, except a few involving extraordinary elements, in which category [this case] is not included. [The Government has] no authority to try a French citizen charged with crime in that country (China), even though the victim should happen to be an American. . . . "[60] The Supreme Court later declared that jurisdiction in criminal matters rests solely with the legislative and judicial branches of government of the state or country in which the crime is committed.[61] The Court has also held that a local criminal statute "has no territorial operation and [a party] cannot be indicted [in the United States] for what he did in a foreign country."[62]

---

the premeditation and conspiracy to commit murder occurred in Arizona); State v. Streater, 559 A.2d 473, 456-77 (N.J. 1989); *cf.*, Moreno v. Baskerville, 452 S.E.2d 653 (Va. 1995) (jurisdiction rejected, because no effect or element occurred in Virginia).

57 Huntington v. Attrill, 146 U.S. 657, 669 (1892); *cf., The Antelope,* 23 U.S. (10 Wheat.) 66, 123.

58 The Schooner Exch. v. McFaddon, 11 U.S. (7 Cranch) 116, 136 (1812).

59 *The Antelope*, 23 U.S. (10 Wheat.) 66, 123.

60 MS Dept. of State, file No. 226/16 (Sept. 17, 1906) ("Our . . . [consular officials] can have no authority to try a French citizen charged with crime in that country (China), even though the victim should happen to be an American. . . .") (quoted in 2 GREEN HACKWORTH, DIGEST ON INTERNATIONAL LAW 179 (1941)). Any acceptance of jurisdiction under the circumstances of this case would have been based on the passive personality-principle. *See* discussion of Passive-Personality, *infra*.

61 *Huntington*, 146 U.S. at 669. *See also* Brown v. U.S., 35 App. D.C. 548, 557 (1910) (the courts of one state shall not execute the criminal law of another); Stewart v. Jessup, 51 Ind. 413, 416 (1875) (a person is not subject to conviction and punishment in this state for a crime committed outside the state).

62 U.S. v. Nord Deutscher Lloyd, 223 U.S. 512, 517-18 (1912). This has been modified by recent expansion of the protective principle and other theories. *E.g.*, U.S. v. Layton, 509 F. Supp. 212 (N.D. Cal. 1981), discussed *infra*. 18 U.S.C. § 1116; U.S. v. Yunis, 681 F. Supp. 896 (D.D.C. 1988), *rev'd* 859 F.2d 953 (D.C. 1988); Abramovsky, *supra* note 26.

Jurisdiction over wholly extraterritorial crime would be improper under such a strict territorial approach. Although jurisdiction over such crime could obtain upon a nonterritorial basis, such as the protective principle, the territorial nature of criminal law is so important to the idea of sovereignty that when crime occurs on another nation's soil, jurisdiction generally is not asserted without the consent of the nation on whose soil it occurred. Priority generally goes to the state on whose territory the crime has actually occurred. Where a crime "actually occurs," however, is quite complex. It occurs either where a constituent element or a significant impact occurs. Conflicts of jurisdiction are inevitable.

Continental systems essentially follow the territorial principle as well. The French Civil Code, for example, provides that "the laws of police and security oblige all those who reside in the territory."[63] On its face, this article of the Civil Code appears to make legislative jurisdiction dependent on residence in France, but it has been interpreted to provide authority for jurisdiction over any offense committed within French territory.[64] French commentators have described the traditional territorial theory as follows: "[t]o affirm the territoriality of criminal law (*lex loci delicti*) is to proclaim that penal law applies to all individuals whatever their nationality or that of their victims, who have committed an offense on the territory of the State in which the law is in force; a *contrario*, that law is refused all application outside the same territory."[65] French application of the negative aspect of the territorial principle has not been as strict as that quote would suggest. France and other continental nations recently have extended jurisdiction to more offenses committed beyond their territory.

The Lotus Case: The Permanent Court of International Justice decided probably the most famous international case involving objective territoriality, the *Lotus* case.[66] Turkey prosecuted and convicted the French pilot of the *Lotus,* a French flag merchant vessel. The French ship had collided with a Turkish vessel, the *Boz-Kourt*, causing much property damage and the loss of eight Turkish lives. France objected to the Turkish criminal prosecution, claiming that customary international law prohibited prosecution for the pilot's actions aboard the French vessel. They claimed that an officer of a ship on the high seas can be held to obey only the laws and regulations of the flag state. Both sides submitted the dispute to the Permanent Court of International Justice. The French argued that Turkey had to prove that international law allowed criminal jurisdiction. They also argued that international law prohibited Turkey from asserting jurisdiction simply on the basis of the nationality of the victims, *i.e.*, that the passive-personality principle was not sufficient to

---

63 C. CIV. art. 3, ¶ 1 (author's translation).

64 *See* PIERRE BOUZAT & JEAN PINATEL, TRAITÉ DE DROIT PÉNAL 1301 (2d ed. 1970); ROGER MERLE & ANDRE VITU, TRAITÉ DE DROIT CRIMINEL 355-56 (4th ed. 1989). *See also* TERRORISM, DRUGS, *supra* note 1, at Ch. 3. French law also recognizes other nonterritorial theories of jurisdiction, such as the nationality theory (*personnalité active*), the passive-personality theory *(personnalité-passive)*, the protective principle *(protection des intérêts fondamentaux*), and the universality theory *(la compétence universelle).* These are applied as exceptions to the territorial principle. *See also* C. PR. PÉN. §§ 689-96.

65 Author's translation: "*Affirmer la Térritorialité de la répression (lex loci delicti), c'est proclamer que la lois pénale s'applique a tous les individus quelle que soit leur nationalité ou celle de leurs victimes, qui ont commit une infraction sur le térritoire de l'Etat ou cette lois est en vigeur; a contrario, on refuse a cette loi toute application en dehors de ce meme térritoire*." MERLE & VITU, *supra* note 64, at 372 n.1 (supporting the quoted statement).

66 The *S.S. "Lotus"* case (France v. Turkey), 1927 P.C.I.J. (ser. A) No. 9 (judgement of Sept. 7, 1927). *See* Manley O. Hudson, *The Sixth Year of the Permanent Court of International Justice*, 22 AM. J. INT'L L. 1, 8 (1928).

support Turkey's assertion of jurisdiction.[67] The Court declined to decide the passive-personality issue, but held that France actually had the burden to prove that international law prohibited Turkish jurisdiction. France failed to meet its burden. France was unable to prove the existence of a rule of customary international law prohibiting the Turkish assertion. The Court noted in dicta that jurisdiction could be predicated on the fact that the effects had occurred on the Turkish flag vessel.[68]

France was not opposed to the notion of objective territoriality per se; France had long adhered to it. French opposition was based on the application of the theory to a ship on the high seas. The French argued essentially that ascribed nationality (of the vessel) predominated over territoriality under the circumstances;[69] that from a practical standpoint in maritime matters, the law of the flagship state must govern the captain of a vessel.[70] But the effect of the pilot's conduct had caused harmful results on the Turkish vessel; international law at the time did not prohibit Turkish jurisdiction.[71] The *Lotus* case shows the difficulty in setting a priority for the bases of jurisdiction. The French point of view may be appropriate for unintentional conduct, not for intentional crimes such as murder. Jurisdiction is appropriate in the injured forum at least in cases of intentional violence. Terrorism, for example, planned in one state, perpetrated on a vessel or airliner, prompts both objective and subjective territoriality as well as the protective principle, nationality, universality, and even the passive-personality theories. Which should have priority? The issues are difficult and were present in the *Case Concerning Questions of Interpretation and Application of the 1971 Montreal Convention Arising from the Aerial Incident Over Lockerbie*.[72] Setting a hierarchy is difficult. Where there is question about the likelihood of vigorous prosecution, it can be argued that the state where the violence occurred, where the victims were nationals, or the state that was the focus of the attempted intimidation, coercion, and influence all should have priority. Perhaps all of these states retain concurrent jurisdiction. This raises issues of *non bis in idem*, *aut dedere aut judicari* and many others.[73] Thus, in the case of the *Achille Lauro,*[74] primary jurisdiction obtained in Italy, the flag-state

---

67 *Lotus,* 1927 P.C.I.J. (ser. A.) No. 9, at 26.

68 *Id.* at 27. *See also* RESTATEMENT (SECOND) OF THE FOREIGN RELATIONS LAW OF THE U.S. § 30 (1965) (reporter's note), describing the *Lotus* case and its holding. This type of jurisdiction is sometimes called the "floating territorial principle." *See* William Empson, *The Application of Criminal Law to Acts Committed Outside the Jurisdiction,* 6 AM. CRIM. L. Q. 32, 32 (1967); B.J. George, *Extraterritorial Application of Penal Legislation,* 64 MICH. L. REV. 609, 613 (1966). The position of the French government and that of the dissent in the *Lotus* case was that the law of the flagship ought to govern the actions of the pilot. That position later was adopted by two major international conventions relating to navigation on the high seas. *See* Brussels International Convention for the Unification of Certain Rules Relating to Penal Jurisdiction in Matters of Collisions or Other Incidents of Navigation (1952), *reprinted in* 4 SINGH, BRITISH SHIPPING LAWS 3111 (1983); Geneva Convention on the High Seas, April 28, 1958, 13 U.S.T. 2312, T.I.A.S. No. 5200, 450 U.N.T.S. 82. *See also* U.S. v. Williams, 589 F.2d 210, 212 n.1 (noting that the Geneva Convention on the High Seas "is a codification of international law"), *aff'd* 617 F.2d 1063, 1090 (5th Cir. 1980).

69 *Lotus,* 1927 P.C.I.J. (ser. A) No. 9, at 25; *see* THE INTERNATIONAL LEGAL SYSTEM, *supra* note 1, at 140, 166-68, 290.

70 *Id.*

71 *Lotus,* 1927 P.C.I.J. (ser. A) No. 9.

72 Libyan Arab Jamahiriya v. U.S.A. (request for Indication of Provisional Measures), [1992] I.C.J.REP. 231; 31 I.L.M. 662 (1992).

73 *See* BASSIOUNI & WISE, *supra* note 44.

74 *See* N.Y. TIMES, June 15, 1985, at A1, col. 6; N.Y. TIMES, Oct. 10, 1985, at A1, col. 6.

of the ship on which the crime occurred, but others retain jurisdiction.[75] Similar issues arise in relation to jurisdiction of the Ad Hoc Tribunals for the crimes in the former Yugoslavia and Rwanda.[76] The objective and subjective territoriality principles have been adopted and applied broadly.[77] If any material element of an offense or any of its significant effects jurisdiction obtains. A clear territorial nexus is required.[78]

Subjective Territoriality

Objective and subjective territoriality are closely related; both often obtain simultaneously. While subjective territoriality requires an element of the offense to occur within the asserting state, objective territoriality obtains when the effect or result of criminal conduct impacts on the asserting state, but the other elements of the offense take place wholly beyond its territorial boundaries.[79] The classic example is presented in European coursebooks. Defendant shoots a gun in Italy, wounding a person in France, who travels to Switzerland where he succumbs to his wounds.[80] Commentators were split for years on the issue of which country should have jurisdiction.[81] Prior to 1959, French courts often

---

75 When U.S. fighter planes intercepted an Egyptian jetliner carrying the *Achille Lauro* hijackers (later to be convicted by the Italian judicial system, N.Y. TIMES, Oct. 11, 1985, at A1, col. 6), they either committed kidnaping or hijacking—an act of violence—of their own, or they have a claim of justification. The only justification could be that the Egyptian government or jetliner pilot consented to the taking, or were participating in the alleged hijackers' escape. *See* TERRORISM, DRUGS, *supra* note 1, at Chs. 1, 2. *But see* the *Letelier* case, where the court stated flatly that "there is no discretion to commit, or to have one's officers or agents commit an illegal act. . . . Whatever policy options may exist for a foreign country, it has not discretion to perpetrate conduct designed to result in the assassination of an individual or individuals, act that is clearly contrary to the precepts of humanity as recognized in both national and international law." Letelier v. Republic of Chile, 488 F. Supp. 665, 673 (D.D.C. 1980).

76 *See* discussion *infra*.

77 *See* TERRORISM, DRUGS, *supra* note 1, at Ch. 4, for discussion of similar German notions of the ubiquity theory and "vicarious administration of justice."

78 *E.g.*, C. PR. PÉN. arts. 689-96.

79 Harvard Research, *supra* note 36, at 387.

80 Example presented in MERLE & VITU, *supra* note 64, at 384, and in most of the works cited in this note. Many of the cases in which the objective territorial theory applies are of the type the French denominate "simple offenses" (*des infractions simple*). *Id.* (discussing this entire subject in depth). A simple offense is one in which the prohibited conduct is constituted by one material element (actus reus/criminal result) that is realized instantaneously. *Id.* An example is intentional killing of a human being. *Id.* The jurisdictional problem presented by the hypothetical in the text is that the act is done in one state, its immediate effect (impact of bullet) occurs on another state, and its result (the crime of murder) is consummated in a third. Jurisdiction would obtain in all three states. The first on the basis of subjective territoriality, the second on the basis of both objective and subjective territoriality, and the latter on the basis of objective territoriality. A complex offense (*des infractions complexes)*, *id.* at 381, on the other hand, is one in which there is a chain of distinct acts and mental states related to those acts, such as the common crime of fraud, in which a combination of two distinct constituent elements must be established: the use of fraudulent methods to obtain funds or property, and the taking of the funds or property. *Id.* *See* Robert, *Compétence térritorial: délit commis en France et a l'étranger,* 1967 REV.SCI.CRIM.ET DR.PÉN.COMP. 879, 880. Articles 689-696 of the Code de procédure pénale allow the assertion of jurisdiction on the objective territorial theory for both the *infraction simple* and the *infraction complêxe*. *See* C. PR. PÉN. arts. 689-696.

81 MERLE & VITU, *supra* note 64, at 384-86 (citing and discussing the cases and split of authority). Other commentators believe that jurisdiction to try the case should rest both with the place of action and with the place of result. For many years, French case law favored jurisdiction in the place of the result. For example, jurisdiction was held to apply only in the place of the receipt of a letter sent for purposes of espionage. In the *Schwartz* case, Decision of Feb. 25, 1911, 1915 S. Jur. I 171 (Cass. Crim.) jurisdiction was allowed when a letter was sent from abroad to France in order to obtain secret information. Jurisdiction in the place of reception of the letter was

approved jurisdiction in cases in which the result or the effects of the offense took place in France, in spite of a doctrinal tendency to favor the place of the action.[82] Now it is clear that jurisdiction obtains in all of the states. The subjective territorial theory obtains when at least one material or constituent element of an offense occurs within a state. It is not necessary that the offense be consummated in a state for jurisdiction to obtain. Article 693 of the French Code *de procédure pénal*, for example, provides that an offense is considered to have been committed on French territory when "an act characterizing one of its elements occurs [there]."[83] Article 693 embodies a long tradition of French jurisprudence that applies various fictions to expand "territorial jurisdiction."[84] Actual and material elements must occur

---

deemed appropriate on the basis of the objective territorial principle. It was not uncommon, however, for concurrent jurisdiction to be considered valid in the place of the action, the place of the immediate goal of the action and the place of the result. For example, when a spy joined the French Military Service in France (material act) to discover secrets and to deliver them abroad, jurisdiction obtained in France on the subjective territorial (and possibly the protective principle). Crim., 27 Juillet 1933, D.P., 1933.1.159, note G.L.

[82] For example, in cases of offenses occurring in the press, jurisdiction nearly always was taken when the illegal publications were published and printed abroad but distributed and sold in France. *E.g.*, Decisions of Apr. 30, 1908, S.Jr. I 553 (Cass. Crim.) (note Roux). During the 1930's, concurrent jurisdiction was considered valid with preemption by the first tribunal to take the case. *Delest* Case, Decision of May 16, 1936, 1936 D.P. II 314 (Cass. Crim.). Mercier favored concurrent jurisdiction of the courts in the place of the action, the immediate goal and the place of the result, with the tribunal to which the action is first brought preempting the others. Mercier, *Le conflit des lois pénales*, 1931 REV. DR. INT'L ET DE LÉG.COMP. 439. Many decisions admit concurrent jurisdiction in the place of the action and the place of the result. *See, e.g.*, Decision of Aug. 3, 1937, 1937 S. Jr. I. 360 (Cass. Crim.) (the tribunal of the place of origin and receipt of threatening telephone calls was considered competent). The same was true in a case of murder threats by correspondence, in Le Havre, Decision of Nov. 11, 1887, 1888 S. Jur. II (Trib. Corr.). See additional cases and discussion in MERLE & VITU, *supra* note 64, at 383-86. The British have had a similar academic and judicial discussion involving what have been called the terminatory and initiatory theories of jurisdiction. It is essential that a significant effect (objective territoriality) or a material element (subjective territoriality) occur within the territory of the asserting state.

[83] C. PR. PÉN. art. 693 (author's translation): "*un acte caracterisant un de ses éléments constitutifs a été accompli . . .*").

[84] Fictions used were *connexité and indivisibilité:* the offenses committed outside the territory were deemed to be connected to or indivisible from the elements that have occurred in France. Fayard, *La localisation international de l'infraction,* 1968 REV. SCI. CRIM. ET DR. PÉN. COMP. 753; Robert, *Compétence Térritorial, supra* note 80, at 880; Lagarde, *Note re Decision* of Oct. 10, 1959, 1960 Dalloz 300 (Cass. Crim. 1959); Lauress & Signolle, *Obs. re Decision* of 25 Sept. 1948 SEM. JUR. 4788. Art. 693 was inspired partly be the *infraction complêxe* (complex offense). The complex offense assumes a chain of distinct acts (elements) that culminate in the principle crime. The classic example is the basic swindle in which a combination of two distinct constituent elements establishes the offense: the use of fraudulent methods to obtain funds of property, and the taking or receipt of the funds or property. If one of the elements occurs in France, jurisdiction over the entire offense is allowed under art. 693. The pretext is that the element committed in France is inherently connected to or indivisible from the element or the result that occurs elsewhere. MERLE & VITU, *supra* note 64, at 381-84 (citing cases and authorities); Légal, *Chroniques de Jurisprudence*, 1967 REV. SOC. CRIM. ET DR. PÉN. COMP. 171. The connection may be real or fictional, depending on the case. *See* Segui v. Min. Pub., Decision of July 27, 1933, 1933 D.P.I. 159 (Cass. Crim.). Any act or omission that occurs in France and is regarded by a French tribunal as a constituent element of the offense may be prosecuted in France as a consummated offense if the act or omission is considered criminal under French law and if the offense is consummated abroad, or if the act that occurs abroad would be perceived by foreign authority to be an attempt to commit an offense. The same fiction, further abstracted, has applied to allow French jurisdiction over some offenses committed entirely outside French territory. Thus, offenses committed entirely abroad are deemed to be connected to other offenses committed in whole or in part in France, thereby rendering the extraterritorial offenses subject to French jurisdiction. French case law and commentary have applied that broad scope of territorial jurisdiction, notwithstanding the fact that art. 693, which mentions only the constituent elements of one offense, does not explicitly envisage that application. As an example, consider the offense of receiving stolen property abroad, which takes place entirely outside French territory—where the property is received. Jurisdiction on the territorial principle will nevertheless obtain if some of the property received was

within the territory. An agreement to import or export narcotics[85] or to commit terrorism, or to transport weapons from or through a state for purposes of terrorism may all provide subjective territorial jurisdiction over the offense, even if it occurs elsewhere.

U.S. law also provides jurisdiction over offenses consummated outside U.S. territory when a constituent element occurs therein.[86] The U.S. federal system has provided fertile ground for the development of both the subjective and objective territorial principles. Indeed, maintenance of a strictly applied territorial principle in the U.S. would make prosecution for many crimes very difficult, due to the complex, variegated federal/state jurisdictional scheme of criminal law and procedure. Application of objective and subjective territoriality mitigated difficulties that could arise under this system.[87]

U.S. states have applied the subjective theory of jurisdiction to acts consummated in sister states and foreign countries.[88] The need is obvious and the application is not inconsistent with the language of the Sixth Amendment, which provides that a person must have his or her trial in the state and district wherein their crime shall have been committed."[89] In addition, U.S. law adopted the early common law rule allowing jurisdiction

---

stolen in France. *See, e.g.,* Decision de 2 Juillet 1932.2.532 (Cass. Crim.) (receiving stolen property abroad); *Conceptual Framework, supra* note 31, at 692 n.23 and accompanying text. British courts often categorize crimes as "conduct crimes" or "result crimes" in order to rationalize taking or rejecting jurisdiction over crimes. *See* Treacy v. Dir. of Pub. Prosecutions, 1971 A.C. 537, 543 (1970) (defining blackmail as a conduct crime, thus creating jurisdiction if any of its elements occur in England). Murder on the other hand, is a result crime, over which English courts will have jurisdiction if "any part of the proscribed 'result' takes place in England." Secretary of State for Trade v. Markus, 1976 A.C. 35, 61 (1975). Some examples relating to cases antedating the promulgation of art. 693, and cited by Harvard Research, *supra* note 36, at 499, are *Defamation*: Clunet (1901), 990, and Sirey (1908), I, 553; *Espionage*: Clunet (1912), 1162: *Extortion:* Clunet (1855), 443; *Fraud:* Decision of Dec. 18, 1908, Sirey (1913), I, 116; Decision of Aug. 31, 1911, *Rev. de Dr. Int. Prive* (1912) 360; Tribunal d'Avignon, Oct. 23, 1911, Clunet (1912) 827; Tribunal de Bayonne, Dec. 29, 1887, Clunet (1887) 517; *Revelation of Trade Secrets*: Sirey (1904), I, 105. General commentaries relating to the application of jurisdiction in situations of the type envisage by art. 693 include: BOUZAT & PINATEL, *supra* note 64, at 898-901 (and cases cited therein); HENRI DONNEDIEU DE VABRES, TRAITÉ ELÉMENTAIRE DE DROIT CRIMINEL ET DE LÉGISLATION PÉNALE COMPARÉE 826 (2d ed. 1943); HENRI DONNEDIEU DE VABRES, LES PRINCIPES MODÈRNE DU DROIT PÉNAL INTERNATIONAL 43-45, 47-48 (1928); MERLE & VITU, *supra* note 64, at 365, et seq. *See also Costa* case, 1969 *Juris-Classeur Périodique, La Semaine Juridique* (J.C.P. II) No. 16011 (violation *des bonnes moeurs,* to photograph nude women in France and attempt to send undeveloped film to Sweden); *Légal La Localisation de délit complêx,* 1970 REV. SCI. CRIM. ET DR. PÉN. COMP. 84.

85 *See, e.g,* U.S. v. Jurado-Rodriguez, 907 F. Supp. 568 (E.D.N.Y. 1995).

86 *E.g.*, State v. Willoughby, 862 P.2d 1319, 1328, 1329-31 (Ariz. 1995) (subjective territorial jurisdiction obtained for Arizona over a murder committed in Mexico, where the premeditation and conspiracy to commit murder occurred in Arizona); State v. Streater, 559 A.2d 473, 456-77 (N.J. 1989); *cf.*, Moreno v. Baskerville, 452 S.E.2d 653 (Va. 1995) (jurisdiction rejected, because no effect or element occurred in Virginia). *Cf.*, Itobe Ltd. v. LEP Group, PLC, 54 F.3d 118, 122 (2d Cir. 1995) (applies conduct test in Securities law arena).

87 Harvard Research, *supra* note 36, at 484. *See also, e.g., Willoughby*, 862 P.2d 1319, 1328, 1329-31; Keen v. State, 504 So.2d 396, (Fla. 1987) (". . . when one of the essential elements of the offense occurs in Florida, Florida courts have the power to try the defendant").

88 *E.g., Willoughby*, 862 P.2d at 1328, 1329-31 (subjective territorial jurisdiction obtained for Arizona over a murder committed in Mexico, where the premeditation and conspiracy to commit murder occurred in Arizona); *Streater,* 559 A.2d at 456-77 (N.J. 1989); *Jurado-Rodriguez,* 907 F. Supp. at 563*; cf., Moreno*, 452 S.E.2d 653 (jurisdiction rejected, because no effect or element occurred in Virginia).

89 U.S. CONST. amend. VI; *cf.* U.S. v. Jackalow, 66 U.S. (1 Black) 484 (1851) (for a circuit court to have jurisdiction of a crime not committed within its district, the defendant first must have been apprehended within that district and the offense must not have been committed within any other state or federal jurisdiction); 18 U.S.C. § 3238 (1969) (the jurisdiction of all offenses occurring on the high seas or elsewhere out of any state or federal jurisdiction shall be in the district in which the offender is apprehended). Judicial decisions have approved assertion of jurisdiction where any element of an offense occurs within the state. *E.g.,* People v. Botkin, 132 Cal. 231, 64

over U.S. participation in offenses committed by cohorts abroad or participation abroad in offenses consummated here.[90]

Objective Territoriality in the United States[91]

Objective territoriality[92] obtains when a significant effect or result of the offense occurs within a nation's territory.[93] U.S. law traditionally has allowed jurisdiction when the conduct

P. 286 (1901); State v. Sheehan, 33 Idaho 553, 196 P. 532 (1921); People v. Zayas, 217 N.Y. 78, 111 N.E. 465 (1916); People v. Licenziata, 199 A.D. 106, 191 N.Y.S. 619 (1921); *Willoughby*, 862 P.2d at 1328, 1329-31 (subjective territorial jurisdiction obtained for Arizona over a murder committed in Mexico, where the premeditation and conspiracy to commit murder occurred in Arizona); *Streater*, 559 A.2d at 456-77. *Cf.*, *Moreno,* 452 S.E.2d 653 (jurisdiction rejected, because no effect or element occurred in Virginia). *See* additional cases and statutes reviewed in Wendell Berge, *Criminal Jurisdiction and the Territorial Principle*, 30 MICH. L. REV. 238 (1931). Some cases construing newer statutes similar to the old New York laws are: People v. Utter, 24 Cal. App. 3d 535, 101 Cal. Rptr. 214 (1972), *aff'd in part, rev'd in part,* 34 Cal. App. 3d 366, 108 Cal. Rptr. 909 (1973); Conners v. Turner, 508 P.2d 1185 (Utah 1973), and cases cited in Schwab, "*Have Crime, Will Travel: Borderlines and Criminal Jurisdiction,*" 50 S.B.J. 30 (1975). Jurisdiction also will lie when an offense is commenced outside a state's territory but consummated within, or when an offense is committed completely outside the territory, if the effect or result of the offense occurs within the state. The theory behind the application of jurisdiction thus moves from subjective territoriality to objective territoriality. The Model Penal Code encourages an expansive application of both the subjective and objective theories for assertion of territorial jurisdiction. MODEL PENAL CODE § 1.03 (1980). The comments to § 1.03 of the Model Penal Code explain that where conduct within the territory of the forum state causes harm outside that state, jurisdiction will usually be allowed, if the conduct within the state, standing alone, would constitute an attempt to commit the offense charged. MODEL PENAL CODE § 1.03 commentary (1980). In *Botkin*, 132 Cal. 231, 64 P. 286, for example, the California courts convicted a person of murder for mailing poisoned candy from California to his victim, who received the candy, ate it and died in Delaware.

[90] I.F. WHARTON, WHARTON'S CRIMINAL LAW § 333 (12th ed. 1932) and cases cited therein.

[91] *See, e.g.*, Strassheim v. Daily, 221 U.S. 280, 285 (1911) (jurisdiction may lie when offense is committed entirely outside the state, but intended effect or result occurs within it). *See also* Harvard Research, *supra* note 36, at 387.

[92] John Bassett Moore stated: "The principle that a man who, outside of a country willfully puts in motion a force to take effect in it is answerable to the place where the evil is done, is recognized in the criminal jurisprudence of all countries." John Bassett Moore, *Report on Extraterritorial Crime and the Cutting Case*, 1887 FOR. REL. 757, 771. Another noted jurist stated similarly: "The setting in motion outside of a State of a force which produces as direct consequences an injurious effect therein, justifies the territorial sovereign in prosecuting the actor when he enters its domain." 1 CHARLES HYDE, INTERNATIONAL LAW 422 (2d ed. 1945) (referring to general rights of property and contracts). Congress has also developed a broad "special maritime and territorial jurisdiction." In the Federal Aviation Act of 1958, § 902(k)(1), former 49 U.S.C. § 1472(k)(1), promulgated to accommodate and incorporate the Hijacking and Sabotage aboard aircraft treaties. Former section 1472(k)(1), provided: "[w]hoever, while aboard an aircraft within the special aircraft jurisdiction of the United States, commits an act which, if committed within the special maritime and territorial jurisdiction [of the U.S.] . . . shall be punished." The legislation incorporating the above noted conventions, has recently been held to allow jurisdiction to be asserted over child sexual abuse, done by a foreign national, aboard a foreign airliner, which was in international airspace, but, given that it was on its way to the United States, was in the "special maritime and territorial jurisdiction." U.S. v. Georgescu, 723 F. Supp 912, 913 (E.D.N.Y. 1989) (applying, *inter alia*, former 49 U.S.C. § 1472(k)(1)). Legislation now in 42 U.S.C. § 46501, *et seq.*, discussed *infra* at note 252 and accompanying text.

[93] *E.g.*, *Strassheim*, 221 U.S. at 285 (Holmes, J.) ("[a]cts done outside a jurisdiction, but intended to produce and producing detrimental effects within it, justify a State in punishing a cause of the harm as if he had been present at the effect, if the State should succeed in getting him within its power"); State v. Doyen, 1996 WL 115902 (Vt. 1996) (custodial interference causing harm within state); People v. McLaughlin, 606 N.E.2d 1357, 1358-59 (N.Y. 1992); Rios v. State, 733 P.2d 242, 249 (Wyo. 1987); People v. Harvey, 435 N.W.2d 456, 457 (Mich.App. 1989) (parental kidnaping); *In re Schwartz*, Judgment of Feb. 25, 1911, 1915 S. I. 171 (Cass. Crim., France) (jurisdiction allowed when letter was sent from abroad to France to obtain secret information); C. PR. PÉN.

giving rise to the offense has occurred extraterritorially, so long as a significant harmful effect takes place within U.S. territory.[94] The objective territorial theory is not appropriate for asserting jurisdiction over thwarted extraterritorial conspiracies.[95] Probably the most frequently cited U.S. decision enunciating objective territoriality is *Strassheim v. Daily*,[96] in which Mr. Justice Holmes stated: "[A]cts done outside a jurisdiction, but *intended to produce and producing* detrimental effects within it, justify a state in punishing a cause of the harm as if he had been present at the effect, if the state should succeed in getting him within its power."[97] It is clear from Justice Holmes' opinion and from historical precedent

---

arts. 689 through 689-7 (1996); C. PÉN. arts. 11-6 through 113-11 (1996) (France, allowing jurisdiction on the objective territorial theory). When an element of an offense occurs within the territory, it is the *subjective* territorial theory that justifies jurisdiction. An offense is considered to have occurred on French territory and to provide French jurisdiction when an act characterizing one of its elements is accomplished in France.) It is subjective in the European sense that an element or subjective aspect of the offense, rather than the object, occurred within the territory. United States courts have found jurisdiction where any element of an offense occurs within the state. *E.g.*, *Botkin*, 132 Cal. 231, 64 P. at 287; *Sheehan*, 33 Idaho 553, 196 P. at 534; *Zayas*, 217 N.Y. 78, 111 N.E at 465-66; *Licenziata*, 199 A.D. 106, 191 N.Y.S. at 619, 622. *See also Criminal Jurisdiction and the Territorial Principle*, 30 MICH. L. REV. 238 (1931). Some cases construing newer statutes similar to the old New York laws are: *Utter*, 24 Cal. App. 3d 535, 101 Cal.Rep. at 214, 224; Conners v. Turner, 508 P.2d 1185, (Utah 1973). *See also* additional cases cited in Schwab, *supra* note 89.

94 Generally, it is necessary that legislation provide for jurisdiction over extraterritorial crime. *See* Commonwealth v. Macloon, 101 Mass. 1 (1869) (statutory authority is required for judicial competence in a homicide case in which the victim was wounded on board a British vessel on the high seas but died in Massachusetts). For further discussion and additional authorities, *see U.S. Jurisdiction*, *supra* note 31, at 1123 n.38 and accompanying text. *See also* E.E.O.C. v. Arabian American Oil Co., 499 U.S. 244, 248 (1991) ("*Aramco*") (". . . [unless] the affirmative intention of the Congress is clearly expressed, we must presume [a statute] is primarily concerned with domestic conditions" . . . and holding that extraterritorial jurisdiction obtains *only* on clear and convincing evidence of congressional intention of extraterritorial application); Benz v. Compania Naviera Hidalgo, S.A., 353 U.S. 138, 147 (1957); Foley Bros., Inc. v. Filardo, 336 U.S. 281, 284-85 (1957); Sloan Overseas Fund, Ltd. v. Sapiens Int'l Corp. N.V., 1997 WL 16664 (S.D.N.Y. 1997). The presumption that Congress intended territorial application generally is held not to apply to "criminal statutes which are, as a class, not logically dependent on their locality for the Government's jurisdiction, but are enacted because of the right of the Government to defend itself against obstruction, or fraud wherever perpetrated . . ." U.S. v. Bowman, 260 U.S. 94, 98 (1922); U.S. v. Vasquez-Velasco, 15 F.3d 833, 839 (9th Cir. 1994). U.S. v. Felix-Gutierrez, 940 F.2d 1200, 1205 n.3 (9th Cir. 1990). The problem in all of these cases is the determination of which is "the evil effect" or result which will allow the assertion of jurisdiction. *See also* Hunter v. State, 40 N.J.L. 495 (1878); State v. Lang, 108 N.J.L. 98, 154 A. 864 (1931). U.S. courts in civil matters have not moved away from the so-called pure "effects" theory of jurisdiction which was initially asserted and accepted by analogizing to the objective territorial principle in international law. *See* the development of the rule in Int'l Shoe Co. v. Washington, 326 U.S. 310 (1945), and the retrenchment of the rule in World Wide Volkswagen Corp. v. Woodson, 444 U.S. 286 (1980); Kulko v. Superior Court, 436 U.S. 84 (1978); *see also* Note, *The Long-Arm Reach of the Courts Under the Effect Test After Kulko v. Superior Court*, 65 VA. L. REV. 175 (1979). Jurisdiction in criminal matters, on the other hand, is expanding to cover extraterritorial offenses more comprehensively. *See also* European Court of Justice which applied the *subjective and objective territoriality theories* to anticompetitive behavior of wood pulp producers: ". . . constituent elements of the offense, and more especially its effects" occurred within national territory, "provides jurisdiction as a matter of both [European] Community and public international law." *Wood Pulp Judgement*, joining cases 89, 104, 114, 116, 117 and 125-29/85, European Court of Justice, 27 Sept. 1988 [*"pratiques concertées entre entreprises établies dans des pays tiers portant sur les prix de vente à des acheteurs établis dans la Communauté"*]; discussed in *Recent Developments, European Community Law: The Territorial Scope of Application of EEC Antitrust Law—The Wood Pulp Judgement*, 30 HARV. INT'L L.J. 195 (1989); THE INTERNATIONAL LEGAL SYSTEM, *supra* note 1, at 158.

95 The subjective territorial principle is appropriate to assert jurisdiction over a conspiracy when an element of the offense has occurred within the asserting state, even when the crime is consummated abroad.

96 Strassheim v. Daily, 221 U.S. 280 (1911).

97 *Id.* at 285 (emphasis added). The Supreme Court in *Strassheim* cites the following cases as supporting the objective territorial principle historically: American Banana Co. v. United Fruit Co., 213 U.S. 347, 356 (1909);

that the objective territorial principle is not designed to apply when parties merely intend their criminal activity to take effect within territorial boundaries, but contemplates those cases in which the intended effects actually occur within those boundaries.[98] Lately, however, some U.S. courts have applied the objective territorial theory more expansively, applying it when there is no more than intent to impact on U.S. territory.[99] It has been expanded beyond territoriality. This has been done mainly to accommodate assertion of jurisdiction over thwarted extraterritorial narcotics conspiracies.[100] The territorial theories allow prescriptive jurisdiction and enforcement jurisdiction via extradition. In extradition practice, however, the objective territorial principle sometimes does not function as it would appear logically that it should. Even though extradition treaties usually state that extradition will be allowed for listed offenses committed within the requesting state's jurisdiction and even though the objective territorial theory would extend "territory" to cover offenses occurring abroad, extradition treaties provide that if the offense also occurred within the territory of the requested state, that state may prosecute first and extradite later. Extradition treaties generally also contain a *non bis in idem* clause. What this clause actually means in terms of protecting the defendant is open to question, however.[101] Finally, extradition treaties require that the offense charged be one that would trigger jurisdiction in the requested state as well as that of the requesting state under the circumstances involved.[102]

Simpson v. State, 92 Ga. 41, 17 S.E. 984, 985 (1893); *Macloon,* 101 Mass. 1, 6, 18, 100 Am. Dec. 89; Commonwealth v. Smith, 93 Mass. (11 Allen) 243, 256, 259 (1865); *see also* U.S. v. King, 532 F.2d 505 (9th Cir. 1976); Rivard v. U.S., 375 F.2d 882 (5th Cir. 1967); U.S. v. Layton, 509 F. Supp. 212, 216 (N.D. Cal. 1981); People v. Fea, 37 N.Y.2d 70, 390 N.E.2d 286, 288-89, 416 N.Y.S. 2d 778, 780-81 (1979).

[98] For detailed analysis of traditional and more recent expansive U.S. application of the objective territorial theory, *see U.S. Jurisdiction, supra* note 31, at 1123-32.

[99] *See* RESTATEMENT (THIRD), *supra* note 23, § 402; U.S. v. Wright-Barker, 784 F.2d 161 (3d Cir. 1986) (conspiracy of at least eight persons to import narcotics, 23 tons of marijuana, into the U.S. from a vessel on the high seas—200 miles off the New Jersey coast) (cited and discussed in Cecil J. Olmstead, *Restatement: Jurisdiction, Symposium on the RESTATEMENT (THIRD),* 14 YALE J. INT'L L. 468, 471 n.19 (1989) (noting how the citation of the Restatement by the Wright-Barker Court, and later citation of *Wright-Barker* by the Restatement (3d) was a prime example of mutual bootstrapping); *see also* U.S. v. Stuart, 109 S.Ct 1183, 1197, (1989) (Scalia, J., concurring); U.S. v. Marino-Garcia, 679 F.2d 1373, 1380-81 (applying a "nexus" theory along with the objective territorial theory and the protective principle), *reh'g denied,* 685 F.2d 1389 (11th Cir. 1982), *cert. denied,* 459 U.S. 1114 (1982); U.S. v. Conroy, 589 F.2d 1258 (5th Cir. 1979); U.S. v. Postal, 589 F.2d 862 (5th Cir. 1979); U.S. v. Cadena, 585 F.2d 1252 (5th Cir. 1978); *King,* 552 F.2d 833, *cert. denied,* 430 U.S. 966 (combining nationality principle with the intent to cause an effect theory).

[100] U.S. v. Winter, 509 F.2d 975, 982 (5th Cir. 1975), *reh'g denied,* 588 F.2d 100 (5th Cir. 1979) (since federal narcotics conspiracy law does not require an overt act, jurisdiction based on the objective territorial theory obtains, even though no effect has occurred on U.S. territory). *See also Cadena,* 585 F.2d 1252. *See* Mark Rosenthal, *Jurisdictional Conflicts Between Sovereign Nations,* 19 INT'L L. 487, 487-92 (1985); *Jurisdictional Considerations, supra* note 30, at 312, 317.

[101] *E.g.,* U.S. v. Jurado-Rodriguez, 907 F.Supp. 568 (E.D.N.Y. 1995), where defendant was convicted and punished in Luxembourg for money laundering (a continuing narcotics trafficking offense) and then was extradited to the U.S. upon a proviso that he "not be prosecuted upon facts that had been used to convict him in Luxembourg. The issue was what the term "facts" in the Luxembourg extradition order meant. *See* discussion below.

[102] Nevertheless, extradition when jurisdiction was based on the objective territoriality theory has been allowed on occasion. In Hammond v. Sittel, 59 F.2d 683 (9th Cir. 1930), the accused had forged a check drawn on a Canadian bank and had deposited it in his account in California. The court concluded that Canada had jurisdiction over the offense because the harmful effect actually occurred in that country. The court declared: "The Supreme Court in the decision from which we have quoted [Ford v. U.S., 273 U.S. 593 (1927)] shows the desirability of surrendering a person for trial who puts in motion forces which operate to consummate a crime within the territory of the demanding nation . . . and there is no reason to suppose that the treaty was intended to exclude such a class of offenders. . . . " In Sternaman v. Peck, 83 F. 690 (2d Cir. 1897), the court extradited a

The territorial theories, therefore, have been extended liberally to mitigate the evils that would arise from a strictly territorial approach to jurisdiction.[103] As long as the offense itself, its significant effects, or any of its constituent elements actually occur within the sovereign territory of the forum state, jurisdiction obtains and extradition will be available. Difficulties may arise, however, when a claim of jurisdiction is based on some theory other than territoriality, or when the claimed "territorial basis" is strained beyond that deemed proper by the another state. Some recent United States cases have put such a strain on the objective territorial theory.[104]

Objective territoriality clearly is not the proper vehicle for assertion of jurisdiction over any act of terrorism or narcotics conspiracy that has not actually had an impact within the territory of the United States, although that is the theory chosen by recent decisions. Neither properly provides a basis for jurisdiction over thwarted extraterritorial conspiracies. The objective territoriality theory is inappropriate, even if the object of the conduct were U.S. citizens or interests. There are other traditional bases of jurisdiction, however, that may be appropriate, including the universality theory,[105] the protective principle, and the passive-personality theory.[106] European jurisprudence and doctrine are clear that the objective territoriality theory does not provide jurisdiction over thwarted extraterritorial *attempts* or conspiracy: "we cannot go so far as to assimilate the result which would have occurred here to one that has actually occurred here."[107]

The territorial theories are not sufficient for jurisdiction over wholly extraterritorial offenses such as terrorism, narcotics trafficking or money laundering. When the offense takes place totally abroad and no effect actually occurs within the territory, territoriality cannot apply. The protective principle might be the more appropriate basis for jurisdiction over extraterritorial terrorism. What theory should apply to the other offenses? Terrorist

---

woman to Canada where her husband had died after she had poisoned him in New York. *In Ex parte Davis*, 54 F.2d 723 (9th Cir. 1931), the court allowed extradition to Mexico in a case where the action culminated in the death of an individual in California. The court recognized as appropriate the Mexican application of the subjective territoriality principle and decided not to apply the objective territoriality principle to assert United States jurisdiction, thus approving extradition to Mexico on the ground that the necessary elements to complete the offense were consummated in the requesting state. It is likely that the court actually did not wish to burden itself with a difficult case in which most of the evidence and the strongest interest in prosecution rested with the requesting state. Many decisions are based on such practical considerations rather than on some theoretical principle of jurisdiction. In reality, however, that was a proper use of discretion and not a derogation from the double criminality condition, as Mexico was asserting a theory of jurisdiction recognized by United States law. *See* Quinn v. Robinson, 783 F.2d 776 (9th Cir. 1986) (jurisdiction sought under, among other, an objective territoriality theory), *cert. denied,* 107 S. Ct 271 (1986); U.S. v. Layton, 509 F. Supp. 212, 216 (N.D Cal. 1981) (jurisdiction asserted on the basis of the objective territorial and protective principles).

[103] *U.S. Jurisdiction, supra* note 31, at 1128 n.53.

[104] *Id.* at 1130-32 (discussing those cases).

[105] *See* discussion *infra.*

[106] *See infra.*

[107] MERLE & VITU, *supra* note 64, at 383 n.2, 398, 400; *see also* Decision of Dec. 9, 1933, 1934 J. DR. INT'L, 898; Législation and the *cour de cassation* have made an exception for situations representing a more dangerous risk to security, sovereignty or governmental function (via the protective principle) (*Les atteintes aux intérêts fondamentaux de l'Etat français*); CODE LA SANTÉ PUBLIQUE, arts. 626, 627 (implicitly recognizing what is developed below as a hybrid theory of jurisdiction). U.S. jurisdiction over RICO offenses, securities fraud and the like are usually determined on the basis of one of two alternative tests: (1) the "conduct test" (subjective territoriality) and (2) the "effects test" (objective territoriality). *See, e.g.,* ITOBA Ltd. v. Lep Group, 54 F.3d 118, 121-22 (2d Cir. 1995), *cert. denied,* 116 S.Ct. 702 (1996); North South Fin. Corp. v. Al-Turki, 100 F.3d 1046, 1051 (2d Cir.1997).

violence is by definition purposeful, malicious and aimed at a state's innocent citizens for the purpose of intimidation or procuring some political or military end. Such violence has an impact on a state's security, sovereignty and important governmental interests.[108] The same cannot be said of drug trafficking or money laundering. Indeed, U.S. Courts have clearly rejected that proposition.[109] The universality principle, which allows the assertion of jurisdiction over certain offenses, even though they have no effect on the territory, security or sovereignty of the asserting state, may also often be appropriate to address the growing problems of terrorism today. It has not been accepted, however, by the U.S. Government for narcotics trafficking or money laundering.[110] These crimes and pertinent bases of jurisdiction are analyzed below.

The Protective Principle

While the objective and subjective territorial theories require a territorial nexus, the protective principle provides jurisdiction over offenses committed wholly outside the forum state's territory, when the offense poses a danger of causing an adverse effect on a state's security, integrity, sovereignty or important governmental function.[111] Most incidents of terrorism and other crimes against humanity[112] will trigger jurisdiction in the object state based on the protective principle. This may be true even if the conduct is aimed at or has an impact on individual nationals, as long as the violence is designed to intimidate, influence,

---

[108] *See, e.g.,* U.S. v. Vasquez-Velasco, 15 F.3d 833, 839 (9th Cir. 1994) (murder of two U.S. national tourists in Mexico to enhance standing in Guadalajara Cartel seriously obstructed functioning of U.S. Government —also jurisdiction per RICO); U.S. v. Felix-Gutierrez, 940 F.2d 1200, 1204 (9th Cir. 1991); *see also* U.S. v. Cotten, 471 F.2d 744, 751 (9th Cir.), *cert. denied,* 411 U.S. 936 (1974). It may also be argued that certain types of conduct in which one takes violent action, knowing there is a high degree of risk to innocents, may be termed terrorism. Such risk-taking with the lives and well-being of innocent people is similar to conduct punished as felonious reckless homicide in substantive criminal law. For example, if an official orders a pilot to bomb a section of a town wherein it is believed that an enemy training facility or sanctuary might be hidden, hoping that no innocent civilians will be killed or injured, although knowing the high degree of risk to those *hors de combat,* such conduct might be considered criminal if the military value of the military target is insignificant compared to the risk to noncombatants. This may be classic depraved-heart murder. *See* ROLLIN PERKINS & RONALD BOYCE, CRIMINAL LAW 59-61 (3d ed. 1982) (defining and analyzing depraved-heart murder or wanton and willful disregard of unreasonable human risk). *See also, e.g.,* U.S. v. Yousef, 927 F.Supp. 673 (S.D.N.Y. 1996) (conspiracy to blow-up aircraft within special U.S. aircraft jurisdiction).

[109] *E.g.,* U.S. v. Juda, 46 F.3d 961 (9th Cir. 1995).

[110] *See* TERRORISM, DRUGS, *supra* note 1, at 117-24, 137-49 and authority therein. But it has been applied to hijacking and even conspiracy to sabotage aircraft. *See, e.g.,* U.S. v. Yunis, 681 F. Supp. 896 (D.D.C. 1988) (hijacking); *Yousef,* 927 F. Supp. at 681; U.S. v. Rezaq, 899 F. Supp. 697, (709 D.D.C. 1995).

[111] Harvard Research described the traditional principle: A state has jurisdiction with respect to any crime committed outside its territory by an alien against the security, territorial integrity or political independence of that state, provided that the act or omission which constitutes the crime was not committed in exercise of a liberty guaranteed the alien by the law of the place where it was committed. Harvard Research, *supra* note 36, at 543. An important motive in any assertion of jurisdiction over territorial crimes is the protection of the forum state. That is true whatever theory of jurisdiction is asserted. *See id.* at 1132-39. *E.g.,* U.S. v. Pizzarusso, 388 F.2d 8 (2d Cir. 1968), *cert. denied,* 392 U.S. 938 (1968); *cf.,* U.S. v. Gabriel, 920 F. Supp. 498, 501 (S.D.N.Y. 1996) (obstruction of justice and aircraft safety); *Vasquez-Velasco,* 15 F.3d at 839 (murder of two U.S. national tourists in Mexico to enhance standing in Guadalajara Drug Cartel seriously obstructed functioning of U.S. Government—also jurisdiction per RICO); *Felix-Gutierrez,* 940 F.2d at 1204.

[112] M. CHERIF BASSIOUNI, CRIMES AGAINST HUMANITY (1994).

or to extort some concession from the state or to threaten its security or sovereignty and important governmental function.[113]

The focus of the protective principle is the nature of the interest that is or that may be injured, rather than the place of the harm or the place of the conduct. This distinction was clearly articulated in *U.S. v. Pizzarusso,* where an alien was convicted of knowingly making false statements under oath in a visa application to a U.S. consul in Canada.[114] The fact that the accused ultimately entered the U.S. was not an element of the offense.[115] The court was careful to point out that the violation of 18 U.S.C. § 1546 took place entirely in Canada. The crime's effect on U.S. sovereignty supported the prosecution under the protective principle.[116] The court defined the protective principle as "[the authority to] prescribe a rule of law attaching legal consequences to conduct outside [the state's] territory that *threatens* its security as a state or the operation of its governmental functions, provided the conduct is generally recognized as a crime under the law of states that have reasonably developed legal systems."[117] Lying to a consular officer in Canada constituted "an affront to the very sovereignty of the United States [and had] a deleterious influence on valid governmental interests."[118]

The protective principle is the only accepted theory that allows jurisdiction over conduct that poses a *potential* threat to certain interest or functions of the asserting state. It is *limited* to recognized and stated interests or functions.[119] Most national penal codes recognize this principle and its limitations.[120] There may be some overlap between the objective territoriality and the protective principles. When a crime's effect actually infringes on the sovereignty or integrity of a state or impinges upon some governmental function, either or both of the theories may be appropriate, depending on whether the effect actually falls upon some territorial situs. It may be said that the objective territorial theories are distinctions within and expansions of the territorial principle, while the protective principle is an exception to it, as the latter does not require an actual territorial effect.

French law provides a prototype example of the protective principle in the context of reaction to terrorism. France traditionally, with some exceptions, did not assert jurisdiction over aliens who committed crimes outside French territory.[121] French law, however,

---

113 If the conduct is perpetrated or promoted by one government against another state's nationals or against some dissident or other group, it is state terrorism or an act of war that will trigger the universality theory of jurisdiction, discussed *infra*.

114 *Pizzarusso*, 388 F.2d at 8.

115 *Id.* at 9.

116 *Id.* at 10.

117 *Id.* at 10 (emphasis added) (quoting RESTATEMENT (SECOND) § 33).

118 *Id. See also U.S. Jurisdiction, supra* note 31, at 1137 n.72. The RESTATEMENT (THIRD), *supra* note 23, § 402(3), recognizes the protective principle and provides that jurisdiction pursuant to the principle will obtain for: "[c]ertain conduct [performed] outside its [the asserting state's] territory by persons not its nationals which is directed against the security of the state or certain interests." If lying to a consular office to obtain a passport is sufficient, then killing or kidnaping a state's national to intimidate or influence his or her government certainly is. *See also* U.S. v. Layton, 509 F. Supp. 212 (N.D. Cal. 1981) (employing protective principle in convictions of conspiracy to murder and aiding and abetting the murder of a U.S. congressman, wounding an American diplomat and aiding in connection with their investigation of cult activities at Jonestown, Guyana).

119 *See Pizzarusso*, 338 F.2d at 8; U.S. v. Egan, 501 F. Supp. 1252, 1257-58 (S.D.N.Y. 1980).

120 *See, e.g.,* French law discussed *infra. See also* Harvard Research, *supra* note 36, at 543, 547-51; Sahovic & Bishop, *The Authority of the State: Its Range with Respect to Persons and Places, in* MANUAL OF PUBLIC INTERNATIONAL LAW 311, 363-64 (Max Sorensen ed., 1968).

121 E.g., in the famous *Fornage* case, 84 J. du Palais 229 (Cass. Crim. 1873), a Swiss national was indicted

explicitly allows jurisdiction over extraterritorial acts by aliens which threaten the "general interests of the Republic, [including state security and that of its diplomatic or consular posts and agents]."[122] Such offenses are "punishable in the same manner as an infraction committed within . . . [French] territory."[123] The basis for jurisdiction is the protective principle, an exception to the territorial theory.[124]

Early drafts of the U.S. Omnibus Anti-Terrorism Act of 1986 aimed at providing jurisdiction over terrorism committed extraterritorially against Americans were too broad.

---

in France for larceny committed in Switzerland. On appeal, the judgment of the lower court was quashed because jurisdiction was not allowed to extend to offenses committed outside the territory by foreigners who, by reason of such acts, are not justiciable by the French tribunals. The Court held that the right to punish emanates from the right of sovereignty, which does not extend beyond the limits of the territory; that, except in the cases specified in Article 7 of the Code d'Instruction Criminelle, the provision of which is founded on the right of legitimate self-defense, the French tribunals are without power to judge foreigners for acts committed by them in a foreign country, that their incompetence in this regard is absolute and permanent; that it can be waived neither by the silence or the consent of the accused; that it exists always the same at every stage of the proceedings. *Id.* at 230.

[122] *See* former C. PR. PÉN. art. 689, et seq.; current C. PR. PÉN. art. 689-3; C. PÉN. art. 113-10. *See also* Bigay, *Les dispositions nouvelles de compétence des jurisdictions françaises a l'égard des infractions commises a l'étranger,* 1976 Dalloz-Sirey, *Législation* [D.S.L.] 51-52. French law allows jurisdiction for extraterritorial offenses committed by (nationality theory), against (passive-personality theory) French nationals, *see* discussions of those bases, *infra*, and for those very grave crimes that all states have an interest in prosecuting, under the universality theory, *infra*.

[123] C. PR. PÉN. art. 689-1: "Principals (including accomplices) of offenses committed extraterritorially may be prosecuted and adjudged by French jurisdictions, either when, in conformity with the dispositions of Book I of the Code Pénal [*quoted infra*] or pursuant to another legislative text, French law is applicable, or when an international convention provides competence to French jurisdiction to hear the offense." The articles of the Code de procédure pénale which follow (arts. 689-1 through 689-7) go through the pertinent international conventions. C. PÉN. arts. 113-6 through 113-11 (effective 1994), cover the other offenses committed extraterritorially. They include: C. PÉN. art 113-6: ". . . all *crimes* committed by a French national . . . all *délits* committed by a French national, if [punishable in the place in which it was committed] . . . This article is applicable, even if the person's nationality is obtained after the commission." Art. 113-7: ". . . all *crimes* and all *délits* punishable with imprisonment committed by a French national or a foreigner [against] a victim who is a French national at the time of the offense." Art. 113-8: "[prosecution pursuant to arts. 113-6 through 113-7 is allowed] only upon the demand of the *ministère public.* This must be preceded by a complaint by the victim or those having [the victim's right to do so] or an official denunciation by the authorities in the state in which the offense was committed." Article 113-9 provides for double jeopardy protection when there has been conviction and sentencing for the same facts. Article 113-10 provides French jurisdiction over *des crimes ou délits* considered offenses against the fundamental interests of the nation, punished in Title I of Book IV, counterfeiting, and all *crimes or délits* against French diplomatic or consular agents (or locals) committed abroad. Article 113-11 covers offenses aboard non-French aircraft, when the perpetrator or the victim is French, when the aircraft lands in French territory after the commission of the offense, when the aircraft has been given or rented to a person who has his principal place of business in France or if his residence is in French territory. (author's translation). These articles are effective after Jan. 1, 1994.

[124] In numerous cases, jurisdiction has been asserted over offenses fitting the protective principle. *E.g., Rivière Case,* 13 REVUE DE DROIT INTERNATIONALE PRIVE 543 (Cass. Crim. 1917) (treason); *In re Glass,* 1858 D.P. IV 339 (Trib. Corr. de Boulogne sur Mer) (alien outside French territory obtained false French passport); *In re Urios,* 1920 Bull. Crim. No. 26. 34 (Cass. Crim.) (alien, outside French territory, endangered French national security), *cited in* 2 HACKWORTH, *supra* note 60, at 203, and Delaume, *supra* note 55, at 176 n.8. With art. 694, the French legislature introduced a scheme that provides clear, if rather broad, application of the protective principle. In the 1930's, French judicial application of the protective principles was criticized as being "inadmissible in principle and in excess of anything which international law permits." Harvard Research, *supra* note 36, at 558. Professor Garcia-Mora also severely criticized any overbroad application of the protective principle because of the likelihood of wide-ranging discretion by the prosecuting state causing unjust, politically oriented judgements. Manuel R. Garcia-Mora, *Criminal Jurisdiction Over Foreigners for Treason and Offenses Against the Safety of the State Committed Upon Foreign Territory,* 19 U. PITT. L. REV. 567, 588 (1958). The U.S. now asserts it just as extensively.

They could be read to cover any criminal violence against U.S. nationals.[125] Ultimately, Congress attempted to make the Act apply strictly to terrorist violence by including the following limitation:

> No prosecution for any offense described in this section shall be undertaken by the United States except on written certification of the Attorney General or the highest ranking subordinate of the Attorney General with responsibility for criminal prosecutions that, in the judgement of the certifying official, such offense was intended to coerce, intimidate, or retaliate against a government or a civilian population.[126]

Although not explicitly articulated, the essence of this legislation is the protective principle, perhaps combined with the universality theory. U.S. jurisprudence provided theoretical underpinnings for the legislation. The 1978 murder of Representative Leo Ryan in Guyana, for example, had provided a federal district court with a vehicle to apply and analyze both the objective territorial and the protective principles. In *U.S. v. Layton*,[127] defendant was charged with conspiracy to murder a U.S. congressman;[128] aiding and abetting the murder

---

[125] 18 U.S.C. § 2331. Chapter 113A, "*Extraterritorial Jurisdiction Over Terrorist Acts Abroad Against U.S. Nationals*," provides in § 2331(a) for reaching "whoever kills a national of the United States, while such national is outside the United States, . . . if the killing is a murder, . . . voluntary manslaughter, and involuntary manslaughter . . ." In § 2331(e), the Act provides: "[n]o prosecution for any offense described in this section shall be undertaken by the United States except [when] . . . in the judgement of the certifying official, such offense was intended to coerce, intimidate, or retaliate against a government or a civilian population." The legislative history comments to the Act provide: "[T]he committee of conference does not intend that chapter 113A reach nonterrorist violence inflicted upon American victims. Simple barroom brawls or normal street crime, for example, are not intended to be covered by this provision." H.R. Rep. No. 494, 99th Cong., 2d Sess., at 87 (1986), *reprinted in* 1986 U.S. CODE CONG. & ADMIN. NEWS 1865, 1960 (legislative history). Earlier drafts did not include the limitation relating to terroristic violence, see H.R. 4288, 99th Cong., 1st Sess. (1986) (The Omnibus Anti-Terrorism Act of 1986); H.R. 4294, 99th Cong., 1st Sess. (1985); S. 1429, 98th Cong., 2d Sess. (1985) (The Terrorist Prosecution Act of 1985). The intent is clearly to apply the protective or universality principles or both, rather than the passive-personality. TERRORISM, DRUGS, *supra* note 1, at 92, 119, 122, 137, 148, 202, 216; Rosalyn Higgins, PROBLEMS & PROCESS: INTERNATIONAL LAW AND HOW TO USE IT, 66-69 (1994), *citing my prior version of this instant Chapter* and my chapter *Jurisdictional Issues & Conflicts of Jurisdiction, in* LEGAL RESPONSES TO INTERNATIONAL TERRORISM, U.S. PROCEDURAL ASPECTS 131-81 (Bassiouni ed. 1988).

[126] 18 U.S.C. § 2332 (c) (Supp. 1996). This is also interesting in that it allows the Attorney General to decide *which* terrorists to pursue. Hostage taking takes a similar tack. 18 U.S.C. § 1203 (Hostage Taking), which reads: ". . . whoever, *whether inside or outside the United States,* seizes or detains or threatens to kill, to injure, or to continue to detain another person in order to compel a third person or a governmental organization to do or abstain from doing any act as an explicit or implicit condition for the release . . . or attempts to do so, shall be punished. . . . It is not an offense under this section if the conduct . . . occurred outside [the U.S.] unless. . . . the offender or person seized or detained is a national of the United States; . . . the offender is found in the United States; or the governmental organization sought to be compelled is the Government of the United States. . . ." The Hostage Act provides that: "(a) . . . [W]hoever, whether inside or outside the United States, seizes or detains and threatens to kill, to injure, or to continue to detain another person in order to compel a third person or governmental organization to do or abstain from doing any act as an explicit or implicit condition for the release of the person detained, or attempts to do so, shall be punished by imprisonment for any term of years or for life. (b)(1) It is not an offense under this section if the conduct required for the offense occurred outside the United States unless—(A) the offender or the person seized or detained is a national of the United States; (B) the offender is found in the United States; or (C) the governmental organization sought to be compelled is the Government of the United States . . ." 18 U.S.C. § 1203(a).

[127] U.S. v Layton, 509 F. Supp. 212 (N.D. Cal. 1981).

[128] *See* 18 U.S.C. § 351(d) (as amended) (proscribing conspiracy to kill or kidnap members of Congress, among other officials). Section (i) provides extraterritorial jurisdiction.

of a U.S. congressman;[129] conspiracy to murder an internationally protected person;[130] and aiding and abetting in the attempted murder of such a person.[131] The district court found that it had subject-matter jurisdiction over all counts.[132]

The court relied in part on "[t]he objective territorial principle, which allows countries to reach acts committed outside territorial limits, but intended to produce, and producing, detrimental effects within the nation."[133] There was no actual impact on U.S. territory, although the effects of the murder might have been felt in Washington, D.C., or in Northern California where Congressman Ryan served. The effect of the killing definitely ended Congressman Ryan's ability to continue functioning as a representative of his district. It impaired an important governmental function. It also infringed upon the official extraterritorial functions of a member of Congress, and impacted on U.S. sovereignty. The court saw this application, noting that "[t]he alleged crimes certainly had a *potentially* adverse effect upon the security or governmental functions of the nation, thereby providing the basis for jurisdiction under the protective principle."[134] The court held that an attack upon a member of Congress, participating in his or her official duties, wherever it occurs, equally threatens the free and proper functioning of government.[135] This was different from other homicides because "[c]ongressmen were singled out for protection because of the position they hold in our constitutional government, because their protection is important to the integrity of the national government and therefore serves an important interest of the government itself."[136] Thus, explained the court, if Congress assigns its members to function in the arena of foreign relations, they must often travel abroad. If it were possible to escape jurisdiction by attacking members of Congress while abroad, there would be clear obstruction and injury to the governmental function, sovereignty, and integrity.[137] The court

---

129 *See id.* at § 351(a) ("whoever kills a member of Congress [or other officials] . . . shall be punished").

130 18 U.S.C. § 1116 (murder or manslaughter of foreign officials, official guests, or internationally protected persons). Layton was also charged in connection with the wounding of a diplomat, the American deputy chief of mission in Guyana. *Layton,* 509 F. Supp. at 214.

131 *See* 18 U.S.C. § 1116(a)(2) (providing that "whoever kills or attempts to kill a foreign official guest, or internationally protected person shall be punished as provided under sections 1111, 1112, and 1113 of this title"). *See* additional implementing legislation, including: 18 U.S.C. § 1117 (proscribing conspiracy to murder an internationally protected person); 18 U.S.C. § 1201(a)(4) (kidnaping an internationally protected person); 18 U.S.C. 878 (proscribing threats and extortion committed against foreign officials, official guests, or internationally protected persons); 18 U.S.C. § 112(a) (punishing, assaulting, striking, wounding, imprisoning and violence against an internationally protected person); 18 U.S.C. § 112(b) (a crime to intimidate, coerce, threaten, or harass a foreign official, official guest or to obstruct a foreign official in the performance of his duties). *See also* U.S. v. Birk, 797 F.2d 199, *reh'g denied* 802 F.2d 455, *cert. denied* 107 S. Ct. 672 (1986); U.S. v. Benitez, 741 F.2d 1312 (11th Cir. 1984), *cert. denied,* 105 S. Ct 2679 (1984) (jurisdiction over assault upon and attempted murder of U.S. DEA agents).

132 The *Layton* court held that "the courts of the United States have repeatedly upheld the power of Congress to attach extraterritorial effect to its penal statutes, particularly where they have been applied to citizens of the United States." 509 F. Supp. at 215 (citing Blackmer v. U.S., 284 U.S. 421, 437 (1932); U.S. v. Baker, 609 F.2d 134, 135 (5th Cir. 1980); U.S. v. King, 552 F.2d 833, 850-51 (9th Cir. 1976), *cert. denied,* 430 U.S. 966 (1977)). The court believed that jurisdiction would be appropriate under the following theories: objective territoriality; protective principle; nationality; and passive-personality. 509 F. Supp. at 216.

133 509 F. Supp. at 215 (citing Strassheim v. Dailey, 221 U.S. 280, 285 (1911)); U.S. v. Fernandez, 496 F.2d 1294, 1296 (5th Cir. 1974).

134 509 F. Supp. at 216.

135 *Id.* at 116 -220.

136 *Id.*

137 *Id.*

held that Congress is free to extend jurisdiction extraterritorially if it wishes.[138] The court explained: "Courts have generally inferred such jurisdiction for two types of statutes: (1) statutes which represent an effort by the government to protect itself against obstructions and frauds; and (2) statutes where vulnerability of the United States outside its own territory to the occurrence of the prohibited conduct is sufficient because of the nature of the offense to infer reasonably that Congress meant to reach those extraterritorial acts." The application of the protective principle is apt only if the violence is designed to intimidate the government or presents a potential danger to U.S. sovereignty, security, integrity or to an important governmental function.

The murders and other acts of violence in *Layton* were extraterritorial acts of terrorism. They were directed against government officials, so the protective principle was appropriate. They also constituted specific crimes against "internationally protected persons" proscribed by international treaty and incorporated by statute.[139] Until the promulgation of the Omnibus Anti-Terrorism Act, however, U.S. law did not provide jurisdiction over attacks on citizens not considered "internationally protected persons" even if committed to intimidate the government or to gain a military or political advantage. The Anti-Terrorism Act was promulgated to ensure jurisdiction in such cases.[140]

---

[138] *Id.* at 216, 218, 224. *See also* E.E.O.C. v. Arabian American Oil Co., 499 U.S. 244, 248 (1991) ("*Aramco*") (". . . [unless] the affirmative intention of the Congress is clearly expressed, we must presume [a statute] is primarily concerned with domestic conditions . . ." and holding that extraterritorial jurisdiction obtains *only* on clear and convincing evidence of congressional intention of extraterritorial application); Benz v. Compania Naviera Hidalgo, S.A., 353 U.S. 138, 147 (1957); Foley Bros., Inc. v. Filardo, 336 U.S. 281, 284-85 (1957); Sloan Overseas Fund, Ltd. v. Sapiens Int'l Corp. N.V., 1997 WL 16664 (S.D.N.Y. 1997). *See also* Skirotes v. Florida, 313 U.S. 69, 73-74 (1941), wherein the Supreme Court combined the protective and nationality principles as follows: "[A] criminal statute dealing with acts that are *directly injurious to the government,* and are capable of perpetration without regard to particular locality, is to be construed as applicable to citizens of the U.S. upon the high seas or in a foreign country, though there be no express declaration to that effect." (emphasis added). *See also* U.S. v. Cotten, 471 F.2d 744, 750 (9th Cir. 1973) (jurisdiction over theft of government property overseas), *cert. denied,* 411 U.S. 936 (1973); Stegeman v. U.S., 425 F.2d 984, 986 (9th Cir. 1970) (jurisdiction allowed violations of bankruptcy laws relating to the concealment of assets, as the statute "was enacted to serve *important interests of government,* not merely to protect individuals who may be harmed by prohibited conduct.") (emphasis added) *cert. denied,* 400 U.S. 873 (1970); *Fernandez*, 496 F.2d at 1294. In U.S. v. Pizzarusso 388 F.2d 8, 10-11 (2d Cir. 1968), the court determined that congress intended to apply the laws there in question extraterritorially. In making this decision, the court explained that the status implicitly and necessarily suggested an extraterritorial application. The government has the right and capacity to protect itself. In U.S. v. Bowman, 260 U.S. 94, 98-99, 102 (1922), the integrity of the U.S. Treasury was involved, when the defendants conspired to defraud a corporation in which the U.S. government had a significant interest. The participants' nationality played a significant role in *Bowman*, as the conviction of the three U.S. nationals was affirmed on the ground that they were "certainly subject to such laws as [Congress] might pass to protect itself and its property." *But see* U.S. v. Juda, 46 F.3d 961 (9th Cir. 1995) (protective principle alone is not a sufficient nexus).

[139] *See, e.g.*, Convention on the Prevention and Punishment of Crimes Against Internationally Protected Persons Including Diplomatic Agents, done at New York, Dec. 14, 1973, *entered into force,* Feb. 20, 1977, 28 U.S.T. 1975; T.I.A.S. 8532; 1034 U.N.T.S. 167; 351(a) ("whoever kills a member of Congress . . .); 351(d) (proscribing conspiracy to kidnap members of Congress).

[140] Former 18 U.S.C. § 2331 (1986) (jurisdiction over extraterritorial violence). For current law, *see* 18 U.S.C. §§ 2331-2339 (A & B) (Supp. 1996). Section 2332 (1996) provides: ". . . [W]hoever kills a national of the United States, while such national is outside the United States, shall — (1) if the killing is murder (as defined in § 1111(a)), [be punished with fine, plus imprisonment, or death]. . . . Extraterritorial attempt or conspiracy to murder a U.S. national are also punished, as is other violence intended to cause serious bodily injury. The limitation requiring written authorization of the Attorney General or highest ranking subordinate with responsibility for criminal prosecutions, certifying that the violence was intended to coerce, intimidate, or retaliate against a government or civilian population, is found in § 2332(d).

The jurisdictional theory applied was the protective principle combined with aspects of the passive-personality and possibly the universality theories. In sum, we have now considered three theories of jurisdiction. The subjective territorial theory provides for jurisdiction over crimes in which a material element has occurred within the territory. The objective territorial theory obtains when a significant effect of the offense impacts on the territory. The protective principle, on the other hand, provides for jurisdiction over offenses committed wholly outside the territory of the forum state, but only applies when the offense threatens the state's security, integrity, sovereignty or important governmental function. The objective and subjective territorial theories are extensions of the territorial principle, while the protective principle is an exception to it.

Continental countries have always maintained a clear distinction between objective-subjective territoriality and the protective principle. Continental law explicitly recognizes the protective principle and allows jurisdiction to be asserted over: (1) acts that threaten the general interest of the republic, including the security of the state and its diplomatic or consular posts or agents, or counterfeiting the seal or national currency;[141] (2) offenses against French nationals;[142] and (3) those very grave crimes that all states have an interest in prosecuting.[143] The *Fornage* case[144] shows the French traditional emphasis on territoriality, but provides an exception for the protective principle. A conviction of a Swiss national for larceny committed in Switzerland was quashed by the Cour de cassation because:

> [J]urisdiction cannot extend to offenses committed outside the territory by foreigners who, by reason of such acts, are not justiciable by the French tribunals; seeing that, indeed, the right to punish emanates from the right of sovereignty, which does not extend beyond the limits of the territory; that, except in the cases . . . founded on the right of legitimate self-defense, French tribunals are without power to judge foreigners for acts committed by them in a foreign country; that their incompetence in this regard is absolute and permanent; that it can be waived neither by the silence or the consent of the accused; that it exists always the same at every state of the proceedings.[145]

As previously noted, there are expansive exceptions to this refusal to assert jurisdiction over crimes of aliens committed abroad.

The authority for the protective type exceptions in Article 694 of the *Code de procédure pénal*, which since July 11, 1975, has provided: "every alien who, outside the territory of the Republic, commits, either as author or as accomplice, a crime or a *délit* against the security of the State or of counterfeiting the seal of the State or national currency in circulation, or a crime against French diplomatic or consular agents or poses is to be prosecuted and adjudged according to the disposition of French law, whether he is arrested in France or the

---

141 Former C. PR. PÉN. art. 694. Currently in C. PÉN. art. 113-10 (1994).

142 The Law of July 11, 1975, No. 75-624, extended the previously recognized but rather exiguously applied passive personality jurisdiction. C. PR. PÉN. art. f113-7 (1994), *supra* note 122, continues this jurisdiction.

143 This is the universality theory. *See infra*.

144 THE INTERNATIONAL LEGAL SYSTEM, *supra* note 1; the *Fornage* case, 84 J. du Palais 229 (1873) (*Cour de Cassation*) (cited and discussed in 2 JOHN B. MOORE, INTERNATIONAL LAW DIGEST 261-63 (1906)); and Delaume, *supra* note 55, at 176 n.8.

145 The *Fornage* case, 84 J. du Palais at 230 (author's translation).

Government obtains his extradition. . . ."[146] This is continued in the new *Code de procédure pénale*, articles 689, et seq., and in the *Code pénal* articles 113-6 through 113-11.

Thus, article 694 permits the prosecution and punishment of certain exceptional offenses committed outside French territory. Its purpose is to protect basic French national interests in cases "for which foreign governments may only have an imperfect appreciation."[147] Those offenses may be prosecuted just as if they had been committed in French territory.[148] The use of the language "punishable in the same manner as an infraction committed within this [French] territory" shows that the French understand that the protective principle is an exception to the territorial theory.[149]

Nationality Principle Theory

In addition to extending territoriality via subjective and objective territoriality, and making exceptions to it via the protective principle, extraterritorial jurisdiction may be asserted on the basis of the nationality principle. Jurisdiction based on the nationality of the perpetrator is a generally accepted principle of international law.[150] The nationality principle plays an important part in the law of most countries. In fact, this theory of jurisdiction is the second most important of the five theories in terms of its worldwide application. Traditional international law provides that nationals of a state remain under its sovereignty and owe their allegiance to it, even though traveling or residing abroad. Professor Hall states: "[t]he authority possessed by a state community over its members being the result of the personal relation existing between it and the individuals of which it is formed; its laws travel with them wherever they go, both in places within and without the jurisdiction of other powers. A state cannot enforce its laws within the territory of another state; but its subjects remain

---

[146] Author's translation.

[147] Bigay, *supra* note 122. The changes made by the law of July 11, 1975, which modified the old Article 694 of the C. PR. PÉN. were rather profound in two ways. First, competence was extended for extraterritorial conduct endangering diplomatic or consular posts or agents. Second, the law equalized the treatment of French and foreign nationals with regard to the protective principle, making it clear that the legislation was recognizing the protective principle and not merely utilizing the nationality theory of jurisdiction. *Id.* C. PR. PÉN. art. 694.

[148] Former C. PR. PÉN. art. 694, § 2, current C.PR.PÉN. arts. 689, et seq., and C. PÉN. arts. 113-6, et seq. discussed more fully in note 122, *supra.*

[149] In 1917, a French national was convicted of entering into a commercial transaction with an Austrian (enemy) firm while he was residing in Portugal. The accused was convicted in absentia, though his conduct, which took place in Portugal, did not violate Portuguese law. *Rivière Case*, 13 REVUE DE DROIT INTERNATIONALE PRIVÉ 543 (Cass. Crim. 1917). Of course, that case represented treason, which also is based on the nationality principle. French case law abounds in convictions of aliens who have violated or who have committed acts that threaten to harm French national security or sovereignty as well. *E.g.*, *In re Glass*, 1858 D.P. IV 339 (Trib. Corr. de Boulogne sur Mer), where the defendant, an Englishman, while outside French territory obtained a French passport by using a false name and providing false information. In Trios, the *Cour de Cassation* upheld a lower court's assertion of jurisdiction and application of French law to a Spanish national who, while in Spain, violated French national security by maintaining correspondence with France's enemies. *In re Urios*, 1920 Bull. Crim. No. 26, 34 (Cass. Crim.) (cited in HACKWORTH, *supra* note 60, at 203, and Delaume, *supra* note 55, at 176 n.8). With the promulgation of article 694, the French legislature introduced a scheme that provides clear, if rather broad, application of the protective principle. In the 1930's, French judicial application of the protective principle was criticized by U.S. commentators as being "inadmissible in principle and in excess of anything which international law permits." Harvard Research, *supra* note 36, at 558 (cited with criticism reemphasized in Note, *Extraterritorial Jurisdiction and Jurisdiction Following Forcible Abduction: A New Israeli Precedent in International Law,* 72 MICH. L. REV. 1087, 1095 (1974)).

[150] Harvard Research, *supra* note 36, at 519.

under an obligation not to disregard them, their social relations for all purposes as within its territory are determined by them, and it preserves the power of compelling observance by punishment if a person who has broken them returns within its jurisdiction."[151] The state has legal authority under international and domestic law, based on that allegiance, to assert criminal jurisdiction over actions of one of its nationals deemed criminal by its laws.[152]

Although the nationality principle of jurisdiction is universally recognized, there are differences in its application.[153] U.S. practice is not opposed in principle to nationality jurisdiction, depending on the crime.[154] On the other hand, jurisdiction on the basis of the nationality of the victim has not been accepted, except in certain "specific" and "exceptional" situations, such as offenses threatening national security, or trafficking in narcotics.[155] France, on the other hand, asserts nationality jurisdiction in a substantially more comprehensive manner.

Continental countries insist on the active personality principle. For many, the rule is constitutional. They maintain that nationality is a link so strong that the national state may prosecute any of its nationals for offenses they commit anywhere in the world. Most require that the offense be punishable in the place where it was committed as well. They feel that jurisdiction is required to maintain their sovereignty over their nationals and in maintaining their respect around the world by punishing their own wrongdoers. They maintain a concomitant exception to extraditing their nationals. If a continental nation refuses extradition, it has an obligation to prosecute the perpetrator.[156] This notion has its roots in the writings of Grotius, "*aut dedere—aut punire.*"[157] Some argue that prosecution is secondary to extradition: "*primo dedere—secundo prosequi,*"[158] except in cases of the

---

[151] W. E. HALL, INTERNATIONAL LAW 56 (8th ed. 1924).

[152] This evolved from the need of international law theorists, jurists and positivists during the 19th and early 20th Centuries, to render states responsible for their nationals. TERRORISM, DRUGS, *supra* note 1, at Ch. 3. *See* Blackmer v. U.S., 284 U.S. 421 (1932). *See also, e.g.*, 21 U.S.C. § 955a(b), (making it unlawful for any citizen of the United States on board any vessel intentionally to possess a controlled substance with intent to distribute).

[153] British law recognizes jurisdiction on the basis of the nationality of the accused in some instances: "[T]he general rule of English law is that offenses committed by British subjects out of England are not punishable by the criminal law of this country. We need not explore the origin of this doctrine . . . [I]t depends partly on the law of nations which would regard an offense committed on the soil of one nation as, at least primarily, the concern of the sovereign of that country, but one can also see the procedural difficulty which would have occurred to a medieval lawyer who would be unable to understand how the jury presentment consisting of persons taken from the vicinage could have knowledge of crimes committed abroad sufficient to present them to the sovereign's courts . . . [C]ertainly from the reign of Henry VII, this rule has been subject to statutory exceptions. Crimes of the present day which can be tried in England though committed abroad are treason, homicide, bigamy and offenses against the Foreign Investment Act, 1870. There may be others, but these instances will suffice." Regina v. Page, [1953] 2 All. ER. 1335, 1356.

[154] *E.g.,* U.S. v. Bowman, 260 U.S. 94 (1922); U.S. v. Boshell, 952 F.2d 1101 (9th Cir. 1991) (U.S. nationals for possession of marijuana); U.S. v. Juda, 46 F.3d 961 (9th Cir. 1995); U.S. v. Thomas, 893 F.2d 1066, 1969 (9th Cir. 1990).

[155] *E.g.*, 21 U.S.C. § 955a(b), makes it unlawful for any citizen of the United States on board any vessel intentionally to possess a controlled substance with intent to distribute.

[156] DEITRICH OEHLER, INTERNATIONALES STRAFRECHT 497 (2d ed. 1983) (cited in Otto Lagodny, *The European Convention on the Suppression of Terrorism: A Substantial Step to Combat Terrorism?,* 60 U.COLO. L. REV. 583, 587 (1989)).

[157] Lagodny, *supra* note 156, at 587.

[158] *Id.*

"nationality principle" where extradition is always forbidden. This does not appear clear-cut, however.[159]

Europeans have important reasons for asserting jurisdiction over nationals who have committed offenses outside national territory.[160] The French explain, for example, that because a nation's nationals have the benefit and protection of their nationality and owe allegiance to their country, they should be answerable to the national jurisdiction for any offense they commit. Furthermore, any offense committed by a French national abroad actually injures France's reputation and respect in the world. Most persuasively, they argue that if the country of their nationality did not have the authority to assert jurisdiction, nationals who have committed extraterritorial offenses might be immune from prosecution anywhere. A national who has committed an extraterritorial offense, but who has returned to his country before the foreign authorities have caught up with him, is exempt from extradition. The French Law of March 10, 1927, for example, prohibits extradition of nationals.[161] Thus, were it not for the Continental principle of jurisdiction based on the nationality of the perpetrator, a person could remain in his or her own nation and be immune from any prosecution.[162]

Although continental countries maintain a very broad application of the nationality principle, its application, except in certain exceptional and specific circumstances, is subsidiary to jurisdiction asserted by the state in which the offense is committed. France will assert jurisdiction only if the accused escapes from foreign justice.[163] By contrast, protective principle jurisdiction is not subsidiary. Also, jurisdiction will be asserted in those instances whether or not foreign jurisdiction is applicable, or even if foreign justice has been met.

---

159 *See* BASSIOUNI & WISE, *supra* note 44; Christopher L. Blakesley, *Review Essay,* 62 REVUE INTERNATIONALE DE DROIT PÉNAL 367 (1996).

160 MERLE & VITU, *supra* note 64, at 394.

161 Extradition Law of Mar. 19, 1927, 1927 D.P. IV 3, 265, available in C. PR. PÉN. Discussed in detail in TERRORISM, DRUGS, *supra* note 1, in Ch. 4. Virtually all European states provide similarly for national exemption from extradition. Israel recently amended its law to extend jurisdiction on the basis, among others, of the nationality principle. *See* 1978 Laws of the State of Israel No. 881, at 52 (Jan. 12, 1978); *see also* S. Z. Feller, *Jurisdiction Over Offenses With a Foreign Element, in* 2 A TREATISE ON INTERNATIONAL CRIMINAL LAW 5, 32-48, and 69-71 (M. Cherif Bassiouni & Ved P. Nanda, eds., 1973); Theodor Meron, *Nonextradition of Israeli National and Extraterritorial Jurisdiction Reflections on Bill No. 1306,* 13 ISR. L. REV. 215, 215-22 (1978).

162 *See, e.g.,* OEHLER, *supra* note 156; Jurgen Meyer, *Agreements and Disagreements Over International Criminal Law, in* Harvard Symposium on International Cooperation in Criminal Matters (June 16-18, 1988); *see also,* e.g., BOUZAT & PINATEL, *supra* note 64, at 1325; MERLE & VITU, *supra* note 64, at 412-14; IVAN SHEARER, EXTRADITION IN INTERNATIONAL LAW 94 (1971); *cf.,* Jurgen Meyer, *German Criminal Law Relating to International Terrorism,* 60 U. COLO. L. REV. 571 (1989); Otto Lagodny, *The European Convention on the Suppression of Terrorism: A Substantial Step to Combat Terrorism?,* 60 U. COLO. L. REV. 583, 586-88 (1989). The Extradition Law of Germany is the *Gesetz uber die Internationale Rechtshilfe in Strafsachen,* BGB1.I 2071 (1982) (discussed in Otto Lagodny, *Grundrechte als Auslieferungs-Gegenrechte,* [1988] NJW, Heft 35, p. 2146-50; and in Otto Lagodny, *Die Rechtsstellung des Auszuliefernden in der Bundesrepublik Deutschland, Reihe: Beitraege und Materialien aus dem Max-Planck-Institut fur Auslaendisches und Internationales Strafrecht*).

163 MERLE & VITU, *supra* note 64, at 412-13. Thus France applies a type of "rule of reasonableness." *See* RESTATEMENT (THIRD), *supra* note 23, § 403.

Continental Extradition and Nationality

Extradition treaties originally provided that "neither party shall be bound to deliver up its own citizens or subjects under the stipulations of this Convention."[164] The exemption of nationals from extradition follows from notions of nationality jurisdiction. Continental nations see it as very important and nonnegotiable.[165] Antiquity saw citizens of the Greek city states, the Italian cities, and Rome, as well as other great civilizations, exempt their citizens from extradition.[166] Native American tribes refused to deliver up their denizens.[167] French history in this regard exemplifies that of Europe. The extradition treaties between France and her adjacent neighbors in the mid-18th Century contained provisions exempting nationals.[168] Napoleon contradicted the rule by issuing a decree that French nationals could be extradited, but the decree was never executed.[169]

French law, like that of other Continental nations, provides for jurisdiction over virtually every serious offense[170] committed by French nationals[171] outside French territory, as long as its punishable in the state of commission. The French Minister of Justice formally promulgated a *circulaire* in 1841, prohibiting the extradition of nationals.[172] Although

---

164 1909 Extradition Treaty between France and the U.S., 37 Stat. 1526, T.I.A.S. No. 872, art. V. On the issue of the extradition of nationals generally, see TERRORISM, DRUGS, *supra* note 1, at Ch. 3, 4; SHEARER, *supra* note 162, at 34.

165 *See* T. Stein, *Extradition Issues,* Jurgen Meyer, and Deitrich Oehler, papers presented at the *Harvard Conference on International Cooperation in Criminal Matters*, on file HARV. J. INT'L L. Of the total of 163 extradition treaties printed in the League of Nations Treaty Series and the first 550 volumes of the United Nations Treaty Series, 98 except the national of the requested State absolutely, 57 give to the requested state a discretionary right to refuse to surrender its nationals, while only eight provide for extradition regardless of the nationality of the fugitive. SHEARER, *supra* note 162, at 96, app. II.

166 SHEARER, *supra* note 162, at 95.

167 Crimes committed by members of the tribe against outsiders were usually not considered to be crimes, and "extradition" was refused. The most severe penalty for intra-tribal crimes was banishment, however.

168 A. AUPECLE, L'EXTRADITION ET LA LOI DE 10 MARS 1927 15 (Paris, 1927) (unpublished thesis in Columbia University School of Law Library) [hereinafter cited as AUPECLE].

169 BILLOT, TRAITÉ DE L'EXTRADITION 70-72 (1874). *See also* SHEARER, *supra* note 162, at 104.

170 C. PR. PÉN. art. 689. French penal law divides criminal acts into three categories: *crimes*, *délits* and *contraventions*. These are roughly equivalent to felonies, misdemeanors, and infractions or administrative offenses. Herzog, *Compétences des Jurisdictions Pénales pour les Infractions Commises a l'Etranger*, *in* VIITH CONGRÊS DE DR. COMP., CONTRIBUTIONS FRANÇAISE 545 (Uppsala ed., 1966).

171 Nationality in France is determined as of the day of the prosecution, not the day of the commission of the crime. C. PÉN. art. 113-6 (1994); *Serlute* Case, 1898 Clunet 1058 (the basic French decision on this issue). Assertion of jurisdiction is not automatic, however. There are conditions that must first be met. None of the conditions applies when the offender commits a crime that threatens the national security of treasury, or a crime against a diplomatic or consular agent or post. There are two types of conditions: *conditions communes*, which apply both to *crimes* and to *délits* and *conditions spéciales*, which apply only to *délits*. Discussed in MERLE & VITU, *supra* note 64, at 394-98. There are three *conditions communes* that must be met before nationality jurisdiction may be asserted: (1) former art. 689 of the Code de procédure pénale required and current Code pénal art. 113-9 (1994), make it clear that France does not enforce the public order of other nations. *Etcheverry* case, 1886 S. Jur. II 166 (Cour d'Appel, Pau) (French national cannot be prosecuted in France for counterfeiting foreign currency in a foreign country); (2) the accused must not have definitively fulfilled the requirements of the foreign state's justice for the crime committed there. C. PR. PÉN. art. 692; *see In re Moisdon*, 1890 Dalloz, Jurisprudence [D. Jur.] I 138 (Cass. Crim.) (defendant convicted and punished for a crime against public morals in Belgium and, therefore, could not be prosecuted in France for that crime); (3) the statute of limitations must not have run. In sum, if the *conditions communes* are met, a French national may be prosecuted for any crime committed abroad.

172 *Circulaire du Ministre de la Justice,* Apr. 4, 1841, para. 2 (cited in SHEARER, *supra* note 162, at 104 n.5).

France subsequently negotiated extradition treaties with Great Britain and the United States without including the exemption of nationals clause, France has never extradited one of her nationals.[173] Its law specifically exempts French citizens from extradition.[174]

The Nationality Principle in the United States

The United States Supreme Court recognized early in its history the existence of the power to punish offenses committed extraterritorially by the U.S. nationals.[175] Congress never has made a general rule relating to extraterritorial jurisdiction,[176] however. Thus, any extraterritorial application of statute is an exception to the territorial principle and general rule. Nevertheless, U.S. case law has approved jurisdiction over nationals who commit crimes abroad even though the appropriate statute did not explicitly declare that it applied extraterritorially. Nationality often appears to play a significant role in the application of U.S. legislation to extraterritorial conduct. Jurisdiction has been approved, for example, in the case of an extraterritorial violation of a penal clause in an absentee voting statute.[177] Nationality jurisdiction also has triggered prosecution of American nationals assisting in the illegal immigration of alien contract laborers[178] and trafficking in controlled substances on the High Seas.[179] Even a murder committed by a U.S. national on the uninhabited Guano island was prosecuted.[180] Courts have upheld a contempt judgment for failure to comply with a subpoena that had been served abroad by a consular officer[181] and sustained jurisdiction

---

173 SHEARER, *supra* note 162, at 104; BILLOT, *supra* note 169, at 73; these were the last French extradition treaties that did not contain the exemption in some form. Both treaties were negotiated in 1843.

174 Extradition Law of 1927, art. 5, ¶ 1.

175 Rose v. Himley, 8 U.S. 143, 166 (4 Cranch) 240, 279 (1808) (dictum); *see also* Chief Justice Marshall's speech, Livingston's Resolution, United States House of Representatives, quote in Appendix, 18 U.S. (5 Wheat.) 129 Note I (1829); *Henfield's* case, 11 F. Cas. 1099 (C.C.D.Pa. 1793) (No. 6360). In addition to the traditional (essentially territorial) function of keeping the peace, one of the functions of a municipal criminal justice system simply is to control its citizens' conduct—to prohibit and attempt to limit conduct deemed to be socially harmful. This may be contrasted with a policy of keeping the king's peace, which obviously is the essence of territoriality. That function may be considered necessary and apt whether the conduct occurs within or without the state's territory. There have been periods in history in which the determinative factor for jurisdiction was citizenship or noncitizenship of the accused offender. Feller, *supra* note 161, at 5, 12, 30-32.

176 Note, *Extraditional Jurisdiction—Criminal Law,* 13 HARV. INT'L L.J. 346, 348-49 (1972). The Supreme Court attempted to lay down a general rule of statutory interpretation with regard to extraterritorial offenses in U.S. v. Bowman, 260 U.S. 94 (1922). It has not become a general rule, however. Certain statutes expressly and specifically apply to offenses committed by nationals outside the prosecuting state's territory. For example, 18 U.S.C. § 953 punishes unauthorized attempts by United States nationals, "wherever they may be," to influence a foreign government in its relations with the United States. 18 U.S.C. § 953.

177 State v. Maine, 16 Wis. 421 (1863).

178 U.S. v. Craig, 28 F. 795, 801 (1886).

179 21 U.S.C. § 955a(b), makes it unlawful for any citizen of the United States on board any vessel intentionally to possess a controlled substance with intent to distribute.

180 Jones v. U.S., 137 U.S. 202 (1890). Interestingly, the same philosophy as that which motivates continental countries to apply nationality jurisdiction—namely the accused's likelihood of escaping justice altogether—motivated U.S. jurisdiction.

181 Blackmer v. U.S., 284 U.S. 421, 441 (1932). In this case, a U.S. citizen residing in France was held in contempt of court for failing to comply with subpoena to be a witness in a criminal trial. The Act of July 4, 1926, ch. 762, 44 Stat. 835 (codified at 28 U.S.C. §§ 711-718 (1926) (current version at 28 U.S.C. § 1783 (1982)), provided that the court could issue a subpoena to be served personally by the United States Consul and that a contempt fine of up to $100,000 could be levied for refusal to comply and failure to show cause why it should not be levied. The Supreme Court found that the hearing for contempt, done with the accused in absentia, did not

to require income tax payment by nationals domiciled abroad.[182] Sometimes the same act committed by an alien and a national might be punishable only against the national.[183] Nationality jurisdiction, where it is deemed appropriate, is applicable even though the national also is a national of the state in which the offense is committed.[184]

The U.S. Supreme Court declared its basic attitude toward nationality jurisdiction in the case of *U.S. v. Bowman*: "The three defendants who were found in New York [but who committed the criminal acts while in Brazil] were citizens of the United States and were certainly subject to such laws as it might pass to protect itself and its property. Clearly it is no offense to the dignity of right of sovereignty of Brazil to hold them for this crime against the Government to which they owe allegiance."[185] And again, in *Blackmer v. U.S.*,[186] the Supreme Court stated: "[w]ith respect to such an exercise of authority, there is no question of international law, but solely of the purport of the municipal law which establishes the duties of the citizen in relation to his own government."[187]

Thus the nationality theory of jurisdiction has been an important basis of jurisdiction in the United States as well as on the continent. Its application in the U.S. is not as expansive as that in Europe, however. There is no general principle that U.S. criminal law be applied to nationals wherever they may be. In fact, the crimes to which the nationality principle has been extended often have been those that indicate a strong protectionist motive. For example, in *Bowman*, jurisdiction was extended to cover extraterritorial fraudulent acts committed by a national because the conduct was "directly injurious to the government and against which the government has the right to defend itself."[188] Nationals are "certainly subject to such laws as [the U.S.] might pass to protect itself."[189]

---

violate due process and that jurisdiction extended to U.S. citizens abroad. It also found that the U.S. Consul could serve subpoenas in order to satisfy due process requirements without any treaty agreement. With regard to extraterritorial application of United States legislation, the Court found that, unless intent to the contrary was manifest, application of legislation to acts committed abroad was a matter of judicial construction, not of legislative power. The Court was able to enforce the order because the defendant had property within the territory of the United States that could be attached. 284 U.S. at 441. *Cf.* FED. R. CIV. P. 45(e)(2) (28 U.S.C. § 2072); FED. R. CRIM. P. 17(e)(2). In U.S. v. First National City Bank, 396 F.2d 897 (2d Cir. 1968), a branch of Citibank in Germany was under a U.S. subpoena to produce documents. The branch risked civil liability if it complied with the subpoena to produce documents. The court held that it has jurisdiction over branches of United States companies on the basis of the nationality principle. Nationality was determined by the place of incorporation. The court applied a balancing approach to decide whether to assert jurisdiction. The court weighed the plaintiff's interest in receiving the documents against the defendant's interest in avoiding civil liability. The court also had to consider delicate diplomatic interests. The decision went against Citibank, although it may have been different had the German penalty been criminal instead of civil.

182 Cook v. Tait, 265 U.S. 47 (1924).

183 U.S. v. Bowman, 260 U.S. 94 (1922).

184 Kawakita v. U.S., 343 U.S. 717 (1952); Coumas v. Superior Court, 31 Cal. 2d 682, 192 P.2d 449 (1948).

185 *Bowman,* 260 U.S. at 102.

186 284 U.S. 421.

187 *Id.* at 437.

188 *Bowman,* 260 U.S. at 102.

189 *Id.* at 102; *see also Blackmer*, 284 U.S. at 437 ("wherever public interest requires").

The Passive-Personality Theory

The passive-personality theory provides a state with competence to prosecute and punish perpetrators of criminal conduct that is aimed at or harms the nationals of the asserting state. In Europe today, the passive-personality theory, which provides for jurisdiction to be asserted by the state of the victim's nationality, is on the ascendancy. This principle developed and was very widespread during the Middle Ages, especially in Italy. The notion was that, since criminal law has as its essential object to protect the public and private interests, the victim's national law and justice had the best appreciation of just what protection ought to be afforded.[190] German criminalists of the 19th Century promoted the notion of *Realsystem*, a combination of the passive-personality and the protective principle theory. It emphasized the protection of the state—injury to a victim injured state.[191]

Passive-personality on the continent went into desuetude during the 19th Century heyday of positivism. It rebounded in the mid-20th Century. Jurisdiction based on the passive-personality theory was recognized only for a short period during World War II, when French law provided that French courts had jurisdiction to prosecute either war crimes,[192] or any *infraction* committed in territory occupied by enemy forces against French citizens or any war crime against any soldier serving France.[193] The passive-personality theory arose definitively with regard to air travel. The French Code de l'aviation civile, provides jurisdiction when a *crime* or *délit* is committed against a French victim aboard a non-French airplane.[194] Finally, the Law of July 11, 1975, added article 689-1 to the Code of Criminal Procedure, providing jurisdiction to prosecute under French law and to punish any foreign national who commits a crime, in which the victim is a French national.[195] This is now covered by *Code pénal* articles 113-6, et seq., and *Code de procédure pénale* articles 689, et seq. The promulgation of Code of Criminal Procedure article 689-1 in 1975,[196]

190 MERLE & VITU, *supra* note 64 (citing Donnedieu de Vabres, *Les Principes Modèrnes du Droit Penal International* at 56, et seq. (1928)); Donnedieu de Vabres, *Le Système de la Personnalité Passive ou de la Protection des Nationaux*, 1950 REVUE INTERNATIONALE DE DROIT PÉNAL 511, et seq.

191 MERLE & VITU, *supra* note 64, at 374 (citing Schultz, *Compétence des Juridictions Pénales pour les Infractions Commises à l'Etranger*, 1936 REV. SCI. CRIM. ET DR. PÉN. COMP. 331, et seq.).

192 Ord., Aug. 28, 1944, art. 1.

193 Ord., Nov. 9, 1944, art. 2; MERLE & VITU, *supra* note 64, at 400-01. This jurisdiction was primary, not subsidiary.

194 *Id.* at 401; C. AV. CIV. art. L. 121-8.

195 C. PR. PÉN. art. 689-1.

196 C. PR. PÉN. art. 689-1 provides: "[a]ny foreigner who, beyond the territory of the Republic, is guilty of a crime, either as author or accomplice, may be prosecuted and convicted in accordance with the disposition of French law, when the victim of the crime is a French national." (author's translation). The title of this chapter of the code was expanded from simply crimes and délits committed abroad (*des crimes et délits commis a l'étranger*) to include contraventions. Articles 689-1, et seq. of the C. PR. PÉN. now provides for French jurisdiction over offenses in application of any international convention. It will allow French jurisdiction for crimes, délits and contraventions committed abroad for which an international convention attributes jurisdiction to France. France has entered into many such conventions in the past several years. *E.g.*, the Hague Convention of Dec. 16, 1970, for the Repression of Aircraft Hijacking, 22 U.S.T. 1641, T.I.A.S. No. 7192, 860 U.N.T.S. 105, *see* C. PR. PÉN. art. 689-6; the Montreal Convention of Sept. 23, 1971, on the Repression of Illicit Acts Against Civil Aviation Security, 24 U.S.T. 664, T.I.A.S. No. 7570, 974 U.N.T.S. 177 (C. PR. PÉN. 689-6 through 689-9); and the Additional Protocol of Mar. 25, 1972, to the Convention Unique sur les Stupéfiants (Single Convention to Narcotic Drugs), Mar. 30, 1961, 18 U.S.T. 1407, T.I.A.S. No. 6298, 520 U.N.T.S. 204. The French legislature promulgated the these articles to accommodate treaties and to legislate any indispensable complements. With regard to the precursors to these articles, *see generally* Bigay, *supra* note 122.

expanded French authority to assert jurisdiction over extraterritorial offenses committed against its nationals. Article 689-1 incorporates the principle of passive-personality to all "*crimes.*" It provided that every alien who is either principal or accomplice in a crime (as opposed to a *délit*) committed outside French territory may be prosecuted and adjudged on the basis of French law if the victim of the crime is a French national.[197] The legislative expansion of the passive-personality principle was opposed forcefully. The opponents feared that broad application of jurisdiction based on the nationality of the victim would cause confusing, concurrent and competing jurisdiction.[198] The proponents of the new law prevailed, however, by arguing that there was no such danger, because French jurisdiction would be subsidiary to that of any country in which the offense occurs, except in cases involving national security.[199] Thus if it is not a matter of national security, France will not take jurisdiction unless the country in which the offense occurs fails to do so.

This does leave some problem of concurrent jurisdiction. When the offense impinges on national security, France claims primary jurisdiction. A state on whose territory the offense actually occurred, however, would probably do the same. If a dispute developed over which state ought to have primary jurisdiction in such a circumstance, the state on whose territory the harm actually occurred would likely prevail under international law. That state could acquiesce to the state whose national security was compromised. In addition, the latter state would still retain jurisdiction and could seek extradition after justice was satisfied in the former.

The factors that motivated the French Legislature to promulgate this new law included the quickly developing international penal law[200] and, most importantly, the events at the Hague in 1974, where French hostages were taken and French property was damaged at the French Consulate General. These events illustrated in dramatic fashion that French law as it stood in 1974 would have inhibited and possibly precluded the prosecution of the offenders, even if their persons were obtained by extradition, which was unlikely at the time because of the political nature of the offenses.[201] The paramount motive for the new law, however, was the legislators' belief that the republic's laws should provide for prosecution

---

197 C. PR. PÉN. art. 689-1.

198 *See* statement in opposition by J.P. Cot in the Assemblée Nationale, arguing that, as in the past, the passive-personality principle should be applied only when French social order is troubled. Discussed in Bigay, *supra* note 122, at 52.

199 Mr. Cot's objections were countered by Mr. Foyer and by the *garde des Sceaux*, arguing that there would be no confusion, noting that the principle was already working in Law No. 121-8 of the *Code de l'aviation civil* as precedent for the new article, C. AV. CIV. art. L. 121-8 (1973). In addition, they presented other European examples: article 7 of the German Penal Code provided for application to acts injuring German nationals if the acts are punishable in the place they occurred or if no other authority takes jurisdiction; article 10 of the Italian Penal Code provided for jurisdiction over acts committed by foreigners abroad that injure Italy or one of its citizens, when the offense is punishable under Italian law by perpetual hard labor or imprisonment for one year or more. Discussed in Bigay, *supra* note 122, at 52. *Compare* C. AV. CIV. art. L. 282-4-1.

200 *See, e.g.*, treaties listed and discussed in the section on the Universality Principle. In 1985, the French promulgated *loi No. 85-1407, du 30 Déc. 1985*, providing jurisdiction to prosecute and punish anyone who commits [anywhere] crimes or delicts that constitute torture, as provided by article 1 of the Convention Against Torture and Other Cruel, Inhuman or Degrading Treatment, done at New York, Dec. 10, 1984, U.N. Doc. A/39/708 (1984). In 1987, the French promulgated *loi No. 87-541, du 16 Juillet 1987* to apply the European Convention For the Repression of Terrorism and other anti-terrorism conventions, allowing French jurisdiction over the conduct prohibited by those treaties and made criminal in the *Code pénal*.

201 *See* Bigay, *supra* note 122, at 51-52.

and punishment for crimes against its citizens when the *lex loci delicti* has failed to do so.[202] Terrorism has prompted the expansion of extraterritorial jurisdiction.

The passive-personality theory traditionally has been anathema to U.S. law and practice. The Restatement (Second) provided the traditional repudiation: "[A] state does not have jurisdiction to prescribe a rule of law attaching a legal consequence to conduct of an alien outside its territory merely on the ground that the conduct affects one of its nationals."[203] The U.S. government has vigorously protested assertions of jurisdiction based on this theory. The *Cutting* case[204] provided the most famous protest. Cutting, a U.S. national, was seized by Mexican authorities during a visit to that country. He was jailed, pending prosecution for criminal libel allegedly perpetrated in Texas against a Mexican national.[205] The U.S. Secretary of State protested the assertion of jurisdiction, arguing that the passive-personality theory was improper under traditional principles of international law:

> [T]he assumption of the Mexican Tribunal, under the law of Mexico, to punish a citizen of the United States for an offense wholly committed and consummated in his own country against its laws was an invasion of the independence of this Government.
>
> . . .
>
> [I]t is not now, and has not been contended, by this Government . . . that if Mr. Cutting had actually circulated in Mexico a libel printed in Texas, in such a manner as to constitute a publication of libel in Mexico within the terms of Mexican law, he could not have been tried and punished for this offense in Mexico.
>
> As to the question of international law, I am unable to discover any principle upon which the assumption of jurisdiction made in Article 186 of the Mexican Penal Code can be justified. . . . [I]t has consistently been laid down in the United States as a rule of action that citizens of the United States cannot be held answerable in foreign countries for offenses that were wholly committed and consummated either in their own country or in other countries not subject to the jurisdiction of the punishing state. . . . [T]o say that he may be tried in another country for this offense, simply because its object happens to be a citizen of that country, would be to assert that foreigners coming to the United States bring hither the penal laws of the country from which they came, and thus subject citizens of the United States in their own country to an indefinite criminal responsibility.[206]

---

[202] Compared to other states of Europe, France was late in developing the passive personality principle to this extent. *See e.g.*, THE PENAL CODE OF SWEDEN, part I, ch. 2 § 3(3), at 15 (G.O.W. Mueller ed., T. Sellin trans. 1972).

[203] RESTATEMENT (SECOND) OF THE FOREIGN RELATIONS LAW OF THE UNITED STATES § 30(2) comment *e* (1965). This has not been changed in RESTATEMENT (THIRD) §§ 402-03, *supra* note 23.

[204] *Cutting* case, 1887 FOR. REL. 751 (1888) (*reported in* JOHN B. MOORE, INTERNATIONAL LAW DIGEST 232-40 (1906)); *see also* THE INTERNATIONAL LEGAL SYSTEM, *supra* note 1, at Ch.3.

[205] *Cutting* case, *supra* note 204, at 229.

[206] *Id.* at 228-42 (quoting cable, Mr. Brayard, Sec. of State, to Mr. Connery, Chargé to Mexico, Nov. 1, 1887, 1887 For. Rel. 751). It was important that the alleged criminal conduct had occurred on United States territory. In 1940, in the *Fiedler* case, similar to *Cutting*, the Counsel for the Department of State instructed the American Consul General in Mexico City as follows: "This Government continues to hold the views which [are] expressed to the Mexico Government in the *Cutting* case. . . . This Government continues to deny that, according to the principles of international law, an American citizen can be justly held in Mexico to answer for an offense committed in the United States, simply because the object of that offense happens to be a Mexican citizen, and it remains that according to the principles of international law, the penal laws of a State, except with regard to

Although the passive-personality theory today is gaining recognition internationally,[207] it is not necessary to adopt it to address growing contemporary problems with terrorist violence. Although the Omnibus Diplomatic Security and Anti-Terrorism Act of 1986 and the current *Anti-Terrorism laws* have language suggesting the passive-personality theory,[208] they are better interpreted as employing the protective principle which articulates that the purpose of the Act is to provide jurisdiction, prosecution and punishment of extraterritorial terrorism.[209]

Universal Jurisdiction, With a Focus on Terrorism

International law provides that there are certain offenses for which any nation obtaining personal jurisdiction over an accused may prosecute. These offenses are condemned by virtually all domestic law.[210] Therefore, any nation that gets hold of the accused has an obligation to extradite or to prosecute. Though there is some difficulty regarding what "prosecute" means, it means at least to bring one's prosecutorial mechanism to bear on an accused.[211]

---

nationals thereof, have extraterritorial force. Accordingly, it is desired that your office should refrain from recognizing the above quoted provisions of Mexican law in the event that another American citizen shall be detained in Mexico charged with an offense committed within the jurisdiction of the United States." 6 MARJORIE M. WHITEMAN, DIGEST OF INTERNATIONAL LAW 103-04 (1968) (quoting *In re Fiedler*, Dept. of State File 312.1121, Feb. 9, 1940).

[207] Although § 402 of the RESTATEMENT (THIRD), *supra* note 23, is equivocal as to whether it rejects or accepts the passive-personality theory, when it is read along with comment *e* it appears to indicate that this theory is acceptable. Given the wider acceptance of this principle, it would be difficult to say that international law bars a broad application of it.

[208] Omnibus Diplomatic Security and Anti-Terrorism Act of 1986, P.L. 99-399, 100 Stat. 853 (1986) (§ 1202, inserting ch. 113A into 18 U.S.C. as § 2331: "(a) Homicide—Whoever kills a national of the United States, while such national is outside the United States [and] (c) whoever outside the United States engages in physical violence—(1) with the intent to cause serious bodily injury to a national of the United States . . ."); Ahmad v. Wigen, 726 F. Supp 389, 399 (E.D.N.Y. 1989) ("The United States recognizes nationality of the victim as a basis for criminal jurisdiction.") (citing 18 U.S.C. § 2331). *See also* 18 U.S.C. § 2332 (Supp. 1996), and 18 U.S.C. § 1203 (Supp. 1996).

[209] *Id. See* discussion of Protective Principle, *supra.*

[210] The positivistic theory is that certain conduct is considered criminal by virtually all domestic criminal justice systems or has been made an international crime by the combination of the domestic law of nations and so many or so pervasive international conventions that virtually all nations abide by its norms and feel bound as a matter of international law to do so. In 1985, the French promulgated *loi No. 85-1407, du 30 Déc. 1985*, providing jurisdiction to prosecute and punish anyone who commits [anywhere] crimes or delicts that constitute torture, as provided by article 1 of the Convention Against Torture and Other Cruel, Inhuman or Degrading Treatment, done at New York, Dec. 10, 1984, U.N. Doc. A/39/708 (1984). In 1987, the French promulgated *loi No. 87-541, du 16 Juillet 1987* to apply the European Convention For the Repression of Terrorism and other anti-terrorism conventions, allowing French jurisdiction over the conduct prohibited by those treaties and made criminal in the *Code pénal.*

[211] BASSIOUNI & WISE, *supra* note 44; Demjanjuk v. Petrovsky, 776 F.2d 571, 581-82 (6th Cir. 1985) (extradition decision explicitly recognizing the universality principle), *cert denied*, 106 S. Ct. 1198 (1986); HUGO GROTIUS, 2 DE BELLI AC PACIS LIBRIS TRES 504 (F. Kelsey trans., 1925); *Federal Jurisdiction, supra* note 35, at 211-12; *European Convention, infra* note 225, at 586-87 (*aut dedere—aut punire; or primo dedere—secundo prosequi*).

Perhaps the most ancient offense of universal interest is piracy,[212] a crime that may be considered an analogue to terrorism or part of the set of terrorist offenses. Like piracy, several other crimes are so universally condemned that international conventions have been aimed at eliminating them and have provided universal jurisdiction to do so. These include slave trade,[213] war crimes,[214] crimes against humanity,[215] hijacking and sabotage of civil

---

212 With regard to universal jurisdiction over piracy, Hackworth wrote: "It has long been recognized and well settled that persons and vessels engaged in piratical operations on the high seas are entitled to the protection of no nation and may be punished by any nation that may apprehend or capture them." HACKWORTH, *supra* note 60, at 681. *See also* MERLE & VITU, *supra* note 64, at 374-75. The 1958 Geneva Convention on the High Seas provides that: "[o]n the high seas, or in any other place outside the jurisdiction of any State, every State may seize a pirate ship or aircraft, or a ship taken by piracy and under the control of pirates, and arrest the persons and seize the property on board. The courts of the State which carried out the seizure may decide upon the penalties to be imposed, and may also determine the action to be taken with regard to the ships, aircraft or property, subject to the rights of third parties acting in good faith." Geneva Convention on the High Seas, Apr. 28, 1958, art. 19, 13 U.S.T. 2312, T.I.A.S. No. 5200, 450 U.N.T.S. 82 [hereinafter Geneva Convention on the High Seas]. *See also The Marianna Flora,* 24 U.S. (11 Wheat.) 1, 40 (1826) ("Pirates may, without doubt, be lawfully captured on the ocean by the public or private ships of every nation: for they are, in truth, common enemies of all mankind, and, as such, are liable to the extreme rights of war."); Edwin D. Dickinson, *Is the Crime of Piracy Obsolete*?, 38 HARV. L. REV. 334 (1925). *But see* ALFRED P. RUBIN, THE LAW OF PIRACY (1988) (ultimately concluding that "there is no public international law of piracy." *Id.* at 343, 344.

213 The modern legal movement to abolish slave trade began with the Paris Peace Treaties of 1814 and 1815 and the Congress of Vienna in 1815. M. Cherif Bassiouni & Ved P. Nanda, *The Crime of Slavery and Slave Trade, in* 1 INTERNATIONAL CRIMINAL LAW 325 n.12 (M. Cherif Bassiouni ed., 1986); Geneva Convention on the High Seas, *supra* note 212, arts. 13, 22. *See* United Nations Conference on Plenipotentiaries on a Supplementary Convention of the Abolition of Slavery, the Slave, the Slave Trade, and Institutions and Practices Similar to Slavery, Aug. 13-Sept. 4, 1956, Final Act and Supp. Conv., U.N. Doc. E/ CONF. 24/20 (cited in *The Crime of Slavery and Slave Trade, supra* this note, at 331 n.40); Geneva Convention Relative to Protection of Civilian Persons in Time of War, Aug. 12, 1949, 6 U.N.T.S. 3516, T.I.A.S. No. 3365, 75 U.N.T.S. 287, arts. 40, 51, 95.

214 *See, e.g.*, Geneva Convention for the Amelioration of the Condition of the Wounded and Sick in Armed Forces in the Field, Aug. 12, 1949, 6 U.S.T. 3114, T.I.A.S. No. 3362, 75 U.N.T.S. 31; Geneva Convention for the Amelioration of the Condition of Wounded, Sick and Shipwrecked Members of Armed Forces at Sea, Aug. 12, 1949, 6 U.S.T. 3217, T.I.A.S. No. 3363, 75 U.N.T.S. 85; Geneva Convention Relative to the Treatment of Prisoners of War, Aug. 12, 1949, 6 U.S.T. 3316, T.I.A.S. No. 3364, 75 U.N.T.S. 135; Geneva Convention Relative to the Protection of Civilian Persons in Time of War, Aug. 12, 1949, 6 U.N.T. 3516, T.I.A.S. No. 3365, 75 U.N.T.S. 287 [hereinafter Geneva Conventions]. *See also In re Yamashita*, 327 U.S. 1 (1945); U.S. v. Calley, 22 C.M.A. 534, 48 C.M.R. 19 (1973); YORAM DINSTEIN & MALA TABORY, WAR CRIMES IN INTERNATIONAL LAW (1996); W. MICHAEL REISMAN & CHRIS ANTONIOU (eds.), THE LAWS OF WAR: A COMPREHENSIVE COLLECTION OF PRIMARY DOCUMENTS ON INTERNATIONAL LAWS GOVERNING ARMED CONFLICT (1994); IAN BROWNLIE, INTERNATIONAL LAW AND THE USE OF FORCE BY STATES, Ch. IX (1963); TELFORD TAYLOR, NUREMBERG AND VIETNAM: AN AMERICAN TRAGEDY, at Chs. 6, 7 (1970); James E. Bond, *Application of the Law of War to Civil Conflicts*, 3 GA. J. INT'L & COMP. L. 345 (1973); Anthony A. D'Amato, *Is International Law Really "Law"?* 79 NW. U.L. REV. 1293 (1984-85); Anthony A. D'Amato, *Public International Law as a Career,* 1 AM. U. J. INT'L L. & POL'Y 13 (1986); Anthony A. D'Amato et. al., *War Crimes and Vietnam: The "Nuremberg Defense" and the Military Service Register,* 57 CAL. L. REV. 1055, 1086 (1969); Taubenfeld, *The Applicability of the Laws of War in Civil War, in* LAW AND CIVIL WAR IN THE MODERN WORLD 499 (John N. Moore ed., 1974). In addition, in the U.S., jurisdiction over war crimes and genocide obtain for *civil damages*, under the Alien Tort Act, 28 U.S.C. § 1350 and the Torture Victim Protection Act of 1991, Pub. L. No. 102-256, 106 Stat. 73 (1992), 28 U.S.C. 73 (1992) (not providing jurisdiction per se, but jurisdiction obtains via 28 U.S.C. § 1331, the general federal question jurisdiction statute); *see, e.g.*, Kadic v. Karadzic, 70 F.3d 232 (2d Cir. 1995); Mushikiwabo v. Baryagwiza, 1996 WL 164496 (S.D.N.Y. 1996) (Rwanda slaughter).

215 *See* Convention on the Non-Applicability of Statutory Limitations to War Crimes and Crimes Against Humanity, Nov. 26, 1968, 754 U.N.T. 73; European Convention on the Non-Applicability of Statutory Limitation to Crimes Against Humanity and War Crimes, Jan. 25, 1974, E.T.S. 82, 22 EUR. Y.B. 371, 7 H.R.J. 707; Principles of International co-operation in the detection, arrest, extradition and punishment of persons guilty of war crimes and crimes against humanity, 14 U.N. GAOR at 448, U.N. Doc. A/Res/3074 (XXVIII). *See also* BASSIOUNI, *supra*

aircraft,[216] genocide,[217] and apartheid.[218] There is a growing trend to include traffic in narcotic drugs.[219] This history, these treaties as well as others, and the domestic criminal law of all states, when considered as a whole, make it clear that terrorism—including hostage taking or kidnaping[220] or wanton violence against innocent civilians—is really a composite term including all of these separate universally condemned offenses, and thus triggers the universality theory of jurisdiction. Recently, many multilateral treaties have condemned

---

note 112.

[216] *See* Convention on Offences and Certain Other Acts Committed on Board Aircraft, Sept. 14, 1963, 20 U.S.T. 2941, T.I.A.S. No. 6768, 704 U.N.T.S. 219, *entered into force* in U.S. Dec. 4, 1969, (regulates international jurisdiction over offenses committed on board aircraft). *See also* Han-Heinrich. Jescheck, *Development & Future Prospects, in* 1 INTERNATIONAL CRIMINAL LAW 83, 96 (Bassiouni ed., 1986) [hereinafter *Development*]. The Convention contains no penal, extradition or mutual-assistance provisions. *Id.* Moreover, the state of aircraft's registration is always competent to prosecute. *Id. See also* Convention for the Suppression of Unlawful Acts against the Safety of Civil Aviation, Sept. 23, 1971, 24 U.S.T. 565, T.I.A.S. No. 7570, 974 U.N.T.S. 177, *entered into force* in U.S. Jan. 26, 1973; Convention for the Suppression of Unlawful Seizure of Aircraft, Dec. 16, 1970, 22 U.S.T. 1641 T.I.A.S. No. 7192, 860 U.N.T.S. 105, *entered into force* in U.S. Oct. 14, 1971; Law of July 5, 1972, No. 72-623, 92 Gazette du Palais (Legislation) 360 (1972), *discussed infra*. *See generally* THE INTERNATIONAL LEGAL SYSTEM, *supra* note 1, at Chs. 3, 4; M. CHERIF BASSIOUNI, INTERNATIONAL TERRORISM & POLITICAL CRIMES (1973); JOHN MURPHY, PUNISHING TERRORISTS: THE LEGAL FRAMEWORK FOR POLICY INITIATIATIVES Ch. 1 (1985); M. Cherif Bassiouni, *Extradition Reform Legislation in the United States: 1981-1983*, 17 AKRON L. REV. 495 (1984); M. Cherif Bassiouni, *Terrorism, Law Enforcement, and the Mass Media: Perspectives, Problems, Proposals,* 72 J. CRIM. L. & CRIMINOLOGY 1 (1981); B.J. George, *Criminal Law Aspects of Legislation on the Prevention, Control and Suppression of Terrorism, International Terrorism, in* LEGAL RESPONSES TO INTERNATIONAL TERRORISM, *supra* note 2. *See generally* U.S. v. Yousef, 927 F. Supp. 673, 677-80 (S.D.N.Y. 1996); U.S. v. Rezaq, 899 F. Supp. 697, 609 (D.D.C. 1995) ("the legislative history of the [Antihijacking Act] provides a strong indication that Congress indeed intended criminal jurisdiction over extraterritorial hijacking offenses."); U.S. v. Marzouki, 899 F. Supp. 697, 708, 709 (D.C.D.C. 1995); U.S. v. Yunis, 681 F. Supp. 896, 1092 (D.D.C. 1988).

[217] Convention on the Prevention and Punishment of the Crime of Genocide, Dec. 9, 78 U.N.T.S. 277, [hereinafter Genocide Convention]. The United States government, although instrumental in developing the convention, took until 1986 to obtain the advice and consent of the Senate (*ratification)*. *See Aggression Against Authority, supra* note 35, at 293, and authorities cited therein; Jordan Paust, *Congress and Genocide: They're Not Going to Get Away With It,* 11 MICH. J. INT'L L. 90 (1989) (providing the authority supporting the notion that genocide is *crimen contra omnes*, over which universal jurisdiction and responsibility obtain—that its prohibition is a peremptory norm; a *jus cogens* principle, allowing no derogation by domestic law, treaty or custom).

[218] International Convention on the Elimination of All Forms of Racial Discrimination, *opened for signature,* Mar. 7, 1966, 660 U.N.T.S. 195; International Convention on the Suppression and Punishment of the Crime of *Apartheid*, G.A. Res. 3068, 28 U.N. GAOR Supp. No. 30 at 74, U.N. Doc. A/9030 (1973). *See also* M. Cherif Bassiouni, *International Criminal Law Conventions by Crime, in* 1 INTERNATIONAL CRIMINAL LAW 137, 148 (M. Cherif Bassiouni ed., 1986); *Aggression Against Authority, supra* note 35, at 289-90.

[219] Convention Against Illicit Traffic in Narcotic Drugs and Psychotropic Substances, done at Vienna, Dec. 20, 1988, U.N. Doc. E/CONF.82/15, of Dec. 19, 1988, *reprinted in* 28 I.L.M. 493 (1989), was signed by some 106 countries, including the U.S. *See* U.S. DEPT. JUSTICE, BUREAU OF NARCOTICS & DANGEROUS DRUGS, A STUDY OF INTERNATIONAL CONTROL OF NARCOTICS & DANGEROUS DRUGS (1972). This study includes texts of 12 international agreements, dating from 1909 to 1972, concerning control of narcotics. Discussed in Bruce Zagaris, *U.N. Drug Convention Signed,* 5 INT'L ENF. L. REP. 80-87 (Mar. 1989); Protocol (with Annex) amending the Agreements, Conventions and Protocols on Narcotic Drugs, Dec. 11, 1946, 61 Stat. 2230, T.I.A.S. No. 1671, 12 U.N.T.S. 179; Single Convention on Narcotic Drugs, Mar. 30, 1961, 18 U.S.T. 1407, T.I.A.S. No. 6298, 520 U.N.T.S. 151.

[220] *See, e.g.*, Convention on the Prevention and Punishment of Crimes Against Internationally Protected Persons, Including Diplomatic Agents, Dec. 14, 1973, 28 U.S.T. 1975, T.I.A.S. No. 8532, *entered into force* by U.S. Feb. 20, 1977; Convention Against the Taking of Hostages, Dec. 18, 1979, G.A. Res. 34/146, 34 U.N. GAOR Supp. (No. 46) at 245, U.N. Doc. A/34/46 (1979). *See also* M. Cherif Bassiouni, *The Crime of Kidnapping and Hostage Taking, in* 1 INTERNATIONAL CRIMINAL LAW 475 (M. Cherif Bassiouni ed. 2d ed., 1998).

various international offenses that could be characterized as terrorism.[221] Moreover, all nations condemn, prosecute and punish terrorist violence, when perpetrated against them or their nationals.

Early this century, there have been attempts by international convention to explicitly proscribe terrorism.[222] In 1970, the United Nations General Assembly imposed a duty on states "to refrain from organizing, assisting or participating in acts of civil strife or terrorist acts in another state or acquiescing in organized activities within its territory directed towards the commission of such acts, when the acts . . . involve a threat or use of force."[223] Thus, the combination and correlation of treaties condemning all conduct amounting to terrorism creates a composite and widely recognized set of crimes subject to the universality theory of jurisdiction.[224]

---

[221] *See* all the treaties listed in TERRORISM, DRUGS, *supra* note 1, at nn.185-93. *See also* Geneva Convention on the High Seas, Apr. 28, 1958, art. 19, 13 U.S.T. 2312, T.I.A.S. No. 5200, 450 U.N.T.S. 82. *See also The Marianna Flora*, 24 U.S. (11 Wheat.) 1, 40 (1826) ("Pirates may, without doubt, be lawfully captured on the ocean by the public or private ships of every nation: for they are, in truth, common enemies of all mankind, and, as such, are liable to the extreme rights of war."); Edwin D. Dickinson, *Is the Crime of Piracy Obsolete*?, 38 HARV. L. REV. 334 (1925). U.N. Conference on Plenipotentiaries on a Supplementary Convention of the Abolition of Slavery, the Slave, the Slave Trade, and Institutions and Practices Similar to Slavery, Aug. 13-Sept. 4, 1956, Final Act and Supp. Conv., U.N. Doc. E/ CONF. 24/20 (cited in *The Crime of Slavery and Slave Trade, supra* note 213, at 186 n.40).

[222] The 1934 assassination of King Alexander I of Yugoslavia, in Marseilles, prompted the Convention for the Prevention and Punishment of Terrorism, League of Nations Doc. 1.546(I) M.383(I) 1937 V (1938), *opened for signature* Nov. 16, 1937; Convention for the Creation of an International Criminal Court, League of Nations, 1.Doc. C.547(1) M.384(1) 1937 V (1938), *opened for signature* Nov. 16, 1937, *reprinted in* 3 INTERNATIONAL CRIMINAL LAW 497 (M. Cherif Bassiouni ed., 1986); 1 ROBERT A. FRIEDLANDER, TERRORISM: DOCUMENTS 253 (1979) [hereinafter TERRORISM: DOCUMENTS]. *See also* 7 MANLEY O. HUDSON, INTERNATIONAL LEGISLATION 862 (1941); CONTROL OF TERRORISM: INTERNATIONAL DOCUMENTS 19 (Yonah Alexander et. al., eds., 1979). Neither convention was ever entered into force. *See Development, supra* note 216; Draft Code of Offences Against the Peace and Security of Mankind, 9 U.N. GAOR Supp. (No.9) at 9, U.N. Doc. A/2693 (1954) (envisaging punishment by one state of support for terrorist activities to be committed in another state).

[223] Declaration of Principles of International Law Concerning Friendly Relations and Co-operation Among States in Accordance with the Charter of the Charter of the United Nations, GA Res. 2625, 25 U.N. GAOR Supp. (No. 18) at 122-24, U.N. Doc. A/8082 (1970), *reprinted in* TERRORISM: DOCUMENTS, *supra* note 222, at 469. Another proposed U.N. provision, Draft Convention for the Prevention and Punishment of Certain Acts of International Terrorism, 26 U.N. GAOR (No. 26), U.N. Doc. A/C.6/L. 850 (1972), *reprinted in* TERRORISM: DOCUMENTS, *supra* note 222, at 487, has never been adopted. *Development, supra* note 216, at 94 nn.43-44; Arthur W. Rovine, *The Contemporary International Legal Attack on Terrorism,* 3 ISR. Y.B. HUM. RTS. 9, 27 (1973). The latter Draft Convention would have provided for binding cooperation among the parties, aimed at prophylaxis, extradition, and prosecution, as well as a duty to abstain from organizing, instigating, or participating in terrorist conduct.

[224] Terrorism was not included as a separate and distinct offense among the international crimes enumerated in either the Draft International Criminal Code, *see* M. CHERIF BASSIOUNI, INTERNATIONAL CRIMINAL LAW: A DRAFT INTERNATIONAL CRIMINAL CODE 49 (1980), or the Draft Statute for an International Criminal Court, BENJAMIN FERENCZ, AN INTERNATIONAL CRIMINAL COURT—A STEP TOWARD WORLD PEACE 360 (1980). The reason they do not provide an abstract definition is because terrorism consists of separate crimes universally condemned as criminal. In a recent study relating to the possible creation of an international or regional criminal court, it was noted that it may be wise to follow Professor Bassiouni's suggestion that it may not be appropriate to use the term *terrorism*, because it seems to have been appropriated by propagandists on all sides. Also, the term only makes sense for criminal law purposes when it contains specific, material elements. These elements differ, of course, depending on the type of *terrorism* that is being prosecuted. On the other hand, the term could be utilized, if it is demystified and given substantive elements. This would avoid its abuse and obfuscation. If we could have a convention that lists specific terroristic offenses, each with proper elements, and establish an international or regional criminal court to prosecute these offenses, it would actually assist in the battle against terrorism and erode the opportunity for propagandists to appropriate the terminology. It would be clear that *terrorism* is a generic

The European Convention on the Suppression of Terrorism,[225] signed in 1977 under the auspices of the Council of Europe,[226] provides that certain acts are not to be covered by the political-offense exception to extradition and that the listed conduct is to be considered extraditable and punishable in the signatory states.[227] The state obtaining custody of a person who has allegedly engaged in the specified violent conduct is obligated to prosecute or extradite that person.[228] It further provides that the substantive laws of the party states, including those relating to criminal jurisdiction, must be adjusted to fulfill the obligation to prosecute or extradite.[229] The European Convention does not define terrorism in the abstract, but recognizes a body of core offenses that are universally condemned and recognized as terrorism. The problem with the Convention relates to its approach to the political-offense exception.[230]

It has become accepted that the Laws of War prohibit torture or execution of prisoners or noncombatants during wartime.[231] All such conduct is universally condemned and triggers

---

term meant to apply to the specific list of offenses in the convention. It may be, as suggested by some at the Symposium, that the Tribunal ought not to cover terroristic offenses because it would be "taking on too much" and could lend itself to propandistic manipulation.

[225] European Convention on the Suppression of Terrorism, *opened for signature* Jan. 27, 1977, E.T.S. No. 90, 25 EUR. Y.B. 289 [hereinafter Europ. Terrorism Conv.], *reprinted in* 15 I.L.M. 1272-76 (1976).

[226] The political-offense exception developed out of principles of asylum and sovereignty. It requires that extradition be denied if the offense charged is political in nature. It prevents a victorious regime from using an extradition treaty to round up political enemies and allows a nation to refuse to participate in a "victor's justice." TERRORISM, DRUGS, *supra* note 1, at 75-86; 263-85; Christine van den Wyngaert, THE POLITICAL OFFENSE EXCEPTION TO EXTRADITION (1980); Blakesley, *Evisceration of the Political Offense Exception to Extradition,* 15 DEN. J. INT'L L & POL'Y 109, 110-18 (1986) [hereinafter *Evisceration*].

[227] The Convention excludes from coverage of the political-offense exemption from extradition the use of a bomb, grenade, rocket, automatic firearm, letter bomb, or parcel bomb if the use endangers private persons. European Convention, *supra* note 225, at art 1. Article 13, however, allows parties to reserve the right to consider article 1 offenses as political. *Id.* at art. 13; TERRORISM, DRUGS, *supra* note 1, at 75-86, 263-85; Colm Campbell, *Extradition to Northern Ireland: Prospects and Problems*, 52 MOD. L. REV 585, 595 (1989). *See also Evisceration, supra* note 226, at 116 n.30; Valerie Epps, *The Political Offense Exception in the U.S. Extradition, in* LEGAL RESPONSES TO INTERNATIONAL TERRORISM, *supra* note 2; Christopher Pyle, *The November Treaty Approved, in* LEGAL RESPONSES TO INTERNATIONAL TERRORISM, *supra* note 2. Christine van den Wyngaert, *The Political Offense Exception to Extradition: How to Plug the Terrorists' Loophole Without Departing from Fundamental Human Rights,* 19 ISR. Y.B. HUM. RTS. 297 (1989); M. Cherif Bassiouni, INTERNATIONAL EXTRADITION IN U.S. LAW & PRACTICE 502-83 (3d ed. 1996).

[228] Europ. Terrorism Conv., *supra* note 225, at art. 7. A state may refuse to assist or extradite if it has substantial grounds to believe that the requesting state has made the request in order to prosecute or punish the person on account for any of these reasons. *Id.* at art. 8. *See* TRANSNATIONAL TERRORISM: CONVENTIONS & COMMENTARY 120-29 (Richard Lillich ed., 1982); *Development, supra* note 216, at 94.

[229] Europ. Terrorism Conv., *supra* note 225, at art. 6.

[230] *See* TERRORISM, DRUGS, *supra* note 1, at Ch. 2.

[231] The universal nature of jurisdiction over terrorism is evidenced by the various international conventions which cover the conduct defined as terrorism in TERRORISM, DRUGS, *supra* note 1, at Chs. 1, 2. *E.g.,* Convention on the Prevention and Punishment of Crimes Against Internationally Protected Persons, Including Diplomatic Agents, *supra* note 220; Convention Against the Taking of Hostages, *supra* note 220; the 1949 Geneva Conventions, *supra* note 214; Protocol I, Additional to the Geneva Conventions of Aug. 12, 1949 and Relating to the protection of Victims of International Armed Conflicts, *opened for signature* Dec. 12, 1977, U.N. Doc. A/32/144 (1977), *reprinted in* 72 AM. J. INT'L L. 457-509 (1978) [hereinafter Protocol I] and *in* PROTECTION OF WAR VICTIMS: PROTOCOL I TO THE GENEVA CONVENTION (Howard Levie ed., 1979) (with many related background documents); Protocol II, Additional to the Geneva Conventions of Aug. 12, 1949, U.N. Doc. A/32/144 (1977) [hereinafter Protocol II]; European Convention, *supra* note 225; Convention to Prevent and Punish the Acts of Terrorism Taking the Form of Crimes Against Persons and Related Extortion that are of International Significance, Feb. 2, 1971, O.A.S. Doc. A6/doc. 88, rev. 1 corr. 1, 27 U.S.T. 3949, T.I.A.S. No. 8431 [hereinafter

universality jurisdiction. Universal condemnation of and jurisdiction over terrorist-violence during peacetime is no less real or valid. It is ludicrous to suggest that war crimes, or similar crimes against humanity, are not universally condemned simply because some states refuse to prosecute or extradite when they are sympathetic with the cause behind the violence. War crimes and crimes against humanity are analogous to terrorism and such acts that have been uniformly condemned.[232] All nations and groups consider it criminal when committed against them.

It is worth noting that some proponents of "realism" in international relations argue that such offenses are committed with impunity by some nations or groups and, therefore, they are not really international crimes.[233] This is especially true, they add, when the nation is at war or pressed by what looks like danger to national survival, so the only rule of law is actually *Raison d'Etat*. They add that the only time these offenses seem to be prosecuted is upon a victor's justice. We also noted that in reality, this misses the point of law. Just because groups or individuals under domestic systems "get away" with violating certain laws because they have the power to "get away with it," does not mean that what they are not violating the law. Similarly, under international law, using violence against innocents such as noncombatants, or their relative peacetime analogues, to fulfill some military, political, religious, or philosophical purpose, may often occur with seeming impunity. Nevertheless, it is condemned conduct. Whether it be called a war crime during "belligerency," "state terrorism" or a crime against humanity when a state participates in or promotes it while there is no "belligerency" during relative peacetime, it is criminal terrorism. When the conduct is performed by private individuals, as members of groups or independently, it is also criminal and may be called "private terrorism," whether or not the ends sought happen to be public,

---

O.A.S. Terrorist Conv.]; Convention on the Physical Protection of Nuclear Material, *opened for signature* Mar. 3, 1980, *reprinted in* 18 I.L.M. 1419, 1422-31 (1979); U.N. Resolution Regarding Terrorism, 27 U.N. GAOR (2114th Gen. Mtg.) (Agenda Item 92) at 20, U.N. Doc. A/8968 (1972) (U.S. voted against it for not being strong enough), 68 U.S. DEP'T OF STATE BULL. 81 (1973)). *See generally* 1 INTERNATIONAL CRIMINAL LAW, Chs. 1, 2, 3 (M. Cherif Bassiouni ed., 1986); G.I.A.D. Draper, *The Modern Pattern of War Criminality*, ISR. Y.B. HUM. RTS. 9 (1976); Perry Gulbrandsen, *Humanitarian Law of Armed Conflicts*, *in* 1 A TREATISE ON INTERNATIONAL CRIMINAL LAW 368 (M. Cherif Bassiouni and Ved. P. Nanda eds., 1973). *See also* Convention on the Non-Applicability of Statutory Limitations to War Crimes and Crimes Against Humanity, Nov. 26, 1968, 754 U.N.T.S. 73; Europ. Non-App. Stat. Limit. Conv., *supra* note 215. *But see* Yoram Dinstein, *International Criminal Law*, 5 ISR. Y.B. HUM. RTS. 55, 71 (1975) (doubting that there are crimes *against*, as opposed to *under* international law) (cited in *Development*, *supra* note 216, at 88 n.24). *See also* M. Cherif Bassiouni, *International Criminal Law Conventions by Crime*, in 1 INTERNATIONAL CRIMINAL LAW 137 (M. Cherif Bassiouni ed., 1986).

[232] *See, e.g.*, 1 INTERNATIONAL MILITARY TRIBUNAL, TRIAL OF THE MAJOR WAR CRIMINALS BEFORE THE INTERNATIONAL MILITARY TRIBUNAL 11, 17 (1947) (crimes against humanity include: "murder, extermination, enslavement, deportation and other inhuman acts against any civilian population, or persecution on political, racial or religious grounds, when such acts are done or such persecutions are carried on in execution of on in connection [sic] with any crime against peace or any war crime"). *See also* Geneva Conventions, *supra* note 214; Protocols I and II, *supra* note 231. Christopher L. Blakesley, *Atrocity and Its Prosecution*, *in* WAR CRIMES: A SYNTHESIS OF INTERNATIONAL AND NATIONAL APPROACHES (1997); Dinstein & Tabory, *supra* note 214; BASSIOUNI, *supra* note 112.

[233] Discussed in TERRORISM, DRUGS, *supra* note 1, at Chs. 1, 2.

or even "just" ends.[234] It is all international crime, and for the purposes of this chapter, it triggers universal jurisdiction.

The 1977 Geneva Protocol I[235] codifies and develops international humanitarian law applicable to armed conflicts. It was signed by the United States in that same year, but has since been criticized and apparently deemed unacceptable by the Reagan administration which did not submit it to the Senate for its advice and consent nor did the Bush administration.[236] Parts of the protocol represent a significant amelioration in international law relating to protecting innocents. Article 51, for example, explicitly prohibits indiscriminate attacks against innocent civilians, and includes most terrorist acts.[237]

One can criticize the Protocols for a basic confusion between humanitarian rules for protecting victims during armed conflict (*jus in bello*) and rules aimed at determining the status of parties to conflict (*jus ad bellum*). To the extent that the Protocols make *jus in bello* dependent on *jus ad bellum* they exclude coverage and protection in certain circumstances.[238] The *jus in bello* originally were undertaken as a matter of self interest, but had the effect of protecting victims within the embattled state, no matter what "morality" of their "side" happened to be fighting for.[239] This was before morally totalitarian notions (fighting to make the world safe for democracy; to make it safe for communism; safe for whatever monolithic ideology) and notions of total war (required by the morally totalitarian notions) changed the rules to apply them only when the conflict was "of an international character."[240] Protocols I and II made the humanitarian rules applicable to more conflicts, not to all of them. To the extent that application of the rules is dependent on an ideologically based litmus test, it was unfortunate.

[234] There have been prosecutions. First Lt. William Calley was prosecuted in 1971 by a military court for killing approximately 400 civilians in Mar., 1968, near My Lai, during the Vietnam conflict. U.S. v. Calley, 22 C.M.A. 534, 48 C.M.R. 19 (1973). The conviction was reversed, however, because he was denied the opportunity to confront his accusers and compulsory process of witnesses, as required by the Sixth Amendment to the United States Constitution. Calley v. Callaway, 382 F. Supp. 650 (M.D. Ga. 1974), *rev'd*, 519 F.2d 184 (5th Cir. 1975), *cert. denied*, 425 U.S. 911 (1976). *See also In re Yamashita*, 327 U.S. 1 (1946) (sanctioning trial of enemy aliens by military commission for offenses of war); *Development, supra* note 216, at 89 n.28.

[235] Protocol I, *supra* note 231. *See* George H. Aldrich, Commentary, *Progressive Development of the Laws of War: A Reply to Criticisms of the 1977 Geneva Protocol I*, 26 VA. J. INT'L L. 693 (1986) [hereinafter Aldrich].

[236] *See* Aldrich, *supra* note 235, at 694; Guy B. Roberts, *The New Rules for Waging War: The Case Against Ratification of Additional Protocol I*, 26 VA. J. INT'L L. 109 (1986).

[237] *See* Protocol I, *supra* note 231, at art. 51. The Protocol was warmly welcomed by the U.S. government in 1977. Aldrich, *supra* note 235, at 699 (citing U.S. Delegation to the Diplomatic Conference on the Reaffirmation and Development of International Humanitarian Law Applicable in Armed Conflicts, Sept. 8, 1977). *See also* George H. Aldrich, *Forward* to 1 Protection of Victims, Protocol 1, *supra* note 231, at xi. However, it was apparently not so well accepted by some advisors to the Reagan Administration. *See* Aldrich, *supra* note 235, at 699, 712-14; Roberts, *supra* note 236, at 149-52. *See Evisceration, supra* note 226; THE INTERNATIONAL LEGAL SYSTEM, *supra* note 1, at 860-62.

[238] *See* Alfred P. Rubin, *International Law and the Use of Force by National Liberation Movements*, 13 THE FLETCH. F. 410, 414 (1989).

[239] *Id.* at 411.

[240] *See* 1949 Geneva Conventions, *supra* note 214, at art. 3.

Other international conventions proscribing genocide,[241] apartheid,[242] and hostage taking, provide additional impetus toward the recognition that terrorism fits within the universality theory of jurisdiction. The United Nations Conventions Against Taking of Hostages provides for the prosecution or extradition of any person who commits the offense of hostage-taking, without reference to motive or identity of the victim.[243] Some states have also taken measures to establish jurisdiction over the crime of hostage-taking and to provide appropriately severe penalties.[244] The conventions relating to aircraft hijacking and sabotage provide examples of how universal jurisdiction is established. The Hague Convention for Suppression of Unlawful Seizure of Aircraft[245] creates universal jurisdiction in that all contracting parties have jurisdiction over unlawful acts of taking seizure or control of aircraft, and the party obtaining custody of the alleged hijackers is obligated to prosecute or extradite them.[246] All parties are to promulgate laws to punish "severely" the prohibited conduct.[247] Priorities of jurisdiction are also established.[248] The Montreal Convention[249] extends the Hague Convention beyond hijacking and unlawful control of aircraft to include acts of sabotage.[250]

---

241 *See generally* THE INTERNATIONAL LEGAL SYSTEM, *supra* note 1, at 755-64. Genocide is directly punishable under international law and may be prosecuted and jurisdiction obtained on the basis of the universality principle. This is so despite the fact that the Genocide Convention inexplicably and in contrast to the Geneva Conventions adopted the territorial and not the universality principle. *See Development, supra* note 216, at 90. The Supreme Court of Israel had noted that: "Article VI [of the Genocide Convention] imposes upon the parties contractual obligations with future effect, that is so say, obligations committed . . . within their territories in the future. This obligation, however, has nothing to do with the universal *power* vested in every State to prosecute for crimes of this type committed in the past—a power which is based on *customary* international law." Attorney General v. Eichmann, 36 I.L.R. 18 (D. Ct. Jerusalem 1961), *aff'd*, 36 I.L.R. 277, 304 (S. Ct. Isr. 1962). *See also* Dinstein, *supra* note 231, at 60-62; *Aggression Against Authority, supra* note 35, at 293, and references cited therein. For an excellent study of Nazi War crimes and transnational criminal law, *see* Steven Lubet & Jan Stern Reed, *Extradition of Nazis from the U.S. to Israel: A Survey of Issues in Transnational Criminal Law,* 22 STAN. J. INT'L L. 1 (1986).

242 The *Apartheid Convention* declares apartheid to be a crime against humanity. International Convention on the Suppression and Punishment of *Apartheid, supra* note 218. The Convention imposes a duty to punish acts of apartheid, with jurisdiction based in the universality principle.

243 Conv. Against Taking of Hostages, *supra* note 220. *See also* Conv. Prevention of Crimes Against Int'l Protected Persons, *supra* note 220.

244 *E.g.*, § 239b 85 StGB (1986) (German statute prosecuting and providing punishment for hijacking); French C. PÉN. art. 113-11; C. AV. CIV. arts. L 121-7 through L 121-9 (crimes against aircraft); French C. PR. PÉN. art. 689-6, et seq. (incorporating European Convention against Terrorism and International Convention prohibiting violence against internationally protected persons); art. 689-4 (incorporating the Conv. on the Physical Protection of Nuclear Material).

245 Convention for Suppression of Unlawful Seizure of Aircraft, Dec. 16, 1970. 22 U.S.T. 1641, T.I.A.S. No. 7192, 860 U.N.T.S. 105 (*entered into force* in U.S. Oct. 14, 1971) [hereinafter Hague Convention], *reprinted in* 65 AM. J. INT'L L. 440 (1971).

246 *Id.* at arts. 1, 4.

247 *Id.* at art. 2.

248 The state of the aircraft's registration and the state in which it landed, if the criminal act occurred in the air, are made "primary jurisdictions." Other states are so-called "substitutionary jurisdictions" to assert jurisdiction in the case that the primary jurisdiction cannot or will not assert it. *Id.* at art. 8. Some states have enacted domestic legislation incorporating these notions. *See, e.g.*, 85 StGB art. 316c (Germany).

249 Convention for the Suppression of Unlawful Acts Against the Safety of Civil Aviation, Sept. 23, 1971, 24 U.S.T. 565, T.I.A.S. No. 7570, 974 U.T.S. 177 (*entered into force* in U.S. Jan. 26, 1973).

250 *Id.* at art. 1. Contracting parties are required to promulgate laws to punish severely the condemned conduct and to establish jurisdiction for cases of primary competence, such as when the offense is committed on the state's territory or against or on board an aircraft registered in the state, or when the aircraft lands, with the alleged perpetrator aboard, on the state territory. *Id.* at arts. 3, 4.

Domestic legislation has been promulgated to accommodate these conventions, notably, for example, in Europe[251] and in the United States.[252] The U.N. Convention Against

[251] *E.g.*, French law condemns crimes committed aboard maritime vessels and aircraft. *See, e.g.*, C. PÉN. art. 113-11; and C. PR. PÉN. arts. 689-5, 689-6, 689-7. French law provides jurisdiction over infractions committed aboard airplanes registered in France, or those committed against such planes, even if committed outside French territory. C. PR. PÉN. arts. 689-5 through 689-7. French law provides jurisdiction over any *crime* or a *délit* committed aboard or against a plane which is not registered in France when the author or the victim was a French national, when the plane lands in France after the commission of the *crime* or *délit*, or when the infraction was committed aboard a plane while rented without crew to a person who has his principal place of business or, lacking this, his permanent residence in France. C. PÉN. art. 113-11(1)-(3). Moreover, where the accused or an accomplice is found in France, jurisdiction obtains for infractions relating to *détournement* (forced off course, hijacking) of a plane that is not registered in France and over every other act of violence against the passengers or the crew committed by the alleged hijacker in the commission of [literally, in direct relationship to] the offense.

[252] 49 U.S.C. § 46502 (*Aircraft Piracy*) (as amended 1994, 1996), provides jurisdiction for prosecution and punishment for aircraft piracy both inside and outside the "*special aircraft jurisdiction of the United States.*"

> (a) In special aircraft jurisdiction—(1) . . . (A) "aircraft piracy" means seizing or exercising control of an aircraft in the special aircraft jurisdiction of [the U.S.] by force, violence, threat of force or violence, or any form of intimidation, and with wrongful intent.
>
> (B) an attempt to commit aircraft piracy is in the special aircraft jurisdiction of [the U.S.] although the aircraft is not in flight at the time of the attempt if the aircraft would have been in the special aircraft jurisdiction of [the U.S.] had the aircraft piracy been completed.
>
> (2) An individual committing or attempting or conspiring to commit aircraft piracy—(A) shall be imprisoned for at least 20 years; or (B) notwithstanding [18 U.S.C. § 3559(b)], if the death of another individual results from the commission or attempt, shall be put to death or imprisoned for life.
>
> (b) Outside special aircraft jurisdiction—(1) An individual committing or conspiring to commit an offense (as defined in the Convention for the Suppression of Unlawful Seizure of Aircraft) on an aircraft in flight outside the special aircraft jurisdiction of the [U.S.]—(A) shall be imprisoned . . .
>
> (2) There is jurisdiction over the offense in paragraph (1) if—(A) a national [of the U.S.] was aboard the aircraft; (B) an offender is a national of the [U.S.]; or (C) an offender is afterwards found in the [U.S.] . . .

See U.S. v. Yousef, 927 F. Supp. 673, 677-80 (S.D.N.Y. 1996) (conspiracy to bomb civil aircraft within special U.S. aircraft jurisdiction—18 U.S.C. § 32(a)); U.S. v. Rezaq, 899 F. Supp. 697, 709 (D.D.C.1995) ("legislative history of [Anti-hijacking Act] provides a strong indication that Congress . . . intended to provided extended criminal jurisdiction over extraterritorial hijacking offenses."); U.S. v. Dixon, 592 F.2d 329, 339-40 (6th Cir. 1979) elements of proof required in an air-piracy charge are seizure or exercise of control of an aircraft; by force, violence, or intimidation, or threat thereof; with wrongful intent; and while in the special aircraft jurisdiction of the U.S.), *cert. denied,* 441 U.S. 951 (1979). A related provision, 49 U.S.C. § 1472(1), proscribes carrying or placing of attempting to place weapons, loaded firearms, and explosive or incendiary devices aboard aircraft, including in the baggage. *See also* U.S. v. Bradley, 540 F. Supp. 690, 692-93 (D.Md. 1982) (the offense is committed when the device or weapon is carried or otherwise place on the aircraft, whether or not injury occurs). Also, United States special aircraft jurisdiction is defined 49 U.S.C. § 46501(2),(3), which provides that jurisdiction obtains for any of the following aircraft in flight:

> (A) a civil aircraft of the United States
>
> (B) an aircraft of the armed forces of the United States
>
> (C) another aircraft in the United States.
>
> (D) another aircraft outside the United States—
>
> (i) that has its next scheduled destination or last place of departure in the United States, if that aircraft next lands in the United States; or (ii) on which an individual commits an offense (as defined in the Convention for the Suppression of Unlawful Seizure of Aircraft), if the aircraft lands in the United States with the individual still on the aircraft; or (iii) against which an individual commits an offense (as defined in subsection (d) or (e) of article I, § I of the Convention for the Suppression of Unlawful Acts against the Safety of Civil Aviation) if the aircraft lands in the U.S. with the individual still on the aircraft.
>
> (E) any other aircraft leased without crew to a lessee whose principal place of business is in the United States or, if the lessee does not have a principal place of business, whose permanent residence is in the U.S.
>
> (3) an individual commits an offense (as defined in the Convention for the Suppression of Unlawful Seizure of Aircraft) when the individual, when on an aircraft in flight—
>
> (A) by any form of intimidation, unlawfully seizes, exercises control of, or attempts to seize or exercise

the Taking of Hostages similarly provides, in strong language, for prosecution and extradition of offenders.[253]

The responsibility to desist from promoting or committing terrorism and actively to combat it devolves on all nations universally because terrorism consists of universally condemned conduct.[254] Although no one multilateral treaty explicitly states as much, it is clear that the universality principle would apply to much of today's terrorist activities.

The theory of jurisdiction actually applied by the United States Omnibus Antiterrorism Act of 1986 is the protective principle. The Act provides that if violence is perpetrated against a United States national, United States jurisdiction will obtain only when the violence is "intended to coerce, intimidate, or retaliate against a government or a civilian population."[255] Violence not aimed at these political or military purposes, or which does not otherwise infringe on United States sovereignty, does not trigger United States jurisdiction.

International law condemns terrorism and provides bases for all nations to assert jurisdiction over its perpetration and its perpetrators, whether they are state functionaries or rebel groups.[256] Most of the world population does not wish to be victims or executioners. International and domestic law can equip us to extricate ourselves from the "infernal dialectic" of violence; they provide the means whereby we may avoid accepting or participating in, even by acquiescence, oppression, or the slaughter of innocents. It is error of the highest order to accept the ideologues' argument that because some nations or rebel groups participate in oppression and terror-violence, it is inevitable and therefore necessary to combat it with like conduct. Self-defense under the rule of law does not include the use of innocent civilians as tools.[257]

---

control of, the aircraft; or

(B) is an accomplice of an individual referred to in sub-clause (A) of this clause.

Added by Pub. L. 103-272, § 1(e), 1994, 108 Stat. 1240.

The legislation incorporating the above noted crimes aboard aircraft conventions, has been held to allow jurisdiction over child sexual abuse committed by a foreign national aboard a foreign airliner which was in international airspace, but given that it was on its way to the U.S., was in the "special maritime and territorial jurisdiction." U.S. v. Georgescu, 723 F. Supp 912, 913 (E.D.N.Y. 1989) (applying, *inter alia,* 49 U.S.C. § 1472(k)(1).

[253] The Convention provides that: "The State Party in the territory of which the alleged offender is found shall if it does not extradite him, be obliged, without exception whatsoever and whether or not the offence was committed in its territory, to submit the case to its competent authorities for the purpose of prosecution, through proceedings in accordance with the law of that State. Those authorities shall take their decision in the same manner as in the case of any ordinary offence of a grave nature under the law of that state." International Convention Against the Taking of Hostages, 34 U.N. GAOR Supp. (No. 46) at 246, art. 8, U.N. Doc. A/34/46 (1979), *reprinted in* 18 I.L.M. 1456-63 (1979). *See* Joseph J. Lambert, TERRORISM & HOSTAGES IN INTERNATIONAL LAW: A COMMENTARY ON THE HOSTAGES CONVENTION OF 1979 (1990); Christopher L. Blakesley, *Book Review,* 90 A.J.I.L. 346 (1996).

[254] TERRORISM, DRUGS, *supra* note 1, at Chs. 1, 2; *see* ROBERT A. FRIEDLANDER, TERROR-VIOLENCE: ASPECTS OF SOCIAL CONTROL (1983); Robert A. Friedlander, *The Origins of International Terrorism: A Micro Legal-Historical Perspective,* 6 ISR. Y.B. HUM. RTS. 49 (1976); Robert A. Friedlander, *The Enforcement of International Criminal Law: Fact or Fiction?,* 17 CASE W. RES. J. INT'L L. 79, 88 (1985); *Federal Jurisdiction, supra* note 35, at 223-27.

[255] 18 U.S.C. § 2331.

[256] *See* RICHARD A. FALK, REVOLUTIONARIES & FUNCTIONARIES: THE DUAL FACE OF TERRORISM (1988).

[257] ALBERT CAMUS, NEITHER VICTIMS NOR EXECUTIONERS 27 (Dwight MacDonald trans., 1972); Robert A. Friedlander, *Terrorism and National Liberation Movements: Can Rights Derive From Wrongs?,* 13 CASE W. RES. J. INT'L L. 281, 282 n.3. But in this, we must still try to overcome, by rectifying wrongs done in the past or currently being perpetrated, the tendency to allow inertia to make executioners or victims of us all. Consider also, Thomas Merton, *The Plague of Albert Camus: A Commentary and Introduction,* (originally in pamphlet, Seabury

There is a tendency today to believe that there is no international law, that it cannot be enforced and, concomitantly, that there is a need to fight terrorism with like action. In such a conflict, both sides consider the other to be terrorists and each regards its conduct as "freedom fighting." But there is a point beyond which any government or any freedom fighter clearly commits crime, a point reached when they use innocent civilians as the means to achieve their ends. All nations accept this in principle, and both international law and the domestic law of virtually every nation substantively condemn terrorism so defined. International and domestic law provide jurisdiction over that conduct and its perpetrators according to a hierarchy of jurisdiction based on the traditional jurisdictional theories. Jurisdiction will obtain for a given state depending on whether the terrorism occurred within or had an impact on its territory; whether it damaged or threatened to damage the state's national security or other governmental interest; or whether the terrorism had an impact upon one of the state's nationals for the purpose of intimidation or achieving some military or political purpose. If no other state seeks to assert jurisdiction, any state may obtain jurisdiction over the perpetrators of such violence, based on the universality theory.

Even if violence is of a terrorist nature and is perpetrated against a country's nationals, it may be that another nation has a higher priority of jurisdiction. This would be true, for example, when the violence occurs on that nation's territory. The definition of the crime must clearly be tied to the definition of terrorism provided in this chapter and the priorities of jurisdiction must be set out as described herein. Thus, in the *Achille Lauro* affair, for instance, Italy had primary jurisdiction pursuant to the territorial theory of jurisdiction. The United States would have had subsidiary jurisdiction on the basis of the protective principle or the passive-personality theory. Had the perpetrators escaped Italian jurisdiction and been captured by some other nation, that nation would have had the right, indeed, the obligation, to prosecute or to extradite the fugitives on the basis of the universality theory.

The U.S. Government has tended lately to extend its enforcement and adjudicatory jurisdiction beyond the bounds allowed by international law, in a manner that amounts to arrogant international vigilantism. The famous *Alvarez-Machain, Fawaz Yunis*, and *Noriega*

Press, 1968), *reprinted in* THOMAS MERTON, THE LITERARY ESSAYS OF THOMAS MERTON (Brother Patrick Hart ed., 1981) ("Man's drive to destroy, to kill, or simply to dominate and to oppress comes from the metaphysical void he experiences when he finds himself a stranger in his own universe. He seeks to make that universe familiar to himself by using it for his own ends, but his own ends are capricious and ambivalent. They may be life-affirming, they may be expressions of comprehension and of love, or they may be life-denying, armored in legalism and false theology, or perhaps even speaking the naked language of brute power. In any case, the message of Camus is that man cannot successfully seek the explanation of his existence in abstractions: instead of trying to justify his life in terms of abstract formulas, man must create meaning in his existence by living in a meaningful way."). *See also* Albert Camus, *Appeal for a Civilian Truce in Algeria* (lecture given in Algiers in February 1956), *in* ALBERT CAMUS, RESISTANCE, REBELLION AND DEATH 131, 135, 137 (J. O'Brien trans., 1960). "[Even] [i]f murder is in the nature of man, the law is not intended to reproduce that nature." Albert Camus, *Reflections on the Guillotine*, *in id.*, at 174, 198.

decisions[258] are prime examples. The attempt to claim that invasion and abduction are legal set a dangerous precedent.

Overview of the Application of Jurisdictional Bases to Terrorism, Drug Trafficking, and Other International Crimes

With regard to terrorism, the protective principle appears to be an appropriate basis for jurisdiction. Because terrorist violence is by definition purposeful, malicious and aimed at a state's innocent citizens for the purpose of intimidation or achieving some political or military end, such violence clearly has an impact on state's sovereignty, national security, or important governmental interest.[259] There is generally no need to call upon the more controversial and less accepted passive-personality theory.[260] The universality principle allows the assertion of jurisdiction over certain offenses, even though they have no effect on the territory, security or sovereignty of the asserting state, may also often be appropriate to address the growing problems of terrorism today.

Although the universality, protective, and passive-personality theories are all potentially applicable, they are less widely accepted and cause problems of concurrent and competing jurisdiction. Priorities for states having concurrent jurisdiction may be set to avoid diplomatic problems and conflicts of jurisdiction. This is no easy task, however. Any effective prioritization must consider the policy and purposes of each of the jurisdictional bases. Should priority be given to the state on whose territory a material element of the crime occurs or to the state upon which it actually has an impact? Should a state whose security, or important governmental functions or interests are damaged have priority? Should the state

---

258 U.S. v. Alvarez-Machain, 504 U.S. 655 (1992); U.S. v. Yunis, 681 F. Supp. 896 (D.D.C. 1988), *rev'd* 859 F.2d 953 (D.C. Cir. 1988); Abramovsky, *supra* note 26, at 201. It is shocking to note that the Clinton Administration has revived the silly and dangerous policy of allowing forcible abduction from foreign countries, when those countries refuse "to cooperate" in extradition procedures. *See U.S. OKs Kidnapping Terrorists: directive apparently declassified in error*, CHIC. TRIB., Feb. 5, 1997 at §1 col. 1. This "non-cooperation" apparently includes refusal to extradite because one's law or constitution prohibits it (for nationals, for example). This policy makes a mockery of the rule of law, promotes terrorism (we can do it so it is good), and endangers all Americans as they travel abroad. Other nations may now abduct U.S. nationals claiming that they have violated that nation's laws; how can the U.S. protest abduction of U.S. nationals, when we do the same!? *See Iranian Law which allows this*, discussed in THE INTERNATIONAL LEGAL SYSTEM, *supra* note 1, at 206-09.

259 *See* TERRORISM, DRUGS, *supra* note 1, at Chs. 1, 2; *see also* notes 183-227, *infra* and accompanying text. It may also be argued that certain types of conduct in which one takes violent action, knowing there is a high degree of risk to innocents, may be termed terrorism. Such risk-taking with the lives and well-being of innocent people is similar to conduct punished as felonious reckless homicide in substantive criminal law. For example, if an official orders a pilot to bomb a section of a town wherein it is believed that an enemy training facility or sanctuary might be hidden, hoping that no innocent civilians will be killed or injured, although knowing the high degree of risk to those *hors de combat,* such conduct might be considered criminal if the military value of the military target is insignificant compared to the risk to noncombatants. *See* ROLLIN PERKINS & RONALD BOYCE, CRIMINAL LAW 59-61 (3d ed. 1982) (defining and analyzing depraved heart murder or wanton and willful disregard unreasonable human risk).

260 The State of Israel applied the passive-personality theory as a basis for asserting jurisdiction over Adolf Eichmann, deciding that it was most appropriate to assert based solely on the national character of the victims. Attorney General v. Eichmann, 36 I.L.R. 18 (D. Ct. Jerusalem 1961), *aff'd*, 36 I.L.R. 277 (S. Ct. Isr. 1962). *See* Jeffrey Allan McCredie, *Contemporary Uses of Force Against Terrorism: The U.S. Response to Achille Lauro—Questions of Jurisdiction and Its Exercise,* 16 GA. J. INT'L & COMP. L. 435, 438 (1986); Helen Silving, *In re Eichmann: A Dilemma of Law and Morality,* 55 AM. J. INT'L L. 307 (1961). *See* LOUIS HENKIN, HOW NATIONS BEHAVE: LAW AND FOREIGN POLICY 209 (1968).

of the victim's nationality enjoy a preference (in cases of terrorism)? Should a state which obtains custody of an alleged perpetrator of a universal crime have the obligation to extradite or can it prosecute pursuant to the universality theory?[261] Thus, it is far from clear that the bases of jurisdiction are hierarchical. Attempting to establish a hierarchy is highly problematical. Perhaps the best that can be done is to allow for an obligation either to prosecute or to extradite or otherwise cooperate.[262]

Extension of the Bases of Jurisdiction over Extraterritorial Crime in the United States

There has been a tendency recently to expand jurisdiction over extraterritorial crime in a manner inconsistent with these fundamental international law principles. Some U.S. judicial decisions have expanded the objective and subjective territoriality theories beyond any actual effect upon or connection with U.S. territory. For example, the territorial theory has been applied to thwarted extraterritorial narcotics or other conspiracies, even when no overt act, element, or any effect has occurred there.[263] They have failed to perceive or have been reticent to apply or articulate a clear distinction between the protective and objective territoriality principles. The cases and the Restatement (Third)[264] expand the objective territorial principle, providing in section 402(1)(c) that jurisdiction over an extraterritorial crime will obtain when the crime "has or is intended to have substantial effect within [U.S.] territory."[265]

---

[261] This hierarchy of jurisdiction is an application of the "rule of reasonableness" to the crime of terrorism. *See* RESTATEMENT (THIRD), *supra* note 23. The Restatement adopts the traditional bases of jurisdiction over extraterritorial crime, *id* § 402, and posits the rule of reasonableness as a means of *limiting* the assertion of jurisdiction in the international context. *Id.* § 403. The rule of reasonableness requires that even when an appropriate traditional basis for jurisdiction exists, assertion will not be proper if it is exorbitant or unreasonable. Assertion of jurisdiction. *Id.* Using the terminology of private international law or the conflicts of law, the rule of reasonableness is an attempt to determine the proper forum when two or more states have a traditional basis for asserting jurisdiction.

[262] BASSIOUNI & WISE, *supra* note 44.

[263] *See, e.g.,* U.S. v. Winter, 509 F.2d 975 (5th Cir. 1975), provides a good example of how this erroneous perception has been developed or rationalized. There, the court admitted that in Ford v. U.S., 273 U.S. 593 (1927) and Rivard v. U.S., 375 F.2d 882 (5th Cir. 1967), illegal contraband had actually been imported into the U.S.—thus establishing a harmful effect. The court, however, discounted the distinction as being without significance under the facts of the case because the conspiracy had been thwarted before importation could occur, and "because it is immaterial to the commission of the crime of conspiracy whether the object of the conspiracy is achieved." *Winter*, 509 F.2d at 982 (quoting U.S. v. Carlton, 475 F.2d 104, 106 (5th Cir. 1973)). The court said that "[a]n overt act, seeming innocent in itself yet in furtherance of the conspiracy, is sufficient under the law of conspiracy. We see no reason why it should be any different for jurisdictional purposes, to the extent that proof of an overt act is required." *Id. See also* U.S. v. Cadena, 585 F.2d 1252 (5th Cir. 1978). The result, of course, is appropriate, but the objective territorial principle is not the appropriate theoretical vehicle to accomplish it. *See U.S. Jurisdiction, supra* note 31, at 1135 n.65 (1982) (additional cases and discussion). *See also, e.g.,* U.S. v. Wright-Barker, 784 F.2d 161 (3d Cir. 1986) (conspiracy of at least eight persons to import narcotics, 23 tons of marijuana, into the United States from a vessel on the high seas—200 miles off the New Jersey coast) (citing Restatement (3d)); *see also* U.S. v. Stuart, 109 S. Ct 1183, 1197, (1989) (Scalia, J., concurring); U.S. v. Toyota Motor Corp., 569 F. Supp. 1158, 1162-64 (C.D. Cal. 1983) (wrongly stating that the Restatement (3d) (articulated international law on the subject of jurisdiction); Compagnie Europeenne des Petroles S.A. v. Nederaland B.V., No. 82/716 (D.Ct. Neth. Sept. 17, 1982) (trans. at 22 I.L.M. 366 (1983).

[264] RESTATEMENT (THIRD) §§ 402 (1) (c), 403.

[265] *Id.* (emphasis added). Reporter's note 8, following § 403, incorrectly relies on some of the cases discussed herein, e.g., those in the section of this chapter on the territoriality theories, to promote the notion that objective territorial jurisdiction obtains when there is simply an intent to have an impact on U.S. territory. This

Applying objective territoriality in this way is wrong. In some of the cases, however, other theories would have been appropriate. It is perfectly appropriate to provide jurisdiction over thwarted extraterritorial conspiracies, but not on the basis of *objective territoriality*. The issue is whether a thwarted extraterritorial conspiracy (to sabotage an aircraft or to violate U.S. narcotics laws, for example) triggers one of the bases. Did an element of the crime occur within the U.S.? If co-conspirators worked in the U.S. this would be sufficient. Did some drugs enter the U.S.? If so, this is sufficient. If there was no subjective or objective territoriality basis, did the thwarted conspiracy sufficiently threaten U.S. sovereignty, security or other important governmental interest?[266] Are narcotics conspiracies sufficient to indicate universal jurisdiction?

The trend of U.S. courts to expand territorial jurisdiction began seriously with the Supreme Court's incorrect statement in *Ford v. U.S.*[267] that the objective territoriality applied to circumstances in which no territorial effect has occurred. Several British subjects were convicted of conspiracy to violate U.S. liquor laws, where they had been on board a British vessel on the high seas (about 25 miles off the coast of San Francisco).[268] The Court misused the term, objective territoriality, under circumstances in which subjective territoriality would have applied. The conspiracy itself had its situs within U.S. territory; there were conspirators within and without U.S. borders, and four overt acts took place in the U.S.[269] A fully thwarted extraterritorial conspiracy, by definition, has no effect within the territory. It is an inchoate offense and has no effects at all, until the substantive offense to which the parties were conspiring is accomplished. The purpose of the crime of conspiracy is to prevent the effects from occurring by attaching a sanction to the undesirable consorting very early in its development. It is the potential effects that we wish to prevent. The objective territorial theory is not the appropriate vehicle for this prophylaxis. Conspiracies are crimes deemed by our jurisprudence to be bad in themselves. The question is where does this harm occur? Does it occur on the territory where the planned substantive offense is to take place, or

---

section of the chapter updates and elaborates my exposure of that error in *United States Jurisdiction, supra* note 31, at 1141-51. The RESTATEMENT (THIRD) may be viewed as creating a new basis of jurisdiction pursuant to the "Rule of Reasonableness" (similar to that in conflict cases) which finds the state with the most significant interest in the crime to be the proper one for jurisdiction. On the other hand, the Rule of Reasonableness is written into the Restatement as a mechanism of limitation, not expansion, unless the ostensible adoption of the bases of jurisdiction is merely a subterfuge to promote a new single theory of jurisdiction over extraterritorial crime: the rule of reasonableness. Jurisdiction over any conspiracy, of course, depends on whether jurisdiction exists as to the underlying substantive charge. *See, e.g.*, U.S. v. Yousef, 927 F. Supp. 673, 682 (S.D.N.Y. 1996) (conspiracy to bomb aircraft and to murder U.S. citizens).

266 A thwarted extraterritorial conspiracy to bomb U.S. citizens or interests within the "special U.S. aircraft jurisdiction" is appropriate under certain circumstances, but not on the basis of objective territoriality. *See, e.g.*, *Yousef*, 927 F. Supp. at 682 (conspiracy to bomb aircraft in the special U.S. aircraft jurisdiction and to murder certain U.S. citizens). The *protective principle* works well here, as does the *universality theory*, as it runs through the *Hijacking and Sabotage Conventions, supra*; U.S. v. Evans, 667 F. Supp. 974, 980 (S.D.N.Y. 1980) ("international law permits jurisdiction under . . . theories [of *extraterritoriality*] even if the act or conspiracy at issue is thwarted before ill effects are actually felt in the target state"). Jurisdiction over the conspiracy, of course, depends on whether jurisdiction exists over the underlying substantive offense. *Yousef*, 927 F. Supp. at 682 (citing U.S. v. Bowman, 260 U.S. 94, 96 (1922)); U.S. v. Cotten, 471 F.2d 744 (9th Cir.), *cert. denied* 411 U.S. 936 (1973).

267 Ford v. U.S., 273 U.S. 593 (1927).

268 *Id.* Convention for Prevention of Smuggling of Intoxicating Liquors, Jan. 23, 1924, U.S.—Great Britain, 43 Stat. 1761, T.S. 685, 12 Bevans 414. The Supreme Court said that jurisdiction obtained by virtue of the treaty and could not be asserted, except under the auspices of the treaty. *Ford, supra,* 273 U.S. at 597.

269 *Ford,* 273 U.S. at 620.

where the agreement or other material element takes place? Surely, it would be a strain on the objective territoriality theory to suggest that this "harm" has impacted on the intended state the moment the agreement is made outside the territory.[270] Yet this is what the language in *Ford*, the Restatement (Third), and more recent cases suggest. Although the Court used the term, this is not objective territoriality. The cases cited by the Court as supporting objective territoriality indicate that the Court did not really understand jurisdictional theory. All of the cases cited were based on an actual effect having occurred on the territory.[271] U.S. courts subsequently have taken the erroneous *Ford* dicta and its confused analysis as authority for the proposition that objective territorial jurisdiction obtains over extraterritorial conspiracies in which no element nor any harmful effects have been caused.

If a potential effect triggers jurisdiction, some theory other than objective territoriality needs to be asserted. This would depend on the substantive offense that is the object of the conspiracy. If, for example, it is an offense that threatens sovereignty or national security, the protective principle applies (no effect is needed).

Rocha v. U.S.[272] is another incorrect application of the objective territorial theory. Although the *Rocha* facts were perfect for the application of the protective theory, the Ninth Circuit Court of Appeals felt constrained to state a territorial basis. An accused alien had made false statements to a consular official abroad. The accused's conduct violated the integrity of important governmental operations and was an insult to its sovereignty. Nevertheless, the appellate court explained that a major reason for its assertion of jurisdiction was the fact that U.S. territory had been adversely impacted when the defendant entered illegally. The offense, however, was complete when the false statements were made to a consular official.[273]

A federal trial court in California felt similarly constrained in *U.S. v. Archer*:[274] It assumed jurisdiction to convict an alien of perjury to a consular official: "[the fraud] consists in having corruptly secured an advantage, and in harming the U.S. The fraud is not in the act, but in the result [the advantage or harm] to be attained."[275] Even though the court argued well that offenses violating the sovereignty of the U.S. may be punished as an exception to the territorial principle, it claimed that "the offense was not committed in a foreign territory [but in the U.S.]."[276]

The confusion or misapplication of the objective territorial theory has been taken to greater lengths recently, especially in cases relating to thwarted extraterritorial conspiracy

---

270 Many non-U.S. jurists object to this aspect.

271 Lamar v. U.S., 240 U.S. 60 (1916); Strassheim v. Daily, 221 U.S. 280 (1911); Benson v. Henkel, 198 U.S. 1 (1905) (a bribe was offered in California, but received in D.C., where jurisdiction over the subject matter was properly asserted, on the basis of the objective territoriality principle); *In re Palliser*, 136 U.S. 257 (1890) (jurisdiction was deemed proper in the place where a letter was received over an offense perpetrated by letter); Simpson v. State, 92 Ga. 41, 17 S.E. 984 (1893); Commonwealth v. Macloon, 101 Mass. 1 (1869).

272 Rocha v. U.S., 288 F.2d 545 (9th Cir.), *cert. denied*, 366 U.S. 948 (1961).

273 This is discussed in detail in *United States Jurisdiction, supra* note 31, at 1141-51; and in TERRORISM, DRUGS, *supra* note 1, at Ch. 3.

274 U.S. v. Archer, 51 F. Supp. 708 (S.D. Cal. 1943).

275 *Id.* at 710.

276 *Id.* This would also be alright if the Court meant on embassy or consular grounds. *See* U.S. v. Rodriguez, 182 F. Supp. 479, 491-92 (S.D. Cal. 1960). *See also* U.S. v. Baker, 136 F. Supp. 546, 549 (S.D.N.Y. 1955), wherein the court refused jurisdiction because, "providing false information to a consular officer abroad" does not occur within the territorial jurisdiction of the United States. The court did not recognize the protective principle as a basis for taking jurisdiction.

to import narcotics. Courts have perceived the problem in two or three conceptual forms. First, as in the *Ford* case,[277] they have construed the facts to find that a conspiracy had its situs in the territory, because an element of the conspiracy actually took place within the territory. This is classic subjective territoriality, not objective territoriality as they have claimed.[278] The subjective territorial theory is a valid vehicle for the assertion of jurisdiction over conspiracies which culminate or are thwarted abroad, as long as a constituent element occurs within the territory. If an overt act in furtherance of a conspiracy is "a constituent element" of the crime, and such occurs within the territory, the subjective territorial principle properly applies.[279]

Where no harmful effects actually occur within the territory—no contraband actually smuggled in, for example—the objective territorial principle cannot be the proper theory. If no element of the crime has occurred on the asserting state's territory, the subjective territoriality theory does not apply. A conspiracy in U.S. law is not only an inchoate offense, it is also a completed crime. The completed conspiracy has its own intrinsic harmful effect where that conspiracy takes place. Although the place of the conspiracy's intended impact clearly has a strong interest in stopping it from occurring, the objective territorial theory is not the vehicle. A basis of jurisdiction that is *actually extraterritorial*, such as universality or the protective principle may work, but not a territorial theory.

The courts have confused objective and subjective territoriality and have confused the substantive elements of conspiracy (agreement) with the jurisdictional requirements of the objective territorial theory (an actual effect). An overt act may be a constituent element of the crime of conspiracy, but it is not a harmful effect, which is the requirement of the objective territorial principle.[280] It is proper to consider the conspiracy to have occurred in

---

[277] Ford v. U.S., 273 U.S. 593, 619 (1927).

[278] *See, e.g.*, U.S. v. Harper, 617 F.2d 35 (4th Cir. 1980); U.S. v. Coats, 611 F.2d (4th Cir. 1979); U.S. v. Perez-Hererra, 610 F.2d 289 (5th Cir. 1980). Only U.S. v. Wright-Barker, 784 F.2d 161 (3d Cir. 1986), applies territoriality where there is no territorial nexus at all.

[279] *See, e.g., Perez-Herrera,* 610 F.2D 289; U.S. v. Cadena, 585 F.2d 1252 (5th Cir. 1978); U.S. v. Winter, 509 F.2d 975 (5th Cir.), *cert. denied sub nom.*, Parks v. U.S., 423 U.S. 825 (1975); Marine v. U.S., 352 F.2d 174 (5th Cir. 1965). *See also Ford,* 273 U.S. 593; Rivard v. U.S., 375 F.2d 882 (5th Cir. 1967). In *Ford* and *Rivard,* significant harmful effects had actually occurred within U.S. territory so the objective territorial theory was proper.

[280] *Winter,* 509 F.2d 975, provides a good example of how this erroneous perception has been developed or rationalized. The Fifth Circuit Court of Appeals (in *Winter*) admitted that in *Ford,* 273 U.S. 593, and in *Rivard,* 375 F.2d 882, illegal contraband had actually been imported into the U.S.—thus establishing a harmful effect. In *Winter*, however, the court discounted the distinction as being without significance under the facts of the case because the conspiracy had been thwarted before importation could occur, and "because it is immaterial to the commission of the crime of conspiracy whether the object of the conspiracy is achieved." *Winter,* 509 F.2d at 982. The court said, "[a]n overt act, seeming innocent in itself yet in furtherance of the conspiracy, is sufficient under the law of conspiracy." *Id.* The court continued, "[w]e see no reason why it should be any different for jurisdictional purposes to the extent that proof of an overt act is required." *Id. See also* some of the reasoning in *Cadena,* 585 F.2d 1252; U.S. v Postal, 589 F.2d 862 (5th Cir. 1979); U.S. v. Williams, 617 F.2d 1063, 1076 (5th Cir. 1980); U.S. v. Marino-Garcia, 679 F.2d 1373 (11th Cir. 1982), *cert. denied,* 103 S.Ct. 748 (1983) (U.S. has jurisdiction to prosecute person on board stateless vessel on the high seas for possession of marijuana with intent to distribute it in violation of 21 U.S.C § 955(a); U.S. v. Michelena-Orovio, 719 F.2d 738, 753 (5th Cir. 1983), *cert. denied,* 465 U.S. 1104 (1984) ("These cases hold that the government need not prove any overt act within the U.S. in order to convict a defendant of conspiracy to possess marijuana with intent to distribute it as long as there is sufficient evidence that the conspiracy was to be consummated within U.S. territory"); U. S. v. Quemener, 789 F.2d 145, 156 (2d Cir. 1986) (holding that jurisdiction based on the objective territorial principle obtained when a British boat was seized on the high seas carrying a cargo of drugs, deemed to be intended for U.S. importation. The Court erroneously stated that the objective territorial theory approves jurisdiction when there is an "intent to cause effects

all places where a constituent element occurs. To say, however, that a conspirator's overt act triggers the traditional objective territorial theory of jurisdiction is to confuse an element of the crime with its effect. U.S. federal narcotics conspiracy law requires no overt act.[281] Combining the confusion, courts have reasoned that, since no overt act is required to commit a conspiracy to import narcotics into the U.S., the objective territorial principle will apply to assert jurisdiction over such a conspiracy, even though no overt act or any effect has occurred, as long as the parties intended such an impact.[282] Certainly, if the substantive definition of the offense does not require an overt act, the crime occurs without one. It is quite another thing, however, to claim that the lack of an overt act equals an effect. Yet this is what the courts do when they hold that the objective territorial principle is the basis of jurisdiction. To hold that the intended effect of an inchoate offense is an actual effect is to consider what would have happened with what actually occurred. Jurisdiction may be asserted when there is no territorial impact, but only based on other, nonterritorial, bases of jurisdiction.

This conceptual problem developed out of the "war on drugs." Expansion of jurisdiction was seen as a more efficient way to effectuate U.S. laws proscribing conspiracies to import illegal drugs into the U.S. Obviously, as the crime of conspiracy itself is designed to be a tool of prophylaxis, it must have an extraterritorial application if it is to regulate importation. The courts reasoned correctly that the Congress intended narcotics conspiracy laws to have an extraterritorial application.[283] *U.S. v. Brown*[284] is a prototypical decision. It poses the conceptual problem and suggests a solution. Defendant, a U.S. citizen member of the military stationed in Germany, was convicted of conspiracy to import heroin into the U.S. from Germany. He conspired with others to use U.S. Army mail to import heroin into the U.S. The parties to the conspiracy actually sent packages, which they believed to contain heroin, to the U.S. The packages, however, actually contained corn starch and dextrose. Thus, while no importation of narcotics occurred, a conspiracy to import heroin into the U.S. did occur and was proved. It occurred in Germany, however. No overt act (of the conspiracy to import heroin) occurred within the U.S. Although there was an effect (of cornstarch and dextrose entering U.S. territory), this impact was benign. Defendant argued that for jurisdiction to obtain, there would have to be a detrimental effect which was intended to occur and which actually did occur on U.S. territory or, alternatively, that defendant's conduct be proved to pose potential damage to important U.S. governmental interests. The defense claimed that neither the impact nor the required potential danger occurred. The

---

within the U.S." Interestingly, the Court also noted that the pertinent statute, [21 U.S.C. §§ 955(a)(d), 955(c), 955(a)(h)], "unambiguously provides that these sections are intended to reach acts of possession . . . committed outside the territorial jurisdiction of the U.S." It is strange that the court considers a statute that it applies to *extraterritorial* conduct is based on the objective *territorial* principle. Objective territoriality *is territoriality*! The Court also noted: "[C]ongress is not bound by international law. If it chooses to do so, it may legislate with respect to conduct outside the U.S., in excess of limits posed by international law . . ."

281 21 U.S.C. §§ 846, 963.

282 *See, e.g.*, U.S. v. Mann, 615 F.2d 668, 671 (5th Cir. 1980); *Postal*, 589 F.2d at 886 n.39. The RESTATEMENT (THIRD), *supra* note 23, § 402 (1)(c), has recognized this same notion. Some of the reasoning in *Cadena*, 585 F.2d 1252; *Williams*, 617 F.2d at 1076; *Marino-Garcia*, 679 F.2d 1373 (U.S. has jurisdiction to prosecute person on board stateless vessel on the high seas for possession of marijuana with intent to distribute it in violation of 21 U.S.C § 955(a)); *Michelena-Orovio*, 719 F.2d 738, 753.

283 *See, e.g.*, U.S. v. Layton, 509 F. Supp. 212 (N.D. Cal. 1981).

284 U.S. v. Brown, 549 F.2d 954 (4th Cir. 1977), *cert. denied*, 430 U.S. 949 (1977).

Fourth Circuit held that, even though what was actually imported happened to be benign, "the conspiracy alleged implicated a crime which would produce detrimental effects within this nation and affront this denouncement of the possession and trafficking in drugs like those contemplated in this case."[285] The Court cited *Strassheim v. Daily*, the classic case representing the objective territorial principle, as authority.[286] *Strassheim* had held that an offense committed abroad whose harmful effects are intended to and do occur within U.S. territory provides jurisdiction on that theory. The *Brown* court also cited *U.S. v. Pizzarusso*,[287] as authority for objective territoriality. Both *Strassheim* and *Pizzarusso*, however, actually held that objective territoriality cannot apply unless an impact occurs on the territory of the asserting state. *Strassheim* insisted on an actual effect and *Pizzarusso* rejected objective territoriality for that reason and applied the *protective principle*, because there was only potential damage arising from the offense. The *Pizzarusso* Court made it clear that when there was danger or potential damage *to national security, integrity, sovereignty, or governmental operations*, the protective theory, not objective territoriality applies.

The Fourth Circuit in *Brown*, after citing *Strassheim* and *Pizzarusso*, applied *U.S. v. Bowman*,[288] which is a nationality principle case combined with notions of protective principle. The Supreme Court in *Bowman* had noted that, "certain crimes [such as conspiracy to defraud a corporation in which the U.S. is the sole stockholder] are such that to limit their locus to the strictly territorial jurisdiction would be greatly to curtail the scope and usefulness of the statute and open a large immunity for frauds as easily committed by citizens on the high seas and in foreign countries as at home."[289] The Court in *Bowman* considered the nationality of the defendant(s), as well as the damage to governmental operations as key features of its allowing jurisdiction. The defendant had conspired extraterritorially to defraud the paying corporation, of which the U.S. Government was the sole shareholder.[290] The Supreme Court in *Bowman* articulated the purpose and ambit of the protective principle. It cited U.S. Code sections relating to "offenses against the operation of the government,"[291] which necessarily, due to the nature of the crimes involved, are designed to provide U.S. jurisdiction, when acts are done which are intended to damage the function of government.[292] The Court went on to analogize the conspiracy to defraud a corporation in which the U.S. Government was the sole shareholder to those "offenses against the operation of the government."[293] Thus, the theory of jurisdiction invoked in *Bowman* is clearly a combination of the nationality and the protective principles. Furthermore, the court explicitly rejected any need for or the use of a territoriality theory. Thus, the *Brown* court's use of *Bowman* as authority for the objective *territoriality* theory

---

285 *Id.*

286 Strassheim v. Dailey, 221 U.S. 280 (1911). *See also* M. CHERIF BASSIOUNI, INTERNATIONAL EXTRADITION IN UNITED STATES LAW AND PRACTICE 373-74 (3d ed. 1996).

287 U.S. v. Pizzarusso, 338 F.2d 8 (2d Cir. 1968).

288 U.S. v. Bowman, 260 U.S. 94 (1922).

289 *Id.* at 98.

290 *Id.* at 95-96.

291 *Id.* at 98-99.

292 *Id.* at 99.

293 *Id.* at 102. Thus, it is a proper application of jurisdiction over extraterritorial crime, based on a properly applicable theory of jurisdiction. *See also* U.S. v. Yousef, 927 F. Supp. 673, 682 (S.D.N.Y. 1996).

is inapt. Yet, the *Brown case* was intended to be and is now cited as an objective territoriality case.[294] This is wrong.

In *U.S. v. Ricardo*,[295] the Fifth Circuit affirmed convictions for conspiracy to import marijuana into the U.S.,[296] although the conspiracy, which took place entirely abroad (no overt acts within the U.S.), was thwarted before any marijuana was imported. Objective territoriality was the indicated territorial basis.[297] The court reasoned that: (1) the law does not require an overt act to be alleged or proved in order to convict a person of conspiracy to import marijuana; (2) the Fifth Circuit has always adhered to the principle of objective territoriality, "which attache[s] criminal consequences to extraterritorial acts that are intended to have effect in the sovereign territory, at least where overt acts within the territory can be proved;"[298] and (3) ". . . [i]mplicit in the statutes is the notion that the proscribed prohibitions apply extraterritorially,"[299] and ". . . when the statute itself does not require proof of an overt act, jurisdiction attaches upon a mere showing of intended territorial effects."[300] Similarly, the Fifth Circuit, in *U.S. v. Michelena-Orovio*,[301] held, "the government need not prove any overt act within the United States in order to convict a defendant of conspiracy to possess marijuana with intent to distribute it as long as there is sufficient evidence that the conspiracy was to be consummated within United States territory."

U.S. v. Mann[302] continued the erroneous notion that objective territoriality applies to extraterritorial conspiracies and is appropriate under the objective territorial theory even though no effect actually occurs within U.S. territory. In *Mann*, the defendants were convicted of conspiracy to import marijuana into the U.S.[303] The Court declared that it was not necessary for the government to prove an overt act under the controlled substance conspiracy statutes[304] because, "[w]hen a conspiracy statute does not require proof of overt acts, the requirement of territorial effect may be satisfied by evidence that the defendants intended their conspiracy to be consummated within the nation's borders."[305] The court then

---

294 *E.g.*, U.S. v. Perez-Herrera, 610 F.2d 289, 290-92 (5th Cir. 1980) (the opinion actually suggests that the protective principle is the appropriate one, but then, exhibits its weak conceptualization by citing Strassheim v. Daily, the classic objective territoriality case). *Cf.*, U.S. v. Endicott, 803 F.2d 506, 514 (9th Cir. 1986); U.S. v. Evans, 667 F. Supp. 974, 981-82 (S.D.N.Y. 1987) (no overt act needed and jurisdiction obtains for extraterritorial conspiracy to violate Arms Export Control Act, 22 U.S.C. §§ 2753, 2778).

295 U.S. v. Ricardo, 619 F.2d 1124 (5th Cir. 1980).

296 *See* 21 U.S.C. §§ 846, 963.

297 *Ricardo,* 619 F.2d 1124 (citing U.S. v. Mann, 615 F.2d 668, 671 (5th Cir. 1980)). *See also* U.S. v. Michelena Orovio, 719 F.2d 738, 753 (5th Cir. 1983) (". . . the government need not prove any overt act within the U.S. in order to convict a defendant of conspiracy to possess marijuana with intent to distribute it as long as there is sufficient evidence that the conspiracy was to be consummated within U.S. territory.") (citing *Ricardo,* 619 F.2d 1124; U.S. v. Baker, 136 F. Supp. 546, 549 (S.D.N.Y. 1955)).

298 *Ricardo,* 619 F.2d 1124 (citing U.S. v. Postal, 589 F.2d 862, 885 (5th Cir. 1979). This is an incorrect statement of the objective territorial principle. Jurisdiction may be appropriate under the facts described in the statement, but on the basis of the subjective, not objective, territorial theory.

299 *Id.* at 1128 (citing U.S. v. Cadena, 585 F.2d 1252 (5th Cir. 1978)).

300 *Id.* at 1120. Thus the court asserted jurisdiction over the conspiracy, because its aim was to import narcotics into the U.S. Jurisdiction was approved, even though no overt act or effect occurred on United States territory, because no overt act is required as an element of the crime.

301 *Michelena-Orovio*, 719 F.2d at 753, *cert. denied*, 465 U.S. at 1104.

302 *Mann*, 615 F.2d at 668.

303 21 U.S.C. §§ 846, 963.

304 *Mann,* 615 F.2d at 671; 21 U.S.C. § 846, conspiracy to possess marijuana with intent to distribute it; and 21 U.S.C. § 963, conspiracy to import marijuana.

305 *Mann,* 615 F.2d at 671 (citing U.S. v. Postal, 589 F.2d 862, 886 n.39 (5th Cir. 1979)).

stated that any other rule would make it too difficult to enforce our laws and would "conflict with the purpose of the objective view of jurisdiction."[306] The court is correct that unless jurisdiction can be asserted to apply to these inchoate offenses, "it will be difficult to enforce them."[307] On the other hand, the simple belief that jurisdiction ought to be asserted does not establish territorial jurisdiction. The court was either unaware of the existence and scope of other theories of jurisdiction or it felt that they would not apply, so it transubstantiated an intent to impact into an actual territorial effect.

The Sufficient Nexus Test

The *sufficient nexus test* provides that jurisdiction over territorial crime in the U.S. could obtain only when a sufficient nexus between defendants and the U.S. exists, sufficient to satisfy due process fairness standards.[308] Few circuits have adopted the test, however. In 1993 the Third Circuit declined to follow the Ninth Circuit's lead. In *U.S. v. Martinez-Hidalgo*, the court held that the U.S. could prosecute under the Maritime Drug Law Enforcement Act (MDLEA), a nonresident alien on a stateless vessel sailing outside U.S. territorial waters, regardless of whether the ultimate destination of the drugs was U.S territory.[309]

On February 2, 1995, the Ninth Circuit decided *U.S. v. Juda.*[310] A ship captured by the U.S. Coast Guard on the high seas, some 530 miles west of Vancouver, British Columbia was found to have hashish on board. The crew consisted of U.S. citizens and one U.S. resident alien. The crew had set the ship afire and were rescued by the Coast Guard. Some

---

306 *Id. See also Michelena Orovio,* 719 F.2d at 753 (". . . the government need not prove any overt act within the United States in order to convict a defendant of conspiracy to possess marijuana with intent to distribute it as long as there is sufficient evidence that the conspiracy was to be consummated within United States territory.") (citing U.S. v. Ricardo, 619 F.2d 1124 (5th Cir. 1980) (incorrect authority, as accused parties were aboard a U.S. vessel); U.S. v. Marino-Garcia, 679 F.2d 1373 (11th Cir. 1982), *cert. denied,* 103 S. Ct. 748 (1983); U.S. v. Jonas, 639 F.2d 200, 205 (5th Cir. 1981); U.S. v. DeWeese, 632, F.2d 1267, 1271 (5th Cir. 1980); U.S. v. Arra, 630 F.2d 836 (1st Cir. 1980); which held that, as long as the parties intend that the conspiracy be consummated within the United States territorial boundaries, the jurisdictional requirements are met. *See also* U.S. v. Willis, 639 F.2d 1335 (5th Cir. 1981) (no discussion at all of the problem of jurisdiction); U.S. v. Espinosa-Cerpa, 630 F.2d 328 (5th Cir. 1980) (no mention of jurisdictional problem); U.S. v. Perez-Hererra, 610 F.2d 289, 290-92 (5th Cir. 1980); U.S. v. Streifel, 507 F. Supp. 480, 483 (S.D.N.Y. 1981).

307 615 F.2d at 67.

308 *See, e.g.,* U.S. v. Juda, 46 F.3d 961 (9th Cir.), *writ denied,* 115 S. Ct. 2632 (1995); U.S. v. Medjuck, 48 F.3d 1107 (9th Cir. 1995) ("[W]e require only [for constitutional extraterritorial jurisdiction over crime] that Congressional intent of extraterritorial scope be clear and that application of the statute to the acts in question not violate due process . . . [which is] not offended as long as there is a sufficient nexus between the conduct and the U.S.); U.S. v. Caicedo, 47 F.3d 370 (9th Cir. 1995); U.S. v. Davis, 905 F.2d 245 (9th Cir. 1990) (rejects the protective principle by itself as being sufficient); U.S. v. Khan, 35 F.3d 426 (9th Cir. 1994); U.S v. Aikins, 923 F.2d 650 (9th Cir. 1990). *But see* U.S. v. Howard-Arias, 679 F.2d 363 (1982) ("[p]rosecutions for possession of controlled substances prior to the enactment of the *Marijuana on the High Seas Act* required proof of intent to distribute the illegal drugs within the United States. The very intent of the Marijuana on the High Seas Act was to eliminate that requirement and to facilitate prosecution of smugglers both native and foreign who were apprehended on the high seas."); *Marino-Garcia,* 679 F.2d. 1373 (stateless vessels); U.S. v. Alvarez-Mena, 765 F.2d 1259 (5th Cir. 1985) (no nexus required regarding activities on a stateless vessel in international waters, which receives no protection of international law, per 21 U.S.C. 955a(a)—possession of a controlled substance with intent to distribute).

309 U.S. v. Martinez-Hidalgo, 993 F.2d 1052 (3d Cir. 1993).

310 *Juda,* 46 F.3d at 961.

hashish was recovered before the boat sank. The boat was declared a stateless vessel after the Captain's claims of British registry were denied by Great Britain. The men were convicted by the U.S. District Court for the Northern District of California under the MDLEA. The Ninth Circuit stated: "[t]he MDLEA prohibits drug activity by 'any person on board a vessel of the United States, or on board a vessel subject to the jurisdiction of the United States or a resident alien of the United States on board any vessel. A vessel subject to the jurisdiction of the United States includes a stateless vessel, *e.g.* a vessel without nationality.'" The Court held that the plain meaning of the statutory language allows for ". . . prosecution in the United States regardless of the destination of the drugs." Nothing in the language of the statute limits its application to defendants who possess drugs intended for distribution in the U.S. However, the Court found sufficient nexus on the basis of defendants' nationality and the fact that substantial elements of the offense (the hatching and development of the conspiracy) actually occurred within the U.S.[311] The court determined that Juda's activities in the U.S., including his arranging for the purchase of the vessel, securing its crew, and organizing the operation provided a sufficient nexus to support the constitutional application of U.S. laws to the defendants.[312]

The Court also held that its assertion of jurisdiction was fully consistent with international law principles, including: the active personality principle (nationality jurisdiction)—"[u]nder international law, a nation may generally assert jurisdiction over its citizens;"[313] "jurisdiction extends to individuals arrested on board a stateless vessel."[314]

The Continent and Jurisdiction Over Extraterritorial Conspiracies

It is interesting to evaluate whether some Continental theories of jurisdiction would approve the expansion of the objective territorial theory of jurisdiction to accommodate the assertion of jurisdiction over a thwarted extraterritorial narcotics conspiracy.[315] French doctrine and jurisprudence have rejected the application of the objective territorial theory over thwarted conspiracies, as well as that of universality and the protective principle. It appears, however, that there may be a trend to allow application of the universality theory or protective principle for such assertion.[316]

Generally, French law does not conceive of the crime of conspiracy to commit a crime as it is known in United States law, unless the combination or *association* is designed to commit crimes against the security of the republic or to violate French laws against the use, sale and importation of narcotics.[317] The French have made specific legislative exception for

---

311 *Id.*

312 *Id.*

313 *Id.* at 967.

314 *Alvarez-Mena*, 765 F.2d at 1265-66. The active personality principle, however, requires that a crime be committed. Mere transportation of drugs on the high seas is not criminal unless it can be shown that the drugs were intended for sale or use in the United States or some other country where their use or possession is illegal.

315 The French development is considered in detail in TERRORISM, DRUGS, *supra* note 1.

316 TERRORISM, DRUGS *supra* note 1, at Ch. 3; International Conference on Extradition, Italian Ministry of Justice (Dec. 4-9, 1989). Discussion and correspondence with eminent continental jurists in relation to the Conference on New Horizons in International Criminal Law, Institut Superieur International des Sciences Criminelles, held May 7-12, 1984, Noto, Italy.

317 The French notion of conspiracy focuses on general combinations or associations to plan crimes (the most serious of French offenses) in the plural. C. PR. PÉN. art. 265. The law does not contemplate conspiracy to

these offenses. Although the protective principle clearly is the jurisdictional basis for asserting jurisdiction over crimes against the security of the republic, including association for that purpose.[318] The legislation on narcotics does not state a jurisdictional basis.

International Criminal Tribunals and Jurisdiction

The Ad Hoc Tribunals for the Former Yugoslavia and Rwanda

Jurisdictional and related issues for the recent developments of the international tribunals for crimes against humanity in the former Yugoslavia and in Rwanda present interesting issues. A brief analysis follows. Articles 1, 6, 8, 9, and 10 of the Bosnia Tribunal Statute apply to jurisdiction. The Bosnia Tribunal's First Annual Report noted that its jurisdiction differed from that of the Nuremberg and Tokyo Tribunals in two basic respects. First, the Bosnia Tribunal has jurisdiction over war crimes and over crimes against humanity, in particular, genocide. Crimes against peace are not within the purview of the tribunal. The Bosnia Tribunal is empowered to adjudicate crimes perpetrated in the course of both inter-state wars and internal strife.[319]

Croatia, Bosnia & Herzegovina, and the Republic of Yugoslavia (Serbia and Montenegro): Articles 24 and 25 of the U.N. Charter require members to abide by Security Council decisions when it acts consistently with its authority. Does the fact that some nations violate this rule with impunity mean that it is not law? This may be *the* question crucial to the continued authority of international legal order, especially when the very nation(s) or group(s) at which the Ad Hoc Tribunal is aimed, seem to be flaunting their impunity. Does this matter in theory? In practice? Is there a difference?[320] The statute is based on a "decision" of the Security Council, not merely a recommendation. A decision requires action under U.N. Charter article 39. Proponents would argue that both customary international law and general principles, in addition to the prescription of the Charter provide authority.

Termination of the Tribunals' mandates: The "life-span" of the Bosnia tribunal is "linked to the restoration and maintenance of international peace and security in the territory of the former Yugoslavia, and Security Council decisions related thereto."[321] If this means that the

---

commit a specific offense unless it reaches the level of an attempt, but rather the combination or association of individuals to commit crimes. The notion was developed to combat combinations of anarchists or underworld gangs. French legislation has established a few exceptional conspiracies to commit specific crimes: CODE DE LA SANTÉ PUBLIQUE art. L. 627 (conspiracy to violate narcotics laws); C. PR. PÉN. arts. 689-1 through 689-5; and C. PÉN. arts. 450-1 through 450-3 (*association de malfaiteurs* to commit offenses that incur at least ten years of imprisonment, including crimes against the security of the state and many narcotics offenses). *See also* C. PÉN. art. 132-71 (*Bande Organisé*). The expansive use of conspiracy in the United States is frowned upon by the European jurists. *See also* BOUZAT & PINATEL, *supra* note 64, at 773, 803.

[318] C. PR. PÉN. art. 689-1 through 689-5 (1994).

[319] Tribunal to Prosecute Crimes Against Humanity in the Territory of the Former Yugoslavia, First Annual Report (*quoted in* M. CHERIF BASSIOUNI & PETER MANIKAS, THE LAW OF THE INTERNATIONAL CRIMINAL TRIBUNAL FOR THE FORMER YUGOSLAVIA 296 (1996)).

[320] *See, e.g.*, TERRORISM, DRUGS, *supra* note 1, at Ch. 1, 2; Anthony D'Amato, *Is International Law Really Law*, *in* INTERNATIONAL LAW: PROCESS & PROSPECTS 1 (1987).

[321] Report of the Secretary-General Pursuant to ¶ 2 of Security Council Resolution 808 (1993, U.N. Doc. S/25704 (3 May 1993)), at ¶ 28 [hereinafter Secretary-General's Report on Yugo Tribunal]; *see* Christopher L. Blakesley, *Comparing the Ad Hoc Tribunal for Crimes Against Humanitarian Law in the Former Yugoslavia and the Project for an International Criminal Court prepared by the International Law Commission*, 67 REVUE INTERNATIONALE DE DROIT PÉNAL 139 (1996).

Tribunal will cease to exist when "peace" is "*restored*," it is problematical, for certainly prosecutions will be ongoing or planned for the future. The better approach is to interpret the term "*maintenance*" of peace, meaning that the Tribunal will continue to function to help promote and maintain peace through justice, even after "peace" is "restored." Once "peace" is restored, will the *Tribunals* have authority to continue? Continuation depends on whether the mandate calls simply for restoration or for restoration and maintenance of peace. Articles 41 and 42 seem to provide authority to continue. Article 42 empowers the Security Council to restore and maintain peace and security. This certainly ought to include the power to create a war crimes tribunal which would help restore or maintain peace. This seems not only to extend the mandates in time, but also to include the obligation to make the tribunals effective.[322] Jurisdiction of the Bosnia Tribunal was limited to the prosecution of persons responsible for "serious violations of international humanitarian law occurring in the territory of the former Yugoslavia, since 1991."[323] For Rwanda, it is to cover genocide and other crimes against humanity committed in Rwanda between January 1, 1994, and December 31, 1994.[324] The Report de-emphasized any precedential value of the ad hoc tribunals on the establishment of a permanent international criminal court or an international criminal jurisdiction.[325]

Territorial and temporal competence of the Bosnia Tribunal are limited to conduct since January 1, 1991, in the territory of the former Yugoslavia.[326] The Rwanda Statute provides jurisdiction to prosecute persons responsible for genocide and other serious violations of international law, committed in the territory of Rwanda and "Rwandan citizens responsible for genocide . . . committed in the territory of neighboring states, between 1 January 1994 and 31 December 1994. . ."[327]

---

322 *See* Ruth Wedgwood, *War Crimes in the Former Yugoslavia: Comments on the International War Crimes Tribunal,* 34 VA. J. INT'L L. 271, 274 (1994).

323 Secretary-General's Report on Yugo Tribunal, *supra* note 321, ¶ 12 ("The Security Council's decision in resolution 808 (1993) to establish an international tribunal is circumscribed in scope and purpose; the prosecution of persons responsible for serious violations of international humanitarian law committed in the territory of the former Yugoslavia since 1991. The decision does not relate to the establishment of an international criminal jurisdiction in general nor to the creation of an international criminal court of a permanent nature, issues which are and remain under active consideration by the International Law Commission and the General Assembly"). *See also id.* ¶¶ 1, 4. In addition to the reports of France, Italy, and CSCE, the Secretary-General took into account suggestions or comments presented formally or informally, since the adoption of S.C. Resolution 808, by the following nations: Australia, Austria, Belgium, Brazil, Canada, Chil, China, Denmark, Egypt (on behalf of the members of the Organization of the Islamic Conference (OIC) and members of the Contact Group of OIC on Bosnia and Herzagovina), Germany, Iran, Ireland, Italy, Malasia, Mexico, Netherlands, New Zealand, Spain, Sweden, Switzerland, Turkey, United Kingdom of Great Britain and Northern Ireland, the United States, and Yugoslavia. The International Committee of the Red Cross (ICRC), Amnesty International, *Association International des Jeunes Avocats*, Ethnic Minorities Barristers' Association, *Fédération Internationale des Femmes des Carrières Juridiques,* International Criminal Police Organization, Jacob Blaustein Institut for the Advancement of Human Rights, Lawyers Committee for Human Rights, National Alliance of Women's Organizations, and Parliamentarians for Global Action, and observations from international colloquia and individual experts in the field of human rights. *Id.* ¶ 14.

324 *See* Rwanda Statute, *infra* note 327, at arts. 2-8. Discussed in detail, *infra.*

325 Secretary-General's Report on Yugo Tribunal, *supra* note 321, ¶ 12; *see* Virginia Morris & Michael Scharf, *The Precedential Value of the International Criminal Tribunal,* paper presented at the ISISC Conference, Siracusa, Italy, Dec. 4-8, 1994.

326 Secretary-General's Report on Yugo Tribunal, *supra* note 321, ¶¶ 60-63.

327 S.C. Res. 955, *Establishing the International Tribunal for Rwanda* (and Annex, which contains the Statute) (Nov. 8, 1994), Statute, art. 1 (Competence of the Tribunal), 33 I.L.M. 1598 (1994) [hereinafter Rwanda

Bosnia Statute, Article 7 and Rwanda, Article 6: "1. A person who planned, instigated, ordered, committed or otherwise aided and abetted in the planning, preparation or execution of a crime referred to in articles 2 to 5 of the present Statute, shall be individually responsible for the crime. 2. The official position of any accused person, whether as Head of State or Government or as a responsible Government official, shall not relieve such person of criminal responsibility nor mitigate punishment. 3. The fact that any of the acts referred to in articles 2 to 5 of the present Statute were committed by a subordinate does not relieve his superior of criminal responsibility if he knew or had reason to know that the subordinate was about to commit such acts or had done so and the superior failed to take the necessary and reasonable measures to prevent such acts or to punish the perpetrators thereof. 4. The fact that an accused person acted pursuant to an order of a Government or of a superior shall not relieve him of criminal responsibility, but may be considered in mitigation of punishment if the International Tribunal determines that justice so requires."

Prescriptive Jurisdiction—Competence of the Ad Hoc Tribunals

Jurisdiction Ratione materiae in General

Nullum crimen sine lege:[328] Although both statutes ostensibly include *nullum crimen sine lege*, its content raises questions. Elements of the offense indicated by the treaty language, custom, or general principles of international law may be too vague to allow prosecution consistent with human rights norms. Some elements of offenses are not clear. Thus, the principle is not served. Criminal law of most nations requires more explicit and specific iteration of the elements to be proved. Bosnia and Rwanda Statutes articles 1 and 2 and the commentary thereto provide some of the elements of the proscribed conduct, although there are still deficiencies. Bosnia Article 1 proscribes "serious violations of international humanitarian law committed in the territory of the former Yugoslavia since 1991 . . ."[329] The Commentary provides:

> [T]he international tribunal shall prosecute persons responsible for serious violations of international humanitarian law. . . . While there is international customary law which is not laid down in conventions, some of the major conventional humanitarian law has become part of customary international law.
>
> In the view of the Secretary-General, the application of the principle *nullem crimen sine lege* requires that the international tribunal should apply rules . . . which are beyond any doubt part of customary law so that the problem of adherence of some but not all States to specific conventions does not arise. . . .

Statute]; *see also* Larry D. Johnson, *The International Tribunal for Rwanda*, 67 REVUE INTERNATIONALE DE DROIT PÉNAL 211 (1996).

[328] This ancient principle of international law is part of the natural law and positivism. *See* HUGO GROTIUS, TREATING OF THE RIGHTS OF WAR AND PEACE 384, 385 (Evats trans., 1945); EMERICH DE VATTEL, THE LAW OF NATIONS: OR PRINCIPLES OF THE LAW OF NATURE, APPLIED TO THE CONDUCT AND AFFAIRS OF NATIONS AND SOVEREIGNS (Pomroy trans., 1805); TERRORISM, DRUGS, *supra* note 1, at 43, 224, 276.

[329] Serbian and Muslim conflict in the region actually began at least as far back as 1463, when the Ottoman Turks conquered the territory.

> The part of conventional international humanitarian law which has beyond doubt become part of international customary law is the law applicable in armed conflict as embodied in: the Geneva Conventions of August 12, 1949 for the Protection of War Victims; the Hague Convention (IV) Respecting the Laws and Customs of War on Land and the Regulations annexed thereto of October 18, 1907; the Convention on the Prevention and Punishment of the Crime of Genocide of December 9, 1948; and the Charter of the International Military Tribunal of August 8, 1945 [Nuremberg] [footnotes omitted].

This is correct, but it does not go far enough. It is necessary to define clearly the particular offense and to provide each of its elements. Bosnia articles 2-5 and Rwanda articles 2-4 are much better than the concomitant proscriptions in the ILC Draft. Vagueness is a potentially disastrous deficiency. Rescue efforts are under way.[330]

Conventions, General Principles, and Customary International Law:

The sources of law and prescriptive jurisdiction for the ad hoc tribunals involve concentric circles of overlapping, possibly antagonistic, or redundant jurisdiction. They involve extremely complicated elements of proof and concomitant jurisdictional prerequisites.[331] Treaty law, general principles of a *jus cogens* nature, and customary international law provide the legal sources proscribing conduct that most of us instinctively consider criminal. Crimes covered include: crimes against humanity, genocide, violations of the customary law of war, and grave breaches of the Geneva Conventions. The Bosnia Statute makes no mention of Common article 3 or Protocols I and II. Article 3 of the Bosnia Statute, however, refers to the "violations of the laws or customs of war." This term has traditionally referred to violations of humanitarian law in international armed conflict, essentially those offenses stemming from the IVth Hague Convention of 1907 and its annexed Regulations.[332] Madeline Albright, U.S. Ambassador to the U.N., has argued that Article 3 of the Bosnia statute (violations of the laws and customs of war) is broad enough to cover common article 3 offenses.[333] International law is not limited to crimes against the peace or war crimes, as the judges at Nuremberg worried.[334] Control Council Law No. 10, provided that "[a]trocities and offences, including but not limited to murder, extermination, enslavement, deportation, imprisonment, torture, rape, or other inhumane acts committed against any civilian population, or persecutions on political, racial or religious grounds [are punishable]."[335] Klaus Barbie and Paul Touvier were prosecuted for crimes against humanity

---

[330] *See* Committee of Experts: international criminal court, meeting in Italy under the auspices of the Association Internationale de Droit Pénal and the Max Planck Institute for Foreign and International Penal Law, June 24-27, 1995.

[331] *See* Wedgwood, *supra* note 322, at 271.

[332] The statute of the International Criminal Tribunal for the Former Yugoslavia (ICTFY) is part of the Secretary-General's Report, *supra* note 321, and incorporates by reference Security Council Resolution 827, S.C. Res. 827, U.N. SCOR, 48th Sess., 3217th mtg., U.N. Doc. S/Res/827 (May 25, 1993).

[333] Ambassador Albright, *Statement*, U.N. Doc. S/PV.3217, at 15 (25 May 1993) (quoted in Theodor Meron, *War Crimes in Yugoslavia and the Development of International Law*, 88 AM. J. INT'L L. 82 (1994)).

[334] Meron, *supra* note 333, at 85.

[335] Amnesty International, *supra* note 323, at 14. *Cf.*, U.S. jurisdiction for tort liability in torture cases, *see* The Torture Victim Protection Act, 28 U.S.C. § 1350 (1992); The Alien Tort Act, 28 U.S.C. 1350; Abebe-Jira v.

independent of any crimes against the peace or war crimes.[336] Conduct covered by these rules may be the most common humanitarian law violations. To allow them to go unpunished due to a hiatus would be tragic. They do seem to be covered by customary international law or general principle.[337]

Both statutes articulate categories of "crimes" in violation of customary international law. Does customary international law cover rape of female combatants or noncombatants, rape or castration of males, slaughter of civilians, detention of villagers under inhumane conditions?[338] The statutes provide jurisdiction over violations of the "laws or customs of war." Listing these offenses may not be absolutely necessary, but would be beneficial to establish clearly the scope of jurisdiction in such internecine war.[339] The statutes explicitly list crimes against humanity, the Rwanda statute being more explicit. They also cover persons responsible for crimes when committed in armed conflict, whether international or internal, when directed against any civilian population.

Geneva Common article 3 covers rape, as do both ad hoc statutes.[340] Crimes against humanity were explicitly recognized in the Nuremberg Charter, Judgement, and in Control Council Law No. 10. These rules have become part of customary international law and, indeed, articulate "general principles of law recognized by civilized nations."[341] In the conflict in the territory of the former Yugoslavia, such inhumane acts have taken the form of so-called "ethnic cleansing" and widespread and systematic rape and other forms of sexual assault and forced impregnation, including enforced prostitution.[342] The tribunal has authority to prosecute persons responsible for the indicated crimes when committed in an armed conflict, whether international or internal in character, and directed against any civilian population: murder, extermination, enslavement, deportation, imprisonment, torture, rape, persecutions on political, racial and religious grounds, and other inhumane acts.[343]

Rwanda Statute, articles 3 and 4 explicitly cover both common article 3 and Protocol II.[344] Circumstances required jurisdiction over offenses in internal armed conflict, through Common Article 3 and Additional Protocol II.[345] The Rwanda Commission of Experts

---

Newego, 72 F.3d 844 (11th Cir. 1996); Hilao v. Marcos, 1996 WL 721218 (9th Cir., Hawaii 1996); Kadic v. Karadzic, 70 F.3d 232 (2d Cir. 1995); Xuncax v. Gramajo, 886 F. Supp. 162, 175 (D. Mass. 1995); Theodore R. Posner, *Alien Tort Claims Act—Genocide—War Crimes—Violations of International Law by Non-State Actors: Kadic v. Karadzic, 70* F.2d 232 (2d Cir.1996), *cert. denied* 64 U.S.L.W. 3832 (June 18, 1996), 90 A.J.I.L. 658 (1996); *see also* Note, Evelyn Mary Aswad, *Torture By Means of Rape*, 84 GEO. L.J. 1913 (1996).

336 *Id.*; *see also Justice* case (Case 3), under Control Council Law No. 10.

337 *See* Jordan Paust, *Applicability of International Criminal Laws to Events in the Former Yugoslavia*, 9 AM. U.J. INT'L L.& POL. 499, 504 (1994); Jordan Paust, *Customary International Law: Its Nature, Sources and Status of Law of the United States,* 12 MICH. J. INT'L L. 59, 64-67, and authority in n.42 (1990); TERRORISM, DRUGS, *supra* note 1, at Chs. 1, 2; THE INTERNATIONAL LEGAL SYSTEM, *supra* note 1, at Chs. 3, 16, 17.

338 Wedgwood, *supra* note 322, at 272.

339 *Id.*

340 *See* ¶ 47 of S/25704. *See* letter from Frank C. Newman to Professor Blakesley, Sept. 21, 1993.

341 *See* ¶ s b & c, *Statute of the International Court of Justice*.

342 Secretary-General's Report, *supra* note 321, ¶ 48.

343 *Id.* ¶ 49, indicating art. 5 of the Statute.

344 *See* Rwanda Statute, *supra* note 327, art. 4.

345 *See id.*; Amnesty International, *supra* note 323, at 12-13; *cf., Corfu Channel* case, I.C.J. Rep. 1949, at 22, ¶ 215; *Case Concerning Military and Paramilitary Activities in and Against Nicaragua* (Nicaragua v. U.S.), ¶ 218.

concluded that crimes against humanity committed there need not be connected to crimes against the peace or war crimes.[346]

Analysis of the Content of Humanitarian Law and Catalogue of Offenses. Rwanda, Statute Articles 2-4; Bosnia Articles 2-5. Is there a common core of crimes?

The Bosnia and Rwanda statutes provide a partial list. The common core of crimes could include grave breaches of the four Geneva Conventions of August 12, 1949, and the Protocols Additional to the Geneva Conventions of August 12, 1949. The Bosnia statute, however, fails to include acts prohibited by Common Article 3 of the Geneva Conventions or by Protocol II relating to the Protection of Victims of Non-International Armed Conflict. The Rwanda Statute adds both Common article 3 and Protocol II.

Offenses in violation of "general international law"—or a common core of crimes. The inclusion of offenses against "*general international law*" is controversial. The "common core" includes offenses, "under a norm of international law accepted and recognized by the international community as a whole as being of such a fundamental character that its violation attracts the criminal responsibility of individuals."[347] The Ad Hoc statutes attempted to be specific and to provide some definition and scope to this concept. More is required, however, as some of the offenses still have limited, vague, and defective definition. Problems of specificity of criminal law elements and definition are similar to those in the some 22 categories of international crimes, in 314 international instruments enacted between 1815 to date, none of which properly defines the offenses proscribed or provides their elements.[348] Often, international criminal law conventions in the past were negotiated by international lawyers, whose expertise does not extend to matters of criminal law. An *actus reus,* a *mens rea,* which combine to cause a specifically prohibited social harm must explicitly be included. It is debatable whether customary international law or general principles derived from the clarification of national law suffices.

Article 4 of Rwanda Statute provides "[t]he Tribunal . . . shall have the power to prosecute persons committing or ordering to be committed serious violations of Article 3 common to the Geneva Conventions of August 12, 1949 for the Protection of War Victims, and of Additional Protocol II thereto of June 8, 1977. These violations shall include, but shall not be limited to: '(a) violence to life, health and physical or mental well-being of persons, in particular murder as well as cruel treatment such as torture, mutilation or any form of corporal punishment; (b) collective punishments; (c) taking of hostages; (d) acts of terrorism; (e) outrages upon personal dignity, in particular humiliating and degrading treatment, rape, enforced prostitution and any form of indecent assault; (f) pillage; (g) the passing of sentences and the carrying out of executions without previous judgement pronounced by a regularly constituted court, by affording all the judicial guarantees which

346 *Commission of Experts on Rwanda, Preliminary Report of the Independent Commission of Experts Established in Accordance with S.C. Resolution 935* at 26-27 (Sept. 29, 1994) (reported in Amnesty International, *supra* note 323, at 15).

347 For elaboration on a *common core of crimes, see* TERRORISM, DRUGS, *supra* note 1, at Chs. 1, 3; IAN BROWNLIE, PRINCIPLES OF PUBLIC INTERNATIONAL LAW 305 (1990); M. CHERIF BASSIOUNI, CRIMES AGAINST HUMANITY IN INTERNATIONAL CRIMINAL LAW 501-27 (1992); Int'l Committee of the Red Cross, Commentary on the Additional Protocols of June 8, 1977 to the Geneva Conventions ¶ 3539 (1987).

348 *See* TERRORISM, DRUGS, *supra* note 1, at 137-49, 215-16.

are recognized as indispensable by civilized peoples; (h) threats to commit any of the foregoing acts.'"

Geneva Conventions' Common article 3 (1) prohibits, as a minimum, in relation to internal armed conflict: "(a) violence to life and person, in particular murder of all kinds, mutilation, cruel treatment and torture; (b) taking of hostages; (c) outrages upon personal dignity, in particular humiliating and degrading treatment; (d) the passing of sentences and carrying out of executions without previous judgement pronounced by a regularly constituted court, affording the judicial guarantees which are recognized as indispensable by civilized peoples." This conduct is prohibited, with special reference to "[p]ersons taking no active part in the hostilities, including members of armed forces who have laid down their arms and those placed *hors de combat* by sickness, wounds, detention or any other cause, shall in all circumstances be treated humanely, without any adverse distinction founded on race, colour, religion or faith, sex, birth or wealth or any other similar criteria."

Additional Protocol II prohibits: (1) [making civilians] "object of attack [article 13(2)]; (2) [making] acts or threats of violence [with the] primary purpose [being to] spread terror among the civilian population [article 13(2)]; (3) starvation of the civilian population as a method of combat [article 14]; (4) acts of terrorism [article 4(2)(d)]; (5) hostage taking [article 4(2)(c)]; and (6) unlawful deportation or transfer of civilians [article 17]." The Bosnia Statute proscribes wanton destruction of cities and towns and the bombardment of undefended towns, when the devastation is not justified by military necessity.[349] But what does this mean in practice? Did Sarajevo and Vihaj lend cover to militia who attacked Bosnian Serb troops at night or with guerilla tactics? Did military necessity allow attacks upon areas where such forces might be hiding? Would sniper fire felling civilians and bombardment of civilian parts of town establish beyond doubt that the snipers and the bombardment were not aimed at military targets? What about snipers killing U.N. peacekeeping forces? What is "wanton destruction?"[350]

Elaboration on Issues of Jurisdiction Rationae Materiae—Bosnia

Article 1, provides, "[t]he International Tribunal shall have the power to prosecute persons responsible for serious violations of international humanitarian law committed in the territory of the former Yugoslavia since 1991. . . ."[351] This authority derives from the mandate set out in paragraph 1 of S.C. Resolution 808 (1993). *Humanitarian Law* has traditionally included the Hague and Geneva rules. *Article 2* lists punishable offenses including, committing or ordering to be committed grave breaches of the relevant Geneva Convention: "(a) willful killing; (b) torture or inhumane treatment, including biological experiments; (c) wilfully causing great suffering or serious injury to body or health; (d) extensive destruction and appropriation of property not justified by military necessity and carried out unlawfully and wantonly [apparently it must be both wanton and unlawful]; (e) compelling a prisoner of war or a civilian to serve in the forces of a hostile power; (f)

---

349 *See* Wedgwood, *supra* note 322, at 272.

350 *Id.; see* critique of many aspects of military necessity in TERRORISM, DRUGS, *supra* note 1, at Chs. 1, 2.

351 Report of the Secretary General on Yugo Tribunal, *supra* note 321, at arts. 1-5; *see also id.* ¶¶ 33-49.

wilfully depriving a prisoner of war or a civilian of the rights of fair and regular trial;[352] (g) unlawful deportation or transfer or unlawful confinement of a civilian; and (h) taking civilians as hostages." Article 2 specifically proscribes "biological experiments" and protects "civilians." "Civilians" are protected whether the conflict is legally internal or international.[353] Laws of War: Bosnia Statute, Article 3 specifies that the Tribunal has jurisdiction to prosecute "violations of the laws or customs of war," lists illustratively: (a) employment of poisonous weapons or other weapons calculated to cause unnecessary suffering; (b) wanton destruction of cities, towns or villages, or devastation not justified by military necessity; (c) attack or bombardment, by whatever means, of undefended towns, villages, dwellings, or buildings; (d) seizure of, destruction or wilful damage done to institutions dedicated to religion, charity and education, the arts and sciences, historic monuments and works of art and science; (e) plunder of public or private property." Article 3 is derived from Hague IV, articles 23-23, and expanded by custom.

Bosnia Article 5 and Rwanda Article 3 (Crimes Against Humanity) provide that "[t]he . . . Tribunal shall have the power to prosecute persons responsible for the following crimes when committed in armed conflict, whether international or internal in character, and directed against any civilian population: (a) murder; (b) extermination; (c) enslavement; (d) deportation; (e) imprisonment; (f) torture; (g) rape; (h) persecutions on political, racial and religious grounds; (i) other inhumane acts." These offenses are derived from Nuremberg Charter article 6, but add rape and torture. Articles 2-5 of the Bosnia Ad Hoc Statute, in order to be more specific, provide for it to have jurisdiction over grave breaches of the Geneva Conventions of 1949, violations of the laws or customs of war, genocide, and crimes against humanity.[354] The Statutes take some license with the term "crimes against humanity," adding some to the list that are not included in the Geneva Convention (IV). Is the phrase "other inhumane acts" still vague? Does this license pose a potential violation of the principle or legality or *nullum crimen sine lege*? It is necessary that whatever conduct is covered be clearly and explicitly "proscribed by relevant international law."[355] The Secretary General's Report notes that only crimes which have clearly and undoubtedly become part

---

[352] The potential for inconsistency here is obvious. Certain defendants were prosecuted in a Bosnian military court and were convicted after confessing. Their confessions, however, were not corroborated and were withdrawn. Also, the defendants claimed that they confessed under torture and repeated beating. Defendant's claims seemed to be corroborated by medical evidence. Will there be prosecution of those who were responsible for the "fairness" of the trial by a Bosnian military court of two Bosnian Serbs. *See Bosnia Convicts and Sentences to Death 2 Serbs,* 9 INT'L L. REP. 147 (No.9, April 1993); John F. Burns, *2 Serbs Shot for Killings and Rapes*, N.Y. TIMES, Mar. 31, 1993, at A6, col. 4; David B. Ottaway, *Bosnia Convicts 2 Serbs in War Crimes Trial,* THE WASH. POST., March 31, 1993, at A21, col. 1. Of course, there is less danger of these sorts of abuses in the ad hoc tribunals, but they must be vigilant. Fairness of the trials must be ensured. Will prosecution for unfair trials apply to all sides? Individuals in U.N. Forces or in the employ of the Tribunal have sufficient power to abuse it. The system should ensure the sanction of those who so abuse their power. *See generally Atrocity and Its Prosecution, supra* note 232; *cf.,* PROSECUTING INTERNATIONAL CRIMES (Roger Clark & Madeline Sann, eds. 1996).

[353] *See* Christopher Joyner, *Strengthening Enforcement of Humanitarian Law: Reflections on the International Tribunal for the Former Yugoslavia,* paper presented at Conference on "Strengthening Enforcement of Humanitarian Law," Duke University School of Law, Mar. 10-11, 1995.

[354] On crimes against humanity, *see generally* BASSIOUNI, *supra* note 112; and Roger Clark, *Crimes Against Humanity, in* THE NUREMBERG TRIAL AND INTERNATIONAL LAW (Ginsburgs & Kudraiavstev eds., 1990); PROSECUTING INTERNATIONAL CRIMES, *supra* note 352.

[355] *See, e.g., Ex Parte Quirin*, 317 U.S. 1, 27-31 (1942) (quoted in the I.M.T. at Nuremberg, Opinion & Judgement, *reprinted at* 44 AM. J. INT'L L. 172, 220 (1947)).

of customary law may be prosecuted.[356] How much this helps any *nullem crimen sine lege* problem is still open to debate; but it is intended to include the law applicable in armed conflict as embodied in the Geneva Conventions of August 12, 1949 (for the protection of War Victims) the Hague Convention (IV) of October 18, 1907 (Respecting the Laws and Customs of War on land and the Regulations annexed thereto).[357] The Convention on the Prevention and Punishment of the Crime of Genocide of December 9, 1948[358] and the Charter of the Military Tribunal of August 8, 1945 are also included.[359]

Rape and other violence-sex offenses:[360] Bosnia article 2 and Rwanda, article 3 provide that the "[t]ribunal shall have the power to prosecute persons responsible for the following crimes, when committed as part of a widespread or systematic attack against any civilian population on national, political, ethnic, racial or religious grounds: (a) murder; (b) extermination; (c) enslavement; (d) deportation; (e) imprisonment; (f) torture; (g) rape; (h) persecutions on political, racial and religious grounds; and (i) other inhumane acts." Rape was not listed in the Nuremberg Charter indictment or judgment but was listed in Control Council Law No. 10, which further deleted "in execution of in connection with any crime within the jurisdiction of the Tribunal." Furthermore, "namely" was deleted and the phrase, "[a]trocities and offenses included but not limited to [murder, etc.]" was substituted. Crimes against humanity include crimes aimed at any civilian population and are prohibited regardless of whether they are committed in an international or internal armed conflict.[361] Other inhumane acts of a very serious nature, proscribed by relevant international law, refer to such crimes as wilful killing, torture or rape, committed as part of a widespread or systematic attack against any civilian population or political, racial or religious grounds. Does "very serious," as found in Bosnia Statute, differ from "serious?" Does article 5's phrase "in armed conflict" mean during armed conflict? Why did part (1), the introductory paragraph of the Bosnia Statute's article 5 use the term "crimes" instead of "atrocities and offenses" and "directed against" instead of "committed against," and why did it delete in (2) "including but not limited to?"

In June 1994 a United Nations panel found the "ethnic cleansing" and related "rape" are "war crimes" and legally constitute genocide.[362] Historically, rape was seen as one of the awful by-products of war and generally not prosecuted as a crime. No rape charges were brought at Nuremberg. Rape has now been indicated as a crime against humanity, but never as a "grave breach" under article 147 the 4th Geneva Convention. During World War II, it was seen as part of "military necessity," as the Japanese leadership felt that their fighting

---

356 Secretary-General's Report on Yugo Tribunal, *supra* note 321, ¶¶ 34, 35.

357 Convention (No.IV) Respecting the Laws and Customs of War on Land with Annex of Regulations, done at The Hague, Oct. 18, 1907, *entered into force*, Jan. 26, 1910, T.S. No. 539.

358 Convention on the Prevention and Punishment of the Crime of Genocide, 78 U.N.T.S. 277 (Dec. 9, 1948).

359 Charter of the International Military Tribunal, 59 Stat. 1544 (1945). The Secretary-General's Report, *supra* note 321, spells out these various offenses in ¶¶ 37-49.

360 *See generally* M. Cherif Bassiouni, *Sexual Violence: An Invisible Weapon of War in the Former Yugoslavia*, An Occasional Paper, DePaul International Human Rights Law Institute (1996); MASS RAPE: THE WAR AGAINST WOMEN IN BOSNIA-HERZEGOVINA (Alexandra Stiglmayer ed., 1994); Krishna Patel, *Recognizing the Rape of Bosnian Women as Gender-Based Persecution*, 60 BROOK. L. REV. 929 (1994).

361 Secretary-General's Report, *supra* note 321, ¶ 47.

362 *See* N.Y.L.J., vol. 211, No. 106, p. 1, col. 1 (June 3, 1994).

men needed "satisfaction," so they enslaved 200,000 Korean women for that purpose.[363] Rape, however, is explicitly listed as an offense in both ad hoc statutes. The Rwanda statute goes further in its article 4, proscribing: "(e) [o]utrages upon personal dignity, in particular humiliating and degrading treatment, rape, enforced prostitution and any form of indecent assault." Rape charges will be brought in both Ad Hoc Tribunals with vigor as crimes against humanity. Blinking at or promoting rape may render one a principal as an aider and abettor. Forced prostitution was listed in the Rwanda statute, but forced impregnation was not listed explicitly as an offense. The Bosnia statute explicitly listed only rape. Nevertheless, their criminality is implicit. Both are evidence of rape or other sexual assault. Failure to list these crimes separately may suggest a weakness in drafting. On the other hand, one might have worried that listing offenses made an exhaustive, not illustrative list.[364] Expansive listing is the common law drafter's predilection. It is not necessarily good drafting. We now must be careful to make it clear that listing some specific offenses should not suggest that others are excluded. The statute allows prosecution for forced impregnation, just as it allows prosecution for rape and other sexual assaults.

Some interest groups and individuals sometimes make hyperbolic, straw-man arguments, which may impress constituencies, but are not always accurate. Some actually have suggested, for example, that the drafters of the tribunal statutes, which actually promote prosecution of rape and other "sexual" offenses, are actually part of a cabal to diminish these offenses as crimes against humanity. The innuendo is that even those who have explicitly and vigorously promoted prosecuting these crimes against humanity are tainted with the same evil as rapists over the centuries, because they did not make forced pregnancy an explicit and separate offense.[365] Rape and other "sexual" violence must be punished.[366] The Rules of Procedure and Evidence show how far the tribunals are ready to go to convict. Rule 96, on evidence in cases of sexual assault, provides: "[i]n cases of sexual assault: (i) no corroboration of the victim's testimony shall be required;[367] (ii) consent shall not be allowed as a defense; (iii) prior sexual conduct of the victim shall not be admitted into evidence." The drafters, the prosecutors and the tribunals certainly seem to take their obligation to prosecute these horrible offenses seriously. Forced pregnancy actually was added in later drafts of the Rwanda statute. Even without that, forced pregnancy is certainly evidence of

---

[363] *See, e.g.*, David Boling, *Mass Rape, Enforced Prostitution, and the Japanese Imperial Army: Japan Eschews International Legal Responsibility?* 32 COLUM. J. TRANSNAT'L L. 533 (1995); TERRORISM, DRUGS, *supra* note 1, at Ch. 1, where we see that slaughter of whole towns (destruction of children, women, older-folks, animals, plants) were also allowed under military necessity.

[364] *See* Rachael Pine, *Pregnancy as Evidence of a Crime*, 94 NAT'L L.J. 15, col.1 (Jan. 24, 1994). Ms. Pine, who might have a career or ideological interest in hinting that even those who are for the first time explicitly and vigorously prosecuting rape as a crime against humanity, are evil because of their failure to have forced pregnancy listed as a separate crime. This goes a bit far. The writer's own title, *Pregnancy as Evidence of a Crime*, may suggest some lack of clear thinking or even promotion of purist ideology or personal interest over successful prosecution.

[365] *See, e.g.*, *id.* at 153.

[366] *See, e.g.*, Blakesley, *supra* note 232; Blakesley, *Report for the International Law Association, on Jurisdiction, Offenses, and Triggering Mechanisms for the War Crimes Tribunals*, 25 DEN. J. INT'L L. & POL'Y. 233 (1997); *Prosecuting and Defending Violations of Genocide and Humanitarian Law: The International Tribunal for the Former Yugoslavia*, 88 ASIL Annual Meeting, at 239, 243, 254 (1994); Christopher L. Blakesley, *Comparing the I.L.C. and Bosnia Tribunals*, 66 REVUE INTERNATIONALE DE DROIT PÉNAL (1995); Cheryl Benard, *Rape as Terror: The Case of Bosnia*, 6 TERRORISM & POL. VIOLENCE 29 (1994); Note, *No Justice, No Peace: Accountability for Rape and Gender-Based Violence in the Former Yugoslavia*, 5 HASTINGS W.L.J. 89 (1994).

[367] This likely includes no need for either physical or testimonial corroboration.

rape or at least some other sexual assault amounting to genocide. Proper "civilian drafting" provides a general principle which allows deduction and the resolution of specific cases.

The Statutes proscribe systematic or mass violations of human rights, genocide, torture, and "exceptionally serious war crimes." The language utilized, however, is vague and inconsistent. The articles incorporate by reference the criminal law weaknesses in those treaty "offenses." The statutes generally fail to specify the mental state required. They fail to specify adequately the nature and scope of defenses. It may be that municipal law around the world has improved on the vagueness problems. This requires the argument to be made that these municipal refinements have become general international law. Depending on the breadth and consistency of these refinements, some may have helped create general principles of international law. If the law of most nations defines certain conduct as criminal and establishes its elements in a consistent fashion, a general principle exists. It is binding as much as if it were promulgated by a legislature. This form of analysis and development is important to give meaning to the so-called "common core of crimes" that would be subject to prosecution before the Tribunal.[368] The elements of the specific offense charged, therefore, may be established by reference to customary international law and general principles determined by a comparative analysis of the law of all states. If this is so, the statutes themselves are in violation of human rights law. Thus, national law or state practice are important not only for the omnipresent question of what is international law.

Genocide: Bosnia, Article 4, and Rwanda article 2: "1. The International Tribunal shall have the power to prosecute persons committing genocide as defined in paragraph 2 of this article or of persons committing any of the other acts enumerated in paragraph 3 of this article. 2. Genocide means any of the following acts committed with intent to destroy, in whole or in part, a national, ethical, racial or religious group as such: (a) killing members of the group; (b) causing serious bodily or mental harm to members of the group; (c) deliberately inflicting on the group conditions of life calculated to bring about its physical destruction in whole or in part; (d) imposing measures intended to prevent births within the group; (e) forcibly transferring children of the group to another group. 3. The following acts shall be punishable: (a) genocide; (b) conspiracy to commit genocide; (c) direct and public incitement to commit genocide; (d) attempt to commit genocide; (e) complicity in genocide." Article 5 covers "crimes against humanity," which includes as the last item on the list, "other inhumane acts."[369]

Although very important on the merits, prosecution of genocide will be difficult. Ruth Wedgwood correctly notes that genocide and crimes against humanity are difficult.[370] Judges feel trepidation as they face cases which become geometrically more difficult each time one adds another vague element of proof.[371] The tribunals should not feel constrained to limit jurisdiction to crimes against humanity to those committed "in execution of or in connection with" crimes against peace and conventional war crimes.[372] It is difficult to prove the "specific intent" element of "to destroy, in whole or in part" of a religious, ethnic, national, or racial group.[373] It is also difficult to prove that a given commander specifically intended

[368] Elucidation of this idea is found in TERRORISM, DRUGS, *supra* note 1, at Ch. 1.

[369] Rwanda Statute, *supra* note 327, at art. 5 (i).

[370] *See* Wedgwood, *supra* note 322, at 276.

[371] *Id.*

[372] *Id.; The Formulation of the Nuremberg Principles*, 1950 U.N.Y.B. 852, 852-57.

[373] *Id.;* note the U.S. reservations and understandings relating to the Convention on Genocide, 28 I.L.M.

to destroy, in whole or in part, an indicated group, when for example his soldiers "ran amok" killing Muslim and ethnic civilians. Generally, there will be no contemporaneous statements from the commanders or from the soldiers as to which group was massacred.[374] Proving specific intent to kill is one thing; proving the specific invidious intent required for genocide is another. Currently, however, the defect of inefficient definition of international crime and controversy over how jurisdiction will obtain, perturbs any claim that there exists any common core of crimes over which an international tribunal would have jurisdiction.

More problems defining genocide: Paragraph 2 defines "genocide," not unexpectedly, to mean "any of the following acts committed with intent to destroy, in whole or in part, a national, ethnical, racial or religious group."[375] This definition is vague. This is a concern that cannot be ignored, because here we are not just merely providing aspirational rhetoric, but providing for offenses that will end-up putting individuals behind bars for life. The statutes proscribe mental harm as a form of genocide. Mental harm occurs, but its scope as genocide is problematical. Drafting must be more precise or a mechanism must be found to render definition clear. When a rhetorical or ideological purpose risks failure of the intent of the statutes—fair prosecution and conviction—it must be modified or interpreted in a way that resolves the human rights deficiencies. It would be unfortunate if those who feel that the mere drafting of a statute satisfies the need for pretense in obtaining justice succeeded. The statutes must not be allowed to be mere window-dressing or a means to allow the authorities with responsibility to pretend that they are doing something. Failure to take fully into account the requirements of criminal law and human rights protections for a fair trial poses a serious danger to success. Care must be taken to ensure that the cause of justice under humanitarian law will not severely be set back. The courts must not be allowed either to fail to convict the guilty or to become a mockery of justice as "kangaroo courts." Fortunately, the judges and prosecutors are serious individuals with a keen understanding of both aspects of the justice/fairness dichotomy. Perhaps they will be able to succeed in achieving justice with fairness.

Concurrent Jurisdiction and non-bis-in-idem—Common articles 8 and 9 and 9 and 10

The statutes provide concurrent jurisdiction between the Tribunal and national courts.[376] Both statutes also require domestic courts to defer to the primacy of the Ad Hoc Tribunals. The Tribunals' jurisdiction is primary, so that at any stage of the procedure, the Tribunal may formally request the national court(s) to defer to the Tribunal's competence.[377] Bosnia Statute Article 9 reads: "1. The International Tribunal and national courts shall have concurrent jurisdiction to prosecute persons for serious violations of international humanitarian law committed in the territory of the former Yugoslavia, since 1 January 1991. 2. The International Tribunal shall have primacy over national courts. At any stage of the procedure, the International Tribunal may formally request national courts to defer to the

---

7879, 782 (1989).

[374] *Id.*

[375] Rwanda Statute, *supra* note 327, at art. 2, ¶ 2.

[376] Secretary-General's Report on Yugo Tribunal, *supra* note 321, ¶¶ 64-65; *see U.N. Secretary General Issues Draft War Crimes Tribunal Statute*, 9 INT'L ENF. L. REP. 172, 174 (No. 5, May 1993). *See discussion in* Bassiouni, Yugoslavia Tribunal , *supra* note 319, at 306.

[377] Secretary-General's Report on Yugo Tribunal, *supra* note 376.

competence of the International Tribunal in accordance with the present Statute and the Rules of Procedure and Evidence of the International Tribunal." Rwanda Statute, Article 7 reads: "[t]he territorial jurisdiction of the [Tribunal] shall extend to the territory of Rwanda, including its land surface and airspace as well as to the territory of neighbouring states in respect of serious violations of international humanitarian law committed by Rwandan citizens." Article 8 reads: "1. The International Tribunal for Rwanda and national courts shall have concurrent jurisdiction to prosecute persons [as indicated in article 7], as well as to Rwandan citizens for such violations committed in the territory of neighbouring states, between 1 January 1994 and 31 December 1994. 2. The International Tribunal shall have primacy over national courts of all states. At any stage of the procedure, "the International Tribunal for Rwanda may formally request national courts to defer to its competence in accordance with the present Statute and the Rules of Procedure and Evidence of the International Tribunal for Rwanda."

Primacy includes capacity to retry a person, even if he or she has been convicted in a national court. [Articles 9(2) (Rwanda) and 10(2) (Bosnia) and Procedure and Evidence Rules 12 and 13]. This is not necessarily inconsistent with general notions of double jeopardy or *non-bis-in-idem*, but it does give one pause.[378] Bosnia article 10 and Rwanda article 9 require that no person shall be tried by a national court when he has already been tried in the tribunal.[379] The primacy of the Tribunal's jurisdiction is limited. Bosnia article 10(2) and Rwanda article 9(2) provide that subsequent trial by the international tribunal is allowed only when: (a) the act for which he was tried in the national court was an ordinary crime; or the national proceedings were not impartial or independent, were designed to shield the accused from the international tribunal, or the case was not diligently prosecuted. Should the Tribunal decide to assume jurisdiction over a person who has already been convicted by a national court, the former should take into consideration the extent to which any penalty imposed by the national court has already been served.[380] The key point seems to be not the characterization of the offense, but the nature of the criminal conduct and its punishability under international law. In considering the penalty to be imposed on a person convicted of a crime under the statute, the tribunal ". . . shall take into account the extent to which any penalty imposed by a national court on the same person for the same act has already been served."[381]

Protection of Human Rights: It is important that an accused not be "shielded from international criminal responsibility." There also may be some situations in which the international tribunal will be more protective of the human rights of the accused than would be a national court, which may not be "impartial" or "well-disposed." Take, for example, the worries of Justice Jackson, the Chief U.S. prosecutor during the Nuremberg Trials, noted above, and the recent trials of two Bosnian Serbs sentenced to death for war crimes in Bosnia Herzegovina.[382] The defendants were convicted after confessing, although their

---

[378] If the defendant has been convicted by the Tribunal, however, the latter has the authority under Rule 13, *mutatis mutandis,* to "request the national permanently to discontinue its proceedings."

[379] Secretary-General's Report on Yugo Tribunal, *supra* note 321, ¶ 66.

[380] *Id.* ¶ 67.

[381] Rwanda Statute, *supra* note 327, at art. 9.

[382] *See Bosnia Convicts and Sentences to Death 2 Serbs,* 9 INT'L ENF. L. REP. 147 (No. 9, Apr., 1993); John F. Burns, *2 Serbs to be Shot for Killings and Rapes*, N.Y. TIMES, March 31, 1993, at A6, col.4; David B. Ottaway, *Bosnia Convicts 2 Serbs in War Crimes Trial,* THE WASH. POST, March 31, 1993,at A21, col. 1.

confessions were not corroborated, and the defendants claimed that they had been given under torture and repeated beatings. Scars and markings found on their bodies were consistent with the claims of torture. The *ad hoc tribunals* would do well to guard against even the impression of impropriety or unfairness. Also, substantive defenses to war crimes and other international crimes should be maintained.[383] Basic notions of fairness and human rights in investigation, prosecution, and trial are paramount. If we are not scrupulous in protecting the individuals accused from abuses and deprivation of civil liberties, ultimately we will condemn the viability of an international criminal tribunal.

Conclusion

If the courts are to avoid confusion and our government is to avoid diplomatic difficulties in matters of extradition[384] and international judicial cooperation, a coherent and consistent approach to jurisdiction over the extraterritorial crimes needs to be developed.

Our purpose is to foster a proper understanding of the bases of extraterritorial jurisdiction, to promote a coherent application of those bases and to manifest the interrelationship between the philosophical ideals and notions presented in Chapters 1 and 2 and the interesting academic and practical problems of jurisdiction over extraterritorial crime. The United States recently has been attempting to expand its power abroad. Not incidentally, broad expansion of jurisdiction over extraterritorial crime has occurred. The expansion of jurisdiction is not necessarily bad, although unprincipled expansion leads to the functional abrogation or propagandistic appropriation of the rule of law. Jurisdiction becomes a procedural mechanism to accommodate philosophical and political prerogatives. Some of the expansion by United States Courts abetted by the Restatement (Third) and the Executive Branch is unfortunate. Not only does it manifest a tendency to international anarchy (we do what we have the power to do), but it also threatens certain domestic constitutional protections. It is all part of the same mentality. Its abuse is anti-conceptual, anti-rule of law and dangerous in the long run.[385]

The hybrid approach articulated herein is designed to instigate a debate on the conceptual problem created by recent case law and the Restatement Draft approach to extraterritorial jurisdiction and to propose a possible solution. The suggested approach utilized the combination of the protective and universal principles (limited by the rule of reasonableness) to allow jurisdiction over thwarted extraterritorial narcotics conspiracies or other inchoate crimes, although no effect actually occurred within the target state's territory, so long as the crime related to a universally recognized, significant state interest and had progressed far enough towards fruition to establish both the intended goals of the conspiracy and the fact that the impact or effect of the crime would have been certain to occur had intervention not prevented it. This chapter also provides the scholar, judge, and practitioner with a guide to the complexities of jurisdiction in relation to international criminal law and procedure.

---

383 Defenses analyzed in Anthony A. D'Amato, *National Prosecution for International Crimes*, *in* 3 INTERNATIONAL CRIMINAL LAW 169, 172-78 (M. Cherif Bassiouni ed., 1987).

384 The relationship of these notions on extradition is analyzed in *Conceptual Framework*, *supra* note 31.

385 Thus, a supremely practical study of *jurisdiction over extraterritorial crime* presents evidence of the moral and philosophical values presented and discussed in Chapters 1, 2, TERRORISM, DRUGS, *supra* note 1.

The desired result might be achieved in at least three ways: by applying the hybrid approach as an additional avenue through which to assert jurisdiction; by making an exception to the objective territorial theory to allow jurisdiction to be asserted over thwarted extraterritorial narcotics conspiracies with certain limitations; or by candidly abrogating the traditional bases and theories of jurisdiction and replacing them with the rule of reasonableness as the sole basis of jurisdiction over extraterritorial crime. The latter two approaches incorporate the traditional bases of jurisdiction and their hybrid combination as manifestations or aspects of reasonableness. The dangers of uncertainty, unpredictability and incoherence that are concomitant of such a revolutionary abrogation of traditional theory are significant and must be considered. Nevertheless, a frank adoption of any one of these approaches would be a significant improvement over the current approach, which leaves the law in a state of confusion, risking diplomatic dispute and denial of extradition.

Adoption of the hybrid approach or a recognition of its viability, would benefit extradition practice and diplomatic relations. It is hoped that this study will focus attention on the problem of extraterritorial jurisdiction and will foster a solution that will be conceptually sound while allowing sufficient flexibility to meet the needs of society in combating modern crime.

Immunities and Exceptions

B.J. George Jr.

Jurisdiction Over Embassies, Consulates, International Organizations and Their Personnel, and Armed Forces Stationed Abroad

History and Background of Diplomatic Immunity

A basic principle of international criminal law is that each state has full power to regulate the conduct of persons physically present within its territory and to punish those who contravene its penal legislation or doctrines.[1] Nevertheless, under customary international law there may have been a principle, or perhaps a practice, recognizing that diplomats or emissaries, and perhaps their family members and servants, were exempt from the exercise of criminal jurisdiction, although not from the abstract coverage of the criminal law. In other words, diplomats and those accompanying them were expected to comply with a receiving state's criminal laws but, if they did not, they were not to be prosecuted.[2]

Three alternative theories or justifications for the concept have emerged over the generations. The first is that of "extraterritoriality," which holds that the space used by diplomatic personnel constitutes an enclave of the sending state within the receiving state's territory.[3] Perhaps the closest surviving vestige of this theory in United States law is the treatment of some Native American tribal lands as if they were enclaves of independent nations within United States territory.[4] In this approach the receiving state's jurisdiction over diplomatic areas appears to be recognized, insofar at least as protection of those enclaves and their occupants from harm is concerned.[5] But, it fails to reflect the asserted receiving state's power to prosecute for treasonous acts against the sovereignty of the receiving state.[6]

The second theory is that a diplomat personifies or represents the sending sovereign or nation, and thus should be as exempt from the exercise of the receiving state's jurisdiction as the foreign sovereign himself, herself or itself would be.[7] This theory bears a rather close relationship to the first, but is not necessarily limited to diplomatic premises within the receiving state.

---

1 *See generally* B.J. George, *Jurisdictional Bases for Criminal Legislation and Its Enforcement,* 1983 MICH. Y.B. INT'L L. 3, 3-4.

2 *See* L.C. Green, *Trends in the Law Concerning Diplomats*, 1981 CAN. Y.B. INT'L L. 132, 132-33. The concept of diplomatic immunity appears to have been rooted in the issuance of safe conducts to emissaries, covering their travel to, sojourn in and return from a receiving state. *See* Margaret Buckley, *Origins of Diplomatic Immunity in England,* 21 U. MIAMI L. REV. 349, 349 (1966). The practice may have become institutionalized first in Renaissance Italy, *id.* at 349-50, and gained at least limited recognition in English practice. *Id.* at 350-51.

3 *See* Albert H. Garretson, *The Immunity of Representatives of Foreign States,* 41 N.Y.U. L. REV. 67, 70 (1966).

4 *See e.g., United States v. Wheeler*, 435 U.S. 313 (1978); George, *supra* note 1, at notes 33-39 and accompanying text.

5 *See infra* notes 158-88 and accompanying text.

6 *See* Buckley, *supra* note 2, at 351-55; *infra* notes 62-64 and accompanying text.

7 *See* Garretson, *supra* note 3 at 70.

The third theory, that of functional necessity, is currently the best recognized of the three; it probably evolved from the representative character theory.[8] It focuses on the functional necessity of diplomatic privileges and immunities if the purposes of embassies, missions and diplomats are to be accomplished within a receiving state.[9] Its importance is attested by its endorsement as a principal objective of the Vienna Convention on Diplomatic Relations.[10] It also appears to have been the principal basis for long-standing United States recognition of the immunity of diplomatic agents to the exercise of federal and state jurisdiction.[11]

Diplomatic immunity was first recognized in American law in the case of *Republica v. De Longchamps*,[12] but became controlling federal law through early federal legislation.[13] The 1790 law, as interpreted by federal courts over nearly 200 years, accorded full civil and criminal immunity from United States jurisdiction for diplomatic agents, their family members, members of their administrative and technical staffs (but not *their* family members), members of their service staff (but not their family members), and their private servants.[14] This quite sweeping legislation accorded greater immunity than the Vienna Diplomatic Convention[15] provided, a state of affairs viewed as unacceptable after the United States ratified the Convention in 1972. Consequently, Congress adopted the Diplomatic Relations Act of 1978, which repealed the 1790 statute and adopted the scope of immunity for members of missions and their families set forth in the Convention.[16] Hence, the Convention governs the contemporary United States law of diplomatic immunity.

---

[8] *See id.*

[9] *Id.*

[10] See Vienna Convention on Diplomatic Relations, Preamble para 5, April 18, 1961, 23 U.S.T. 3227, T.I.A.S. No. 7502, 500 U.N.T.S. (*entered into force* with respect to the United States Dec. 13, 1972) ("Realizing that the purpose of such privileges and immunities is not to benefit individuals but to ensure the efficient performance of the functions of diplomatic missions as representing states.") [hereinafter Vienna Diplomatic Conv.]

[11] Letter of Secretary of State Elihu Root, March 16, 1906, *in* 4 GREEN HAYWOOD HACKWORTH, DIGEST OF INTERNATIONAL LAW 513-14 (1942).

[12] 1 U.S. (1 Dall.) 111 (1784). De Longchamps assaulted the secretary of the French legation, who in turn beat De Longchamps severely. De Longchamps was then convicted under Pennsylvania law for having violated the law of nations. The trial court held that whenever a diplomat is attacked in any way, "his freedom of conduct is taken away, [and] the business of his Sovereign cannot be transacted." *Id.* at 117. *See* Comment, *A New Regime of Diplomatic Immunity: The Diplomatic Relations Act of 1978*, 54 TUL. L. REV. 661, 664-66 (1980).

[13] Act of April 30, 1790, ch. 9, 1 Stat. 117 (codified as 22 U.S.C.§ 252-254 (1976)), repealed by Diplomatic Relations Act, Pub. L. No. 95-393, 92 Stat. 808 (Dec. 29, 1978). *See* Tulane Law Review Comment, *supra* note 12, at 665-67.

[14] *See generally* H.R. REP. No. 95-526, 95th Cong. 1st Sess. 2 (1977); S. REP. NO. 95-1108, 95th Cong. 1st Sess. 1-2 (1978); S. REP. NO. 95-958, 95th Cong., 1st Sess. 1-3 (1978); Tulane Law Review Comment, *supra* note 12, at 665-67. The federal statute used as its model the English Diplomatic Privileges Act, 1708, 7 Anne ch. 12. *See* Buckley, *supra* note 2, at 357-60.

[15] Vienna Diplomatic Conv., *supra* note 10. *See infra* notes 64-76 and accompanying text.

[16] 22 U.S.C. § 254a (1994). The same privileges and immunities are accorded missions of nonparties to the Convention. *Id.*§ 254b. The President, on the basis of reciprocity, may either contract or expand the coverage otherwise contemplated in the Convention. *Id.* § 254c. The President has delegated the authority under § 254c (and the liability insurance provisions of §254e) to the Secretary of State, without presidential ratification. Exec. Order No. 12, 101, 43 Fed. Reg. 54, 195 (1978).

The Vienna Diplomatic Convention is the controlling source of international law in this area because, as of January 1, 1996, 173 states have adopted it.[17] Although it recognizes that customary international law continues to govern questions not regulated expressly by its provisions,[18] the comprehensive character of its coverage seemingly relegates to history the traditional doctrines to be found in sources antedating its adoption. Therefore, the ensuing text uses its provisions as a foundation stone for discussion of diplomatic immunities and exceptions from criminal jurisdiction.[19]

Immunity of Foreign States From Forum Jurisdiction

The doctrine of sovereign immunity, as recognized in international law, means that a state or state instrumentality is immune from the jurisdiction of the courts of another state, except in case of activities of the kind that may be carried on by private persons.[20] For example, a state is not immune in cases arising out of its commercial activity.[21] On the other hand, a state is not immune from the *prescriptive* jurisdiction of another state, except with respect to diplomatic and consular activities, as discussed below. In carrying on activities in another state, a state is thus obliged to observe the laws of that state[22] and when its activities are of private character, the state does not enjoy immunity from adjudication.[23] That means that forum criminal law can extend to activities by foreign trading and other commercial entities, even though government-owned or operated within the forum nations.[24] Obviously, problems of sovereign immunity are of only peripheral concern in criminal justice administration.

Diplomatic Immunity—Persons Covered

Diplomatic agents of a state who are accredited to and accepted by another state are immune from civil and criminal processes of that state as well as from the exercise of prescriptive jurisdiction by that state with respect to the exercise of their official functions.[25]

---

17 UNITED STATES DEPARTMENT OF STATE, TREATIES IN FORCE: A LIST OF TREATIES AND OTHER INTERNATIONAL AGREEMENTS OF THE UNITED STATES IN FORCE ON JANUARY 1, 1996 345-46 (1996)[hereinafter TREATIES IN FORCE]. The Government of Taiwan also has adhered to the Convention, although that entity is not a formal participant of the United Nations. *Id* at 346 n.3.

18 Vienna Diplomatic Conv., *supra* note 10, Preamble para. 6 ("Affirming that the rules of customary international law should continue to govern questions not expressly regulated by the provisions of the present Convention . . ." *Id.*).

19 English statutes implementing the Convention are Diplomatic Privileges Act, 1964 c. 81, and Diplomatic and Other Privileges Act, 1971 c. 64.

20 RESTATEMENT (THIRD) OF FOREIGN RELATIONS LAW OF THE UNITED STATES § 451 (1987) [hereinafter RESTATEMENT (THIRD)]. "A state instrumentality includes a corporation, association, or other jurisdical person a majority of whose shares or other ownership interests are owned by the state, even when organized for profit." *Id.* §452 cmt.a.

21 *See id.* § 453.

22 *See* § 461 cmt. a.

23 *Id.*

24 One should distinguish the problems created by the United States efforts to give extraterritorial reach to the enforcement of federal antitrust and securities legislation. *See* George, *supra* note 1, at 15-18. There is no problem, however, in invoking such regulatory legislation concerning activities within the United States.

25 RESTATEMENT (THIRD) *supra* note 20, §464. *See also* Vienna Diplomatic Conv., *supra* note 10, arts. 29 (freedom from arrest or detention) and 31 (immunity from criminal, civil, and administrative jurisdiction).

This immunity extends to "diplomatic agents,"[26] the chief of whom is the head of the mission.[27] The members of the mission staff with diplomatic rank[28] are also within the span of immunity, as are members of the administrative and technical staff of a mission.[29] A mission's personnel may include as well members of a mission service staff performing clerical and caretaking functions.[30] A basic principle under the Vienna Diplomatic Convention is that diplomatic staff members should be nationals of a sending state;[31] nationals of a receiving state may be so appointed only with the consent of their government, subject to revocation at will.[32] Members of the administrative, technical or service staff of a mission or family members of a diplomatic agent or mission staff member do not enjoy immunity if they are nationals of the receiving state or have been admitted as permanent residents of that state.[33]

A head of a mission must be presented through accreditation to a receiving state for its approval.[34] That state can refuse its *agreement* without being obliged to indicate its grounds.[35] In the instance of other members of a mission, family members and private servants, advance approval by the receiving state is not expected or authorized.[36] Instead, a sending state at some time should notify the appropriate receiving state agency (the Department of State when the United States is the receiving state) of the fact of appointment of members of missions and termination of their assignments[37] and is encouraged to give prior notice of their arrival and final departure.[38] Notice of arrival and final departures of family members also must be given,[39] as well as the arrival and final departure of private servants in the employ of mission members.[40]

---

26 Defined in the Vienna Diplomatic Conv., *supra* note 10, at art. 1(e)(as "the head of the mission or a member of the diplomatic staff of the mission.").

27 As designated by the sending state to undertake that assigned duty. Vienna Diplomatic Conv., *supra* note 10, art. 1(a).

28 *Id.* arts. 1(d), 29.

29 *Id.* arts. 1(f), 29, 37(2).

30 *Id.* arts. 1(g), 37(3) (concerning acts in the performance of their duties). Private servants or employees of members of a mission are exempt only from payment of receiving state income taxes; otherwise, they are subject to receiving state law. *Id.* art. 37(4).

31 *Id.* art. 8(1).

32 *Id.* art. 8(2). The consent may be withdrawn at any time. *Id.* The same holds true of mission members who are nationals of a third state without dual nationality in the sending state. *Id.*

33 *Id.* art. 37.

34 *Id.* art. 4(1).

35 *Id.* art. 4(2). Two or more states may accredit one person as the head of the mission unless a receiving state objects, *id.* at art. 6, and a single state may designate one individual as head of missions to two or more receiving states unless one of the latter objects. *Id.* art. 5(1).

36 *See id.* art. 7 ("Subject to the provisions of Articles 5, 8, 9 and 11, the sending State may freely appoint the members of the mission."). However, a receiving state may require advance approval of military, naval or air attaches. *Id.*

37 *Id.* art. 10(1)(a).

38 *Id.* art. 10(2).

39 *Id.* art. 10(1)(b). Notice should be given where appropriate of the fact that a person has become or ceased to be a family member of a member of the mission. *Id.*

On the scope of privileges and immunities for family members of members of diplomatic missions, *see* Patrick J. O'Keefe, *Privileges and Immunities of the Diplomatic Family,* 25 INT'L & COMP. L.Q. 329 (1976).

40 Vienna Diplomatic Conv., *supra* note 10, art. 10(1)(c). This should include the fact that a private servant is leaving a mission member's employ. *Id.* Notification extends to the engagement or discharge of persons resident in the receiving state as members of a mission or private servants eligible for privileges and immunities. *Id.* art. 10(1)(d).

The Department of State maintains a diplomatic list ("Blue List") of all diplomatic officers and their spouses, and a list of other diplomatic personnel and the private servants of diplomatic officers ("White List").[41] A State Department listing is presumptive evidence that a given individual holds diplomatic status,[42] as contrasted with an official certification by the department to a court, which has conclusive effect.[43]

Immunity according sending-state personnel within a receiving state also must be extended to those who are in transit through a nation on their way to a receiving state.[44]

Diplomatic Immunity—Nations Covered

The Vienna Diplomatic Convention delineates the nations, the diplomatic missions of which are covered by immunity principles, in the sense that it binds all states which ratify it[45] except as they note reservations to its coverage.[46] Congress has gone beyond the requirements of the Convention to accord the privileges and immunities established through the Convention to missions, family members of mission members and diplomatic couriers of nonmember states.[47] In addition, the United States adopted an unprecedented agreement as an aftermath to the diplomatic recognition by the United States of the People's Republic of China and the incidental termination of relations with the Republic of China (Taiwan). Under the general authorization of 1979 legislation,[48] the federal government sponsored an agreement between the American Institute in Taiwan[49] and the Taiwanese Coordination

---

41 *See* RESTATEMENT (THIRD), *supra* note 20, §464, Reporter's Note 1. The listing is accomplished through sending state notices to the Department of State. *Id.*

42 *Id.* (citing authorities).

43 *Id.* (citing authorities).

44 Vienna Diplomatic Conv., *supra* note 10, art. 40(1)-(2). *See* RESTATEMENT (THIRD), *supra* note 20, § 464, Reporters' Note 11 (citing authorities); *Regina v. Guildhall Magistrates' Court,* Ex parte Jarret-Thorpe, *London Times* (Q.B. Div. Ct., Oct. 5, 1977)(immunity is extended to family members during travel to or from receiving state, whether accompanying diplomat or traveling separately, on the basis of Diplomatic Privileges Act, 1964, art. 40).

45 *See supra* note 19 and accompanying text, concerning the number of ratifying states. Efforts by adherents to the self-proclaimed "Republic of New Africa," which has asserted sovereignty over the states of Mississippi, Alabama, Louisiana, Georgia and South Carolina, to claim diplomatic immunity have been rejected summarily by federal courts. *See e.g., United States v. James*, 528 F.2d 999, 1016 (5th Cir.), *cert. denied,* 429 U.S. 959 (1976); *United States v. Lumumba*, 578 F.Supp. 100, 103 (S.D.N.Y. 1983).

46 At least 23 states have entered one or more reservations. TREATIES IN FORCE, *supra* note 17, at 345-46. *See* Note, *Murder in the Casbah or The Effect of Morocco's Jurisdictional Reservation to the Vienna Convention on Diplomatic Relations,* 11 INT'L L. & POL. 299 (1978).

47 22 U.S.C. §254b (1994). Under the provisions of 22 U.S.C.§ 288h (1994), diplomatic privileges and immunities have been extended to the Commission of the European Communities mission to the United States and its members.

48 Taiwan Relations Act of 1979, Pub. L. No. 96-8, 93 Stat. 14 (1979), 22 U.S.C.§§ 3301 *et seq.* (1994). The President is authorized to extend to the Taiwan instrumentality and its appropriate personnel those privileges and immunities necessary for the effective performance of their functions. 22 U.S.C. § 3309(c) (1994). See RESTATEMENT (THIRD), *supra* note 20,§ 464 Reporters' Note 1. Congress empowered the President to extend the privileges and immunities of a diplomatic mission and its members to the Liaison Office of the People's Republic of China, 22 U.S.C. § 288i (1994). That was accomplished through Executive Order No. 11,771, 39 Fed. Reg. 10,415 (March 9, 1974).

49 A nonprofit corporation incorporated in the District of Columbia and staffed by United States government employees on temporary leave. *See* Note, *International Agreements: United States-Taiwan Relations,* 22 HARV. INT'L L.J. 451 n.1 (1982) [hereinafter *United States-Taiwan Relations*].

Council for North American Affairs[50] which set up various privileges, exemptions and immunities for the two entities.[51] Under this agreement, personal diplomatic immunity is extended to staff members of the two organizations, limited to acts in the course of official duties;[52] it does not extend to staff activities of a personal nature or to family members under any circumstances.[53]

Diplomatic Immunity—Duration of Immunity

An immune status is generated at the time of appointment[54] and continues for a reasonable period of time after termination of that status, appropriate to completing arrangements to leave the receiving state.[55] If the individual remains in the receiving state after expiration of that period, he or she can be prosecuted or proceeded against for other than official acts done within the scope of authority during the period of immunity,[56] because while the immunity affects the power to charge and adjudicate, it does not entirely limit legislative competence to prescribe.[57]

Diplomatic Immunity—Activities Covered

As noted, the prohibition against legislating and enforcing extends to acts and omissions of mission heads and members relating to their official functions.[58] This may be characterized as the substantive law dimension of diplomatic immunity. Those functions comprise, generally; (a) representing the sending state within the receiving state; (b)

---

50 A private corporation registered in Taiwan with offices in Taiwan and Washington, D.C., recognized by President Carter under 22 U.S.C. § 3309(c) (1994), as Taiwan's unofficial instrumentality to conduct its unofficial relations with the United States. Exec. Order No. 12, 143, 44 Fed. Reg. 37, 191 (1979). *See United States-Taiwan Relations, supra* note 49, at 451 n. 2.

51 Executed Oct. 2, 1980. *See generally United States-Taiwan Relations, supra* note 49, at 451.

52 Art. V(e). *See United States-Taiwan Relations, supra* note 49, at 453.

53 *Id.* at 454.

54 Vienna Diplomatic Conv., *supra* note 10, art. 13, notes that the head of a mission is considered to have taken up his or her official functions at the time of either presentation of credentials or notification of arrival coupled with presentation of a true copy of those credentials to the Department of State ("Ministry of Foreign Affairs," in Convention usage). However, art. 13 is significant chiefly in terms of precedence of heads of various sending state missions under arts. 16-17; it does not affect the basic (and traditional) premise that immunity attaches once an accredited or appointed mission head or member actually enters the territory of a receiving state, or has his or her appointment notified if already present in the receiving state. *Id.* art. 39(1).

55 *See id.* art. 39(2) ("When the functions of a person enjoying privileges and immunities have come to an end, such privileges and immunities shall normally cease at the moment when he leaves the country, or on expiry of a reasonable period in which to do so, but shall subsist until that time, even in case of armed conflict."). *See also* RESTATEMENT (THIRD), *supra* note 20, § 464 Reporters' Note 10.

If a mission member dies in office, family members continue to enjoy the privileges and immunities to which they are entitled under Vienna Diplomatic Conv., *supra* note 10, art. 37(1)-(2), for a reasonable period while they leave the receiving state. *Id.* art. 39(3).

56 *Id.* art. 39 (a).

57 Jurisdiction to prescribe law can extend to anything not relating to "acts or omissions in the exercise of . . . official functions" or other law that would not be incompatible with the agent's diplomatic status. RESTATEMENT (THIRD), *supra* note 20, § 464. Otherwise, diplomatic agents are subject to criminal law and traffic regulations, even though they cannot be proceeded against during a period of immunity. *See* RESTATEMENT (THIRD), *supra* note 20, § 464 at 26, cmt c.

58 *See* RESTATEMENT (THIRD), *supra* note 20, § 464.

protecting the interests of the sending state and its nationals within the receiving state, within the limits of international law; (c) negotiating with the receiving state government; (d) ascertaining, through lawful means, conditions and developments in the receiving state and reporting on them to the sending state; and (e) promoting friendly relations between the two states, including economic, cultural and scientific relations.[59] Presumably, a receiving state determines whether a plea of immunity is properly advanced.[60] A sending state, if dissatisfied with a receiving state's assertion of jurisdiction, can protest through diplomatic channels.

Diplomatic Immunity–Freedom from Arrest

An important dimension of diplomatic immunity is freedom from arrest or detention by authorities of a receiving state. This is specific under the Vienna Diplomatic Convention.[61] However, this should not affect the ability of representatives of a receiving state to exercise forms of protective custody when, for example, a person holding diplomatic status is under the influence of a substance or mentally incompetent, and thus in a position of jeopardy if left to his or her own devices.[62] The same should hold true if the objective of noncriminal arrest or detention is for the protection of third persons.[63]

Diplomatic Immunity–Freedom from Criminal Prosecution

The basic premise underlying diplomatic immunity is that diplomatic agents enjoy immunity against the exercise of criminal jurisdiction by a receiving state.[64] This includes offenses directed against a receiving state,[65] whether or not that conforms to customary

---

[59] Vienna Diplomatic Conv., *supra* note 10, art. 3(1). A diplomatic mission also may perform consular functions. *Id.* art. 3(2). Because the listed functions are, *inter alia*, an *ejusdem generis* approach properly may be taken to make a determination of whether nonlisted activities also may lie within the scope of immunity. *See generally* RESTATEMENT (THIRD), *supra* note 20, §464 Reporters' Note 2.

[60] *See infra* notes 96-97 and accompanying text, concerning the mode of asserting immunity in American proceedings. An illustration is *People v. Leo*, 96 Misc. 2d 408, 407 N.Y.S.2d 941 (Crim. Ct. 1978) (disallowing a claim of diplomatic immunity advanced by a Tanzanian national employed by the United Nations, charged with having assaulted an unwanted visitor in his home).

[61] Vienna Diplomatic Conv., *supra* note 10, art. 29. *See also* RESTATEMENT (THIRD), *supra* note 20, § 464 & cmt. d.

[62] This is implicit in the terms "arrest or detention" in Vienna Diplomatic Conv., *supra* note 10, art. 29. It seems also to be recognized generally. *See* RESTATEMENT (THIRD), *supra* note 20, § 464 cmt. d.

[63] *See* RESTATEMENT (THIRD), *supra* note 20, § 464 cmt. d.

[64] Vienna Diplomatic Conv., *supra* note 10, art. 31(1); RESTATEMENT (THIRD), *supra* note 20, § 464 & cmt. e.

[65] Although diplomatic personnel have a duty not to interfere in the internal affairs of a receiving state, *see* Vienna Diplomatic Conv., *supra* note 10, art. 41(1); RESTATEMENT (THIRD), *supra* note 20,§ 464 Reporters' Note 3; Green, *supra* note 2, at 149-51, this does not affect the sweep of the general immunity in Vienna Diplomatic Conv., *supra* note 10, art. 31(1).

On espionage prosecutions against citizens of Bulgaria and the U.S.S.R. who were not found to enjoy protected diplomatic status, *see United States v. Kostadinov*, 734 F.2d 905 (2d Cir.), *cert. denied,* 105 S. Ct. 246 (1984); *United States v. Enger*, 472 F. Supp. 490 (D.N.J. 1978); Note, *A Comparison and Analysis of Immunities Defenses Raised by Soviet Nationals Indicted Under United States Espionage Laws,* 6 BROOK. J. INT'L L. 259 (1980).

international law principles.[66] Traffic violations are included,[67] which has created a significant source of friction between diplomatic personnel and states and localities in which large numbers of foreign diplomatic personnel have been stationed. Nevertheless, privileged mission staff members cannot be arrested or brought into court, no matter how serious a traffic law contravention they may have committed. At most, it seems possible to ticket for infractions, for example, parking and speeding violations, and forward the process for payment of penalties to the mission to which an offender is posted.[68]

Diplomatic Immunity—Privilege Against Giving Evidence

In contrast to the immunity accorded diplomatic agents from the exercise of criminal jurisdiction[69] and most exercises of civil and administrative jurisdiction,[70] the convention creates a form of privileges: "A diplomatic agent is not obliged to give evidence as a witness."[71] In contrast to the necessity of waiver by a sending state before immunity from the exercise of criminal, civil or administrative jurisdiction evaporates,[72] the discretion to invoke or relinquish the privilege appears to lie with the diplomatic agent. But he will usually need to obtain the consent of his state before he may yield his privilege not to testify.[73]

Waiver of Diplomatic Immunity

The immunity against exercise of criminal, civil or administrative jurisdiction is that of a sending state itself and not of a diplomatic agent of that state.[74] Consequently, even though

---

66 *See supra* note 6 and accompanying text.

67 RESTATEMENT (THIRD), *supra* note 20,§ 464 Reporters' Note 8.

68 *See id* (" . . . it is increasingly accepted that the issuance of a traffic "ticket" is not a violation of his immunity and the ticket may be forwarded to the foreign mission for payment." *Id.*).

69 Vienna Diplomatic Conv., *supra* note 10, art. 31(1); *see supra* notes 67-71 and accompanying text.

70 Vienna Diplomatic Conv., *supra* note 10, art. 31(1) (except a real action against private immovable property, other than property held on behalf of a sending state for purposes of a mission is situated in a receiving state's territory; actions concerning succession when a diplomatic agent is involved as executor, administrator, heir or legatee as a private person and not on behalf of the sending state; and actions relating to professional or commercial activity exercised by a diplomatic agent within a receiving state outside the scope of the agent's official functions). Only in such instances may measures of execution be taken concerning a diplomatic agent, and even then those measures are not to infringe the inviolability of the agent's person or residence. *Id.* art. 31(3). *See* RESTATEMENT (THIRD), *supra* note 20, § 464 *&* cmt. f.

71 Vienna Diplomatic Conv., *supra* note 10, art. 31(2). *See also* RESTATEMENT (THIRD), *supra* note 20, § 464 & cmt. f; *infra* note 218 and accompanying text (consular immunity).

72 *See infra* notes 77-83 and accompanying text.

73 RESTATEMENT (THIRD), *supra* note 20, § 464 cmt. f. Those cases which are concerned with the possibility of a submission to countersuit under Convention art. 32(3), seem of limited relevancy to criminal proceedings. Be that as it may, however, efforts to use subpoenas duces tecum and like process against the official property and papers of missions and diplomatic agents contravene the direct protection accorded to such property under the Convention. *See infra* notes 112-13 and accompanying text.

74 RESTATEMENT (THIRD), *supra* note 20, § 464 cmt. j ("Immunities under this section [§464], even when they relate to private acts, are not the personal rights of the individual agent, but are countered by international law or the sending state. " *Id.*); §464 Reporters' Note 15. Article 32 (1) of the Vienna Diplomatic Conv., *supra* note 10, prescribes that "the immunity from jurisdiction of diplomatic agents. . . may be waived by the sending State." No provision exists in the Convention for the agent's waiver of the immunity in the absence of his state's prior consent. *See* RESTATEMENT (THIRD), *supra* note 20, § 464 cmt. j.

an agent is amenable to the exercise of receiving state competence, that competence cannot be asserted in the face of a sending state's refusal to waive immunity.[75] Moreover, a sending state, under international law principles, has no obligation to waive its immunity, even though a serious crime is involved and a receiving state has asked specifically for a waiver.[76]

A sending state may, of course, choose to waive immunity,[77] but that waiver must be express.[78] The implication to be drawn from the language of Article 32(2) of the Convention that blanket waivers are unacceptable is obvious in the context of crimes by sending state diplomatic agents, because a blanket advance authorization might well embody an assumption that those agents will commit criminal offenses. American courts are reluctant to acknowledge that possibility as an acceptable premise.[79] Accordingly, criminal jurisdiction should be assertable only on the basis of a clear indication by the sending state that it wishes to waive the immunity of the individual involved.[80]

---

[75] The sending state has no obligation to waive immunity. *See* RESTATEMENT (THIRD), *supra* note 20, § 464 cmt. j. If the sending state elects not to waive immunity, it may recall the agent. *Id.* In the event that it does not do so, however, the receiving state may declare the agent *persona non grata* and ask that he be recalled. *Id.* If the agent is not recalled or does not leave the receiving state within a reasonable time, the receiving state may refuse to continue to recognize him as a member at the sending state's mission and deny him diplomatic immunities.§ 464 cmt.b. *See also* Vienna Diplomatic Conv., *supra* note 10, art. 9.

[76] *See* RESTATEMENT (THIRD), *supra* note 20, § 464 cmt. j

[77] Vienna Diplomatic Conv., *supra* note 10, art. 32(1) ("immunity . . . may be waived by the sending State"). Several cases recently arose in which the United States as the receiving state has requested waivers of immunity. In the case of a Russian and a Belarussian diplomat charged in New York County with driving while intoxicated, resisting arrest, harassment and disorderly conduct, the State Department plans to seek a waiver of diplomatic immunity from the sending states. *See U. S. Department of State Daily Press Briefing,* June 5, 1997, M2 PRESSWIRE, *available in* LEXIS, NEWS LIBRARY. In the case of a Georgian diplomat charged with involuntary manslaughter and aggravated assault for a drunk driving accident which resulted in the death of a teenager, the United States sought and received from Georgia, the sending state, a waiver of the diplomat's immunity. *See* Bill Miller, *U.S. Officially Asks Georgia to Waive Diplomat's Immunity,* THE WASHINGTON POST, Feb. 12, 1997, at B1, *available in* LEXIS, NEWS LIBRARY; Scott Bowles, *Diplomat's Immunity is Waived,* THE WASHINGTON POST, Feb 16. 1997, at A1, *available in* LEXIS, NEWS LIBRARY. In connection with that waiver, Nicholas Burns, State Department spokesman said "This is an unusual case . . . there are very few instances in diplomatic history where a government has lifted diplomatic immunity in a case like this, where the charges are so serious." Scot Bowles, *Diplomat's Immunity is Waived,* THE WASHINGTON POST, Feb. 16, 1997, at A1. In other recent cases arising from traffic accidents and drunk driving involving a Kyrgyzs diplomat and a wife of an Ukrainian diplomat, the State Department also sought waivers of immunity. *See U. S. To Seek Waiver of Immunity for Ukrainian,* REUTERS NORTH AMERICAN WIRE; April 14, 1997, available in LEXIS, NEWS LIBRARY *U. S Department of State Daily Press Briefing,* M2 PRESSWIRE, Apr. 14 & Apr. 15,1997, *available in* LEXIS, NEWS LIBRARY.

Publicity of cases like these led to the introduction of the Diplomatic Immunity Reform Bill in May 1997 in Congress. The Bill calls on the State Department to pursue waivers of immunity when diplomats commit crimes in the U. S. and should the sending state refuse to grant the waiver, the Bill would oblige the sending state to prosecute the diplomat under its own laws. *See* Ken Foskett, *Diplomatic Immunity under Fire,* THE ATLANTA JOURNAL AND CONSTITUTION, May 22, 1997, at 9A, *available in* LEXIS, NEWS LIBRARY.

[78] *Id.* art. 32(2) ("Waiver must always be express"). Silence on the part of a mission will not suffice. *See* RESTATEMENT (THIRD), *supra* note 20, § 464 Reporters' Note 15 (citing civil authorities).

[79] Thus, royal or executive clemency in the form of a pardon cannot be exercised in advance of the commission of a criminal act, but only after the act has been committed. *See generally Schick v. Reed,* 419 U.S. 256 (1974); Luis Kutner, *A Legal Note on the Nixon Pardon: Equal Justice vis-à-vis Due Process,* 9 AKRON L. REV. 243, 244 (1975). Nor will the Supreme Court allow would-be Federal Civil Rights Act [42 U.S.C. §§ 1983, 1985 (1994)] class action plaintiffs to assume that they or others like them will commit future crimes and thus be subject to unlawful police action. *See City of Los Angles v. Lyons,* 461 U.S. 95, 102-03 (1983) (discussing *O'Shea v. Littleton,* 414 U.S. 488, 493-97 (1974)).

[80] Waiver can be accomplished concerning civil counterclaims if a diplomatic agent otherwise enjoying immunity initiates a proceeding. Vienna Diplomatic Conv., *supra* note 10, art. 32(3). This has no application to American criminal proceedings because private persons cannot initiate private prosecutions. The Convention, art.

As noted previously,[81] because the immunity extends not to the power to legislate or prescribe, but exclusively to the power to charge and adjudicate if a diplomatic agent or protected family member or servant chooses to remain within the receiving state after the termination of his or her employment or assignment, and a reasonable time for leaving the receiving state has expired, there is no bar under the Convention or principles of customary international law to exercising criminal jurisdiction.[82]

The immunity of a diplomatic agent against exercise of the receiving state's criminal jurisdiction does not extend to the assertion of the sending state's criminal competence, a premise acknowledged in the Convention.[83] Whether that can be done, of course, depends on whether the penal law of the sending state reflects the exercise of legislative competence based on the nationality of an offending diplomatic agent or the impact of a criminal act within a receiving state on a protected interest of the sending state.[84] If a sending state will not waive and cannot assert its own powers to prosecute, adjudicate and punish, a diplomatic agent will enjoy a freedom from criminal law controls, a situation hardly conducive to either international or national order.

The Power to Expel Immune Offenders

Under the Vienna Diplomatic Convention a receiving state can notify that the head of a mission or any member of the diplomatic staff is *persona non grata;*[85] no reason need be

32(4), provides that a separate waiver is required for execution of judgment in connection with a civil or administrative matter. Although the language of the Convention is not precise on the point, one may assume that quasi-criminal or civil *in rem* forfeitures based on a transaction, some aspects of which contravene receiving state criminal statutes, would have to be subject of an express waiver under art. 32(1)-(2), even though immunity from the exercise of criminal prosecution powers has already been waived under those provisions.

A federal statute, 8 U.S.C. §1257 (1994), requires resident aliens who accept employment with a foreign mission in the United States to waive all "rights, privileges, exceptions and immunities under any law or any executive order which would otherwise accrue" to them, other than those immunities which United States nationals enjoy in respect of official acts. This statute, by its language, would seem not to allow a blanket waiver of immunity from criminal prosecutions, in the United States nationals benefit from the provisions of Convention art. 31(1) until the United States waives immunity under art. 32(1)-(2); a resident alien has the same protection.

United States practice requires that the Secretary of State waive immunity for the country's diplomatic agents upon the express request of the chief of a mission. *See* RESTATEMENT (THIRD), *supra* note 20, § 464 Reporters' Note 15.

See generally O'Keefe, *supra* note 39, at 346-47.

[81] *See supra* notes 59-60 and accompanying text.

[82] *See supra* note 78; Vienna Diplomatic Conv., *supra* note 10, art.9; RESTATEMENT (THIRD), *supra* note 20, § 464 cmt. b. However, this is true only of offenses not based on acts done in the course of diplomatic activities. Immunity for acts of the latter character remains intact permanently. Vienna Diplomatic Conv., *supra* note 10, art. 39(2).

[83] Vienna Diplomatic Conv., *supra* note 10, art. 31(4).

[84] *See* George, *supra* note 1, at 3-4. Federal criminal law has little, if any, application to criminal acts by United States diplomatic agents committed abroad. In addition, federal courts apply a presumption of exclusively domestic or internal application of penal law which can be rebutted only through proof of a clear expression of congressional intent to provide for extraterritorial application. *See United States v. Mitchell*, 533 F.2d 996, 1001-05 (5th Cir. 1977); George, *supra* note 1, at 6. Whether multiple prosecutions in both sending and receiving states are possible turns on whether the law of the state which proceeds second recognizes a *non bis in idem* principle governing either prosecution or punishment.

[85] Vienna Diplomatic Conv., *supra* note 10, art. 9 (1). *See also* RESTATEMENT (THIRD), *supra* note 20, §464 cmt. b; Green, *supra* note 2, at 152-54; J.G. Fennessy, *The 1975 Vienna Convention on the Representation of States in Their Relations With International Organizations of a Universal Character*; 70 AM. J. INT'L L. 62,67-

given for that action.[86] Upon receipt of such a declaration, the sending state must either recall the individual or terminate his or her functions with the mission.[87] After a reasonable time has elapsed for a person declared *non grata* to leave the receiving state, immunity is destroyed and the receiving state may arrest and prosecute the formerly immune offender.[88]

United States Jurisdiction in Immunity Matters

Under the federal Constitution,[89] the judicial power of the United States extends to all cases affecting ambassadors, other public ministers and consuls, and the Supreme Court has original jurisdiction over them.[90] In 1978, Congress gave the Supreme Court "original but not exclusive" jurisdiction over all actions or proceedings to which ambassadors, other public ministers, consuls, or vice-consuls of foreign states are parties[91] and at the same time allotted to federal district courts jurisdiction exclusive of state courts over civil actions and proceedings against members of missions or their family members.[92] The concurrent jurisdiction thus created would govern only noncriminal matters; original criminal jurisdiction would seem, therefore, still to rest with the Supreme Court, assuming a sending state should waive immunity in a criminal matter.[93] Because that seemingly has not happened, there is no criminal precedent on the point.[94]

---

70 (1976). This is an appropriate response to, *e.g.*, a terrorist act committed by diplomatic agents of foreign states who are immune to receiving state criminal prosecution. *See* RESTATEMENT (THIRD), *supra* note 20, §464 cmt.b.

86 Vienna Diplomatic Conv., *supra* note 10, art. 9(1).

87 *Id.* art. 9(1). It may select whichever alternative it prefers under the circumstances. *Id.*

88 *Id.* art. 9(2), providing that if a sending state refuses or fails within a reasonable period to carry through its obligation to recall or terminate diplomatic status, a receiving state may refuse to recognize the person concerned as a member of the mission." *See Regina v. Palacios,* [1984] 1 O.A.C. 356 (Ct. App.), confirming under the Vienna Diplomatic Conv., *supra* note 10, at arts. 10 & 39, that a diplomatic agent charged with violating the Canadian government had been notified by Palacios' government of the withdrawal of his diplomatic status, followed by a one-week visit to the United States and a return to Canada. Because Palacious had not yet had a reasonable time to leave, the criminal charges brought against him were properly dismissed on the basis of his assertion of immunity.

Because the competence to prescribe has remained intact throughout a period of immunity, *see supra* notes 59-60 and accompanying text, at least concerning acts done in furtherance of diplomatic mission responsibilities, *see supra* note 85, the power to prosecute, adjudicate and sanction revives when Convention art. 9(2) concepts come into play. At that time, also, a receiving state may notify a sending state that it refuses to recognize the diplomatic agent as a member of the sending state's mission. Vienna Diplomatic Conv., *supra* note 10, art. 43(b).

If a receiving state only requests that a diplomatic agent be withdrawn, without declaring him or her *persona non grata,* the individual continues to function and enjoy immunity until he or she actually is withdrawn by the sending state.

One should note that the termination of diplomatic relations, including occasions of armed conflict between sending and receiving states, does not destroy diplomatic privileges and immunities of non-nationals of a receiving state's mission. Vienna Diplomatic Conv., *supra* note 10, art. 39(2). A receiving state must allow them and their families to depart at the earliest possible moment and, if necessary, provide means of transportation for them and their property. *Id.* art. 44.

89 U.S. CONST. art. III, § 2.

90 *Id.*

91 28 U.S.C. § 1251(b)(1) (1994).

92 *Id.* § 1351. *See* RESTATEMENT (THIRD), *supra* note 20, § 464 Reporters' Note 16.

93 *See supra* notes 81-83 and accompanying text.

94 However, there have been recent cases where the U.S. State Department sought waivers of immunity from the sending states and which may result in criminal prosecutions of the diplomatic agents in the United States. *See supra* note 80 (listing such cases).

If a criminal prosecution or civil action has been brought against an individual entitled to immunity under the Convention, the appropriate action is dismissal based on the defendant's motion or suggestion, or other appropriate procedural action established by law or procedural rules.[95] The congressional enactment governs state prosecutions as well as federal.[96]

Immunity of Diplomatic Premises and Property

A receiving state must facilitate recognized sending states' acquisition of premises appropriate to their mission[97] and accommodations for their mission staff members.[98] Once premises have been established, a receiving state must hold them inviolable and its representatives cannot enter the state without consent by the mission head.[99] Nevertheless, consent may be presumed in case of fire and other emergencies.[100] Moreover, mission premises are not viewed as beyond a receiving state's power to prescribe, so that zoning, safety and other regulatory measures may be enforced,[101] and persons not protected by diplomatic or consular immunity may be prosecuted for their criminal acts committed on mission premises.[102]

The Convention cautions that mission premises are not to be used in ways incompatible with mission functions delineated by the convention or other rules of international law or special agreements in force between sending and receiving states.[103] That raises delicate issues if a sending state mission accords diplomatic asylum by accepting fugitives or refugees within its premises and refuses entry to representatives of the receiving state for

---

[95] 22 U.S.C. § 254d (1994). *See Regina v. Palacios*, [1984] 1 O.A.C. 356 (Ct. App.), discussed *supra* note 91, which rejected a prosecution effort to obtain mandamus to override a trial court dismissal of charges based on a claim of diplomatic immunity.

[96] U.S. CONST. art. II, § 3, cl. 1 (presidential power to receive ambassadors and other public ministers), in relation to *id.* art. I, § 8, cl. 18 (necessary and proper legislation to carry into execution "all other powers vested by this Constitution in the Government of the United States").

[97] Vienna Diplomatic Conv., *supra* note 10, art. 21(1) (facilitate the acquisition or assist in some other way). However, sending states may not establish mission offices away from the primary location of a mission without the express consent of the receiving state. Vienna Diplomatic Conv., *supra* note 10, art. 12. A mission and its head have the right to display the flag and emblem of the sending state on premises, including the residence of the head of mission, and on vehicles. *Id.* art. 20.

[98] Vienna Diplomatic Conv., *supra* note 10, art. 21(2) ("where necessary").

[99] *Id.* at art. 22(1). *See* RESTATEMENT (THIRD), *supra* note 20, § 466.

Inviolability extends to the private residence of a diplomatic agent. Vienna Diplomatic Conv., *supra* note 10, art. 30(1).

If a sending state's mission abuses the concept of inviolability of diplomatic premises, a receiving state of course may declare offending members *persona non grata, see supra* notes 88-90 and accompanying text, or even break diplomatic relations, sanctions which usually assure appropriate use of diplomatic premises. *See* RESTATEMENT (THIRD), *supra* note 20, § 466 cmt.a.

[100] *See* RESTATEMENT (THIRD), *supra* note 20, § 466, cmts. a &c.

[101] *Id.*

[102] *United States v. Garcia*, 456 F. Supp. 1358 (D.P.R. 1978) (Congress can penalize crimes of violence committed against consular officials on consular premises).

[103] Vienna Diplomatic Conv., *supra* note 10, art. 41(3). Those functions are delineated in *id.* at art. 3; *see supra* notes 61-63 and accompanying text.

purposes of arresting and removing them. The position of the *Restatement (Second)*[104] in 1965 was that a right of asylum did not exist in international law.[105] The *Restatement (Third)*, however, reports a different position.[106] "The inviolability of the premises of a diplomatic mission or a consular post precludes officials of the receiving state from entering to arrest a person who seeks asylum there.[107] And while the *Restatement (Third)* notes that sending states have usually denied diplomatic asylum to "ordinary fugitives from justice or military service," it is now "accepted practice" to grant asylum "to refugees from political or religious repression, to others claiming refuge on humanitarian grounds . . . or to particular refugees accused of crime who might not receive a fair trial."[108]

The immunity and claim to protection of a diplomatic agent extends as well to tangible property,[109] including means of transportation.[110]

Immunity of Diplomatic Documents and Archives

The papers and correspondence of diplomatic agents must also enjoy inviolability,[111] as must mission archives and documents.[112] This means that they cannot be seized or inspected, without consent, by any representative of a receiving state.[113] This extends to

---

[104] RESTATEMENT (SECOND) OF FOREIGN RELATIONS LAW OF THE UNITED STATES (1965) at 244, Reporters' Note 2. "Notwithstanding its significant status in certain states, a right to grant diplomatic asylum does not appear to be generally recognized by international law." *Id.*

[105] *See id.* at 244-45 (listing authorities supporting the conclusion that such had been the United States view of international law).

[106] *See* RESTATEMENT (THIRD), *supra* note 20, § 466 cmt.b.

[107] *Id.*

[108] *Id.* & Reporters' Note 3.

[109] Vienna Diplomatic Conv., *supra* note 10, arts. 22(3) (mission premises), 30(1) (private residence of diplomatic agent), 30(2) (private property of diplomatic agent).

[110] *Id.* art. 22(3) (means of transport). On the status of government-owned and -operated vessels, Rosalyn Higgins, *Recent Development in the Law of Sovereign Immunity in the United Kingdom,* 71 AM. J. INT'L L. 423 (1977).

[111] Vienna Diplomatic Conv., *supra* note 10, art. 30(2); RESTATEMENT (THIRD), *supra* note 20, § 466. Messages in code or cipher are protected in the course of transit. *See* Vienna Diplomatic Conv., *supra* note 10, arts. 27(1), 40(3). Federal employees who obtain unauthorized access to codes and correspondence between a foreign government and its mission in the United States commit a federal felony. 18 U.S.C. § 952 (1994) (punishment by a fine of not more than $10,000, imprisonment for not more than 10 years, or both).

[112] Vienna Diplomatic Conv., *supra* note 10, art. 24. Archives include "all papers, documents, correspondence, books, films, tapes and registers, together with ciphers and codes, card indexes, and the articles of furniture intended for their safekeeping or storage." RESTATEMENT (THIRD), *supra* note 20, § 466. cmt. e, deriving the definition from Vienna Convention on Consular Relations art. 1(k), Apr. 24, 1963, 21 U.S.T. 77, 596 U.N.T.S. 261 (*entered into force* with respect to the United States Dec. 24, 1969) [hereinafter Vienna Consular Conv.] (definition of "consular archives").

[113] *See* Vienna Diplomatic Conv., *supra* note 10, art. 27(2).

diplomatic couriers within the territory of a receiving state[114] or a third party state through which they pass.[115]

Inviolability of Communications

In simpler times when communications were written and dispatched in diplomatic pouches or transmitted by diplomatic agents who had received oral instructions, the immunity just described sufficed. With the development of wire and radio communications, however, new concepts of inviolability had to be developed and accorded them. The concern was reflected in the 1965 *Restatement (Second)*[116] statement that a receiving state is not to "prescribe or enforce any rule interfering with its official communication with the sending state other than a rule with respect to operation of a wire transmitter."[117] The current *Restatement (Third)*[118] uses the general term "communications," but continues to note that installation and operation of wireless transmitters are subject to approval by a receiving state.[119]

The position of the federal courts is that warrantless electronic surveillance of foreign agents does not violate the fourth amendment[120] as long as it is not directed against domestic dissidents.[121] In 1978, Congress quite comprehensively regulated foreign intelligence surveillance by United States authorities, in the Foreign Intelligence Surveillance Act.[122]

---

[114] Vienna Diplomatic Conv., *supra* note 10, art. 27(3) ("the diplomatic bag shall not be opened or detained"). Packages constituting a diplomatic bag must bear visible external marks of their character and may contain only diplomatic documents or articles intended for official use. *Id.* art. 27(4). Diplomatic couriers must be provided with official documents including their status and the number of packages constituting the diplomatic bag; they cannot be subjected to any form of arrest or detention. *Id.* art. 27(5). Diplomatic couriers can be designated *ad hoc*, but their immunities cease when they have delivered the diplomatic bags in their charge. *Id.* art. 27(6). Diplomatic bags may be entrusted to captains of commercial aircraft scheduled to arrive at an authorized port of entry, and are to be given official documents indicating the number of packages constituting the diplomatic bag (although this does not make them diplomatic couriers); a recipient diplomatic mission may send an emissary to take direct possession of the diplomatic bag from the aircraft captains. *Id.* art. 27(7). *See also* RESTATEMENT (THIRD), *supra* note 20, § 466. cmt.f & Reporters' Note 6.

[115] As long as a third state has granted diplomatic couriers a visa or other permission to enter and pass through, it must accord them inviolability and other needed immunities, Vienna Diplomatic Conv., *supra* note 10, art. 40(1)-(2), and must accord diplomatic bags in transit the same inviolability and protection that a receiving state is bound to accord. *Id.* art. 40(3). That extends as well to instances in which couriers are physically present within a third party state because of *force majeure*. *Id.* art. 40(4).

[116] *Supra* note 104, § 77(3).

[117] *Id.*

[118] *Supra* note 20, § 466.

[119] Vienna Diplomatic Conv., *supra* note 10, art. 27(1) ("the mission may install and use a wireless transmitter only with the consent of the receiving State.") *See also* RESTATEMENT (THIRD), *supra* note 20, § 466 cmt.f.

[120] *Katz v. United States*, 389 U.S. 347, 358 n.23 (1967); *United States v. Butenko*, 494 F.2d 593 (3d Cir.), *cert. denied*, 419 U.S. 881 (1974); *United States v. Brown*, 484 F.2d 418 (5th Cir. 1973).

[121] *United States v. United States District Court*, 407 U.S. 297 (1972).

[122] 50 U.S.C. §§ 1801-1811 (1994). The constitutional basis for the enactment is found in the *Katz* language, 389 U.S. at 358 n. 23, indicating that Congress might enact special legislation governing foreign intelligence cases with less stringent requirements than govern domestic eavesdropping (now regulated by 18 U.S.C. §§ 2510-2520 (1994)).

Key classifications under the statute are "foreign powers,"[123] "agents of foreign powers"[124] and "United States persons."[125] Under certain circumstances, foreign intelligence information[126] can be obtained without advance authorization; the President may authorize the Attorney General to acquire foreign intelligence information for up to one year if the Attorney General certifies in writing under oath[127] that electronic surveillance[128] will be directed only at the acquisition of contents of communications transmitted through communications channels used exclusively between or among foreign powers, or the acquisition of technical information (other than spoken communications of individuals) from property or premises under the exclusive control of a foreign power, that there is no substantial likelihood that the result will be acquisition of the contents of any communication to which a United States person is a party, and that minimization requirements[129] will be

---

[123] Defined as a foreign government or its component, whether recognized by the United States or not, a faction of one or more foreign states not substantially composed of United States persons, an entity acknowledged by one or more foreign governments as under their direction, a group engaged in international terrorism (defined in 50 U.S.C. §1801(c)(1994)) or activity preparatory to it, a foreign-based political organization not substantially composed of United States persons, or an entity directed or controlled by one or more foreign governments. *Id.* §1801(a).

[124] Defined as anyone other than a United States person who acts in the United States as an officer or employee of a foreign power or member of an international terrorist group, or who on behalf of a foreign power engages in clandestine intelligence activities in the United States (including accessories), and anyone, including a United States person, who knowingly engages in clandestine intelligence activities amounting to a federal crime, on behalf of a foreign government or at the direction of a foreign intelligence service or network, or who commits sabotage (defined in *id.* § 1801(d) through cross reference to 18 U.S.C. § 2151 *et seq.* (1994), or who aids or conspires with such persons. *Id.*§ 1801(b).

[125] Defined as a United States citizen or alien admitted for permanent residence, an unincorporated association composed substantially of such persons, or a U.S. corporation. *Id.* §1801(i). Associations and corporations qualifying as foreign powers under §1801(a)(1)-(3) are not United States persons. *Id.*

[126] Defined as information relating to the ability of the United States to protect itself against actual or potential attack or grave hostile acts, sabotage, or international terrorism by a foreign power or agent of a foreign power, or clandestine intelligence activity by such entities, and information with respect to a foreign power or foreign territory which related to U.S. national defense or security or conduct of U.S. foreign affairs. *Id.* §1801(e). If a United States person is involved, the information must be necessary to the American purpose. *Id.*

[127] Certifications must be retained for at least 10 years. 50 U.S.C.A §1805(g) (West Supp. 1997).

[128] Defined for all purposes as (1) acquisition by electronic, mechanical or other surveillance device of wire or radio communications to which a United States person in the United States is a party, provided the individual is targeted under circumstances supporting a reasonable expectation of privacy which would impel a warrant for law enforcement purposes, (2) any acquisition of information involving a United States person in the United States if there is no consent, (3) intentional acquisition of contents of radio communications concerning which there is a reasonable expectation of privacy so that a warrant otherwise would be necessary for law enforcement purposes, if both sender and all intended recipients are within the United States, and (4) installation or use of surveillance devices in the United States to monitor other than a wire or radio communication under circumstances in which there is a reasonable expectation of privacy mandating a warrant for law enforcement purposes. 50 U.S.C. §1801(f).

[129] Minimization under the statute means (1) specific procedures adopted by the Attorney General reasonably designed to avoid acquisition, retention and dissemination of nonpublic information concerning nonconsenting United States persons (consistent with the needs of the United States to obtain, produce and disseminate foreign intelligence information), (2) procedures requiring that information not otherwise public, and not foreign intelligence information, not be disseminated so as to identify a United States person without the latter's consent, unless identity is necessary to understand foreign intelligence information or assess its importance, (3) procedures allowing for retention and dissemination of evidence of crimes committed or about to be committed, needed for law enforcement purposes, and (4) procedures which ensure that such information may not be obtained for longer than 24 hours unless an authorizing court order is obtained or unless the information supports a determination by the Attorney General that the information indicates a threat of death or serious bodily harm to someone. *Id.* §1801(h).

met.[130] Surveillance must comply with the terms of such a certification.[131] Communications carriers are required to assist when requested to do so by the Attorney General, at their prevailing rates, while maintaining necessary security precautions.[132]

In all other circumstances, judicial authorization has to be solicited before electronic surveillance can be conducted. The President must first, in writing, authorize the Attorney General to approve applications for such surveillance.[133] An application is to be submitted in writing by a federal officer, under oath or affirmation, to a judge of the special court.[134] An application must follow a legislatively prescribed format.[135] Hearings are to be held on an application as expeditiously as possible and recorded under circumstances compatible with security.[136] A recipient judge may require an applicant to furnish other information not attached to an application.[137] All proceedings, of course, are *ex parte*.[138] If an application is

---

130 50 U.S.C.A. § 1802 (a) (1) (West Supp. 1997).

131 50 U.S.C. §1802(a)(2). Certificates must be filed under security conditions with a special court created under the act, *id.*, §1802(a)(3), and must remain sealed unless an application for an authorizing order is submitted and the certificate is needed to determine the lawfulness of surveillance. *Id.* The court is composed of seven federal district judges from seven different judicial circuits, publicly designated by the Chief Justice, 50 U.S.C.A. §1803(a)(West Supp.1997), who serve seven-year rotating terms. 50 U.S.C. §1803(d).

Emergency surveillance not within the certification procedure can be conducted by authorization of the Attorney General, but retroactive judicial authorization must be sought within 24 hours, 50 U.S.C.A. §1805(West Supp. 1997).

132 50 U.S.C. § 1802(a)(4).

133 50 U.S.C.A. § 1802 (West Supp. 1997).

134 An application cannot be submitted to a second judge after having been rejected by another judge. 50 U.S.C.A. § 1803(a) (West Supp. 1997).

135 Applications must include (1) the identity of the applicant federal officer, 50 U.S.C.A.§1804(a)(1) (West Supp 1997); (2) the fact of presidential authorization to the Attorney General and the latter's approval of the application, *id.* § 1804(a)(2); (3) the identity, if known, or a description of the target of electronic surveillance, *id.* § 1804(a)(3); (4) a statement of facts and circumstances relied on by the applicant to support a belief that the target is a foreign power, *id.* § 1804(a)(4); (5) a statement of proposed minimization procedures, *id.* § 1804(a)(5); (6) a detailed description of the nature of the information sought and the type of communications or activities to be placed under surveillance, *id.*§ 1804(a)(6); (7) a certification by executive branch officials (defined to include the Assistant to the President for National Security Affairs or executive branch officials designated by the President from persons employed in national security or defense, appointed by the President with advice and consent of the Senate, *id.* §1804(a)(7)) that the information is foreign intelligence information, that the surveillance is intended to obtain such information, that the information cannot reasonably be obtained through other normal investigative techniques, the statutory designation of the category of information sought and the basis for the certification, *id.* (although the basis for certification need not be given if the target is a foreign power and its facilities [*Id.* §1804(b)]); (8) a statement of the means of surveillance to be used and any physical entry required to conduct surveillance. *Id.* § 1804(a)(8) (although this is not required for surveillance of facilities under the exclusive control of a foreign power, *id.* 1804(b), but enough must be indicated to allow evaluation of minimization procedures); (9) a statement of facts of all earlier applications under the statute involving any of the persons, places and facilities specified in the application, and the action taken on each previous application, *id.* §1804(a)(9); (10) a statement of the time required for surveillance and the basis for a belief that additional information of the same type will be obtained so that the authorizing order should not lose its effect when described information has been obtained initially, *id.* §1804(a)(10); (11) if more than one device is to be used, the coverage of each device and the minimization elements applicable to the information secured through each, *id.* §1804(a)(11) (a requirement not applicable to facilities under the exclusive control of a foreign power, *id.* §1804(b)); and (12) other affidavits or certificates required by the Attorney General in connection with the application, *id.* §1804(c).

136 *Id.* §1803(c). Security measures are to be established by the Chief Justice in consultation with the Attorney General and Director of Central Intelligence. *Id.*

137 50 U.S.C. § 1804(d).

138 *Id.* § 1805(a).

denied, a written statement is to be incorporated in a record, which at the motion of the government must be transmitted to a special appellate court[139] created under the statute.[140]

Before issuing an order, the special court judge has to enter findings paralleling the required elements of an application; a burden of persuasion at the level of probable cause attaches to certain of the elements.[141] An order must specify certain legislatively mandated matters.[142] An extension order may be obtained for the same period appropriate for an original order, based on a new application and showing.[143]

Certain activities are not considered to be subject to the statutory requirements: (1) electronic surveillance to acquire foreign intelligence information for a period not to exceed fifteen calendar days after Congress has declared war;[144] (2) tests to determine capabilities of surveillance equipment, as long as no contents[145] are disclosed other than to testing personnel and are destroyed before or immediately at termination of testing;[146] (3) detection

---

139 50 U.S.C.A. § 1803(West Supp. 1997).

140 The appellate tribunal is composed of three district or circuit judges designated by the Chief Justice; one is denominated the chief judge, *id.* § 1803(b). If the tribunal determines that denial was proper, it in turn prepares a written statement of reasons for its decision which is transmitted under seal to the Supreme Court, which is empowered to review the decision. *Id.*

141 50 U.S.C.§1805(a)(3). That extends to the elements of foreign power or foreign-power agent status and use or imminent use of facilities by a foreign power or foreign-power agent; no United States person may be determined to be a foreign power or foreign-power agent solely on the basis of first amendment-protected activities. *Id.*

142 These include (1) the identity, if known, or description of the target of surveillance, *id* § 1805(b)(1)(A); (2) the nature and location of each place or facility at which surveillance will be directed, *id.* § 1805(b)(1)(B); (3) the type of information to be acquired and type of communications or activities to be subjected to surveillance, *id.* §1805(b)(1)(C) (although this is not needed concerning places or facilities under the exclusive control of a foreign power, *id.* §1805(c)); (4) the means by which electronic surveillance will be conducted and whether physical entry will required, *id.* § 1805(1)(D) (but this does not govern facilities under the exclusive control of a foreign power, but enough must be indicated to describe the information sought, object of surveillance and type of surveillance procedure, and the need for physical entry, *id.* §1805(c); an order can direct a communications common carrier, lessor, custodian or other specified person to assist in its execution in a way suitable to reduce inconvenience to other patrons to a minimum, at standard rates, under suitable conditions, *id.* § 1805(b)(2)(B)-(D); (5) the period of time approved for surveillance, *id.* §1805(b)(i)(E); this may be the time necessary to accomplish the purposes of the order but not to exceed 90 days, *id.* § 1805(d)(1), unless a foreign power is involved, in which case the period may be one year or a lesser time set forth in the order, *id.* and § 1801(a)(1)-(3); and (6) if multiple devices will be used, the coverage authorized for each and the minimization requirements of each, *id.* § 1805(b)(1)(F) (but this does not apply to orders applicable to foreign-controlled facilities, *id.* §1805(c)). An order must direct that minimization procedures will be followed, *id.* § 1805 (b)(2)(A), and the issuing judge may assess compliance with minimization requirements. *Id.* §1805(d)(3).

143 50 U.S.C.A. § 1805(d)(2)(West Supp. 1997). The court also may review compliance with minimization procedures during the original period, *id.* § 1805(d)(3). The period of an extension order may be up to one year as long as there is probable cause to believe that no communication of an individual United States person will be acquired during that time. *Id.* § 1805(d)(2).

144 *Id.* § 1811. The President through the Attorney General can authorize surveillance under such circumstances. *Id.*

145 Defined for all purposes in the statute as information concerning the identity of parties to communications or the existence, substance, purport or meaning of communications. 50 U.S.C. § 1801(a).

146 *Id.* §1805(f)(1). The Attorney General must authorize in advance testing for more than 90 days. *Id.*

of unlawful surveillance activities;[147] and (4) training electronic surveillance personnel in the use of equipment if training cannot otherwise be accomplished.[148]

The statutory emphasis on minimization is intended to control nonessential dissemination of material obtained through surveillance. For that reason, otherwise privileged communications are to retain that character and may be disclosed only for lawful purposes.[149] The Attorney General must give advance authorization for use of the material in criminal prosecutions.[150] A special form of discovery[151] is available to an aggrieved person.[152]

The principal remedy available to an aggrieved person is a motion to suppress in federal or state court where surveillance-derived evidence may be used. However, unlawful surveillance is a felony,[153] and civil liability is provided for.[154]

It is doubtful that any other nation in the world has enacted or will enact such sweeping legislative and judicial regulation of the foreign intelligence surveillance activities allowed under international law. One can only assume that in times of imminent war or overt hostilities, the statute will be repealed swiftly.[155] Meanwhile, it is difficult to determine the extent to which federal authorities actually have resorted to the statute, because of the high degree of secrecy which the statute dictates for data relating to it.

The Right of Diplomatic Agents to Receiving State Protection

The Vienna Diplomatic Convention[156] requires receiving states to take all appropriate steps to prevent attacks on the person, freedom or dignity of diplomatic agents.[157] A failure

---

147 *Id.* § 1805(f)(2). This must be conducted under circumstances in which consents cannot be obtained from persons incidentally subjected to surveillance, must be limited to efforts to detect existence and capability of equipment, and cannot be used other than to convict for eavesdropping violations or to protect information from unauthorized surveillance. *Id.*

148 50 U.S.C.A. § 1805(f)(3) (West Supp. 1997). This is acceptable only if consents from persons incidentally to be subjected to surveillance cannot reasonably be expected; the surveillance must be the minimum necessary for training, and no contents of communications can be retained or disseminated, but instead must be destroyed as soon as reasonably possible. *Id.*

149 *Id.* § 1806(a).

150 *Id.* § 1806(b).

151 *Id.* § 1806(c) (federal proceedings), (d) (state proceedings).

152 Defined for purposes of the statute as one who is the target of or whose communications or activities have been subject to electronic surveillance. *Id.* § 1801(k).

153 *Id.* § 1809. Jurisdiction is federal if a federal officer or employee is a defendant. *Id.* A defendant can assert the protection of authorizing judicial process executed in the course of official duties. *Id.*

154 *Id.* § 1810. Recovery extends to actual damages or liquidated damages in the amount of $100 per day of unlawful activity or $1,000 (whichever is greater), reasonable attorney fees and litigation costs reasonably incurred, *Id.* (patterned on the basic federal eavesdropping statute, 18 U.S.C. § 2520 (1994).

155 Congress has retained general supervisory control over the matter, perhaps in violation of separation of powers theory. The Attorney General is to report semiannually to the House and Senate Select Committees on intelligence an assessment of compliance with minimization standards. 50 U.S.C. § 1802(a)(2), and surveillance activities conducted under the law. 50 U.S.C.A. § 1808 (West Supp. 1997). Each April the Attorney General also is to transmit to Congress and the Administrative Office of the United States Courts a report for the preceding calendar year covering the total number of applications for orders and extension orders and the number granted, modified or denied. *Id.* § 1807. The designated congressional committees are to report to their respective chambers about implementation of the statute, including recommendations for amendment or repeal. *Id.* §1808(b).

156 Vienna Diplomatic Conv., *supra* note 10, art. 29.

157 *Id. See Also* RESTATEMENT (THIRD), *supra* note 20, § 464 Reporters' Note 6.

to do so creates a measure of state responsibility to see that appropriate remedies are available. Federal law prohibits acts of murder,[158] manslaughter,[159] attempted murder or manslaughter,[160] kidnaping,[161] assault,[162] or intimidation[163] against a foreign official,[164] internationally protected person[165] or official guest.[166] Conspiracies to commit these offenses are also punishable.[167] If an offender is actually found in a place subject to federal

---

[158] 18 U.S.C.A. §§1111, 1116 (a) (West Supp. 1997) (first-degree murder is punishable by death or by imprisonment for life, and second-degree murder by any term of years or life. *Id.* § 1111(b)).

[159] *Id.* §§1112, 1116 (voluntary manslaughter is punishable by fine or imprisonment for not more than ten years, and involuntary manslaughter by a fine or imprisonment for not more than six years or both. *Id.* § 1112 (b)).

[160] *Id.* §§ 1111, 1112, 1116(a). Attempted murder is punishable by a fine, imprisonment for not more than twenty years, or both. *Id.* §1113. Attempted manslaughter is punishable by a fine, imprisonment for not more than seven years, or both. *Id.*

[161] *Id.* § 1201(4) (punishable by imprisonment for any term of years of life and if death results, punishable by death or life imprisonment). Attempts to kidnap protected persons are criminal and punishable by imprisonment for not more than 20 years. *Id.* § 1201(d). Conspiracies implemented by at least one overt act are punishable by any term of years or for life. *Id.* § 1201(c).

[162] *Id.* § 112(a) The basic punishment is a fine, imprisonment for not more than three years, or both, but if a deadly or dangerous weapon is used, the sanction is a fine, imprisonment for not more than ten years, or both. *Id. See United States v. Gan*, 636 F.2d 28 (2d Cir. 1980), *cert. denied,* 451 U.S. 1029 (1981) (conviction based on throwing paint on United States and Soviet representatives to the U.N.).

[163] *Id.* § 112(b)("intimidates, coerces, threatens, or harasses . . . obstructs" or attempts to do so). The punishment is a fine, imprisonment for not more than six months, or both. *Id.* The provision is not to be construed so as to abridge first amendment rights. *Id.* §112(d).

Indirect protection of status is accomplished, at least in some instances, by the prohibition against falsely assuming or pretending to be a diplomatic, consular or other official of a duly-accredited foreign government and obtaining or attempting to obtain money, paper, documents or other things of value, with intent to defraud. *Id.* 915 (punishable by a fine, imprisonment for not more than ten years, or both*)*. *Id.*.

[164] Defined in *id.* § 1116(b)(3) as "(a) a Chief of State or the political equivalent, President, Vice President, Prime Minister, Ambassador, Foreign Minister, or other officer of Cabinet rank or above of a foreign government or the chief executive officer of an international organization, or any person who has previously served in such capacity, and any member of his family, while in the United States; and (b) any person of foreign nationality who is duly notified to the United States as an officer or employee of a foreign government or international organization, and who is in the United States on official business, and any member of his family whose presence in the United States is in connection with the presence of such officer and employer. *Id.*

"Foreign government" is defined as the government of a foreign country "irrespective of recognition by the United States" *Id.* §1116(b)(2). It includes as well any government, faction or body of insurgents within a country with which the United States is at peace. *Id.* §11.

An international organization is a public organization designated as such as 22 U.S.C. §288 (1994), or created by treaty or other agreement under international law "as an instrument through or by which two or more foreign governments engage in some aspect of their conduct of international affairs," 18 U.S.C. §1116(b)(5) (1994).

Protected family members include spouses, parents, brothers or sisters, children, persons to whom a foreign official or internationally protected person stands in loco parentis, or any other person living in the official's or internationally protected person's household and related to him or her by blood or marriage, 18 U.S.C. §1116(b)(1).

[165] Defined in 18 U.S.C. §1116(b)(4) as: (a) a Chief of State or the political equivalent, head of government or Foreign Minister whenever such person is in a country other than his own and any member of his family accompanying him; or (b) any other representative, officer, employee, or agent of the United States government, a foreign government, or international organization who at the time and place concerned is entitled pursuant to international law to special protection against attack upon his person, freedom, or dignity, and any member of his family then forming part of his household. *Id. See supra* note 164 for definitions of terms incorporated in the above definition.

[166] Defined in 18 U.S.C.§ 1116(b)(6) as "a citizen or national of a foreign country present in the United States as an official guest of the Government of the United States pursuant to designation as such by the Secretary of State."

[167] 18 U.S.C.A. § 1117 (West Supp. 1997) (punishable by imprisonment for any term of years or for life).

jurisdiction,[168] he or she may be tried in an appropriate federal court without regard to the place where the offense was committed or the nationality of the victim or defendant.[169] This is a relatively rare reflection in American criminal law of the protected interest and passive personality principles.

The Attorney General can request assistance in enforcement of the murder and assault provision from any federal, state or local agency including the United States armed forces,[170] a departure from the usual strictures of the Posse Comitatus Act.[171] Congress's expressed intent was that the federal criminal provisions not occupy the field and thus preclude the exercise of state criminal jurisdiction over crimes against diplomatic agents committed within a state's territorial boundaries.[172] The result is concurrent federal and state jurisdiction.[173] Because of the important federal interests affected by crimes of this nature, however, it is unlikely that federal authorities frequently will invoke the so-called *Petite* policy[174] to withdraw federal charges in favor of state prosecution.

The Vienna Diplomatic Convention[175] requires that the premises[176] and property[177] of diplomatic agents be held inviolable.[178] Federal statutes penalize damage to or destruction of property within the United States of a foreign government, international organization, foreign official or official guest,[179] trespass on[180] or refusal to depart from[181] protected premises,[182] or violent attacks on official premises, private accommodations or means of transport if they are likely to endanger a protected individual's person or liberty.[183] These crimes are governed by the venue and enforcement provisions described above.[184]

The United States' position, as an aggrieved sending state, achieved world wide prominence during the seizure of the United States Embassy in Tehran, Iran, in 1980 and 1981. The United States litigated before the International Court of Justice the issue of the

---

168 Defined in *id.* §§ 5, 7; 49 U.S.C. § 1301(38) (1994).

169 18 U.S.C. §§ 112 (e), 1116(c), 1201(e) (1994).

170 *Id.* §§ 112(f), 1116(d), 1201(f).

171 *Id.* § 1385 (making it a federal felony to use any part of the Army or Air Force to assist in enforcement of civilian law except as otherwise authorized by Congress).

172 Pub. L. No. 94-467 § 10; Pub. L. No. 92-539§ 2; Pub. L. No. 92-539 § 3; Pub. L. No. 88-493§ 5.

173 *See* George, *supra* note 1, at notes 44-45, 85-87 and accompanying text.

174 Named after *Petite v. United States*, 361 U.S. 529 (1960), and *see Rinaldi v. United States*, 434 U.S. 22 (1977). Administrative policy is to withhold or withdraw federal prosecutions duplicative of state prosecutions arising from a single transaction, unless federal law enforcement will likely be more effective than state prosecution.

175 Vienna Diplomatic Conv., *supra* note 10, arts. 22(2), 30(1), 30(2).

176 *Id.* arts. 22(1), (3), 30(1).

177 *Id.* arts. 22(3), 30(2).

178 *See also* RESTATEMENT (THIRD), *supra* note 20, § 464 Reporters' Note 6, § 466 & 466 Reporters' Note 2.

179 18 U.S.C. A. § 970(a) (West Supp. 1997) (punishable by a fine, imprisonment for not more than five years, or both). The definitions of the terms used in the section are set forth in *supra* notes 166-168.

180 *Id.* § 970 (b)(1)(1982) (punishable by a fine, imprisonment for not more than six months, or both). Acts must be done intentionally (willfully) "with intent to intimidate, coerce, threaten or harass." *Id.* § 970(b).

181 *Id.* § 970(b)(2) (same punishment). The intent and motivation requirements are the same as for entries. *Id.* § 970(b).

182 Buildings must be used or occupied for official business or for diplomatic, consular or residential purposes, *id.* § 970(b), by a foreign government, international organizations, foreign official or official guest, as defined in *id.* § 1116(b). *Id.* § 970(c). *See supra* notes 169-71.

183 *Id.* §112(a)(punishable as an assault, *see supra* note 166).

184 *See supra* notes 172-173 and accompanying text.

violations of international law generated by the seizure of embassy and other diplomatic premises and the holding hostage of diplomatic and consular personnel, and obtained a judgement holding Iran responsible under international law to keep the hostages safe, to release them, to restore U.S. diplomatic premises to its control and to protect and respect privileges and immunities founded in international law.[185] The outcome of the affair, although useful in establishing specific, contemporary international precedent, demonstrates how utterly dependent diplomatic missions are on the goodwill and motivation on the part of receiving state officials to protect them.

Immunity and Privileges of Consular Personnel

(a) *Persons covered*—Consular officers[186] must be designated by a sending state and accepted by a receiving state. The head of a consular post[187] must be designated by a sending state. The head of a consular post is accepted by a receiving state through issuance of an *exequatur*,[188] while the appointment of other consular staff members is handled through notification to the receiving state government.[189] A sending state must notify a receiving state's ministry for foreign affairs (the Department of State in the United States) of the appointment, arrival, change in status or departure of members of a consular post,[190] family members of a member of a consular post forming part of his or her household,[191] and private staff members,[192] as well as the engagement or discharge of persons resident in the receiving state as members of a consular post or private staff.[193] The provisions apply to honorary

---

185 Case Concerning United States Diplomatic and Consular Staff in Tehran (*U.S. v. Iran*), (1980) I.C.J. 3; (May 24). *See also* RESTATEMENT (THIRD), *supra* note 20, § 464 Reporters' Note 6; M. Cherif Bassiouni, *Protections of Diplomats under Islamic Law*, 74 AM. J. INT'L L. 609 (1980); Green, *supra* note 2; Leo Gross, *The Case Concerning United States Diplomatic and Consular Staff in Tehran: Phase of Provisional Measures*, 74 AM. J. INT'L L. 395 (1980); Amir Rafat, *The Iran Hostage Crisis and the International Court of Justice: Aspects of the Case Concerning United States Diplomatic and Consular Staff in Tehran*, 10 DENV. J. INT'L L. & POL'Y. 425 (1981); Note, *The Case Concerning United States Diplomatic and Consular Staff in Tehran*, 11 CAL. W. INT'L L. J. 543 (1981).

186 Defined in Vienna Consular Conv., *supra* note 112, art. 1(1)(d), as persons, including the head of a consular post, entrusted in that capacity with the exercise of consular functions.

187 Defined in *id.* Art. 1(1)(d) as the person charged with the duty of acting in that capacity.

188 *Id.* art. 12(1). A receiving state need give no reasons for refusing to issue an *exequatur*. *Id.* art. 12(2). A nominated head of a consular post is not to commence functioning until an *exequatur* has been issued. *Id.* art. 12(3), unless the receiving state grants admission provisionally. *Id.* art. 13. Procedures governing acting heads of consular posts are delineated in *id.* art. 15.

A receiving state can declare a nominated head of consular post *persona non grata* before or after his or her arrival to assume official duties. *Id.* art. 23(1).

A person can be appointed, with the consent of a receiving state, to serve as consular officer for two or more states. *Id.* arts. 8, 18.

189 *Id.* art. 19(2), A sending state can request issuance of an *exequatur* for such persons. *Id.* § 19(3), and a receiving state can require *exequaturs* for them under its own law. *Id.* art. 19(4).

Notice should be given enough in advance that a receiving state can exercise its right under *id.* art. 23(1) to declare a nominee unacceptable. *Id.* art. 19(2).

190 *Id.* art. 24(1)(a). "Members of the consular post" means consular officers, consular employees and members of the service staff. *Id.* art. 1(1)(g). Consular employees are defined in *id.* art. 1(1)(e), and members of the service staff in *id.* art. 1(1)(f).

191 *Id.* art. 24(1)(b).

192 *Id.* art. 24(1)(c). "Members of the private staff" is defined in *id.* art. 1(1)(i).

193 *Id.* art. 24(a), (d).

consuls, who serve part time and often are either nationals of or permanent residents in a receiving state.[194]

Third states are to recognize the protected status of consular personnel as they pass to and from the receiving state to which they are assigned.[195]

(b) *Duration of Consular privileges and immunities*—Protection begins from the moment a designee arrives within the territory of a receiving state or, if he or she is already physically present at the time of appointment, at entry into performance of consular duties.[196] It ends at the termination of the functions of the member of a consular post[197] and physical departure from the receiving state of one who no longer has consular status.[198] If the person remains within the receiving state, protected status ends after whatever period would have been reasonably appropriate for departure.[199]

(c) *Activities covered*—The list of consular functions is quite lengthy,[200] but comprehends the protection of the political, commercial, economic, cultural and scientific interests of the sending state, safeguarding the various interests of sending state nationals, executing and attesting various documents and approving travel documents for entry into the receiving state. Under certain circumstances, consular officers can be authorized, with received state consent, to perform diplomatic acts.[201] Immunity persists concerning consular acts even though thereafter the consular official responsible ceases to function in that official capacity.[202]

(d) *Freedom from arrest or detention*—Consular officers have a slightly diminished freedom from arrest in comparison to diplomatic personnel;[203] they can be arrested and detained, but only for "grave crime" and pursuant to "a decision by the competent judicial authority."[204] Presumably, the latter requirement is satisfied through a probable cause determination underlying issuance of an arrest warrant.[205] In other cases, they must remain in the community until a final judgement of conviction has been entered.[206] Honorary

---

194 *See* RESTATEMENT (THIRD), *supra* note 20, § 465 Reporters' Note 10.

195 Vienna Consular Conv., *supra* note 112, art. 54(1).

196 *Id.* art. 53(1). Family members gain protection at the same time as the member of the consular post to which they are related, or from their physical entry into the receiving state if they arrive later. *Id.* art. 53(2).

197 *See id.* art. 25, based on a withdrawal of appointment by a receiving state, *id.* arts. 24(1), 25(a), or a declaration that a consular officer is *persona non grata*, *id.* art. 23(1), or other staff member is unacceptable. *Id.*

198 *Id.* art. 53(3).

199 *Id.* Family members of a deceased member of a consular post enjoy privileges and immunities until they depart the receiving state, or a reasonable time has elapsed. *Id.* art. 53(4).

200 *See id.* art. 5.

201 *Id.* art. 17. Diplomatic acts are delineated in Vienna Diplomatic Conv., *supra* note 10, art. 3. *See supra* notes 61-62 and accompanying text.

202 Vienna Consular Conv., *supra* note 112, art. 53(4).

203 *See supra* notes 64-66 and accompanying text (discussing diplomatic agents' freedom from arrest or detention).

204 Vienna Consular Conv., *supra* note 112, art. 41(1). *See also* RESTATEMENT (THIRD), *supra* note 20, § 465 (2)& §465 cmt. 2. If a member of a consular staff is arrested, detained pending trial or prosecuted, the receiving state must notify the head of the consular post unless the latter is the accused, in which event the sending state must be informed through diplomatic channels. Vienna Consular Conv., *supra* note 112, art. 42.

205 In the U.S., preconviction detention is governed by fourth amendment probable cause requirements. *Gerstein v. Pugh*, 420 U.S. 103 (1975). This should be a sufficient basis for compliance with international law expectations as well.

206 Vienna Consular Conv., *supra* note 112, art. 41(2).

consuls, however, may be arrested and detained like persons not enjoying consular immunity.[207]

(e) *Exemption from Criminal Prosecution*—Consular officers are immune to prosecution only with respect to acts performed in the exercise of consular functions.[208] They can be prosecuted for all other crimes and must appear before "competent authorities;"[209] receiving state authorities, however, must afford proper respect to them as sending state officials, hamper the exercise of their consular functions as little as possible, and give notice of the fact of prosecution.[210] If a consular officer is lawfully detained pending adjudication, proceedings must be carried forward with minimum delay.[211]

(f) *Liability to give testimony*—Consular officials are not immune to process calling them to be witnesses in judicial or administrative proceedings and are not, with one exception, to decline to testify.[212] The exception covers testimony concerning matters connected with the exercise of consular functions or production of official correspondence and documents reflecting those functions.[213] This appears to cover criminal as well as civil proceedings.

(g) *Waiver*—The same general principles governing waiver of diplomatic immunity[214] apply to waiver of whatever immunity consular officials enjoy.[215] Accordingly, only a sending state may waive privileges and immunities of a consular official.[216]

---

207 *Id.* art. 58 (which does not include art. 41 among the provisions applicable to honorary consuls). However, notice must be given or arrest, preconviction detention or initiation of prosecution to the head of the consular post in the receiving state, or to the sending state if the honorary consul is the head. *Id.* arts. 42, 58(2).

208 Art. 43(1). That immunity attaches according to official status at the time an act was performed and survives a subsequent termination of official status, without time limitation. *Id.* art. 53(4). These provisions govern honorary consuls. *Id.* art. 58(2). *See also* RESTATEMENT (THIRD), *supra* note 20, § 465 (1)(6).

209 Vienna Consular Conv., *supra* note 112, art. 41(3), applicable to honorary consuls. *Id.* art. 58(2). An example is *Silva v. Superior Court*, 52 Cal. App. 3d 269, 125 Cal. Rptr. 78 (1975) (Mexican consul is not immune to prosecution for criminal solicitation of business for an attorney, since acts were not within the scope of consul's official duties).

210 Vienna Consular Conv., *supra* note 112, art. 41(3). Honorary consuls enjoy a similar duty of respect. *Id.* art. 63.

211 *Id.* art. 42. *See supra* note 209. *See also* RESTATEMENT (THIRD), *supra* note 20, § 465 (2).

212 *Id.* art. 44(1). A receiving state authority requiring a consular officer to testify should avoid interference with the performance of consular functions, and if possible should use deposition practice. *Id.* art. 44(2) ("take such evidence at his residence or at the consular post or accept a statement from him in writing"). *See also* RESTATEMENT (THIRD), *supra* note 20, § 465 cmt.e & Reporters' Note 7.

If a consular officer declines to testify, no coercive measure or penalty may be invoked against him or her. Vienna Consular Conv., *supra* note 112, art. 44(2). *See*, however, *Illinois Commerce Comm'n v. Salamie*, 54 Ill. App. 3d 465, 369 N.E.2d 235 (1977) (honorary consul, an American citizen, was required to give testimony unless it related to official functions and could be sanctioned for refusal).

213 Vienna Consular Conv., *supra* note 112, art. 44(3). This covers honorary consuls as well. *Id.* art. 58(2).

214 *See supra* notes 77-87 and accompanying text.

215 *See* RESTATEMENT (THIRD), *supra* note 20, § 465 Reporters' Note 11.

216 Vienna Consular Conv., *supra* note 112, art. 45(1). The waiver must be sent by express and conveyed in writing to the receiving state. *Id.* art. 45(2).

(h) *Immunity of consular premises and property*—Consular premises[217] are to be inviolable to the extent they are used for consular purposes.[218] This is a narrower protection than is afforded diplomatic premises and property.[219]

(i) *Immunity of consular documents and archives*—Consular archives and documents must be inviolate,[220] as must consular bags and their contents.[221]

(j) *Protection of communications*—The protection afforded consular communications and correspondence is essentially that governing diplomatic communications.[222] Receiving states must allow freedom of communication for all official purposes, and correspondence must be respected as inviolable.[223] As noted,[224] consular bags and packages have equivalent protection against interception and inspection to diplomatic courier pouches.[225]

(k) *Right to receive state protection*—Receiving states are required to take all appropriate steps to prevent attacks on the person, freedom or dignity of consular officers,[226] including, to a more limited extent, honorary consular officials.[227] The federal statutes described earlier[228] serve by their express terms to protect consular officials. Similar requirements of protection[229] apply to consular premises,[230] including those occupied by honorary consuls.[231] Federal criminal law implements the Convention.[232]

---

217 Receiving states must accord full facilities for performance of consular functions, *id.* art. 28, and accommodations for staff. *Id.* art. 30. A sending state has the right to use its flag and national emblem on consular premises, having due regard to receiving state laws and regulations. *Id.* art. 29.

218 *Id.* art. 31(1)-(2). They can be entered by representatives of the receiving state only with the consent of the head of the consular post or designee, or of the head of the sending states diplomatic mission. *Id.* art. 31(2). Consent may be presumed in instances of fire or other disaster requiring prompt protective action. *Id.* Consular premises headed by an honorary consul are subject to the same protections. *Id.* art. 59.

219 *See supra* notes 100-113 and accompanying text (discussing inviolability of diplomatic premises). *See also* RESTATEMENT (THIRD), *supra* note 20, § 465 Reporters' Note 1(immunities of diplomatic missions and consular posts compared).

220 Vienna Consular Conv., *supra* note 112, art. 33. *See also* RESTATEMENT (THIRD), *supra* note 20, § 466. Inviolability extends to consular archives and documents in the control of an honorary consul, but they must be kept separate from other documents and, in particular, the private correspondence of the head of a consular post or anyone working with him, and from materials, books or documents relating to their profession or trade. *Id.* art. 61.

221 *Id.* art. 35(3)-(4). However, consular bags or packages may contain only official correspondence and documents or articles intended exclusively for official use. *Id.* art. 35(4). If receiving state authorities believe a bag contains something else, they may request that the bag or package be opened in their presence by an authorized sending state representative. If the request is refused by sending state authorities, the receiving state authorities may return the bag to its place of origin. *Id.* art. 35(3).

The exchange of consular bags between two consular posts headed by honorary consular officers in different states is allowable only with the consent of the two receiving states concerned. *Id.* art. 58(4).

222 *See supra* notes 119-59 and accompanying text (discussing inviolability of diplomatic communications).

223 Vienna Consular Conv., *supra* note 112, art. 35(1). Honorary consuls are included. *Id.* art. 58(1).

224 *See supra* note 227.

225 This protection extends during passage through third states. Vienna Consular Conv., *supra* note 112, art. 54(3).

226 *Id.* art. 40.

227 *Id.* art. 64 ("duty to accord to an honorary consular officer such protection as may be required by reason of his official position").

228 *See supra* notes 162-177 and accompanying text.

229 *See supra* notes 179-189 and accompanying text.

230 Vienna Consular Conv., *supra* note 112, art. 31(3). *See also* RESTATEMENT (THIRD), *supra* note 20,§ 466 § 466 Reporters' Note 2.

231 Vienna Consular Conv., *supra* note 112, art. 59.

232 *See supra* notes 183-188 and accompanying text.

Privileges and Immunities of Representatives of International Organizations

The creation of the United Nations and the establishment of its various functions and premises in several countries, including the United States, brought with it a necessity to expand and modernize older doctrines governing the privileges of personnel and premises of international organizations.[233] That was reflected in the adoption of the Convention on Privileges and Immunities of the United Nations,[234] to which the United States subscribes, as do most nations in the world.[235] The privileges and immunities afforded the United Nations and its subsidiary organs, as well as its permanent personnel, generally correspond to those delineated earlier for diplomats.[236]

The United Nations as a juridical personality[237] is immune to every form of legal process directed at its property and assets, unless it waives that immunity in a specific case.[238] More significantly, the United Nations' premises, wherever located, are to be held inviolable and not subjected to any form of search, requisition, confiscation, expropriation or other form of interference.[239] In terms of criminal law enforcement, that would preclude the issuance or execution of search warrants or administrative search warrants. United Nations archives and documents enjoy commensurate protections.[240] The United Nations also is to have no less favorable a right to protection of its official communications than is accorded by a

---

[233] *See generally* RESTATEMENT (THIRD), *supra* note 20, §467 (Privileges and Immunities of International Organizations); § 468 (Immunity of Premises, Archives, Documents, and Communications of International Organizations); § 469 (Immunity of Officials of International Organizations).

[234] Feb. 13, 1946, 21 U.S.T. 1418, 1 U.N.T.S. 16 (*entered into force* with respect to the United States Apr. 29, 1970) [hereinafter U.N. Privileges Conv.].

[235] As of January 1,1996, 137 states were parties to the United Nations Conventions. TREATIES IN FORCE, *supra* note 17, at 449-50.

[236] *See supra* notes 61-76 and accompanying text.

[237] U.N. Privileges Conv., *supra* note 234, § 1.

[238] *Id.* § 2. A waiver of immunity, however, does not extend to execution measures against property or assets. *Id. See generally* RESTATEMENT (THIRD), *supra* note 20, § 467 cmt.e & § 467 Reporters' Note 3. The claim to inviolability includes the expectation that a receiving state will provide protection for U.N. property. *See* RESTATEMENT (THIRD), *supra* note 20, § 467 Reporters' Note 3.

On claims to asylum on international organization premises *see id.* Reporters' Note 4.

With the exception of taxation and duties measures under U.N. Privileges Conv., *supra* note 234, § 7, the immunity is against the exercise of jurisdiction to enforce, not competence to prescribe. *See id.* § 467 cmt. c. On waiver, *see id.* §467 cmt. e & Reporters' Note 7.

[239] U.N. Privileges Conv., *supra* note 234, § 3; Agreement Between the United Nations and the United States of America Regarding the Headquarters of the United Nations, 61 Stat. 3416, T.I.A.S. No. 1676 § 9 (June 26, 1947) (*entered into force* with respect to the United States Nov. 27, 1947) [hereinafter U.N. Headquarters Agreement]. The U.N. headquarters district is defined in the U.N. Headquarters Agreement § 1(a) and annex 1, as modified by supplemental agreements of Feb. 9, 1966, 17 U.S.T. 2319, T.I.A.S. No. 6176; Aug. 28, 1969, 20 U.S.T. 2810, T.I.A.S. No. 6750; Dec. 10, 1980, T.I.A.S. No. 9955.

The United States is obligated to exercise due diligence to ensure the tranquility of the headquarters district through police protection, U.N. Headquarters Agreement §16.

The U.N. has undertaken to prevent the headquarters district from becoming a refuge for persons seeking to avoid arrest under United States federal, state or local law, extradition by the United States or another country, or service of legal process. *Id.* art. 9(b). It can expel or exclude persons who violate its regulations adopted under *id.* §10, and such persons are then subject to prosecution under applicable state or federal laws. *Id.*

See generally RESTATEMENT (THIRD), *supra* note 20, § 468 cmt. c. & Reports' Note 5.

[240] U.N. Headquarters Agreement, *supra* note 239, § 4. *See* RESTATEMENT (THIRD), *supra* note 20, § 468.

receiving state to diplomatic missions,[241] and is to be free from receiving state censorship.[242] It may use diplomatic couriers and courier bags with the same protections given generally to those forms of communication.[243]

Officials of the United Nations[244] are immune against exercises of jurisdiction relating to their written and spoken words and to their acts performed in their official capacity.[245] However, only the families of senior officials of the United Nations are accorded equivalent protections.[246] The United Nations has undertaken to cooperate with member governments in seeing that its officials and employees do not abuse their privileges and immunities and thus frustrate the proper administration of justice and breach police regulations.[247]

The immunity envisioned in the convention is that of the United Nations itself, so that waiver is the prerogative of that body and not an individual official.[248] However, the Secretary-General has the "right and duty" to waive immunity if a failure to do so would impede the course of justice.[249]

Representatives[250] of United Nations' members to that body itself and to conferences it convenes are to enjoy immunity from civil and criminal process for spoken or written words and acts done by them in their capacity as representatives,[251] as well as from personal arrest or detention and seizure of personal baggage during their sojourns and travels to and from places of meeting.[252] Their papers and documents are to be inviolable,[253] and they have the right to use codes and to receive papers or correspondence by courier or in sealed bags.[254] The protection afforded their mission premises in the United States does not come directly from the Convention but from the United Nations Headquarters Agreement[255] and

---

241 U.N. Privileges Conv., *supra* note 234, § 9. *See* RESTATEMENT (THIRD) *supra* note 20,§ 468 Reporters' Note 8; *supra* notes 117-20 and accompanying text. The basis for a U.N. communications system is U.N. Headquarters Agreement, *supra* note 239, § 4.

242 U.N. Privileges Conv., *supra* note 234, § 11(a). It may also use codes. *Id.* §10.

243 *Id.*§ 10. *See supra* notes 117-118, 228-229 and accompanying text.

244 Under U.N. Privileges Conv., *supra* note 234, § 17, the Secretary-General specifies the categories of U.N. officials covered by privileges and immunities and submits them to the General Assembly. After submission, the categories are to be communicated to the governments of all U.N. members, and the names of officials within them will be communicated from time to time to those governments. *See* RESTATEMENT (THIRD), *supra* note 20, § 469 cmt.e.

245 U.N. Privileges Conv., *supra* note 234, § 18(a). *See* RESTATEMENT (THIRD), *supra* note 20, § 469, §469 cmts. b&c, §469 Reporters' Notes 1 &4 (citing instances of prosecutions in the United States raising issues of official status and scope of official duties).

246 U.N. Privileges Conv., *supra* note 234, § 19, restricted protection to the spouses and minor children of the Secretary-General and U.N. assistant secretaries-general. *See* RESTATEMENT (THIRD), *supra* note 20, § 469 cmt. d.

247 U.N. Privileges Conv., *supra* note 234, § 21.

248 U.N. Privileges Conv., *supra* note 234, § 20. The Secretary-General has the exclusive right to waive, unless he is the one protected by immunity, in which case the Security Council holds the power of waiver. *Id. See also* RESTATEMENT (THIRD), *supra* note 20, § 469 cmt.f & Reporters' Note 7.

249 U.N. Privileges Conv., *supra* note 234, § 20.

250 Defined in the U.N. Privileges Conv., *supra* note 234, § 16 to include delegates, deputy delegates, advisers, technical experts and secretaries of delegations.

251 *Id.* § 11(a). The immunity against prosecution or action rests on official status at the time of the act, and continues to exist even though an individual ceases to represent a member state. *Id.* §12. *See generally* RESTATEMENT (THIRD), *supra* note 20,§ 470.

252 U.N. Privileges Conv., *supra* note 234, § 11(a).

253 *Id.* § 11(b).

254 *Id.* § 11(c).

255 U.N. Headquarters Agreement, *supra* note 239, § 15.

implementing federal legislation,[256] which provides them with equivalent protections afforded diplomatic premises generally.[257] The immunities are those of the member states, not individuals, so that only a sending state can waive them.[258]

Experts on missions for the United Nations, if not otherwise officials of that body covered under Article V of the Convention, are protected to the extent that privileges and immunities are necessary for the independent exercise of their functions during the period of their assignment, including mission-connected travel.[259] Those immunities include freedom from legal process concerning written or spoken words or acts performed in the course of a mission,[260] and from personal arrest and detention or seizure of personal baggage.[261] Their papers and documents must be held inviolable,[262] and for purposes of their communication with the United Nations, they may send and receive papers or correspondence by couriers or in sealed bags.[263] Because these privileges and immunities are accorded for the benefit of the United Nations itself, only the Secretary-General may waive them in individual cases.[264]

---

256 61 Stat. 756 (Aug. 4, 1947), appearing in 22 U.S.C. § 287 (1994).

257 *See supra* notes 100-113 and accompanying text.

258 U.N. Privileges Conv., *supra* note 234, § 14. However, members are under a duty to waive immunity in any case in which, in a member's opinion, continued reliance on immunity would impede the course of justice. *Id.* The privileges and immunities delineated in § 11 do not apply if a representative is, or was at the time of the act complained of, a national of the state wishing to prosecute or sue. *Id.* § 15.

259 *Id.* § 22. The "experts on mission" status has also been extended to military forces engaged in U.N. operations. *See* Steven J. Lepper, *The Legal Status of Military Personnel in United Nations Peace Operation: One Delegate's Analysis*, 18 HOUS. J. INT'L L 359, 368 (1996) (citing a letter from the U.N. Legal Adviser expressing the U.N. view "that U.S. aircrews flying missions in support of the United Nations Protective Force (UNPROFOR) in Bosnia-Herzegovina are Experts on Mission.") *Id.*

The Convention on the Safety of United Nations and Associated Personnel (Dec. 9, 1994), 34 I.L.M.482 (1995), which contains provisions for unimpeded transit of U.N. and associated personnel to and from the host state (art. 5), for their freedom from interrogation and prompt release should they be captured or detained (art.8) is not yet in force (only 13 states out of 22 needed for its *entry into force*, having ratified it thus far). Once it will *enter into force*, however, it will extend its protection, *inter alia,* to "persons engaged or deployed by the Secretary-General of the United Nations as members of the military, police or civilian components of a United Nations operation," (art. 1 (a)(i)) including operations "for the purpose of maintaining or restoring international peace and order." Art.1 (c)(i).

260 *Id.* § 22(b). Immunity continues even though the individual at the time of prosecution or suit is no longer serving as a U.N. expert. *Id.*

261 *Id.* § 22(a).

262 *Id.* § 22(c).

263 *Id.* § 22(d).

264 *Id.* § 23. The Secretary-General is under a duty to waive if reliance on immunity would impede the course of justice and can be waived without prejudice to the U.N. *Id.*

The immunities of other organizations than the United Nations, and their representatives and officials, are governed by treaties and implementing legislation.[265] In general, they correspond to those described above.

The status of trade missions and representatives of governmental trade organizations is determined by international agreement.[266] If an office has not been accorded the formal status of a diplomatic mission, however, criminal prosecutions can be maintained against mission personnel who violate domestic law.[267] The same holds true for special missions of various types.[268]

Jurisdiction Over Visiting Armed Forces Under Status of Forces Agreements

Historical Status of Visiting Forces

The traditional international law governing the amenability of visiting military and naval personnel to the exercise of receiving state criminal jurisdiction has been a matter of debate. The United States position for many years was based on statements in an early United States Supreme Court decision, *Schooner Exchange v. McFaddon*,[269] in which the American plaintiffs in a maritime libel action asserted ownership of a French public armed

---

265 Congress has accorded general authority to the President to extend, withhold or withdraw privileges, exemptions and immunities from international organizations with which the United States has entered into a treaty or which Congress has recognized as an international organization. 22 U.S.C. § 288 (a) (1994). Revocation can be based on abuse by an international organization or its officers and employees of such privileges, exemptions and immunities. *Id.* A current list of organizations so recognized may be found appended to the statute. *See* 22 U.S.C.A. § 288(West Supp.1997).

The property and assets of international organizations are accorded the same exemption from suit and "every form of judicial process" as foreign governments enjoy, unless the organizations waive it. 22 U.S.C. § 288a(b) (1994). Property and assets are exempt from search and confiscation (absent waiver), and their archives are to be inviolable. *Id.* § 228a(c). Representatives of foreign governments in or to international organizations, and officers and employees of such organizations, are "immune from suit and legal process relating to acts performed by them in their official capacity and falling within their functions as such representatives, officers, or employees," unless the immunity is waived by the foreign government or international organization. *Id.* § 288d.

Privileges and immunities are contingent on (1) notification to and acceptance by the Secretary of State appointed as representative, officer or employee; (2) designation by the Secretary of State to that effect before formal notification; or (3) notification to the Secretary of State that an individual is a member of an accredited individual's family or suite, or a servant. *Id.* § 288e(a). No additional immunities are to be enjoyed by such persons beyond those provided in the federal statute. *Id.* § 288e(c). If the Secretary of State determines that an individual no longer is entitled to privileges or immunities, he or she is to inform the foreign government or international organization of that decision. *Id.* § 288e(b). After the person affected has had a reasonable time (as the Secretary of State determines) to leave the country, he or she ceases to be protected. *Id.* The Secretary of State may withhold or withdraw recognition on the basis of a failure on the part of a foreign government to grant reciprocal protections to United States citizens. *Id.* § 288f.

On the conflicting views in Canada and the United States concerning the status of the International Joint Commission, *see* Note, *The Legal Status of the International Joint Commission under International and Municipal Law*, 1978 CAN.Y.B. INT'L L. 276.

266 *See* Vladimir S. Pozdniakov, *The Legal Status of Soviet Trade Representations Abroad*, 5 DENV. J. INT'L L. & POL'Y. 261 (1975).

267 *See e.g., United States v. Kostadinov*, 734 F.2d 905 (2d Cir.), *cert. denied*, 105 S.Ct. 246 (1984) (assistant counselor in Bulgarian trade office in New York did not have diplomat status and could be prosecuted for espionage).

268 *See* Michael H. Ryan, *The Status of Agents on Special Mission in Customary International Law*, 1978 CAN.Y.B. INT'L L. 157.

269 11 U.S. (7 Cranch) 116 (1812).

ship after the vessel had been forced by a storm to seek shelter in an American port. The Supreme Court sustained a district court dismissal of the libel on the basis that armed vessels of a friendly foreign nation are not within the jurisdiction of federal courts. Chief Justice Marshall noted in dictum that a "grant of free passage" to armed forces of a friendly power "implies a waiver of all jurisdiction over the troops, during their passage, and permits the foreign general to use that discipline, and to inflict those punishments which the government of his army may require."[270] No specific right of passage had to be granted a foreign naval vessel because "the ports of a friendly nation are considered as open to the public ships of all powers with whom it is at peace."[271] From this, influential American writers drew an inference that visiting forces should be considered immune from the exercise of receiving state jurisdiction, unless by treaty the sending state waives that immunity.[272] That theory often has been referred to as the concept of foreign territorial immunity, or the "law of the flag" principle.[273]

The competing theory, which prevails under contemporary international law, is that every sovereign has jurisdiction over criminal acts done within its territory, but that permission to a foreign power to station armed forces within receiving state territory creates not exclusive,[274] but concurrent jurisdiction. That principle must be acknowledged as the controlling law today, probably because it has been embodied explicitly in the many status-of-forces agreements according to which criminal cases against service personnel, civilian components and dependents are disposed of.[275] It appears as well to be the position accepted by the United States Supreme Court in *Wilson v. Girard*,[276] in which it perceived no federal constitutional or statutory grounds on the basis of which to compel the recovery and return to United States military jurisdiction of a service person, primary jurisdiction over whom had been waived by the President and Secretaries of Defense and State to Japanese authorities under the Japan-United States Mutual Security Treaty.[277]

---

270 *Id.* at 139-40.

271 *Id.* at 141.

272 *See* Archibald King, *Jurisdiction Over Friendly Foreign Armed Forces*, 36 AM. J. INT'L L. 539 (1942). *See also* Archibald King, *Further Developments Concerning Jurisdiction Over Friendly Foreign Armed Forces*, 40 AM. J. INT'L L. 257 (1946).

273 *See generally* Walter F. Brown, *Criminal Jurisdiction Over Visiting Naval Forces Under International Law*, 24 WASH. & LEE L. REV. 9 (1967); Edmund H. Schwenk, *Jurisdiction of the Receiving State Over Forces of the Sending State Under the NATO Status of Forces Agreement*, 6 INT'L LAW 525, 527-29 (1972); D.S. Wijewardane, *Criminal Jurisdiction Over Visiting Forces With Special Reference to International Forces*, 1965 BRIT. Y.B. INT'L LAW 122, 122-29; Note, *The Law of the Flag, the Law of Extradition, the NATO Status of Forces Agreement and Their Application to Members of the United States Army National Guard*, 15 VAND. J. TRANSNAT'L L. 179, 185-91 (1982) [hereinafter Vanderbilt Note].

274 Wijewardane, *supra* note 273, notes that states have not asserted exclusive criminal jurisdiction over visiting forces based on the territorial principal. *Id.* at 129. *But see* Schwenk, *supra* note 273, at 529 (asserting that a receiving state has exclusive jurisdiction unless it agrees by treaty to recognize concurrent jurisdiction).

275 *See generally* Wijewardane, *supra* note 273, at 129-32; Vanderbilt Note, *supra* note 273, at 183-85.

276 345 U.S 524 (1957). *See infra* notes 318-323 and accompanying notes.

277 Currently, Treaty of Mutual Cooperation and Security Between the United States and Japan, Jan. 19, 1960, 11 U.S.T. 1632, 1652, T.I.A.S. No. 4509, 4510 (*entered into force* with respect to the United States on June 23, 1960). This superseded Administrative Agreement Under Article III of the Security Treaty Between the United States and Japan, Feb. 28, 1952, 3 U.S.T. 3341, T.I.A.S. No. 2492 (*entered into force* with respect to the United States April 28, 1952), which was in force when the *Girard* case arose.

Status-of-Forces Agreements Affecting Criminal Jurisdiction Over Visiting Armed Forces

By far the most influential source of international law on the matter of receiving state criminal jurisdiction over sending-state forces and their dependents has been the Status of Forces Agreement under the North Atlantic Treaty,[278] governing North Atlantic Treaty Organization (NATO) forces. Its provisions have been incorporated by reference in certain other multilateral or bilateral agreements,[279] the most frequently invoked of which has been the treaty with the Federal Republic of Germany, because of the relatively large numbers of United States service personnel and their dependents stationed in that country.[280]

The NATO agreement enjoins all members of a visiting force[281] and its civilian component to respect a receiving state's laws.[282] If they do not, Article VII of the treaty establishes baselines for exercise of criminal jurisdiction:

---

[278] Agreement Between the Parties to the North Atlantic Treaty Regarding the Status of Their Forces, June 19, 1951, 4 U.S.T. 1792, 199 U.N.T.S. 67,(*entered into force* with respect to the United States Aug. 23, 1953)[hereinafter NATO SOFA]. The signatories are Belgium, Canada, Denmark, France, Germany, Greece, Italy, Luxembourg, The Netherlands, Norway, Portugal, Spain, Turkey, United Kingdom and United States.

[279] *E.g.*, Agreement Regarding Status of United States Forces in Australia, May 9, 1963, 14 U.S.T. 506, T.I.A.S. No. 5349; Agreement Regarding Application of North Atlantic Treaty Status of Forces Agreement to United States Forces at Leased Bases, United States-Canada, April 28-30, 1952, 5 U.S.T. 2139, T.I.A.S. No. 3074; Agreement Regarding Status of United States Forces in Egypt, July 26, 1981, T.I.A.S. No. 10,238; Agreement Regarding Status of United States Forces in Greece, Sept. 7, 1956, 7 U.S.T. 2556, T.I.A.S. No. 3649; Agreement Regarding Status of United States Forces in Grenada (effected by exchange of notes at St. George's March 12-13, 1984; entered into force March 13, 1984), 84 Dep't of State Bull, No 2087, p. 87 (1984); Annex to the Agreement Regarding United States Personnel and Property in Iceland, May 8, 1951, 2 U.S.T. 1534, T.I.A.S. No. 2295; Panama Canal Treaty, Implementation of Article IV, Agreement Between the United States and Panama, Sept. 7, 1977, art. VI, T.I.A.S. No. 10,032; United States-Philippines Agreement Concerning Military Bases, July 9, 1966, 61 Stat. 4019, T.I.A.S. No. 6084, 22 U.S.T. 1469, T.I.A.S. No. 6127, (*entered into force* with respect to the United States Feb. 9, 1967), and agreed minutes, 17 U.S.T. 1768, T.I.A.S. No. 6127; Agreement Regarding the Status of United States Forces in Turkey, June 23, 1954, 5 U.S.T. 1465, T.I.A.S. No. 3020.

United States military personnel in the Sudan are accorded diplomatic immunity. Agreement Regarding the Status of United States Military Personnel in the Sudan, Nov. 12 & Dec. 27, 1981, T.I.A.S. No. 10,322. The United States-Thailand Mutual Defense Assistance Agreement, Oct. 17, 1950, 3 U.S.T. 2675, T.I.A.S. No. 2434 (*entered into force* with respect to the United States Oct. 17, 1950) art. VII (2), makes all personnel assigned under the agreement diplomatic personnel, protected by the usual privileges and immunities, but does not mention military personnel expressly.

[280] *See* Agreement Regarding the Status of Forces in the Federal Republic of Germany, Aug. 3, 1959, 14 U.S.T. 531, 481 U.N.T.S. 262 (*entered into force* with respect to the United States July 1, 1963): Agreement Regarding the Status of United States Forces in the Federal Republic of Germany, Aug. 3, 1959, 14 U.S.T. 689 T.I.A.S. No. 5352; Agreement Amending the Agreement Regarding the Status of Forces in the Federal Republic of Germany, Oct. 21 1971, 24 U.S.T. 2355, T.I.A.S. No. 7759. *See* William A. Crawford, *The Air Force Local Liaison Authority for Criminal Offenses in Germany*, 9 JAG L. REV. 11 (May-June 1967).

[281] NATO SOFA, *supra* note 278, defines "force" as "the personnel belonging to the land, sea or air armed services of one Contracting Party when in the territory of another Contracting Party in the North Atlantic Treaty area in connection with their official duties," unless modified by independent agreement. *Id.* art. I(1)(a).

[282] Civilian component means "the civilian personnel accompanying a force of a Contracting Party who are in the employ of an armed service of that Contracting Party, and who are not stateless persons, nor nationals of any State which is not a Party to [NATO], nor nationals, of, nor ordinarily resident, in the State in which the force is located." *Id.* art. I(1)(b).

(1) Military authorities of a sending state[283] can exercise within the territory of a receiving state all criminal and disciplinary jurisdiction conferred on them by sending state law, covering all persons subject to sending state law.[284]
(2) Receiving state authorities have jurisdiction over the members of a force or civilian component and their dependents[285] with respect to offenses committed in receiving state territory and punishable under its laws.[286]
(3) Sending state military authorities may exercise exclusive jurisdiction over persons subject to sending state military law concerning offenses, including offenses relating to its security,[287] punishable under sending state law, but not that of the receiving state.[288]
(4) Receiving state authorities can exercise exclusive jurisdiction over members of a force or civilian component and their dependents concerning offenses, including those related to the security of the receiving state, punishable by its laws but not the law of the sending state.[289]

Although the third and fourth alternatives, by their terms, rest on exclusive and not concurrent jurisdiction, the first and second clearly foster concurrent jurisdiction. Therefore, Article VII sets out criteria according to which concrete cases can be disposed of:

(1) Sending state military authorities have priority in the exercise of criminal jurisdiction over a member of a force or civilian component in relation to (a) offenses solely against the property or security of that state, or against the person or property of another member of the force or civilian component of that state or of a dependent; or (b) offenses arising out of an act or omission done "in the performance of official duty."[290]
(2) Receiving state authorities have a primary right over all other offenses.[291]
(3) If the state with the primary right to prosecute decides not do so, it is to notify authorities of the other state as soon as practicable. The authorities of the state with jurisdictional priority are enjoined, however, to give "sympathetic consideration" to a request from the other government for a waiver of rights if the latter government considers "waiver to be of particular importance."[292]
(4) None of the rules, however, is to allow military authorities of a sending state to exercise jurisdiction over persons who are nationals of or ordinarily resident in the receiving state unless they are members of the sending state armed forces.[293]

---

283 Defined as those authorities of a sending State who are empowered by its law to enforce the military law of that State with respect to members of its forces or civilian components." *Id.* art. I(1)(f).

284 *Id.* art. VII(1)(a).

285 Defined as the spouse of a member of a force or civilian component, or a child dependent on him or her for support. *Id.* art. I(1)(c).

286 *Id.* art. VII(2)(a).

287 Security offenses against a state include treason, *id.* art. VII(c)(i); and sabotage, espionage or violation of any law relating to official secrets of that state, or secrets relating to the national defense of that state, *id.* art. VII(c)(ii).

288 *Id.* art. VII(2)(a).

289 *Id.* art. VII(2)(b).

290 *Id.* art. VII(3)(a). *See generally* Will H. Carroll, *Official Duty Cases Under Status of Forces Agreements: Modest Guidelines Toward a Definition,* 12 JAG L. REV. 284 (1970).

291 NATO SOFA, *supra* note 278, art. VII(3)(b).

292 *Id.* art. VII(3)(c).

293 *Id.* art. VII(4).

To effectuate the allocation of criminal jurisdiction under the treaty, sending and receiving states agree to assist each other in arresting offenders and turning them over to authorities of the state which will exercise jurisdiction,[294] to aid in the investigation of the case and the transfer of evidence to the prosecuting authority,[295] and to notify one another of the disposition of cases in which there is concurrent jurisdiction.[296]

Whatever may be the minimum procedural protections which international law requires criminal tribunals to accord nationals of other nations, the NATO agreement establishes certain procedural safeguards to sending state personnel tried in receiving state courts:[297] (1) a prompt and speedy trial; (2) notice in advance of trial of the specific charges; (3) confrontation by prosecution witnesses; (4) compulsory process for defense witnesses if they are within receiving state jurisdiction; (5) legal representation of the defendant's choice, or free or assisted legal representation under the conditions prevailing at the time in the receiving state; (6) services of an interpreter if the accused person desires; (7) a right of communication with a representative of the sending state government; and (8) the attendance of proceedings of a representative of the sending state government if receiving state procedural rules allow.

The death penalty is not to be carried out by the sending state within the territory of a receiving state which does not allow capital punishment.[298] If a receiving state adjudicates a sending force person guilty, it can enforce a sentence of imprisonment within its own borders if it wishes.[299] In addition, receiving state authorities should give "sympathetic consideration" to requests from sending state authorities for assistance in confining a convicted person within receiving state territory.[300]

The NATO agreement contains a *non bis in idem* provision prohibiting a second state from prosecuting after an acquittal, a conviction followed by service of sentence, or pardon, based on the same offense within the territory of the receiving state.[301] That does not bar, however, a military proceeding based on a violation of sending state disciplinary rules.[302]

---

294 *Id.* art. VII(5)(a). Receiving state authorities must notify sending state military authorities when a member of a force or civilian component, or a dependent, has been arrested. *Id.* art. VII(5)(b). A sending state may keep an accused member of a force or civilian component in custody until a receiving state with jurisdiction institutes charges. *Id.* art. VII(5)(c). *See generally* Stratton Health, *Status of forces Agreements as a Basis for United States Custody of an Accused,* 49 MIL. L. REV. 45(1970).

Military police of a sending state have the right to police camps, establishment or other premises occupied under the agreement, and have an obligation to maintain order and security on those premises, NATO SOFA, *supra* note 280, art. 10(a). Outside such premises, however, military police can be employed only as arranged with receiving state authorities, for the purpose of maintaining discipline and order among members of sending state forces. *Id.* art. 10(b).

295 *Id.* art. VII (6)(a). The transmitting authority, however, may require return of objects at a time which it specifies. *Id.*

296 *Id.* art. VII(6)(b).

297 *Id.* art. VII (9).

298 *Id.* art. VII(7)(a).

299 This is a corollary to the power to prosecute under the territorial principle. *See supra* notes 1, 278-281 and accompanying text.

300 NATO SOFA, *supra* note 278, art. VII(7)(b).

301 *Id.* art. VII(8).

302 *Id.*

United States Experience Under Status of Forces Agreements

The principal concern which emerged in public debate concerning United States ratification of the NATO agreement, other than the abstract question of international law theory,[303] was that U.S. service personnel would not receive a fair trail (judged according to federal constitutional standards) in receiving state courts. Accordingly, the Senate, while rejecting the so-called Bricker amendment[304] which would have insisted on exclusive United States court-martial jurisdiction over U.S. service personnel, attached certain "understandings" to its ratification of the agreement.[305]

One was that the provisions of Article VII did not constitute a precedent for future agreements. That premise has been long abandoned, as attested by the many status-of-forces agreements entered into in ensuing years.[306] The second was that, if a United States service person was to be tried by receiving state authorities, the commander of United States forces in the receiving state was to examine the laws of the host country to ascertain their consonance with U.S. constitutional safeguards for criminal defendants. If the commander envisioned danger that an accused individual would not enjoy or would be denied those rights, he or she was to request a waiver of receiving state jurisdiction. If a waiver was not forthcoming, the commander was to request the Department of State to press the request through diplomatic channels.[307] The third was that a United States representative, appointed by the chief of the United States diplomatic mission in the receiving state with the advice of the senior United States military representative in that country, was to attest receiving state trials to observe compliance with Article IX procedural standards.[308]

Whatever validity the senatorial fears may have had then, status-of-forces agreements have been implemented in many criminal cases abroad in which U.S. military personnel, civilian employees and dependents have been the defendants.[309] Constitutional concerns

---

303 *See supra* notes 276-278 and accompanying text.

304 Named after is sponsor, Senator John Bricker. *See* Vanderbilt Note, *supra* note 273, at 203-04.

305 The text as transmitted by the United States to other signatory states appears in 4 U.S.T. 1792, 1828-29 (1953) [hereinafter Senate Resolution].

306 *See supra* notes 283-284.

307 Senate Resolution, *supra* note 305, para.2-3. The executive branch also was required to notify the Armed Services Committees of the House and Senate. *Id.* Para.3.

308 *Id.* para. 4. Failure to comply with NATO SOFA, *supra* note 278, art IX requirements was to be reported to the commanding officer of the United States forces in the country, who then was to request the Department of State to take "appropriate action"; the executive branch was required to notify the congressional committees mentioned *supra* note 309. Senate Resolution, *supra* note 305, para 4.

309 A number of well publicized cases involving SOFA arose with respect to U.S. troops stationed in Japan. Those U.S. servicemen were tried and convicted in Japan for a September 1995 abduction and rape of a 12-year-old girl. *See Okinawa Rape Ruling,* MAINICHI DAILY NEWS, Mar. 9,1996, at 2, *available in* LEXIS, NEWS LIBRARY. Pursuant to the SOFA, which obliges U.S. authorities to hand over criminal suspects to the Japanese authorities only after indictment, U.S. military authorities refused the request of the Japanese police to surrender the three accused servicemen to Japanese custody. *See* Edward W. Desmond, *Rape of an Innocent, Dishonor in the Ranks,* TIME, Oct. 2, 1995, at 51. Only after the Japanese authorities prepared an indictment did they secure custody of the three servicemen. *See Rape Trial Date Set for U.S. Servicemen in Japan,* REUTERS N. AM. WIRE, Oct.13, 1995, *available in* LEXIS, NEWS LIBRARY. The nature of the crime and the SOFA provisions governing custody of suspected criminals led to a public outcry for change in Japan. *See U.S. Servicemen Charged in Okinawa Rape,* FACTS ON FILE WORLD NEWS DIGEST, Oct.12, 1995, *available in* LEXIS, NEWS LIBRARY. This resulted in an agreement between the U.S. and Japan that may enable Japanese authorities to take into custody before indictment U.S. servicemen suspected of having committed serious crimes. *See U.S. Agrees to Turn Over Suspects Before Indictment,* JAPAN TIMES WEEKLY, Nov.6,1995, at 3, *available in* LEXIS, NEWS LIBRARY. According to the

were rejected (if not necessarily allayed) by the Supreme Court approval, in *Wilson v. Girard*,[310] of the implementation of such agreements. In that case, Girard, while participating in field exercises in Japan, killed a Japanese woman by discharging a firearm at her.[311] United States military authorities at first claimed that he acted in "performance of official duty," and disagreed with the contention of Japanese prosecuting authorities that Girard's act did not further the discharge of those duties and thus was a criminal act over which Japan had primary jurisdiction.[312] Nevertheless, because under the agreement the authorities of a state with primary jurisdiction are to give "sympathetic consideration" to a request from authorities of the other state to waive primacy, the President confirmed the joint conclusion of the Secretaries of State and Defense that Girard should be surrendered for trial by Japanese courts.[313] Girard sued for *habeas corpus* against the Secretary of Defense to require his return to United States military custody.[314]

The Supreme Court, *per curiam*, ruled that the writ properly had been denied by the federal district court.[315] The treaty delineated the circumstances under which Japan had waived its jurisdiction based on the territorial principle and the procedures embodied in the agreement had been followed. There was no constitutional or federal statutory barrier to the implementation of that policy.

The *Girard* case settled the constitutional issue of SOFA-based surrender of U.S. armed forces personnel and their dependents for receiving state trial, as far as lower federal courts have been concerned. To illustrate, in *Holmes v. Laird*,[316] the District of Columbia Circuit Court of Appeals refused to bar the surrender of U.S. soldiers to West German authorities for service of sentence, despite the claim that they had not received all the procedural

---

agreement, U.S. authorities will give "sympathetic consideration" to Japanese requests for custody in cases involving serious crimes. *Id.* This provision is similar to the one that covers U.S. troops in Germany. *See* Nicholas D. Kristof, *U.S. Gives Way to Japan on Accused Servicemen,* INT'L HERALD TRIBUNE, Oct.26,1995. In South Korea, on the other hand, U.S. servicemen charged with crimes are held in U.S. custody until the completion of their trial and sentencing. *See S. Korea to Take Over U.S. Soldier on Indictment,* JAPAN ECONOMIC NEWSWIRE, Jan. 17, 1996, *available in* LEXIS, NEWS LIBRARY. The first case that arose under the new SOFA application rules in Japan involved a U.S. serviceman accused of cutting the throat of a Japanese woman and robbing her of her purse. *See Japan-U.S. Status of Forces Agreement,* JIJI PRESS TICKER SERVICE, July 19, 1996, *available in* LEXIS, NEWS LIBRARY. Upon the request of the Japanese authorities and pursuant to the "sympathetic consideration" provision U.S. authorities surrendered the suspect to the Japanese before indictment. *See U.S. Sailor Sentenced to 13 Years in Prison*, JIJI PRESS TICKER SERVICE, Dec. 4,1996, *available in* LEXIS, NEWS LIBRARY. The serviceman was subsequently convicted of attempted murder and robbery and sentenced to 13 years in prison, by a Japanese court. *See U.S. Seaman Gets 13 Years for Brutal Robbery,* MAINICHI DAILY NEWS, Dec.5, 1996, at 16, *available in* LEXIS, NEWS LIBRARY. Another U.S. sailor was recently transferred to Japanese custody following indictment charging him with attempted rape and assault. *See U.S. Sailor Indicted in Japan for Attempted Rape,* REUTERS WORLD SERVICE, Apr. 15, 1997, *available* in LEXIS, NEWS LIBRARY.

For cases of SOFA implementation in Germany and South Korea, *see U.S. Soldier is Given Life in German Prison for Rape and Murder,* THE HOUSTON CHRONICLE, Dec. 2, 1995, at 32; David Holley, *S. Korean Case Shows why U.S. Protective of Soldiers' Rights,* THE COMMERCIAL APPEAL (MEMPHIS), Jan.14, 1996, at 6A; *GI Arrested in South Korea and Charged with Attempted Rape*, L.A. TIMES, Jan.11, 1996, at A6.

[310] 534 U.S. 524 (1957).

[311] *Id.* at 526.

[312] *Id.* at 529.

[313] *Id.*

[314] *Id.* at 526.

[315] *Id.* at 530.

[316] 459 F.2d 1211 (D.C. Cir.), *cert. denied,* 409 U.S. 869 (1972). *See also Starks v. Seamans*, 339 F.Supp. 1200 (E.D. Wis. 1972) (refusing to bar the Secretary of the Air Force from surrendering Starks, then stationed in Taiwan, to the Taiwanese government for service of sentence based on a drug offense conviction).

safeguards to which they would have been entitled under U.S. constitutional law and the status-of-forces agreement itself. The treaty expressly provides that all differences arising in its implementation are to be settled without recourse to any outside jurisdiction,[317] which settled the matter as far as the federal judiciary was concerned.

In *Matter of Burt,*[318] the Seventh Circuit found no federal due process barrier to a transfer through extradition proceedings of former servicemen to West Germany for civilian trial on murder charges. West Germany had waived its primary claim to jurisdiction over the off-duty crime on the understanding that the two defendants would be tried by U.S. authorities. Because the principal evidence against them had become inadmissible as a result of the intervening decision *of Miranda v. Arizona,*[319] military prosecutors felt it was no longer possible to court-martial the two, and they were given dishonorable discharges. For some years, the extradition treaty between the United States and West Germany did not allow for the extradition of nationals of one country for trial in the other, thus barring the surrender of the two defendants for West German trial. In the revised extradition treaty of 1978,[320] however, each country obligated itself to surrender its own nationals for trial by the other, whether offenses had been committed before or after the effective date of the treaty. On that basis, the federal government honored a West German request for the defendants' surrender. The court of appeals sustained the surrender, even though Burt claimed that he would be denied the speedy trial guaranteed him under the status-of-forces agreement.[321] The delay in Burt was the fault of the United States, not West Germany as the prosecuting state. In any event, the court held that the sole recourse against a treaty violation would be diplomatic and not judicial.[322]

Federal Trials of Members of a Force and Civilian Components

As noted, if members of a visiting force or its civilian component are either within the primary jurisdiction of the sending state, or jurisdiction has been waived by the receiving state, the sending state is under a responsibility to proceed to adjudication and to notify the receiving state of the outcome.[323] That poses no problem as long as an accused person is on active duty as a member of the United States armed forces; a court-martial can try the matter.[324] However, once a person has been discharged from active duty, it violates his or her federal constitutional rights for authorities to order a recall to active duty and institute court-martial proceedings.[325]

Moreover, since court-martial procedure does not embrace the right to jury trial required under the sixth amendment to the Constitution, the Supreme Court has barred that form of

---

317 NATO SOFA, *supra* note 278, art. 16.

318 737 F.2d 1477 (7th Cir. 1984).

319 384 U.S. 436 (1966) (holding inadmissible, in the absence of valid warnings and waiver of rights, confessions obtained in the absence of counsel and evidence derivative from them).

320 32 U.S.T. 000, T.I.A.S. No. 9785 (effective as to the United States on Aug. 29, 1980).

321 *See* NATO SOFA, *supra* note 278, art. VII(9)(a).

322 737 F.2d at 1487-88.

323 *See supra* note 297 and accompanying text.

324 *See e.g., Marymont v. Joyce,* 352 F.Supp. 547 (W.D. Ark. 1972) (denying *habeas corpus* to convicted court-martial defendant serving his sentence in the United States; the offense was murder in England of Marymont's wife).

325 United States *ex rel. Toth v. Quarles,* 350 U.S. 11 (1955).

trial for both civilian employees[326] and civilian dependents of service personnel.[327] Because no federal criminal statute covers the criminal acts of persons in those categories committed outside the territorial jurisdiction of the United States, they cannot be prosecuted for their crimes in federal district courts where jury trial is available, and Congress has not established extraterritorial courts other than in occupied West Berlin.[328]

In light of this constitutional limitation on fulfillment of the United States obligation under its status-of-forces agreements of adjudicating civilian employee and dependent criminal offenses, the only alternative to functional criminal immunity for those classes of defendants is a waiver of American jurisdictional claims in favor of the exercise of criminal jurisdiction by the receiving state. This makes the position adopted by the United States Supreme Court highly anomalous, indeed pyrrhic; the Court barred the exercise of court-martial jurisdiction because of the want of juries in military courts, but thereby impelled a surrender to receiving state authorities of persons in the classes it wished to protect. However, those states, certain common-law nations aside, do not allow for jury trial in the form we know it. One can only wish that reality had held sway over theory in United States Supreme Court thinking, so that civilian employees and dependents could have been tried under U.S. military authority.[329] Nevertheless, the Court's decisions stand unimpaired, leaving it to American military authorities to forestall a form of functional asylum by ceding jurisdiction to receiving states, at least until Congress extends the reach of federal criminal laws to acts by American nationals in receiving state territory.[330]

* * * *

EDITOR'S NOTE

The immunity of diplomats and Heads of State from prosecution or international crimes has never been definitively settled. The Nuremberg and Tokyo War Crime Trials (*see* Vol. III) prosecuted persons who could have been deemed includable in the "immuned" category

---

326 *McElroy v. United States ex rel.* Guagliardo, 361 U.S. 281 (1960) (noncapital offenses); *Grisham v. Hagan*, 361 U.S. 278 (1960) (capital offense).

327 *Kinsella v. United States ex rel.* Singleton, 361 U.S. 234 (1960)(noncapital offenses); *Reid v. Covert*, 354 U.S.1 (1957) (capital crime).

328 *See United States v. Tiede*, 86 F.R.D. 227 (U.S. Court for Berlin, 1979), in which an alien on trial for hijacking a domestic airliner from Poland to West Berlin was afforded a jury trial. *See generally* H. STERN, JUDGEMENT IN BERLIN 232-357(1984) (by the federal judge who presided over the trial proceedings). The Supreme Court in *Reid v. Covert,* 354 U.S. 1(1957), characterized *In re Ross,* 1940 U.S. 453 (1891), which had upheld the conviction by the American consular court in Yokahama, Japan, of a British seaman serving on an American vessel who had murdered a shipmate in Yokohama port, as "a relic from an earlier era." 354 U.S. at 12. That would appear to preclude widespread use of extraterritorial, nonmilitary courts to try civilian employees and defendants.

329 The Court's decision created analogous problems during United States civilian administration of the Ryukyu Island before their reversion to Japan. *See* B.J. George, *The United States in the Ryukyus: The Insular Cases Revised,* 39 N.Y.U. L. Rev. 785,793-94 (1964).

330 In the Comprehensive Crime Control Act of 1984, Pub. L. No. 98-473, §1210 (Oct.12,1984), Congress added a new 18 U.S.C.§ 7(7), which extends the special maritime and territorial jurisdiction of the United States to "any place outside jurisdiction of any nation with respect to an offense by or against a national of the United States." Although an interesting extension of federal jurisdiction to cover crimes by and against United States nationals, the restriction of location to places outside the jurisdiction of the United States (Congress had in mind the Antarctic, ice floes, unclaimed islands, or the moon) makes it essentially useless to reach civilian employees and dependents since their crimes are by hypothesis committed within receiving state jurisdiction.

and established the principle of Non-Immunity of Heads of State in accordance with the precedent established in the Treaty of Versailles (1919) Art. 227 which set forth the prosecution of Kaiser Wilhelm II (*see* BASSIOUNI, THE PROSECUTION OF INTERNATIONAL CRIMES AND THE ESTABLISHMENT OF AN INTERNATIONAL CRIMINAL COURT, Vol. III). Recent problems of terrorism and traffic in drugs raised the question of limiting diplomatic immunity.

United States Legislative Approach to Extraterritorial Jurisdiction in Connection with Terrorism

Roman Boed

Introduction

This chapter examines the U.S. legislative approach to extraterritorial jurisdiction in connection with terrorism and concludes that recent legislative activity expanded the extraterritorial reach of U.S. laws beyond limits presently recognized in international law and beyond the contemplation of relevant international instruments. In its final section, this chapter considers various limits on the exercise of extraterritorial jurisdiction and suggests that those limits are unlikely to restrict the application of U.S. antiterrorist laws abroad.

Controlling the extraterritorial reach of U.S. statutes must begin with legislative work. Namely, amending some of the statutes analyzed here to rely on jurisdiction aimed at protecting the state itself from terrorist attacks, rather than U.S. nationals abroad. This amendment would not diminish whatever protection U.S. antiterrorist statutes offer to U.S. nationals abroad, as most terrorist acts affecting such nationals would likely be aimed at them in the first place, because of their U.S. nationality and would thus trigger the protective jurisdiction of the United States. Such an amendment would, however, make U.S. antiterrorist laws consistent with doctrine and more acceptable to other states. Because the laws thus amended would be more acceptable, they would also be more enforceable and, in the end, the goal of combating terrorism would be better served.

This chapter is primarily concerned with prescriptive extraterritorial jurisdiction, the legal capacity of a state to prescribe penal laws applicable extraterritorially. It is an inquiry from the point of view of international law and whatever authorizations for or challenges to such capacity there may be in the domestic legal system are not addressed here. Consequently, selected U.S. antiterrorism statutes are analyzed in this chapter against the doctrinal background of international law, including against relevant provisions of international treaties. To initiate the analytical process, section II reviews jurisdictional principles recognized in international law and in the practice of states, and section III examines jurisdictional provisions of relevant conventions. Section IV contains an analysis of U.S. laws aimed at extraterritorial terrorist acts. The chapter closes with a consideration of issues that are implicated in a state's exercise of extraterritorial jurisdiction.

Jurisdictional Principles Relevant to Combating Terrorism

The Territorial Principle

The competence of a state to prescribe laws governing conduct and status of persons in its territory is generally recognized as one of the aspects of state sovereignty.[1] This is simply

[1] In the *S.S. Lotus Case*, the Permanent Court of International Justice stated: "[A]ll that can be required of a State is that it should not overstep the limits which international law places upon its jurisdiction; within these limits, its title to exercise jurisdiction rests in its sovereignty." 1927 P.C.I.J. (ser. A) No. 9, at 19. *See also* Harvard

because states have the prerogative of control over their territories and the people present in them.[2] The *Restatement (Third) of Foreign Relations Law of the United States* stipulates that "a state has jurisdiction to prescribe law with respect to . . . (a) conduct that, wholly or in substantial part, takes place within its territory; (b) the status of persons, or interests in things present within its territory; (c) conduct outside its territory that has or is intended to have substantial effect within its territory."[3] And thus, the *Restatement (Third)* evinces the state's capacity to prescribe laws applicable not only to conduct or persons actually present in its territory, but also in cases when extraterritorial conduct would have a *substantial effect* in the state. Both of these applications of the territorial principle, respectively referred to as subjective and objective applications, appear to be accepted by states and, in principle, are not controversial.[4]

The Nationality Principle

The nationality principle of jurisdiction, sometimes referred to as the active personality theory of jurisdiction, is another principle that flows out of state sovereignty, nationality being an aspect of sovereignty.[5] This principle entails jurisdiction over crimes committed by a state's nationals abroad. The *Restatement (Third)* recognizes the nationality principle as one of the bases of jurisdiction to prescribe. In section 402(2), the *Restatement (Third)* stipulates that a state has jurisdiction to prescribe law with respect to "the activities,

---

Research In International Law, *Draft Convention on Jurisdiction with Respect to Crime*, 29 AM. J. INT'L L. 439, 467-68 (Supp. 1935)[hereinafter Harvard Research]; IAN BROWNLIE, PRINCIPLES OF PUBLIC INTERNATIONAL LAW 298 (4th ed. 1990); D. W. Bowett, *Jurisdiction: Changing Patterns of Authority over Activities and Resources*, 1982 BRIT. Y.B. INT'L L. 1, 1.

2 *See e.g.*, Harvard Research, *supra* note 1, at 480; Michael Akehurst, *Jurisdiction in International Law*, 1972-73 BRIT. Y.B. INT'L L. 145, 152.

3 RESTATEMENT (THIRD) OF FOREIGN RELATIONS LAW OF THE UNITED STATES § 402 (1987)[hereinafter RESTATEMENT (THIRD)]. It should also be noted that the *Restatement (Third)* recognizes limitations on jurisdiction to prescribe. *See id.* § 403. In general, a state may not exercise its prescriptive jurisdiction over a person or conduct with connections to another state when this would be unreasonable. *Id.* § 403(1). Section 403(2) of the *Restatement (Third)* gives guidance on determining when an exercise of jurisdiction is unreasonable.

> Whether exercise of jurisdiction over a person or activity is unreasonable is determined by evaluating all relevant factors, including, where appropriate:
> (a) the link of the activity to the territory of the regulating state, *i.e.*, the extent to which the activity takes place within the territory, or has substantial, direct, and foreseeable effect upon or in the territory;
> (b) the connection, such as nationality, residence, or economic activity, between the regulating state and the person principally responsible for the activity to be regulated, or between that state and those whom the regulation is designed to protect;
> (c) the character of the activity to be regulated, the importance of the regulation to the regulating state, the extent to which other states regulate such activities, and the degree to which the desirability of such regulation is generally accepted;
> (d) the existence of justified expectations that might be protected or hurt by the regulation;
> (e) the importance of the regulation to the international political, legal, or economic system;
> (f) the extent to which the regulation is consistent with the traditions of the international system;
> (g) the extent to which another state may have an interest in regulating the activity; and
> (h) the likelihood of conflict with regulation by another state.

Id. § 403(2).

4 *See, e.g.*, RESTATEMENT (THIRD), *supra* note 3, § 402 cmt. c; Harvard Research, *supra* note 1, at 480-503; CHRISTOPHER L. BLAKESLEY, TERRORISM, DRUGS, INTERNATIONAL LAW, AND THE PROTECTION OF HUMAN LIBERTY 103-17 (1992); BROWNLIE, *supra* note 1, at 300-01; Akehurst, *supra* note 2, at 152-55.

5 *See, e.g.*, BROWNLIE, *supra* note 1, at 303.

interests, status, or relations of its nationals outside as well as within its territory."[6] The practice of states indicates acceptance of this jurisdictional principle.[7]

The Protective Principle

Under the protective principle, states claim jurisdiction over acts committed against their security interests by aliens abroad.[8] The *Restatement (Third)*, in this regard, restates the jurisdictional competence of a state to prescribe law with respect to "certain conduct outside its territory by persons not its nationals that is directed against the security of the state or against a limited class of other state interests."[9] The protective principle is similar to the subjective application of the territorial principle of jurisdiction in that it covers conduct outside the state's territory, but it is distinguishable from the principle of subjective territoriality in that it only extends to aliens and only to conduct threatening the state as such.[10]

The state's competence to proscribe extraterritorial conduct aimed at its very existence derives from its interest to protect itself and thus has been accepted in the practice of states despite the lack of territorial or nationality nexus.[11] The generally advanced justification for prescriptive jurisdiction based on the protective principle is the inadequacy of domestic laws addressing domestic conduct threatening the security or integrity of other states.[12] Because the interest sought to be protected by this jurisdictional principle is the security of the state, the protective principle is of particular relevance to combating extraterritorial acts of terrorism against a state.[13]

---

6 RESTATEMENT (THIRD), *supra* note 3, § 402(2).

7 *Id.* § 402 cmt. e; Harvard Research, *supra* note 1, at 519-23; BLAKESLEY, *supra* note 4, at 125; BROWNLIE, *supra* note 1, at 303; Akehurst, *supra* note 2, at 156-57; Geoffrey R. Watson, *Offenders Abroad: The Case for Nationality-Based Criminal Jurisdiction*, 17 YALE J. INT'L L. 41, 67, 69 (1992).

8 The *Harvard Research* stated the protective principle in the following way:

> A State has jurisdiction with respect to any crime committed outside its territory by an alien against the security, territorial integrity or political independence of that State, provided that the act or omission which constitutes the crime was not committed in exercise of a liberty guaranteed the alien by the law of the place where it was committed.

Harvard Research, *supra* note 1, at 543.

9 RESTATEMENT (THIRD), *supra* note 3, § 402(3).

10 The *Restatement (Third)* notes that "[t]he protective principle may be seen as a special application of the effects principle . . . but it has been treated as an independent basis of jurisdiction." *Id.* § 402 cmt. f.

11 The *Harvard Research* noted that the basis for protective jurisdiction is "the nature of the interest injured rather than the place of the act or the nationality of the offender." It then continued, "[w]ith the exception of the jurisdiction universally recognized over nationals abroad and over pirates . . . legislation enacted in reliance upon the protective principle constitutes the most common extension of penal jurisdiction to offences committed abroad." Harvard Research, *supra* note 1, at 543. *See also* BROWNLIE, *supra* note 1, at 304 ("Nearly all states assume jurisdiction over aliens for acts done abroad which affect the security of the state . . ." *Id.*); Akehurst, *supra* note 2, at 158 ("The principle is well established. . . ." *Id.*).

12 *See* Harvard Research, *supra* note 1, at 552 ("There is justification for the enactment of penal legislation based upon the protective principle in the inadequacy of most national legislation punishing offences committed within the territory against the security, integrity and independence of foreign States." *Id.*); IAN CAMERON, THE PROTECTIVE PRINCIPLE OF INTERNATIONAL CRIMINAL JURISDICTION 31 (1994) ("The *raison d'etre* of the protective principle is quite simply the fact that state A cannot really rely upon state B to protect A's vital interests, or to protect them to the extent which A considers necessary or desirable." *Id.*).

13 *See* BLAKESLEY, *supra* note 4, at 117-18 ("Most acts of terrorism . . . aimed at a particular state or government, will trigger jurisdiction in the object state based on the protective principle." *Id.*); Jordan J. Paust, *Federal Jurisdiction Over Extraterritorial Acts of Terrorism and Nonimmunity for Foreign Violators of International Law Under the FSIA and the Act of State Doctrine*, 23 VA. J. INT'L L. 191 (1983) ("The protective

While the principle itself is well established in state practice, the spectrum of conduct covered by it is not well defined.[14] The *Harvard Research* defined the range of conduct covered by the protective principle as crimes "against the security, territorial integrity or political independence" of a state[15] and "falsification or counterfeiting, or an uttering of falsified copies or counterfeits, of the seals, currency, instruments of credit, stamps, passports, or public documents" issued by a state.[16] The *Restatement (Third)* in a much broader (and vaguer) statement included in the scope of the protective principle conduct against the "security of the state" as well as conduct "against a limited class of other state interests."[17] According to the *Restatement (Third)*, conduct threatening to "other state interests" includes the traditional categories of counterfeiting and falsification of state documents as well as "perjury before consular officials, and conspiracy to violate the immigration or customs laws."[18]

The lack of definition of the range of conduct encompassed by the protective principle and the principle's malleability[19] could lead to the principle's justification of a wide-ranging exercise of extraterritorial jurisdiction.[20] After all, if "perjury before consular officials"[21] comes within the ambit of threats to the "security, territorial integrity or political independence"[22] of the state, so will many other kinds of conduct which may not threaten the existence or foundations[23] (such as territorial integrity or political independence) of the state.[24] The danger from an aggressive exercise of jurisdiction to prescribe extraterritorially applicable laws under the protective principle is conflict between states.[25] Since the conduct covered by the protective principle is, by definition, extraterritorial and is carried out by an alien, it is very likely that at least one other state (but possibly more) will have jurisdiction

---

principle is another useful basis for jurisdiction over extraterritorial acts of terrorism." *Id.* at 209). Paust also notes that commentators view the protective principle as related to the self-defense of a state and observes that "it would not be unreasonable to recognize the application of the protective principle to any violation of article 2(4) of the U.N. Charter as elaborated to preclude acts of state terrorism or the toleration, aiding, and abetting of international terrorism." *Id.* at 210.

14 *See* Akehurst, *supra* note 2, at 158; Bowett, *supra* note 1, at 10.

15 Harvard Research, *supra* note 1, at 543.

16 *Id.* at 561. Commentators such as Feller view the *ratione materiae* of the protective principle as "offenses against the security of the state and its political regime, against its territorial integrity and independence, against its prestige, or against its economic stability, and other offenses of this kind directed against the state as such." S.Z. Feller, *Jurisdiction Over Offenses With a Foreign Element*, *in* 2 A TREATISE ON INTERNATIONAL CRIMINAL LAW 5, 26 (M. Cherif Bassiouni & Ved P. Nanda eds., 1973).

17 RESTATEMENT (THIRD), *supra* note 3, § 402(3).

18 *Id.* § 402 cmt. f.

19 Cameron notes that "the protective principle is uniquely flexible" and that "its scope appears to be capable of almost infinite expansion." CAMERON, *supra* note 12, at 33.

20 Paust warns that "[t]here is a danger in pushing the protective theory too far, however, and I suspect that the better view is that actual effects should be felt, before the protective principle could properly be seen to apply." Paust, *supra* note 13, at 210.

21 RESTATEMENT (THIRD), *supra* note 3, § 402 cmt. f.

22 Harvard Research, *supra* note 1, at 543.

23 Feller notes that "[i]n the case of the protective principle, the offense affects *the very foundations of the state itself.*" Feller, *supra* note 16, at 29 (emphasis added).

24 Of course, the requirement of reasonableness in the exercise of jurisdiction to prescribe is a limitation on the exercise of jurisdiction under the protective principle as well as under the territorial and nationality principles. *See* RESTATEMENT (THIRD), *supra* note 3, § 403.

Paust notes that "[t]he national interest at stake, when viewed in the context, should be of real significance." Paust, *supra* note 13, at 210.

25 *See* CAMERON, *supra* note 12, at 32.

over it. Cameron envisions two conceivable jurisdictional conflicts in this context.[26] First, when two (or more) states would seek to exercise jurisdiction over a person for the same conduct.[27] Second, when a state would seek to exercise jurisdiction over extraterritorial conduct that would not be criminal in the state where it was committed.[28]

The Passive Personality Principle

The passive personality principle embodies the proposition that "a state may apply law—particularly criminal law—to an act committed outside its territory by a person not its national where the victim of the act was its national."[29] Like the protective principle, the passive personality principle addresses extraterritorial conduct by aliens. But the two principles may be distinguished from one another by the type of conduct to which they are directed. While the protective principle is, in general, concerned with conduct aimed at the state itself, the passive personality principle, in its pure form, encompasses extraterritorial offences against a state's nationals, as individuals.[30]

The passive personality principle is said to stem from the state's interest to protect its nationals.[31] While this is a legitimate interest when safeguarded domestically, its extraterritorial extension is questionable.[32]

Perhaps not surprisingly then, the passive personality theory of extraterritorial jurisdiction has not traditionally enjoyed support in the practice of states or among commentators.[33] Significantly, the passive personality principle was not included in the Draft Convention on Jurisdiction with Respect to Crime,[34] largely because the drafters believed

---

26 *See* CAMERON, *supra* note 12, at 32-33.

27 *Id.* at 32.

28 *Id.* at 32-33.

29 RESTATEMENT (THIRD), *supra* note 3, § 402 cmt. g.

30 Feller, *supra* note 16, at 29.

31 *Id.* at 28.

32 The *Harvard Research* notes "[o]f all principles of jurisdiction having some substantial support in contemporary national legislation, [the passive personality principle] is the most difficult to justify in theory." Harvard Research, *supra* note 1, at 579. It is not difficult to see why. Extension of extraterritorial jurisdiction for the protection of a state's nationals, if exercised, would constitute an interference in domestic matters of other states. Certainly, the principle of non-intervention should always be considered with respect to an exercise of extraterritorial jurisdiction, on whatever grounds. But the protection of a national abroad (as distinguished from the protection of national interests going to the safety or integrity of the state itself), in particular, would seem not to justify interference in the domestic matters of other states.

Cameron argues that the principle of non-intervention applies to the area of jurisdiction, and that "it is applicable *a fortiori* to criminal law, which represents an even greater intervention in internal affairs [than antitrust law matters where non-intervention has been applied to the area of jurisdiction]." CAMERON, *supra* note 12, at 345. The reporters of *Restatement (Third)* similarly noted that "the exercise of criminal (as distinguished from civil) jurisdiction in relation to acts committed in another state may be perceived as particularly intrusive." RESTATEMENT (THIRD), *supra* note 3, § 403 Reporters' Note 8.

Gilbert observes that the exercise of the passive personality principle represents "a very broad assertion of jurisdiction which may interfere with the sovereign status of the State where the crime occurred." Geoff Gilbert, *Crimes Sans Frontieres: Jurisdictional Problems in English Law*, 1992 BRIT. Y.B. INT'L L. 415, 418.

33 Brownlie, for example, refers to this principle as "the least justifiable, as a general principle, of the various bases of jurisdiction." BROWNLIE, *supra* note 1, at 303. Higgins noted that the passive personality principle has been "always uncertain and never really consolidated in general international practice." Rosalyn Higgins, *The General International Law of Terrorism*, *in* TERRORISM AND INTERNATIONAL LAW 13, 24 (Rosalyn Higgins & Maurice Flory eds., 1997). *See, e.g.*, Gilbert, *supra* note 32, at 418-19; Paust, *supra* note 13, at 202.

34 *See* Harvard Research, *supra* note 1, at 579 ("[T]he principle finds no place in the present Convention." *Id.*).

that "[u]nless circumscribed by important safeguards and limitations, it is unlikely that [the passive personality principle] can be made acceptable to an important group of States."[35] The *Restatements (Second)* and *(Third) of Foreign Relations Law of the United States* have also omitted the passive personality principle from the paragraphs restating permissible bases of prescriptive jurisdiction. The *Restatement (Second)* explicitly stated: "A State does not have the jurisdiction to prescribe a rule of law attaching legal consequence to conduct of an alien outside its territory merely on the ground that the conduct affects one of its nationals."[36] But *Restatement (Third)*, while not including the principle in its restatement of bases of jurisdiction to prescribe, comments that the passive personality principle "is increasingly accepted as applied to terrorist and other organized attacks on a state's nationals by reason of their nationality, or to assassination of a state's diplomatic representatives or other officials."[37] In such circumstances, however, it seems that more is being protected than just the national as an individual. A terrorist attack against a national of a particular state "by reason of [his] nationality" may be considered an attack against the state of the individual's nationality. Consequently, jurisdiction over such attack really derives from the protective theory and not from the passive personality principle.[38]

The Universality Principle

The universality principle stands for the proposition that some conduct is so offensive to the international community of states, "harming not only those against whom [it is] directed, but the international community generally,"[39] that all states may claim jurisdiction over the conduct despite lack of any connection with it.[40] The *Restatement (Third)* restates the universality principle in the following way: "A state has jurisdiction to define and prescribe punishment for certain offenses recognized by the community of nations as of universal concern."[41] The justification for basing extraterritorial jurisdiction upon this principle is that each state has an interest in protecting the community of states as a whole. Consequently, pursuant to this principle, each state may act to control conduct that would be harmful to the community of states, regardless of where such conduct takes place.[42]

---

35 *Id.*

36 RESTATEMENT (SECOND) OF FOREIGN RELATIONS LAW OF THE UNITED STATES § 30(2) (1965).

37 RESTATEMENT (THIRD), *supra* note 3, § 402 cmt. g. Lambert makes a similar observation: "States seem increasingly willing to accept the [passive personality] principle in connexion with terrorist offences." JOSEPH J. LAMBERT, TERRORISM AND HOSTAGES IN INTERNATIONAL LAW 154 (1990).

38 Cameron observes that "[t]he *Restatement (Third)* appears to reconcile the new U.S. position towards the passive personality principle with its former opposition to it by incorporating it into the protective principle." CAMERON, *supra* note 12, at 230. Brownlie also acknowledges that certain applications of the passive personality principle fall under the protective or universality principles. BROWNLIE, *supra* note 1, at 303. Similarly, Gilbert notes: "[T]he open-ended nature of the passive personality principle makes it difficult to accept it for even the purpose of combating terrorist crimes such as hijacking or offences against diplomats, especially since jurisdiction over such crimes may be upheld on the basis of the more widely accepted protective principle." Gilbert, *supra* note 32, at 419.

39 Higgins, *supra* note 33, at 24.

40 Brownlie defines this principle as one "allowing jurisdiction over acts of non-nationals where the circumstances, including the nature of the crime, justify the repression of some types of crime as a matter of international public policy." BROWNLIE, *supra* note 1, at 304.

41 RESTATEMENT (THIRD), *supra* note 3, § 404.

42 Cameron compares the universality principle to the protective principle by noting that while the protective principle is to protect the interests of particular individual states, the universality principle "is to protect the interests of the international community." CAMERON, *supra* note 12, at 81.

While the principle as such seems accepted in international law, it is not agreed which types of conduct it encompasses. The only conduct that has been unquestionably included in the scope of the universality theory is piracy.[43] The *Restatement (Third)* also lists "slave trade, attacks on or hijacking of aircraft, genocide, war crimes, and perhaps certain acts of terrorism" as conduct that a state may proscribe and punish under the universality theory.[44] As to conduct that would be the proper subject of antiterrorism laws, it is still debated whether terrorism and attacks on or hijacking of aircraft are the types of conduct liable to jurisdiction under the universality principle.[45]

---

43 *See, e.g.*, RESTATEMENT (THIRD), *supra* note 3, § 404 (listing piracy among offences subject to universal jurisdiction); Harvard Research, *supra* note 1, at 563 ("A State has jurisdiction with respect to any crime committed outside its territory by an alien which constitutes piracy by international law." *Id.*). *See, e.g.*, Akehurst, *supra* note 2, at 160; Bowett, *supra* note 1, at 11; Harold G. Maier, *Jurisdictional Rules in Customary International Law*, *in* EXTRATERRITORIAL JURISDICTION IN THEORY AND PRACTICE 64, 68 n. 172 (Karl M. Meessen ed., 1996).

44 RESTATEMENT (THIRD), *supra* note 3, § 404.

45 Higgins, for example, states: "Contrary to popular belief, terrorism is not subject to universal jurisdiction—some degree of connection with the event is required." Higgins, *supra* note 34, at 24. Blakesley, on the other hand, states: "International treaties as well as the domestic criminal law of all states, when considered as a whole, make it clear that *terrorism*—including hostage taking or kidnaping or wanton violence against innocent civilians—is really a composite term including all of these separate universally condemned offenses, and thus *triggers the universality theory of jurisdiction.*" BLAKESLEY, *supra* note 4, at 140 (emphasis added). The *Restatement (Third)* may shed some light on this difference in opinions. "There has been wide condemnation of terrorism but international agreements to punish it have not, as of 1987, been widely adhered to, principally because of inability to agree on a definition of the offense." RESTATEMENT (THIRD), *supra* note 3, § 404 cmt. a. But the reporters of the *Restatement* continued: "Universal jurisdiction is increasingly accepted for certain acts of terrorism, such as assaults on the life or physical integrity of diplomatic personnel, kidnaping, and indiscriminate violent assaults on people at large." *Id.*

Extending universal jurisdiction over attacks on or hijacking of aircraft seems to be more accepted than extending universality to terrorism. The *Restatement (Third)* specifically includes attacks on or hijacking of aircraft in its enumeration of offences falling under the scope of the universal principle. RESTATEMENT (THIRD), *supra* note 3, § 404. *See also* BLAKESLEY, *supra* note 4, at 146; BROWNLIE, *supra* note 1, at 305 ("hijacking . . . *probably* subject to universal jurisdiction" *Id.*) (emphasis added); Akehurst, *supra* note 2, at 161 ("there is doctrinal authority for the view that [hijacking] is subject to universal jurisdiction"); David Freestone, *International Cooperation against Terrorism and the Development of International Law Principles of Jurisdiction*, *in* TERRORISM AND INTERNATIONAL LAW 43, 60 (Rosalyn Higgins & Maurice Flory eds., 1997) ("There is already strong, and growing, doctrinal support for the view that universality jurisdiction for hijacking is already customary." *Id.*); Maier, *supra* note 43, at 68 n. 172. On the other hand, Bowett was skeptical that hijacking falls under universal jurisdiction. "It would, indeed, be surprising if hijacking were truly a case of universal jurisdiction, for many States have declined to treat it as a crime, or to adhere to [the relevant convention]." Bowett, *supra* note 1, at 13. The fact that as of the beginning of 1996, 154 states were parties to the 1970 Hague Convention for the Suppression of Unlawful Seizure of Aircraft, however, puts the relevance of Bowett's argument for the present into question. UNITED STATES DEPARTMENT OF STATE, A LIST OF TREATIES AND OTHER INTERNATIONAL AGREEMENTS OF THE UNITED STATES IN FORCE ON JANUARY 1, 1996 326-27 (1996) [hereinafter LIST OF TREATIES].

Indeed, it is difficult to understand why aircraft hijacking would not be considered a proper subject of the universality theory. Akehurst points out that "[t]he policy reasons which justify universal jurisdiction over piracy justify it equally in the case of hijacking." Akehurst, *supra* note 2, at 162. "Hijacking threatens international communications to the same extent as piracy; it is an attack on international order and injures the international community as a whole, which means that all States have a legitimate interest in repressing it." *Id.*

Jurisdictional Principles Contained in Conventions Relevant to Combating Terrorism

A survey of twelve international and regional instruments relevant to the fight against terrorism[46] shows that together they contain all the jurisdictional principles discussed previously.[47] Individually, eight of the 12 instruments considered here incorporate the territoriality principle, six incorporate the nationality principle, five incorporate the protective principle, four incorporate the passive personality principle, and ten incorporate the universality principle.[48] The individual instruments have been categorized into thematic groups and their jurisdictional provisions are excerpted below.

---

[46] To limit the scope of this chapter (but not the substantive discussion of extraterritorial jurisdiction), only the following themes under the umbrella of combating "terrorism" are considered here: aviation safety, safety of maritime navigation and fixed platforms, suppression of crimes against internationally protected persons, suppression of hostage-taking, safety of nuclear materials, and suppression of "terrorism" as that term is used in the two regional conventions specifically addressed to this task. For a thorough discussion of international terrorism and its varied components, *see* LEGAL ASPECTS OF INTERNATIONAL TERRORISM (Alona E. Evans & John F. Murphy eds., 1978).

[47] The following instruments have been considered here:

1. Convention on the High Seas, Apr. 28, 1958, 13 U.S.T. 2312, 450 U.N.T.S. 82;
2. Convention on Offences and Certain Other Acts Committed on Board Aircraft, Sept. 14, 1963, 20 U.S.T. 2941, 704 U.N.T.S. 219 [hereinafter Tokyo Convention];
3. Convention for the Suppression of Unlawful Seizure of Aircraft, Dec. 16, 1970, 22 U.S.T. 1641, 860 U.N.T.S. 105 [hereinafter Hague Highjacking Convention];
4. Convention to Prevent and Punish Acts of Terrorism Taking the Form of Crimes Against Persons and Related Extortion that are of International Significance, Feb. 2, 1971, 27 U.S.T. 3949 [hereinafter OAS Terrorist Convention];
5. Convention for the Suppression of Unlawful Acts Against the Safety of Civil Aviation, Sept. 23, 1971, 24 U.S.T. 564, 974 U.N.T.S. 177 [hereinafter Montreal Convention];
6. Convention on the Prevention and Punishment of Crimes Against Internationally Protected Persons, including Diplomatic Agents, Dec. 14, 1973, 28 U.S.T. 1975, 1035 U.N.T.S. 167 [hereinafter Int'l Protected Persons Convention];
7. European Convention on the Suppression of Terrorism, Jan. 27, 1977, 1137 U.N.T.S. 93, 15 I.L.M. 1272 [hereinafter Euro. Terrorism Convention];
8. Convention on the Physical Protection of Nuclear Material, Oct. 26, 1979, T.I.A.S. No. 11,080, 18 I.L.M. 1419 [hereinafter Nuclear Material Convention];
9. International Convention Against the Taking of Hostages, Dec. 17, 1979, T.I.A.S. No. 11,081, 1316 U.N.T.S. 205 [hereinafter Conv. Against Taking of Hostages];
10. Protocol for the Suppression of Unlawful Acts of Violence at Airports Serving International Civil Aviation, Supplementary to the [Montreal Convention], Feb. 24, 1988, 27 I.L.M. 628 [hereinafter Protocol to the Montreal Convention];
11. Convention for the Suppression of Unlawful Acts Against the Safety of Maritime Navigation, Mar. 10, 1988, 27 I.L.M. 668 [hereinafter IMO Convention]; and
12. Protocol for the Suppression of Unlawful Acts Against the Safety of Fixed Platforms Located on the Continental Shelf, Feb. 24, 1988, 27 I.L.M. 668, 685 [hereinafter IMO Protocol].

[48] That a treaty relies on the universality principle of jurisdiction may be inferred from, *inter alia,* its imposition upon states parties of a duty to extradite or prosecute (*aut dedere aut judicare*) the offender. *See, e.g.,* BLAKESLEY, *supra* note 4, at 137 ("International law provides that there are certain offenses for which any nation obtaining personal jurisdiction over an accused person may prosecute . . . so that any of the 'community' of nations has an obligation to extradite or to bring their prosecutorial mechanism to bear on [the] accused person found in their hands." *Id.*). *See generally* M. CHERIF BASSIOUNI & EDWARD M. WISE, AUT DEDERE AUT JUDICARE: THE DUTY TO EXTRADITE OR PROSECUTE IN INTERNATIONAL LAW (1995) ("[*Aut dedere aut judicare*] is a condition for the effective repression of offenses which are universally condemned." *Id.* at 24).

Another indication of the universality principle in a treaty is the treaty's recognition of jurisdictional competence over extraterritorial offences regardless of the offender's nationality. *See, e.g.,* OSCAR SCHACHTER, INTERNATIONAL LAW IN THEORY AND PRACTICE 268 (1991); Kenneth C. Randall, *Universal Jurisdiction Under International Law*, 66 TEX. L. REV. 785, 819 (1988).

Conventions Dealing with Aviation Safety

The four principal instruments that comprise the conventional international law relating to the suppression of conduct jeopardizing the safety of aircraft in flight and its passengers and cargo, unlawful seizure of aircraft, sabotage of aircraft, and unlawful acts of violence at airports are, respectively: the Tokyo Convention,[49] the Hague Highjacking Convention,[50] the Montreal Convention,[51] and the Protocol to the Montreal Convention.[52]

The Tokyo Convention, which has 148 states parties,[53] permits the states to exercise criminal jurisdiction over offences within its scope on the grounds of the territorial, nationality, passive personality, and protective principles.[54] The wide acceptance of this Convention indicates that, as between states parties to it, even the more controversial jurisdictional principle of passive personality is acceptable in combating offences against the safety of aircraft in flight and its passengers and cargo.[55] Although the Convention itself does not list the universality principle as grounds for the exercise of jurisdiction, commentators have suggested that the wide acceptance of this Convention may provide universal jurisdiction for achieving its aims.[56]

The Hague Highjacking Convention and the Montreal Convention, each with 154 state-parties,[57] explicitly provide for jurisdiction based on the territorial principle.[58] Furthermore,

---

[49] *See supra* note 47, item 2.

[50] *See supra* note 47, item 3.

[51] *See supra* note 47, item 5.

[52] *See supra* note 47, item 10.

[53] LIST OF TREATIES, *supra* note 46, at 325-26.

[54] The relevant provision is article 4:

> A Contracting State which is not the State of registration [of the aircraft] may not interfere with an aircraft in flight in order to exercise its criminal jurisdiction over an offence committed on board except in the following cases:
>
> (a) the offence has effect on the territory of such State;
>
> (b) the offence has been committed by or against a national or permanent resident of such State;
>
> (c) the offence is against the security of such State . . .

Tokyo Convention, *supra* note 47, art. 4.

[55] Freestone, *supra* note 45, at 59. *But see* Abraham Abramovsky, *Extraterritorial Jurisdiction: The United States Unwarranted Attempt to Alter International Law in* United States v. Yunis, 15 YALE J. INT'L L. 121, 129 (1990) ("[s]ince it is the only article which relies solely on the nationality of the victim, absent any other nexus to the contracting state, it is unclear whether article 4(b) [the passive personality-based provision] was ever intended to stand on its own." *Id.*).

[56] *See* BLAKESLEY, *supra* note 4, at 138-39; Freestone, *supra* note 45, at 60.

[57] LIST OF TREATIES, *supra* note 45, 326-27, 327-28.

[58] The Hague Highjacking Convention provides:

> Each Contracting State shall take such measures as may be necessary to establish jurisdiction over the offence . . . in the following cases:
>
> (a) when the offence is committed on board an aircraft registered in that State;
>
> (b) when the aircraft on board which the offence is committed lands in its territory with the alleged offender still on board. . . .

Hague Highjacking Convention, *supra* note 47, art. 4(1).

The Montreal Convention provides:

> Each Contracting State shall take measures as may be necessary to establish its jurisdiction over the offences in the following cases:
>
> (a) when the offence is committed in the territory of that State;
>
> (b) when the offence is committed against or on board an aircraft registered in that State;
>
> (c) when the aircraft on board which the offence is committed lands in its territory with the alleged offender still on board. . . .

Montreal Convention, *supra* note 47, art. 5(1).

the Hague Highjacking Convention and the Montreal Convention, as supplemented by its Protocol, require the states parties to either extradite or prosecute alleged offenders[59] and have been said to rely on the universality principle of extraterritorial jurisdiction.[60]

It has also been argued that with respect to hijacking, the core offence in this group, universal jurisdiction applies as a matter of custom.[61] Should this indeed be the case, any state, whether or not party to the conventions discussed above, could exercise universal jurisdiction over the offence of unlawful seizure of aircraft.

Conventions Dealing with Safety of Maritime Navigation and Fixed Platforms

First in this category is the 1958 Geneva Convention on the High Seas[62] which has 61 state-parties.[63] In article 19, this Convention creates universal jurisdiction over piracy[64] and thus formalizes the traditional practice of exercising jurisdiction on such basis over this offence.[65]

---

59 The Hague Highjacking Convention provides:

> Each Contracting State shall likewise take such measures as may be necessary to establish its jurisdiction over the offence in the case where the alleged offender is present in its territory and it does not extradite him. . . .

Hague Highjacking Convention, *supra* note 47, art. 4(2). The Convention further stipulates:

> The Contracting State in the territory of which the alleged offender is found shall, if it does not extradite him, be obliged, without exception whatsoever and whether or not the offence was committed in its territory, to submit the case to its competent authorities for the purpose of prosecution.

Id. art. 7.

The Montreal Convention, as supplemented by its Protocol, has identical requirements to those excerpted above from the Hague Highjacking Convention. *See* Montreal Convention, *supra* note 47, art. 5(2); Protocol to the Montreal Convention, *supra* note 47, art. III.

60 *See* RESTATEMENT (THIRD), *supra* note 3, § 404 Reporters' Note 1 (Offenses Subject to Universal Jurisdiction); BLAKESLEY, *supra* note 4, at 138-39; Abramovsky, *supra* note 55, at 129 ("The operative jurisdictional principle throughout the [Tokyo, Hague, and Montreal] conventions . . . is the Universality principle." *Id.*); Freestone, *supra* note 45, at 50.

Bowett, however, questions whether the jurisdictional provision in article 4(2) of the Hague Highjacking Convention ("Each Contracting State shall likewise take such measures as may be necessary to establish its jurisdiction over the offence in the case where the alleged offender is present in its territory and it does not extradite him. . . .") establishes universal jurisdiction. *See* Hague Highjacking Convention, *supra* note 47, art. 4(2). He argues: "If this [art. 4(2)] establishes a universal jurisdiction, what is the point of setting out the narrower heads of jurisdiction in the first paragraph [art. 4(1) containing jurisdictional provisions grounded in the territorial theory]?" Bowett, *supra* note 1, at 13 n. 59. This argument could be extended to the same provision of the Montreal Convention, as supplemented by its Protocol. *See* Montreal Convention, *supra* note 47, art. 5(2); Protocol to the Montreal Convention, *supra* note 47, art. III.

61 *See* Freestone, *supra* note 45, at 60. "There is already strong, and growing, doctrinal support for the view that universality jurisdiction for hijacking is already customary. The very wide adherence to the hijacking conventions—Tokyo, The Hague and Montreal—suggests that for hijacking at the very least the right to try on the basis of universality has now moved into the realm of customary law." *Id.*

62 *See supra* note 47, item 1.

63 LIST OF TREATIES, *supra* note 45, at 391.

64 The Convention specifically provides:

> On the high seas, or in any other place outside the jurisdiction of any State, every State may seize a pirate ship or aircraft, or a ship taken by piracy and under the control of pirates, and arrest the persons and seize the property on board. The courts of the State which carried out the seizure may decide upon the penalties to be imposed, and may also determine the action to be taken with regard to the ships, aircraft or property, subject to the rights of third parties acting in good faith.

Convention on the High Seas, *supra* note 47, art. 19.

65 *See supra* note 43 (listing sources noting the traditional application of universal jurisdiction to piracy).

Second in this category are two instruments promulgated by the International Maritime Organization, the IMO Convention and Protocol,[66] each of which has 32 state-parties.[67] The IMO Convention covers offences threatening the safety of navigation such as, for example, hijacking a ship or endangering safe navigation through violence against the ship or a person or cargo aboard the vessel.[68] The Convention requires state-parties to establish jurisdiction over the included offences based on the territorial and nationality theories[69] and, in a nod to the universality principle, further requires state-parties to establish jurisdiction over the offences in cases "where the alleged offender is present in its territory and it does not extradite him to any of the States Parties."[70] Additionally, in a separate provision, the Convention permits state-parties to rely on the protective and passive personality principles in establishing jurisdiction over the included offences. Given that the impetus for drafting the Convention was the *Achille Lauro* incident, it should not be surprising that the members of the IMO agreed to permit the use of the traditionally disfavored jurisdictional principle of passive personality.[71]

The IMO Protocol essentially extends the included offences of the IMO Convention to fixed platforms. Under the Protocol, it is thus proscribed, *inter alia*, to seize a fixed platform by force, threat, or intimidation, to perpetrate violence against a person on a fixed platform, and to damage or destroy a fixed platform. The Protocol also contains jurisdictional provisions identical to those of the IMO Convention. States parties are thus to establish jurisdiction over the included offences under the territorial, nationality, or universality theories, and may also rely on the protective and passive personality principles.[72]

---

[66] *See supra* note 47, items 11 & 12.

[67] LIST OF TREATIES, *supra* note 45, at 398.

[68] *See* IMO Convention, *supra* note 47, art. 3 (listing included offences).

[69] The IMO Convention provides:

> Each State Party shall take such measures as may be necessary to establish its jurisdiction over the offences . . . when the offence is committed:
>
> (a) against or on board a ship flying the flag of the State at the time the offence is committed; or
>
> (b) in the territory of that State, including its territorial sea; or
>
> (c) by a national of that State.

IMO Convention, *supra* note 47, art. 6(1).

[70] *Id.* art. 6(4). Article 10(1) of the IMO Convention incorporates the *aut dedere aut judicare* principle. *Id.* art. 10(1). Freestone notes that the 1988 IMO Conference on maritime Safety that adopted the Convention accepted with readiness the universality theory of jurisdiction for the offences included in the IMO Convention. Freestone, *supra* note 45, at 60.

[71] *See generally* Glen Plant, *Legal Aspects of Terrorism at Sea*, *in* TERRORISM AND INTERNATIONAL LAW 68, 69 (Rosalyn Higgins & Maurice Flory eds., 1997). *See also* G. Gilbert, *The 'Law' and 'Transnational Terrorism'*, 1995 NETHERLANDS Y.B. INT'L L. 3, 13-14 (criticizing the reactive approach of the world community of states to combating terrorism).

Indeed, 32 states at the drafting conference voted for jurisdiction based on the nationality of the victim, while only four states voted against including this jurisdictional basis in the Convention, and three states abstained from voting on this point. Malvina Halberstam, *Terrorism on the High Seas: The Achille Lauro, Piracy and the IMO Convention on Maritime Safety*, 82 AM. J. INT'L L. 269, 294 (1988).

[72] The Protocol specifically provides:

> 1. Each State Party shall take such measures as may be necessary to establish its jurisdiction over the offences . . . when the offence is committed:
>
> (a) against or on board a fixed platform while it is located on the continental shelf of that State; or
>
> (b) by a national of that State;
>
> 2. A State Party may also establish its jurisdiction over any such offence when: . . .
>
> (b) during its commission a national of that State is seized, threatened, injured or killed; or
>
> (c) it is committed in an attempt to compel that State to do or abstain from doing any act.

IMO Protocol, *supra* note 47, art. 3. Additionally, the *aut dedere aut judicare* provision of the IMO Convention

Convention Dealing with Safety of Internationally Protected Persons

The International Protected Persons Convention[73] seeks to protect heads of state, heads of government, ministers of foreign affairs, and other state and international organizations officials and their families entitled to special protection under international law[74] from attacks (or threats thereof) against them and their offices and homes. The states that drafted the Convention noted in its preamble that "the commission of such crimes is a matter of grave concern to the international community" creating a "serious threat" to relations among states.[75]

Consequently, then, the Convention requires state-parties to establish jurisdiction over the proscribed conduct on territorial, nationality, and protective grounds. In as much as the Convention requires state-parties to establish jurisdiction over the included offences in cases when the alleged offender is present in their territory and is not extradited to another state, the Convention also resorts to the universality theory in creating jurisdictional competence of its state-parties.[76]

Finally, some commentators suggest that the Convention also invokes jurisdictional competence on the basis of the nationality of the victim by requiring extension of jurisdiction to cases "when the crime is committed against an internationally protected person . . . who enjoys his status as such by virtue of functions which he exercises on behalf of [the] State."[77] In advancing this argument, its authors must assume that the protected person is a national of the state that would exercise jurisdiction in a case involving him. While the protected person is likely to be a national of that state, this need not necessarily be the case.[78]

Convention Dealing with the Taking of Hostages

The international convention for the suppression of hostage taking[79] has 73 state-parties. The Convention recognizes that the taking of hostages is a manifestation of international terrorism and that it is "of grave concern to the international community."[80] The Convention defines the offence of hostage taking as seizure and detention of a person "in order to

---

is incorporated in the Protocol by reference. *See id.* art. 1(1).

73 *See supra* note 47, item 6. The Int'l Protected Persons Convention has 91 state-parties. LIST OF TREATIES, *supra* note 46, at 441-42.

74 Int'l Protected Persons Convention, *supra* note 47, art.1 (defining "internationally protected person").

75 *Id.* preamble.

76 *See id.* art. 3(2). The Convention also contains the *aut dedere aut judicare* requirement. *Id.* art. 7. *See also* RESTATEMENT (THIRD), *supra* note 3, § 404 Reporters' Note 1 (including the Int'l Protected Persons Convention in a discussion of "offenses subject to universal jurisdiction" and noting its *aut dedere aut judicare* provision); BLAKESLEY, *supra* note 4, at 140 (listing the Int'l Protected Persons Convention as encompassing offences that trigger the universality theory of jurisdiction).

77 Int'l Protected Persons Convention, *supra* note 47, art. 3(1)(c). Cameron and Freestone, for example, assert that the Convention incorporates the passive personality principle. *See* CAMERON, *supra* note 12, at 77, 230 n. 95; Freestone, *supra* note 45, at 59. *Accord* Halberstam, *supra* note 72, at 297 n. 116.

78 Particularly since the Convention includes as protected persons "members of family." A case could materialize, for example, involving an alien spouse of a state official. In such a case, extension of jurisdictional competence pursuant to the passive personality principle (under which jurisdiction may extend only to offences against nationals) would be impossible.

79 *See supra* note 47, item 9.

80 Conv. Against Taking of Hostages, *supra* note 47, preamble.

compel a third party, namely, a State, [or] an international intergovernmental organization . . . to do or abstain from doing any act as [a] . . . condition for the release of the hostage."[81]

State-parties are obliged to extend jurisdiction over hostage taking based on the territorial, nationality, and protective principles.[82] The Convention also allows, but does not require, passive personality-based jurisdiction.[83] Finally, the Convention mandates universal jurisdiction "over . . . offences . . . in cases where the alleged offender is present in [the] territory [of the particular state] and it does not extradite him."[84]

Convention Dealing with Safety of Nuclear Material

The Convention on the Protection of Nuclear Material[85] has been in force since 8 February 1987 and presently has 48 state-parties.[86] The Convention aims to promote safe storage, transport, and use of nuclear material;[87] and to this end, *inter alia*, requires states parties to criminalize certain conduct, including theft, embezzlement, and an unlawful demand for nuclear material, and a threat to use nuclear material with the intent to compel a state, an international organization, or any person, to do or to refrain from doing

---

81 *Id.* art. 1.

82 The Convention specifically provides:

> Each State party shall take such measures as may be necessary to establish its jurisdiction over any of the offences . . . which are committed:
>
> (a) In its territory or on board a ship or aircraft registered in that State;
>
> (b) By any of its nationals . . .
>
> (c) In order to compel that State to do or to abstain from doing any act; . . .

Id. art. 5(1).

Lambert points out that "[j]urisdiction based on the status of the State as the compelled party [art. 5(1)(c)] is similar to jurisdiction based on the 'protective principle." LAMBERT, *supra* note 37, at 151.

83 The Convention provides:

> Each State Party shall take such measures as may be necessary to establish its jurisdiction over any of the offences . . . which are committed: . . .
>
> (d) With respect to a hostage who is a national of that State, *if that State considers it appropriate*.

Id. art. 5(1)(d) (emphasis added).

Abramovsky understands this provision to extend only to cases when the exercise of jurisdiction pursuant to the passive personality principle would be reasonable, "that is only where a sufficient nexus exists between a hostage-taking incident and a nation's interests." Abramovsky, *supra* note 55, at 129. When a nation's interests are engaged in a hostage-taking incident, however, would the protective principle embodied in article 5(1)(c) of the Convention not be the proper jurisdictional ground? At any rate, Abramovsky points out that article 14 of the Convention represents a limitation on the potentially unrestricted exercise of passive personality jurisdiction. Article 14 provides: "Nothing in this Convention shall be construed as justifying the violation of the territorial integrity or political independence of a State in contravention of the Charter of the United Nations." Conv. Against Taking of Hostages, *supra* note 47, art. 14.

84 *Id.* art. 5(2). The Convention also contains an explicit *aut dedere aut judicare* requirement. *See id.* art. 8(1). *See also* RESTATEMENT (THIRD), *supra* note 3, § 404 Reporters' Note 1 (including the Conv. Against Taking of Hostages in a discussion of "offenses subject to universal jurisdiction" and noting its *aut dedere aut judicare* provision); BLAKESLEY, *supra* note 4, at 140 (listing the Conv. Against Taking of Hostages as encompassing offences that trigger the universality theory of jurisdiction); LAMBERT, *supra* note 37, at 133, 155-56 ("[In this provision the Convention requires] the establishment of 'subsidiary' jurisdiction, based on the principle of universality." *Id.* at 133).

85 *See supra* note 47, item 8.

86 LIST OF TREATIES, *supra* note 45, at 406.

87 *See* Nuclear Material Convention, *supra* note 47, preamble.

something.[88] Under the Convention, each state party is to establish jurisdiction over the proscribed acts on the grounds of territoriality, nationality, and universality.[89]

Regional Anti-Terrorism Conventions

The Organization of American States and the Council of Europe promulgated, in 1971 and 1977 respectively, regional conventions aimed at the suppression of terrorism.[90] The OAS Terrorist Convention, with 11 state-parties,[91] designates as "common crimes of international significance" the offences of "kidnaping, murder, and other assaults against the life or personal integrity of those persons to whom the state has the duty to give special protection according to international law, as well as extortion in connection with those crimes."[92] The OAS Convention calls upon state-parties to cooperate in preventing and punishing the included terrorism offences, including by criminalizing them in their domestic penal laws,[93] and to either extradite or prosecute alleged offenders.[94] The Convention does not stipulate jurisdictional bases upon which state-parties may or must base their competence over the included offences, but its inclusion of the explicit *aut dedere aut judicare* provision[95] indicates that universality is a permissible jurisdictional basis under it.[96]

The European Terrorism Convention, with 29 state-parties,[97] is principally concerned with facilitating extradition in cases involving terrorist offences[98] in order "to ensure that the perpetrators of such acts do not escape prosecution or punishment."[99] To this end it eliminates the political offence exception to extradition for the offences within its scope[100] and obliges state parties to establish jurisdiction over the offences in cases when the alleged offender is in their territory and is not extradited.[101] The Convention's jurisdictional

---

88 *Id.* art. 7.

89 The Convention specifically provides:

1. Each State Party shall take such measures as may be necessary to establish its jurisdiction over the offences set forth in article 7 in the following cases:

(a) when the offence is committed in the territory of that State or on board a ship or aircraft registered in that State;

(b) when the alleged offender is a national of that State.

2. Each State Party shall likewise take such measures as may be necessary to establish its jurisdiction over these offences in cases where the alleged offender is present in its territory and it does not extradite him. . .

Id. art. 8.

The Convention also contains an explicit *aut dedere aut judicare* requirement. *See id.* art. 10.

90 *See supra* note 47, items 4 & 7.

91 LIST OF TREATIES, *supra* note 45, at 441.

92 OAS Terrorist Convention, *supra* note 47, art. 2.

93 *Id.* art. 8(d).

94 *Id.* art. 5.

95 *Id.*

96 *See supra* note 48.

97 As of 12 June 1997. Per information posted on the Council of Europe web page <http://www.coe.fr>.

98 Under the Euro Terrorism Convention that is those offences within the scope of the Hague and Montreal Conventions, and "a serious offence involving an attack against the life, physical integrity or liberty of internationally protected persons, including diplomatic agents . . . an offence involving kidnaping, the taking of a hostage or serious unlawful detention . . . an offence involving the use of a bomb, grenade, rocket, automatic firearm or letter parcel bomb if this use endangers a person; [and] . . . an attempt to commit any of the foregoing offences or participation as an accomplice. . . ." Euro Terrorism Convention, *supra* note 47, art. 1.

99 *Id.* preamble.

100 *Id.* art.1.

101 *Id.* art. 6.

provision is somewhat different from those contained in the other instruments reviewed here and consequently merits a closer look. The Convention stipulates that when the alleged offender is in a territory of a state and that state "does not extradite him after receiving a request for extradition from a Contracting State whose jurisdiction is based on a rule of jurisdiction existing equally in [its] law," it is to establish its jurisdiction over the offence.[102] One of the preconditions for the requested state's move to establish jurisdiction over the particular offence thus is that the requesting state must have jurisdictional competence over the offence grounded in the same jurisdictional principle as the requested state. This provision does not indicate jurisdictional bases that may be appropriate in connection with the included offences.[103] But, in a now familiar pattern, the Convention contains an explicit *aut dedere aut judicare* provision which indicates that jurisdictional competence over the included offences may be based on the universality principle.[104]

The foregoing discussion of the jurisdictional principles recognized in international law and the jurisdictional provisions of conventions relevant to combating terrorism forms a background for an analysis of jurisdictional principles contained in U.S. laws relevant to combating terrorism.

Jurisdictional Principles Contained in U.S. Laws Relevant to Combating Terrorism

This section considers the U.S. legislative approach to extraterritorial criminal jurisdiction in connection with terrorist offences. The U.S. legislators' most recent pronouncements on extraterritorial criminal jurisdiction for offences of concern in this chapter are contained in the Antiterrorism and Effective Death Penalty Act of 1996.[105] The 1996 Act includes section 721, Clarification and Extension of Criminal Jurisdiction over Certain Terrorism Offenses Overseas, which addresses extraterritorial jurisdiction over aircraft piracy,[106] destruction of aircraft or aircraft facilities,[107] violence at international airports,[108] murder of foreign officials and certain other persons,[109] protection of foreign officials and certain other persons,[110] threats and extortion against foreign officials and certain other persons,[111] kidnaping of internationally protected persons,[112] and biological weapons.[113] While these specific jurisdictional provisions are set out and analyzed below, it bears noting at this point that they rely on nationality, protective, passive personality, and universality principles of extraterritorial jurisdiction. It is thus quite clear that U.S.

---

102 *Id.* art. 6(1).

103 Freestone comments that the "object of this clause was probably to maximize jurisdiction without forcing States to accept new principles." Freestone, *supra* note 45, at 56.

104 *See id.* art. 7.

105 Pub. L. No. 104-132, 110 Stat. 1214 (1996) [hereinafter the 1996 Act].

106 Amending 49 U.S.C.§ 46502(b) (1994).

107 Amending 18 U.S.C.§ 32(b) (1994).

108 Amending 18 U.S.C.§ 37(b)(2) (1994).

109 Amending 18 U.S.C.§ 1116 (1994).

110 Amending 18 U.S.C.§ 112 (1994).

111 Amending 18 U.S.C.§ 878 (1994).

112 Amending 18 U.S.C.§ 1201(e) (1994).

113 Amending 18 U.S.C.§ 178 (1994).

legislators have now overcome their traditional reluctance to prescribe laws reaching beyond U.S. borders when the task at hand is combating terrorism.[114]

The 1996 Act, *inter alia*, also criminalized certain acts of terrorism transcending national boundaries,[115] modified and expanded the weapons of mass destruction statute,[116] expanded the scope and jurisdictional bases of nuclear material prohibitions,[117] and criminalized certain uses of chemical weapons of mass destruction.[118]

Most of the relevant provisions of the 1996 Act have their origins in 1995 draft legislation, the Omnibus Counterterrorism Act of 1995,[119] proposed by the Clinton Administration to Congress, and in the Comprehensive Antiterrorism Act of 1995[120] prepared by Representative Hyde. The 1995 Omnibus Act contained, for example, a section on acts of terrorism transcending national boundaries,[121] a section on clarification and extension of criminal jurisdiction over certain terrorism offences overseas,[122] a section dealing with nuclear material prohibitions,[123] and an expansion of the weapons of mass destruction statute.[124] Similarly, the 1995 Comprehensive Act addressed, *inter alia*, acts of terrorism transcending national boundaries,[125] extension and clarification of jurisdiction over certain overseas terrorism offences,[126] expansion and modification of the weapons of mass destruction statute,[127] and expansion of nuclear material prohibitions.[128]

Both of the 1995 draft laws noted above essentially stemmed from the belief that "[i]nternational terrorism remains a serious and deadly problem which threatens the interests of the United States both overseas and within its territory"[129] and the conclusion that "[t]he Nation's security interests are seriously impacted by terrorist attacks carried out overseas against United States Government facilities, officials and other American citizens present in foreign countries."[130] One of the 1995 bills' stated purposes thus was to address acts of international terrorism "within the United States, or directed against the United States or its nationals anywhere in the world."[131] In light of these statements it is not surprising that the

---

114 *See, e.g.*, Bruce Zagaris & Jay Rosenthal, *United States Jurisdictional Considerations in International Criminal Law*, 15 CAL. W. INT'L L.J. 303, 307 (1985) ("Traditionally, the United States . . . [has] at least theoretically denied the ability of a State to assert criminal jurisdiction outside of its territory against a non-national." *Id.*).

115 1996 Act, *supra* note 111, § 702. Codified in 18 U.S.C.A. § 2332(b) (West Supp. 1997).

116 *Id.* § 725. Codified in 18 U.S.C.A. § 2332(a) (West Supp. 1997).

117 *Id.* § 502. Codified in 18 U.S.C.A. § 831 (West Supp. 1997).

118 *Id.* § 521. Codified in 18 U.S.C.A. § 2332(c) (West Supp. 1997).

119 H.R. 896, 104th Cong. (1995) [hereinafter the 1995 Omnibus Act].

120 H.R. 1710, 104th Cong. (1995) [hereinafter the 1995 Comprehensive Act].

121 1995 Omnibus Act, *supra* note 125,§ 101.

122 *Id.* § 103.

123 *Id.* § 501.

124 *Id.* § 602.

125 1995 Comprehensive Act, *supra* note 126, § 104.

126 *Id.* § 106.

127 *Id.* § 107.

128 *Id.* § 401.

129 1995 Omnibus Act, *supra* note 125, § 3(a)(1).

130 *Id.* § 3(a)(3). Representative Hyde's Report on the 1995 Comprehensive Act noted that because of the visible position of the United States in the world, "[t]errorists hope that their attacks on U.S. citizens or U.S. military personnel will bring publicity and attention to their cause" and stated that "the bill is a recognition that there is a need to update certain criminal statutes . . . so as to respond to the serious and growing threat of terrorism." H.R. REP. NO. 104-383, at 37, 42 (1995).

131 1995 Omnibus Act, *supra* note 125, § 3(b)(1) (emphasis added).

1995 bills, and later the 1996 Act, extended extraterritorial criminal jurisdiction over terrorist offences.

But even before that, Congress exercised its jurisdictional competence in the area of terrorism, for example, in the Omnibus Diplomatic Security and Antiterrorism Act of 1986,[132] which notably created extraterritorial jurisdiction over terrorist acts abroad against U.S. nationals,[133] and in the Comprehensive Crime Control Act of 1984,[134] which contained implementing legislation for the Convention Against Taking of Hostages,[135] the Act for the Prevention and Punishment of the Crime of Hostage-Taking,[136] and the implementing legislation for the Montreal Convention,[137] the Aircraft Sabotage Act.[138]

The following discussion of U.S. extraterritorial criminal jurisdiction relevant to combating terrorism is divided into thematic groups mirroring those in the preceding section: offences against aviation safety, offences against maritime safety, offences against the safety of internationally protected persons, hostage-taking, offences against the safety of nuclear material, and other terrorist offences. Within each group, criminal jurisdictional provisions of the relevant U.S. law(s) are set out and analyzed in light of international law doctrine on extraterritorial jurisdiction,[139] and in light of relevant international instrument(s),[140] if any.

Offences against Aviation Safety

The representative offences in this thematic group are aircraft piracy,[141] aircraft sabotage,[142] and violence at international airports.[143] The U.S. statutes that set out these offences rely on, in addition to territoriality, the universality, nationality, and passive personality theories of jurisdiction.

The aircraft piracy statute[144] is a part of the U.S. implementing legislation for the Hague Highjacking Convention[145] which has been in force since 1971.[146] The statute originated in a 1994 law designed to revise the "Transportation" title of the U.S. Code.[147] The jurisdictional provisions of the 1994 aircraft piracy statute mirrored those of the Hague

---

132 Pub. L. No. 99-399, 100 Stat. 853 (1986) [hereinafter the 1986 Omnibus Act].

133 *Id.* § 1202. Codified in 18 U.S.C.A. § 2332 (West Supp. 1997). Until the passage of the 1986 Omnibus Act, federal law only prohibited extraterritorial murder of or assault on U.S. officials and diplomats. H.R. CONF. REP. NO. 99-783, at 87 (1986), *reprinted in* 1986 U.S.C.C.A.N. 1926, 1960.

134 Pub. L. No. 98-473, 98 Stat. 1837 (1984).

135 *See supra* note 47, item 9.

136 Pub. L. No. 98-473, 98 Stat. 1837, 2186 (1984). Codified in 18 U.S.C.A. § 1203 (West Supp. 1997).

137 *See supra* note 47, item 5.

138 Pub. L. No. 98-473, 98 Stat. 1837, 2187 (1984). Codified in 18 U.S.C.A. § 32 (West Supp. 1997).

139 *See supra* § II (discussing international law doctrine on extraterritorial jurisdiction). Note, however, that it has been argued that public international law cannot restrict the capacity of the U.S. Congress to promulgate laws with extraterritorial effect even if such legislation would be contrary to international law doctrine or even to international legal obligations of the United States. A. Mark Weisburd, *Due Process Limits on Federal Extraterritorial Legislation?* 35 COLUM. J. TRANSNAT'L L. 379, 381-82 (1997).

140 *See supra* § III (discussing jurisdictional principles contained in conventions relevant to combating terrorism).

141 49 U.S.C.A. § 46502 (West Supp. 1997).

142 18 U.S.C.A. § 32 (West Supp. 1997).

143 18 U.S.C.A. § 37 (West Supp. 1997).

144 49 U.S.C.A. § 46502.

145 *See supra* note 47, item 3.

146 LIST OF TREATIES, *supra* note 45, at 326.

147 Pub. L. No. 103-272, 108 Stat. 745, 1240 (1994).

Highjacking Convention, that is the statute provided for jurisdiction based on territoriality and universality.[148] The 1996 Act,[149] however, extended the extraterritorial jurisdiction under the aircraft piracy statute beyond jurisdiction based on universality to include jurisdiction based on the U.S. nationality of the offender and of the victim.[150] The 1996 amendments thus embraced the nationality and passive personality theories of extraterritorial jurisdiction and in this departed from the extraterritorial jurisdictional provisions of the parent text, the Hague Highjacking Convention.[151]

The 1996 Act similarly extended the extraterritorial jurisdictional provisions of the aircraft sabotage[152] and violence at international airports[153] statutes beyond the provisions of the Montreal Convention[154] and Protocol[155] that these statutes implement in U.S. law. The aircraft sabotage statute originated in the Aircraft Sabotage Act[156] included in the Crime Control Act of 1984.[157] The legislative history shows that the Aircraft Sabotage Act was to fully implement the Montreal Convention,[158] including its jurisdictional provisions which are based on territoriality and universality.[159] Consequently, the Aircraft Sabotage Act extended territorial and universality-based jurisdiction over the offence of destruction of aircraft or aircraft facilities.[160] The 1996 Act, however, expanded the extraterritorial reach of the aircraft sabotage statute beyond the reach of the Montreal Convention and the original text of the Aircraft Sabotage Act to include the exercise of extraterritorial jurisdiction over U.S. nationality perpetrators and victims of aircraft sabotage.[161]

---

[148] The 1994 statute criminalized aircraft piracy (as therein defined) in the "special aircraft jurisdiction of the United States" (as defined in § 46501(2)) and outside such jurisdiction provided that the offender is "later found in the United States." § 46502(b)(1).

Compare these provisions to arts. 4(1) and 4(2) of the Hague Highjacking Convention. *See supra* notes 59 & 60 (setting out the text of the provisions).

[149] *See supra* note 110.

[150] The extraterritorial provision of the piracy statute now reads:

There is jurisdiction over the offense . . . if—

(A) a national of the United States was aboard the aircraft;

(B) an offender is a national of the United States; or

(C) an offender is afterwards found in the United States.

49 U.S.C.A. § 46502(b)(2).

[151] Of course, this is not prohibited by the Hague Highjacking Convention. The Convention specifies that it "does not exclude any criminal jurisdiction exercised in accordance with national law." Hague Highjacking Convention, *supra* note 47, art. 4(3).

[152] 18 U.S.C.A. § 32.

[153] 18 U.S.C.A. § 37.

[154] *See supra* note 47, item 5.

[155] *See supra* note 47, item 10.

[156] Pub. L. No. 98-473, §§ 2011-2015, 98 Stat. 1837, 2187 (1984).

[157] Pub. L. No. 98-473, 98 Stat. 1837 (1984).

[158] *See* S. REP. NO. 619, at 1 (1984). The Convention entered into force for the U.S. on 26 Jan. 1973. *See* LIST OF TREATIES, *supra* note 45, at 327.

[159] *See supra* notes 59 & 60 (setting out the jurisdictional provisions).

[160] *See* § 2012, Pub. L. No. 98-473, 98 Stat. 2187. *See* S. REP. NO. 619, at 5 (showing the lawmakers' intent to mirror the Convention's jurisdictional provisions in U.S. law).

[161] The aircraft sabotage statute now provides that "[t]here is jurisdiction over an offense under this subsection if a national of the United States was on board, or would have been on board the aircraft; an offender is a national of the United States; or an offender is afterwards found in the United States. 18 U.S.C.A. § 32(b). Note, however, that the Montreal Convention "does not exclude any criminal jurisdiction exercised in accordance with national law." Montreal Convention, *supra* note 47, art. 5(3).

The violence at international airports statute originated in the Violent Crime Control and Law Enforcement Act of 1994[162] and was to implement the Protocol to the Montreal Convention under U.S. law.[163] Consistent with the Protocol, the statute, as enacted in 1994, prescribed jurisdiction over the offence of violence at international airports based on territorial and universality principles.[164] The 1996 Act, however, added nationality and passive personality-based extraterritorial jurisdiction to the original text of the statute,[165] again evidencing the broadening of the U.S. lawmakers' exercise of prescriptive jurisdiction.

In commenting on section 721 of the 1996 Act, the provision that expanded the jurisdictional bases of the three statutes discussed in this group to include nationality and passive personality grounds, the lawmakers stated: "The United States has a legitimate interest in punishing anyone who injures a U.S. national, and also retains an interest in punishing its own citizens for crimes committed against foreign nations, or foreign nationals."[166] While a state's competence to prescribe laws governing the conduct of its citizens abroad[167] is uncontroverted in international law,[168] its competence to regulate conduct of aliens abroad if such conduct would harm its nationals, that is its competence to prescribe law pursuant to the passive personality principle, is questionable.[169] Let us recall that *Restatement (Second)* denied that a state has jurisdiction to prescribe "merely on the grounds that the conduct [in question] affects one of its nationals."[170] Exercise of prescriptive jurisdiction is doctrinally more acceptable when the impetus for the exercise is the desire to protect the interests of the state (protective theory), rather than protect the individual as such (passive personality theory). This analysis is consistent with the restatement of law in the *Restatement (Third)*. There, passive personality is not included as a valid jurisdictional basis, but the reporters observed that the passive personality principle "is increasingly accepted as applied to terrorist and other organized attacks on a state's nationals *by reason of their nationality*."[171] A terrorist attack against nationals of a state because of their nationality is, of course, a valid subject for protective jurisdiction. This is because such an attack is really an attack on the state rather than an attack against the individuals. But the U.S. lawmakers did not justify their expansion of jurisdictional grounds in section 721 of the 1996 Act on the protective grounds; rather, legislative history of this

---

162 Pub. L. No. 103-322, § 60021, 108 Stat. 1796, 1979 (1994).

163 The Protocol *entered into force* for the U.S. on 18 Nov. 1994. *See* LIST OF TREATIES, *supra* note 45, at 328.

164 The statute provided:

> There is jurisdiction over the prohibited activity . . . if—
>
> (1) the prohibited activity takes place in the United States; or
>
> (2) the prohibited activity takes place outside the United States and the offender is later found in the United States.

Pub. L. No. 103-322, § 60021, 108 Stat. 1980.

165 The violence at international airports statute now provides jurisdiction if: "(1) the prohibited activity takes place in the United States; or (2) the prohibited activity takes place outside the United States and (A) the offender is later found in the United States; or (B) an offender or a victim is a national of the United States . . ." 18 U.S.C.A. § 37(b).

166 H.R. CONF. REP. NO. 104-518, at 122 (1996).

167 *See supra* § II.B (discussing the nationality principle).

168 *See e.g., supra* note 7 (citing authorities in support of this proposition).

169 *See supra* note 32 (citing problems with the exercise of passive personality jurisdiction) and note 33 (listing commentators skeptical of the exercise of jurisdiction under this principle).

170 RESTATEMENT (SECOND), *supra* note 36, § 30(2).

171 RESTATEMENT (THIRD), *supra* note 3, § 402 cmt. g (emphasis added).

section reflects their reliance on a pure passive personality theory.[172] In section 721, the lawmakers did not eclipse their jurisdictional competence so that it would extend only to aliens' extraterritorial acts against U.S. nationals *because of their nationality*, rather they granted the U.S. the power of "punishing anyone who injures a U.S. national,"[173] apparently for any reason, as long as it is in connection with one of the included offences. The recent inclusion of the passive personality grounds of extraterritorial jurisdiction in the U.S. statutes on aircraft piracy, aircraft sabotage, and violence at international airports goes beyond the jurisdictional grounds set out in the relevant conventions and is at odds with international law doctrine.[174]

It remains to be seen whether the U.S. Government will interpret the amendments relating to U.S. nationality victims as extending only to proscribed extraterritorial acts by aliens against U.S. nationals *because of their U.S. nationality* or whether it will take these amendments at face value and use them against aliens for proscribed extraterritorial acts against, or also affecting, U.S. nationals, irrespective of their nationality. At any rate, it would have been preferable[175] if the jurisdictional provisions relating to U.S. victims targeted only acts that the U.S. could justifiably reach under the protective theory, which is well accepted in the practice of states and in doctrine.[176] A simple amendment of the provisions basing extraterritorial jurisdiction on U.S. nationality would cure the present doctrinal problem: the jurisdictional basis of offences against U.S. nationals should be limited to offences aimed or committed against U.S. nationals *because of their nationality.*

Offences against the Safety of Maritime Navigation and Fixed Platforms

The two representative offences in this category are violence against maritime navigation[177] and violence against maritime fixed-platforms.[178] Both of these statutes originated in the Violent Crime Control and Law Enforcement Act of 1994[179] and constitute

---

172 *See* H.R. CONF. REP. NO. 104-518, at 122.

173 *Id.*

174 In a testimony before the U.S. House Judiciary Committee in connection with the Comprehensive Antiterrorism Act of 1995, Abraham Sofaer, a distinguished scholar and senior fellow of the Hoover Institution, and a former official in the Reagan Administration, stated about the then-proposed jurisdictional provisions which have since been incorporated into the 1996 Act:

> Most of the extraterritorial provisions conferring jurisdiction are sound, and needed. *I doubt, however, that the mere fact that a U.S. national was or 'would have been' aboard an aircraft that is attacked* [referring to the current jurisdictional provision from the aircraft sabotage statute, 18 U.S.C. § 32(b)—*see supra* note 167 setting out the full text of the provision] *is a sufficient basis for jurisdiction.* Even if it is technically sufficient, it would seem preferable as a matter of comity and practicality to restrict the cases in which the U.S. asserts jurisdiction to those in which the American national is actually targeted because he or she is an American.

Testimony of Abraham D. Sofaer, George P. Schultz Distinguished Scholar and Senior Fellow, the Hoover Institution, Stanford University, on the Comprehensive Antiterrorism Act of 1995 before the Committee on the Judiciary, House of Representatives, June 12, 1995, 104th Cong. 1st Sess. (1995), *available in* LEXIS (emphasis added) [hereinafter Sofaer Testimony].

175 *See* Sofaer Testimony, *supra* note 180 ("it would seem preferrable as a matter of comity and practicality to restrict the cases in which the U.S. asserts jurisdiction to those in which the American national is actually targeted because he or she is an American."). *See also infra* section V (discussing problems with a broad exercise of extraterritorial jurisdiction).

176 *See supra* note 11 and accompanying text (discussing acceptance of the protective principle).

177 18 U.S.C.A. § 2280 (West Supp. 1997).

178 18 U.S.C.A. § 2281 (West Supp. 1997).

179 Pub. L. No. 103-322, 108 Stat. 1796 (1994).

the U.S. implementing legislation for the IMO Convention and Protocol.[180] The original text of these statutes created jurisdiction over the included offences on the bases of territoriality, universality, nationality, protected interest, and passive personality[181] and the 1996 Act left this unchanged.[182]

It may be recalled that the IMO Convention and Protocol call on state-parties to establish jurisdiction based on territoriality, universality, and nationality, and that these instruments also allow states to establish jurisdiction pursuant to the protective and passive personality theories.[183] The jurisdictional provisions of the U.S. statutes concerning violence against maritime navigation and maritime fixed-platforms are thus consistent with the terms of the international instruments these statutes implement.

Nevertheless, the validity of the statutes' passive personality jurisdiction is questionable in view of the current doctrine.[184] The comments made above in connection with the use of passive personality jurisdiction in statutes dealing with aviation safety are relevant here as well.[185] What is particularly troubling about the inclusion of the passive personality grounds in the maritime safety statutes is that these statutes, unlike the aviation safety statutes, also contain the protective jurisdictional basis. This may indicate that the lawmakers did not intend passive personality-based jurisdiction to arise only in cases where a U.S. national would be affected by the proscribed conduct *because of his nationality*, since then there

---

[180] *See supra* note 47, items 11 & 12. Both instruments entered into force for the United States on 6 March 1995. *See* LIST OF TREATIES, *supra* note 45, at 398.

[181] *See* Pub. L. No. 103-322, § 60019, 108 Stat. 1796, 1975-78.

[182] The jurisdictional provision of the violence against maritime navigation statute presently reads:

> There is jurisdiction over the activity prohibited in subsection (a)— (1) . . . if—
>
> (A) such activity is committed—
>
> (i) against or on board a ship flying the flag of the United States at the time the prohibited activity is committed;
>
> (ii) in the United States; or
>
> (iii) by a national of the United States . . . ;
>
> (B) during the commission of such activity, a national of the United States is seized, threatened, injured or killed; or
>
> (C) the offender is later found in the United States after such activity is committed;
>
> (2) in the case of a ship navigating or scheduled to navigate solely within the territorial sea or internal waters of a country other than the United States, if the offender is later found in the United States after such activity is committed; and
>
> (3) in the case of any vessel, if such activity is committed in an attempt to compel the United States to do or abstain from doing any act.

18 U.S.C.A. § 2280(b).

The jurisdictional provision of the violence against maritime fixed platforms statute presently reads:

> There is jurisdiction over the activity prohibited in subsection (a) if—
>
> (1) such activity is committed against or on board a fixed platform—
>
> (A) that is located on the continental shelf of the United States;
>
> (B) that is located on the continental shelf of another country, by a national of the United States . . . ;
>
> (C) in an attempt to compel the United States to do or abstain from doing any act;
>
> (2) during the commission of such activity against or on board a fixed platform located on a continental shelf, a national of the United States is seized, threatened, injured or killed; or
>
> (3) such activity is committed against or on board a fixed platform located outside the United States and beyond the continental shelf of the United States and the offender is later found in the United States.

18 U.S.C.A. § 2281(b).

[183] *See supra* notes 69-71 and 74 (setting out the jurisdictional provisions of the IMO instruments).

[184] *See supra* note 32 (citing problems with the exercise of passive personality jurisdiction) and note 33 (listing commentators skeptical of the exercise of jurisdiction under this principle).

[185] *See supra* notes 175-178 and accompanying text.

would be jurisdiction under the protective principle, but rather suggests that jurisdiction would exist in *any* case of the proscribed conduct involving a U.S. national. Should the latter interpretation be accepted in practice, it would allow for a broad extraterritorial application of these statutes.[186]

Offences against the Safety of Internationally Protected Persons

Until the amendments of section 721 of the 1996 Act,[187] the offences included in this group carried extraterritorial jurisdiction based only on universality. For example, the kidnaping statute[188] provided for extraterritorial jurisdiction only in cases where the victim of the offence was an internationally protected person and the alleged offender was present in the United States.[189] If these conditions were met, there was jurisdiction "irrespective of the place where the offense was committed or the nationality of the victim or the alleged offender."[190] The statutes dealing with protection of foreign officials, official guests, and internationally protected persons,[191] threats and extortion against foreign officials, official guests, or internationally protected persons,[192] and murder or manslaughter of foreign officials, official guests, or internationally protected persons[193] contained the same jurisdictional provision for universal jurisdiction in cases involving internationally protected persons as the kidnaping statute.[194]

The 1996 Act expanded the extraterritorial jurisdiction over these offences so that the United States has jurisdiction over them "if (1) the victim is a representative, officer, employee, or agent of the United States, (2) an offender is a national of the United States, or (3) an offender is afterwards found in the United States" provided that the victim "is an internationally protected person outside the United States."[195] The statutes concerned with the safety of internationally protected persons thus now rely on, in addition to territoriality and universality, the nationality and protective principles of jurisdiction.

This is in accordance with the International Protected Person Convention[196] which obliges state-parties to establish jurisdiction over the included offences on territorial,

---

[186] *See infra* section V (discussing problems with a broad exercise of extraterritorial jurisdiction). *See also* Sofaer Testimony, *supra* note 179 ("it would seem preferrable as a matter of comity and practicality to restrict the cases in which the U.S. asserts jurisdiction to those in which the American national is actually targeted because he or she is an American.").

[187] *See supra* note 110.

[188] 18 U.S.C.A. § 1201 (West Supp. 1997).

[189] *See* Act for the Prevention and Punishment of Crimes Against Internationally Protected Persons, Pub. L. No. 94-467, § 4, 90 Stat. 1997, 1998 (1976) (prior to 1996 amendment). *See also* H. REP. NO. 94-1614, at 6 (1976).

[190] Act for the Prevention and Punishment of Crimes Against Internationally Protected Persons, Pub. L. No. 94-467, § 4(e), 90 Stat. 1997, 1998 (1976) (prior to 1996 amendment).

[191] *See* Act for the Prevention and Punishment of Crimes Against Internationally Protected Persons, Pub. L. No. 94-467, § 5, 90 Stat. 1997, 1999 (1976) (prior to 1996 amendment).

[192] *See* Act for the Prevention and Punishment of Crimes Against Internationally Protected Persons, Pub. L. No. 94-467, § 8, 90 Stat. 1997, 2000 (1976) (prior to 1996 amendment).

[193] *See* Act for the Prevention and Punishment of Crimes Against Internationally Protected Persons, Pub. L. No. 94-467, § 2, 90 Stat. 1997 (1976) (prior to 1996 amendment).

[194] *See supra* note 192.

[195] *See* 18 U.S.C.A. § 1201(e) (West Supp. 1997); 18 U.S.C.A. § 112(e) (West Supp. 1997); 18 U.S.C.A. § 878(d) (West Supp. 1997); 18 U.S.C.A. § 1116(c) (West Supp. 1997).

[196] *See supra* note 47, item 6. The Convention has been in force for the United States since 20 Feb. 1977. *See* LIST OF TREATIES, *supra* note 45, at 441.

nationality, universality, and protective grounds.[197] As noted earlier,[198] some commentators also suggest that the International Protected Persons Convention invokes jurisdictional competence on the basis of the nationality of the victim by calling for jurisdiction "when the crime is committed against an internationally protected person . . . who enjoys his status as such by virtue of functions which he exercises on behalf of that State."[199] This argument suffers from relying on an assumption which does not necessarily hold true: that "the internationally protected person . . . who enjoys his status as such by virtue of functions which he exercises on behalf of [a] State"[200] is a national of that state.[201] For this reason, it is preferable to take the vague language of the International Protected Persons Convention on this point to mean that there is to be jurisdiction over proscribed acts committed against internationally protected persons because of the *functions* they exercise on behalf of the particular state irrespective of their nationality. Under this understanding, what is really being protected are the state's interests rather than the person as such.

Whatever construction one finds more convincing, this provision of the International Protected Persons Convention is not one indubitably representing the protective or the passive personality theory of jurisdiction.[202] But, as jurisdiction under this provision of the International Protected Persons Convention vests over acts against a person who enjoys his status because of the *functions* that he performs on behalf of the state, the impetus for this provision seems to be more like that inherent in the protective theory rather than that underlying the passive personality theory.

The U.S. lawmakers did not correct this imprecision of the International Protected Persons Convention in their 1996 amendments of the jurisdictional provisions of the statutes relating to the safety of internationally protected persons. As noted above, the amendments added jurisdiction over the included offences, *inter alia*, "if . . . the victim is a representative, officer, employee, or agent of the United States."[203] This could not be said to be a passive personality-based provision since, for example, one need not be a national of the United States to be its agent. But, the provision is also not stated clearly in protective terms as it does not tie the offence against the person to his functions on behalf of the state.[204]

At any rate, if one interprets this provision to represent the protective principle of extraterritorial jurisdiction, the jurisdictional provisions of the U.S. statutes dealing with offences against the safety of internationally protected persons are consistent with the International Protected Persons Convention and with doctrine. Should the practice under the statutes' jurisdictional provisions reach extraterritorial acts against U.S. nationality,

---

197 *See supra* notes 79 & 80 and accompanying text (setting out and discussing the Convention's jurisdictional provisions).

198 *See supra* notes 81 & 82 and accompanying text.

199 Int'l Protected Persons Convention, *supra* note 47, art. 3(1)(c).

200 *Id.*

201 *See supra* note 82 and accompanying text (elaborating on this point).

202 Cameron finds that this assertion of jurisdiction is grounded in a hybrid of the protective and passive personality principles. *See* CAMERON, *supra* note 12, at 77.

203 18 U.S.C.A. § 1201(e); 18 U.S.C.A. § 112(e); 18 U.S.C.A. § 878(d); 18 U.S.C.A. § 1116(c).

204 For example, an offence could be perpetrated against a person as such, irrespective of his functions on behalf of the U.S., although that person could be a representative, officer, employee, or agent of the U.S.

Of course, in practice, it can be difficult to ascertain whether an offence was perpetrated because of a person's functions on behalf of a state or, indeed, because of his nationality. *See, e.g.*, CAMERON, *supra* note 12, at 77.

internationally protected persons irrespective of such persons' functions on behalf of the United States, this would contravene doctrine.[205]

Hostage-Taking

The U.S. implementing legislation for the Convention Against Taking of Hostages,[206] the Act for the Prevention and Punishment of the Crime of Hostage-Taking,[207] incorporated in the Comprehensive Crime Control Act of 1984,[208] created extraterritorial jurisdictional bases over the offence of hostage-taking.[209] Pursuant to the Hostage-Taking Act, the United States has jurisdiction over an extraterritorial act of hostage-taking if "(A) the offender or the person seized or detained is a national of the United States; (B) the offender is found in the United States; (C) the governmental organization sought to be compelled is the Government of the United States."[210] This jurisdictional provision has not been amended, including by the 1996 Act, and extraterritorial jurisdiction over the offence of hostage-taking thus remains based on nationality, passive personality, universality, and protected interest.[211]

These jurisdictional provisions are consistent with the Convention Against Taking of Hostages. The Convention obliges states parties to establish jurisdiction over the offence of hostage-taking[212] under the territorial, nationality, protective, and universality principles of jurisdiction.[213] The Convention also allows, but does not require, states to establish passive personality-based jurisdiction over the offence.[214]

Some commentators understand the passive personality-based grounds permitted under the Convention to be valid only in cases when there is "a sufficient nexus" between the offence and the nation's interests.[215] But in a case with such a sufficient nexus, there already would be jurisdiction under the protective principle and there would be no need to invoke jurisdiction based on passive personality. Indeed, no requirement of a sufficient nexus to a state's interests when a state would wish to rely on the passive personality theory is included in the Convention.

---

205 It would not, however, violate the terms of the Int'l Protected Persons Convention since the Convention expressly "does not exclude any criminal jurisdiction exercised in accordance with internal law." Int'l Protected Persons Convention, *supra* note 47, art. 3(3).

206 *See supra* note 47, item 9. The Conv. Against Taking of Hostages *entered into force* for the United States on 6 Jan. 1985. *See* LIST OF TREATIES, *supra* note 45, at 442.

207 Pub. L. No. 98-473, §§ 2001-2003, 98 Stat. 1837, 2186 (1984) [hereinafter Hostage-Taking Act].

208 Pub. L. No. 98-473, 98 Stat. 1837 (1984).

209 *See* 18 U.S.C.A. § 1203(a) (West Supp. 1997) (defining the offence).

210 Pub. L. No. 98-473, § 2002, 98 Stat. 2186.

211 *See* 18 U.S.C.A. § 1203(b)(1) (West Supp. 1997) (setting out the jurisdictional provisions). Interestingly, President Reagan's message transmitting a draft of the Hostage Taking Act to Congress identified the extraterritorial jurisdictional principles involved in the draft legislation as: "the well-accepted territorial, personal, and passive personality bases for the exercise of legislative jurisdiction under international law." H.R. DOC. NO. 211 (1984), *reprinted in* Marian Nash Leigh, Current Development, *Four Bills Proposed by President Reagan to Counter Terrorism*, 78 AM. J. INT'L L. 915, 919 (1984).

212 *See* Conv. Against Taking of Hostages, *supra* note 47, art. 1 (defining the offence).

213 *See supra* notes 87 & 89 and accompanying text (setting out the jurisdictional provisions).

214 *See supra* note 88 and accompanying text (setting out this optional jurisdictional basis).

215 *See supra* note 88; Abramovsky, *supra* note 55, at 129.

The U.S. practice under the hostage-taking statute shows that the United States, also, does not see any such requirement in the Convention.[216] The passive personality jurisdictional basis in the hostage-taking statute thus evinces potential for a broad application of the statute by the United States, and consequently for jurisdictional conflict with other states.[217]

Offences against the Safety of Nuclear Material

In 1982, the U.S. Congress passed implementing legislation for the Nuclear Material Convention,[218] the Convention on the Physical Protection of Nuclear Material Act.[219] Since this legislation was intended to mirror the Convention,[220] it contained jurisdictional grounds over the included offences identical to those in the Convention. Consequently, pursuant to the Act, the United States has jurisdiction over the covered offences on territorial, nationality, and universality grounds. The legislative history shows that the lawmakers were reluctant to exercise prescriptive extraterritorial jurisdiction in the Act, but that, in the end, they felt justified by the Convention to rely on the universality principle. The Judiciary Committee's report submitted with the legislation stated:

> Ordinarily, the United States is reluctant to exercise its jurisdiction in the circumstances . . . when all the conduct comprising the offense was committed in another country, and the defendant entered the United States at a later point in time. In this case, the Committee chose to provide for extraterritorial Federal criminal jurisdiction because of the nature of the conduct and the fact that the exercise of jurisdiction is recognized under principles of international law. . . . The universality principle is generally accepted in the international community in the case of internationally recognized crimes. In this context, the Convention provides that international recognition.[221]

Fourteen years later, the lawmakers did not feel similarly constrained in extending the reach of the U.S. nuclear material statute abroad, and by an amendment of the statute contained in the 1996 Act extended jurisdiction over the covered offences pursuant to the passive personality principle. This extension of extraterritorial criminal jurisdiction reflects the recent U.S. trend to reach, with its antiterrorist laws, "all situations, anywhere in the world where a United States national is the victim of an offense or where the perpetrator or victim of the offense is a 'United States corporation or other legal entity.'"[222] Indeed, this was the justification cited for the 1996 amendment of the nuclear material statute by its drafters. The legislative history of this amendment does not hint at restricting the application

---

[216] *See* United States v. Yunis, 681 F. Supp. 896 (D.D.C. 1988), *aff'd*, 924 F.2d 1086 (D.C. Cir. 1991) (holding that the U.S. had jurisdiction over an alien defendant who hijacked a foreign airliner with three U.S. nationals on board absent any other nexus to the U.S.). *See generally* Abramovsky, *supra* note 55 (discussing the *Yunis* case).

[217] *See infra* section V (discussing problems with a broad exercise of extraterritorial jurisdiction).

[218] *See supra* note 47, item 8. The Convention *entered into force* for the United States on 8 Feb. 1987. *See* LIST OF TREATIES, *supra* note 45, at 406.

[219] Pub. L. No. 97-351, 96 Stat. 1663 (1982).

[220] *See* H.R. REP. NO. 97-624, at 1 (1982) ("The primary purpose of the bill . . . is to implement the [Nuclear Material Convention]" *Id.*).

[221] H.R. REP. NO. 97-624, at 9-10 (1982) (citations omitted).

[222] H.R. DOC. NO. 104-31, at 100 (1995).

of the statute to instances when a U.S. national is the victim of the offence *because of his nationality*. Rather, the lawmakers' statements show that the statute is meant to apply to any included offence involving a U.S. national, whether or not the offence was perpetrated against that person because of his nationality. Adding jurisdiction over the included offences based purely on the U.S. nationality of the victim goes beyond the jurisdictional provisions of the Nuclear Material Convention that the statute implements in U.S. law and is at odds with doctrine. In yet another respect, the amendments contained in the 1996 Act thus set the stage for a scenario of a broad extraterritorial application of a criminal statute by the United States and invite jurisdictional conflict with other states.[223]

Other Terrorist Offences

This group of offences consists of those included in the "Terrorism" chapter of title 18 of the U.S. Code. The included offences in the "Terrorism" chapter that are relevant here, because the U.S. has extraterritorial penal jurisdiction over them, are homicide of a U.S. national outside the U.S.,[224] physical violence against a U.S. national outside the U.S.,[225] use of weapons of mass destruction,[226] acts of terrorism transcending national boundaries,[227] and the use of chemical weapons. The extraterritorial reach of each offence is discussed in turn below.

The Omnibus Diplomatic Security and Antiterrorism Act of 1986[228] added to the U.S. statutes chapter 113A, entitled Extraterritorial Jurisdiction Over Terrorist Acts Abroad Against United States Nationals. Under the heading Terrorist Acts Abroad Against United States Nationals, the 1986 Omnibus Act created the offences of homicide of, and physical violence against, a U.S. national while such national is outside the U.S. This seemingly passive personality provision was, however, tempered by the requirement that any prosecution of these offences proceed only after "written certification of the Attorney General or the highest ranking subordinate of the Attorney General with responsibility for criminal prosecutions that, in the judgement of the certifying official, such offense was intended to coerce, intimidate, or retaliate against a government or a civilian population."[229]Therefore, the extraterritorial reach of the statute is limited to circumstances invoking the state's protective interest. The lawmakers noted that they did not intend this statute to "reach nonterrorist violence inflicted upon American victims"[230] and specified that "[s]imple barroom brawls or normal street crime, for example, are not intended to be covered

---

223 *See infra* section V (discussing problems with a broad exercise of extraterritorial jurisdiction). *See also* Sofaer Testimony, *supra* note 179 ("it would seem preferable as a matter of comity and practicality to restrict the cases in which the U.S. asserts jurisdiction to those in which the American national is actually targeted because he or she is an American.").

224 18 U.S.C.A. § 2332(a) (West Supp. 1997).

225 18 U.S.C.A. § 2332(c) (West Supp. 1997).

226 18 U.S.C.A. § 2332a (West Supp. 1997).

227 18 U.S.C.A. § 2332b (West Supp. 1997).

228 Pub. L. No. 99-399, 100 Stat. 853 (1986).

229 Pub. L. No. 99-399, § 1202, 100 Stat. 896-897. This provision is now codified in 18 U.S.C.A. § 2332(d) (West Supp. 1997).

230 H.R. CONF. REP. NO. 99-783, at 87 (1986).

by this provision."[231] The 1996 Act[232] did not alter the jurisdictional provisions of this statute.

It is well accepted that terrorism is a threat to the state as such and that, consequently, every state has the right to protect itself against it. Because this statute permits extraterritorial reach of the U.S. only in circumstances involving a violent extraterritorial act against a U.S. national *in order to coerce, intimidate or retaliate against a government or civilian population*, that is, in circumstances which may be characterized as terrorism, it is acceptable from the point of view of doctrine.[233]

The weapons of mass destruction statute prohibits, with respect to extraterritorial conduct, use, threats, attempts, and conspiracies to use a weapon of mass destruction, including biological agents, against a national of the United States or by a U.S. national, or against property used by the U.S. Government. This statute has its origin in the Violent Crime Control and Law Enforcement Act of 1994. The 1994 law made it a crime to use a weapon of mass destruction against a U.S. national abroad, against any person in the United States, and against any property anywhere that is used by the U.S. Government. The statute, in its present form,[234] employs the nationality,[235] passive personality,[236] and perhaps to some extent, the effects (objective application of the territoriality principle),[237] and protective principles of jurisdiction.[238]

Though the use of the nationality principle to reach proscribed extraterritorial conduct by a state's own nationals is accepted in doctrine,[239] the use of the passive personality principle, generally, is not. Where, as in this statute, the lawmakers made no attempt to limit the exercise of jurisdiction to cases when the nationals are targeted specifically because of their nationality, the jurisdictional provision is unfounded in view of current doctrine. As noted earlier in connection with other statutes,[240] such a jurisdictional provision also has the potential for causing conflict with other states.[241]

The 1996 Act added a group of new offences to the "Terrorism" chapter of the U.S. Code. Section 702 of the 1996 Act, entitled Acts of Terrorism Transcending National Boundaries,[242] made it an offence, *inter alia*, to kill, kidnap, or assault any person in the United States[243] or to create a risk of bodily injury by destroying or damaging any structure or property in the U.S. "or by attempting or conspiring to destroy or damage any structure,

---

231 *Id.*

232 *See supra* note 110.

233 *See, e.g.*, RESTATEMENT (THIRD), *supra* note 3, § 402(3); Harvard Research, *supra* note 1, at 543. *See also supra* note 243 (noting the potential application of this statute in a case when the U.S. is not the state intended to be affected by the proscribed conduct).

234 It was amended by section 725 of the 1996 Act. *See supra* note 110, § 725.

235 18 U.S.C.A. § 2332a(b).

236 18 U.S.C.A. § 2332a(a)(1).

237 *See supra* § II.A (discussing the territorial principle).

238 18 U.S.C.A. § 2332a(a)(3).

239 *See supra* § II.B (discussing the nationality principle).

240 *See supra* notes 180, 191, 222, 231.

241 *See infra* section V (discussing problems with a broad exercise of extraterritorial jurisdiction). *See also* Sofaer Testimony, *supra* note 179 ("it would seem preferable as a matter of comity and practicality to restrict the cases in which the U.S. asserts jurisdiction to those in which the American national is actually targeted because he or she is an American.").

242 Pub. L. No. 104-132, § 702. Codified as 18 U.S.C.A. § 2332b (West Supp. 1997).

243 18 U.S.C.A. § 2332b(a)(1)(A) (West Supp. 1997).

conveyance, or other real or personal property within the United States."[244] The jurisdictional bases for these offences include circumstances when "the victim, or intended victim, is the United States Government, a member of the uniformed services, or any official, officer, employee, or agent of the legislative, executive, or judicial branches, or of any department or agency, of the United States."[245] The statute specifies that there is extraterritorial federal jurisdiction over any included offence, including any threat, attempt, or conspiracy to commit such an offence. Since the exercise of extraterritorial jurisdiction under this statute is tied to acts targeting the U.S. Government,[246] that is, the state as such, it is consistent with doctrine under the protective theory.[247]

The 1996 Act also added a new offence: the use of chemical weapons. This statute criminalizes the use of chemical weapons in the United States or against U.S. nationals or U.S. Government property abroad. It thus relies on the territorial, protective, and passive personality theories of jurisdiction. While as repeated above,[248] the territorial and protective principles are not problematic in view of doctrine; reliance upon the passive personality principle engenders the risk of jurisdictional conflict with other states.[249]

The foregoing survey reveals that U.S. laws relevant to combating terrorism rely on the nationality, protective, passive personality, and universality principles of extraterritorial jurisdiction. For the purposes of discerning the U.S. lawmakers' position on extraterritorial jurisdiction, at least in connection with antiterrorism laws, it is noteworthy that the 1996 Act,[250] evincing the lawmakers' most recent activity in this area, added passive personality jurisdiction to several existing statutes[251] and created a new offence over which the U.S. has extraterritorial jurisdiction based on the U.S. nationality of the victim. The lawmakers' recent ventures into combating terrorism thus show that the passive personality principle is presently their favorite jurisdictional weapon.

While several relevant treaties to which the United States is a state party mandate or permit reliance on this principle,[252] it is still disfavored in doctrine. Moreover, even when the U.S. statutes confer passive personality-based extraterritorial jurisdiction pursuant to treaties, and are not in contravention of the relevant treaties, they do not limit the exercise of jurisdiction under them to offences in states parties to those treaties. The possibility thus exists that a particular U.S. antiterrorism statute will be used to proceed extraterritorialy against an alien accused of proscribed conduct against a U.S. national abroad, although the state in whose territory the conduct will have taken place is not a party to the treaty involved.

---

244 18 U.S.C.A. § 2332b(a)(1)(B) (West Supp. 1997).

245 18 U.S.C.A. § 2332b(b)(1)(C) (West Supp. 1997).

246 *See supra* note 264. *See also* H.R. CONF. REP. NO. 104-518, at 120 (1996) (discussing jurisdictional grounds).

247 *See generally supra* § II.C (discussing the protective principle).

248 *See generally supra* §§ II.A & II.C (discussing the territorial and protective principles of jurisdiction).

249 *See infra* section V (discussing problems with a broad exercise of extraterritorial jurisdiction). *See also* Sofaer Testimony, *supra* note 180 ("it would seem preferable as a matter of comity and practicality to restrict the cases in which the U.S. asserts jurisdiction to those in which the American national is actually targeted because he or she is an American.").

250 *See supra note* 110.

251 *See supra* notes 155 (passive personality jurisdiction added to the aircraft piracy statute, 49 U.S.C.A. § 46502); 166 (passive personality jurisdiction added to the aircraft sabotage statute, 18 U.S.C.A. § 32(b)); 170 (passive personality jurisdiction added to the violence at international airports statute, 18 U.S.C.A. § 37(b)); 221 (passive personality jurisdiction added to the nuclear material statute, 18 U.S.C.A. § 831(c)).

252 *See supra* notes 54 (Tokyo Convention); 71 (IMO Convention); 74 (IMO Protocol); 88 (Conv. Against Taking of Hostages).

In these cases, and in cases where the jurisdictional provisions of a U.S. statute are not grounded in a treaty, the extraterritorial exercise of jurisdiction by U.S. authorities can be judged only by doctrine. It can only be repeated again that doctrine disfavors reliance on the passive personality principle.[253]

The lawmakers would have done better had they based extraterritorial jurisdiction on the protective principle, which is relatively well-accepted, and which, in any case, would likely operate to reach most extraterritorial terrorist acts harming, or threatening to harm, U.S. nationals abroad. Simply linking the extraterritorial jurisdiction to offences against U.S. nationals *because of their nationality* would diminish the threat of an overbroad application of U.S. laws abroad and would make the laws doctrinally justifiable and more acceptable to other states.

Conclusion: Some Issues to be Considered in Connection with the Exercise of Extraterritorial Penal Jurisdiction

In conclusion it must be noted that an overbroad extraterritorial application of U.S. criminal laws, such as that allowed by the passive personality principle now incorporated into many U.S. antiterrorist statutes, engenders risk of conflict with other states. This is because one state's exercise of extraterritorial jurisdiction normally intrudes upon another state's territorial sovereignty. Naturally, such conflict cannot be helpful to the long-term interests of the United States.

Abramovsky suggests that the United States should limit the extraterritorial application of its criminal laws for the following reasons: "the danger of provoking reciprocal conduct from unfriendly nations, the danger of setting unsound precedent for other nations to follow, and respect for relations among nations."[254] To these reasons may be added another, a problem of representation: aliens with little or no contact with the United States may be affected by U.S. laws enacted by a government in which they are not represented.[255]

This chapter has focused on *prescriptive* jurisdiction, on the power of a state to prescribe the law, rather than on its capacity to enforce it. Generally, the mere act of prescribing a law does not lead to a conflict with other states. This is because the exercise of prescriptive jurisdiction by itself constitutes no extraterritorial action. However, when a state that has the means to enforce its laws abroad prescribes laws that may have extraterritorial reach, "the potential for conflict is rife."[256] Nadelmann elaborates on this point:

> The ability of the United States government to demand foreign recognition of its claims to extraterritorial jurisdiction greatly exceeds that of any other government. Its unparalleled networks of law enforcement, diplomatic, and intelligence agents provide numerous means to further United States interests globally. At the same time, most foreign governments and multinational corporations have sufficient interests in, and contacts with, the United States to be susceptible to a wide variety of United States

---

[253] *See supra* notes 32-36 and accompanying text (discussing the position of the principle in doctrine and citing commentators' views).

[254] Abramovsky, *supra* note 55, at 138.

[255] *See* Weisburd, *supra* note 144, at 428.

[256] *See*, Ethan A. Nadelmann, *Negotiations in Criminal Law Assistance Treaties*, 33 AM. S. INT'L L. 467 (1985).

> pressures, ranging from domestic law enforcement actions to economic sanctions. Most foreign governments thus have a good reason to fear the United States government's assertions of extraterritorial jurisdiction over violations of its antitrust, export control, money laundering, tax, and even drug and terrorism statutes. Today, many of the more serious conflicts between the United States and its allies over criminal justice issues focus on precisely these extraterritorial assertions.[257]

It is for this reason, the viability of enforcement of U.S. laws abroad, that this chapter now considers in more detail some of the international law principles which may theoretically limit the exercise of extraterritorial penal jurisdiction and consequently the potential for conflict between the United States and other states.

These principles are the equality of states, territorial sovereignty, and non-intervention. Essentially, these principles represent aspects of state sovereignty. The principle of sovereign equality of states is acknowledged in the United Nations Charter which, in article 2(1), states that "[t]he Organization is based on the principle of sovereign equality of states."[258] The principle of sovereign equality of states implies that states pay due respect to each others' jurisdictional rights; that is that one state not trespass upon the jurisdictional rights of another state.[259]

The principle of territorial sovereignty is acknowledged in article 2(4) of the U.N. Charter: "All members shall refrain in their international relations from the threat or use of force against the territorial integrity or political independence of any state, or in any other manner inconsistent with the Purposes of the United Nations."[260] Unauthorized exercise of enforcement jurisdiction by one state in the territory of another[261] may be understood to constitute use of force against the territorial integrity of another state. An exercise of prescriptive jurisdiction which may lead to such enforcement may be considered a threat of force against the territorial integrity of a state, particularly when, as in the case of the United States, such threat is credible.[262]

The principle of non-intervention may be gleaned from article 2(7) of the U.N. Charter: "Nothing contained in the present Charter shall authorize the United Nations to intervene in matters which are essentially within the domestic jurisdiction of any state. . . ."[263] This principle has been restated in the 1970 United Nations Declaration on Principles of International Law concerning Friendly Relations and Co-operation among States in Accordance with the Charter of the United Nations which reads: "No State . . . has the right to intervene, directly or indirectly, for any reason whatever, in the internal or external affairs

---

257 *Id.* Cameron warns that "a lack of restraint in enforcement jurisdiction together with a growing sphere of prescriptive jurisdiction is a dangerous combination, especially when the country in question is the most powerful in the world." CAMERON, *supra* note 12, at 295.

258 U.N. CHARTER art. 2, para. 1.

259 *See* Bowett, *supra* note 1, at 16; Freestone, *supra* note 45, at 48.

260 U.N. CHARTER art. 2, para. 4.

261 Bowett lists seizure of property and arrest by one state in the territory of another state as examples of such exercise of enforcement jurisdiction. Bowett, *supra* note 1, at 16.

262 On the credibility of such a threat emanating from U.S. legislation *see supra* note 285.

263 U.N. CHARTER art. 2, para. 7.

of any other State. . . ."[264] The unauthorized exercise of enforcement jurisdiction by one state in the territory of another would constitute an intervention in the affairs of that state.[265]

Freestone, however, suggests that it may be difficult to rely upon the non-intervention principle in the case of extraterritorial terrorist offences. Indeed, the Reagan Administration found another principle in the U.N. Charter to dismiss the non-intervention argument in cases of extraterritorial terrorist offences. The Administration's argument was that an extraterritorial attack on a U.S. national because of his nationality was an attack on the United States and consequently, that article 51 of the U.N. Charter gave the U.S. the right to defend itself. Article 51 provides: "Nothing in the present Charter shall impair the inherent right of individual or collective self-defence if an armed attack occurs against a Member of the United Nations, until the Security Council has taken measures necessary to maintain international peace and security."[266] For the purposes of this chapter, it is important to note that the Administration limited its right to self-defence to cases involving an attack on a U.S. national *because of his nationality*, a circumstance considered here to come under the protective theory, and did not suggest that self-defence under article 51 would be an appropriate response to extraterritorial attacks against U.S. nationals irrespective of their nationality.[267]

These three international law principles, sovereign equality of states, territorial sovereignty, and non-intervention, should, at least in theory, operate to limit the extraterritorial exercise of jurisdiction. Another limitation on such jurisdictional exercise comes from the rule of reasonableness. Since no prescribed method exists in international law for choosing among competing basis of extraterritorial jurisdiction,[268] the rule of reasonableness may be used to resolve jurisdictional conflict. The difficulty with resorting to the rule of reasonableness to decide jurisdictional conflicts in terrorism cases which may well implicate political policies of the states involved, is that the entity that would apply the rule would be a domestic court. Schachter observed that in such circumstances, "it becomes almost impossible for the courts in either country to balance the conflicting interests in terms of what is reasonable."[269]

Moreover, the rule of reasonableness is most likely not a rule of international law, but a manifestation of comity. When a state relies on comity, it defers to another state on a particular point with the expectation that that state will yield to it on a similar point in the future. But given the relatively strong position of the United States in the world, it cannot be left solely to comity to keep the extraterritorial application of U.S. laws in check. Nor, for that matter can it be assumed that the vague and, in this context, practically

---

264 G.A. Res. 2625, U.N. GAOR, 25th Sess., U.N. Doc. A/RES/2625 (1970).

265 Commenting on the intersection of the principle of non-intervention with jurisdiction, Bowett said: "The principle of non-intervention, therefore, would prohibit what is in effect the exercise of a prerogative, sovereign power by one State in the territory of another." Bowett, *supra* note 1, at 17. *See also* CAMERON, *supra* note 12, at 343-46 (discussing the principle of non-intervention and its relevance to issues of extraterritorial jurisdiction). *See generally supra* note 32 (discussing the passive personality theory and the rule of non-intervention).

266 U.N. CHARTER art. 51.

267 Yet the 1996 Act relies on the passive personality theory of extraterritorial jurisdiction. *See supra* notes 273 & 274 (listing offences over which the U.S. has extraterritorial jurisdiction under the passive personality theory).

268 *See e.g.*, Akehurst, *supra* note 2, at 168.

269 SCHACHTER, *supra* note 48, at 264. Cameron concurs in this view on the grounds that the process of balancing required by the rule "can never be impartial." CAMERON, *supra* note 12, at 336. *See also* CAMERON, *supra* note 12, at 335-36 (discussing criticisms of the rule of reasonableness).

unenforceable principles of international law (sovereign equality of states, territorial sovereignty, and non-intervention) will limit the reach of the U.S. antiterrorist statutes discussed above. Only an amendment of the statutes, for example favoring the protective principle of extraterritorial jurisdiction over the now-preferred (and dangerously broad) passive personality principle, can limit their reach.

While it is necessary for the world community of states to guard and fight against terrorism, it is not in the interest of that community to splinter itself in that fight over jurisdictional conflicts. This basic point should be a strong inducement to states to heed the international law principles and doctrine reviewed here and to combat terrorism with due regard for each other's rights. In the end, this will benefit not only the community as a whole, but, indeed, each member of that community, no matter how weak or mighty, and terrorism will face a stronger challenge.

The European Union and the Schengen Agreement

Bert Swart

Introduction

For a long time, the Council of Europe has been the leading forum for developing mutual cooperation in criminal matters between European states. Its achievements in this field are of fundamental and lasting importance. However, in recent years, the Council increasingly has had to share that position with the European Union and it may well, in the future, lose preeminence to the Union. One of the reasons for this is that the Council, by accepting the countries of Eastern Europe as members, now has expanded its membership to almost 40 states while that of the Union is limited to15.[1] Another reason is that the goals of the Union are considerably more ambitious than those pursued by the Council. According to Article A of the Treaty on European Union, the Union aims at nothing less than creating an ever-closer union among the peoples of Europe.

The European Union was created by the Treaty on European Union, signed on 7 February 1992 at Maastricht and entered into force on 1 November 1993. The Treaty, often referred to as the Maastricht Treaty, rests on what is commonly called a "three-pillar structure." The First Pillar, covered by Titles II-V of the Treaty, encompasses the European Communities of which the European Community (formerly the European Economic Community) is the most important one.[2] The Second Pillar, provided for in Title V, is concerned with a common foreign and security policy. The provisions of Title V recast earlier provisions on European Political Cooperation in the 1986 Single European Act. Finally, there is the Third Pillar, created by Title VI, which deals with cooperation in the fields of justice and home affairs. Its provisions provide an exclusive legal basis as well as an organizational framework for cooperation in these fields, replacing older and unstructured forms of cooperation existing before the Treaty on European Union came into force.[3] In June 1997, during an intergovernmental summit in Amsterdam, the governments of the Member States decided to revise the Treaty in a number of respects.[4] This so-called Treaty of Amsterdam was signed on 2 October 1997 but has not yet entered into force. One of the technical consequences of revision is that the provisions of the Treaty on European Union and those of the Treaty establishing the European Community have been renumbered.[5]

---

[1] Until January 1995, the Member States were Belgium, Denmark, the Federal Republic of Germany, France, Greece, Ireland, Italy, Luxembourg, the Netherlands, Portugal, Spain and the United Kingdom. On that date, Austria, Finland and Sweden became full members.

[2] The other two are the European Coal and Steel Community and the European Atomic Energy Community. This chapter will concentrate on the European Community.

[3] *Cf.* Julian J.E. Schutte, *Judicial Cooperation Under the Union Treaty, in* THE THIRD PILLAR OF THE EUROPEAN UNION 181-91 (Jeorg Monar & Robert Morgan eds., 1994).

[4] Treaty of Amsterdam amending the Treaty on European Union, the Treaties establishing the European Communities and certain related acts, 1997 O.J. (C 340/1). For a useful guide, *see* ANDREW DUFF, THE TREATY OF AMSTERDAM (1997).

[5] For the consolidated versions of both treaties, *see* 1997 O.J. (C 340/145) and (C 340/173).

Article C[6] of the Maastricht Treaty declares that the Union shall be served by a single institutional framework. Its components are the (European) Council, the European Commission, the European Parliament and the Court of Justice of the European Communities. However, their respective roles vary from Pillar to Pillar. The European Communities are international organizations with distinct supranational features. The fact that they constitute a new legal order in international law has been emphasized by the Court of Justice on many occasions. By contrast, cooperation between the Members States in the Second and Third Pillars has a predominantly intergovernmental character. Consequently, the roles of Commission, Parliament and Court are much less significant here. The complicated structure of the Union is a source of controversies that also affect criminal law and cooperation in criminal matters in a number of ways.

The European Union not only provides an important framework for cooperation in criminal matters between its members. Cooperation also serves the purpose of protecting the interests of the Union as a separate entity, notably that part of it that constitutes the European Communities. Moreover, within the European Communities vertical cooperation between Member States and the institutions of the Communities plays a part as vital as horizontal cooperation between the Member States. It usually takes the form of cooperation in administrative rather than criminal matters. Finally, with the Union aiming to integrate 15 different national societies, the fundamental question arises of whether and to what extent it will succeed in harmonizing national laws and policies of Member States in the area of criminal justice.

The First Pillar and Criminal Law

Initially, the goals of the European Communities were primarily, though not exclusively, economic. Soon, however, a process of expanding the scope of the European Community started, and its pace accelerated in the1980s and the 1990s. The 1986 Single European Act and the Maastricht Treaty have considerably enlarged the areas in which the Community may become active. The catalogue of Community activities in Article 3 of the EC Treaty rose from 11 to 20 items. As the scope of Community law widens, one may even wonder whether it knows any limits *ratione materiae*. Now that Article 7a[7] of the EC Treaty, introduced by the Single European Act, aims at the achievement of an internal market without internal borders, there probably is hardly any form of human behavior that does not, in one way or another, affect the Community if it acquires a transnational character or produces transnational effects. As a result of these changes, Community law has ventured into such areas as insider dealing, money laundering, the manufacturing of drugs, the acquisition and possession of weapons and the export of cultural goods, areas that used to belong to the exclusive competence of the Member States.[8]

---

[6] Article 3 in the Consolidated version.

[7] Article 14 in the Consolidated version.

[8] *See* Directive 89/592 of 13 October 1989 coordinating regulations on insider dealing, 1989 O.J. (L 334) 30; Regulation 3677/90 of 13 December 1990 laying down measures to discourage the diversion of certain substances to the illicit manufacture of drugs and psychotropic substances, 1990 O.J. (L 357) 1; Directive 91/308 of 10 June 1991 on prevention of the use of the financial system for the purpose of money laundering, 1991 O.J. (L 166) 77; Directive 91/447 of 18 June 1991 on control of the acquisition and possession of weapons, 1991 O.J. (L 256) 51; Regulation 3911/92 of 9 December 1992 on the export of cultural goods, 1992 O.J. (L 359)1; Directive 92/101 of

In order to enforce its rules, the Community lays down two systems of enforcement at its disposal. One may be named the direct system, the other the indirect system. The direct system is, for the most part, limited to the area of competition; investigating violations and imposing sanctions are primarily matters for Community institutions. It is the European Commission that investigates and imposes sanctions; appeal lies with the Court of Justice. Sanctions include fines and periodic penalty payments. In this system, the role of Member States is limited to providing assistance to the Commission in its investigations and in enforcing its decisions.[9] Meanwhile, in the vast majority of cases it is incumbent on Member States to enforce Community law themselves. Their duty to do so is based on Article 5 of the EC Treaty.[10] As far as fraud against the Community is concerned, this duty now also follows from Article 209a, introduced by the Maastricht Treaty.[11]

It has always been an article of faith for most Member States that the Community lacks competence in criminal matters.[12] While they have a duty to enforce Community law, they do not recognize a general obligation to do so by making use of the instruments of their criminal justice systems. According to the case law of the Court of Justice, criminal legislation and rules of criminal procedure are matters for which, in principle, the Member States are still responsible. It is not for the Community to compel Member States to criminalize infringements of Community law,[13] nor to tell them how they should structure their mutual cooperation in criminal matters in order to repress infringements.[14] While the Court seems to allow for exceptions to these principles, there is no Regulation or Directive that has even attempted to limit the discretion of Member States in either field. Recently, the exclusive competence of Member States has acquired explicit constitutional underpinnings in the EC Treaty. Both Article 116 and 209a, as revised by the Treaty of Amsterdam, now state that measures to be taken in the field of customs cooperation and fraud against the Community shall not concern the application of national criminal law or the national administration of justice.[15] Cooperation in criminal matters is, moreover, safely locked away from the Community by the present Articles K.3 and K.9 of the Maastricht Treaty, provisions that pertain to the Third Pillar.

A closer look at Community law reveals that things are not quite what they seem to be. Indeed, the relationship between Community law and criminal law is much stronger than is often thought. First, the Court of Justice in 1988 held that any penalty provided for in national law must be effective, proportionate and dissuasive, regardless of whether a Member State considers it to be a criminal or an administrative penalty. Moreover, while the choice of penalties remains within the discretion of Member States, they must nevertheless ensure that infringements of Community law are penalized under conditions, both procedural and substantive, which are analogous to those applicable to infringements of national law of a

---

14 December 1992 on the manufacture and placing on the market of certain substances used in the illicit manufacture of narcotic drugs and psychotropic substances, 1992 O.J. (L 370)76.

[9] *Cf. e.g.*, CHRISTOPHER HARDING, EUROPEAN INVESTIGATIONS AND SANCTIONS (1993).

[10] Article 10 in the Consolidated version.

[11] Article 280 in the Consolidated version.

[12] On the subject *see* Janet Dine, *European Community Criminal Law?* CRIMINAL L. REV. 246-254 (1993); Hanna G. Sevenster, *Criminal Law and EEC Law*, 29 COMMON MKT. L. REV. 24-70 (1992); and JOHN A.E. VERVAELE, FRAUD AGAINST THE COMMUNITY (1992).

[13] *Cf. e.g.*, Case 203/80, Casati, E.C.R. 2595 (1981).

[14] Case 1/78, Draft Convention on the International Atomic Energy Agency, E.C.R. 2191 (1978).

[15] Articles 135 and 280 in the Consolidated version.

similar nature and importance.[16] This so-called assimilation principle limits quite dramatically the freedom of Member States to make their own choices. It has now been incorporated in Article 209a of the EC Treaty where fraud against the Community is concerned and applies also to cooperation between Member States and Community institutions in enforcing Community rules. Second, it is no longer disputed that the Community may prescribe the imposition of so-called administrative penalties by Member States and give rules as to their application.[17] What is important here is that the concept of administrative penalties in the case law of the Court is unusually broad and covers sanctions that, from a perspective of national law and human rights treaties would rather be considered to be criminal penalties because of their punitive and deterrent purpose.[18] This again considerably limits the freedom of action of Member States.

The Court's case law has had a major influence on the shaping of two general instruments concerning fraud against the Communities in 1995. Council Regulation 2988/95 on the protection of the European Communities' financial interests, adopted on 18 December 1995, provides a general framework for imposing administrative measures and penalties on persons who have or might have caused financial harm to the Communities by disregarding their rules.[19] The second instrument is a Convention on the protection of the European Communities' financial interests, signed by the Member States on 26 July 1995.[20] As criminal law remains outside Community competence, this convention has been drawn up within the Third Pillar. The Convention obliges Member States to criminalize intentional infringements of Community law that impair the financial interests of the Communities in the same manner as they have criminalized similar infringements of national law. Sanctions should be effective, proportionate and dissuasive. Serious fraud cases should be liable to imprisonment of such duration that extradition is a possibility between Member States. A number of rather timid provisions are concerned with jurisdiction, extradition, mutual assistance and *ne bis in idem*. Meanwhile, a Protocol to the Convention has been adopted.[21] It obliges Member States to criminalize and repress acts of corruption that involve national and Community officials and damage or are likely to damage the European Communities' financial interests. In 1997, a Second Protocol was adopted.[22]

Schengen and the European Union

Among other things the Single European Act of 1986, in a number of aspects the predecessor of the Treaty on European Union, represents an attempt by the Member States of the European Communities to provide a new stimulus to the achievement of a truly common market. In what is now Article 7a of the EC Treaty, this market is defined as a "space without internal frontiers in which the free circulation of goods, persons, services and capital is

---

[16] Case 68/88, Commission v. Greece, E.C.R. 2965, 2984-2985 (1989).

[17] Case 240/90, Germany v. Commission, E.C.R. I-5381, 5431 (1992).

[18] *Cf.* Öztürk v. Germany, 21.2 Eur. Ct. Hum. Rts. (ser/ A) at 85 (1984), and Bendenoun v. France, 24.2 Eur. Ct. Hum. Rts. (ser/A) at 284 (1994).

[19] 1995 O.J. (L 312) 1.

[20] 1995 O.J. (L 316) 48.

[21] Protocol to the Convention on the protection of the European Communities' financial interests, adopted on 27 September 1996, O.J. (C 313/1).

[22] Second Protocol to the Convention on the protection of the European Communities' financial interests, adopted on 19 June 1997 O.J. (C 221/11).

ensured."[23] At first glance, the definition seems to imply a total abolition of border control at the inner borders of the Member States. The United Kingdom, however, has always maintained that the provision does not apply to nationals from third countries crossing internal borders. While the Member States have devoted, before and after the Maastricht Treaty, considerable energy to harmonizing their immigration and asylum laws and policies, free movement of persons has not yet been realized in full within the area of the European Union. Several problems still remain unresolved, among them a dispute between Spain and the United Kingdom over the status of Gibraltar.

Meanwhile, even before the Single Act was adopted, France and Germany, soon joined by the Benelux countries, took the initiative of abolishing border controls between them in preparation of future developments at a European level. Their initiative resulted in the Agreement on the gradual abolition of checks at their common borders, signed at Schengen on 14 June 1985.[24] Compensatory measures to cope with the consequences of totally abolishing controls are the substance of the Convention applying the Schengen Agreement of 19 June 1990.[25] The actual lifting of border controls was achieved in 1995. In the meantime, most other members of the European Union have acceded to both instruments.[26]

While originally Schengen was meant to create a provisional structure only, the Treaty of Amsterdam will make it a permanent one. On the one hand, Protocol 3 to the Treaty on European Union and the Treaty establishing the European Community on the application of certain aspects of Article 7a of the EC Treaty to the United Kingdom and Ireland now officially accepts the fact that Member States are unable to reach an agreement on the interpretation of Article 7a. On the other hand, Member States adopted Protocol 2 to the same treaties, integrating the Schengen *acquis* into the framework of the European Union. The main consequences of this Protocol are that Schengen has now, in an institutional sense, become a concern of the European Union and that those Member States who signed the Schengen Agreement are, within the institutional framework of the Union, authorized to establish closer cooperation among themselves within the scope of the Schengen Agreement and related agreements.

The compensatory measures envisaged in the Schengen Convention relate to immigration law and criminal law.[27] As far as criminal law is concerned the largest part of the Convention, comprising more than 50 articles and divided into seven different chapters, is devoted to matters of police and security.

Certainly the most important and interesting chapter is the one on police cooperation. In Article 39 the Contracting Parties undertake to ensure that their police authorities shall, in compliance with national law, render each other assistance. The duty to assist not only covers assistance in investigating crimes that have been committed but applies to other police activities as well. Written information may not be used by the requesting authorities as

---

[23] Article 14 in the Consolidated version.

[24] Unofficial English translations have been published in 33 EUR. Y.B. 18-25 (1985) and 30 I.L.M. 73-83 (1991).

[25] For an unofficial English translation, *see* 30 I.L.M. 84-147 (1991).

[26] Austria, Greece, Italy, Portugal and Spain. The five countries of the Nordic Council are currently negotiating their accession.

[27] For an analysis, *see* David O'Keeffe, *The Schengen Convention: A Suitable Model for European Integration?*, 11 Y.B. EUR. L., 185-219 (1991); Julian J.E. Schutte, *Schengen: Its Meaning for the Free Movement of Persons in Europe,* 28 COMMON MKT. L. REV. 549-570 (1991); and A.H.J. Swart, *Police and Security in the Schengen Agreement and the Schengen Convention, in* SCHENGEN, INTERNATIONALIZATION OF CENTRAL CHAPTERS OF THE LAW ON ALIENS, REFUGEES, PRIVACY, SECURITY AND THE POLICE (Henri Meijers ed., 1991).

evidence of a criminal offence without the consent of the authorities of the requested state. This provision is supplemented by Article 46 allowing the spontaneous provision of information, *i.e.,* without prior request, if this may help in preventing future crimes and in preventing offences against or threats to public order and security. Articles 40-43 and 73 deal with various forms of operational cooperation: cross-border observation, cross-border pursuit of suspects and monitored delivery of narcotic drugs. They have been partly inspired by the 1960 Benelux Convention on Transferring Border Checks[28] and regulate these matters in considerable detail. Other provisions of the chapter on police cooperation deal, among other things, with improving communications between police authorities and with liaison officers. All in all, the chapter on police cooperation, however limited its scope may still be, represents an innovative attempt to lay down a coherent body of rules in an area that, so far, has been neglected in traditional instruments on international cooperation in criminal matters. A general duty of police forces to assist each other may also contribute to eliminating a number of illegal practices that quite often violate national sovereignty.

The chapters on mutual assistance, extradition and transfer of the execution of criminal sentences, although important for everyday practice, are less innovative. Basically, they are concerned with achieving equal standards of cooperation between the parties on the basis of already existing Council of Europe and Benelux conventions. In between these chapters is a separate chapter on the application of the *non bis in idem* principle. Its provisions are largely copied from the 1987 Convention on Double Jeopardy, concluded between the Member States of the European Communities.

Harmonization of legislation and policies with respect to drugs and firearms is dealt with in two other chapters. These topics were among the most controversial during negotiations and their application continues to divide the Contracting Parties.[29] They are partly agreements to disagree. National differences in legislation and policies are accepted in so far as they relate to the treatment of drug addicts, demand control of and surveillance of retail trade in narcotic drugs. However, where they have transnational consequences they become matters of common concern.

Probably the most innovative part of the Schengen Convention are the chapters on the Schengen Information System. The system consists of a central database containing computerised information on wanted persons or objects which is made available to national law enforcement agencies. The information relates to such categories of persons as those wanted for arrest for the purpose of extradition, witnesses, persons summoned to appear before the judicial authorities in connection with criminal proceedings, persons who are to be notified of a sentence and persons with respect to whom discreet surveillance or specific checks are desired. The system also contains information on objects sought for the purpose of seizure as evidence in criminal proceedings. Information with respect to each category of persons or goods is fed into the system with a distinct purpose. For instance, information on suspects wanted by the judicial authorities is entered with a view to their provisional arrest preceding extradition, information on persons who are to be discreetly surveyed or specifically checked to obtain information about their movements or behavior. Data entered into the system may not be used for other purposes than those indicated in various provisions. The Convention

---

[28] *Cf.* Coen Mulder & Bert Swart, *The Benelux and Nordic Countries, infra,* Chapter 11.

[29] When border control was actually lifted in 1995 France invoked the escape clause in Article 2 of the Convention, partly out of dissatisfaction with Dutch drug policies.

contains numerous provisions on data protection and data security. The Schengen Information System has served as a model for similar but more extensive information systems in the Convention on the use of information technology for customs purposes and the Convention on the establishment of a European Police Office, recently adopted by the Member States of the European Union.

Cooperation in the Fields of Justice and Home Affairs

The Third Pillar of Maastricht, providing a structure for cooperation between the Union Members in the fields of justice and home affairs, has been preceded by a period of some 20 years of cooperation between them outside the framework of the European Communities. Two fora existed to develop cooperation: Trevi and the European Political Cooperation.

During a meeting in Rome, close to the fountains of Trevi, the Ministers of Justice and Home Affairs of the European Communities decided in 1976 to consult each other regularly on matters of internal security. Soon two working groups were established. One was concerned with various aspects of international terrorism, the other with the organization, equipment and training of police forces. In later years, third and fourth working groups were created, dealing with various international crimes and with studying measures to compensate for the abolition of border controls envisaged by the Single European Act. During its existence the Trevi group has dealt with an enormous variety of topics. More than 40 decisions were taken, few of which have been published due to the secretive nature of the decision-making process. When the Maastricht Treaty entered into force the activities of this forum were integrated into the Third Pillar.[30]

A second platform for cooperation was provided by the regular meetings of the Ministers of Foreign Affairs of the European Communities within the framework of the European Political Cooperation. While the Trevi group was concerned with practical matters mainly, here the emphasis lay on drafting conventions. Between 1979 and 1993, six different conventions on cooperation in criminal matters have been adopted. Some of them are intended to supplement existing conventions of the Council of Europe. This is the case of the Agreement on the Application of the European Convention on the Suppression of Terrorism, Dublin, 4 December 1979, and the Agreement on the Application of the Convention on Transfer of Sentenced Persons, Brussels, 25 May 1987. Others may be considered watered-down versions of Council of Europe instruments, created because these conventions had been ratified by few Member States. Unlike their counterparts of the Council of Europe, the Convention on Transfer of Proceedings in Criminal Matters, Brussels, 6 November 1990, and the Convention on the Enforcement of Foreign Criminal Sentences, Brussels, 13 November 1991, do not create obligations to cooperate. They merely aim at facilitating cooperation. Finally, the Convention on Double Jeopardy, Brussels, 25 May 1987, and the Convention on the Simplification and Modernization of Methods of Transmitting Extradition Requests, Donostia-San Sebastian, 20 May 1989, venture into areas not covered by Council of Europe instruments or at least not completely. As all six conventions require ratification by the states who were

---

[30] For an analysis of police cooperation *see, e.g.*, THE INTERNATIONALIZATION OF POLICE COOPERATION IN WESTERN EUROPE (Cyrille Fijnaut ed., 1993); HEINER BUSCH, GRENZENLOSE POLIZEI? NEUE GRENZEN UND POLIZEILICHE ZUSAMMENARBEIT IN EUROPA (1995); BILL HEBENTON & TERRY THOMAS, POLICING EUROPE: COOPERATION, CONFLICT AND CONTROL (1995).

members of the European Communities at the date of their adoption, none has yet entered into force. With the exception of the terrorism convention, however, they all provide for their provisional application between Member States who have ratified them.[31]

The main purpose of the provisions of the Third Pillar of the Maastricht Treaty is to express a determination to develop closer cooperation between the Member States in justice and home affairs and to give it a more orderly and systematic structure.[32] These provisions have been throughly revised by the Treaty of Amsterdam.

Article K.1[33] of the Maastricht Treaty indicates nine areas of common interest where close cooperation between Member States should be achieved. Apart from asylum and immigration policies and the crossing of borders they include drug addiction, fraud with international implications, judicial cooperation in civil and criminal matters and customs and police cooperation. The Treaty of Amsterdam aims at transferring cooperation in asylum and immigration matters as well as judicial cooperation in civil matters to the First Pillar. The scope of the Third Pillar will thus be limited to police and judicial cooperation in criminal matters.

Obviously, the word "cooperation" refers to mutual assistance in individual cases involving a transnational element. However, a much wider meaning has to be given to it. Cooperation may also consist in solving or easing problems that arise from the fact that Member States have different legislation or pursue different policies in the area of justice and home affairs. This opens the perspective of their approximation or harmonization. The new Articles K.1 and K.3 of the Treaty of Amsterdam explicitly declare harmonization to be one of the objectives of cooperation.[34] Moreover, as is apparent from various provisions, cooperation need not necessarily be limited to legal cooperation but may take a wide variety of forms between the authorities of the Member States. Finally, the open character of the Third Pillar is reinforced by the fact that the Treaty defines the goals of cooperation in the vaguest terms only. The final goal is to create an ever-closer union among the peoples of Europe. In the (very) long term, this might even lead to criminal justice being organized on a federal basis.

To a considerable extent, the subject-matter of the Third Pillar is also covered by the First Pillar. This is notably true for drug addiction, fraud against the Communities and customs matters since Articles 129, 209a and 9-37 of the EC Treaty explicitly refer to them.[35] Moreover, the Single European Act and the Maastricht Treaty have expanded the ambit of the European Community considerably. Conflicts of competence between Union institutions are the results.

Article K.3 lists the legal instruments that Member States may use: joint positions, joint actions and conventions. A joint position seems to be a statement of an agreed policy or

---

[31] None of the conventions have been published in the OFFICIAL JOURNAL OF THE EUROPEAN COMMUNITIES.

[32] For an analysis, *see* I.D. Hendry, *The Third Pillar of Maastricht: Cooperation in the Fields of Justice and Home Affairs*, 1993 GERMAN Y.B. OF INT'L L. 295-327.

[33] Article 29 in the Consolidated version.

[34] Articles 29 and 31 in the Consolidated version. Article K.1 speaks of "approximation, where necessary, of rules on criminal matters in the Member States, in accordance with the provisions of Article K.3(e)." According to Article K.3(e) common action on judicial cooperation in criminal matters shall include *inter alia*, "progressively adopting measures establishing minimum rules relating to the constituent elements of criminal acts and to penalties in the fields of organized crime, terrorism and drug trafficking." However, in a separate Declaration to this provision it is stated that this shall not have the consequence of obliging a Member State whose legal system does not provide for minimum sentences to adopt them.

[35] Articles 152, 280 and 23-31 in the Consolidated version.

standpoint of the Member States. As is apparent from Article K.5, it may be used in the Union's contacts with international organizations and at international conferences in particular. The meaning of the term "joint action" is not clear, as Member States do not agree on the question of when it may be binding on them. Joint positions, joint actions and conventions must be adopted unanimously. In actual practice Member States have frequent recourse to resolutions, recommendations, decisions, statements and conclusions that do not create legal obligations. The Treaty of Amsterdam will simplify matters considerably. A new Article K.6, distinguishes between common positions, framework decisions and other decisions, and conventions.[36] Framework decisions and other decisions shall be binding upon the Member States but shall not entail direct effect.

Another innovation introduced by the Treaty of Amsterdam is to be found in a new Article K.12.[37] It authorizes Member States which intend to establish closer cooperation between themselves to do so subject to a number of conditions. Cooperation within the Schengen framework, discussed above, provides an example here.

At the end of 1997, Member States had agreed on six conventions, two protocols and an agreement on criminal and related matters.

The first and simplest of them is the Convention on simplified extradition procedures between the Member States of the European Union, signed on 10 March 1995.[38] It introduces the surrender of persons with their consent at a Union level. Surrender may take place on the basis of a request for provisional arrest of the person, thus making formal extradition requests superfluous. This convention is the first modest result of the desire of Member States to facilitate extradition between them.

On 26 July 1995, the Member States signed the Convention on the use of information technology for customs purposes.[39] On the basis of this convention a central computerized Customs Information System will be set up by the customs administrations of Member States. The system should enable them to assist each other in preventing, investigating and prosecuting serious violations of national laws in the application of which they have total or partial competence. The convention not only covers traditional customs offences but also money laundering originating from international drug trafficking. A parallel system is envisaged where infringements of Community rules are concerned. That, however, will be based on a Regulation, the European Community being competent in the matter.[40]

The third most important and most spectacular convention is the Convention on the establishment of a European Police Office (Europol Convention), also signed on 26 July 1995.[41] It fulfills a promise made in Article K.1 of the Maastricht Treaty and the Declaration on police cooperation attached to the Treaty. The contents of this complex convention can only be briefly outlined here. Essentially, Europol is an organization for exchanging information, whether in pure or in enriched form. Information that may be provided to all

---

[36] Article 34 in the Consolidated version.

[37] Article 40 in the Consolidated version.

[38] 1995 O.J. (C 78) 1. For the Explanatory Report, *see* 1996 O.J. (C 375/4).

[39] 1995 O.J. (C 316/ 33). For the Agreement on the provisional application of the Convention, adopted on the same day, *see* 1996 O.J. (C 316/58).

[40] Regulation 515/97 on mutual assistance between the administrative authorities of the Member States and cooperation between the latter and the Commission to ensure the correct application of the law on customs and agricultural matters, 1997 O.J. (L 82/1).

[41] 1995 O.J. (C 316/1).

public bodies in the Member States which are responsible under national law for preventing and combating criminal offences as well as, subject to more restrictive conditions, to third states and international bodies.

Article 2 of the convention and the Annex thereto indicate the crimes with respect to which Europol may collect, analyze and disseminate information. Eventually, Europol will be made competent for terrorist crimes, unlawful drug trafficking and "other" serious forms of international crimes. Its competence will also extend to illegal money-laundering activities in connection with these crimes as well as criminal offences related to these serious forms of international crime. Article 2 limits Europol's competence by requiring that there are factual indications that an organized criminal structure is involved and two or more Member States are affected by these crimes. At the date of entry into force, however, Europol will be competent for unlawful drug trafficking, trafficking in nuclear and radioactive substances, illegal immigrant smuggling, trade in human beings and motor vehicle crime only. At a later date it may be made competent for terrorist offences and the 18 different categories of international crimes listed in the Annex. As is apparent from Article 2 and the Annex, the concept of international crime refers to the transnational character of crimes rather than to their status under customary or conventional international law. Most of the crimes covered by the Convention are not international crimes in the latter sense.

To fulfill its tasks, Europol will have a computerised system of information that consists of three parts. The first component is the information system. Article 7 of the Convention defines it as a system with a restricted and precisely defined content which allows rapid reference to the information available to the Member States and Europol. It contains a limited amount of data on persons suspected or convicted of crimes for which Europol is competent as well as on persons concerning whom there are serious grounds for believing that they will commit such offences. In limiting the types of data that may be stored, the system resembles the Schengen Information System. However, the use of data disseminated by Europol is not restricted to a specific and limited purpose. The second computerised system consists of "work files." The purpose of these files is to analyze series of events or groups of persons in order to acquire a deeper understanding of certain phenomena and developments. This will be done on the basis of comprehensive information, *i.e.,* all information that Europol is able to collect from Member States or from third states and third bodies. Obviously, this system will enable Europol to act as a criminal intelligence agency at a European level. The sensitive nature of the information stored explains why access to the system has been limited. Coupled to the work files is an index system enabling those who are entitled to consult it to verify whether the files might contain information that is relevant to them.

In 1991, while work on drafting the Europol Convention had not yet begun, the Member States decided to create a provisional structure for exchanging information on drug-trafficking offences. This structure, the European Drugs Unit, essentially consists of members of national police forces sitting together and exchanging information on the basis of their national laws. The Unit's own databases may contain non-personal data only. In 1994 and 1996 its ambit was expanded to cover illegal trafficking in nuclear and radioactive substances, crimes involving clandestine immigrant networks, traffic in human beings, illicit vehicle trafficking, and related money-laundering offenses. Its statute is now determined by the Joint Action concerning the Europol Drugs Unit, adopted on 10 March 1995, as amended in 1996.[42]

---

[42] 1995 O.J. (L 62/1) and 1996 O.J. (L 342/2).

The fourth convention to have been adopted is the 1995 Convention on the protection of the European Communities' financial interests. It is accompanied by two Protocols. The Convention and the Protocols have already been discussed above.

Another convention is the 1996 Convention relating to extradition between the Member States of the European Union.[43] Its purpose is to supplement the provisions of the 1957 European Convention on Extradition, the 1977 European Convention on the Suppression of Terrorism, the 1990 Convention applying the Schengen Agreement, and the 1962 Benelux Convention on Extradition and Mutual Assistance in Criminal Matters, as well as to facilitate their application. Among other things, the Convention represents an attempt of the Member States to abandon a number of traditional principles of extradition law. In this respect, special mention should be made of Articles 5 and 7. Pursuant to Article 5, no offence may be regarded as a political offence, an offence connected with a political offence or an offence inspired by political motives. Article 7 requires the Member States not to refuse extradition on the ground that the person claimed is a national of the requested Member State. However, reservations may be made to both provisions, as well as to a number of other provisions. It remains, therefore, to be seen whether the attempt to break new ground will succeed or fail. It is worth noting here that the extradition convention is the first convention ever to have been concluded within the framework of the European Political Cooperation and the European Union which permits Member States to enter reservations to its provisions.[44]

The sixth and latest convention is the 1997 Convention on the fight against corruption involving officials of the European Communities or officials of Member States of the European Union.[45] It closely resembles the Second Protocol to the Convention on the protection of the European Communities' financial interests. However, while the scope of the Protocol is limited to acts which damage or are likely to damage the European Communities' financial interests, the Convention covers all acts of (active or passive) corruption.

At the end of 1997, negotiations were still pending on a convention on judicial assistance in criminal matters, a convention on mutual assistance between the national customs administrations, and a convention on the implementation of decisions on the withdrawal of drivers' licenses.

During negotiations on the various conventions Member States were deeply divided on the question of whether the Court of Justice should be given jurisdiction in disputes relating to their interpretation and application. In the case of three conventions, special protocols have been adopted to settle the matter.[46] They all introduce a system of opting in; Member States may declare that they accept the jurisdiction of the Court of Justice to give preliminary rulings on the interpretation of the Convention. The Treaty of Amsterdam now approaches the problem in a more general manner. A new Article K.7[47] grants jurisdiction to the Court of Justice to give preliminary rulings on the validity and interpretation of framework decisions

---

[43] Adopted on 27 September 1996 O.J. (C 313/11). For the Explanatory Report, *see* 1997 O.J. (C 191/13).

[44] For an analysis, *see* G. Vermeulen & T. Vander Beken, *Extradition in the European Union: State of the Art and Perspectives*, 4 EUR. J. CRIME, CRIM. L & CRIM. JUST. 200-225 (1996).

[45] Adopted on 26 May 1997, 1997 O.J. (C 195/1).

[46] *Cf.* the Protocol on the interpretation, by way of preliminary rulings, by the Court of Justice of the European Communities of the Convention on the establishment of a European Police Office, 1996 O.J. (C 299/1), and similar protocols to the Convention on the protection of the European Communities' financial interests and the Convention on the use of information technology for customs purposes, 1997 O.J. (C 151/1) and 1997 O.J. (C 151/15).

[47] Article 35 in the Consolidated version.

and decisions on the interpretation of conventions established under Title VI and interpretation of the measures implementing them, provided that the Member State concerned has declared that it accepts the jurisdiction of the Court.

Drawing up conventions is only part of the activities deployed by the European Union. In recent years a number of joint actions, recommendations and resolutions have also been adopted by the Member States. The joint action concerning the Europol Drugs Unit has already been mentioned. Among the more important other joint actions one may mention are: joint actions on liaison magistrates and liaison officers,[48] on racism and xenophobia,[49] on the approximation of the laws and practices to combat drug addiction and illegal drug trafficking,[50] and on trafficking in human beings and sexual exploitation of children.[51] Resolutions in the area of criminal justice include a resolution on the interception of telecommunications,[52] a resolution on the effective uniform application of Community law and on penalties applicable for breaches of Community law,[53] a resolution on the protection of witnesses in the fight against international organized crime,[54] resolutions on measures to address drug tourism problems and on sentencing for serious illicit drug trafficking,[55] and a resolution on individuals who cooperate with the judicial process in the fight against international organized crime.[56] Moreover, numerous initiatives have been taken within the framework of the Third Pillar to promote mutual cooperation at practical levels. Finally, the Union is developing close contacts with groups of third states, whether Eastern European, Mediterranean or Latin American, in various areas of international cooperation in criminal matters.

---

[48] Joint Action of 22 April 1996 concerning a framework for the exchange of liaison magistrates to improve judicial cooperation between the Member States of the European Union, 1996 O.J. (L 105/1), and Joint Action of 14 October 1996 providing a framework for the initiatives of the Member States concerning liaison officers, 1996 O.J. (L 268/2).

[49] Joint Action of 15 July 1996 concerning action to combat racism and xenophobia, 1996 O.J. (L 185/5). It requires Member States to criminalize hate speech.

[50] Joint Action of 17 December 1996 concerning the approximation of the laws and practices of the Member States of the European Union to combat drug addiction and to prevent and combat illegal drug trafficking, 1996 O.J. (L 342/6).

[51] Joint Action of February 24, 1997 concerning action to combat trafficking in human beings and sexual exploitation of children, 1997 O.J. (L 63/2).

[52] Adopted on 17 January 1995, not published.

[53] Adopted on 29 June 1995, 1995 O.J. (C 188) 1.

[54] Adopted on 23 November 1995, 1995 O.J. (C 327) 5.

[55] Adopted on 29 November 1996, 1996 O.J. (C 375/3), and on 20 December 1996, 1997 O.J. (C 10/3).

[56] Adopted on 20 December 1996, 1997 O.J. (C 10/1).

Section III

Extradition

Law and Practice of the United States

M. Cherif Bassiouni

Introduction

Extradition is the oldest form of inter-state cooperation in criminal matters, but it is not a substitute for other modalities of inter-state cooperation.[1] International extradition in the United States is the process by which a person found in one country is rendered to another for trial or punishment.[2] It is a process regulated mainly by treaty, but also by statute, federal common law, and subject to constitutional requirements.

The processes of extradition in the United States involve the executive, legislative, and judicial branches of the federal government. Each of these has a defined constitutional role in the making, the execution, and the interpretation of treaties. The interrelationship of the three branches of government in extradition is dictated by the constitutional grant of powers to the various branches of government and by the constitutional doctrine of separation of powers.

---

[1] *See* M. CHERIF BASSIOUNI, INTERNATIONAL EXTRADITION: U.S. LAW AND PRACTICE (3rd rev. ed. 1996) (hereinafter BASSIOUNI, EXTRADITION). *See also* MICHAEL ABBELL & BRUNO A. RISTAU, INTERNATIONAL JUDICIAL ASSISTANCE, VOLS. 4, 5 (1990); John G. Kester, *Some Myths of U.S. Extradition Law*, 76 GEO. L. J. 1441 (1988). For a U.S. historical perspective, *see* 6 MARJORIE WHITEMAN, DIGEST OF INTERNATIONAL LAW (1963) (hereinafter WHITEMAN DIGEST); JOHN B. MOORE, A TREATISE ON EXTRADITION AND INTER-STATE RENDITION (2 vols. 1891) (hereinafter MOORE, EXTRADITION). For general texts, *see* IVAN SHEARER, EXTRADITION IN INTERNATIONAL LAW (1971), and SATYA D. BEDI, INTERNATIONAL EXTRADITION IN LAW AND PRACTICE (1966). For a European perspective, *see* Dominique Poncet, The European Approach, *infra* Chapter 8; THEO VOGLER, AUSLIEFERUNG AND GRUNDGESETZ (1969); ANDRÉ BILLOT, TRAITÉ DE L'EXTRADITION (1874). For a common law perspective, *see* ALUN JONES, JONES ON EXTRADITION (1995); V. E. HARTLEY-BOOTH, BRITISH EXTRADITION LAW AND PRACTICE (1980); SIR EDWARD G. CLARKE, A TREATISE UPON THE LAW OF EXTRADITION (1866). *See also,* Christopher L. Blakesley, *The Practice of Extradition from Antiquity to Modern France and the United States: A Brief History*, 4 B.C. INT'L & COMP. L. REV. 39 (1980).

Extradition is defined as:

> [a] process by which, in accordance to treaty provisions and subject to its limitations, one state requests another to surrender a person charged with a criminal violation of the law of the requesting state who is within the jurisdiction of the requested state, for the purpose of answering criminal charges, standing trial or executing a sentence arising out of the stated criminal violation.

WHITEMAN DIGEST, *supra* this note, at 727-28; *See also* Terlinden v. Ames, 184 U.S. 270 (1902). As one author stated:

> [Extradition] includes not only modes by which a state effects the return of a fugitive offender to the demanding state against whose laws he may have committed some offense, but also the acts or processes by which one sovereign state, in compliance with a formal demand, prepares to surrender to another state for trial the person of criminal character who has sought refuge in its boundaries.

SATYA D. BEDI, EXTRADITION IN INTERNATIONAL LAW AND PRACTICE 16 (1968).

[2] BASSIOUNI, EXTRADITION, *supra* note 1; In 1902, the United States Supreme Court articulated the generally accepted definition when it held: "[e]xtradition may be sufficiently defined to be the surrender by one nation to another of an individual accused or convicted of an offence outside of its own territory, and within the territorial jurisdiction of the other, which, being competent to try and punish him, demands the surrender." Terlinden v. Ames, 184 U.S. 270, 289 (1902). In its introductory note to its section on extradition, the American Law Institute defines it as "the process by which a person charged with or convicted of a crime under the law of one state is arrested in another and returned for trial or punishment." RESTATEMENT (THIRD) OF THE FOREIGN RELATIONS LAW OF THE UNITED STATES § 475 preface (1987).

Extradition in the United States is statutorily based on treaties. Treaties are made by the executive branch subject to the "advice and consent" of the Senate.[3] The authority to enter extradition treaties and to request or grant extradition rests exclusively with the executive branch by virtue of its constitutional power to conduct foreign relations.[4] This power is only limited by the Senate's power to "advise and consent" to treaties[5] that the executive branch submits to it and by the authority of Congress to enact legislation defining the substantive requirements and procedures to be followed by United States courts.

The federal judiciary has the prerogative of interpreting and applying treaties and federal legislative enactments in accordance with the applicable provisions of the United States Constitution. The judiciary, however, cannot enjoin, prohibit, or mandate the executive's negotiation of an agreement or a treaty, nor can it enjoin or mandate the executive's exercise of discretion to request a relator's extradition or to refuse to grant extradition, although the terms of the applicable treaty have been satisfied.[6] The judiciary, however, has the authority to enjoin the federal government from extraditing a person if the extradition is in violation of the Constitution, U.S. laws, or the applicable treaty.[7] In the event of a conflict between an extradition treaty and a constitutional provision, the latter prevails, and in the event of a conflict between a treaty and statutory provisions, the later in time prevails under domestic U.S. law.[8] Extradition treaties are deemed self-executing; consequently, United States legislation is complementary to treaties rather than substitutive of them.[9]

The first stage in the extradition process is the existence of a legal basis upon which the United States may request or grant extradition. While there are several such bases, *i.e.*, treaties, whether bilateral or multilateral, reciprocity, comity, and national legislation, the United States relies essentially on bilateral treaties. Nothing, however, prevents the United States from relying on multilateral treaties. In fact, the United States has ratified a number of multilateral treaties containing extradition provisions.[10] Furthermore, the United States can request extradition from a state with which no extradition treaty exists on the basis of reciprocity or comity.

While United States legislation requires that a treaty must exist before extradition can be granted,[11] and the Supreme Court has frequently referred to the need for a treaty in order

---

3 U.S. CONST. art. 2, § 2; *see also* United States v. Curtiss-Wright Export Co., 299 U.S. 304, 318-21 (1936).

4 *Id.*

5 *See also* M. Cherif Bassiouni, *Reflections on the Ratification of the International Covenant on Crime and Political Rights by the United States Senate,* 42 DEPAUL L. REV. 69 (1993) and various authorities cited.

6 *See* Terlinden v. Ames, 184 U.S. 270 (1902); United States v. Rauscher, 119 U.S. 407 (1886); Shapiro v. Secretary of State, 499 F.2d 527 (D.C. Cir. 1974); Jhirad v. Ferrandina, 536 F.2d 478 (2d Cir.), *cert. denied,* 429 U.S. 833 (1976); Wacker v. Bisson, 370 F.2d 552 (5th Cir.), *cert. denied,* 387 U.S. 936 (1967); United States v. Orsini, 424 F. Supp. 229 (E.D.N.Y. 1976), *aff'd,* 559 F.2d 1206 (2d Cir. 1977); United States v. Salzmann, 417 F. Supp. 1139 (E.D.N.Y.), *aff'd,* 548 F.2d 395 (2d Cir. 1976).

7 *See* Valentine v. United States *ex rel.* Neidecker, 299 U.S. 5 (1936).

8 *See* MOORE, EXTRADITION *supra,* note 1 at 97; and *see also* LOUIS HENKIN, FOREIGN AFFAIRS AND THE CONSTITUTION (1972).

9 *See* WHITEMAN DIGEST *supra* note 1, at 734.

10 *See generally* 1 M. CHERIF BASSIOUNI, INTERNATIONAL CRIMINAL LAW, CONVENTIONS AND THEIR PENAL PROVISIONS (1997) [hereinafter ICL CONVENTIONS].

11 18 U.S.C. § 3181 *et seq.* (1985).

for extradition to be granted,[12] there is nothing in the Constitution that mandates this requirement.

Legislative History

The first legislative act concerning extradition was the Act of August 12, 1848.[13] The Act provided that extradition of persons from the United States could be performed only pursuant to a treaty, and set forth the procedure to be followed by judges or commissioners. Since 1848-1984, the following legislation was passed: Act of August 12, 1848;[14] Act of June 22, 1860;[15] Act of March 3, 1869;[16] Act of June 19, 1876;[17] Act of August 3, 1882;[18] Act of June 6, 1900;[19] Act of June 28, 1902;[20] Act of March 22, 1934;[21] Act of June 25, 1948;[22] Act of May 24, 1949;[23] and Act of October 17, 1968.[24] Thus in 100 years the original Act was amended in a piecemeal fashion ten times.

Between 1981-84 several unsuccessful legislative efforts for a major reform were undertaken, while between 1984-1996 additional partial amendments were made to the statute, and established related provisions which appeared in other legislation.[25] Overall

---

[12] Valentine v. United States *ex rel.* Neidecker, 229 U.S. 5 (1936); Factor v. Laubenheimer, 290 U.S. 276 (1933); United States v. Rauscher, 119 U.S. 407 (1886). In *Rauscher* the Court stated:

> It is only in modern times that the nations of the earth have imposed upon themselves the obligation of delivering up these fugitives from justice to the states where their crimes were committed, for trial and punishment. This has been done generally by treaties.... Prior to these treaties, and apart from them . . . there was no well-defined obligation on one country to deliver up such fugitives to another, and though such delivery was often made, it was upon the princip[le] of comity. . . . [It] has never been recognized as among those obligations of one government towards another which rest upon established principles of international law.

Id. at 411.

[13] Ch. 167, 9 Stat. 302.

[14] Ch. 167, § 5, 9 Stat. 302, 303.

[15] Ch. 184, 12 Stat. 84.

[16] Ch. 141, §§ 1-3, 15 Stat. 337.

[17] Ch. 133, 19 Stat. 59.

[18] Ch. 378, §§ 1-6, 22 Stat. 215.

[19] Ch. 93, 31 Stat. 656.

[20] Ch. 1301 (judicial), 32 Stat. 419, 475.

[21] Ch. 73, §§ 1-4, 48 Stat. 454.

[22] Ch. 645, 62 Stat. 822.

[23] Ch. 139, 63 Stat. 96.

[24] Pub. L. No. 90-578, Title III, § 301(a)(3), 82 Stat. 1115.

[25] *See also* M. Cherif Bassiouni, *Extradition Reform Legislation in the United States: 1981-83*, 17 AKRON L. REV. 495 (1984). Later amendments include Nov. 10, 1986, Pub. L. 99-646, § 87(c)(6), 100 Stat. 3623 (conforming amendment, authorizing extradition from countries occupied or controlled by U.S. for sexual abuse); Nov. 14, 1986, Pub. L. 99-654, § 3(a)(6), 100 Stat. 3663 (conforming amendment, same); Nov. 18, 1988, Pub. L. 100-690, Title VII, § 7087, 102 Stat. 4409 (authorizing government to obtain an arrest warrant for foreign fugitive whose specific whereabouts are not known); Nov. 21, 1990, Pub. L. 101-623, § 11(a), 104 Stat. 3350, 3356 (giving the Secretary of State the authority to extradite U.S. Nationals, whether treaty authorizes such power or not); Nov. 29, 1990, Pub. L. 101-647, Title XVI, § 1605, 104 Stat. 4843 (authorizing issuance of an arrest warrant for fugitive about to enter U.S.); Oct. 11, 1996, Pub. L. 104-294, Title VI, § 601(f)(9), 110 Stat. 3500 (technical amendment); Pub. L. 104-132, Title IV, § 443(b), 110 Stat. 1281 (amending § 3184 to authorize magistrate to consider case arising under new § 3181(b), extradition of aliens for certain crimes without a treaty); on April 24, 1996, the President signed into law the Anti-Terrorism and Death Penalty Act of 1996, Pub. L. 104-132, 110 Stat. 1280. Title IV, § 443(a) of that act amended § 3181 to allow the government to extradite non-U.S. nationals, citizens or permanent residents on the basis of comity, regardless of whether a treaty exists or not, provided (1) the crime for

legislative reform was not, however, successful.[26]

The 1848 Act can be traced to the landmark case of *In re Robbins*,[27] decided in 1799. In that case, President Adams granted England's request that the United States extradite an individual charged in England for a murder he had allegedly committed while in the British navy. Robbin's defense was that he had been impressed into British service, and that he had escaped during the other crew members' mutiny in which the ship's officers had been killed. Many individuals in the United States perceived this to be a justifiable act for which punishment was wholly inappropriate, such that Robbins should not have been returned to England.[28] Although the exact term "political offense exception" was not used at the time,

---

which extradition is requested was a crime of violence, as defined by 18 U.S.C. § 16, against a U.S. national in a foreign country; (2) that the Attorney General certifies in writing that the crime would have been a crime if committed in the U.S.; and (3) the offense is not a political offense. This fundamental change in U.S. extradition law is discussed throughout this paper. For the text of the provision, *see supra*, note 13. The Act also imports the definition of "national of the United States from 8 U.S.C. § 1101(a)(22), the Immigration and Nationality Act. Between 1981 and 1984, primarily in response to three cases concerning the "political offense exception," Matter of Mackin, 80 Cr. Misc. 1 (S.D.N.Y.) Aug. 13, 1981), *aff'd.* United States v. Mackin, 668 F.2d 122 (2d Cir. 1981; *In re* McMullen, No. 2-78-1899 M.G. (N.D. Cal. May 11, 1979), and Eain v. Wilkes, 641 F.2d 504 (7th Cir.), *cert. denied,* 454 U.S. 894 (1981). The amendments were aimed at expanding executive discretion and limiting the judiciary's ability to refuse to allow extraditions. They also contained several technical improvements. The amendments also would have codified some existing case law and answered some of the unsettled problems facing the courts. For a comprehensive analysis of these efforts, *see* BASSIOUNI, EXTRADITION *supra* note 1, at 36-49. The statute and rules concerning extradition are as follows: authorizing extradition, § 3181; circumstances under which provisions relating to the surrender of persons to a foreign country apply, § 3181; rendition of fugitives from one of the several states or U.S. territory found in same, § 3182; transportation of fugitive under § 3182, § 3194; rendition of juveniles from one of the several states, U.S. territory or possession or District of Columbia to same, §§ 5001, 5032; rendition of fugitives from one of the several states or U.S. territory or possession found in extraterritorial jurisdiction of the United States, § 3183; extraterritorial jurisdiction of the U.S. defined, § 3042; provisional arrest and detention of fugitive under § 3042 and § 3183, § 3187; rendition of fugitive from country under control of United States who flees to the United States, § 3185; rendition of fugitive from foreign country to United States, § 3184; authority of Secretary of State to order extradition of U.S. citizen even where treaty does not obligate U.S. to extradite its citizens, § 3196; appointed agent's authority over fugitive received from foreign government, § 3193; Secretary of State has authority to appoint agent to receive fugitive from foreign government, Exec. Order No. 11517, 35 Fed. Reg. 4937 (1970), *reprinted in* § 3193; protection of accused delivered by foreign government, § 3192; Secretary of State's authority to surrender fugitive to foreign government, agent of foreign government, § 3186; foreign agent's authority over fugitive, § 3186; Federal Rules of Criminal Procedure not applicable to proceedings on extradition and rendition of fugitives, Rule 54(b)(5); Federal Rule of Evidence not applicable to proceedings on extradition and rendition of fugitives, Rule 1101(b)(3); authentication of foreign legal documents, § 3190; authentication satisfied by certification of foreign legal documents by foreign countries principal diplomatic or consular officer in the U.S., § 3190; payment of fees and costs, including witnesses, § 3195; requirement of the place and character of extradition hearing, § 3189; two calendar months is the maximum time the government may detain a person detained for rendition to a foreign country, § 3188; discharge of prisoner detained over statutory maximum time, § 3188; escape, retaking accused, § 3186; procuring attendance at extradition hearing of witnesses for indigent fugitives, § 3191; habeas corpus remedy, 28 U.S.C. § 2241; criminal offense to resist extradition agent, § 1502; rendition and judicial assistance to the International Tribunals for the former Yugoslavia and Rwanda, § 3181, historical and statutory notes; requirement that extradition of drug traffickers be a priority issue of United States mission in major illicit drug producing or transit countries, § 3181, historical and statutory notes; updating extradition treaties with major drug producing countries, § 3181, historical and statutory notes.

[26] *See* M. Cherif Bassiouni, *Extradition Reform Legislation in the United States: 1981-83,* 73 AKRON L. REV. 495 (1984).

[27] 27 F. Cas. 825 (No. 16,175) (D.S.C. 1799).

[28] *See* 10 ANNALS OF CONGRESS 580-640 (1800), reprinted following *In re* Robbins, 27 F. Cas. 825, 833-70 (No. 16,175) (D.S.C. 1799).

the underlying concept was already recognized in customary international law.[29]

The legal basis for Robbins' surrender was President Adams' order that he be arrested and returned to England. In reviewing that order, the federal district court, sitting in Charleston, South Carolina, in *habeas corpus* proceedings, relied on the President's directions through the Secretary of State, even though neither Jay's Treaty with England[30] (which was the treaty basis for the request) nor national legislation formed a legal basis for such action.[31] President Adams' decision in the highly publicized extradition of Robbins was considered one of the reasons for his failure to be re-elected as President.[32] The political controversy and legal irregularities of Robbins were not soon forgotten. In 1848, similar factors were brought to the forefront of public attention in the *Metzger* case,[33] which prompted Congress to enact the 1848 Extradition Act.[34] Similarly, the 1981-84 Extradition Reform Acts (which have not been enacted) have been prompted primarily by three highly publicized *causes célebrès* in which the "political offense exception" was at issue: *Matter of Mackin*,[35] *In re McMullen*,[36] and *Eain v. Wilkes*.[37] In *McMullen* and *Mackin*, extradition to England was denied on the basis of the "political offense exception." In the *Eain* case, however, the exception was denied and the relator was extradited to Israel.[38] The political controversies giving rise to both the 1848 Act and the 1981-84 Acts is the respective role of the executive, legislative, and judicial branches in granting a foreign state's extradition request. The outcomes, however, were different on these two historic occasions. The 1848 Act was designed to limit executive power so that action such as President Adams' ordering an individual's surrender in *In re Robbins* would be impermissible. The underlying theory

---

[29] For an historical analysis of the "political offense exception," *see* BASSIOUNI, EXTRADITION, *supra* note 1, at 502-587. *See also* CHRISTINE VAN DEN WYNGAERT, THE POLITICAL OFFENSE EXCEPTION TO EXTRADITION (1980).

[30] The Treaty of Amity, Commerce and Navigation with Great Britain (Jay Treaty), 19 Nov. 1794, 8 Stat. 116, T.S. No. 105, *reprinted in* 1 WILLIAM M. MALLOY, TREATIES, CONVENTIONS, INTERNATIONAL ACTS, PROTOCOLS AND AGREEMENTS BETWEEN THE UNITED STATES OF AMERICA AND OTHER POWERS, 1776-1909 490 (1910).

[31] *In re Robbins*, 27 F. Cas. at 827.

[32] MOORE, EXTRADITION *supra* note 1, at 550-51.

[33] *In re* Metzger, 17 F. Cas. 232 (No. 9,511) (S.D.N.Y. 1847). In *Metzger*, France requested that the United States extradite an individual charged with forgery in France. The judicial determination of Metzger's extraditabilty was made by Judge Betts in chambers, who found his extradition in order. The decision prompted considerable discussion over whether judicial review could be performed in chambers as opposed to in open court.

[34] Ch. 167, § 5, 9 Stat. 302, 303; *see In re* Kaine, 55 U.S. (14 How.) 63, 68 (1852) (noting "[t]hat the eventful history of Robbin's case had a controlling influence . . . especially on Congress, when it passed the act of 1848, is, as I suppose, free from doubt.").

[35] 80 Cr. Misc. 1 (S.D.N.Y. Aug. 13, 1981), *aff'd*, United States v. Mackin, 668 F.2d 122 (2d Cir. 1981). In *Mackin*, the United Kingdom's request that a member of the Provisional Irish Republican Army be extradited to the United Kingdom in order to face prosecution for the charge of attempted murder and related offenses he allegedly committed against a British soldier (dressed in civilian clothes), standing in a Belfast bus station, was denied on the grounds that these charges were "political offenses" for which extradition could not be granted.

[36] No. 3-78-1899 M.G. (N.D. Cal. May 11, 1979). In *McMullen*, the United Kingdom's request that a member of the Provisional Irish Republican Army be extradited to the United Kingdom in order to face prosecution for his alleged bombing of a British army installation in England was denied on the grounds that he was being sought for a "political offense" for which extradition could not be granted.

[37] 641 F.2d 504 (7th Cir.), *cert. denied*, 454 U.S. 894 (1981). In *Eain*, Israel's request that an alleged member of the Palestine Liberation Organization be extradited to Israel to be prosecuted for his alleged bombing of a bus in Israel was granted. The court refused to entertain the relator's defense that such actions constituted "political offenses."

[38] *See* BASSIOUNI, EXTRADITION, *supra* note 1, at 495-643 (discussing the political offense exception).

was that the judiciary should have the authority to review executive action so that individual liberty would not be improperly infringed.

The relationship between legislative provisions and treaty provisions is of particular importance in United States extradition law and practice because of the Constitution and the relationship between treaties and legislation.[39] Basically, this relationship can take one of two forms: (1) the legislation can serve as the basis for all or most substantive and procedural matters, while treaties provide for exceptional matters not included in the legislation; or (2) the legislation can serve as a supplement to treaties such that all substantive and procedural matters are regulated primarily by treaties rather than by the legislation. The distinction between these two possible relationships has important ramifications. If the former approach were followed, then national legislation would be controlling with respect to all extradition matters and would regulate both substance and procedure and treaties would be the exception. If the latter approach were followed, however, then national legislation would not be the general rule.[40]

The jurisprudence of the U.S. Courts interpreting and applying the statute and the various treaties has been essentially consistent. The United States Supreme Court, however, has only accepted to review, in 1992, one case in the last 40 years.[41]

Nature of Extradition

In the United States, international extradition is regarded as an exclusive power of the federal government denied to the several states.[42] The power to make treaties rests specifically with the President[43] but is subject to the "advice and consent" of two-thirds of the Senate.[44] The treaty-making power shared by the President and the Senate is limited only by other articles of the Constitution itself or by federal legislation. As the Supreme Court stated in 1890 in *Geofroy v. Riggs*:

> The treaty power as expressed in the Constitution, is in terms unlimited except by those restraints which are found in that instrument against the action of the government or one of its departments, and those arising from the nature of the government itself and of that of the States. It would not be contended that it extends so far as to authorize what the Constitution forbids, or a change in the character of the government or in that of one of the States, or a cession of any portion of the territory of the latter, without its consent. . . . But with these exceptions, it is not perceived that there is any limit to the questions

---

39 *See generally* LOUIS HENKIN, FOREIGN AFFAIRS AND THE CONSTITUTION (1972).

40 *See* 18 U.S.C. § 3181-3196 (1988). There are at present 147 treaties in force, applicable to 103 countries; *see also* IGOR I. KAVASS & ADOLF SPRUDZS, EXTRADITION LAWS AND TREATIES: UNITED STATES (4 vols. 1979; 1995 update).

41 The United States Supreme Court has reviewed few extraditions. The only one between 1952 and 1997 has been *United States v. Alvarez-Machain,* 505 U.S. 655 (1992). In that case, the Court sanctioned law enforcement officials disregard of formal extradition processes by endorsing their use of abduction to apprehend and try suspected criminals. The case of abducted person Dr. Alvarez- Machain was later dismissed. *See e.g.*, Edmund S. McAlister, *The Hydraulic Pressure of Vengence: United States v. Alvarez-Machain and the Case for a Justifiable Abduction,* 43 DEPAUL L. REV. 449 (1994).

42 *See* BASSIOUNI, EXTRADITION, supra note 1, at 33-48; and WHITEMAN DIGEST *supra* note 1, at731-38.

43 U.S. CONST. art. II, § 2.

44 U.S. CONST. art. I, § 10.

which can be adjusted touching any manner which is properly the subject of negotiation with a foreign country.[45]

Thus, the determination of the extent of this treaty-making power requires an analysis of the substantive national rights that are created or proscribed under the terms of the treaty. In 1794, for example, the case of *In re Robbins*[46] raised the question of whether Article III of the Constitution permitted judicial review in extradition proceedings. The issue arose because no statutory provision authorizing the court to act pursuant to presidential mandate existed, nor did the treaty make any provision for a judicial hearing or the manner in which the proceedings were to be undertaken. The President ordered the case heard in the United States District Court. The court held that its judicial power under Article III extended to the interpretation and application of extradition treaties and did not require federal legislation specifically implementing procedures for judicial review in extradition proceedings. Having thereby established its jurisdiction over the subject matter, the court ruled that the terms of the treaty had been satisfied and ordered the relator surrendered to the requesting state.

The central question presented in *Robbins* was whether extradition treaties are self-executing, in reliance on international law doctrine, or non-self-executing and thus require national legislation for their implementation. The debate lasted from 1794 to 1848. During that period, the proponents of the view that extradition treaties are self-executing prevailed and extradition proceedings were adjudicated by federal district courts on request of the President or the Secretary of State. It was not until 1848, as discussed above, that Congress passed the first extradition statute, setting forth that extradition is to be undertaken by virtue of a treaty and subject to judicial proceedings in federal district court in accordance with the provisions of the statute.[47] Since then the federal extradition statute has been revised several times.[48]

Since the resolution of this controversy, the judiciary has determined that the Executive Branch has the authority to do only that which is granted in federal legislation or in an extradition treaty. This constitutional doctrine is founded on the principle that executive prerogative alone cannot dispose of a person's liberty. The government's right to restrict personal freedom in a manner consistent with the Constitution must derive from a treaty which has become part of the law of the land after the Senate's "advise and consent." The United States Supreme Court reiterated this view in 1936, when it declared:

> [A]pplying as we must, our law in determining the authority of the President, we are constrained to hold that this power, in the absence of a statute conferring an independent power, must be found in the terms of the treaty and that, as the treaty with France fails to grant the necessary authority, the President is without power to surrender the respondent.[49]

---

45 133 U.S. 258, 267 (1890); *see also* Reid v. Covert, 354 U.S. 1, 16-17 (1957).

46 *In re Robbins,* 27 F. Cas. 825 (no. 16,175) (D.S.C. 1799).

47 Act of Aug. 12, 1848, ch. 167, 9 Stat. 302 (1898).

48 *See infra* sec. 3.1 (The Relationship of Treaties to National Legislation).

49 Valentine v. United States *ex. rel.* Neidecker, 299 U.S. 5 (1936). In Williams v. Rogers, 499 F.2d 513 (1971), the Eighth Circuit held that *Valentine* meant:

> that the holding there requires only that there be a showing of some authority, whether in the form of congenial dictate or policy, or the provisions of an existing treaty, to provide a legitimate basis for the

As early as 1886, the Supreme Court reemphasized that the treaty-making power shared by the President and the Senate is an exclusive national power when it stated:

> There is no necessity for the states to enter upon relations with foreign nations which are necessarily implied in the extradition of fugitives from justice found within the limits of the state, as there is none why they should in their own name make demand upon foreign nations for the surrender of such fugitives.
>
> At this time of day, and after the repeated examinations which have been made by this Court into the powers of the Federal Government to deal with all international questions exclusively, it can hardly be admitted that, even in the absence of treaties or acts of Congress on the subject, the extradition of a fugitive from justice can become the subject of negotiation between a state of this Union and a foreign government.[50]

Thus, it is firmly established that the various states have no power to negotiate extradition treaties, that international extradition is regarded as an exclusively federal power, and that there can be no extradition under present practice without a treaty. This constitutional doctrine is, however, also at the basis of "Executive Discretion,"[51] which permits the President or whomever he may delegate (*i.e.* the Secretary of State) to refuse to surrender a person who was ordered delivered to a requesting state by the judiciary pursuant to an order entered after a hearing held in accordance with the requirements of Title 18 U.S.C. § 3184.

The relationship between the judiciary and the executive contemplated by the extradition statute has raised separation of powers issues. The statute requires the extraditing judge, a Magistrate or Federal District Court judge to either deny extradition or commit for extradition, and then places the authority to extradite in the hands of the Secretary of State, who may or may not extradite. If the extradition judge does not commit for extradition, the Secretary is barred from extraditing. But if the extradition judge commits for extradition, it may appear as though the judge's decision, if he is acting in his Article III capacity,[52] is being reviewed by the executive branch, in violation of the separation of powers doctrine. This controversy began when a Washington D.C. Federal District Court judge, in *Lobue v. Christopher*,[53] held the extradition statute to be unconstitutional in violation of the separation of powers doctrine and the Appointments Clause. The Court of Appeals for the D.C. Circuit vacated the district court's decision, holding that the lower court did not have jurisdiction

---

surrender of fugitives from justice by this country to another.

Id. at 521. In this case, a United States military person had been reassigned from the United States to a United States base in the Philippines where he had once been and was under indictment by the Philippines courts for the crime of rape. Under the agreement between the United States and the Philippines, the latter had jurisdiction to prosecute for common crimes committed by United States military personnel. The reassignment order was construed by this decision as a form of surrender akin to extradition, but as quoted it apparently need not rest on a treaty.

[50] United States v. Rauscher, 119 U.S. 407, 414 (1886); *see also* WHITEMAN DIGEST *supra* note 1, at 736.

[51] *See* BASSIOUNI, EXTRADITION, *supra* note 1, at 777; *see infra* sec. 16 (Executive Discretion and Conditional Discretion); *see also* discussion of Lobue and other cases in sec. 3 above.

[52] Article III "nourishes two intersecting values in our constitutional system: first, it protects the institutional integrity of the judiciary by safeguarding its independence against encroachment by the political branches; second, it guarantees litigants the personal right to have their claims adjudicated by judges cloakes with that independence" Austin v. Healy, 5 F.3d 598, 602 (2nd Cir. 1993).

[53] 893 F. Supp. 65 (D.C. 1995).

to entertain *Lobue's* claim.[54] A number of cases ensued, with relators challenging the constitutionality of their potential certification, based on *Lobue*.[55] None, however, followed *Lobue*.

In *Lo Duca v. United States*,[56] the Second Circuit Court of Appeals refused to follow the appellate decision in *Lobue*, repudiating it on its merits. The *Lo Duca* court held that the statute was constitutional under the separation of powers doctrine and the Appointments Clause of the United States Constitution. It held, basically, that the extradition statute did not violate the separation of powers doctrine because the statute and its legislative history and case law revealed that extradition magistrates were not acting in their capacity as Article III Federal Court judges.[57] The court also, somewhat cryptically, reasoned that the extradition judge, in following the statute, does not make a decision to extradite that can be reviewed by the Secretary of State, but merely one which the Secretary of State examines to instruct him as to the case, so that he can make his own determination of whether to surrender or not on the basis of "Executive Discretion." Indeed, after the judicial determination is reached, the Secretary of State has the authority on behalf of the President to exercise "Executive Discretion" in surrendering or not the person found extraditable, or in conditioning extradition.

The Relationship of Treaties to National Legislation

As stated above extradition treaties are deemed self-executing and are therefore equivalent to an act of the legislature.[58] Thus, they are enforceable without the aid of implementing legislation. As a result, they are part of the municipal law of the United States and are binding upon the judiciary, which is under the same obligation to enforce extradition treaties as it is to enforce the Constitution and the laws of the United States. As the Supreme Court stated in the *Head Money Cases*:

> A treaty is primarily a compact between independent nations. It depends for the enforcement of its provisions on the interest and the honor of the governments which are parties to it. If these fail, its infraction becomes the subject of international negotiations and reclamations, so far as the injured party chooses to seek redress, which may in the end be enforced by actual war. It is obvious that with all this the judicial courts have nothing to do and can give no redress. But a treaty may also contain provisions which confer certain rights upon the citizens or subjects of one of the nations residing in the territorial limits of the other, which partake of the nature of municipal law, and which are capable of enforcement as between private parties in the courts of

---

[54] Lobue v. Christopher, 82 F.3d 1081 (D.C. Cir. 1996) *rehearing denied* (July 1, 1996).

[55] *See* Sandhu v. Bransom, 932 F. Supp. 822, 826 (N.D. Tex. 1996); *In re* Marzook, 924 F. Supp. 565, 570-572 (S.D.N.Y.); *In re* Lin, 915 F. Supp. 206, 211-15 (D. Guam 1995); *In re* Sutton, 908 F. Supp. 631 (E.D. Mo. 1995); *In re* Lang, 905 F. Supp. 1385 (C.D. Cal. 1995); Carreno v. Johnson, 899 F. Supp. 624 (S.D. Fla. 1995).

[56] 93 F.3d 1100, (2nd Cir.) *cert. denied,* 117 S.Ct. *508 (1996).*

[57] Courts have long recognized that federal judges acting under the extradition statute were not acting as Article III judges, Austin v. Healy, 5 F.3d 598 (1993).

[58] Terlinden v. Ames, 184 U.S. 270, 288 (1902); *see also* Foster & Elam v. Neilson, 27 U.S. 253, 314 (1829). *See generally* RESTATEMENT (THIRD) § 111; Richard Cohen, Comment, *Self-Executing Agreements: A Separation of Powers Problem*, 24 BUFFALO L. REV. 137 (1974).

> the country. . . . The Constitution of the United States places such provisions as these in the same category as other laws of Congress by its declaration that "this Constitution and the laws made in pursuance thereof, and all treaties made or which shall be made under authority of the United States, shall be the supreme law of the land." A treaty, then, is a law of the land as an act of Congress is, whenever its provisions prescribe a rule by which the rights of the private citizen or subject may be determined. And when such rights are of a nature to be enforced in a court of justice, that court resorts to the treaty for a rule of decision for the case before it as it would to a statute.[59]

Because extradition treaties and federal legislation regarding extradition carry the same weight and force, conflict between the two raises difficult questions of judicial interpretation and enforcement. Although the courts generally attempt to interpret the two in a manner that avoids inconsistency and conflict, the prevailing view in the United States is that federal legislation which is enacted after the ratification of a self-executing treaty is controlling over conflicting treaty provisions. In its *Head Money Cases* decision, the Supreme Court went on to state:

> But even in this aspect of the case there is nothing in this law which makes it irreparable or unchangeable. The Constitution gives it no superiority over an act of Congress in this respect, which may be repealed or modified by an act of a later date. Nor is there anything in its essential character, or in the branches of the government by which the treaty is made, which gives it this superior sanctity.
>
> A treaty is made by the President and the Senate. Statutes are made by the President, the Senate and the House of Representatives. The addition of the latter body to the other two in making a law certainly does not render it less entitled to respect in the matter of its repeal or modification than a treaty made by the other two. If there be any difference in this regard, it would seem to be in favor of an act in which all three of the bodies participate. And such is, in fact, the case in a declaration of war, which must be made by Congress, and which when made, usually suspends or destroys existing treaties between the nations thus at war.
>
> In short, we are of opinion that, so far as a treaty made by the United States with any foreign nation can become the subject of judicial cognizance in the courts of this country, it is subject to such acts as Congress may pass for its enforcement, modification, or repeal.[60]

The court reaffirmed this view in its interpretation of an extradition treaty in *Grin v. Shine.*[61] There, the relator unsuccessfully argued that the extradition treaty with Russia, which required proof of probable cause by the production of an arrest warrant from the requesting state, should take precedence over subsequent Congressional legislation, which did not require that the arrest warrant be issued by the requesting state. The Court reasoned that:

---

59 Head Money Cases, 112 U.S. 580, 598-99 (1884).

60 *Id.*

61 Grin v. Shine, 187 U.S. 181 (1902).

> [w]hile the treaty contemplates the production of a copy of a warrant of arrest or other equivalent document, issued by a magistrate of the Russian empire, it is within the power of Congress to dispense with this requirement, and we think it has done so by Rev. Stat. sec. 5270. . . . The treaty is undoubtedly obligatory upon both powers, and, if Congress should prescribe additional formalities than those required by the treaty, it might become the subject of complaint by the Russian government and of further negotiations. But notwithstanding such treaty, Congress has a perfect right to provide for the extradition of criminals in its own way, with or without a treaty to that effect, and to declare that foreign criminals shall be surrendered upon such proofs of criminality as it may judge sufficient. *Castro v. De Uriarte*, 16 Fed. Rep. 93 (S.D.N.Y. 1883).[62]

It should be emphasized that the United States' view on this issue is contrary to the practice of many other states. One commentator has noted that:

> in civil law systems international law is generally of superior force to municipal law. Thus, in the event that an extradition treaty should impose an obligation on these countries to extradite a national [for example] this obligation must be discharged, notwithstanding the contrary provisions of municipal law.[63]

It would also appear that the United States' practice of permitting national legislation to supersede treaty obligations would be a breach of treaty obligations, giving rise to state responsibility.[64] Because extradition is in the nature of an international agreement stating the parties' obligations, it is only logical that the precise extent of these obligations should be contained in the treaty. Therefore, regardless of the method by which United States courts resolve a conflict between treaty obligations and Congressional legislation, "by international law it is no defense to plead conflicting municipal law in answer to a breach of an internationally binding obligation."[65]

Treaty Interpretation[66]

In the constitutional scheme of separation of powers and the respective powers granted each branch, the judiciary has the power to interpret treaties.[67]

---

62 *Id.* at 191. The doctrine was affirmed in Charlton v. Kelly, 229 U.S. 447, 465 (1913).

63 IVAN A. SHEARER, EXTRADITION IN INTERNATIONAL LAW 115 (1971).

64 *See* BASSIOUNI, EXTRADITION, *supra* note 1, at 107-109.

65 *Grin,* 187 U.S. at 195. The 1984 Extradition Act maintains the traditional position of the United States that national legislation supersedes treaties. This position was criticized by this writer before the Senate and House Committee hearings on their respective proposed bills. *See* H.R. 5227, 97th Cong. 2d Sess., 128 CONG. REC. H9670 (Daily ed Dec. 15, 1981) [hereinafter *Senate Judiciary Hearings on S. 1639*]; The Extradition Act of 1981: Hearing on S. 1639 Before the Senate Comm. On the Judiciary, 97th Cong. 1st sess. (1981) [*House Judiciary Hearings on H.R. 5227*].

66 *See generally* Vienna Convention on the Law of Treaties, *opened for signature*, May 23, 1969, U.N. Doc. A/CHEF. 39/27 (1969), *reprinted in* 8 I.L.M. 679 (1969) *and in* 63 AM. J. INT'L. L. 875 (1969) [hereinafter Vienna Convention]; T.O. ELIAS, THE MODERN LAW OF TREATIES (1974); LOUIS HENKIN, FOREIGN AFFAIRS AND THE UNITED STATES (1996); FARAD MALEKIN, THE SYSTEM OF INTERNATIONAL LAW (1987).

67 *Head Money Cases*, 112 U.S. 580 (1884), at 598-99. *See also* Charlton v. Kelly, 229 U.S. 447 (1913); The Chinese Exclusion Case, 130 U.S. 581, 602-603 (1889).

In the *Head Money Cases*, the Supreme Court held in 1884:

> A treaty is primarily a compact between independent states. It depends for the enforcement of its provisions on the interest and the honor of the governments which are parties to it. If these fail, its infraction becomes the subject of international negotiations and reclamations, so far as the injured party chooses to seek redress which may in the end be enforced by actual war. It is obvious that with all this the judicial courts have nothing to do and can give no redress. But a treaty may also contain provisions which confer certain rights upon the citizens or subjects of one of the nations residing in the territorial limits of the other, which partake of the nature of municipal law, and which are capable of enforcement as between private parties in the courts of the country. An illustration of this character is found in treaties which regulate the mutual rights of citizens and subjects of the contracting nations in regard to rights of property by descent of inheritance, when the individuals concerned are alien. The Constitution of the United States places such provisions as these in the same category as other laws of Congress, by its declaration that, "this Constitution, and the laws made in pursuance thereof, and all treaties made or which shall be made under the authority of the United States, shall be the supreme law of the land." A treaty, then, is a law of the land, as an act of Congress is, whenever its provisions prescribe a rule by which the rights of the private citizen or subject may be determined. And when such rights are of a nature to be enforced in a court of justice, that court resorts to the treaty for a rule of decision for the case before it as it would to a statute.

The rules of treaty interpretation can be summarized as follows:

1. The purpose of treaty interpretation is to ascertain the plain meaning[68] of the

---

[68] *See* Sumitomo Shoji American, Inc. v. Avagliano, 457 U.S. 176 (1981); Valentine v. United States *ex rel.* Neidecker, 299 U.S. 5 (1936); Factor v. Laubenheimer, 290 U.S. 276 (1933); Hu Yau-Lueng v. Soscia, 649 F.2d 914 (2d Cir. 1981); *In re* Assarsson, 635 F.2d 1237 (7th Cir. 1980); Greci v. Birknes, 527 F.2d 956 (1st Cir. 1976); United States *ex rel.* Bloomfield v. Gengler, 507 F.2d 925 (2d Cir. 1975); United States v. Vreeken, 603 F. Supp. 715 (Utah 1984).

The *Restatement (Third)*, states:

Section 329. General Rule of Interpretation

(1) An international agreement shall be interpreted in good faith in accordance with the ordinary meaning to be given to the terms of the agreement in their context and in the light of its object and purpose.

(2) The context for the purpose of the interpretation of an agreement shall comprise, in addition to the text, including its preamble and annexes:

(a) any agreement relating to the international agreement which was made between all the parties in connection with the conclusion of the agreement;

(b) any instrument which was made by one or more parties in connection with the conclusion of the agreement and accepted by the other parties as an instrument related to the agreement.

(3) There shall be taken into account, together with the context:

(a) any subsequent agreement between the parties regarding the interpretation of the agreement or the application of its provisions;

(b) any subsequent practice in the application of the agreement which establishes the agreement of the parties regarding its interpretation;

(c) any relevant rules of international law applicable in the relations between the parties.

(4) A special meaning shall be given to a term if it is established that the parties so intended.

Section 329 is based on Article 31 of the Vienna Convention on the Law of Treaties, *in* 1 LASSA OPPENHEIM, OPPENHEIM'S INTERNATIONAL LAW (9th ed. 1992).

language that comports with the parties' intentions.[69]

2. Sources of evidence which indicate this are:
    a. Negotiating history[70]
    b. Interpretation of the parties[71]
    c. Subsequent conduct of the parties[72]
3. These sources are then construed according to the following criteria:
    a. Consistent interpretation of the terms[73]
    b. Liberal construction of terms[74]
    c. Rule of liberality[75]
    d. *Expressio unius exclusio est alterius*[76]
    e. *Ejusdem generis*[77]
    f. Retroactive application[78]

---

69 *See* Sumitomo Shoji American, Inc. v. Avagliano, 457 U.S. 176 (1980); Valentine v. United States *ex rel.* Neidecker, 299 U.S. 5 (1936); Ford v. United States, 273 U.S. 593 (1927); United States v. Wiebe, 733 F.2d 549 (8th Cir. 1984); United States v. Kember, 685 F.2d 451 (D.C. Cir. 1982); Caltagirone v. Grant, 629 F.2d 739 (2d Cir. 1980); Escobedo v. United States, 623 F.2d 1098 (5th Cir. 1980); Reed v. Wiser, 555 F.2d 1079 (2d Cir. 1977); Day v. Trans World Airlines, Inc., 528 F.2d 31 (2d Cir. 1975); Denby v. Seaboard World Airlines, Inc., 575 F. Supp. 1134 (E.D.N.Y. 1983); Maschinenfabrik Kern, A.G. v. Northwest Airlines, Inc., 562 F. Supp. 232 (N.D. Ill. 1983).

70 *See* Factor v. Laubenheimer, 290 U.S. 276 (1933); Greci v. Birknes, 527 F.2d 956 (1st Cir. 1976); Day v. Trans World Airlines, Inc., 528 F.2d 31 (2d Cir. 1975).

> The *Restatement (Third)* similarly allows for consideration of supplemental materials. Section 330 states: Recourse may be had to supplementary means of interpretation, including the preparatory work of the international agreement and the circumstances of its conclusion, in order to confirm the meaning resulting from the application of section 329 or to determine the meaning when the interpretation according to section 329:
>
> (a) leaves the meaning ambiguous or obscure; or
>
> (b) leads to a result which in manifestly absurd or unreasonable.

Section 330 is based upon Article 32 of the Vienna Convention, *supra* note 180. Sindona v. Grant, 461 F. Supp. 199 (S.D.N.Y. 1978).

71 *See* Sumitomo Shoji American Inc. v. Avagliano, 457 U.S. 176 (1981); Kolovrat v. Oregon, 366 U.S. 187 (1961); Factor v. Laubenheimer, 290 U.S. 276 (1933); Demjanjuk v. Petrosky, 776 F.2d 571 (6th Cir. 1985); Arnbjornsdottir-Mendler v. United States, 721 F.2d 679 (9th Cir. 1983); Eain v. Wilkes, 641 F.2d 504 (7th Cir. 1981); *Escobedo*, 623 F.2d 1098 (5th Cir. 1957); Ivancevic v. Artukovic, 211 F.2d 565 (9th Cir. 1954).

72 *See* Trans World Airlines, Inc. v. Franklin Mint Corp., 104 S. Ct. 1776 (1984); Terlinden v. Ames, 194 U.S. 270 (1902); Day v. Trans World Airlines, Inc., 528 F.2d 31 (2d Cir. 1975); Argento v. Horn, 241 F.2d 258 (6th Cir. 1957); Ivancevic v. Artukovic, 211 F.2d 565 (9th Cir. 1954); *In re* Extradition of D'Amico, 177 F. Supp. 648 (S.D.N.Y. 1959).

73 *See* Caltagirone v. Grant, 629 F.2d 739 (2d Cir. 1980); Sabatier v. Dabrowski, 453 F. Supp. 1250 (D.C.R.I.), *aff'd*, 586 F. 2d 866 (1st Cir. 1978).

74 *See* Factor v. Laubenheimer, 290 U.S. 276 (1933); Jordan v. Tashior, 278 U.S. 123 (1928); United States v. Wiebe, 733 F.2d 549 (8th Cir. 1984); Brauch v. Raiche, 618 F.2d 843 (1st Cir. 1980); Vardy v. United States, 529 F.2d 404 (5th Cir. 1976); United States *ex rel.* Sakaguchi v. Kaulukukui, 520 F.2d 726 (9th Cir. 1975); Matter of Sindona, 584 F. Supp. 1437 (E.D.N.Y. 1984); Maschinenfabrik Kern, A.G. v. Northwest Airlines, Inc., 562 F. Supp. 232 (N.D.Ill. 1983).

75 *See* Melia v. United States, 667 F.2d 399 (2d Cir. 1981); Handel v. Artukovic, 601 F. Supp. 1421 (C.D. Cal. 1985).

76 *See* Hu Yau-Lueng v. Soscia, 649 F.2d 914 (2d Cir. 1981); United States v. Galanis, 568 F.2d 234 (2d Cir. 1977); *In re* Chan Kam-shu, 477 F.2d 333 (5th Cir. 1973).

77 *See* Factor v. Laubenheimer, 290 U.S. 276 (1933).

78 *See* Galanis v. Pallanck, 568 F.2d 234 (2d Cir. 1977).

g. International law principles regarding treaty interpretation[79]

In addition to the criteria enumerated above, United States courts also rely on customary international law principles in construing the meaning of treaty provisions. The recognition of customary international law is found in the much-quoted language of Mr. Justice Gray in the *Paquette Habana* case:

> International law is part of our law and must be ascertained and administered by the courts of justice of appropriate jurisdiction, as often as questions of right depending on it are duly presented for their determination.[80]

As Professor Henkin has stated: "Like treaties, customary international law is law for the Executive and the courts to apply."[81] The Vienna Convention on the Law of Treaties,[82] although not yet ratified by the Senate, is already recognized as the "authoritative guide to current treaty law and practice."[83] Because the Convention essentially codifies customary international law governing international agreements, the Convention may be used by the United States in interpreting treaties, even though the United States is not a party to the Convention.[84] In fact, United States courts have already treated certain provisions of the Vienna Convention as authoritative.[85]

"General principles of law" are a source of international law. Consequently, they can be used for purposes of treaty interpretation:

> The best evidence that international law has not only accepted but relied on "General Principles" is the Vienna Convention on the Law of Treaties, which contains a number of such "principles" in its rules of treaty interpretation. Although that Convention codifies customary rules of international law, it nonetheless incorporates such principles as good faith and others as part of customary international law, even though their origin is found in "General Principles."[86]

Furthermore, this writer has also stated that:

> "General Principles" have been primarily used to clarify and interpret international law. For example, as Schlesinger notes, "General Principles" must be considered in determining the meaning of treaty terms. Lauterpacht points out that recourse by the ICJ to "General Principles" has constituted "no more than interpretation of existing

---

[79] *See* United States v. Cadena, 585 F.3d 1252 (5th Cir. 1978); Day v. Trans World Airlines, 528 F.2d 31 (2d Cir. 1975); Husserl v. Swiss Air Transportation Co., 351 F. Supp. 702 (S.D.N.Y. 1972).

[80] Paquette Habana, 175 U.S. 677, 700 (1900).

[81] HENKIN, *supra* note 39, at 221.

[82] Vienna Convention, *supra* note 68.

[83] S. EXEC. DOC. L., 92d Cong., 1st sess. 1 (1971).

[84] RESTATEMENT (THIRD) § 325 (interpreting international agreements).

[85] *See* United States v. Cadena, 585 F.2d 1252, 1261 (5th Cir. 1978) (applying Art. 36 to interpret High Seas Convention); Day v. Trans World Airlines, 528 F.2d 31, 33, 36 (2d Cir. 1975) (applying Art. 31 to interpret Warsaw Convention).

[86] M. Cherif Bassiouni, *A Functional Approach to "General Principles" of International Law*, 11 MICH. J. INT'L L. 768, 786-87 (1990) (citation omitted).

> conventional and customary law by reference to common sense and the canons of good faith." This interpretive function is the most widely recognized and applied function of "General Principles" and the one that is evidently the most needed and useful, in contrast to the use of "General Principles" as a method to supplant or remedy deficiencies in conventional and customary international law.
>
> "General Principles" can be utilized to interpret ambiguous or uncertain language in conventional or customary international law, but, foremost, they can be relied upon to determine the rights and duties of States in the contextual, conventional, or customary law. This is particularly the case, for example, with respect to such principles as "good faith" and "equitable performance."
>
> The extent to which one can resort to "General Principles" for interpretative purposes has never been established. Consequently, "General Principles" can logically extend to fill gaps in conventional and customary international law and serve as a supplementary source thereto. From that basis, "General Principles" can be interpreted as a source of law that overreaches other positive sources of international law, and eventually supersedes it.
>
> This interpretative approach can be applied *in extenso*. "General Principles" thus become not only a source of new norms, but also a source of higher law, i.e., *jus cogens*.[87]

For example, with respect to determining double criminality, research may be required in comparative criminal law systems so that "general principles" can be determined and applied.

Since the 1980's, federal judges have tended to be more conservative and federal prosecutor's zeal sometimes stretches the limits of propriety. The combination of these two realities has had a strong impact on the way treaties have been interpreted. Suffice it to note that the Supreme Court, the last bastion of justice and fairness, interpreted the United States-Mexico Treaty[88] as permitting abduction because the treaty did not exclude it.[89]

The Restatement (Third) of Foreign Relations states:

> § 325 Interpretation of International Agreement
>
> (1) An international agreement is to be interpreted in good faith in accordance with the ordinary meaning to be given to its terms in their context and in the light of its object and purpose.
>
> (2) Any subsequent agreement between the parties regarding the interpretation of the agreement, and subsequent practice between the parties in the application of the agreement, are to be taken into account in its interpretation.

This requires examining:

1. Customary international law of interpretation.
2. Context of Agreement.
3. Subsequent practice and interpretation.

---

87 *Id.* at 776-77 (citations omitted).

88 Extradition Treaty, May 4, 1987, 31 U.S.T. 5059, T.I.A.S. No. 9656.

89 *See* BASSIOUNI, EXTRADITION, *supra* note 1, at Ch. IV (discussing Stevens' dissent); McAlister, *supra* note 41.

4. Interpretation of different types of agreements.
5. Recourse to travaux prếparatoires.
6. Interpretation of agreements authenticated in two or more languages.
7. Interpretation by United States courts.[90]

Restatement (Third) section 326 states:

(1) The President has authority to determine the interpretation of an international agreement to be asserted by the United States in its relations with other states.

(2) Courts in the United States have final authority to interpret an international agreement for purposes of applying it.[91]

The Comments and Reporters' Notes to Restatement (Third) section 326 expand upon the relationship between branches of the federal government and the treaty-making process. The elements to be considered are:

1. Presidential authority to interpret.
2. Executive and judicial interpretation.
3. Communication of Executive views to courts.
4. Interpretation as federal law.
5. Subsequent Senate interpretation.
6. Differing interpretations by Executive and courts.
7. Interpretation not a "political question."
8. Interpretation of agreement and determination of international law.
9. Evidence of United States interpretive practice.

The Effects of State Succession and War on United States Extradition Treaties[92]

State Succession

State succession and war cause the United States' treaty obligations regarding extradition to lapse or be suspended either until a new treaty comes into force or until hostilities are ended.

State succession related to how extradition relations arise "when a state or territory covered by such a treaty changes its form of government, or becomes a part of a nation other than that with which the [United States has] the formerly applicable treaty."[93] If the treaty is deemed abrogated by such changes, the United States will not grant an extradition request, because its extradition practice is based exclusively on the existence of a treaty in force.[94]

Generally, the question of state succession arises whenever there is a change in the

---

[90] See RESTATEMENT (THIRD) § 325, Source Note, Comment and Reporters' Notes.

[91] RESTATEMENT (THIRD) *supra* note 90.

[92] Section 3 is substantially based on BASSIOUNI, EXTRADITION, *supra* note 1, at 101-106.

[93] O. John Rogge, *State Succession,* 16 N.Y.L.F. 378 (1970). *See generally* Vienna Convention of Succession of States in Respect of Treaties, U.N. Doc. A/COEF.80/31, as corrected by A/COEF..80/31/Corr.2 of 27 Oct. 1978, *reprinted in* 17 I.L.M. 1488 (1978).

[94] WHITEMAN DIGEST *supra* note 1, at 727.

country's status, rather than in its government. This question recurs whenever former colonies of a given state become independent.[95] Upon gaining independence, several states have voluntarily assumed the treaty obligations applicable to their respective territories and which were formerly binding on the parent state. As an illustration, the Provisional Government of Burma assumed all applicable obligations of the United Kingdom, agreeing with the United States that:

> All obligations and responsibilities heretofore devolving on the Government of the United Kingdom which arise from any valid international agreement shall henceforth, insofar as such instrument may be held to have application to Burma, devolve upon the Provisional Government of Burma. The rights and benefits heretofore enjoyed by the Government of the United Kingdom in virtue of the application of any such international instrument to Burma shall henceforth be enjoyed by the Provisional Government of Burma.[96]

While some newly independent states specifically assume the treaty obligations of the predecessor states,[97] others do not.[98] For example, Israel proclaimed its statehood in 1948. A year later, it announced that the Extradition Treaty of 1931 between the United States and the United Kingdom was not in force with respect to Israel. As a result, the United States and Israel were compelled to negotiate a new extradition treaty. The new treaty was signed in 1962, 13 years after Israel denounced the previous treaty.[99] The Israeli Government's rejection of the treaties applicable to Palestine illustrates the controlling principle operative in such state succession situations: the government of the successor state determines whether or not a given treaty remains effective with that state.[100]

The prevailing position of the United States is that a treaty is in force *sua sponte* and binds the successor state unless that state repudiates it.[101] In *Sabatier v. Dabrowski,*[102] for example, the relator challenged the order certifying his extradition on the grounds that no extradition treaty between Canada and the United States was in force at the time he allegedly committed the offense for which his extradition was requested. In rejecting his contention,

---

[95] *See* Rogge, *supra* note 93, at 383; *see also* State v. Bull, 52 I.L.R. 84 (Sup. Ct., Transvaal Provincial Division 1966) (S. Afr.), where it was held that the extradition treaty between South Africa and Malawi, which became independent following the dissolution of the Federation of Rhodesia and Nyasaland, was in full force and effect.

[96] Treaty between the United Kingdom and Burma Regarding Recognition of Burmese Independence, Oct. 17, 1947, art. 2, 70 U.N.T.S. 184, 186; *see also* WHITEMAN DIGEST *supra* note 1, at 763; Rogge, *supra* note 93, at 383.

[97] Treaty between the United Kingdom and Burma Regarding Recognition of Burmese Independence, *supra* note 96.

[98] Rogge, *supra* note 93, at 374.

[99] Convention relating to Extradition, Dec. 5, 1963, 14 U.S.T. 1707, T.I.A.S. No. 5476, 484 U.N.T.S. 283.

[100] *Harvard Research in International Law, Draft Convention on Jurisdiction with Respect to Crime,* 29 AM. J. INT'L L. 435 (supp. 1935) [hereinafter *Harvard Research*].

[101] *See* Sabatier v. Dabrowski, 586 F.2d 866 (1st Cir. 1978) (concerning Canada's succession to treaty with England); United States v. Paroutian, 299 F.2d 486 (2d Cir. 1962) (concerning Lebanon's succession to treaty with France); Ivancevic v. Artukovic, 211 F.2d 565 (9th Cir.), *cert. denied,* 348 U.S. 818 (1954) (concerning Yugoslavia's succession to treaty with the Kingdom of Serbia); Jhirad v. Ferrandina, 355 F. Supp. 1155 (S.D.N.Y. 1973), *rev'd on other grounds,* 536 F.2d 478 (2d Cir.), *cert. denied,* 429 U.S. 833 (1976) (concerning India's succession to treaty with England).

[102] 586 F.2d 866 (1st Cir. 1978).

the court reasoned as follows:

> Sabatier's major contention is that the offense of armed robbery committed in 1975 is not extraditable under any valid treaty between Canada and the United States. The government seeks to extradite Sabatier under Article X of the Webster-Ashburton Treaty, 8 Stat. 572, T.S. No. 119, signed by Great Britain and the United States in 1842 and incorporated into subsequent conventions with Britain and Canada. It relies on the fact that the weight of authority is "that new nations inherit the treaty obligations of the former colonies." *Jhirad v. Ferrandina*, 355 F. Supp. 1155, 1159-61 (S.D.N.Y.), *rev'd on other grounds*, 536 F.2d 478 (2d Cir.), *cert. denied*, 429 U.S. 833, 97 S. Ct. 97, 50 L.Ed.2d 98 (1976). Sabatier argues that Canada is an exception to this rule and that the Webster-Ashburton Treaty therefore is not applicable. In effect, he would have us hold that no extradition treaty between Canada and the United States covering the offense of armed robbery was effective until 1976, when the current treaty with Canada was ratified by the Senate. This disputes the conduct of the governments of both countries, to which we must give great deference. *Terlinden v. Ames*, 184 U.S. 270, 288, 22 S. Ct. 484, 46 L.Ed. 534 (1902). The history of the relations between the two countries, the terms of the current extradition treaty, the official position of the Department of State, and the relevant rules of law all point to the conclusion that Canada should be regarded as a party to the Webster-Ashburton Treaty and that treaty permits her to seek Sabatier's extradition for an armed robbery committed in 1975. *Cf. Terlinden v. Ames*, 184 U.S. 270, 22 S. Ct. 484, 46 L.Ed. 534 (1902) (treaty with Germany); *Jhirad v. Ferrandina*, 536 F.2d 478 (treaty with India); *Ivancevic v. Artukovic*, 211 F.2d 565 (9th Cir.) *cert. denied*, 348 U.S. 818, 75 S. Ct. 28, 99 L.Ed. 645 (1954) (treaty with Yugoslavia).[103]

Similarly, in *Ivancevic v. Artukovic*,[104] the Ninth Circuit determined that the Treaty of Extradition of 1902 between the United States and Serbia[105] was sufficient legal basis for the relator's extradition to Yugoslavia, which succeeded to the treaty when it became a separate state.[106]

---

103 *Id.* at 868.

104 211 F.2d 565 (9th Cir.), *cert. denied*, 348 U.S. 818 (1954).

105 T.S. No. 406, 32 Stat. 1890 (1902).

106 The court reasoned that:

> [T]he combination of countries into the Kingdom of the Serbs, Croats and Slovenes, and then by internal political action into 'Federal Peoples Republic of Yugoslavia' was formed by a movement of the Slav people to govern themselves in one sovereign nation, with Serbia as the central or nucleus nation. Great changes in the going government were in the planning, and were brought about, but the combination was not an entirely new sovereignty without parentage. But even if it is appropriate to designate the combination as a new country, the fact that it started to function under the Serbian constitution as the home government and under Serbian legations and consular service in foreign countries, and has continued to act under Serbian treaties of Commerce and Navigation and the Consular treaty, is conclusive proof that if the combination constituted a new country it was the successor of Serbia in its international rights and obligations.

211 F.2d at 572-73. The Ninth Circuit again considered the issue of state succession in Arnbjornsdottir-Mendler v. United States, 721 F.2d 679 (1983). The court held that a treaty concluded in 1902 between the United States and Denmark was binding upon Iceland, which in 1902 was part of Denmark, even though Iceland subsequently became an independent state with no ties to Denmark. The court affirmed the applicability and validity of the treaty as applied to Iceland, even though Denmark had terminated the treaty in 1968. The court noted that in the 1918 Act of Union, by which Iceland declared itself a sovereign state, Iceland explicitly accepted all treaty obligations between Denmark and other countries that had been applicable to Iceland. The court also gave weight to the

The issue of state succession arose in connection with the reversion of Hong Kong to China in July 1997, based on the treaty between China and the U.K. The U.S. and the U.K. have an extradition treaty.[107] The question of states succession was raised in *United States v. Lui Kiu-Hong, a/k/a Jerry Lui.*[108] The first circuit held that the U.S.-U.K. treaty as supplemented by the supplementary treaty are applicable to Hong Kong, but the court did not go into the issue of state succession, even though China has rejected the doctrine of state succession. Nevertheless, the court accepted the Government's position that since China, in its revision treaty with the U.K. had accepted to apply the laws in force in Hong Kong at the time of revision, was bound by the extradition treaty.[109]

War

There are widely divergent views in international law regarding war's effect on treaty obligations, ranging from the view that war totally abrogates a treaty to the view that it has no effect on treaty enforcement. Early writers asserted that war *ipso facto* abrogated all treaties between the warring parties.[110] The contemporary view is that whether treaty provisions are annulled by war depends upon the provisions' extrinsic character.[111] It is obvious that war must extinguish certain treaties because of their very nature, such as those of friendship and alliance, whereas it only suspends rather than abrogates treaties contemplating a permanent arrangement of rights.[112]

---

endorsement of the treaty by the governments of both Iceland and the United States.

[107] 28 U.S.T. 227, June 8, 1997. The treaty was made applicable to Hong Kong by an exchange of diplomatic matters on October 21, 1976, 28 U.S.T. 238. The U.S.-U.K. treaty was supplemented on June 25, 1985, with a supplementary treaty, T.I.A.S. No. 12050 which is also applicable to Hong Kong.

[108] 110 F.3d 103 (1997).

[109] Joint Declaration of the Government of the United Kingdom of Great Britain and Northern Ireland and the Government of the Peoples Republic of China on the question of Hong Kong, Dec. 19, 1984, ratified and enacted into force May 27, 1985, T.S. No. 26 (1985). *Id.* art. 3(3).

[110] *See* James J. Lenoir, *The Effect of War on Bilateral Treaties, with Special Reference to Reciprocal Inheritance Treaty Provisions*, 34 GEO. L. J. 129 (1946) (containing, in footnote 9, citations to the views of the earlier writers upon this question). The reasoning in support of this view is expressed in EMMERICH DE VATTEL, THE LAW OF NATIONS, sec. 175, at 877 (trans. of ed. 1758, C. Fenwick, 1916): "Conventions and treaties are broken and annulled when war breaks out between the transacting parties, either because such agreements imply a state of peace, or because each party, having a right to deprive the enemy of his property, may take from him such rights as have been given him by treaties."

[111] In Karnuth v. United States, 279 U.S. 231 (1929), the Supreme Court stated:

> There seems to be a fairly common agreement that, at least, the following treaty obligations remain in force: Stipulations in respect of what shall be done in a state of war; treaties of cession, boundary, and the like; provisions giving the right to citizens or subjects of one of the high contracting powers to continue to hold and transmit land in the territory of the other; and, generally, provisions which represent completed acts. On the other hand, treaties of amity, of alliance, and the like, having a political character, the object of which is to promote relations of harmony between nation and nation, are generally regarded as belonging to the class of treaty stipulations that are absolutely annulled by war.

Id. at 236.

[112] In Society for the Propagation of the Gospel in Foreign Parts v. New Haven, 21 U.S. (8 Wheat.) 464 (1823), the Supreme Court declared:

> But we are not inclined to admit the doctrine urged at the bar, that treaties become extinguished, ipso facto, by war between the two governments, unless they should be revived by an express or implied renewal on the return of peace. Whatever may be the latitude of doctrine laid down by elementary writers on the law of nations, declaring in general terms, in relation to this subject, we are satisfied, that the doctrine contended for is not universally true. There may be treaties of such a nature as to their object and import, as that war will

United States courts have determined that extradition treaties are only suspended rather than abrogated by war. In *Argento v. Horn*,[113] for example, Italy requested the return of an individual who had been convicted *in absentia* and sentenced to life imprisonment in Italy in 1931 for a murder committed there in 1922. The relator challenged his extradition on the grounds that, despite the purported "revival" of the United States' extradition treaty with Italy pursuant to the peace treaty of 1947, the treaty had been abrogated by the outbreak of war and could be replaced only by a new treaty. Therefore, the relator argued, there was no legal authority for his extradition.

The court avoided the theoretical question by basing its decision on a consideration of the "background of the actual conduct of the two nations involved, acting through the political branches of their government."[114] The court found that in light of the peace treaty's provision inviting notification of revival of treaties, the notification by the Department of State of its intention to revive the treaty, and the subsequent conduct of the parties evidencing an understanding that the treaty was in force, the conclusion was that the treaty had been merely suspended during the war, not abrogated by it.[115]

A subsequent landmark decision on the effect of war on extradition treaties is *In re Extradition of D'Amico*.[116] On the application of the Republic of Italy, extradition proceedings were begun against the relator before the United States Commissioner for the Southern District of New York. The Commissioner found that the relator was the same Vito D'Amico who had been convicted *in absentia* in Italy in 1952 for robbery and kidnaping committed in Italy on or about April 15, 1946, and that there was probable cause to believe that D'Amico had committed the crime charged. The Commissioner therefore committed D'Amico to custody pending surrender to the Republic of Italy. D'Amico petitioned for a writ of *habeas corpus,* contending: (1) that the convention between the United States and the Kingdom of Italy of 1868 for the surrender of criminals was abrogated by the outbreak of war between the parties in 1942, and was not validly revived by the notification of the United States to Italy on February 6, 1948; (2) that the revival of the Treaty of 1868 did not make it applicable retroactively to crimes committed during the existence of a state of war between the parties; and (3) that the offense was not committed in territory subject to the jurisdiction of the demanding state because it was committed while the Italian Government was subject to Allied Control.[117] In discharging the writ of *habeas corpus* and remanding

---

> put an end to them; but where treaties contemplate a permanent arrangement of territorial, and other national rights, or which in their terms are meant to provide for the event of an intervening war, it would be against every principle of just interpretation, to hold them extinguished by the event of war. If such were the law, even the treaty of 1783, so far as it fixed our limits, and acknowledged our independence, would be gone, and we should have had again to struggle for both upon revolutionary principles. Such a construction was never asserted, and would be so monstrous as to supersede all reasoning. We think, therefore, that treaties stipulating for permanent rights, and general arrangements, and professing to aim at perpetuity, and to deal with the case of war as well as of peace, do not cease on the occurrence of war, but are, at most, only suspended while it lasts; and unless they are waived by the parties, or new and repugnant stipulations are made, they revive in their operation at the return of peace.

Id. at 494. *See generally* JOHN B. MOORE, DIGEST OF INTERNATIONAL LAW 799 (1901).

[113] 241 F.2d 258 (6th Cir.), *cert. denied*, 355 U.S. 818 (1957).

[114] *Id.* at 262.

[115] *Id.* at 263; *see also* Clark v. Allen, 331 U.S. 503 (1947); Gallina v. Fraser 278 F.2d 77 (2d Cir.), *cert. denied*, 364 U.S. 51 (1960).

[116] 177 F. Supp. 648 (S.D.N.Y. 1959).

[117] *Id.* at 650.

D'Amico to the custody of the United States Marshal, the court concluded that the extradition treaty was merely suspended by the outbreak of war between the parties and was revived by the formal cessation of hostilities. In effect, the court held that an extradition treaty could operate retroactively to apply to offenses committed while the treaty was suspended.[118] It would seem that this decision violates the principle *nulla poena sine lege nullum crimen sine lege.*[119]

The Duty to Extradite and State Responsibility

Under Title 18, Section 3181, of the United States Code, the United States may extradite persons within its territory only pursuant to an extradition treaty between the United States and the state requesting extradition. Under Section 3184, this treaty must be in force when the request for extradition is made.[120] Read in conjunction, these two sections permit surrender of an accused only in accordance with the applicable treaty in force. Although these provisions set forth the requirements to permit the United States' extradition of an individual within its territory, they do not indicate whether satisfaction of these requirements creates a duty to extradite. Furthermore, United States jurisprudence reflects the view that an extradition treaty does not *per se* create an obligation to extradite.[121]

The view that executive discretion negates any duty to extradite under treaty obligations or under customary international law is, however, in contradiction to general international law. According to the doctrine of state responsibility, an internationally wrongful act of a State exists when:

(a) Conduct consisting of an act or omission is attributable to the State under international law, and

(b) That conduct constitutes a breach of an international obligation of the State.[122]

---

118 In support of this view, the court stated, in United States *ex rel.* Oppenheim v. Hecht, 16 F.2d 955 (2d Cir. 1927):

> The status of relations between the demanding nation and the asylum nation at the time of the commission of the offense for which extradition is sought has never been deemed so critical, as we read the cases bearing on this issue; rather it is the status at the time of the demand that is determinative of whether or not extradition will be allowed.

Id. at 956.

119 *See* M. CHERIF BASSIOUNI, SUBSTANTIVE CRIMINAL LAW 25-26 (1978).

120 *See* United States *ex rel.* Donnelly v. Mulligan, 74 F.2d 220, 221 (2d Cir. 1934); *see also* 1 LASSA OPPENHEIM, INTERNATIONAL LAW § 327 (1995).

121 This view is founded on the notion that the State's right to protect its sovereignty and its freedom to provide asylum to whomever it chooses may override the State's obligation under the treaty. *See* 1 OPPENHEIM, *supra* note 120, at 800-01. It is for this reason that the Secretary of State, exercising executive discretion through delegation of this authority by the President, may refuse to extradite a relator despite a judicial determination that extradition would be compatible with the terms of the applicable treaty. *See* BASSIOUNI, EXTRADITION, *supra* note 1, at 777.

122 *See generally The Report of the International Law Commission on the Work of Its 46th Session, 2 May -23 July,* U.N. GAOR, 49th Sess., Supp. (No.10), A/49/10 (1994); IAN BROWNLIE, SYSTEM OF THE LAW OF NATIONS: STATE RESPONSIBILITY (1983); INTERNATIONAL LAW OF STATE RESPONSIBILITY FOR INJURIES TO ALIENS (Richard B. Lillich ed., 1983); *Draft Articles on State Responsibility*, 1984 Y.B. INT'L L. COMM'N 259.

The United States's treaty commitments, whether bilateral or unilateral, are binding international obligations.[123] Under these treaties, the United States is obligated to extradite in accordance with the treaties' terms and conditions those persons who have been charged with or convicted of offenses enumerated in the treaties. The United States' practice of allowing executive discretion to override treaty obligations, therefore, may be in violation of its international duty. Furthermore this view contradicts the emerging customary international law principle of *aut dedere aut judicare*, whereby a state always has a duty to extradite in the absence of prosecution.[124]

The Bases of Extradition

Bilateral Treaties

As stated above, the United States relies on bilateral treaties as the legal basis of extradition,[125] although reliance on multilateral treaties is equally valid though seldom done.[126]

The first international extradition treaty entered into by the United States was with Great Britain in 1794.[127] Article 27 of that treaty states:

> It is further agreed that His Majesty and the United States on mutual requisition, by them respectively, or by their respective ministers or officers authorized to make the same, will deliver up to justice all persons who, being charged with murder or forgery, committed within the jurisdiction of either, shall seek an asylum within any of the countries of the other, provided that this shall only be done on such evidence of criminality as, according to the laws of the place where the fugitive or person so charged shall be found, would justify his apprehension and commitment for trial if the offense had there been committed. The expense of such apprehension and delivery shall be borne and defrayed by those who make the requisition and receive the fugitive.[128]

---

[123] *See* Statute of International Court of Justice, art. 38, 59 Stat. 1055 (1945), T.S. No. 993.

[124] *See* BASSIOUNI, EXTRADITION, *supra* note 1, at 8-10 & Appendix I; *and* M. CHERIF BASSIOUNI & EDWARD WISE, AUT DEDRE AUT JUDICARE (1995). Customary International law applies to the U.S. *See* The Paquette Habana, 175 U.S. 677 (1900); Filartiga v. Peña-Irala, 630 F.2d 876 (2d Cir. 1980); Rand P. Tel-Oren v. Lybia Arab Republic, 726 F.2d 774 (D.C. Cir. 1984) (construing the Alien Tort Act, 28 U.S.C. § 1350); *see also* the Torture Victim Protection Act (TVPA) (limiting the Foreign Sovereign Immunities Act (FSIA) 28 U.S.C. § 1630). For a discussion of the applicability of customary international law, see Jordan J. Paust, *After* Alvarez-Machain: *Abduction, Standing, Denials of Justice, and Unaddressed Human Rights Claims*, 67 ST. JOHN'S L. REV. 551 (1993); Jordan J. Paust, *Customary International Law: Its Nature, Sources and Status of Law of the United States*, 12 MICH. J. INT'L L. 59 (1990); Jordan J. Paust, *Rediscovering the Relationship between Congressional Power and International: Exceptions to the Last in Time Rule and the Primacy of Custom*, 28 VA. J. INT'L L. 393 (1988). *See also* RESTATEMENT (THIRD) §§ 102, 103, & 702.

[125] 119 U.S. 407, 411 (1886); *see also* Factor v. Laubenheimer, 290 U.S. 276 (1933).

[126] *See* WHITEMAN DIGEST *supra* note 1, at 732-3; *see also* RESTATEMENT (THIRD) § 476; *International Procedures for the Apprehension and Rendition of Fugitive Offenders,* 1980 PROC. AM. SOC'Y INT'L L. 277 (remarks of M. Cherif Bassiouni).

[127] The Treaty of Amity, Commerce and Navigation with Great Britain (Jay's Treaty), Nov. 19, 1794, [1795] 8 Stat. 116, T.S. No. 105, *reprinted in* MALLOY, *supra* note 30, at 590; *see also* SAMUEL F. BEMIS, JAY'S TREATY: A STUDY IN COMMERCE AND DIPLOMACY (2d ed. 1965) [hereinafter BEMIS, JAY'S TREATY]. For a discussion of the treaty and its effect on American extradition, see MOORE EXTRADITION *supra* note 1, at 90.

[128] *Id.*

This practice remains a subject of periodic controversy and debate.[129]

Extradition treaties may be deemed declarative of an existing reciprocal relationship or creative of the substantive basis of the very process. The choice of theory relied upon will determine its applicability.[130] As stated by Whiteman:

> Extradition treaties do not, of course, make acts crimes. They merely provide a means whereby a State may obtain the return to it for trial or punishment of persons charged with or convicted of having committed acts which are crimes at the time of their commission and who have fled beyond the jurisdiction of the State whose laws, it is charged, have been violated.[131]

Multilateral Treaties

United States legislation is not explicit as to the type of treaty that may be relied upon as a legal basis for extradition. Thus multilateral treaties can be the legal basis for extradition.[132]

There are two types of multilateral treaties that may serve as the basis for extradition: those treaties which deal exclusively with extradition, and those which deal with international criminal matters and impose on the signatories the duty to extradite the accused or convicted offender.[133]

The United States is a party to two multilateral extradition treaties, the 1933 Montevideo Convention on Extradition[134] and the 1981 Inter-American Convention on Extradition.[135] There are also a number of non-extradition multilateral treaties on international crimes containing an extradition provision,[136] and thus permitting the United States and other signatory states to rely on them as a substitute for bilateral treaties.[137]

---

[129] *See* Symposium, *International Law and Extradition*, 16 N.Y.L.F. 315-525 (1970) [hereinafter Symposium]. *Compare* Alona E. Evans, *Legal Bases for Extradition in the United States*, 16 N.Y.L.F. 525 (1970), *with* Brendan F. Brown, *Extradition and the Natural Law*, 16 N.Y.L.F. 578 (1970) *and* O. John Rogge, *State Succession*, 16 N.Y.L.F. 378 (1970). *See also* M. Cherif Bassiouni, *International Extradition: A Summary of the Contemporary American Practice and a Proposal*," 39 REV. INT'LE DE DROIT PÉNAL 494 (1968), *reprinted in* 15 WAYNE L. REV. 733 (1968); Edward M. Wise, *Prolegomenon to the Principles of International Criminal Law*, 16 N.Y.L.F. 562 (differing from the position of Evans and Rogge, but remaining consistent with his views expressed in *Some Problems of Extradition*, 39 REV. INT'LE DE DROIT PÉNAL 518 (1968), *reprinted in* 15 WAYNE L. REV. 709 (1969)).

[130] Thus, if an extradition treaty is considered a reflection of reciprocal relationships, then it is nullified by the breaking of diplomatic relations between the state parties to the treaty. This is the position of the United States. *See* WHITEMAN DIGEST *supra* note 1, at 769; GREEN HAYWOOD HACKWORTH, DIGEST OF INTERNATIONAL LAW 37 (1944); *see also* BASSIOUNI, EXTRADITION, *supra* note 1, at 35-48.

[131] WHITEMAN DIGEST *supra* note 1, at 753-54.

[132] *See Senate Judicial Hearings on S. 1639, supra* note 40 (remarks of this writer). Section 3199(a)(2) of S. 1639 defines "treaty" as including present and future multilateral treaties ratified by the Senate.

[133] BASSIOUNI & WISE, AUT DEDRE AUT JUDICARE, *supra* note 124.

[134] Convention on Extradition, signed at Montevideo, Dec. 26, 1933, 49 Stat. 3111, T.S. No. 882.

[135] Adopted at Caracas, Feb. 25, 1981, O.A.S. Doc. OEA/Ser.A/36(SEPF), *reprinted in* 20 I.L.M. 723 (1981).

[136] *See see* BASSIOUNI, EXTRADITION, *supra* note 1, at 8-10.

[137] This author has identified 25 categories of international crimes between 1815 and 1996. A number of the treaties relating to these crimes contain an extradition provision on which the parties can rely in the absence of a bilateral treaty. These crimes are: (1) Aggression; (2) War crimes; (3) Unlawful use, production and stockpiling of certain prohibited weapons; (4) Crimes against humanity; (5) Genocide; (6) *Apartheid*; (7) Slavery and slave-

Reciprocity and Comity

There have been several instances where the United States has deviated from the treaty practice. In these instances, extradition was granted or requested on the basis of comity or reciprocity. There are, however, few recorded instances where the United States granted extradition to a requesting state in the absence of a treaty.[138] The most well-known case is probably that of Arguelles, which occurred in 1864.[139] Arguelles, an officer in the Spanish army, had been accused in Spain of selling individuals into slavery for his own personal gain. Although the United States had no extradition treaty with Spain, it granted Spain's extradition request on the basis of comity because the crime was an international one. The Secretary of State defended the decision as follows:

> There being no treaty of extradition between the United States and Spain, nor any act of Congress directing how fugitives from justice in Spanish dominions shall be delivered up, the extradition in the case referred to in the resolution of the Senate is understood by this Department to have been made in virtue of the law of nations and the Constitution of the United States. Although there is a conflict of authorities concerning the expediency of exercising comity towards a foreign government by surrendering, at its request, one of its own subjects charged with the commission of crime within its territory, and although it may be conceded that there is no national obligation to make such a surrender on a demand therefore, unless it is acknowledged by treaty or by statute law, yet a nation is never bound to furnish asylum to dangerous criminals who are offenders against the human race; and it is believed that if, in any case, the comity could with propriety be practiced, the one which is understood to have called forth the resolution furnished a just occasion for its exercise.[140]

Although the United States has rarely granted extradition on the basis of comity or reciprocity, it has on occasion requested extradition on these bases. Usually, its request on the basis of comity has been coupled with the observation that the United States would be unable to reciprocate if the requested state sought extradition from the United States in the absence of a treaty.[141] The United States has resorted to this basis to supplement treaty relations when the applicable extradition treaty does not include, as an extraditable offense, the offense for which the relator has been indicted. For example, in *United States v.*

---

related practices; (8) Torture; (9) Unlawful human experimentation; (10) Piracy; (11) Offenses against international maritime navigation; (12) Unlawful seizure of aircraft, sabotage and related crimes; (13) Attacks against internationally protected persons; (14) Taking of hostages; (15) Unlawful use of the mails (for terror-violence); (16) Drug offenses (international); (17) Destruction and/or theft of national treasures and cultural heritage; (18) Environmental violations; (19) Cutting of submarine cables; (20) International traffic in obscene materials; (21) Counterfeiting (currency); (22) Bribery of foreign public officials; (23) Theft of nuclear materials; (24) Mercenarism; (25) Crimes Against United Nations Personnel. BASSIOUNI, ICL CONVENTIONS, *supra* note 10.

[138] *See* MOORE, EXTRADITION *supra* note 1, at 33-35 (discussing the *Arguelles* case); WHITEMAN DIGEST *supra* note 1, at 744-45 (discussing the *Koveleskie* case).

[139] *See* MOORE, EXTRADITION *supra* note 1, at 33-35.

[140] *Id.* at 35.

[141] For earlier cases where the United States requested extradition on the basis of comity, *see* MOORE, EXTRADITION *supra* note 1, at 41-42.

Fiocconi,[142] Italy surrendered the relators to the United States in an act of comity. The United States' request was not based on its extradition treaty with Italy because the treaty did not list the crime of conspiracy to import heroin, the offense for which extradition was requested, as an extraditable offense.[143] However, Italy granted extradition and surrendered the relators to the United States.[144]

In a few instances occurring in the 1800's, the United States requested extradition with the assurance that it would reciprocate, even though the United States had no extradition treaty with the requested states. For example, in 1855, when the United States requested that Spain extradite an individual charged with murder in New York, it noted that the extradition "would be considered as an act of courtesy which would be appreciated and reciprocated."[145] Similarly, in 1878, the United States requested that Portugal extradite an individual who had been charged with embezzlement in the United States.[146] The Portuguese government responded that it would be willing to comply if the proper documents were provided, and expressed the hope that "if at any time [the Portuguese government] has to address a requisition of like nature to the government of the United States, the same would be received with equal good will."[147] The United States Government answered that "such application will meet with an equally prompt and effectual response. [We] are fully alive to the courtesy shown by [the Portuguese government] in this instance, and will not fail to give a like evidence of its good feeling to any similar application made to it."[148] The relator was extradited to the United States. These commitments of reciprocity were of questionable legal validity in the absence of a treaty, as evidenced by the fact that in 1833 and 1888, when the Portuguese government requested that the United States extradite a fugitive and referred to the case discussed above, the United States refused extradition on the grounds that no treaty existed between Portugal and the United States.[149]

It should be noted, however, that the United States will rely on other forms of *ad hoc* arrangements to secure extradition in the absence of a formal treaty. This has been the case with Egypt, where in at least one case, the United States relied on a "letter of understanding" to obtain the surrender of an Israeli citizen arrested in Egypt at the request of the United States Government.[150] The United States would not be able to surrender anyone from this

---

142 United States v. Fiocconi, 462 F.2d 475 (2d Cir. 1972).

143 *See* BASSIOUNI, EXTRADITION, *supra* note 1, at Ch. VII.

144 The United States also resorted to comity as the basis of its requests when it asked Lebanon to extradite an individual to face charges of drug trafficking, as there was no extradition treaty between Lebanon and the United States at that time. *See* United States v. Paroutian, 299 F.2d 486 (2d Cir. 1962), *aff'd on other grounds*, 319 F.2d 661 (2d Cir. 1963), *cert. denied*, 375 U.S. 981 (1964). Similarly, the United States requested that Italy extradite Settimo Accardi to face prosecution on drug smuggling charges as an act of comity, because its extradition treaty did not include these charges as an extraditable offense. *See* United States v. Accardi, 241 F. Supp. 119 (S.D.N.Y. 1964), *aff'd*, 342 F.2d 697 (2d Cir.), *cert. denied*, 382 U.S. 954 (1965); *see also* Alona Evans, *Legal Bases of Extradition in the United States*, 3 N.Y.L.F. 525, 532-33 (1970). For a Commonwealth position, see Ivan A. Shearer, *Extradition Without a Treaty*, 49 AUSTL. L.J. 116 (1975).

145 *See* MOORE, EXTRADITION *supra* note 1, at 43 (discussing the *Baker* case).

146 *See id.* at 43-45 (discussing the *Angell* case).

147 *Id.* at 45.

148 *Id.*

149 *Id.*

150 *See* United States v. Levy, 947 F.2d 1032 (2d Cir. 1991); United States v. Levy, 1991 U.S. Dist. LEXIS 6332 (E.D.N.Y. May 8, 1991); United States v. Levy, 25 F.3d 146 (2d Cir. June 3, 1994).

country on such a basis, however, as it would violate Title 18 § 3183 requiring a treaty as a pre-condition of extradition.[151]

Status of Forces Agreements

The United States relies on status of forces agreements (SOFAs) as an alternative basis for rendition,[152] but does not consider the practice as part of extradition. SOFAs represent an agreement between the United States and a host state of United States armed forces regarding, *inter alia*, the criminal jurisdiction which either state may have over United States armed services personnel who have allegedly engaged in criminal conduct in the host state. The typical SOFA provides that the United States has the primary right to submit the accused service-person or civilian employee to criminal prosecution if the alleged offense was committed in the performance of official duty or if it was directed against the property or person of the United States military community. All other offenses, on the other hand, are within the primary criminal jurisdiction of the host country. Either state may, however, relinquish its primary jurisdiction to the other state party.[153]

SOFAs also set forth the rendition procedures. Usually, a member of the United States armed services, who is accused of a criminal offense, in the host state will be held in custody by the United States armed forces until the imposition of a criminal sentence by the judiciary of the host state. The detention by United States military authorities is based on the Uniform Code of Military Justice.[154] The convicted service-person is delivered by the United States military authorities to the host state to serve the judicially-imposed sentence.[155]

Surrender of a member of United States armed forces for foreign trial pursuant to a SOFA has been upheld by the United States Supreme Court.[156] A landmark case is *Holmes*

---

[151] *See, e.g.*, United States v. Rauscher, 119 U.S. 407 (1886).

[152] *See generally* James R. Coker, *The Status of Visiting Military Forces in Europe: NATO-SOFA, A Comparison, in* M. CHERIF BASSIOUNI & VED P. NANDA, A TREATISE ON INTERNATIONAL CRIMINAL LAW 115 (1973).

[153] *See, e.g.*, Agreement Between the Parties to the North Atlantic Treaty Regarding the Status of Their Forces, June, 19 1951, 4 U.S.T. 1792, T.I.A.S. No. 2846 [NATO SOFA], art. VII; *see also* William J. Norton, *United States' Obligations Under Status of Forces Agreements: A New Method of Extradition?* 5 GA. J. INT'L & COMP.L.1 (1975).

[154] 10 U.S.C. § 810 (1988).

[155] *See* Norton, *supra* note 153, at 17-18.

[156] *See* Wilson v. Girard, 354 U.S. 524 (1957); *see also* Holmes v. Laird, 459 F.2d 1211 (D.C. Cir.), *cert. denied*, 409 U.S. 869 (1972); Williams v. Rogers, 449 F.2d 513 (8th Cir. 1971), *cert. denied*, 405 U.S. 926 (1972); Cozart v. Wilson, 236 F.2d 732 (D.C. Cir.), *vacated*, 352 U.S. 884 (1956); United States *ex rel.* Stone v. Robinson, 309 F. Supp. 1261 (W.D. Pa.), *aff'd*, 431 F.2d 548 (3d Cir. 1970); Smallwood v. Clifford, 286 F. Supp. 97 (D.D.C. 1968). In Plaster v. United States, 720 F.2d 340 (1983), the Fourth Circuit considered the return of a former United States serviceman to West Germany pursuant to the NATO SOFA. Under that agreement, the United States would retain jurisdiction only over those offenses committed by servicemen on a United States military base or that arose out of the performance of an official duty. Germany could thus claim jurisdiction over Plaster for the crime of murder. However, the treaty allowed Germany to waive its jurisdiction in favor of the United States

In 1959, the United States and Germany signed a Supplementary Agreement to the SOFA Treaty, July 1, 1963, T.I.A.S. No. 5351. The agreement provided, *inter alia*, that Germany would automatically waive its jurisdiction in favor of United States military courts at the request of the United States. Germany could recall its waiver only by notifying the United States within twenty-one days of receipt of a request for waiver.

Plaster, a serviceman, had been suspected of murder in Germany, but had fled to the United States. While in custody for a murder committed in Wisconsin, Plaster allegedly confessed to the German murder. The United States formally notified Germany of its request of a waiver of Germany's jurisdiction. Germany urged the trial of Plaster *v. Laird.*[157] In *Holmes*, American servicemen stationed in Germany requested a United States federal court to enjoin their surrender to Germany to serve criminal sentences imposed upon them by German courts. The servicemen had been convicted of attempted rape and related offenses committed in Germany. Shortly before the pronouncement of the German appellate court decision affirming their convictions, they left West Germany without authorization and returned to the United States. Thereafter, they surrendered to United States Army officials and initiated litigation in a federal district court to prevent their rendition to Germany. They claimed primarily that the German court's failure to provide the procedural guarantees set forth in the applicable SOFA rendered their convictions invalid.

The Holmes court rejected these claims on the grounds that it did not have the authority to review the sufficiency of the German courts' determinations. In reaching this conclusion, the Holmes court relied upon *Neely v. Henkel*,[158] where a United States citizen contended that a federal statute authorizing extradition pursuant to a treaty was unconstitutional because it failed to secure to the accused surrendered to a foreign state for trial in its tribunals those constitutional rights provided in the United States. The *Holmes* court determined that the *Neely* court's rejection of such a claim was controlling:

> What we learn from *Neely* is that a surrender of an American citizen required by treaty for purposes of a foreign criminal proceeding is unimpaired by an absence in the foreign judicial system of safeguards in all respects equivalent to those constitutionally enjoined upon American trials. We do not believe that [this] teaching has been eroded by time, nor that the slight factual differences between the pretrial extradition there and the post-conviction surrender here removes the instant situation from *Neely's* ambit. We conclude, then, that the Constitution erects no barrier to appellant's surrender to the Federal Republic.[159]

The *Holmes* decision demonstrates the similarity between SOFAs and extradition treaties. Although SOFAs and extradition treaties are similar in some respects, there are several important distinctions between them.[160] For example, SOFAs do not require a judicial determination by a United States tribunal before surrender of the national to the host state, nor do they allow the United States executive's exercise of discretion to refuse surrender.[161] Both of these provisions are usually included in extradition treaties, however, and are required by United States legislation.[162] In addition, SOFAs generally cover an entire range of criminal conduct, which permits the host country's exercise of primary jurisdiction. Extradition treaties, on the other hand, are applicable only to those criminal offenses specifically enumerated in the treaty. Furthermore, although an extradition treaty may

---

and another serviceman for the German murder by an American military court, but did not recall its waiver. The Army filed formal court-martial charges against Plaster and the other serviceman. The Army ceased its pursuit of the prosecution when the Supreme Court handed down the *Miranda* decision, thus rendering the confession potentially inadmissible. Ultimately the Army promised Plaster transnational immunity from prosecution for the German murder if he agreed to testify against the other serviceman. Miranda v. Arizona, 396 U.S. 868 (1969).

157 Holmes v. Laird, 459 F.2d 1211 (D.C. Cir.), *cert. denied*, 409 U.S. 869 (1972).

158 Neely v. Henkel, 180 U.S. 109 (1901).

159 *Holmes*, 459 F.2d at 1219.

160 *See generally* Norton, *supra* note 153.

161 *Id.* at 26.

162 18 U.S.C. § 3184 *et seq.* (1996).

prohibit a state's surrender of its own nationals to face prosecution in a foreign state, a SOFA may nevertheless permit such surrender if the accused was a member of the armed forces or a civilian employee of the armed forces when the alleged offense was committed in the host country.

Extradition Requests

The United States as a Requesting State

Requests for extradition from the U.S. usually originate with the prosecuting authority having jurisdiction in the criminal case in question, whether federal or state. Extradition requests are prepared by the Department of Justice's Office of International Affairs, [DOJ/OIA] on the basis of a request from a federal prosecutor, a state governor, state attorney-general, or county prosecutor. Before such a formal request is made, DOJ/OIA will make an informal determination as to whether or not there are sufficient legal grounds for extradition.

Once DOJ/OIA determines that an extradition request can be presented to a foreign government, it will work with the prosecutor in the preparation of the necessary documentation. The extradition documentation will usually consist of an affidavit by the prosecutor stating the charge or charges, summarizing the facts, describing the elements of the offense or offenses charged, and relating these charges to the applicable treaty which makes such an offense or offenses extraditable, and stating that the applicable statute of limitations has not expired. The documents will also contain a copy of the applicable criminal code violation and statute of limitations. A certified copy of the arrest warrant and the indictment, (or information), or judgment of a conviction (whichever is applicable) for each offense for which the accused is sought, will have to be attached. The prosecuting authority will also attach supporting evidence, sufficient to make out a *prima facie* case against the accused and to identify him, usually in the form of an affidavit by a law enforcement officer. The documentation will be reviewed by DOJ/OIA for its compliance with the treaty's requirements and any requirements under the laws of the requested state.

Once the appropriate documentation is completed, DOJ/OIA will forward it to the Department of State, Office of Legal Advisors (DOS/L), who will review the request's implications for foreign policy and political concerns. DOS/L will then prepare the formal request signed by the Secretary of State or his designee to which the documentation is attached, and it is then transmitted to the U.S. embassy in the requested state, which submits the request to the requested state's ministry of foreign affairs, which then forwards it to its ministry of justice, which then forwards it to appropriate prosecuting office or court, depending upon that country's legal system.

The United States as a Requested State

Requests by a foreign state to the United States are submitted through the diplomatic channel to DOS/L, that is, by either the U.S. embassy in the requesting state, or through the requesting state's embassy in Washington, D.C. The foreign embassy will receive the request either from its own ministry of foreign affairs or from its ministry of justice, depending upon each country's internal administrative procedure.

The request and documentation submitted to the U.S. will have to comply with the treaty requirements. All documents must be translated into English and authenticated by the appropriate U.S. consul in the requesting state. DOS/L will then transmit the request to DOJ/OIA for review. If any technical questions arise during the review as to the form or substance of the request, it will be returned to the requesting state either through the same diplomatic channel or informally through the diplomatic representative of the requesting state working with DOS/L and DOJ/OIA.

There is no time limit for extradition requests other than the applicable statute of limitation, as the treaty may provide.

If a relator is requested by more than one country, the applicable treaties may specify the factors the executive must or may take into account to determine which request has priority. These factors are usually jurisdictional, such as in whose territory did the relator commit the offense[163] or the relative seriousness of the crimes charged,[164] before deciding which request should be given priority. Subject to the relevant treaties, the determination of priority is discretionary with the executive.

When the request is deemed in compliance with the applicable treaty, it will be forwarded by DOJ/OIA to the appropriate federal prosecuting authority in the federal district where the person sought is known or believed to be found. If the person's whereabouts are not known, the request will be retained by DOJ/OIA and a fugitive arrest warrant will be sought from the Federal District Court in the District of Columbia. If what is called an "Interpol arrest warrant" already exists and has been delivered to the FBI through the Interpol liaison office (which operates with the FBI), that warrant shall be sent by the FBI to DOJ/OIA, who will then send it to the U.S. Attorney in the federal district wherein the person is to be arrested; and that federal district court will have jurisdiction in the extradition proceedings to follow. If the individual is arrested elsewhere, the federal district court closest to the place of arrest will have jurisdiction, and the proceedings will be conducted in that district court.

---

[163] *See, e.g.*, Multilateral Convention on Extradition, signed at Montevideo, Dec. 26, 1933, art. 7, 49 Stat. 3111, 165 U.N.T.S. 45, which reads:

> [w]hen the extradition of a person is sought by several States for the same offense, preference will be given to the State in whose territory said offense was committed. If he is sought for several offenses, preference will be given to the State within whose bounds shall have been committed the offense which has the greatest penalty according to the law of the surrendering State. If the case is one of different acts which the State from which extradition is sought esteems of equal gravity, the preference will be determined by the priority of the request.

[164] *See, e.g.*, Extradition Treaty between the United States and the United Kingdom and Northern Ireland, Jan. 21, 1977, art. 10, 28 U.S.T. 227, 232-33, T.I.A.S. No. 8468, which provides:

> [i]f the extradition of a person is requested concurrently by one of the Contracting Parties and by another State or States, either for the same offense or for different offenses, the requested Party shall make its decision in so far as its law allows, having regard to all the circumstances, including the provisions in this regard in any Agreements in force between the requesting States, the relative seriousness and place of commission of the offenses, the respective dates of the requests, the nationality of the person sought and the possibility of subsequent extradition to another State.

Provisional Arrest in the United States

Prior to the filing of a formal extradition request a requesting state may, if the applicable treaty permits it, request the provisional arrest of the relator. Provisional arrest is an arrest and detainment made prior to, and in contemplation of, a formal extradition request. Such an order can only be issued by a Federal Judge or U.S. magistrate. The legal basis for such a provisional arrest must be an applicable treaty provision because the extradition statute does not specifically authorize provisional arrest. The rationale for provisional arrest is urgency to avoid risk of flight pending the preparation and transmittal of the extradition request and accompanying documentation by the requesting state. Provisional arrest must nonetheless be supported by "probable cause," without which the arrest would violate the fourth and fifth amendments of the Constitution. In practice, urgency is seldom determined by the Judge or magistrate issuing the arrest warrant, and "probable cause" is hardly established, yet the practice has, so far, eluded constitutional scrutiny.

Existing treaties provide for a period of up to 60 days of provisional arrest, after which, if no formal extradition request is presented, the relator must be released. If the request is presented within the period of time provided by the treaty, the provisional arrest warrant issued by a judge or magistrate will have to be replaced by another arrest warrant based on the extradition complaint prepared by the U.S. on the basis of the request.

The mechanics of provisional arrest are informal. The liaison office of Interpol, usually located within the principal or central law enforcement agency of each Interpol member state, will send a telex or facsimile message to the Interpol liaison office of the state wherein the person is believed to be located. In the U.S., the liaison office is part of the FBI. If the whereabouts of the person sought are unknown, then Interpol Headquarters (Lyon, France) will issue an "international warrant," or an "alert," or both, to all or some of its liaison stations. Such alerts are coded blue or red depending upon the dangerousness of the person sought and the urgency and importance which the requested state attaches to the apprehension of that individual. Immigration and customs agencies will also be advised. Because of the rapidly growing computerization of such agencies and law enforcement in general worldwide, such notifications are promptly recorded in the databases of the different law enforcement agencies, leading to greater effectiveness in tracking and apprehending wanted offenders. There are, regrettably, occasional problems with mistaken identities as well as problems with subsequent removal of erroneous data from these computerized files.

In *Caltagirone v. Grant*[165] the Second Circuit, upholding the need for "probable cause," avoided, nonetheless, reaching the issue of whether the Fourth Amendment also required an independent determination by a judge of "probable cause" based on competent and sufficient evidence. In a recent landmark decision, *Parretti v. United States,* the Ninth Circuit held that the Fourth Amendment requires such a finding for provisional arrest, holding that the "clarity of this (the Fourth Amendment's) language allows for no exceptions, regardless whether the government's purpose in making the arrest is to enforce treaties or our own

---

[165] Caltagirone v. Grant, 629 F.2d 739, 748 (2nd Cir. 1980) (Fourth Amendment and treaty language required Italy to show probable cause to justify provisional arrest); United States v. Williams, 480 F. Supp. 482, 485 (D. Mass.), *rev'd on other grounds*, 611 F.2d 914 (1st Cir. 1979).

domestic law."[166] In practice, however, most courts have accepted something less than "probable cause" for provisional arrest.[167]

The informality of that process and its reliance on law enforcement and intelligence agencies cooperation makes the legal process in the U.S. less than balanced with respect to relators' rights. U.S. judges will only be able to rely on the representations of the Government, which are not always impartial or accurate, and relators will have very little to rely upon in arguing lack of "probable cause" and bail.[168] On occasion, the Government will argue on the basis of oral representations made by the requesting state which subsequently do not turn out to be supported by evidence.

What is particularly troublesome is that the process *de facto* reverses the presumption of innocence as it is otherwise applied in the U.S.'s adversarial and accusatorial system of criminal justice and it therefore raises "due process" issues.[169]

Initiation of the Formal Proceedings

The formal part of the extradition proceedings is the hearing pursuant to section 3184. It is, however, proceeded by a "complaint" filed by the Government and accompanied by the submissions of the requesting state. It is on the basis of the "complaint" and supporting documents that the extradition hearing is held. The Government can rest on these submissions, supplement with additional documentary evidence, or by oral testimony. The relator will file an "answer" to the "complaint" and attach, if he wants, supporting documents. These documents are deemed evidence and cannot contradict the Government's evidence, but only explain it. The relator can also present additional evidence at the hearing and testimony, provided that it is explanatory and not contradictory of the governments's evidence.[170]

Upon filing a "complaint," a magistrate or judge will issue a warrant for the arrest of the relator. The warrant is valid anywhere in the United States, and any federal judicial officer can hear the case even if he did not issue the warrant.[171] If the relator is already in custody under a "Provisional arrest warrant," the warrant issued pursuant to the "complaint" shall

---

166 Parretti v. United States, 122 F.3d 758 (1997). The court reversed the district court's denial of Parretti's *habeas corpus* petition, reasoning that they would not "equate the existence of a foreign arrest warrant with a showing of probable cause."

167 *In re* Russell, 805 F.2d 1215, 1217 (5th Cir. 1986) (holding that while the foreign government did show probable cause to justify provisional arrest, governments may not need to show probable cause to justify provisional arrest).

168 *Leitner*, 784 F.2d at 160 (granting bail in a provisional arrest situation); United States v. Messina, 566 F. Supp. 740, 742 (E.D.N.Y. 1983) (acknowledging a liberalization of the bail standard in provisional arrest). *But see In re* Extradition of Smyth, 976 F.2d 1535 (9th Cir. 1992) (reversing lower court's decision to grant Smyth bail during provisional arrest period; the lower court had relied on the particular facts and the liberalizing trend in provisional arrest bail).

169 Such issues are raised but seldom resolved in favor of the relator. *See* United States v. Leitner, 784 F.2d 159, 160 (2nd Cir. 1986); *In re* Russell, 805 F.2d 1215, 1218 (5th Cir. 1986).

170 The Department of Justice acting through the U.S. Attorney for that District represents the requesting state.

171 Jiminez v. Aristiguieta, 311 F.2d 547, 553 (5th Cir. 1962) (the court held that the warrant was returnable before any justice, judge or magistrate authorized to hear evidence of criminality in extradition cases under 18 U.S.C. § 3184); *In re* Farez, 8 F. Cas. 1007 (C.C.S.D.N.Y. 1870) (No. 4,645), the court held that if the warrant was issued by a commissioner his authority to do so had to appear on the warrant. *See also In re* Henrich, 11 F. Cas. 1143, 1146 (C.C.S.D.N.Y. 1867) (No. 6,369); Pettit v. Walshe, 194 U.S. 205, 217-219 (1904).

substantiate the "Provisional arrest warrant." Once the relator is in custody, an initial hearing prior to the extradition hearing pursuant to section 3184 will take place to verify the identity of the person arrested and also to receive the relator's bail request. Subsequently, a hearing is held pursuant to section 3184 to determine if "probable cause" and other treaty requirements exist to extradite.[172] If the extradition magistrate finds that extradition is warranted, he will issue a warrant placing the relator in detention until the Secretary of State effectuates the surrender of the relator.[173] The court must certify a copy of the Order along with a copy of all testimony in the case to the Secretary of State.[174] Section 3188 requires that the Secretary of State surrender the relator within two calender months (which are tolled by the relator's opposition to effectuate the surrender), otherwise the relator shall be released and that, for all practical purposes, terminates the earlier extradition proceedings. The Secretary of State may then condition extradition or refuse to surrender on the basis of "Executive Discretion."

Extradition proceedings are not deemed criminal proceedings, and such cases are docketed as Miscellaneous. The rules of procedure and evidence applicable to criminal cases are not applicable except for basic "due process" and "fundamental fairness" requirements. The extradition magistrate, who can also be a Federal District Court Judge, does not determine the relator's guilt or innocence and therefore evidence of innocence is not allowed to be presented by the relator.

The Complaint

The Government initiates extradition proceedings by filing a "complaint" with a U.S. magistrate or Federal District Court judge, charging the person sought in accordance with the applicable treaty, with having committed an extraditable offense within the jurisdiction of the requesting state.[175] The "complaint" is akin to an indictment or information,[176] and must therefore inform the relator of the charges against him to allow the relator to argue lack of "probable cause"[177] and to raise any defenses allowed under the treaty.

The following information is to be included in a complaint: the identity of the person sought and relevant personal information; reference to the applicable treaty in force;[178] the nature of the offense charged and that it is extraditable under the terms of the treaty;[179] that

---

172 18 U.S.C. § 3184 (1994).

173 *Id.*

174 *Id.*

175 18 U.S.C. § 3184 (1994).

176 *See* FED. R. CRIM. P. 7. The complaint must satisfy the requirements of the applicable treaty and relevant legislation, and these require that it set forth the basic facts upon which it is founded. It is to that extent akin to any other federal criminal complaint, and it can be amended to comply with these requirements or with any other order by the court requiring more specificity. It is also possible for the Government to amend the complaint after its filing if new charges are brought against the relator. The converse is also true. Whenever the United States is the requesting state, it can amend its original request to take into account a superseding indictment.

177 *In re* Wise, 168 F. Supp. 366, 369 (S.D.Tex. 1967); *Ex parte* Sternaman, 77 F. 595, 596 (C.C.D.C.N.Y. 1896).

178 *See, generally*, Terlinden v. Ames, 184 U.S. 270, 282 (1902); United States v. Rauscher, 119 U.S. 407, 410 (1886); Argento v. Horn, 241 F.2d 258, 259 (6th Cir.), *cert. denied*, 355 U.S. 818, *reh'g denied*, 355 U.S. 885 (1957); Artukovic v. Boyle, 107 F. Supp. 11, 28 (S.D.Cal. 1952); United States v. Stockinger, 269 F.2d 681, 682 (2nd Cir.), *cert. denied*, 361 U.S. 913 (1959).

179 18 U.S.C. § 3184; Yordi v. Nolte, 215 U.S. 227 (1909); Sidali v. INS, 107 F.3d 191 (3rd Cir. 1997).

the offense in question is also a crime under United States federal law or the laws of the state wherein the district court is located (known as the principle of "double criminality");[180] that there are no official treaty defenses; a summary of the factual circumstances of the alleged offense; a showing that "probable cause" exists; reference to the foreign criminal law that has been infringed; reference to the order or warrant of arrest or judgment of conviction.

The following documents must be attached to the complaint: a certified copy of the arrest warrant, charging instrument, or judgment of conviction in the requesting state issued by its competent authorities, showing the offense charged and any other documents on which the complaint is based; a sworn or verified statement by the appropriate foreign legal authority describing the facts and the relevant documents; accompanying affidavits, documents and evidence on the applicable foreign law and the facts alleged.[181]

The foreign documents submitted must be duly certified by the appropriate issuing authority and authenticated by the United States Consul accredited in the requesting state.[182] All foreign documents must also be translated, subscribed or sworn to, and authenticated by the competent United States Consul.

Bail[183]

As stated above, the initial hearing before a U.S. magistrate or judge is to determine whether the person arrested is the one named in the arrest warrant and to allow arguments by the relator for admission to bail. But the bail issue can be raised at any other stage of the proceeding. The Supreme Court has not held so far that the Sixth Amendment to the U.S. Constitution guaranteeing bail is applicable to extradition, but has held that bail can be granted in such cases. In *Wright v. Henkel*, the Supreme Court held that "bail should not ordinarily be granted in cases of foreign extradition," but may be granted in cases of "special circumstances."[184] Federal Courts have recognized their power to grant bail, even though there is no statutory or treaty provision authorizing bail.[185] However, the constitutional presumption in favor of bail afforded defendants in U.S. criminal proceedings is reversed,

---

[180] *Stockinger*, 269 F.2d at 684.

[181] Desmond v. Eggers, 18 F.2d 503, 504 (9th Cir. 1927). *See also* Glucksman v. Henkel, 221 U.S. 508, 514 (1911); Rice v. Ames, 180 U.S. 371, 375-76 (1901). *But see* United States *ex rel.* McNamara v. Henkel, 46 F.2d 84 (S.D.N.Y. 1912) (holding that a complaint based on information and belief made pursuant to a telegraphic request without supporting documents was sufficient, provided the request was made by a person whom the United States authorities were justified in believing). One of the most frequent objections to an extradition complaint based on information and belief is that the information, the certifications, the depositions, etc., are all hearsay. However, such testimony is admissible in the extradition hearing. *Argento*, 241 F.2d at 263.

[182] Any foreign documents presented either to the executive or judicial branch in an extradition proceeding must be authenticated by the principal diplomatic or consular officer of the United States in the requesting state. This officer must certify that the documents are entitled to be received for similar purposes, *i.e.*, as evidence of criminality, in the requesting state. *See* 18 U.S.C. § 3190 (1994), *see also* In re Oteiza y Cortes, 136 U.S. 330, 336 (1890); Grin v. Shine, 187 U.S. 181, 190 (1902); Collins v. Loisel, 259 U.S. 309, 313 (1922); O'Brien v. Rozman, 554 F.2d 780 (6th Cir. 1977); United States v. Galanis, 429 F. Supp. 1215 (D. Conn. 1977).

[183] *See* BASSIOUNI, EXTRADITION, *supra* note 1, at 692-698. For other discussions of bail in U.S. extradition, *see* John G. Kester, *Some Myths of United States Extradition Law*, 76 GEO. L.J. 1441, 1449 (1988); Note, *A Recommended Approach to Bail in International Extradition Cases*, 86 MICH. L. REV. 599 (1987).

[184] Wright v. Henkel, 190 U.S. 40, 63 (1903).

[185] *Id.* at 63; In re Mitchell, 171 F. 289, 290 (C.C.S.D.N.Y. 1909).

with respect to extradition, placing the burden on the relator to prove he is entitled to bail under the applicable standard.[186]

Although being a flight risk is the operative factor in criminal cases, proof that the relator is not a flight risk does not *per se* suffice for bail.[187] The Government has successfully argued in many extradition cases that bail may frustrate the United States' treaty obligations toward the requesting state.

The "special circumstances" test is an ambiguous one, which varies in its application from Circuit to Circuit. A review of the cases indicates some inroads into the presumption against bail.[188] Although flight risk may be the most significant factor, many other factors are also considered, such as the relator's ties to the community[189] and the nature of the crime charged.[190] "Special Circumstances" deal with the relator and with the case itself. They include: complexity of the case and the need of the relator to assist counsel in preparing his defense;[191] projected delay in the extradition hearing;[192] serious health problems of the relator;[193] the probability of defeating the extradition;[194] other extradition cases with similar circumstances in which bail was granted;[195] the overt political nature of motivation of the requested state,[196] and other reasons.[197] In *Parretti v. United States,*[198] the Ninth Circuit held that a Constitutional right to bail exists, but that recent decision departs from the ruling of all other circuits.

---

186 Beaulieu v. Hartigan, 554 F.2d 1, 2 (1st Cir. 1977) ("[u]nlike the situation for domestic crimes, there is no presumption favoring bail. The reverse is rather the case.").

187 Proof that relator is not a flight risk is not, on its own, sufficient to warrant bail in extradition. Salerno v. United States, 878 F.2d 317, 318 (9th Cir. 1989); Kamrin v. United States 725 F.2d 1225, 1228 (9th Cir. 1984).

188 *See, Messina*, 566 F. Supp. at 742, 745 (denying bail)

189 *In Re* Kirby, *et al*, 106 F.2d 855 (9th Cir. 1997); *In re Sutton*, 898 F. Supp. 691, 695 (E.D. Mo. 1995).

190 Magisano v. Locke, 545 F.2d 1228, 1230 (9th Cir. 1976); *Leitner*, 784 F.2d at 160; BASSIOUNI, EXTRADITION, *supra* note 1, at 696.

191 *U.S. v. Taitz*, 130 F.R.D. 442, 445-446 (S.D. Cal. 1990).

192 In the matter of the Requested Extradition of Kirby, et al, 106 F.3d 855 (9th Cir. 1997); Salerno v. United States, 878 F.2d 317 (9th Cir. 1989); United States v. Kin-Hong, 83 F.3d 523, 524 (1st Cir. 1996) (stating that "special circumstances' may include a delayed extradition hearing"); *In re* Extradition of Morales, 906 F. Supp. 1368, 1374-75 (S.D. Cal. 1995) ("special circumstances" existed when, after being held for six months on one charge, the magistrate dismissed the complaint against the relator for lack of probable cause and the United States, at the request of the foreign government, filed a new complaint charging a different offense, thus delaying conclusion of the matter); *McNamara*, 46 F.2d at 84 ("[w]hen the examination day comes and the [government] is not ready to proceed after having had a reasonable opportunity to communicate with the region from whence the request for extradition emanated, it is then time enough to ask for bail").

193 *In re* Extradition of Siegmund, 887 F. Supp. 1383, 1385-86 (D. Nev. 1995); *Taitz*, 130 F.R.D. at 444-45.

194 *Id*; *Salerno*, 878 F.2d at 317; *In re* Extradition of Mainero, 950 F. Supp. 290 (S.D. Cal. 1996).

195 In an unusual case arising out of an PIRA prison break out in 1983, the Ninth Circuit Court of Appeals upheld the district court's bail decision, in part because another alleged PIRA member, in a completely separate proceeding, had received bail. *Kirby*, 106 F.3d at 863 ("[n]onetheless, in a rough sense, the argument that Artt, Brennan, and Kirby should be released on bail to achieve parity with Smyth has some claim to being considered a 'special circumstance.'")

196 *Kirby*, 106 F.3d at 865 ("[w]e are reasonably convinced that a grant of bail will contribute more to promoting harmony between the supporters of the cause of the Catholics in Northern Ireland and those whose interests are otherwise, than would a denial of bail because of any dissatisfaction we might have with the 'special circumstances' upon which the district court relied.")

197 Hu Yau-Leung v. Soscia, 649 F.2d 914 (2nd Cir. 1981) (age and background); *Taitz*, 130 F.R.D. at 445-446 (no facilities to practice religion).

198 *Parette*, 122 F.3d 758.

Discovery

Prior to the extradition hearing, the relator has the right to receive a copy of the extradition "complaint," the requesting state's request and the documentation supporting it. He also has a limited right of discovery in the discretion of the court unless the treaty specifies otherwise. During these proceedings as well as throughout the entire extradition process, the relator has the right to be represented by counsel of choice or to a court appointed counsel if such a person has no means to secure private counsel.

Neither the extradition statute or most treaties allow for discovery of documents, the identification of witnesses, depositions and the like which may be relevant to the relator's committal for extradition. In limited instances, the applicable treaty may contemplate discovery.[199] However, a series of decisions have found that the court retains inherent authority to grant discovery in extradition proceedings.[200] Usually discovery is limited to the issues before the court, and will not encompass the underlying merits of the charge.[201] It is still an open question whether the government must turn over "exculpatory" evidence (defined not as evidence going to innocence, but that favorable to the relator and relevant to issues cognizable in extradition proceedings, e.g. identity) it possesses or has knowledge of to the relator, under the constitutional requirements of *Brady v. Maryland.*[202]

The Extradition Hearing and "Probable Cause."

The extradition hearing is governed by Section 3184. The issue is essentially whether there exists "probable cause" to commit the relator for extradition in accordance with the extradition "complaint," the applicable treaty and U.S. law, and whether any treaty or statutory defenses, exceptions or exclusions apply which would deny extradition. A court will commit a relator for extradition where:

---

199 *See In re* Extradition of McMullen, 1988 U.S. Dist LEXIS 7201 (S.D.N.Y. 1988) (discovery granted under Article 3(a) of the Supplemental Extradition Treaty between the U.S. and U.K.).

200 *See* Koskotas v. Roche, 931 F.2d 169, 175 (1st Cir. 1991); Quinn v. Robinson, 783 F.2d 776, 817 n.41 (9th Cir.), *cert. denied,* 479 U.S. 882 (1986); Jhirad v. Ferrandina, 363 F. Supp. 34, 37 (S.D.N.Y. 1973), *aff'd* 536 F.2d 478 (2nd Cir. 1976); First Nat'l City Bank of New York v. Aristeguieta, 287 F.2d 219, 226 (2d Cir. 1960), *vacated as moot,* 84 S. Ct. 144 (1963). *But see In re* Extradition of Singh, 123 F.R.D. 108, 115-16 (D.N.J.1987).

201 *Koskotas,* 931 F.2d at 175 (discovery is within the discretion of the magistrate and narrow in scope); Jhirad v. Ferrandina, 536 F.2d 478, 484 (same); Emami v. United States Dist. Court for Northern District of California, 834 F.2d 1444, 1452 (9th Cir. 1987) (quoting *Quinn,* 783 F.2d at 817 n.41) (courts should be aware that "extradition proceedings are not to be converted into a dress rehearsal for trial" and discovery limited to "whether the resolution of the contested issue would be appreciably advanced by the requested discovery").

202 Demjanjuk v. Petrovsky, 10 F.3d 338, 353 (6th Cir. 1993) ("[w]e believe Brady should be extended to cover denaturalization and extradition cases where the government seeks denaturalization or extradition based on proof of alleged criminal activities of the party proceeded against") *reh'g en banc denied,* Demjanjuk v. Petrovsky, 1994 U.S. App. LEXIS 3678 (6th Cir.), *cert. denied,* Rison v. Demjanjuk, 115 S. Ct. 295 (1994); Brady v. Maryland, 373 U.S. 83, 87 (1963) (holding that "the suppression by the prosecution of evidence favorable to an accused upon request violates due process where the evidence is material either to guilt or to punishment irrespective of the good faith or bad faith of the prosecution"). However, the evidence is restricted to those issues cognizable in an extradition hearing. *See* Gill v. Imundi, 1994 U.S. Dist. LEXIS 8037 (S.D.N.Y. 1994) (holding that *Demjanjuk* does not necessarily provide broader discovery rights). *But see* In The Matter of the Extradition of Koskotas, 127 F.R.D. 13 (D.C. Mass. 1989); *Singh,* 123 F.R.D. at 112 (holding that *Brady* does not apply to extradition); Merino v. United States Marshal, 326 F.2d 5, 12 (9th Cir. 1963), *cert. denied,* 377 U.S. 997 (1964) (same).

1. There exists a valid extradition treaty in force between the U.S. and the requesting state;[203]
2. The relator is the person sought;
3. The offenses charged are extraditable within the meaning of the treaty;
4. The offense charged satisfies the requirements of "double criminality";
5. There is "probable cause" to believe the relator committed the crimes charged;
6. The documents required are presented in accordance with U.S. law, subject to any treaty requirements; translated and duly authenticated by a United States Consul;
7. Other treaty requirements and statutory procedures are followed.
8. No treaty defense is applicable.

The Supreme Court defined "probable cause" as competent and sufficient legal evidence[204] based on federal standards[205] from which the court could reasonably conclude the relator committed the offense, and not simply that he is suspected of the offense. However, the quantum of evidence required clearly is not that which is sufficient to convict.[206] An extradition hearing is not a mini-trial on the issues of relator's guilt or innocence.

If the requesting state has already convicted the relator of the offense for which extradition is requested, a certified copy of the conviction is usually found to be convincing on its face to the judge determining "probable cause" to commit.[207]

The relator may not argue his innocence or present exculpatory evidence to the underlying charge,[208] but can present evidence that "explains" or "clarifies" the evidence presented by the government in an attempt to demonstrate a lack of "probable cause."[209]

---

203 18 U.S.C. § 3181 (a) (1994).

204 *Collins*, 259 U.S. at 316; Ahmad v. Wigen, 910 F.2d 1063, 1066 (2nd Cir. 1990).

205 There may be an issue of what standard of probable cause to apply, especially where a state's standard is stricter than the federal. Romeo v. Roache, 820 F.2d 540, 545 (1st Cir. 1987) (similar clause in the United States/Canada Extradition Treaty requires Massachusetts' standard of probable cause to apply). *But see* Koskotas v. Roche, 740 F. Supp. 904 (D. Mass. 1990) *aff'd*, Koskotas v. Roche, 931 F.2d 169 (1st Cir. 1991). The United States has changed treaty language that supported an application of the state standard of probable cause. Greci v. Birknes, 527 F.2d 956, 958, 959 (1st Cir. 1976) (interpreting the United States/Italy Extradition Treaty, noting that the U.S. and Italy had changed the language to "ensure that [the construction applying state law] would not be carried forward and that uniform federal law be applied"); *Koskotas*, 740 F. Supp at 913 n.13 (holding that the protocol to the U.S.-Greece extradition treaty served that same purpose as the change in the U.S. Italy treaty in *Greci*). Zanazanian v. United States, 729 F.2d 624-27 (9th Cir. 1984) (self-incriminating statements of co-conspirator sufficient to show probable cause to commit for extradition); Marquez v. Molinari, 1996 U.S. App. LEXIS 8218 (9th Cir. 1996) (same); *Sakaguchi v. Kaulukukui*, 520 F.2d 726, 730 (9th Cir. 1975) (hearsay sufficient); Bozilov v. Seifert, 983 F.2d 140, 143 (9th Cir. 1993) (uncorroborated statement sufficient).

206 The language in the U.S.-Can. Extradition Treaty is typical: "[E]xtradition shall be granted only if the evidence be found sufficient, according to the laws of the place where the person sought shall be found to justify his committal for trial", Extradition Treaty, Dec. 3, 1971, U.S.-Can., 27 U.S.T. 983, T.I.A.S. No. 8237.

207 Spatola v. United States, 925 F.2d 615, 618 (2nd Cir. 1991); Sidali v. I.N.S., 107 F.3d 191 (3rd Cir. 1997).

208 *See* Benson v. McMahon, 127 457, 462-63 (1888); *Glucksman*, 221 U.S. at 512; *Collins*, 259 U.S. at 316; Ward v. Rutherford, 921 F.2d 286, 287 (D.C. Cir. 1990), *cert. dismissed*, 501 U.S. 1225 (1991) (the judicial officer "thus performs an assignment in line with his or her accustomed task of determining if there is probable cause to hold a defendant to answer for the commission of an offense"); In re McMullen, 989 F.2d 603, 611 (2nd Cir.), *cert denied*, 510 U.S. 913 (1993). *See also* M. CHERIF BASSIOUNI, INTERNATIONAL EXTRADITION AND WORLD PUBLIC ORDER 524 (1974).

209 Charlton v. Kelly, 229 U.S. 447, 462 (1913); *Collins*, 259 U.S. at 316; *Sidali*, 107 F.3d at 194-195.

The issue of "probable cause" is frequently linked to that of "double criminality," namely that the crime charged by the requesting state also constitutes a crime under U.S. law, with precedence given to state criminal law, and, following it to federal criminal law.[210]

The procedural and evidentiary rules of the requested state shall apply in extradition proceedings. In the United States, the rules set out in the extradition statute shall apply; however, subsequent treaty provisions control.[211] Although the relator's liberty interests are affected, the United States does not consider extradition subject to procedural and evidentiary rules applicable to criminal proceedings.[212] But the relator does have "due process" rights in all extradition proceedings.[213] Consequently the Federal Rules of Criminal Procedure,[214] and the Federal Rules of Criminal Evidence[215] are generally not applicable.[216]

In summary, the relator:

1. has the right to assistance of counsel,[217] and the court shall appoint counsel for indigent relators.
2. does not have the right to confront witnesses; [218]

---

[210] Court's may use state or federal law or both to ascertain double criminality. *See* Factor v. Laubenheimer, 290 U.S. 276 (1934). This approach exists largely because traditionally states and not the federal government criminalized common crimes. However, the federalization of crime in the United States is so nearly complete as to make the reliance on state law nearly unnecessary to demonstrate double criminality. Marzook v. Christopher (In re Marzook), 924 F. Supp. 565, 573-575 (S.D.N.Y. 1996) (holding that treaty did not require magistrate to look only at state law for determining double criminality, but required analysis of both); *Wright*, 190 U.S. at 58 (treaty's requirement that offense be criminal "under the law of both countries" held to refer to both federal and state law); *Pettit*, 194 U.S. at 217 ("[b]ut as there are no common law crimes of the United States, and as the crime of murder, as such, is not known to the National Government, except in places over which it may exercise exclusive jurisdiction, the better construction of the treaty is, that the required evidence as to the criminality of the charge against the accused must be such as would authorize his apprehension and commitment for trial in that State of the Union in which he is arrested"). *But see* In re Extradition of Locatelli, 468 F. Supp. 568, 572 (S.D.N.Y. 1979) and; Shapiro v. Ferrandina, 478 F.2d 894 (2nd Cir. 1973), *cert. denied*, 414 U.S. 884 (1973), holding that the law of the state where the relator was found applies, and not federal law.

[211] Miner v. Atlass, 363 U.S. 641, 650 (1960).

[212] *See for example* Merino v. United States, 326 F.2d 5 at 12 (9th Cir. 1963).

[213] Due Process Clause entitles the relator to an extradition hearing prior to rendition. Sayne v. Shipley, 418 F.2d 679, 686 (5th Cir. 1969), *cert. denied*, 398 U.S. 903 (1970).

[214] FED. R. CRIM. P. 54 (b) (5) ([t]hese rules are not applicable to extradition and rendition of fugitives. . . .). However, courts may employ the rules by analogy. First National Bank of New York v. Aristeguita, 287 F.2d 219, 223 (2nd Cir. 1969).

[215] FED. R. EVID. 1101 (d) (3) ("[t]he rules (other than respect to privileges) do not apply . . . [to] . . . [p]roceedings for extradition or rendition. . . .").

[216] *See, e.g.*, Desmond v. Eggers, 18 F.2d 503, 504 (9th Cir. 1927); *Merino*, 326 F.2d at 12; Eain v. Wilkes, 641 F.2d 504, 508 7th Cir.), *cert. denied*, 454 U.S. 894 (1981); U.S. v. Kin Hong, 110 F.3d 103 (1st Cir. 1997).

[217] *Romeo*, 820 F.2d at 543; Lopez-Smith v. Hood, 951 F. Supp. 908, 912-913 (D. Ariz. 1996) (court held that "because the Sixth Amendment by its terms applies only to 'criminal prosecutions,' extradition proceedings do not carry the Sixth Amendment right to the assistance of counsel" and therefore no right to effective assistance to counsel). *But see* Matter of Extradition of Artukovic, 628 F. Supp. 1370, 1375 (C.D. Cal. 1986) (Sixth Amendment guarantees right to assistance of counsel in extradition proceedings). There is, however, no case where a relator was denied right to counsel.

[218] Bingham v. Bradley, 241 U.S. 511, 517 (1916) (extradition is intended "to obviate the necessity of confronting the accused with the witnesses against him; . . . [requiring] the demanding government to send its citizens to another country to institute legal proceedings, would defeat the whole object of the treaty"); *Lopez-Smith*, 951 F. Supp at 912-913 (no Sixth Amendment right to confront or cross-examine witnesses in extradition proceedings); Esposito v. Adams, 700 F. Supp. 1470, 1477, *later proceeding*, Esposito v. Adams, 700 F. Supp. 1482 (N.D. Ill. 1988).

3. the extradition statute governs the admissibility of evidence,[219] but judicial precedents are mostly controlling;

4. the government may prove "probable cause" by hearsay evidence,[220] sometimes by unsworn affidavits,[221] and other evidence that may not be admissible in criminal matters.[222] Thus, a person may be extradited on evidence that would be excludable in a criminal proceeding.[223]

5. the government may be able to use the relator's statements gained in violation of the Fifth Amendment;[224]

6. the relator cannot introduce evidence to prove innocence,[225] or even rebut the government's evidence, but may introduce evidence to "clarify" or "explain" the government's evidence;[226]

7. discovery is extremely limited;

8. the relator cannot subpoena evidence or witnesses from the requesting state, and the right of confrontation and cross-examination exists only where the government will present the testimony of a person present in the U.S.;

9. there is no right to a speedy extradition or extradition hearing;[227]

10. the relator's ability to impeach statements or witnesses is severely limited;[228]

---

[219] The admissibility of evidence is controlled by § 3190. *Collins*, 259 U.S. at 317; *Shapiro*, 478 F.2d at 901-02; *Sayne*, 418 F.2d at 685; Escobedo v. United States, 623 F.2d 1098 (5th Cir.), *cert. denied*, 449 U.S. 1036 (1980), *cert. denied sub nom.*, Castillo v. Forsht, 450 U.S. 922, *reh'g denied*, 451 U.S. 934 (1981).

[220] *Esposito*, 700 F. Supp. at 1477 (hearsay evidence and unsworn statements allowed in extradition proceedings); *Shapiro*, 478 F.2d at 902 (evidence may consist of hearsay).

[221] Then v. Melendez, 92 F.3d 851, 855 (9th Cir. 1996).

[222] There is almost no limit on the kind of evidence a magistrate can consider. *Sakaguchi*, 520 F.2d at 730-31 (the judge must "determine whether there is 'any' evidence sufficient to establish reasonable or probable cause" that the fugitive committed the offense charged) (citing Fernandez v. Phillips, 268 U.S. 311, 312, (1925)).

[223] The exclusionary rule, which makes inadmissible certain confessions and evidence gained in violation of the Fourth, Fifth, and Sixth Amendments, as well as *Miranda's* prophylactic protections, does not apply to actions taken by foreign officials acting outside the direction of U.S. agents. United States v. Yousef, 925 F. Supp. 1063, 1076 (S.D.N.Y. 1996); United States v. Lira, 515 F.2d 68, 71 (2nd Cir. 1975) (U.S. law enforcement agencies "can hardly be expected to monitor the conduct of representatives of each foreign government to assure that a request for extradition or expulsion is carried out in accordance with American constitutional standards"). Miranda's exclusionary rule does not apply to evidence obtained by foreign officials since courts reason that its deterrent purpose can have no effect on foreign law enforcement. *Yousef*, 925 F. Supp. at 1076; United States v. Welch, 455 F.2d 211, 212 (2nd Cir. 1972).

[224] *Esposito*, 700 F. Supp. at 1478 (Fifth Amendment's prohibition against self incrimination does not apply to extradition because it is not a criminal case).

[225] Charlton v. Kelly, 229 U.S. 447, 458; Gluckman v. Henkel, 221 U.S. 508, 512 (1911); *Desmond*, 18 F.2d at 505-506.

[226] *Collins*, 259 U.S. at 316; *Sayne*, 418 F.2d at 685.

[227] Yapp v. Reno, 26 F.3d 1562 (11th Cir. 1994) (Sixth Amendment not applicable to extradition proceedings); Martin v. Warden, Atlanta Pen, 993 F.2d 824, 829 (11th Cir.1993) (same); Sabatier v. Dabrowski, 586 F.2d 866, 869 (1st Cir.1978) (same); *Jhirad*, 536 F.2d at 485 n. 9 (same). *But see In re* Extradition of Mylonas, 187 F. Supp. 716, 721 (N.D. Ala. 1960) (judge held that "I am of the opinion that the accused has not been afforded a speedy trial, and that extradition should be denied on that ground"). Both *Martin* and *Yapp* disapproved of *Mylonas*. *Yapp*, 26 F.3d at 1566; *Martin*, 993 F.2d at 829 n.8. However, a person extradited to the U.S. may raise Sixth Amendment speedy trial issues arising out of delay in extradition proceedings. United States v. Manning, 56 F.3d 1188, 1194 (9th Cir. 1995) (30 month delay between defendant's indictment and U.S. extradition request to Israel not sufficient to violate speedy trial right where delay attributable to defendant's fight against extradition).

[228] Eain v. Wilkes, 641 F.2d 504, 511 (7th Cir.), *cert. denied*, 454 U.S. 894 (1981); Bovio v. United States, 989 F.2d 255, 258 (7th Cir. 1993).

11. the relator may be incompetent to stand trial in a U.S. criminal trial, but competent enough to endure an extradition proceeding;[229]

12. there is no double jeopardy or *res judicata* effect if the magistrate finds that the relator is not extraditable[230] and the U.S. can, on behalf of a requesting state, initiate a new "complaint" for extradition even on the basis of the same facts.

Substantive Requirements: Reciprocity, Extraditable Offenses, Double Criminality, Specialty, and Non-Inquiry

Reciprocity

Strict adherence to the principle of reciprocity–the mutuality of rendition and similar criminal processes between respective treaty partners–is not required in the United States. Thus, for instance, the United States will not refuse extradition because the requesting state's theory of jurisdiction over the offense charged is not recognized by U.S. law.[231] Moreover, the U.S. has expressly repudiated the need for reciprocal jurisdiction in several recent treaties. However, when the U.S. is the requesting state, its expanding extraterritorial jurisdiction may conflict with a requested state's understanding and application of jurisdictional principles, and may thwart U.S. extradition efforts.[232] The U.S. will also not insist on reciprocity with respect to extradition of nationals, and the statute specifically permits extradition of U.S. naturals even when the treaty partner does not extradite its own naturals.

---

[229] Although a court may properly inquire into the relator's competence to endure extradition proceedings, it is a much higher standard than in criminal cases. *See Romeo*, 820 F.2d at 553 (generally no due process protection for incompetent relator, who, unless "catatonic, has lost all contact with reality, or is totally unable to communicate" is competent to stand for extradition proceedings); *Charlton*, 229 U.S. at 462; *but see* Matter of Extradition of Artukovic, 628 F. Supp. 1370, 1375 (C.D. Cal. 1986) ("[t]he Sixth Amendment guarantees him [the relator], as all persons before the court in matters affecting life and liberty, the effective assistance of counsel. Meaningful consultation between attorney and client is an essential element of competent representation [citation omitted]. Furthermore, respondent's Fifth Amendment right to a fair hearing requires that he be shown to have . . . minimum competence" [citing Pate v. Robinson, 383 U.S. 375, 385 (1966)].

[230] The Fifth Amendment guaranty against double jeopardy does not apply to extradition, because courts have held that extradition proceedings are not criminal trials. *Collins*, 262 U.S. at 429; United States ex rel. Bloomfield v. Gengler, 507 F.2d 925, 927 (2nd Cir. 1974); *In re* McMullen, 769 F. Supp 1278, 1288 (S.D.N.Y. 1991); Esposito v. Adams, 700 F. Supp. 1470, 1478 (N.D. Ill. 1988).

[231] For a thorough discussion of the applicable theories of jurisdiction —territorial, active personality, passive personality, protected interest, universal—*see* BASSIOUNI, EXTRADITION *supra* note 1, at 295-382, citing various cases, including Matter of Assarsson 635 F.2d 1237 (7th Cir. 1980). Outside of terrorist crimes, the U.S. rarely relies on passive personality theory. Geoffrey R. Watson, *The Passive Personality Principle*, 28 TEX. INT'L L.J. 1 (1993).

[232] *See, e.g.*, orders arising out of the Lockerbie incident. Case Concerning Questions of Interpretation and Application of the 1971 Montreal Convention Arising from the Aerial Incident at Lockerbie (Libyan Arab Jamahiriya v. United Kingdom), Provisional Measures, Order of 14 April 1991, 1992 I.C.J. Reports 3; Case Concerning Questions of Interpretation and Application of the 1971 Montreal Convention Arising from the Aerial Incident at Lockerbie (Libyan Arab Jamahiriya v. United Kingdom), Provisional Measures, Order of 14 April 1992, 1992 I.C.J. Reports 114. *See also*, David M. Kennedy *et al.*, *The Extradition of Mohammed Hamadei*, 31 HARV. INT'L L. J. 5 (1990); Christopher Blakesley, *A Conceptual Framework for Extradition and Jurisdiction over Extraterritorial Crimes*, 4 UTAH L. REV. 685 (1984).

Extraditable Offenses and "Double Criminality"

The crime for which the relator is requested must be stated or contemplated in the applicable legal basis of the process, i.e., the treaty or national legislation; in other words, it must be one of the offenses for which extradition is permitted under the treaty. In the U.S., the courts must first find that a treaty authorizing extradition includes the offense for which the person is requested.[233] Some bilateral extradition treaties list such offenses, but most of them provide for a formula, namely that the offense charged constitutes an offense under the laws of both states and that the offense be punishable by a certain term of imprisonment, usually one year.

The United States, at one time, had followed the practice of listing extraditable offenses in its bilateral extradition treaties, but has largely abandoned this practice.[234] Generally, the U.S. follows the formula approach.[235] In the case of a prior conviction for which extradition is requested, the same formula applies, but the sentence has to be more than one year, or in the case of a fugitive the remaining sentence should also be one year.

Multilateral treaties on specific subjects, i.e., the drugs and hijacking conventions, contain a provision on extradition which can serve as a legal basis for the process.[236] These provisions constitute a declaration of the extraditable offense and are complemented by other provisions of the treaty. Because extraditable offenses are either listed in the applicable treaty, or defined by formula in the treaty, courts will apply liberal principles of treaty interpretation with an aim to finding the offense extraditable.[237] The name or elements of the offense charged need not be the same in the requested state for a court to find the crime extraditable.[238] The Courts will look at the underlying facts to determine whether these facts

---

[233] *Rauscher*, 119 U.S. at 409; *Terlinden* U.S. at 279; *Collins*, 259 U.S. at 311-12; Messina v. United States; 728 F.2d 77 (2nd Cir. 1984), Hu Yau-Leung v. Soscia, 649 F.2d 914, 916-17 (2nd Cir. 1981); Melia v. United States, 667 F.2d 300, 304 (2nd Cir. 1981); Brauch v. Raiche, 618 F.2d 843, 847 (1st Cir. 1980); *Shapiro*, 478 F.2d at 907-913.

[234] However, many treaties retain this approach. *See, e.g.*, Treaty of Extradition, U.S.-U.K., June 8, 1972, art. III, annex, 28 U.S.T. 227, T.I.A.S. No. 8468.

[235] *See, e.g.*, Treaty of Extradition, U.S.-Ital., Oct. 13, 1983, art. II, T.I.A.S. No. 10837; Protocol Amending the Extradition Treaty, Jan. 11, 1988, U.S.-Can., 27 I.L.M. 423.

[236] ICL CONVENTIONS, *supra* note 10.

[237] *Factor*, 290 U.S. at 298-300; *Wright*, 190 U.S. at 57; *Charlton*, 229 U.S. at 475; *Valentine*, 290 U.S. at 293. For some other extradition decisions, *see* In Re Chan Kam Shu, 477 F.2d 333 (5th Cir. 1973); Vardy v. United States, 529 F.2d 404 (5th Cir. 1976); Galanis v. Pallanck, 568 F.2d 234 (2d Cir. 1977); *Hu Yau-Leung*, 649 F.2d at 918. For Supreme Court decisions on general rules of treaty interpretation, *see* United States v. Alvarez-Machain, 504 U.S. 655 (1992); Sumitomo Shoji American. Inc. v. Avagliano, 457 U.S. 176 (1982); Maximov v. United States, 373 U.S. 49 (1963); Kolovrat v. Oregon, 366 U.S. 187 (1961); Jordan v. Tashiro, 278 U.S. 123, 127 (1928); Sullivan v. Kidd, 254 U.S. 433 (1921); Tucker v. Alexandroff, 183 U.S. 424, 437 (1902); *The* Amiable Isabella, 19 U.S. 1 (1821).

[238] *Collins*, 259 U.S. at 311-12; United States v. Sensi, 879 F.2d 888, 895 (D.C. Cir. 1989); *Collins*, 259 U.S. at 312; *Wright*, 190 U.S. at 58; *Glucksman*, 221 U.S. at 513-514; *Kelly*, 241 U.S. at 14; United States v. Casamento, 887 F.2d 1141, 1185 (2nd Cir. 1989), *cert. denied*, 493 U.S. 1081 (1990); *Artukovic*, 784 F.2d at 1356; *Demanjanjuk*, 776 F.2d at 579-80; United States v. Lehder-Rivas, 668 F. Supp. 1523 (M.D. Fla. 1987); *In re* Russell, 789 F.2d 803-04 ("each element of the offense purportedly committed in a foreign country need not be identical to the elements of the similar offense in the U.S."); *Collins*, 259 U.S. at 312 ("[t]he law does not require that the name by which the crime is described in the two counts be the same. . . . "); *Enami*, 834 F.2d at 1449-50; Theron v. United States Marshall, 832 F.2d 492, 496-97 (9th Cir. 1987), *cert. denied,* 486 U.S. 1059 (1988). Treaty provisions also may contain this broad approach. *See, e.g.*, Treaty of Extradition, June 20, 1978, U.S.-F.R.G., 32 U.S.T. 1485, T.I.A.S. No. 9785; *Collins*, 259 U.S. at 312; *Wright*, 190 U.S. at 58; *Brauch*, 618 F.2d

constitute a crime under U.S. law, whether state or federal. The Courts will not seek the existence of comparable legal elements of the offense charged in the laws of both countries.[239]

The requirement of "double criminality" is treaty based.[240] But it is also a customary rule of international law, which is therefore binding on the U.S., even without a treaty requirement. States vary as to the exactitude of this requirement.[241]

"Double criminality" is frequently raised in extradition proceedings, but seldom successfully.[242] However, when the United States is the requesting state, problems of "double criminality" arise in foreign states because some of the U.S.'s modern complex crimes have no specific counterpart in other states, e.g. mail fraud, RICO[243], CCE[244] and CTR.[245]

---

at 851; United States v. Levy, 905 F.2d 326, 328 (10th Cir. 1990), *cert. denied*, 498 U.S. 1049 (1991); *Spatola*, 926 F.2d at 619; Oen Yin-Choy v. Robinson, 858 F.2d 1400, 1404 (9th Cir. 1988), *cert. denied*, 490 U.S. 1106 (1989); *Lo Duca*, 93 F.3d at 1111-12.*Collins*, 259 U.S. at 311-12; *Wright*, 190 U.S. at 58; *Levy*, 905 F.2d at 328; *Spatola*, 925 F.2d at 618-19.

239 *Wright*, 190 U.S. at 58, 60-61; Kelly v. Griffin, 241 U.S. 6, 14 (1916); *Benson*, 127 U.S. at 465; *Collins*, 259 U.S. at 311-12; *Factor*, 290 U.S. at 298-300; United States *ex rel.* DiStefano v. Moore, 46 F.2d 310 (2nd Cir.), *cert. denied*, 283 U.S. 830 (1930); United States v. Stockinger *et al*, 269 F.2d 681 (2nd Cir.), *cert. denied*, 361 U.S. 913 (1959); United States v. Paroutian, 299 F.2d 486 (2d. Cir. 1962); Fiocconi v. Attorney General, 462 F.2d 425 (2nd Cir.), *cert. denied*, 409 U.S. 1059 (1972); Shapiro v. Ferrandina, 478 F.2d 894 (2nd Cir.), *cert. dismissed*, 414 U.S. 884 (1973); United States ex. rel. Sakaguchi v. Kaulukukui, 520 F.2d 726 (9th Cir. 1975); Greci v. Birknes. 527 F.2d 956 (1st Cir. 1976); O'Brien v. Rozmon, 554 F.2d 780 (6th Cir. 1977); Galanis v. Pallanck, 568 F.2d 234 (2nd Cir. 1977); Sindona v. Grant, 619 F.2d 167 (2nd Cir. 1980); Brauch v. Raiche, 618 F.2d 843 (1st Cir. 1980); Caplan v. Vokes, 649 F.2d 1336 (9th Cir. 1981); Cucuzzella v. Kelikoa, 638 F.2d 105 (9th Cir. 1981); *In re* Sindona, 584 F. Supp. 1437, 1447 (E.D.N.Y. 1984); Demjanjuk v. Petrovsky, 776 F.2d 571 (6th Cir. 1985), *cert. denied*, 475 U.S. 1016 (1986); Artukovic v. Rison, 784 F.2d 1354, 1356 (9th Cir. 1986); United States v. Sensi, 879 F.2d 888 (D.C. Cir. 1989); *In re* Extradition of Russell, 789 F.2d 801 (9th Cir. 1986); *In re* Extradition of Manzi, 888 F.2d 204 (1st Cir.), *cert. denied*, 494 U.S. 1017 (1990); Ahmad v. Wigen, 910 F.2d 1063 (2d Cir. 1990).

240 *See, e.g.*, Treaty of Extradition, May 14, 1900, U.S.-Switz., art. II, 31 Stat. 1928, 1929-30.

241 In State of Washington v. Pang, 940 P.2d 1293 (1997), Brazil surrendered a U.S. citizen charged with the crime of arson in the State of Washington, but refused to include in the extradition order the charge of murder (three firefighters having been killed in that arson). Brazil does not have the "felony-murder" that the state of Washington has, whereby an unintentional death arising out of a felony results in a charge of murder for the felon.

242 *See, e.g.*, *Sensi*, 879 F.2d at 893 (dual criminality to commit mail fraud in the U.K. is satisfied if a person succeeds in stealing something, while U.S. law does not require that element); *Bozilov*, 983 F.2d at 143 (crimes charged by foreign government could have been charged as conspiracy in the U.S.); United States v. Riviere, 924 F.2d 1289 (3rd Cir. 1991) (U.S. charge of "departing the U.S. by aircraft in possession of marijuana" [21 U.S.C. § 955] and "exportation of marijuana" [21 U.S.C. § 953] sufficiently analogous to Dominican crime of possession of marijuana to satisfy dual criminality). *But see* United States v. Khan, 993 F.2d 1368, 1372-73 (9th Cir. 1993) (court found that relator's trial for "using a communication facility (e.g. telephone) to facilitate a conspiracy" did not satisfy dual criminality since, while conspiracy was a crime under Pakistan law, Pakistan had extradited the relator on a separate count of conspiracy, and no other analogous crime existed); *In re* Extradition of Mainero, 950 F. Supp. 290 (S.D. Cal. 1996) (under "special circumstances" analysis in bail hearing, court found that relator's charge in Mexico of "carrying a firearm exclusively reserved for the use of the armed forces" for possession of a .38 caliber pistol was not sufficiently analogous to California state law prohibiting the general public, except military and police officials, from possessing certain assault weapons where (1) the California law did not preclude possession of a .38; (2) no other California law prohibited the carrying of .38 without the addition of some other nonjurisdictional element).

243 Racketeer Influenced and Corrupt Enterprise, 21 U.S.C. § 1961. In United States v. Billman, 1996 U.S. App. LEXIS 11657 (4th Cir. 1996), the court recognized France's refusal to extradite for the U.S. crimes of conspiracy and RICO. The French government extradited on the underlying charges of wire and mail fraud, finding them analogous to French crimes.

244 Continuing Criminal Enterprise, 21 U.S.C. § 848 (1994).

245 Reports on Domestic Coins and Currency Transactions, 31 U.S.C. § 5313 (1994).

Requested states may reject an extradition request for lack of "double criminality" where the predicate acts of an offense which otherwise satisfies "double criminality," are themselves non-extraditable or not criminal acts under the requesting state's laws.[246] Although the law of the requested state applies when examining a U.S. request, the expansive U.S. approach to "double criminality" has influenced many countries.[247]

The position of the United States on the subject of "double criminality" has evolved in the last hundred years from one of strict construction of finding the alleged offense criminal in both legal systems, including the consideration that it is the same or substantially the same crime, and that it is prosecutable as well, to one of liberality of construction that the underlying facts constitute a prosecutable offense in the U.S. The increased level of crime in the U.S., and elsewhere, the increased level of transnational crime, the greater international mobility of offenders, and the significant disparity in the criminal laws of the world have combined to produce a more flexible approach that is reflected in the jurisprudence of U.S. courts.

The Rule of Non-Inquiry

United States courts follow the "rule of non-inquiry,"[248] which is also a rule of customary international law whereby courts refuse to examine:

1. the processes by which a requested state secures evidence of "probable cause" to request extradition;[249]
2. whether the relator will receive a fair trial in the requested state;
3. the fairness of procedures under which a requested state secured a criminal conviction;
4. and the potential treatment or punishment a government may impose on a relator if returned to that country.[250]

---

[246] In United States v. Saccoccia, 58 F.3d 574 (1st Cir. 1995) (Switzerland granted extradition for RICO despite the fact that the predicate offenses of CTR are not recognized as crimes in Switzerland).

[247] For an Australian case involving the U.S. and complex crimes, *see* Riley and Butler v. Commonwealth, 260 A.L.R. 106 (Austrl. 1985) (extradition granted for CCE, although having no counterpart in Australian law, where Australian government could have tried relator for the acts or omission underlying CCE); for a Canadian case, *see* Sudur v. United States of America, 25 S.C.R.3d 183 (Can. 1981) (predicate RICO acts of murder, threat to murder, arson, and extortion sufficient to find double criminality, even if RICO has no counterpart in Canadian law); for a U.K. case, *see* United States Government v. McCaffrey, 2 All. E.R., 570 (Eng. 1984) (same for wire fraud and interstate transportation of stolen securities).

[248] See BASSIOUNI, EXTRADITION *supra* note 1, at 486-492; Jacques Semmelman, *Federal Courts, The Constitution and the Rule of Non-Inquiry in International Extradition Proceedings*, 76 CORNELL L. REV. 1198 (1991). Analogous cases on the rule on noninquiry arise in cases construing transfer of prisoner treaties. *See* BASSIOUNI, EXTRADITION *supra* note 1, at 489-492.

[249] Arnbjornsdottir-Mendler v. United States, 721 F.2d 679, 683 (9th Cir. 1983) (the rule of non-inquiry prevents the extradition magistrate from inquiring into the procedures or treatment which awaits a surrendered fugitive in the requesting country"); Peroff v. Hylton, 542 F.2d 1247, 1249 (4th Cir. 1976), *cert. denied*, 429 U.S. 1062 (1977).

[250] *Escobedo*, 623 F.2d at 1107 (court refused to disregard Mexico's evidence supporting probable cause obtained by means of torture); *Ahmed*, 726 F. Supp. at 412-413 (relator alleged that his conviction obtained by confederates coerced confessions and that he faced torture if returned).

More generally, the "rule of non-inquiry" stands opposed to judicial assessment of any ground for denial of extradition that is not enumerated in the treaty or U.S. law.[251] Courts have used the rule to deny a relator's request to block the extradition, despite claims that either the requesting government's actions[252] or lawless conditions[253] in the country may result in the torture or murder of the relator, prosecution for offenses not included in extradition request,[254] or that the relator will face an unfair trial.[255] Courts have also invoked the rule to deny relief based on violation of statute of limitations,[256] speedy trial,[257] speedy extradition,[258] double jeopardy,[259] requesting state's lack of jurisdiction,[260] and requesting state's breach of plea agreement.[261] Recent decisions concerning the reversion of Hong Kong to China have denied relator's claim that their return would subject them to trial in China proper, which would be a violation of the "principle of speciality."[262] Extradition requests based on convictions gained by unfair[263] or *in absentia*[264] proceedings are also protected by the rule. The Supreme Court first set the rule in *Neely v. Henkel*:

> [w]hen an American citizen commits a crime in a foreign country he cannot complain if required to submit to such modes of trial and to such punishment as the laws of that country may prescribe for its own people, unless a different mode be provided for by treaty stipulations between that country and the United States[265]

---

251 Related to the rule of non-inquiry is the rule that courts will not examine the motives behind a requesting state's request for extradition. *In re* Lincoln, 228 F. 70, 74 (E.D.N.Y. 1915) *aff'd per curiam*, 241 U.S. 651 (1916); *Eain*, 641 F.2d at 516

252 *Arnbjornsdottir-Mendler*, 721 F.2d at 683; *Escobedo*, 623 F.2d at 1098; *In re* Singh, 123 F.R.D. 127 (D.N.J. 1987); In the Matter of the Extradition of Sandhu, 1996 U.S. Dist. LEXIS 11828 (order denying motion to introduce evidence of human rights abuses of Sikh minority in India by government).

253 *In re* Manzini, 888 F.2d 204, 206 (1st Cir. 1989); *cert. denied*, (1990); *Sindona*, 619 F.2d at 174-175; Geisser v. United States, 627 F.2d 745 (5th Cir. 1980), *cert. denied*, 450 U.S. 1031 (1981); Peroff v. Hylton, 563 F.2d 1099, 1249 (4th Cir. 1977).

254 Garcia-Guillern v. United States, 450 F.2d 1189, 1192 (5th Cir. 1971), *cert. denied*, 405 U.S. 989 (1972).

255 *In re* Singh, 123 F.R.D. 127, 128-129 (D.N.J. 1987) (claim that trial against relator would be biased); Gallina v. Fraser 278 F.2d 77, 78-79 (2d. Cir. 1960) (relator would unfairly restricted from preventing full defense), *cert. denied*, 364 U.S. 851 (1960); Magisano v. Locke, 545 F.2d 1228, 1230 (9th Cir. 1976) (prosecution based on illegally obtained evidence).

256 Kamrin v. United States, 725 F.2d 1225, *cert. denied*, 469 U.S. 817 (1984).

257 Yapp v. Reno, 26 F.3d 1562, 1567-1568 (11th Cir. 1994).

258 Martin v. Warden, 993 F.2d 824, 829-830 (11th Cir. 1993).

259 In the Matter of the Extradition of Sidali, 899 F. Supp. 1342, 1349 (D.C.N.J. 1995); *In re* Ryan, 360 F. Supp 270, 274 (E.D.N.Y.) *aff'd*, 478 F.2d 1397 (2nd Cir. 1973).

260 *Demjanjuk*, 776 F.2d at 583.

261 United States v. Clark, 470 F. Supp. 976, 979-80 (D. Vt. 1979). However, relator is entitled, as a matter of constitutional right, to enforcement of plea agreements with U.S., where protection from extradition is offered to induce cooperation. Plaster v. United States, 720 F.2d 340, 352 (4th Cir. 1983); Geisser v. United States, 513 F.2d 862, 864 (5th Cir. 1975).

262 United States v. Lui Kin-Hong 110 F.3d 103 (1st Cir. 1997).

263 Holmes v. Laird, 459 F.2d 1211, 1214 (D.C. Cir.), *cert. denied*, 409 U.S. 869 (1972) (application of NATO SOFA treaty).

264 *Gallina*, 278 F.2d at 79; Argento v. Horn, 241 F.2d 258, 263-64 (6th Cir.) *cert. denied*, 355 U.S. 818 (1957); *In re* Mylonas, 187 F. Supp. 716 (N.D. Ala. 1960); *Ex parte* Fudera, 162 F. 591 (S.D.N.Y. 1908), *appeal dismissed sub. nom.*, Italian Gov't v. Asaro, 219 U.S. 589 (1911); *Ex parte* La Mantia, 206 F. 330 (S.D.N.Y. 1913).

265 Neely v. Henkel, 180 U.S. 109, 123 (1901); *Manzini*, 888 F.2d at 206; *Ahmad*, 726 F. Supp. at 413 ("[t]he interests of international comity are ill served by requiring a foreign nation such as Israel to satisfy a United States district judge concerning the fairness of its laws and the manner in which they are enforced. It is the function

Even *habeas corpus* is not a valid means of inquiry into the treatment the relator is expected to receive in the requesting state, although the issue is often raised in that context.[266] However, several U.S. courts have held out the possibility that in a given case they may deny certification because circumstances indicate that sending a relator to face trial or punishment in the requesting state would violate fundamental "due process."[267] Courts faced with a case implicating fundamental "due process" may deny extradition on another ground that, absent the "due process" considerations, the court may not have found sufficient to deny certification.[268]

The legal basis of the "rule of non-inquiry" in the United States is primarily based on the court's obligation to enforce the applicable extradition treaty and to respect the sovereignty of the requesting state.[269] Most treaties, as well as the extradition statute, do not give the court explicit authority to deny extradition based on humanitarian concerns outside of the substantive provisions of the treaty. Thus, concerns that fall outside the provisions of the treaty—which may concern fundamental human rights in the administration of justice—are left to the discretion of the Executive Branch. The Secretary of State may refuse to extradite a person that the court has certified as extraditable for a variety of reasons which the court could not have considered in the face of the "rule of non-inquiry."[270] However, constitutionally based protections may serve as a legally sufficient basis for a court to make exception to the "rule of non-inquiry" in a particular case.[271]

---

of the Secretary of State to determine whether extradition should be denied on humanitarian grounds").

[266] The rule, developed in part on the limitation the Supreme Court, set on the scope of *habeas corpus* review in extradition matters. *Gallina*, 278 F.2d at 79 ("the procedures which will occur in the demanding country subsequent to extradition were not listed as matter of a federal court's consideration"); *In re* Luis Oteizaa y Cortes, 136 U.S. 330, 334 (1890).

[267] The leading case is Gallina v. Fraser 278 F.2d 77, 78-79 (2d. Cir. 1960), *cert. denied*, 364 U.S. 851 (1960), where the court stated in *dicta* that "[w]e can imagine situations when the relator, upon extradition, would be subject to procedures or punishment too antipathetic to a federal court's sense of decency as to require re-examination of the principle set out above." Although no court has utilized the *Gallina* exception to deny certification, several courts have either cited it approvingly or endorsed a similar approach, albeit in *dicta*: Rosado v. Civiletti, 621 F.2d 1179, 1195 (2nd Cir.), *cert. denied*, 449 U.S. 856 (1980) ["the presumption of fairness routinely accorded the criminal process of a foreign sovereign may require closer scrutiny if a relator persuasively demonstrates that extradition would expose him to procedures or punishment 'antipathetic to a federal court's sense of decency'" (citing *Gallina*)]; Saleh v. United States Department of Justice, 962 F.2d 234, 241 (2nd Cir. 1992) (deportation); *Demjanjuk*, 776 F.2d at 583; Prushinowski v. Samples, 734 F.2d 1016, 1019 (4th Cir. 1984); *In re* Extradition of Burt, 737 F.2d 1477, 1487 (7th Cir. 1984); Arnbjornsdottir Mendler v. United States, 721 F.2d 679 (6th Cir. 1983); United States ex. rel. Bloomfield v. Gengler, 507 F.2d 925, 928 (2nd Cir. 1974); United States v. Romano, 706 F.2d 370, 374-375 (1983). *See also*, 1978 DIGEST OF U.S. PRACTICE IN INTERNATIONAL LAW 410-11.

[268] For instance, courts will not pass on the propriety of *in absentia* criminal convictions that serve as the basis for an extradition request. However, the courts may find other grounds upon which to deny extraditabilty. *See* Ex parte Fudera, 162 F. 591 (S.D.N.Y. 1908), *appeal dismissed sub nom.*, Italian Gov't v. Asaro, 219 U.S. 589 (1911), (conviction *in absentia* did not preclude extradition, but court released due to insufficient evidence); Ex parte La Mantia, 206 F. 330 (S.D.N.Y. 1913) (same); *In re* Mylonas, 187 F. Supp. 716 (N.D. Ala. 1960), (conviction *in absentia* did not preclude extradition, but treaty required release because of long delay in government's effort to take relator into custody).

[269] 18 U.S.C. § 3184 (1994). The extradition magistrate must certify the relator as extraditable if she "deems the evidence sufficient to sustain the charge under the provisions of the proper treaty or convention, or under section 3181 (b) (relating to extradition by comity and statute of aliens). . . ."

[270] *Lui Kin-Hong*, 110 F.3d 103.

[271] Constitutional rights, including the right to due process, can trump the government's treaty obligations. Reid v. Covert, 354 U.S. 1 (1957); *Geisser*, 513 F.2d at 869 n.11; *In re* Petition of Geisser, 627 F.2d 745, 750 (5th Cir. 1980), *cert. denied*, 450 U.S. 1030 (1981); *In re* Extradition of Burt, 737 F.2d 1477, 1484 (7th Cir. 1984); Plaster v. United States, 720 F.2d 340, 348 (4th Cir. 1983); *Martin*, 993 F.2d at 829; Geofroy v. Riggs, 133 U.S.

The "rule of non-inquiry" is also based on considerations of separation of power[272] and principles of international comity.[273] Indeed, the Secretary of State's discretion is justified, as a policy matter, by the fact that courts follow the "rule of non-inquiry." Primarily, the "rule" assumes the judiciary's lack of competence or propriety in assessing the fairness of other criminal justice systems—a decision U.S. courts have found to be largely political,[274] and best left to the Executive Branch.[275] In the United States, it is also supported by the limited extraterritorial reach courts have given constitutional protections, which only protect United States citizens from fundamental "due process" violations.[276]

The "rule of non-inquiry" is case-law created, and is not mandated by the constitution.[277]Consequently it may be abrogated by constitutional considerations,[278] statute,[279] or treaty.[280] Thus, a court may decide to abrogate the rule—and deny

---

258, 267 (1890); Doe v. Braden, 57 U.S. (16 How.) 635, 656 (1853).

272 *Lui Kin-Hong*, 110 F.3d 103.

273 *In re* Extradition of Howard, 996 F.2d 1320, 1330 (1st Cir. 1993); Koskotas v. Roche, 931 F.2d 169 (1st Cir. 1991).

274 Courts have implied that the rule of non-inquiry is mandated by the "political question" doctrine. *See* Quinn v. Robinson, 783 F.2d 776, 789-90 (9th Cir.), *cert. denied*, 479 U.S. 882 (1986). The leading case on political questions doctrine in the United States is Baker v. Carr. 369 U.S. 186 (1962).

275 Emami v. United States Dist. Court for Northern District of California, 834 F.2d 1444 (9th Cir. 1987) (stating that while Congress has provided that extraditabilty shall be determined by the judge or magistrate in the first instance, the ultimate decision to extradite is ordinarily a matter within the exclusive purview of the executive); Peroff v. Hylton, 563 F.2d 1099, 1102 (4th Cir. 1977). In *dicta*, the court held that the rule of non-inquiry into the future treatment of the offender in the requesting state applies to the judiciary. The proper forum to raise such questions is the executive branch of the government, since that branch can exercise executive discretion in denying a person's surrender to a foreign state.

276 Reid v. Covert, 354 U.S. 1, 12 (1957); United States v. Curtis-Wright Export Corp, 299 U.S. 304, 318 (1936) ("[n]either the Constitution nor the laws passed in pursuance of it have any force in the foreign territory unless in respect of our own citizens"); *but see supra* note 111. The relator may be entitled to particular constitutional protections incorporated into the applicable treaty, where the parties to the treaty have agreed to the extraterritorial application. *Cf.* Yapp v. Reno, 26 F.3d 1562, 1567 (apparently recognizing, although rejecting such an interpretation of the treaty language at issue, that treaty could incorporate constitutional protections).

277 *In re* Extradition of Howard, 996 F.2d 1320, 1329-1330 n.6 (1st Cir. 1993) (stating that "[t]he government suggests that the Constitution mandates the 'rule of non-inquiry.' We disagree. The rule did not spring from a belief that courts, as an institution, lack either the authority or the capacity to evaluate foreign legal systems. Rather, the rule came into being as judges, attempting to interpret particular treaties, concluded that, absent a contrary indication in a specific instance, the ratification of an extradition treaty mandated 'non-inquiry' as a matter of international comity. No doubt the rule exemplifies judicial deference to executive authority (citations omitted) but it is a deference stemming at least in part from the fact that the executive is the branch which most likely has written and negotiated the document being interpreted").

278 *See supra* notes 115, 110.

279 Fong Yue Ting v. United States, 149 U.S. 698, 714 (1893); Head Money Cases, 112 U.S. 580, 598-99 (1884).

280 The 1985 U.S.-U.K. Supplemental Extradition Treaty, under article 3 (a), abrogated the rule in cases under it by permitting a court to examine the treatment a relator may receive upon surrender. Supplementary Extradition Treaty, June 25, 1985, U.S.-U.K., art. 3(a), S. EXEC. REP. NO. 99-17 (1986). The First Circuit recognized the treaty's right to review in *Howard*, 996 F.2d at 1329-1330. *See also* U.S.-U.K. Supplemental Extradition Treaty, M. Cherif Bassiouni, Testimony Before the Senate Foreign Relations Committee, 99-703 Hearings of Sept. 18, 1985 276-305 (1985); M. Cherif Bassiouni, *The Political Offense Exception Revisited: Extradition Between the U.S. and the U.K. - A Choice Between Friendly Cooperation Among Allies and Sound Law and Policy*, 15 DENV. J. INT'L L. & POL'Y 255 (1987); Michael P. Scharf, *Foreign Courts on Trial: Why U.S. Courts Should Avoid Applying the Inquiry Provisions of the Supplemental U.S.-U.K. Extradition Treaty*, 25 STAN. J. INT'L L. 257 (1988).

extradition—on the basis of international human rights instruments or customary international law.

The "Principle of Speciality"[281]

An extradition order will state the offense for which the relator is to be tried or punished in the requesting state, and that constitutes a limitation on the requesting state which is precluded, save for subsequent approval by the original requested state, to prosecute or punish[282] the relator for any other offense than the one for which extradition was granted. If acquitted or, if convicted and after serving his sentence, the relator must be given a reasonable time to leave the country before prosecution for another crime may begin.[283]

The "principle of speciality" also applies to conditions placed on the extradition and limitations on penalties that the originally requested state may include in extradition order.

The principle is so broadly recognized in international law and practice that it has customary international law status, and applies to treaty-based extraditions as well as to extraditions predicated on other bases.[284] Section 3186 provides that "[t]he Secretary of State may order the person committed under sections 3184 (fugitive from foreign country found in United States) . . . to be delivered to any authorized agent of such foreign government, to be tried for the offense of which charged."[285] Also, section 3192 empowers the President to safeguard any person brought into the United States to face trial "until the final conclusion of his trial for the offenses specified in the warrant of extradition, and until his final discharge from custody or imprisonment for or on account of such offenses, and for a

---

[281] For a thorough discussion of the rule, *see* BASSIOUNI, EXTRADITION, *supra* note 1, at 429-486.

[282] Johnson v. Browne 205 U.S. 309 (1907).

[283] Ever since the Supreme Court decided United States v. Rauscher, 119 U.S. 467 (1886) the jurisprudence of U.S. Courts has consistently recognized and applied what is sometimes called the "principle," "rule" or "doctrine" of "Speciality" or "specialty." The major cases upholding "speciality" after Rauscher are: *In re* Woodall, 57, L.J. 72 (C.A.Cr. 1888); Cosgrove v. Winney, 174 U.S. 64 (1899); Johnson v. Browne 205 U.S. 309 (1907), Green v. United States, 154 F.2d 401 (6th Cir. 1907); Collins v. O'Neil, 214 U.S. 113 (1909); United States v. Paroutrian, 299 F.2d 486 (2nd Cir. 1962); Fiocconi v. Attorney General, 464 F.2d (2nd Cir. 1972); Shapiro v. Ferrandina, 478 F.2d 894 (2nd Cir. 1973), *cert. denied*, 414 U.S. 884 (1973); United States v. Flores, 538 F.2d 939 (2nd Cir. 1976); United States v. Rossi, 545 F.2d 814 (2nd Cir. 1976); United States v. Archhold-Newball, 554 F.2d 665 (5th Cir.), *cert. denied*, 434 U.S. 1000 (1977); Berenguer v. Vance, 473 F. Supp. 1195 (D.C. 1979); Melia v. United States, 667 F.2d 300 (2nd Cir. 1981), United States v Kember, 685 F.2d 451 (D.C. Cir. 1982); United States v. Jetter and Maniccia, 772 F.2d 371 (8th Cir 1983); United States v. Najohn, 785 F.2d 1420 (9th Cir. 1986), *cert. denied*, 479 U.S. 1009 (1986); United States v. Thirion, 813 F.2d 146 (8th Cir. 1987); United States v. Van Cauwenberghe, 827 F.2d 424 (9th Cir. 1987), *cert. denied*, 484 U.S. 1042 (1988); United States v. Cuevas, 847 F.2d 1417 (9th Cir. 1988), *cert. denied*, 489 U.S. 1012 (1989); United States v. Kaufman, 858 F.2d 994 (5th Cir. 1988); *reh'g denied*, 874 F.2d 242 (5th Cir.), *aff'd sub nom.*, Franks v. Harwell, 869 F.2d 1485 (5th Cir.), *cert. denied*, 493 U.S. 895 (1989); United States v. Sensi, 879 F.2d 888 (D.C. Cir. 1989); United States v. Alvarez-Moreno, 874 F.2d 1402 (11th Cir. 1989), *cert. denied*, 494 U.S. 1032 (1990); Peters v. Engor, 888 F.2d 713 (10th Cir. 1989); United States v. Levy, 905 F.2d 326 (10th Cir. 190), *cert. denied*, 498 U.S. 1049 (1991); United States v. Khan, 993 F.2d 1368, 1373-74 (9th Cir. 1993); United States v. Abello-Silva, 948 F.2d 1168 (10th Cir. 1991), *cert. denied*, 113 S. Ct. 107 (1992), *reh'g denied*, 113 S. Ct. 1068 (1993); United States v. Andonian, 29 F.3d 1432 (9th Cir. 1994), *cert. denied*, 115 S. Ct. 938 (1995); United States v. Puentes, 50 F.3d 1567 (11th Cir. 1995); United States v. Saccoccia, 58 F.3d 754 (9th Cir. 1995). In 1992, the Supreme Court reaffirmed the *Rauscher* rule in United States v. Alvarez-Machain, 504 U.S. 655 (1992), although finding no violation in that case.

[284] Fiocconi v. Attorney General, 464 F.2d (2nd Cir. 1972) (rule applies even though Italy extradited relator to the U.S. on the basis of comity). *See also United States v. Levy*, 947 F.2d 1032, 1034 (2nd Cir. 1991).

[285] 18 U.S.C. § 3186 (1994).

reasonable time thereafter. . . ."[286] The leading case in the United States is *United States v. Rauscher*, a Supreme Court case construing the Webster-Ashburton Treaty,[287] a treaty which concerned, *inter alia*, extradition but did not contain a provision on "speciality." In *Rauscher*, the Court held that the relator "shall be tried only for the offence with which he is charged in the extradition proceedings and for which he was delivered up, and that if not tried for that, or after trial and acquittal, he shall have a reasonable time to leave the country. . . ."[288]

The rationale for the doctrine rests on the following factors: (1) the requested state could have refused extradition if it had known that the relator would be prosecuted or punished for an offense other than the one for which extradition was granted; (2) the requesting state would not have had *in personam* jurisdiction over the relator, if not for the requested state's surrender of that person; (3) the requesting state would be abusing the formal processes of the requested state to secure the surrender of the person; (4) the requested state used its processes in reliance upon the representations made by the requesting state and is entitled to the observance of these representations; (5) the relator is entitled to be tried for the crime or crimes for which he was extradited and to be free from prosecutorial abuse once he is within the jurisdictional control of a requested state.

The protections of the principle should apply to persons brought to the United States to stand trial, regardless of the procedures employed to gain their presence, whether rendition is secured by deportation, kidnap,[289] informal demand, or where rendition is gained by false pretenses, the relator should be entitled to the protection of the rule as a prophylactic measure against prosecutorial abuses that could follow illegal rendition.

The "principle of speciality" is both the right of the surrendering state as well as that of the relator. But for those who see extradition as essentially a contract between states where the individual is the object and not the subject of an international agreement, "speciality" is deemed only the right of the contracting states. Thus, under this view, a requested state can freely waive "speciality" or not protest its violation and the individual would have no standing to object to the violation by the requesting state, now the prosecuting state. A more enlightened and modern view is to deem the individual the subject of a legal right with the capacity to have standing to raise the issue, irrespective of the requested state's protest.[290]

---

[286] 18 U.S.C. § 3192 (1994); *Rauscher*, 119 U.S. at 434, where Gray, J., concurred on the grounds that through the Act of March 3, 1869, Ch. 141, §§ 1-3, 15 Stat. 337, codified now as 18 U.S.C. § 3192 ". . . the political department of the government has clearly manifested its will, in the form of an express law (of which any person may prosecuted in any court within the United States has the right to claim the protection), that the accused shall be tried only for the crime specified in the warrant of extradition, and shall be allowed a reasonable time to depart the United States, before he can be arrested or detained for another offense."

[287] Webster-Ashburton Treaty, Aug. 9, 1842, United States-United Kingdom, 8 Stat. 572, T.S. No. 119, *reprinted in* 12 TREATIES AND OTHER INTERNATIONAL AGREEMENTS OF THE UNITED STATES OF AMERICA 1776-1949, at 82 (Charles I. Bevans, ed. 1974).

[288] *Rauscher*, 119 U.S. at 424.

[289] However, this was decidedly not the holding of United States v. Alvarez-Machain, 504 U.S. 655 (1992), where the Supreme Court held that an individual's abduction from Mexico does not violate the U.S.-Mex. extradition treaty and therefore any prosecution resulting from that abduction does not violate the rule of speciality. *Id.* at 659-670.

[290] There is currently a split on this issue between the circuits. For cases holding that an individual does not have standing, absent protest, *see*: United States v. Riviere, 924 F.2d 1289, 1298-1301 (3d Cir. 1991) ("Dominica has exercised its power to surrender Riviere as a matter of comity for charges not listed in the extradition order; Riviere has no basis for objection to its actions"); United States v. Chapa-Garza, 62 F.3d 118, 121 (5th Cir. 1995); United States v. Kaufman, 858 F.2d 994 (5th Cir. 1988); *reh'g denied*, 874 F.2d 242 (5th Cir.),

Allowing a relator to raise the issue without the need for a protest avoids raising the issue to a level of confrontation between states.

The confusion arises from the basic idea that speciality is only intended to protect the interests of the requested state. The Supreme Court, in *Rauscher*,[291] held that the self-executing nature of extradition treaties and statutorily created rights, clearly evidence that a relator has the right to raise "speciality" violations, regardless of any protest by the requesting state. All U.S. extradition treaties and Sections 3186 and 3192 establish the principle, but neither the treaties nor statutory language are dispositive of the issue of standing. So far the First, Second and Seventh Circuits require a protest before giving the relator standing to object. But other Circuits do not.

Application of the rule in the U.S. has met with different outcomes, although the Ninth, Tenth and Eleventh Circuits have been consistently on that issue. Generally, the offenses charged must reflect the offenses listed in the extradition order. Formal differences between the request for extradition and technical variances in an indictment do not violate the principle, which applies to the substantive nature of the crime and the facts supporting it for

---

aff'd sub nom., Franks v. Harwell, 869 F.2d 1485 (5th Cir.), *cert. denied*, 493 U.S. 895 (1989); United States v. Kaufman, 874 F.2d 242, 243 (5th Cir. 1989) (holding that only the offended treaty partner may complain of a breach of the treaty); Demjanjuk v. Petrovsky, 776 F.2d 571, 583-584 (6th Cir. 1985) (expressing doubt that the individual has standing on the grounds that "the right to insist on application of the principle of specialty belongs to the requested state, not to the individual whose extradition is requested") (citation omitted), *cert. denied*, 475 U.S. 1016 (1986); Matta-Ballesteros v. Henman, 896 F.2d 255, 259 (7th Cir.), *cert. denied*, 498 U.S. 878 (1990) ("Treaties are designed to protect the sovereign interest of nations, and it is up to the offended nations to determine whether a violation of sovereign interests has occurred and requires redress"); United States v. Diwan, 864 F.2d 715, 721 (11th Cir.), *cert. denied*, 492 U.S. 921 (1989). For cases holding that an individual has standing based on the treaty, *see*: United States v. Thirion, 813 F.2d 146, 151 n. 5 (8th Cir.1987) (allowing the extradited individual to bring any objections the requested country might have raised); United States v. Najohn, 785 F.2d 1420, 1422 (9th Cir.) (same), *cert. denied*, 479 U.S. 1009 (1986); United States v. Levy, 905 F.2d 326, 328 n. 1 (10th Cir.1990) (extradited individual has standing to claim a violation of the rule of specialty), *cert. denied*, 498 U.S. 1049 (1991); United States v. Puentes, 50 F.3d 1567, 1574 (11th Cir. 1995) (construing *Machain* as ". . . reject(ing) the premise underlying the cases that require the requested nation to object as a condition precedent to the individual's ability to claim the benefits of the rule of specialty"). Not all of the circuits have resolved this issue, *see*: United States v. Saccoccia, 58 F.3d 754, 767 n.6 (1st Cir. 1995) (recognizing the split in the circuits, but disposing of the case on the merits), *cert. denied*, Saccoccia v. United States, 116 S. Ct. 1322 (1996); United States v. Davis, 954 F.2d 182 (4th Cir. 1992).

[291] In *Rauscher*, a case applying the rule of speciality even though no provision existed in the treaty, found the relator had standing based on international law and the extradition statute. *Rauscher*, 119 U.S. at 427-430. In *Alvarez-Machain*, the court, in construing *Rauscher*, recognized that the treaty created the relator's right to raise the protest: "[t]he Extradition Treaty (between the United States and Mexico) has the force of law, and if, as respondent asserts, it is self-executing, it would appear that the court must enforce it on behalf of an individual regardless of the offensiveness of the practice of one nation to the other nations. In *Rauscher*, the Court noted that Great Britain had taken the position in other cases that the Webster-Ashburton Treaty included the doctrine of speciality, but no importance was attached to whether or not Great Britain had protested the prosecution of Rauscher for the crime of cruel and unusual punishment as opposed to murder." United States v. Alvarez-Machain, 504 U.S. 655, 667 (1992). The Court also confirmed this principle of *Rauscher* in Johnson v. Browne, 205 U.S. 309 (1907). Generally, the Supreme Court has held that an individual has a right to raise violations of a treaty: Cook v. United States, 288 U.S. 102 (1933); Factor v. Laubenheimer, 290 U.S. 276 (1933); Ford v. United States, 773 U.S. 276 (1933). Several lower court cases have ascribed to this view: United States *ex. rel.* Donnelly v. Mulligan, 74 F.2d 220 (2nd Cir.1934); Fiocconi v. Attornev General, 462 F.2d 475 (2d Cir. 1972) *cert. denied*, 409 U.S. 1059 (1972); Waits v. McCowan, 516 F.2d 203 (3rd Cir. 1975).

which extradition was granted.[292] One circuit court has held that as long as the relator is charged with an (1) extraditable offense and (2) supported by the facts upon which extradition was granted, the rule is satisfied.[293] Another circuit has held that without an unambiguous representation in the extradition order (or later clarification) by the requested state that prosecution for a particular count is authorized, the rule will bar the court's jurisdiction, regardless of the facts upon which extradition was based.[294]

The rule does not bar the prosecutor from prosecuting additional charges in a superseding indictment provided that the source facts support the additional charges and that the additional charges are of the same legal nature as those contained in the request for extradition.[295] Application of the rule also does not bar the U.S. prosecutor from using evidence of a rule-barred offense in a prosecution for a charge that does not violate the rule.[296]

The proper procedure for a state that wishes to prosecute for another crime, or for a variant of the crime for which the relator was extradited is to request a waiver of the original requested state or to file a request for variance. Such a waiver or supplemental extradition does not necessarily involve the extradited person in subsequent legal proceedings in the original requesting state if the facts alleged remain the same or substantially the same.[297] The relator can, however, oppose such a request in the original requested state under its applicable laws and procedures. The relator also may waive speciality claims, either expressly or by implication.[298]

---

292 *See, e.g.*, United States v. Lehder-Rivas, 955 F.2d 1510 (11th Cir. 1992) (holding that Colombia's failure to refer specifically to the CCE charge in its review of the extradition request did not violate the specialty principle since Colombia specifically included the charge by a divergent name in its order), *cert. denied sub nom.*, Reed v. United States, 113 S. Ct. 347 (1992); *Levy*, 905 F.2d at 328 (considering the totality of circumstances and concluding the variance did not violate the specialty principle); United States v. Rossi, 545 F.2d 814 (2d Cir. 1976), *cert. denied*, 430 U.S. 907 (1977).

293 United States v. Sensi, 879 F.2d 888 (D.C. Cir. 1989). The holding of *Sensi* is somewhat narrowed by the treaty-based speciality rule expressed in the U.S.-U.K. treaty at issue: "[a] person extradited shall not be [prosecuted] . . . for any offense other than an extraditable offense established by the facts in respect of which his extradition has been granted." *Id.* at 895.

294 United States v. Khan, 993 F.2d 1368 (9th Cir. 1993). The *Khan* court specifically rejected the *Sensi* analysis.

295 United States v. Abello-Silva, 948 F.2d 1168 (10th Cir. 1991), *cert. denied*, 113 S. Ct. 107 (1992), *reh'g denied*, 113 S. Ct. 1068 (1993).

296 *See Thirion*, 813 F.2d at 153 (holding that the doctrine of speciality does not alter existing rules of evidence or procedure); United States v. Flores, 538 F.2d 939 (2nd Cir. 1976); McGann v. United States Board of Parole, 488 F.2d 39 (3rd Cir. 1973) (holding that the doctrine does not apply to the method of trial or admissibility of evidence in the requesting state), *cert. denied*, 416 U.S. 958, *reh'g denied*, 417 U.S. 927 (1974); United States v. Paroutian, 299 F.2d 486 (2nd Cir. 1962). This was also the case in Sacoccio v. United States, where evidence of CTR violations was presented even though Switzerland specifically barred prosecution for CTR violations because its legal system did not deem such activity to be a crime. The *Sacoccio* case allows bringing in through the back door what could not be brought in through the front door.

297 *Najohn*, 785 F. 2d at 1422; *Puentes*, 50 F.3d at 1575 (holding that while an extradited individual has standing to raise violations of specialty, he ". . . enjoys this right at the sufferance of the requested nation. As a sovereign, the requested nation may waive its right to object to a treaty violation and thereby deny the defendant standing to object to such an action").

298 *See, e.g.*, United States v. Vreeken, 803 F.2d 1085, 1089 (10th Cir. 1986) (holding that the defendant's failure to raise the rule of speciality in a timely manner precluded him from raising it at all as a bar to prosecution for violations of United States income tax law, when extradition from Canada had been based on charges of wire fraud), *cert. denied*, 479 U.S. 1067 (1987). *See also* United States v. Davis, 954 F.2d 182 (4th Cir. 1992) (holding that the defendant waived his right to appeal on specialty grounds by his failure to object to the government's

As an original requested state, the United States may grant a waiver of the "rule of speciality" based on a formal request from an original requesting state after the relator has been surrendered to that state and is still in its legal custody. In this type of case, the United States has taken the position that no further judicial proceedings are required if the original record contains "probable cause" evidence sufficient to support the additional charge. But, since the question of "probable cause" is to be judicially determined, such a person may judicially challenge that administrative decision.[299] Such a challenge can be by means of *habeas corpus* or by injunction, the later being the exception.

The "principle of speciality" also limits the right of the original requesting state to which the relator was surrendered to re-extradite the relator to another (third state) without first securing the permission of the original requested state.

Grounds for Denial of Extradition: Defenses, Exchanges or Exceptions.

Nature and Basis

Failure to satisfy the requirements of extradition, both substantive and procedural, constitute grounds for denial of extradition. In addition, however, specific grounds also exist in treaties. They are referred to as defenses, exclusions or exceptions to the grant of extradition. These grounds arise out of different reasons and satisfy different purposes and concerns that states have in connection with surrendering persons sought for prosecutorial punishment in another state. These concerns increase whenever the political relations between the state in question are tenuous or not friendly, or when their respective legal systems and authors are radically different. They are:

1. "The political offense exception;"
2. Exclusion for prosecution based on certain discriminatory grounds;
3. Offenses of military or fiscal or economic nature;
4. Exclusion of nationals;
5. Double jeopardy;
6. Applicability of a statute of limitation and extinction of the cause of action by amnesty or pardon;
7. Immunity from prosecution;
8. Exclusions concerning certain penalties and treatment of offenders.

Some national legislation include all or part of these defenses, exclusions and exceptions in order to avoid disparity in treaties. The U.S. does not follow that approach and deals with these issues in its separate lateral treaties. Thus, there is some disparity in application. The U.S.'s bilateral approach is intentional because it permits the U.S. to favor states with which it has friendly relations and to deal guardedly with those which it has less than friendly relations.

---

reference to illegal accounting practices in the initial indictment which were not included in the extradition order).

299 *See* Berenguer v. Vance, 473 F. Supp. 1195, 1198 (D.C. 1979) (recognizing, in certain circumstances, a right to a hearing on subsequent expansion of extradition order).

The "Political Offense Exception"[300]

There are two types of offenses falling within the category of the "political offense exception:" the "purely political offense," and the "relative political offense." There is also an exception to this exception, namely international crimes which are excluded from the "political offense exception."

All U.S. extradition treaties contain a provision concerning the "political offense exception;" but only the "purely political offense" has been consistently applied without question. These are offenses of opinion, political expression or those which otherwise do not involve the use of violence. They include, for example, such offenses as treason and espionage.[301]

The "relative political offense" is one which involves violence as an incidence of the political motivation and goal of the actor, but which does not constitute wanton or indiscriminate violence directed against a protected person, such as civilians. The violence that befalls innocent and unintended targets must therefore be initially directed against a permissible target, incidental to the political motives and goals of the actor, and performed in the context of a civil war, insurrection or uprising. These tests have originally been applied by U.S. courts who borrowed them from earlier English jurisprudence.[302] The more recent jurisprudence of the United States involved a number of cases in which Irish resisters belonging to the Provisional Irish Republican Army (PIRA) and Palestinians involved or thought to be involved in the Palestine Liberation Organization (PLO) or one of its affiliated groups committed acts of violence. While many PIRA cases resulted in the application of

---

300 For a history of the political offense exception to extradition, *see* BASSIOUNI, EXTRADITION, *supra* note 1, at 502-518. *See also* M. Cherif Bassiouni, *Ideological Motivated Offenses and the Political Offense Exception in Extradition A Proposed Juridical Standard for an Unruly Problem*, 19 DE PAUL L. REV. 217 (1969); Manuel R. Garcia-Mora, *The Nature of the Political Offenses. A Knotty Problem of Extradition*, 48 VA. L. REV. 1226 (1962).

301 *See* Chandler v. United States, 171 F.2d 921 (1st Cir.1948), *cert. denied,* 336 U.S. 918 (1949).

302 The cases relied upon by the U.S. were *In re* Castioni (1891) 1 Q.B. 149, 156 (Eng.) ("fugitive criminals are not to be surrendered for extradition crimes if those crimes were incidental to and formed a part of political disturbance"); *In re* Meunier (1894) 2 Q.B. 415 (Eng.). U.S. courts first followed these cases in *In re* Ezeta, 62 F. 972, 999 (C.C.N.D. Cal. 1894) (stating the general rule and citing *Castioni*); Ornelas v. Ruiz, 161 U.S. 502 (1896); Artukovic v. Boyle 107 F. Supp. 11 (S.D. Cal. 1952) (holding no extradition treaty existed between U.S. and Yugoslavia), *rev'd sub nom.*, Ivancevic v. Artukovic, 211 F.2d 565 (9th Cir. 1954) (holding that a valid treaty existed), *on remand sub. nom.*, Artukovic v. Boyle, 140 F. Supp. 245 (S.D. Cal. 1956) (holding that political offense exception precluded extradition), *aff'd sub nom.*, Karadzole v. Artukovic, 247 F.2d 198 (9th Cir. 1957), *rev'd*, 355 U.S. 393 (1958) (holding that a full hearing on political offense issue required), *on remand sub nom.*, United States v. Artukovic, 170 F. Supp. 383 (S.D. Cal. 1959) (insufficient evidence to find guilt but offense would be considered political) [Artukovic was eventually extradited to Yugoslavia in 1986, where he was executed; *see* Artukovic v. Rison, 628 F. Supp. 1370 (C.D. Cal.), *aff'd*, 784 F.2d 1354 (9th Cir. 1986)]; Ramos v. Diaz, 179 F. Supp. 459, 462-63 (S.D. Fla. 1959); Gallina v. Fraser, 177 F. Supp. 856 (D. Conn. 1959), *aff'd*, 278 F.2d 77 (2nd Cir.), *cert. denied*, 364 U.S. 851 (1960); Jimenez v. Aristequieta, 311 F.2d 547 (5th Cir. 1962), *cert. denied*, 373 U.S. 914 (1963); *In re* Gonzalez, 217 F. Supp. 717 (S.D.N.Y. 1963); Garcia-Guillern v. United States, 450 F.2d 1189 (5th Cir. 1971), *cert. denied*, 405 U.S. 989 (1972); In Matter of Sindona, 450 F. Supp. 672 (S.D.N.Y. 1978); Koskotas v. Roche, 931 F.2d 169 (1st Cir. 1991) (no political offense); Ahmad v. Wigen, 910 F.2d 1063 (2nd Cir. 1990) (no political offense); Abu Marzook v. Christopher, 1996 U.S. Dist. LEXIS 15007 (S.D.N.Y. 1996) (not a political offense since Hamas' attacks on purely civilian targets do not meet "incidental" test); *In re* Extradition of Lahoria, 932 F. Supp. 802 (N.D. Tex. 1996), and in the cases cited *infra*.

the exception,[303] the PLO cases did not.[304] U.S. courts' liberal application of the "political offense exception" in PIRA cases served as the impetus for the U.S.-U.K. supplementary extradition treaty,[305] which does not allow its application for violent crimes.[306] Recently, in

---

303 U.S. Courts applied the political offense exception to deny committal for extradition to the U.K. in three of the four major cases involving persons who committed acts of violence in the United Kingdom and Northern Ireland. *In re* McMullen, Magistrates Decisions No. 3-78-1099 M.G. (N.D. Cal., May 11, 1979); Matter of Mackin, No. 86 Cr. Misc. 1, at 47, (S.D.N.Y. Aug. 12, 1981), *appeal dismissed, In re* Mackin, 668 F.2d. 122 (2nd Cir. 1981); Quinn v. Robinson, 783 F.2d 776 (9th Cir.) (found extraditable), *cert. denied*, 479 U.S. 882 (1986); *In re* Doherty, 599 F. Supp. 270 (S.D.N.Y. 1984), *petition denied*, United States v. Doherty, 615 F. Supp. 755 (S.D.N.Y. 1985), *aff'd*, 786 F.2d 491 (2nd Cir. 1986). *See also*, Charles Cantrell, *The Political Offense Exception in International Extradition: A Comparison of the United States, Great Britain, and the Republic of Ireland*, 60 MARQ. L. REV. 777 (1977); and Barbara Ann Banoff & Christopher H. Pyle, *"To Surrender Political Offenders": The Political Offense Exception to Extradition in United States Law*, 16 N.Y.U. J. INT'L L. & POL. 169 (1984). For a critical review of the doctrine and some of its applications, *see* Thomas E. Carbonneau, *The Political Offense Exception to Extradition and Transnational Terrorists: Old Doctrine Reformulated and New Norms Created*, 1 AM. SOC. INT'L L. 1 (1977); William M. Hannay, *International Terrorism and the Political Offense Exception to Extradition*, 18 COLUM. J. TRANSNAT'L L. 381 (1979); and Steven Lubet & Morris Czackes, *The Role of the American Judiciary in the Extradition of Political Terrorists*, 71 J. CRIM. L. & CRIMINOLOGY 193 (1980).

304 Eain v. Wilkes, 641 F.2d 504 (7th Cir. 1981), *cert. denied*, 454 U.S. 894 (1981).

305 Supplementary Extradition Treaty, June 25, 1985, U.S.-U.K., art. 3(a), *reprinted in*, S. EXEC. REP. NO. 99-17 (1986) (Supplementary Treaty). Prior to the treaty amendment, President Reagan unsuccessfully attempted to amend the extradition statute to give the Secretary of State sole discretion to make the political offense exception determination. S. 1639, 97th Cong., 1st Sess., 127 Cong. Rec. 9955 - 61 (daily ed. Sept. 18, 1981). Article 1 of the Supplemental treaty provides that:

> For the purposes of the Extradition Treaty, none of the following shall be regarded as an offense of a political character:
> (a) an offense for which both Contracting Parties have the obligation pursuant to a multilateral international agreement to extradite the person sought or to submit his case to their competent authorities for decision as to prosecution;
> (b) murder, voluntary manslaughter, and assault causing grievous bodily harm;
> (c) kidnaping, abduction, or serious unlawful detention, including taking a hostage;
> (d) an offense involving the use of a bomb, grenade, rocket, firearm, letter or parcel bomb, or any incendiary device if this use endangers any person; and
> (e) an attempt to commit any of the foregoing offenses or participation as an accomplice of a person who commits or attempts to commit such an offense.

The Supplementary Treaty's key substantive provision, Article 3(a), creates a defense to extradition. It provides:

> Notwithstanding any other provision of this Supplementary Treaty, extradition shall not occur if the person sought establishes to the satisfaction of the competent judicial authority by a preponderance of the evidence that the request for extradition has in fact been made with a view to try or punish him on account of his race, religion, nationality or political opinions, or that he would, if surrendered, be prejudiced at his trial or punished, detained or restricted in his personal liberty by reason of his race, religion, nationality or political opinions.

For similar language, *see* Protocol Relating to the Status of Refugees, 19 UST 6223, 606 UNTS 267, 6 ILM 78 (1967), enacted as part of the U.S. Immigration and Nationality Act, 8 U.S.C. § 1158(a) (1988), incorporating §1101(42), and § 1253(h). M. Cherif Bassiouni, *The "Political-Offense Exception" Revisited: Extradition Between the U.S. and the U.K. - A Choice Between Friendly Cooperation Among Allies and Sound Law and Policy*, 15 DENVER J. INT'L L. & POL'Y 255 (1987).

306 Only a few cases have been presented under the Supplemental Treaty, including McMullen, one of the original three protected by the political offense exception. *In re* Extradition of Smyth, 863 F. Supp. 1137 (N.D. Cal. 1994) (finding, under the article 3(a) exception that Smyth could not be committed for extradition); *rev'd and remanded*, United States v. Smyth (*In re* Smyth), 61 F.3d 711, (9th Cir.) (finding Smyth extraditable under supplementary treaty), *amended*, United States v. Smyth (*In re* Smyth), 73 F.3d 887 (9th Cir. 1995), *reh'g en banc denied*, United States v. Smyth (*In re* Smyth), 72 F.3d 1433 (9th Cir.), *cert. denied*, Smyth v. United States, 116 S. Ct. 2558 (1996); United States v. Howard, 1991 U.S. Dist. LEXIS 16729 (D. Mass. 1991) (alleged PIRA member Howard extraditable under the supplementary treaty), *aff'd*, *In re* Howard, 791 F. Supp. 31 (D. Mass. 1992), *aff'd*, *In re* Extradition of Howard, 996 F.2d 1320 (1st Cir. 1993); *In re* McMullen, 1988 U.S. Dist. LEXIS

an effort to combat international terrorism, the U.S. has sought to include a similar limitation on the "political offense exception" in several new treaties, as well as supplementary amendments to existing treaties.[307] The United States Senate has advised the President not to negotiate a limitation on the "political offense exception" with totalitarian or non-democratic regimes.[308] The "political offense exception" has not been found to extend to economic or financial crimes.[309]

While the "political offense exception" continues to attract much interest and attention in light of increased international terrorism, it is seldom granted.[310] The United States, like most countries with a similar legal system, is now accepting the doctrine of the "exception to the exception;" that is, to exclude international crimes from being considered part of the "political offense exception."[311]These international crimes include: aggression; war crimes; unlawful use, production and stockpiling of certain prohibited weapons; crimes against humanity; genocide; *apartheid*; slavery and slave-related practices; torture; unlawful human experimentation; piracy; offenses against international maritime navigation; unlawful seizure of aircraft, sabotage and related crimes; attacks against internationally protected persons; taking of hostages; unlawful use of the mails (for terror-violence); drug offenses (international); destruction and/or theft of national treasures and cultural heritage; environmental violations; cutting of submarine cables; international traffic in obscene materials; counterfeiting (currency); bribery of foreign public officials; theft of nuclear materials; mercenarism; and crimes against United Nations personnel.[312] Recent U.S. treaties have included a provision to the effect that the "political offense exception" will not apply to offenses included in multilateral treaties, conventions or agreements which the U.S. and

---

7201 (S.D.N.Y. 1988), *habeas corpus granted*, *In re* Extradition of McMullen, 769 F. Supp. 1278 (S.D.N.Y. 1991), *aff'd*, McMullen v. United States, 953 F.2d 761 (2nd Cir. 1992), *aff's in part, rev'd in part*, *In re* Extradition of McMullen, 989 F.2d 603 (2nd Cir.), *cert. denied*, McMullen v. United States, 510 U.S. 913 (1993). Another case, still pending on the merits at the time of this writing, is *In re* Kirby. An appeal of bail was heard at 106 F.3d 855 (9th Cir. 1997).

[307] Similar provisions exist in Supplementary Treaty of Extradition to promote the Repression of Terrorism, Mar. 17, 1987, U.S.-Belg., art. 2, 3 and 4, S. TREATY DOC. NO. 104-8 (1995); Second Supplementary Extradition Treaty, Feb. 9, 1988, U.S.-Spain, art. 4, S. TREATY DOC. NO. 102-24 (1992); Supplementary Extradition Treaty, Oct. 21, 1986, U.S.-F.R.G., S. TREATY DOC. NO. 100-6 (1987). However, the provision was not included in the treaty with Jordan. Treaty of Extradition, Mar. 28, 1995, U.S.-Jordan, art. 4, S. TREATY DOC. NO. 104-3 (1995).

[308] Supplementary Extradition Treaty, June 25, 1985, U.S.-U.K., S. EXEC. REP. NO. 99-17 (1985).

[309] *Koskotas*, 931 F.2d at (financial crimes not political offenses); *Sindona*, 619 F.2d at 173 (fraudulent bankruptcy, even if "it resulted from political maneuvering and is pursued for political reasons," not a political offense); Jhirad v. Ferrandina, 536 F.2d 478, 485 (2nd Cir.)) (embezzlement by public official, "not in any sense a political offense"), *cert. denied*, 429 U.S. 833 (1976); *Garcia-Guillern*, 450 F.2d at 1192 (financial crimes by Peruvian public official, not political offenses); *Jimenez*, 311 F.2d at 560 (financial crimes by former chief executive of Venezuela, not political offenses).

[310] *See* CHRISTINE VAN DEN WYNGAERT, THE POLITICAL OFFENSE EXCEPTION IN EXTRADITION (1981); M. CHERIF BASSIOUNI, INTERNATIONAL TERRORISM AND POLITICAL CRIMES (1975). *See also* M. CHERIF BASSIOUNI, U.S. LEGAL RESPONSES TO INTERNATIONAL TERRORISM (1987). It has not been the object of many decisions in the U.S., where the jurisprudence of the courts has been consistent and narrow in granting it. Throughout the history of extradition, from Jay's Treaty of 1794 to 1997, there have been approximately 80 cases involving the "political offense exception," of which 30 were in the last 20 years, and it was granted in less than 10 cases.

[311] *Artukovic*, 247 F.2d at 204-05 (war crimes do not bar application of political offense exception); *Artukovic*, 628 F. Supp. at 1370 (finding Artukovic extraditable, no political offense exception).

[312] These crimes are the subject of a number of international conventions which provide for the duty to prosecute or extradite. *See* BASSIOUNI, EXTRADITION, *supra* note 1, at 566-80; ICL CONVENTIONS, *supra* note 10.

the applicable treaty partner are both parties that include an obligation to extradite or prosecute.[313] There is a growing trend in international relations to give effect to the maxim *aut dedere aut judicare*.[314] Thus, if a state wishes to shield someone from extradition for the "political offense exception," it should assume the duty to prosecute.

Exclusion for Prosecution Based on Certain Discriminatory Grounds

It could be said that this exclusion is an extension of the "political offense exception." It is based on the fact that the requesting state is seeking the relator as a means of persecuting him on the basis of his political, or religious beliefs, or because of his race or religion, or if there is a reasonably well-grounded fear. These grounds are based on the 1967 Protocol Amending the 1951 Refugee Convention, which is embodied in U.S. immigration and naturalization law by virtue of which such a person may obtain political asylum.[315]

There is an interrelationship between the "political offense exception" and exclusion based on certain discriminatory grounds. Usually the former arises exclusively in extradition proceedings while the latter arises in immigration proceedings. Because the question of prosecution arises in the context of asylum proceedings, it is subsequent to the INS statute and relative Federal Regulations. It is therefore an issue determined as part of administrative proceedings, subject to limited judicial review, and about which the government has much discretion. Such a determination does not affect extradition proceedings, nor, vice-versa, do extradition determinations of the applicability of the "political offense exception" affect asylum proceedings. Both follow separate and unrelated tracks, and the findings of either one are not conclusive on the other. Thus, a person may be held non-extraditable on grounds of the "political offense exception" and yet be denied "political asylum."[316] This is an incongruent situation, but it is one that gives the government political leeway to effectuate surrender by means of immigration when extradition fails.

Offenses of a Military and Fiscal Nature

The military offenses exclusion will not be applied to conduct which is also criminal under civilian criminal codes, nor will it block extradition where the conduct amounts to a violation of the laws of war that amount to war crimes.[317]

In recent times, the U.S. has sought to include fiscal and economic offenses in treaties which are usually excluded by other countries. They include: tax evasion and other administrative regulations, such as cash reporting requirements. The U.S. also seeks the inclusion of crimes arising out of economic and financial regulations. The traditional reluctance of countries to refuse to include these offenses, often because states have no

---

313 *See, e.g.*, Treaty of Extradition, Nov. 14, 1994, U.S.-Switz., art. 3 (2), S. TREATY DOC. NO. 104-9 (1995); Treaty of Extradition, Mar. 28, 1995, U.S.-Jordan, art. 4 (2) (b), S. TREATY DOC. NO. 104-3 (1995).

314 *See* BASSIOUNI, EXTRADITION, *supra* note 1, at 8-11. *See* BASSIOUNI & WISE, AUT DEDRE, AUT JUDICARE, *supra* note 124.

315 8 U.S.C.A. § 1101.

316 *See* BASSIOUNI, EXTRADITION, *supra* note 1, at 563-566.

317 Historically, the military offense exception has arisen in relation to those who illegally avoided the draft during the Vietnam war. *See* David A. Tate, *Draft Evasion and the Problem of Extradition*, 32 ALB. L. REV. 337 (1968).

mutual interest in enforcing law peculiar to other state's political-economic system,[318] is breaking down due to increased concerns with organized crime, drug trafficking, money laundering, tax evasion, and violation of currency laws.[319] The U.S., however, includes these crimes as part of other complex crimes like RICO and CCE, which are unknown to other legal systems. Furthermore, the use of such statutes as mail fraud to convict for other crimes has also met with some resistance by other states. Two treaties, respectively with Germany and Switzerland, do not include fiscal offenses and crimes against economic policy.[320]

Exclusion of Nationals

Generally, the U.S. does not refuse extradition simply because the relator is a U.S. national, even if its treaty partners do.[321] Recent U.S. treaties leave the decision to extradite nationals to the discretion of each party, subject to its laws.[322] *Valentine v. United States ex rel. Neidecker*[323] held that the treaties without the express grant did not authorize the executive to extradite U.S. nationals; but in 1990, the Congress adopted Section 3196, a new section of the extradition statute which gives the Secretary of State the authority to extradite U.S. nationals regardless of treaty language.

U.S. treaties partners who invoke discretionary treaty provisions to refuse to extradite their own nationals have served as a consistent source of consternation to the U.S. Congress.[324] Such a denial of extradition should be conditional on the requested state to

---

318 *See* A. N. Sack, *Non-Enforcement of Foreign Revenue Laws in International Law and Practice*, 81 U. PA. L. REV., 559 (1933).

319 *See, e.g.*, United Nations Convention Against Illicit Traffic in Narcotic Drugs and Psychotropic Substances, *opened for signature*, Dec. 20, 1988, *reprinted in* 28 I.L.M. 493; Council of Europe Convention on Laundering, Search, Seizure and Confiscation of the Proceeds from Crime, Nov. 8, 1990, No. 141 Europ. T.S. No. 141, *reprinted in*, 30 I.L.M. 148.

320 Treaty of Extradition, Nov. 14, 1990, U.S.-Switz., art. 3 (3), S. TREATY DOC. NO. 104-9 (1995); Extradition Treaty, June 20, 1978, U.S.-F.R.G., 32 U.S.T. 1485, T.I.A.S. No. 9785. For the celebrated case of Marc Rich and Pinkus Green and the United Sates' efforts to extradite them from Switzerland for economic crimes, *see* THEY WENT THATAWAY: THE STRANGE CASE OF MARCH RICH AND PINCUS GREEN, H. REP. NO. 102-537 (1992).

321 *See* Charlton v. Kelly, 229 U.S. 447 (1913) (holding that absent any treaty language to the contrary, the U.S. may extradite its own nationals) .

322 The following language is typical of treaties negotiated after 1936: "[n]either Contracting Party shall be bound to deliver up its own nationals, but the executive authority of the requested Party shall, if not prevented by the laws of that Party, have the power to deliver them up if, in its discretion, it be deemed proper to do so." Extradition Treaty, May 4, 1978, U.S.-Mex., art. 9, 31 U.S.T. 5059, T.I.A.S. No. 9656. There are currently 29 treaties in force that contain the *Neidecker* language, Valentine v. United States *ex rel.* Neidecker, 299 U.S. 5, 7-12 (1936) (where the court held that the applicable treaties proscription that the parties are not bound to deliver their nationals did not contain a grant of authority to surrender nationals) and Gouveia v. Vokes, 800 F. Supp 241, 244 n.3 (E.D. Penn. 1992) (listing 33 treaties with the same language. The Senate has recently consented to new treaties with Hungary, Bolivia, Belgium, and Switzerland), excluding that language.

323 *Id.*

324 Mexico's practice of refusing to extradite its nationals, in conjunction with its status as a transit state for the U.S.'s illicit drug market, caused a burgeoning practice of informally rendering Mexican Nationals—many of whom also held U.S. citizenship—to the U.S. to stand trial. This practice, often carried out between local DEA agents, Mexican law enforcement, and local federal and state prosecutors and law enforcement agents, was recklessly utilized in the abduction of Dr. Alvarez-Machain, which culminated in the *Machain* decision. However, the political fallout after *Machain* has caused a flurry of formal and informal meetings between the U.S. and Mexican officials with the intent, if not to end the practice, to implement some formality into the process. The most prominent example of this dispute is Mexico. In Escobedo v United States, 623 F.2d 1098, 1106 (5th Cir. 1980) the Court held that even if Mexico never extradited its nationals to the U.S., the U.S. could do so, but that the

prosecute its national under the principle *aut dedere aut judicare.*[325] It is hardly defensible for any state to refuse an otherwise valid extradition request only because the relator is a national. But to do so without subjecting the relator to prosecution, when sufficient grounds exist under national law, is unconscionable. It simply shows that nationals of a given state can commit crimes abroad with impunity if they return to their country of origin before being caught. This practice should be reversed, and in that respect, the U.S. has taken a positive position.

Double Jeopardy

While this defense is at times contained in treaties,[326] it will depend largely on the similarity of the charges for which the relator has been requested and for which he has been already prosecuted, acquitted or convicted. The defense has not been so far based on the Fifth Amendment of the U.S. Constitution insofar as the Constitution has a very limited extraterritorial application.[327] Moreover, the U.S. recognizes the doctrine of "separate sovereigns," meaning that a foreign prosecution for the same crime and/or conduct is not deemed *per se* to violate double jeopardy.[328] The defense is available in the U.S. only if contained in a treaty.

Statute of Limitations, Pardon or Amnesty

Most treaties contain a defense to extradition where the prosecution at issue is barred by the statute of limitations statute of the requested or requesting state. The treaties vary as to whether it is the one or the other of the two states whose statute is to be relied upon, or the longest of both. It is, in the U.S., only a treaty-based defense.[329] One fundamental consideration is when the applicable statute of limitations began to run or whether some intervening fact has tolled the running of the statute of limitations. For instance, a relator's status as a fugitive from justice will toll the statute.[330] Statute of limitations is not, however, a defense for charges of war crimes, crimes against humanity, or genocide.[331] Amnesty or pardon may be defenses to extradition, but only where the applicable treaty provides for it.

---

secretary of state under "Executive Discretion" could deny it.

325 BASSIOUNI & WISE, AUT DEDRE AUT JUDICARE, *supra* note 124.

326 *See* Galanis v. Pallanck, 568 F.2d 234 (2nd Cir. 1977), where the Court held that it was a treaty right; United States *ex. rel.* Bloomfield v. Gengler, 507 F.2d 925 (2nd Cir. 1974); and Gusikog v. United States, 620 F.2d 459 (5th Cir. 1980).

327 *See* United States v. Ryan, 360 F. Supp. 270 (1973); United States v. Martinez. 616 F.2d 185 (5th Cir. 1980), *cert. denied*, 450 U.S. 994 (1981).

328 Blockburger v. U.S., 52 S. Ct. 180 (1932).

329 Hatfield v. Guay, 87 F.2d 358 (1st Cir. 1937); Merino v. United States Marshall, 326 F.2d 5 (9th Cir. 1963); Freedman v. United States, 437 F. Supp. 1252 (N.D. Ga.1977); Jhirad v. Ferrandina, 377 F. Supp. 34 (S.D.N.Y. 1974) and Jhirad v. Ferrandina, 536 F.2d 478 (2nd Cir. 1976), *cert. denied*, 429 U.S. 833 (1976); Caplan v. Vokes, 649 F.2d 1336 (9th Cir. 1981); Garcia Guillern v. United States 450 F.2d 1189 (5th Cir. 1971).

330 United States v. Fowlie, 24 F.3d 1059, 1071-72 (9th Cir. 1994) (one is a fugitive who affirmatively and voluntarily acted with the intent to avoid prosecution, and therefore tolls the statute); United States v. Catino, 735 F.2d 718 (2nd Cir. 1984); Caplan v. Vokes, 649 F.2d 1336 (9th Cir. 1981); *Jhirad*, 536 F.2d at 480.

331 Convention on the Non-Applicability of Statutory Limitations to War Crimes and Crimes Against Humanity, art. 1, Nov. 26, 1968, 754 U.N.T.S. 73.

Immunity from Prosecution

The United States employs grants of immunity from prosecution as part of plea-bargaining in exchange for an accused's cooperation or testimony in another criminal trial.[332] It is a technique not recognized in most other systems of the world, where mandatory prosecutions are the norm. In the context of extradition, the question is whether plea agreements bar extradition where the grant of immunity or plea bargain arose from the same or substantially same conduct as the one on which the criminal charge advanced for extradition. Since usually immunity or plea bargaining are not enumerated defenses in the applicable treaty, the question becomes whether barring extradition on these grounds violates the U.S.'s treaty obligations. Courts have held, however, that, given the constitutional rights a relator gives up to obtain the immunity or bargain,[333] the executive has an obligation to enforce these agreements, despite the possible treaty violation it engenders.[334] When immunity is granted as part of a plea bargain, the U.S. cannot transmit the evidence obtained by virtue of the immunity to the requesting state.[335]

Exclusions Concerning Certain Types of Penalties and Treatment of Offenders.

Certain countries exclude extradition where the death penalty is enforceable for the offense charged. U.S. treaty language is usually discretionary, giving each respective treaty partner the option to refuse to extradite for the death penalty or, if extradition is granted, limit the penalty to a term of years. When the U.S. is the requested state, the "rule of non-inquiry" will prohibit the court from inquiring into the potential treatment of the relator once extradited.[336] Once again, the non-territorial application of the Constitution means that the Eighth Amendment's prohibition against "cruel and unusual" treatment does not protect those who may be extradited to a foreign country. However, the Secretary of State can, based on the applicable treaty, exercise discretion to refuse to surrender the individual, or allow "conditional extradition" (discussed below) and limit the penalty. The United States' continued application of the death penalty can prevent the extradition of individuals to the United States.[337] This law is the case with respect to Italy, which in June 1996 declared that

[332] Geisser v. United States, 513 F.2d 862 (5th Cir. 1975), *on remand*, Petition of Geisser, 414 F. Supp. 49 (S.D. Fla. 1976), *vacated on other grounds*, 554 F.2d 698 (5th Cir. 1977) (recognizing that a breach of a plea agreement may in some instances form the basis for an order enjoining extradition, relying on Santabello v. New York, 404 U.S. 257 (1971)), *appeal after remand*, 627 F.2d 745 (5th Cir. 1980), *cert. denied*, Bauer v. United States, 450 U.S. 1031 (1981); Palermo v. Warden, 545 F.2d 286 (2nd Cir. 1976) (using the first *Geisser* decision to free a defendant who had relied on prosecution's assurance of a limited sentence), *cert. dismissed*, 431 U.S. 911 (1977)

[333] Most significantly, an individual's Fifth Amendment right against self-incrimination.

[334] *See Geisser*, 414 F. Supp. at 52. For similar decisions arising under the Status of Forces Agreement (SOFA) between the United States and West Germany, *see* Plaster v. United States, 720 F.2d 340 (4th Cir. 1983); *In re* Burt, 737 F.2d 1477 (7th Cir. 1984)

[335] United States v. Galanis, 429 F. Supp. 1215 (D. Conn. 1977).

[336] *See, e.g., In re* Sandhu, 1996 U.S. Dist. LEXIS 11828 (S.D.N.Y. Aug. 19, 1996) (court, despite strong evidence that the relator, a Sikh minority in India, would face terrible persecution and possible death upon return to India and the court's apparent reticence given the facts, found the "rule of non-inquiry" to completely bar consideration of requesting country's judicial system).

[337] *See, e.g.*, Soering v. United Kingdom, 11 EUR. HUM. RTS. REP. 439 (1989) ("having regard to the very long period of time spent on death row in such extreme conditions, with the ever present and mounting anguish of awaiting execution of the death penalty . . . [Soering's] extradition to the United States would expose him to

the extradition treaty's provision on allowing extradition where the death penalty could be applied is unconstitutional. Regrettably, that decision of the Constitutional Court of Italy did not take into account the possibility of the U.S. not giving assurances that it would not apply the death penalty. Such a principled decision results in giving a requested person impunity because it is not conditional upon Italy prosecuting under the principle *aut dedere aut judicare*.

Review of Extradition Orders

Neither the governments nor the relator can directly appeal an extradition magistrate's decision. This stems in part from Congress' failure to include a right of appeal in the extradition statute and from the Executive's failure to include it in most treaties.[338] It also stems from two procedural questions that deprive federal courts of appellate jurisdiction over the extradition magistrate's decision: (1) a decision to extradite is not a final judicial order;[339] and (2) an extradition order is not made by a judge acting as an Article III Judge.[340] Thus, an appellate court in the United States cannot exercise appellate review over the decision of an extradition magistrate because they are not exercising Article III powers.[341] By limiting appeal rights, this effectively limits the federal courts' inquiry into the merits of an extradition decision. The only limited review of the extradition magistrate's decision is by way of a petition for a writ of *habeas corpus*.

If an extradition magistrate finds the relator not extraditable, the government cannot have that decision reviewed by any court at any level.[342] However, since the order denying extradition is not a final order, the government can file a new complaint for extradition, even when based on the same or substantially same facts.[343]

A person found extraditable can collaterally attack the order by means of a petition for a writ of *habeas corpus*.[344] *Habeas corpus* review is not, however, an appeal nor a trial *de novo*. Rather, it is limited to the following issues: (1) whether the magistrate had proper

---

a real risk of treatment going beyond the threshold set by Art.3"). Italy's Constitutional Court ruled in June 1997 that the treaty provision applicable to crimes for which the death penalty can apply is unconstitutional. The ruling of the Constitutional Court of Italy excludes even conditional extradition based on assurances by the U.S. that the penalty shall not be applied.

338 The sole exception to this is the 1985 U.S.-U.K. Supplemental Extradition Treaty. Article 3(a) provides for a right to appeal within the meaning of 28 U.S.C. § 1291. *See In re* Extradition of Howard, 996 F.2d 1320 (5th Cir. 1993).

339 28 U.S.C. § 1291; Ahmad v. Wigen, 910 F.2d 1063, 1065 (2nd Cir. 1990); Oen Yin-Choy v. Robinson, 858 F.2d 1400 (9th Cir. 1988) ("[b]ecause a certification of extradition is not a final order, no direct appeal from the decision will lie and review is available only by way of a petition of habeas corpus"); Quinn v. Robinson, 783 F.2d 776, 786 n.3 (9th Cir.), *cert. denied*, 479 U.S. 882 (1986); Collins v. Miller, 252 U.S. 364 (1920); United States v. Bishopp, 286 F.2d 320 (2d Cir 1961); Koskotas v. Roche, 931 F.2d 169, 171 (1st Cir. 1991). *But see* United States v. Bishopp, 286 F.2d at 323-24 (Medina, J., concurring).

340 *See* Austin v. Healy, 5 F.3d 598, 603 (2nd Cir. 1993); *Howard*, 996 F.2d at 1325; *In re* Metzger, 46 U.S. (5 How.) 176, 191 (1847); Lo Duca v. United States, 1996 U.S. App. LEXIS 28746 (2nd Cir. 1996).

341 *Metzger*, 46 U.S. at 191.

342 *In re* Mackin, 668 F.2d 122, 125-30 (2nd Cir. 1981). Nor can the government use mandamus or declaratory judgment to appeal a decision not to certify based on a factual finding. *See* United States v. Doherty, 786 F.2d 491, 497-501 (2d Cir. 1986).

343 *Collins,* 262 U.S. at 429; United States v. Doherty, 786 F.2d 491, 495 (2nd Cir. 1986); Massieu v. Reno, 91 F.3d 416 (3rd Cir.) *Reh'g en banc denied* 1996 U.S. App. LEXIS 25539 (3rd Cir. 1996).

344 28 U.S.C. § 2241 (c) (1) (1994).

jurisdiction; (2) the proper identity of the relator; (3) the existence of a valid treaty; (4) the extraditabilty of the crime charged; (5) the existence of "double criminality;" (6) the existence of "probable cause;" (7) the absence of any grounds for denial of extraditions or the applicability of a treaty defense, exclusion or exception.[345] The court will also review the extradition proceedings for "due process" violations.[346] Petitioners have raised, *inter alia,* issues pertaining to: provisional arrest, denial of bail, double jeopardy/double criminality and specialty, and probable cause violations through *habeas corpus* proceedings.[347] The reviewing court will rule on the questions of law involved in the issues stated above, and will examine the facts only insofar as they relate to these legal issues. The reviewing court will not substitute its judgment to that of the extradition magistrate who heard the case initially unless such judge: failed to properly apply the law or the applicable legal standards; committed error with respect to the sufficiency of the evidence supporting the existence of "probable cause;" failed to apply one of the grounds for denial of extradition; or abused his judicial discretion.

The *habeas corpus* hearing will be held before a Federal District Court judge, who can review the order of an extradition magistrate, even if that extradition magistrate was also a Federal District judge.[348] This situation makes it unlikely that one Federal District Court Judge will overturn another Judge of the same level within the same District Court. Furthermore, it is possible that the same Judge who sat as an extradition magistrate can be the reviewing judge in a *habeas corpus* proceeding. This anomalous situation, like the one described earlier, reduces the chances for an impartial review on *habeas corpus.* If the *habeas corpus* court upholds the order of extradition, the relator can seek review before the U.S. Circuit Court of Appeals, which will review the District Court's *habeas* decision on the same grounds as stated above. If the relator fails to receive a favorable judgment before the Court of Appeals, he may file a motion for a rehearing *en banc*. Finally, the relator may petition the United States Supreme Court for the seldom-granted writ of *certiorari.*

A petition for *habeas corpus* and any eventual petitions by the relator must be accompanied by a petition for an order to stay the original order granting extradition. Otherwise, the government may surrender the relator even while the *habeas corpus* petition is pending. At all levels of review, the question of bail may be reargued either by the relator

---

[345] Terlinden v. Ames, 184 U.S. 270 (1902); Fernandez v. Philips, 268 U.S. 311, 312 (1925); Ornelas v. Quiz, 161 U.S. 502 (1896); Wright v. Henkel, 190 U.S. 40 (1903); Benson v. McMahon, 127 457 (1888).

[346] *See* Matter of Extradition of *Manzi*, 888 F.2d 204, 206 (1st Cir. 1989). In *Manzi*, the court noted that "serious due process" violations could justify *habeas corpus* relief beyond the usual scope, "[i]n considering Manzi's claims, this court recognizes that serious due process concerns may merit review beyond the narrow scope of inquiry in extradition proceedings."

[347] *See* Pfeifer v. United States Bureau of Prisons, 615 F.2d 873 (9th Cir. 1980) (seeking release through a *habeas corpus* proceeding from a federal penitentiary, where relator was serving the remainder of a sentence imposed originally by Mexican officials in a Mexican court for a Mexican crime); Freedman v. United States, 437 F. Supp. 1252 (N.D. Ga. 1977) (grounding jurisdiction upon the federal *habeas corpus* statute, 28 U.S.C. § 2241). The court in *Pfeifer* found the relator was not entitled to *habeas corpus* relief, that "the United States may constitutionally take custody of Americans tried and convicted in foreign countries under procedures that do not comport with the Bill of Rights." 615 F.2d at 297, *citing* 28 U.S.C. § 2256 (Supp. 1978). *See also* United States v. Socaccia, 18 F.3d 795 (9th Cir. 1994) (raising issues on interlocutory appeal of double jeopardy and specialty which was denied on the grounds that these issues can be raised in the course of the appellate process after trial of the defendant who was extradited from Switzerland).

[348] David v. Attorney General, 699 F.2d 411, 416 (7th. Cir. 1983), *cert. denied*, 464 U.S. 832 (1983); *Demjanjuk*, 776 F.2d at 577.

or by the government. An accused may seek a declaratory judgment[349] or mandamus in limited cases. The former,[350] as an alternative to review by means of *habeas corpus*, the latter,[351] only when there is a clear abuse of discretion by the court or the government. Both are rare occurrences.

Executive Discretion and Conditional Extradition

Prior to the 1848 Extradition Act, the President exercised unfettered discretion in extradition.[352] As mentioned previously, Congress enacted the 1848 Act in part to curb the executive's discretion and to empower the courts to protect the relator's liberty interests through the application of the treaty, the statute, and under fundamental due process requirements of the U.S. Constitution. Thus, the 1848 Act partially retained the Executive's discretion, but limits the exercise of that discretion to those relators the extradition magistrate has certified as extraditable. The Executive Branch has no power under the Act to extradite a relator that the extradition magistrate has not certified as extraditable. That situation has not been changed since 1848.

Even before a complaint for extradition is filed, the Executive Branch may exercise discretion and refuse to accept a foreign state's request for extradition.[353] In that case, the issue of whether the U.S. has breached its treaty obligations arises.

As discussed above, an extradition magistrate's order certifying extradition does not necessarily mandate the surrender of the relator. Once the relator is certified, Section 3186, the sole discretion to surrender that person rests with the Secretary of State. U.S. courts have found that the Executive's discretion to decide whether to extradite derives from its constitutional power to conduct foreign relations and is a recognition by Congress of the foreign policy considerations involved.[354] The Secretary of State may review the court's ruling on both the facts and the law, for political or human rights considerations,[355] or for

---

[349] 28 U.S.C. § 2201 (1994).

[350] A declaratory judgment is an adequate procedural for the government and the relator to challenge some aspect of the judicial proceedings, and in the case of the relator, a substitutive means to challenge an extradition order instead of resorting to *habeas corpus*. *See* Wacker v. Bisson, 348 F.2d 602 (5th Cir. 1965).

[351] A party may also resort to mandamus in cases of clear usurpation of power or abuse of discretion. *See In re* Extradition of Ghandtchi, 697 F.2d 1037 (11th Cir. 1983).

[352] Lo Duca v. United States, 93 F.3d 1100, 1103, n.2 (2nd Cir.) *cert. denied*, 117 S.Ct. 508 (1996); Eain v. Wilkes, 641 F.2d 504, 513 n. 13 (7th Cir), *cert. denied,* 454 U.S. 894 (1981); *see* Fong Yue Ting v. United States, 149 U.S. 698, 714 (1893); M. CHERIF BASSIOUNI, INTERNATIONAL EXTRADITION AND WORLD PUBLIC ORDER 505 (1974).

[353] *See, e.g.*, where the Government determined that the defense of "double jeopardy" applied, it denied France's request before going to a hearing in 1978 DIGEST OF UNITED STATES PRACTICE IN INTERNATIONAL LAW 410-11; United States Dep't of State File No. P78 0080-1043.

[354] The first judicial recognition of the executive's discretion to extradite was *In re* Strupp, 23 F. 281 (C.C.S.D.N.Y. 1873). For a historical discussion, see MOORE, EXTRADITION, *supra* note 1, at §§ 361-366. For a more contemporary view, *see* BASSIOUNI, EXTRADITION, *supra* note 1, at 766-776; 4 ABBELL & RISTAU, INTERNATIONAL JUDICIAL ASSISTANCE: CRIMINAL - EXTRADITION, § 13-3-8(2); Note, *Executive Discretion in Extradition*, 62 COL. L. REV. 1313, 1316-25 (1962).

[355] Peroff v. Hylton, 563 F.2d 1099, 1249 (4th Cir. 1977) ("[a] denial of extradition by the Executive may be appropriate when strong humanitarian grounds are present, but such grounds exist only when it appears that, if extradited, the individual will be persecuted, not prosecuted, or subjected to grave injustice.") The executive may consider grounds applicable under Articles 32 and 33 of the 1967 Protocol relating to the Status of Refugees amending the 1951 Refugee Convention, 19 U.S.T. 6223, T.I.A.S. No. 6577, the text of which is embodied in the Immigration and Nationality Act, 8 U.S.C. §§ 1101-1151 (1988).

any other reason, and refuse or grant extradition.[356] Courts, although precluded from judicial action by the "rule of non-inquiry," will often highlight potential human rights concerns as amenable to the Secretary's discretion.[357]

Another way the Secretary may address political or humanitarian concerns is through its discretion to place conditions on the surrender.[358] This authority emanates from section 3186's grant of discretion: the power not to surrender includes the power to conditionally surrender. The judiciary does not have this power.[359] In these cases, the Secretary of State will require from the original requesting state certain assurances before surrendering the extraditable relator,[360] such as the return of the relator to the U.S. upon completion of the legal proceedings or the insistence that the government not try him before a special or military tribunal. This process is also essentially political.

Although not a judicial process, in the exercise of its discretion, the Secretary will often accept written petitions on behalf of the relator. The Secretary's decision is not, however, subject to judicial review nor is it reported in judicial records. Sometimes it is published in some Department of State publication, and sometimes it is "classified."

Finally, the Executive may re-file an extradition request that an extradition magistrate has denied, even when based on the same facts. There is no double jeopardy prohibition, nor is the magistrate's denial deemed to be *res judicata* to a second or any number of future requests.[361] However, subsequent extradition magistrates entertaining the refiled requests cannot disturb findings of fact made by the initial magistrate without new evidence. The process of re-filing requests is, however, the government's indirect way of having another bite of the apple after a denial of extraditabilty. While in practice, the government has re-filed requests on the basis of new evidence or new circumstances, it has abused the process.[362]

---

[356] *See, e.g.*, Escobedo v. United States, 632 F.2d 1098, 1105 (5th Cir.), *cert. denied*, 449 U.S. 1036 (1980).

[357] *See* Yapp v. Reno, 26 F.3d 1562, 1567 (11th Cir. 1994) (indicating that the relator may address her concerns over speedy trial rights to the Secretary of State). In the same case, the court also addressed its concerns to the requesting state. *Id.*

[358] *See* Jimenez v. United States District Court, 84 S. Ct. 14, 19 (1963) (Goldberg, J., chambers opinion) (denying stay and describing conditions on surrender placed by Venezuela).

[359] *See, e.g.*, Emami v. United States Dist. Court for Northern District of California, 834 F.2d 1444, 1453 (9th Cir. 1987); *Demjanjuk*, 776 F.2d at 584.

[360] The United States put conditions on the surrender of Ziyad Abu Eain a case which, but for its political nature, should have resulted in the Secretary denying extradition. *See* Eain v. Wilkes, 641 F.2d 504 (7th Cir. 1981); BASSIOUNI, EXTRADITION, *supra* note 1, at 768-769.

[361] *See* Hooker v. Klein, 573 F.2d 1360 (9th Cir.), *cert. denied*, 439 U.S. 932 (1978). *See also* Collins v. Loisel, 262 U.S. 426 (1923); Artukovic v. Rison, 628 F. Supp. 1370 (C.D. Cal.) (stating prior holding of applicability of political offense exception not bar to subsequent extradition based on separate request), *aff'd*, 784 F.2d 1354 (9th Cir. 1986); *In re* Gonzalez, 217 F. Supp. 717 (S.D.N.Y. 1963); *Ex parte* Schorer, 197 F. 67 (C.C.E.D. Wis. 1912); *In re* Kelly, 26 F. 852 (C.C.D. Minn. 1886).

[362] The United States attempted to extradite Mr. Mario Ruiz Massieu, a former Deputy Attorney General of Mexico who headed the investigation into the assassination of his brother, PRI Presidential candidate Jose Fransisco Ruiz Massieu, to Mexico on charges of intimidation, obstruction of justice, concealment, and embezzlement. Although denied each time because of a lack of evidence to support extradition, the government presented four complaints for extradition and attempted to have Mr. Ruiz deported to Mexico, even though there were no grounds under the Immigration and Nationality Act (INA) for his deportation. The government contended that section 241(a)(4)(C) of the INA [8 U.S.C. § 1251(a)(4)(C)(I)] granted the Secretary of State unfettered authority to deport an alien whose presence adversely effects U.S. foreign policy. The court, however, found that portion of the Act unconstitutional. *Massieu*, 91 F.3d 416.

Surrender of the Relator

Once the relator is certified as extraditable, Section 3186 empowers the Secretary of State to deliver the relator to an authorized agent of the foreign government.[363] The agent of the foreign government is empowered to take custody of the relator and to take him to the territory of the requesting state, but only pursuant to the applicable treaty.[364] Usually, U.S. Marshals will deliver the relator to the agents of the requesting state for travel to that state. The Marshals will often accomplish the surrender of the relator on board the aircraft carrying him to the requesting state. Occasionally, the government will transfer the relator to the requesting state's agents before he can file for a stay of the certification or for *habeas corpus* relief.

The government cannot arbitrarily hold a relator for an unlimited amount of time prior to surrendering him to the requesting state. Section 3188 prohibits the government from holding a relator for more than two calendar months after his commitment for extradition.[365] The two months begins to run after the extradition magistrate "commits" the relator, that is, from the time the extradition magistrate orders him detained for the purpose of extradition.[366] The two months, however, are tolled by any *habeas corpus* actions initiated by the relator,[367] and do not include the actual time needed to remove the relator from the United States.[368] In certain cases, the government may induce the relator to sign a waiver of section 3188.[369] If the relator is still detained after the two calendar months, he may apply to a federal judge of any state for his release,[370] usually in the form of a *habeas corpus* action. The relator is required to notify the Secretary of State of his application for release.[371] However, the section no longer mandates release[372] after the two months, but provides for the right to be released.[373] The government bears the burden of demonstrating why the Court should not release the relator.[374]

Transit Extradition

Occasionally, persons extradited from one country to another must travel through United States territory. While the United States has no involvement in the original extradition proceedings, the state's agent must have legal authority to detain the relator while

---

363 18 U.S.C. § 3186 (1994).

364 *Id.*

365 18 U.S.C. § 3188 (1994).

366 The section applies, and the two months begin to run, "[w]henever any person . . . is committed for rendition to a foreign government . . ." and not upon certification—a purely ministerial action that officially informs the Secretary of State that the judge has found the relator extraditable. *In re* U.S., 713 F.2d 105, 108 n.2 (C.A. Tex. 1983); Barrett v. U.S., 590 F.2d 624 (C.A. Mich. 1978).

367 McElvy v. Civiletti, 523 F. Supp. 42 (D.C. Fla. 1981); *Barrett*, 590 F.2d at 625-626. The two month period begins to run again upon final adjudication of the relator's *habeas* action(s). *McElvy*, 523 F. Supp at 47.

368 18 U.S.C. § 3188 (1994).

369 Courts have upheld such waivers as valid. *McElvy*, 523 F. Supp. at 46-47.

370 18 U.S.C. § 3188 (1994).

371 *Id.*

372 Former section 654 of Title 18 required release after two calendar months. *See In re* Normano, 7 F. Supp 329 (D.C. Mass. 1934).

373 *In re* U.S., 713 F.2d at 108; *Barrett*, 590 F.2d at 626.

374 18 U.S.C. § 3188 (1994).

in the United States. Currently, the extraditions statute does not regulate this procedure. Extradition treaties that deal with transit may require "double criminality" or other conditions for the transit.[375] Certain treaties do grant foreign agents this authority, without any conditions.[376]

Alternatives to Extradition[377]

Abduction and Unlawful Seizure

In the United States, a court is not divested of *in personam* jurisdiction over a person brought before it via an abduction, kidnap or unlawful seizure that violates due process. This is the holding of what is now be called the *Ker-Frisbie-Machain* doctrine, or the U.S. version of *male captus bene detentus*. U.S. courts have therefore given alternatives to extradition that utilize illegal methods to secure an individual's presence the imprimatur of law. It is a doctrine based on the assumption that whatever harm is caused by the abduction adheres to the offended state, a wrong that implicates foreign policy concerns and is therefore best remedied (or not) by the executive branch. It is also based on a policy decision that assumes the benefits of trying those present, before the court, who have may have committed a crime outweigh the costs of principled adherence to the rule of law.

In 1992 the Supreme Court reaffirmed the *Ker-Frisbie*[378] doctrine in *United States v. Alvarez-Machain.*[379] The Court held that the rule of specialty, as found in the 1980 Extradition treaty between U.S. and Mexico, did not divest the trial court of jurisdiction over the relator because U.S. agents, working with the connivance of Mexican officials, abducted and did not extradite the relator. The court reasoned that the treaty: (1) did not express an intent by the parties to limit all renditions to its terms; (2) the parties had not intended Mr. Alvarez-Machain's rendition to be an extradition under the treaty; (3) the treaty did not prohibit abduction; and (4) was not intended to protect the territorial sovereignty of the parties and its terms could not remedy violations of that sovereignty, such as abductions. Thus, the Court held that the abduction did not violate the extradition treaty, and therefore

---

[375] *See, e.g.,* Extradition Treaty, Apr. 27, 1987, U.S.-Belg., art. 17, S. TREATY DOC. NO. 104-7 (1995) (requested state may refuse transit of its own nationals or if the person transited is wanted in that state for crime or punishment); Extradition Treaty, June 27, 1995, U.S.-Bol., art. XV, S. TREATY DOC. NO. 104-22 (1995) (requested state must respond to transit requested from requesting state "unless doing so would compromise that Party's essential interests"). Other treaties put no substantive restrictions on transit. *See, e.g.,* Extradition Treaty, Nov. 14, 1990, U.S. -Switz., art. 20, S. TREATY DOC. NO. 104-9 (1995)

[376] *See* Treaty Between the United States and Great Britain Concerning Reciprocal Rights for United States and Canada in the Conveyance and Wrecking and Salvage, May 18, 1908, art. 1, T.I.A.S. No. 502, 35 Stat. 2035; WHITEMAN DIGEST *supra* note 1, at 1078-80.

[377] BASSIOUNI, EXTRADITION *supra* note 1, at ch. 1.

[378] Ker v. Illinois, 119 U.S. 436 (1886) (government's illegal abduction of defendant from Peru does not necessarily defeat the court's jurisdiction over defendant); Frisbie v. Collins, 342 U.S. 519 (1952) (reaffirming *Ker* in interstate rendition context); Gerstein v. Pugh, 420 U.S. 103, 119 (1975) (reaffirming the rule of *Ker* and *Frisbie* in the context of illegal arrest).

[379] United States v. Alvarez-Machain, 504 U.S. 655 (1992) (abduction of person from foreign country with which the United States has an extradition treaty does not defeat U.S. criminal jurisdiction); McAlister, *supra* note 42.

the *Ker* doctrine applied.[380] Although not legalizing international abduction by government agents, the Court's opinion has the practical effect of removing any consequence for such illegal action.

There are two main exceptions to this rule recognized by U.S. courts. First, a court may refuse to exercise jurisdiction over a relator brought before it by shockingly egregious conduct by U.S. officials or their agents[381] that so violates fundamental notions of due process that a court will not sanction its practice. This is the holding of *United States v. Toscanino*,[382] although no court in a reported decision has applied it to release a relator.[383] Several U.S. courts have refused to recognize the *Toscanino* exception and therefore do not allow evidentiary hearings on claims of outrageous government conduct.[384] The *Toscanino* exception, although still viable, was somewhat eroded by *Machain*. The *Toscanino* court held, in part, that the nearly one-hundred-year-old *Ker* doctrine could not be squared with the Supreme Court's then recently developed due process standards.[385] The Supreme Court

---

380 *See* United States v. Valot, 625 F.2d 308, (9th Cir. 1980) (abduction does not violate extradition treaty). Cases that have followed *Machain* have found that extradition treaties do not prohibit abductions. United States v. Matta-Ballesteros, 71 F.3d 754, 762 (9th Cir. 1995) *reh'g en banc denied, amended*, United States v. Matta-Ballesteros, 98 F.3d 1100 (9th Cir. 1996) (*Alvarez-Machain* controlled in absence of an express provision in the Honduras-U.S. extradition treaty prohibiting kidnaping); United States v. Chapa-Garza, 62 F.3d 118, 120 (5th Cir. Tex. 1995) (court found held that the fact that U.S. Government's request for extradition was pending against Chapa-Garza under the U.S.-Mexico treaty prior to is abduction did not mean he was brought back under the extradition treaty and therefore *Machain* precluded him from claiming its protections); United States v. Baker, 1995 U.S. App. LEXIS 6295 (4th Cir.), *cert. denied*, Baker v. United States, 116 S. Ct. 194 (1995) (expulsion of U.S. citizen from Panama did not violate the U.S.-Panama extradition treaty and therefore did not divest the court of jurisdiction). Some non-U.S. court's have taken a different view. *See, e.g.*, Giry v. Dominican Republic, 95 I.L.R. 321 (U.N.H.R.C. 1990) (government's assistance in abduction and deportation of individual to stand trial in the U.S. violated procedural protection of the U.S.-Dom. extradition treaty).

381 United States v. Lira, 515 F.2d 68, 70 (2nd Cir.) (*Toscanino* does not apply if alleged mistreatment was not at the hands of representatives of the United States government), *cert. denied*, 423 U.S. 847 (1975).

382 United States v. Toscanino, 500 F.2d 267 (2nd Cir. 1974) (defendant's allegations of abduction and torture by or at the direction of U.S. government agents entitled defendant to an evidentiary hearing and, if true, would so offend due process, a federal court may refuse to try him under its supervisory powers over the administration of criminal justice).

383 Courts have limited the holding of *Toscanino* to require the articulation of facts sufficiently egregious to implicate due process. United States *ex rel.* Lujan v. Gengler, 510 F.2d 62, 66 (2nd Cir.), *cert. denied*, 421 U.S. 1001 (1975) (limiting Toscanino to a "complex of shocking governmental conduct sufficient to convert an abduction which is simply illegal into one which sinks to a violation of due process"). In practice this standard is so high that it effectively eviscerates the *Toscanino* exception to the *Ker* doctrine. United States v. Matta-Ballesteros, 71 F.3d 754, 764 (9th Cir. 1995) *reh'g en banc denied, amended*, United States v. Matta-Ballesteros, 98 F.3d 1100 (9th Cir. 1996) (holding that the lower courts finding that the defendant's mistreatment at the hands of U.S. Marshals was not "torture" was not "clearly erroneous," and despite indicting that it would find the defendant's treatment to constitute torture, and therefore, albeit reluctantly, would not exercise its supervisory powers); United States v. Chapa-Garza, 62 F.3d 118, 121 (5th Cir. Tex. 1995) (no *Toscanino* level harm alleged).

384 *See, e.g.*, United States v. Matta, 937 F.2d 567 (11th Cir. 1991); Matta-Ballesteros v. Henman, 896 F.2d 255 (7th Cir.), *cert. denied*, 498 U.S. 878 (1990); United States v. Wilson, 732 F.2d 404 (5th Cir.), *cert. denied*, 469 U.S. 1099 (1984); United States v. Darby, 744 F.2d 1508 (11th Cir. 1984), *reh'g denied, en banc*, 794 F.2d 733 (11th Cir. 1984), *cert. denied*, 471 U.S. 1100 (1985).

385 The *Toscanino* court specifically relied on Rochin v. California, 342 U.S. 165 (1952) (due process bars the government from exploiting its own deliberate lawlessness in bringing the accused to trial). *See* Olmstead v. United States, 277 U.S. 438, 483-85 (1928) (dissent admonishing that the government should not profit from its illegal activity). An abduction does not violate the Fourth Amendment's proscription against unreasonable seizures. United States v. Reed, 639 F.2d 896 (2nd Cir. 1981) (defendant's abduction, at gun point, from Bahamas did not violate fourth Amendment's proscription against unreasonable seizures since it was carried out on a valid warrant based on probable cause).

in *Alvarez-Machain* reaffirmed *Ker's* central holding, despite its earlier due process holdings.

The second exception to the *Ker-Frisbie-Machain* doctrine states that a court may not try an individual rendered for trial via a violation of international law—either convention or customary-based. The Court in *Alvarez-Machain* itself raised the possibility of this exception by expressly noting that it was not deciding whether Mr. Alvarez-Machain's abduction violated international law.[386] However, one post-*Machain* court has held, without analysis, that government -ponsored "kidnaping" does not rise to the level of a peremptory norm of international law that would divest the court of jurisdiction over the person kidnaped.[387] There is no doctrinal reason—in either domestic or international law—for limiting violations that defeat domestic *in personam* jurisdiction to violations of *jus cogens*, although it may reflect a judicial policy that the drastic remedy of exclusion will only apply where the most fundamental norms of international law are violated. Such a requirement would subsume this exception under the *Toscanino* exception, simply adding another source of "due process" considerations[388] rather than enforcement of the United States' international obligations.

Use of Immigration Laws[389]

The government may also use immigration law as a means of surrendering a person to another state, either before extradition proceedings are commenced or after extradition is denied, through the devices of exclusion, deportation, and denaturalization.[390]

Retroactive Application

It is a basic tenet of extradition law that a treaty providing for the extradition of individuals accused of specified crimes does not make an act a crime, but rather merely provides the means by which a state can obtain persons charged with those specified acts in order to try them where the act was committed. As a result, a treaty of extradition which includes a particular crime, but which was passed after the commission of that crime by the accused, still applies to the earlier act unless there is a specific treaty provision to the contrary,[391] thus in effect providing for some form of retroactivity.

The United States Government, in both the executive and judicial branches, has adhered to this basic tenet. In 1933 the Acting Secretary of State sent a telegram to the Chairman of

[386] The *Machain* court explicitly left that question open.

[387] *Matta-Ballesteros*, 71 F.3d at 763 n.5 ("[k]idnaping also does not qualify as a jus cogens norm, such that its commission would be justiciable in our courts even absent a domestic law"); *see also* Committee of U.S. Citizens Living in Nicaragua v. Reagan, 859 F.2d 929, 939-40 (D.C. Cir. 1988) (defining jus cogens).

[388] *See, e.g.*, United States v. Verdugo-Urquidez, 1994 U.S. App. LEXIS 16083 (9th Cir.) *amended, reh'g, en banc, denied*, 1994 U.S. App. LEXIS 20719 (9th Cir. 1994) (in denying that relator's abduction violated international law, court held that "outrageous government conduct is a prerequisite to Verdugo's international law and due process claims"); United States v. De La Pava, 1993 U.S. Dist. LEXIS 1912 (N.D. Ill. 1993) (*Machain* "suggests that due process concerns are triggered with respect to extradition treaties only where those treaties are actually invoked to obtain custody over the accused criminal"), *aff'd sub nom.*, United States v. Munoz-Solarte, 1994 U.S. App. LEXIS 18128 (7th Cir. 1994).

[389] BASSIOUNI, EXTRADITION *supra* note 1, at 167-216.

[390] U.S. v. Doherty, 786 F.2d 491 (2nd Cir. 1986).

[391] WHITEMAN DIGEST *supra* note 1, at 753. For a treaty provisions excluding retroactive effect, *see* Extradition Convention of 1856 between U.S. and Austria-Hungry, art. I, U.S.T. 9, 11 Stat. 691, 692-93.

the American Delegation to the 7th International Conference of American States in Montevideo informing him that extradition treaties applied to a previously committed offense unless the treaty expressly stated otherwise.[392] The Supreme Court reaffirmed this rule in *Factor v. Laubenheimer*,[393] where the Court stated that a later extradition treaty extended to proceedings concerning an offense not included in an previous treaty, regardless of the date of the offense. The Court added that a later treaty also would apply where there had been no previous extradition treaty.

However, this retroactivity provision can also be applied against the government. For example, in *Galanis v. Pollanck*,[394] a treaty of extradition between the United States and Canada contained a double jeopardy provision, which forbade extradition under the treaty where an accused had already been tried for the offense in the United States. The earlier extradition treaty lacked this provision. The defendant argued that the provision applied even to a crime committed before the effective date of the treaty as a result of the retroactivity rule. The Second Circuit agreed, pointing out that the drafters of the treaty must have been aware of this basic rule, and their failure to include a provision excluding retroactive effect manifested their intent to give the article that force.

Conclusion

Extradition has become more frequent to and from the U.S. due to the increased number of national and transnational crimes. It is the most effective way of inter-state cooperation in penal matters.

Although the rights of relators have been recently reduced in U.S. law and practice, mostly due to increase in drug traffic offenses, U.S. legal processes are fair, and indeed more so than in most countries in the world. There are some occasional abuses and miscarriages of justice, but these are few and far between. Indeed, considering the large number of extradition cases adjudicated in the U.S., the occasional wrongly decided case is the exception. The Government however, rightly feels that the extradition process is still too long and cumbersome. In part that may be due more to the lack of experience of certain judges than to other reforms.

The lengthy description of the U.S. extradition process that preceded evidences how fair and legislatic the process is in this country. Notwithstanding its weakness, it is still one that offers better guarantees of "due process" than most countries in the world.

---

[392] M.S. Dept. of State, file 710. G. International Law 5; 1933 FOREIGN REL., vol. IV, p. 185.

[393] 290 U.S. 276 (1933); *see also In re* DiGiancomo, 7 F. Cas. 366 (No. 3,747) (S.D.N.Y. 1874).

[394] 568 F.2d 234 (2d Cir. 1977); *see also* United States v. Flores, 538 F.2d 939 (2d Cir. 1976); BASSIOUNI, EXTRADITION, *supra* note 1, at 598-607.

Appendix 1

18 U.S.C.
CHAPTER 209 -- EXTRADITION

FEDERAL RULES OF CRIMINAL PROCEDURE

Applicable to removed proceedings, see rule 54, Appendix to this title.
Inapplicable to extradition or rendition of fugitives, see rule 54.
Removal proceedings, see rule 40.

CROSS REFERENCES

Removal of offenders against the United States, from district of arrest to district of commission of crime, see section 3042 of this title.

§ 3181. Scope and limitation of chapter

(a) The provisions of this chapter relating to the surrender of persons who have committed crimes in foreign countries shall continue in force only during the existence of any treaty of extradition with such foreign government.

(b) The provisions of this chapter shall be construed to permit, in the exercise of comity, the surrender of persons, other than citizens, nationals, or permanent residents of the United States, who have committed crimes of violence against nationals of the United States in foreign countries without regard to the existence of any treaty of extradition with such foreign government if the Attorney General certifies in writing that --

(1) evidence has been presented by the foreign government that indicates that had the offenses been committed in the United States, they would constitute crimes of violence as defined under section 16 of this title; and

(2) the offenses charged are not of a political nature.

(c) As used in this Section, the term "national of the United States" has the meaning given such term in section 101(a)(22) of the Immigration and Nationality Act (8 U.S.C. 1101(a)(22)).

(June 25, 1948, ch. 645, 62 Stat. 822.)
(As amended Apr. 24, 1996, Pub.L. 104-132, Title IV, §443(a), 110 Stat. 1280.)

HISTORICAL AND REVISION NOTES

Based on title 18, U.S.C., 1940 ed., § 658 (R.S. § 5274).

Minor Changes were made in phraseology. 80th Congress House Report No. 304.

CONVENTION ON EXTRADITION

The United States is a party to the Multilateral Convention on Extradition signed at Montevideo on Dec. 26, 1933, entered into force for the United States on Jan. 25, 1935, 49 Stat. 3111.

Other states which have become parties: Argentina, Chile, Colombia, Dominican Republic Ecuador, El Salvador, Guatemala, Honduras, Mexico, Nicaragua, Panama.

REFERENCES IN TEXT

Section 101(a)(22) of the Immigration and Nationality Act, referred to in subsec. (c), is section 101(a)(22) of Act June 27, 1952, c. 477, 66 Stat. 166, which is classified to section 1101(a)(22) of Title 8, Aliens and Nationality.

AMENDMENTS

1996--Subsec. (a). Pub.L. 104-132, § 443(a)(1), designated existing provisions as subsec. (a).

1996--Subsec. (b), (c). Pub.L. 104-132, § 443 (a)(2), added subsec. (b) and (c).

§ 3182. Fugitives from State or Territory to State, District, or Territory

Whenever the executive authority of any State or Territory demands any person as a fugitive from justice, of the executive authority of any State, District or Territory to which such person has fled, and produces a copy of an indictment found or an affidavit made before a magistrate of any State or Territory, charging the person demanded with having committed treason, felony, or other crime, certified as authentic by the governor or chief magistrate of the State or Territory from whence the person so charged has fled, the executive authority of the State, District or Territory to which such person has fled shall cause him to be arrested and secured, and notify the executive authority making such demand, or the agent of such authority appointed to receive the fugitive, and shall cause the fugitive to be delivered to such agent when he shall appear. If no such agent appears within thirty days from the time of the arrest, the prisoner may be discharged. (June 25, 1948, ch. 645, 62 Stat. 822.)
(As amended Oct. 11, 1996, Pub.L. 104-294, Title VI, § VI, § 601(f)(9), 110 Stat. 3500.)

HISTORICAL AND REVISION NOTES

Based on title 18, U.S.C., 1940 ed., § 662 (R.S. § 5278).

Last sentence as to costs and expenses to be paid by the demanding authority was incorporated in section 3195 of this title.

Word "District" was inserted twice to make section equally applicable to fugitives found in the District of Columbia.

"Thirty days" was substituted for "six months" since, in view of modern conditions, the smaller time is ample for the demanding authority to act.

Minor changes were made in phraseology. 80th Congress House Report No. 304

CROSS REFERENCES

Constitutional provision enforced by this section, see Const. Art. 4, § 2, cl. 2.

Juvenile delinquents, surrender to State authorities, see section 5001 of this title.

Resistance to extradition agent, see section 1502 of this title.

Surrender of youthful offenders to State authorities, see section 5001 of this title.

Transportation of fugitive by receiving agent, see section 3194 of this title.

SECTION REFERRED TO IN OTHER SECTIONS

This section is referred to in sections 3194, 5001 of this title.

AMENDMENTS

1996--Pub.L. 104-294, § 601(f)(9), substituted "District, or" for "District or", wherever appearing.

§ 3183. Fugitives from State, Territory, or Possession into extraterritorial jurisdiction of United States

Whenever the executive authority of any State, Territory, District, or possession of the United States or the Panama Canal Zone, demands any American citizen or national as a fugitive from justice who has fled to a country in which the United States exercises extraterritorial jurisdiction, and produces a copy of an indictment found or an affidavit made before a magistrate of the demanding jurisdiction, charging the fugitive so demanded with having committed treason, felony, or other offense, certified as authentic by the Governor or chief magistrate of such demanding jurisdiction, or other person authorized to act, the officer or representative of the United States vested with judicial authority to whom the demand has been made shall cause such fugitive to be arrested and secured, and notify the executive authorities making such demand, or the agent of such authority appointed to receive the fugitive, and shall cause the fugitive to be delivered to such agent when he shall appear.

If no such agent shall appear within three months from the time of the arrest, the prisoner may be discharged.

The agent who receives the fugitive into his custody shall be empowered to transport him to the jurisdiction from which he has fled. (June 25, 1948, ch. 645, 62 Stat. 822.)

HISTORICAL AND REVISION NOTES

Based on title 18, U.S.C., 1940 ed., § 662c (Mar. 22, 1934, ch. 73, § 2, 48 Stat. 455).

Said section 662c was incorporated in this section and sections 752 and 3195 of this title.

Provision as to costs or expenses to be paid by the demanding authority were incorporated in section 3196 of this title.

Reference to the Philippine Islands was deleted as obsolete in view of the independence of the Commonwealth of the Philippines effective July 4, 1946.

The attention of Congress is directed to the probability that this section may be of little, if any, possible use in view of present world conditions.

Minor changes were made in phraseology.

REFERENCES IN TEXT

For definition of Canal Zone referred to in text, see section 3602(b) of Title 22, Foreign Relations and Intercourse.

CROSS REFERENCES

Provisional arrest, obtained by telegraph, see section 3187 of this title.

SECTION REFERRED TO IN OTHER SECTIONS

This section is referred to in section 3187 of this title.

§ 3184. Fugitives from foreign country to United States

Whenever there is a treaty or convention for extradition between the United States and any foreign government, or in cases arising under section 3181(b), any justice or judge of the United States, or any magistrate authorized so to do by a court of the United States, or any judge of a court of record of general jurisdiction of any State, may, upon complaint made under oath, charging any person found within his jurisdiction, with having committed within the jurisdiction of any such foreign

government any of the crimes provided for by such treaty or convention, or provided for under section 3181(b), issue his warrant for the apprehension of the person so charged, that he may be brought before such justice, judge, or magistrate, to the end that the evidence of criminality may be heard and considered. Such complaint may be filed before and such warrant may be issued by a judge or magistrate of the United States District Court for the District of Columbia if the whereabouts within the United States of the person charged are not known or, if there is reason to believe the person will shortly enter the United States. If, on such hearing, he deems the evidence sufficient to sustain the charge under the provisions of the proper treaty or convention, or under section 3181(b), he shall certify the same, together with a copy of all the testimony taken before him, to the Secretary of State, that a warrant may issue upon the requisition of the proper authorities of such foreign government, for the surrender of such person, according to the stipulations of the treaty or convention; and he shall issue his warrant for the commitment of the person so charged to the proper jail, there to remain until such surrender shall be made. (June 25, 1948, ch. 645, 62 Stat. 822; Oct. 17, 1968, Pub. L. 90-578, title III, § 301(a)(3), 82 Stat. 1115.)
(As amended Nov. 18, 1988, Pub.L. 100-690, Title VII, § 7087, 102 Stat. 4409; Nov. 29, 1990, Pub.L. 101-647, Title SVI, § 1605, 104 Stat. 4843; Apr. 24, 1996, Pub.L. 104-132, Title IV, § 443(b), 110 Stat. 1281.)

HISTORICAL AND REVISION NOTES

Based on title 18, U.S.C., 1940 ed., § 651 (R.S. § 5270; June 6, 1900, ch. 793, 31 Stat. 656). Minor changes of phraseology were made. 80th Congress House Report No. 304.

AMENDMENTS

1996—Pub.L. 104-132, § 443(b), inserted provisions referring to section 3181b, wherever appearing.

1990—Pub.L. 101-647, § 1605, inserted "or, if there is reason to believe the person will shortly enter the United States" after "are not known".

1988—Pub.L. 100-690, § 7087, added "Such complaint may be filed before and such warrant may be issued by a judge or magistrate of the United States District Court for the District of Columbia if the whereabouts within the United States of the person charged are not known." following "heard and considered.".

1968—Pub. L. 90-578 substituted "magistrate" for "commissioner" in two instances.

EFFECTIVE DATE OF 1968 AMENDMENT

Amendment by Pub. L. 90-578 effective Oct. 17, 1968, except when a later effective date is applicable, which is the earlier of date when implementation of amendment by appointment of magistrates and assumption of office takes place or third anniversary of enactment of Pub. L. 90-578 on Oct. 17, 1968, see section 403 of Pub. L. 90-578, set out as an Effective Date of 1968 Amendment note under section 631 of Title 28, Judiciary and Judicial Procedure.

CROSS REFERENCES

Arrest, power of courts and magistrates, see section 3041 of this title.
Surrender of fugitive to agent of foreign government, see section 3186 of this title.

SECTION REFERRED TO IN OTHER SECTIONS

This section is referred to in section 3186 of this title.

§ 3185. Fugitives from country under control of United States into the United States

Whenever any foreign country or territory, or any part thereof, is occupied by or under the control of the United States, any person who, having violated the criminal laws in force therein by the commission of any of the offenses enumerated below, departs or flees from justice therein to the

United States, shall, when found therein, be liable to arrest and detention by the authorities of the United States, and on the written request or requisition of the military governor or other chief executive officer in control of such foreign country or territory shall be returned and surrendered as hereinafter provided to such authorities for trial under the laws in force in the place where such offense was committed.

(l) Murder and assault with intent to commit murder;

(2) Counterfeiting or altering money, or uttering or bringing into circulation counterfeit or altered money;

(3) Counterfeiting certificates or coupons of public indebtedness, bank notes, or other instruments of public credit, and the utterance or circulation of the same;

(4) Forgery or altering and uttering what is forged or altered;

(5) Embezzlement or criminal malversation of the public funds, committed by public officers, employees, or depositaries;

(6) Larceny or embezzlement of an amount not less than $100 in value;

(7) Robbery;

(8) Burglary, defined to be the breaking and entering by nighttime into the house of another person with intent to commit a felony therein;

(9) Breaking and entering the house or building of another, whether in the day or nighttime. with the intent to commit a felony therein;

(10) Entering, or breaking and entering the offices of the Government and public authorities, or the offices of banks, banking houses, savings banks, trust companies, insurance or other companies, with the intent to commit a felony therein;

(11) Perjury or the subornation of perjury;

(12) A felony under chapter 109A of this title;

(13) Arson;

(14) Piracy by the law of nations;

(15) Murder, assault with intent to kill, and manslaughter, committed on the high seas, on board a ship owned by or in control of citizens or residents of such foreign country or territory and not under the flag of the United States, or of some other government;

(16) Malicious destruction of or attempt to destroy railways, trams, vessels, bridges, dwellings, public edifices, or other buildings, when the act endangers human life.

This chapter, so far as applicable, shall govern proceedings authorized by this section. Such proceedings shall be had before a judge of the courts of the United States only, who shall hold such person on evidence establishing probable cause that he is guilty of the offense charged.

No return or surrender shall be made of any person charged with the commission of any offense of a political nature.

If so held, such person shall be returned and surrendered to the authorities in control of such foreign country or territory on the order of the Secretary of State of the United States, and such authorities shall secure to such a person a fair and impartial trial .

(June 25, 1948, ch. 645, 62 Stat. 823; May 24, 1949, ch. 139, § 49, 62 Stat. 96.)

(As amended Nov. 10, 1986, Pub.L. 99-646, § 87(c)(6), 100 Stat. 3623; Nov. 14, 1986, Pub.L. 99-654, § 3(a)(6), 100 Stat. 3663.)

Historical and Revision Notes

1948 Act

Based on title 18, U.S.C., 1940 ed.. § 652 (R.S. § 5270; June 6, 1900, ch. 793, 31 Stat. 656).

Reference to territory of the United States and the District of Columbia was omitted as covered by definitive section 5 of this title.

Changes were made in phraseology and arrangement.

1949 Act

This section [section 49] corrects typographical errors in section 3185 of title 18, U.S.C., by transferring to subdivision (3) the words, "indebtedness, bank notes, or other instruments of public", from subdivision (2) of such section where they had been erroneously included.

Amendments

1949—Subds. (2), (3). Act May 24, 1949, transferred from subd. (2) to subd. (3) the words "indebtedness, bank notes, or other instruments of public".

1987--Par. (12). Pub.L. 99-646 substituted "A felony under chapter 109A of this title" for "Rape". Pub.L. 99-654 made an amendment identical to Pub.L. 99-646.

Effective Date of 1986 Amendment

Amendment of Pub.L. 99-654, effective 30 days after Nov. 14, 1986, see section 4 of Pub.L. 99-654, set out as a note under section 2241 of this title.

Amendment by section 87 of Pub.L. 99-646 effective 30 days after Nov. 10, 1986, see section 87(e) of Pub.L. 99-646, set out as a note under section 2241 of this title.

Cross References

Extradition of fugitives from justice, see section 3042 of this title.

Surrender of fugitive to agent of foreign government, see section 3186 of this title.

Section Referred to in Other Sections

This section is referred to in section 3186 of this title.

§ 3186. Secretary of State to surrender fugitive

The Secretary of State may order the person committed under sections 3184 or 3185 of this title to be delivered by any authorized agent of such foreign government, to be tried for the offense of which charged.

Such agent may hold such person in custody, and take him to the territory of such foreign government, pursuant to such treaty.

A person so accused who escapes may be retaken in the same manner as any person accused of any offense.

(June 25, 1948, ch. 645, 62 Stat. 824.)

Historical and Revision Notes

Based on title 18, U.S.C., 1940 ed., § 653 (R.S. § 5272).

Changes were made in phraseology and surplusage was deleted.

Section Referred to in Other Sections

This section is referred to in section 4114 of this title.

§ 3187. Provisional arrest and detention within extraterritorial jurisdiction

The provisional arrest and detention of a fugitive, under sections 3042 and 3183 of this title, in advance of the presentation of formal proofs, may be obtained by telegraph upon the request of the authority competent to request the surrender of such fugitive addressed to the authority competent to grant such surrender. Such request shall be accompanied by an express statement that a warrant for the fugitive's arrest has been issued within the jurisdiction of the authority making such request charging the fugitive with the commission of the crime for which his extradition is sought to be obtained.

No person shall be held in custody under telegraphic request by virtue of this section for more than ninety days.

(June 25,1948, ch. 645, 62 Stat. 824.)

HISTORICAL AND REVISION NOTES

Based on title 18, U.S.C., 1940 ed., § 662d (Mar. 22, 1934, ch. 73, § 3, 48 Stat. 455).

Provision for expense to be borne by the demanding authority is incorporated in section 3195 of this title.

Changes were made in phraseology and arrangement.

CANAL ZONE

Applicability of section to Canal Zone, see section 14 of this title.

SECTION REFERRED TO IN OTHER SECTIONS

This section is referred to in section 14 of this title.

§ 3188. Time of commitment pending extradition

Whenever any person who is committed for rendition to a foreign government to remain until delivered up in pursuance of a requisition, is not so delivered up and conveyed out of the United States within two calendar months after such commitment, over and above the time actually required to convey the prisoner from the jail to which he was committed, by the readiest way, out of the United States, any judge of the United States, or of any State, upon application made to him by or on behalf of the person so committed, and upon proof made to him that reasonable notice of the intention to make such application has been given to the Secretary of State, may order the person so committed to be discharged out of custody, unless sufficient cause is shown to such judge why such discharge ought not to be ordered.
(June 25,1948, ch. 645, 62 Stat. 824.)

HISTORICAL AND REVISION NOTES

Based on title 18, U.S.C., 1940 ed., § 654 (R.S. § 5273).

Changes in phraseology only were made.

SECTION REFERRED TO IN OTHER SECTIONS

This section is referred to in section 4114 of this title.

§ 3189. Place and character of hearing

Hearings in cases of extradition under treaty stipulation or convention shall be held on land, publicly, and in a room or office easily accessible to the public.
(June 25, 1948, ch. 645, 62 Stat. 824.)

HISTORICAL AND REVISION NOTES

Based on title 18, U.S.C., 1940 ed., § 657 (Aug. 3, 1882, ch. 378, § 1, 22 Stat. 215).

First word "All" was omitted as unnecessary.

SECTION REFERRED TO IN OTHER SECTIONS

This section is referred to in section 4114 of this title.

§ 3190. Evidence on hearing

Depositions, warrants, or other papers or copies thereof offered in evidence upon the hearing of any extradition case shall be received and admitted as evidence on such hearing for all the purposes of such hearing if they shall be properly and legally authenticated so as to entitle them to be received for similar purposes by the tribunals of the foreign country from which the accused party shall have escaped, and the certificate of the principal diplomatic or consular officer of the United States resident in such foreign country shall be proof that the same, so offered, are authenticated in the manner required .

(June 25, 1948, ch. 645, 62 Stat. 824.)

HISTORICAL AND REVISION NOTES

Based on title 18, U.S.C., 1940 ed., § 655 (R.S. § 5271; Aug. 3, 1882, ch. 378, § 5, 22 Stat. 216). Unnecessary words were deleted.

SECTION REFERRED TO IN OTHER SECTIONS

This section is referred to in section 4114 of this title.

§ 3191. Witnesses for indigent fugitives

On the hearing of any case under a claim of extradition by a foreign government, upon affidavit being filed by the person charged setting forth that there are witnesses whose evidence is material to his defense, that he cannot safely go to trial without them, what he expects to prove by each of them, and that he is not possessed of sufficient means, and is actually unable to pay the fees of such witnesses. the judge or magistrate hearing the matter mav order that such witnesses be subpoenaed; and the Costs incurred by the process, and the fees of witnesses, shall be paid in the same manner as in the case of witnesses subpoenaed in behalf of the United States.

(June 25, 1948, ch. 645, 62 Stat. 825; Oct. 17, 1968, Pub. L. 90-578. title III. § 301(a)(3), 82 Stat 1115.)

HISTORICAL AND REVISION NOTES

Based on title 18, U.S.C., 1940 ed., § 656 (Aug. 3, 1882, ch. 378, § 3, 22 Stat. 215). Words "that similar" after 'manner" were omitted as unnecessary.

AMENDMENTS

1968— Pub. L. 90-578 substituted "magistrate" for "commissioner".

EFFECTIVE DATE OF 1968 AMENDMENT

Amendment by Pub. L. 90-578 effective Oct. 17,1968, except when a later effective date is applicable, which is the earlier of date when implementation of amendment by appointment of magistrates and assumption of office takes place or third anniversary of enactment of Pub. L. 90-578 on Oct. 17,1968, see section 403 of Pub. L. 90-578, set out as an Effective Date of 1968 Amendment not under section 631 of Title 28, Judiciary and Judicial Procedure.

FEDERAL RULES OF CRIMINAL PROCEDURE

Witness fees for indigent defendants, generally, see rule 17, Appendix to this title.

SECTION REFERRED TO IN OTHER SECTIONS

This section is referred to in section 4114 of this title.

§ 3192. Protection of accused

Whenever any person is delivered by any foreign government to an agent of the United States, for the purpose of being brought within the United States and tried for any offense of which he is duly accused, the President shall have power to take all necessary measures for the transportation and safekeeping of such accused person, and for his security against lawless violence, until the final conclusion of his trial for the offenses specified in the warrant of extradition, and until his final discharge from custody or imprisonment for or on account of such offenses, and for a reasonable time thereafter, and may employ such portion of the land or naval forces of the United States, or of the militia thereof, as may be necessary for the safe-keeping and protection of the accused.

(June 25, 1948, ch. 645, 62 Stat. 825.)

HISTORICAL AND REVISION NOTES

Based on title 18, U.S.C.,1940 ed., § 659 (R.S. § 5275).

Words "crimes or" before "offenses" were omitted as unnecessary.

§ 3193. Receiving agent's authority over offenders

A duly appointed agent to receive, in behalf of the United States, the delivery, by a foreign government, of any person accused of crime committed within the United States, and to convey him to the place of his trial, shall have all the powers of a marshal of the United States, in the several districts through which it may be necessary for him to pass with such prisoner, so far as such power is requisite for the prisoner's safekeeping.
(June 25, 1948, ch. 645, 62 Stat. 825.)

HISTORICAL AND REVISION NOTES

Based on title 18, U.S.C., 1940 ed., § 660 (R.S. § 5276).

Words " jurisdiction of the" were omitted in view of the definition of United States in section 5 of this title.

Minor changes only were made in phraseology.

EX. ORD. NO. 11517. ISSUANCE AND SIGNATURE BY SECRETARY OF STATE OF WARRANTS APPOINTING AGENTS TO RETURN FUGITIVES FROM JUSTICE EXTRADITED TO UNITED STATES

Ex. Ord. No. 11517, Mar. 19, 1970, 35 F.R. 4937, provided:

WHEREAS the President of the United States. under section 3192 of Title 18, United States Code, has been granted the power to take all necessary measures for the transportation, safekeeping and security against lawless violence of any person delivered by any foreign government to an agent of the United States for return to the United States for trial for any offense of which he is duly accused; and

WHEREAS fugitives from justice in the United States whose extradition from abroad has been requested by the Government of the United States and granted by a foreign government are to be returned in the custody of duly appointed agents in accordance with the provisions of section 3193 of Title 18, United States Code; and

WHEREAS such duly appointed agents under the provisions of the law mentioned above, being authorized to receive delivery of the fugitive in behalf of the United States and to convey him to the place of his trial, are given the powers of a marshal of the United States in the several districts of the United States through which it may be necessary for them to pass with such prisoner, so far as such power is requisite for the prisoner's safekeeping; and

WHEREAS such warrants serve as a certification to the foreign government delivering the fugitives to any other foreign country through which such agents may pass, and to authorities in the United States of the powers therein conferred upon the agents: and

WHEREAS it is desirable by delegation of functions heretofore performed by the President to simplify and thereby expedite the issuance of such warrants to agents in the interests of the prompt return of fugitives to the United States:

NOW, THEREFORE, by virtue of the authority vested in me by section 301 of Title 3 of the United States Code, and as President of the United States, it is ordered as follows:

SECTION 1. The Secretary of State is hereby designated and empowered to issue and sign all warrants appointing agents to receive, in behalf of the United States, the delivery in extradition by a foreign government of any person accused of a crime committed within the United States, and to convey such person to the place of his trial.

SEC. 2. Agents appointed in accordance with section 1 of this order shall have all the powers conferred in respect of such agents by applicable treaties of the United States and by section 3193 of Title 18, United States Code, or by any other provisions of United States law.

SEC. 3. Executive Order No. 10347, April 18, 1952, as amended by Executive Order No 11354, May 23, 1967, is further amended by deleting numbered paragraph 4 and renumbering paragraphs 5 and 6 as paragraphs 4 and 5, respectively.

RICHARD NIXON

CROSS REFERENCES

Powers of United States marshals. see section 3053 of this title.

United States marshals generally, see section 561 et seq. of Title 28, Judiciary and Judicial Procedure.

§ 3194. Transportation of fugitive by receiving agent

Any agent appointed as provided in section 3182 of this title who receives the fugitive into his custody is empowered to transport him to the State or Territory from which he has fled.
(June 25. 1948. ch. 645.62 Stat. 825).

HISTORICAL AND REVISION NOTES

Based on title 18, U.S.C., 1940 ed., § 663 (R.S. § 5279).

Last sentence of said section 663, relating to rescue of such fugitive, was omitted as covered by section 752 of this title, the punishment provision of which is based on later statutes. (See reviser's note under that section.)

Minor changes were made in phraseology.

§ 3195. Payment of fees and costs.

All costs or expenses incurred in any extradition proceeding in apprehending, securing, and transmitting a fugitive shall be paid by the demanding authority.

All witness fees and costs of every nature in cases of international extradition, including the fees of the magistrate, shall be certified by the judge or magistrate before whom the hearing shall take place to the Secretary of State of the United States, and the same shall be paid out of appropriations to defray the expenses of the judiciary or the Department of Justice as the case may be.

The Attorney General shall certify to the Secretary of State the amounts to be paid to the United States on account of said fees and costs in extradition cases by the foreign government requesting the extradition, and the Secretary of State shall cause said amounts to be collected and transmitted to the Attorney General for deposit in the Treasury of the United States.
(June 25, 1948, ch. 645, 62 Stat. 825; Oct. 17, 1968, Pub. L. 90-578, title III, § 301(a)(3), 82 Stat. 1115).

HISTORICAL AND REVISION NOTES

Based on title 18, U.S.C., 1940 ed., §§ 662, 662c, 662d, 668 (R.S. § 5278, Aug. 3 1882, ch. 378, § 4,22 Stat. 216; June 18, 1902, ch. 1301, § 1, 32 Stat. 475; Mar. 22, 1934 ch. 73, §§ 2, 3, 48 Stat. 455).

First paragraph of this section consolidates provisions as to costs and expenses from said sections 662, 662c, and 662d.

Minor changes were made in phraseology and surplusage was omitted.

Remaining provisions of said sections 662, 662c, and 662d of title 18, U.S.C., 1940 ed., are incorporated in sections 752, 3182, 3183, and 3187 of this title.

The words "or the Department of Justice as the case may be" were added at the end of the second paragraph in conformity with the appropriation acts of recent years. See for example act July 5, 1946, ch. 541, title II, 60 Stat. 460.

AMENDMENTS

1968—Pub. L. 90-578 substituted "magistrate" for "commissioner" in two instances.

EFFECTIVE DATE OF 1968 AMENDMENT

Amendment by Pub. L. 90-578 effective Oct. 17, 1968, except when a later effective date is applicable, which is the earlier of a date when implementation of amendment by appointment of magistrates and assumption of office takes place or third anniversary of enactment of Pub. L. 90-578 on Oct. 17, 1968, see section 403 of Pub. L. 90-578 set out as an Effective Date of 1968 Amendment note under section 631 of Title 28, Judiciary and Judicial Procedure.

CANAL ZONE

Applicability of section to Canal Zone, see section 14 of this title.

§3196. Extradition of United States citizens.

If the applicable treaty or convention does not obligation the United States to extradite its citizens to a foreign country, the Secretary of State may, nevertheless, order the surrender to that country of a United States citizen whose extradition has been requested by the country if the other requirements of that treaty or convention are met.

(Added Pub. L. 101-623, §11(a), Nov. 21, 1990, 104 Stat. 3356.)

Appendix 2

Extradition Treaty Between the Government of the United States of America and the Government of the Republic of Italy*

The Government of the United States of America and the Government of the Republic of Italy,

Recognizing their close cooperation in the repression of crimes;

Desiring to make such cooperation even more effective;

Seeking to conclude a new Treaty for the reciprocal extradition of offenders;

Have agreed as follows:

ARTICLE 1

Obligation to Extradite

The Contracting Parties agree to extradite to each other, pursuant to the provisions of this Treaty, persons whom the authorities of the Requesting Party have charged with or found guilty of an extraditable offense.

ARTICLE II

Extraditable Offenses

1. An offense, however denominated, shall be an extraditable offense only if it is punishable under the laws of both Contracting Parties by deprivation of liberty for a period of more than one year or by a more severe penalty. When the request for extradition relates to a person who has been sentenced, extradition shall be granted only if the duration of the penalty still to be served amounts to at least six months.

2. An offense shall also be an extraditable offense if it consists of an attempt to commit, or participation in the commission of, an offense described in paragraph 1 of this Article. Any type of association to commit offenses described in paragraph 1 of this Article, as provided by the laws of Italy, and conspiracy to commit an offense described in paragraph 1 of this Article, as provided by the laws of the United States,. shall also be extraditable offenses.

* The Italian Constitutional Court declared on 25 June 1996 that Article IX of the Treaty (concerning extradition in cases where the death penalty could be applied) to be unconstitutional. The Court held that Article IX of the Treaty violated the "absolute right to life" guaranteed by Articles 2 and 27, para. 4 of the Italian Constitution. The Court surprisingly rejected all past precedents and similar practices of other European jurisprudence that adequate guarantees offered by a requesting state could be deemed sufficient to allow extradition. In the *Venezia* case, the Court rejected out of hand any guarantees offered by the U.S. not to seek the death penalty and not to carry it out in the event of a conviction. The Court held that such guarantees were incompatible with the "absolute right to life" guaranteed by the Italian Constitution. The Court did not, however, elaborate on the reasons why an absolute guarantee of not applying the death penalty by the U.S. would not be sufficient to displace the "absolute right to life." A reasonable interpretation is that the Court deemed that the U.S. could either not offer such an absolute guarantee, or that Italy could not enforce it.

The *Sentenza* (decision) number 223 of 25 June 1996 was deposited with the clerk of the Court on 26 June 1996 and published on 3 July 1996 in the *Ggazzetta Ufficiale, serie speciale numbero* 27. Also reprinted with commentary by Judge Di Chiara in *Foro Italiano*, I, c. 2586 (1996). For a critical comment, *see* Mario Pisani, *Pena di Morte ed Estradizione nel Trattato Italia - USA: il caso Venezia,* INDICE PENALE XXX-3, p. 671 (1996). Author's note: This article appeared in the last issue of *Indice Penale*'s 30 year life.This valuable criminal law journal which served an important scholarly function had been directed by Professor Pisani. Its absence will be missed by Italian and comparative criminal law researchers.

3. When extradition has been granted for an extraditable offense, it shall also be granted for any other offense specified in the request even if the latter offense is punishable by less than one year's deprivation of liberty, provided that all other requirements for extradition are met.
4. The provisions of this Article apply whether or not the offense is one for which United States federal law requires proof of an element, such as interstate transportation,. the use of the facilities of interstate commerce, or the effects upon such commerce, since such an element is required for the sole purpose of establishing the jurisdiction of United States federal courts.

ARTICLE III
Jurisdiction

When an offense has been committed outside the territory of the Requesting Party, the Requested Party shall have the power to grant extradition if its laws provide for the punishment of such an offense or if the person sought is a national of the Requesting Party.

ARTICLE IV
Extradition of Nationals

A Requested Party shall not decline to extradite a person because such a person is a national of the Requested Party.

ARTICLE V
Political and Military Offenses

1. Extradition shall not be granted when the offense for which extradition is requested is a political offense, or if the person whose surrender is sought proves that the request for surrender has been made in order to try or punish him or her for a political offense.
2. For the purpose of the application of paragraph 1 of this Article, an offense with respect to which both Contracting Parties have the obligation to submit for prosecution or to grant extradition pursuant to a multilateral international agreement, or an offense against the life, physical integrity or liberty of a Head of State or Government or a member of their respective families, or any attempt to commit such an offense, will be presumed to have the predominant character of a common crime when its consequences were or could have been grave. In determining the gravity of the offense and its consequences, the fact that the offense endangered public safety, harmed persons unrelated to the political purpose of the offender, or was committed with ruthlessness shall, in particular, be taken into account.
3. Extradition shall not be granted for offenses under military law which are not offenses under ordinary criminal law.

ARTICLE VI
Non Bis in Idem

Extradition shall not be granted when the person sought has been convicted, acquitted or pardoned, or has served the sentence imposed, by the Requested Party for the same acts for which extradition is requested.

ARTICLE VII
Pending Proceedings for the Same Acts

Extradition may be refused if the person sought is being proceeded against by the Requested Party for the same acts for which extradition is requested.

Article VIII
Lapse of Time

Extradition shall not be granted when the prosecution, or the enforcement of the penalty, for the offense for which extradition has been requested has become barred by lapse of time under the laws of the Requesting Party.

Article IX
Capital Punishment

When the offense for which extradition is requested is punishable by death under the laws of the requesting Party and the laws of the requested Party do not provide for such punishment for that offense, extradition shall be refused unless the requesting Party provides such assurances as the requested Party considers sufficient that the death penalty shall not be imposed, or, if imposed, shall not be executed.

Article X
Extradition Requests and Supporting Documents

1. Requests for extradition shall be made through the diplomatic channel.
2. All requests for extradition shall be accompanied by:

(a) documents, statements or other information which set forth the identity and probable location of the person sought, with, if available, physical description, photographs and fingerprints;

(b) a brief statement of the facts of the case, including the time and location of the offense;

(c) the texts of the laws describing the essential elements and the designation of the offense for which extradition is requested;

(d) the texts of the laws describing the punishment for the offense: and

(e) the texts of the laws describing the time limit on the prosecution or the execution of the punishment for the offense.

3. A request for extradition which relates to a person who has not yet been convicted shall also be accompanied by:

(a) a certified copy of the arrest warrant or any order having similar effect:

(b) a summary of the facts of the case, of the relevant evidence and of the conclusions reached, providing a reasonable basis to believe that the person sought committed the offense for which extradition is requested: in the case of requests from Italy such a summary shall be written by a magistrate, and in the case of requests from the United States it shall be written by the prosecutor and shall include a copy of the charge: and

(c) documents establishing that the person sought is the person to whom the arrest warrant or equivalent order refers.

4. A request for extradition which relates to a person who has been convicted shall, in addition to those items set forth in paragraph 2 of this Article, be accompanied by:

(a) a copy of the judgment of conviction, or, in the case of the United States, if the person has been found guilty but not yet sentenced, a statement by a judicial officer to that effect;

(b) if the penalty has been pronounced, a copy of the sentence and a statement as to the duration of the penalty still to be served; and

(c) documents establishing that the person sought is the person convicted.

5. If the person sought has been convicted in absentia or in contumacy, all issues relating to this aspect of the request shall be decided by the Executive Authority of the United States or the competent authorities of Italy. In such cases, the Requesting Party shall submit such documents as are described in paragraphs 2, 3 and 4 of this Article and a statement regarding the procedures, if any, that would be available to the person sought if he or she were extradited.
6. The documents which accompany an extradition request shall be made available in English and Italian by the Requesting Party.
7. The documents which accompany an extradition request shall be admissible into evidence when:

(a) in the case of a request from the United States, they are certified by a judge, magistrate or other United States official and are sealed by the Secretary of State;

(b) in the case of a request from Italy, they are signed by a judge or other Italian judicial authority and are certified by the principal diplomatic or consular officer of the United States in Italy.

ARTICLE XI

Additional Documentation

1. If the Requested Party considers that the documentation furnished in support of a request for extradition is incomplete or otherwise does not conform to the requirements of this Treaty, that Party shall request the submission of necessary additional documentation. The Requested Party shall set a reasonable time limit for the submission of such documentation, and shall grant a reasonable extension of that time limit upon an application by the Requesting Party setting forth the reasons requiring the extension.

2. If the person sought is in custody and the additional documentation submitted is incomplete or otherwise does not conform to the requirements of this Treaty, or if such documentation is not received within the period specified by the Requested Party, that person may by discharged from custody. Such discharge shall not prejudice the re-arrest and the extradition of the person sought if a new request and the additional documentation are delivered at a later date.

ARTICLE XII

Provisional Arrest

1. In case of urgency, either Contracting Party may apply for the provisional arrests of any person charged or convicted of an extraditable offense. The application for provisional arrest shall be made either through the diplomatic channel or directly between the United States Department of Justice and the Italian Ministry of Grace and Justice, in which case the communication facilities of the International Criminal Police Organization (Interpol) may be used.

2. The application shall contain: a description of the person sought including, if available, the person's nationality; the probable location of that person; a brief statement of the facts of the case including, if possible, the time and location of the offense and the available evidence; a statement of the existence of a warrant of arrest, with the date it was issued and the name of the issuing court; a description of the type of offenses, a citation to the sections of law violated and a maximum penalty possible upon conviction, or a statement of the existence of a judgment of conviction against that person, with the date of conviction, the name of the sentencing court and the sentence imposted, if any; and a statement that a formal request for extradition of the person sought will follow.

3. On receipt of the application, the Requested Party shall take the appropriate steps to secure the arrest of the person sought. The Requesting Party shall be promptly notified of the result of its application.

4. Provisional arrest shall be terminated if, within a period of 45 days after the apprehension of the person sought, the Executive Authority of the Requested Party has not received a formal request for extradition and the supporting documents required by Article X.

5. The termination of provisional arrest pursuant to paragraph 4 of this Article shall not prejudice the re-arrest and extradition of the person sought if the extradition request and the supporting documents are delivered at a later date.

ARTICLE XIII

Decision and Surrender

1. The Requested Party shall promptly communicate to the Requesting Party through the diplomatic channel its decision on the request for extradition.

2. The Requested Party shall provide reasons for any partial or complete rejection of the request for extradition and a copy of the court's decision, if any.

3. When an extradition request has been granted, the competent authorities of the Contracting Parties shall agree on the time and place of the surrender of the person sought. If, however, that person is not

removed from the territory of the Requested Party within the agreed time, that person may be set at liberty, unless a new date for surrender has been agreed upon.

ARTICLE XIV
Deferred Surrender and Temporary Surrender

After a decision on a request for extradition has been rendered in the case of a person who is being proceeded against or is serving a sentence in the Requested Party for a different offense, the Requested Party shall have the authority to:

(a) defer the surrender of the person sought until the conclusion of the proceedings against that person or the full execution of any punishment that may be or may have been imposed; or

(b) temporarily surrender the person sought to the Requesting Party solely for the purpose of prosecution. A person so surrendered shall be kept in custody while in the Requesting Party and shall be returned to the Requested party at the conclusion of the proceedings against that person, in accordance with conditions to be determined by mutual agreement of the Contracting Parties.

ARTICLE XV
Requests for Extradition Made by Several States

The Executive Authority of the Requested Party, upon receiving requests from the other Contracting Party and from one or more other States for the extradition of the same person, either for the same offense or for different offenses, shall determine to which State it will extradite that person. In making its decision, the Executive Authority shall consider all relevant factors, including:

(a) the place in which the offence was committed;

(b) the gravity of the respective offenses, where the requesting States are requesting extradition for different offenses;

(c) the possibility of re-extradition between the requesting States; and

(d) the order in which the requests were received.

ARTICLE XVI
Rule of Specialty and Re-Extradition

1. A person extradited under this Treaty may not be detained, tried or punished in the Requesting Party except for:

(a) the offense for which extradition has been granted or when the same facts for which extradition was granted constitute a differently denominated offense which is extraditable;

(b) an offense committed after the surrender of a person; or

(c) an offense for which the Executive Authority of the United State or the competent authorities of Italy consent to the person's detention, trial or punishment.

For the purpose of the subparagraph, the Requested Party may require the submission of the documents called for in Article X.

2. A person extradited under this Treaty may not be extradited to a third State unless the surrendering Party consents.

3. Paragraphs 1 and 2 of this Article shall not prevent the detention, trial or punishment of an extradited person in accordance with the laws of the Requesting Party, or the extradition of that person to a third State, if:

(a) that person leaves the territory of the Requesting Party after extradition and voluntarily returns to it; or

(b) that person does not leave the territory of the Requesting Party within 30 days of the day on which that person is free to leave.

ARTICLE XVII

Simplified Extradition

If the person sought irrevocably agrees in writing to surrender to the Requesting Party after having been advised by a judge or competent magistrate of the right to formal proceedings and the protections afforded under this Treaty, the Requested Party may surrender the person without formal proceedings.

ARTICLE XVIII

Surrender of Articles, Instruments. Objects and Documents

1. All articles, instruments, objects of value, documents and other evidence relating to the offense may be seized and surrendered to the Requesting Party, Such property may be surrendered even when extradition cannot be effected. The rights of third parties in such property shall be duly respected.
2. The Requested Party may condition the surrender of the property upon satisfactory assurance from the Requesting Party that the property will be returned to the Requested Party as soon as practicable, and may defer its surrender if it is needed as evidence in the Requested Party.

ARTICLE XIX

Transit

1. Either Contracting Party may authorize transit through its territory of a person surrendered to the other by a third State. The Contracting Party requesting transit shall provide the transit State, through the diplomatic channel, a request for transit which shall contain a description of the person and a brief statement of the facts of the case.
2. No authorization for transit shall be required when air transportation is used and no landing is scheduled in the territory of the other Contracting Party. If an unscheduled landing occurs in the territory of that Contracting Party, it shall detain the person being transited not less than 96 hours while awaiting a request for transit pursuant to paragraph I of this Article.

ARTICLE XX

Assistance and Representation

The United States Department of Justice shall advise, assist and represent the Republic of Italy in any proceedings in the United States arising out of a request for extradition made by the Republic of Italy.

The Italian Ministry of Grace and Justice, through all means permitted by its legal system, shall advise, assist and provide for the representation of the United States of America in any proceedings in Italy arising out of a request for extradition made by the United States of America.

ARTICLE XXI

Expenses

The Requesting Party shall pay the expenses related to the translation of documents and the transportation of the person sought from the city where confined to the Requesting Party. The Requested Party shall pay all other expenses related to the provisional arrest, extradition request and proceedings. Any expenses related to transit under Article XIX shall be borne by the Requesting Party.

The Requested Party shall make no pecuniary claim against the Requesting Party arising out of the arrest, detention or surrender of persons sought under the terms of this Treaty.

ARTICLE XXII

Scope of Application

This Treaty shall apply to offenses committed before as well as after the date this Treaty enters into force.

ARTICLE XXIII
Denunciation

Either Contracting Party may terminate this Treaty at any time by giving written notice to the other Contracting Party. Termination shall be effective six months after the date of receipt of such notice.

ARTICLE XXIV
Ratification and Entry into Force

1. This Treaty shall be subject to ratification. The instruments of ratification shall be exchanged at Washington as soon as possible.
2. This Treaty shall enter into force immediately upon the exchange of the instruments of ratification.
3. Upon the entry into force of this Treaty, the Treaty on Extradition between the United States of America and the Republic of Italy, signed at Rome on January 18, 1973, and the Supplementary Protocol, signed at Rome on November 9, 1982, shall cease to have effect; however, extradition proceedings pending in a Requested Party at the time this Treaty enters into force shall be subject to the prior Treaty, except that Article II of this Treaty should also be applicable to such proceedings. Article XIV of this Treaty shall also apply to persons found extraditable under the prior Treaty.

DONE at Rome, this thirteenth day of October, 1983 in duplicate in the English and Italian languages, both equally authentic.

FOR THE GOVERNMENT OF
THE UNITED STATES OF AMERICA

FOR THE GOVERNMENT OF
THE REPUBLIC OF ITALY

The European Approach

Dominique Poncet and Paul Gully-Hart

Legal Framework of Extradition in Europe[1]

Multilateral Conventions

The European Convention on Extradition

The European Convention on Extradition, which was opened for signature on December 13, 1957, and entered into force on April 18, 1960,[2] was elaborated under the auspices of the Council of Europe.[3] It is a highly successful regional convention forming the procedural framework for more extraditions than any other multilateral treaty and by the end of 1994, 26 states ratified it. The Convention provides for extradition without proof of a *prima facie* case and gives parties the discretion to refuse to extradite their nationals. It repeals the clauses of previously concluded treaties, conventions or bilateral arrangements regarding extradition between the contracting states. Member States can enter bilateral or multilateral agreements between themselves with a view to supplementing the clauses of the European Convention or in order to facilitate their implementation.[4]

The most significant development over the past years has been the ratification of the European Convention by the United Kingdom. In accordance with the Criminal Justice Act of 1988[5] and the Extradition Act of 1989, the Government of the United Kingdom has been conferred with the capacity to enter into agreements with foreign states which will not require the requesting state to demonstrate a *prima facie* case against the fugitive. Thus, the main obstacle to the ratification of the European Convention by the United Kingdom was removed and the United Kingdom ratified the Convention on February 13, 1991. The change in the United Kingdom's extradition policy was considered necessary not only in the formal sense for ratification of the European Convention, but to prevent the United Kingdom from becoming a haven for fugitive criminals. The United Kingdom Government sympathized with the claims made by some European states that the *prima facie* requirement presented so great an obstacle to obtaining the return of wanted persons that they were deterred from even seeking extradition in some cases.

---

1 For a comparison to the U.S. approach, *see* M. Cherif Bassiouni, *Law and Practice of the United States*, *supra*, Chapter 7.

2 European Convention on Extradition, Europ. T.S. No. 24 [hereinafter Euro. Extradition Conv.].

3 The Euro. Extradition Conv. is one of the kingpins in the complex European system of mutual assistance instruments made up of at least 15 Conventions and Additional Protocols and a score of Resolutions and Recommendations drawn up by the Council of Europe.

4 Art. 26 of Euro. Extradition Conv. does not limit the possibility for contracting parties to formulate reservations. The Committee of Ministers of the Council of Europe in Resolution (78) 43 (Oct. 25, 1978) made clear that it was aware of this and recommended that contracting parties "limit the range of reservations that they have formulated or withdraw them, in light of the solutions provided by the Additional Protocols."

5 *See* Colin Warbrick, *The Criminal Justice Act 1988 (1) The New Law on Extradition*, 4 CRIM. L. REV. 14 (1989); *see also* ALUN JONES, JONES ON EXTRADITION (1995).

With the collapse of the Iron Curtain in 1989/1990, several East European states have joined—or are in the process of joining—the Council of Europe, which will grant them access to the network of European Treaties in matters of international criminal cooperation.[6] Bulgaria, Hungary, the Czech Republic and Slovakia have already ratified the European Convention.

The main features of the European Convention may be summarized as follows:

1. Extradition is not restricted to a list of offences (enumerative system) but should encompass any offence which is serious enough to justify the surrender of the fugitive (eliminative system).[7]

2. The dual criminality rule is implicitly required[8] by the Convention as the offence should be punishable under the laws of both the requesting and requested state.

3. The Convention makes provision for the so-called political offence exception.[9] Extradition is also excluded for military offences.[10] Regarding tax matters, the Convention and its Second Additional Protocol endeavor to promote extradition for tax offences, thus taking into account the harmonization of European tax legislation.[11]

4. The Convention has attempted, but so far without much success, to permit the extradition of nationals;[12] each state is granted the discretion to refuse extradition provided it ensures the prosecution of nationals in the domestic courts.

5. Extradition will not be granted if the fugitive has been definitively tried by the courts of the requested state. This rule has been extended by the First Additional Protocol to judgments rendered by the courts of third State which are parties to the Convention.[13]

6. The Convention has endeavored to settle the problems raised by conflicts of jurisdiction between Member States.[14]

7. Member States are authorized by the Convention to deny extradition where the fugitive is exposed to the death penalty.[15]

8. As mentioned before, no evidence of guilt or probable cause is required by the state requested to surrender the fugitive.[16]

9. The Convention encourages the idea that extradition is not as much an act of sovereignty as it is a measure of international cooperation between like-minded states.

---

[6] All Members of the Council of Europe are expected to ratify the European Convention on Human Rights (Europ. T.S. No. 5) which represents a collective guarantee at a European level of a number of principles set out in the Universal Declaration of Human Rights supported by international judicial machinery making decisions which must be respected by contracting states.

[7] *See* Euro. Extradition Conv., *supra* note 2, at Art. 2.

[8] *See id.* at Art. 2: "shall give rise to extradition those facts punished by the laws of the requesting party and of the requested party. . . ."

[9] *Id.* at Art. 3 ¶¶ 1, 2.

[10] *Id.* at Art. 4.

[11] *Id.* at Art. 5, *see also* Second Additional Protocol to the European Convention of 1978, Europ. T.S. No. 98, § II [hereinafter Euro. Conv. 2d. Add. Prot. Extradition].

[12] Euro. Extradition Conv., *supra* note 2, at Art. 6.

[13] *Id.* at Art. 9; *see also* Additional Protocol to the European Convention of 1978, Europ. T.S. No. 86, § II [hereinafter Euro. Conv. Add. Prot. Extradition].

[14] Euro. Extradition Conv., *supra* note 2, at Art. 7.

[15] *Id.* at Art. 11.

[16] This used to be the main difference between the Convention and Common Law. Pursuant to the provisions of the Extradition Act 1989, the United Kingdom has been able to ratify the Euro. Extradition Conv., *supra* note 2.

Although the rule is that a request for extradition should be processed through diplomatic channels, other means of communication may be arranged by direct agreement between two or more parties. Section V of the Second Additional Protocol to the Convention provides that requests are to be addressed by the Ministry of Justice of the requesting state to the Ministry of Justice of the requested state. Interpol plays an important role in forwarding requests for provisional arrest with a view to extradition.[17]

10. Extradition is subject to the rule of speciality.[18]

The European Convention has been complemented by two Additional Protocols. The Additional Protocol of 1975,[19] ratified by 12 states, recognizes that the political offence exception should not apply to crimes against humanity or to war crimes. The protection of a person against whom a final judgement has been rendered is reinforced to the extent that the extradition of that person should not be granted if the judgment resulted in acquittal, if the term of imprisonment has been completely enforced or has been the subject of a pardon or an amnesty, or if the court convicted the offender without imposing a sanction. Wider domestic provisions relating to the effect of *ne bis in idem* attached to foreign criminal judgements has been reserved.

The Second Additional Protocol,[20] ratified by 18 states, allows extradition for tax offences. The rights for the fugitive sentenced *in absentia* are safeguarded to the extent that where a contracting party requests from another contracting party the extradition of a person for the purpose of enforcing a sentence imposed by a judgment rendered *in absentia*, the requested party may refuse to extradite if the proceedings leading to the judgement did not satisfy the minimum rights of a defense recognized as due to everyone charged with a criminal offence. However, extradition will be granted if the requesting party gives an assurance that the fugitive will be afforded the right to a retrial which safeguards his rights of defense and is considered sufficient by the requested state.

The Nordic Union

In order to achieve the highest possible degree of equality of treatment between Scandinavian nationals, the Scandinavian countries (Denmark, Finland, Iceland, Norway and Sweden) have adopted uniform legislation. The Nordic scheme is compatible with the European Convention, although it requires the requesting state to provide sufficient evidence of guilt. Other features of the Scandinavian reciprocal legislation have been expressed in the form of reservations towards certain clauses of the Extradition Convention. For instance, foreigners domiciled in any one of the Nordic states are considered nationals of those states and therefore benefit from the rule relating to the non-extradition of nationals.

It is fair to mention that, in the light of this successful regional framework in dealing with matters of criminal policy, representatives of the Nordic countries have, in many ways, promoted efforts to elaborate internationally accepted standards for criminal policy and criminal justice and to implement these standards. Examples of these endeavors are found

---

17 Euro. Extradition Conv., *supra* note 2, at Art. 16 ¶ 3.
18 *Id.* at Art. 14.
19 Euro. Conv. Add. Prot. Extradition, *supra* note 13.
20 Euro. Conv. 2d Add. Prot. Extradition, *supra* note 11.

at the level of the United Nations congresses on the prevention of crime and the treatment of offenders.[21]

The Benelux Extradition Treaty of June 27, 1962[22]

The clauses of the Treaty between The Netherlands, Belgium and Luxembourg are very similar to those of the European Convention. It is a simplified trilateral agreement which deals with extradition and mutual assistance in criminal matters. Because of the special arrangements made between the Benelux countries, The Netherlands, upon ratification of the European Convention, rejected Article 28, paragraph 1 and paragraph 2 (whereby the Convention prevails over bilateral agreements), and also reserved the future right to derogate from those same provisions in order to accommodate any arrangement under the auspices of the European Union.

The European Union

On September 27, 1996, at an informal Council Meeting in Dublin, the Justice Ministries of the European Union agreed and signed a Convention relating to extradition between Member States.[23] This Convention responds to the European Council's concerns that the progressive abolition of checks at the borders between the states of the E.U. will diminish the security of European citizens and that additional guarantees were required for organized and systematic cooperation among E.U. members. The Convention supplements and improves the operation of the European Convention and, in certain respects, the European Convention on the Suppression of Terrorism. The new Convention considerably increases the number of circumstances likely to give rise to extradition and lowers the threshold for extraditable offences. Hence, extradition will be granted for offences which are punishable, under the law of the requesting E.U. member, by deprivation of liberty or a detention order for a maximum period of at least 12 months and, under the law of the requested E.U. Member, by deprivation of liberty for a maximum period of at least six months. One of the other features of the E.U. Convention is that it extends extradition to offences classified as a conspiracy or an association to commit offences of a sufficiently serious nature, even if the law of the requested state does not provide for the same facts to be an offence. This is an exception to the Rule of Dual Criminality. However, the intention of the conspiracy or association must be to commit terrorist acts, within the meaning of Articles 1 and 2 of the European Convention on the Suppression of Terrorism, or offences which are considered to be particularly serious, such as offences directed against the life, physical integrity or liberty of a person, or creating a collective danger for persons (for instance drug trafficking and other forms of organized crime or other acts of violence).

---

[21] *See* Raimo Lahti, *Sub-regional Criminal Policy: The Experience of the Nordic Countries, in* SCANDINAVIAN CRIMINAL POLICY AND CRIMINOLOGY 1986-1990, 93-99 (Norman Bishop ed., 1990).

[22] Traité d'extradition et d'entraide judiciaire en matière pénale entre le Royaume de Belgique, le Grand-Duché de Luxembourg et le Royaume des Pays-Bas, 27 juin 1962, approuvé par la loi du 1er juin 1964, *Moniteur Belge*, October 24, 1964.

[23] Convention Relating to Extradition between the Member States of the European Union, press release from the Informal Council Meeting of Justice and Home Affairs Ministers in Dublin on Sept. 26-27, 1996; *see* 12 INT'L ENFORCEMENT L. REP. 436-37 (1996).

The Convention also lays down the general rule that no offence should be considered by the requested state to be a political offence; Member States are allowed to make reservations to this rule provided that the reservation does not relate to acts of terrorism or to conspiracy to commit such acts. In addition, the Convention provides that extradition may not be denied on the grounds that the person claimed is a national of the requested E.U. Member State. This rule could not be applied immediately by all the E.U. Member States since the extradition of nationals is, in some of them, forbidden under their Constitution. A mechanism is provided in the Convention whereby the reservation to this rule made by E.U. members will be valid for five years. Beyond that period, reservations may be upheld or amended so as to facilitate the conditions for surrender or withdrawn.

Other provisions in the Convention concern fiscal offences, lapse of time, amnesty, re-extradition to another E.U. member, transit and the exchange of information.

The E.U. Agreement shall enter in force upon its ratification by the last Member State of the Union. It is the second Convention on Extradition that has been adopted since the entry into force of the Treaty on European Union; the first, which was signed on March 10, 1996, concerned the establishment of a simplified extradition procedure which applies only where the fugitive gives his consent to his surrender.[24]

The Schengen Agreement of June 19, 1990

Historically the Schengen Agreement is based on an agreement signed between France and Germany on July 13, 1984 (the Sarrebrück Agreement) regarding the progressive abolition of checks at the borders between the two states. The three Benelux countries became involved in the same process and the talks between the five states led to the signing of the first Schengen Agreement on June 14, 1985. This initial agreement prepared the way for open internal borders between the five. The Convention applying the 1985 Schengen Agreement was signed on June 19, 1990.[25] Italy (November 27, 1990), Spain and Portugal (June 25, 1991) and Greece (November 6, 1992) have also joined this Agreement. Austria[26] signed the Agreement on April 28, 1995. At this juncture, five states of the Nordic Union have entered into the Schengen process. Norway and Iceland, who are not members of the European Union, have signed an Agreement of Cooperation with the Schengen countries. The integration of the Scandinavian States in the Schengen process should be completed by the year 2000.

---

[24] Christine Van Den Wyngaert & G. Stessens, *Mutual Legal Assistance in Criminal Matters in the European Union, in* CHANGES IN SOCIETY, CRIME AND CRIMINAL JUSTICE IN EUROPE: CHALLENGE FOR A CRIMINOLOGICAL EDUCATION AND RESEARCH: 2 INTERNATIONAL ORGANIZED AND CORPORATE CRIME 137-76 (Cyrille Fejnaut, Johan Goethals et al. eds., 1996); *see also* D. Richard, *Une contribution européenne aux tendances actuelles du droit extraditionnel: la Convention du 27 septembre 1996, in* LA SEMAINE JURIDIQUE, 3988, ÉDITION GÉNÉRALE N 1, 1-7 (1997).

[25] *See* Y. Gautier, *Accords de Schengen, in* EDITIONS DU JURIS-CLASSEUR 1996, EUROPE FASCICULE 140, DROIT INTERNATIONAL FASCICULE 408; *see also* Jacqueline Costa-Lascoux, *De Schengen à Maastricht: Libertés et contrôles dans l'Europe des citoyens, in* MÉLANGES OFFERTS À GEORGES LEVASSEUR 1992, 129-38 (1992); *see also* Cryille Fijnaut, *The Schengen Treaties and European Police Cooperation*, EUR. J. CRIME. L. & CRIM. JUST. 37-56 (1993).

[26] Austria has encountered considerable difficulties in supervising its borders with East European countries. According to Government statistics, more than 10,000 illegal immigrants have been arrested in 1996 at the eastern borders of Austria, an increase of 61 percent from the 1995 figures.

The largest title of the 1990 Schengen Convention is devoted to police and security. The signing countries have engaged in a lengthy debate on the basic principles upon which cooperation and harmonization in the field of criminal law should be based. The foremost issue is the autonomy of the national criminal justice system; each national system is a product of a long historical development and operates within a specific cultural context. This issue concerns substantive criminal law, prosecution policy and sentencing policy. The well-publicized debate on Dutch drug policy in relation to that of neighboring countries provides a striking illustration of this theme. A further matter of concern is the procedural implication of Schengen. International assistance in criminal matters requires cooperation between the relevant national legal authorities and this raises the question of how such cooperation between government agencies and police forces should be controlled and supervised in the interest of the process of law.

The Schengen Convention contains certain provisions dealing with extradition. These provisions elaborate on agreements already in existence between the contracting parties (Article 59). In Article 60, Belgium (which has not ratified the European Convention) undertakes to consider requests for extradition by France and Germany on the basis of the European Convention. In accordance with Article 61, France has accepted to mitigate the requirement of qualified dual criminality in relation to the other Schengen states. While the requirement under French Law that the offence carries a penalty of at least two years imprisonment remains valid, no more than a penalty of at least one is required under the law of the requesting state. Article 62 provides for regulation of some aspects of the Statute of Limitations, amnesty and offences which can only be prosecuted after a complaint has been lodged. Article 63 is of greater significance as the extradition of offenders in relation to indirect taxation becomes compulsory. Article 64 states that registration in the Schengen Information System (SIS) shall be deemed a request for provisional arrest which may lead to extradition. Article 65 facilitates extradition to the extent that requests for extradition need no longer follow the diplomatic route.[27]

EUROPOL

The European Police Organization, known as EUROPOL,[28] is achieving success in assisting in the identification, investigation, and prosecution of international criminal cases, even though the Convention establishing EUROPOL has not yet been ratified. At present, EUROPOL's scope is quite limited. It can exchange and analyze information that EUROPOL members provide. It is not able to start investigations and cannot develop its own data banks of criminal activities. The substantive criminal areas it can handle include only trafficking of drugs, nuclear materials, illegal immigration networks and vehicle theft. Once the Convention establishing EUROPOL is ratified, EUROPOL will be able to compile its own data and to develop relationships with non-European Union organizations. The current trend is to encourage international task forces to investigate and prosecute specific types of offences.

---

27 *See* Bert (A. H. J.) Swart, *Police and Security in the Schengen Agreement and Schengen Convention*, *in* SCHENGEN INTERNATIONALIZATION OF CENTRAL CHAPTERS OF THE LAW ON ALIENS, REFUGEES, PRIVACY, SECURITY AND THE POLICE, 96-109 (1991).

28 13 INT'L ENFORCEMENT L. REP. 107, 281 (1997); Emma Tucker, *EUROPOL Team is Clearly on the Case*, FINANCIAL TIMES, Feb. 8-9, 1997, at 2 col..

Other Sources of Extradition Law

Bilateral Conventions

It is not possible within the limited scope of this discussion to draw up a list of the main bilateral treaties between European states nor to examine their characteristics.

As a general rule, the conclusion of treaties on extradition has preceded, historically, the enactment of domestic legislation. As a result, domestic legislation tends to conform to the general principles of extradition law which is derived from international agreements on extradition. The pattern of extradition law is quite the opposite in the United Kingdom because very few treaties had been negotiated before the Extradition Act of 1870. Conventions concluded after this date are strictly in accordance with the Act. Hence the requirement of lawful surrender, which implies that the surrender of fugitive criminals means surrender in accordance with the provisions of the Extradition Act; any other arrangement would not be lawful.[29]

The number of bilateral treaties between European states is decreasing due to the great number of Member States to the European Convention. In accordance with Article 28 of the European Convention, the main purpose of bilateral agreements is to supplement the provisions of the European Convention or to facilitate the application of the principles contained therein.[30]

Domestic Laws

In the Civil Law System (as opposed to the United Kingdom), a principle which is generally recognized is that Treaty obligations supersede domestic legislation, which should be considered as auxiliary and subsidiary in relation to international conventions. The preeminence of international law, whether conventional or customary, is recognized by practically all the states of Western Europe. The French Law on Extradition of 1927 must abide by contrary clauses in the Treaty[31] and french law is applicable only when there exists no convention or in order to make up for *lacunæ* in the Treaty. Article 1 of the Swiss Act on International Mutual Assistance in Criminal Matters which entered into force on January 1, 1983, explicitly reserves the international conventions that bind Switzerland. Article 10 of the Italian Constitution states that Italy undertakes to conform to the "generally recognized principles of International Law" which includes compliance with international treaties. Problems of interpretation have nevertheless arisen over the existence or the extent of these "generally recognized principles."[32]

General Principles of International Law

---

[29] V. E. HARTLEY-BOOTH, 1 BRITISH EXTRADITION LAW AND PRACTICE 17 (1980).

[30] For instance, Switzerland has supplemented its extradition arrangements with Germany and Austria through the ratification of additional accords regulating technical issues such as the designation of the competent authorities to issue a warrant of arrest, the direct communication of extradition requests through the Ministries of Justice, the procedural acts which are likely to interrupt the Statute of Limitation, etc.

[31] CLAUDE LOMBOIS, DROIT PÉNAL INTERNATIONAL 543-44, ¶ 419 (2d ed. 1979).

[32] GUILO CATELANI & DANIELE STRIANI, L'ESTRADIZIONE 44-45, 105-09 (1983).

Certain principles of Extradition Law have met with such a broad consensus that they should be considered as Customary Rules of International Law which should prevail over conflicting provisions of the Treaty or domestic legislation (*jus cogens*).

These principles appear to be the following:

1. The rule of dual criminality,[33] which requires that the conduct stated in the request for extradition should be punishable under the laws of the requesting and the requested states. In our opinion the binding nature of the rule is limited to the elements constituting the offence and does not pertain to the circumstances affecting the punishability of the offender, such as lapse of time, the requirement that a complaint should be filed prior to prosecution, the insanity of the offender and amnesty.

2. The rule of speciality,[34] to the extent that the requesting state is precluded from prosecuting, trying or convicting the extradited person for offences other than those which have given rise to extradition and which are prior to them, unless by consent of the requested state or of the extradited person.

3. The political offence exception, although there are considerable differences of opinion as to the extent of this defence to extradition.[35] It is quite clear that the non-discrimination rule contained in Article 3, paragraph 2 of the European Convention is of a binding nature.[36] According to this provision, the political offence exception extends to cases where the requested party has substantial grounds for believing that the request for extradition for an ordinary criminal offence has been made for the purpose of prosecuting or punishing a person on account of his race, religion, nationality or political opinion, or that that person's position may be prejudiced for any of these reasons.

4. Extradition should be denied where the fugitive is in serious danger of being tried by a "tribunal d'exception," *e.g.*, an *ad hoc* tribunal, of being subjected to inhuman or degrading treatments[37] or where the criminal justice system in the requesting state falls short of the

---

33 Dual criminality is based partly on the principle of reciprocity and partly on the rule "*nulla poena sine lege*" (also referred to as the rule of legality); M. CHERIF BASSIOUNI, INTERNATIONAL EXTRADITION AND WORLD PUBLIC ORDER 322 (1974); IVAN ANTHONY SHEARER, EXTRADITION IN INTERNATIONAL LAW 23 (1971).

34 Speciality is one of the traditional rules of extradition law: the rule appears for the first time in the Extradition Treaty concluded between France and Luxembourg in 1844; *see* BASSIOUNI, *supra* note 33, at 352; ALBERT BILLOT, TRAITÉ DE L'EXTRADITION 552 (1874); FRANCO MOSCONI & MARCO PISANI, LE CONVENZIONI DI ASSISTENZA GIUDIZIARIA 84-88 (1984); Hans Schultz, *Les principes du droit d'extradition traditionnel*, *in* COUNCIL OF EUROPE PUBLICATIONS: ASPECTS JURIDIQUES DE L'EXTRADITION ENTRE ETATS EUROPÉENS (1970).

35 CHRISTINE VAN DEN WYNGAERT, THE POLITICAL OFFENCE EXCEPTION TO EXTRADITION (1980); P. Gully-Hart, *Loss of Time through Formal and Procedural Requirements in International Cooperation*, *in* 33 PRINCIPLES AND PROCEDURES FOR A NEW TRANSNATIONAL CRIMINAL LAW, REPORTS AND MATERIALS FROM THE MAX PLANCK INSTITUTE 257-58 (Albin Eser & Otto Lagodny eds., 1991).

36 *See* Recommendation No. R(80)9 of the Committee of Ministers to member States concerning extradition to States not party to the European Convention on Human Rights adopted on June 27, 1980; Member States are recommended to apply the provisions of Art. 3 ¶ 2 of the European Convention to States which are not party to that Convention and, further, to comply with any interim measures which may be suggested by the European Commission of Human Rights under Rule 36 of its Rules of Procedure; *see also* C. Rouiller, *L'évolution du concept de délit politique en droit de l'entraide internationale en matière pénale*, REVUE PÉNALE SUISSE 40-41 (1986).

37 *See* Schultz, *supra* note 34, at 14-15; Schultz considers that the existence of a "tribunal d'exception" must entail *pars pro toto* the refusal to extradite where the principles of procedure applied by the requesting state do not meet the requirements of due process of law; *see also* DOMINIQUE PONCET & PHILIPPE NEYROUD, L'EXTRADITION ET L'ASILE POLITIQUE EN SUISSE 30-31 (1976); and Resolution XI, Tenth International Congress on Penal Law (Rome 1969), *printed in* LA REVUE DE SCIENCE CRIMINELLE ET DE DROIT COMPARÉ 216 (1970).

basic rights and guarantees contemplated in the European Convention of Human Rights and Fundamental Freedoms or the United Nations Covenant on Civil and Political Rights.

5. The *ne bis in idem* rule[38] to the extent that an offender cannot be sentenced twice for the same offence.

Declarations of Reciprocity

To achieve international cooperation between states some kind of arrangement, whether formal or informal, whether general or *ad hoc,* is necessary between the states involved. The arrangement may be based on a treaty, bilateral or multilateral, or on the application with respect to the requesting state of the requested state's domestic extradition legislation. In any event, some level of agreement must be reached between the two states acknowledging that the fugitive should be surrendered provided that certain prerequisites are met. Inherent in any such arrangement is the potential for reciprocity.[39] Reciprocity is explicit in a treaty where each party has agreed to surrender up fugitives to the other on the understanding that its requests will also be honored. In *ad hoc* arrangements, designed to meet the situation where the fugitive is found in a state with which the requesting state does not possess general extradition relations, a special agreement may be reached whereby the requested state will extract an understanding that in similar circumstances its request for extradition will be considered. Many European countries provide for a Declaration of Repricocity in such circumstances, for instance France, Germany, Austria, Belgium and Switzerland.[40]

Although there are increasing doubts as to whether the rule of reciprocity should constitute a legal requirement for extradition, reciprocity continues to play a significant role in the practice of extradition. It renders extradition possible without excessive formalities in the absence of a treaty. It may also be relied upon to complement a treaty where the offence for which extradition is requested falls outside of the scope of the treaty, but is nevertheless permitted by the domestic laws of the requested state. In addition, the rule of reciprocity extends to the interpretation and application of treaties in order to ensure that they provide the same rights and obligations for each of the contracting parties. The fact that certain Member States have made a large number of reservations to the European Convention has created an undeniable disparity between the contracting parties. As no state should be compelled to enter into unilateral commitments, the requested state should be left with the option of applying reciprocity in such cases.[41]

---

[38] *See* the U.N. Covenant on Civil and Political Rights, Art. 14(7); *see also* the Euro. Extradition Conv., *supra* note 2, at Art. 9; the Euro. Conv. Add. Prot. Extradition, chapter II; BASSIOUNI, *supra* note 33, at 452-59.

[39] G. GILBERT, ASPECTS OF EXTRADITION LAW 17-19 (1991).

[40] *See* for instance Art. 8 of the Swiss Federal Act on International Mutual Assistance in Criminal Matters, which provides that the Swiss authorities may require a guarantee of reciprocity *if it is deemed necessary*; 20 I.L.M. 1339 (1981).

[41] The Euro. Extradition Conv. does not specifically reserve the application of the rule of reciprocity in such a case but nevertheless the rule of reciprocity has been interpreted in order to re-establish equal rights and obligations between the contracting parties.

The Formal and Substantial Requirements of Extradition

Formal Requirements

Evidence and Extradition Hearings

Generalities

The first step in any extradition proceeding is to inform the arresting authorities in the requested state of the fugitive's presence. There are two means of achieving this communication. The first involves the formal request through diplomatic or governmental channels for the issuance of a warrant for the fugitive's surrender.[42] Such a request must be backed up by sufficient evidence to convince the government department responsible for criminal matters, or a member of the judiciary, that arresting the fugitive and holding an extradition hearing is appropriate.[43] Secondly, the requesting state may make an application directly to a judge for a warrant of arrest, known as the provisional warrant, to be issued; this procedure is followed more particularly in the United Kingdom.[44] Once arrested, it would be unusual for the fugitive to be granted bail before the extradition hearing, and as a result, the fugitive may have to spend long periods in pre-trial custody.

The second stage in the extradition process consists of forwarding a fully-motivated request for the fugitive's extradition to the authorities of the requested state.[45] Normally the request is submitted to a local court or magistrate, or in some cases to the government itself, with the opportunity for the individual concerned to seek a judicial review. Extradition hearings do not determine the guilt or innocence of the fugitive, only his susceptibility to surrender. The hearing differs between civil and common law states, the latter usually requiring proof of a *prima facie* case, although—as we have already seen—this requirement has now been abandoned by the United Kingdom in its extradition dealings under the European Convention.[46]

Having finished the hearing and any appeal, the process enters its final administrative phase. Assuming that the courts have agreed to the fugitive's surrender, it is left to the executive branch to make its own decision on a case before authorizing extradition.[47] To this

---

42 *See* Euro. Extradition Conv., *supra* note 2, at Art. 16 ¶ 3: "A request for provisional arrest shall be sent to the competent authorities of the requested State either through the diplomatic channel or direct by post or telegraph or though Interpol or by any other means affording evidence in writing or accepted by the requested State."

43 Under the Euro. Extradition Conv., procedural requirements at the stage of provisional arrest have become somewhat relaxed: it is usually sufficient to state the offence or offences for which a warrant of arrest has been issued by the requesting state.

44 On these matters *see* GILBERT, *supra* note 39, at 35-36.

45 Treaties and domestic law usually provide for a period of time in which the supporting documentation should be forwarded to the requested state; *see* for instance Euro. Extradition Conv., *supra* note 2, at Art. 16 ¶ 4.

46 *See supra* note 4.

47 In France, the opinion of the Court unfavorable to extradition is binding upon the Government; if however the Court's opinion is favorable, the Government nevertheless has the discretionary power to refuse to give effect to the request; the same rule applies in Belgium, *see* Christine Van Den Wyngaert, *La Belgique et l'exception politique en matière d'extradition*, in 59 REVUE DE DROIT PÉNAL ET DE CRIMINOLOGIE, 833-63 (1970).

extent, extradition may be described as an act of government which is usually subject to judicial review or judicial authorization.[48]

Article 22 of the European Convention merely provides that "the proceedings with a regard to extradition and provisional arrest shall be governed solely by the law of the requested party."

However, the Committee of the Council of Europe has enhanced the judicial nature of extradition proceedings.[49] The contracting parties must ensure that the person whose extradition is sought has the right to be heard by a judicial authority and to be assisted by the lawyer of his own choosing, and must submit to a judicial authority the control of his custody for the purpose of extradition as well as the conditions of his extradition. There is no doubt that due process of law requirements should be extended to international cooperation procedures. There is a growing concern, however, that the function of determining issues arising under requests for international cooperation should be assigned to constitutionally impartial organs. The acceleration of international cooperation procedures should not be obtained at the expense of appropriate judicial review, particularly if the freedom or important civil rights of an individual are at stake.[50]

Proceedings in the requested state need not be unnecessarily lengthy. The main task of the court or of the competent government agency is to enforce treaty obligations or, as the case may be, to enforce domestic legislation providing for mutual assistance in favor of the requesting state. The requested state is not the appropriate forum for discussing the merits or the strength of the case against the defendant. Mutual cooperation in criminal matters implies that the authorities of the requested state should, as a matter of principle, trust the judicial system of the requesting state and its ability to comply with adequate standards of a fair trial. This presumption of good faith in inter-state cooperation may obviously be rebutted in the light of clear evidence that the requesting state does not afford the basic rights and guarantees to which the defendant is entitled under existing international human rights instruments.[51]

---

48 *See* for instance Belgium: Law of Oct. 1, 1833 (replaced by the Law of Mar. 15, 1874); Denmark: Law of June 9, 1967; Federal Republic of Germany: Law of Dec. 23, 1929 (replaced by the Law of Dec. 23, 1982); France: Mar. 10, 1927; Greece: Code of Penal Procedure of Aug. 17, 1950, Arts. 436-61; Ireland: Extradition Act of July 19, 1965; Luxembourg: Law of Dec. 31, 1841 (replaced by the Law of Mar. 13, 1870); the Netherlands: Law of Apr. 6, 1875 (replaced by the Law of Aug. 13, 1949 and replaced again by the Law of Mar. 9, 1967); United Kingdom: Extradition Act of 1870 (replaced by Extradition Act 1989); Switzerland: Law of Jan. 22, 1892 (replaced by the Law of Mar. 20, 1981). Only Switzerland and Spain seem to admit today that a judicial decision is binding upon the government.

49 *See* Resolution (75) 12 of May 21, 1975 and Recommendation (80) 7 of June 27, 1980 of the Committee of Ministers of the Council of Europe.

50 *See* Gully-Hart, *supra* note 35, at 256.

51 Rouiller, *supra* note 36, at 41.

Pre-hearing Detention

One of the major practical issues in extradition cases is the time a fugitive may have to spend in prison waiting for the extradition process to run its course. It is often assumed that the alleged fugitive offender has fled to the asylum state. Another consideration is that if the fugitive takes advantage of his release to flee from the asylum state prior to his extradition, the requesting state may legitimately raise the issue of a breach by the requested state of its obligations under the Treaty. For these reasons, it is unusual for a fugitive to be released prior to the extradition hearing if there is a serious chance that he could leave the requested state. However, the detained fugitive is entitled to argue abusive process if, after having made a request for his release, he is not granted the benefit of an adversarial proceeding. While no right not to be extradited exists under the European Convention of Human Rights,[52] a fugitive should not be detained for an unreasonable length of time under Article 5 (3) ECHR. Further under Article 5 (1) (f) ECHR, the Commission has held that extradition proceedings must be conducted with "requisite diligence."[53]

Under the European Convention, there is a provision for two periods after which the release of the fugitive should be ordered should the formal submission of the request be delayed: after a period of 18 days from the arrest, release may be ordered; or a period of 40 days from the arrest, at the end of which release is compulsory. There is no *res judicata*: a new arrest remains possible if the request for extradition arrives later.[54]

In addition to the above-mentioned legal safeguards, the fugitive is entitled to a judicial review of the lawfulness of his detention pending extradition proceedings. He must be informed as soon as possible and in a language that he understands, of the request for extradition and the guarantees afforded by the extradition procedure; it must be possible for his defense against the request for extradition to be heard and, if necessary, he must be given legal aid.[55]

The Decision to Extradite and Its Enforcement

Although extradition itself is a prerogative of the government, the judiciary will examine the legal requirements set forth in the Treaty or in domestic legislation. Where the fugitive consents to extradition, surrender will be enforced without formalities provided, however, that consent has been given freely. In most domestic legislation, consent by the fugitive does not limit the discretionary power exercised by the government. In the event of consent, the Council of Europe has recommended a summary procedure in view of the speedy surrender of the fugitive (Resolution (80) 7, of June 27, 1975). The European Union has established a simplified extradition procedure where the fugitive gives his consent to his surrender.[56]

---

[52] *See* Application 1983/63, X v. the Netherlands, 8 Y.B. EUR. CONV. ON H.R. 288; Application 2143/1964, X v. Austria & Yugoslavia Yearbook, 7 Y.B. EUR. CONV. ON H.R. 314; Application 3110/67, X v. Germany 11 Y.B. EUR. CONV. ON H.R. 494.

[53] *See* Sanchez-Reisse v. Switzerland, Application 9862/82, EUR. CT. H. R. (Oct. 21, 1986).

[54] *See* Euro. Extradition Conv., *supra* note 2, at Art. 16 ¶ 5: Release shall not prejudice re-arrest and extradition if a request for extradition is received subsequently.

[55] *See* Resolution and Recommendation, *supra* note 49.

[56] *See supra* note 24.

Under Article 18 of the European Convention, the requested party shall inform the requesting party of its decision with regard to the extradition and reasons shall be given for any complete or partial rejection. If the request is agreed to, the requesting party shall be informed of the place and date of surrender and of the length of time for which the person claimed was detained with a view to surrender. As in the case of provisional arrest, two periods are provided for: a first period of 15 days, after which the requested state may release the fugitive and a second period of 30 days, after which release by the requested state is compulsory.

The Extradition Convention has provisions for both deferred and conditional surrender of the extradited person. In the first case,[57] the surrender of the individual can be postponed so that he may be prosecuted by the requested party or serve a sentence issued in respect of another offence. In the second event,[58] the requested party, instead of deferring surrender, may temporarily extradite the fugitive to the requesting party on conditions to be determined by common consent.

Article 20 of the Extradition Convention provides that, at the request of the requesting party, the requested party shall seize and hand over, to the extent allowed by its legislation, such property as may serve as evidence as well as property which, resulting from the offence, may have been found in the possession of the fugitive at the time of the arrest or that may have been discovered later. Property may be handed over even where extradition has been granted but is not enforceable, for instance, because a fugitive has died or has fled the asylum state.[59] Any rights the requested party or third parties may have acquired over the property are reserved. Further, the Council of Europe has recommended that the contracting parties take into consideration the interests of the victim of the offence in obtaining the speedy restitution of property (Resolution (75) 12 of May 21, 1975).

Extradition Crimes, Jurisdiction and Dual Criminality

Extradition Offenses

Extradition law has developed two systems to determine extradition offenses. If the enumerative approach is adopted, the Extradition Treaty and the relevant domestic legislation list all defences for which surrender might be granted; if the offense is not listed, then there is no extraditable offence and the fugitive will not be surrendered. The drawbacks of the enumerative system are well-known. First, treaties which resort to the enumerative system are often old and do not take into account new forms of criminality, such as drug trafficking, aircraft hijacking or terrorism. Second, a certain number of serious offences may have been omitted in the list. Where it is not possible to supplement the Convention by means of a Declaration of Reciprocity, the fugitive will not be extradited. A further complaint against the enumerative method is that it is restrictive, and that any offences added after the conclusion of the Treaty have to be the subject of time-consuming supplementary treaties.

---

57 *See* Euro. Extradition Conv., *supra* note 2, at Art. 19 ¶ 1.

58 *See id.* at Art. 19 ¶ 2.

59 *See* for instance Gelli v. Federal Office of Police Matters *published in* THE OFFICIAL REPORTER OF DECISIONS OF THE SUPREME COURT OF SWITZERLAND, vol. 112 1b at 610-33 (1986).

The alternative is the eliminative approach, which usually defines extradition crimes in terms of a minimum penalty. The European Convention has adopted this approach, providing in Article 2 section 1 that extraditable offences are those which are punished by the laws of the requesting state and of the requested state with a sentence or a detention order for a maximum of one year. If a sentence or a detention order is passed, it should be, at least, for four months. The requested state has the option of granting extradition for offenses which do not comply with this requirement provided the request for extradition is made for several different charges. This rule is justified by the fact that if an individual is to be surrendered for a serious offense anyway, it follows logically that he should also be prosecuted for minor offenses which would not have entailed extradition if taken individually. Article 2 section 3 of the Convention allows those countries which have adopted the enumerative system in their domestic laws to make a reservation by excluding offences for which extradition would not be authorized by domestic law. Israel has made use of this provision. Switzerland withdrew the reservation it had made in this respect as a result of the entry into effect on January 1, 1983, of the Federal Act of March 20, 1981, on International Mutual Assistance in Criminal Matters. The United Kingdom has converted to the eliminative approach with the logical result that the number of extraditable crimes has been greatly increased.[60]

Jurisdiction

Three different situations should be contemplated in regard to jurisdiction. The offense may have been committed on the territory of (1) the requesting state (2) the requested state or (3) a third-party state.

The first situation generates no particular problems. The traditional approach of common law states was to acknowledge only territorial jurisdiction, and this is reflected in bilateral treaties with the United Kingdom or the United States.[61] European states usually apply the principle of ubiquity, whereby a crime is deemed to have occurred in the place where the perpetrator acted or in the place where the statutorily proscribed harm occurred.[62]

For a long period of time, the second situation received a simple and rigid response: extradition was denied because of the judicial sovereignty of the requested state. European Extradition Law and practice have significantly mitigated this rule. Unlawful conduct on the territory of the requested state is sometimes the continuation or the outcome of criminal conduct initiated abroad. In addition, the surrender of the fugitive may favor his social rehabilitation if, as a result of his extradition, he will be tried by the courts of the state of which he is a national. Where the center of gravity of the defence is located in the requesting

---

60 *See* GILBERT, *supra* note 39, at 39, 72 (author's note): for instance under the Extradition Act 1989, "One can now return a fugitive who has allegedly committed that notorious international crime purporting to act as a spiritualistic medium for reward, contrary to paragraph 1 Fraudulent Mediums Act 1951."

61 It has been suggested that U.S. law generally does not allow jurisdiction under circumstances in which the result of a crime occurs abroad. While this may have been true in the past, expansion of and exceptions to territorial theory recently have eroded rigid notions of territoriality; *see, e.g.*, Christopher Blakesley, *A Conceptual Framework for Extradition and Jurisdiction over Extraterritorial Crimes*, 1984 UTAH L. REV. 685; Christopher Blakesley & Otto Lagodny, *Finding Harmony Amidst Disagreement over Extradition, Jurisdiction, the Role of Human Rights, and Issues of Extraterritoriality Under International Criminal Law*, 24 VAND. J. OF TRANSNAT'L L. 14-15 (1991).

62 *See* for instance, the German Criminal Code § 9 ¶ 1; the Swiss Criminal Code, Art. 7.

state and, particularly, where co-defendants will be prosecuted and tried by the courts of that state, it is often opportune that international cooperation should prevail over a rigid assertion of judicial sovereignty by the requested state. This issue is not resolved by the European Convention; Article 7 gives discretion to Member States to apply their domestic legislation in respect to offenses which fall within the jurisdiction of the requested state. Greece, the Netherlands and Switzerland have made a reservation in this respect. The Netherlands, concerned as to reciprocity, reserves the possibility of not granting extradition where the requesting state would be authorized to refuse extradition in similar circumstances. Switzerland, which had declared that it would deny extradition pursuant to Article 7 of the European Convention, withdrew its reservation effective January 1, 1983. Austria, without formulating a reservation, declared that extradition would only be granted to the extent that the fugitive should be extradited on account of another offence and that it was opportune for the passing of the sentence and its enforcement that all offences be tried by the courts of the requesting state.

It is certainly more rational to transfer all proceedings to the same court where co-defendants are to be tried by that court, or if investigations have been initiated at an early stage in the requesting state resulting in substantial evidence already being available. There is usually no advantage for the defendant to face several trials in different jurisdictions, as sentencing guidelines provide for a more lenient global sentence where the accused is tried in the same court for all the offences for which he has been charged. The requirement of rational and expeditious proceedings in one single forum should prevail over assertions of judicial sovereignty by the requested party. Switzerland, Germany and Austria, for instance, have privileged the criteria of rational proceedings in bilateral arrangements for the purpose of completing the European Convention and facilitating its application.[63]

One way of resolving the problem is for the state where the offense occurred to transfer the proceedings to the other state under the European Convention on the Transfer of Proceedings in Criminal Matters. This Convention has been ratified only by Austria, Denmark, the Netherlands, Norway, Sweden and Turkey and its scope of application is therefore limited.

The third situation involves an offense perpetrated within the jurisdiction of a third-party state. Extradition will be subjected to a requirement of dual jurisdiction evocative of the dual criminality rule: extradition is granted if the laws of the requested state authorize the prosecution of the offense of the same kind committed outside its territory; thus, extradition will depend very much on the extraterritorial jurisdiction in the requested state.[64] Most civil law states have extended the jurisdiction of their criminal law system to offences which are perpetrated outside their territory under the protective principle (the offense poses a threat to the integrity, sovereignty or government functions of the state), the passive personality principle (a state is competent to prosecute and punish perpetrators of criminal conduct which harms or is intended to harm a national of the asserting state) and the active

---

[63] *See* the Arrangements between Switzerland and Austria for the purpose of completing and facilitating the application of the Euro. Extradition Conv. reached on June 13, 1972, Art. III; *see also* the Arrangements of a similar nature between Switzerland and Germany reached on Nov. 13, 1969, Art. III.

[64] *See* Euro. Extradition Conv., *supra* note 2, at Art. 7 ¶ 2; in order to weaken the impact of the objection to extradition founded on the jurisdiction of the requested state, this rule is expressed in a negative way: "Extradition may only be refused if the Law of the requested State does not allow prosecution for the same category of offence when committed outside of its territory. . . ."

personality principle (a state may prosecute any of its nationals for offenses they commit anywhere in the world so long as the offense is punishable in the place where it was committed and under national law).[65]

Dual Criminality

One of the main planks of extradition practice is the principle of dual criminality. This rule purports to achieve two different purposes: to ensure the lawfulness of any form of deprivation of liberty according to the laws of the requested state on the ground that no individual may be arrested or detained on account of facts which are not punishable under the laws of that state and to preserve the rule of reciprocity in international mutual assistance proceedings.[66] Although there is a broad consensus on the necessity of maintaining the rule of dual criminality,[67] different national approaches to this rule may be perceived as a barrier to the effective implementation of international extradition arrangements.[68]

There are at least three different theories in relation to the dual criminality rule:

(a) According to one definition, dual criminality embraces all elements which may affect not only the legal definition of the offense, but also the punishability of the conduct itself which includes the prerequisites of prosecution (for instance, the filing of a complaint).

(b) A second theory is based on all the facts that support the accusation in the requesting state. All the constituent elements of the offense allegedly committed in the requesting state must be encompassed by a specific statute of the criminal law in the requested state.

(c) According to a third theory, it is sufficient that the conduct described in the request for extradition is punishable according to the laws of the requesting and the requested states. It does not matter whether the offense described in the request is, as such, unknown under the laws of the requested state. In the same way, there is no requirement that the law of the requested state should include a specific statute containing all the constituent elements of the alleged offense.

The general recognition of this last theory would certainly facilitate and accelerate the examination of requests for extradition. In other words, the emphasis should be on the fugitive's conduct, not on the precise requirements of the criminal laws of each state in some search for equivalence.[69]

---

65 One good example of broad extraterritorial jurisdiction is the German Penal Code which, provides for jurisdiction over extraterritorial crimes where a special connecting factor exists with the German State, such as the need to protect certain domestic or international legal interests; the important domestic legal interests would include planning a war of aggression, treason, endangering external security, abduction; the important international legal interest would include crimes involving atomic energy, explosives and radiation, attacks on air traffic, unauthorized dealings in narcotics, dissemination of pornography, encouraging prostitution, counterfeiting, and economic subsidy fraud; *see* German Penal Code §§ 3-7.

66 *See* Schultz, *supra* note 34, at 13; *see* SHEARER, *supra* note 33, at 137.

67 *See* BASSIOUNI, *supra* note 33, at 325.

68 *See* GILBERT, *supra* note 39, at 47; this issue has often been discussed in Swiss legal literature.

69 For a more general discussion *see* HANS SCHULTZ, SCHWEIZERISCHES AUSLIEFERUNGSRECHT 325-26 (1953); J.L. COLOMBINI, LA PRISE EN CONSIDÉRATION DU DROIT ÉTRANGER DANS LE JUGEMENT PÉNAL 85-86 (1983); W. De Capitani, *Internationale Rechtshilfe: Eine Standortbestimmung*, 100 REVUE DE DROIT SUISSE, II, 391 (1981); *see* GILBERT, *supra* note 39, at 48-49.

Regarding the requirements of punishability, practically all treaties contain provisions dealing with lapse of time by virtue of a statute of limitation. Article 10 of the European Convention provides that extradition will not be granted if the sentence for the offense has lapsed according to the legislation in either the requesting or the requested party.

Another requirement of punishability is amnesty, which is specifically contemplated in chapter IV of the Second Additional Protocol to the European Convention of March 17, 1978, providing that extradition is denied when amnesty is granted in the requesting state.

The Political Offense Exception

It is widely accepted that there is no internationally accepted definition of the term "political offense" and that no international criteria exist for the application of the rule. No universal definition exists since the political offense exception is built on a complex rationale in which arguments of a very different nature are intertwined: (1) the *political argument* that States should remain neutral vis-à-vis political conflicts in other states, therefore extradition of political opponents is to be *a priori* refused; (2) the *moral argument* based on the premise that resistance to oppression is legitimate and that political crimes can therefore be justified; and (3) the *humanitarian argument*, whereby a political offender should not be extradited to a state in which he risks an unfair trial. In relation to extradition, the word "political" means noncriminal and may result in immunity from prosecution and punishment of the offender, thus having an effect similar to justification and excuses —excluding punishability of the offender's acts—in domestic criminal law.[70]

As a matter of consequence, legal writers tend to categorize the concept of political offence. A political offense may be classified as pure or relative, and a relative offense may be a *délit complexe* or a *délit connexe*. A pure political offense is one affecting the political organization of the state, such as treason, sedition or espionage. A *délit complexe* is a category of relative political offense covering acts which are directed at both the political order and private rights. A *délit connexe* is a second category of relative political offense which is not in itself an act directed against a political system but which is closely connected with another act which is so directed (for instance, the theft of guns in order to prepare for an armed rebellion).[71]

Article 3, paragraph 1 of the European Convention prevents extradition from taking place if the offense for which it has been requested is viewed by the asylum state as a political offense. Article 3, paragraph 2 has established a nondiscrimination clause in providing that the concept of political offense should be extended to a request for extradition for an ordinary criminal offense that has been made for the purpose of prosecuting or punishing a person on account of his race, religion, nationality or political opinion, or whose position may be prejudiced for any of these reasons.

There is a general trend towards restricting, if not excluding altogether, the applicability of the political offense exception in respect to violent criminal acts. The 1977 European Convention on the Suppression of Terrorism provides that, for the purposes of extradition,

---

[70] *See* VAN DEN WYNGAERT, *supra* note 35, at 368-428; *see also* M. Cherif Bassiouni, *Ideologically Motivated Offences and the Political Offence Exception in Extradition: A proposed juridical standard for an unruly problem*, 19 DE PAUL L. REV. 217 (1969).

[71] For a general discussion on the theory of the political offense exception to extradition, *see* GILBERT, *supra* note 39, at 113-65.

certain offenses enumerated in Article 1 of the Convention (aircraft hijacking, particularly odious acts such as murder, the taking of hostages, the use of explosives) will never be deemed political and that other offences listed in Article 2 (certain serious acts of violence other than those defined in Article 1) may not be considered as political, whatever their content or their political motive. For those states which have ratified the Convention without reservation, the exemptions apply *per se:* the possibility to apply the political offense exception is altogether ruled out. States which have made a reservation are bound by a normative exception formula: they retain the right to consider the offenses listed in the Convention as political crimes, but undertake to apply a number of normative criteria when appreciating the nature of the offense. These criteria will relate to the seriousness of the act, such as whether it created a collective danger for the life, physical integrity or liberty of the person involved, whether it reached persons foreign to the motives behind it or whether particularly perfidious or cruel means were used for its accomplishment.[72]

The 1975 Additional Protocol to the European Convention provides (in chapter 1) that for the application of Article 3 of the Convention, political offenses shall not be considered to include crimes against humanity as specified in the 1948 Genocide Convention and war crimes as specified in the 1949 Geneva Red Cross Conventions. The explanatory report on the Additional Protocol describes this development as a "current trend towards defining political offences and regarding certain crimes as so abominable that no immunity could be granted."

As mentioned above, the new framework of extradition designed by the European Union has endeavored to abolish altogether the political offense exception in relations between Member States, such a drastic measure being predicated on their common interests, the similarities of their judicial systems, the fact that they are all bound by the European Convention on Human Rights and Fundamental Freedoms, and given the fact that the provisions on free trade and freedom of movement in the Treaty of Rome prohibit regarding other Member States as "foreign countries" in the proper sense.

In the light of these developments, it has been suggested that humanitarian and political aspects are inextricably interwoven and that for the purpose of avoiding political decisions made by national courts, it could be preferable to replace the political offense exception by the above-mentioned nondiscrimination clause. The underlying rationale is that the fundamental issue is whether a fugitive will obtain a fair trial or whether he is likely to be persecuted or prejudiced in any way on account of circumstances which are unrelated to the offence itself. The proper test would then be whether the requesting state will uphold internationally recognized standards for a fair trial in its proceedings against the fugitive.[73]

---

[72] Christine Van Den Wyngaert, *The Political Offence Exception to Extradition: How to plug the 'terrorists' loophole' without departing from fundamental human rights, in* INTERNATIONAL REVIEW OF PENAL LAW 300-01 (1991). Half of the states which are parties to the European Convention on the Suppression of Terrorism have used the option of reservation

[73] Albin Eser, *Common Goals and Different Ways in International Criminal Law, Reflections from a European Perspective*, 31 HARV. INT'L L.J. 125-26 (1990); Otto Lagodny, *Grundkonstellationen des Internationalen Strafrechtes*, 101 ZEITSCHIFT FÜR DIE GESAMTE STRAFRECHTSWISSENSCHAFT 987 (1989); Bert (A.H.J.) Swart, *Human Rights and the Abolition of Traditional Principles, in* 33 PRINCIPLES AND PROCEDURES FOR A NEW TRANSNATIONAL CRIMINAL LAW, REPORTS AND MATERIALS FROM THE MAX PLANCK INSTITUTE 505-06 (Albin Eser & Otto Lagodny eds., 1991).

Military Offenses

Extradition is usually refused for military offenses. The European Convention provides in Article 4 that "extradition for offences under military law which are not offences under ordinary criminal law is excluded from the application of the Treaty." It is noteworthy, however, that the Benelux Accord provides that military desertion is not considered a political offense.

Under Article 4 (*in fine*) of the French Extradition Statute of 1927 (which reflects common practice throughout Europe), the exemption does not apply to offenses perpetrated by members of the armed forces where the offences would be considered by French Law to be common offenses subject to the ordinary provisions of criminal legislation.

The exemption is therefore based on the nature of the offense (for instance refusal to serve in the armed forces or desertion) and not on the military status of the person accused or convicted for having committed an offense.[74]

In accordance with chapter I of the Additional Protocol to the European Convention, the military offense exception does not extend to genocide or war crimes.[75]

Fiscal Offenses

Fiscal offenses were traditionally excluded from those crimes which are extraditable either through an explicit provision[76] or by omission from the list of extraditable offences.[77] The rationale for denying extradition in tax matters was that prosecution for tax offences involves the financial interests of the state, thereby raising a certain amount of suspicion as to the impartiality of the proceedings and, by analogy, to the political offence exception. Another reason is that it is easy to challenge the rule of double criminality inherent in practically all extradition procedures on account of the extreme diversity of tax laws from one state to another.

The trend has now been reversed. To a large extent tax laws have been standardized throughout Western Europe, and the appearance of taxes of an identical nature (for instance, VAT) have to some extent undermined the basis of traditional objections to the non-extraditability of tax offenders. The welfare state has prompted governments to be more interventionist and an increasing part of tax revenue is allocated to the improvement of social security or the implementation of the welfare state.[78]

Article 5 of the European Convention does not settle the issue of tax offenses but allows extradition if parties so decide among themselves, provided that extradition complies with

---

[74] *See* M.D. Wims, *Reexamining the Traditional Exceptions to Extradition, in* INTERNATIONAL REVIEW OF PENAL LAW (EXTRADITION) 327-330 (1991).

[75] If the military offense overlaps an offense for which extradition is normally authorized, Scandinavian countries will only grant extradition on the condition that the accused person will not be sentenced for having breached the military law of the requesting state.

[76] *See* Euro. Extradition Conv., *supra* note 2, at Art. 5.

[77] For instance, the Norwegian Government had to withdraw an extradition request to the United Kingdom in 1983 because tax fraud was not a ground for extradition in the Anglo-Norwegian Treaty; *see* GILBERT, *supra* note 39, at 55.

[78] *See* for instance a contribution by T. Stein *in* THE COMMONWEALTH REVIEW OF EXTRADITION ARRANGEMENTS 31 (1982) (available from the Commonwealth Secretariat).

standard requirements including the double criminality rule. Fiscal offenses extend to tax, duty, customs and exchange offenses.

Chapter II of the Second Additional Protocol of March 17, 1978, gives Article 5 of the main Convention a more mandatory form: extradition shall take place irrespective of any arrangements between the contracting parties whenever the fiscal offense, under the law of the requesting state, corresponds, under the law of the requested state, to an offense of the same nature. The rule of double criminality has been relaxed to the extent that extradition may not be refused on the grounds that the law of the requested party does not impose the same kind of tax or duty or does not contain a tax, duty, customs or exchange regulation of the same kind as the law of the requesting party. It is enough that an act of the same nature as that underlying the request for extradition would be punishable in the requested state. For instance, a person who intentionally evades a tax in the requesting state by giving inaccurate information in a document which serves as a basis for a decision concerning the amount of that tax may be extradited if the same kind of deliberate misleading of tax authorities is punishable under the law of the requested state, irrespective of the nature of the tax involved.[79]

Other Defenses to Extradition

Nationality of the Fugitive

Civil law states do not usually extradite their nationals. Many parties to the European Convention have used the optional ground provided by the Treaty to deny extradition of nationals, including at least six Member States of the European Union (Germany, Denmark, Spain, France, Greece and Luxembourg). As mentioned above, the recent Convention of the European Union on Extradition will remove nationality as an obstacle to the surrender of fugitives, subject to a five-year period enabling Member States of the Union to adapt their domestic legislation.[80] The notion of nonextradition of nationals has lost some of its sacrosanct aura, at least within the framework of European treaties.[81] There is room for argument that the best way for a state to protect its nationals is not to assert exclusive jurisdiction over them (regardless of where the offence was committed), but to give them the opportunity to serve their sentence within their own country. The European Convention on the Transfer of Sentenced Persons (open for signature on March 21, 1983, ratified by 18 States, including the U.S. and Canada),[82] is predicated on this principle. In the Dutch Extradition Act of 1988, the Netherlands has provided the possibility of extraditing a Dutch national for the purpose of standing trial in the requesting state, provided that the requesting state guarantees that the person, should he be later sentenced, will be able to serve that

---

79 *See* Explanatory Report to Euro. Conv. 2d Add. Prot. Extradition ¶ 17.

80 *See supra* note 24.

81 *See* Peter Wilkitzki, *Defences, Exceptions and Exemptions in the Extradition Law and Practice in the Criminal Policy of the Federal Republic of Germany, in* INTERNATIONAL REVIEW OF PENAL LAW (EXTRADITION) 286-89 (1991).

82 Austria, Cyprus, Denmark, Norway, Sweden and Turkey.

sentence in the Netherlands.[83] Switzerland subjects extradition of its nationals to the written consent of the fugitive.[84]

The Italian Constitution has opened another breach in the rule of nonextradition of nationals by stating that the immunity of Italian citizens to extradition is subject to international agreements of which Italy is a party.[85] Hence, Article IV of the Treaty between Italy and the United States of America of October 13, 1993, which provides that "the requested party may not refuse extradition of a person solely on the grounds that this person is a citizen of the requested party." [86]

It is now common ground in the European framework of extradition that whenever extradition is denied on account of the nationality of the fugitive, the requested party shall, at the request of the requesting party submit the case to its competent authorities in order that proceedings may be taken if they are considered appropriate; for that purpose, the files, information and exhibits relating to the offence should be transmitted to the requested state.[87]

In the event of conflicting requests of extradition, the European Convention takes into account the nationality of the fugitive as one of the criteria for deciding where the fugitive should be returned.[88]

The Death Penalty

There has been a growing trend over the past 30 years to abolish the death penalty, although it is far from being eradicated. The demise of the death penalty is most visible in Western Europe. Protocol no. 6 to the European Convention for the Protection of Human Rights and Fundamental Freedoms (ECHR), abolishing the death penalty in peace-time, was adopted in April 1983 and has been ratified by 18 Members of the Council of Europe. It is recognized as the first international instrument to abolish the death penalty, and Europe now exports its philosophy by refusing extradition to states where capital punishment still exists.[89]

---

83 The extradition of nationals is only permitted if the person involved would be able to serve his sentence in the Netherlands; for this reason, two treaties are required in so far as the extradition of a national is concerned: one which provides for extradition and the other which provides for the transfer of the sentenced person to the Netherlands for the purpose of enforcing the sentence. This "double treaty condition" makes it impossible to extradite Dutch nationals to countries which are not yet party to the European Convention on the International Validity of Criminal Judgements of 1970 or to the European Convention on the Transfer of Sentenced Persons of 1983.

84 *See* the Swiss Federal Act on International Mutual Assistance in Criminal Matters which came into force on Jan. 1, 1983; *see supra* note 40.

85 In a case of one *Locatelli*, the Italian Supreme Court considered that, in the light of Art. 6 of the Euro. Extradition Conv., extraditions of nationals is the rule and the refusal to extradite, the exception. As a matter of consequence, the extradition of Locatelli, who had dual Swiss and Italian nationality, was granted; *see* the judgement of Jan. 18, 1978 of the Supreme Court of Italy in Giust. Pen., III at 354 (1978).

86 *See* Mario Pisani, *Italia-Stati Uniti d'America: Appunti sul nuovo Trattato di Estradizione* 18 L'INDICE PENALE 398-404 (1984).

87 The rule *aut dedere aut punire* is established by Art. 6 of the Euro. Extradition Conv.

88 Art. 17 of Euro. Extradition Conv. provides: "If extradition is requested concurrently by more than one State, either for the same offence or for different offences, the requested party shall make its decision having regard to all circumstances and especially the relative seriousness and place of commission of the offences, the respective dates of the requests, the nationality of the person claimed and the possibility of subsequent extradition to another State."

89 The death penalty can be said to be incompatible with the regional standard of criminal justice that has developed in the Council of Europe; *see* Christine Van Den Wyngaert, *Rethinking the Law of International Criminal Cooperation: the Restrictive Function of International Human Rights through Individual-Oriented Bars,*

The ECHR itself does not prohibit the death penalty, which is considered as an admissible exception to the right to life under Article 2, paragraph 1 ECHR. It is now accepted that the death penalty, although ostensibly permitted, might raise issues under other provisions of the ECHR embodying general principles of international law. In *Kirkwood v. United Kingdom*,[90] the European Commission of Human Rights first considered the possibility that the imposition of the death penalty by the requesting state in extradition proceedings could breach Article 3, ECHR which prohibits inhuman and degrading treatment. The Commission held that this possibility could not be ruled out as a matter of principle, but Kirkwood's application was declared inadmissible because he had not demonstrated that detention on "death row" in the United States of America was inhuman and degrading treatment within the meaning of Article 3. In the later decision of *Soering v. United Kingdom*, the European Court of Human Rights held that a lengthy wait on "death row," to which the surrendered person would be subject in Virginia, constitutes an inhuman or degrading punishment or treatment under Article 3, ECHR.[91]

It is therefore not surprising that this general European perception towards the death penalty has been reflected in extradition law.[92] Article 11 of the European Convention states that, when the offence is punishable by death under the law of the requesting party but not that of the requested party or the death penalty is not normally carried out by the latter party, "extradition may be refused unless the requesting party gives such assurance as the requested party considers sufficient that the death penalty will not be carried out."[93]

The adequacy of the assurance given by the requesting state is likely to be challenged if the independence of the judiciary in the requesting state makes the guarantee less of a certainty than the fugitive would like.[94] In addition, the discretion to refuse extradition where the fugitive would face a death penalty if surrendered may be vested in the executive rather than in the courts. It should be noted in this respect that the British Extradition Act of 1989 provides the fugitive with an express right to seek judicial review of the Home Secretary's order for return after making representations to the latter concerning the likelihood of the death penalty being imposed.[95]

Double Jeopardy (Ne Bis In Idem)

There is no doubt that the rule on *ne bis in idem*, which provides that a person should not be convicted and punished twice for the same offence, is a widely acknowledged rule

---

in 33 PRINCIPLES AND PROCEDURES FOR A NEW TRANSNATIONAL CRIMINAL LAW, REPORTS AND MATERIALS FROM THE MAX PLANCK INSTITUTE 496 (Albin Eser & Otto Lagodny eds., 1991).

90 Kirkwood v. United Kingdom, application no. 10479/1983, *in* DECISIONS AND REPORTS OF THE EUROPEAN COMMISSION OF HUMAN RIGHTS 184 (1985).

91 Soering v. United Kingdom, judgement of the Eur. Ct. Hum. Rts. July 7, 1989, publications Eur. Ct. Hum. Rts., series A, vol. 161; nevertheless, even in this case the fugitive was extradited once the U.S. had given assurances that Soering would not be executed.

92 For a general discussion, *see* WILLIAM A. SCHABAS, THE ABOLITION OF THE DEATH PENALTY IN INTERNATIONAL LAW 211-49 (1993).

93 *See* for instance the practice followed by the French Conseil d'état in the decision of Oct. 15, 1993 *re Joy Davis-Aylor in La Semaine Juridique* (JCP) 1994 at Ed. G. II 22257: "The assurances given by the requesting State should not necessarily be that the death penalty will be excluded, but rather that it will not be enforced."

94 *See* GILBERT, *supra* note 39, at 99-100.

95 *See* 1989 Extradition Act, §§ 12, 13.

of international law based on elementary considerations of justice.[96] It seems established that the rule is not limited to a sentence duly enforced nor to a judgement of acquittal, but extends to earlier phases of the proceedings.[97] Thus, bilateral extradition treaties generally allow extradition to be denied where the requested state has decided either not to institute or to terminate proceedings conducted on its territory. Article 9 of the European Convention endorses this broad approach by providing that extradition shall not be granted if final judgment has been passed by the competent authorities of the requested state upon the person claimed in respect of the events for which extradition is requested and, further, extradition may be refused if the competent authorities of the requested party have decided either not to institute or to terminate proceedings in respect of the same offense.

It soon became apparent that Article 9 was incomplete, as it did not contemplate the eventuality of a judgment or a trial taking place in a third-party state. Chapter II of the Additional Protocol of October 15, 1975 remedied this shortcoming by providing that the extradition of a person against whom a final judgment has been rendered in a third State, party to the Convention, for the offense in respect of which the request was made, shall not be granted:

(a) if the judgment resulted in his acquittal;
(b) if the term of imprisonment has been completely enforced or has been wholly, or with respect to the part not enforced, the subject of a pardon or an amnesty;
(c) if the court convicted the offender without imposing a sanction.

Even if one of these circumstances arises, extradition will be optional (and not obligatory) in two situations where the requesting state might have a special interest in bringing a prosecution. The first situation applies to cases where the offense is directed against either a person or an institution having public status in the requesting state (for instance espionage, counterfeiting, taking of bribes). The second situation relates to cases where the offense was committed completely or partly in the territory of the requesting state.[98]

The Netherlands and Luxembourg have reserved the possibility of not granting extradition requested for the enforcement of a judgment rendered *in absentia* in respect of which no appeal is possible, if extradition would mean that the fugitive would be compelled to serve a sentence without having been able to exercise the minimum rights of defense guaranteed by Article 6 ECHR.[99]

The legal principle underlying this reservation led to the adoption of chapter III of the Second Additional Protocol to the European Convention (March 17, 1978) which provides a specific procedure whereby the requested party may refuse extradition:

---

96 *See* the International Covenant of Civil and Political Rights, Art. 14 ¶ 12; The Inter-American Convention on Human Rights of 1969 Art. 8 ¶ 4; *see* BASSIOUNI, *supra* note 33, at 452, 458; *see* HARTLEY-BOOTH, *supra* note 29, at 60-63; *see* CATELANI & STRIANI, *supra* note 32, at 86.

97 *See* Jean-François Flauss, *Le Principe "ne bis idem" dans le cadre de la convention européenne des droits de l'homme, bilan et perspectives, in* LE DROIT PÉNAL ET SES LIENS AVEC LES AUTRES BRANCHES DU DROIT, MÉLANGE EN L'HONNEUR DU PROFESSEUR JEAN GAUTHIER, REVUE PÉNALE SUISSE 271-86 (1996).

98 Explanatory report, Euro. Conv. Add. Prot. Extradition, ¶ 28.

99 *See* C. Rouiller, *L'extradition du condamné par défaut: illustration des rapports entre l'ordre constitutionel et autonome le "Jus cogens" et le droit des traités, in* DE LA CONSTITUTION, ETUDES EN L'HONNEUR DE JEAN-FRANÇOIS 647-59 (Aubert et al., eds., 1996).

> if, in its opinion, the proceedings leading to the judgement did not satisfy the minimum rights of defence recognized as due to everyone charged with a criminal offence. However, extradition shall be granted if the requesting State gives an assurance considered sufficient to guarantee to the person claimed the right to a retrial which safeguards the rights of defence. This decision will authorize the requesting party either to enforce the judgement in question if the convicted person does not make an opposition or, if he does, to take proceedings against the person extradited. [100]

Statute of Limitation

Most domestic laws and extradition treaties follow the traditional doctrine and proceed from the assumption that extradition is not permissible if, given the existence of similar facts in the requested state, prosecution of the offense or enforcement of the penalty would be barred by lapse of time in that state. This approach appears to be an extension of the dual criminality rule and is predicated on the rationale that the fugitive should not be surrendered on account of an offense for which he would not be punishable under the laws of the requested state. It may be argued that this rationale is losing momentum in the light of the obvious need to increase international cooperation in criminal matters. Germany for instance, in the extradition treaties which it has signed with the United States of America and Australia, has agreed that a contracting party may not deny a request for extradition based on lapse a of time in the requested state.[101] Nevertheless, Article 10 of the European Convention explicitly forbids extradition when the person claimed has, according to the law of either the requesting or the requested party, become immune by reason of a time lapse from prosecution or punishment. An unresolved issue is whether procedural acts which can interrupt the time limitation in the requesting state should have the same legal effect in the requested state.

Extradition and Human Rights

Human Rights Provisions Applicable to Extradition

In addition to the individual-oriented defenses provided by extradition treaties, human rights protections are now available to fugitives from sources other than the established principles of extradition law. It has been argued that in view of the greater protection which is afforded under the so-called "Soering" approach within the Council of Europe, it may be more beneficial for the fugitive to rely on human rights provisions than on the current defenses and exceptions arising from the Treaty and/or the domestic law of the requested state. It is now widely accepted that it is not beyond the bounds of possibility that surrendering a fugitive to another state might lead to a violation of that person's fundamental rights.[102]

---

[100] *See* MOSCONI & PISANI, *supra* note 34, at 96-97; these authors point out to the uncertainty in respect of the authorities of the requesting state who would be competent to give "assurances" likely to be judged sufficient by the requested state.

[101] Wilkitzki, *supra* note 81, at 283.

[102] *See* Van Den Wyngaert, *supra* note 89, at, 489-503.

As mentioned above, the imposition of the death penalty is not *per se* recognized as a violation of international law, although it has been argued that the death penalty is incompatible with the regional standard of criminal justice which has developed within the Council of Europe. All Member States have *de jure* or *de facto* abolished the death penalty and the Sixth Additional Protocol to the ECHR prohibits the death penalty in peace-time.[103] For states-parties to that protocol, extradition on account of capital offenses where there is a substantial risk of a death penalty being carried out would be contrary to the protocol.[104] Those states which have not ratified the protocol cannot rely on this instrument as a basis to refuse extradition. If the death penalty in the requesting state involves the so-called "death row" phenomenon, extradition could probably be denied on the grounds delineated in the *Soering* judgment of the European Court of Human Rights.

Although the protection against cruel and unusual treatment or punishment does not, as such, belong to the traditional exceptions to extradition, there is no doubt that a fugitive may rely on Article 3, ECHR which provides for an absolute prohibition of torture as well as for the prohibition of inhuman or degrading treatment or punishment. In a recent landmark judgment delivered by the European Court in a matter connected with an order for deportation, the Court determined that expulsion could engage the responsibility of the requested state under Article 3 ECHR in the presence of substantial grounds shown for believing that there would be a real risk to the deportee of torture or inhuman or degrading treatment or punishment in the requesting country.[105] There is no doubt that this would apply equally to extradition.

Nevertheless, the European Commission of Human Rights has clearly decided that Article 3, ECHR does not guarantee a right not to be extradited for a political offense, although there is an obvious overlap between the political offense exceptions' offshoot, the discrimination clause (under Article 3, paragraph 2 of the European Convention) and the torture/cruel and unusual treatment or punishment clause in the ECHR. This overlap is highlighted by recommendation number R(80)9 of the Committee of Ministers of the Council of Europe of June 27, 1980, not to grant extradition where a request for extradition emanates from a state not party to the ECHR and where there are substantial grounds for believing that the request has been made for the purpose of prosecuting or punishing the person concerned on account of his race, religion, nationality or political opinion, or that his position may be prejudiced for any of these reasons.

Extradition might raise delicate issues where the fugitive is in serious danger of being tried by a "tribunal d'exception" or of being subjected to a criminal justice system which is inconsistent with the basic guarantees contemplated in Article 6 ECHR. The ECHR itself does not grant the fugitive a right not to be extradited, and the guarantees afforded by its Article 6 are not directly applicable to extradition. The requested state will have to determine, in the light of its domestic legislation, whether strict compliance with

---

[103] On Apr. 28, 1993, Protocol No. 6 was signed by representatives of Austria, Belgium, Denmark, France, Germany, Luxembourg, the Netherlands, Norway, Portugal, Spain, Sweden and Switzerland. Greece and Italy signed a little later followed by Iceland in 1985; Finland, Liechtenstein and San Marino signed in 1989, Hungary in 1990 and Czechoslovakia and Malta in 1991. It came into force on Feb. 1, 1985.

[104] Art. 1 of Protocol No. 6 establishes three principles: the death penalty shall be abolished, no one may be condemned to death, and no one may be executed; *see* WILLIAM A. SCHABAS, THE ABOLITION OF THE DEATH PENALTY IN INTERNATIONAL LAW 238-48 (1993).

[105] *See* Chahal v. United Kingdom, Eur. Ct. of Hum. Rts. (Nov. 15, 1996).

internationally acknowledged standards of a fair trial should prevail over a treaty obligation to extradite. In the absence of a treaty, the requested state is obviously at freedom to subject extradition and other forms of mutual assistance in criminal matters to adequate assurances that the requesting state will meet the internationally recognized standards of a fair trial.[106] There is room for argument that these standards have now become part and parcel of international law and are indeed embodied in international instruments such as the UN Covenant on Civil and Political Rights.[107] An indirect protection is granted by Article 3 of the Second Additional Protocol to the European Convention whereby the requested state may refuse to extradite a person for the purpose of carrying out a sentence or detention order rendered against him *in absentia* if "in its opinion, the proceedings leading to the judgement did not satisfy the minimum rights of defence recognised as due to everyone charged with a criminal offence." The same Article further provides that "extradition shall be granted if the requesting party gives an assurance considered sufficient to guarantee to the person claimed the right to a retrial which safeguards the rights of defence." The practical implication is that the person whose extradition is being sought for the enforcement of the sentence *in absentia* enjoys a higher level of protection than the fugitive who has participated in the proceedings which have led to his judgment. In the first case, the requested state will be in a position to make an assessment of the proceedings conducted in the requesting state in the light of its own perception of the minimum rights of defense.[108]

Another human rights' protection which has been frequently overlooked so far is the defense based on the principle of legality which may be found in Article 7 ECHR. According to this principle, no one shall be held guilty of any criminal offense on account of any act or omission which did not constitute a criminal offense under national or international law at the time when it was committed. There is no doubt that the principle of legality is an internationally recognized principle of international law which has been embodied in modern human rights instruments (cf. Article 15 of the International Covenant on Civil and Political Rights). The principle of legality ranks among the absolute rights and no derogation is possible. Therefore, the fugitive alleging that the dual criminality test has been violated in extradition proceedings may attempt to rely on Article 7, ECHR in order to consolidate his legal position.[109]

---

[106] Examples of this evolution can be seen in the laws of certain European countries; for instance Switzerland's Law on International Mutual Assistance in Criminal Matters of Mar. 20, 1981; Austria's Law on Extradition and Mutual Assistance in Criminal Matters of Dec. 4, 1979 and Germany's Law on International Mutual Assistance in Criminal Matters of Dec. 12, 1982, which have adopted the principle that extradition shall be denied if the proceedings in the requesting state are contrary to the European Convention on Human Rights; the Swiss Statute contains a general reference to the European Convention on Human Rights and has been recently amended to reflect also the fair trial provisions in the International Covenant on Civil and Political Rights (Art. 2 a). The Austrian Statute refers to Arts. 3, 6 of the Euro. Extradition Conv. (¶ 19). The German Statute contains no explicit reference to the Euro. Extradition Conv., but it is deemed to be implied in the terms of ¶ 73, *see* T. VOGLER ET AL., GESETZ ÜBER DIE INTERNATIONALE RECHTSHILFE IN STRAFSACHEN (IRG - Kommentar), § 73 ¶ 33 (1984).

[107] *See* for instance The United Nations' Model Convention on Extradition, Art. 3 (g) (La Havana, 1990) which contains an explicit exception to extradition in this respect.

[108] *See* Rouiller, *supra* note 99, at 652-53.

[109] *See* Van Den Wyngaert, *supra* note 89, at 493: she points out that a minimum requirement should be that the conduct is an offense under the *lex loci delicti*; the problems which this requirement may raise with respect to the universality principle as a theory of jurisdiction are resolved by the exception to the principle of legality contained in Art. 7 ¶ 2 of the European Convention on Human Rights and in Art. 15 ¶ 2 of the International Covenant on Civil and Political Rights.

The Procedural Protection Granted by the ECHR

The ECHR provides a remedy whereby a fugitive on the point of being extradited may attempt to delay the enforcement of the order of extradition. The ECHR does not provide for interim relief through an injunction, but rule 36 of the Rules of Procedure of the European Commission of Human Rights may indicate "any interim measure the adoption of which seems desirable in the interests of the parties or the proper conduct of the proceedings before it." The Commission may only convey to the requested state that it wishes a stay in the domestic proceedings and cannot issue an order to that effect. Recommendation no. R(80)9 of the Committee of Ministers has invited Member States to comply with any interim measure which the European Commission might indicate under Rule 36 of its Rules of Procedure, as, for instance, a request to stay extradition proceedings pending a decision on the matter. Most Member States of the ECHR have indicated their willingness to follow that recommendation. However, it might seem strange that having accepted the concept of an individual petition under Article 25 ECHR, the contracting parties were not able to agree to mandatory interim orders.[110]

The Applicability of Human Rights Standards to Extradition Proceedings

The issue is whether and to what extent the fugitive can complain that proceedings taken with a view to extradition do not comply with his right to liberty under Article 5, ECHR or his right to a fair trial under Article 6, ECHR. Extradition proceedings are usually not considered as criminal proceedings (but rather as administrative proceedings) and, as a matter of consequence, the fair trial rules which normally apply to criminal proceedings under domestic law cannot be relied upon. Fair trial rights under the ECHR apply to proceedings concerning the determination of civil rights and obligations or of any criminal charge (Article 6 paragraph 1, ECHR) and to persons "charged with a criminal offence" (Article 6 paragraphs 2 and 3, ECHR). The European Commission's case law is not particularly clear. The Commission has held that Article 6 does not apply to extradition hearings because there is no final determination of guilt or innocence. However, it seems difficult to argue that Article 6 paragraph 3, ECHR, which grants basic rights to "everyone charged with a criminal offence" does not apply as it is obvious that a fugitive is charged with a criminal offense. The Commission's approach appears to be that an extradition hearing does not deal with the criminal offense charged, but merely with its extraditability.[111] The scope of Article 6, ECHR in extradition proceedings remains a hotly disputed issue.[112]

The matter is somewhat different in respect of the protection of personal liberty contained in Article 5, ECHR. Since Article 5, paragraph 1 (f) lists extradition and deportation among the permissible grounds of deprivation of liberty, an arrested fugitive is entitled under Article 5 paragraph 4, ECHR to take proceedings by which the lawfulness of his detention shall be decided speedily by a court and his release ordered if the detention is not lawful. The European Commission and the European Court have somewhat extended the

110 *See* GILBERT, *supra* note 39, at 81-83.

111 Application 10227/82 v. Spain (1984), 6 E.H.R.R. 581; Application 10292/82 v. Spain (1984), in 6 E.H.R.R. at 146.

112 *See* GILBERT, *supra* note 39, at 90; *see also* Van Den Wyngaert, *supra* note 89, at 500-03.

protection granted to a fugitive by Article 5 by encompassing certain rights which are inherent to Article 6, ECHR. Article 5 paragraph 4, ECHR has been used to test the fairness of the proceedings that are available to the arrested person. Although the procedural rights of the fugitive under Article 5, paragraph 4 are not identical to those which may be invoked by a defendant in criminal proceedings under Article 6, paragraph 3, the Commission and Court have in some instances transposed parts of Article 6, paragraph 3 into Article 5.[113]

The Committee of Ministers of the Council of Europe has issued guidelines[114] in respect of extradition proceedings. Irrespective of the administrative or judicial nature of those proceedings, the person concerned:

(a) should be informed, promptly and in a language which he understands, of the extradition request and the facts on which it is based, of the conditions and the procedure of extradition and, where applicable, of the reasons for his arrest;

(b) should be heard on the arguments which he invokes against his extradition;

(c) should have the possibility to be assisted in the extradition procedure; if he has not sufficient means to pay for the assistance, he should be given it free.

These procedural facilities, which are no more than recommendations[115] to Member States of the ECHR, echo some of the fair trial rights contained in Article 6, but are tailored to suit the requirements of extradition law.

The Rule of Speciality

The principle of speciality (or specialty), widely acknowledged as part of the basic rules of extradition law, provides that a fugitive shall only be tried in the requesting state for those offences for which he was surrendered. The rule of speciality's main function is to ensure compliance with other principles of extradition law (*e.g.*, reciprocity and dual criminality) The principle of speciality not only protects the fugitive's rights—to the extent that it prevents the fugitive being requested for one offense and tried for another—but also upholds the contractual nature of the agreement between the two states in that the requesting state has to accept that the requested state has granted extradition for the specified offenses and no others.[116]

Under Article 14 of the European Convention, the principle implies that:

---

[113] *See* Sanchez-Reisse v. Switzerland, Eur. Ct. Hum. Rts. (Oct. 21, 1986).

[114] Recommendation No. R(80)7 of the Committee of Ministers to Member States of the Council of Europe concerning the practical application of the Euro. Extradition Conv.

[115] These provisions lack the binding, *erga omnes* effect of provisions contained in international human rights instruments.

[116] *See* Schultz, *supra* note 34, at 20; IVAN BROWNLIE, PRINCIPLES OF PUBLIC INTERNATIONAL LAW 315 (1987); GIULIO CATELANI & DANIELE STRIANI, L'ESTRADIZIONE 64 (1983); L. Sbolci, *Il Principio di specialità dell'estradizione nel diritto internazionale, in* RIVISTA DI DIRITTO INTERNAZIONALE 749-50 (1980); *see* SHEARER, *supra* note 33, at 146; ROBERT LINKE ET AL., INTERNATIONALES STRAFRECHT, COMMENTARY ON THE AUSTRIAN LAW ON INTERNATIONAL MUTUAL ASSISTANCE IN CRIMINAL MATTERS OF 4TH DECEMBER 1979 42 (1981); *see also* Dominique Poncet & Paul Gully-Hart, *Le principe de la spécialité en matière d'extradition, in* INTERNATIONAL REVIEW OF PENAL LAW (EXTRADITION) 200-01 (1991).

A person who has been extradited shall not be proceeded against, sentenced or detained with a view to the carrying out of a sentence or detention order for any offence committed prior to his surrender other than that for which he was extradited, nor shall he be for any other reason restricted in his personal freedom.

Article 15 of the European Convention adds a further protection to the effect:

[T]hat the requesting party shall not surrender to another party or to a third State a person surrendered to a requesting party and sought by the said other party or third State in respect of offences committed before his surrender.

It is therefore clear that the principle of speciality imposes restrictions on the sovereignty of the requesting state. In determining the scope of the rule of speciality, the facts underlying the request for extradition are of great importance. Speciality allows the fugitive to be prosecuted for any charge made out by the facts supporting the request for extradition regardless of any difference in the legal qualification of those facts in the requesting and requested state. However, if the legal qualification is amended by the requesting state after the surrender of the fugitive, Article 14, paragraph 3 of the European Convention provides that the extraditee may be prosecuted or punished only if extradition would be granted in respect of the constituent elements of the newly qualified offence.

Measures of prosecution which could also be taken in the extraditee's absence are not covered by the Rule of Speciality, and these would include, for example, measures which are necessary according to the law of the requesting state to interrupt the statute of limitation without affecting the fugitive's personal freedom. The rationale of this exception to speciality is that the sovereignty of the requesting state should not be restricted to a greater extent than if extradition had not taken place at all. The protection granted by speciality is not unlimited in time nor in its scope and should therefore not be viewed as an absolute defense to extradition. The requesting state's undertakings under the rule of speciality do not apply in the following circumstances:

1. The requested state subsequently agrees to extend the extradition order to other offenses, provided that a request for such extension is made by the requesting state and that the surrendered fugitive is afforded the opportunity of stating his views and/or raising objections in respect of that request.[117]

2. The fugitive voluntarily remains in the requestings following his release beyond a certain lapse of time (Article 14 paragraph 1 (b), of the European Convention provides for a period of 45 days).

3. The fugitive returns to the requesting state after having left it or is extradited there by a third State.

---

[117] *See* for instance Art. 22 ¶ 2 of the French Law on Extradition of Mar. 10, 1937 which provides that the explanations given by the surrendered person may be completed by a freely chosen or state-appointed lawyer; Israel has made a specific reservation to the Euro. Extradition Conv. for the purpose of obtaining that the wanted person is given an opportunity to be represented in the proceedings aiming at extradition for other offences.

In domestic law, the speciality of extradition can have the meaning of a legal obstacle in proceedings conducted against the surrendered defendant. Several European states have ensured in their legislation that speciality has to be observed *ex officio* and at any stage of the proceedings (see for instance, Article 72 of the German Law on International Mutual Assistance in Criminal Matters; Article 721 of the Italian Code of Criminal Proceedings; Article 38 of the Swiss Federal Act on International Mutual Assistance in Criminal Matters). In addition, the rule of speciality prohibits the full enforcement of a sentence if extradition has not been granted for all the offenses underlying the sentence. In order to comply with its undertakings under the rule of speciality, the requesting state should therefore determine if and to what extent the sentence should be enforced.

The Yugoslav War Crimes Tribunal[118]

Generalities

On February 22, 1993, the United Nations' Security Council decided to set up an *ad hoc* International Tribunal to try serious violations of humanitarian law committed during the conflicts in the former Yugoslavia after 1991. The creation of this Tribunal reiterates the principle clarified at the Nuremberg and Tokyo War Crimes Tribunals, reaffirmed in United Nations' General Assembly resolutions and embodied in several UN Conventions, that individuals are criminally responsible for any act which constitutes a crime under international law, even if internal law does not criminalize the same act or even authorizes it. These international crimes include crimes against humanity, war crimes, torture, genocide, slavery and apartheid. The Tribunal sits in the Hague (the Netherlands).

The Tribunal, now referred to as the International Criminal Tribunal for the Former Yugoslavia (ICTY) has *inter alia* indicted and issued arrest warrants for a Bosnian Serb leader and his top military commander on charges of genocide, crimes against humanity and war crimes. On November 29, 1996, the ICTY meted out its first sentence (10 years of imprisonment) to a 25 year-old ethnic Croat who confessed to participating in an execution squad and killing scores of unarmed men. The defendant had been convicted for crimes against humanity.[119]

Several important decisions have already been made by the Tribunal's Trial Chamber as well as by its Appeals Chamber on issues relating to the lawfulness of Security Council actions in establishing the Tribunal, the ICTY's primacy over national courts and its jurisdiction to adjudicate alleged offenses regardless of the type of conflict (internal or international) in which they were committed.[120]

Judicial Assistance to the Yugoslav War Crimes Tribunal

The Judges of the ICTY have issued guidelines designed to help states to implement the obligations deriving from Security Council resolutions on the ICTY. These guidelines

---

118 The most authoritative compilation in this matter is M. CHERIF BASSIOUNI (WITH THE COLLABORATION OF PETER MANIKAS), THE LAW OF THE INTERNATIONAL CRIMINAL TRIBUNAL FOR THE FORMER YUGOSLAVIA (1996); *see also* KARINE LESCURE, LE TRIBUNAL PÉNAL INTERNATIONAL POUR L'EX-YOUGOSLAVIE (1994).

119 *See* 13 INT'L ENFORCEMENT L. REP. 29 (1997).

120 *See* 11 INT'L ENFORCEMENT L. REP. 452 (1995).

indicate areas of national law which may need to be amended by states in order to comply with the appropriate Security Council resolutions. Resolution 827 of May 25, 1993, establishes the statute of the Yugoslav War Crime Tribunal whereas Resolution 955 of the November 8, 1994, establishes the statute of the similar War Crimes Tribunal set up to deal with war crimes perpetrated in Rwanda.

The statute relating to the ICTY states that it is the duty of state to cooperate fully with Tribunal requests and sets forth the obligation to defer to the jurisdiction of the ICTY any criminal proceeding pending before the national authority. There is a further obligation for the national prosecution authorities to use their best endeavors to ensure prompt arrest of any person against whom an arrest warrant has been issued. States should provide a legal basis for provisional arrest and are under a general obligation to provide "other forms of assistance." This should include an obligation for persons in a given state who are summoned by a judge or a trial chamber of the ICTY to appear as a witness or an expert to comply with that summons, and further to supply relevant data from police files.

Several European countries have already enacted implementing legislation. The Danish Act of December 21, 1994, deals *inter alia* with the deferral of a criminal case to the Tribunal and with the transfer of the accused to the Hague.[121] In Ireland, Section 56 of the Criminal Justice Act, 1994, no. 15 mandates the Irish government to include provisions in Irish Law on cooperation for International War Crimes Tribunals. Switzerland's implementing legislation entered into force on December 22, 1995, and is drafted in accordance with the structure of the Swiss Act on International Mutual Assistance in Criminal Matters. That general act is applicable unless the act implementing the Security Council resolutions provides differently. All forms of assistance included in the General Act on International Assistance can also be rendered to International Tribunals. One interesting feature is that Switzerland is the only country to stipulate that information and evidence shall be sent spontaneously to International Tribunals (including the ICTY).[122] Austria has enacted legislation which came into force on June 1, 1996.[123] In the U.K., the United Nations (International Tribunal) (Former Yugoslavia) Order 1996 came into force on March 15, 1996. The Order enables the United Kingdom to cooperate with the International Criminal Tribunal for the former Yugoslavia in the investigation and prosecution of persons accused of committing the crimes for which the Tribunal has jurisdiction and the punishment of persons convicted of such crimes.[124]

---

[121] Danish Act on Criminal Proceedings before the International Tribunal for the Prosecution of Persons Responsible for War Crimes committed in the Territory of the Former Yugoslavia, Act No. 1099 of Dec. 21, 1994 *entered into force* on Jan. 1, 1995.

[122] *Arrêté fédéral relatif à la coopération avec les Tribunaux internationaux chargés de poursuivre les violations graves du droit international humanitaire* of Dec. 21, 1995, *entered into force* on Dec. 22, 1995.

[123] *Bundersgesetz über die Zusammenarbeit mit den Internationalen Gerichten* (Federal Act on the Cooperation with International Tribunals; *see* O. Triffter, *Österreichs Verpflichtungen zur Durchsetzung des Volkstrafrechts, in* ÖSTERREICHISCHE JURISTENZEITUNG 321-46 (1996).

[124] *Published in* STATUTORY INSTRUMENTS 1996, No. 716; *see also* 12 INT'L ENFORCEMENT L. REP. 366 (1996).

Appendix 3

European Convention on Extradition

European Treaty Series.
No. 24

The Governments signatory hereto, being Members of the Council of Europe,

Considering that the aim of the Council of Europe is to achieve a greater unity between its Members;

Considering that this purpose can be attained by the conclusion of agreements and by common action in legal matters;

Considering that the acceptance of uniform rules with regard to extradition is likely to assist this work of unification,

Have agreed as follows:

Article 1
Obligation to Extradite

The Contracting Parties undertake to surrender to each other, subject to the provisions and conditions laid down in this Convention, all persons against whom the competent authorities of the requesting Party are proceeding for an offense or who are wanted by the said authorities for the carrying out of a sentence or detention order.

Article 2
Extraditable Offences

1. Extradition shall be granted in respect of offences punishable under the laws of the requesting Party and of the requested Party by deprivation of liberty or under a detention order for a maximum period of at least one year or by a more severe penalty. Where a conviction and prison sentence have occurred or a detention order has been made in the territory of the requesting Party, the punishment awarded must have been for a period of at least four months.
2. If the request for extradition includes several separate offences each of which is punishable under the laws of the requesting Party and the requested Party by deprivation of liberty or under a detention order, but of which some do not fulfil the condition with regard to the amount of punishment which may be awarded, the requested Party shall also have the right to grant extradition for the latter offences.
3. Any Contracting Party whose law does not allow extradition for certain of the offences referred to in paragraph 1 of this Article may, in so far as it is concerned, exclude such offences from the application of this Convention.
4. Any Contracting Party which wishes to avail itself of the right provided for in paragraph 3 of this Article shall, at the time of the deposit of its instrument of ratification or accession, transmit to the Secretary-General of the Council of Europe either a list of the offences for which extradition is allowed or a list of those for which it is excluded and shall at the same time indicate the legal provisions which allow or exclude extradition. The Secretary-General of the Council shall forward these lists to the other signatories.
5. If extradition is subsequently excluded in respect of other offences by the law of a Contracting Party, that Party shall notify the Secretary-General. The Secretary-General shall inform the other signatories. Such notification shall not take effect until three months from the date of its receipt by the Secretary-General.

6. Any Party which avails itself of the right provided for in paragraphs 4 or 5 of this Article may at any time apply this Convention to offences which have been excluded from it. It shall inform the Secretary-General of the Council of such changes, and the Secretary-General shall inform the other signatories.
7. Any Party may apply reciprocity in respect of any offences excluded from the application of the Convention under this Article.

ARTICLE 3
Political Offences

1. Extradition shall not be granted if the offence in respect of which it is requested is regarded by the requested Party as a political offence or as an offence connected with a political offence.
2. The same rule shall apply if the requested Party has substantial grounds for believing that a request for extradition for an ordinary criminal offence has been made for the purpose of prosecuting or punishing a person on account of his race, religion, nationality or political opinion, or that that person's position may be prejudiced for any of these reasons.
3. The taking or attempted taking of the life of a Head of State or a member of his family shall not be deemed to be a political offence for the purposes of this Convention.
4. This Article shall not affect any obligations which the Contracting Parties may have undertaken or may undertake under any other international convention of a multilateral character.

ARTICLE 4
Military Offences

Extradition for offences under military law which are not offences under ordinary criminal law is excluded from the application of this Convention.

ARTICLE 5
Fiscal Offences

Extradition shall be granted, in accordance with the provisions of this Convention, for offences in connection with taxes, duties, customs and exchange only if the Contracting Parties have so decided in respect of any such offence or category of offences.

ARTICLE 6
Extradition of Nationals

1. (a) A Contracting Party shall have the right to refuse extradition of its nationals.

(b) Each Contracting Party may, by a declaration made at the time of signature or of deposit of its instrument of ratification or accession, define as far as it is concerned the term "nationals" within the meaning of this Convention.

(c) Nationality shall be determined as at the time of the decision concerning extradition. If, however, the person claimed is first recognised as a national of the requested Party during the period between the time of the decision and the time contemplated for the surrender, the requested Party may avail itself of the provision contained in subparagraph (a) of this Article.

2. If the requested Party does not extradite its national, it shall at the request of the requesting Party submit the case to its competent authorities in order that proceedings may be taken if they are considered appropriate. For this purpose, the files, information and exhibits relating to the offence shall be transmitted without charge by the means provided for in Article 12, paragraph 1. The requesting Party shall be informed of the result of its request.

ARTICLE 7
Place of Commission

1. The requested Party may refuse to extradite a person claimed for an offence which is regarded by its law as having been committed in whole or in part in its territory or in a place treated as its territory.

2. When the offence for which extradition is requested has been committed outside the territory of the requesting Party, extradition may only be refused if the law of the requested Party does not allow prosecution for the same category of offence when committed outside the latter Party's territory or does not allow extradition for the offence.

ARTICLE 8

Pending Proceedings for the Same Offences

The requested Party may refuse to extradite the person claimed if the competent authorities of such Party are proceeding against him in respect of the offence or offences for which extradition is requested.

ARTICLE 9

Non Bis in Dem

Extradition shall not be granted if final judgment has been passed by the competent authorities of the requested Party upon the person claimed in respect of the offence or offences for which extradition is requested. Extradition may be refused if the competent authorities of the requested Party have decided either not to institute or to terminate proceedings in respect of the same offence or offences.

ARTICLE 10

Lapse of Time

Extradition shall not be granted when the person claimed has according to the law of either the requesting or the requested Party, become immune by reason of lapse of time from prosecution or punishment.

ARTICLE 11

Capital Punishment

If the offence for which extradition is requested is punishable by death under the law of the requesting Party, and if in respect of such offence the death-penalty is not provided for by the law of the requested Party or is not normally carried out, extradition may be refused unless the requesting Party gives such assurance as the requested Party considers sufficient that the death-penalty will not be carried out.

ARTICLE 12

The Request and Supporting Documents

1. The request shall be in writing and shall be communicated through the diplomatic channel. Other means of communication may be arranged by direct agreement between two or more Parties.
2. The request shall be supported by:

(a) the original or an authenticated copy of the conviction and sentence or detention order immediately enforceable or of the warrant of arrest or other order having the same effect and issued in accordance with the procedure laid down in the law of the requesting Party;

(b) a statement of the offences for which extradition is requested. The time and place of their commission, their legal descriptions and a reference to the relevant legal provisions shall be set out as accurately as possible; and

(c) a copy of the relevant enactments or, where this is not possible, a statement of the relevant law and as accurate a description as possible of the person claimed, together with any other information which will help to establish his identity and nationality.

ARTICLE 13

Supplementary Information

If the information communicated by the requesting Party is found to be insufficient to allow the requested Party to make a decision in pursuance of this Convention, the latter Party shall request the necessary supplementary information and may fix a time limit for the receipt thereof.

ARTICLE 14

Rule of Speciality

1. A person who has been extradited shall not be proceeded against, sentenced or detained with a view to the carrying out of a sentence or detention order for any offence committed prior to his surrender other than that for which he was extradited, nor shall he be for any other reason restricted in his personal freedom, except in the following cases:

(a) When the Party which surrendered him consents. A request for consent shall be submitted, accompanied by the documents mentioned in Article 12 and a legal record of any statement made by the extradited person in respect of the offence concerned. Consent shall be given when the offense for which it is requested is itself subject to extradition in accordance with the provisions of this Convention;

(b) when that person, having had an opportunity to leave the territory of the Party to which he has been surrendered, has not done so within 45 days of his final discharge, or has returned to that territory after leaving it.

2. The requesting Party may, however, take any measures necessary to remove the person from its territory, or any measures necessary under its law, including proceedings by default, to prevent any legal effects of lapse of time.

3. When the description of the offense charged is altered in the course of proceedings, the extradited person shall only be proceeded against or sentenced in so far as the offence under its new description is shown by its constituent elements to be an offense which would allow extradition.

ARTICLE 15

Re-Extradition to a Third State

Except as provided for in Article 14, paragraph 1 (b), the requesting Party shall not, without the consent of the requested Party, surrender to another Party or to a third State a person surrendered to the requesting Party and sought by the said other Party or third State in respect of offences committed under his surrender. The requested Party may request the production of the documents mentioned in Article 12, paragraph 2.

ARTICLE 16

Provisional Arrest

1. In case of urgency the competent authorities of the requesting Party may request the provisional arrest of the person sought. The competent authorities of the requested Party shall decide the matter in accordance with its law.

2. The request for provisional arrest shall state that one of the documents mentioned in Article 12, paragraph 2 (a), exists and that it is intended to send a request for extradition. It shall also state for what offence extradition will be requested and when and where such offense was committed and shall so far as possible give a description of the person sought.

3. A request for provisional arrest shall be sent to the competent authorities of the requested Party either through the diplomatic channel or direct by post or telegraph or through the International Criminal Police Organisation (Interpol) or by any other means affording evidence in writing or accepted by the requested Party. The requesting authority shall be informed without delay of the result of its request.

4. Provisional arrest may be terminated if, within a period of 18 days after arrest, the requested Party has not received the request for extradition and the documents mentioned in Article 12. It shall not,

in any event, exceed 40 days from the date of such arrest. The possibility of provisional release at any time is not excluded, but the requested Party shall take any measures which it considers necessary to prevent the escape of the person sought.

5. Release shall not prejudice re-arrest and extradition if a request for extradition is received subsequently.

ARTICLE 17

Conflicting Requests

If extradition is requested concurrently by more than one State, either for the same offence or for different offences, the requested Party shall make its decision having regard to all the circumstances and especially the relative seriousness and place of commission of the offences, the respective dates of the requests, the nationality of the person claimed and the possibility of subsequent extradition to another State.

ARTICLE 18

Surrender of the Person to be Extradited

1. The requested Party shall inform the requesting Party by the means mentioned in Article 12, paragraph 1 of its decision with regard to the extradition.
2. Reasons shall be given for any complete or partial rejection.
3. If the request is agreed to, the requesting Party shall be informed of the place and date of surrender and of the length of time for which the person claimed was detained with a view to surrender.
4. Subject to the provisions of paragraph 5 of this Article, if the person claimed has not been taken over on the appointed date, he may be released after the expiry of 15 days and shall in any case be released after the expiry of 30 days. The requested Party may refuse to extradite him for the same offense.
5. If circumstances beyond its control prevent a Party from surrendering or taking over the person to be extradited, it shall notify the other Party. The two Parties shall agree a new date for surrender and the provisions of paragraph 4 of this Article shall apply.

ARTICLE 19

Postponed of Conditional Surrender

1. The requested Party may, after making its decision on the request for extradition, postpone the surrender of the person claimed in order that he may be proceeded against by that Party or, if he has already been convicted, in order that he may serve his sentence in the territory of that Party for an offense other than that for which extradition is requested .
2. The requested Party may, instead of postponing surrender, temporarily surrender the person claimed to the requesting Party in accordance with conditions to be determined by mutual agreement between the Parties.

ARTICLE 20

Handing Over of Property

1. The requested Party shall, in so far as its law permits and at the request of the requesting Party, seize and hand over property:

(a) which may be required as evidence or

(b) which has been acquired as a result of the offence and which, at the time of the arrest, is found in the possession of the person claimed or is discovered subsequently.

2. The property mentioned in paragraph 1 of this Article shall be handed even if extradition, having been agreed to, cannot be carried out owing to the death or escape of the person claimed.
3. When the said property is liable to seizure or confiscation in the territory of the requested Party, the latter may, in connection with pending criminal proceedings, temporarily retain it or hand it over on condition that it is returned.

4. Any rights which the requested Party or third parties may have acquired in the said property shall be preserved. Where these rights exist, the property shall be returned without charge to the requested Party as soon as possible after the trial.

ARTICLE 21
Transit

1. Transit through the territory of one of the Contracting Parties shall be granted on submission of a request by the means mentioned in Article 12, paragraph 1, provided that the offense concerned is not considered by-the Party requested to grant transit as an offense of a political or purely military character having regard to Articles 3 and 4 of this Convention.
2. Transit of a national, within the meaning of Article 6, of a country requested to grant transit may be refused.
3. Subject to the provisions of paragraph 4 of this Article, it shall be necessary to produce the documents mentioned in Article 12, paragraph 2.
4. If air transport is used, the following provisions shall apply:

(a) when it is not intended to land, the requesting Party shall notify the Party over whose territory the flight is to be made and shall certify that one of the documents mentioned in Article 12, paragraph 2 (a) exists. In the case of an unscheduled landing, such notification shall have the effect of a request for provisional arrest as provided for in Article 16, and the requesting Party shall submit a formal request for transit;

(b) when it is intended to land, the requesting Party shall submit a formal request for transit.

5. A Party may, however, at the time of signature or of the deposit of its instrument of ratification of, or accession to, this Convention, declare that it will only grant transit of a person on some or all of the conditions on which it grants extradition. In that event, reciprocity may be applied.
6. The transit of the extradited person shall not be carried out through any territory where there is reason to believe that his life or his freedom may be threatened by reason of his race, religion, nationality or political opinion.

ARTICLE 22
Procedure

Except where this Convention otherwise provides, the procedure with regard to extradition and provisional arrest shall be governed solely by the law of the requested Party.

ARTICLE 23
Language to be Used

The documents to be produced shall be in the language of the requesting or requested Party. The requested Party may require a translation into one of the official languages of the Council of Europe to be chosen by it.

ARTICLE 24
Expenses

1. Expenses incurred in the territory of the requested Party by reason of extradition shall be borne by that Party.
2. Expenses incurred by reason of transit through the territory of a Party requested to grant transit shall be borne by the requesting Party.
3. In the event of extradition from a non-metropolitan territory of the requested Party the expenses occasioned by travel between that territory and the metropolitan territory of the requesting Party shall be borne by the latter. The same rule shall apply to expenses occasioned by travel between the non-metropolitan territory of the requested Party and its metropolitan territory.

ARTICLE 25

Definition of "Detention Order"

For the purposes of this Convention the expression "detention order" means anv order involving deprivation of liberty which has been made by a criminal court in addition to or instead of a prison sentence.

ARTICLE 26

Reservations

1. Any Contracting Party may, when signing this Convention or when depositing its instrument of ratification or accession make a reservation in respect of any provision or provisions of the Convention.
2. Any Contracting Party which has made a reservation shall withdraw it as soon as circumstances permit. Such withdrawal shall be made by notification to the Secretary-General of the Council of Europe.
3. A Contracting Party which has made a reservation in respect of a provision of the Convention may not claim application of the said provision by another Party save in so far as it has itself accepted the provision.

ARTICLE 27

Territorial Application

1. This Convention shall apply to the metropolitan territories of the Contracting Parties.
2. In respect of France, it shall also apply to Algeria and to the overseas Departments and, in respect of the United Kingdom of Great Britain and Northern Ireland, to the Channel Islands and to the Isle of Man.
3. The Federal Republic of Germany may extend the application of this Convention to the Land of Berlin by notice addressed to the Secretary-General of the Council of Europe, who shall notify the other Parties of such declaration.
4. By direct arrangement between two or more Contracting Parties, the application of this Convention may be extended, subject to the conditions laid down in the arrangement, to any territory of such Parties, other than the territories mentioned in paragraphs 1, 2 and 3 of this Article, for whose international relations any such Party is responsible.

ARTICLE 28

Relations Between this Convention and Bilateral Agreements

1. This Convention shall, in respect of those countries to which it applies, supersede the provisions of any bilateral treaties, conventions or agreements governing extradition between any two Contracting Parties.
2. The Contracting Parties may conclude between themselves bilateral or multilateral agreements only in order to supplement the provisions of this Convention or to facilitate the application of the principles contained therein.
3. Where, as between two or more Contracting Parties, extradition takes place on the basis of a uniform law, the Parties shall be free to regulate their mutual relations in respect of extradition exclusively in accordance with such a system notwithstanding the provisions of this convention. The same principle shall apply as between two or more Contracting Parties each of which has in force a law providing for the execution in its territory of warrants of arrest issued in the territory of the other Party or Parties. Contracting Parties which exclude or may in the future exclude the application of this Convention as between themselves in accordance with this paragraph shall notify the Secretary-General of the Council of Europe accordingly. The Secretary-General shall inform the other Contracting Parties of any notification received in accordance with this paragraph.

ARTICLE 29

Signature, Ratification and Entry into Force

1. This Convention shall be open to signature by the Members of the Council of Europe. It shall be ratified. The instruments of ratification shall be deposited with the Secretary-General of the Council.

2. The Convention shall come into force 90 days after the date of deposit of the third instrument of ratification.

3. As regards any signatory ratifying subsequently the Convention shall come into force 90 days after the date of the deposit of its instrument of ratification.

ARTICLE 30

Accession

1. The Committee of Ministers of the Council of Europe may invite any State not a Member of the Council to accede to this Convention, provided that the resolution containing such invitation receives the unanimous agreement of the Members of the Council who have ratified the Convention.

2. Accession shall be by deposit with the Secretary-General of the Council of an instrument of Accession, which shall take effect 90 days after the date of its deposit.

ARTICLE 31

Denunciation

Any Contracting Party may denounce this Convention in so far as it is concerned by giving notice to the Secretary-General of the Council of Europe. Denunciation shall take effect six months after the date when the Secretary-General of the Council received such notification.

ARTICLE 32

Notifications

The Secretary General of the Council of Europe shall notify the Members of the Council and the Government of any State which has acceded to this Convention of

(a) the deposit of any instrument of ratification or accession,

(b) the date of entry into force of this Convention;

(c) any declaration made in accordance with the provisions of Article 6, paragraph 1, and of Article 21, paragraph 5;

(d) any reservation made in accordance with Article 26, paragraph 1;

(e) the withdrawal of any reservation in accordance with Article 26, paragraph 2;

(f)any notification of denunciation received in accordance with the provisions of Article 31 and by the date on which such denunciation will take effect.

In witness whereof the undersigned, being duly authorised thereto have signed this Convention.

Done at Paris, this 13th day of December 1957, in English and French, both texts being equally authentic, in a single copy which shall remain deposited in the archives of the Council of Europe. The Secretary-General of the Council of Europe shall transmit certified copies to the signatory Governments.

Appendix 4

Additional Protocol to the European Convention on Extradition

European Treaty Series
No. 86

The member States of the Council of Europe, signatory to this Protocol,

Having regard to the provisions of the European Convention on Extradition opened for signature in Paris on 13 December 1957 (hereinafter referred to as "the Convention") and in particular Articles 3 and 9 thereof;

Considering that it is desirable to supplement these Articles with a view to strengthening the protection of humanity and of individuals,

Have agreed as follows:

CHAPTER I

Article 1

For the application of Article 3 of the Convention, political offences shall not be considered to include the following:

(a) the crimes against humanity specified in the Convention on the Prevention and Punishment of the Crime of Genocide adopted on 9 December 1948 by the General Assembly of the United Nations;

(b) the violations specified in Article 50 of the 1949 Geneva Convention for the Amelioration of the Condition of the Wounded and Sick in Armed Forces in the Field, Article 51 of the 1949 Geneva Convention for the Amelioration of the Condition of Wounded, Sick and Shipwrecked Members of Armed Forces at Sea, Article 130 of the 1949 Geneva Convention relative to the Treatment of Prisoners of War and Article 147 of the 1949 Geneva Convention relative to the Protection of civilian Persons in Time of War;

(c) any comparable violations of the laws of war having effect at the time when this Protocol enters into force and of customs of war existing at that time, which are not already provided for in the above-mentioned provisions of the Geneva Conventions.

CHAPTER II

Article 2

Article 9 of the Convention shall be supplemented by the following text, the original Article 9 of the Convention becoming paragraph 1 and the under-mentioned provisions becoming paragraphs 2, 3 and 4:

"2. The extradition of a person against whom a final judgment has been rendered in a third State. Contracting Party to the Convention, for the Offence or Offences in respect of which the claim was made, shall not be granted:

(a) if the afore-mentioned judgment resulted in his acquittal;

(b) if the term of imprisonment or other measure to which he was sentenced:

(i) has been completely enforced;

(ii) has been wholly, or with respect to the part not enforced, the subject of a pardon or an amnesty;

(c) if the court convicted the offender without imposing a sanction.

3. However, in the cases referred to in paragraph 2, extradition may be granted:

(a) if the offence in respect of which judgment has been rendered was committed against a person, an institution or any thing having public status in the requesting State;

(b) if the person on whom judgment was passed had himself a public status in the requesting State;

(c) if the offence in respect of which judgment was passed was committed completely or partly in the territory of the requesting State or in a place treated as its territory.

4. The provisions of paragraphs 2 and 3 shall not prevent the application of wider domestic provisions relating to the effect of *ne bis in idem* attached to foreign criminal judgments."

CHAPTER III

Article 3

1. This Protocol shall be open to signature by the member States of the Council of Europe which have signed the Convention. It shall be subject to ratification, acceptance or approval. Instruments of ratification, acceptance or approval shall be deposited with the Secretary General of the Council of Europe.
2. The Protocol shall enter into force 90 days after the date of the deposit of the third instrument of ratification, acceptance or approval.
3. In respect of a signatory State ratifying, accepting or approving subsequently, the Protocol shall enter into force 90 days after the date of the deposit of its instrument of ratification, acceptance or approval.
4. A member State of the Council of Europe may not ratify, accept or approve this Protocol without having, simultaneously or previously, ratified the Convention.

Article 4

1. Any State which has acceded to the Convention may accede to this Protocol after the Protocol has entered into force.
2. Such accession shall be effected by depositing with the Secretary General of the Council of Europe an instrument of accession which shall take effect 90 days after the date of its deposit.

Article 5

1. Any State may, at the time of signature or when depositing its instrument of ratification, acceptance, approval or accession, specify the territory or territories to which this Protocol shall apply.
2. Any State may, when depositing its instrument of ratification, acceptance, approval or accession or at any later date, by declaration addressed to the Secretary General of the Council of Europe, extend this Protocol to any other territory or territories specified in the declaration and for whose international relations it is responsible or on whose behalf it is authorised to give undertakings.
3. Any declaration made in pursuance of the preceding paragraph may, in respect of any territory mentioned in such declaration, be withdrawn according to the procedure laid down in Article 8 of this Protocol.

Article 6

1. Any State may, at the time of signature or when depositing its instrument of ratification, acceptance, approval or accession, declare that it does not accept one or the other of Chapters I or II.
2. Any Contracting Party may withdraw a declaration it has made in accordance with the foregoing paragraph by means of a declaration addressed to the Secretary General of the Council of Europe which shall become effective as from the date of its receipt.
3. No reservation may be made to the provisions of this Protocol.

Article 7

The European Committee on Crime Problems of the Council of Europe shall be kept informed regarding the application of this Protocol and shall do whatever is needful to facilitate a friendly settlement of any difficulty which may arise out of its execution.

Article 8

1. Any Contracting Party may, in so far as it is concerned, denounce this Protocol by means of a notification addressed to the Secretary General of the Council of Europe.
2. Such denunciation shall take effect six months after the date of receipt by the Secretary-General of such notification.
3. Denunciation of the Convention entails automatically denunciation of this Protocol.

Article 9

The Secretary General of the Council of Europe shall notify the member States of the Council and any State which has acceded to the Convention of:

(a) any signature;

(b) any deposit of an instrument of ratification, acceptance, approval or accession;

(c) any date of entry into force of this Protocol in accordance with Article 3 thereof;

(d) any declaration received in pursuance of the provisions of Article 5 and any withdrawal of such a declaration;

(e) any declaration made in pursuance of the provisions of Article 6, paragraph 1;

(f) the withdrawal of any declaration carried out in pursuance of the provisions of Article 6, paragraph 2;

(g) any notification received in pursuance of the provisions of Article 8 and the date on which denunciation takes effect.

In witness whereof, the undersigned, being duly authorised thereto, have signed this Protocol.

Done at Strasbourg, this 15th day of October 1975, in English and in French, both texts being equally authoritative, in a single copy which shall remain deposited in the archives of the Council of Europe. The Secretary-General of the Council of Europe shall transmit certified copies to each of the signatory and acceding States.

Appendix 5

Second Additional Protocol to the European Convention on Extradition

European Treaty Series
No. 98

The member States of the Council of Europe, signatory to this Protocol,

Desirous of facilitating the application of the European Convention on Extradition opened for signature in Paris on 13 December 1977 (hereinafter referred to as "the Convention") in the field of fiscal Offenses;

Considering it also desirable to supplement the Convention in certain other respects,

Have agreed as follows:

CHAPTER I

Article 1

Paragraph 2 of Article 2 of the Convention shall be supplemented by the following provision:

"This right shall also apply to Offenses which are subject only to pecuniary sanctions."

CHAPTER II

Article 2

Article 5 of the Convention shall be replaced by the following provisions:

"*Fiscal offenses*

1. For Offenses in connection with taxes, duties, customs and exchange extradition shall take place between the Contracting Parties in accordance with the provisions of the Convention if the Offense, under the law of the requested Party, corresponds to an Offense of the same nature.
2. Extradition may not be refused on the ground that the law of the requested Party does not impose the same kind of tax or duty or does not contain a tax, duty, customs or exchange regulation of the same kind as the law of the requesting Party."

CHAPTER III

Article 3

The Convention shall be supplemented by the following provisions:

"*Judgments in absentia*

1. When a Contracting Party requests from another Contracting Party the extradition of a person for the purpose of carrying out a sentence or detention order imposed by a decision rendered against him in absentia, the requested Party may refuse to extradite for this purpose if, in its opinion, the proceedings leading to the judgment did not satisfy the minimum rights of defense recognised as due to everyone charged with criminal offense. However, extradition shall be granted if the requesting Party gives an assurance considered sufficient to guarantee to the person claimed the right to a retrial which safeguards the rights of defense. This decision will authorise the requesting Party either to enforce the judgment in question if the convicted person does not make an opposition or, if he does. to take proceedings against the person extradited.

2. When the requested Party informs the person whose extradition has been requested of the judgment rendered against him in absentia, the requesting Party shall not regard this communication as a formal notification for the purposes of the criminal procedure in that State."

CHAPTER IV

Article 4

The Convention shall be supplemented by the following provisions:

"*Amnesty*

Extradition shall not be granted for an offence in respect of which an amnesty has been declared in the requested State and which that State had competence to prosecute finder its own criminal law."

CHAPTER V

Article 5

Paragraph 1 of Article 12 of the Convention shall be replaced by the following provisions:

"The request shall be in writing and shall be addressed by the Ministry of Justice of the requesting Party to the Ministry of Justice of the requested Party; however, use of the diplomatic channel is not excluded. Other means of communication may be arranged by direct agreement between two or more Parties."

CHAPTER VI

Article 6

1. This Protocol shall be open to signature by the member States of the Council of Europe which have signed the Convention. It shall be subject to ratification, acceptance or approval. Instruments of ratification, acceptance or approval shall be deposited with the Secretary General of the Council of Europe.
2. The Protocol shall enter into force 90 days after the date of the deposit of the third instrument of ratification, acceptance or approval.
3. In respect of a signatory State ratifying, accepting or approving subsequently. the Protocol shall enter into force 90 days after the date of the deposit of its instrument of ratification, acceptance or approval.
4. A member State of the Council of Europe may not ratify, accept or approve this Protocol without having, simultaneously or previously ratified the Convention.

Article 7

1. Any State which has acceded to the Convention may accede to this Protocol after the Protocol has entered into force.
2. Such accession shall be effected by depositing with the Secretary General of the Council of Europe an instrument of accession which shall take effect 90 days after the date of its deposit.

Article 8

1. Any State may, at the time of signature or when depositing its instrument of ratification, acceptance, approval or accession, specify the territory or territories to which this Protocol shall apply.
2. Any State may, when depositing its instrument of ratification, acceptance, approval or accession or at any later date, by declaration addressed to the Secretary General of the Council of Europe, extend this Protocol to any other territory or territories specified in the declaration and for whose international relations it is responsible or on whose behalf it is authorised to give undertakings.
3. Any declaration made in pursuance of the preceding paragraph may, in respect of any territory mentioned in such declaration, be withdrawn by means of a notification addressed to the Secretary General of the Council of Europe. Such withdrawal shall take effect six months after the date of receipt by the Secretary General of the Council of Europe of the notification.

Article 9

1. Reservations made by a State to a provision of the Convention shall be applicable also to this Protocol, unless that State otherwise declares at the time of signature or when depositing its instrument of ratification, acceptance, approval or accession.
2. Any state may, at the time of signature or when depositing its instrument of ratification, acceptance, approval or accession, declare that it reserves the right:

(a) not to accept Chapter I;

(b) not to accept Chapter II, or to accept it only in respect of certain offenses or certain categories of the offenses referred to in Article 2;

(c) not to accept Chapter III, or to accept only paragraph I of Article 3;

(d) not to accept Chapter IV;

(e) not to accept Chapter V.

3. Any Contracting Party may withdraw a reservation it has made in accordance with the foregoing paragraph by means of a declaration addressed to the Secretary General of the Council of Europe which shall become effective as from the date of its receipt.
4. A Contracting Party which has applied to this Protocol a reservation made in respect of a provision of the Convention or which has made a reservation in respect of a provision of this Protocol may not claim the application of that provision by another Contracting Party; it may, however, if its reservation is partial or conditional claim, the application of that provision in so far as it has itself accepted it.
5. No other reservation may be made to the provisions of this Protocol.

Article 10

The European Committee on Crime Problems of the Council of Europe shall be kept informed regarding the application of this Protocol and shall do whatever is needful to facilitate a friendly settlement of any difficulty which may arise out of its execution.

Article 11

1. Any Contracting Party may, in so far as it is concerned, denounce this Protocol by means of a notification addressed to the Secretary General of the Council of Europe.
2. Such denunciation shall take effect six months after the date of receipt by the Secretary-General of such notification.
3. Denunciation of the Convention entails automatically denunciation of this Protocol.

Article 12

The Secretary General of the Council of Europe shall notify the member States of the Council and any State which has acceded to the Convention of:

(a). any signature of this Protocol;

(b) any deposit of an instrument of ratification, acceptance, approval or accession;

(c) any date of entry into force of this Protocol in accordance with Articles 6 and 7;

(d) any declaration received in pursuance of the provisions of paragraphs 2 and 3 of Article 8;

(e) any declaration received in pursuance of the provisions of paragraph 1 of Article 9;

(f) any reservation made in pursuance of the provisions of paragraph 2 of Article 9;

(g) the withdrawal of any reservation carried out in pursuance of the provisions of paragraph 3 of Article 9;

(h) any notification received in pursuance of the provisions of Article 11 and the date on which denunciation takes effect.

In witness whereof the undersigned, being duly authorised thereto, have signed this Protocol.

Done at Strasbourg, this 17th day of March 1978, in English and in French, both texts being equally authoritative, in a single copy which shall remain deposited in the archives of the Council of Europe. The Secretary General of the Council of Europe shall transmit certified copies to each of the signatory and acceding States.

Appendix 6

European Convention on the Suppression of Terrorism

European Treaty Series
No. 90

The member States of the Council of Europe, signatory hereto,

Considering that the aim of the Council of Europe is to achieve a greater unity between its Members;

Aware of the growing concern caused by the increase in acts of terrorism;

Wishing to take effective measures to ensure that the perpetrators of such acts do not escape prosecution and punishment;

Convinced that extradition is a particularly effective measure for achieving this result,

Have agreed as follows:

Article 1

For the purposes of extradition between Contracting States, none of the following offenses shall be regarded as a political offense or as an offense connected with a political offence or as an offense inspired by political motives:

(a) an offense within the scope of the Convention for the Suppression of Unlawful Seizure of Aircraft, signed at The Hague on 16 December 1970;

(b) an offense within the scope of the Convention for the Suppression of Unlawful Acts against the Safety of Civil Aviation, signed at Montreal on 23 September 1971;

(c) a serious offense involving an attack against the life, physical integrity or liberty of internationally protected persons, including diplomatic agents;

(d) an offense involving kidnaping, the taking of a hostage or serious unlawful detention;

(e) an offense involving the use of a bomb, grenade, rocket, automatic firearm or letter or parcel bomb if this use endangers persons;

(f) an attempt to commit any of the foregoing offenses or participation as an accomplice of a person who commits or attempts to commit such an offense.

Article 2

1. For the purposes of extradition between Contracting States, a Contracting State may decide not to regard as a political offense or as an offense connected with a political offense or as an offense inspired by political motives a serious offense involving an act of violence, other than one covered by Article 1, against the life, physical integrity or liberty of a person.
2. The same shall apply to a serious offense involving an act against property. other than one covered by Article 1, if the act created a collective danger for persons.
3. The same shall apply to an attempt to commit any of the foregoing offenses or participation as an accomplice of a person who commits or attempts to commit such an offence.

Article 3

The provisions of all extradition treaties and arrangements applicable between Contracting States, including the European Convention on Extradition, are modified as between Contracting States to the extent that they are incompatible with this Convention.

ARTICLE 4

For the purposes of this Convention and to the extent that any offence mentioned in Article 1 or 2 is not listed as an extraditable offence in any extradition convention or treaty existing between Contracting States, it shall be deemed to be included as such therein.

ARTICLE 5

Nothing in this Convention shall be interpreted as imposing an obligation to extradite if the requested State has substantial grounds for believing that the request for extradition for an offence mentioned in Article 1 or 2 has been made for the purpose of prosecuting or punishing a person on account of his race, religion, nationality or political opinion, or that that person's position may be prejudiced for any of these reasons.

ARTICLE 6

1. Each Contracting State shall take such measures as may be necessary to establish its jurisdiction over an offence mentioned in Article 1 in the case where the suspected offender is present in its territory and it does not extradite him after receiving a request for extradition from a Contracting State whose jurisdiction is based on a rule of jurisdiction existing equally in the law of the requested State.
2. This Convention does not exclude any criminal jurisdiction exercised in accordance with national law.

ARTICLE 7

A Contracting State in whose territory a person suspected to have committed an offence mentioned in Article 1 is found and which has received a request for extradition under the conditions mentioned in Article 6, paragraph 1, shall, if it does not extradite that person, submit the case, without exception whatsoever and without undue delay, to its competent authorities for the purpose of prosecution. Those authorities shall take their decision in the same manner as in the case of any offense of a serious nature under the law of that State.

ARTICLE 8

1. Contracting States shall afford one another the widest measure of mutual assistance in criminal matters in connection with proceedings brought in respect of the offences mentioned in Article 1 or 2. The law of the requested State concerning mutual assistance in criminal matters shall apply in all cases. Nevertheless this assistance may not be refused on the sole ground that it concerns a political offence or an offence connected with a political offence or an offence inspired by political motives.
2. Nothing in this Convention shall be interpreted as imposing an obligation to afford mutual assistance if the requested State has substantial grounds for believing that the request for mutual assistance in respect of an offence mentioned in Article 1 or 2 has been made for the purpose of prosecuting or punishing a person on account of his race, religion, nationality or political opinion or that that person's position may be prejudiced for any of these reasons.
3. The provisions of all treaties and arrangements concerning mutual assistance in criminal matters applicable between Contracting States, including the European Convention on Mutual Assistance in Criminal Matters, are modified as between Contracting States to the extent that they are incompatible with this Convention.

ARTICLE 9

1. The European Committee on Crime Problems of the Council of Europe shall be kept informed regarding the application of this Convention.
2. It shall do whatever is needful to facilitate a friendly settlement of any difficulty which may arise out of its execution.

ARTICLE 10

1. Any dispute between Contracting States concerning the interpretation or application of this Convention, which has not been settled in the framework of Article 9, paragraph 2, shall, at the request of any Party to the dispute, be referred to arbitration. Each Party shall nominate an arbitrator and the two arbitrators shall nominate a referee. If any Party has not nominated its arbitrator within the three months following the request for arbitration, he shall be nominated at the request of the other Party by the President of the European Court of Human Rights. If the latter should be a national of one of the Parties to the dispute, this duty shall be carried out by the Vice-President of the Court or, if the Vice-President is a national of one of the Parties to the dispute, by the most senior judge of the Court not being a national of one of the Parties to the dispute. The same procedure shall be observed if the arbitrators cannot agree on the choice of referee.
2. The arbitration tribunal shall lay down its own procedure. Its decisions shall be taken by majority vote. Its award shall be final.

ARTICLE 11

1. This Convention shall be open to signature by the member States of the Council of Europe. It shall be subject to ratification, acceptance or approval. Instruments of ratification, acceptance or approval shall be deposited with the Secretary General of the Council of Europe.
2. The Convention shall enter into force three months after the date of the deposit of the third instrument of ratification, acceptance or approval.
3. In respect of a signatory State ratifying, accepting or approving subsequently, the Convention shall come into force three months after the date of the deposit of its instrument of ratification, acceptance or approval.

ARTICLE 12

1. Any State may, at the time of signature or when depositing its instrument of ratification, acceptance or approval, specify the territory or territories to which this Convention shall apply.
2. Any State may, when depositing it instrument of ratification, acceptance or approval or at any later date, by declaration addressed to the Secretary General of the council of Europe, extend this Convention to any other territory or territories specified in the declaration and for whose international relations it is responsible or on whose behalf it is authorised to give undertakings.
3. Any declaration made in pursuance of the preceding paragraph may, in respect of any territory mentioned in such declaration, be withdrawn by means of a notification addressed to the Secretary General of the Council of Europe. Such withdrawal shall take effect immediately or at such later date as may be specified in the notification

ARTICLE 13

1. Any State may, at the time of signature or when depositing its instrument of ratification, acceptance of approval, declare that it reserves the right to refuse extradition in respect of any offense mentioned in Article I which it considers to be a political offence, an offense connected with a political offense or an offense inspired by political motives, provided that it undertakes to take into due consideration, when evaluating the character of the offense, any particularly serious aspects of the offense, including:

(a) that it created a collective danger to the life, physical integrity or liberty of persons; or
(b) that it affected persons foreign to the motives behind it; or
(c) that cruel or vicious means have been used in the commission of the offense.

2. Any State may wholly or partly withdraw a reservation it has made in accordance with the foregoing paragraph by means of a declaration addressed to the Secretary General of the Council of Europe which shall become effective as from the date of its receipt.
3. A State which has made a reservation in accordance with paragraph 1 of this article may not claim the application of Article 1 by any other State; it may, however, if its reservation is partial or conditional, claim the application of that article in so far as it has itself accepted it.

ARTICLE 14

Any Contracting State may denounce this Convention by means of a written notification addressed to the Secretary General of the Council of Europe. Any such denunciation shall take effect immediately or at such later date as may be specified in the notification.

ARTICLE 15

This Convention ceases to have effect in respect of any Contracting State which withdraws from or ceases to be a Member of the Council of Europe.

ARTICLE 16

The Secretary General of the Council of Europe shall notify the member States of the Council of:

(a). any signature;

(b) any deposit of an instrument of ratification, acceptance or approval;

(c) any date of entry into force of this Convention in accordance with Article 11 thereof;

(d) any declaration or notification received in pursuance of the provisions of Article 12:

(e) any reservation made in pursuance of the provisions of Article 13, paragraph 1;

(f) the withdrawal of any reservation effected in pursuance of the provisions of Article 13, paragraph 2;

(g) any notification received in pursuance of Article 14 and the date on which denunciation takes effect;

(h) any cessation of the effects of the Convention pursuant to Article 15.

In witness whereof, the undersigned, being duly authorised thereto, have signed this Convention.

Done at Strasbourg, this 27th day of January 1977, in English and in French, both texts being equally authoritative, in a single copy which shall remain deposited in the archives of the Council of Europe. The Secretary General of the Council of Europe shall transmit certified copies to each of the signatory States.

Section IV

Judicial Assistance and Mutual Cooperation in Penal Matters

Inter-State Cooperation in Penal Matters Within the Council of Europe Framework

Ekkehart Müller-Rappard*

Introduction

The Institutional Framework of the Council of Europe

The international treaty providing for the establishment of the Council of Europe, i.e. the Council's Statute, was signed in London on May 5, 1949, in the aftermath of the Second World War and at the beginning of the so-called Cold War, by ten Western European states and, upon ratification by seven of them, entered into force on August 3, 1949. The Council of Europe is a regional intergovernmental organization, the seat of which is at Strasbourg, France. Its Members are the states parties to its Statute. According to the latter, it consists of two organs: the Committee of Ministers, which is composed of representatives of the Governments of the Member States and functions as the decision-making body; and the Parliamentary Assembly, the deliberative organ, which consists of representatives elected or appointed by the national parliaments from among their own members. The Secretariat which serves these two organs of the Council of Europe includes a permanent staff of some 1,200 people at present. The Council of Europe is financed by the governments of its Member States, the respective contributions being assessed according to a scale taking into account both their gross domestic product and the size of their population. In 1996, the Organization's ordinary budget amounted to approximately US$150 million.

The aim of the Council of Europe, according to Article 1 of its Statute, is to achieve a greater unity between its Members for the purpose of safeguarding and realizing the ideals and principles which are their common heritage and facilitating their economic and social progress. This aim is to be pursued through the organs of the Council by discussion of questions of common concern and by agreements and common action in economic, social, cultural, scientific, legal and administrative matters and in the maintenance and further realization of human rights and fundamental freedoms. Except for matters relating to national defense which are excluded from its scope, the Council of Europe's competence thus extends to practically all aspects of European affairs. This is evidenced by the wide range of its intergovernmental program of activities which, together with the corresponding credits, is approved once a year by the Committee of Ministers.

When this Committee considers the action required to further the aim of the Council of Europe with regard to a particular matter, including the follow-up to proposals of new activities recommended by the Parliamentary Assembly to the Committee of Ministers, it has at its disposal essentially three working methods: the mutual exchange of information on specific questions of common concern; the elaboration and adoption of policy statements which propose a common course of action to be followed and which are addressed to the

* This article constitutes a revision and update to the January 1996 article *The European System* in the 1986 edition of INTERNATIONAL CRIMINAL LAW, Volume II, pp. 95-119. Any personal views expressed in this article reflect those of its author and therefore cannot commit, in any way, the Council of Europe.

member governments in form of a Recommendation by the Committee of Ministers; and the preparation and conclusion of conventions and agreements, for example, the European multilateral treaties, which the Member States are, however, entirely free to sign and ratify. In other words, although the multilateral treaties negotiated within the institutional framework of the Council of Europe represent a general European consensus on a given topic, these so-called European conventions must generally first be transferred into domestic law in order to become effective in the Member States, and they are therefore legally binding only for those states which have indeed accepted, usually by way of their ratification, to commit themselves to respect the legal obligations laid down in such treaties. In fact, as regards the approximately 160 European conventions adopted so far, it is rare for a European convention to be ratified by all Member States because of the wide range of subjects covered in the various conventions, the differences which still remain in the Member States' socio-economic and legal systems, as well as the fact that more than one-third of its present Members have acceded to the Council of Europe only recently, that is within the last five years.

It is to be recalled, in this respect, that every Member State of the Council of Europe must accept the principles of the rule of law and the enjoyment by all persons within its jurisdiction of human rights and fundamental freedoms, and collaborate sincerely and effectively in the realisation of the aim of the Council of Europe as specified in the above-mentioned Article 1 of the Statute. Any European state which is deemed to be able and willing to fulfil these conditions may be invited to become a Member of the Council of Europe. In January 1996 the Council of Europe had 38 Member States, several newly independent states of the former Yugoslavia and the ex-U.S.S.R, including Russia, having moreover applied for future accession to the Council of Europe. Following the chronological order in which they ratified or acceded to the Statute (the respective dates are indicated in parentheses), the present 38 Member States are: Denmark (7/14/49), Sweden (7/20/49), United Kingdom (7/26/49), Norway (7/30/49), Ireland (8/2/49), Italy (8/3/49), Luxembourg (8/3/49), France (8/4/49), Netherlands (8/5/49), Belgium (8/8/49), Greece (8/9/49), Iceland (3/7/50), Turkey (4/13/50), Germany (7/13/50), Austria (4/16/56), Cyprus (5/24/61), Switzerland (5/6/63), Malta (4/29/65), Portugal (9/22/76), Spain (11/24/77), Liechtenstein (11/23/78), San Marino (11/16/88), Finland (5/5/89), Hungary (11/6/90), Poland (11/26/91), Bulgaria (5/7/92), Estonia (5/14/93), Lithuania (5/14/93), Slovenia (5/14/93), Czech Republic (6/30/93), Slovakia (6/30/93), Romania (10/7/93), Andorra (11/10/94), Latvia (2/10/95), Albania (7/13/95), Moldova (7/13/95), the former Yugoslav Republic of Macedonia (11/9/95) and Ukraine (11/9/95).

It clearly appears from this enumeration that the Council of Europe has become the most representative and truly pan-European organization, including already all the Western European states and committed, since early 1990, to accept as well all the Eastern European and Central European states which are ready to submit to the obligations set out in its Statute. This newly developing West-East cooperation within the institutional framework of the Council of Europe prompted the Governments of the United States of America and of Japan to apply, in mid-1995, for permanent observer status at the Council of Europe. Yet, whatever the political merits of the sudden vast extension of the Council towards the east, it is obvious that the multiple attempts at "integrating the East" into the essentially western European framework of the Council bring about a fundamental change of both the nature and the priorities of its ongoing activities and present, too, a considerable challenge at the technical level. Even assuming that the Council's values are shared alike by all its present Member States, it appears, indeed, that certain standards set by the Council in the past cannot be achieved by all of them at the same time. The only question being whether some standards may be lowered, if not dispensed with altogether, for a short-term transition period, or whether double standards will prevail at the Council also in the long term—notwithstanding any official monitoring by the Parliamentary Assembly and the Committee of Ministers of the Member States' compliance with the commitments entered into before or upon their accession to the Council of Europe.

Context, Methods and Content of European Cooperation in Penal Matters

Until fairly recently, the Council's intergovernmental annual program of activities was divided into nine major fields, Field VIII being entitled: "co-operation in the legal field, including the harmonisation of national legislation and practice in specific legal sectors, the prevention of crime and the treatment of offenders." The numerous government expert committees which carried out these legal activities usually culminating in the elaboration of a European convention or a Committee of Ministers' Recommendation to the Member States, were co-ordinated by two steering committees which still exist today: the European Committee on Legal Co-operation (CDCJ) which handles matters of civil, commercial, administrative and international law, and the European Committee on Crime Problems (CDPC) which deals with matters of criminal law and procedure, prison matters and the treatment of offenders, criminological research and crime policy issues, and, last but not least, inter-state cooperation in penal matters. It is only the latter, i.e. the government experts' work concerning the inter-state cooperation in the prevention and prosecution of crime and the treatment of sentenced offenders, which will be discussed here. In this respect, the term "penal" matters, rather than that of "criminal" matters, is used in order to indicate that the scope of the cooperation set up and including, for instance, mutual administrative information with a view to the prevention of certain offenses, reaches well beyond the traditional "judicial assistance in criminal matters." Moreover, the term "inter-state" cooperation, rather than that of "intergovernmental" cooperation, is used in order to underline that, although the work is carried out by the government experts co-operating within the Council of Europe framework, the parties to the European Conventions prepared by these experts are the contracting states and the cooperation provided for by these conventions might be requested not only from the governmental authorities but also from non-governmental entities of the states-parties concerned.

The European inter-state cooperation in penal matters considered hereafter is based on a large number of multilateral conventions and agreements, prepared and concluded within the Council of Europe framework over the last 40 years, and on an even greater number of resolutions or recommendations which were adopted by its Committee of Ministers with a view to facilitating the practical application of these conventions by the states-parties.[1] To date, 20 European treaties deal exclusively with the Member State's cooperation in penal matters; they are, in the chronological order of their adoption, the following:

---

[1] For a compilation of the relevant texts, *see* EKKEHART MÜLLER-RAPPARD & M. CHERIF BASSIOUNI, EUROPEAN INTER-STATE CO-OPERATION IN CRIMINAL MATTERS (2d ed. 1991).

- European Convention on Extradition of 1957[2]
- European Convention on Mutual Assistance in Criminal Matters of 1959[3]
- European Convention on the Supervision of Conditionally Sentenced or Conditionally Released Offenders of 1964[4]
- European Convention on the Punishment of Road Traffic Offences of 1964[5]
- European Convention on the International Validity of Criminal Judgements of 1970[6]
- European Convention on the Repatriation of Minors of 1970[7]
- European Convention on the Transfer of Proceedings in Criminal Matters of 1972[8]
- European Convention on the Non-applicability of Statutory Limitations to Crimes against Humanity and War Crimes of 1974[9]
- Additional Protocol to the European Convention on Extradition of 1975[10]
- European Convention on the International Effects of Deprivation of the Right to Drive a Motor Vehicle of 1976[11]
- European Convention on the Suppression of Terrorism of 1977[12]
- Additional Protocol to the European Convention on Information on Foreign Law of 1978[13]
- Second Additional Protocol to the European Convention on Extradition of 1978[14]
- Additional Protocol to the European Convention on Mutual Assistance in Criminal Matters of 1978[15]
- European Convention on the Control of the Acquisition and Possession of Firearms by Individuals of 1978[16]
- European Convention on the Transfer of Sentenced Persons of 1983[17]
- European Convention on the Compensation of Victims of Violent Crimes of 1983[18]
- European Convention on Offences relating to Cultural Property of 1985[19]
- European Convention on Laundering, Search, Seizure and Confiscation of the Proceeds from Crime of 1990[20]

---

2 Europ. T.S. No. 24 (1957) [hereinafter Euro. Extradition Conv].
3 Europ. T.S. No. 30 (1959) [hereinafter Euro. Mutual Assistance Conv.].
4 Europ. T.S. No. 51 (1964) [hereinafter Euro. Supervision Conv.].
5 Europ. T.S. No. 52 (1964) [hereinafter Euro. Road Traffic Conv.].
6 Europ. T.S. No. 70 (1970) [hereinafter Euro. Conv. Int'l Val. Crim. Judg.].
7 Europ. T.S. No. 71 (1979) [hereinafter Euro. Minors Conv.].
8 Europ. T.S. No. 73 (1972) [hereinafter Euro. Trans. Proc. Conv.].
9 Europ. T.S. No. 82 (1974) [hereinafter Euro. Non-app. Stat. Limit. Conv.].
10 Europ. T.S. No. 86 (1975) [hereinafter Euro. Conv. Add. Prot. Extradition].
11 Europ. T.S. No. 88 (1976) [hereinafter Euro. Driving Conv.].
12 Europ. T.S. No. 90 (1977) [hereinafter Euro. Terrorism Conv.].
13 Europ. T.S. No. 97 (1978) [hereinafter Euro. Conv. Add. Prot. Infor.].
14 Europ. T.S. No. 98 (1978) [hereinafter Euro. Conv. 2d Add. Prot. Extradition].
15 Europ. T.S. No. 99 (1978) [hereinafter Euro. Conv. Add. Prot. Mutual Assistance].
16 Europ. T.S. No. 101 (1978) [hereinafter Euro. Firearms Conv.].
17 Europ. T.S. No. 112 (1983) [hereinafter Euro. Conv. Tran. Sent. Per.].
18 Europ. T.S. No. 116 (1983) [hereinafter Euro. Victims Conv.].
19 Europ. T.S. No. 119 (1985) [hereinafter Euro. Conv. Cultural Prop.].
20 Europ. T.S. No. 141 (1990) [hereinafter Euro. Conv. Money Laundering].

- Agreement on Illicit Traffic by Sea, implementing Article 17 of the [1995] United Nations Convention against Illicit Traffic in Narcotic Drugs and Psychotropic Substances, of 1995[21]

It is not the aim of this article to explain these 20 treaties in great detail. Indeed, even though this might be a worthwhile exercise, it has been carried out already several times both in the official commentaries on these treaties and in the regular Council of Europe publications on "the activities in the field of crime problems."[22] This article rather aims at a review and synthesis of these treaties with a view to highlighting some major horizontal and vertical developments which have occurred in the field of European inter-state cooperation in penal matters well before the opening up of the Council of Europe to eastern and central Europe.

During this period ranging from 1955 to 1990, the relations between the then-Council of Europe Member States underwent profound changes resulting in their ever-increasing interdependence and interpenetration. In particular, massive migrations of foreign workers moving North or East from either South or West, mass tourism flowing from North to South or West, as well as many technological, organizational, social and economic developments led, as far as crime was concerned, to a new factual situation: crime had become more mobile, organized and complex and surely more international and/or transnational in aspect than in the past. This new type of crime could not adequately be controlled and dealt with on the basis of the traditional principle regarding criminal jurisdiction because this principle, by providing essentially for the territoriality of criminal law, still reflects the out-dated concept of the co-existence of independent sovereign nations. When the highly interdependent northern, western and southern European states embarked upon the search of common solutions to their transnational crime problems, they had thus little alternative but to opt for vast and intensive mutual cooperation—irrespective of some restrictions which were put in the way of such cooperation in the past by the glorious concept of national sovereignty.

This new common approach led, first of all, from the traditional bilateral to a newly established multilateral cooperation in the fight against crime. At a second stage, the traditional methods of cooperation, namely extradition and mutual assistance in criminal matters, were complemented by two entirely new devices: the transfer of proceedings in criminal matters and the enforcement of foreign judgments in criminal matters. These four principal methods of inter-state cooperation in penal matters were firmly established already by mid-1972, as well as the following two main criteria for their alternative or cumulative use in a concrete case: the requirements and interests of a proper administration of justice (favoring prosecution and trial in the state of the commission of the offense, generally best-suited to that effect), on the one hand, and, on the other hand, the objective of social rehabilitation of the sentenced offender (favoring the enforcement of the sentence in the state of the offender's residence). In a third stage, between 1972 and 1990, the scope of the European cooperation in this matter was considerably extended: the major technical and legal obstacles, in particular the "classical" grounds for refusal of cooperation, were reduced, if not altogether dispensed with, and the content or object of inter-state cooperation

---

[21] Europ. T.S. No. 156 (1995) [hereinafter U.N. Sea Traffic Conv.].

[22] *See, e.g.*, Council of Europe, Activities in the Field of Crime Problems, (1956-76), (1975-80), (1980-85), (1985-90), (1990-95).

in the fight against crime was enlarged so as to include, too, in this term various measures, such as mutual information, aiming at the prevention of crime as well as certain measures for the compensation of victims of crime. The overall objective pursued during this period remains the consolidation and improvement of the cooperation procedures already established. In this respect, the conclusion of more than a dozen new multilateral treaties and the adoption of numerous recommendations on the practical application of the earlier European conventions surely reflect not only the ever-increasing need, but also the existing difficulties of establishing an adequate system of European mutual cooperation in penal matters and of adapting such a system to new circumstances, including deeper European integration and the ensuing greater mobility of people.

From this point of view, it is quite evident that the Council of Europe's opening up to eastern and central Europe has led to a new and still ongoing stage starting with Hungary's accession to the organization in late 1990. This last stage is characterized by the attempts at integrating the new eastern and central European Member States into the existing Council of Europe network and at building up in this way a truly pan-European system of inter-state cooperation in penal matters. There are many good and obvious reasons for believing that this is a very difficult task the implementation of which will require much time, besides a lot of political and technical support at all levels in the states concerned.

One of the rather technical reasons which makes this integration endeavor so difficult now, stems from the fact that the mutual cooperation system established by 1990 is the result of a lengthy piecemeal approach and is applied only in part, only by the states parties, and not by all the Member States to the same extent. When, in the light of the following survey of the Council of Europe's conventions on penal matters, this author evaluates their application and practical relevance, he will therefore renew his plea for a consolidated comprehensive approach in this matter, for example, the elaboration and adoption of a comprehensive code on European mutual cooperation in penal matters.

Survey of the Council of Europe's Treaties on Penal Matters

1951-1959: Initiation of Multilateral Treaties

During the first stage of development, between 1951 and 1959, cooperation efforts within the framework of the Council of Europe took up, at a multilateral level, the subjects and methods already well established by the practice of bilateral cooperation in penal matters among Member States, that is, extradition and mutual (judicial) assistance. This evolved from the belief that the adoption of common rules in these two fields was likely to assist the unification, thus contributing to one of the aims of the Council of Europe, the attainment of greater unity among its members.[23] The first two European conventions in this field, that on extradition of 1957[24] and that on mutual assistance of 1959[25] therefore contain principles according to which the new multilateral treaties shall, in respect of those countries to which they apply, supersede the provisions of any bilateral treaties, conventions or agreements

---

[23] *See, e.g.*, Euro. Extradition Conv., *supra* note 2, at pmbl.; and Euro. Mutual Assistance Conv., *supra* note 3, at preamble.

[24] Euro. Extradition Conv., *supra* note 2.

[25] Euro. Mutual Assistance Conv., *supra* note 3.

governing either extradition[26] or mutual assistance in criminal matters[27] between any two contracting parties. Yet, these two conventions do not really go beyond the limits and scope as set by the bilateral agreements then in force among Member States.

Thus, according to general practice prevailing at the time, extradition was not granted for political offenses[28] or for military offenses; it was granted for fiscal offenses only if the contracting Parties had decided to by a previous arrangement,[29] and a contracting party had the right to refuse extradition of its nationals.[30] Furthermore, extradition requests are to be communicated through diplomatic channels, although other means of communication could be arranged by direct agreement between two or more parties.[31]

Regarding this last procedural aspect, the Mutual Assistance Convention is less formal, since it allows communication through the channels of the ministries of justice of the contracting parties. It even provides for direct transmissions between the judicial authorities concerned of certain requests for investigation and of other information in the case of urgency.[32] Nevertheless, even though, according to Article 1 of this convention, the contracting parties undertake to afford each other the widest measure of mutual assistance in respect of offenses the punishment of which, at the time of the request for assistance, falls within the jurisdiction of the judicial authorities of the requesting party, assistance may be refused. This occurs not only if the execution of the request is considered likely to prejudice certain essential interests of the requested party,[33] but also when the latter has, for instance, reserved the right (and several contracting parties have indeed done so) to make the execution of certain letters rogatory dependent on the condition that the offence motivating such letters rogatory is an extraditable offense in the requested state.[34]

In other words, the various traditional exceptions to extradition provided for in the Extradition Convention of 1957 constitute restrictions on the multilateral European cooperation, which are all the more decisive and serious because of the clear interdependence of the Extradition Convention and the Mutual Assistance Convention of 1959; thus, the fairly wide scope of the latter may be considerably reduced following a restrictive application of the Extradition Convention.

Since, in the late 1950s, the mere harmonization of the bilateral rules in force at the time did not allow a close multilateral cooperation to be achieved in the penal field, it became necessary in the 1960s to go beyond this first stage, when the Council of Europe Member States became convinced of both the necessity of their mutual cooperation in ensuring more effective methods of the fight against crime committed in their territories, and the need to pursue a common crime policy aimed at the protection of society.[35]

---

26 Euro. Extradition Conv., *supra* note 2, at Art. 28.
27 Euro. Mutual Assistance Conv., *supra* note 3, at Art. 26.
28 Euro. Extradition Conv., *supra* note 2, at Art. 3.
29 *Id.* at Art. 5.
30 *Id.* at Art. 6.
31 *Id.* at Art. 12.
32 Euro. Mutual Assistance Conv., *supra* note 3, at Art. 15.
33 *Id.* at Art. 2(b).
34 *Id.* at Art. 5(1)(b).
35 *See, e.g.*, Euro. Road Traffic Conv., *supra* note 5, at preamble; Euro. Conv. Int'l Val. Crim. Judg., *supra* note 6, at preamble.

1961-1971: Period of Innovation

During the second stage, lasting from 1961 to 1971, the objectives and methods of European inter-state cooperation in the penal field were entirely revised. During this period of innovation, new solutions and methods were devised taking into account that crime had become more mobile and, thus, contained more and more international or transnational aspects and characteristics.

The context of this development has already been indicated:[36] increased mobility of people, following the improvement of transportation and communication, and the economic expansion in the early 1960s resulting in mass tourism of northerners to the south and in mass migrations of foreign workers from south to north; interdependence and interpenetration of the western European society; change of fundamental values and social patterns, including the disruption of the larger family unit, the decline of the role of schools and churches, the challenge by youth of society at large and of the work ethic; technological and organizational developments, including the increased use of computers and other sophisticated technical devices and the frequent establishment of multinational corporations.

These new methods and principles of inter-state cooperation in the penal field are already incorporated in the European Convention on the Punishment of Road Traffic Offences of 1964[37] and remarkably justified in the explanatory report thereto. It states the consideration that:

> [T]he law at present does not entirely ensure that penalties will be enforced against drivers from some other country who are guilty of offences against traffic regulations. Extradition is hedged about with conditions, laid down by municipal law or by treaty, that can rarely be satisfied. Further, the principle of territorial jurisdiction which governs most national criminal law prevents the State of residence of the driver from proceeding against him for traffic offences committed in another country or enforcing sentences pronounced by foreign courts. Thus, when proceedings are taken in the State where the offence is committed the offender cannot be punished after he has returned to his country of residence. The proceedings remain in abeyance or are concluded by a sentence which is not likely to be enforced. Moreover, the authorities in one country are naturally apprehensive that a person who causes a road accident may return to his own country to escape the consequences, and they will take measures to detain him in their own territory, which may cause him unnecessary inconvenience and are justified only because there is no enforceable international law.[38]

With a view to removing these difficulties, the Road Traffic Convention provides for the "addition of a European jurisdiction to national jurisdiction" by "departing in two ways from the principle of territoriality which by tradition settles the question of the competent court and the applicable criminal law."[39] On the one hand, the convention provides that the state where the offender is ordinarily resident (the state of residence) shall be competent to

---

36 *See supra* Introduction Part B.

37 *Supra* note 5.

38 European Committee on Crime Problems, Council of Europe, Explanatory Report on the European Convention on the Punishment of Road Traffic Offences, p. 7 (1970).

39 *Id.* at 7-8.

prosecute, at the request of the state where the offence has been committed (state of offense), for a road traffic offense committed in the territory of that state[40] whatever the nationality of the offender and/or of the victim. This is the newly established principle of transfer of proceedings in criminal matters, according to which the state of offense may present a request for proceedings to the State of residence which, upon such a request, shall have competence to prosecute under its own criminal law an offense to which the law of the other state is applicable.

On the other hand, the convention provides that the authorities of the state of residence shall be competent, when requested by the state of offense, to enforce sentences pronounced for a road traffic offence in that state.[41] This is the newly established principle of the enforcement of foreign judgments (or of the international validity of criminal judgments), according to which the state of offense may present a request for enforcement of a sanction, imposed by its authorities, to the state of residence which, upon such a request, shall be competent to enforce under its law the sanction imposed in the state of offense.[42]

In other words:

> [T]he Convention extends the competence of the State of residence and makes it possible for the State of offence either itself to institute proceedings against an offender in the usual way and eventually to request the State of residence to enforce the sentence, or to request the State of residence to institute proceedings, whatever the nationality of the offender or of the victim. The State of residence for its part is obliged to act on the request for proceedings or enforcement made by the State of offence [and to decide thereon according to its own law], all possible precautions being taken to avoid dual proceedings or dual enforcement.[43]

The punishment, in the territory of one contracting state, of road traffic offenses committed in the territory of another one is subject to formal requirements as well as to various substantive conditions including, for instance, the grounds on which the state of residence shall or may refuse a request for enforcement.[44] Rather than examining these provisions in detail, it is sufficient in the present context to stress that the elaboration of the Road Traffic Convention already seems to be influenced by the concern that a road traffic offender not be detained in the state of offense merely because he may return to his country of residence (this "may cause him unnecessary inconvenience") and that sentences be enforced preferably in the state of residence.

The European Convention on the Supervision of Conditionally Sentenced or Conditionally Released Offenders,[45] which was opened for signature on the same day as the Road Traffic Convention, constitutes a second illustration of the extension of European cooperation in penal matters. Indeed, it established a system whereby conditional measures such as suspended sentence, probation, or early release which take effect concurrently with

---

40 Euro. Road Traffic Conv., *supra* note 5, at Art.3.
41 *Id.* at Art. 8.
42 Euro. Conv. Int'l Val. Crim. Judg., *supra* note 6.
43 Explanatory Report, *supra* note 38, at 7-8.
44 Euro. Road Traffic Conv., *supra* note 5, at Art. 9.
45 Euro. Supervision Conv., *supra* note 4.

or subsequent to a sentence pronounced by one contracting party, may be carried out on the territory of another.[46]

The reasons invoked for dealing with this matter are fairly similar to those given in support of the enforcement of convictions for road traffic offenses committed and sentenced abroad: financial reasons, humane aspects, equity and better prevention of recidivism. According to the arguments contained in the explanatory report on this convention, conditional measures are at present "a recognised part of the penal system, and are used to provide better protection against crime while at the same time lightening the financial burden of prison costs and aid to prisoners' families."[47]

However:

> [W]here foreigners or persons residing abroad are concerned, courts are reluctant to pass a sentence which is not certain to be put into effect in another country. In consequence, offenders who would normally have qualified for suspended sentence or probation are either given a term of confinement, kept in prison until their sentence expires, or released only in order to be expelled from the country.[48]

In the past, "very few cases were involved: but today there is so much coming and going between different countries of Europe that a more equitable system has become essential." It consists of "making available across frontiers those methods of individual amendment and social rehabilitation which have proved successful on a national scale. Its aim will be not only to supervise released offenders but also to give such assistance as may be necessary to ensure their rehabilitation in their country of residence."[49]

This indicates the emergence of the principle of the social rehabilitation of the offender in his state of residence and its first, selective application in a special convention on inter-state cooperation.

This principle will later become the leitmotiv for the elaboration of several other European conventions as well as the decisive criterion for their application in specific cases. This principle results essentially from the postulate of having a rational and efficient application of a common crime policy in Western Europe. Indeed, since crime policy has come to lay greater emphasis upon the treatment of the offender, "it would seem that resocialization is often considerably facilitated when the sanctions imposed upon the offender are carried out in his State of residence rather than in the State of the offence and judgement."[50] This policy, moreover, "is also rooted in humane considerations, in particular the understanding of the detrimental influences upon a prisoner of difficulties in

---

46 European Committee on Crime Problems, Council of Europe, Explanatory Report on the European Convention on the Supervision of Conditionally Sentenced or Conditionally Released Offenders, p. 7 (Strasbourg, 1970). *See also* Euro. Supervision Conv., *supra* note 4, at preamble ¶ 4 and Art. 1 (the contracting parties undertake to grant each other mutual assistance for the social rehabilitation of offenders either in the form of simple supervision of the offender, or supervision and, in case of revocation of the conditional suspension, enforcement of the sentence, or assumption of entire responsibility for enforcing the sentence).

47 Explanatory Report, *supra* note 46, at 7.

48 *Id.*

49 *Id.*

50 European Committee on Crime Problems, Council of Europe, Explanatory Report on the European Convention on the International Validity of Criminal Judgements, p. 13 (Strasbourg, 1970). The elaboration of the Convention on the Transfer of Sentenced Persons, *supra* note 17, is largely prompted by similar considerations.

communication by reason of language barriers, alienation from local culture and habits and the absence of contact with relatives and friends."[51]

The European Convention on the Repatriation of Minors of 1970[52] does not contain any new principles regarding European cooperation in the penal field and, moreover, is not confined to mutual assistance with a view to officially imposed transfer of delinquent minors. Indeed, according to this convention, a contracting state may be requested to repatriate a minor if his presence in the territory of the requested state is either against the will of the person having parental authority or incompatible with a measure of protection or re-education taken in the requesting state, or if his presence in the territory of the requesting state is necessary because of the institution of proceedings in that state. A state may also repatriate a minor when it deems that his presence in its territory is incompatible with the interests of the state or of the minor, provided that its legislation authorizes removal of the minor from its territory.

By the mid-1960s,

> the need for effective mutual assistance in this particular sphere [was] all the more evident since young people [were] travelling more and more, either as tourists or in connection with their work, and arrangements for their protection [had] developed greatly. It [was] mainly for these reasons that a multilateral European Convention [was] required making possible the officially imposed transfer of minors from the territory of one Contracting Party to that of another.[53]

The European Convention on the International Validity of Criminal Judgements,[54] which was opened for signature on May 28, 1970 (the same day as the European Convention on the Repatriation of Minors), is inspired by two regional arrangements: the one provided for between the five Nordic countries,[55] and the one envisaged between the three Benelux countries. This convention follows up and extends the new methods and principles of inter-state cooperation, established by the Road Traffic and Supervision Conventions,[56] in order to make them more widely applicable.[57] Accordingly, "a Contracting State shall be competent to enforce a sanction imposed in another Contracting State which is enforceable in the latter State" although "this competence can only be exercised following a request by the other Contracting State."[58]

A necessary prerequisite for the establishment of such a system, which departs from the classical concept of national sovereignty and the principle of territoriality referred to above, is the mutual confidence in legal systems prevailing in the Member States of the Council of Europe, as well as the common desire of these states to make a joint effort to fight crime at

---

51 Explanatory Report, *supra* note 50, at 13.

52 Euro. Minors Conv., *supra* note 7.

53 European Committee on Crime Problems, Council of Europe, Explanatory Report on the European Convention on the Repatriation of Minors, p. 8 (Strasbourg, 1971) (By dealing at the same time with civil, criminal and administrative procedures in respect to minors, this Convention might have been an unrealistic attempt of a comprehensive solution. This could explain why the Convention has only been ratified by two Member States).

54 Euro. Conv. Int. Val. Crim. Judg., *supra* note 6.

55 Denmark, Iceland, Norway, Sweden and Finland.

56 Euro. Road Traffic Conv., *supra* note 5.

57 Explanatory Report (Euro. Conv. Int'l Val. Crim. Judg.), *supra* note 50, at 13-14.

58 Euro. Conv. Int'l Val. Crim. Judg., *supra* note 6, at Art. 3.

an international level.[59] It is, therefore, not surprising that the explanatory report expressly confirms, regarding the conditions for enforcement, that

> the decision must have been rendered in full observation of the fundamental principles of the Convention on Human Rights, notably Article 6, which lays down certain minimum requirements for court proceedings. Though it is not expressly stated in the text, there was complete agreement that it was unthinkable to acknowledge the outcome of a trial as a valid judgment if it fell short of basic democratic requirements.[60]

The European Convention on the International Validity of Criminal Judgements, which does establish such an enforcement scheme (the Enforcement Convention), is very elaborate and detailed. The reasons for this are the fundamental concept behind it, that is, the assimilation of a foreign judgment to a judgment emanating from the courts of the enforcing state. This assimilation is applied in three different respects: the enforcement of European criminal judgments;[61] the international effect of European criminal judgments,[62] including the *ne bis in idem* effect; and the taking into consideration of foreign judgments. No attempt will be made to summarize these highly complex legal provisions, as the main concern of this article is to examine the underlying broad concepts of the expanding scope of western European cooperation in penal matters.

The same considerations and comments apply, *mutatis mutandis*, to the second "general" convention drafted during this period and relating to the other method of inter-state cooperation established by the Road Traffic Convention. This other method is the transfer of proceedings and organization of competence (or redistribution of jurisdiction), with a view to ensuring that proceedings will be conducted and that the sentence will be pronounced in the state best suited to prosecute, according to the general criterion of the proper administration of justice.

The European Convention on the Transfer of Proceedings in Criminal Matters[63] (the Prosecution Convention), opened for signature on May 15, 1972, gives tangible expression to the "spirit of mutual confidence" of the Member States "desiring to supplement the work which they have already accomplished in the field of criminal law with a view to arriving at more just and efficient sanctions"[64] by granting any contracting state "competence to prosecute under its own criminal law any offence to which the law of another Contracting State is applicable."[65] However, similar to the relevant restriction in the Enforcement Convention, this competence "may be exercised only pursuant to a request for proceedings presented by another Contracting State."[66] In such a case, the requesting state "can no longer prosecute the suspected person for the offence in respect of which the proceedings have been requested. . . ."[67] and additionally the requesting state is "obliged to recognise the effect

---

59 Explanatory Report (Euro. Conv. Int'l Val. Crim. Judg.), *supra* note 50, at 19-20.
60 *Id.* at 15.
61 Euro. Conv. Int'l Val. Crim. Judg., *supra* note 6, at Arts. 2-52.
62 *Id.* at Arts. 53-57.
63 Euro. Trans. Proc. Conv., *supra* note 8.
64 *Id.* at preamble, ¶¶ 3, 4.
65 *Id.* at Art. 2(1).
66 *Id.* at Art. 2(2).
67 *Id.* at Art. 21(1).

of *ne bis in idem*" of any final and enforceable criminal judgment pronounced in this matter by the requested state.[68]

Furthermore, in accordance with the second objective of the Prosecution Convention, to ensure the organization of criminal proceedings on the international level, "in particular, by avoiding the disadvantages resulting from conflicts of competence,"[69] the transfer of proceedings is established as one of the principal means for the appropriate solution of positive conflicts of jurisdiction.[70]

Such conflicts can arise when several states claim jurisdiction over an offense by reason of the place of commission (conflicts of territorial jurisdiction) or on other grounds if the offense was committed in foreign territory (such as the active or passive personality principle, or universal jurisdiction, or jurisdiction based on the protection of the sovereignty or the security of the state). However, as set out in the explanatory report, "the weight to be given in each case to conflicting considerations cannot be decided by completely general rules.[71] The decision must be taken in the light of the particular facts of each case. By attempting in this way to arrive at an agreement between the various states concerned,[72] it will be possible to avoid the difficulties which they would encounter by a prior acceptance of a system restricting their power to impose sanctions."[73]

If, in the absence of such an agreement, a final and enforceable criminal judgment has been rendered against a person, he cannot be prosecuted, sentenced or subjected to enforcement of a sanction in another contracting state for the same act according to the detailed regulations of the convention[74] on the principle *ne bis in idem*.

1972-1990: Extension and Improvement of the Mutual Cooperation in Penal Matters

During the third stage, the consolidation period, which began in the early 1970s, the foundation for European cooperation in penal matters has been extended and improved with a view to a more general and coherent application of the schemes already established. This aim was achieved by the elaboration and adoption of a whole series of new legal instruments providing either for (1) an extension of the scope of the penal conventions, or (2) a restriction on the many exceptions they contain regarding the undertaking of multilateral cooperation, or (3) a simplification of the procedures they provide to that end.

The Road Traffic Convention of 1964 was thus complemented by the conclusion of the European Convention on the International Effects of Deprivation of the Right to Drive a

---

68 *Id.* at Art. 35.

69 *Id.* at preamble, ¶ 4.

70 *Id.* at Art. 30(1).

71 *E.g.*, the state in which the act was committed should have priority to prosecute the offender. *See also* European Committee on Crime Problems, Council of Europe, Explanatory Report on the European Convention on the Transfer of Proceedings in Criminal Matters (Strasbourg, 1970), where at page 15, it explains:

> The assumption that it is normally most appropriate to prosecute an offence where it has been committed is not justified. Rehabilitation of the offender which is increasingly given weight in modern penal law requires that the sanction be imposed and enforced where the reformative aim can be most successfully pursued, that is normally in the State in which the offender has family or social ties or will take up residence after the enforcement of the sanction. On the other hand, it is clear that difficulties in securing evidence will often be a consideration militating against the transmission of proceedings from the State where the offence has been committed to another State. . . .

72 As to which state should take action against the perpetrator of a given offence.

73 Explanatory Report, *supra* note 71, at 15.

74 Euro. Trans. Proc. Conv., *supra* note 8, at Art. 35.

Motor Vehicle[75] and then by the adoption of several resolutions and recommendations of the Committee of Ministers regarding road traffic offenses and the application of this specific convention.[76] The "Guidelines for offenses to be included in a European Highway Code," published in 1979 and based on these texts, were intended to serve as a guide to Member States regarding any future changes in national legislation on this matter.

Furthermore, the Second Additional Protocol to the Extradition Convention[77] provides for the extension of extradition "to offences in connection with taxes, duties, customs and exchange," while stipulating that extradition for such fiscal offenses "may not be refused on the ground that the law of the requested Party does not impose the same kind of tax or duty or does not contain a tax, duty, customs or exchange regulation of the same kind as the law of the requesting Party."[78] Similarly, the Additional Protocol to the Mutual Assistance Convention[79] extends the application of this convention to fiscal offenses[80] while also adding that the optional requirement of dual criminal liability shall be considered fulfilled in this context "if the offence is punishable under the law of the requesting Party and corresponds to an offence of the same nature under the law of the requested Party."[81] Fiscal offenses have been greatly increasing recently and can no longer remain excluded from a system of cooperation based on a common crime policy and mutual confidence of the Member States.

Various other restrictions or exceptions to European cooperation, which were foreseen in some of the earlier European conventions, had already been reduced or abolished in the same spirit of solidarity. Thus, one European convention[82] provides for the non-applicability of statutory limitations to crimes against humanity and to the most serious violations of the laws and customs of war.[83] Moreover, the First Protocol to the Extradition Convention excludes such crimes from the concept of political offences so as to ensure that extradition for such offenses cannot be refused on that ground either.[84]

The refusal of extradition and of mutual assistance on the ground that the offense is regarded by the requested party as a political offense or an offense connected with a political offense has been considerably restricted by the provisions of Resolution (74)3 and of the European Convention on the Suppression of Terrorism,[85] which is precisely based on this resolution. This convention expresses very clearly in its preamble the Member States'

---

[75] This Convention could be particularly useful for neighboring states with frequent transfrontier road traffic, which are not already Parties to the Euro Conv. Int'l Val. Crim. Judg., *supra* note 6. When a driving deprivation is ordered as a consequence of a road traffic offense which took place in the territory of a contracting party other than the party which issued the driving license or the party where the offender is habitually resident, the former party shall notify the latter accordingly. The notified party may order the driving deprivation, which it would have deemed useful, had the road traffic offense occurred in its own territory.

[76] Committee of Ministers, Council of Europe, Resolutions and Recommendations R(73)7 (1973), R(75)24 (1975), R(77)29 (1977), R(78)42 (1978), R(79)5 (1979).

[77] Euro. Conv. 2d Add. Prot. Extradition, *supra* note 14.

[78] *Id.* at Art. 2(2). This same Protocol provides in Art. 1 for the extension for accessory extradition "to offences which are subject only to pecuniary sanctions."

[79] Euro. Conv. Add. Prot. Mutual Assistance, *supra* note 15.

[80] *Id.* at Art. 1.

[81] *Id.* at Art. 2. (in accordance with Art. 3 of this Protocol, the Euro. Mutual Assistance Conv., *supra* note 3, shall also apply to the enforcement of sentences and similar measures).

[82] Euro. Non-app. Stat. Limit. Conv., *supra* note 9.

[83] *Id.* at Art. 1. These are war crimes specified in certain international instruments and other comparable violations of the laws of war. It should be stressed that most national legislations contain this principle and that this Convention was not to be retroactive. This may explain why the Convention has been ratified by only one state.

[84] Euro. Conv. Add. Prot. Extradition, *supra* note 10, at Art. 1.

[85] Euro. Terrorism Conv., *supra* note 12.

conviction that "extradition is a particularly effective measure" for ensuring that the perpetrators of acts of terrorism do not escape prosecution and punishment. Nevertheless, it still allows a state to avoid the automatic extradition in such cases[86] by providing that there is no obligation to extradite "if the requested State has substantial grounds for believing that the request for extradition . . . has been made for the purpose of prosecuting or punishing a person on account of his race, religion, nationality or political opinion, or that that person's position may be prejudiced for any of these reasons."[87] Moreover, a state may reserve the right to refuse extradition in regard to any offense covered by the convention provided it takes into due consideration, when evaluating the character of the offense, any particularly serious aspects thereof.[88] In such a case, however, the requested state which does not extradite shall submit the case without exception and delay to its competent authorities for the purpose of prosecution. This is the requirement of the principle *aut dedere aut judicare* which, although already incorporated into the Extradition Convention of 1957,[89] has been considerably strengthened and completed in Articles 6 and 7 of the Terrorism Convention.

In addition to the above-mentioned supplementary European treaties eliminating or reducing the grounds for refusing inter-state cooperation, in particular for fiscal and political offenses, some Council of Europe legal instruments restrict also the grounds for refusing such cooperation in case of judgments *in absentia*.[90] If one adds to all this various provisions in the newly adopted legal instruments, which aim at the simplification of the channels of communication[91] in these inter-state cooperation procedures, one cannot, at first sight, avoid the impression of a permanent trend and continuing consensus among the Member States to agree to whatever appears to be required in order to make their common fight against transnational crime as efficient and as effective as possible.

Next to the obvious trend towards greater efficiency in the protection and repression of all transnational offenses, which is supported in particular by the various enforcement agencies belonging to the ministries of interior, there appears, however, as well a distinct concern, often voiced by representatives of the ministries of justice: it is their concern that the expending European cooperation in penal matters be firmly subordinated to the requirements and interests of a proper administration of justice, as reflected in the relevant provisions of the European Human Rights Convention.[92] Thus, the principle of *ne bis in idem* as well as amnesty given by the requested state are additional grounds for mandatory refusal of extradition requests.[93] Moreover, Member States are expressly recommended to reduce remand in custody pending extradition proceedings. And the Committee of Ministers of the Council of Europe also recommended to the Member States that they not extradite to

---

86 *Id.* at Art. 1.

87 *Id.* at Art. 5.

88 *Id.* at Art. 13.

89 Euro. Extradition Conv., *supra* note 2, at Art. 6(2).

90 *E.g.*, Council of Europe, Committee of Ministers Resolution R(75)11 and Euro. Conv. 2d Add. Prot. Extradition, *supra* note 14, at Art. 3.

91 Euro. Conv. 2d Add. Prot. Extradition, *supra* note 14, at Art. 5 and Committee of Ministers Recommendation R(82)1 (1982).

92 Convention for the Protection of Human Rights and Fundamental Freedoms, Europ. T.S. No. 5 (1950).

93 Euro. Conv. Add. Prot. Extradition, *supra* note 10, at Art. 2 and Euro. Conv. 2d Add. Prot. Extradition, *supra* note 14, at Art. 4.

states which do not comply with the requirements of the European Human Rights Convention.[94]

The Convention on the Transfer of Sentenced Persons[95] is an illustration of efforts undertaken with a view to simplifying and improving certain cooperation methods, subject to any human rights requirements applicable in this matter. Indeed the Enforcement Convention[96] and, prior to it, the Road Traffic Convention[97] and the Supervision Convention[98] already envisioned the possibility of foreigners undergoing conviction in their state of residence. Under the Transfer of Sentenced Persons Convention, however, "transfer may be requested by either the sentencing State or the administering State"[99] while the person concerned[100] may express to either state his interest in being transferred under this convention,[101] but cannot be transferred unless, *inter alia*, he or, exceptionally, his legal representative, consents thereto.[102] In other words, the person to be transferred is no longer the mere object of certain inter-state dealings—as in case of an extradition request—but he becomes a full partner in the proceedings concerning his eventual transfer and, as such, a new subject of international treaty law.

The very active participation of Canada and the United States of America in the elaboration of this convention could be considered as the beginning of an extension of some parts of this inter-state cooperation beyond European frontiers. Indeed, following its ratification by Canada and the U.S., two more non-European States, namely the Bahamas and Trinidad-Tobago, have acceded in the meantime to the Transfer Convention,[103] while other non-European states have also applied for authorization to do so in the future. This is surely a remarkable new development since Israel was so far the only non-European state showing its interest in the European mutual cooperation in penal matters by acceding many years ago to the European Conventions on Extradition and Mutual Assistance.

Be that as it may, the widely shared interest in the application and smooth functioning of the Transfer Convention has already led to the preparation and adoption of three Committee of Ministers' recommendations on the matter.[104] The first one deals in particular with the states-parties' obligation under Article 4, paragraph 1, of the Convention, according to which "any sentenced person to whom this Convention may apply shall be informed by the sentencing State of the substance of this Convention." The two subsequent

---

94 *See,* in the context of mutual assistance, Recommendations and Resolutions R(71)43 (1971), R(77)36 (1977), and R(80)8 (1980). In the context of extradition, *see* Recommendations and Resolutions R(7512 (1975), R(78)43 (1978), R(80)7 (1980), and R(80)9 (1980).

95 Euro. Conv. Tran. Sent. Per., *supra* note 17.

96 Euro. Conv. Int'l Val. Crim. Judg., *supra* note 6.

97 Euro. Road Traffic Conv., *supra* note 5.

98 Euro. Supervision Conv., *supra* note 4.

99 Euro. Conv. Tran. Sent. Per., *supra* note 17, at Art. 2(3).

100 This is, by definition, a national of the administering state, imprisoned, with at least six months left to serve, as a result of his commission of a criminal offense in the sentencing state, as this Convention is limited to sentences involving the deprivation of liberty. The Convention also provides for continued enforcement in Art. 10 and for conversion of sentence in Art. 11.

101 Euro. Conv. Tran. Sent. Per., *supra* note 17, at Art. 2(2).

102 *Id.* at Art. 3(d).

103 It should be recalled that, although it is not (yet) a Council of Europe Member State, Bosnia-Herzegovina has acceded to several Council of Europe treaties, including the Transfer Convention referred to above.

104 Committee of Ministers (Council of Europe), Recommendation R(84)11 of June, 1984, Recommendation R(88)13 of September, 1988, and Recommendation R(92)18 of October, 1992.

recommendations constitute attempts at tackling various practical difficulties which have arisen mainly from the fact that the modalities for the processing of transfer requests, including the spelling out of any grounds for refusal, were left to inter-state practice and that, moreover, contracting states to the Transfer Convention are entitled under its Article 3, paragraph 3, to exclude the application of either the continued enforcement procedure or the conversion of sentence procedure. This led to the recommendation of increased standardization in this matter, including standard texts providing information in a language the prisoner understands, national guidelines concerning the criteria to be met when making a decision whether to accept or to refuse a request for transfer, and updated lists containing all required information on the persons responsible in each state-party for the operation of the convention.[105]

There is another fairly recent trend in the work and priorities of the government experts meeting within the Council of Europe framework: European cooperation in penal matters tends to be expanding to certain matters merely connected with the fight against crime, such as the prevention of crime and relief from the prejudice suffered as the result of crime.

For example, the Firearms Convention[106] provides for the (preventive) control of cases in which a firearm[107] situated in one contracting party is either sold, transferred or otherwise disposed of to a person resident in the territory of another contracting party,[108] or is transferred permanently and without change in the possession thereof to the territory of another contracting party.[109] In these cases, the former party is to notify the latter as expeditiously as possible of a number of details of the transfer,[110] and the convention also provides for an elaborate system of double authorization as a prerequisite for the acquisition of firearms in such cases.[111] The harmonization of national legislations relating to firearms is, moreover, the aim and object of a recommendation adopted by the Committee of Ministers of the Council of Europe in late 1984.[112]

According to the Victims Convention,[113] contracting states undertake to provide, either in their legislation or in their administrative arrangements, for a method to compensate, from public funds if compensation is not fully available from other sources, victims of intentional and violent offenses who have suffered bodily injury or impairment of health, and to compensate the dependents of persons who have died as a result of such crime.[114] The convention retains the principle of territoriality and requires the contracting state in whose territory the offense is committed, to contribute to compensation of its own nationals and also of foreigners who are nationals of other parties or are permanent residents and nationals of Council of Europe Member States.[115] Besides the minimum requirements for such compensation schemes, there is the undertaking that information about the scheme is made available to potential applicants[116] as well as the multilateral cooperation proviso that the

---

105 *See* the Appendices to R(84)11 and R(92)18.
106 Euro. Firearms Conv., *supra* note 16.
107 *Id.* at App. I.
108 *Id.* at Art. 5.
109 *Id.* at Art. 6.
110 *Id.* at Arts. 8, 9.
111 *Id.* at Art. 10.
112 Committee of Ministers, Council of Europe Recommendation R(84)23 (December, 1984).
113 Euro. Victims Conv., *supra* note 18.
114 *Id.* at Art. 2.
115 *Id.* at Art. 3.
116 *Id.* at Art. 11.

contracting states give each other "the maximum possible assistance in connection with the matters covered by this Convention."[117]

The new concern about the prevention of crime and the reparation of prejudice from crime at the European level constitutes a certain change, if not a departure from the original objective of European cooperation, *i.e.* to improve and harmonize the legal basis required first of all for the prosecution of transnational crime. There appears yet another, entirely new trend in this cooperation since the mid-1980s. It consists of the preparation and adoption of new multilateral, special conventions by which the four, previously established, general cooperation methods were more or less combined and made applicable to certain categories of offenses considered particularly damaging or dangerous to society at large. This new trend is illustrated by the last three multilateral treaties negotiated within the institutional framework of the Council of Europe, which relate essentially to the illicit traffic in works of art and the illicit traffic in narcotic drugs.

The European Convention on Offences relating to Cultural Property[118] was opened for signature on June 23, 1985. It constitutes a "special" convention in which four "general" conventions, on extradition, on mutual assistance, on transfer of enforcement and on transfer of prosecution, are "jointly" applied to a specific category of offenses: those relating to cultural property, as set out in Appendix III to this convention. This convention, therefore, contains essentially the same rules as those in the four "general" conventions mentioned above, though, as in most test cases, the rules are restricted to Western European cooperation with a view to restoring possession to the lawful owner of cultural property found in the territory of one party which had been removed from the territory of another party subsequent to an offense relating to cultural property committed in the territory of any party.[119]

Insofar as the convention was prompted by the Member States' explicit recognition of "their common responsibility and solidarity in the protection of the European Cultural heritage," it contains a detailed enumeration and specification of the categories of cultural property and of the offenses which are, or may fall, within its scope.[120] Moreover, the convention imposes on the states-parties the obligation to take appropriate measures with a view both to "enhancing public awareness of the need to protect cultural property" and "to co-operating in the prevention of offences relating to cultural property and the discovery of cultural property removed subsequent to such offenses."[121] The regulations on the restitution of cultural property[122] and, in particular, on the solution of plurality of proceedings,[123] as well as the prohibition of *ne bis in idem*, reflect the principles already established in the general conventions referred to. However, while the government experts preparing and negotiating the text of this convention thus achieved their task of applying all the pertinent, existing, general cooperation methods to this particular category of offenses, they could not, as requested, agree as well on a new common European legal standard concerning "the settlement of problems inherent in the concept of 'bona fide owner,' transnational restitution

---

117 *Id.* at Art. 12.

118 Euro. Conv. Cultural Prop., *supra* note 19.

119 *Id.* at Art. 6 (such a party may be either the first party or the second party or any other contracting party).

120 *Id.* at preamble ¶ 6, and Arts. 2, 3.

121 *Id.* at Arts. 4, 5.

122 *Id.* at Arts. 6-11.

123 *Id.* at Arts. 13-19.

and prescription."[124] The convention leaves this matter to the domestic law of the state-parties by providing explicitly in its Article 8, paragraph 2, in fine: "Restitution of the property in question is however subject to the conditions laid down in the law of the requested Party." This might explain the fact that, although the convention has been signed in the meantime by half-a-dozen Member States particularly threatened and/or suffering from illicit removal of cultural property from their territories, no state had ratified this convention by mid-January 1996. In this respect, the second recent special convention relating to a particular category of offenses has been more supported in practice.

The Convention on Laundering, Search, Seizure and Confiscation of the Proceeds from Crime of November 8, 1990,[125] was prompted by the wish to grasp the enormous financial profits of those involved in the illicit traffic of narcotic drugs, and to combat more efficiently the supply for drug abuse and to reduce the risk and scope of organized crime at the international level. However, from the start, the European government experts entrusted with the preparation of this convention were requested to consider search, seizure and confiscation of the proceeds from any crime, and not only from illicit drug traffic, and to examine in this context, in addition to the applicability of the already existing European penal law conventions, also the ongoing work of the Council of Europe's so-called Pompidou Group and of the United Nations, in particular the United Nations Convention against Illicit Traffic in Narcotic Drugs and Psychotropic Substances, concluded in Vienna in December, 1988. Australia, Canada and the United States of America participated in the drafting and negotiation, right from the beginning, and this, including the understanding that the convention be open in the future to accession by other non-Member States, is the reason why this convention (like the one on transfer of sentenced persons mentioned above) is not entitled "European."

Insofar as the Laundering Convention aims at the establishment, at a more restricted regional level, of an improved mechanism of international cooperation together with a complete set of all the rules required to that effect, it contains many detailed provisions, starting with the measures to be taken at national level as a prerequisite to international cooperation. They include legislative and other measures necessary to enable state-parties to identify and trace property which is liable to confiscation, to prevent any disposal thereof and, to confiscate such property.[126] They also include the states-parties' obligation to criminalize the various laundering offences in their domestic law. In this respect, Article 3 of the 1988 U.N. Convention provided only for the criminalization of intentional (a) conversion or transfer of property, (b) concealment or disguise, and (c) acquisition, possession or use of assets known to be derived from specific drug offenses. This approach is followed by Article 6 of the (European) convention, although the latter applies to proceeds from any crime and contains, moreover, in paragraph 3 the option of criminalizing laundering also where the offender "a. ought to have assumed that the property was proceeds; b. acted for the purpose of making profit; c. acted for the purpose of promoting the carrying out of further criminal activity." This kind of approach is hardly conducive to a new standard practice by all states concerned and might even fall short of what is required for effective international cooperation in this field: if knowledge, intent or purpose is a

---

[124] *See* Explanatory Report to this Convention (Council of Europe, Strasbourg, 1985), p. 2, note 2, "Terms of reference of the Select Committee," *in fine*.

[125] Euro. Conv. Money Laundering, *supra* note 20.

[126] *Id.* at Arts. 2-4.

required element of money-laundering offenses and if international cooperation is restricted to the intentional commission of such offenses, there will be serious difficulties and all sorts of legal obstacles to such cooperation whenever it does not concern *prima facie* cases, i.e. offenses where the intentional element "may be inferred from objective, factual circumstances."[127]

From this point of view, the various principles of international cooperation, set out in chapter III of the Convention, are of particular importance. They include *inter alia* the states-parties' obligation to enact legislation enabling them to comply, under certain conditions, with both requests from other states-parties for confiscation of certain assets or property derived from such assets and requests for investigative assistance and provisional measures with a view to confiscation.[128] In case of a request for confiscation, the requested party shall either "enforce a confiscation order made by a court of a requesting party" or "submit the request to its competent authorities for the purpose of obtaining an order of confiscation and, if such order is granted, enforce it."[129]

The long list of grounds for refusal of such cooperation in Article 18 of the Convention as well as the frequent reference to the applicability of the domestic law of the requested party indicate rather clearly that international cooperation against laundering offences is not yet a routine matter of inter-state practice. The Convention contains, however, a noteworthy provision in its Article 15, which might become in the long run a major incentive for more forthcoming cooperation on the part of the states requested to that effect: unless otherwise agreed by the sarties concerned, "any property confiscated by the requested Party shall be disposed of by that party in accordance with its domestic law(!)" Yet, this rule might also prompt certain states to abstain from requesting the assistance of other states for the mere "fear" that huge amounts of illegally acquired funds moved out of their territory will be confiscated abroad and never returned.

Another interesting aspect of this Convention is the fact that its effective application requires considerable cooperation at national level between the enforcement agencies and the banking and financial sectors. Notwithstanding the traditional principle of bank secrecy,[130] banks and other financial institutions are indeed obliged henceforth to report certain suspicious financial transactions of their customers and to take a whole series of preventive measures aiming at the reduction of the risks of money laundering, such as the application of the "know your customer" rule, the habit of record keeping, and the improvement of the standards of the business and professionals conducting financial operations. In fact, the enhancement of the role of the financial system in both prevention and repression is likely to become the key element of a new multifaceted strategy against money laundering.

The Sea Traffic agreement[131] is the latest multilateral cooperation treaty in penal matters concluded within the Council of Europe framework and constitutes another attempt at improving, at the regional level, certain provisions of the 1988 U.N. Convention against illicit drug traffic. This follows, indeed, from the latter's Article 17, paragraph 9, which provides that "the Parties shall consider entering into bilateral or regional agreements or

---

127 *Id.* at Art. 6 ¶ 2c.

128 *Id.* at Art. 7 ¶ 2.

129 *Id.* at Art. 13 ¶ 1.

130 *Id.* at Art. 4 ¶ 1.

131 U.N. Sea Traffic Conv., implementing Article 17 of the United Nations Convention against Illicit Traffic on Narcotic Drugs and Psychotropic Substances, *supra* note 21.

arrangements to carry out, or to enhance the effectiveness of, the provisions of this article," which contains on its part a whole series of rules relating to illicit (drug) traffic by sea. The European treaty concluded to that effect is therefore essentially an "implementation agreement" conditioned on the prior ratification of the 1988 U.N. Convention, and there exists thus quite a difference between this agreement and the "free-standing" Laundering Convention referred to above.

Be that as it may, the Sea Traffic agreement concentrates on the following kind of scheme already envisioned by Article 17 of the 1988 U.N. Convention: a party to this agreement (the intervening state) is in possession of information leading it to believe that a vessel on the high seas belonging to another party (the flag state) is engaged in, or is used for, the commission of a drugs trafficking offense. The intervening state then requests confirmation of registry from the flag state and, if confirmed, the latter's authorization to intervene on board the vessel, to search it and, if evidence of involvement in illicit traffic is found, to take appropriate action with respect to the vessel, persons and cargo on board. Notwithstanding the basic obligation to cooperate to the fullest extent possible, the flag state which has preferential jurisdiction in such a situation, is entitled to refuse its cooperation in certain circumstances or to subject it to certain conditions, in particular the condition of the intervening state's responsibility for the planned action, its liability for any damages resulting therefrom and its obligation to eventually return the vessel, cargo, arrested persons and evidence to the flag state. Moreover, there might occur as well a situation where the flag state suspects that a vessel flying its own flag is engaged in illicit drug traffic, and therefore requests the assistance of another party better suited to that effect, in suppressing the use of this vessel for that purpose.

With a view to solving these main questions, the Sea Traffic agreement contains a comprehensive set of specific rules which are based to a large extent on the experience gathered from the negotiation and application of the preceding European penal law conventions, in particular those on mutual assistance and on transfer of proceedings and on money laundering. However, in accordance with the particular subject matter, there are also some entirely new principles governing this kind of inter-state cooperation, such as the rule of proportionality, which is reflected in particular in the provisions entitled "operational safeguards,"[132] or the rules concerning the "exercise of preferential jurisdiction," which provide *inter alia* that certain measures taken by the intervening state "may be deemed to have been taken as part of the procedure of the flag State" where the latter has made known its wish to exercise itself its preferential jurisdiction.[133]

The above-mentioned trend, which led over the last 15 years to the elaboration and adoption of some fairly comprehensive special conventions whereby the four general methods of European inter-state cooperation were applied to particular categories of offenses and/or offenders, would seem to raise two major questions. The first question is, of course, whether the conclusion of some of these new special conventions was required because of new, unforeseen circumstances and developments in transnational crime, or whether this was due to the failure of full and large-scale application of the general conventions establishing the European system of inter-state cooperation in penal matters. Be that as it may, if there

---

[132] *Id.* at Art. 12 ¶ 1, which reads as follows: "In the application of this Agreement, the Parties concerned shall take due account of the need not to endanger the safety of life at sea, the security of the vessel and cargo and not to prejudice any commercial or legal interest. . . ."

[133] *Id.* at Art. 14 ¶ 5.

is, as it appears, a distinct trend to replace the earlier general conventions by new special conventions, this prompts a second question: will this new trend not diminish considerably both the interest to ratify the general conventions for states not yet having done so and the likelihood of their full application as a matter of daily routine by most, if not all Council of Europe Member States? With a view to replying to these two questions, a closer evaluation of the significance of these European penal law conventions as a whole and of their over-all application in practice is surely required.

Evaluation of the Application of the European Penal Law: Conventions and Perspectives for the Future

There can be no doubt that, through the European Committee on Crime Problems (CDPC), the Council of Europe has made a considerable theoretical contribution to the many problems which the increasing transnational crime has created for its Member States. The solutions proposed by the government experts preparing and negotiating these European penal law conventions are based, essentially, on the assumption of the Member States' resolve to actively pursue a common and rational crime policy, on the one hand, and, on the other, on the assumption of the Member States' mutual trust and confidence in each other's legal system and standards. There is also no doubt that the scope of the European mutual cooperation in penal matters has been considerably extended over the years and that the modalities, methods and procedures of such cooperation were constantly improved. Yet, the crucial test of any mutual cooperation system is, of course, whether there is some tangible proof that it "fits" and can be applied and that it is, indeed, generally used in practice. This depends, first of all, on the state of ratification by the Member States of the various multilateral treaties establishing the European system. For this reason, the over-all ratification of these treaties by the Member States appears as the obvious criterion for evaluating their practical significance.

It appears from the appended state of ratification of the 20 European penal law conventions referred to above that by the end of January, 1996, only five of them have been ratified by more than 20 of the present 38 Member States: these are the multilateral treaties on extradition (27 ratifications), on mutual assistance (24 ratifications), on terrorism (23 ratifications), on information on foreign law (24 ratifications) and on the transfer of sentenced persons (28 ratifications). The three additional protocols to the Extradition and to the Mutual Assistance Conventions, for example, European Treaty Series Numbers 86, 98 and 99, have been ratified respectively, by 14, 20 and 17 Member States. As regards the remaining 12 treaties, four have not yet entered into force (European Treaty Series Numbers 71, 82, 119, 156) and none of the eight treaties which have entered into force has been ratified up to now by a mere dozen Member States. It is true that all these treaties have been signed, moreover, by many other Member States expressing, thereby, their intention to also ratify them in future, but, in the light of past practice and experience, this is no genuine indication that many more ratifications will indeed take place within the near future. From this point of view, too, one might reasonably conclude that the over-all state of ratification of these European penal law conventions is rather disappointing and surely well below the level expected at the time of their conclusion.

Insofar as Member States never ratify at the same time a given European treaty, there exists, too, a considerable difference among the states-parties as regards the date from when they are subject to the application of the treaty concerned. Furthermore, many contracting states have made important reservations regarding the application of some of the European treaties ratified by them. It follows that, such as it was established, the European system of inter-state cooperation in penal matters can neither be applied by all Member States—due to the failure of some of them to ratify all the relevant treaties—nor be applied to its full extent by all the states-parties to certain treaties—due to the decision of some of them to reserve, i.e. to exclude as far as they themselves are concerned, the application of certain parts of the treaties ratified by them. The limited applicability—*ratione materiae*, *ratione personae* and *ratione temporis*—of these treaties implies that their actual application in European inter-state practice is necessarily restricted, too.

There are several objective explanations, if not entirely convincing justifications, as regards the surprisingly low level of ratification of the European penal law conventions. First of all, the 15 states which have acceded to the Council of Europe over the last five years and which are all, but one, eastern and central European states, need obviously some time for profound and vast changes in their domestic law and practice to enable them to ratify a significant number of these European treaties. Similarly, because any national ratification process usually takes some time, one can hardly expect the two European treaties concluded within the last five years to be ratified already by a very large number of states—even if the fight against illicit drugs traffic and, in particular, money laundering is allegedly considered a high political priority all over Europe.

Second, it must be recalled in this respect that states which have already ratified all the "general" conventions, including those on transfer of enforcement and on transfer of proceedings, have no need, from a theoretical point of view, to ratify as well some "special" conventions such as the Supervision Convention, the Road Traffic Offences Convention, the Deprivation of Driver's Licence Convention and even the Transfer of Sentenced Persons Convention—unless they wish to cooperate with states which are only parties to some of these special conventions. Similarly, some states-parties to such special conventions will only consider ratification of certain general conventions if, on that basis, they wish to cooperate with other states which are only parties to such general conventions.

Third, it might well be that the objectives pursued in the preparation of several European conventions were either too ambitious or overtaken by subsequent events and/or developments in the domestic law and practice of the Member States, which led some of them to conclude that their ratification of these conventions was of no particular practical interest and urgency, the conventions going either too far or not far enough. This might explain why the Repatriation of Minors Convention, the convention on statutory limitations and the Cultural Property Convention have not been ratified by the minimum number of states required for these conventions to enter into force. It might explain as well why the two, innovative, general conventions of the early 1970s, that on the transfer of enforcement and that on the transfer of prosecution, have been ratified so far by only nine and ten states, respectively. The latter two treaties, it should be recalled, were concluded a quarter of a century ago in the firm belief that they reflected genuine modern crime policy, and in the earnest hope that they become the very pillars of future Western European cooperation in penal matters. Did they fall victim to the persisting principle of national sovereignty they were supposed to overcome in certain respects? Or is the failure of their full and large-scale ratification and application due to the "fading myth" of the principle of "social rehabilitation in the State of residence," which prompted to some extent their preparation? The latter explanation appears *prima facie* contradicted by the great "success" of the Transfer of Sentenced Persons Convention.

In the light of this, another, fourth explanation of the relatively low level of overall ratification of the European penal law conventions could thus rest on the following, rather astonishing "discovery:" in practice, transnational crime in Europe is far from being important and alarming enough nowadays to warrant serious inter-state cooperation if such cooperation implies either the modification of sacred national traditions or restrictions to the sovereign power of prosecution and punishment. Yet, such an explanation would be at variance with the fact that transfer of proceedings as well as transfer of enforcement are methods of inter-state cooperation which were built again into the more recent European penal law conventions and are intended, indeed, for wide future use. For the same reason, it would be difficult to argue that the two main assumptions and fundamental prerequisites for European cooperation in penal matters, that is, the Member States' resolve to actively pursue a common and rational crime policy and their mutual trust and confidence in each other's legal standards—even in case of fiscal and political matters—are less well established than expected and that this might explain the apparent difficulty of rallying in some states enough political support by the executive and legislative authorities for enacting the national legislation required for the ratification of these European treaties. Unless this becomes a real political priority, the heavy workload of national parliaments, the frequent absence of clear-cut parliamentary majorities and government priorities, and the considerable technical work required in the ministerial departments for the enabling legislation to be enacted will all contribute to the continuing postponement of the ratification of these conventions.

There is yet another, last explanation which seems more plausible to this author: most practitioners, including police officers, prosecutors, judges, attorneys and even many government officials called upon to prepare the enabling legislation prior to the ratification on an international treaty, either ignore the great potential of the established European cooperation system or consider this system far too complicated and piecemeal to wish it to be fully implemented in the domestic law and practice by the speedy ratification of all the European treaties concerned. The absence of permanent and concerted pressure by the practitioners of inter-state cooperation is all the more relevant in this respect because, as indicated above, Member States are entirely free to decide, according to each state's national interests and domestic law requirements, whether or not to ratify anyone of the treaties concluded within the Council of Europe's institutional framework. In practice, states will only then ratify an international treaty dealing, for instance, with fiscal offences or with the illicit traffic in cultural property, when they have a well-known and genuine interest to do so and are likely to get something worthwhile out of its ratification.

Be that as it may, it remains to be stressed that the very aim of multilateral cooperation is, or should be, that the solutions worked out in common be applied jointly by all those who participated in the preparation and negotiation process. This, after all, is the reason why the conventions are elaborated in common in a lengthy and expensive process consisting of six to eight meetings of government experts from all the Member States, why the conventions contain the possibility of reservations for states which cannot accept all the obligations foreseen, and why the final texts agreed upon by the government experts as well as the opening of the conventions for signature are subject to qualified majority votes at the political level of the Council's Committee of Ministers.

There still exists, moreover, at least officially, a consensus among the Member States that these treaties are intended to be ratified by all of them and that each of them is called upon under the Council's general rules and practice, at least to consider how and when to do so. This is reflected in the standing practice of the European Committee on Crime Problems (CDPC) to proceed, at each of its annual plenary sessions, to a general exchange of views on signatures and ratifications of these Conventions and to a detailed examination of one specifically selected European treaty with regard to which the national delegations from the states which have not yet ratified the treaty under consideration, have to indicate any progress on the matter in their corresponding legislative procedures or their specific difficulties impeding ratification of the treaty concerned. This also explains why the CDPC has set up a permanent "Select Committee on the Operation of European Conventions in the Penal Field (PC-R-OC)" and entrusted the latter with the detailed examination of all these treaties with a view to the smooth functioning of the established system of mutual cooperation. In this general context the government experts continue the preparation of new legal instruments, such as additional protocols to the existing conventions and, as the case may be, Committee of Ministers' recommendations on their practical application, which are aimed at both the application and the ratification of these treaties by all Member States.

Similar efforts are undertaken by the Council's Parliamentary Assembly which, at regular intervals, tends to remind the governments of the Member States which have not yet ratified certain conventions of the need to do so in the foreseeable future. Yet, despite these "institutional" calls at intergovernmental and at parliamentary level for general and speedy ratification of all the relevant European treaties, the pace of their over-all ratification is very slow, indeed, and is likely to remain slow also in the future for the various reasons explained above.

In addition to the fact that the pace of over-all ratification of the European conventions in penal matters is so far rather disappointing and likely to remain slow in future, there is another reason, already referred to, for justified concern about the future application of this European cooperation system. The number of legal instruments, i.e. the multilateral treaties and official recommendations on their practical application, upon which this system is based, is steadily increasing and the same is true as regards the national reservations and/or declarations by which some of the states-parties exclude the application of parts of the system as far as they are concerned. This entails that the whole system becomes more cumbersome and complex and that the practical application of the relevant treaties will become more difficult, too—to the point where, in the not too remote a future, the effective functioning of the whole European cooperation structure might be at risk, even if the over-all ratification rate were to increase significantly. An obvious illustration of such difficulties is the coordination between, and practical choice of, general and special conventions concluded at different times and yet applicable to the same subject matter in a concrete case. Indeed, as regards the European penal law conventions, the mere reference to the sacred maxims *lex specialis derogat generali* and *lex posterior derogat priori* is no longer of much use, particularly where a given matter between two states is dealt with in several general and special conventions to all of which the states concerned are parties: it might well be that the general convention was concluded after the relevant special convention, or that the special convention is less specific than the preceding general convention, and that there is therefore no sound theoretical or practical criterion for choosing between two equally applicable international treaties in a specific case.

In the search for new remedies to these difficulties and for alternative solutions to the present piecemeal approach to European inter-state cooperation in penal matters, this author has pleaded persistently in favor of the merger of the relevant special and general conventions, including their additional protocols, and the redrafting of the combined new texts in the light of the various recommendations on the practical application of these treaties. By considerably simplifying the application of all the treaties concerned, such an approach would surely enhance their wider ratification, improved implementation and smooth functioning. This kind of approach was in fact examined by the CDPC in the early 1970s, but finally rejected, *inter alia*, for the fear that as long as such a merger exercise is not completed, the Member States which await the eventual outcome of such a merger may no longer wish to ratify those European treaties to which they are not yet a party.

As it turned out, the over-all ratification rate did not improve as hoped for in the late 1970s; instead, the number of newly adopted legal instruments in this field increased considerably and reinforced thus the above-mentioned concerns about the theoretical and practical difficulties the expanding European cooperation system would face as regards its application in future.

For these reasons, this author felt compelled, when he was put again in charge of the Secretariat of the CDPC in the early 1980s, to renew his plea for a consolidated comprehensive approach within the Council of Europe framework to inter-state cooperation in penal matters. The argument in favor of such an approach was much reinforced by the fact that similar steps had been or were being taken at the national level in three Member States: Austria, the Federal Republic of Germany and Switzerland were enacting comprehensive national legislation on international mutual assistance and cooperation in penal matters and this kind of national legislation, essentially based on the provisions in the relevant European treaties, could serve as well as a model for a comprehensive codification on the matter within the institutional framework of the Council of Europe—just as, at an earlier stage, the Scandinavian and Benelux legislations had served as a reference and as guidelines for the preparation of the corresponding European penal law conventions.

Moreover, in the light of the earlier failure in this respect, an exhaustive feasibility study had been completed already by a few eminent legal experts and scholars particularly interested in this matter. Thanks to the generous hospitality of the International Institute of Higher Studies in Criminal Sciences and the intellectual leadership of its President, Professor M. Cherif Bassiouni, these experts had met twice under the author's chairmanship in Siracusa, Italy, in May 1984 and in March 1986, and prepared a "preliminary draft of a comprehensive (European) Convention on inter-State cooperation in the penal field." This draft text, which has already been explained and published elsewhere,[134] streamlines and restructures all the relevant, existing European legal instruments while taking great care that the gist of the obligations contained in the latter as well as any exceptions thereto be faithfully reproduced in the new text so as to ensure that states subject to the new text would keep the same rights and obligations regarding mutual cooperation in penal matters as they used to have according to the treaties ratified by them so far. In other words, this text is restricted to a mere six, fairly short chapters: a general chapter on common provisions, applicable to all the four principal methods of inter-state cooperation in the penal field; four special chapters relating to these methods, i.e. extradition, mutual assistance, transfer of

---

[134] *See* MÜLLER-RAPPARD & BASSIOUNI, *supra* note 1, at 1661-88.

supervision and enforcement of foreign criminal judgments, and transfer of prosecution; and another general chapter containing the final clauses, in particular on the co-existence of the already existing European treaties and the newly proposed comprehensive European convention and on the latter's ratification and entry into force. According to the crucial proviso in this respect, a state might become a party to only that part of the new convention which corresponds, so to say, to the European treaties which it has ratified already.

This work was supported first by the "Third Conference on Crime Policy," held at the Council of Europe's headquarters in March, 1985, and then endorsed (in Resolution No. 3) by the "Fifteenth Conference of European Ministers of Justice," which took place at Oslo in June 1986. Acting upon the latter's recommendation, in September 1996 the Committee of Ministers of the Council of Europe instructed the CDPC to undertake the elaboration of a draft comprehensive European convention on inter-state cooperation in the penal field. A progress report on this matter was presented to the Sixteenth Conference of European Ministers of Justice, held in Lisbon in 1988, which, by its Resolution No. 5, recommended then the Council's Committee of Ministers "to accord high priority to this activity (and) to provide all necessary facilities to the Committee of Experts entrusted with the elaboration of the comprehensive convention, to enable it to complete its work as soon as possible."

Yet, despite all this very high-level support, the ongoing drafting work was stopped in June 1994 after almost a dozen meetings of the Select committee concerned, i.e. the PC-OC, and only shortly before the PC-OC, enlarged to all Member States, was to meet for the purpose of preparing its final draft of the so-called comprehensive convention! The official "administrative" reason for this decision was the Council of Europe's lack of financial resources at a time when priority had to been given to the smooth integration into the Council of newly, democratically reformed states of eastern and central Europe. Another more "substantive" ground was the difficulty to foresee whether the draft convention would be adopted by the Committee of Ministers in due course and then be ratified by a significant number of Member States. Since this author had by then again left the CDPC's secretariat, he can only guess about the pertinence of such a reason and the implied lack of governmental support for the speedy and successful conclusion of all the efforts undertaken so far. It would seem, *inter alia*, that several newly admitted Member States had started ratifying some of the existing European penal law conventions and that there was again a certain concern about such a trend being slowed down or interrupted by the ongoing "merger exercise." Be that as it may, the elaboration of a comprehensive European convention on inter-state cooperation in the penal field was not excluded definitely, but merely postponed in 1994: the CDPC has agreed, indeed, to review the matter at a future session, but not later than 1998, in the light of new developments, and this could imply that the merger exercise is taken up again and hopefully concluded by the end of the 1990s.

In this respect, the author is firmly convinced that, in case of an emerging pan-European inter-state cooperation in penal matters, the reasons mentioned above for the elaboration of a comprehensive general convention on the matter will be reinforced and drastically increased insofar as the existing piecemeal system will become ever more complicated and complex, in particular for the government officials in eastern and central Europe who are not familiar with such a system they are called upon to apply in practice. An illustration of this point of view might be the obvious difficulty to come to grips with money laundering, which is allegedly of major concern to all the present Member States. If, in a concrete case, the mutual assistance requested according to the Laundering Convention does not relate to an offense which, *prima facie*, has been committed intentionally in the requested state, the latter's authorities may or will refuse such a request according to their reading and implementation of Article 6 of this convention, notwithstanding all the principles in its subsequent articles in favor of the widest possible mutual cooperation. The requesting state may then have to rely on the pertinent provisions in the Mutual Assistance Convention and face another difficulty if the requested state has made certain declarations and reservations regarding the latter's application or has not yet ratified the relevant additional protocol thereto extending the obligation of mutual assistance to certain fiscal and financial matters. The difficulty of selecting an adequate legal basis for mutual cooperation in such a case and the likelihood of subsequent complicated, bilateral negotiations may even prompt the requesting state's authorities to abandon the case. Is this not a decisive argument for wishing to simplify, streamline and structure the existing cooperation system and to replace it by the adoption of a comprehensive, general convention on European inter-state cooperation in penal matters?

Securing Evidence Abroad: A European Perspective

Dionysios D. Spinellis

Introduction

The Problems

Criminal offenses affecting more than one country have increased in the last decades. International commerce, tourism and the mobility of the labor force have all contributed to this increase. However, it is the internationally organized crimes and the economic crimes which are producing the most difficult legal problems.

Courts and judicial authorities investigating and trying such cases often face the fact that evidence lies beyond the border of the state in which they function, requiring these authorities to find ways to take or gather evidence abroad.

This effort may be understood in a strict sense: the court or judicial authority concerned, or an official sent by them, may travel to the foreign country where the evidence is located and perform all the acts necessary in order to compile the evidence.

Taking evidence abroad may also be understood in a broader sense: it comprises the whole procedure by which a court or a judicial authority procures from a foreign country the information needed in order to prove or disprove the facts concerning the offense under investigation. It is in this broader sense that the subject is discussed here.

The task of taking evidence abroad or from abroad results in certain legal problems. First, courts and other judicial authorities usually have jurisdiction only within the territory of the state to which they belong. This problem may be solved, however, by provisions in the national laws prescribing ways in which such courts and authorities may proceed in order to take evidence abroad or from abroad.

The second and the most serious problem results from the international law principle according to which any exercise of power by one state on the territory of another state is prohibited, unless a rule to the contrary exists.[1] Therefore, the states have a right to prohibit any procedural acts engaged in by foreign authorities in the taking or securing of evidence on their own territory. In some countries the performance of procedural acts by foreign authorities, or on their behalf, is considered as usurpation of the sovereign functions of the local government, which in some cases is a criminal offense.[2]

A third problem arises when considering the taking of evidence abroad and the possible impact of this action on a person's individual rights. It may be argued that limiting all

---

[1] *See* Geck, *Hoheitsakte auf fremdem Staatsgebiet*, *in* 3 STRUPP-SCHLOCHAUER, WÖRTERBUCH DES VÖLKERRECHTS 795 (1962) and references to court decisions cited therein; D. NORDMANN, DIE BESCHAFFUNG VON BEWEISMITTELN AUS DEM AUSLAND DURCH STAATLICHE STELLEN 58-59 (1979) [hereinafter NORDMANN]; K.F. NAGEL, BEWEISAUFNAHME IM AUSLAND 18-19 (1988) [hereinafter NAGEL]. It is also provided expressly in some national laws. *See, e.g.*, § 59 of Austrian Law "über die Auslieferung und die Rechtshilfe" of 4-12-79 [hereinafter Austrian ARHG].

[2] A classical example is Art. 271 of the Swiss Penal Code, *see infra* note 9. About incidents in which usurpation of sovereign rights of one state led to its reaction, *see* Jones, *International Judicial Assistance: Procedural Chaos and a Program for Reform*, 62 YALE L.J. 520 (1953); Tigar & Doyle, *International Exchange of Information in Criminal Cases*, 1983 MICH. Y.B. INT'L LEGAL STUD. 62; NORDMANN, *supra* note 1, at 43.

procedural acts concerning an individual to those used in a certain territory corresponds to a right of such individual to be subject to the procedures only of a certain jurisdiction.[3] Other rights of the defendant, for example his right to confront the witnesses against him or his right to a personal secrecy sphere (such as attorney-client privilege), have also been invoked on certain occasions.[4]

Finally, a fourth problem is whether and to what extent evidence taken abroad under circumstances different from those provided by the normal procedure of the investigating court or other authority can be accepted and fully relied on by the court.

The Possible Solutions

The problems delineated above may be solved in one of the following ways:

(1) The court or other judicial authority needing the evidence located in the territory of another state may ask the corresponding authorities of that state to take or collect the evidence for them and in some way make it available to them. This is the procedure of letters rogatory and is sometimes called "active" judicial assistance.[5]

(2) The court or judicial authority may also address letters rogatory to its own consular authorities, which would then perform the necessary acts on behalf of the requesting authority. This course, however, is legally possible only if the state where the consular authorities are functioning either expressly permits it or silently tolerates it. Some authors have called this "passive" judicial assistance.[6]

(3) The court or judicial authority investigating the case may send one of its members or a designated official to the other country in order to perform the required procedural acts in the foreign territory.

It is obvious that in this procedure, like those described above, some form of cooperation from the state where the evidence is taken is desirable and in most cases necessary. It may take the form of either active or passive judicial assistance in the above sense. These methods of assistance belong to the so-called "small" or "other" judicial assistance,[7] that, together with extradition, constitute judicial assistance in the broad sense.

(4) Additionally, the investigating authorities may use any of several ways to proceed on their own, trying to make evidence from abroad available to them directly, without

---

3 Novella Galantini, *La Cooperazione Internazionale per la ricerca e l' acquisizione della prova, in* ARGOMENTI DI PROCEDURA PENALE INTERNAZIONALE 41, 66 (O. Doniniani ed., 1982) [hereinafter Galantini].

4 *See* Gerhard O. W. Mueller, *International Judicial Assistance in Criminal Matters, in* INTERNATIONAL CRIMINAL LAW 412 (Gerhard O.W. Mueller & Edward M. Wise eds., 1965) [hereinafter Mueller & Wise]; Markees, *The Difference in Concept Between Civil and Common Law Countries as to Judicial Assistance and Cooperation in Criminal Matters, in* 2 A TREATISE ON INTERNATIONAL CRIMINAL LAW 180-81 (M. Cherif Bassiouni & Ved P. Nanda eds., 1973).

5 Mueller & Wise, *supra* note 4, at 41. Antonio Brancaccio, *Metodi di Cooperazione e Assistenza Giudiziaria, in* DIRITTO PENALE INTERNAZIONALE 95 (1979) [hereinafter Brancaccio], using a distinction made by Italian jurists, calls it "bound" assistance. On the relation of the terms "judicial assistance" and "judicial cooperation," *see* Heinrich Grótzner, *International Judicial Assistance and Cooperation in Criminal Matters, in* 2 A TREATISE ON INTERNATIONAL CRIMINAL LAW 191 (M. Cherif Bassiouni & Ved P. Nanda eds. 1973) [hereinafter Grótzner].

6 Mueller & Wise, *supra* note 4, at 41; Brancaccio, *supra* note 5, at 96 calls it "free" judicial assistance.

7 In German: "'kleine' oder 'sonstige' Rechtshilfe," in French: "autres formes d' entraide" or "petite entraide." The term "other" is preferable to the term "small"; Robert Linke, *Aktuelle Fragen der Rechtshilfe in Strafsachen, in* NEUE ZEITSCHRIFT FÜR STRAFRECHT 416 (1982); NAGEL, *supra* note 1, at 35-36.

contacting the authorities of the foreign country. These ways include the use of consular authorities or a designated official, but without any assistance either passive or active on the part of the state where the evidence is taken. In this same category one may also include acts of individuals acting on commission of the investigating court or authority, but without any cooperation or assistance from the authorities of the state where the evidence is located.

(5) Finally, one can envisage a last possibility. Instead of taking the evidence abroad, the court or other judicial authority may bring the means of evidence to its own country. This method includes summonses to appear directed to witnesses, experts, or the accused person, transfer of persons in custody to the territory where the hearing takes place, and similar acts. However, this method is not covered by the subject of this article, since no evidence is taken abroad. This is rather just preparatory work, done to allow evidence to be taken in the country of the court or judicial authority.

Provisions Governing the Taking of Evidence Abroad

Provisions governing the procedure by which investigating authorities take evidence abroad and the method of making requests for judicial assistance by foreign states are contained in international treaties and conventions as well as in the national laws of many countries.

National laws often include provisions regulating these matters in the Codes of Penal Procedure[8] or in special laws.[9]

Additionally, most states have entered into bilateral treaties with other states, providing ways to facilitate the taking of evidence abroad in criminal matters. These treaties govern judicial assistance in both civil and criminal matters or only in all criminal matters, which usually includes extradition.[10]

---

[8] *See e.g.*, Arts. 457-461 of the Greek code of penal procedure [hereinafter Greek CPP]; and Arts. 723-729 of the Codice di procedura penale (Italian code of penal procedure) [hereinafter Italian CPP].

[9] *See e.g.*, the French Law of Mar. 10, 1927, "relative a l' extradition des ιtrangers," *reprinted in* DALLOZ, CODE DE PROCEDURE PENAL ET CODE DE JUSTICE MILITAIRE, 570-577 (1992-1993) [hereinafter French Law of Mar. 10, 1927], especially Arts. 28-35; the German *Gesetz όber die Internationale Rechtshilfe in Strafsachen* vom Dec. 23, 1982, *reprinted in* UHLIG & SHOMBURG, GESETZ ÓBER DIE INTERNATIONALE RECHTSHILFE IN STRAFSACHEN (1983), [hereinafter German IRG]; the Austrian ARHG, *reprinted in* ROBERT LINKE, ET. AL., INTERNATIONALES STRAFRECHT (1981); the Swiss *Bundesgesetz όber internationale Rechtshilfe in Strafsachen* of Mar. 20, 1981, cited after an English translation by Frei & Syssmann, edited by the Federal Office for Police Matters [hereinafter Swiss IMAC]; 28 U.S.C. § 1782 (1970); the United Kingdom Extradition Acts of 1870, §24 and 1873, § 5 [the latter hereinafter U.K. Extradition Act 1873] the Evidence (Proceedings in Other Jurisdictions) Act, 1975 § 5 [hereinafter U.K. Evidence Act 1975] and the Criminal Justice (International Cooperation) Act 1990, [hereinafter cited as U.K. Criminal Justice Act 1990]; the Canada Evidence Act, Can. Rev. Stat. § 43 (1970).

[10] Among the bilateral treaties the one between the United States and Switzerland, Treaty on Mutual Assistance in Criminal Matters, May 25, 1973, United States-Switzerland, 27 U.S.T. 2019, (1974 Bundesblatt II 592), [hereinafter U.S.-Swiss MLAT] deserves special mention, since it is the first such treaty between a common law country and a civil law one. Greece has entered into several bilateral treaties, especially with (former) socialist states or non-European states. The ones mentioned below are still in force, while some others, valid until recently, have been superseded by the adhesion of the corresponding country to the European Convention. These treaties have been ratified by Greek Laws and are published in the Government Gazette [hereinafter GG]: They are the treaties with: (former) Yugoslavia (still valid in the successor states), Greek Law 4009/59 (GG 238/59); Romania, Greek Law 429/74 (GG 178/74); Poland, Greek Law 1184/81 (GG 198/81); The (former) Soviet Union, (still valid in the successor states), Greek Law 1242/82 (G 44/82); Syria, Greek Law 1450/84 (GG 87/84); Albania, Greek law 2311/95 (GG 119/95); Tunisia, Greek Law 2312/95 (GG 120/95); [these treaties are hereinafter Greece-Yugoslavia Treaty, etc.].

A special kind of bilateral agreement is the "Lockheed Agreements", which have been concluded between the authorities of the United States and the authorities of various other states. It must be noted that these were not general agreements for mutual assistance in criminal matters between these states, but only provided for the exchange of technical evidence and for cooperation arrangements of limited scope between law enforcement authorities.[11]

Judicial assistance in taking evidence is also provided for by various multilateral conventions, one of the most important being the European Convention on Mutual Assistance in Criminal Matters of 1959 (European Convention).[12]

Among the other multilateral Conventions including provisions on judicial assistance in criminal matters, the following two are also worth mentioning: The Benelux "Treaty Concerning Extradition and Mutual Assistance in Criminal Matters" of June 27, 1962[13] and the "Convention Applying the Schengen Agreement" done on June 19, 1990 (hereinafter Schengen Agreement).[14]

Another framework of multilateral agreement on judicial cooperation is the so-called "Commonwealth scheme" between the Commowealth countries. This does not create binding international obligations, but rather an agreed set of recommendations for legislative implementation by each government.[15]

Some authors have raised the question whether a general international customary rule exists obligating states to render judicial assistance mutually, even without previous agreement. This question should be answered in the negative.[16] In the absence of such agreements or national laws, judicial assistance is to be granted only voluntarily, out of comity or courtesy, and often on the condition of reciprocity.[17]

National laws usually state that they are applicable only in the absence of international treaties or customs, or only if and to the extent that international agreements do not provide otherwise.[18] In the case where a treaty provision is applicable, national laws are of a

---

[11] Their exact title was: "Procedures for Mutual Assistance in Administration of Justice in Connection with the Lockheed Aircraft Corporation Matter." It should be noted that they also applied to bribery cases connected with other multinational corporations; *see* Bruno K. Ristau, *International Cooperation in Penal Matters: The Lockheed Agreements, in* MICH. Y.B. INT'L LEGAL STUD., 91-93 n.23; Francesco D. Riccioli, *L'accordo fra Italia e Stati Uniti etc.*, in LA RIVISTA DI DIRITTO INTERNAZIONALE 541 (1977); *see also* Brancaccio, *supra* note 5, at 97.

[12] Europ. T.S. No. 30 [hereinafter Euro. Mutual Assistance Conv.].

[13] Julian J. Schutte, *The European Market of 1993: Test for a Regional Model of Supranational Criminal Justice or of Interregional Cooperation in Criminal Law*, 3 CRIM. L.F. 77-80 (1991).

[14] About which *see* Schutte, *supra* note 13, at 80-82.

[15] David McClean, *Mutual Assistance in Criminal Matters: The Commonwealth Initiative*, 14 COMMONWEALTH L. BULL. 841-52 (1988).

[16] Brancaccio, *supra* note 5, at 192-93; Galantini, *supra* note 3, at 46; NORDMANN, *supra* note 1, at 33 and cited references; NAGEL, *supra* note 1, at 88-89.

[17] Moore, *Judicial Cooperation in the Taking of Evidence Abroad*, 8 TEX. INT'L L.J. 57 (1973); NORDMANN, *supra* note 1, at 33; De Capitani, *Internationale Rechtshilfe. Eine Standortbestimmung*, 115 ZEITSCHRIFT FÜR SCHWEIZERISCHES RECHT 381, 388 (1981); *see also* the "classical" definition of letters rogatory in the decision *The Signe*, 37 F. Supp. 819, 820 (E.D. La. 1941), *cited in* 12 TEX. INT'L L.J. 107, n.1 (1977) and NORDMANN, *supra* note 1, at 30, n.10.

[18] Italian CPP, *supra* note 8, at Art. 696 § 2; French Law of Mar. 10, 1927, *supra* note 9, at Art. 1. In the Greek CPP, *supra* note 8, at Arts. 457, 458 it is simply provided that international treaties and customs are also to be complied with. In case of conflict with provisions of common internal law, treaties that have been ratified by law prevail, GREEK CONST., Art. 28. Therefore, the internal law plays a subsidiary and supplementary role. The same is expressly provided by the Swiss IMAC, *supra* note 9, at Art. 1 § 1. *See also* De Capitani, *supra* note 17,

subsidiary and supplementary character. The European Convention provides that it supersedes the provisions of other treaties, conventions or bilateral agreements governing mutual assistance in criminal matters.[19] Therefore, in states that are parties to the European Convention, the priority of provisions on mutual assistance is as follows: In the first place the European Convention applies. Second, the bilateral agreements and obligatory international customs, if any, would apply.[20] Third, where no agreements exist, national laws and international comity apply.

In the remainder of this article, the procedure of taking evidence abroad with a view to the various systems of rules already referred to is discussed. The coexistence of so many different legal texts does not make it an easy task for one who attempts a systematic approach to this matter. The variety of legal systems in the various countries, and in particular the differences between common-law and civil-law systems, are factors that make this task more difficult. Since an exhaustive report within the scope of this article is impossible, only the most important regulations included in the legal texts available to the author are mentioned.

Who Requires the Evidence

Regarding requesting authorities, some national laws refer to "foreign tribunals" or "courts;"[21] others provide more generally for foreign judicial authorities,[22] while still others do not mention which authorities of the foreign state are competent to request assistance.[23] The European Convention refers to "judicial authorities"[24] as opposed to administrative authorities, but it also provides that each contracting party may by declaration define what authorities it will deem judicial.[25] From the declarations made by the various states it is seen that courts, investigating judges or magistrates, public prosecutors, and sometimes even chiefs of police are considered judicial authorities. Bilateral agreements very often use the term "judicial authorities," while the Lockheed Agreements often refer to "law enforcement agencies."[26] Therefore, the problem of whether letters rogatory may emanate from police

---

at 384; the Austrian ARHG, *supra* note 9, § 1; *see* Linke, *supra* note 7, at 417.

19 *See* Euro. Mutual Assistance Conv., *supra* note 12, at Art. 26 ¶ 1. Exceptions are provided, where bilateral agreements or other arrangements are more favorable to international cooperation, *id* at Art. 15 ¶ 7; or govern specific matters, *id* at Art. 16 and Art. 26 ¶ 2.

20 *See e.g.*, Italian CPP, *supra* note 8, at Art. 696; Mueller, *supra* note 4.

21 This used to be especially true with respect to the legislation of common law countries. *See, e.g.*, 28 U.S.C. § 1782 (1970); U.K. Extradition Act of 1870, *supra* note 9, § 24, the U.K. Extradition Act 1873, *supra* note 9, § 5 and the U.K. Evidence Act 1975, *supra* note 9, § 5; and Canada Evidence Act, Can. Rev. Stat., § 43 (1970). About the concept that previously prevailed in many countries regarding assistance from judge-to-judge, *see* Grótzner, *supra* note 5, at 189, 193- 94. More recently, however, there is a tendency to broaden the concept of the requesting authorities: U.K. Criminal Justice Act 1990, *supra* note 9, § 4(1)(a) and (b), *see also* U.S. Court of Appeals, D.C. Civ. Mar. 17, 1989 decision giving a broad interpretation to 28 U.S.C. § 1782 to include the U.K. Crown Service: 83 AM. J. INT'L L. 929 (1989).

22 Greek CPP, *supra* note 8, at Art. 458.

23 The Swiss IMAC, *supra* note 9, is an example. However, the provision that allows a possibility of appealing to a judge is useful, *id.* at Art. 1 § 3. Not specific is the wording of Italian CPP, *supra* note 8, at Art. 723 § 1.

24 Euro. Mutual Assistance Conv., *supra* note 12, at Art. 1.

25 *Id.* at Art. 24.

26 *See* Ristau, *supra* note 11, at 91; and Riccioli, *supra* note 11, at 541. *See also* Brancaccio, *supra* note 5, at 97-98 about the differences between the American and Italian negotiators of the Lockheed Agreement on the character of the U.S. Attorney General.

authorities is not solved in the same way by the various countries and the various texts. However, the general trend is to extend the use of letters rogatory to authorities other than just courts or tribunals.

It is important to note that in this regard the judicial authorities that investigate a criminal case are not only courts and investigating judges or magistrates but also public prosecutors and other authorities acting under their supervision.[27] It should also be noted that as a rule the laws of common law countries are more restrictive in this respect, giving authority only to courts or tribunals.[28] The activity and mutual cooperation of police authorities is not considered in this context[29] unless they are acting as auxiliaries of a public prosecutor, in which case the assistance will be requested under the authority of the prosecutor.

In the remainder of this article these various authorities will be referred to as "requesting authority" or as "investigating authority," as the case may be.

What Evidence May be Taken

Many national laws provide that in criminal proceedings all forms of evidence are permitted,[30] and it is possible that any one of them may be located abroad. However, situations in which the need for taking evidence abroad usually arises concern the hearing of witnesses, the interrogation of defendants, confrontations, reports on the scene of an offense, house visits, searches of premises, seizure of pieces of evidence or of specimens of handwriting for purposes of comparison by experts, procuring of other testing material

---

27 In some countries the public prosecutors are regarded as administrative authorities. *See* Committee on Crime Problems, Council of Europe, *Explanatory Report to the European Convention for Mutual Assistance in Criminal Matters*, 11 (1969).

28 *See, e.g.*, 28 U.S.C. § 1782 (1980), which refers to a "foreign or international tribunal;" U.K. Extradition Act of 1870, *supra* note 9, § 24 and U.K. Extradition Act of 1873, *supra* note 9, § 5 and the U.K. Evidence Act 1975, *supra* note 9, § 5 and Canada Evidence Act, Can. Rev. Stat. § 43 (1970) speak about a "court of tribunal." However, the more recent U.K. Criminal Justice Act 1990, § 4(1) includes "prosecuting authorities" and "any other authority which appears to him (the Secretary of State) to have the function of making requests of the kind to which this section applies." Most civil law countries apply broad concepts. *See, e.g.*, Greek CPP, *supra* note 8, at Art. 457 which provides for requests of "judicial authorities." The same broad wording is used by Italian CPP, *supra* note 8, at Art. 696 § 1, while Art. 30 of the French Law of Mar. 20, 1927, *supra* note 9, refers generally to "foreign authorities." The German IRG, *supra* note 9, § 59 specifies clearly that it is irrelevant whether the assistance is to be granted to a court or to another authority. The Austrian ARHG, *supra* note 9, § 50.2 speaks of "a court, a public prosecutor or an authority acting in the execution of penalties and measures." Further the Swiss IMAC, *supra* note 9, at Art. 75, provides that assistance may be requested by authorities who are "competent to investigate offenses" and also in other proceedings.

In spite of some hesitation, *see, e.g.*, Brancaccio, *supra* note 5, at 99 and Galantini, *supra* note 3, at 53, it is now accepted in most countries that the problem of taking evidence abroad concerns all judicial authorities both in the trial and pre-trial (investigative) phases. *See* Galantini, *supra* note 3. *See also* Jean Claude Lombois, DROIT PENAL INTERNATIONAL, Nz. 501, at 547 (1st ed. 1971); Mueller, *supra* note 4, at 414; and De Capitani, *supra* note 17, at 390. *See also* Euro. Mutual Assistance Conv., *supra* note 12, at Art. 24 which provides that each state may determine which authorities it considers "judicial." It is also significant that in the United States the courts have recently accepted that judicial assistance may be granted to bodies other than tribunals (foreign investigating magistrates, prosecutors) provided they enforce the process of a court. *See In re* Letter Rogatory from the Tokyo District, Tokyo, 539 F.2d 1216 (9th Cir. 1976) and *In re* Letters Rogatory from The Justice Court, Dist. of Montreal, Canada, 523 F.2d 562 (6th Cir. 1975).

29 Cooperation through Interpol cannot be considered as a form of judicial assistance.

30 *See e.g.*, Code de procédure pénale (French Code of Penal Procedure) [hereinafter C. PR. PÉN.], Art. 427; Greek CPP, *supra* note 8, at Art. 179.

for expert opinions, submission and verification of records or accounts, examination of experts, and collection of information as to the character of the defendant. Also, information on criminal records and other similar information should be included in this broad meaning of evidence.

Procedure of Letters Rogatory and Other Requests to Authorities of Other States

"Letters rogatory" is a mandate given by a judicial authority of a state where criminal proceedings are pending to a foreign judicial authority to perform one or more specified procedural acts in order to assist such proceedings.[31]

Scope of Application of this Procedure

The necessity of taking evidence abroad may occur both in the pre-trial phase of a criminal proceeding and during the trial. The texts, however, vary with respect to the scope of their application. The European Convention is applicable to proceedings in respect of offenses, the punishment for which is subject to the jurisdiction of the judicial authorities of the requesting party.[32] Bilateral treaties usually include similarly broad wording.[33] The scope of application of some national laws is described by reference to requests of "judicial authorities" and for "acts of instruction."[34] Other laws refer to "criminal proceedings abroad,"[35] or may even refer to other proceedings that are related to them.[36]

The acts required in the procuring of evidence that may be the object of letters rogatory are in some texts described in general terms;[37] in others, these acts are specifically

---

[31] Different definitions are given by the decision *The Signe*, 37 F. Supp. 819, 820 (E.D. La. 1941); *see also* Galantini, *supra* note 3, at 46 and Dussaix, *Some problems arising from the practical application from the judicial point of view of the European Convention on Mutual Assistance in Criminal Matters*, *in* EUROPEAN COMMITTEE ON CRIME PROBLEMS, COUNCIL OF EUROPE, PROBLEMS ARISING FROM THE PRACTICAL APPLICATION OF THE EUROPEAN CONVENTION ON MUTUAL ASSISTANCE IN CRIMINAL MATTERS 37, 41 (1971).

[32] Euro. Mutual Assistance Conv., *supra* note 12, at Art. 1 ¶ 1. This provision is interpreted in its broadest sense to include petty offenses and "Ordnungswidrigkeiten" (offenses punishable by fines imposed by administrative authorities, where the accused has a right of appeal to the ordinary court. Such offenses are provided by the legislation of certain countries, *e.g.*, Germany, Austria, Italy and Portugal. *Cf. also* Art. 50(a) of the Schengen Agreement).

[33] For example, the expressions "criminal matters" or "criminal affairs" are used in the bilateral treaties of judicial assistance in civil and criminal matters between Greece and other states, *supra* note 10.

[34] Greek CPP, *supra* note 8, at Art. 458; Italian CPP, *supra* note 8, at Art. 723 § 1 ("un autoritŕ straniera") and 727 § 1 ("dei giudici e dei magistrati del pubblico ministero").

[35] Swiss IMAC, *supra* note 9, at Art. 1(b); German IRG, *supra* note 9, § 59(1), (2).

[36] Austrian ARHG, *supra* note 9, § 50.

[37] The French Law of Mar. 10, 1927, *supra* note 9, refers generally to letters rogatory. The Swiss IMAC, *supra* note 9, at Art. 63 refers to acts necessary for proceedings carried out abroad in criminal matters. An indicative enumeration follows in Swiss IMAC, § 2. The Austrian ARHG, *supra* note 9, § 50 speaks of judicial assistance to a foreign authority. The German, IRG, *supra* note 9, § 59.2 speaks of "every support." The Euro. Mutual Assistance Conv., *supra* note 12, at Art. 1, refers to the widest measure of mutual assistance and speaks of procuring evidence or transmitting articles to be produced in evidence, Euro. Mutual Assistance Conv., Art. 3 ¶ 1. *See also* treaties mentioned by Levasseur & Andre Decocq, *Commission Rogatoire*, *(matiore penale)*, *in* 1 DALLOZ, ENCYCLOPEDIE JURIDIQUE, RIPERTOIRE DE DROIT INTERNATIONAL 356, No. 5 (1968); [hereinafter Levasseur & Decocq, *Commission Rogatoire*].

enumerated.[38] However, even in the latter the enumeration should be interpreted as exemplary only, and not exclusive of acts which are not expressly mentioned.[39]

Conditions Concerning the Offense

The offense for which the evidence is to be collected must usually fulfill certain conditions,[40] however, the various texts differ in this respect. One condition provided in some of them is that the act must be regarded as an offense by the law of both the requesting and the requested state, i.e. the condition of *double criminality*.[41] On the other hand, some modern texts do not include this condition,[42] while others require it only if compulsory measures have to be taken,[43] such as the summoning of witnesses under the threat of sanctions.

A further condition provided by some texts is that the offense for which evidence is requested must not belong to one of the three categories of offenses for which extradition can be refused: namely political, military and fiscal. The consequences, however, in the event that the offense belongs to one of these categories are not the same in all the texts containing these provisions and not the same with respect to all these categories. The European Convention and some other legal texts, for example, provide that they do not apply to military offenses[44] or to political offenses at all.[45] In the case of offenses that the requested party considers political, or offenses connected with a political or fiscal offense, some texts provide that assistance may be refused.[46]

---

38 *See* Greek CPP, *supra* note 8, at Art. 457; and Italian CPP, *supra* note 8, at Art. 96, 723, 727 (including also a general term: "rogatorie internazionali"). *See also* Greece-Yugoslavia Treaty, *supra* note 10, at Art. 35; Greece-U.S.S.R. Treaty, *supra* note 10, at Art. 3; Greece-Syria Treaty, *supra* note 10, at Art. 6 ¶ 2. Greece-Albania Treaty, *supra* note 10, at Art. 4. *See also* Levasseur & Decocq, *Commission Rogatoire*, *supra* note 37, (discussing similar treaties between France and other countries).

39 *See also* Levasseur & Decocq, *Commission Rogatoire*, *supra* note 37.

40 The Lockheed Agreements, due to their very limited character, were applicable only to ongoing or impending criminal investigations involving allegation of bribery of foreign officials by specific American multinational corporations. *See* Ristau, *supra* note 11, at 92.

41 *See e.g.*, Austrian ARHG, *supra* note 9, § 51, No. 1, Italian CPP Art. 724 § 5(b). The Greek CPP *supra* note 9, at Art. 458 § 3 may reach the same result by permitting the Minister of Justice to refuse the request if the conditions of extradition set forth in Arts. 437-438 are not met. Double criminality is one of these conditions, Greek CPP, Art. 437. The double criminality requirement is also provided as an optional ground of refusal of assistance in the Schengen Agreement Art. 51(a).

42 *See e.g.*, Euro. Mutual Assistance Conv., *supra* note 12, (unless reservation is made). The U.K. Criminal Justice Act 1990, *supra* note 9, makes it optional to refuse assistance if the offense relates to a fiscal offense (with exceptions). *See also* Brian De Schutter, *International Criminal Cooperation the Benelux Example*, *in* A TREATISE ON INTERNATIONAL CRIMINAL LAW 249, 253 (M. Cherif Bassiouni & Ved P. Nanda eds., 1973) and the German IRG, *supra* note 9, § 59. *See also* UHLIG & SCHOMBURG, *supra* note 9, § 59 No. 101.

43 *See e.g.*, Swiss IMAC, *supra* note 9, at Art. 64(c)(1); and Greece-Syria Treaty, *supra* note 10, at Art. 14(c)(2). *See also* reservations to the Euro. Mutual Assistance Conv. by several states under Art. 5 of the Convention. A complex method of enumeration of offenses and consideration of criminality under Swiss Law uses the U.S.-Swiss MLAT, *supra* note 10, at Art. 4 § 2(a), and *see* De Capitani, *supra* note 17, at 392-93; Bloem, *Treaty on Mutual Assistance in Criminal Matters between the United States and Switzerland*, 7 VAND. J. TRANSNAT'L L. 469, 474 (1974) Leonard Frei & Stefan Trechsel, *Origins and Application of the U.S. - Switzerland Treaty on Mutual Assistance in Criminal Matters*, 31 HARV. INT' L L. J. 84 (1990).

44 Euro. Mutual Assistance Conv., *supra* note 12, at Art. 1 ¶ 2.

45 U.K. Extradition Act of 1873, *supra* note 9, § 5; French Law of Mar. 20, 1927, *supra* note 9, at Art. 30.

46 Euro. Mutual Assistance Conv., *supra* note 12, at Art. 2(a). The same is provided indirectly in the Greek CPP, *supra* note 8, at Art. 458 § 3; *see also supra* note 35; and the Austrian ARHG, *supra* note 9, § 51 referring to the conditions of extradition. However, in the opinion of the author, letters rogatory for evidence should not be

Some modern national laws, however, reveal a trend to limit or abolish these restrictions altogether.[47]

Conditions Concerning the Prosecution of the Offense

Some national laws provided the condition that "proceedings have to be initiated," but this condition is not stressed in recent texts.[48]

The *rule of speciality* is also provided in some texts.[49] This means that the evidence taken by the authority of the requested state in response to letters rogatory may be used in the requesting state only for the investigation and trial of the offense for which such evidence has been requested.

Some texts provide that judicial assistance may be denied when the requested state is itself involved in the case for which assistance is requested. This involvement may entail only the fact that according to the law of the requested state, its courts have jurisdiction to prosecute and punish the offender.[50] Other texts, in accordance with the principle *ne bis in idem*, provide that proceedings must be already pending in the requested state or a third state regarding the offense to which the request refers, or that a final judgment on the merits has been delivered.[51]

In some regulations it is provided that the judicial assistance may be denied if, according to the law of the requesting state, or the requested state, or the state in which the offense has been committed, a fact has occurred which constitutes a legal ground for extinguishing the criminal nature of the offense, such as amnesty, statute of limitations or similar reasons.[52]

---

necessarily treated in the same way as extradition, since the former may result in evidence favorable for the defendant. *See also* Brancaccio, *supra* note 5, at 100. By contrast, the Schengen Agreement Art. 50 §§ 1 and 2 provides that the parties to it shall grant judicial assistance in certain categories of fiscal offenses.

[47] For instance, the Swiss IMAC, *supra* note 9, at Art. 63 § 5 provides that assistance shall be permitted in one or more of these categories of offenses if this will exonerate a person pursued. With respect to fiscal and economic offenses, Art. 3 § 3 provides that assistance may be granted if the subject of the proceedings is a tax fraud. See in regard to this concept and similar ones that must be distinguished from it, De Capitani, *supra* note 17, at 396-401. Finally, in Art. 3 § 2 it provides that the plea that an act is of a political character shall not be taken into account in cases of genocide, hijacking planes or other such crimes. The German IRG, *supra* note 9, § 59(3) does not mention conditions other than the ones under which German courts or authorities would grant assistance to each other. Therefore this law does not make judicial assistance dependent on the character of the offense, UHLIG & SCHOMBURG, *supra* note 9, § 59, No. 101.

[48] The U.K. Criminal Justice Act 1990, *supra* note 9, § 4(3), provides it only with respect to fiscal offenses and subject to exceptions. Otherwise, it is sufficient that a criminal investigation is being carried out (§ 4(1)).

[49] *See e.g.*, Greek CPP, *supra* note 8, at Art. 458 § 3: assistance may be refused if extradition is not allowed. This is the case when it is probable that the person extradited will be prosecuted for an offense different from the one for which extradition or assistance is requested. The Swiss IMAC, *supra* note 9, at Art. 67 § 1(2) makes any further use of information obtained subject to approval by the Federal Office. *See also* U.S.-Swiss MLAT, *supra* note 10, at Art. 5 ¶ 1, and Swiss reservation under Art. 2 of the Euro. Mutual Assistance Conv., *supra* note 12.

[50] *See e.g.*, Greek CPP, *supra* note 8, at Arts. 458 § 3, 438(b).

[51] *See e.g.*, Swiss IMAC, *supra* note 9, at Art. 4 (request shall not be granted) and Art. 66 (assistance may be denied). *See also* reservations under Art. 2 of the Euro. Mutual Assistance Conv. by Norway, Denmark, Netherlands, Switzerland, Sweden, Belgium, Luxembourg and Finland.

[52] Compare Greek CPP, *supra* note 8, at Art. 438(d), taken in conjunction with Art. 457 § 1(c). The Euro. Mutual Assistance Conv. does not mention this condition. In serious cases, however, where the prosecution of an offense already barred seems unjust, the *ordre public* clause may be invoked; *see* De Capitani, *supra* note 17, at 417.

Either expressly or by reference to the provisions governing extradition,[53] some texts allow their authorities to refuse to render judicial assistance if the defendant is a national of the requested state. This condition, however, is seldom invoked as a ground for refusal.

In some texts the *principle of proportionality* as a condition of granting judicial assistance is either expressly provided or implicitly invoked.[54] It means that the requested authority may grant the assistance requested, provided that the harm caused by it, especially to private interests, is not out of proportion to the purpose for which assistance is requested. More specifically the measure requested must be convenient, necessary and not avoidable by the use of a milder measure.[55]

A negative prerequisite included in almost all the texts is that the request is not one that would be likely to prejudice such general principles as the sovereignty, security, *ordre public* or other essential interests of the requested country.[56] These conditions are of a general character and can be interpreted freely by the competent authorities of the requested state.

It is reasonable to assume that once all the substantial conditions provided for by the system of rules of a certain text are fulfilled, the granting of judicial assistance is obligatory for the requested state. However, this is so only where international conventions and treaties exist.[57] National laws often provide that they do not confer a right to demand judicial assistance.[58]

While it is evident that international agreements obligating states to grant judicial assistance are based on reciprocity,[59] in situations where no such agreement exists, states

---

53 *See e.g.*, Greek CPP, *supra* note 8, at Arts., 458 § 3, 438(a); Greece-Yugoslavia Treaty, *supra* note 10, at Art. 35 § 2.

54 Expressly in Swiss IMAC, *supra* note 9, at Art. 4, and implied in Art. 74 § 1. Implicitly it is applicable in as much as the national laws in general govern the manner in which letters rogatory are executed and this principle is recognized by the laws of certain states.

55 *See* De Capitani, *supra* note 17, at 415-16.

56 This is the wording of the Euro. Mutual Assistance Conv., *supra* note 12, at Art. 2(b), of the Schengen Agreement Art. 51(b) and of most bilateral treaties, *see*, *e.g.*, U.S.-Swiss MLAT, *supra* note 10, at Art. 3 ¶ 1(a). *Cf.*, De Capitani, *supra* note 17, at 412; and numerous treaties between France and other countries. *Cf.*, Levasseur & Decocq, *Entraide judiciaire (matiore penale)*, in I DALLOZ, ENCYCLOPEDIE JURIDIQUE, REPERTOIRE DE DROIT INTERNATIONAL 751, No. 25 (1968) [hereinafter Levasseur & Decocq, *Entraide Judiciaire*]; Greece-Yugoslavia Treaty, *supra* note 10, at Art. 34 § 1; Greece-Rumania Treaty, *supra* note 10, at Art. 6; Greece-Poland Treaty, *supra* note 10, at Art. 13 § 1; Greece-U.S.S.R. Treaty, *supra* note 10, at Art. 12; and Greece-Syria Treaty, *supra* note 10, at Art. 14 § 1(a). Similar provisions are also included in national laws: Swiss IMAC, *supra* note 9, at Art. 1 § 2; German IRG, *supra* note 9, § 73; Austrian ARHG, *supra* note 9, § 51 (in conjunction with §§ 2 and 3); Italian CPP, *supra* note 8, at Art. 723 §§ 1 and 2. On the interpretation given to these clauses in various countries *see* De Capitani, *supra* note 17, at 412 and Levasseur & Decocq, *Entraide Judiciaire*, *supra* this note, at No. 25.

57 Of course the *ordre public* clause and the other general clauses mentioned above give the requested state wide latitude in refusing assistance. But it can only do this by invoking these principles and as a rule it has to *motivate* the refusal.

58 Express provision to this effect is included in Swiss IMAC, *supra* note 9, at Art. 1 § 4; and the Austrian ARHG, *supra* note 9, § 50; *see* LINKE, ET. AL., *supra* note 9, at 68; German IRG, *supra* note 9, § 59; *see also* UHLIG & SCHOMBURG, *supra* note 9, at 165 and French Law of Mar. 10, 1927 *supra* note 9, at Art. 30; *see also* Levasseur & Decocq, *Entraide Judiciaire, supra* note 56, at No. 7 which are also interpreted in this way. The wording of U.K. Extradition Act 1873, *supra* note 8, § 5 and U.K. Criminal Justice Act 1990 § 4(2) ("may"); 28 U.S.C. § 1782 ("may"); Canada Evidence Act, Can. Rev. Stat., § 43 (1970) ("may in its own discretion"), lead to the same interpretation. The wording of Greek CPP, *supra* note 8, at Art. 458 § 3 and Italian CPP, *supra* note 8, at Art. 723 § 1 is such that, as this author interprets them, if none of the obstacles contained in them can be invoked, the requested state is obliged to grant the assistance. *See* Brancaccio, *supra* note 5, at 100 who states that Italian courts had accepted this view previously but now reject any legal obligation theory.

59 *See, e.g.*, Euro. Mutual Assistance Conv., *supra* note 12, at Art. 23 ¶ 3 which is based on this principle.

usually grant their judicial assistance on the condition that the requesting state guarantees reciprocity.[60]

Procedure in General

International Stage: If no special provisions of international agreements provide otherwise, letters rogatory and other requests for assistance must generally be transmitted through diplomatic channels.[61]

This mode of communication permits a better appreciation of *ordre public* grounds for refusal of the request[62] and reduces the risk of errors and other irregularities. Yet this mode is cumbersome and time consuming.[63] For this reason the possibility of communication between Ministries of Justice and even directly between the authorities concerned is sometimes preferred.[64]

The European Convention provides for communication between the Ministries of Justice of the states concerned, and, in certain cases of urgency, for communication between the judicial authorities of the requesting and the requested parties.[65] Similar provisions are included in many bilateral treaties.

In certain countries, due to local legal conditions, it may be preferable to forward the request directly to the court concerned through the local consular authorities of the requesting country.[66]

Most texts have similar provisions concerning the contents of the requests for judicial assistance in taking evidence abroad. According to these provisions, requests must indicate the authority making the request, the object and the reason for the request and, where possible, the identity and the nationality of the person concerned.[67] In certain texts it is provided that information concerning the offense which is the object of the investigation shall also be included.[68] This is a reasonable prerequisite for several reasons, one of them being that it would not be possible to determine whether there were any grounds for refusal of assistance, based on the character of the offense, without such information.

The object of the request is to have the requested evidence collected. The reasons for the request are the circumstances for which the taking of evidence in the territory of the requested state is necessary. It should be noted that before requesting such judicial assistance, the requesting authority must have adequate suspicion with respect to the offense and the person concerned. The act requested should be aimed toward corroborating a

---

60 Italian CPP, *supra* note 8, at Art. 723 § 4, Greek CPP, *supra* note 8, at Art. 461 § 2. *See also* Jones, *supra* note 2, at 532-34; De Capitani, *supra* note 17, at 418.

61 *See e.g.*, Italian CPP, *supra* note 8, at Art. 727 § 1; and Greek CPP, *supra* note 8, at Art. 457.

62 Levasseur & Decocq, *Entraide Judiciaire*, *supra* note 56, at No. 31.

63 *Id.*

64 *See* De Schuter, *supra* note 42, at 253, 255. *See also* Galantini, *supra* note 3, at 49-51, and Brancaccio, *supra* note 5, at 101 (discussing the various systems of communication).

65 Euro. Mutual Assistance Conv., *supra* note 12, at Art. 15; also Schengen Agreement Art. 53 § 1.

66 *See* Mueller, *supra* note 4, at 480, referring to the practice in the United States (at least as of 1965).

67 Euro. Mutual Assistance Conv., *supra* note 12, at Art. 14 and treaties referred to *infra* note 68.

68 For example, the treaties between Greece and Rumania *supra* note 10, at Art. 12; Greece-U.S.S.R. Treaty, *supra* note 10, at Art. 5, Greece-Syria Treaty, *supra* note 10, at Art. 8. Greece-Albania Treaty, *supra* note 10, at Art. 5. Also the treaties between France and other countries mentioned by Levasseur & Decocq, *Entraide Judiciaire*, *supra* note 56, at No. 39. *See also* U.S.-Swiss MLAT, *supra* note 10, at Art. 29 ¶ 1(a) and Swiss IMAC, *supra* note 9, at Art. 28 § 1(c).

suspicion against an identified offender with regard to clearly described circumstances. Therefore, the request should be based on certain already existing evidence and not used as a means for deciding whether any grounds for suspicion exist or whether pieces of evidence exist. Requests for so-called "fishing expeditions," for example, "to find out whether an offense has been committed" or "if a bank officer or a bank has any information which would make worthwhile the submission of a formal request . . ."[69] should not be the object of letters rogatory.

The texts usually include provisions concerning the language in which the request should be made.

In some states a court decision or an order of a court or another authority[70] is necessary before the request is granted. The court or the other authority then determines whether the conditions provided in the applicable provisions are fulfilled.[71]

Internal stage: As a rule, the procedure by which letters rogatory are executed is governed by the law of the requested state (*locus regit actum*). This is reasonable, since the commissioned judges or officers are most familiar with their own procedure while they are usually unfamiliar with the procedure of the requesting state.

A problem sometimes raised is whether this procedure is a criminal or an administrative one. Against the first view, that it is a criminal procedure, it can be argued that there is no criminal case pending in the requsted state, even though the criminal procedure of such state is intended to regulate such cases. On the other hand, the administrative procedures are totally irrelevant to the criminal character of the matter. The most convincing view is that the judicial assistance is a procedure *sui generis*, by which evidence is taken in aid of a criminal proceeding pending before a foreign court. Therefore, the *criminal* procedure rules of the requested state are the most appropriate ones for these cases, because they regulate similar domestic matters.[72]

The act of taking the evidence requested may not be permitted or feasible, in whole or in part, according to the domestic provisions of the requested state. National laws and treaties provide in these cases the following alternatives: If the act is not permitted or is

---

69 *See* De Capitani, *supra* note 17, at 433; Dussaix, *supra* note 31, at 41. Besides, treaties provide for "specified" procedural acts, e.g. Greece-Syria Treaty, *supra* note 10, at Art. 6. The U.S.-Swiss MLAT, *supra* note 10, at Art. 1 ¶ 2 provides that the initiating state must have a reasonable suspicion that an offense has been committed; *see also* Bloem, *supra* note 43, at 474. On the limits of "pre-trial discovery" or "fishing expeditions" in England and Canada, *see* Moore, *supra* note 17, at 68.

70 These orders may be subject to appeals. On such appeals under Swiss law *see* De Capitani, *supra* note 17, at 464-74.

71 Italian CPP, *supra* note 8, at Art. 724 provides that such a procedure is necessary in all cases (with the exception of the service of summons to witnesses). According to German IRG, *supra* note 9, §§ 60 and 61, a distinction is made between the authority competent to approve the request (usually a court, in case of refusal, a higher court) and the authority competent to execute it. Greek CPP, *supra* note 8, at Art. 458 § 3 only grants to the Minister of Justice the authority to refuse the request following an opinion of the appellate court (in camera). The Austrian ARHG, *supra* note 9, § 55, provides that a court is competent both to approve and to grant the request. In the U.S., 18 U.S.C. § 1782 provides that the district court may order a person to give his testimony or produce documents before a person appointed by the court. A similar provision is included in the Canada Evidence Act, Can. Rev. Stat. § 43, (1970). In the U.K. the Secretary of State or in Scotland the Lord Advocate nominate a court to receive the evidence requested, U.K. Criminal Justice Act 1990, *supra* note 9, § 4(2). By Swiss IMAC, *supra* note 9, at Art. 78, the Federal Office for Police Matters examines whether the request meets the formal requirements; *see also* De Capitani, *supra* note 17, at 419.

72 *See* De Capitani, *supra* note 17, at 420-21; Grótzner, *supra* note 5, at 194, and Markees, *supra* note 4, at 175.

impossible under national laws, then the assistance must be refused.[73] If the act is only partly permitted, it may be performed only in part, for example, a witness may testify only on matters not falling under his professional secrecy as a doctor, lawyer, or clergyman. If the act is both feasible and permitted under the domestic law, it is executed in the manner provided by such law. Other issues to be decided on the basis of national law include the extent of the rights of the parties, including the question of who should be considered as a party to the judicial proceedings. Also, decisions regarding restrictions on the taking of evidence based on national interests, human dignity, personal and financial privacy, and professional secrecy should be based on national law.[74]

Under some legal systems, the restrictions based on personal and financial privacy and professional secrecy are related to the requirement of banking secrecy, which in certain countries is particularly protected. This is especially true in Switzerland. However, in criminal proceedings before a Swiss federal tribunal this secrecy requirement does not prevent the banker from testifying; he is required to testify, but only in regard to facts directly related to the matter being investigated.[75] This same rule is applicable if he is interrogated in compliance with letters rogatory of a foreign authority.[76] With respect to taxation offenses, judicial assistance may be granted only in cases of duty or tax fraud, and only then may the banker be required to testify.[77]

Sometimes the requesting country may express the desire that in taking evidence certain additional procedures are observed. Such a desire should be respected as far as possible because the evidence is to be used in the courts of the foreign state, and it should be taken in a manner acceptable to them. In these cases the requested authority should comply with this desire, provided that the procedures are, though not prescribed by its domestic law, at least not incompatible with it. An example of this is the oath of witnesses and experts, which is expressly provided in several treaties.[78]

A problem may arise with regard to the presence of the person accused, or other parties, at the examination of a witness or expert by an investigating judge. In some states the parties to the proceedings have the right to be present in all acts of investigation,[79] and in others this is a constitutionally guaranteed condition of every examination of witness.[80] In other countries the presence of the parties during interrogations before the investigating judge is

---

73 *Cf.* Italian CPP, *supra* note 8, at Art. 723 §§ 1 and 2, 724 § 5, and Greek CPP, *supra* note 8, at Art. 458 § 1. *See* German IRG, *supra* note 9, § 59. 3, and Austrian ARHG, *supra* note 9, § 51.1, No. 3; Schengen Agreement Art. 51(b).

74 Italian CPP, *supra* note 10, at Art. 723 § 2. Markees, *supra* note 4, at 180-83 invokes the need to weigh the opposing interests and apply the proportionality principle according to the law of each country.

75 *See* Jean-Luc Aubert, *Quelques Aspects de la Portee du Secret Bancaire au Droit Penal Interne dans l' Entraide Judiciaire Internationale*, 1984 REVUE PENALE SUISSE 173; and Tigar & Doyle, *supra* note 2, at 64.

76 *See* Aubert, *supra* note 75, at 176-77.

77 *See* Swiss IMAC, *supra* note 8, at Art. 3 § 3; and Aubert, *supra* note 75, at 178-79.

78 *See* Euro. Mutual Assistance Conv., *supra* note 12, at Art. 3 ¶¶ 2, 3; more general clauses are included in the U.S.-Swiss MLAT, *supra* note 10, at Art. 9 ¶ 2; several treaties between France and other states referred to by Levasseur & Decocq, *Entraide Judiciaire*, *supra* note 56, at No. 45; the Greece-Rumania Treaty, *supra* note 10, at Art. 6; and also the Swiss IMAC, *supra* note 9, at Art. 765(b).

79 This is so in Switzerland. *See* De Capitani, *supra* note 17, at 446. *See also* Swiss IMAC, *supra* note 9, at Art. 65(a).

80 *See, e.g.*, U.S. CONST. amend. VI. *Cf.* the *Archina* case reported in Mueller, *supra* note 4, at 412.

not provided.[81] In such cases the general principle should apply, and the presence of the parties should be permitted if this is not incompatible with the law of the requested state.[82] In deciding on this incompatibility issue, the requested state should not demand or expect that its legal concepts be accepted by the requesting state[83] unless the difference in concepts would amount to an *ordre public* issue.[84]

Another important question concerning the procedure for the taking of evidence is whether foreign officials, representing the authorities of the requesting state, may be present at the various proceedings without taking any active part in them. If such proceedings take place in a public hearing there is no problem. Often, however, proceedings take place in the office of an investigating judge or another commissioned person, where only the persons provided by the law are present.[85] Therefore, the presence of foreign officials is an additional procedure which is to be followed only under the conditions mentioned above.[86] It should be noted, however, that some practical problems may be created by such presence. For instance, the foreign officials may be used later in their country as hearsay witnesses, when such testimony is permitted, based on their participation in the foreign proceeding. Additionally, they could testify with respect to cases other than the one prompting the request for assistance, and in this way the rule of speciality could be circumvented.[87] Therefore, in order to avoid such eventualities, corresponding guarantees should be undertaken by the requesting state.

A different problem would be whether the foreign officials could take an active role in the proceedings for taking evidence abroad, such as questioning the witnesses or experts, or studying files in order to select the documents connected with the case. Practical considerations may be invoked in favor of such participation. These officials are more familiar with the case being investigated than the commissioned judge or other officer of the foreign country who has a rather incomplete knowledge of the case based only on the letters rogatory. Moreover, if these officials are the judges who are trying the case, this practice is helpful in assuring that the principle of *immediacy of evidence* is observed. This active participation is not provided in the domestic law of many states or in bilateral treaties and thus would not be permitted. In some other states it is expressly provided in international agreements to which they are a party,[88] or it may be permitted by special act of the requested

---

[81] *See, e.g.*, Greek, CPP, *supra* note 8, at Art. 97 § 1 which provides that the parties may be present with counsel in every procedural act during the pre-trial phase of the proceedings, but not at the examination of witnesses and of the accused persons. In view of the above provision Greece has made a reservation to Arts. 4 and 11 of the Euro. Mutual Assistance Conv..

[82] *See* now Italian CPP, *supra* note 8, at Art. 725 § 2.

[83] *See* Grótzner, *supra* note 5, at 203, and Mueller, *supra* note 4, at 412, who refers to the *Archina* case, in which a court had upheld a contrary view.

[84] This should not be the case in the author's opinion in regard to the provision in the Greek CPP, *supra* note 8, at Art. 97 § 1. An argument in favor of this view is, that in Art. 219 § 2 of the Greek CPP the presence of parties at the examination of witnesses before the investigating judge is provided exceptionally, if they will not be able to testify at the hearing.

[85] *See, e.g.*, Greek CPP, *supra* note 8, at Art. 97 and *supra* note 81.

[86] Euro. Mutual Assistance Conv., *supra* note 12, at Art. 4 provides this expressly on the condition that the requested state permits it. Two additional treaties which Switzerland has concluded with Germany and Austria provide for an obligation of the requested state to permit the presence of foreign officials and even their right to ask complementary questions, *cf.* De Capitani, *supra* note 17, at 443. But, Greece has made a reservation with regard to this Article, believing that it is incompatible with Art. 97 of Greek CPP. *See also supra* notes 81 and 84.

[87] *See* De Capitani, *supra* note 17, at 440.

[88] Such are the "Lockheed" Agreements.

states. Since the involvement of foreign officials in these proceedings is an exercise of authority on the territory of that state, permission to be present and actively participate should be granted by a central authority of the requested state. Finally, in some countries the active participation is simply permitted by silent toleration.[89] A variation of this practice is that the court of the state where the case is pending travels abroad to take the evidence, without any assistance of the requested state other than its permission (passive assistance).[90]

The Various Procedures for Taking Evidence

Witnesses and Experts

The most common case of evidence taken in compliance with letters rogatory is the examination of witnesses. An important question is whether a witness who is unwilling to appear and give testimony may be compelled to do so. Several legal texts, by referring to the examination of witnesses provisions applicable in domestic proceedings, accept implicitly that coercion may be used in judicial assistance proceedings.[91] Other texts provide that compulsory measures may be used under certain conditions, such as when the double criminality condition is fulfilled or if the testimony would help exonerate the person pursued.[92]

The rules of the domestic laws determine whether the witness shall testify on oath or not. However, it may be provided that the requested state shall comply with the desire of the requesting state that the testimony is given on oath.[93]

Domestic provisions concerning professional secrecy or other reasons for which testimony may be refused also apply in these proceedings.[94] A request, which would entail the violation of this secrecy privilege may be considered as contrary to the *ordre public* of the requested state.

Experts are heard as witnesses in the common law states, while in the civil law states they are appointed by the court or the investigating magistrate. Under some domestic laws, experts submit their expert opinion in writing.[95] Therefore, in conformity with the above

---

[89] On precedents and experiences in Switzerland, *see* De Capitani, *supra* note 17, at 441-42. In trials against Nazi criminals it has been arranged between Germany and Israel that a judge or even a whole mixed tribunal would travel to Israel in order to participate in the interrogation of witnesses. A similar arrangement exists in Czechoslovakia. *See* NORDMANN, *supra* note 1, at 40-41. *See also* Krómpelman, *Bericht óber ein Kolloquium anlδsslich der konstituierenden Sitzung des Kuratoriums des Max-Planck-Instituts fór auslδndisches und internationales Strafrecht*, 79 ZEITSCHRIFT FÓR DIE GESAMTE STRAFRECHTSWISSENSCHAFT 390, 392-93 (1967).

[90] *See* Brancaccio, *supra* note 5, at 96.

[91] *See* the wording as to the application of the provisions of Greek CPP, *supra* note 8, at Art. 458 § 1(2); likewise, Italian CPP, *supra* note 8, at Art. 725 § 2. A different view supports Brancaccio, *supra* note 5, at 102 unless express provisions of treaties provide otherwise. *See also* Greece-Rumania Treaty, *supra* note 10, at Art. 16 (expressly), and treaties between Greece and the other countries mentioned *supra* note 10 (indirectly); the treaties referred to in Levasseur & Decocq, *Commission Rogatoire*, *supra* note 37, at Note 22 between France and other countries provide that witnesses are compelled to appear only after they refused to comply with a simple administrative notice to do so.

[92] *See, e.g.*, Swiss IMAC, *supra* note 9, at Art. 64.

[93] *See, e.g.*, Euro. Mutual Assistance Conv., *supra* note 12, at Art. 3 ¶ 2.

[94] *See* 28 U.S.C. § 1782 (a)(2) (1970). *See also* Markees, *supra* note 4, at 181.

[95] Greek CPP, *supra* note 8, at Art. 198 (in the pre-trial phase, while at trial it may be expressed orally); Italian CPP, *supra* note 8, at Art. 227 § 5 provides a written expertise in certain cases. *See also* Grótzner, *supra* note 5, at 204.

principle the examination of the expert will be made according to the *lex fori*. However, in this case special desires of the requesting state may be considered, such as a request that certain questions be put to the expert.

Examination of the Accused Person

Although it is doubtful whether the examination of the accused person can be considered as "evidence,"[96] it may still be the object of letters rogatory.[97] However, such an examination in some states is inadmissible as contrary to the principle of self incrimination.[98] Where it is permitted, it is accepted that no compulsive measures may be taken against the accused who refuses to be examined. Many states would consider it incompatible with the principles of their law if this examination would take the form of a testimony on oath.[99]

Local Inspection

The local inspection of certain places, such as the scene of an offense, is expressly provided by some legal instruments,[100] while others include it under the general concept of "acts of investigation."

Although local inspection may be performed by the commissioned judicial officer, the presence of officers of the authority of the requesting state is also of great importance, since it is this latter authority that must ultimately form a judgment relating to the places visited. If these officers do not attend the inspection, they will have only the report made by the commissioned foreign authority on which to base their decision.

A similar argument can be made relating to the inspection of documents and records conducted by the foreign authority alone, or in cooperation with an officer of the requesting state.[101]

Delivery of Articles to be Produced in Evidence, Especially of Documents and Records

The delivery of such articles is in certain cases provided expressly[102] within the general term of "acts of investigation." This type of evidence would include anything that has been used to commit the offense and anything that appears to be a product of it (*instrumenta vel producta sceleris*). Further, testing material for expert opinions such as blood samples, fingerprints, and specimens of handwriting, as well as documents and records of any kind must be included here.

If the articles or documents are in the possession of the requested authorities, they may be delivered without difficulty. It is sometimes provided that delivery will take place only

---

96 *See* Greek CPP, *supra* note 8, at Art. 178 which mentions among other forms of evidence only the confession of the accused, which has no specific evidentiary value, but must be weighed by the court. But, note that examination and confession of the accused are not the same.

97 *See* Grótzner, *supra* note 5, at 204, and Dussaix, *supra* note 31, at 41.

98 *See* Grótzner, *supra* note 5, at 204 with reference to U.S. CONST. amend. V.

99 *See* Grótzner, *supra* note 5, at 205.

100 *See, e.g. supra* note 35.

101 *See* NORDMANN, *supra* note 1, at 32.

102 *See, e.g.*, the treaties mentioned *supra* note 10; *see also* Greek CPP, *supra* note 8, at Art. 461 (on the condition of reciprocity).

on the condition that the delivered articles shall be returned to the requested authority.[103] In the case of documents, photostatic copies may be sent.

If, however, the articles or documents are still in private hands, letters rogatory must be sent asking the requested authority to either order the person in possession to produce them[104] or to seize them if the person refuses to comply with the order.[105]

Search and Seizure

Often the requesting authority combines the request for delivery of evidence with an application for a search warrant and for the seizure of certain articles, if they are found. Some national laws permit the requested authority to determine whether and to what extent the seized objects are of significance to the investigation of the requesting authority and to comply with the request only if the objects are significant.[106]

Sometimes national laws appear more "cooperative" than others: the German IRG Art. 67 provides that such articles may be seized by the local authorities even before receiving the request of the foreign state.

The European Convention provides for search and seizure in Article 5. This article permits reservations, so that the contracting parties can make the execution of such letters rogatory dependent on all or any of the following conditions: double criminality, the extraditable character of the offense, and the conformity of the requested act with the law of the requested party.

In cases of seizure of objects and documents the main question is always how to safeguard the rights of private persons. Since the delivered property must be returned to the requested state after being used for evidentiary purposes,[107] it can be claimed by such persons when it is returned.

Other Evidence, Especially Interception of Communications

As already mentioned, most legal texts do not enumerate specifically the forms of judicial assistance that will be granted, and, with respect to the texts which do so, it is accepted that this enumeration is not exclusive. Therefore, any other procedure for taking evidence not expressly mentioned may be delegated to the foreign authorities by letters rogatory.

The interception of communications is one act that may yield evidence, and may be the object of letters rogatory. In the framework of the European Convention, which does not specifically deal with such requests, problems of practical application have arisen. Some states apply Article 3, paragraph 1 of the European Convention, considering that any provisions in the law of the requested party are included within the words "in the manner provided for by its laws," and thus reserve the right to refuse requests of this kind on constitutional and other grounds. Other states comply with such requests on the basis of the

---

103 Greek CPP, *supra* note 8, at Art. 461 and Austrian ARHG, *supra* note 9, § 52(1).

104 *See, e.g.*, 28 U.S.C. § 1782 (a) (1970).

105 *See* Dussaix, *supra* note 31, at 42. Under 28 U.S.C. § 1782 (a) delivery may be compelled by a *subpoena duces tecum. See also* Grótzner, *supra* note 5, at 207.

106 Swiss IMAC, *supra* note 9, at Art. 74 § 1. The principle of proportionality also plays a role here. *See also* De Capitani, *supra* note 17, at 436.

107 Euro. Mutual Assistance Conv., *supra* note 12, at Art. 6 ¶ 2.

general obligation of Article 1. Finally, there are states in which such requests are considered as "letters rogatory for search and seizure of property" to which Article 5 is applicable.

Recommendation No. R (85) 10 of the Council of Europe[108] sets forth certain rules which should govern the mutual assistance in criminal matters in respect to letters rogatory for the interception of telecommunications. It includes provisions on reasons for refusal of the assistance, on addititonal contents of the request and on conditions of the execution of such letters rogatory concerning the use of the records. These provisions are not legally binding upon the member states, but they usually influence their legislations and the treaties.

More difficulties may be encountered by the use of letters rogatory for search and seizure related to bodily searches such as the taking of blood samples, handwriting specimens and fingerprints. Here the principle of proportionality in conjunction with the principles of human dignity must be considered in each case.

Criminal Records

The information received as the result of a request for extracts from and information related to judicial records can also be considered as evidence in a broad sense, since it helps the court to form an opinion on the personality of the accused person prior to sentencing. This obligation is expressly provided in Article 13, paragraph 1 of the European Convention. It is also found in many bilateral treaties.[109]

Other Information

The request may direct the requested authority to order a person or a legal entity to provide certain information in writing. In particular, banks may be ordered to give information concerning their customers. It is doubtful whether such written information is an acceptable form of evidence[110] however, it can have some other practical value. It can, for instance, provoke additional letters rogatory for the examination of witnesses and the production of documents.

Letters Rogatory to Consular Authorities

Under certain conditions, requests to take evidence abroad may be directed to the consular authorities of the requesting state that are present in the country where the evidence is located. The Vienna Convention on Consular Relations of 1963, Article 5(j) provides that consular authorities have the power to execute letters rogatory or commissions to take evidence for the courts of the sending state in accordance with international agreements; and

---

108 Adopted by the Committee of Ministers on June 28, 1985.

109 *See, e.g.*, Greece-Poland Treaty, *supra* note 10, at Art. 53 § 3; Greece-U.S.S.R. Treaty, *supra* note 10, at Art. 53; Greece-Syria Treaty, *supra* note 10, at Art. 47.

110 The Greek CPP, *supra* note 8, at Art. 178 enumerates only the "principal" forms of evidence; therefore other ones, not mentioned there, are not excluded. Whether written information of that kind may be considered as a "document" or as a kind of "written testimony without oath" is an open issue. For views of courts and legal scholars in Switzerland, where the problem has been discussed, *see* De Capitani, *supra* note 17, at 435.

in the absence of such agreements, in any other manner compatible with the laws and regulations of the receiving state.[111]

This course presupposes that the state where the consular authority is accredited approves or at least tolerates such proceedings. Some states permit them generally, without special approval being required each time.[112] Other states consider this action as a violation of their sovereignty. However, international treaties often allow the contracting parties to have witnesses, experts and accused persons examined by their own consular authorities if the persons to be examined are their own nationals, and no coercion is used on persons or things in order to take the evidence.[113]

Taking Evidence Abroad Directly

The procedures of international judicial assistance and the use of the consular authorities have certain disadvantages, as they are complicated and time-consuming. The most important problem associated with these procedures, however, is that the granting of judicial assistance depends on so many conditions, thus leaving the matter virtually within the control and sole discretion of the requested state. Besides, international treaties do not exist in many cases, or the existing treaties do not apply.

Therefore, it is not surprising that investigating authorities in various countries have attempted, with varying results, to produce evidence from abroad directly, that is without any kind of cooperation from the state where the evidence is located.

By the Use of Coercion

There have been cases in the past in which officers of one state have tried to procure evidence in the territory of a foreign state without the express permission or silent acquiescence of the latter. Such cases have not always been clearly criminal cases. They have been concerned with various forms of investigation on such matters as: currency offenses, the loyalty of the United States consular staff, custom duties violations, and conformity with banking or taxation laws.[114] These cases are of interest here because the problems would be the same even if they concerned clearly criminal offenses.

First, according to one opinion, if international agreements exist, only the procedures provided in the agreements should be followed;[115] however, it may also be argued that such a procedure is simply the preferred one among several allowable alternatives.

---

[111] Vienna Convention on Consular Relations and Optional Protocol on Disputes, Apr. 24, 1963, 21 U.S.T. 77, 596 U.N.T.S. 261 (entered in force Mar. 19, 1967). Greece has ratified it in Greek Law 90/1975, GG/150/1975. *See also* NORDMANN, *supra* note 1, at 30; Brancaccio, *supra* note 5, at 96, National Laws on consular services include corresponding provisions.

[112] For instance, the United States permit them even if the witness is an American citizen. *See* Mueller, *supra* note 4, at 420.

[113] *See, e.g.*, the treaties between France and other countries mentioned in Levasseur & Decocq, *Commission Rogatoire*, *supra* note 37, at No. 25.

[114] For a detailed report of such cases *see* NORDMANN, *supra* note 1, at 43-47. For other cases *see* Tigar & Doyle, *supra* note 2, at 61-63. However, the cases reported by them do not fall directly within the framework of this article to the extent that they consider the compelling of evidence abroad to be brought before the domestic authority.

[115] *See* NORDMANN, *supra* note 1, at 48. This view is based on an interpretation based on the rules of the Vienna Convention on the Law of Treaties of May 23, 1969 (ratified by Greek Law 402/1974, GG/141/1974).

If no international agreements exist, acts of investigation of this kind may be considered as violations of the obligation to respect foreign sovereignty or territorial jurisdiction. However, while this obligation is generally recognized as part of the international customary law, it is questionable as to what acts constitute a violation of this obligation.

It is evident initially that any kind of coercion definitely constitutes such a violation. Coercion here includes both physical force, such as the taking of documents against the resistance of their possessor, and the threat of detrimental consequences for noncompliance with the demands of the investigating officers.[116]

Without Use of Coercion

A more difficult problem than that discussed above is whether acts of investigation carried out without the use of any coercion, or even with the consent of the persons concerned, may violate the territorial jurisdiction of the state in which they are performed. *Example*: In proceedings for tax evasion before a court, the defendant consents to allow officers commissioned by this court to go and examine his bank accounts abroad.

Opinions on this problem differ. In the United States this practice might appear normal and routine,[117] but other countries such as Switzerland, Germany,[118] and several others consider it contrary to international law. Also, the decisions of international courts support this latter view.[119] In support of this view point it has been pointed out that the territorial jurisdiction of a state cannot be disposed of by the consent of a private person.[120]

Therefore, attempts of officials from one state to perform any acts of investigation in a foreign state without permission of the latter, may be considered as a violation of the principle of territoriality and may arouse reactions of many kinds from the foreign state. This applies even in cases in which the official performs such acts not by invoking his official capacity, but by appearing as a private person. Such a change of roles is simply seen as a way of circumventing the legal obstacles associated with functioning in an official capacity and should not be permitted.[121]

---

[116] *See* NORDMANN, *supra* note 1, at 51-55, where these arguments are made, and are invoked in each of the cases reported by him either by courts or by other authorities which have dealt with them; *see also* Klaus Tiedemann, *Privatdienstliche Amtshandlungen im Ausland—strafprozessuales Verwertungsverbot? in* FESTSCHRIFT FÜR BOCKELMANN 822 (1979).

[117] *See* Jones, *supra* note 2, at 520, *see also* NORDMANN, *supra* note 1, at 58.

[118] *See* Tiedemann, *supra* note 116, at 823 and additional references cited therein; and NORDMANN, *supra* note 1, at 58. In Switzerland these incidents are considered such serious violations of the sovereignty that they have been made criminal offenses. More specifically, Art. 271 of the Swiss Penal Code provides that:

> Whoever, on Swiss territory, without being authorized so to do, takes on behalf of a foreign state any action ascribable to public powers; whoever would take such action on behalf of a foreign party or another foreign organization; whoever encourages such action, shall be punished by imprisonment (3 days to 3 years) and in serious cases by severe imprisonment (1 year to 20 years).

As a result of the above provision the criminal liability exists irrespective of the eventual willingness of the person concerned to testify, or to produce documents.

[119] *See* Geck, *supra* note 1, at 795; Suzanne Bastid, *Les problomes territoriaux dans la jurisprudence de la Cour Internationale de Justice*, *in* III RECUEIL DES COURS, ACADIMIE DE DROIT INTERNATIONAL, 386-90 (1963); and NORDMANN, *supra* note 1, at 58-59, with reference to the "*Lotus* case" and other cases.

[120] *See* NORDMANN, *supra* note 1, at 59.

[121] *See* Tiedemann, *supra* note 116, at 823-24.

Value of Evidence Obtained in This Way

Evidence procured abroad by any of the procedures described above creates further problems regarding its value before the court trying the case.

It is obvious, especially when the acts are performed by persons other than the members of the court (foreign officials or consular officers), that the evidence procured constitutes a breach of the principles of immediacy,[122] orality and continuous procedure that govern the criminal procedures of most states. Since, however, these principles are not provided without exceptions,[123] the taking of evidence abroad may be considered as one of these exceptions. However, with regard to these principles, the taking of evidence abroad by the court itself or in its presence constitutes the lesser irregularity.

On the other hand, since the taking of evidence abroad by the investigating authority may violate the territoriality principle, it is questionable whether evidence thus obtained may be used by the trying court. Since this principle constitutes a general rule of international law, which in many countries is considered as part of and sometimes even superior to national law,[124] a view has been expressed that courts of such countries may be required to reject this kind of evidence.[125]

Conclusion

Based on the considerations discussed, one may draw the conclusion that ways in which taking evidence abroad is possible without the risk of violating the principles of international law are only those that secure the cooperation of the country where the evidence is located.

Mutual assistance of some kind, either active or passive, cannot be avoided. It is up to the states which are members of the international community to regulate this assistance by international agreements so that it becomes prompt and effective.

---

[122] The principle of immediacy means *inter alia* that evidence should be taken by the deciding court directly from the source of evidence; *see* ZISSIADIS, 1 PENAL PROCEDURE 68 (1975) (in Greek); PETERS, STRAFPROZESS 266 (1966); CLAUS ROXIN, STRAFVERFAHRENSRECHT 287 (20th ed., 1987); Brancaccio, *supra* note 5, at 100, while evidence taken by means of letters rogatory comes to the knowledge of the court in the form of a written document (report or record).

[123] *See, e.g.*, Greek CPP, *supra* note 8, at Art. 354, which provides that if a witness cannot appear before the court, he may be examined by a commissioned judge in the place of his domicile and his written deposition is then read during the trial. Similar provisions are included in the German CPP § 251.

[124] *See, e.g.*, German Basic Law (Grundgesetz), Art. 25; Greek Constitution Art. 28; Italian Constitution Art. 10.

[125] *See* Tiedemann, *supra* note 116, at 826-27, basing his arguments on the obligation of states to redress the consequences of violations of international law.

Appendix 7

European Convention on Mutual Assistance in Criminal Matters

European Treaty Series
No. 30

Preamble

The governments signatory hereto, being members of the Council of Europe,

Considering that the aim of the Council of Europe is to achieve greater unity among its Members;

Believing that the adoption of common rules in the field of mutual assistance in criminal matters will contribute to the attainment of this aim;

Considering that such mutual assistance is related to the question of extradition, which has already formed the subject of a Convention signed on 13th December 1957,

Have agreed as follows:

CHAPTER I
General provisions

Article 1

1. The Contracting Parties undertake to afford each other, in accordance with the provisions of this Convention, the widest measure of mutual assistance in proceedings in respect of offences the punishment of which, at the time of the request for assistance, falls within the jurisdiction of the judicial authorities of the requesting Party.
2. This Convention does not apply to arrests, the enforcement of verdicts or offences under military law which are not offences under ordinary criminal law.

Article 2

Assistance may be refused:

(a) if the request concerns an offence which the requested Party considers a political offence, an offence connected with a political offence, or a fiscal offence;

(b) if the requested Party considers that execution of the request is likely to prejudice the sovereignty, security, ordre public or other essential interests of its country.

CHAPTER II
Letters rogatory

Article 3

1. The requested Party shall execute in the manner provided for by its law any letters rogatory relating to a criminal matter and addressed to it by the judicial authorities of the requesting Party for the purpose of procuring evidence or transmitting articles to be produced in evidence, records or documents.
2. If the requesting Party desires witnesses or experts to give evidence on oath, it shall expressly so request, and the requested Party shall comply with the request if the law of its country does not prohibit it.
3. The requested Party may transmit certified copies or certified photostat copies of records or documents requested, unless the requesting Party expressly requests the transmission of originals, in which case the requested Party shall make every effort to comply with the request.

Article 4

On the express request of the requesting Party the requested Party shall state the date and place of execution of the letters rogatory. Officials and interested persons may be present if the requested Party consents.

Article 5

1. Any Contracting Party may, by a declaration addressed to the Secretary General of the Council of Europe, when signing this Convention or depositing its instrument of ratification or accession, reserve the right to make the execution of letters rogatory for search or seizure of property dependent on one or more of the following conditions:

(a) that the offence motivating the letters rogatory is punishable under both the law of the requesting Party and the law of the requested Party;

(b) that the offence motivating the letters rogatory is an extraditable offence in the requested country;

(c) that execution of the letters rogatory is consistent with the law of the requested Party.

2. Where a Contracting Party makes a declaration in accordance with paragraph 1 of this article, any other Party may apply reciprocity.

Article 6

1. The requested Party may delay the handing over of any property, records or documents requested, if it requires the said property, records or documents in connection with pending criminal proceedings.

2. Any property, as well as original records or documents, handed over in execution of letters rogatory shall be returned by the requesting Party to the requested Party as soon as possible unless the latter Party waives the return thereof.

CHAPTER III

Service of writs and records of judicial verdicts -
Appearance of witnesses, experts and prosecuted persons

Article 7

1. The requested Party shall effect service of writs and records of judicial verdicts which are transmitted to it for this purpose by the requesting Party.

Service may be effected by simple transmission of the writ or record to the person to be served. If the requesting Party expressly so requests, service shall be effected by the requested Party in the manner provided for the service of analogous documents under its own law or in a special manner consistent with such law.

2. Proof of service shall be given by means of a receipt dated and signed by the person served or by means of a declaration made by the requested Party that service has been effected and stating the form and date of such service. One or other of these documents shall be sent immediately to the requesting Party. The requested Party shall, if the requesting Party so requests, state whether service has been effected in accordance with the law of the requested Party. If service cannot be effected, the reasons shall be communicated immediately by the requested Party to the requesting Party.

3. Any Contracting Party may, by a declaration addressed to the Secretary General of the Council of Europe, when signing this Convention or depositing its instrument of ratification or accession, request that service of a summons on an accused person who is in its territory be transmitted to its authorities by a certain time before the date set for appearance. This time shall be specified in the aforesaid declaration and shall not exceed 50 days.

This time shall be taken into account when the date of appearance is being fixed and when the summons is being transmitted.

Article 8

A witness or expert who has failed to answer a summons to appear, service of which has been requested, shall not, even if the summons contains a notice of penalty, be subjected to any punishment or measure of restraint, unless subsequently he voluntarily enters the territory of the requesting Party and is there again duly summoned.

Article 9

The allowances, including subsistence, to be paid and the traveling expenses to be refunded to a witness or expert by the requesting Party shall be calculated as from his place of residence and shall be at rates at least equal to those provided for in the scales and rules in force in the country where the hearing is intended to take place.

Article 10

1. If the requesting Party considers the personal appearance of a witness or expert before its judicial authorities especially necessary, it shall so mention in its request for service of the summons and the requested Party shall invite the witness or expert to appear.

The requested Party shall inform the requesting Party of the reply of the witness or expert.

2. In the case provided for under paragraph 1 of this article the request or the summons shall indicate the approximate allowances payable and the traveling and subsistence expenses refundable.

3. If a specific request is made, the requested Party may grant the witness or expert an advance. The amount of the advance shall be endorsed on the summons and shall be refunded by the requesting Party.

Article 11

1. A person in custody whose personal appearance as a witness or for purposes of confrontation is applied for by the requesting Party shall be temporarily transferred to the territory where the hearing is intended to take place, provided that he shall be sent back within the period stipulated by the requested Party and subject to the provisions of Article 12 in so far as these are applicable.

Transfer may be refused:

(a) if the person in custody does not consent,

(b) if his presence is necessary at criminal proceedings pending in the territory of the requested Party,

(c) if transfer is liable to prolong his detention, or

(d) if there are other overriding grounds for not transferring him to the territory of the requesting Party.

2. Subject to the provisions of Article 2, in a case coming within the immediately preceding paragraph, transit of the person in custody through the territory of a third State, Party to this Convention, shall be granted on application, accompanied by all necessary documents, addressed by the Ministry of Justice of the requesting Party to the Ministry of Justice of the Party through whose territory transit is requested.

A Contracting Party may refuse to grant transit to its own nationals.

3. The transferred person shall remain in custody in the territory of the requesting Party and, where applicable, in the territory of the Party through which transit is requested, unless the Party from whom transfer is requested applies for his release.

Article 12

1. A witness or expert, whatever his nationality, appearing on a summons before the judicial authorities of the requesting Party shall not be prosecuted or detained or subjected to any other

restriction of his personal liberty in the territory of that Party in respect of acts or convictions anterior to his departure from the territory of the requested Party.

2. A person, whatever his nationality, summoned before the judicial authorities of the requesting Party to answer for acts forming the subject of proceedings against him, shall not be prosecuted or detained or subjected to any other restriction of his personal liberty for acts or convictions anterior to his departure from the territory of the requested Party and not specified in the summons.

3. The immunity provided for in this article shall cease when the witness or expert or prosecuted person, having had for a period of fifteen consecutive days from the date when his presence is no longer required by the judicial authorities an opportunity of leaving, has nevertheless remained in the territory, or having left it, has returned.

CHAPTER IV
Judicial records

Article 13

1. A requested Party shall communicate extracts from and information relating to judicial records, requested from it by the judicial authorities of a Contracting Party and needed in a criminal matter, to the same extent that these may be made available to its own judicial authorities in like case.

2. In any case other than that provided for in paragraph 1 of this article the request shall be complied with in accordance with the conditions provided for by the law, regulations or practice of the requested Party.

CHAPTER V
Procedure

Article 14

1. Requests for mutual assistance shall indicate as follows:
   (a) the authority making the request,
   (b) the object of and the reason for the request,
   (c) where possible, the identity and the nationality of the person concerned, and
   (d) where necessary, the name and address of the person to be served.

2. Letters rogatory referred to in Articles 3, 4 and 5 shall, in addition, state the offence and contain a summary of the facts.

Article 15

1. Letters rogatory referred to in Articles 3, 4 and 5 as well as the applications referred to in Article 11 shall be addressed by the Ministry of Justice of the requesting Party to the Ministry of Justice of the requested Party and shall be returned through the same channels.

2. In case of urgency, letters rogatory may be addressed directly by the judicial authorities of the requesting Party to the judicial authorities of the requested Party. They shall be returned together with the relevant documents through the channels stipulated in paragraph 1 of this article.

3. Requests provided for in paragraph 1 of Article 13 may be addressed directly by the judicial authorities concerned to the appropriate authorities of the requested Party, and the replies may be returned directly by those authorities. Requests provided for in paragraph 2 of Article 13 shall be addressed by the Ministry of Justice of the requesting Party to the Ministry of Justice of the requested Party.

4. Requests for mutual assistance, other than those provided for in paragraphs 1 and 3 of this article and, in particular, requests for investigation preliminary to prosecution, may be communicated directly between the judicial authorities.

5. In cases where direct transmission is permitted under this Convention, it may take place through the International Criminal Police Organisation (Interpol).
6. A Contracting Party may, when signing this Convention or depositing its instrument of ratification or accession, by a declaration addressed to the Secretary General of the Council of Europe, give notice that some or all requests for assistance shall be sent to it through channels other than those provided for in this article, or require that, in a case provided for in paragraph 2 of this article, a copy of the letters rogatory shall be transmitted at the same time to its Ministry of Justice.
7. The provisions of this article are without prejudice to those of bilateral agreements or arrangements in force between Contracting Parties which provide for the direct transmission of requests for assistance between their respective authorities.

Article 16

1. Subject to paragraph 2 of this article, translations of requests and annexed documents shall not be required.
2. Each Contracting Party may, when signing or depositing its instrument of ratification or accession, by means of a declaration addressed to the Secretary General of the Council of Europe, reserve the right to stipulate that requests and annexed documents shall be addressed to it accompanied by a translation into its own language or into either of the official languages of the Council of Europe or into one of the latter languages, specified by it. The other Contracting Parties may apply reciprocity.
3. This article is without prejudice to the provisions concerning the translation of requests or annexed documents contained in the agreements or arrangements in force or to be made between two or more Contracting Parties.

Article 17

Evidence or documents transmitted pursuant to this Convention shall not require any form of authentication.

Article 18

Where the authority which receives a request for mutual assistance has no jurisdiction to comply therewith, it shall, ex officio, transmit the request to the competent authority of its country and shall so inform the requesting Party through the direct channels, if the request has been addressed through such channels.

Article 19

Reasons shall be given for any refusal of mutual assistance.

Article 20

Subject to the provisions of Article 10, paragraph 3, execution of requests for mutual assistance shall not entail refunding of expenses except those incurred by the attendance of experts in the territory of the requested Party or the transfer of a person in custody carried out under Article 11.

CHAPTER VI

Laying of information in connection with proceedings

Article 21

1. Information laid by one Contracting Party with a view to proceedings in the courts of another Party shall be transmitted between the Ministries of Justice concerned unless a Contracting Party avails itself of the option provided for in paragraph 6 of Article 15.

2. The requested Party shall notify the requesting Party of any action taken on such information and shall forward a copy of the record of any verdict pronounced.
3. The provisions of Article 16 shall apply to information laid under paragraph 1 of this article.

CHAPTER VII
Exchange of information from judicial records

Article 22

Each Contracting Party shall inform any other Party of all criminal convictions and subsequent measures in respect of nationals of the latter Party, entered in the judicial records. Ministries of Justice shall communicate such information to one another at least once a year. Where the person concerned is considered a national of two or more other Contracting Parties, the information shall be given to each of these Parties, unless the person is a national of the Party in the territory of which he was convicted.

CHAPTER VIII
Final provisions

Article 23

1. Any Contracting Party may, when signing this Convention or when depositing its instrument of ratification or accession, make a reservation in respect of any provision or provisions of the Convention.
2. Any Contracting Party which has made a reservation shall withdraw it as soon as circumstances permit. Such withdrawal shall be made by notification to the Secretary General of the Council of Europe.
3. A Contracting Party which has made a reservation in respect of a provision of the Convention may not claim application of the said provision by another Party save in so far as it has itself accepted the provision.

Article 24

A Contracting Party may, when signing the Convention or depositing its instrument of ratification or accession, by a declaration addressed to the Secretary General of the Council of Europe, define what authorities it will, for the purpose of the Convention, deem judicial authorities.

Article 25

1. This Convention shall apply to the metropolitan territories of the Contracting Parties.
2. In respect of France, it shall also apply to Algeria and to the overseas Departments, and, in respect of Italy, it shall also apply to the territory of Somaliland under Italian administration.
3. The Federal Republic of Germany may extend the application of this Convention to the Land of Berlin by notice addressed to the Secretary General of the Council of Europe.
4. In respect of the Kingdom of the Netherlands, the Convention shall apply to its European territory. The Netherlands may extend the application of this Convention to the Netherlands Antilles, Surinam and Netherlands New Guinea by notice addressed to the Secretary General of the Council of Europe.
5. By direct arrangement between two or more Contracting Parties and subject to the conditions laid down in the arrangement, the application of this Convention may be extended to any territory, other than the territories mentioned in paragraphs 1, 2, 3 and 4 of this article, of one of these Parties, for the international relations of which any such Party is responsible.

Article 26

1. Subject to the provisions of Article 15, paragraph 7, and Article 16, paragraph 3, this Convention shall, in respect of those countries to which it applies, supersede the provisions of any treaties, conventions or bilateral agreements governing mutual assistance in criminal matters between any two Contracting Parties.
2. This Convention shall not affect obligations incurred under the terms of any other bilateral or multilateral international convention which contains or may contain clauses governing specific aspects of mutual assistance in a given field.
3. The Contracting Parties may conclude between themselves bilateral or multilateral agreements on mutual assistance in criminal matters only in order to supplement the provisions of this Convention or to facilitate the application of the principles contained therein.
4. Where, as between two or more Contracting Parties, mutual assistance in criminal matters is practised on the basis of uniform legislation or of a special system providing for the reciprocal application in their respective territories of measures of mutual assistance, these Parties shall, notwithstanding the provisions of this Convention, be free to regulate their mutual relations in this field exclusively in accordance with such legislation or system. Contracting Parties which, in accordance with this paragraph, exclude as between themselves the application of this Convention shall notify the Secretary General of the Council of Europe accordingly.

Article 27

1. This Convention shall be open to signature by the members of the Council of Europe. It shall be ratified. The instruments of ratification shall be deposited with the Secretary General of the Council.
2. The Convention shall come into force 90 days after the date of deposit of the third instrument of ratification.
3. As regards any signatory ratifying subsequently the Convention shall come into force 90 days after the date of the deposit of its instrument of ratification.

Article 28

1. The Committee of Ministers of the Council of Europe may invite any State not a member of the Council to accede to this Convention, provided that the resolution containing such invitation obtains the unanimous agreement of the members of the Council who have ratified the Convention.
2. Accession shall be by deposit with the Secretary General of the Council of an instrument of accession which shall take effect 90 days after the date of its deposit.

Article 29

Any Contracting Party may denounce this Convention in so far as it is concerned by giving notice to the Secretary General of the Council of Europe. Denunciation shall take effect six months after the date when the Secretary General of the Council received such notification.

Article 30

The Secretary General of the Council of Europe shall notify the members of the Council and the government of any State which has acceded to this Convention of:

(a) the names of the signatories and the deposit of any instrument of ratification or accession;

(b) the date of entry into force of this Convention;

(c) any notification received in accordance with the provisions of Article 5 - paragraph 1, Article 7 - paragraph 3, Article 15 - paragraph 6, Article 16 - paragraph 2, Article 24, Article 25 - paragraphs 3 and 4, Article 26 - paragraph 4;

(d) any reservation made in accordance with Article 23, paragraph 1;

(e) the withdrawal of any reservation in accordance with Article 23, paragraph 2;

(f) any notification of denunciation received in accordance with the provisions of Article 29 and the date on which such denunciation will take effect.

In witness whereof the undersigned, being duly authorised thereto, have signed this Convention.

Done at Strasbourg, this 20th day of April 1959, in English and French, both texts being equally authoritative, in a single copy which shall remain deposited in the archives of the Council of Europe. The Secretary General of the Council of Europe shall transmit certified copies to the signatory and acceding governments.

Additional Protocol to the European Convention on Mutual Assistance in Criminal Matters

European Treaty Series
No. 99

The member States of the Council of Europe, signatory to this Protocol,

Desirous of facilitating the application of the European Convention on Mutual Assistance in Criminal Matters opened for signature in Strasbourg on 20th April 1959 (hereinafter referred to as "the Convention") in the field of fiscal offences;

Considering it also desirable to supplement the Convention in certain other respects,

Have agreed as follows:

CHAPTER I

Article 1

The Contracting Parties shall not exercise the right provided for in Article 2.a of the Convention to refuse assistance solely on the ground that the request concerns an offence which the requested Party considers a fiscal offence.

Article 2

1. In the case where a Contracting Party has made the execution of letters rogatory for search or seizure of property dependent on the condition that the offence motivating the letters rogatory is punishable under both the law of the requesting Party and the law of the requested Party, this condition shall be fulfilled, as regards fiscal offences, if the offence is punishable under the law of the requesting Party and corresponds to an offence of the same nature under the law of the requested Party.
2. The request may not be refused on the ground that the law of the requested Party does not impose the same kind of tax or duty or does not contain a tax, duty, customs and exchange regulation of the same kind as the law of the requesting Party.

CHAPTER II

Article 3

The Convention shall also apply to:

(a) the service of documents concerning the enforcement of a sentence, the recovery of a fine or the payment of costs of proceedings;

(b) measures relating to the suspension of pronouncement of a sentence or of its enforcement, to conditional release, to deferment of the commencement of the enforcement of a sentence or to the interruption of such enforcement.

CHAPTER III

Article 4

Article 22 of the Convention shall be supplemented by the following text, the original Article 22 of the Convention becoming paragraph 1 and the below-mentioned provisions becoming paragraph 2:
"2. Furthermore, any Contracting Party which has supplied the above-mentioned information shall communicate to the Party concerned, on the latter's request in individual cases, a copy of the convictions and measures in question as well as any other information relevant thereto in order to enable it

to consider whether they necessitate any measures at national level. This communication shall take place between the Ministries of Justice concerned."

CHAPTER IV

Article 5

1. This Protocol shall be open to signature by the member States of the Council of Europe which have signed the Convention. It shall be subject to ratification, acceptance or approval. Instruments of ratification, acceptance or approval shall be deposited with the Secretary General of the Council of Europe.
2. The Protocol shall enter into force 90 days after the date of the deposit of the third instrument of ratification, acceptance or approval.
3. In respect of a signatory State ratifying, accepting or approving subsequently, the Protocol shall enter into force 90 days after the date of the deposit of its instrument of ratification, acceptance or approval.
4. A member State of the Council of Europe may not ratify, accept or approve this Protocol without having, simultaneously or previously, ratified the Convention.

Article 6

1. Any State which has acceded to the Convention may accede to this Protocol after the Protocol has entered into force.
2. Such accession shall be effected by depositing with the Secretary General of the Council of Europe an instrument of accession which shall take effect 90 days after the date of its deposit.

Article 7

1. Any State may, at the time of signature or when depositing its instrument of ratification, acceptance, approval or accession, specify the territory or territories to which this Protocol shall apply.
2. Any State may, when depositing its instrument of ratification, acceptance, approval or accession or at any later date, by declaration addressed to the Secretary General of the Council of Europe, extend this Protocol to any other territory or territories specified in the declaration and for whose international relations it is responsible or on whose behalf it is authorised to give undertakings.
3. Any declaration made in pursuance of the preceding paragraph may, in respect of any territory mentioned in such declaration, be withdrawn by means of a notification addressed to the Secretary General of the Council of Europe. Such withdrawal shall take effect six months after the date of receipt by the Secretary General of the Council of Europe of the notification.

Article 8

1. Reservations made by a Contracting Party to a provision of the Convention shall be applicable also to this Protocol, unless that Party otherwise declares at the time of signature or when depositing its instrument of ratification, acceptance, approval or accession. The same shall apply to the declarations made by virtue of Article 24 of the Convention.
2. Any State may, at the time of signature or when depositing its instrument of ratification, acceptance, approval or accession, declare that it reserves the right:

(a) not to accept Chapter I, or to accept it only in respect of certain offences or certain categories of the offences referred to in Article I, or not to comply with letters rogatory for search or seizure of property in respect of fiscal offences;

(b) not to accept Chapter II;

(c) not to accept Chapter III.

3. Any Contracting Party may withdraw a declaration it has made in accordance with the foregoing paragraph by means of a declaration addressed to the Secretary General of the Council of Europe which shall become effective as from the date of its receipt.
4. A Contracting Party which has applied to this Protocol a reservation made in respect of a provision of the Convention or which has made a reservation in respect of a provision of this Protocol may not claim the application of that provision by another Contracting Party; it may, however, if its reservation is partial or conditional claim the application of that provision in so far as it has itself accepted it.
5. No other reservation may be made to the provisions of this Protocol.

Article 9

The provisions of this Protocol are without prejudice to more extensive regulations in bilateral or multilateral agreements concluded between Contracting Parties in application of Article 26, paragraph 3, of the Convention.

Article 10

The European Committee on Crime Problems of the Council of Europe shall be kept informed regarding the application of this Protocol and shall do whatever is needful to facilitate a friendly settlement of any difficulty which may arise out of its execution.

Article 11

1. Any Contracting Party may, in so far as it is concerned, denounce this Protocol by means of a notification addressed to the Secretary General of the Council of Europe.
2. Such denunciation shall take effect six months after the date of receipt by the Secretary General of such notification.
3. Denunciation of the Convention entails automatically denunciation of this Protocol.

Article 12

The Secretary General of the Council of Europe shall notify the member States of the Council and any State which has acceded to the Convention of:

(a) any signature of this Protocol;

(b) any deposit of an instrument of ratification, acceptance, approval or accession;

(c) any date of entry into force of this Protocol in accordance with Articles 5 and 6;

(d) any declaration received in pursuance of the provisions of paragraphs 2 and 3 of Article 7;

(e) any declaration received in pursuance of the provisions of paragraph 1 of Article 8;

(f) any reservation made in pursuance of the provisions of paragraph 2 of Article 8;

(g) the withdrawal of any reservation carried out in pursuance of the provisions of paragraph 3 of Article 8;

(h) any notification received in pursuance of the provisions of Article 11 and the date on which denunciation takes effect.

In witness whereof the undersigned, being duly authorised thereto, have signed this Protocol.

Done at Strasbourg, this 17th day of March 1978, in English and in French, both texts being equally authoritative, in a single copy which shall remain deposited in the archives of the Council of Europe. The Secretary General of the Council of Europe shall transmit certified copies to each of the signatory and acceding States.

Sub-Regional Arrangements: The Benelux and the Nordic Countries

Coen Mulder and Bert Swart

Introduction

Within Europe there are some sub-regional arrangements between neighboring states that have some affinities, particularly as to their legal systems. At present there are two such sub-regional arrangements. They are among the Benelux countries and among the Nordic countries.

Mutual Cooperation among the Benelux Countries

Belgium, the Netherlands and Luxemburg, the three countries of the Benelux, have a long-standing tradition of mutual cooperation that goes back to before World War II. Their intensified efforts to cooperate during the postwar period culminated in the adoption of the Treaty on the Benelux Economic Union in 1958, establishing the Benelux as an international organization. Unlike the European Communities, the Union has a strictly intergovernmental structure. However, in 1965 a Benelux Court of Justice was created and charged with settling disputes about the interpretation of Benelux conventions and other instruments. Meanwhile, cooperation between the three countries has never been limited to mere economic matters. For instance, in 1948 the three governments established a Commission for the Study of Unification of Law. The Commission was charged with the general task of drafting proposals for harmonization and unification of national laws by means of either conventions or model laws.

The purpose of the Benelux Economic Union is to create an area in which persons, goods, capital and services circulate freely. Three conventions created to implement that purpose have a special significance for cooperation in criminal matters. The first is the 1960 Convention on transferring border checks of persons to the external frontiers of the Benelux, creating a free travel area within the Benelux. The second is the 1969 Benelux Convention on cooperation between administrative and judicial authorities in matters pertaining to the Benelux Economic Union. It establishes a structure for combating infringements of Union law. Finally, one may mention the 1970 Benelux Convention on arms and ammunition which, however, has not been ratified by Belgium.

Other conventions have been adopted outside the framework of the Union. The most important one is the 1962 Benelux Convention on extradition and mutual assistance in criminal matters, together with its 1974 Protocol. Of lesser importance are the 1968 Benelux Convention on the execution of criminal sentences and the 1974 Benelux Convention on transfer of proceedings in criminal matters. Not having been ratified by all three countries, they have not yet entered into force. Of the few model laws that have been created in the area of criminal law, we may mention here the 1962 model law on perjury before international courts. According to this model law it is a crime under national law for anyone to commit perjury before an international court, provided that court has been established on the basis of an international agreement to which the Benelux country is a party.

The best way to assess the significance of the various Benelux conventions on cooperation in criminal matters is to compare them with the corresponding conventions that have been drafted by the Council of Europe during the same period.[1] As the three countries of the Benelux have been members of the Council of Europe from the beginning, it comes as no surprise that the Benelux and European conventions share the same structure and the same philosophy. Specific differences between the two sets of instruments usually consist of the Benelux conventions establishing further reaching obligations to cooperate and more easily relinquishing national sovereignty for the sake of cooperation. Obviously, within a small group of neighboring countries consensus on a higher level is easier to achieve. But one must also realize that abolishing checks of persons at common borders requires special compensatory measures in the area of cooperation.[2]

In its approach, the Benelux Convention on extradition and mutual assistance is basically similar to the 1957 European Convention on Extradition. However, the thresholds for extraditing suspects and convicted persons in Article 2 of the Benelux Convention are considerably lower than those contained in Article 2 of the European Convention. The diplomatic procedure is completely eliminated where extradition requests are concerned. Article 19 of the Benelux Convention provides for extradition without a full court hearing if the requested person consents to his surrender. In practice, surrender on the basis of this provision has become the rule rather than the exception.

More innovative is the Benelux Convention where mutual assistance is concerned and here the differences with the 1959 European Convention on Mutual Assistance in Criminal Matters are more pronounced. As a rule, requests for assistance may be made and acted upon by judicial authorities directly. As a rule too, the authorities of the requesting state are allowed to be present at the execution of their request by the authorities of the requested state. Articles 27-29 allow law enforcement officers engaged in pursuing a suspect in order to arrest him to continue their pursuit within the territory of another Benelux country over a distance of ten kilometers. These provisions, compensating for the abolition of checks at the inner borders are among those which served as a model for the 1990 Schengen Convention.[3] Also worth mentioning is Article 34, which makes it a criminal offence for witnesses and experts residing in the requested state not to appear before a court of the requesting state. In addition, Article 25a provides for the temporary transfer of a person in custody for testimonial purposes without the person's consent. Both provisions may be partly explained by the small geographical distances within the Benelux.

The Benelux conventions on transfer of proceedings and execution of criminal sentences are very similar to the 1972 European Convention on the Transfer of Proceedings in Criminal Matters and the 1970 European Convention on the International Validity of Criminal Judgements. One may note here that both Benelux conventions have abolished the requirement of double criminality for specific categories of offences. The Benelux convention on

---

[1] *See infra* Muller-Rappard, chapter 9; Oehler, chapter 17; Schutte, chapter 18; Poncet & Gully-Hart, chapter 8.

[2] For a more detailed discussion of the work of the Benelux in the 1960s, *see* B. de Schutter, *International Criminal Law in Evolution: Mutual Assistance between the Benelux Countries,* 14 NEDERLANDS TIJDSCHRIFT VOOR INTERNATIONAAL RECHT 382-410 (1967).

[3] *See infra* Bert Swart, *European Union and Schengen* ch.6.

the execution of criminal sentences is remarkable in two respects. Articles 25-29 provide for a system of 'partial decisions.' On the basis of these provisions courts in the state where the offence has been committed may, after conviction, refrain from imposing punishment themselves and leave that to the courts of the state where the convicted person resides. This is perhaps the most radical consequence that has been drawn from the rehabilitative philosophy that used to inspire the makers of European and Benelux conventions so strongly in the past. Another striking provision is Article 36. It entitles the convicted person to oppose the execution of a custodial sentence in his state of residence on the ground that he prefers to undergo punishment in the sentencing state. This may entail a form of self-surrender to the authorities of that state.

Probably the most interesting and innovative Benelux convention is that on cooperation between administrative and judicial authorities in matters pertaining to the Benelux Economic Union. This convention is concerned with infringements of Benelux rules, i.e. with offences of an economic or fiscal nature. Article 9 of the Benelux Convention introduces the concept of what one may call Benelux offences: infringement of Benelux rules are not only punishable in the country where they have been committed but also in the two other countries. Articles 10-15 establish a system of priority of jurisdiction and transfer of proceedings. Articles 16-24 are concerned with mutual cooperation in criminal matters. The obligation to provide assistance is unconditional. Moreover, in allowing authorities of one country to carry out investigations in another country, the Convention goes considerably further than the Benelux convention on extradition and mutual assistance in criminal matters. It is interesting to compare the Convention with the Convention on the protection of the European Communities' financial interests adopted within the European Union in 1995.[4] Compared to the 26-years older Benelux Convention, the European Union Convention is a rather timid instrument.

In retrospect, the 1950s and 60s were the heydays of the Benelux. After the 1974 Convention on the transfer of proceedings in criminal matters, no new conventions or model laws have been introduced. Interesting projects, like those on territorial and extraterritorial jurisdiction and on the rights of victims in criminal proceedings, have borne no fruits. For a long time now the countries of the Benelux have abandoned the thought that cooperation and harmonization between them might be expanded further. This is partly due to the fact that even between these three countries harmonization and unification of law have proven to be particularly arduous and sensitive matters where criminal law is concerned. On the other hand, the European Community, covering the same ground as the Benelux Economic Union, has shown itself to be a far more powerful and dynamic organization. Finally, where cooperation in criminal matters is concerned the Benelux has always had to compete with the Council of Europe, while in recent years the European Union has become the center of developments.

This is not to deny the importance of what has been achieved within the Benelux. In so far as the various Benelux conventions on cooperation in criminal matters have more to offer than the corresponding conventions of the Council of Europe, they remain of great practical significance to the Benelux countries themselves. Moreover, they have had a significant influence on the drafting of various Council of Europe instruments[5] and, even more so, on

---

4 *See id.*

5 *Cf.* F. THOMAS, DE EUROPESE RECHTSHULPVERDRAGEN IN STRAFZAKEN (1980).

the 1990 Schengen Convention.[6] Finally, in some respects they may still serve as an example where the progressive development of international cooperation is concerned.

Mutual Cooperation Among The Nordic Countries

Within Europe, the Nordic council provides an example of a coherent system of international cooperation in criminal matters which functions well in practice. The five members of the Nordic Council are Denmark, Iceland, Norway, Finland and Sweden and their more or less autonomous territories.[7] The Nordic Council is an organization of their national parliaments. It was established in 1952 and is involved in various fields such as the labor market, the environment, culture, education, etc. In 1962, cooperation within the Nordic Council resulted in the Helsinki Nordic Cooperation Treaty, which is considered the formal basis of Nordic cooperation in criminal matters.[8] This Agreement was preceded by the Nordic Passport Control Agreement[9] of 1957, which created a free travel area between the five countries.

Cooperation in criminal matters between the Nordic States and the Nordic Passport Agreement have been operational for more than thirty years now. However, there are some significant differences between the five countries as regards both substantive criminal law and criminal procedure. The Nordic states can be divided into two groups: Denmark, Norway and Iceland on the one hand, Sweden and Finland on the other. The first three have adopted the opportunity principle in their codes of criminal procedure, while the structure of criminal procedure is virtually the same in all three. The police and public prosecution departments are organized similarly. Sweden and Finland on the other hand, have adopted the principle of legality and the police and public prosecution are separate organizations in both countries. The differences between the two groups are not merely of a historical or doctrinal nature. There are also fundamental differences in criminal policies. In general, one could say that in Sweden and Finland the emphasis is more on prevention of crime and in Denmark, Norway and Iceland more on retribution. Compared to the similarities, the differences between the Nordic states are relatively small, but they are highly relevant to the way in which Nordic cooperation in criminal law matters is organized. All instruments of cooperation contain rules of conflict, usually between Danish/Norwegian/Icelandic law on the one hand and Swedish/Finnish law on the other.

---

6 *Cf.* Julian J.E. Schutte, *The European Market of 1993: A Test for a Regional Model of Supranational Criminal Justice or for Inter-Regional Cooperation? in* PRINCIPLES AND PROCEDURES FOR A NEW TRANSNATIONAL CRIMINAL LAW 387 note 407-408 (Albin Eser & Otto Lagodny eds., 1992).

7 For Denmark the Færøer and Greenland, for Finland Åland.

8 *Cf.* Raimo Lahti, *Sub-Regional Cooperation in Criminal Matters: The Experience of the Nordic Countries, in* PRINCIPLES AND PROCEDURES FOR A NEW TRANSNATIONAL CRIMINAL LAW 305-310 (Albin Eser & Otto Lagodny eds., 1992).

9 *See* Henning Fode, *Cooperation on Law Enforcement, Criminal Justice and Legislation in Europe, Nordic Experience, in* FREE MOVEMENT OF PERSONS IN EUROPE 63-64 (Henry G. Schermers et al. eds., 1993).

Jurisdiction

There are significant differences[10] between the Nordic states as regards jurisdiction over criminal offences committed by a non-national outside the territory of a Nordic state. Under certain circumstances, however, all Nordic states do have jurisdiction over inhabitants of other Nordic states or over offenses which have been committed in other Nordic states. This enables them to make a choice between extradition, transfer of criminal proceedings and transfer of criminal sentences in specific cases, since the Nordic state on whose territory the offender resides prosecuted will almost always have jurisdiction. Conflicts of jurisdiction may in theory arise because more than one state will have jurisdiction in any single case. In practice, however, such conflicts do not occur because a decision to prosecute offences committed outside the state's territory will usually only be made after authorization from a higher authority. The rule then applies that the weaker the tie with the state's territory the higher the authority has to be. Sometimes the authority deciding on exercising jurisdiction is the Minister of Justice or the government.

The territoriality principle also takes priority in another way. The Nordic regulations almost always assume a request from the competent prosecuting authority. The competent prosecuting authority is the public prosecutor within whose jurisdiction the offence was committed. If the offence has a foreign aspect to it because the suspect is foreign, the evidence or the witnesses are abroad or the suspect resides abroad, the locally competent prosecutor decides whether, and what kind of assistance he will ask of the other country. One of the characteristics of Nordic cooperation is that the regulations assume that the locally competent prosecutor will first informally contact his colleague in the Nordic state which is supposed to render the assistance. There are few clues on what interests the prosecutor is to take into consideration and in which circumstances, except for the agreement on transfer of criminal proceedings that will be discussed in more detail later.

Extradition

The Nordic states extradite on the basis of their extradition laws. An extradition treaty is not required and between the Nordic states extradition treaties no longer apply. Each Nordic state has two extradition laws, a uniform Nordic extradition law and a general extradition act. The uniform Nordic extradition laws apply to extradition to other Nordic states only.

The uniform Nordic extradition laws and the general extradition acts differ as regards conditions and procedure. The uniform Nordic laws contain far fewer conditions for extradition than the general acts and the procedure is simpler, especially because in practice the choice is usually made to resort to summary proceedings. The uniform Nordic extradition laws date from about 1960 and replaced the totally outdated bilateral extradition agreements between the Nordic states. The conditions for extradition and the grounds for refusal as incorporated in the various uniform Nordic extradition laws are virtually the same. However, extradition procedures vary from country to country.

---

[10] The most recent and complete comparison of the jurisdiction regulations can be found in a Note from the Nordic Council and the Nordic Council of Ministers: Straffrättslig jurisdiktion i Norden (Criminal jurisdiction in Nordic countries), Nord 1992:17, København 1992.

A far-reaching simplification of extradition conditions has primarily been achieved by abandoning mutual international extradition obligations. Instead, there is only an unwritten moral obligation to meet the reasonable request of a civilized country. That there is no duty to extradite is apparent in, for example, Article 1 of the Norwegian Uniform Nordic Extradition Law. This provision stipulates that a person who is suspected of, has been formally accused of or convicted for an offense in Denmark, Finland, Iceland or Sweden, and who resides in Norway, may be extradited in accordance with the stipulations of the Law. The word "may" precludes any obligation. In practice, requests for extradition from another Nordic state are almost always granted since they are always preceded by consultations which prevent prospectless requests. Mutual trust between the Nordic states also explains that extradition requests will hardly ever be denied, but should this trust in any given case be absent, there is no obligation included in the law.

The reverse side of the coin is that there are few grounds for refusal. A number of special stipulations apply to nationals. Thus, for example, the Norwegian Uniform Nordic Extradition Law states that Norwegians may not be extradited for offenses committed entirely on Norwegian territory. Nor may they be extradited for political offences. Double criminality is required in cases of political offenses only. There are no other grounds for refusal related to the nature of the offense. Extradition for purely military or purely fiscal offenses is, therefore, certainly possible. There are also hardly any grounds for refusal related to the requested person himself, but some conditions may be set as regards the treatment of the extradited person and it may be required that he be returned after trial. The penalty imposed will then be executed in Norway, pursuant to the uniform Nordic Law on the transfer of sentences. Furthermore, the principle of *ne bis in idem* applies. The rule of speciality applies but is easily breached and has little practical value these days.

The procedure for dealing with extradition requests pursuant to the uniform Nordic extradition laws is very simple. The request is sent directly to the competent authority in the other Nordic state, as is a request for provisional arrest. The Norwegian situation may again serve as an example of the simplicity of the procedure. If the requested person is traced in Norway and apprehended, he has to be brought before the competent court of first instance within 24 hours. The court will ask him whether he objects to his extradition. If the person consents, the public prosecutor may surrender him immediately. If he does object, however, the court of first instance will investigate whether all legal conditions for extradition have been met and subsequently take a well-argumented decision. Appeal against this decision is open to a higher court. If the court considers extradition lawful, the Ministry of Justice decides whether it is expedient. The procedure is not the same in all Nordic states. In Denmark for instance, the Ministry of Justice takes the first decision after which the person concerned may appeal against it before a court.

Judicial Assistance and Police Cooperation

Mutual judicial assistance and police cooperation are so tightly interwoven within the Nordic framework that to make a distinction in this context serves no purpose. In Denmark, Norway and Iceland the public prosecutions office and the police are one single organization. The chief prosecutor in a district is also the head of the police. The persons involved in judicial assistance and police cooperation, therefore, are physically the same. Theoretically, and in contrast to extradition, the European Convention on Mutual Assistance in Criminal Matters and its Additional Protocol also apply between the Nordic states unless a Nordic regulation deviates from them. In practice, the number of deviations is so large that there are actually two concurring regimes for judicial assistance: one as regards the other Nordic states and one as regards third countries. The Nordic "exceptions" to the European regulations consist of two agreements, uniform laws on the hearing of witnesses and national legislation and implementing regulations.

The Agreement between Denmark, Finland, Iceland, Norway and Sweden on judicial assistance in the service of writs and the gathering of evidence dates from 1974.[11] Article 1 allows the competent authorities of the Nordic States to approach each other directly in applying for and in lending assistance. The Agreement furthermore contains rules on how requests are to be made as well as on translation of requests and the costs thereof. The matter is regulated in more detail by an executive agreement concluded between the highest police authorities of the Nordic states in 1972.[12] As the executive agreement lacks international status, its main principles were later incorporated in the 1974 Agreement. Like the 1974 Agreement, the executive agreement establishes the principle of direct contact between the competent authorities. Higher authorities need be consulted only if requests have to be registered or if complications, such as language problems, arise. Its provisions mainly give specific rules for specific situations, such as what documents should be included in a request for assistance, how surrender of a person should be effected and how a missing person should be traced. There is no provision on exchanging information in the agreement. National laws apply here. They allow for providing information to the authorities of other Nordic countries unless specific provisions on keeping information confidential apply to the situation. In actual practice, information is generously provided, both on request and spontaneously. Standing working groups of Nordic officials, including police and fiscal and tax authorities, play an important role here.[13]

The uniform laws deal with the testifying by witnesses before courts in other Nordic countries. They have created what is usually called the "Nordic duty to testify" and apply in civil and administrative as well as in criminal proceedings. A witness has to appear before a court in another Nordic country if the importance of the case and the importance of his testimony so require. The duty to appear is determined according to the law of the court, before which the witness is summoned. A witness may refuse to testify according to the law of his state of residence as well as that of the state that requests his presence in court.

Transfer of proceedings

Most Nordic states are parties to the European Convention on Transfer of Proceedings in Criminal Matters.[14] However, they do not apply it in their mutual relations. Transfer of

---

[11] Overenkomst mellom Finland, Danmark, Island, Norge og Sverige om gjensidig rettshjelp gjennom forkynning og bevisopptak, København 1974.

[12] Politisamarbeidsavtalen av 1972 (Agreement on police cooperation of 1972).

[13] For instance, the standing working group of police and customs authorities on combating illegal drug smuggling. It establishes full operational cooperation in investigating transborder smuggling and sends Nordic liaison officers to non-Nordic states.

[14] Denmark, Norway on Sweden are parties. Iceland has signed the convention but has not yet ratified it. However, ratification is expected to occur shortly. The Finnish position in the matter is not known.

proceedings between the Nordic States takes place pursuant to the Agreement on prosecution in another Nordic State than the State where the offence was committed.[15] This agreement was concluded by the highest public prosecutors of the Nordic states in 1970 and amended in 1972. It has no more than eight Articles and contains provisions on:

- when transfer of proceedings is considered expedient;
- the way in which a request for transfer of proceedings must be made;
- what information a request for transfer of proceedings must contain;
- in what language the request may be made;
- to what authority the request must be directed;
- the legal consequences of transfer and of refusal of transfer.

Articles 7 and 8 of the Agreement contain indications regarding the way in which the distribution mechanism works and some rules of conflict. Paragraph 7 stipulates that the authorities of a Nordic state may not prosecute offenses committed in another Nordic state without notifying the competent authorities of that state. According to paragraph 8 of the Agreement, conflicts over the implementation of the Agreement have to be resolved via consultation and consensus.

The Agreement on transfer of proceedings is one of the major successes of Nordic cooperation. In contrast with many other European countries, transfer of proceedings is daily routine in the Nordic states.[16] In simple cases, usually involving a confessing suspect from another Nordic state, transfer of proceedings occurs by making a phone call and faxing the indictment and related documents to the authorities in the requested state. In intricate or sensitive cases consultations take place at a higher level, sometimes even between the highest ranking prosecutors of the states concerned. The final decision on whether or not proceedings will be transferred is based on practical considerations. The Agreement on transfer contains a number of suggestions in the matter. Thus, for instance, transfer of proceedings is the best option according to Articles 1 and 2 of the Agreement if:

- the suspect lives or resides in another Nordic state and special interests make it preferable that he should be tried and sentenced in that state;
- extradition of the suspect to the state where the offense was committed is undesirable or impossible;
- the suspect is prosecuted in another Nordic state for other offenses and combining all cases against him offers practical advantages.

Transfer of proceedings is generally not thought to be desirable if complications in obtaining evidence may arise. In practice, this also includes consideration of the interests of victims and witnesses.

---

[15] Samarbeidsavtale om rettsforfolgning in annet nordisk land enn der den strafbare handlingen er begatt av 6. februar 1970, endret 12. oktober 1972.

[16] *See* HOLGER ROMANDER, OM ÖVERFÖRING AV ÅTAL INOM NORDEN 376-377 (1984)(On transfer of proceedings between Nordic countries).

Transfer of execution of sentences

Transfer of execution of sentences between Nordic states has been possible since 1948 when the Agreement on the transfer of sentences was concluded. It provided for the transfer of execution of noncustodial sentences only. This agreement has been replaced by uniform laws at the beginning of the 1960s. These uniform laws, providing also for transfer where custodial sentences are concerned, have identical provisions on the matter. Much later, other laws where adopted aiming at the implementation of the European Convention on the International Validity of Criminal Judgements and the European Convention on the Transfer of Sentenced Persons. They provide a basis for transferring execution of sentences in relation to non-Nordic states. As the uniform Nordic laws do not enable transfer of execution of all types of sanctions, the general laws also serve as a basis for transfer between Nordic countries in specific situations. An example is the transfer of custodial measures applied on mentally disturbed offenders.

Pursuant to the uniform Nordic laws, financial penalties, prison sentences, supervision of provisionally convicted persons and supervision of provisionally released prisoners may be transferred. As with all other Nordic regulations the uniform Nordic laws on transfer of execution do not impose any obligation to transfer or accept transferral. However, the rationale underlying these regulations is that a reasonable request from a civilized country should not be denied. One highly remarkable feature of uniform Nordic legislation on transfer of sentences is that it has no requirement of double criminality, not even as regards the transfer of prison sentences.[17] Thus it may occur that a Dane who was sentenced in Norway for publishing pornography is imprisoned in Denmark, although in Denmark publishing pornography is not an offense.

Transfer of execution of sentences between Nordic states is in practice a purely administrative matter conducted by the enforcement authorities concerned. The convicted person may lodge an appeal with the court which will then review whether the legal conditions for transfer of execution have been met. A system of continued enforcement applies to the transfer of prison sentence. A prison sentence imposed in one Nordic state will be executed in full in the executing state without conversion of sentence. This procedure runs into problems if the maximum punishments differ substantially between the Nordic states, as for instance in the case of possession of a certain amount of cannabis. When the general laws on transfer of execution were introduced, a number of Nordic states voiced a clear preference for a conversion of sentence procedure. In some instances this preference has been included in the general law itself, sometimes in the Explanatory Memorandum. Proposals for the revision of the uniform Nordic laws on transfer of sentences do, therefore, sometimes include conversion of sentence procedure, especially as regards prison sentences.[18]

---

[17] Per Ole Träskman, *Should we take the Condition of Double Criminality Seriously? in* DOUBLE CRIMINALITY, STUDIES IN INTERNATIONAL CRIMINAL LAW 135-154, 144 (Nils Jareborg ed., 1989).

[18] *See* Lene Ravn, *Er det nordiske samarbejdsmodel forældet (Is the Nordic model of cooperation outdated)? in* KRIMINALISTIK INSTITUTS ÅRBORG 1994 325-331 (redigeret af Flemming Balvig og Annika Snare, 1995).

Conclusion

These two examples of sub-regional arrangements evidence the proposition that countries which have similarities and affinities particularly as to their legal systems, tend to develop greater cooperation.

The United States Treaties on Mutual Assistance in Criminal Matters

Alan Ellis and Robert L. Pisani *

Introduction

As international borders shrink, permitting criminals and their ill-gotten gains to move more freely, more concern has been focused within the United States on the problems of transnational crime and ways to combat it. For want of jurisdiction, and due to the limitations that sovereignty places on law enforcement, officials (including courts) in the United States must seek information about criminal activities from the state where evidence or persons related to the investigation, including the accused, are located.

However, the traditional manner of seeking judicial assistance from a foreign country, that of letter rogatory,[1] is a cumbersome and time-consuming process involving the passing of letters rogatory and subpoenas through their respective courts as well as foreign justice ministries and embassies.[2] Private local counsel must also be hired, often at great expense, to press the claims of the requesting countries.[3] Moreover, letters rogatory rely on comity, creating no duty to provide information or assistance.[4] The difficulty in obtaining foreign evidence or testimony material to a U.S. investigation has been an additional source of frustration to U.S. officials,[5] who have on occasion resorted to attempts to enforce U.S.

---

* This article has been revised and updated from the first edition by David S. Gualtieri.

[1] BLACK'S LAW DICTIONARY 1050 (rev. 4th ed. 1968) defines letters rogatory as "(t)he medium whereby one country, acting through one of its courts, requests another thereto and entirely within the latter's control, to assist the administration of justice in the former country." For the form of a letter rogatory, *see* JAMES W. MOORE ET. AL., 4 MOORE'S FEDERAL PRACTICE 28:05; *see* also UNITED STATES ATTORNEY MANUAL, Tit. 9, ch. 4. at 77.

[2] *See* Bruce Zagaris, *Developments in International Judicial Assistance and Related Matters*, 18 DENV. J. INT'L L. & POL'Y 339, 351-52 (1990).

[3] *See* MUTUAL LEGAL ASSISTANCE WITH THE REPUBLIC OF COLOMBIA, S. EXEC. REP. NO. 97-35, 97th Cong., 1st Sess., at 8 (1981)[hereinafter COLOMBIAN REPORT].

[4] For a discussion of how MLATs limit the discretion of federal courts, as opposed to non-MLAT requests under 28 U.S.C. § 1782, *see generally* Michael Abbell, *Obtaining Evidence in the U.S. in Criminal Cases Through the Use of Compulsory Process, in* THE ALLEGED TRANSNATIONAL CRIMINAL (R. Atkins ed., 1995).

[5] Letters rogatory cannot be used prior to the grand jury stage of a criminal proceeding; a court may only issue a letter rogatory if it has a criminal proceeding pending before it. Some countries will not permit the use of a letter rogatory even at the grand jury stage. Bruce Zagaris, *International Tax and Related Crimes: Gathering Evidence, Comparative Ethics, and Related Matters* in THE ALLEGED TRANSNATIONAL CRIMINAL 364 (R. Atkins ed., 1995). *See also* William J. Snider, *Developments in Criminal Law and Criminal Justice: International Cooperation in the Forfeiture of Illicit Drug Proceeds*, 6 CRIM. L.F. 377, 384-85 (1995) (discussing the drawbacks of letters rogatory).

subpoenas in foreign jurisdictions[6] and the use of extra-legal methods such as the "kidnaping" of information[7] in order to achieve their ends.

Treaties on mutual legal assistance in criminal matters (MLATs)[8] offer a solution to many of these problems by creating binding obligations and greatly enhancing judicial cooperation. The rapid proliferation of these treaties over the past several years is a response to dramatic changes in the realm of international criminal law enforcement.

A discussion of these treaties is especially timely for three reasons. First, the international legal community has responded to serious threats of increasingly sophisticated transnational criminality. Terrorism, organized crime, arms smuggling and other serious forms of criminality present numerous international law enforcement challenges. However, drug trafficking, money laundering, and the perceived need to strike at the financial base of criminal organizations, have resulted in an increased need for the modality of mutual legal assistance as well as dramatic changes to the system of interstate cooperation in penal matters.

For example, legal assistance obligations, including a requirement to immobilize the proceeds of crime,[9] have been included in substantive international criminal law treaties, most importantly the 1988 United Nations Convention Against Illicit Traffic in Narcotic Drugs and Psychotropic Substances[10] and the Council of Europe's 1990 Convention on Laundering, Search, Seizure and Confiscation of the Proceeds from Crime.[11] The

---

[6] A good example of the difficulties which U.S. authorities face in attempting to enforce U.S. subpoenas in foreign jurisdictions is provided in the Marc Rich case, which involved the investigation of Marc Rich and Company, A.G., a Swiss Corporation, and two U.S. nationals who were alleged to have engaged in transfer-pricing involving a U.S. oil-trading company and its Swiss parent. *See* Marc Rich & Co., A.G. v. United States of America, 707 F.2d 663 (2nd Cir. 1983), *cert. denied* 103 S. Ct. 3555 (1983); Marc Rich & Co., A.G. v. United States of America, 736 F.2d 864 (2nd Cir. 1984), discussed *infra* at note 166 et. seq. *See also The Marc Rich Saga: Extraterritorial Application of U.S. Law—A Growing Legal and Diplomatic Problem*, paper presented by Bruce Zagaris at New Horizons in International Criminal Law. Conference sponsored by International Institute for the Study of Higher Criminal Sciences, Siracusa, Italy, May 6-11, 1984. *See also* Bruce Zagaris et. al., *The U.S. and U.K. Lock Horns Over a U.S. Transfer-Pricing Criminal Investigation,* 44 TAXES INT'L, 11-18 (June, 1983); *U.S. Court of Appeals Orders a Swiss Corporation With No U.S. Office to Deliver Documents to a U.S. Grand-Jury in New York City in a Criminal Transfer-Pricing Investigation*, excerpts from *In Re Grand-Jury Proceedings: U.S. v. Marc Rich and Co. AG,* 44 TAXES INT'L, 11-18 (June 1983); Bruce Zagaris, *Mark Rich Caves In*, 46 TAXES INT'L, 55-57 (Aug. 1983); Bruce Zagaris, *Mark Rich and Similar Cases Prompt Other Countries to Assert Their Sovereignty*, 48 TAXES INT'L, 3-6 (Oct. 1983); Bruce Zagaris, *Developments in International Enforcement*, 49 TAXES INT'L, 3-4 (Nov. 1983).

[7] *See* Michael E. Tigar & Austin J. Doyle Jr., *International Exchange of Information in Criminal Cases, in* MICHIGAN YEARBOOK OF INTERNATIONAL LEGAL STUDIES, TRANSNATIONAL ASPECTS OF CRIMINAL PROCEDURE 77-78 (1983).

[8] Primarily outside the United States, the term "mutual assistance" has been used to describe this modality, thereby avoiding limitations inherent in the terms mutual legal assistance and judicial assistance which restrict the forms of assistance to the law enforcement or judicial arms of government. *See generally* Ethan A. Nadelmann, *Negotiations in Criminal Law Assistance Treaties,* 33 AM. J. INT'L. L. 467 (1985).

[9] One scholar has referred to the application of the modalities of interstate cooperation as "immobilization," which consists of: "identifying individuals who engage in criminal activity, finding and arresting them, gathering the evidence necessary to indict and convict them, and finally imprisoning them," as well as identifying, seizing, and forfeiting the criminal's assets. ETHAN A. NADELMANN, COPS ACROSS BORDERS 5 (1993).

[10] United Nations Convention Against Illicit Traffic in Narcotic Drugs and Psychotropic Substances, U.N. Doc. E/CONF.82/15 Corr. 1 and Corr. 2, 28 I.L.M. 493 (Done at Vienna Nov. 25-Dec. 20, 1988) (Opened for signature Dec. 20, 1988; *entered into force* Nov. 1990) [hereinafter U.N. Drug Convention]. Over one hundred nations are party to this treaty, including the United States.

[11] *Done at* Strasbourg 8 November 1990, No. 141 Europ. T.S. No. 141, 30 I.L.M. 148 *reprinted in* EKKEHART MÜLLER-RAPPARD & M. CHERIF BASSIOUNI, II EUROPEAN INTER-STATE CO-OPERATION IN CRIMINAL

significance of this mode of interstate cooperation is also highlighted by the United Nations Model Treaty on Mutual Assistance in Criminal Matters and its Optional Protocol on the freezing and seizing of illicit proceeds.[12]

Second, since the explosion of drug trafficking in the 1980s the United States has aggressively expanded its law enforcement reach abroad, even beyond its efforts to conclude MLATs with countries of special concern (*e.g.*, states in "bank secrecy" jurisdictions with significant connections to drug trafficking and money laundering). Third, the United States and other countries must now face emerging forms of transnational criminality occasioned by the end of the Cold War. A unique example of this is the international smuggling of nuclear materials from Russia and the republics of the former Soviet Union which has spurred the United States to seek cooperative arrangements with many eastern European states, especially those of the former Soviet Union.[13]

More than one dozen bilateral U.S. MLATs are currently in force and at the disposal of law enforcement authorities.[14] The United States concluded the first of these treaties with

---

MATTERS 1405 (rev'd 2d ed. 1993) (*entered into force* March 1, 1991) [hereinafter COE Convention].

An unusual example that demonstrates the extent of his trend is that legal assistance obligations are also contained in international arms control agreements. For example Article VII of the 1993 Chemical Weapons Convention requires State Parties to provide the "appropriate form of legal assistance" in the investigation and prosecution of acts that States Parties must penalize under the treaty. This minimalist approach neither enumerates what a State Party must provide, nor addresses the several procedural issues that MLATs typically cover. THE CONVENTION ON THE PROHIBITION OF THE DEVELOPMENT, PRODUCTION, STOCKPILING AND USE O CHEMICAL WEAPONS AND ON THEIR DESTRUCTION, *opened for signature* January 13, 1993, 32 I.L.M. 800, *entered into force* Apr. 29, 1997, Art. VII(2). For an analysis of the possible interpretations o this obligation, *see* BARRY KELLMAN ET AL., MANUAL OR NATIONAL IMPLEMENTATION OF THE CHEMICAL WEAPONS CONVENTION Ch. 10 (1993).

[12] G.A. Res. 45/117 (14 Dec. 1990) [hereinafter U.N. Model MLAT]. This model treaty is part of a package of model treaties on interstate cooperation in penal matters adopted at the Eighth United Nations Congress on the Prevention of Crime and the Treatment of Offenders. The other treaties include: Model Treaty on Extradition, G.A. Res. 45/116, U.N. GAOR, 45th Sess., Supp No. 49A, at 211, U.N. Doc. A/45/49 (1991); Model Treaty on the Transfer of Proceedings in Criminal Matters, G.A. Res. 45/118, U.N. GAOR, 45th Sess., Supp No. 49A, at 219, U.N. Doc. A/45/49 (1991); Model Treaty on the Transfer of Supervision of Offenders Conditionally Sentenced or Conditionally Released, U.N. GAOR, 45th Sess., Supp No. 49A, at 221, U.N. Doc. A/45/49 (1991); and Model Treaty for the Prevention of Crimes that Infringe on the Cultural Heritage of Peoples in the Form of Movable Property, U.N. Doc A/CONF.144/28/Rev. 1 (1991). For a discussion of all of these agreements *see* Roger S. Clark, *Crime: The U.N. Agenda on International Cooperation in the Criminal Process*, 15 NOVA L. REV. 475 (1991); Eduardo Vetere, *The Role of the United Nations Working for More Effective International Cooperation in* PRINCIPLES AND PROCEDURES FOR A NEW TRANSNATIONAL CRIMINAL LAW 713 (Albin Eser & Otto Lagodny eds., 1992) (summary of recent U.N. initiatives in the field and relevant documents). To enhance these agreements' utility, the Crime Prevention and Criminal Justice Branch of the United Nations has drafted two manuals to assist states in implementing the model treaties on mutual assistance and extradition.

[13] For a discussion of this new phenomenon and how the modalities of interstate cooperation in penal matters can be applied to address it, *see generally* Barry Kellman & David S. Gualtieri, *Barricading the Nuclear Window: A Legal Regime to Curtail Nuclear Smuggling*, 3 U. ILL. L. REV. 667 (1996). The U.S. is attempting to cultivate "talking partners" to gather evidence and investigate suspected incidents. James F. Collins, Senior Coordinator, Office of the Ambassador-at-Large for the Newly Independent States, Crime in the New Independent States: The U.S. Response, Testimony before the Senate Select Comm. on Intelligence (Apr. 3, 1995). The United States Dept. of State credits much of the success in combating international terrorism to the fact that "U.S. intelligence and law enforcement agencies have an active network of cooperative relationships with counterparts in scores of friendly countries." United States Department of State, Office of the Coordinator for Counterterrorism, PATTERNS OF GLOBAL TERRORISM: 1994 (May 1995) (full text available over the World Wide Web at (gopher://dosfan.lib.uic.edu) [hereinafter Dep't of State, PATTERNS OF GLOBAL TERRORISM].

[14] This article will not discuss the more limited mutual assistance treaties known collectively as the "Lockheed Agreements." For a discussion, *see* Bruno A. Ristau, International Cooperation in Penal Matters: The 'Lockheed Agreements.' *in*, TRANSNATIONAL ASPECTS OF CRIMINAL PROCEDURE 85-104 (R. Atkins eds., 1995).

Switzerland in 1973.[15] Since then, MLATs with the following countries have entered into force: Argentina,[16] the Bahamas,[17] Canada,[18] the Cayman Islands,[19] Italy,[20] Jamaica,[21] Mexico,[22] Morocco,[23] the Netherlands,[24] Panama,[25] the Philippines,[26] Spain,[27] Thailand,[28] Turkey,[29] the United Kingdom and Northern Ireland,[30] and Uruguay.[31] MLATs with

---

15 Treaty With the Swiss Confederation on Mutual Assistance in Criminal Matters, May 25, 1973, 27 U.S.T. 2019, T.I.A.S. 8302, *entered into force* Jan. 23, 1977.

16 Treaty on Mutual Legal Assistance in Criminal Matters, Dec. 4, 1990, S. Treaty Doc. No. 18, 102d Cong. 1st Sess., *entered into force* Feb. 9, 1993.

17 Treaty Between the United States and the Commonwealth of the Bahamas on Mutual Legal Assistance in Criminal Matters, Aug. 18, 1987, S. Treaty Doc. No. 16, 100th Congress, 2d Sess., *entered into force* July 18, 1990.

18 Treaty Between the United States and the Government of Canada on Mutual Legal Assistance, Mar. 18, 1985, *reprinted in* 24 ILM 1092, S. Treaty Doc. No. 14, 100th Congress, 2d Sess., *entered into force* Jan. 24, 1990.

19 Treaty Between the United States and the United Kingdom of Great Britain and Northern Ireland Concerning the Cayman Islands Relating to Mutual Legal Assistance in Criminal Matters, *reprinted in* 26 I.L.M. 537, July 3, 1986, S. Treaty Doc. No. 8, 100th Congress, 2d Sess., *entered into force* Mar. 19, 1990. For a thorough discussion of the Cayman Treaty, *see* MUTUAL ASSISTANCE IN CRIMINAL AND BUSINESS REGULATORY MATTERS xxix-xxiii (W.C. Gilmore ed., 1995).

20 Treaty Between the United States of America and the Italian Republic on Mutual Assistance in Criminal Matters, Nov. 9, 1982, *reprinted in* 24 I.L.M. 1536, Sen. Treaty Doc. No. 25, 98th Congress, 2d Sess., *entered into force* Nov. 13, 1985.

21 Treaty Between the Government of the United States and the Government of Jamaica on Mutual Assistance in Criminal Matters, July 7, 1989, S. Treaty Doc. No. 102-16, 102d Cong., 1st Sess., *entered into force* July 25, 1995.

22 Treaty Between the United States and the Government of Mexico on Mutual Legal Assistance in Criminal Matters, S. Treaty Doc. No. 13, 100th Congress, 2d Sess., *entered into force* May 3, 1991.

23 Convention Between the United States and the Kingdom of Morocco on Mutual Assistance in Criminal Matters, Oct. 17, 1983, Sen. Treaty Doc. No. 24, 98th Cong., 2d Sess., *entered into force* June 23, 1991.

24 Treaty on Mutual Legal Assistance Between the United States of America the Kingdom of the Netherlands, June 12, 1981, T.I.A.S. No. 10374, *entered into force* Sept. 15, 1983.

25 Treaty on Mutual Legal Assistance Between the United States of America and Panama, Apr. 11, 1991, Treaty Doc. No. 102-15, 102d Cong., 1st Sess., *entered into force* Sept. 6, 1995. For an article by article analysis of this treaty *see* Bruce Zagaris, *International Tax and Related Crimes: Gathering Evidence, Comparative Ethics, and Related Matters, in* THE ALLEGED TRANSNATIONAL CRIMINAL 365-80 (R. Atkins ed., 1995).

26 Treaty Between the Government of the United States of America and the Government of the Philippines on Mutual Legal Assistance in Criminal Matters, Nov. 13, 1994, S. Treaty Doc. No. 104-18 (1994). Instruments of ratification were exchanged on Nov. 22, 1996. *Philippines, U.S. Exchange Extradition Treaty*, Xinhua News Agency, Nov. 22, 1996 (NEXIS Curnws file).

27 Treaty on Mutual Legal Assistance in Criminal Matters Between the United States and the Kingdom of Spain, Nov. 20, 1990, S. Treaty Doc. No. 21, 102d Cong., 2d Sess., *entered into force* June 30, 1993.

28 Treaty Between the United States and Government of the Kingdom of Thailand on Mutual Assistance in Criminal Matters, Mar. 19, 1987, S. Treaty Doc. No. 18, 100th Congress, 2d Sess., *entered into force* June 10, 1993.

29 Treaty on Extradition and Mutual Assistance in Criminal Matters Between the United States of America and the Republic of Turkey, June 7, 1979, 32 U.S.T. 3111, T.I.A.S. No. 989, *entered into force* June 1, 1981.

30 Treaty Between the Government of the United States of America and the Government of the United Kingdom of Great Britain and Northern Ireland on Mutual Legal Assistance in Criminal Matters, July 6, 1994, S. Treaty Doc. No. 104-2 (1994). The treaty was ratified by both parties in December 1996. *Home Secretary and U.S. Attorney General Ratify Anti-Crime Treaty*, M2 Presswire, Dec. 4, 1996 (NEXIS Curnws file).

31 Treaty Between the United States of America and the Government of the Oriental Republic of Uruguay, May 6, 1991, Treaty Doc. No. 102-16, 102d Cong., 1st Sess., *entered into force* Apr. 15, 1994. For an article by article analysis of this treaty, as well as a comparison with other U.S. MLATs, *see generally* Didier Opertti, *Juridical Mutual Cooperation in Criminal Matters: The Latest Trends in the Inter-American System and the Bilateral Treaties Between the United States and Latin-American Countries*, 39 NETHERLANDS INT'L L. REV. 89 (1992).

Austria,[32] Belgium,[33] Colombia,[34] Hungary,[35] Nigeria,[36] the Republic of Korea,[37] and Poland[38] have been signed but are not yet in force.

The United States has also entered into several interim executive agreements that cover only drug offenses with the United Kingdom over the Turks and Caicos Islands,[39] Montserrat,[40] Anguilla[41] and the British Virgin Islands.[42] In addition, the U.S. has entered into interim executive agreements providing formal liaison procedures for exchange of evidence with Haiti,[43] Great Britain[44], and Nigeria.[45] Similar agreements with Colombia, Hong Kong, and the Netherlands (covering Aruba and the Dutch Antilles) provide for asset forfeiture and the sharing of proceeds.[46] Finally, the U.S. has entered into negotiations with, among others, Russia, Germany, Australia, Sweden, and Israel in the hopes of concluding MLATs.

---

32 Treaty Between the Government of the United States of America and the Government of the Republic of Austria on Mutual Legal Assistance in Criminal Matters, Feb. 23, 1995, S. Treaty Doc. No. 104-21 (1995).

33 Treaty Between the United States of America and the Kingdom of Belgium on Mutual Legal Assistance in Criminal Matters, Jan. 28, 1988, S. Treaty Doc. No. 16, 100th Congress, 2d Sess. (1988). Advice and consent of the United States Senate on Oct. 24, 1989.

34 Treaty on Mutual Legal Assistance with the Republic of Colombia, Aug. 20, 1980, Treaty Doc. No. 97-11, 97th Cong., 1st Sess. (1981). Advice and consent of the Senate, Dec. 2, 1981. This treaty, one of many points of friction over law enforcement between Colombia and the United States, has been a dead letter in the Colombian Congress for years and is not likely to come into force. *See* ETHAN A. NADELMANN, COPS ACROSS BORDERS 348-49 (1993). *See also* James K. Knapp, *Mutual Assistance Treaties as a Way to Pierce Bank Secrecy,* 20 CASE W. RES. J. INT'L L. 413, n.31 (1988).

35 Treaty Between the Government of the United States of America and the Government of the Republic of Hungary on Mutual Legal Assistance in Criminal Matters, Dec. 1, 1994, S. Treaty Doc. No. 104-20 (1994).

36 Treaty with Nigeria on Mutual Legal Assistance in Criminal Matters, Sept. 13, 1989, Treaty Doc. No. 102-26, 102d Cong., 2d Sess.

37 Treaty Between the United States of America and the Republic of Korea on Mutual Legal Assistance in Criminal Matters, Nov. 23, 1993, S. Treaty Doc. No. 104-1 (1995) (transmitted to the United States Senate Jan. 12, 1995).

38 Treaty Between the United States of America and the Republic of Poland on Mutual Assistance in Criminal Matters, July 10, 1996, S. Treaty Doc. 105-12 (1996) (Read the first time in the Senate July 8, 1997).

39 *See* Exchange of Letters concerning the Turks and Caicos Islands and any Matter Related to any Activity Referred to in the Single Convention on Narcotic Drugs (1961), as amended, Sept. 6, 1986, United States-United Kingdom, D.S.B. 6.87.

40 *See* Exchange of Letters concerning Montserrat and Matters Related to any Activity Referred to in the Single Convention on Narcotic Drugs (1961), as amended May, 14, 1987 United States-United Kingdom. D.S.B. 8.87.

41 *See* Exchange of Letters concerning Anguilla and Matters Related to any Activity Referred to in the Single Convention on Narcotic Drugs (1961), as amended Mar. 11, 1987 United States-United Kingdom. D.S.B. 6.87.

42 *See* Exchange of Letters concerning the British Virgin Islands and any Matter Related to any Activity Referred to in the Single Convention on Narcotic Drugs (1961), as amended, Apr. 14, 1987, United States-United Kingdom, D.S.B. 9.87.

43 *See* Agreement on Procedures for Mutual Assistance in Law Enforcement Matters, Aug. 15, 1987. United States - Haiti.

44 *See* Interim Executive Agreement Concerning the Investigation of Drug Trafficking Offenses and the Seizure and Forfeiture of Proceeds and Instrumentalities of Drug Trafficking, Feb. 9, 1988. United States - Great Britain.

45 *See* Agreement on Procedures for Mutual Assistance in Law Enforcement Matters, Nov. 2, 1987, United States - Nigeria.

46 William J. Snider, *Developments in Criminal Law and Criminal Justice: International Cooperation in the Forfeiture of Illicit Drug Proceeds,* 6 CRIM. L. F. 377, 384 (1995) and sources cited therein. Exchanges of notes cover forfeiture and sharing with the Cayman Islands, Ecuador, and Mexico. *Id.*

This chapter contains three additional sections. The second section discusses the legal and diplomatic circumstances that gave rise to the perceived need for the first MLAT with Switzerland. That section also discusses how U.S. initiatives fit into the global scheme to improve mutual legal assistance in criminal matters, particularly how changes to the landscape of transnational criminality have necessitated such improvements. The fourth section considers several legal issues that have been raised by the application of MLATs, including charges that MLAT procedures violate criminal procedural rights.

Background

For many years, U.S. judicial authorities were reluctant to grant judicial assistance in criminal matters. Such reluctance was based on a number of factors, including concern over the old conflict of law rule that the criminal law of one nation will not give effect to the criminal law of another,[47] the more general doubt about the common law duty or power of courts to grant judicial assistance to foreign courts in criminal matters, and the right of the accused to be confronted by the witness against him. There may have been additional reasons for this reluctance, including the fact that judicial authorities in the United States were merely ignorant or suspicious of foreign tribunals.[48] Mueller, writing in 1962, stated that "as far as criminal cases are concerned, the U.S. common law doctrine is to the effect that the power to execute letters rogatory or a commission issued by a foreign court 'is confined to civil suits and does not extend to criminal proceedings; criminal law being strictly local and a subject to which the comity of states does not extend.'"[49]

Problems of International Judicial Assistance and the Need for the First MLAT

The initial U.S. basis for judicial assistance to proceedings in foreign countries was set out by the Act of March 2, 1855, stating that "Where letters rogatory have be(en) addressed, from any court of a foreign country to any circuit court of the United States, and a United States commissioner designated by said circuit court to make the examination of Witnesses in said letters mentioned, said commissioner shall be empowered to compel the witness to appear and depose in the same manner as to appear and testify in court."[50] A later Act of March 3, 1863, largely made the 1855 Act obsolete and limited judicial assistance to certain civil actions by permitting "testimony of any witness residing within the United States to be used in any suit *for the recovery of money or property* depending in any court in any foreign country with which the United States are at peace, and in which the government of such foreign country shall be a party or shall have an interest. . . ."[51] (emphasis added). The same

47 *The Antelope*, 23 U.S. (10 Wheat.) 66 (1825).

48 One authority seemed to feel it was a little of all of these factors. *See* Gerhard O. W. Mueller, *International Judicial Assistance in Criminal Matters*, 7 VILL. L. REV. 196, 197, 198 (1962).

49 Mueller, supra note 48, at 204 (citing *In the Matter of Jenckes*, 6 R.I. 18,21(1859)).

50 Act of Mar. 2, 1855, ch. 140 § 2, 9 Stat 630.

51 Act of Mar. 3, 1863, ch. 95, 1, 12 Stat. 769. Jones, writing in 1953, noted that ironically the original 1855 Act was enacted to enable a federal circuit court to examine a witness on behalf of a French *juge d'instruction*, which is a magistrate sitting in a preliminary criminal proceeding, but that the subsequent enactment of the 1863 Act limiting assistance to money suits in which the government had an interest not only made the 1855 Act obsolete, but also severely limited the assistance U.S. courts could offer. *See* Harry L. Jones, *International Judicial Assistance: Procedural Chaos and a Program for Reform*, 62 YALE L.J. 540-541 (1953). Jones felt that

act also permitted letters rogatory to be used by U.S. courts for use in foreign countries, permitting them to be returned through the "ministers or consuls of the U.S. nearest the place where said letters or commission shall have been executed."[52]

The next major revision of the U.S. law on international judicial assistance[53] occurred in 1948 and permitted "the deposition of any witness residing within the United States to be used *in any civil action* pending in any court in a foreign country . . . (to) be taken before a person authorized to administer oaths designated by the district court of any district where the witness resides or may be found."[54] (emphasis added). This broadened the law to include any civil action and dropped the requirement that the United States "be a Party or have an interest" in the suit. However, Congress apparently meant to allow such inquiries with regard to other proceedings as well, because the next year the phrase "civil action" was struck out of the law and the phrase "judicial proceeding" inserted in lieu thereof.[55]

The 1948 and 1949 amendments represented the beginnings of a change in U.S. attitudes toward international judicial assistance. A decade earlier, in 1938, the Department of Justice and the Harvard Law School's Research in International Law Project published critiques of the problems in obtaining international judicial assistance, the Harvard Project going so far as to publish a draft treaty on International Judicial Assistance.[56] The American Bar Association passed a resolution in 1950 urging the federal government to "draf(t) treaties and tak(e) other such action as may appear advisable to codify and improve

---

it was not until the adoption of the 1949 amendment permitting assistance in "judicial proceedings" that Congress once again clearly indicated that criminal matters were to be included in such assistance. *Id.*

52 *See supra* note 41, at §4. The U.S. was required to either be a party or have an interest in the matter.

53 Earlier amendments permitted the witness to answer only to the specific questions contained in the letters rogatory (Act of Mar. 3, 1873, Ch. 245, §1, 17 Stat. 581, a right which could be waived upon consent of the Parties); granted the right against self-incrimination with respect to answering questions contained in the letters rogatory (Id. §2, such right to be secured "either under the laws of the State or Territory within which such examination is had, or any other, foreign State"); and permitted commissioners of circuit courts of the United States to whom letters rogatory had been addressed to compel witnesses to "appear and depose in the same manner as witnesses may be compelled to appear and testify in courts" (Act of Feb. 27, 1877, Ch. 69, 19 Stat. 241). This amendment was precisely the wording of the original 1855 legislation and was subsequently appended to the Revised Statutes §875 (2d. Ed., 1878). One year later, the *Revised Statutes* §§4071-4073 drew on the 1863 and 1873 Acts and set forth more limited circumstances in which a foreign government could seek the aid of U.S. courts, i.e., suits involving money or property in which the foreign nation was a party or had an interest. The statutes remained separate but apparently equal until 1948 when they were revised and consolidated into 28 USC §1781 *et. seq.* (62 Stat. 949). *See In re Letters Rogatory From the Justice Court, District of Montreal, Canada*, 523 F.2d note 5 at 564 (1975). Later, when circuit courts were abolished, this power passed to the newly created district courts (Act of Mar. 3, 1911, Ch. 231, §291, 36 Stat. 1167).

By 1926 the courts were permitted to issue subpoenas through consular officers to U.S. citizens abroad who refused to appear in a foreign court pursuant to a letters rogatory issued by a U.S. court in order to compel them to appear. Act of July 3, 1926, Ch. 762, §1, 44 Stat 835. The same Act permitted U.S. courts to issue subpoenas through consular officers to U.S. citizens abroad who were needed as witnesses at a criminal trial commanding the witness to appear at the said court at a specified date and time. If the witness refused to appear as directed, the court was empowered to issue an order directing the witness to appear and show cause why he should not be held in contempt. The court was also permitted to seize property of the witness to be held to satisfy any judgment that may be rendered against him, and such person was subject to a maximum fine of $100,000 upon a finding of contempt. Id. §4-§7.

54 Act of June 25, 1948, ch. 646, 62 Stat 949. *See also* Howard E. Martin, *International Judicial Assistance, Letters Rogatory, Federal Courts Are to Grant Assistance Only To Those Foreign Bodies That Qualify As Tribunals Under 28 USC §1782*, 9 TEX. INT'L L.J. 108 (1974).

55 Act of May 24, 1949, ch.139, §93, 63 Stat. 103.

56 Harvard Law School, Research in International Law, *Draft Convention on Judicial Assistance*, 33 AM. J. INT'L. L., (Supplement), 1939; *see also* Jones, *supra* note 51, at 558 (1953).

international procedures in civil and criminal matters."[57] In the early 1950s, the U.S. military adhered to the North Atlantic Treaty Organization's Status of Forces Agreement.[58] The treaty requires mutual assistance between the host and visiting country, including investigation in criminal matters. However, the treaty is restricted to offenses committed by members of the military.

In 1958, in response to increasing problems with international judicial assistance, Congress established the Commission and Advisory Committee on International Rules of Judicial Procedure to study means of improving such assistance.[59] The commission proposed and Congress later passed an entire revision of the statutes governing international judicial assistance.[60] U.S. courts were empowered to "order service upon (a resident of the district) of any document issued in connection with a proceeding in a foreign or international tribunal."[61] The new law also permitted the Department of State to receive and transmit letters rogatory.[62] No distinction was made between civil and criminal cases for the purposes of the State Department's handling of the requests for judicial assistance. Most important of all, it was made clear under a revised Section 1782 of Chapter 28 that judicial assistance may be sought not only to compel testimony and statements but also to require the production of documents and other tangible evidence:

> The district court of the district in which a person resides or is found may order him to give his testimony or statement or to produce a document or other thing for use in a proceeding in a foreign or international tribunal, including criminal investigations conducted before formal accusation. The order may be made pursuant to a letter rogatory issued, or request made, by a foreign or international tribunal or upon the application of any interested person and may direct that the testimony or statement be given, or the document or other thing be produced, before a person appointed by the court.[63]

Up until this time the U.S. Department of State would not aid in the transmission of requests from a foreign court, including letters rogatory; such requests had to be forwarded directly to the appropriate courts via consular officers of the country in which the letters rogatory were to be used.[64]

Though the 1964 amendments unquestionably "broadened and liberalized" United States practice in international judicial assistance,[65] letters rogatory have been consistently criticized as being "cumbersome, time consuming and extremely limited";[66] the cost of

---

[57] 75 ABA Rep. 150 (1950), *quoted in* Jones, *supra* note 41, at note 146.

[58] Agreement between the parties to the North Atlantic Treaty regarding the status of their forces. Signed at London, June 19, 1951, 4 U.S.T. 1792, 199 U.N.T.S. 67 (entered into force for the United States Aug. 23, 1953).

[59] Act of Sept. 2, 1958, P.L. No. 85-906, §2, 72 Stat. 1743.

[60] Act of Oct. 3, 1964, P.L. No. 88-619, 78 Stat. 995.

[61] *Id.* §4, 28 U.S.C. 1696 (1996).

[62] *Id.* §8, 28 U.S.C. 1781 (1996).

[63] *Id.* §9, 28 U.S.C. 1782 (1996).

[64] Mueller, *supra* note 48, at 202.

[65] *See* S. REP. 1580, 1964, *reproduced in,* 1964 U.S.C.C.A.N. 3782. *See also, In Re* Letters Rogatory From Tokyo District Tokyo, Japan, 539 Fed. 2d 1216 (9th Cir. 1976).

[66] COLOMBIAN REPORT, *supra* note 3, at 2; Treaty on Mutual Legal Assistance With the Kingdom of the

hiring an attorney to press foreign letters rogatory has been described as "astronomical" and "one of the major stumbling blocks to obtaining evidence abroad."[67] One authority has noted that "foreign letters rogatory are often unsatisfying, if not incomprehensible to U.S. lawyers because investigating magistrates are accustomed to writing for a reader who is another investigating magistrate,"[68] and that, "[b]y the same token, American letters rogatory are especially opaque to foreign judges, who do not have an inkling of the American law or procedure."[69]

Problems have also arisen concerning the wording of the statutes. The 1964 amendment to 28 U.S.C. §1782 replaced the language "any judicial proceeding pending in any court in a foreign country" with "in a proceeding in a foreign or international tribunal." Considerable debate and litigation has occurred over the precise meaning of the phrase "tribunal;" judicial pronouncements have indicated that the assistance sought must be for use in a foreign judicial tribunal, and cannot be a merely administrative proceeding.[70] Additionally, the wording of 28 U.S.C. §1782 indicates that such assistance is at the court's discretion, a fact that has been upheld by the courts.[71] Such rulings have not been looked upon favorably either by foreign bodies seeking assistance or by U.S. authorities concerned about the principle of comity.

In the past, U.S. courts did not look with favor upon the use of letters rogatory to secure evidence for introduction in criminal investigations or cases.[72] However, since 1975 requests

---

Netherlands, S. EXEC. REP. No. 97-36, 97th Cong., 1st Sess., at 2 (1981) [hereinafter Netherlands Report]; Convention on Mutual Legal Assistance With the Republic of Morocco, S. EXEC. REP. No. 98-35, 98th Cong., 2nd Sess., 2 (1984) [hereinafter Moroccan Report]; Mutual Legal Assistance Treaty With Italy, S. EXEC. REP. No. 36, 98th Cong., 2nd Sess., at 2 (1984) [hereinafter Italian Report].

[67] Colombian Report, *supra* note 51, at 8.

[68] Larry Chamblee, *International Legal Assistance in Criminal Cases, in* 1 TRANSNATIONAL LITIGATION: PRACTICAL APPROACHES TO CONFLICTS AND ACCOMMODATIONS 188 (1984) [hereinafter TRANSNATIONAL LITIGATION].

[69] *Id.*

[70] *In Re* Letters Rogatory Issued by Director of Inspection of the Government of India, 385 F.2d 1017 (2d Cir. 1967) (Superintendent of Exchange Control of Colombia not a "tribunal" since he acts in government interest); *In re* Letters of Request to Examine Witnesses From the Court of Queen's Bench for Manitoba, Canada, 488 F.2d 511 (9th Cir. 1973) (Canadian Commission of Inquiry not a "tribunal" since its work is unrelated to judicial or quasi-judicial controversies); *In Re* Letters Rogatory From Tokyo District, Tokyo, Japan, 539 Fed. 2d 1216 (9th Cir. 1976) (Tokyo District Court is entitled to international judicial assistance despite contention that Court, while not acting as an adjudicatory body, was not a "tribunal"); Fonseca v. Blumenthal 620 F.2d 322 (2d Cir. 1980) (Indian Income Tax officer not a "tribunal" since he acts in government interest). *See also* Note, *Judicial Assistance: Obtaining Evidence in the United States, Under 28 USC §1782 for Use in a Foreign or International Tribunal*, 5 B. C. INT'L & COMP. L. REV. 175-193 (1982). The mutual assistance treaties circumvent this problem by authorizing U.S. courts to use all of their usual powers to issue subpoenas or any other process in order to satisfy a request for assistance under the treaties. *See*, e.g., Colombian Treaty Art. 4(1); Italian Treaty Art. 4(1); Turkish Treaty Art. 25(4), Moroccan Treaty Art. 3(1), requiring the requested State to do everything in their power to execute the request.

[71] *In Re* Request for Judicial Assistance from Seoul District Criminal Court Seoul, Korea, 555 F.2d. 720 (C.A. Cal. 1977); *In Re* Letters Rogatory From Tokyo District, Tokyo, Japan, 539 Fed. 2d 1216 (9th Cir. 1976).

Other problems with letters rogatory have included the lack of an internationally accepted model to specify the requisite information, inadequate oversight of their execution by diplomatic personnel, a lack of specified procedures for taking testimonial evidence in the requested State, and a lack of mandatory procedures regarding authentication of foreign public documents. *See* Michael Abbell, *International Assistance in Criminal Investigations and Prosecutions, in,* PRACTICING LAW INSTITUTE, EXTRATERRITORIAL DISCOVERY IN INTERNATIONAL LITIGATION 227, 231-32 (1984).

[72] *See In Re* Letters Rogatory From First District Judge of Vera Cruz, 36 F. 306 (CCSDNY, 1888); *In Re*

for execution of letters rogatory have definitively applied to criminal as well as civil matters.[73] By then, the 1964 amendments had been in place for some time. And because of the lack of judicial precedent granting letters rogatory in a criminal case, reliance was made wholly upon the legislative history and intent.[74] The Court of Appeals, in granting the request, noted that the Senate Report on the 1964 amendments stated that the enactment of the word "tribunal" in place of "court" indicated that "assistance should be available, in the court's discretion, in connection with criminal proceedings abroad."[75]

In 1962, the Council of Europe's European Convention on Mutual Assistance in Criminal Matters came into force.[76] The European Convention played a major role in assisting the United States to draft the Swiss Treaty and subsequent MLATs. A Conference on International Judicial Assistance, which was attended by a number of U.S. and Italian authorities, was held in Italy in August 1961. That conference adopted a resolution urging the creation of a bilateral research commission to consider utilization of the principles embodied in the European Convention with a view toward the making of a Convention for Judicial Assistance in Criminal Matters between the United States and Italy.[77]

Despite these good intentions, no serious negotiations were initiated until a series of criminal prosecutions in the United States in the 1960s revealed that Swiss bank secrecy laws were being used to protect a variety of illegal activities, including avoidance of U.S. security laws, evasion of U.S. taxes, and the financing of organized crime activities.[78]

One of the cornerstones of Swiss law is its strong concern for the privacy of the individual, a concern which extends to banking transactions, including those of foreigners. At that time, unauthorized disclosure of financial information created civil and criminal liability under the Swiss Federal Banking Law.[79] The Swiss Penal Code also prohibited disclosure of business secrets, including disclosure to foreign authorities.[80] While an earlier treaty, the 1951 U.S.-Swiss Convention for the Avoidance of Double Taxation With Respect to Taxes on Income,[81] permitted U.S. authorities to obtain information necessary to prevent

---

Letters Rogatory of Republic of Colombia, 4 F. Supp. 165 (SDNY 1933); *In Re* Letters Rogatory From Examining Magistrate of Tribunal of Versailles, France, 26 F. Supp. 852 (D. Md. 1939). Chamblee has noted that amendments to the U.S. statutes in 1948 and 1949 provided the authority to grant assistance in criminal matters. Chamblee, *supra* note 68, at 210.

73 *In Re* Letters Rogatory From Justice Court, District of Montreal, Canada, 383 F. Supp. 857 (E.D. Mich. 1974), *aff'd.* 523 F.2d. 562 (6th Cir. 1975).

74 *Id.* at 565. This was also the procedure of the lower court which could find no precedent where a letter rogatory had been granted in a criminal case, *supra* note 73, at 858.

75 *Supra* note 73, at 565, quoting the Senate Report.

76 European Convention on Mutual Assistance in Criminal Matters, EUROP. T.S. No. 30 (*entered into force* June 12, 1962) [hereinafter Euro. Mutual Assistance Conv.]. A Protocol was signed and came into effect on Apr. 12, 1982. The European Convention in turn was based in part on bilateral treaties concluded between member states of the Council. *See The Antelope*, 23 U.S. 194.

77 Sheldon D. Elliott, Conference on International Judicial Assistance (Judicial Assistance Series, Institute on Judicial Administration), 9-U-14 (1961), at 13, *cited in The Antelope*, 23 U.S. 223.

78 Treaty With the Swiss Confederation on Mutual Assistance in Criminal Matters, [hereinafter Swiss Report] S. EXEC. REP. No. 29, 94th Cong., 2d Sess., at 1 (1976).

79 *See* Tigar & Doyle, *supra* note 4, at 64; Walter Meier, *Banking Secrecy in Swiss and International Taxation*, 7 INT'L LAW. 19, n. 16 (1973); James H. Bloem, *Criminal Law* Treaty on Mutual Assistance in Criminal Matters Between the United States and Switzerland, 7 VAND. J. TRANSNAT'L L. 469, n. 1 (1974); Paul W. Johnson, *Judicial Assistance, Criminal Procedure, Treaty With Switzerland Affects Banking Secrecy Law, Provisions Against Organized Crime Set New Precedent*, 15 HARV. J. INT'L L. 360-64 (1974).

80 Tigar & Doyle, *supra* note 4, at 64; Meier, *supra* note 59, at note 5.

81 Convention for the Avoidance of Double Taxation With Respect to Taxes on Income, signed at

fraud against U.S. tax laws, few disclosures of tax fraud have been made under the convention, and it has been of no assistance in other criminal matters.[82] With the growing concern of U.S. prosecutorial interests extending beyond fiscal offenses and into the area of white collar crime and transactions of multinational corporations, the United States sought to negotiate a broader treaty.

In November 1968, discussions began with Swiss authorities on these issues.[83] An impasse soon developed over the Swiss reluctance to compromise their views on fiscal privacy in matters they did not consider a crime, such as tax evasion. The impasse was resolved when the United States dropped its request for information on tax evaders.[84] The Treaty on Mutual Assistance in Criminal Matters was signed in May 1973 and came into force in January 1977.[85] Perhaps because of the complicated banking laws involved in the negotiations and the fact that it was the first mutual assistance in criminal matters treaty negotiated by the United States, the Swiss-U.S. treaty is the longest and most complicated of any of U.S. MLATs.

New Challenges to International Law Enforcement—The Increased Need for Mutual Legal Assistance on the International Plane

Mutual Legal Assistance on the International Plane

The U.S. experience with MLATs has both influenced and been influenced by developments on the international legal plane. The need for effective inter-state cooperation in penal matters has become a central theme of international law enforcement, as evidenced by the proliferation of bilateral, regional and multilateral legal assistance agreements. Requirements for the provision of mutual legal assistance have become features of major international criminal law treaties, most notably the 1988 United Nations Drug Convention and the Council of Europe's 1990 Laundering Convention. Perhaps even more indicative of the international community's recognition of the importance of this modality is the adoption, in 1990, of the United Nations Model Treaty on Mutual Assistance in Criminal Matters. Each of these instruments will be briefly introduced to place the United States' bilateral MLAT agenda in its proper global context.

Washington May 24, 1951, Art 16, 2 U.S.T. 1751, 126 U.N.T.S. 227, (*entered into force* Sept. 27, 1951). *See also* Tigar & Doyle, *supra* note 4, at 65. The Convention has been discussed extensively elsewhere and need not concern us here. *See* Meier, *supra* note 59; *see also* Mario Kronauer, *Information Given for Tax Purposes From Switzerland to Foreign Countries Especially to the United States for the Prevention of Fraud and the Like in Relation to Certain American Taxes*, 30 TAX L. REV. 47 (1974).

[82] *See* Bloem, *supra* note 59, at 473.

[83] Treaty With The Swiss Confederation on Mutual Assistance in Criminal Matters, S. EXEC. REP. No. 29, 94th Cong., 2d Sess., at 1(1976).

[84] *Id.*, at 2. The Treaty, however, was amended in 1983 by changes in the Swiss legislation to allow for legal assistance in cases of tax or customs fraud for individuals other than organized crime figures. *See infra* note 119 and accompanying text.

[85] Of course, many other difficult matters had to be dealt with including the conflict of law problem between the procedures and philosophies of civil and common law countries. *See* Curt Markees, *The Difference in Concept Between Civil and Common Law Countries As To Judicial Assistance and Cooperation in Criminal Matters, in* 2 A TREATISE ON INTERNATIONAL CRIMINAL LAW 171-188 (M. Cherif Bassiouni & Ved P. Nanda eds., 1973).

The United Nations Drug Convention, which requires states to criminalize nearly every conceivable facet of the production, cultivation, distribution, sale or possession of illicit drugs, including money laundering related to drug offenses,[86] contains extensive legal assistance obligations.[87] Article 7 of the Convention requires parties to provide the "widest measure of mutual legal assistance" in investigations, prosecutions and judicial proceedings related to Article 3(1) violations. The Drug Convention provides a nonexhaustive list of the types of mutual legal assistance to be provided, including: taking evidence or statements from persons, effecting service of judicial documents, executing searches and seizures, examining objects and sites, providing information and evidentiary items; providing records and documents, including bank, financial, corporate or business records; and identifying or tracing proceeds, instrumentalities or other things for evidentiary purposes.[88] Requested parties may provide any other type of assistance allowed by domestic law.[89]

To overcome the hindrance of business and bank confidentiality which has undermined mutual legal assistance and efforts to suppress money laundering, parties cannot decline assistance based on bank secrecy laws.[90] This provision may bolster existing and future legal assistance treaties, especially since the obligations of states under existing treaties are not affected by this Convention.[91] If states are not party to a bilateral or multilateral legal assistance treaty, then the mutual legal assistance provisions will apply. Even if the states are party to such a treaty, they may agree to apply the provisions of the Convention.[92]

Another multilateral development with significant implications for mutual legal assistance in the U.S. and other countries is the 1990 Council of Europe Laundering Convention. This multilateral instrument, which is open to accession by like-minded states that are not members of the Council of Europe, integrates several of the modalities of

---

[86] U.N. Drug Convention Art. 3.

[87] For a discussion of the treaty's restricted scope of covered offenses *see* M. Cherif Bassiouni, *Effective National and International Action Against Organized Crime and Terrorist Criminal Activities* 4 EMORY INT'L L. REV. 9, 37 (1990).

[88] U.N. Drug Convention Art. 7(2)(a)-(g).

[89] *Id.* at Art. 7(3). The obligations under Article 7, and some of the confiscation provisions of Article 5, create a "miniature mutual legal assistance treaty." Because methods of acquiring admissible evidence vary from country to country, it was impossible to negotiate legal assistance provisions as detailed and comprehensive as those in bilateral or regional agreements. Thus, while the U.N. Convention contains many of the "key elements of mutual legal assistance relations, " it does not, and could not, contain more detailed procedures. *See Report of the United States Delegation to the United Nations Conference for the adoption of a Convention Against Illicit Traffic in Narcotic Drugs and Psychotropic Substances*, Executive Report 101-15, 101st Cong., 1st Sess *reprinted in* INTERNATIONAL EFFORTS TO COMBAT MONEY LAUNDERING 98, 127 (W.C. Gilmore ed., 1992). This lack of specificity, however, will inevitably result in countries interpreting their legal assistance obligations differently according to national law. This limitation in the U.N. Convention contrasts with the greater comprehensiveness and detail of regionally motivated multilateral instruments like the Laundering Convention and the Draft Inter-American Convention on Mutual Assistance in Criminal Matters. Issues of interpretation will be diminished under these instruments.

[90] *Id.* at Art. 7(5). *See* Bruce Zagaris, *Developments in International Judicial Assistance and Related Matters*, 18 DENV. J. INT'L L. & POL'Y 339, 346 (1990).

[91] U.N. Drug Convention Art. 7(6).

[92] *Id.* at Art. 7(7). An important explanatory document relating to this treaty and other United Nations initiatives in this area is *Money Laundering and Associated Issues: The Need for International Cooperation*, U.N. Doc. No. E/CN.15/1992/4/Add.5 [hereinafter U.N. Money Laundering Report]. For a more thorough discussion of this treaty *see generally* William C. Gilmore, Dirty Money: The Evolution of Money Laundering Counter-Measures 61-69 (1995); David P. Stewart, *Internationalizing The War on Drugs: The U.N. Convention Against Illicit Traffic in Narcotic Drugs and Psychotropic Substances,* 18 DENV. J. INT'L L. & POL'Y 387 (1990).

interstate cooperation to accomplish its primary goal of confiscating the proceeds of crime. Unlike the United Nations Drug Convention, the Council of Europe Convention was formulated with reference, in principle, to all serious offenses that generate large profits; it is not directed particularly at drug trafficking.[93]

The Laundering Convention requires parties to criminalize money laundering[94] and consists of four chapters. Chapter II (dealing with measures to be taken at the national level) and Chapter III (concerning international cooperation) require parties to enact legislation and other measures necessary to: (1) confiscate instrumentalities and proceeds of crime;[95] (2) identify and trace property liable to confiscation (investigative measures);[96] (3) prevent the transfer or disposal of such property (provisional measures);[97] (4) empower its courts or authorities to order the availability of bank, commercial or financial records and requiring that no party may deny a request on grounds of bank secrecy;[98] and (5) ensure that interested parties affected by confiscation or provisional measures have effective legal remedies in order to preserve their rights.[99]

The Convention's format is somewhat unique and differs from an MLAT in that each section concerns a form of assistance (investigative assistance, provisional measures, or confiscation) and each section begins with an obligation to assist followed by the method of execution (as governed by the law of the requested state). Each party must also enact legislation to enable it to comply with requests for investigation, preliminary measures and confiscation. With this format, the Laundering Convention integrates a mutual legal assistance requirement with a procedure so that there can be no confusion as to what type of assistance a party must render upon receipt of a confiscation request. Upon request, parties must afford each other the widest possible measure of assistance in identifying and tracing proceeds and instrumentalities liable to confiscation, and any assistance must be carried out in accordance with the domestic law of the requested state.[100]

The final international development, the United Nations Model Treaty, is an important tool in the development of the types of bilateral agreements the United States has been able to conclude.[101] The treaty is intended to popularize these types of agreements and is, therefore, a negotiating aid that contains widely agreed-upon provisions that can be adopted in bilateral and multilateral conventions and which can enhance states' abilities to harmonize

---

[93] Article 1(e) of the Euro. Money Laundering Conv. defines a "predicate offense" as "any criminal offense as a result which proceeds were generated that may become the subject of an offense as defined in Article 6 of this Convention." For a discussion of the scope of covered offenses, *see* Explanatory Report on the Convention on Laundering, Search, Seizure and Confiscation of the Proceeds From Crime, Strasbourg, ISBN 92-871-1933-3, ¶ 8 (1991) *reprinted in* EKKEHART MÜLLER-RAPPARD & M. CHERIF BASSIOUNI, II EUROPEAN INTER-STATE CO-OPERATION IN CRIMINAL MATTERS 1419 (rev'd 2d ed. 1993).

[94] *Id.* at Art. 6.

[95] *Id.* at Art. 2(1).

[96] *Id.* at Art. 3.

[97] *Id.*

[98] *Id.* at Art. 4(1).

[99] *Id.* at Art. 5.

[100] For a more detailed description of the treaty's provisions, *see generally* Hans G. Nilsson, *The Council of Europe Laundering Convention: A Recent Example of a Developing International Criminal Law*, 2 CRIM. L. F. 419, 429-31 (1991). *See also* INTERNATIONAL EFFORTS TO COMBAT MONEY LAUNDERING (W. C. Gilmore ed., 1992) (Introduction discussing Laundering Convention in context of other international initiatives); William C. Gilmore, *International Responses to Money Laundering: A General Overview*, Conference Paper: The Money Laundering Conference, M.L 92(10), at 9 (Strasbourg, Sept. 28-30, 1992).

[101] *See* DAVID MCCLEAN, INTERNATIONAL JUDICIAL ASSISTANCE 254-70 (1992).

their national legal schemes with international obligations to cooperate in penal matters despite differences in legal systems. Although there are some significant differences,[102] the structure and content of this model treaty closely resembles many of the U.S. MLATs discussed below. It provides for similar forms of assistance,[103] the establishment of a central authority,[104] similar (although more expansive) grounds for refusing a request,[105] and similar procedures for making and executing requests.[106]

As with most other agreements on cooperation in penal matters, the U.N. Model Treaty provides that the law of the requested state will govern the execution of requests, except that procedures specified by the requesting state will be followed to the extent permitted by the law of the requested state.[107] The treaty's procedures for taking evidence from witnesses, including persons in custody,[108] and executing searches and seizures[109] are also similar to many bilateral MLATs. Significant in its own right, the Model Treaty's Optional Protocol on the freezing and seizing of illicit proceeds is discussed below.

The Expansion of U.S. Law Enforcement and the Second Generation of U.S. MLATs

The proliferation of MLATs concluded at the insistence of the United States is part of a larger expansion of U.S. law enforcement onto the territory of foreign states.[110] There may be no more dramatic symbol of the coming era of international law enforcement than the opening of an FBI office in Moscow in July 1994, one of 24 such FBI outposts on foreign soil. The office will be situated on U.S. Embassy premises, and two FBI agents will be under direct supervision of the U.S. ambassador. Its main function will be to exchange information with Russian law enforcement authorities.[111] FBI and State Department funds have also

---

102 For instance, unlike most recent U.S. MLATs, the Model Treaty specifies that the requesting state must have jurisdiction over the offense being investigated. U.N. Model MLAT Art. 1(1).

103 Art. 1(2).

104 Art. 3.

105 Art. 4 recognizes the following grounds for refusal: (1) the request, if granted, would prejudice the sovereignty, security, *ordre public*, or other public interest; (2) the offense is of a political or military nature; (3) there are substantial grounds to believe the request has been made to prosecute a person on account of that person's race, sex, religion, nationality, ethnic origin, or political opinion or to prejudice that person's position for any of those reasons; (4) the request relates to an offense already subject to investigation or prosecution in the requested state; (5) prosecution in the requesting state would amount to double jeopardy in the requested state; or (6) the assistance requested would contradict the requested state's law had the offense been investigated in its own jurisdiction. For instance, a requested state, under its domestic law, may not be able to fulfill a request to intercept telecommunications or conduct DNA sampling. Other possible grounds for refusal might include objections to the nature of the penalty (*e.g.* capital punishment), requirements of double criminality, and expiration of applicable statutes of limitation.

106 Arts. 5 and 6.

107 *See* Article 6.

108 Arts. 11-15.

109 Art. 17.

110 For an exhaustive discussion of this issue, including the role of MLATs in this process, *see generally* ETHAN A. NADELMANN, COPS ACROSS BORDERS (1993). No other nation extends its criminal legislation abroad as far as the United States. It should be noted that both Australia and Canada have an aggressive strategy of concluding bilateral MLATs. MUTUAL ASSISTANCE IN CRIMINAL AND BUSINESS REGULATORY MATTERS xix (W. C. Gilmore ed., 1995).

111 Wendy Sloane, *FBI's Moscow Mission: The Mob, Nuclear Theft*, CHRISTIAN SCI. MON., July 5, 1994, at 6. FBI officials have begun to forge relationships with Russia, Slovakia, Czech Republic, Hungary, Poland, Lithuania, and Ukraine. *See also* Daniel Klaidman, *FBI Chief Stakes Claim on Realm of James Bond*, RECORDER,

helped establish the International Law Enforcement Academy in Budapest, Hungary, modeled after the FBI training Academy in Quantico, Virginia.[112]

The expansion of U.S. law enforcement and the concomitant expansion in interstate cooperation in penal matters is so extensive that the possibility now exists that law enforcement will encroach upon the areas of intelligence gathering and national security.[113] Perhaps once thought impossible, the United States and Russia have concluded an executive agreement on cooperation in criminal matters and are currently negotiating an MLAT.[114]

Basic Provisions of the Mutual Legal Assistance Treaties Negotiated by the United States

This section surveys the major provisions of the bilateral U.S. MLATs that have entered into force and are currently in use.[115] With the exception of the Swiss and Turkish treaties, and a few MLATs that also contain extradition procedures, the U.S. MLATs are very consistent and contain the same core provisions. Accordingly, rather than discuss each article of each treaty, this section discusses representative provisions in a selection of MLAT's. Those treaties with an established history of use (*e.g.*, those with Switzerland and Turkey) will be discussed most intensively. MLATs concluded more recently (*e.g.*, those with the Bahamas and the Cayman Islands) will be considered to the extent they illustrate the important trends in treaty negotiation and developments in the area of mutual legal assistance. Some deviations in MLATs not yet in force will also be discussed.

It must be remembered that while the core provisions of the U.S. MLATs are very similar, the terms of an MLAT must also be tailored to the specific needs of the two states. For instance, the MLAT with Canada provides for wide assistance and cooperation due to the shared border and the large volume of cases.[116] Briefly, other examples include: 1) the

July 18, 1995 at 7.

[112] James F. Collins, Senior Coordinator, Office of the Ambassador-at-Large for the New Independent States, Crime in the New Independent States: The U.S. Response, Testimony before the Senate Select Comm. on Intelligence (Apr. 3, 1995). FBI Director Louis B. Freeh has cited the repeated incidents of nuclear smuggling in eastern Europe as a reason for "a centrally located school where we can develop a network of police partners in countries" where these relationships do not now exist. David Johnston, *Strength is Seen In a U.S. Export: Law Enforcement*, N. Y. TIMES, Apr. 17, 1995, at A8.

[113] For example, the United States CIA is in a turf battle with the FBI over this issue. *See* Charles Hanley, *On Alert: Smugglers Make Nuclear Disaster a Threat Ever -Present*, THE SUNDAY GAZETTE MAIL, Mar. 26, 1995, at 1A. Foreign policy authority may be shifting to the FBI, according to Richard Holbrooke, Assistant Secretary of State for European Affairs: "We are in a new phase of foreign policy. The CIA and Defense Department issues that have predominated during the Cold War have receded. The FBI is moving to the forefront of this new foreign policy." The FBI implements its new investigative responsibilities through the National Security Threat List, focusing on crimes such as nuclear smuggling that are important to U.S. security. Fed. News Serv., Feb. 14, 1995.

[114] Agreement Between the United States and Russia on Cooperation in Criminal Law Matters, June 30, 1996, State Dept. No. 96-38, 1995 WL 831037 (Treaty) *entered into force* Feb. 5, 1996. *See also Joint Statement by Yeltsin and Clinton on Cooperation in Promoting the Rule of Law and Combating Crime*, U.S. Newswire, Sept. 29, 1994; *Russia and U.S. Prepare Agreement on Mutual Legal Assistance*, ITAR-TASS, Sept. 21, 1994. Additional agreements with Belarus and Ukraine have been proposed. James F. Collins, Senior Coordinator, Office of the Ambassador-at-Large for the New Independent States, Crime in the New Independent States: The U.S. Response, Testimony before the Senate Select Comm. on Intelligence (Apr. 3, 1995).

[115] These include MLATs with: Argentina, the Bahamas, Canada, the Cayman Islands, Italy, Jamaica, Mexico, Morocco, the Netherlands, Panama, Spain, Thailand, Turkey, and Uruguay.

[116] *See* Bruce Zagaris, *Dollar Diplomacy: International Enforcement of Money Movement and Related Matters - A United States Perspective*, 22 GEO. WASH. J. INT'L. LAW & ECON. 465, 498 (1989) and sources cited

focus on bank secrecy in the Swiss MLAT; 2) the conclusion of an MLAT with Belgium that makes special consideration for that nation's financial status and legal system; and 3) the focus on inbound investment found in MLATs concluded with offshore "banking secrecy" jurisdictions (the Bahamas, the Cayman Islands, the Dutch Antilles, Panama, etc.).[117]

General Provisions

These straightforward, self-executing agreements typically consist of approximately 20 articles. While the wording of the treaties differs, their main elements do not.[118] All provide for a broad range of assistance in criminal matters, including: (1) executing requests relating to criminal matters; (2) taking of testimony or statement of persons; (3) effecting the production, preservation and authentication of documents, records, or articles of evidence; (4) returning to the requesting party any objects, articles or any other property or assets belonging to it or obtained by the accused through offenses; (5) serving judicial documents, writs, summonses, records of judicial verdicts and court judgements or decisions; (6) effecting the appearance of a witness or expert before a court of the requesting party; (7) locating persons; and (8) providing judicial records, evidence and information.[119] In addition, since 1985, all U.S. MLATs in force contain a provision permitting the freezing and eventual confiscation of the proceeds of crime.

All the treaties provide that the contracting parties shall provide mutual assistance in criminal investigations and proceedings,[120] implying that assistance will be rendered regardless of whether any charges have been filed. The stated desire to provide assistance in criminal investigations and proceedings indicates that such assistance could be made available at both the investigatory and trial stages; this would include grand jury proceedings in the United States.[121] The more recent treaties contain no requirement that the matter under investigation in the requesting state be one which falls or would fall within the jurisdiction of that state.[122] Earlier treaties, such as those with Switzerland and Turkey, contain such a provision.[123]

---

therein.

117 *Id.* at 498-499 and sources cited therein.

118 After the Swiss Treaty came into effect, a much simplified model treaty was drafted by the Department of State. *See* Marian Nash Leich, 1978 DIGEST OF UNITED STATES PRACTICE IN INTERNATIONAL LAW 859-65 (1980). However, this model is no longer used in MLAT negotiations. MUTUAL ASSISTANCE IN CRIMINAL AND BUSINESS REGULATORY MATTERS xix, n. 126 (W. C. Gilmore ed., 1995).

119 *See e.g.,* Swiss Treaty, Art. 1(4), 11, 16, 19, 20, 22; Turkish Treaty Art. 21; Netherlands Treaty Arts. 1 and 2; Italian Treaty Art. 1; Moroccan Treaty Art. 1. *See also* Netherlands Report, *supra* note 66, at 1, Italian Report, *supra* note 66, at 1; Moroccan Report, *supra* note 66, at 1: Letter of Transmittal of President Jimmy Carter to the Senate concerning the Treaty with the Republic of Turkey on Extradition and Mutual Assistance in Criminal Matters, S. EXEC. REP. No. 18. U.S. Senate 96th Cong., 1st Sess., Washington, DC, US GPO, 1979, at III [hereinafter Turkish Report].

120 *See, e.g.,* U.S.-Swiss MLAT Treaty Art. 1(1)(a); U.S.-Netherlands MLAT Art. 1(1); U.S.-Turkish MLAT Art. 21(2); U.S.-Italian MLAT Art. 1(1); U.S.-Moroccan MLAT Art. 1(1); U.S.-Bahamas Treaty Art. 1(1) (assistance provided in the "investigation, prosecution and suppression of offenses and in proceedings connected therewith").

121 *See, e.g.,* Swiss Treaty Art. 31(2); Italian Report, *supra* note 66, at 1; Moroccan Report, *supra* note 66, at 1.

122 *See* Moroccan Report, *supra* note 51, at 3.

123 Swiss Treaty Art. 1(1); Turkish Treaty Art. 21(2).

On the United States side, the treaties are all intended to be self-executing, relying on the existing authority of the federal courts, particularly 28 U.S.C. §1782.[124] The treaties amend and supplement existing law in matters such as creating discretionary authority to provide confidential information in the possession of the government, creating a right of safe conduct, creating a legal authority to hold persons in custody, creating a hearsay exception for chain of custody evidence, and removing the discretion to refuse to issue subpoenas for testimony and tangible evidence presently in 28 U.S.C. §1782.[125]

Limitations on Assistance

The U.S. MLATs consistently include the same limitations on assistance (or, put another way, permissible grounds for refusing a request for assistance). The limitations on assistance are very similar to limitations contained in extradition agreements or other instruments of inter-state cooperation in penal matters. The MLATs currently in force allow judicial assistance to be refused if the execution of the request would prejudice the security or other essential interests of the requested state.[126] Assistance can typically be denied if the offense is a purely military or political offense;[127] some treaties recognize only one of these exceptions.[128]

---

[124] Turkish Report, *supra* note 119, at v; Message From the President of the United States Transmitting the Treaty on Mutual Legal Assistance Between the United States of America and the Kingdom of the Netherlands, Together with a Related Exchange of Notes, S. TREATY DOC. No.16, 97th Cong., 1st Sess., at v.; Swiss Report, *supra* note 78, at 5. *But See* note *infra* at 127.

[125] Netherlands Report, *supra* note 51, at 11-12. Additionally, Articles 18 and 20 of the U.S.-Swiss MLAT concerning business records and testimony to authenticate documents created new evidentiary rules in providing for the admissibility in evidence in U.S. courts. These articles are based on the foreign official records provision of 28 U.S.C.1741, 18 U.S.C. 3491, et. seq., 28 U.S.C 1732, and Rule 44(a)(2) of the Federal Rules of Civil Procedure. *See Treaty With the Swiss Confederation on Mutual Assistance in Criminal Matters,* Senate Executive Report No. 29, 94th Cong., 1st Sess., 1976, at 5 (Statement of John C. Keeney, Deputy Assistant Attorney General, Criminal Division Department of Justice).

[126] *See, e.g.,* Swiss Treaty Art. 3(1)(a); Turkish Treaty Art. 22(1)(b); Netherlands Treaty Art. 10(1)(a); Italian Treaty Art. 5(1)(a); Moroccan Treaty Art. 2(1)(a); Bahamas Treaty Art. 3(1)(a); Jamaican Treaty Art. 2(1)(a) *cf.* European Convention Art. 2(b). "Security or other essential interests" could include, *inter alia*, national security information, disclosure of the identity of a key informant, and disclosure of trade or other business secrets which might cause economic damage to third parties. Italian Report, *supra* note 66, at 5. The Swiss Implementing Legislation permits Swiss authorities to appoint a commission of experts to determine if the essential interests of Switzerland would be prejudiced by the granting of a request. Swiss Implementing Legislation, Art. 6(1).

[127] *See e.g.,* U.S.-Turkish MLAT Art. 22(1); U.S.-Italian MLAT Art. 5(l)(b); U.S.-Bahamas Treaty Art. 3(1)(b); Uruguay MLAT Art. 5(1)(b) *cf.* Euro. Mutual Assistance Conv. Art. 1(2), 2(a). Exactly what constitutes a political offense is elaborated upon in the U.S.-Turkish MLAT, but only in a negative manner: (T)he following offenses shall not be considered political offenses or offenses connected with a political offense: (a) Offenses for which investigations and proceedings are obligatory for the Contracting Parties under multilateral international agreements; and (b) Offense against a Head of State or a Head of Government or members of their families." U.S.-Turkish MLAT Art. 22(2). The Netherlands Report states that the delegates "appreciate that the United States adheres to the narrower 'British view' of political offenses, while the Netherlands adheres to the broader 'Swiss view'." Netherlands Report, *supra* note 51, at 11.

[128] Netherlands Treaty Art. 10(1)(b) (only political offense exception); Moroccan Treaty Art. 2(1)(b) (only military offense exception); Spanish Treaty 3(1)(a) (only military offense exception). The lack of an absolute bar to assistance in "political offense" cases in the Moroccan treaty was mitigated somewhat in the Executive Report to the Senate, which stated that "the tradition of withholding our assistance from a foreign country prosecuting persons for improper political purposes is so firmly rooted in our country that we would view the "public order" exception as a basis for denying assistance should the occasion arise." Moroccan Report, *supra* note 66, at 4.

A request may generally be refused if it does not conform with the provisions of the treaty in question.[129] Execution of a request may be postponed or denied under most treaties if it would interfere with an ongoing investigation or legal proceeding in the requested state.[130] Conditions may be placed on the assistance given in lieu of denial of a request.[131] Finally, some treaties permit the denial of assistance if executing the request would facilitate the prosecution of an individual on account of his race, religion, nationality, or political opinions.[132]

Scope of Covered Offenses

This issue potentially limits the application of many MLATs, particularly with respect to nontraditional offenses that are somewhat peculiar to U.S. law such as RICO, CCE, conspiracy, money laundering, and structuring (the breaking up of transactions into non-reportable amounts). These nontraditional offenses are often unknown or nonexistent in foreign legal systems. This limitation is especially ironic in that, by aggressively seeking MLATs with money laundering havens, the United States most often seeks the aid of MLAT's in the prosecution of RICO, CCE and money laundering offenses—where tracing the paper trail to offshore banks and companies is critical to the detection of either the offense itself or the proceeds of illicit activity. Similarly, some treaties limit their scope to permit the denial of assistance where the offense in question is a fiscal offense or is tax-related.[133]

The scope of covered offenses depends, to a great extent, on how the doctrine of "double criminality" (requiring that the offenses in question be punishable under the laws of both parties[134]) is applied to a particular request for assistance. Double criminality is specifically required under some MLATs;[135] however, this is not the case with the more recent treaties, such as those with Italy, the Cayman Islands, and Argentina, under which

---

[129] *See, e.g.,* Swiss Treaty Art. 31(1); Netherlands Treaty Art. 10(l)(d); Italian Treaty Art. 5(1)(c); Moroccan Treaty Art. 2(1)(c); Canadian Treaty Art. V(1)(a); Jamaica Treaty Art. 5 (2) (permitting objection for non-conforming requests).

[130] *See, e.g.,* Netherlands Treaty Art. 10(2); Italian Treaty Art. 5(3); Moroccan Treaty Art. 2(3); Jamaican Treaty Art. 2(4); Argentina Treaty Art. 5(4).

[131] *See,* e.g., Swiss Treaty Art. 3(2); Netherlands Treaty Art. 10(2); Italian Treaty Art. 5(2); Moroccan Treaty Art. 5(2).

[132] U.S.-Bahamas Treaty Art. 3(1)(d); *see also* U.S.-Korean MLAT Art. 3(1)(b).

[133] *See, e.g.,* U.S.-Cayman Islands Treaty Art. 3(1)(a) (assistance does not extend to "any matter which relates . . . to the regulation, including the imposition, calculation, and collection, of taxes"); U.S.-Uruguay MLAT Art. 5(1)(c) (exception for tax offenses inapplicable with respect to "willful" false declarations).

[134] Shearer defines double criminality as "an act . . . (which) constitutes a crime according to the laws of both the requesting and requested States." IVAN A. SHEARER, EXTRADITION IN INTERNATIONAL LAW 137 (1971).

[135] The U.S.-Swiss MLAT contains a Schedule listing 35 categories of offenses which constitute crimes in both countries and to which the parties would be required to lend assistance. In addition to common law crimes such as murder, theft, and rape, the Schedule also lists forgery and counterfeiting, drug violations, gambling and bookmaking operations, fraud in relation to running a business, and other crimes including conspiracy to commit such offenses. U.S.-Swiss MLAT Art. 4. The double criminality and listing in the Schedule of offenses requirement are both waived in the case of organized crime investigations. Assistance can also be given even if the offense is not listed in the schedule, provided dual criminality exists and the requested state finds the offense to be of sufficient gravity to warrant assistance. *See also, e.g.,* U.S.-Bahamas Treaty Art. 2(1); U.S.-Jamaica MLAT Art. 1(3) (requested state has discretion to deny assistance where conduct would not constitute an offense in the requested state).

assistance must be rendered regardless of whether the act under investigation is an offense in the requested state.[136] Under such a standard, RICO, CCE and money laundering would rarely pass muster because these are not criminal offenses in most other states.

Generally, MLAT's adopt a broad interpretation of dual criminality by not requiring that all elements of the offense be present in order to grant assistance.[137] Negotiators, however, most often try to ensure that the treaty will cover even more offenses than a broad dual criminality standard. They are usually successful because it is generally considered more controversial and drastic to arrest and surrender a person (as is the case with extradition) than it is to secure and transmit evidence or testimony.[138]

The Turkish, Canadian, Belgian, Italian, Bahamas and Dutch MLATs, for example, are generally quite broad—even granting assistance in tax matters under certain circumstances (usually where the fiscal offense is related to drug trafficking or organized crime).[139] The Cayman MLAT permits assistance with respect to a very wide range of offenses.[140]

The Swiss Treaty, by contrast, lists a number of offenses for which requests for assistance "shall not apply" under the treaty. These include political and military offenses, extradition requests, execution of judgments in criminal matters, anti-trust laws, and violations with respect to taxes, customs duties, governmental monopoly charges or exchange control regulations, except insofar as they relate to certain offenses enumerated in the schedules.[141] However, the nonapplicability of requests for assistance in political, antitrust, and fiscal cases does not apply when the object of the investigation is an organized

---

136 While "double criminality" is the accepted rule for extradition treaties, a somewhat different theory has been applied to MLAT's. *See* Knapp, *supra* note 27, at 418-419. *See* U.S.-Italian MLAT Art. 1(3). However, dual criminality is a prerequisite to obtaining a search warrant, which will be used to obtain documents and records in that country since Italy lacks a process equivalent to a subpoena *duces tecum*. Italian Report, *supra* note 51, at 8. U.S.-Cayman Islands Treaty Art. 1(3); U.S.-Argentina MLAT Art. 1(3).

137 Knapp, *supra* 34, at 420.

138 *Id.*

139 *Id.*

140 Article 19 (3) of the Cayman Treaty ("Definitions") provides for the following offenses:

(a) offenses meeting the dual criminality standard;

(b) all forms of "racketeering" conduct (painstakingly defined in Article 19(b));

(c) all offenses related to narcotics activity(a catch-all provision designed to encompass conspiracy and CCE offenses);

(d) the use of fraud in concocting a tax shelter scheme;

(e) false statements to tax authorities concerning tax matters arising from the unlawful proceeds of a criminal offense;

(f) failure to make a currency transaction report arising from unlawful proceeds (designed to reach money laundering offenses);

(g) insider trading;

(h) fraudulent securities practices;

(i) bribing a foreign official;

(j) mail fraud;

(k) any offense later agreed to in a diplomatic note ; and

(l) any attempt or conspiracy to commit any of the above offenses

See Cayman Treaty art. 19(3)(a)-(l). Although limited to the provisions of (d) and (e), this agreement reaches a significant number of tax offenses. *See* Knapp, *supra* note 34, at 421; MUTUAL ASSISTANCE IN CRIMINAL AND BUSINESS REGULATORY MATTERS xxii (W.C. Gilmore, ed. 1995) (noting unique flexibility of Cayman Treaty) *cf.* Bahamas MLAT, Art. 2 (providing briefer and less explicit definitions of offenses but, arguably, reaching the same offenses as the Cayman MLAT).

141 Swiss Treaty Art. 2(1).

criminal group.[142] Information may also be refused to the extent that it relates to the prosecution of a person for acts of which he has been acquitted or convicted by a final judgment of a court in the requested state.[143]

Civil and Administrative Matters

In addition to mutual assistance in criminal matters, many MLATs explicitly or implicitly permit mutual assistance in civil and administrative investigations and proceedings.[144] The obligation arises under many treaties because of the broad definition of "proceedings" to include "any court or administrative agency in a hearing which could result in an order imposing forfeiture of fruits or instrumentalities" of criminal offenses.[145] The emphasis on administrative investigations indicates that agencies in foreign countries could share with the United States such data as the movement of suspected drug traffickers, which was one of the prime objectives of the treaties.[146] Including these proceedings also helps the U.S. to enforce civil *in rem* forfeitures. The Panama MLAT, for example, allows a requested state to provide assistance to an administrative agency performing an adjudicatory function, perhaps concerning the imposition of sanctions, that is ancillary to a matter covered by the treaty.[147]

---

[142] Swiss Treaty Art. 2(2); *see also infra* note 115 and accompanying text.

[143] U.S.-Swiss MLAT Art. 3(1). The U.S.-Netherlands MLAT also allows a request to be denied to the extent that "the person is immune from prosecution for the offense for which assistance is requested by reason of the laws of the Requested State relating to prior jeopardy." The U.S.-Netherlands MLAT Art. 10(c).

[144] *See e.g.,* U.S.-Netherlands MLAT Art. 11(2); U.S.-Italian MLAT Arts. 1(2) and 8(3); U.S.-Morocco MLAT Art. 7(2); U.S.-Swiss MLAT Art. 1(1); U.S.-Mexican MLAT Art. 1; U.S.-Jamaican MLAT Art. 1(2),(5); U.S.-Argentina MLAT Art. 1(2) *cf.* U.S.-Turkish MLAT Art. 23(1). *See also* Netherlands Report, *supra* note 51, at 1. For another example of legal assistance with respect to administrative matters, *see, e.g., Council of Europe: European Convention on the Obtaining Abroad of Information and Evidence in Administrative Matters, done at Strasbourg,* Mar. 15, 1978, *reprinted in* 17 I.L.M. 805 (1978); *Council of Europe: European Convention on the Service Abroad of Documents Relating to Administrative Matters, done at Strasbourg,* Nov. 24, 1977, *reprinted in* 17 I.L.M. 265 (1978); *European Convention on Mutual Assistance-Administrative Tax Matters,* (*opened for signature* at Strasbourg, 25 Jan. 1988), 27 I.L.M. 1160 (1980). Mutual assistance in administrative matters may even be provided in the context of a treaty ostensibly covering mutual assistance in criminal matters. For example, Article 22 of the *European Convention on Mutual Assistance in Criminal Matters,* ETS No. 30, *entered into force* Jun. 12, 1962, provides for the exchange of information from judicial records whether that information pertains to criminal or administrative matters. *See also Convention on Service Abroad of* Judicial and Extrajudicial Documents in Civil or Commercial Matters ("Hague Service Convention"), done at The Hague Nov. 15, 1965, 20 U.S.T.361, 658 U.N.T.S.163 (*entered into force* for the United States February 10,1969); Convention on the Taking of Evidence Abroad in Civil or Commercial Matters, done at The Hague Mar. 18, 1970, 23 U.S.T. 2555 (*entered into force* for the United States Oct. 7,1972). These Conventions also allow procedures to be followed under the terms of the Conventions rather than utilizing the provisions of 28 USC §1781 and 28 USC § 1782, respectively.

[145] Bahamas Treaty Art. 2(3)(c). *See also* Jamaican Treaty Art. 1(5)(c).

[146] *See* Italian Report, *supra* note 66, at 2; Moroccan Report, *supra* note 66, at 1, 2. *See also* Knapp, *supra* note 34, at 405, 422.

[147] U.S.-Panama MLAT Art. 2(3)(e). *See also* Bruce Zagaris, *International Tax and Related Crimes: Gathering Evidence, Comparative Ethics, and Related Matters, in* THE ALLEGED TRANSNATIONAL CRIMINAL 366 (R. Atkins ed., 1995).

Competent Authorities

All MLATs require that a central authority in each state will administer and implement the treaty. These "competent authorities" or "central authorities" are permitted to communicate directly with each other, rather than through diplomatic channels,[148] and are responsible for transmitting each request to its appropriate federal or state agency, court or other authority for execution. The competent authorities are usually the appropriate heads of the justice ministries of the respective countries. In the United States, the Attorney General delegated such responsibility to the Assistant Attorney General of the Criminal Division, who re-delegated that authority to the Criminal Division's Office of International Affairs.[149]

Contents and Execution of a Request

Requests made under the treaty are generally to be made in writing;[150] requests in "another form" are permitted under the more recent MLATs in urgent circumstances.[151] The competent officials of the requested state are directed to do everything in their power to execute a request.[152] All the treaties have similar requirements for what the contents of a request for assistance shall contain, including: the name of the authority conducting the investigation, the subject matter of the investigation, a description of the evidence sought and the purpose for which it is sought, applicable legal provisions (with their texts) and the name and location of any persons being sought. The treaties also specify information that a request must include to the extent necessary or possible, such as: information on the identity and whereabouts of the person to be located or served and information on that person's relationship to the proceedings, a description of the place or person to be searched and of the articles to be seized, and a list of questions to be asked during the taking of evidence.[153]

---

[148] The competent authority for the United States under all the treaties is the Attorney General or his designees; counterparts in other states include, *inter alia*: for the Swiss, the Division of Police of the Federal Department of Justice and Police in Bern, U.S.-Swiss MLAT Art. 28(1); for the Turkish, the Ministry of Justice, U.S.-Turkish MLAT Art. 38; for the Netherlands, the Minister of Justice of the Netherlands or the Minister of Justice of the Netherlands Antilles, U.S.-Netherlands MLAT Art. 14; for the Italians, the Minister of Grace and Justice, U.S.-Italian MLAT Art. 2(2); for the Moroccans, Minister of Justice or person designated by him, U.S.-Morocco MLAT Art. 3(2); for the Canadians the Minister of Justice or his designees, U.S-Canadian MLAT art. I; for the Spanish the Ministry of Justice or persons designated by it, U.S.-Spanish MLAT Art. 2(2).

[149] *See Order No. 918-80, 28 CFR 0.64-1 (1983).*

[150] *See, e.g.,* U.S.-Cayman Islands Treaty Art. 4(1).

[151] *See, e.g.,* Argentina Treaty Art. 4(1); Uruguay Treaty Art. 6(1).

[152] *See, e.g.,* Swiss Treaty Art. 9(3); Turkish Treaty Art. 25(4); Italian Treaty Art. 4(1); Moroccan Treaty Art. 5(1). However, the treaties are not intended or understood to authorize the use of the grand jury in the United States for the collection of evidence abroad. Moroccan Report, supra note 30, at 5. The Swiss Treaty, Art. 31(2), states that, "in the case of a request by Switzerland this paragraph shall authorize the use of grand juries to compel the attendance and testimony of witnesses and the production of documents, records and articles of evidence." However, according to officials at the Department of Justice, Office of International Affairs Criminal Division, discussions were held between the Justice Department and the American Bar Association at the time of the Senate hearing on the Swiss Treaty, and the Justice Department agreed that the use of grand juries to collect evidence in Swiss cases would constitute an abuse of the grand jury and that they would not utilize this provision of the Treaty. Under the provisions of 28 USC §1782, judges possess similar investigatory powers.

[153] Most all treaties have two categories for what the contents of a request should contain, one category

Because the main function of an MLAT, and its main advantage over letters rogatory, is to obtain evidence in a manner admissible in the requesting state, most MLATs provide that requests can be executed in a manner prescribed by the requesting state. Under many MLATs the procedures specified by the requesting state will be followed unless they are incompatible with, or expressly prohibited by, the law of the requested state.[154] Completed requests are to be returned to the requesting state together with all the documents, information and evidence obtained.[155]

Availability of Records

MLATs generally require the requested state to provide publicly available, duly authenticated, government documents or records to the requesting state.[156] In the U.S., the Freedom of Information Act[157] provides guidance in determining if government files are "publicly available"; however, a record would not be deemed available to the public solely because it is available to a specific individual under the Privacy Act.[158] Non-publicly available records are to be provided to the same extent and under the same conditions as they would be available to the requested state's law enforcement officials; the requested state may exercise discretion as to whether such information is released.[159] Where the contracting states

---

for information which a request "shall" contain, another for information which a request shall contain "to the extent necessary and possible." *Cf.* Turkish Treaty art. 24; Netherlands Treaty Art. 13; Italian Treaty Art. 3; Moroccan Treaty Art. 4(2) and 4(3); Swiss Treaty Art. 29; European Treaty Article 14(1); Uruguay Treaty Art. 6 (2) and 6(3).

[154] *See, e.g.,* Turkish Treaty Art. 25(2); Netherlands Treaty Art. 12(2); Italian Treaty Art. 4(2) and accompanying Memorandum of Understanding; Moroccan Treaty Art. 5(3); Swiss Treaty Art. 9(2). Under the Swiss, Turkish, and Netherlands Treaties, search and seizure may only be executed according to the laws of the requested State. Swiss Treaty Art. 9(2); Turkish Treaty Art. 27; Netherlands Treaty Art. 6(1); cf. European Convention Art. 7(1); Thailand Treaty Art. 5(3); Spanish Treaty Art.5(3); Uruguay Treaty Art. 7(3). Accordingly, where necessary or possible, the requesting state must provide information with respect to the manner in which testimony or a statement is taken and a description of particular procedures to be followed. *See, e.g.,* Uruguay Treaty Art. 6(3)(e), (f).

There is some precedent for executing a request in the form of a letter rogatory using procedures for obtaining evidence not provided for by local procedural law, at least in Italy. See Gori-Montanelli and Botwinik. *International Judicial Assistance, Italy,* 9 INT'L LAW. 722 (1975).

[155] *See, e.g.,* U.S.-Swiss MLAT Art. 32(1); U.S.-Turkish MLAT Art. 39(2); U.S.-Netherlands MLAT Art. 15(1); U.S.-Italian MLAT Art. 6(1). Requests for originals are made in the U.S.-Netherlands MLAT Art. 15(2); U.S.-Italian MLAT Art. 6(2).

[156] *See, e.g.,* Swiss Treaty Art. l9; Turkish Treaty Art. 26; Netherlands Treaty Art. 4(l); Italian Treaty Art. 12(2)-(3); Moroccan Treaty Art. 11(1); Mexican Treaty Art.10 (1), (3); Spanish Treaty Art. 9(1),(3); Uruguay Treaty Art. 14. The authentication procedures differ from treaty to treaty; the most recent treaties have a form appended to the treaty. *See* Swiss Treaty Art. 18(4) (chain certification); Netherlands Report, *supra* note 66, at 6 (authentication to be done in any manner stated in the request); Italian Treaty Art. 12(3) (Central Authority certification of authenticity). The Turkish and Moroccan Treaties are silent as to authentication procedures, however under Article 25(2) and Art. 5(3), respectively, procedures specified by the requesting State may be followed as long as it is not prohibited under the laws of the requested State, thus permitting the United States to follow procedures in Rule 902(3) of the Federal Rules of Evidence. Moroccan Report, *supra* note 66, at 6.

[157] 5 U.S.C. §552 (1996).

[158] 5 U.S.C. §552 (1996).

[159] *See, e.g.,* Swiss Treaty Art. 16(1); Turkish Treaty Art. 26(b); Netherlands Treaty Art. 4(2); Italian Treaty Art. 12(2); Moroccan Treaty Art. 11(2); Mexican Treaty Art.10 (2); Spanish Treaty Art. 9(2) *cf.* European Convention Art. 13.

lack a process equivalent to a subpoena *duces tecum*, search and seizure will be used to obtain necessary business documents.[160]

Search and Seizure

MLATs require a requested state to conduct searches and seizures at the request of the requesting state if the request contains enough information to justify such action under the laws of the requested state.[161] A request from one country to the United States would thus have to be supported by probable cause for the action requested; a corresponding evidentiary standard, under the law of the requested state, would be required for a request from the United States.

Most treaties provide an exception to the U.S. hearsay rule whereby the requested state must provide certificates relating to the chain of custody of records, documents and articles seized; the identity of the object seized and the integrity of its condition. According to the terms of the MLATs, these certifications are to be admissible in evidence as proof of the matters asserted therein.[162]

Immobilization and Forfeiture of Assets

The requirement to trace, immobilize, and confiscate criminal proceeds has emerged as a powerful new modality of inter-state cooperation and is, perhaps, the single most important development in U.S. MLAT policy. In addition to the provisions of the United Nations Drug Convention and the Council of Europe Laundering Convention previously discussed, the growing importance of this modality worldwide is illustrated by the adoption by the Eighth United Nations Congress on the Prevention of Crime and the Treatment of Offenders of a Model Treaty on Mutual Assistance in Criminal Matters that includes an Optional Protocol related to "proceeds of crime."[163] The obligation to immobilize illicit proceeds is most often operationalized through the terms of a legal assistance agreement. Accordingly, before

---

160 *See* U.S.-Netherlands MLAT Art. 5; U.S.-Turkish MLAT Art. 27; U.S.-Italian MLAT Art. 13(1); U.S.-Morocco MLAT Art. 13; Italian Report, supra note 51, at 8; *cf.* U.S.-Swiss MLAT Art. 18.

161 *See, e.g.,* Turkish Treaty Art. 27; Netherlands Treaty Art. 6(1); Italian Treaty Art. 13(1), Moroccan Treaty Art. 13; implied in Swiss Treaty Art. 31(2); Thailand Treaty Art. 11; Mexican Treaty Art.12; Argentina Treaty Art.13. This was the subject of an exchange of diplomatic notes between the negotiations of the Netherlands Treaty agreeing that requests for search and seizure based on "fiscal offenses" such as taxes, duties, customs and exchange will be "judiciously invoked." *See* letter of 12 June 1981 from Thomas J. Dunnigan to Ministerie Van Buitenlandre Zaken, and reply letter of 12 June 1981 from Ministerie Zaken to Mr. Dunnigan, reproduced as an Annex to the Netherlands Treaty, at 11-15. The delegates also agreed to limit searches and seizures to cases where the alleged criminal acts constitute crimes in both countries for imprisonment for more than one year, or if less, is specified in the Annex to the Treaty. This is the only place in the Netherlands Treaty where the concept of dual criminality comes into play.

162 *See* U.S.-Netherlands MLAT Art. 6(5); U.S.-Italian MLAT Art. 13(2); U.S.-Mexican MLAT Art.12(2); U.S.-Argentina MLAT Art.14(2). The Executive Reports state that these are "narrow exceptions" to the hearsay rule. See Netherlands Report, *supra* note 51, at 4.

163 G.A. Res. 45/117 (1990) *reprinted in* Eighth United Nations Congress on Crime Prevention and the Treatment of Offenders (Havana, Cuba, Aug.-Sept. 1990) A/Conf.144/28/Rev. 1 at 77-89. "Proceeds of crime" is defined as "any property suspected, or found by a court, to be property directly or indirectly derived or realized as a result of the commission of an offence or to represent the value of property and other benefits derived from the commission of an offence." *Id.* Optional Protocol, ¶ 1.

addressing very similar requirements of U.S. MLATs, it will be instructive to see how this requirement has been addressed at the multilateral level.

The Optional Protocol deals with assistance related to the enforcement of orders authorizing the tracing, seizing and confiscating of proceeds of crime.[164] Forms of assistance to be provided by a requested state include: tracing proceeds of crime within its jurisdiction, investigating financial dealings, and securing evidence to assist in the recovery of the proceeds of crime.[165] Where suspected proceeds of crime are located, the requested state must take measures to prevent the dealing in, transfer, or disposal of the assets pending a final, judicial determination in relation to those proceeds.[166] These procedures will be conducted in accordance with the law of the requested state.[167] Similarly, a requested state must, to the extent allowed by its law, give effect to a final order of confiscation made by a court of the requesting state.[168] Any measure taken under the Protocol must protect the rights of *bona fide* third parties.[169]

Beginning with the Italian MLAT, several of the most recent U.S. MLATs contain provisions relating to the immobilization and forfeiture of proceeds of crime.[170] The Moroccan Treaty raises a distinction once common in this area in that only "narcotics-related assets" can be immobilized and confiscated.[171]

---

164 *See UN Money Laundering Report*, *supra* note 92, at ¶ 72 for a discussion of how this initiative is related to other international efforts to control the proceeds of crime.

165 Optional Protocol, ¶¶ 2-3.

166 *Id.* ¶ 4.

167 *Id.*

168 *Id.* ¶ 5.

169 *Id.* ¶ 6.

170 U.S.-Italian MLAT Arts. 1(2)(g), 18. U.S.-Italian MLAT Art. 18 provides:

Immobilization and Forfeiture of Assets

1. In emergency situations, the Requested State shall have authority to immobilize assets found in that state which are subject to forfeiture.

2. Following such judicial proceedings as would be required under the laws of the Requested State, that State shall have the authority to order the forfeiture to the Requesting State of assets immobilized pursuant to paragraph 1 of this Article.

The forfeiture provisions were contingent on implementing legislation, and U.S. inactivity for a number of years was a point of contention. *See* Nadelmann, *supra* note 27, at 494. A provision in the Anti-Drug Abuse Act of 1986 eradicated the problem. 18 U.S.C. § 981 provides statutory authority 1) to forfeit the proceeds of a foreign drug trafficking offense and 2) when authorized by a treaty, to sell the property and transfer the proceeds to a foreign country (at least where there has been joint participation in the investigation leading to the proceeds). *See* Knapp, *supra* note 27, at 423 for a discussion of how proceeds should be disposed of once confiscated by the requested state.

171 U.S.-Morocco MLAT Art. 12. Criminal narcotics matters include: (a) intentionally committing any offense against the laws relating to cultivation, production, manufacture, extraction, preparation, custody, possession, offering, offering for sale, distribution, purchase, sale, delivery on any terms whatsoever, brokerage, dispatch in transit, transport, importation and exportation of dangerous drugs as defined in the laws of each of the two States; and (b) any set of conspiracy relating to the offenses mentioned in subparagraph (a) above including any association of criminals any supplying of financial operations or services, together with any punishable attempt to commit these offenses. U.S.-Morocco MLAT Art. 12(3). *See also supra* note 23. U.S.-Morocco MLAT Art. 12. Criminal narcotics matters include: (a) intentionally committing any offense against the laws relating to cultivation, production, manufacture, extraction, preparation, custody, possession, offering, offering for sale, distribution, purchase, sale, delivery on any terms whatsoever, brokerage, dispatch in transit, transport, importation and exportation of dangerous drugs as defined in the laws of each of the two States; and (b) any set of conspiracy relating to the offenses mentioned in subparagraph (a) above including any association of criminals any supplying of financial operations or services, together with any punishable attempt to commit these offenses. U.S.-Morocco MLAT Art. 12(3). *See also supra* note 52.

The forfeiture provisions in the U.S. MLATs are far simpler than those outlined in the Optional Protocol. Under the most recent treaties, if a treaty party becomes aware of the proceeds of crime located in another treaty party, it may inform the other party. If that other state has jurisdiction over the matter, it must present the information to the authorities for a determination of whether any action is appropriate. These authorities must issue their decision, pursuant to the laws of their country, and inform the other state of the action taken.[172] MLAT parties are further required to assist each other in forfeiting the proceeds of crime to the extent permitted by domestic law.[173] Some of the treaties address the manner in which the forfeited assets will be disposed or shared by the two parties.[174]

Serving Documents

The competent authority of the requested state is empowered to cause service of any document transmitted for the purpose of service by the requesting state.[175] Request for service of documents requiring the appearance of a person before authorities in the requesting state must be transmitted a reasonable time before the scheduled appearance.[176] Proof of service will be returned as specified in the request. Some MLAT's, including those with Panama, the Cayman Islands, and the Bahamas, expressly do not require the requested state to serve a subpoena;[177] others restrict the power of the requesting state to take action to compel a personal appearance in its territory.[178]

Taking Testimony in the Requested State

A person in the requested state from whom evidence is sought can be compelled to testify and produce documents, records or articles in the same manner and to the same extent as in criminal investigations or proceedings in the requested state.[179] The treaties specify that if the witness asserts a claim of privilege, immunity or incapacity under the law of the requesting state, the testimony will nevertheless be taken and the assertion will be resolved by authorities in the requesting state.[180] The treaties generally permit the presence of the

---

[172] *See, e.g.,* Bahamas Treaty Art. 14(1); Argentina Treaty Art. 16(1).

[173] *See, e.g.,* Bahamas Treaty Art. 14(2); Argentina Treaty Art. 16(2). The Argentina and Cayman Treaties explicitly provides that the scope of assistance includes "immobilizing" proceeds of crime. Argentina Treaty Art. 1(2)(g); Cayman Treaty Art. 1(2)(g).

[174] *See, e.g.,* U.S.-Panama MLAT Art. 14; U.S.-Spanish MLAT Art. 16(3); U.S.-Argentina MLAT Art. 17(3).

[175] *See,* e.g., Swiss Treaty Art. 22(1); Turkish Treaty Art. 30(1); Netherlands Treaty Art. 3(1); Italian Treaty Art. 11(1); Moroccan Treaty Art. 15(1); Canadian Treaty Art. XI.

[176] *See,* e.g., Swiss Treaty Art. 22(3); Turkish Treaty Art. 29(2); Netherlands Treaty Art. 3(2); Italian Treaty Art. 11(2); Moroccan Treaty Art. 15(2); Thailand Treaty Art. 10(2); similar provision in European Convention Article 7(3). The Swiss, Turkish and Italian Treaties require 30 days advance notice for a personal appearance. The authority of the United States to serve subpoenas on its own nationals under 28 U.S.C.1783 is not affected by the Treaties. Italian Report, *supra* note 66, at 7.

[177] U.S.-Panama MLAT Art. 17 (1); U.S.-Cayman Islands Treaty Art.13(1); U.S.-Bahamas Treaty Art. 17(1).

[178] *See* U.S.-Thailand MLAT Art. 10(4).

[179] *See, e.g.,* Swiss Treaty Art. 10(1); Turkish Treaty Art. 25(3); Netherlands Treaty Art. 14; Italian Treaty Art. 14; Moroccan Treaty Art. 8(1); Cayman Treaty Art. 8(1); Argentina Treaty art. 8(1).

[180] *See, e.g.,* U.S.-Swiss MLAT Art. 10(1); U.S.-Turkish MLAT Art. 25(3); U.S.-Netherlands MLAT Art. 14; U.S.-Italian MLAT Art. 4; U.S.-Morocco MLAT Art. 8(5); U.S.-Cayman Islands Treaty Art. 8(2); U.S.-

accused, counsel for the accused, and any other person specified in the request to be present.[181]

Taking Testimony in the Requesting State

Where testimony is to be taken in the requesting state requiring the witness to travel from the requested state, the procedures differ depending on whether the witness is in custody. With respect to persons not in custody, where testimony is required to execute a request under the treaty, the requesting state may ask the requested state to "invite" the individual to appear before the appropriate authorities in the requesting state.[182] The individual will be informed of the kind and amount of expenses that the requesting state will pay to him.[183] The person invited to testify cannot be compelled to accept the invitation.[184]

The treaties permit a person who has been detained in the requested state to be sent to the requesting state to testify providing that both the person and the central authority of the requested state consent.[185] The person must be returned to the sending state as soon as possible, and no later than the date when he would have completed his sentence in the sending state. Prisoners must also receive credit toward their sentence for time served in the requesting state.[186] The requesting state must keep the transferred person under custody

---

Argentina MLAT Art. 8(4).

[181] *See, e.g.,* U.S.-Swiss MLAT Art. 12(2) (permitting presence of the defendant and/or his counsel with the consent of the requesting stated U.S.-Turkish MLAT Art. 25(5); U.S.-Netherlands MLAT Art. 5(3); U.S.-Italian MLAT Art. 14(3); U.S.-Morocco MLAT Art. 8(4); see also Swiss Law on International Judicial Assistance in Criminal Matters, Art, 21(2).

[182] *See, e.g.,* Netherlands Treaty Art. 3(2); Italian Treaty Art. 15(1); Moroccan Treaty Art. 9, Cayman Treaty, Art. 11; Spanish Treaty Art. 10 (also incorporating safe conduct requirement).

[183] The response of the individual will be communicated promptly to the requesting state. *See, e.g.,* Cayman Treaty Art. 11.

[184] *But see* U.S.-Italian MLAT Art. 15(1). The U.S.-Italian MLAT compels that person to appear and testify in the requesting state by means of the procedures for compelling appearances and testimony of witnesses in the Requested State. U.S.-Italian MLAT Art. 15; *see also infra* note 174 and accompanying text. The requirement to appear and testify under the U.S.-Italian MLAT also differs from the Euro. Mutual Assistance Conv. Art. 8.

[185] Once again, the Italian Treaty does not give the detainee the option to refuse to testify. Italian Treaty Art. 16(1).

[186] *See* U.S.-Swiss MLAT art. 26(2); U.S.-Turkish MLAT Art. 32(1); U.S.-Netherlands MLAT Art. 7(1); U.S.-Cayman Islands Treaty Art. 11; U.S.-Spanish MLAT Art. 11(1)-(3); similar provision in the Euro. Mutual Assistance Conv. Article 11(1). The U.S.-Netherlands MLAT also allows a person detained in the requesting State to be present in the requested State for purposes of confrontation which is understood here in the civil law sense of allowing persons giving conflicting versions of the facts to be brought before a judicial officer. This was apparently added to allow for the procedural law of the Netherlands. Netherlands Report, *supra* note 51 at 9.

A few treaties provide that the requesting state shall not decline to return a transferred person solely because such person is a national of that state. U.S.-Swiss MLAT Art. 26(5); Turkey Treaty Art. 32(4); U.S.-Netherlands MLAT Art. 7(4); U.S.-Italian MLAT Art. 16(3)(c).

The U.S.-Swiss MLAT specifically states the rights of a detained individual testifying in the requesting state. If such person agrees to appear before the requesting state under the U.S.-Swiss MLAT he or she may not be compelled to give testimony or produce documents if under the law in either state he or she has the right to refuse. U.S.-Swiss MLAT Art. 25(1). However, such person may be compelled to testify in the United States if a right to refuse to give testimony or produce evidence is not established, the facts sought are those a bank would be required to keep secret or are manufacturing or business secrets. The person is not in any way connected with the offense which is the basis of the request if the following conditions are met: (1) the request concerns the investigation or prosecution of a serious offense; (2) the disclosure is of importance for obtaining or providing facts which are of substantial significance for the investigation or proceeding; and (3) reasonable but unsuccessful efforts have been made in the United States to obtain the evidence or information in other ways. U.S.-Swiss MLAT Art. 25(2); Art.

unless the requested state authorizes his release;[187] this also has the effect of creating the legal authority for holding a prisoner transferred under the treaty in custody in the United States.[188] Some treaties specify that the requested state need not initiate extradition procedures in order to have the person returned.[189]

A defendant in custody in one state who seeks for purposes of confrontation to be present at judicial proceedings in the other state may be transported to that state, and shall be held and returned under circumstances similar to the transfer of a detained person as outlined above.[190] In these articles the word "confrontation" is used in the United States constitutional sense, to provide a mechanism for affording a defendant the right to confront a witness against him where the witness is not willing to travel to the requesting state.[191] Once again, the requested state may not decline to return the person transferred because such person is a national of that state.[192]

Safe Conduct

Persons transferred under the above circumstances cannot be subject to service of process, detained, or subject to any restriction of liberty with respect to any act or conviction that preceded the person's departure from the territory of the requested state.[193] However, under some treaties, a person summoned before a proceeding in the requesting state to answer for acts forming the subject of proceedings against him is permitted similar safe conduct but only with respect to acts which are not specified in the request.[194] Safe conduct is provided only with respect to acts which preceded the person's departure from the requested state; subsequent crimes committed in the requesting state, such as perjury, can be prosecuted.[195] Moreover, safe conduct ceases altogether if shortly after receiving official notification that his presence is no longer required (10 or 15 days), the person has not left the territory or having left has voluntarily returned.[196]

10(2).

What precisely constitutes a "serious offense" under the U.S.-Swiss MLAT was the subject of an exchange of letters between the chief negotiators of the Treaty. *See* letter of May 25, 1973 from Dr. Albert Weitnauer, Ambassador of Switzerland to Shelly Cullom Davis, Ambassador of the United States and the reply letter of May 25, 1973 of Ambassador Davis to Ambassador Weitnauer. Reproduced in the U.S.-Swiss MLAT at 123-6.

187 U.S.-Swiss MLAT Art. 26(4); U.S.-Turkish MLAT Art. 32(3); U.S.-Netherlands MLAT Art. 7(3); U.S.-Italian MLAT Art. 16(3)(a).

188 Netherlands Report, *supra* note 51 at 5; U.S.-Italian MLAT Art. 16(3)(a).

189 *See* U.S.-Netherlands MLAT Art. 18(3); U.S.-Italian MLAT Art. 16(3)(c); U.S.-Bahamas Treaty Art. 10(3)(c); U.S.-Spanish MLAT Art. 11(3)(c).

190 *See* Swiss Treaty Art. 26(1); Turkish Treaty Art. 33; Netherlands Treaty Art. 8; Italian Treaty Art. 16(2)l Thailand Treaty Art. 12(2).

191 *See* Netherlands Report, *supra* note 51, at 9.

192 *See* U.S.-Swiss MLAT Art. 26(5): U.S.-Netherlands MLAT Art. 8(3); U.S.-Italian MLAT Art. 16(3)(c)

193 *See, e.g.*, U.S.-Swiss MLAT Art. 27(1); U.S.-Turkish MLAT Art. 34(2); U.S.-Netherlands MLAT Art. 9(1); U.S.-Italian MLAT Art. 17(1); U.S.-Morocco MLAT Art. 10; U.S.-Thailand MLAT Art. 17 (1); U.S.-Jamaican MLAT Art. 13 (1); identical provision in Euro. Mutual Assistance Conv. Article 12(1).

194 U.S.-Swiss MLAT Art. 27(2); U.S.-Turkish MLAT Art. 34(2); U.S.-Netherlands MLAT Art. 9(2) identical provision in European Article 12(2).

195 Netherlands Report, *supra* note 51, at 10; U.S.-Italian MLAT Art. 17(l)(b)

196 *See, e.g.*, U.S.-Swiss MLAT Art. 27(3); U.S.-Turkish MLAT Art. 34(3); U.S.-Netherlands MLAT Art. 9(3); U.S.-Italian MLAT Art. 17(2); U.S.-Morocco MLAT Art. 10(2); U.S.-Thailand MLAT Art. 17 (2); U.S.-Jamaican MLAT Art. 13 (2); *cf.* European Treaty Art. 12(3) (immunity ceases 15 days from date such person's presence is not needed). The U.S.-Netherlands MLAT also permits a person appearing as a witness in the requesting

Costs

The requested state is generally required to render assistance without cost to the requesting state. However, most of the treaties require expenses associated with the execution of a request to be paid by the requesting state.[197]

Limitations on Use

Evidence obtained under the treaties generally cannot be used for purposes other than for those stated in the request without the prior consent of the requested state.[198] The treaties also provide that when necessary the requested state may require that evidence and information provided be kept confidential in accordance with stated conditions, except to the extent that disclosure is necessary as evidence in a public proceeding.[199] Several MLATs permit the use of information and evidence for specified purposes, without the consent of the requested state, after the information has been made public in a proceeding related to the case that was the subject of the request.[200]

Other Treaties and Domestic Laws

The treaties provide that assistance and procedures under the treaties shall not prevent or restrict any assistance or procedures provided under other international conventions or

---

state to refuse to testify when such person has an obligation or right to do so under the laws of the requested state and the testimony relates to protected information. Under the law of the Netherlands such persons can include the police, physicians, clergymen, social workers, notaries, tax inspectors, various types of public employees (including intelligence officials) accounts, and attorneys. Netherlands Report, *supra* note 51, at 10.

197 Some treaties (*e.g.*, those with Turkey and Italy) require allowances for a witness or expert invited to appear in the requesting party as well as expenses involved in the transfer and return of detained persons to be paid by the requesting state. U.S.-Turkish MLAT Art. 41; U.S.-Italian MLAT Art. 7. The U.S.-Netherlands MLAT specifies that transfers of persons in custody be paid by the requesting state. U.S.-Netherlands MLAT Art. 17(2). The U.S.-Swiss MLAT permits reimbursement to the requested state for travel expenses, fees of experts, costs of stenographic reporting by other than salaried government employees, costs of interpreters, costs of translation, and fees of private counsel. U.S.-Swiss MLAT Art. 34(1). The U.S.-Morocco MLAT requires the requesting state to pay all of the costs incurred in execution of the request with the exception of legal fees incurred when execution requires judicial or administrative action. U.S.-Morocco MLAT Art. 6. The U.S.-Jamaican MLAT requires consultation between the central authorities where expenses of an extraordinary nature will be required to execute a request U.S.-Jamaican MLAT Art. 7(3).

198 U.S.-Netherlands MLAT Art. 11(2); U.S.-Italian MLAT Art. 8(3); U.S.-Morocco MLAT Art. 7(2). A long list of exceptions are enumerated to this limitation in the U.S.-Swiss MLAT, including where individuals involved in the initial proceeding are suspected of having committed another offense for which assistance is mandatory where persons are suspected of being accessories to the offense or where the persons are suspected of organized crime connections. U.S.-Swiss MLAT Article 5(2); *see also* Johnson, *supra* note 59, at 353-54.

The U.S.-Turkish MLAT provides that such evidence may be used in an investigation relating to an offense other than the offense for which assistance was granted provided the purpose falls within the scope of the treaty. U.S.-Turkish MLAT art. 23(2).

199 Swiss Treaty Art. 15: Netherlands Treaty Art. 11(1); Italian Treaty Art. 8(1); Moroccan Treaty Art. 7(1); Moroccan Report *supra* note 66, at 7. Under some MLATs, the Central Authority of the requesting state can also request that the application for assistance and its supporting documentation be kept confidential. When requests cannot be executed without breaking confidentiality, the requesting state must be so informed so that it can determine if it nevertheless wishes to go forward. *See, e.g.,* Bahamas Treaty Art. 7(3).

200 *See, e.g.,* U.S.-Bahamas Treaty Art. 7(4); U.S.-Argentina MLAT Art. 7(3) (permitting use of information already made public "for any purpose").

arrangements or under the internal laws of the contracting parties.[201] Provisions of previously existing agreements between the United States and the respective countries are thus left intact.[202]

A "first resort" requirement has been included in many recent U.S. MLATs in response to objections of prospective treaty partners to the use by the U.S. of coercive self-help tactics to obtain evidence and information located abroad.[203] These provisions typically prohibit states from using compulsory procedures, such as a grand jury subpoena, without first using the legal assistance procedures of the treaty.[204] Some MLATs specify the amount of time that must elapse before denial of a request or unreasonable delay in executing a request will justify resorting to compulsory measures.[205] A separate Memorandum of Understanding has been concluded with Switzerland to require "first resort" to MLAT procedures and to discourage unilateral compulsory measures.[206]

---

[201] U.S.-Swiss MLAT Art. 38(1); U.S.-Turkish MLAT Art. 42(2); U.S.-Netherlands MLAT Art. 18(1); U.S.-Italian MLAT Art. 19(1); U.S.-Morocco MLAT Art. 16(1); U.S.-Bahamas Treaty Art. 18(1); U.S.-Jamaican MLAT Art. 19. More limited statements concerning lack of a right of any person to take action in a criminal proceeding to suppress or exclude evidence (U.S.-Netherlands MLAT Art. 18(1); U.S.-Bahamas Treaty Art. 18(3)) and activities of INTERPOL not being affected by treaty (U.S.-Italian MLAT Art. 19(2)) are also included.

[202] This would include, *inter alia*, the 1988 U. N. Drug Convention; the Protocol Amending the Single Convention on Narcotic Drugs 1961 done at Geneva Mar. 25, 1972, 26 U.S.T. 1939, (*entered into force* for the United States Aug. 8, 1975); the Executive Agreement with Turkey on Mutual Assistance in Connection with the Lockheed Aircraft Corporation and the McDonnell Douglas Corporation, signed at Washington July 8, 1976, 27 U.S.T. 3419 (*entered into force* July 8, 1976), extensions July 8 and 15, 1980, T.I.A.S. 9810, and Aug. 7 and Dec. 21, 1982; Convention for the Avoidance of Double Taxation and the Prevention of Fiscal Evasion With Respect to Taxes on Estates and Inheritances With Protocol United States-Netherlands 22 U.S.T. 247(*entered into force* Feb. 3, 1971); Procedures for Mutual Assistance in the Administration of Justice in Connection with the Lockheed Aircraft Corporation Matter United States-Netherlands. 27 U.S.T. 1064 (*entered into force* Mar. 29, 1976), related agreement, Mar. 21, 1979, 30 U.S.7. 2500; Procedures for Mutual Assistance in the Administration of Justice in Connection with the Lockheed Aircraft Corporation Matter United States-Italy, 27 U.S.T. 3437 (*entered into force* Apr. 12, 1976); Convention for the Avoidance of Double Taxation and the Prevention of Fiscal Evasion With Respect to Taxes on Estates and Inheritances United States-Italy, 7 U.S.T. 2977 (*entered into force* Oct. 26, 1956). Convention for the Avoidance of Double Taxation and the Prevention of Fiscal Evasion With Respect to Taxes on Income United States-Italy,.7 U.S.T. 2999 (*entered into force* Oct. 26, 1956); Procedures for Mutual Assistance in the Administration of Justice in Connection with the Lockheed Aircraft Corporation Matter United States-Colombia 27 U.S.T. 1059 (*entered into force* Apr. 22,1976), related agreements July 7 and 15, 1980, T.I.A.S. 9809 and August 28 and September 10, 1980 T.I.A.S. 9860; Convention for the Avoidance of Double Taxation and the Prevention of Fiscal Evasion With Respect to Taxes on Income United States-Morocco, T.I.A.S. 10194 (*entered into force* Dec. 30, 1981); Convention for the Avoidance of Double Taxation With Respect to Taxes on Income United States-Switzerland,, 2 U.S.T. 1751 (*entered into force* Sept. 27, 1951).

[203] Such techniques include the issuance of extraterritorial subpoenas on foreign bank records abroad. *See* Bruce Zagaris, *International Tax and Related Crimes: Gathering Evidence, Comparative Ethics, and Related Matters*, *in* THE ALLEGED TRANSNATIONAL CRIMINAL 374 (R. Atkins ed., 1995) citing *Proceedings of a National Security Conference on Strengthening the Rule of Law in the War Against Drugs and Narco-Terrorism*, 15 NOVA L. REV. 795, 805 (1991). For a discussion of how this issue was addressed in the Cayman Treaty *see* MUTUAL ASSISTANCE IN CRIMINAL AND BUSINESS REGULATORY MATTERS xxii-xxiii (W.C. Gilmore ed., 1995).

[204] Canadian Treaty Art. IV; Panama Treaty Art. 18(2); Bahamas Treaty Art. 18(2); Cayman Treaty Art. 17.

[205] Canadian Treaty Art. IV(3) (30 days); Cayman Treaty Art. 17(4) (90 days after receipt of the request for assistance and at least 45 days after giving written notice to the requested state).

[206] U.S.-Switzerland Memorandum of Understanding on Mutual Assistance in Criminal Matters and Ancillary Administrative Proceedings, 1978, *reprinted in* 27 I.L.M. 480 (1988).

Rights of Private Parties

The treaties are not intended for use by nongovernmental parties; private individuals may not invoke the treaty in order to obtain evidence from the other country for use in solely private matters.[207] Nor do the treaties give rise to any right on the part of the defendants to obtain judicial relief or to suppress or exclude evidence through the treaties except as specified.[208] Private parties may continue to use letters rogatory where applicable.[209] The due process implications of this limitation are discussed more fully *infra.*

Denunciation

All of the treaties contain standard diplomatic language concerning the procedure for termination of the respective treaty, requiring that either state give six months notice of intent to terminate.[210]

Special Provisions of the Swiss Treaty

The United States was especially interested in investigating organized crime cases,[211] and Articles 6 through 8 of the Swiss Treaty deal with this topic. If the two states can agree that the investigation concerns organized crime figures, a concept tortuously defined in Article 6,[212] then the requested state shall provide compulsory assistance "even if the

---

[207] U.S.-Netherlands MLAT Art. 18(2); U.S.-Italian MLAT Art. 1(4): U.S.-Morocco MLAT Art. 1(3); U.S.-Cayman Islands Treaty Art. 1(3) ("The provisions of this Treaty shall not create any right on the part of any private person to obtain, suppress, or exclude any evidence, or to impede the execution of a request."); U.S.-Panama MLAT Art. 1(3); U.S.-Spanish MLAT Art. 1(4).

[208] Netherlands Treaty Art. 18(2); Moroccan Treaty Art. 16(2); implied in Italian Treaty Art. 1(4); Swiss Treaty Art. 37(1) contains similar provisions but with numerous exceptions. A defendant may not take any private action with regard to failure on the part of one of the Parties to comply with the terms of the Treaty; he or she is limited to informing the Central Authority of the other state which may or may not require an explanation or take action. Swiss Treaty Article 37(3) and exchange of letters between Ambassador Weitnauer and Davis dated May 25, 1973 and reproduced on pages 110-120 of the Swiss Treaty; *see also* Moroccan Report, *supra* note 66 at 12.

[209] Swiss Treaty Art. 38(1) Turkish Treaty Art. 42(2); Netherlands Treaty Art. 18(1); Italian Treaty Art. 19(1); Moroccan Treaty Art. 16(1); *see also* Italian Report supra note 66 at 3; Moroccan Report, *supra* note 66, at 11. In Fustok v. Banque Populaire Suisse. 546 F. Supp. 506 (Second Dist. N.E 1982). the Court ruled that plaintiff, a nonresident foreign citizen, could obtain information via letters rogatory for use in a Swiss proceeding to the extent that documents or witnesses located in New York possess some information relevant to plaintiff s claims.

[210] *See, e.g.,* U.S.-Swiss MLAT Art. 41(3); U.S.-Turkish MLAT Art. 44(4); U.S.-Netherlands MLAT Art. 21(1); U.S.-Italian MLAT Art. 21; U.S.-Morocco MLAT Art. 18.

[211] *See* testimony of John C. Keeney, *supra* note 93, at 4.

[212] Article 6 states:

[T]he term organized criminal group refers to an association or group of persons combined together for a substantial or indefinite period for the purposes of obtaining monetary or commercial gains or profits for itself or for others wholly or in part by illegal means and of protecting its illegal activities against criminal prosecution and which in carrying out its purposes in a methodical and systematic manner:

a. at least in part of its activities commits or threatens to commit acts of violence or other acts which are likely to intimidate and are punishable in both States; and

b. either:

(1) strives to obtain influence in politics or commerce especially in political bodies or organizations public administrations the judiciary in commercial enterprises employers associations or trade unions or other employees association; or

investigation or proceeding in the requesting State concerns acts which should not be punishable under the law in the requested State, or which are not listed in the Schedule, or neither."[213] Here, income tax violations are also included as an offense for which the requested state shall furnish compulsory assistance, but only if the person investigated is "reasonably suspected" of being a high-level person in the organization, the available evidence is insufficient to prosecute the person without the information requested, and the information provided will substantially assist in the prosecution of the person under investigation.[214] The nonapplicability of requests for assistance in political, antitrust, or fiscal cases does not apply to the investigation of an organized crime group.[215]

Swiss bank records can also be obtained for use in criminal prosecutions in the United States, since the Swiss Treaty requires production of business documents in the requested state at the request of the requesting state.[216] An exchange of letters upon the signing of the Swiss Treaty stated that "It is the understanding of the United States government that Swiss bank secrecy and Article 273 of the Swiss Penal Code shall not serve to limit the assistance provided for by this Treaty, except as provided by paragraph 2 of Article 10."[217] In the words of one of the U.S. negotiators, "When the conditions of the Treaty have been met, bank secrecy is no bar to assistance."[218] The Swiss Law on International Judicial Assistance in Criminal Matters altered the traditional Swiss reluctance to offer international assistance in fiscal cases by allowing "a request for judicial assistance. . . [to] be granted if the subject of the proceeding is a tax fraud."[219]

Legal Challenges to the Use of MLATs

Litigation Under the Treaties

Few published cases concern the MLATs in force. In one case, *Cardenas v. Smith*,[220] a nonresident alien who alleged that her assets had been frozen in Switzerland as a result of information supplied by the United States under the Swiss Treaty brought action against the U.S. Attorney General for declaratory judgment, injunction and damages under the Administrative Procedure Act.[221] The U.S. District Court for the District of Columbia held

---

> (2) associates itself formally or informally with one or more similar associations or groups at least one of which engages in the activities described in subparagraph b(1).

U.S.-Swiss MLAT art. 6(3).

213 *Id.* at Art. 7(1).

214 *Id.* at Art. 7(2).

215 *Id.* at Art. 2(2).

216 *Id.* at Art. 18.

217 Exchange of notes between Shelly Cullom Davis and Dr. Albert Weitnauer, Bern, May 25, 1973, *reproduced in* U.S.-Swiss MLAT.

218 *See* Testimony of John C. Keeney, *supra* note 93, at 5. In this regard, the U.S.-Swiss MLAT was well ahead of the curve as major initiatives such as the U.N. Drug Convention and the Council of Europe Laundering Convention have adopted the same requirement. Oddly, subsequent U.S. MLATs, including those with reputed laundering and tax havens, have not incorporated a similar requirement.

219 Swiss Law, *supra* note 119, at Art. 3(3).

220 Cardenas v. Smith, 555 F. Supp. 539 (D.C.1982).

221 The relevant section of the Administrative Procedures Act is as follows: This chapter [5 U.S.C. §701 *et. seq.*] applies, according to the provisions thereof except to the extent that, (1) statutes preclude judicial review; or (2) agency action is committed to agency discretion by law. 5 U.S.C. §701(a) (1980).

that it had no basis for applying due process standards on behalf of the alien with respect to matters not under the court's control (i.e., the Swiss bank account).[222] More at point, the court held that the Swiss Treaty specifically precluded review when a Swiss account was frozen, except a review under Swiss law. The procedures of the Administrative Procedures Act therefore did not apply.

In another case, *U.S. v. Johnpoll*, use was made of the Swiss Treaty in order to gather evidence which led to the conviction of Johnpoll for conspiracy to transport stolen securities.[223] Johnpoll alleged that the terms of the Swiss Treaty had been violated because U.S. prosecutors had made use of the Swiss evidence in order to attempt to convict Johnpoll of additional customs offenses which were not covered under the terms of the treaty.[224] The Second Circuit Court of Appeals ruled that "As long as the evidence was used to prosecute violations covered by the Treaty, the government was not precluded from also prosecuting other related non-treaty offenses. . . ."[225] The Court also took note of the fact that under Article 37(a) of the Treaty Johnpoll was expressly barred from asserting any right to suppress or exclude evidence gathered under the treaty."[226]

The lack of published cases may at first seem surprising, given the large number of requests for international judicial assistance made through the U.S. Justice Department, especially from the Swiss government. Swiss and U.S. authorities process approximately 100 requests for assistance per year, many involving the seizure and forfeiture of proceeds of crime in Swiss bank accounts.[227] The United States has, in general, made three times more requests for judicial assistance than the Swiss.[228] The use of the treaty has generally been very successful and has led to scores of federal and state convictions.[229] A recent use of the treaty resulted in the seizure from Zurich bank accounts of US$150 million in drug money sought by U.S. officials.[230]

However, the lack of published cases should not be taken to mean that there are no issues capable of litigation. One possible explanation is that, as with extradition cases, many

---

[222] The Court however left open the possibility that damages could be collected under the Federal Tort Claims Act though compliance with the terms of the Act was not alleged by defendant.

[223] U.S. v. Johnpoll, 739 F.2d 702 (2nd Cir. 1984).

[224] *Id.*, at 714. The customs offenses were dismissed by the district court. *Id.*

[225] *Id.*

[226] *Id.*

[227] ETHAN A. NADELMANN, COPS ACROSS BORDERS 340 (1993). According to an earlier article approximately 75% of the requests made to the Swiss government by the United States were for the purpose of obtaining Swiss business or banking records. Lionel Frei and Leonard H. Ralston, *Swiss-American Cooperation in Criminal Investigations*, FBI LAW ENFORCEMENT BULLETIN, January 1982, at 22.

[228] This figure applies to the first eight years that the treaty has been in force (1977-85). *See* Exec. Rep. 100-30, 100th Cong., 2d Sess. September 26, 1988, Bahamas MLAT Report at 1. *See also* Knapp, *supra* note 34, at 414 (for the first six years the United States made 202 requests to Switzerland's 65 requests).

[229] During the first six years that the treaty was in force, the evidence obtained contributed to over 145 convictions. Notably, mutual assistance from Switzerland contributed to the fraudulent transactions and money laundering convictions of Michele Sindona (United States v. Sindona, 636 F.2d 792 (2d Cir. 1980) *cert. denied* 451 U.S. 912 (1981)) and mobster Anthony Giacalone (United States v. Giacalone, No. S 80 Cr. 123 S.D.N.Y. indictment filed February 6, 1980). These convictions were facilitated by access to Swiss bank and business records. *See* Knapp, *supra* note 34, at 415.

[230] *Most Effective Forms of International Cooperation for the Prevention and Control of Organized Transnational Crime at the Investigative, Prosecutorial and Judicial Levels*, U.N. Doc. E/CONF.88/4, September 1, 1994 (background document to the World Ministerial Conference on Organized Transnational Crime) at ¶ 68 (*citing U.S. Swiss MLAT Yields $150 Million Seizure in Swiss Bank*, Money Laundering Alert, May 1994 at 3).

may choose not to contest the request either because they lack the financial resources or because they feel that litigation in this country would be fruitless. Another reason might be that "the receipt and execution of requests are usually matters shrouded in secrecy and the parties affected are unaware of any order made until the order is served and perhaps execution completed."[231]

Yet, while a number of cases involving mutual assistance have been litigated in Switzerland as high as the Swiss Federal Council, they appear to be a small percentage of the whole.[232] One commentator has speculated that potential U.S. defendants may be failing to retain proper Swiss counsel and to alert third parties to their rights under Swiss law.[233]

One unpublished case raises a number of interesting questions concerning the process by which search and seizure is carried out under the Netherlands Treaty. In *United States ex. rep Public Prosecutor of Rotterdam, Netherlands v. Richard Jean Van Aalst,*[234] a defendant's premises were searched pursuant to a search warrant issued by a U.S. magistrate in Orlando, Florida based on an affidavit signed by a Special Agent of the Drug Enforcement Administration. On a Motion for Evidentiary Hearing to Suppress Evidence and/or Return of Property, the defendant alleged that the cablegram received from Dutch authorities to the U.S. Department of Justice requesting a search of defendant's property was not a judicial statement under oath before a judge in the Netherlands, as required under Article 4 of the treaty. The defendant further alleged that the search warrant did not contain probable cause and did not meet the legal requirements for a search warrant under the Federal Rules of Criminal Procedure and federal case law. Finally, the defendant alleged that Section 4 of Article 6 of the treaty is unconstitutional in that it has taken judicial powers away from the judicial branch in an act by the executive branch.[235] The original request for a hearing, as well as a subsequent request for a rehearing, was denied by the judge.[236]

Another explanation for the dearth of published cases is a tendency for the Justice Department to avoid their use in complex cases where the defendants may raise objections under local law that could delay the obtaining of evidence for a year or more. The government has complained bitterly about these delays in the past.[237] In another unpublished

---

[231] MUTUAL ASSISTANCE IN CRIMINAL AND BUSINESS REGULATORY MATTERS xxiii (W.C. Gilmore ed., 1995) citing P.T. Georges, *Mutual Legal Assistance—The Bahamian and Cayman Islands Treaties, in* ACTION AGAINST TRANSNATIONAL CRIMINALITY: PAPERS FROM THE 1992 OXFORD CONFERENCE ON INTERNATIONAL AND TRANSNATIONAL CRIME 134 (1993).

[232] *See* Chamblee, *supra* note 53, at 204; Statement of Mark M. Richard, Deputy Assistant Attorney General, Criminal Division, before the Subcommittee on Criminal Justice House Judiciary Committee Concerning Foreign Evidence Rules Amendments, Apr. 25,1984, Appendix, at 2-5; Swiss Supreme Court Opinion Concerning Judicial Assistance in the Santa Fe Case, 22 I.L.M. 785 (1983).

[233] Richard S. Shine, *Transnational Litigation in Criminal Matters: A Case Study of the Interconex Prosecution, in* TRANSNATIONAL LITIGATION, *supra* note 53, at 561.

[234] United States District Court, Middle District of Florida, Orlando Division Case No. 84-67MISC-018.

[235] Article 6 paragraph 4 of the U.S.-Netherlands MLAT states that: A request to the United States for a search and seizure shall be accompanied by a statement made under oath before or by judge in the Kingdom of the Netherlands, which shall establish good cause to believe that an offense has taken place or is about to take place and that evidence of the offense is to be found on the persons or the premises to be searched. and shall provide a precise description of the persons or premises to be searched. Such a statement shall be considered in the United States in lieu of an affidavit sworn before a United States judicial officer.

[236] Personal communication to the authors by Jeff Kay, Esquire, July 15, 1984.

[237] Foreign Evidence Rules Amendments, H.R. 5406 and S. 1762, Hearings Before the Subcommittee on Criminal Justice, Committee on the Judiciary, House of Representatives, Apr. 25, 1984. (Testimony of Mark Richard, Assistant Attorney General, Criminal Division Department of Justice).

case, *United States of America v. George N. Meros et al.*,[238] a U.S. magistrate granted a motion to take depositions in Switzerland pursuant to Rule 15(c) of the Federal Rules of Criminal Procedure. When defendants hired Swiss counsel to challenge the taking of the depositions, the United States filed a Motion for Injunction seeking to prevent the defendant and his counsel from taking any action in Switzerland which would interfere with the taking of the depositions. The magistrate subsequently issued the order and enjoined the defendants and their U.S. counsel from asserting any rights under Swiss law or in any way interfering with the taking of the depositions. The Assistant U.S. Attorney relied partially on the argument that such motions were causing delays in obtaining evidence abroad.[239]

In another unpublished case, *U.S. v. Carver et al.*,[240] the U.S. District Court Judge ordered that the defendants "shall not, either directly or indirectly, attempt to frustrate this Court's order granting leave to take depositions or this Court's requests for international judicial assistance to the jurisdictions of Bermuda, Liechtenstein, and Switzerland by seeking to re-litigate in those jurisdictions the propriety of this Court's orders, including any issue properly within the scope of Rule 15, Federal Rules of Criminal Procedure."[241] The Judge went on to state that any attempt to so frustrate the execution of the court's orders may constitute a waiver of the right to confrontation.

Despite these pronouncements, the Comprehensive Crime Control Act of 1984 specifically envisions and anticipates that parties will challenge the taking of evidence in foreign countries.[242] The Foreign Evidence section of the act attempts to ameliorate several difficulties United States authorities have been having with regard to gathering evidence abroad, including establishing an exception to the hearsay rule regarding the authenticity of foreign business records, creating an exception to the Speedy Trial Act to specifically exclude reasonable periods of delay resulting from efforts to obtain evidence from abroad for use at trial, and extending the statute of limitations for the time needed to obtain information from abroad (but in no case for more than three years).[243] The law also requires any party that submits a pleading or other document to a court in a foreign country in opposition to an official request for evidence to serve notice on the other party at the same time. S. Cass Weiland, Chief Counsel for the Committee on Government Affairs of the Senate Permanent Subcommittee on Investigations, noted in discussing the legislation prior to its enactment that: "Nothing can or would be done to prohibit the subject's access to

---

238 United States of America v. George N. Meros et al., United States District Court, Middle District of Florida, Tampa Division, Case No. 84-76-CR-T-8.

239 United States v. Carver, et. al. Criminal No. 81-342 (D.D.C. Nov. 10, 1981) (authentication of documents held up for four years by defendants filing appeals in Swiss court); United States v Johnpoll, 739 F.2d. 702 (2nd Cir. 1984) (two-year delay in obtaining evidence under U.S.-Swiss MLAT) *See supra* note 186 and accompanying text); Marc Rich & Co., A. G. v. United States, 707 F.2d 663 (2nd Cir. 1983) *cert. denied* 103 S. Ct. 3555 (1983) (one-year delay in obtaining documents); U.S. v . Friedland, 660 F.2d.919 (3rd Cir. 1981) (delay in excess of one year to obtain bank records in Switzerland).

When the Assistant Attorney General felt that the defendant was not complying with the term of the Order, he filed a Motion requesting the court to issue a bench warrant and an Order to Show Cause why the defendants and their attorneys should not be held in criminal contempt. The Motion was dismissed by the court. United States of America v. George N. Meros et. al., *supra* note 163.

240 U.S. v. Carver. et. al., Criminal No. 81-342 (D.D.C. Nov. 10 1981).

241 *Id.* at 4.

242 H.J. Res. 648, Title II, ch. XII, Part K, P.L. 98-473 Oct. 4, 1984, 98th Cong., 2d Sess.

243 Foreign Evidence Rules Amendments, H.R. 5406 and S. 1762 (Hearings Before the Subcommittee on Criminal Justice Committee on the Judiciary House of Representatives Apr. 25, 1984).

foreign courts but it is reasonable to require him to give notice of his action to his litigation opponent in the United States, be it the government or a private litigant."[244]

At the same time, U.S. courts are more sympathetic to the issuance of subpoenas to obtain foreign bank and tax information regardless of the conflict of law questions involved and regardless of the fact that procedures compatible with foreign law are often available.[245]

Ironically, U.S. courts have bristled at attempts by foreign courts to limit the rights of appellants here through injunctions in foreign courts. The controversy surrounding Laker Airways provides a case in point. In 1982 Laker filed an antitrust suit in U.S. courts against six major airlines and two other corporations, charging them with a predatory scheme to drive it out of business.[246] The four foreign airlines named as defendants in the suit then filed suit in the Court of Queen's Bench in London, seeking a declaration of nonliability to Laker and an order enjoining Laker permanently from continuing its action in the United States. They later were granted a permanent injunction in the Court of Appeal after the Secretary of State for Trade and Industry issued an order under the British Protection of Trading Interests Act.[247] The U.S. District Court for the District of Columbia, upon reviewing the proceedings to date, lamented "the increasing intrusiveness of the English orders"[248] and after noting that the plaintiff was now effectively precluded from asserting his rights under U.S. law, the court appointed an *amicus* to advise it on the means by which the lawsuits could be revived.[249] Though the British injunction was eventually dissolved by the House of Lords,[250] the Laker case represents precisely the reverse of the situation in the Meros and Carver cases, where U.S. courts prevented defendants from asserting rights guaranteed under foreign law.

---

[244] S. Cass Weiland, *Legislative Perspective on Problem of Transnational Evidence Gathering, in,* TRANSNATIONAL LITIGATION, *supra* note 53, at 580.

[245] *See Courts Aid Officials Efforts to Get Offshore Bank Data of U.S. Firms,* WALL ST. J., July 24, 1984; *see also* Marc Rich & Co., A. G. v. United States of America 707 F.2d 663 (2nd Cir. 1983), *cert. denied, 103 S. Ct. 3555 (*1983); United States v. Bank of Nova Scotia 691 F.2d. 1384 (11th Cir. 1982) *cert. denied,* 103 S. Ct. 3086 (1983); United States v. Vetco, Inc., 644 F.2d 1324, *modified,* 691 F.2d 1281 (9th Cir. 1981) *cert. denied* 454 U.S. 1098 (1981); United States v. Field 532 F.2d 404 (5th Cir. 1976) *cert. denied,* 429 U.S. 940, 97 S. Ct.354, 50 L.Ed. 309 (1976); Securities and Exchange Commission v. Banca Della Svizzera Italiana, 92 F.R.D. 119 (S.D.N.Y.1981); *In re* Grand Jury No.81-2, 550 F. Supp. 29 (W.D. Mich. N.D.1982); *but see Societe Internationale Power Participations Industry v. Rogers 357 U.S. 197,* 78 S. Ct. 1087, 2 L.Ed. 2d 1255 (1958) (dismissal of plaintiff's complaint could not be imposed where plaintiff had acted in good faith, was unable to comply because of foreign law and was entitled to a hearing on the merits with regard to particulars alleged in suit); United States v. First National Bank of Chicago, 699 F.2d 341 (7th Cir. 1983) (Court denied enforcement of an IRS summons directed to First National Bank seeking disclosure of records which were located in Greece and concerned Greek nationals). U.S. courts have generally employed a balancing test in determining whether they should exercise jurisdiction over foreign documents. *See* RESTATEMENT (SECOND) OF FOREIGN RELATIONS LAW OF THE UNITED STATES (1965) §40; RESTATEMENT (REVISED) OF THE FOREIGN RELATIONS LAW OF THE UNITED STATES (Tentative Draft No. 3 1982) §420.

[246] *See United States: Judicial Proceedings in Antitrust Action of Laker Airways Limited,* 53 I.L.M. 517 (1984). Four other airlines were subsequently added as defendants. *Id.* note 3 at 590.

[247] *Id.*, at 518. The British Protection of Trading Interests Act appears at 21 I.L.M., 834 (1982). Other countries have also enacted similar protective legislation to guard against encroachments of extraterritorial jurisdiction including France, Australia, Canada, and Germany. *See Foreign Blocking Statutes, in* TRANSNATIONAL LITIGATION, *supra* note 68, at 1329.

[248] *Id.*, at 596.

[249] *Id.*

[250] United States of America v. George N. Meros et. al., United States Court of Appeals for the Eleventh Circuit C.A. No. 84-3721, Motion for Stay Pending Appeal at 45.

At least one government, Switzerland, has lodged several objections to what they perceive to be the overly aggressive stance of the Justice Department in pursuing evidence abroad. In a controversy involving Credit Suisse, for example, the New York branch of that company resisted a U.S. District Court judge's order to turn over evidence, causing the judge to threaten to freeze the assets of the New York branch office until a compromise was reached.[251] In a tax evasion scheme involving Marc Rich and Co., A.G., U.S. officials successfully subpoenaed documents directly rather than through the Swiss Treaty, causing the Swiss government to call a news conference at the United Nations to protest the maneuver and to file an *amicus curiae* brief on Rich's behalf.[252] The Swiss are dearly disturbed that, at least in some instances, the United States is not following the terms of the agreements on mutual assistance worked out over the last decade.[253] The Swiss government, in filing its *amicus curiae* brief in the *Marc Rich* case, noted that "Despite repeated assurances from the Government of Switzerland that a request for intergovernmental assistance would likely lead to release of most of the documents within a short period of time, the United States prosecutors have refused to make any such request."[254] Criticism of the U.S. government's handling of that case has extended as high as the Swiss Federal Council.[255] "First resort" requirements in the more recent U.S. MLATs and side agreements with other states address this problem directly.[256]

Potential Conflicts with Criminal Procedural Rights

Several potential problems inhere whenever law enforcement measures such as MLATs are drafted from a prosecutorial perspective.[257] Though MLATs contain some procedural

---

[251] *See* SEC v. American Institute Counselors Inc. et. al., FED. SEC. L. REP. (CCH) 95 388 (D.D.C. Dec. 30 1975). *See also* Note, *Extraterritoriality: Swiss Supreme Court Refuses United States Request for Information Concerning Insider Trading,* 25 HARV. INT'L L. J. n. 19 (1984).

[252] *See War Breaks Out Over a Rich Man's Tax Return,* ECONOMIST, Sept. 24, at 83 (1983); *amicus curiae* brief of Swiss government in Marc Rich & Co., A. G. v. United States of America 736 F.2d. 864 (2nd Cir. 1984) Docket 84-6033.

[253] *See* Letter of Anton Heger Ambassador of Switzerland to Judge Leonard B. Sand, *in re* Grand Jury Investigation of March Rich and Co. A.G. dated Sept. 19, 1983, *reprinted in,* TRANSNATIONAL LITIGATION, *supra* note 53, at 744. Dr. Lionel Frei, Chief, Section of International Assistance and Police Matters of the Federal Department of Police in Bern, Switzerland has expressed the view that if conflicts of law arise they should be solved by mutual consultations and compromise and not by unilateral action. Lionel Frei, *Swiss Secrecy Laws and Obtaining Evidence from Switzerland, in* TRANSNATIONAL LITIGATION, *supra* note 53, at 33.

Besides the U.S.-Swiss MLAT, an agreement was also negotiated concerning assistance in insider trading that was outside the scope of the U.S.-Swiss MLAT. *See* Switzerland-United States: Memorandum of Understanding to Establish Mutually Acceptable Means for Improving International Law Enforcement Cooperation in the Field of Insider Trading, Aug. 31, 1982, 22 I.L.M. 1 (1983).

Other countries have also expressed concerns about unilateral actions by U.S. authorities. *See e.g.*, Serge April and Johnathan T. Fried, *Compelling Discovery and Disclosure in Transnational Litigation: A Canadian View*, 16 N.Y U. J. INTL L. & POL. 961 (1984).

[254] *Amicus curiae* brief of Swiss government in Marc Rich & Co. A. G. v. United States of Americas, *supra* note 174, at 8. The brief also noted that Swiss law prohibited the production of documents other than through an official request of intergovernmental assistance. *Id.*, at 17.

[255] *See* text accompanying note 202.

[256] *See* text accompanying note 121.

[257] In responding to the criticism that MLATs procedures are not available to the defendants, Justice Department officials have readily admitted that these treaties are "frankly intended to be law enforcement tools.' Statement of Mark M. Richard, U.S. Senate Report, Mutual Legal Assistance Treaty Concerning the Cayman

safeguards, concerns persist over several potential conflicts between the evidence gathering procedures under MLATs and criminal procedural rights. In exercising their authority under these treaties, both requesting and requested states will be subject to several limitations, including: (1) limitations contained in the treaties themselves, including permissible grounds for refusing to grant a request;[258] (2) statutory and constitutional requirements in the requested state; and (3) limitations imposed by international human rights norms and standards.

There are three basic concerns with MLATs under U.S. law. First, the evidence-gathering procedures have been criticized as impermissibly amending the Federal Rules of Evidence, particularly with respect to prohibitions against hearsay testimony and authentication requirements. Second, requirements for taking testimony in the requested state have been criticized as violative of the Sixth Amendment's requirement that criminal defendants be permitted to confront the witnesses against them. Third, and by far the most important, is the fact that private parties, including defendants, are prohibited from using MLATs to obtain assistance and are instead relegated to the use of letters rogatory.

U.S. authorities must consider the hearsay rule, provisions on authentication, and the confrontation rights of the defendant if the evidence is being gathered for trial purposes.[259] Two legal practitioners, Tigar and Doyle,[260] note that under Article 12 of the Swiss Treaty the Swiss government's right to withhold portions of records as being subject to overriding concerns over secrecy may cause problems regarding the admissibility of the records in question. Exclusion of the witness and his counsel from the proceedings raises further questions under the federal "rule of completeness"[261] and also perhaps under the public trial and confrontation clauses.[262] Exceptions to the hearsay rule may pose significant problems if the defendant seeks to cross-examine the custodian of such a document to determine

---

Islands, 101st Cong., 1st Sess., Exec. Report No. 101-8 (1989) at 272-5 cited in ETHAN A. NADELMANN, COPS ACROSS BORDERS 381, n. 198 (1993).

[258] As noted above, MLATs grant states the discretion to refuse to grant a request if the request violates certain well-established principles of legality. For instance, under most MLATs, requests can be refused if the action sought would be contrary to the fundamental principles of the legal system of the requested state, the request is based on a political or fiscal offense, the request violates the principles of dual criminality or *ne bis in idem*, or if the request is contrary to the *ordre public* or other essential interests of the requested state. It is important to note that all grounds for refusal are discretionary or optional. A state is not obligated to refuse a request for assistance, even if a violation of legal protections is imminent. *See* Christine Van den Wyngaert, *Rethinking the Law of International Cooperation: The Restrictive Function of International Human Rights Through Individual-Oriented Bars*, *in* PRINCIPLES AND PROCEDURES FOR A NEW TRANSNATIONAL CRIMINAL LAW 489 (Eser & Lagodny eds., 1992) (discussing the distinction and differences in effectiveness between bars to assistance contained in inter-state cooperation agreements and relying on fundamental human rights as codified in international agreements).

[259] FED. R. OF EVID. 801-04 (hearsay) 901-03 (authentication and identification).

[260] Tigar & Doyle, *supra* note 4, at 67-68.

[261] The rule of completeness is codified in Rule 106 of the Federal Rules of Evidence: When a writing or recorded statement or part thereof is introduced by a party an adverse party may require him at that time to introduce any other part or any other writing or recorded statement which ought in fairness to be considered contemporaneously with it.

[262] The Sixth Amendment to the U.S. Constitution provides:

> In all criminal prosecutions the accused shall enjoy the right to a speedy and public trial, by an impartial jury of the State and district wherein the crime shall have been committed, which district shall have been previously ascertained by law, and to be informed of the nature and cause of the accusation; to be confronted with the witnesses against him; to have compulsory process for obtaining witnesses in his favor and to have the Assistance of Counsel for his defense.

U.S. CONST, amend. 6.

whether it in fact meets the business records standard as defined in Federal Rule of Evidence 803(6).

Finally, and perhaps most importantly, there remains the question of the availability of legal assistance treaties, and their vast improvements over letters rogatory, to private parties. The more recent MLATs specifically state that they are not intended for use by private persons, including defendants.[263] Thus, defendants cannot use an MLAT to obtain evidence or seek other assistance.[264] The treaties also deny defendants the opportunity to challenge or exclude evidence under the treaties.[265] A defendant or other affected person who seeks to prevent the execution of a request that would violate the MLAT or who claims that the requested state has violated the terms of the treaty in executing the request can only apply to the government authorities, and not to its courts.[266]

While the government may gain access to certain records to prosecute a defendant, it is not at all clear that the government could be compelled to make a request for information that contained exculpatory evidence.[267] Theoretically, a defense attorney can request the relevant U.S. court to instruct the Department of Justice to make a request for the defense, at least under the Swiss Treaty.[268] However, such requests are possible only after the indictment has been endorsed and only if the court approves.[269] Additionally, the defense must comply with the terms of the treaty in making such requests, including describing the need for the evidence sought, raising the possibility that the defense will be required to reveal much of its strategy even if it can gain access to the treaty.[270] In one case, *U.S. v. Sindona,*[271] a request for assistance under the treaty with Switzerland was made by the defense and the court ordered that it should be complied with or the case would be dismissed. The Department of Justice complied with the request.

In applying these new modalities, states and their law enforcement bodies are also governed by human rights norms and standards which arise from treaty obligations, regional obligations, customary international law and general principles of international law.[272] National governments are bound to respect human rights under a framework of international human rights instruments consisting of, *inter alia*: the European Convention for the

---

263 See, e.g., Cayman Treaty art. 1(3) ("The provisions of this Treaty shall not create any reght on the part of any privte person to obtain, suppress, or exclude any evidence, or to impede the executin of a request."); Panama Treaty art. 11(3); Spanish Treaty art. 1(4).

264 Bruce Zagaris, *International Tax and Related Crimes: Gathering Evidence, Comparative Ethics, and Related Matters, in* THE ALLEGED TRANSNATIONAL CRIMINAL 377 (R. Atkins ed., 1995).

265 *See supra* note 125 and accompanying text.

266 Bruce Zagaris, *International Tax and Related Crimes: Gathering Evidence, Comparative Ethics, and Related Matters, in* THE ALLEGED TRANSNATIONAL CRIMINAL 377 (R. Atkins ed., 1995).

267 However, if pursuant to a request initiated by the defendant or the United States, the government would be obligated to disclose any exculpatory material to the defense upon request. Failure to do so, under *Brady v. Maryland*, 373 U.S. 83 (1963), is a violation of due process where the evidence is material to guilt or innocence. Presumably, it makes no difference through what means the government gains possession of such *Brady* material.

268 Swiss MLAT Art. 28(2); *see also* Frei, *supra* note 177, at 17.

269 Frei, *supra* note 177, at 17.

270 Swiss MLAT Art. 29; Frei, *supra* note 177, at 17

271 U.S. v. Sindona, 636 F.2d at 892 (2d Cir. 1980). *See also* William S. Kenney, *Structures and Methods of International and Regional Cooperation in Penal Matters,* 29 N.Y. L. SCH. L. REV. 65 (1984).

272 Although a complete discussion of these issues is beyond the scope of this chapter, a brief discussion of several potential individual rights issues is warranted. Differences in national legal traditions and the ambiguities of international human rights law mean that the possible rights issues raised herein will be dealt with in a manner that is appropriate for each country as it deals with legal assistance requests.

Protection of Human Rights and Fundamental Freedoms,[273] the American Convention on Human Rights,[274] the American Declaration of the Rights and Duties of Man,[275] and the African Charter on Human and Peoples' Rights.[276] There also exist United Nations instruments, such as the Universal Declaration on Human Rights[277] and the International Covenant on Civil and Political Rights.[278]

Criminal suspects and defendants will have the right to invoke the provisions of these treaties to the extent that a party seeking or providing legal assistance is a signatory to a relevant human rights instrument. For example, requests for inter-state cooperation or confiscation under many of the U.S. MLATs with OAS members will be subject to the requirements of the American Convention. Defendants may also be entitled to protections to the extent that such treaties and the subsequent practice of states have brought the protection of human rights into the ambit of customary international law.

States will be required to provide certain forms of mutual legal assistance, such as executing searches and seizures and tracing the proceeds of crime. These law enforcement activities will, necessarily, entail additional infringement on individual privacy rights,[279] particularly in light of the ability of government agencies to search massive databases and financial records by means of computers.[280] Apart from adopting the legal standards of the requested state, MLATs contain no independent obligation to respect the privacy expectations of defendants.[281] The information required for a valid request for assistance will not necessarily enable the authorities of the requested state to establish reasonable suspicion or to assess whether the assistance sought would be permissible if it were carried out in the requesting state. Coupled with the treaties' liberal standards with respect to the admissibility of evidence seized abroad, the lack of a reasonable suspicion standard might encourage law enforcement officials in states with strict prohibitions against unreasonable searches and seizures to try to execute searches in other states based on a lesser showing than would be required for a domestic search.[282]

---

[273] Nov. 4, 1950, 218 U.N.T.S. 221, Europ. T.S. No. 5 and its Eight Protocols.

[274] O.A.S. Off. Rec. OEA/Ser. L/V/II. 23 Doc. 21 Rev. 6, *opened for signature* Nov. 20, 1969, *entered into force* July 18, 1978.

[275] Adopted by the Ninth International Conference of American States (Mar. 30-May 2, 1948), O.A.S. Off. Rec. OEA/Ser.L/V/I.4 Rev. (1965).

[276] Done at Banjul, June 26, 1981, entered into force Oct. 21, 1986, O.A.U. Doc. CAB/LEG/67/3 Rev. 5, *reproduced in* 21 I.L.M. 59 (1982).

[277] Dec. 10, 1948, U.N.G.A. Res. 217A (III), 3 U.N. GAOR 71, U.N. Doc., A/810.

[278] Dec. 16, 1966, U.N.G.A. Res. 2200 (XXI), 21 U.N. GAOR, Supp. (No. 16) 52, U.N. Doc. A/6316.

[279] The right to privacy is an international human right. Most countries recognize this right under constitutional, statutory or judge-made law. The right to privacy is also enshrined in many international human rights agreements. *See, e.g.,* The Universal Declaration of Human Rights, art. 12 ("no one shall be subject to arbitrary interference in his privacy, family, home, or correspondence. . ."); International Covenant on Civil and Political Rights, Art. 17 ("no one shall be subjected to arbitrary or unlawful interference with his privacy. . ."); European Convention for the Protection of Human Rights and Fundamental Freedoms, Art. 8 ("Everyone has the right to respect for his private and family life, his home and correspondence.").

[280] *See* generally Comment, *The Right to Financial Privacy Versus Computerized Law Enforcement: A New fight in an Old Battle*, 86 NORTHWESTERN UNIV. L. REV. 1169 (1992)

[281] Some MLATs do, however, permit a requested state to deny assistance where the request does not establish reasonable grounds for believing that the offense has been committed or that the information sought relates to the offense and is located in the requested state. This provision first appeared in the 1986 MLAT with the U.K. concerning the Cayman Islands. *See, e.g.,* Cayman Treaty Art. 3(2)(c); Panama Treaty Art. 3(1). A denial of assistance on this basis is not, however, obligatory.

[282] Another possible rights issue concerns the infringement of these initiatives upon financial privacy rights.

Other rights concerns raised by MLATs could generically be described as "due process" issues. Due process of law is protected by domestic law in most countries and must be provided under international human rights instruments.[283] Several aspects of MLATs could threaten the due process rights of criminal defendants and innocent third parties, especially requirements for the freezing and seizing of proceeds of crime that inadequately protect the property interests of criminal defendants and *bona fide* third parties.

None of the MLATs specifies a minimum burden of proof, such as an authenticated copy of a restraining order issued by a court of the requesting state, before assets can be restrained. The requirement that a requested state merely have "jurisdiction" over the matter in order to petition its authorities is easily met and vague. As a result, assets may be frozen and placed beyond the defendant's reach without the benefit of a hearing (either before or after the seizure) in the requested state if the law of the requested state does not require a hearing or other procedural safeguards. Under these terms, a state party could probably request seizure of assets based solely upon the investigation of a suspect.[284] Unlike the United Drug Convention and the Council of Europe Laundering Convention,[285] U.S. MLATs do not specifically recognize, let alone protect, the interests of *bona fide*, innocent third parties in property subject to seizure and forfeiture.

Another closely held tenet of international human rights law and the domestic law of most nations is that a defendant is presumed innocent until proven guilty in criminal proceedings.[286] However, the sometimes quasi-criminal nature of confiscation and the focus on the *res* rather than the defendant, creates an ambiguity that undermines the presumption

---

When providing legal assistance or executing provisional measures under an MLAT, states might lift their bank secrecy requirements and provide access to financial information, which threatens to place the interests of law enforcement above the legitimate and once undisputed right to financial privacy. Of course, no one would advocate that drug traffickers and money launderers have the right to conduct their illicit dealings in utter private. But legitimate rationales support the traditions of bank secrecy and financial privacy, and these interests must be weighed fairly against the government's crime-fighting objectives. According to one commentator: "Secrecy laws have served to shield persons from financial loss in countries plagued by instability, weak currency and run-away inflation rates. Secrecy laws have also served to protect wealthy individuals or those who promote unpopular political causes by allowing them to hide their assets to avoid the threat of kidnaping or persecution." *See also* Peter Schroth, *Bank Confidentiality and the War on Money Laundering in the United States*, 42 AM. J. COMP. L. 369, 369 (1994) (arguing that the war on drugs and money laundering has eroded universally accepted rights to financial privacy and bank confidentiality: "Since 1970, the steadily escalating indirect war on drug traffickers has been conducted almost without regard to privacy, property rights, the costs to financial institutions and government. . . .").

[283] *See, e.g.*, European Convention for the Protection of Human Rights and Fundamental Freedoms, Art. 5 and 6; American Declaration of the Rights and Duties of Man, Art. XXVI ("every person accused of an offense has the right to be given an impartial and public hearing. . . ").

[284] The confiscation provisions are less objectionable because confiscation requires some form of adjudication of guilt in the requesting state and is, therefore, based on more than mere suspicion. Confiscation is, however, potentially objectionable when it interferes with a defendant's right to secure legal counsel or if his assets are confiscated without due process.

[285] *See* COE Convention Art. 22 (requiring the requested party to recognize any judicial decision with respect to property rights claimed by third parties, and permitting a requested state party to refuse a request for confiscation if third parties were not given adequate opportunity to assert their interests in the property to be confiscated).

[286] *See, e.g.*, American Convention on Human Rights, Art. 8 (2). ("Every person accused of a criminal offense has the right to be presumed innocent so long as his guilt has not been proven according to law."); African Charter on Human and Peoples' Rights, Art. 7 (1)(b) ("Every individual shall have the right to have his cause heard. This comprises . . . the right to be presumed innocent until proved guilty by a competent court or tribunal;"); Universal Declaration of Human Rights, Art. 11 (1) ("Everyone charged with a penal offense has the right to be presumed innocent until proved guilty according to law. . . .").

of innocence. Under civil forfeiture laws, the property is presumed guilty; but under criminal forfeiture, as is contemplated by MLATs, the property ought to be presumed innocent. This has not proven to be the case.[287] Once the government proves that there is reason to believe that property could be subject to forfeiture, the burden of proof is shifted from the government to the criminal defendant to prove that the assets are not tied to wrongdoing.[288]

Finally, the inaccessibility of MLAT procedures to private persons might so hinder the preparation of a defense as to diminish a defendant's internationally recognized right to a fair trial.[289] At the very least, this situation creates an imbalance in the equality of arms that is suspect under international human rights standards.

Conclusion

United States' treaties on mutual assistance in criminal matters represent a step forward in international relations in that they offer rules and procedures that greatly simplify previous practices and offer an alternative to questionable techniques such as the kidnaping of information in foreign countries and attempting to enforce U.S. subpoenas in foreign jurisdictions. Their continuing proliferation would seem to assure that the concerns of Dr. Gerhard Mueller expressed thirty five years ago that "American courts neither give nor receive (nor ask for) adequate judicial assistance in criminal matters" will at last be addressed. [290]

---

[287] One commentator has noted that an international standard is emerging whereby assets can be subjected to forfeiture based on "indicia" of wrongdoing: "This notion of indicia—that which is or might be wrong, not under fact-finding standards, but under skewed presumptions—is paramount in dealing with international drug trafficking and money laundering problems. In this context, the standard of the United States forfeiture laws, now being incorporated in the international arena, will not protect any legitimate business person from persecution."

[288] This shifted burden is complicated by the fact that the owner is required to prove a negative (i.e., the lack of a nexus). Once currency enters the stream of commerce, and is commingled with other proceeds, it is exceedingly difficult, if not impossible, to prove that a specific portion of the proceeds has not been tainted by illegality. The U.S. MLATs do not provide defendants, or a potentially innocent third party, with a sufficient opportunity to show that proceeds are not tainted.

[289] *See, e.g.*, Universal Declaration of Human Rights, Art. 10 ("Everyone is entitled in full equality to a fair and public hearing by an independent and impartial tribunal, in the determination of his rights and obligations and of any criminal charge against him."); art. 11 ("Everyone charged with a penal offense has the right to be presumed innocent until proved guilty according to law in a public trial at which he has all the guarantees necessary for his defence."); European Convention for the Protection of Human Rights and Fundamental Freedoms, Art. 6(1) ("everyone is entitled to a fair and public hearing within a reasonable time by an independent and impartial tribunal established by law."); American Convention on Human Rights, Art. 8.

[290] Mueller, *supra* note 38, at 197.

Appendix 9

Senate Report on the Treaty on Mutual Legal Assistance Between the United States of America and the Kingdom of the Netherlands

November 20 (legislative day, November 2),1981.—

Mr. Percy, from the Committee on Foreign Relations submitted the following

REPORT

[To accompany Treaty Doc. No 97-16]

The Committee on Foreign Relations, to which was referred the Treaty on Mutual Legal Assistance Between the United States of America and the Kingdom of the Netherlands, together with a related exchange of notes, signed at The Hague on June 12, 1981, having considered the same, reports favorably thereon without reservation and recommends that the Senate give its advice and consent to ratification thereof.

Purpose

The treaty articulates the general obligation of the parties to render assistance in criminal matters and specifically includes criminal investigations in this category to make it clear that assistance will be rendered whether or not formal charges have been filed. Unlike the Colombian Mutual Legal Assistance Treaty, considered by the Committee, the Mutual Legal Assistance Treaty with the Kingdom of the Netherlands does not extend to civil or administrative matters. However, as expressed in Article 11, paragraph 2 of the treaty, the parties do not rule out the use of evidence or information obtained under this treaty for criminal investigations and proceedings other than that for which assistance is originally requested or for civil or administrative proceedings.

The kinds of assistance specifically provided for under the treaty include but are not necessarily limited to:

(a) locating persons;
(b) serving documents;
(c) providing records;
(d) taking the testimony or statements of persons;
(e) producing documents;
(f) executing requests for search and seizure; and
(g) transferring persons in custody for testimonial purposes.

Background

The traditional procedures for obtaining evidence from foreign countries (See 22 U.S.C. 1782) is by the cumbersome, time-consuming and extremely limited process of letters rogatory.[1]

The mutual legal assistance treaties recently negotiated with Colombia and the Netherlands cover mutual assistance in criminal matters and represent the third and fourth of their kind for the United States. The first was the Treaty on Mutual Assistance in Criminal Matters Between the United States

[1]"Letters rogatory are the medium, in effect, whereby one country speaking through one of its courts, requests another country, acting through its own courts and by methods of court procedure peculiar thereto and entirely within the latter's control, to assist the Administration of justice in the former country: such request being made, and being usually granted. by reason of the comity existing between nations in ordinary peaceful times." The Signe. Tiedmonn v. She Signe et ol.. 37 F. Supp. 819, 820 (E.D La 1941).

and Switzerland; the second was the Treaty on Extradition and Mutual Assistance in Criminal Matters with Turkey.

One commentator writing about the Swiss treaty noted:

"The United States has shown a new pragmatic willingness to engage in concerned action in order to fill the growing need for an international practice with respect to legal assistance in criminal matters. The United States is thus moving to fulfill its obligations as a member of the world community as well as to extend the reach of its own proceedings."[2]

Many of the provisions in the new agreements derive from the Swiss and Turkish treaties.

The new treaties are intended to meet the diverse needs of the numerous enforcement agencies that may be involved in criminal proceedings. Where mutually agreeable, informal procedures will be employed to obtain evidence and/or testimony. Where informal procedures are inappropriate formal requirements have been established through which the treaties objectives of legal assistance can be achieved.

Both treaties will address a variety of criminal activities, including drug trafficking, fraud, the avoidance of American securities law, evasion of American taxes, and the financing of organized crime. In this context, both the Departments of State and Justice believe that mutual legal assistance treaties provide an effective mechanism for U.S. enforcement agencies seeking the assistance of foreign governments in obtaining information related to pending investigations or proceedings in the United States.

Summary of Major Provisions

Double Criminality

Double Criminality is required in the Dutch treaty only as it relates to requests for searches and seizures. In such cases, the alleged criminal act must constitute a crime in both the Netherlands and the United States and be punishable in both countries by imprisonment for more than one year. (Article 6)

Since the U.S. and the Netherlands operate under different legal traditions and systems, it was made clear during negotiations that the requirement of dual criminality should not erect technical barriers that would impede providing assistance contemplated by the treaty. Consequently, the Departments of Justice and State have informed the committee that: "the proper approach to interpretation of the dual criminality requirement is to look to the harm the criminal statutes of each country are intended to prevent, rather than the particular wording of the Requesting country's law, which may have no meaning in the jurisprudence of the Requested country."

Competent Authority

Article 14 of the treaty provides that all requests for assistance be made and executed through a Competent Authority being for each Party the senior official in the Department or Ministry of Justice. In the case of the United States, the Attorney General has been designated as the Competent Authority because the Treaty is primarily concerned with criminal investigation and litigation. Thus, in its role as the primary law enforcement agency in the U.S., the Justice Department will advise and assist state and federal prosecutors and law enforcement agencies in making requests pursuant to the treaty.

Discretionary Authority to Release Records

Under Article 4 of the treaty, the requested State is granted discretionary authority to release to the Requesting State records maintained in government files to the same extent that such records would be available to the domestic law enforcement or judicial authorities of the Requested State. The exchange of diplomatic notes makes it clear that discretion to refuse to provide information or records

---

[2]Johnson, Paul W., "Judicial Assistance-Criminal Procedure," Harvard *International Law Journal,* pp. 349-364, at p.350.

should be exercised sparingly. Moreover, should a government agency resist providing records, it must demonstrate specific harm caused by such disclosure.

As for the disclosure of tax records and information, the exchange of diplomatic notes indicates that such records and information are within the scope of Article 4. Disclosure will be allowed to the same extent, and under the same conditions as in the Requested State.

Testimony of Persons in Custody

Articles 7 and 8 of the treaty make it possible under certain circumstances for a person in custody to be a witness in either the Requested or Requesting State. Article 7 provides for transfer of the person to the Requesting State if the transferee consents, is kept in custody throughout his stay in the Requesting State, is promptly returned to the Requested State once his testimony has been completed, and the Requested State has no reason to deny the transfer. In the case of a person who is in custody in the Requesting State, Article 8 provides that the person may be present at the deposition of a government witness located in the Requested State so long as the prisoner is kept in custody pending the taking of testimony or other proceedings and is speedily returned to the Requesting State at the conclusion of the proceedings.

Searches and Seizures on Behalf of the Requesting State

Article 6 provides that the Requested State is limited in its requests for searches and seizures by the Requested State to offenses which are crimes in both countries and punishable by imprisonment for more than one year. This is the only provision of the treaty which preserves the requirement of double criminality.

Requests made to the Dutch authorities for search and seizure in fiscal cases must be approved by the Minister of Finance and will be approved to the same extent as under Dutch domestic law. Fiscal cases involve taxes, custom duties, or monetary exchange control.

Exception to the Hearsay Rule

Article 6 of the treaty provides a narrow exception to the hearsay rule for information on the chain of custody to the effect that a record will be kept of every transfer of an article seized and that those records will be admissable as evidence of the truth of the facts they assert.

Refusal of Assistance

Article 10 of the treaty specifies instances in which assistance may be refused including where it may adversely effect the "essential public interests" or security of the Requested State or where the request relates to a matter considered a political offense by the Requested State. It is anticipated that these provisions will rarely be invoked and only where there is a demonstrable need for refusing compliance.

Committee Action and Recommendations

The Committee on Foreign Relations held a public hearing on the Mutual Legal Assistance Treaty with the Kingdom of the Netherlands on November 10, 1981, at which time Mr. Daniel McGovern, Deputy Legal Advisor, Department of State; Mr. Joseph Linneman, Deputy Assistant Secretary for International Narcotics Matters, Department of State; and Mr. Michael Abbell, Director of the Office of International Affairs, Criminal Division, Department of Justice testified in its support. No witnesses were heard opposing the Treaty or seeking reservations thereto. Each witness testified that the Treaty will serve significant law enforcement objectives by enabling U.S. law enforcement agencies to obtain more effective assistance in investigating and prosecuting a wide range of criminal activities, such as drug trafficking, fraud, tax evasion, and sophisticated business and financial transactions of organized crime.

On November 17,1981, the Committee on Foreign Relations considered the Mutual Legal Assistance Treaty with the Kingdom of the Netherlands in open session. At that time the Committee, by voice vote of a quorum of the Committee present, ordered it reported favorably to the Senate for its advice and consent.

Section-by-Section Analysis

The U.S. Delegation composed of representatives from the Departments of State and Justice has provided the Committee with the following section-by-section analysis of the Treaty.

Changes in the new treaty

The mutual legal assistance treaty derives in form and substance from that originally concluded with Switzerland. However, there are several innovations in our new treaty with the Netherlands. These include:

1. *Double criminality*—The treaty requires double criminality only with respect to requests for searches and seizures. In the case of searches and seizures the subject offense must be punishable in both countries for a period in excess of one year or less If the offense is listed in the annex to the treaty (Article 6). (Note: Double criminality requirement is eliminated entirely in U.S.-Colombian treaty).
2. *Release of Government information*—The treaty provides discretionary authority to an agency of the Requested State to release to a foreign law enforcement authority records maintained in government files to the same extent that they would be available to domestic law enforcement or judicial authorities (Article 4). (Note: Same innovation is found in U.S.-Colombian treaty, Article 14)
3. *Giving testimony abroad*—The treaty allows a person in custody in one country to be a witness in the other. Such assistance requires the consent of the person and is discretionary with the Requested State (Article 7). The innovation is that the provision creates the legal authority for holding a prisoner transferred under the treaty in custody in the United States. (Note: Similar provision found in U.S.-Colombian treaty, Article .)
4. *Searches and seizures*—The treaty allows the Requested State to make searches and seizures on behalf of Requesting State (Article 6). The request for such assistance must contain information which would justify the issuance of a search warrant under the law of the Requested State. Searches and seizures as noted above are limited to offenses which are crimes in both countries and punishable by imprisonment for more than one year or less if the offense is listed in the Annex to the treaty. The treaty will allow a judge in the United States to consider testimony given in the other country as evidence of probable cause for the issuance of a search warrant. (Note: Similar but less stringent provision found in U.S.-Colombian treaty, Article 15).
5. *Hearsay exception*—To assure that evidence received as a result of a request for search and seizure may be admissible in a United States court, the treaty creates a narrow exception to the hearsay rule for information on the chain of custody (Article 6). The Dutch agreement provides that evidence seized shall be received into evidence without additional proof.

Additional Comments

ARTICLE I

Article 1 states the general obligation to render assistance in criminal matters. It specifically covers criminal investigations to make it clear that assistance will be rendered regardless whether there have been any charges filed. This is necessary because evidence from abroad is often needed in order to make an informed decision whether criminal charges should be brought.

ARTICLE 2

Locating persons is a very commonly needed form of assistance. By obligating themselves to make "thorough efforts," the Parties undertake to make the same efforts on behalf of the Requesting State as they would on their own behalf to find persons the Requesting State believes to be in the Requested State.

ARTICLE 3

Although service of documents is a form of international assistance which the United States rarely needs in criminal cases, other countries often need service of documents. It was explained to the

Netherlands delegation that a "reasonable time before the scheduled appearance" will vary from jurisdiction to jurisdiction within the United States, since each Federal district has its own rules concerning the time a person is allowed to respond to service of documents. In the Netherlands, documents will be served by police officers, who take oath of office requiring them to truthfully report the facts relating to service of process. The delegations agreed that this oath of office would obviate the need for a sworn affidavit of service.

ARTICLE 4

Article 4 is designed to strike a balance between the desirability of maximizing assistance and maintaining the integrity of government held information which cannot be disclosed for either legal or important policy reasons.

The first paragraph of Article 4 deals with publicly available records. The intention of the United States delegation was that this paragraph would cover records such as those available under the Freedom of Information Act to the public at large. It is not intended to cover information not available to the public, but available to a specific individual under the Privacy Act. The purpose of this paragraph is to avail the Requesting Country of the knowledge of officials of the Requested Country concerning how and where to seek public records. These records will be authenticated in any manner stated in the request.

The exchange of diplomatic notes explains Paragraph 2 of Article 4 more fully. The intent of the delegations is that discretion to refuse to give information will be exercised sparingly. Where a Government agency resists giving requested records, it must demonstrate specific harm.

The diplomatic note makes it clear that this treaty is a "convention relating to the exchange of tax information" within the meaning of 26 U.S.C. 6103(k)(4), under which the disclosure of tax information is authorized. Paragraph 2 is intended to create discretionary power to make disclosure of non-tax information in the possession of the government under this treaty in the absence of other express authority.

The fact that certain evidence or information may be in the possession of the government, and might be sought under this article, is not intended to preclude a request to obtain it from its source under Article 5 or Article 6.

ARTICLE 5

Article 5 is intended to avail the Requesting State of the compulsory process of the Requested State. The treaty supersedes existing law (28 U.S.C. 1782) to the extent of making the issuance of the necessary subpoenas compulsory rather than discretionary with the court.

Paragraph 1 prevents assistance from being barred by the assertion in the Requested State of claims of privilege under the laws of the Requesting State. This avoids the unnecessary litigation of questions of foreign law. The privilege may be asserted when the evidence is sought to be introduced in the Requesting State. In this way, questions of privilege will always be decided by the courts most competent to deal with them.

Paragraphs 2 through 4 are designed to accommodate the Sixth Amendment right to confrontation by permitting the presence of the accused or counsel for the accused at the execution of a request for the taking of testimony to be introduced at the trial. Nothing in this treaty is intended to expand the right to confrontation so as to prevent the government from obtaining information. Testimony may be taken without confrontation before or after charges are brought. Whether or not such testimony may be used in a criminal trial is the question which involves the right to confrontation. Nothing in these paragraphs is intended to impose an obligation on the government of either party to pay for the defendant's travel or any other expenses connected with his assertation of his right to confrontation.

Under the Continental law system, testimony is taken in response to questioning by an examining magistrate rather than attorneys for the parties. Because some magistrates in the Netherlands may insist on retaining the exclusive right to question witnesses, Paragraph 4 is designed to permit the parties, at the very least, to propose questions to the magistrate to be asked of the witness.

Article 5 contemplates that all the incidents of giving testimony in the Requested State, including the sanctions for contempt and perjury, shall apply.

ARTICLE 6

As stated in the portion of the diplomatic note relating to Article 6, the delegations agreed to limit searches and seizures to cases where the alleged criminal acts constitute crimes in both the Netherlands and the United States, punishable in both countries by imprisonment for more than one year. This is the only place in the treaty where the notion of dual criminality comes into play.

Paragraph 1 makes an exception to the requirements that the offense be punishable by a sentence of more than one year in both countries for offenses listed in the annex. The purpose for the annex is to accommodate the need for search and seizure in certain crimes which are misdemeanors under the law of the one or both of the Parties.

Paragraph 2 manifests the delegations' intention that the requirements of dual criminality will not erect technical and insubstantial objections based on technical differences between the two Parties' legal approaches to prohibiting certain conduct. Obviously, the wording of different countries' statutes prohibiting certain kinds of conduct will be different even if there were a common language, just as the individual states of the United States have differing criminal laws on the same subject. It was the intention of the delegations that the treaty be interpreted liberally to maximize the assistance available under it. The proper approach to interpretation of the dual criminality requirement is to look to the harm the criminal statutes of each country are intended to prevent rather than the particular wording of the Requesting Country's law, which may have no meaning in the jurisprudence of the Requested Country.

The delegations dealt with one such technical difference specifically in the second sentence of Paragraph 2. United States Federal criminal statutes are necessarily based on powers granted the Federal government in the Constitution, such as the power to regulate interstate commerce and the mails. The delegations agree that the essence of the offenses of mail fraud and wire fraud in violation of Title 18 U.S.C. 1341 and 1343 is fraud, taking or scheming to take another person's property by false representations. Similarly, interstate transportation of stolen property, 18 U.S.C. 2314, will be considered by the Netherlands analogous to their possession of stolen property statute.

Since the subpoena *duces tecum* is unknown in the practice of the Netherlands, the compulsion of documents is done only through orders for search and seizure. Thus while Netherlands requests for the production of documents may be handled under Article 5, United States requests for the production of documents must always meet the additional requirements of Article 6.

Paragraph 4 imposes the obligation to state in every request the requirements for authentication of documents. With respect to other objects obtained by search and seizure, this paragraph requires that documentary evidence of the chain of custody be made by the authorities of the Requested Country, and requires the courts of the Requesting Country to admit this evidence of chain of custody. In this respect, the treaty is intended to create a narrow exception to the hearsay rule for chain of custody evidence made by the authorities of the Netherlands in the execution of a request by the United States for search and seizure.

The diplomatic notes interpreting Article 6 reflect the understanding of the Parties with respect to two important matters of procedure, one under Netherlands procedure and one under United States procedure.

Under Netherlands procedure, any request for search and seizure in a "fiscal"[3] case must be approved by the Minister of Finance. This is the "established administrative practice" referred to in the second paragraph of the portion of the diplomatic notes dealing with Article 6. The Netherlands delegation states that the Netherlands authorities will authorize search and seizure pursuant to a request under the treaty in the same circumstances where they would approve it in a domestic case.

The fourth paragraph of this portion of the diplomatic note makes it clear that requests by the Netherlands for search and seizure will be treated uniformly in the United States regardless of the type of offense. This paragraph also paraphrases the constitutional and statutory requirements for search and seizure in the United States. The language of Paragraph 1 of Article 6, stating that "the Requested

[3]A "fiscal" matter is one involving taxes, customs duties, or monetary exchange control.

State shall execute requests for search and seizure in accordance with its law and practices . . ." is not intended to require that an affiant come from the Netherlands to comply with Rule 41(c)(1). Rather, the last sentence of Paragraph 4 provides that a sworn statement made by or before a judicial officer in the Netherlands be accepted in lieu of an affidavit "sworn to before the federal Magistrate or state judge" as prescribed in Rule 41(c)(1).

ARTICLE 7

Article 7 is designed to deal with the situation where a person in custody in one country is needed as a witness in the other. It is intended to extend the jurisdiction of the Requested State to the prisoner during the entire procedure. Although this form of assistance requires the consent of the person in custody and is discretionary with the Requested State, Paragraph 1c implies an obligation for the Requested State to articulate any reason it may have to deny the transfer. Paragraph 3 of Article 7 is intended to create the legal authority for holding a foreign prisoner in custody of the United States so that he may not obtain his release through a habeas corpus action.

The use of the word "confrontation" in Paragraph 1 is not used in the common law sense, but in the civil law sense. Under civil law practice, "confrontation" is a procedure wherein persons giving conflicting versions of the facts are brought before a judicial officer who questions them to resolve the differences. The inclusion of the word "confrontation" in Paragraph 1 is intended to accommodate those cases where the Netherlands will find it necessary to request a prisoner from the United States whose version of the facts conflicts with that of a witness in the Netherlands.

Paragraph 3 of Article 18 makes it clear that the transfer of persons under Article 7 and Article 8 is not to be considered an extradition procedure and the rules governing extradition, whether in treaty or domestic law, particularly the rule of speciality, have no application.

ARTICLE 8

Article 8 is designed to accommodate the situation where the State requesting judicial assistance sends a person in custody to the Requested State. It is intended to extend the jurisdiction of the Requesting State to the prisoner during the entire procedure. In this article the word "confrontation" is used in the United States constitutional sense. The purpose of the article is to provide a mechanism for affording a defendant the right to confront a witness against him where the witness is not willing to travel to the Requesting State pursuant to Article 9. It is not intended to expand or limit the scope of that right, and it is not intended to create an obligation on the part of the government to pay for the travel or any other expenses of a defendant who chooses to exercise the right.

The Netherlands may use this article for "confrontation" in the civil law sense, that is, when a person in custody in the Netherlands gives a version of the facts different from a witness located in the United States. In such a case the Netherlands may send the prisoner to the United States.

Paragraph 2, like Paragraph 3 of Article 7, creates the legal authority for holding the transferred person in custody.

As with Article 7, provisions of extradition laws and extradition treaties do not apply.

ARTICLE 9

Article 9 provides assurance to a person voluntarily appearing as a witness or for confrontation that there is not an ulterior motive for requesting his presence. This article makes it clear that requests for witnesses are not to be used as a pretext for obtaining personal jurisdiction over persons for other purposes. Thus, a person summoned under Article 3 (or a person responding to a less formal request for his presence), or a person transferred under Articles 7 or 8 will have the safe conduct protection afforded by this Article. Naturally, this Article is not intended to override the obligation to keep a person in custody under Articles 7 or 8.

Paragraph 3 prevents any permanent immunity from resulting from this article. Notice, in fact, is all that is required to trigger the running of the ten-day grace period.

Paragraph 2 is a provision which permits the safe conduct privilege to attach to a person summoned as a defendant. It provides an assurance for a person outside the country that if he enters the country, he will be prosecuted only upon the charges stated in the request. This prevents a summons for a minor offense being used as a pretext for obtaining personal jurisdiction over a person in order to prosecute him for a more serious offense. However, Paragraph 3 makes it very clear that permanent immunity is not conferred on a person coming to the Requested State under Paragraph 2.

The safe conduct applies only to acts which preceded the person's departure from the Requested State. Thus, if the person commits an offense while in the jurisdiction of the Requested Country or en route, he may be prosecuted, convicted, and sentenced.

Since a person appearing in the Requesting State under this treaty always does so voluntarily, he is permitted by Paragraph 4 to assert testimonial privileges under the law of the Requested State, whence he came. Under the law of the Netherlands, matters of testimonial privilege can be matters of public law as well as private law. That is there are criminal statutes prohibiting the disclosure of information obtained by certain professionals in the course of their employment.

These include the police, physicians, clergymen, social workers, notaries, tax inspectors, various types of public employees (including intelligence personnel), accountants and attorneys. Bankers and journalists do not have privileges under the law of the Netherlands. To eliminate the difficulty of the Requesting State's having to decide a question of privilege under the law of the Requested State, Paragraph 4 requires the verification by the Justice officials of the Requested State of the existence of a privilege. As a practical matter, most questions of privilege will be anticipated and resolved before the person consents to travel.

ARTICLE 10

Article 10 sets forth the provisions for denying or postponing the execution of a request. It will be a very rare case when the execution of a request will prejudice the security of either country and the intent of the delegations is that the "essential public interests" exception is to be sparingly used, only when there is a demonstrable need.

The idea of refusing assistance on the basis that a matter is considered a political offense is born of extradition treaties. However, since extradition is perhaps the most extreme form of assistance in criminal cases, the "political offense" grounds for refusing assistance under this treaty should not be invoked as readily as in extradition. The delegations appreciate that the United States adheres to the narrower "British view" of political offenses, while the Netherlands adheres to the broader 'Swiss view."

ARTICLE 11

Since the primary thrust of the treaty is for assistance with a view towards prosecution of criminal offenses, Paragraph 1 of Article 11 does not permit the Requested Country to impose conditions of confidentiality on information provided under this treaty which will interfere with its use at trial. This paragraph is intended as a general proposition, and does not preclude the Requesting Country from accepting more stringent confidentiality requirements on a case by case basis.

Paragraph 2 reflects the understanding of the Parties that this treaty is primarily for the purpose of assistance in criminal investigations and prosecutions and is not to be used as a pretext for requesting assistance for other purposes. Nevertheless, the Parties do not rule out the use of evidence or information obtained under this treaty for criminal investigations and proceedings other than that for which assistance is originally requested or for civil or administrative proceedings.

ARTICLE 12

The first paragraph of Article 12 recognizes that the executive authorities of each government may be able to satisfy some requests completely, while judicial authority will be needed for others. The requirement for promptness recognizes the need for expeditious handling of matters relating to criminal investigations and proceedings. Paragraph 2 reflects the intention of the Parties to use existing domestic law to the extent that it is available to further this treaty's purposes, which are to provide expedient and effective international assistance in criminal investigations and proceedings. In addition, the treaty is intended to create new legal authority where needed and provide the rules of decision for the courts of each Party. On the United States side, this treaty is intended to be self-executing. It is intended to amend and supplement existing law in matters such as creating discretionary authority to provide confidential information in the possession of the government, creating a right of safe conduct under Article 9, creating legal authority to hold persons in custody under Articles 7 and 8, creating a hearsay exception for chain of custody evidence, permitting a judge in the United States to consider testimony given in the Netherlands as evidence of probable cause for the issuance of a search warrant, eliminating the problem of litigating foreign privileges in U.S. courts, and removing the discretion to refuse to issue subpoenas for testimony and tangible evidence presently in 28 U.S.C. 1782. The second sentence of Paragraph 2 reflects the Netherlands acceptance of the concept of following foreign procedures in the execution of foreign requests, which is already embodied in the law of the United States in 28 U.S.C. 1782.

ARTICLE 13

The purpose of Paragraph 1 of Article 13 is to set forth the minimum requirements for requests to be made under the treaty. The intention of the Parties is that requests be as simple and as straightforward as possible. The purpose of the requests is to inform a foreign official, in non-technical terms (which will survive translation by a layman) of the need for his assistance in an investigation or proceeding under foreign laws and procedures which are unfamiliar to him. The requirement of legalization, the certification of signatures on traditional requests for international legal assistance, has been eliminated.

ARTICLE 14

Article 14 provides that the central Competent Authority for each jurisdiction be the senior official in the Department or Ministry of Justice. A central authority is necessary to administer the treaty to insure consistency in its interpretation, to provide a definitive and responsive channel of communication in criminal and judicial matters, and to bring into play the greatest possible experience in international legal assistance in every case. Justice officials are designated as the Competent Authorities because the treaty is primarily concerned with criminal investigation and litigation. As the prosecuting agency, the Department of Justice has an overview of all criminal investigations whether performed by agencies such as the Federal Bureau of Investigation or Drug Enforcement Administration within the Justice Department, or by agencies such as the Customs Service, Internal Revenue Service, or the Bureau of Alcohol, Firearms and Tobacco in the Treasury Department, or by independent agencies such as the Interstate Commerce Commission or Securities and Exchange Commission. As the litigating agency, Justice is responsible for the admissibility and sufficiency of evidence and is the agency most immediately concerned with, and organizationally responsive to, the needs of prosecutors.

In its role as the primary law enforcement agency in the United States, the Department of Justice will advise and assist State and Federal prosecutors and law enforcement agencies in making requests under the treaty. Because of its central interests in the furtherance of the treaty, it will determine both the sufficiency of requests and the propriety of making a request in any particular case.

ARTICLE 15,16

Articles 15 and 16 are self-explanatory.

Annex

The Annex of the treaty lists the offenses which will be exceptions to the requirement that crimes covered by Article 6 must be punishable by more than one year's imprisonment.

Provided the acts alleged are punishable in both countries, the Parties' agreement to list an offense obliges both parties to entertain requests for search and seizure for that offense, regardless of the severity of the penalty.

ARTICLE 194

Article 194 of the Criminal Code of the Netherlands describes conduct which would be punishable in the United States by criminal contempt and perjury laws.

ARTICLE 272

The United States does not have a general confidentiality law. However, there are many provisions of the United States law requiring certain kinds of information to be kept confidential. (See e.g. Rule 6, F.R. Crm. P.,18 U.S.C 1902, 18 U.S.C. 1905 through 1908, 5 U.S.C. 552a(i)(1), 26 U.S.C. 6103.) The United States will have to approach dual criminality with respect to this article on a case by case basis to determine if there is a law prohibiting the kind of conduct described in the Netherlands request.

ARTICLE 328 *BIS*

This article has no clear and complete counterpart in U.S. law, but appears to cover conduct which could violate the antitrust laws and the trade laws. Certainly, if the "fraudulent act" were a secret combination in restraint of trade, it would be covered by antitrust laws. Title 16 U.S.C. 52 prohibits false advertising and Section 54 establishes the penalties. There may be state laws which correspond more closely to Article 328 *bis*. Requests by the Netherlands under Article 328 *bis* will have to be examined on a case by case basis to determine if dual criminality exists. It is also possible that conduct proscribed by Article 328 *bis* rises to the level of fraud which would be prohibited by 18 U.S.C. 1341 or 1343.

ARTICLE 328 *TER*

Article 328 *ter*, Paragraph (1) prohibits the acceptance of bribes by employees other than public employees. Paragraph (2) prohibits the offer of such a bribe. These statutes are described by Netherlands lawyers as "commercial bribery" laws. The essence of the offenses appears to be prejudice to an employer from the unfaithful actions of an employee or agent.

We cannot be certain that we will be able to afford assistance to the Netherlands when they ask for a search and seizure in a commercial bribery case. One U.S. District Court has denied extradition, stating that there is no Federal prohibition against commercial bribery and a majority of the states have not enacted commercial bribery statutes. *See Freedman v. U.S.*, 437 F. Supp.1252 (N.D. Ga. 1977).

The intention of the Parties was to provide for search and seizure assistance with respect to investigations under the Foreign Corrupt Practices Act. Of course, the Netherlands does not have an analogous law, prohibiting the payment of bribes to officials of foreign countries, but stated that such conduct would be included within the prohibition of their commercial bribery statues. Since commercial bribery is not a felony in the Netherlands, it is listed in the Annex for it to be included under Article 6.

ARTICLE 336

There is no mirror image of Article 336 in the law of the United States. However, publishing a false balance sheet could constitute fraud in violation of 18 U.S.C. 1341 or 1343, or securities fraud in violation of 15 U.S.C. 77q, or state laws governing businesses. As with previous articles, we have to look at Dutch requests on a case by case basis to determine whether the conduct would be punishable under the law of the United States.

U.S. Offenses

The only offense under United States law listed in the annex is 26 U.S.C. 7203, which prohibits willful failure to pay any tax, to make any return, to keep any records or supply any information at the time required by law. It is listed because it is one of three most important criminal provisions in the tax code, but carries a maximum penalty of one year's imprisonment.

Entry Into Force

The treaty shall enter into force 30 days after the exchange of the instruments of ratification. The treaty shall apply both with respect to acts committed before or after its entry into force.

As regards the Kingdom of the Netherlands, the present treaty shall apply to the territory of the Kingdom in Europe and to the Netherlands Antilles, unless the instrument of ratification of the government of the Kingdom of the Netherlands, referred to in Article 19, shall otherwise provide.

The Kingdom of the Netherlands reserves the right to declare at the time of ratification that this treaty shall not apply to requests for assistance relating to fiscal offenses addressed to the Netherlands Antilles. This reservation may at any time be wholly or partially withdrawn through an exchange of diplomatic notes between the Contracting Parties.

Either Contracting Party may terminate the treaty at any time by giving notice to the other Party and the termination shall be effective six months after the date of receipt of such notice.

Termination of the treaty by the Government of the Kingdom of the Netherlands may be limited to one of the constituent parts of the Kingdom.

Resolution of Ratification

Resolved (two-thirds of the Senators Present concurring therein), that the Senate advise and consent to the ratification of the Treaty on Mutual Legal Assistance Between the United States of America and the Kingdom of the Netherlands, together with a related exchange of notes, signed at the Hague on June 12, 1981.

Gathering Evidence from and for the United States

Bruce Zagaris

Introduction

Globalization has facilitated the ease with which criminals move goods, capital, and persons internationally. As a result prosecutors, investigating magistrates, and defense counsel increasingly need to gather evidence in order to effectively participate in investigations.

This paper discusses the laws and procedures to gain evidence in criminal cases for and from the U.S.

Motivations Behind the Requests

The motivations behind requests for information from the U.S. differ greatly. In the *Marcos* and *Duvalier* cases, newly-elected governments requested financial information about the prior investment activities and hidden assets of deposed political leaders who were suspected of fraud and corruption. Many other cases in countries other than the U.S. have sought information to recover assets, from Ceaucescu in Romania and Johnny O'Halloran, a former minister in Trinidad & Tobago. These cases also concerned political corruption.

Some requests have concerned "flight capital," money that is exported to the U.S. in violation of exchange control and/or reporting laws and regulations by businessmen seeking a more secure investment environment than their own country. These same foreign persons often may have been the subject of criminal tax investigations for not reporting the income from the money exported.

The increased availability of forfeiture provisions may provide motivation for transnational investigations.

The request for financial information may come from individuals in the private sector looking for information to support attacks on their competitors in business or politics. These individuals may wish to show that the money exporters have violated the laws of their country or are "bad" or immoral. If these individuals are clever and have sufficient resources, they may be able to use public record information to ascertain whether the large movements of capital to the U.S. may be evidence of tax violations in their country.

Similarly, the motivations of the U.S. and state government prosecutors for obtaining foreign evidence in a form admissible in criminal and quasi-criminal cases has grown dramatically in recent years.

Coercive Means of Obtaining Information

The U.S. has used at least nine different methods of coercion to obtain documentary information or evidence situated abroad, to obtain testimony from witnesses resident or located abroad, and to secure the transfer of private assets to the U.S.[1] The coercive means of obtaining information include the following:

1. compelling testimony of U.S. nationals or residents located abroad through subpoenas issued by federal courts and notwithstanding potential violations of the laws of many civil law countries;
2. compelling the production of documents located abroad of a target or defendant when a U.S. court has personal jurisdiction over the alleged wrongdoer, the documents or other tangible evidence is in the possession, custody, or control of the alleged wrongdoer or a related entity; and the production of the evidence is not protected by an evidentiary privilege;
3. compelling the production of documents located abroad from a third party that is not a target of the investigation or a defendant in the prosecution;
4. compelling through a subpoena a foreign witness in the U.S. to testify;
5. compelling the production of documents from foreign entities by a subpoena *duces tecum* of an officer or custodian over whom the U.S. has personal jurisdiction;
6. compelling "consents" to disclose third-party records as means to overcome bank secrecy;
7. compelling defendant not to seek a foreign blocking order;
8. compelling the repatriation of assets to pay a fine or taxes or for purposes of forfeiture; and
9. imposing a tax levy on a bank in the U.S. for funds of a taxpayer located in a foreign branch.

In April 1985, the Department of Justice issued an instruction requiring federal prosecutors planning to seek the issue of a subpoena for bank, business or commercial records reasonably believed to be in a foreign country, to obtain the agreement of the Office of International Affairs of the Criminal Division before taking such action. It also set forth the considerations to determine whether such a subpoena should be authorized:

(a) The availability of alternative methods for obtaining the records in a timely manner, such as mutual assistance treaties, tax treaties or letters rogatory.
(b) The indispensability of the records to the success of the investigation or prosecution.
(c) The need to protect against the destruction of records located abroad and to protect the ability to prosecute for contempt or obstruction of justice for such destruction.

In addition, prosecutors must consult with the Office of International Affairs before they bring proceedings relating to the enforcement of subpoenas for records located abroad. They must also obtain the OIA's concurrence before they serve a subpoena *ad testificandum*

---

[1] For additional discussion *see* Bruce Zagaris, *International Tax and Related Crimes: Gathering Evidence, Comparative Ethics and Related Matters, in* THE ALLEGED TRANSNATIONAL CRIMINAL 315, 357-64 (Richard D. Atkins ed., 1995); M. ABBELL & B. RISTAU, 3 INTERNATIONAL JUDICIAL ASSISTANCE—CRIMINAL OBTAINING EVIDENCE Ch. 5 (1990).

on an officer of or an attorney for a foreign bank or corporation who is temporarily in or passing through the U.S. when the testimony sought relates to the officer's or attorney's duties in connection with the operation of the bank or corporation.

Letters Rogatory

Background

The term "letters rogatory" refers to a request by one court to another court in an independent jurisdiction that a witness be examined upon interrogatories sent with the request. Internationally, letters rogatory is "the medium whereby one country, speaking through one of its courts, requests another country, acting through its own courts and by methods of the requested court procedure and entirely within the latter's control to aid the administration of justice in the former country."[2] Originally, the concept was based entirely on the comity of courts towards each other. More recently, it is founded in international conventions and local statutes.

Until the 1960s, the U.S. was reluctant to grant assistance in criminal matters. The reluctance was based on the view that the criminal law of one country should not give effect to the criminal law of another country,[3] the fear that the accused would not be able to confront witnesses against him, and the suspicion that an accused might not receive fair treatment in a foreign tribunal.[4]

While a statute providing for U.S. judicial assistance to proceedings in foreign countries was enacted in 1855,[5] it has been amended several times.[6]

In 1964, significant amendments were enacted.[7] The current statute allows the Department of State to receive and transmit letters rogatory.[8] Before this amendment, requests had to be forwarded directly to the appropriate courts through consular officers of the requesting state.[9]

Current law provides for judicial assistance to compel testimony and statements and the production of documents and other tangible evidence.[10] The 1964 law also authorized a U.S. court of the district in which a person resides to order service upon him of any papers issued in connection with a proceeding in a foreign or international tribunal.[11]

---

2 *The Signe*, 37 F. Supp. 819, 820 (D.C. La. 1941).

3 *The Antelope*, 23 U.S. [10 Wheat.] 66 (1825).

4 For a discussion of the former reluctance of U.S. courts to provide judicial assistance in criminal matters, *see* G. Mueller, *International Judicial Assistance in Criminal Matters*, 7 VILL. L. REV. 196-98 (1962).

5 Act of Mar. 2, 1855, Ch. 140, §2, 9 Stat. 630.

6 Act of Mar. 3, 1863, Ch. 95, § 1, 12 Stat. 769; Act of June 25, 1948, Ch. 646, 62 Stat. 949.

7 Act of Oct. 3, 1964, Pub. L. No. 88-619, 78 Stat. 995.

8 28 U.S.C. § 1781. The U.S. Department of Justice screens and then submits the requests. Courts seem to defer to the Department, apparently expecting it to use judgment in not submitting a request in a circumstance where a defendant would not receive due process in the requesting country's proceeding. Otherwise, the U.S. court must make some type of *de novo* finding each time the defendant and contesting party raises the issue of unfairness of the criminal procedure in the requesting country.

9 Mueller, *supra* note 4, at 202.

10 28 U.S.C. § 1782.

11 28 U.S.C. § 1696.

28 U.S.C. § 1782

Compulsory Cooperation

In most criminal cases, an individual with evidence that one party seeks does not want to cooperate voluntarily. Hence, the party seeking the evidence may obtain an order from the appropriate U.S. district court compelling cooperation.[12] Much litigation has been the result over the application and interpretation of 28 U.S.C. § 1782, which provides as follows:

> (a) The district court of the district in which a person resides or is found may order him to give his testimony or statement or to produce a document or other thing for use in a proceeding in a foreign or international tribunal. The order may be made pursuant to a letter rogatory issued, or request made, by a foreign or international tribunal or upon the application of any interested person and may direct that the testimony or statement be given or the document or other thing be produced, before a person appointed by the court. By virtue of his appointment, the person appointed has power to administer any necessary oath and take the testimony or statement. The order may prescribe the practice and procedure which may be in whole or in part the practice and procedure of the foreign country or the international tribunal, for taking the testimony or statement or producing the document or other thing. To the extent that the order does not prescribe otherwise, the testimony or statement shall be taken, and the document or other thing produced, in accordance with the Federal Rules of Civil Procedure.

A person may not be compelled to give his testimony or statement or to produce a document or other thing in violation of any legally applicable privilege.

Voluntary Cooperation

Under Section 1782(b), a person who voluntarily agrees to give evidence can do so "before any person and in any manner acceptable to [the witness]."[13] Two purposes are served: (1) it emphasizes to foreign countries the freedom the U.S. gives voluntary evidence-taking; and (2) it safeguards such voluntary procedures.[14] These provisions allow a foreign litigant to obtain evidence in the U.S. in a method convenient to the witness and also acceptable to the foreign tribunal. In a civil-law jurisdiction, an attorney who obtains evidence by circumventing the judiciary risks criminal sanctions even when a witness provides evidence voluntarily.[15]

---

12 Subject matter jurisdiction for section 1782 actions lies in the U.S. district courts. 28 U.S.C. § 1782. Venue lies in the district court "of the district in which [the witness] resides or is found." *Id.*

13 28 U.S.C. § 1782(b).

14 1964 U.S. Code Cong. & Admin. News 3790.

15 *See e.g.*, Paul Gully-Hart, *Obtaining Evidence in the Civil Law System*, *in* THE ALLEGED TRANSNATIONAL CRIMINAL 277-78 (Richard D. Atkins ed., 1995); Deutsch, *Judicial Assistance: Obtaining Evidence in the United States under 28 U.S.C. § 1782, for Use in a Foreign or International Tribunal*, 5 B.C. INT'L & COMP. L. REV. 175, 178 n.14 (1982).

Construction

The key goals of the 1948 and 1964 amendments were to facilitate the ability of the U.S. government and courts taking more of a leadership role in providing judicial assistance with the hope that the unilateral example of the U.S. would set an example for the rest of the world.[16] As a result, U.S. courts have given a liberal interpretation to the statute when they have applied it.

The Initiator of a Request

A U.S. court may order compulsory cooperation "pursuant to a letter rogatory issued, or request made, by a foreign or international tribunal or upon the application of any interested person." The phrase "interested person" includes both persons designated under foreign law to seek evidence and parties to foreign or international litigation.[17] Several cases denied foreign requests for assistance under letters rogatory based on the fact that the requests did not emanate from the proper entity. For the most part, these cases relied on the fact that the requesting body and the person that would use the information did not separate the investigatory from the adjudicatory arm.[18]

Several more recent cases have upheld the right of foreign officials to obtain evidence at the investigatory stage on the basis that ultimately the evidence would be used in an adjudicatory proceeding.[19]

Application of Right to Financial Privacy

An important issue raised in some letters rogatory requests is the applicability of the Right to Financial Privacy Act of 1978 (Privacy Act).[20] In the *Young* case, the court held that although the Privacy Act applies in cases in which the U.S. Government brings a request, it does not apply in cases where a foreign tribunal or interested person requests financial information under the letters rogatory statute.[21] The *Young* case signifies a further erosion of financial privacy, especially insofar as foreign investors are concerned. It means that the level of protection against government intrusions is different and weaker when the requester is a foreign government than when the requester is the U.S. government. It appears that only new legislation can correct the two levels of protection under the Privacy Act.

---

16 *See e.g.*, comments on legislative history in Amram, *Public Law 8-619 of October 3, 1964 — New Developments in International Judicial Assistance in the United States of America*, D.C. B.J. 32-33 (Jan. 1965). *See also In re* Request for Judicial Assistance from Seoul Dist. Criminal Court, Seoul, Korea, 428 F. Supp. 109 (C.D. Cal.), *aff'd*, 555 F.2d 720 (9th Cir. 1977).

17 1964 U.S. Code Cong. & Admin. News 3789.

18 1978 U.S. Code Cong. & Admin. News 9307.

19 Young v. United States Department of Justice, No. 87 Civ. 8307 (JFK) (S.D.N.Y. filed Nov. 28, 1988) (Kennan, J.); *In re* Letter Request from the Crown Prosecution Service of the United Kingdom, 683 F. Supp. 841 (D. D.C. 1988), *aff'd* 870 F.2d 686 (D.C. Cir. 1989); *In re* Request for Assistance from Ministry of Legal Affairs of Trinidad and Tobago, 648 F. Supp. 4646 (S.D. Fla. 1986), *aff'd* 848 F.2d 1151 (11th Cir. 1988), *cert. denied* 109 S. Ct. (1989).

20 12 U.S.C. § 3401 *et seq.*

21 *Young, supra* note 19.

Lack of Proceeding Before a Foreign Court

Letters rogatory may be used by prosecutors in common law countries to compel testimony of witnesses in the U.S. even though no proceeding is pending before a foreign court if: (a) there is a *bona fide*, pending criminal investigation in connection to which the testimony is sought; (b) the testimony is sought for the purpose of using it in a proceeding before a court in the requesting state if charges are brought; and (c) criminal proceedings are very likely to be started in the near future or are within reasonable contemplation.[22]

While a U.S. Court cannot consider whether the evidence sought would be admissible in a trial in the requesting state,[23] the procedures used in taking the evidence should be consistent with the intent to use the evidence in judicial proceedings, especially since Section 1972 is not intended to allow evidence gathering for use solely in a preliminary police investigation.[24]

Type of Evidence Discoverable and Discovery Procedures

Evidence sought in a letters rogatory request must be discoverable under the laws of the requesting state before a U.S. court will grant assistance.[25] In a civil case the House of Lords has held that a party could use whatever discovery procedures are available to it under the laws of the U.S., even though those procedures are much wider than British discovery procedures.[26]

Appointment of Commissioner

Once letters rogatory are granted, the U.S. court will appoint a commissioner who may be a magistrate, a prosecutor, or some other person. A commissioner lacks the authority to refuse to execute the request.[27]

A commissioner appointed may be an "interested party" or an attorney for an "interested party."[28]

---

[22] *In re* Request for International Judicial Assistance, Brazil, 946 F.2d 702, 706 (2d Cir. 1991) (adjudicative proceedings must be "imminent—very likely to occur and very soon to occur;" *In re* Request for Assistance from Ministry of Legal Affairs of Trinidad and Tobago, 848 F.2d 1151, 1155-56 (11th Cir. 1988), *cert. denied*, 488 U.S. 1005 (1989) (judicial "proceeding is very likely to occur" and the request is not a "fishing expedition" or a "vehicle for harassment"); *In re* Letter of Request from Crown Prosecution Service, 870 F.2d 686, 689-92 (D.C. Cir. 1989) ("reliable indications of the likelihood that proceedings will be instituted within a reasonable time" or were within "reasonable contemplation"). *See also In re* Letters Rogatory from Tokyo District, 539 F.2d 1216, 1218-19 (9th Cir. 1976).

[23] *In re* Letters Rogatory from Seoul District Criminal Court, 555 F.2d 720, 723-23 (9th Cir. 1977); *In re* Letters Rogatory from Tokyo District, 539 F.2d 1216, 1219 (9th Cir. 1976).

[24] *In re* Request from Crown Prosecution Service, *supra* note 19, at 693.

[25] *In re* Request for Assistance from Ministry of Legal Affairs of Trinidad and Tobago, 848 F.2d 1151, 1156 (11th Cir. 1988), *cert. denied*, 488 U.S. 1005 (1989); John Deere Ltd. v. Sperry Corp, 754 F.2d 132, 136 (3rd Cir. 1985).

[26] South Carolina Insurance Co. v. Assurantie Maatschappij, N.V. 3 All E.R. 487 [1987].

[27] *In re* Request for Assistance from Seoul District Criminal Court, 428 F. Supp. 109, 112 (N.D. Cal.), *aff'd* 555 F.2d 720 (9th Cir. 1977).

[28] *In re* Request for Judicial Assistance from Haiti, 6698 F. Supp. 403, 407 (S.D. Fla. 1987) (private lawyer representing government of Haiti on a contingency fee in a civil case authorized to serve as commissioner in taking evidence in connection with a related Haitian criminal case).

Illustrative Cases

The Young Case

In late 1988 the U.S. District Court for the Southern District of New York held that the Privacy Act does not restrict access to customer records by requests emanating from foreign governments.[29]

The case developed from a request in 1986 by the Attorney General of Bermuda, who sought assistance under Section 1782 in gaining access to the records of a Chemical Bank branch in Manhattan relating to an investigation of currency violations in Bermuda and presented a letter rogatory to the court.[30] The request produced the requested records and certain affidavits of Chemical employees which were transmitted to Bermuda. Based on this information, an indictment was filed by the Bermudian government on August 13, 1987, against Roderick and Sybil Young, charging them with making false statements for the purpose of buying foreign currency and exporting foreign currency notes without permission of the Controller. They were convicted and sentenced to imprisonment and fined. They then sued the U.S. Department of Justice and Chemical Bank, alleging that the acts of the U.S. Attorney's Office constituted a violation of the Privacy Act and Section 1782(a).

In dismissing the complaint, Judge Keenan concluded that the Privacy Act's restrictions on the federal government's access to customer records do not apply to foreign letters rogatory. The reasoning was based on the language and history of the Privacy Act.[31] The U.S. Attorney's Office, acting as Commissioner, had not procured financial information within the meaning of the Privacy Act because it had acted as a representative of a foreign tribunal and not in its own individual capacity.[32] Judge Keenan rejected the contention that a federal district court is a "government authority" within the meaning of the Privacy Act, noting that the statutory term is defined as an "agency or department of the United States" and U.S. courts are not "government authorities" within the Privacy Act.[33]

The district court rejected the argument that the Bermuda Attorney General is not a "tribunal" within the meaning of Section 1782, noting that there would be an impartial judge to weigh the evidence and citing another Section 1782 case that allowed applications for judicial assistance from an "interested person" and not just "tribunals."[34]

Judge Keenan rejected plaintiff's argument that Section 1782 requires a proceeding be "pending" before a foreign tribunal when the request for letters rogatory is made and the argument that the U.S. Attorney's Office was illegally retaining copies of the financial records it obtained for the Bermuda Attorney General and that such records could be used against them in a future proceeding in a U.S. court. The court stated that if the U.S.

---

29 *Young, supra* note 19, discussed in 5 INT'L ENFORCEMENT L. REP. (June, 1989).

30 *In re* Request for International Judicial Assistance from the Attorney General of Bermuda, M19-118 (S.D. N.Y. 1987).

31 The court also cited as authority *In re* Letter of Request for Judicial Assistance from the Tribunal Civil de Port-Au-Prince, Republic of Haiti, 669 F. Supp. 403 (S.D. Fla. 1987).

32 For authority the court cited Republic of Haiti v. Crown Charters, Inc., 667 F. Supp. 839, 847-48 (S.D. Fla. 1987).

33 *See e.g.*, Doe v. Bd. of Prof'l Responsibility of the D.C. Court of Appeals, 717 F.2d 1424 (D.C. Cir. 1983).

34 *In re* Request for Assistance from Ministry of Legal Affairs of Trinidad and Tobago, 648 F. Supp. 464 (S.D. Fla. 1986), *aff'd* 848 F.2d 1151 (11th Cir. 1988), *cert. denied* 109 S.Ct. 784 (1989); 1964 U.S. Code Congr. & Admin. News 3789.

Government wants to engage in its own investigation into the plaintiffs' criminal activity, the grand jury process is available to the Justice Department. The court observed that grand jury subpoenas are exempt from the requirements of the relevant portions of the Privacy Act.[35] The reason is that grand juries "operate under judicial scrutiny."[36]

Crown Prosecution (Ward) Case

In the *Crown Prosecution* (*Ward*) case, U.S. Courts enforced the letters rogatory procedure for taking of evidence in aid of foreign criminal proceedings arising out of the Guinness PLC securities fraud case in England.[37] The decision illustrates the liberal way in which the letters rogatory statute is interpreted.

The Crown Prosecution Service of the U.K. had requested judicial assistance concerning criminal proceedings against Ernest Saunders, the former chairman of Guinness PLC (Guinness). Saunders was charged with obstructing justice and destruction and falsification of documents. According to the letter, the Guinness share-support scheme involved the receipt of questionable payments by insiders, including Thomas J. Ward, an attorney in the District of Columbia and a Guinness director. In particular, one of the alleged payments was the purchase of a Watergate South apartment in Washington, D.C., by Guinness insider Sir Isadore Jack Lyons of London. However, the transferee of record on the documents for the sale of Lyons' apartment was Ward.

Upon receiving the letter rogatory by diplomatic note, the State Department transmitted it to the Office of International Affairs (OIA), Criminal Division, U.S. Department of Justice, which in turn referred it to the U.S. Attorney's Office for the District of Columbia. In response to the U.S. Attorney's *ex parte* application, the district court on January 21, 1988, appointed Robert R. Chapman, Assistant U.S. Attorney, and John E. Harris, OIA Associate Director at the time, as Commissioners of the Court and instructed them to obtain evidence from witnesses pursuant to the letter of request and to transmit it to the crown Prosecution Service.

Ward contested the order by moving in the district court to quash the appointment of the Commissioners and the subpoenas issued by them. Ward's motion was based mainly on the theory that the evidence was not sought "for use in a [judicial] proceeding" as required by Section 1782, but was sought by Scotland Yard for use in a police investigation with no "proceeding in a . . . tribunal" yet pending.[38]

The district court held that the statute does not require a pending judicial proceeding at the time assistance is sought under Section 1782. On March 21, 1988, the court denied Ward's motion.[39]

---

35 12 U.S.C. § 3414(i).

36 1978 U.S. Code Cong. & Admin. News 9307.

37 *In re* Letter Request from the Crown Prosecution Service of the United Kingdom, 683 F. Supp. 841 (D.D.C. 1988), *aff'd* 870 F.2d 686 (D.C. Cir. 1989); 5 INT'L ENFORCEMENT L. REP. 142 (1989).

38 On Feb. 2, 1988, the U.K. had issued an arrest warrant for violations of the Theft Act 1968.

39 *In re* Letter of Request from the Crown Prosecution Service of the U.K., 683 F. Supp. 841 (D.D.C. 1988). For an earlier discussion of the case after oral argument occurred in the appellate process, *see* B. Zagaris & S. Gardner, *U.S. Circuit Court Considers Letters Rogatory from Scotland Yard*, 5 INT'L ENFORCEMENT L. REP. 12 (Jan. 1989).

One year later, the U.S. Court of Appeals for the District of Columbia affirmed the district court's judgement.[40] In rejecting Ward's appeal, the appellate court held that there does not have to be "pending" judicial proceedings for a foreign prosecutor to obtain assistance as an "interested person" under 28 U.S.C. § 1782. In the instant case, the court noted, proceedings were within "reasonable contemplation" and hence the district court properly denied the motion to quash.[41] The court also ruled that the Crown Prosecution Service was an "interested person" within the meaning of Section 1782. The court relied on both scholarly comment[42] and decisions for the proposition that a legal affairs ministry, attorney general, or other prosecutor fit the "interested person" requirement.[43]

The court also ruled that as in the *Trinidad and Tobago* case,[44] the district court must fulfill the factual requirement that a proceeding is very likely to occur before it grants an order. The appellate court stated that, to protect against abuse, the district court should insist on reliable indications of the likelihood that proceedings will be initiated within a reasonable time.

During the pendency of the appeal, in December 1988, a 65-count indictment was lodged with the Central Criminal Court (Old Bailey) charging seven defendants, including Saunders and Lyons, with multiple criminal offenses. Although not indicted, Ward was named as a co-conspirator in three of the counts, and was also identified in two other counts. On August 28, 1990, Saunders, Lyons, and two others were convicted by a London jury of conspiracy, false accounting, and theft.[45]

Mutual Legal Assistance Treaties (MLATs)

To avoid the cumbersome, slow, *ad hoc*, and discretionary nature of the letters rogatory process,[46] many countries have concluded treaties on mutual legal assistance in criminal matters.[47]

The U.S. has 15 MLATs in force. The MLATs in force are with: Argentina, the Bahamas, Canada, the Cayman Islands (also extended to include Anguilla, the British Virgin

---

40 The appellate court did rule that Ward, as a potential target of the British investigation, had standing to assert a violation of § 1782.

41 The appellate court did remand the case to the district court for further proceedings to ensure that the evidence was taken in a way appropriate "for use in a [judicial] proceeding" in the U.K. The Court further stated that the district court should be guided by a submission from the Crown Prosecution Service, describing the form appropriate for a British court, as distinguished from a police investigation.

42 The court relied partly on the remarks of Professor Hans Smit, who explained that an interested person is intended "to include not only litigants before foreign or international tribunals, but also foreign and international officials as well as any other person . . . [who] possesses] a reasonable interest in obtaining assistance." Hans Smit, *International Litigation under the United States Code*, 65 COLUM. L. REV. 1015, 1027 (1965).

43 *Trinidad and Tobago*, *supra* note 19; Young, *supra* note 19; *In re* Letter Rogatory from the Public Prosecutor's Office at the Regional Ct. of Hamburg, Fed. Republic of Germany, Misc. No. M-1988, slip. op. at 4 (S.D.N.Y. June 21, 1988).

44 For a discussion of the case, *see* Zagaris & Razdan, *Florida Bankers Are Concerned about Judicial Assistance to Law Enforcement Officials in the Absence of a Treaty and a Court Request*, 4 INT'L ENFORCEMENT L. REP. 366 (Nov. 1988).

45 Forman, *Former Guinness Chairman Is Sentenced to Five-Year Term for Role in Takeover*, WALL ST. J., Aug. 29, 1990, at A4.

46 The letters rogatory process can take up to three years in some cases. *See* L. Davis, *House Subcommittee Holds Hearings on Telemarketing Fraud and International Enforcement Efforts to Combat It*, 6 INT'L ENFORCEMENT L. REP. 336, 338 n.6 (1990).

47 *See supra*, Chapter 12.

Islands, Turks & Caicos, and Montserrat), Italy, Jamaica, Mexico, Morocco, the Netherlands, Panama, Spain, Switzerland, Thailand, Turkey, and Uruguay.

Ten MLATs have been signed and not ratified. They are with: Austria, Barbados, Belgium, Colombia, Hungary, Korea, Nigeria, the Philippines, Trinidad and Tobago, and the U.K. The U.S. has also signed but not ratified an MLAT with the OAS.

The U.S. has concluded a pre-MLAT Executive Agreement with Russia. It has an *ad hoc* agreement with the U.K. on cooperating on fraud and financial crime in the Caribbean dependencies of Britain.

The U.S. is close to concluding MLATs with Luxembourg. In a novel initiative, the U.S. has negotiated in parallel and is close to concluding an MLAT with the countries of the Organization of East Caribbean States (*e.g.*, Antigua and Barbuda, Dominica, Grenada, St. Kitts, St. Lucia, and St. Vincent).

The U.S. has been a comparative latecomer to concluding MLATs. It did not have any MLATs until the Swiss treaty was signed in May 19, 1973, and came into force in January 1977, after lengthy negotiations that started in 1968.

MLATs provide for a wide variety of assistance: service of documents, provision of records, locating persons, taking of the testimony or statements of persons, production of documents, execution of requests for search and seizure, forfeiture of criminally obtained assets, and transfer of persons in custody for testimonial purposes. Most importantly, under the MLATs, evidence must be transmitted in a form that is admissible in the requesting state's courts.

Assistance in Investigations

The MLATs clarify a situation that has created much dispute in the use of letters rogatory by obligating the contracting parties to provide mutual assistance in criminal investigations as well as in "proceedings." Hence, a contracting party that is merely investigating a case in an early stage of the investigation can obtain assistance from the U.S. The MLATs are self-executing in the U.S. They amend and add to federal law on issues such as the creation of a right of safe conduct, the conferral of authority to detain persons in custody, the creation of a hearsay exception for chain-of-custody evidence, the removal of discretion to refuse to issue subpoenas for testimony and tangible evidence, and the U.S. right to disclose confidential information to a requesting country.

Use of a Central Authority

While letters rogatory must be made through the courts in both countries with the involvement of various foreign ministries, justice ministries, and in some cases embassies, MLATs are much more expeditious, partly because there is a direct link through a "central authority" in each country to process requests for assistance.

The Attorney General is the central authority for the U.S. under all the U.S. MLATs. The Attorney General has delegated his duties as central authority to the Assistant Attorney General in charge of the Criminal Division, who has, in turn, subdelegated his authority to the Deputy Assistant Attorneys General and the Director of the Criminal Division's Office of International Affairs in the Criminal Division of the Department of Justice, pursuant to regulations.[48]

OIA handles all requests under an MLAT, both outgoing and incoming. It is charged with receiving and seeing to the execution of incoming requests from foreign countries for investigative or evidence-gathering assistance in the U.S. The Office consults with appropriate officials in the Justice and State Departments, as well as officials in other agencies as necessary, when required to make discretionary determinations under the treaties in novel, unusual, or sensitive situations.

Procedural Requirements

The MLATs provide that a request for assistance must contain the name of the authority conducting the investigation, the subject after of the investigation, a description of the evidence sought, the purpose for which it is sought, and the name and location of any persons being sought. The documents from the requesting state do not have to be authenticated or legalized. Normally, requests are executed pursuant to the laws of the requesting state. Procedures may be executed pursuant to the laws of the requesting state, provided such procedures are not specifically forbidden by the requested state's laws.[49] The requested state must return the completed requests to the requesting state, together with all the documents, information and evidence obtained.[50]

The requested state may cause service of any document transmitted for this purpose by the requesting state. A request for service of documents that require the appearance of a person before authorities in the requesting state must be transmitted a reasonable time before the scheduled appearance.[51] Under 28 U.S.C. § 1783, the U.S. can issue subpoenas to its own nationals.

Compulsion of Testimony or Documents

The MLATs provide that a person from whom evidence is sought may be compelled to testify and produce documents, records, or articles in the same way and to the same extent

---

[48] Directive No. 81, 44 F.R. 18661, Mar. 29, 1979, as amended at 45 F.R. 6541, Jan. 29, 1980, 48 F.R. 54595, Dec. 6, 1983.

[49] U.S.-Turkish MLAT, 32 U.S.T. 3111, T.I.A.S. No. 9891, Art. 25(2); U.S.-Netherlands MLAT, T.I.A.S. No. 10734, Art. 12(2); U.S.-Colombian MLAT, S. Treaty Doc. No. 11, 97th Cong., 1st Sess. (1981), Art. 4(2); U.S.-Italian MLAT, S. Treaty Doc. No. 25, 98th Cong., 2d Sess. (1984), Art. 2(2) and the accompanying Memorandum of Understanding; U.S.-Moroccan MLAT, S. Treaty Doc. No. 24, 98th Cong., 2d Sess. (1984), Art. 5(3); U.S.-Swiss MLAT, 27 U.S.T. 2019, T.I.A.S. No. 8302, Art. 9(2). The Swiss, Turkish, and Netherlands MLATs provide that search and seizure may be executed only according to the laws of the requested state. U.S.-Swiss MLAT, at Art. 9(2); U.S.-Turkish MLAT, at Art. 27; U.S.-Netherlands MLAT, at Art. 6(1); *cf.* European MLAT, Art. 7(1).

[50] U.S.-Swiss MLAT, *supra* note 49, at Art. 32(1); U.S.-Turkish MLAT, *supra* note 49, at Art. 39(2); U.S.-Netherlands MLAT, *supra* note 49, at Art. 15(1); U.S.-Columbia MLAT, *supra* note 49, at Art. 6(1); U.S.-Italian MLAT, *supra* note 49, at Art. 6(1).

[51] U.S.-Swiss MLAT, *supra* note 49, at Art. 22(3); U.S.-Turkish MLAT, *supra* note 49, at Art. 29(2); U.S.-Netherlands MLAT, *supra* note 49, at Art. 3(2); U.S.-Colombian MLAT, *supra* note 49, at Art. 19; U.S.-Italian MLAT, *supra* note 49, at Art. 11(1); U.S.-Moroccan MLAT, *supra* note 49, at Art. 15(1).

as in criminal investigations or proceedings in the requested state.[52] The requested state must compel testimony unless the person has the right to refuse under the laws of the requested state.[53] Under some U.S. MLATs, testimonial privileges under the laws of the requesting state do not apply in the execution of the request.[54]

The U.S.-Italian MLAT provides that a U.S. citizen can be removed to Italy to testify with respect to a criminal investigation, and it permits U.S. authorities to subpoena persons within the Italian jurisdiction. If one refuses, the person becomes subject to the same sanctions under U.S. law as if he had failed to appear in similar circumstances in the U.S.[55] However, the sanctions cannot include removal of that person to Italy. An apparently open question is the testimonial privileges of the witness while he or she testifies in Italy and the procedures for the resolution of disputes that could arise in the course of testifying.

Safe Conduct to Testify

The MLATs provide safe conduct to persons transferred to testify in the requested state concerning any act or conviction preceding the person's departure from the territory of the requested state.[56] Under some MLATs, a person summoned before a proceeding in the requesting state to answer for acts forming the subject of proceedings against him is permitted similar safe conduct, but only with respect to acts that are not specified in the request.[57]

Safe conduct is provided only for acts that preceded the person's travel from the requested state. If a person commits subsequent crimes in the requesting state, such as perjury, she or he can be prosecuted.[58] Safe conduct stops ten days after the person receives official notification that his or her presence is no longer required if the person has not departed the territory or returns.[59]

---

52 U.S.-Swiss MLAT, *supra* note 49, at Art. 10(2); U.S.-Turkish MLAT, *supra* note 49, at Art. 25(3); U.S.-Netherlands MLAT, *supra* note 49, at Art. 5(1); U.S.-Colombian MLAT, *supra* note 49, at Art. 9(1); U.S.-Italian MLAT, *supra* note 49, at Art. 11(2); U.S.-Moroccan MLAT, *supra* note 49, at Art. 15(2).

53 U.S.-Swiss MLAT, *supra* note 49, at Art. 10(1); U.S.-Turkish MLAT, *supra* note 49, at Art. 25(3); U.S.-Netherlands MLAT, *supra* note 49, at Art. 5(1); U.S.-Colombian MLAT, *supra* note 49, at Art. 9(1); U.S.-Italian MLAT, *supra* note 49, at Art. 14(1); U.S.-Moroccan MLAT, *supra* note 49, at Art. 8(1).

54 *Id.*

55 A court may deem the failure to obey a subpoena a contempt of court, FED. R. CRIM. P. 17(g)(1984), FED. R. CIV. P. 45(f) (1984). *See also* NATIONAL LAWYERS GUILD, REPRESENTATION OF WITNESSES BEFORE FEDERAL GRAND JURIES 444 (1982).

56 U.S.-Swiss MLAT, *supra* note 49, at Art. 27(1); U.S.-Turkish MLAT, *supra* note 49, at Art. 34(2); U.S.-Netherlands MLAT, *supra* note 49, at Art. 9(1); U.S.-Colombian MLAT, *supra* note 49, at Art. 13(1); U.S.-Italian MLAT, *supra* note 49, at Art. 17(2); U.S.-Moroccan MLAT, *supra* note 49, at Art. 10.

57 U.S.-Swiss MLAT, *supra* note 49, at Art. 27(2); U.S.-Turkish MLAT, *supra* note 49, at Art. 34(2); U.S.-Netherlands MLAT, *supra* note 49, at Art. 9(2).

58 U.S.-Italian MLAT, *supra* note 49, at Art. 17(1)(b); Treaty on Mutual Legal Assistance with the Kingdom of the Netherlands, Exec. Rep. No. 8736, 97th Congress, 1st Session, 1981, at 10; Treaty of Mutual Legal Assistance with the Republic of Colombia, Exec. Rep. No. 897-35, 97th Congress, 1st Session, 1981, at 13.

59 U.S.-Swiss MLAT, *supra* note 49, at Art. 27(3); U.S.-Turkish MLAT, *supra* note 49, at Art. 34(3); U.S.-Netherlands MLAT, *supra* note 49, at Art. 9(3); U.S.-Colombian MLAT, *supra* note 49, at Art. 13(2); U.S. Italian MLAT, *supra* note 49, at Art. 17(2); U.S.-Moroccan MLAT, *supra* note 49, at Art. 10(2).

Production of Records

The MLATs permit the requested state to provide publicly available government documents or records to the requesting state, if duly authenticated.[60] Non-publicly available records must be provided only to the same extent and under the same conditions as they would be available to the requested state's law enforcement officials. The requested state may exercise discretion as to whether such information is released.[61]

The MLATs permit a requesting state to obtain assistance in search and seizure requests from the requested state. Such a request must contain such information as would justify such action under the laws of the requested state.[62] A request for search and seizure by the U.S. should be accompanied by a showing of probable cause.

Exceptions

Under the MLATs a requested state can refuse judicial assistance if the execution of the request would prejudice its security or other essential "interests."[63] Under many MLATs a requested state can deny a request for assistance if the offense is a purely military or political offense.[64] The Dutch MLAT permits the U.S. to deny a request for assistance if it is a political offense. The Moroccan treaty permits the U.S. to deny a request if it is a military offense.[65] In addition, all the U.S. MLATs authorize denial of a request if the request does not conform with the provisions of the treaty in request.[66]

Use of MLATs Not Allowed for Defendants and Third Parties

The more recent U.S. MLATs provide that they are intended only for use by the governments. Private individuals may not use the treaty to obtain evidence from the other country for use in solely private matters.[67] Under the Swiss, Dutch, Moroccan, and the proposed Colombian MLATs, the defendants do not have any right to obtain judicial relief

---

60 U.S.-Swiss MLAT, *supra* note 49, at Art. 19; U.S.-Turkish MLAT, *supra* note 49, at Art. 26; U.S.-Netherlands MLAT, *supra* note 49, at Art. 4(1); U.S.-Colombian MLAT, *supra* note 49, at Art. 14(1); U.S.-Italian MLAT, *supra* note 49, at Art. 12(3); U.S.-Moroccan MLAT, *supra* note 49, at Art. 11(1).

61 U.S.-Swiss MLAT, *supra* note 49, at Art. 16(1); U.S.-Turkish MLAT, *supra* note 49, at Art. 26(b); U.S.-Netherlands MLAT, *supra* note 49, at Art. 4(2); U.S.-Colombian MLAT, *supra* note 49, at Art. 14(1); U.S.-Italian MLAT, *supra* note 49, at Art. 12(2); U.S.-Moroccan MLAT, *supra* note 49, at Art. 11(2).

62 U.S.-Swiss MLAT, *supra* note 49, at Art. 27; U.S.-Netherlands MLAT, *supra* note 49, at Art. 6(1); U.S.-Colombian MLAT, *supra* note 49, at Art. 15(1); U.S.-Italian MLAT, *supra* note 49, at Art. 13(1); U.S.-Moroccan MLAT, *supra* note 49, at Art. 13.

63 U.S.-Swiss MLAT, *supra* note 49, at Art. 3(1); U.S.-Turkish MLAT, *supra* note 49, at Art. 22(1)(b); U.S.-Netherlands MLAT, *supra* note 49, at Art. 10(1)(a); U.S.-Colombian MLAT, *supra* note 49, at Art. 5(1)(a); U.S.-Italian MLAT, *supra* note 49, at Art. 5(1)(a); U.S.-Moroccan MLAT, *supra* note 49, at Art. 2(1)(a).

64 U.S.-Netherlands MLAT, *supra* note 49, at Art. 10(1)(b).

65 U.S.-Moroccan MLAT, *supra* note 49, at Art. 2(1)(b).

66 U.S.-Swiss MLAT, *supra* note 49, at Art. 21(1); U.S.-Netherlands MLAT, *supra* note 49, at Art. 10(1)(d); U.S.-Colombian MLAT, *supra* note 49, at Art. 4(4)(a); U.S.-Italian MLAT, *supra* note 49, at Art. 5(1)(c); U.S.-Moroccan MLAT, *supra* note 49, at Art. 2(1)(c).

67 U.S.-Netherlands MLAT, *supra* note 49, at Art. 18(2); U.S.-Colombian MLAT, *supra* note 49, at Art. 1(4); U.S.-Italian MLAT, *supra* note 49, at Art. 1(4); U.S.-Moroccan MLAT, *supra* note 49, at Art. 1(3).

or to suppress or exclude evidence through the treaties except as specified.[68] Private parties may use letters rogatory where available.[69]

Counsel for defendants can ask the U.S. court conducting a criminal proceeding to order the Department of Justice to make a request for the defense, provided the MLAT makes such a motion appropriate. For example, under the Swiss treaty, such requests can be made.[70] Defense counsel must comply carefully with the MLAT provisions when she or he makes such requests. Counsel must show the need for the evidence sought under the risk of disclosing its strategy even if it does succeed in gaining access to the treaty.[71] In at least one case under the Swiss treaty, the court ordered that either the government comply with a request for assistance under the Swiss treaty or the case would be dismissed.

In one unpublished case, a request for search and seizure from the U.S. by the Netherlands was challenged. A search warrant was issued by a U.S. magistrate in Orlando, Florida, on the basis of an affidavit signed by a Special Agent of the Drug Enforcement Administration.[72] The defendant moved to have a hearing to suppress the evidence, alleging that the cablegram from Dutch authorities requesting a search of the defendant's property was not a judicial statement under oath before a judge in the Netherlands, as required under Article 4 of the U.S.-Dutch MLAT. The defendant also argued that the search warrant did not contain probable cause and did not satisfy the legal requirements for a search warrant under the Federal Rules of Criminal Procedure and federal case law. The defendant also alleged that Article 6(4) of the MLAT was unconstitutional because it has taken judicial powers away from the judicial branch in an act by the executive branch. The court denied the request for both a hearing and a rehearing.

Coverage of RICO and Other New Crimes

One of the principal goals of the U.S. in negotiating newer MLATs is to include within the treaties modern offenses, such as Racketeer Influenced and Corrupt Organizations Act (RICO), Continuing Criminal Enterprises (CCE), money laundering, and white collar crimes, including tax offenses. The individual MLATs reflect negotiating priorities and exigencies of the time of negotiations. For example, when the Thai and Canadian MLATs were negotiated in the early 1980s, the Department of Justice had some experience in implementing the MLATs with Switzerland, Italy, Turkey, and the Netherlands and refined its objectives accordingly.

---

68 U.S.-Netherlands MLAT, *supra* note 49, at Art. 18(2); U.S.-Colombian MLAT, *supra* note 49, at Art. 1(5); U.S.-Italian MLAT, *supra* note 49, at Art. 1(4) (implied only); U.S.-Moroccan MLAT, *supra* note 49, at Art. 16(2); U.S.-Swiss MLAT, *supra* note 49, at Art. 37(1) (similar provisions, but with exceptions). If the defendant believes that one of the parties have violated the MLAT, he or she can only inform the central authority of the other state, which may or may not require an explanation or act.

69 U.S.-Swiss MLAT, *supra* note 49, at Art. 38(1); U.S.-Turkish MLAT, *supra* note 49, at Art. 42(2); U.S.-Netherlands MLAT, *supra* note 49, at Art. 18(1)(a); U.S.-Colombian MLAT, *supra* note 49, at Art. 21(1)(a); U.S.-Italian MLAT, *supra* note 49, at Art. 5(1)(a); U.S.-Moroccan MLAT, *supra* note 49, at Art. 2(1)(a).

70 U.S.-Swiss MLAT, *supra* note 49, at Art. 28(2); Frei, *Swiss Secrecy Laws and Obtaining Evidence from Switzerland*, *in* 1 TRANSNATIONAL LITIGATION: PRACTICAL APPROACHES TO CONFLICTS AND ACCOMMODATIONS 17 (Fedders et al., eds., 1984).

71 U.S.-Swiss MLAT, *supra* note 49, at Art. 29; Frei, *supra* note 70, at 17.

72 *See* Ellis & Pisani, *supra* note 47, at 173-74, discussing United States ex. rel. Public Prosecutor of Rotterdam, Netherlands v. Richard Jean Van Aalst, Case No. 84-67-MISC-018 (M.D. Fla. 1984).

Most recent experience and changes in U.S. domestic law have led to further modifications in the U.S. negotiating objectives. For example, all of the MLATs have provisions that will enable the U.S. to implement recently enacted U.S. law providing for the transfer of an equitable share of certain forfeited property to other countries.[73]

Limited Coverage of MLATs with Offshore Jurisdictions

The U.S. MLATs with the Cayman Islands, the Bahamas, and Panama apply to offenses that are crimes in both the U.S. and the other treaty partners and are punishable by more than one year's imprisonment, but excludes certain tax matters. In the U.S.-Cayman MLAT, no information may be sought relating directly or indirectly to the imposition, calculation, or collection of taxes unless this involves the unlawful proceeds of a crime covered by the treaty.

The crimes covered by the U.S.-Bahamas MLAT are even narrower than the U.S.-Cayman MLAT: only certain enumerated crimes, which must be a crime in both countries and be punishable by one year's imprisonment or more. The grounds for a requested state to refuse a request is much broader than in the proposed U.S.-Cayman MLAT and in other U.S. MLATs.

Executive Agreements (MINI-MLATs)

Narcotics Agreements

Starting with the 1984 Agreement with the Cayman Islands,[74] the U.S. has negotiated several executive agreements providing for mutual assistance concerning matters "connected with, arising from, related to, or resulting from any narcotics activity."[75] These agreements have been made with a wide variety of countries. They are limited to narcotics cases and offenses arising from narcotics trafficking (*e.g.*, tax crimes). They apply to investigations and prosecutions. Some of them, such as the Cayman agreement, are not reciprocal and cannot be used by the other party to obtain assistance from the U.S.

Executive Agreements Related to Corruption

Between 1976 and 1982, the U.S. concluded executive agreements, known as the "Lockheed Agreements," to obtain evidence from other countries in joint criminal investigations and prosecutions of "sensitive payments" in violation of the Foreign Corrupt Practices Act.[76] These agreements provide for sharing investigative information, providing

---

[73] 18 U.S.C. § 981(i)(1).

[74] Supplementary Agreement of July 26, 1984, to the Single Convention on Narcotic Drugs 1961.

[75] For a discussion of the U.S.-Turks and Caicos agreement, *see* Bruce Zagaris, *International Enforcement Matters-Money Movement and Related Matters*, *in* 1 FIFTH ANNUAL INTERNATIONAL INSTITUTE ON INTERNATIONAL TAXATION 4.48-50 (Fla. Bar Jan. 15-16, 1987); for a discussion of the U.S.-Cayman agreement, *see* Bruce Zagaris, *Exchange of information Outside Tax Agreements*, *in* INTERNATIONAL EXCHANGE OF TAX INFORMATION RECENT DEVELOPMENTS 63, 94-98 (R. Gordon & B. Zagaris eds., 1985).

[76] For a discussion of the "Lockheed Agreements," *see* B. Ristau, *International Cooperation in Penal Matters: The "Lockheed Agreements,"* (TRANSNATIONAL ASPECTS OF CRIMINAL PROCEDURE) 1983 MICH. Y.B. OF INT'L LEGAL STUD. 85-106.

assistance, and safeguarding the confidentiality of information resulting from the investigations.

Unlike MLATs, the Lockheed Agreements do not obligate the requested state to furnish assistance to the requesting state. Rather, the requesting state must use letters rogatory to obtain assistance requiring compulsory measures. The requested state is simply obligated to execute these requests for assistance in a diligent manner.

Other Mini-Executive Agreements and MOUs

The U.S. has concluded many executive agreements and Memoranda of Understanding (MOUs) on diverse subjects, including: securities enforcement cooperation; commodities futures enforcement cooperation; anti-trust enforcement cooperation; mutual assistance in tax matters; tax information exchange agreements; and customs enforcement cooperation.

Summary and Conclusion

Globalization mandates continued reassessment of U.S. evidence-gathering statutes and treaties, executive agreements, and MOUs. A major new mechanism is the growing role of international organizations in setting standards and facilitating the preparation and elaboration of new agreements and harmonized legislation.

The next major U.S. initiative will come in the form of a legislative initiative against international organized crime. First announced on October 22, 1996, in a set of speeches to the U.N. General Assembly by President Clinton, executive order and presidential directive, on May 22, 1996, President Clinton is expected to announce additional initiatives that will increase efforts by the U.S. to expand jurisdiction, gain access to evidence, and deny rights of organized criminals to gain and use evidence in U.S. litigation.

In the future, major tasks will be for the U.S. and its treaty partners to ensure that the law and law enforcement keep pace with technological developments and that increased law enforcement does not unduly sacrifice the rule of law.

Appendix 10

Foreign Documents—Title 28 U.S.C.

§ 1740. Copies of consular papers

Copies of all official documents and papers in the office of any consul or vice consul of the United States, and of all official entries in the books or records of any such office authenticated by the consul or vice consul, shall be admissible equally with the originals. (June 25, 1948, ch. 646, 62 Stat. 947.)

HISTORICAL AND REVISION NOTES

Based on title 28, U.S.C., 1940 ed., § 677 (R.S. § 896; Apr. 5, 1906, ch. 1366, § 3.34 Stat. 100).

Words "authenticated by the consul or vice consul" were substituted for "certified under the hand and seal of such officer", for clarity. Words "in the courts of the United States", were omitted after "admissible". Such papers should be so admitted in all courts consistently with sections 1738 and 1739 of this title.

See also Rule 44 of the Federal Rules of Civil Procedure.

Changes were made in phraseology.

FEDERAL RULES OF CIVIL PROCEDURE

Authentication of copy of official record see rule 44 Appendix to this title.

Effect of rule 44 on former section 677 of this title, see note by Advisory Committee under rule 44.

FEDERAL RULES OF CRIMINAL PROCEDURE

Criminal cases, proof of official record, see rule 27, Title 18, Appendix, Crimes and Criminal Procedure.

§ 1741. Foreign official documents

An official record or document of a foreign country may be evidenced by a copy, summary, or excerpt authenticated as provided in the Federal Rules of Civil Procedure. (June 25, 1948, ch. 646, 62 Stat. 948; May 24, 1949, ch. 139, § 92(b), 62 Stat 103; Oct. 3, 1964, Pub. L. 88-619, § 5(a) 78 Stat. 996.)

HISTORICAL AND REVISION NOTES

1948 ACT

Based on title 28, U.S.C., 1940 ed. § 695e (June 20, 1936, ch. 640, § 6, 49 Stat 1563).

Words "Nothing contained in this section shall be deemed to alter, amend, or repeal section 689 of this title," at the end of section 695e of title 28, U.S.C., 1940 ed., were omitted. Although significant in the original Act, such words are unnecessary in a revision wherein both sections in question, as revised, are enacted at the same time.

See also Rule 44 of the Federal Rules of Civil Procedure.

Section 695e-1 of title 28, U.S.C., 1940 ed., providing for certification of Vatican City Documents will be incorporated in title 22, U.S.C., Foreign Relations and Intercourse.

Changes were made in phraseology.

1949 ACT

This section corrects a typographical error in section 1741 of title 28, U.S.C.

AMENDMENTS

1964—Pub. L. 88-619 substituted "An official record or document of a foreign country may be evidenced by a copy, summary, or excerpt authenticated as provided in the Federal Rules of Civil Procedure" for "A copy of any foreign document of record or on file in a public office of a foreign country or political subdivision thereof, certified by the lawful custodian thereof, shall be admissible in evidence when authenticated by a certificate of a consular officer of the United States resident in such foreign country, under the seal of his office, that the copy has been certified by the lawful custodian", in the text, and "official documents" for "documents, generally copies" in the catchline.

1949—Act May 24, 1949

§ 1781. Transmittal of letter rogatory or request

(a) The Department of State has power, directly, or through suitable channels–

(1) to receive a letter rogatory issued, or request made, by a foreign or international tribunal, to transmit it to the tribunal, officer, or agency in the United States to whom it is addressed, and to receive and return it after execution; and

(2) to receive a letter rogatory issued, or request made, by a tribunal in the United States, to transmit it to the foreign or international tribunal, officer, or agency to whom it is addressed, and to receive and return it after execution.

(b) This section does not preclude–

(1) the transmittal of a letter rogatory or request directly from a foreign or international tribunal to the tribunal, officer, or agency in the United States to whom it is addressed and its return in the same manner; or

(2) the transmittal of a letter rogatory or request directly from a tribunal in the United States to the foreign or international tribunal, officer, or agency to whom it is addressed and its return in the same manner.

(June 25, 1948, ch. 646, 62 Stat. 948; Oct. 3, 1964, Pub. L. 88-619, § 8(a), 78 Stat. 996.)

HISTORICAL AND REVISION NOTES

Based on title 28, U.S.C., 1940 ed., § 653 (R.S. § 875; Feb. 27, 1877, ch. 69, § 1, 19 Stat. 241; Mar. 3, 1911, ch. 231, § 291, 36 Stat. 1167).

Word "officer" was substituted for "commissioner" to obviate uncertainty as to the person to whom the letters or commissioned may be issued.

The third sentence of section 653 of title 28, U.S.C., 1940 ed., providing for admission of testimony "so taken and returned" without objection as to the method of return, was omitted as unnecessary. Obviously, if the method designated by Congress is followed, it cannot be objected to.

The last sentence of section 653 of title 26, U.S.C., 1940 ed., relating to letters rogatory from courts of foreign countries, is incorporated in section 1782 of this title.

The revised section extends the provisions of section 653 of title 28, U.S.C., 1940 ed., which applied only to cases wherein the United States was a party or was interested, so as to insure a uniform method of taking foreign depositions in all cases.

Words "courts of the United States" were inserted to make certain that the section is addressed to the Federal rather than the State courts as obviously intended by Congress.

Changes were made in phraseology.

AMENDMENTS

1964—Pub. L. 88-619 substituted provisions authorizing the Department of State to transmit a letter rogatory or request by a foreign or international tribunal, or by a tribunal in the United States, to the tribunal, officer or agency in the United States or its foreign or international counterpart, to whom addressed, and to return it after execution, and providing that this section does not preclude direct transmission of letters rogatory or requests between interested tribunals, officers or agencies of foreign, international and of United States origin, for provisions authorizing United States ministers or consuls, whenever a United States court issues letters rogatory or a commission to take a deposition, to receive the executed letters or commissions from foreign courts or officers, endorse them with the place and date of receipt and any change in the deposition, and transmit it to the clerk of the issuing court in the same manner as his official dispatches, in the text and "Transmittal of letter rogatory or request" for "Foreign witnesses" in the catchline.

FEDERAL RULES OF CIVIL PROCEDURE

Persons before whom depositions may be taken in foreign countries, see rule 28 Appendix to this title.

§ 1782. Assistance to foreign and international tribunals and to litigants before such tribunals

(a) The district court of the district in which a person resides or is found may order him to give his testimony or statement or to produce a document or other thing for use in a proceeding in a foreign or international tribunal. The order may be made pursuant to a letter rogatory issued, or request made, by a foreign or international tribunal or upon the application of any interested person and may direct that the testimony or statement be given, or the document or other thing be produced, before a person appointed by the court. By virtue of his appointment, the person appointed has power to administer any necessary oath and take the testimony or statement. The order may prescribe the practice and procedure, which may be in whole or part the practice and procedure of the foreign country or the international tribunal, for taking the testimony or statement or producing the document or other thing. To the extent that the order does not prescribe otherwise, the testimony or statement shall be taken, and the document or other thing produced, in accordance with the Federal Rules of Civil Procedure.

A person may not be compelled to give his testimony or statement or to produce a document or other thing in violation of any legally applicable privilege.

(b) This chapter does not preclude a person within the United States from voluntarily giving his testimony or statement, or producing a document or other thing, for use in a proceeding in a foreign or international tribunal before any person and in any manner acceptable to him.

(June 25, 1948, ch. 646, 62 Stat. 949; May 24, 1949, ch. 139, § 93,63 Stat 103; Oct. 3, 1964, Pub. L. 88-619, § 9(a), 78 Stat. 997.)

HISTORICAL AND REVISION NOTES

1948 ACT

Based on title 28, U.S.C., 1940 ed., §§ 649-653, 701, 703, 704 (R.S. §§ 871-875, 4071, 4073, 4074; Feb. 27, 1877, ch. 69, § 1, 19 Stat. 241; Mar. 3, 1911, ch. 231, § 291, 36 Stat. 1167; June 25, 1936, ch. 804, 49 Stat. 1921).

Section 649-652 of title 28, U.S C., 1940 ed., applied only to the District of Columbia and contained detailed provisions for issuing subpoenas, payment of witness fees and procedure for ordering and taking depositions. These matters are all covered by Federal Rules of Civil Procedure, Rules 26-32.

Provisions in sections 649-652 of title 28, U.S.C.,1940 ed., relating to the taking of testimony in the District of Columbia for use in State and Territorial courts were omitted as covered by section 14-204 of the District of Columbia Code, 1940 ed., and Rules 26 et seq., and 46 of the Federal Rules of Civil Procedure.

Only the last sentence of section 653 of title 28, U.S.C., 1940 ed., is included in this revised section. The remaining provisions relating to depositions of witnesses in foreign countries form the basis of section 1781 of this title.

Sections 701, 703, and 704 of title 28, U.S.C., 1940 ed., were limited to "suits for the recovery of money or property depending in any court in any foreign country with which the United States are at peace, and in which the government of such foreign country shall be a party or shall have an interest."

The revised section omits this limitation in view of the general application of the last sentence of section 653 of title 28, U.S.C., 1940 ed., consolidated herein. The improvement of communications and the expected growth of foreign commerce will inevitably increase litigation involving witnesses separated by wide distances.

Therefore the revised section is made simple and clear to provide a flexible procedure for the taking of depositions. The ample safeguards of the Federal Rules of Civil Procedure, Rules 26-32, will prevent misuse of this section.

The provisions of section 703 of title 28, U.S.C.,1940 ed., for punishment of disobedience to subpoena or refusal to answer is covered by Rule 37(b)(1) of Federal Rules of Civil Procedure.

The provisions of section 704 of title 28, U.S.C., 1940 ed., with respect to fees and mileage of witnesses are covered by Rule 45(c) of Federal Rules of Civil Procedure.

Changes were made in phraseology.

1949 ACT

This amendment corrects restrictive language in section 1782 of title 28, U.S.C., in conformity with original law and permits depositions in any judicial proceeding without regard to whether the deponent is "residing" in the district or only sojourning there.

REFERENCES IN TEXT

The Federal Rules of Civil Procedure, referred to in subsec. (a), are set out in the Appendix to this title.

AMENDMENTS

1964—Pub. L. 88-619 substituted provisions which empowered district courts to order residents to give testimony or to produce documents for use in a foreign or international tribunal, pursuant to a letter rogatory, or request, of a foreign or international tribunal or upon application of any interested person, and to direct that the evidence be presented before a person appointed by the court, provided that such person may administer oaths and take testimony, that the evidence be taken in accordance with the Federal Rules of Civil Procedure unless the order prescribes using the procedure of the foreign or international tribunal, that a person may not be compelled to give legally privileged evidence, and that this chapter doesn't preclude a person from voluntarily giving evidence for use in a foreign or international tribunal, for provisions permitting depositions of witnesses within the United States for use in any court in a foreign country with which the United States was at peace to be taken before a person authorized to administer oaths designated by the district court of the district where the witness resides or is found, and directing that the procedure used be that generally used in courts of the United States, in the text, and "Assistance to foreign and international tribunals and to litigants before such tribunals" for "Testimony for use in foreign countries", in the catchline.

1949—Act May 24,1949 struck out the word "residing" following "witness", and substituted "judicial proceeding" for "civil action" following "to be used in any".

CROSS REFERENCES

Fees of witnesses in the United States courts, see section 1821 of this title.

Letters rogatory from United States courts, see section 1781 of this title.

§ 1783. Subpoena of person in foreign country

(a) A court of the United States may order the issuance of a subpoena requiring the appearance as a witness before it, or before a person or body designated by it, of a national or resident of the United States who is in a foreign country, or requiring the production of a specified document or other thing by him, if the court finds, that particular testimony or the production of the document or other thing by him is necessary in the interest of justice, and, in other than a criminal action or proceeding, if the court finds, in addition, that it is not possible to obtain his testimony in admissible form without his personal appearance or to obtain the production of the document or other thing in any other manner.

(b) The subpoena shall designate the time and place for the appearance or for the production of the document or other thing. Service of the subpoena and any order to show cause, rule, judgment, or decree authorized by this section or by section 1784 of this title shall be effected in accordance with the provisions of the Federal Rules of Civil Procedure relating to service of process on a person in a foreign country. The person serving the subpoena shall tender to the person to whom the subpoena is addressed his estimated necessary travel and attendance expenses, the amount of which shall be determined by the court and stated in the order directing the issuance of the subpoena. (June 25,1948, ch. 646, 62 Stat. 949; Oct. 3, 1964, Pub. L. 88-619, § 10(a), 78 Stat. 997.)

HISTORICAL AND REVISION NOTES

Based on title 28, U.S.C., 1940 ed., §§ 711,712, and 713 (JULY 3, 1926, ch. 762, §§ 1-3, 44 Stat. 835).

Word "resident" was substituted for "or domiciled therein." (See reviser's note under section 1391 of this title.)

Words "or any assistant or district attorney acting under him," after "Attorney General" in section 712 of title 28, U.S.C, 1940 ed., were omitted, since, in any event, the approval of the Attorney General would be required. (See section 507 of this title.)

Changes were made in phraseology.

REFERENCES IN TEXT

The Federal Rules of Civil Procedure, referred to in subsec. (b), are set out in the Appendix to this title.

AMENDMENTS

1964—Pub. L. 88-619 amended section generally, and among other changes, authorized a United States court to issue a subpoena to require the appearance of a witness before it or a person or body designated by it, and the production of documents or other tangible evidence, when necessary in the interest of justice, and in other than criminal actions or proceedings, if the court finds, in addition, that its not possible to obtain admissible evidence in any other manner, and provided that the procedure relating to the subpoena shall be in accordance with the Federal Rules of Civil Procedure, and deleted provisions which authorized the issuance of a subpoena when a personally notified individual failed to appear to testify pursuant to letter rogatory, or failed to answer any question he would have to answer in any examination before the court or if such person was beyond United States jurisdiction.

Foreign Service of Process Letters Rogatory and Judicial Assistance in the United States—Title 28 U.S.C.

§1696. Service in foreign and international litigation

(a) The district court of the district in which a person resides or is found may order service upon him of any document issued in connection with a proceeding in a foreign or international tribunal. The order may be made pursuant to a letter rogatory issued, or request made, by a foreign or international tribunal or upon application of any interested person and shall direct the manner of service. Service pursuant to this subsection does not, of itself, require the recognition or enforcement in the United States of a judgement, decree, or order rendered by a foreign or international tribunal.

(b) This section does not preclude service of such a document without an order of court.
(Added Pub. L. 88-619, § 4(a). Oct. 3, 1964, 78 Stat. 995.)

§ 1781. Transmittal of letter rogatory or request

(a) The Department of State has power, directly, or through suitable channels—

(1) to receive a letter rogatory issued, or request made, by a foreign or international tribunal, to transmit it to the tribunal, officer, or agency in the United States to whom it is addressed, and to receive and return it after execution; and

(2) to receive a letter rogatory issued, or request made, by a tribunal in the United States, to transmit it to the foreign or international tribunal, officer, or agency to whom it is addressed, and to receive and return it after execution.

(b) This section does not preclude—

(1) the transmittal of a letter rogatory or request directly from a foreign or international tribunal to the tribunal, officer, or agency in the United States to whom it is addressed and its return in the same manner; or

(2) the transmittal of a letter rogatory or request directly from a tribunal in the United States to the foreign or international tribunal, officer, or agency to whom it is addressed and its return in the same manner.
(June 25, 1948, ch. 646, 62 Stat. 948; Oct. 3, 1964, Pub. L. 88-619, § 8(a), 78 Stat. 996.)

HISTORICAL AND REVISION NOTES

Based on title 28, U.S.C., 1940 ed., § 653 (R.S. § 875 Feb. 27, 1877, ch. 69. § 1, 19 Stat. 241; Mar. 3,1911, ch. 231, § 291, 36 Stat. 1167).

Word “officer” was substituted for “commissioner” to obviate uncertainty as to the person to whom the letters or commissioned may be issued.

The third sentence of section 653 of title 28, U.S.C., 1940 ed., providing for admission of testimony “so taken and returned” without objection as to the method of return, was omitted as unnecessary. Obviously, if the method designated by Congress is followed, it cannot be objected to.

The last sentence of section 653 of title 26, U.S.C., 1940 ed., relating to letters rogatory from courts of foreign countries, is incorporated in section 1782 of this title.

The revised section extends the provisions of section 653 of title 28, U.S.C., 1940 ed., which applied only to cases wherein the United States was a party or was interested, so as to insure a uniform method of taking foreign depositions in all cases.

Words “courts of the United States” were inserted to make certain that the section is addressed to the Federal rather than the State courts as obviously intended by Congress.

Changes were made in phraseology.

AMENDMENTS

1964—Pub. L. 88-619 substituted provisions authorizing the Department of State to transmit a letter rogatory or request by a foreign or international tribunal, or by a tribunal in the United States, to the tribunal, officer or agency in the United States or its foreign or international counterpart, to whom addressed, and to return it after execution, and providing that this section does not preclude direct transmission of letters rogatory or requests between interested tribunals, officers or agencies of foreign, international and of United States origin, for provisions authorizing United States ministers or consuls, whenever a United States court issues letters rogatory or a commission to take a deposition, to receive the executed letters or commissions from foreign courts or officers, endorse them with the place and date of receipt and any change in the deposition, and transmit it to the clerk of the issuing court in the same manner as his official dispatches, in the text and "Transmittal of letter rogatory or request" for "Foreign Witnesses" in the catchline.

FEDERAL RULES OF CIVIL PROCEDURE

Persons before whom depositions may be taken in foreign countries, see rule 28, Appendix to this title.

§ 1782. Assistance to foreign and international tribunals and to litigants before such tribunals

(a) The district court of the district in which a person resides or is found may order him to give his testimony or statement or to produce a document or other thing for use in a proceeding in a foreign or international tribunal. The order may be made pursuant to a letter rogatory issued, or request made, by a foreign or international tribunal or upon the application of any interested person and may direct that the testimony or statement be given, or the document or other thing be produced, before a person appointed by the court. By virtue of his appointment, the person appointed has power to administer any necessary oath and take the testimony or statement. The order may prescribe the practice and procedure, which may be in whole or part the practice and procedure of the foreign country or the international tribunal, for taking the testimony or statement or producing the document or other thing. To the extent that the order does not prescribe otherwise, the testimony or statement shall be taken, and the document or other thing produced, in accordance with the Federal Rules of Civil Procedure.

A person may not be compelled to give his testimony or statement or to produce a document or other thing in violation of any legally applicable privilege.

(b) This chapter does not preclude a person within the United States from voluntarily giving his testimony or statement, or producing a document or other thing, for use in a proceeding in a foreign or international tribunal before any person and in any manner acceptable to him.

(June 25, 1948, ch. 646, 62 Stat. 949; May 24, 1949, ch. 139, § 93, 63 Stat. 103; Oct. 3, 1964, Pub. L. 88-619, § 9(a), 78 Stat. 997.)

HISTORICAL AND REVISION NOTES

1948 ACT

Based on title 28, U.S.C., 1940 ed., §§ 649-653, 701, 703, 704 (R.S. § 871-875, 4071, 4073, 4074; Feb. 27, 1877, ch. 69, § 1, 19 Stat. 241; Mar. 3, 1911, ch. 231, § 291, 36 Stat. 1167; June 25, 1936, ch. 804, 49 Stat. 1921).

Sections 649-652 of title 28, U.S.C., 1940 ed., applied only to the District of Columbia and contained detailed provisions for issuing subpoenas, payment of witness fees and procedure for ordering and taking depositions. These matters are all covered by Federal Rules of Civil Procedure, Rules 26-32.

Provisions in sections 649-652 of title 28, U.S.C., 1940 ed., relating to the taking of testimony in the District of Columbia for use in State and Territorial courts were omitted as covered by section 14-204 of the District of Columbia Code, 1940 ed., and Rules 26 et seq., and 46 of the Federal Rules of Civil Procedure.

Only the last sentence of section 653 of title 28, U.S.C., 1940 ed., is included in this revised section. The remaining provisions relating to depositions of witnesses in foreign countries form the basis of section 1781 of this title.

Sections 701,703, and 704 of title 28, U.S.C., 1940 ed., were limited to "suits for the recovery of money or property depending in any court in any foreign country with which the United States are at peace, and in which the government of such foreign country shall be a party or shall have an interest."

The revised section omits this limitation in view of the general application of the last sentence of section 653 of title 28, U.S.C., 1940 ed., consolidated herein. The improvement of communications and the expected growth of foreign commerce will inevitably increase litigation involving witnesses separated by wide distances.

Therefore the revised section is made simple and clear to provide a flexible procedure for the taking of depositions. The ample safeguards of the Federal Rules of Civil Procedure, Rules 26-32, will prevent misuse of this section.

The provisions of section 703 of title 28, U.S.C., 1940 ed., for punishment of disobedience to subpoena or refusal to answer is covered by Rule 37(b)(1) of Federal Rules of Civil Procedure.

The provisions of section 704 of title 28, U.S.C., 1940 ed., with respect to fees and mileage of witnesses are covered by Rule 45(c) of Federal Rules of Civil Procedure.

Changes were made in phraseology.

1949 ACT

This amendment corrects restrictive language in section 1782 of title 28, U.S.C., in conformity with original law and permits depositions in any judicial proceeding without regard to whether the deponent is "residing" in the district or only sojourning there.

REFERENCES IN TEXT

The Federal Rules of Civil Procedure, referred to in subsec. (a), are set out in the Appendix to this title.

AMENDMENTS

1964—Pub. L. 88-619 substituted provisions which empowered district courts to order residents to give testimony or to produce documents for use in a foreign or international tribunal, pursuant to a letter rogatory, or request, of a foreign or international tribunal or upon application of any interested person, and to direct that the evidence be presented before a person appointed by the court, provided that such person may administer oaths and take testimony, that the evidence be taken in accordance with the Federal Rules of Civil Procedure unless the order prescribes using the procedure of the foreign or international tribunal, that a person may not be compelled to give legally privileged evidence, and that this chapter doesn't preclude a person from voluntarily giving evidence for use in a foreign or international tribunal, for provisions permitting depositions of witnesses within the United States for use in any court in a foreign country with which the United States was at peace to be taken before a person authorized to administer oaths designated by the district court of the district where the witness resides or is found, and directing that the procedure used to be that generally used in courts of the United States, in the text, and "Assistance to foreign and international tribunals and to litigants before such tribunals" for "Testimony for use in foreign countries," in the catchline.

1949—Act May 24, 1949, struck out word "residing" following "witness," and substituted "judicial proceeding" for "civil action" following "to be used in any."

CROSS REFERENCES

Fees of witnesses in the United States courts, see section 1821 of this title.

Letters rogatory from United States courts, see section 1781 of this title.

§ 1783. Subpoena of person in foreign country

(a) A court of the United States may order the issuance of a subpoena requiring the appearance as a witness before it, or before a person or body designated by it, of a national or resident of the United States who is in a foreign country, or requiring the production of a specified document or other thing by him, if the court finds, that particular testimony or the production of the document or other thing by him is necessary in the interest of justice, and, in other than a criminal action or proceeding, if the court finds, in addition, that it is not possible to obtain his testimony in admissible form without his personal appearance or to obtain the production of the document or other thing in any other manner.

(b) The subpoena shall designate the time and place for the appearance or for the production of the document or other thing. Service of the subpoena and any order to show cause, rule, judgement, or decree authorized by this section or by section 1784 of this title shall be effected in accordance with the provisions of the Federal Rules of Civil Procedure relating to service of process on a person to whom the subpoena is addressed his estimated necessary travel and attendance expenses, the amount of which shall be determined by the court and stated in the order directing the issuance of the subpoena.

(June 25, 1948, ch. 646, 62 Stat. 949; Oct. 3, 1964, Pub. L. 88-619, § 10(a), 78 Stat. 997.)

HISTORICAL AND REVISION NOTES

Based in title 28, U.S.C., 1940 ed., §§ 711, 712, and 713 (July 3, 1926, ch. 762, §§ 1-3, 44 Stat. 835).

Word "resident" was substituted for "or domiciled therein." (See reviser's note under section 1391 of this title.)

Words "or any assistant or district attorney acting under him," after "Attorney General" in section 712 of title 28, U.S.C., 1940 ed., were omitted, since, in any event, the approval of the Attorney General would be required. (See section 507 of this title.)

Changes were made in phraseology.

REFERENCES IN TEXT

The Federal Rules of Civil Procedure, referred to in subsec. (b), are set out in the Appendix to this title.

AMENDMENTS

1964—Pub. L. 88-619 amended section generally, and among other changes, authorized a United States court issue a subpoena to require the appearance of a witness before it or a person or body designated by it, and the production of documents or other tangible evidence, when necessary in the interest of justice, and in other than criminal actions or proceedings, if the court finds, in addition, that it is not possible to obtain admissible evidence in any other manner, and provided that the procedure relating to the subpoena shall be in accordance with the Federal Rules of Civil Procedure, and deleted provisions which authorized the issuance of a subpoena when a personally notified individual failed to appear to testify pursuant to letter rogatory, or failed to answer any question he would have to answer in any examination before the court or if such person was beyond United States jurisdiction and the testimony was desired by the Attorney General in a criminal proceeding, provided that the subpoena issued to any United States counsul, that the counsul make personal service of the subpoena and of any order, rule, judgement or decree, that be make return of the subpoena and tender expenses to the witness, and substituted "person" for "witness" in the catchline.

Based on title 28, U.S.C., 1940 ed., §§ 714, 715, 716, 717, and 718 (July 3, 1926, ch. 762, §§ 4-8, 44 Stat. 836).

Sections 714-718 of title 28, U.S.C., 1940 ed., were consolidated, since all relate to contempt by a witness served personally in a foreign country.

The last sentence omits specific reference to section 118 of title 28, U.S.C., 1940 ed., now incorporated in section 1655 of this title, which provides for the method of opening judgements rendered on publication of process. (See also Rule 60(b) of the Federal Rules of Civil Procedure.)

Changes were made in phraseology.

AMENDMENTS

1964—Pub. L. 88-619 amended section generally, and among other changes, authorized the court to order a person to show cause for failing to produce a document or other thing in subsec. (a), provided that a copy of the order to show cause shall be served in accordance with section 1783(b) of this title, and deleted provisions requiring the marshal making levy or seizure to forward to any United States consul in the country where the witness may be, a copy of the order and a request for its personal service, and to cause publication of the order in the district where the issuing court sits, in Subset (c), and deleted provisions in subsec. (d) permitting any judgement rendered upon service by publication only to be opened for answer within one year.

FEDERAL RULES OF CIVIL PROCEDURE

Civil cases, contempt for failure to obey subpoena, see Rule 45, Appendix to this title.

FEDERAL RULES OF CRIMINAL PROCEDURE

Criminal cases, contempt for failure to obey subpoena, see Rule 17, Title 18, Appendix, Crimes and Criminal Procedure.

SECTION REFERRED TO IN OTHER SECTIONS

This section is referred to in section 1783 of this title.

[§ 1785. Repealed. Pub. L. 88-619, § 12(a), Oct. 3,1964, 78 Stat. 998]

Section, act June 25, 1948, ch. 646, 62 Stat. 950, provided a privilege against self-incrimination on examination under letters rogatory. See section 1782(a) of this title.

Section V

Transfer of Prisoners

International Perspective[1]

Mohamed Abdul-Aziz

Introduction

A foreign prisoner is a convicted person who is incarcerated in a territory of a state other than his home country. The term foreigners is a very broad term which comprises several varied groups of people whose social, economic, political, family and psychological characteristics are completely different. Foreigners originate from various cultural circles. When they arrive in the country of their new residence, they bring with them their customs and religious belief; few are able or willing to leave these at the borders. Foreigners, like racial, national and religious minorities often become groups of marginal, outcast, "second class" citizens. It's why conflict between assimilation and acculturation results in delinquency and predisposes a youth toward criminal behavior. The more that is known about the members of such minorities, the better the situation of those serving their time in prison is understood; the clearer and more comprehensible the motives for their behavior and the sources of their delinquency, the easier it should be to find the right remedy for their situation. The difficult situations of foreign prisoners are the results not only of their legal status, but also of their treatment by the prison staff and their relationships with native inmates.[2] A better understanding of their plight gave rise to and a real impetus for the development of modern instrument, both international and domestic, for the enforcement of foreign penal judgements. The question is to know whether foreign offenders are discriminated against as compared to native offenders, when a sanction is imposed. A problem of particular importance is whether foreign offenders are "second class" prisoners or not. A particularly intriguing problem is the scope of proposed and possible adjustments of a prison and a prison system to the specific needs of foreign inmates. These problems include the scope of persons eligible for transfer and the methods of delineating it, conditions for transfer, as well as the procedure for transfer and the system of its adaptation of a foreign sentence at the domestic level.

To what extent, if any, does the fact that a defendant is a foreigner influence the decisions made in the criminal proceedings? This question is of particular importance today when the choice of sentence cannot be determined simply by the nature of the crime committed, but must take into account the offender's individual circumstances.[3] Cultural differences between the home and host countries, along with the language barrier, present the major problem in prosecuting and trying foreign defendants. Imprisonment is a very unnatural condition. It also has a negative influence on people imprisoned in their home

---

1 The views presented herein are not those of the United Nations or the Crime Prevention and Criminal Justice Division, United Nations Office at Vienna.

2 MICHAL PLACHTA, *Foreign Offenders in Prison: A Social and Legal Problem*, *in* TRANSFER OF PRISONERS UNDER INTERNATIONAL INSTRUMENTS AND DOMESTIC LEGISLATION 5 (1993) [hereinafter TRANSFER OF PRISONERS].

3 MICHAL PLACHTA, *Sentencing Policy Towards Foreigners*, *in* TRANSFER OF PRISONERS, *supra* note 2, at 49.

country who have their families and habitual milieu not far from the institution. These negative effects become more serious and potentially more destructive when the person is, or feels himself to be, alien to the environment. One of the main sources of problems by an alien during his imprisonment stem from the language barrier. Real troubles appear where the prisoner and the prison administration's officials do not share a common tongue; even where some understanding of a common tongue exists, communication remains imperfect and uncertain. At the same time, explanation of legal rights may often be impossible without the services of an interpreter, whose duties in these matters impose a heavy burden on him. The interpreters must be very sensitive to the different connotations ascribed to the legal terms in various legal systems in order to avoid misunderstanding. For the linguistically handicapped prisoner who is without family or friends, social isolation places a heavy burden on his personality. Apart from language problems, there are other problems which stem from the prisoner's different cultural milieu, religious beliefs and customary norms.[4]

In this article, an attempt will be made to deal with the issue of the transfer of foreign prisoners based on the work of the United Nations, intergovernmental and nongovernmental organizations, and of the findings of research conducted by experts in this field.

Role of the United Nations

Since its inception, the United Nations has been concerned with the development of international standards, norms and guidelines in the field of crime prevention and criminal justice. Such standards represent internationally agreed upon norms that provide a yardstick against which countries can gauge their current policies and desirable reforms. They are useful training material for countries eager to modernize the criminal justice systems and upgrade the capabilities of their personnel.[5]

Background

In the context of its discussion of the issue of the treatment of offenders, the Fifth United Nations Congress on the Prevention of Crime and the Treatment of Offenders recommended that "in order to facilitate the return to their domicile of persons serving sentences in foreign countries, policies and practices should be developed by utilizing regional cooperation and starting with bilateral arrangements." Following this recommendation, the United Nations Secretariat elaborated some basic provisions for the transfer of prisoners for consideration by the Sixth United Nations Congress on the Prevention of Crime and the Treatment of Offenders. Given the importance of the matter, the Sixth Congress urged Member States "to consider the establishment of procedures whereby such transfers of offenders may be affected," recognizing that any such procedures can only be undertaken with the consent of both the sending and the receiving states and either with consent of the prisoner or in his interest. As the expert body of the United Nations at that time, the Committee on Crime Prevention and Control was requested by the

---

[4] MICHAL PLACHTA, *Foreigners in Prison: a "Second Class" Prisoner?*, *in* TRANSFER OF PRISONERS, *supra* note 2, at 69-86.

[5] *See Crime Prevention and Criminal Justice, Report of the Secretary-General*, ¶ 18, U.N. Doc. A\50\432 (1995).

Congress to give priority to the development of a model agreement on the transfer of offenders with a view to presenting it to the General Assembly for consideration.

At its eighth session, the Committee considered a draft model agreement on the transfer of foreign prisoners and recommendations on the treatment of foreign prisoners and decided to submit it to the Seventh Congress for consideration and adoption. At the Seventh Congress, while general approval was expressed for the development of such a model agreement, it was interesting to note that some delegations expressed concern about some of the points contained therein, in particular as regards the requirement that the consent of the prisoner should be obtained for a transfer. It was pointed out, however, that the model agreement only served as a model for the conclusion of new instruments on the transfer of prisoners and would not in any way affect existing bilateral and multilateral agreements on the transfer of foreign prisoners.[6] After thorough consideration, the Congress adopted the model agreement and invited Member States, if they have not established treaty relations with other Member States in the matter of the transfer of foreign prisoners to their own countries, or if they wish to revise existing treaty relations, to take into account, whenever doing so, the Model Agreement on the Transfer of Foreign Prisoners.

The purpose of the Model Agreement is to provide Member States with a model on which bilateral and regional agreements can be elaborated and applied between states, thus facilitating the transfer of foreign prisoners to their home countries. It provides general principles, taking into account the diversity of legal systems worldwide and bearing in mind that penal policies continue to develop as modern crime and criminals respect no borders.

In its Resolution 13, the Seventh United Nations Congress on the Prevention of Crime and the Treatment of Offenders invited member states to take further steps to improve the methods of international cooperation in criminal matters by considering the conclusion of agreements on the transfer of supervision of foreign offenders who have been conditionally sentenced or conditionally released. The Congress requested the Committee on Crime Prevention and Control to study this subject and consider the possibility of formulating a model agreement on the transfer of supervision of foreign offenders who are conditionally sentenced or conditionally released, with a view to submitting it to the General Assembly for consideration. The drafting of the draft model agreement was a common effort of the Committee, the Interregional Preparatory Meeting for the Eighth Congress and of the International Expert Meeting on the United Nations and Law Enforcement held at Baden, Austria, November 16-19, 1987. The draft was considered by the Eighth Congress, which recommended it for approval by the General Assembly.

At its forty-fifth session, the General Assembly adopted the Model Treaty on the Transfer of Foreign Offenders Conditionally Sentenced or Conditionally Released (General Assembly Resolution 45/119). The Assembly invited Member States, if they have not established treaty relations with other states in relation to this matter, or if they wish to revise existing treaty relations, to take into account the Model Treaty. Its main thrust is to provide states with a framework flexible enough to allow offenders on probation, parole or under suspended sentence to return to their country of origin or to move to another country by transferring the responsibility for supervision to the party concerned.

---

6 REPORT OF THE SEVENTH UNITED NATIONS CONGRESS ON THE PREVENTION OF CRIME AND THE TREATMENT OF OFFENDERS, Milan, Aug. 26-Sept. 6, 1985, U.N. Doc. A/ CONF.121/22/Rev.1 (1986).

Model Agreement on the Transfer of Foreign Prisoners

The United Nations Secretariat prepared explanatory notes on the Model Agreement with a view to providing clarifications on the thrust of its various pronouncements.[7]

General principles: Provision 1 reflects the declared objective of the Agreement, as set forth in its Preamble: to develop mutual co-operation between states in the field of criminal justice in order to facilitate the return of foreign prisoners to their home countries to serve their sentences. It should be noted that the Agreement takes no position on whether a prisoner should be transferred to the country of nationality or to the country of residence, if they are different. Thus, it leaves it to the administering state to accept also non-nationals residing in its territory. In any case, the transfer should be effected at the earliest possible stage with a view to continuing the enforcement of the sentence in the administering state.

Provision 2 states that transfer of prisoners is an agreement of states in a single case and is based on mutual confidence. No state has an obligation to request a transfer, or to grant a transfer at the request of another country. If, however, two states agree to such a transfer, that agreement alone is the basis for international co-operation, although the consent of the prisoner should not be excluded.

Provision 3 underlines another important condition for transfer, namely the requirement of double criminality (dual criminal liability), which is one of the general principles not only regarding a transfer of prisoners but also regarding extradition or mutual assistance in criminal matters. It implies that the offense for which the sanction is imposed in the sentencing state must also be an offence according to the legislation of the administering state. This condition might be interpreted in the same way as for traditional extradition and mutual assistance, where it has been applied for many years. For the condition of dual criminal liability to be fulfilled, it is not necessary that the criminal offence should be precisely the same under both the law of the administering and the law of the sentencing state. There may be differences in the wording and legal classification. The basic idea is that the essential constituent elements of the offense should be comparable under the law of both states. The wording of the Model Agreement classifies the principles of dual criminal liability further by indicating that the offence has to fall within the competence of judicial authorities. Thus, punishment imposed by administrative authorities would in no case, even if it amounted to deprivation of liberty, fall within the scope of such a transfer agreement.

In accordance with Provision 4, the decision concerning a transfer lies within the sole competence of the states concerned. Since a transfer agreement is an international instrument, the only subjects with the authority to take a decision are the sovereign states, which have to agree on the means, requirements and circumstances for such cooperation. These states should, however, take into due consideration the wishes of the prisoner and his close relatives regarding a repatriation.

Provision 5 underlines the fact that the Model Agreement is based on the voluntary transfer, as embodied in most regional and bilateral arrangements, and as recommended by the Sixth United Nations Congress. In particular, the requirement that prisoners must consent to the transfer ensures that transfers are not used as a method of expelling prisoners, or as a means of disguised extradition. Moreover, since prison conditions vary considerably from

---

[7] *See Model Agreement on the Transfer of Foreign Prisoners and Recommendations for the Treatment of Foreign Prisoners, Note by the Secretariat,* U.N. Doc. A/ CONF.121/10.

country to country, and the prisoner may have very personal reasons for not wishing to be transferred, it seems preferable to base the proposed model agreement on the consent requirement.

Provision 6 stresses a basic right of a sentenced person who may be eligible for a transfer. He or she should be informed of the possibilities and the legal consequences of such a transfer, to enable him or her to decide whether to express interest in a transfer. In accordance with the Standard Minimum Rules for the Treatment of Prisoners, such information should be given in a language that the prisoner can understand. The prisoner should be informed also whether he or she might be prosecuted for offenses committed before the transfer. As this depends also on the domestic law of the administering state, that state should be involved in the information procedure.

Provision 7 demonstrates the flexibility of the Model Agreement, which leaves it to the discretion of the states concerned to decide whether the transfer should be effected to the country of the prisoner's nationality or residence. In any case, the transfer should take place only with the expressed free will or consent of the prisoner. Such consent should refer to the transfer itself and also to the state to which the transfer is to be effected. The requirement of the prisoner's consent to his or her transfer corresponds to the primary purpose of this instrument, that is, to facilitate the resocialization of offenders; transferring a prisoner against his or her will may not accomplish this goal.

As the sentenced person's consent to his or her transfer is one of the basic elements of the transfer mechanism, it seems necessary that, in accordance with Provision 8, the sentencing state should not only ensure that the consent is given voluntarily and with full knowledge of the legal consequences that the transfer would entail for the person concerned (Provision 6), but that the administering state also should have an opportunity to verify that the consent is given in accordance with these conditions. Such verification can be effected with the assistance of the diplomatic or consular corps, or any other official agreed upon between the states concerned.

Provision 9 extends the application of the Model Agreement to measures involving deprivation of liberty of persons detained in institutions for mentally disturbed offenders who cannot be held responsible for the commission of their offenses. It also applies to offenders who, after being sentenced, become mentally disturbed and, therefore, unable to determine their will freely. The reference to the person's legal representative is not meant to imply that the representative must be legally qualified; it includes any person duly authorized by the law of either the sentencing or the administering state to represent the sentenced person, for example, a parent or somebody authorized to give such a consent. However, it should be required that the legal representative takes a decision after due contact with the sentenced person.

Other requirements: Provision 10 spells out another requirement for lodging a request for transfer or initiating such a request, namely, that the sentence should be final and definitive and have executive force. Thus, all available remedies must have been exhausted, or the time-limit for such remedies must have expired without the parties having availed themselves of them. Moreover, a suspended sentence cannot be given as a reason for requesting a transfer. This provision does not, however, preclude the possibility of a later review of the sentence in the sentencing state, in the light of newly produced evidence.

Considering that procedures for a transfer of prisoners and time, in accordance with Provision 11 the Model Agreement proposes a flexible time-limit for its application: in general, the person should, at the time of request, have to serve at least six months of the sentence. This limit seems appropriate in view of the aim of the transfer, namely the social resettlement of the offender. States may, however, agree between themselves also to use the transfer instrument in cases where the rest of the enforceable sanction is lower than six months. Provision 12 stresses the need to take a timely decision on the question of a transfer without any delay.

Provision 13 underlines the fact that the requirement of *ne bis in idem* comprises the most important effect of a transfer on the jurisdiction of the administering state: that state shall be bound by the conviction of the sentencing state and, thus, may not try the transferred person again for the criminal act for which the sentence underlying the transfer was imposed.

Procedural regulations: According to Provision 14, any competent judicial or administrative authority may decide on a request for transfer. Whereas the administering state is clearly bound by the facts established by the sentencing court, the Agreement provides for two alternative procedures regarding the imposed sanction, following two different practices existing in different Member States:

(a) The continued enforcement of the sentence, either immediately or through a court or administrative order (principle 15); and

(b) the conversion of the sentence, also known as the *exequatur* procedure.

In the continued enforcement procedure, pursuant to Provision 15, the length of imprisonment as imposed in the sentencing state is, in principle, to be enforced in the administering state. A restricted adaptation is, however, also included in this procedure: where sanctions imposed in the sentencing state exceed the maximum penalties of the administering state, the maximum penalty of the administering state is to be applied.

In accordance with Provision 16, the conversion of sentence procedure is based on the assumption that the sentencing country transfers its responsibility regarding the execution of the sentence to the receiving country. The administering state is bound by the facts as they derive explicitly or implicitly from the foreign judgment, but it has the right, on the basis of the sentence, to reduce further the imposed sanction following current sentencing practices. Such adaptation is, however, restricted in the model agreement by excluding the substitution of a fine for imprisonment. In any case, no aggravation of the prisoner's penal situation is permitted.

Irrespective of which procedure is followed in a given case, Provision 17 stipulates that the administering state is bound by the establishment of facts by the sentencing court, as far as they are explicitly stated or appear from the judgment. The reason for this is that, even when using the conversion procedure, this does not imply a modification of the judgment. The administering state has no freedom to evaluate differently the facts on which the judgment is based; this applies to objective facts relating to the commission of the act and its results, as well as to subjective facts relating, for example, to premeditation and intent on the part of the convicted person. Consequently, the competence for a review of the sentence lies with the sentencing state. Provision 18 applies to the sentence already served in the sentencing state as well as to provisional detention served prior to conviction or prior to detention served during transit.

Provision 19 underlines the importance of the principle of nonaggravation. It stresses that the penal situation of the prisoner must in no case be aggravated. This rule refers not only to the length of the sentence, which must not exceed that imposed in the sentencing state, but also to the kind of sanction to be enforced: thus it must not be harsher than that imposed in the sentencing state; for example, forced labor could not be substituted for imprisonment. The principle of nonaggravation also implies that the administering state cannot enforce a minimum penalty for the same offense under its own laws if the sanction already imposed in the sentencing state is less than this minimum. Moreover, the conditions in the states concerned regarding conditional release should be taken into due consideration for the benefit of the prisoner.

Provision 20 draws a line between the two types of costs. It does not regulate the question of enforcement expenses. It is to be understood that both states should bear these costs as far as they incur on their territory. As to transportation and transit costs, the Agreement suggests that these costs should be borne by the administering state, unless otherwise agreed by both the sentencing and the administering states.

Enforcement and pardon: Provision 21 should be understood in a wide sense. It is meant to include regulations of treatment and prison regime and it also refers to rules concerning eligibility for conditional release. In this latter respect, however, the competent authorities should take into consideration any more favorable conditions in the sentencing state so as to avoid aggravation of the prisoner's situation. Whereas Provision 21 renders the administering state only solely responsible for the enforcement of the sentence, Provision 22 underlines that pardon and amnesty may be granted by both the sentencing and the administering states.

Final clauses: In accordance with Provisions 23 to 26 the Agreement, and the agreements based on it, should also be applicable to sentences that have been passed or that have become final before the entry into force of such agreements, thus enlarging its scope for the benefit of the prisoner. Although the Agreement includes, for the sake of completeness, a preamble and final clauses referring to bilateral solutions only, it is intended to be used also for multilateral negotiations.

Recommendations for the Treatment of Foreign Prisoners

The Model Agreement specified a number of safeguards, the implementation of which would grant the convicted and unconvicted person in a foreign state important rights in the process of his or her transfer to the country of origin. These include the right to be informed of a transfer possibility with his or her consent and not to be forced to agree on a step which does not correspond to his or her own wish. The right to be assisted in all stages of applying the transfer procedure in a timely manner, with full protection against any aggravation or any consequences of the execution of the enforcement of the sentence in the receiving state. In order to provide further assistance to foreign prisoners, the Committee on Crime Prevention and Control elaborated a set of recommendations for the treatment of foreign prisoners, which were adopted by the Seventh United Nations Congress.

In formulating these recommendations, the Committee took into account the fact that among the foremost measures for alleviating the problems of foreign prisoners abroad, including those whose transfer cannot be effected, would be the provision of information and contacts, the intensification of the role of consular authorities and the international co-operation of probation and rehabilitation services.

One way of lessening tension and uncertainty and of preventing foreign prisoners from feeling isolated that is employed in various countries is to give them information in their own language, or in one that they can understand, on prison regulations and regimes, the law and legal procedure, their right to legal representation and to assistance from their consul, and on channels of information that can answer any pertinent question they may have. It may not always be sufficient to supply the information in writing, as some prisoners may be illiterate. Thus, another way of assisting prisoners is to provide interpreters, not only at the trial but at any other time when important questions may arise. It could also be of great benefit to foreign prisoners to be visited by other nationals living in the vicinity, who could serve as volunteers in order to help overcome prisoner's isolation.

Other means of helping foreign prisoners include the facilitation of communication with prison staff, the provision of access to medical and religious services and the encouragement of personal contacts with the outside world and, in particular, with the prisoner's family. Consideration could be given to possible ways of compensating foreign prisoners for the lack of visits from relatives. Efforts could further be made to modify possible restrictions in order to make foreign literature and newspapers available to prisoners. It is also important that consulates and the diplomatic corps should give effective material and nonmaterial assistance to foreign prisoners abroad; this may be done in co-operation with probation agencies in the home country, but only if the prisoners wish to receive such assistance.

Several of the issues referred to are mainly relevant with respect to foreigners whose stay in the host country is only temporary, and who will eventually return to their country of origin after they have served their sentence, or who are eligible for transfer to their country of origin to serve their sentence there. Prisoners who will remain in the country of imprisonment indefinitely after their release are in a different category altogether. Many of them may be members of minority groups, or of groups whose social and economic position is weak; many may come from noticeably different cultural backgrounds and sometimes may be subject to discrimination. Their integration into society may be far from problem-free, and the same would be true for their families. For all these reasons, it would be best to arrange programs for them in prison in order to familiarize them with the prevailing culture and teach them subjects that will help to improve their prospects in an otherwise often alien society.

Model Treaty on the Transfer of Supervision of Offenders Conditionally Sentenced or Conditionally Released

The transfer of supervision of conditionally sentenced or conditionally released offenders to the offenders' home countries, and the need for further international or bilateral agreements effectively facilitating such transfers are important steps towards intensified international cooperation in criminal justice matters. In drawing on the experience gained from pertinent existing conventions, treaties and agreements, the Model Treaty was finalized, taking into account the traditions and cultural identity of Member States. It sets out, on the basis of general consensus, principles accepted by the international community so that favorable consideration could be given to their use within the framework of national legislation and practice. It also focuses on the purpose of the institution of the transfer of supervision and the need for a clear differentiation between various forms and solutions, and the diversity of the legal and technical problems involved.

In its Preamble, the Model Treaty stresses the fact that the social rehabilitation of offenders and the increased application of alternatives to imprisonment would be promoted by facilitating the supervision of conditionally sentenced or conditionally released foreign offenders in their state of ordinary residence. In terms of scope, the Model Agreement applies to conditions imposed on foreign offenders by: (a) prosecutors, where they use their discretion not to initiate or continue proceedings, combining this decision with specific conditions; (b) courts, as part of that sentence; (c) courts or the administration, as part of that decision to grant the release of an offender; and (d) the competent authority, as part of this decision to grant the release of an offender by way of pardon. The authority that would be competent to decide on the transfer of supervision in the requested state could be a judicial body or, for practical reasons an administrative organ, in particular the one that it is already responsible for the supervision of the enforcement of sentences. There are also reasons, however, supporting the competence of a court to decide the issue in view of the need for due process, and the fact that transfer of supervision may sometimes require the conditions imposed in a sentence to be adapted to some extent. The question which arises regarding the status of the sentence in the administering country is whether an offender should be considered a recidivist if he or she commits a new offense, since an earlier sentence involving supervision has been enforced by the administering state. Normally, sentences imposed by foreign courts are not considered in this connection. The situation might be different if the latter sentence would be enforced in the administering country, due to the fact that the authorities responsible for the enforcement would have records of this enforcement.[8]

The Model Treaty is applicable if, according to a final court decision, a person has been found guilty of an offense and has been placed on probation without sentence having been pronounced; given a suspended sentence involving deprivation of liberty; and given a sentence, the enforcement of which has been modified (parole) or conditionally suspended, in whole or in part, either at the time of the sentence or subsequently. The sentencing state where the decision was taken may request the administering state to take responsibility for applying the terms of the transfer of supervision. The Model Treaty sets out the procedure for such a process, including the grant for refusal in case the administering state refuses acceptance of a request for transfer of supervision. It also spells out the effects of such a transfer on the sentencing and administering state, as well as on the sentencing person, including the guaranteeing of relevant rights of parties concerned. It also contains provisions on pardon and amnesty.

[8] *See Supervision of Foreign Offenders Who Have Been Conditionally Sentenced or Conditionally Released, Preliminary Report of the Secretary-General,* U.N. Doc. E/AC.57/1988/7.

Transfer of Prisoners at the Bilateral, Regional and Multilateral Levels

Transfer of Prisoners at the Bilateral Level

There is an extensive international network of bilateral treaties in existence dealing with the Transfer of Penal Sanctions. The United States, for example, has such treaties with Bolivia,[9] Canada,[10] France,[11] Mexico,[12] Panama,[13] Peru,[14] Thailand[15] and Turkey.[16] Canada also has similar treaties with France,[17] Mexico,[18] Panama[19] and Peru.[20] These are but a few examples of the many treaties of this type in existence. Although there are distinctions between them, most bilateral prisoner transfer treaties follow a similar format. The following paragraphs set out some of the main provisions of such treaties.

In general the bilateral treaties require that the prisoner to be transferred be a national of the receiving state (for example, U.S.-France, Art. 2 (b); U.S.-Mexico, Art. II(2)). Another fundamental requirement is that of double criminality. The U.S.-France treaty, for example, requires that "the offense . . . be punishable as a crime under the law of both States" (Art. 2 (a)).

Almost all the bilateral treaties demand the consent of the prisoner before a transfer can be performed (for example, U.S.-France, Art. 2 (c)). This consent must generally be given with full knowledge of the consequences of the transfer (for example, U.S.-France, Art. 12 (2)). By containing no obligation on either state to consent to a transfer, all the bilateral treaties effectively require the consent of both states to each transfer. Although they set forth specific criteria to be considered before granting the transfer, these factors are generally so broad that both states have a wide margin of discretion as to whether to accept or not the request for transfer. Article 5 of the U.S.-France treaty, for example, sets out general reasons upon which a refusal may be based.

Many of the treaties require one or both states to inform the offender of his/her eligibility to obtain a transfer. For example, the U.S.-France treaty makes this an obligation of the sentencing state (for example, U.S.-France, Art. 8). The bilateral treaties also regulate the period after transfer. It is the sentencing state which retains the right to pardon the

---

9 Treaty on the Execution of Penal Sentences, Feb. 10, 1978, U.S.-Bolivia, 30 U.S.T. 796, T.I.A.S. No. 9219 (becoming effective on Aug. 17, 1978).

10 Treaty on the Execution of Penal Sentences, Mar. 2, 1977, U.S.-Canada, 30 U.S.T. 6263 (effective on July 19, 1978).

11 Convention on the Transfer of Sentenced Persons, Jan. 28, 1983, U.S.-France, 35 U.S.T. 2847 (*entered into force* Feb. 1, 1985).

12 Treaty on the Execution of Penal Sentences, Nov. 25, 1976, U.S.-Mexico, 28 U.S.T. 7399.

13 Treaty on the Execution of Penal Sentences, Jan. 11, 1979, U.S.-Panama, 32 U.S.T. 1565 (effective on June 17, 1980).

14 Treaty on the Execution of Penal Sentences, July 6, 1979, U.S.-Peru, 32 U.S.T. 1471 (effective on July 21, 1980).

15 Treaty on Cooperation in the Execution of Penal Sentences, Oct. 29, 1982, U.S.-Thailand, S. TREATY DOC. No. 98-8, 1 1st Sess. (1983).

16 Treaty on the Enforcement of Penal Judgements, June 7, 1979, U.S.-Turkey, 32 U.S.T. 3187 (effective on June 1, 1981).

17 Canada-France of Feb. 9, 1979.

18 Canada-Mexico, Nov. 22, 1977 (effective on Mar. 29, 1979).

19 Canada.-Panama., signed on Mar. 6, 1980.

20 Canada.-Peru (effective on July 1, 1980).

offender or grant amnesty, the receiving state being obliged to comply with such orders. The receiving state, however, acquires the power to grant parole or conditional release according to its own laws (for example, U.S.-France, Art. 9). This is in contrast to the European multilateral convention, under which both the sentencing and receiving states retain the right to pardon (the Convention on the Transfer of Sentenced Persons, Art. 12). Many of the bilateral treaties require that regular status reports be given during the post-transfer period, or at least require that such reports be furnished on request by the sentencing state (for example, U.S.-France, Art. 16).

All the treaties also provide that the sentencing state has ". . . the sole right to decide on any action for review of the conviction or sentence" (U.S.-France, Art. 7). In general, the sentencing state retains jurisdiction over the conviction and sentence, while the receiving state has jurisdiction over the execution of the sentence and all related matters.[21]

The bilateral treaties also often contain a minimum time which must remain to be served by the prisoner. In some treaties this is six months; however, the U.S.-France treaty requires that "at the time of the request for transfer the sentenced person has left to serve a period of at least one year" (Art. 2(e)). There is also the common requirement that the sentence be final (for example, U.S.-France, Art. 2 (d)) and any appeal has been disposed of, or the time for appeal has elapsed.[22] Also the bilateral treaties generally only apply to sentences involving deprivation of liberty (for example, U.S.-France, Art. 1(c)).

There are normally provisions excluding transfers for people convicted of certain types of offenses, such as violations of immigration laws or "political" offences. The U.S.-France treaty, for example, excludes purely military offences (Art. 3).

The bilateral treaties also follow the general rule of prisoner transfer treaties by forbidding the receiving state from aggravating, by its nature or duration, the penalty imposed by the sending state (for example, U.S.-France, Art. 9(3)).

Also, as a general rule, the costs of transfer and subsequent detention are the responsibility of the receiving state (for example, U.S.-France, Art. 10).

As to which party, between the sending state, the receiving state and the offender, makes the initial transfer request, this differs from treaty to treaty. Under the U.S.-Mexico treaty for example, it is contemplated that the sentencing state will initiate the process. Offenders, however, may also petition for consideration of transfer themselves.[23] The U.S.-Canadian treaty establishes a system whereby offenders make transfer applications to the detaining state.[24] The U.S.-France treaty allows a transfer request to be submitted by either the sentencing or administering state or by the prisoner, who can make the application to either state (Art. 11).

Transfer of Prisoners at the Regional and Multilateral Levels

The Convention on the Transfer of Sentenced Persons: One of the main multilateral instruments dealing with international prisoner transfers is the Convention on the Transfer

---

21 *See infra*, Chapter 19.

22 *Id.* at 243.

23 *Id.* at 244-45.

24 *Id.* at 245.

of Sentenced Persons.[25] In addition to European civil law countries, the U.K., Canada, the U.S. and representatives from the Commonwealth Secretariat contributed to the drafting of the Convention. This ensured that it would be acceptable to common law countries in their relations among themselves as well as in relations with civil law countries. The convention was not intended to supersede the European Convention on the International Validity of Criminal Judgements (Euro. Conv. Int'l Val. Crim. Judg), but rather to supplement it.

It differs from that convention in five main ways: (1) It provides a simplified, less cumbersome procedure; (2) a transfer may be requested not only by the sentencing state, but also by the state of which the prisoner is a national; (3) the transfer is subject to the prisoner's consent; (4) the convention does not oblige contracting states to comply with a request for transfer, nor does it require that grounds for refusal be given; (5) the convention is applicable only for sanctions involving deprivation of liberty, as opposed to the full range of sanctions covered by the Euro. Conv. Int'l Val. Crim. Judg. Although the Convention was prepared under the auspices of the Council of Europe, it is open to accession by non-European democratic states.[26] The U.S. and Canada were in fact actively involved in the elaboration of the text.

Important features of the Convention include Article 2, which sets out the general principles of the Convention. It specifies that "[t]ransfer may be requested by either the sentencing State or the administering State" (Art. 2(3)). This is one significant way in which this Convention differs from the Euro. Conv. Int'l Val. Crim. Judg., the latter allowing only the sentencing state to make the request.

However, under Article 2 (1), states-parties undertake only ". . . to afford each other the widest measure of co-operation in respect of the transfer of sentenced persons. . . ." Thus, Member States are under no obligation to consent to a request for transfer. This choice remains discretionary. The requested state is not required to give grounds for refusal either. The convention, in fact, contains no "real" binding commitment. It rather sets out the procedure by which prisoner transfers will be conducted. In this way too, it differs from the Euro. Conv. Int'l Val. Crim. Judg., which obliges contracting states to comply with a request for transfer.

The Convention, although not giving the prisoner the "right" to apply for a transfer, does allow him/her to ". . . express his interest to the sentencing State or to the administering State in being transferred under [the] Convention" (Art. 2(2)). The formal request is then made by one of these states to the other.

The Convention is only applicable to persons serving sentences which involve a "deprivation of liberty ordered by a court . . . on account of a criminal offence" (Art. 1(a)). It is also only applicable "if, at the time . . . of the request for transfer, the sentenced person has at least six months . . . to serve or if the sentence is indeterminate" (Art. 3(1)(c)).

---

[25] Convention of the Transfer of Sentenced Persons of 1983, *opened for signature* Mar. 21, 1983, Europ. T.S. No. 112 (*entered into force* July 1, 1985). As at Sept. 16, 1996, there were 35 Member States to this convention. These were: Austria, the Bahamas, Belgium, Bulgaria, Canada, Croatia, Cyprus, the Czech Republic, Denmark, Finland, France, Germany, Greece, Hungary, Iceland, Ireland, Italy, Lithuania, Luxembourg, Malta, Netherlands, Norway, Poland, Portugal, Romania, Slovakia, Slovenia, Spain, Sweden, Switzerland, Trinidad and Tobago, Turkey, the Ukraine, the U.K. and the U.S.. In addition, at that date, Estonia and Liechtenstein had signed, but not yet ratified the Convention.

[26] As of Sept. 16, 1996, there were five Member States which were not members of the Council of Europe: the Bahamas, Canada, Croatia, Trinidad and Tobago and the United States.

However, the Convention allows this requirement to be waived in exceptional cases (Art. 3(2)).

Article 3 sets out other conditions which must be fulfilled before a transfer can be performed. The most fundamental of these being that both states agree to the transfer (Art. 3(1)(f)). Another condition is that the prisoner must consent to the transfer, or, his/her legal representative, if he/she is incapable of giving consent (Art. 3(1)(d)). This latter condition is only natural given that the main goal of the transfer is to benefit the prisoner through resettlement in his/her home country. This resocialization goal would clearly not be met if the prisoner were transferred to another country against his/her will. Consent is particularly important considering that the receiving state is able to further prosecute the sentenced person for offences other than the ones for which he/she is currently imprisoned. By requiring his/her consent, he/she may thus choose whether to submit to any such proceedings or not. This is in contrast to the Euro. Conv. Int'l Val. Crim. Judg. which provides for a rule of speciality, but does not require the prisoner's consent. The rule of speciality means that the transferred person cannot be prosecuted for other crimes by the state to which he/she is sent.

Article 7 provides a mechanism to ensure that the consent of the prisoner is truly voluntary. It requires that "[t]he sentencing state . . . afford an opportunity to the administering State to verify . . . that the consent is given . . . voluntarily and with full knowledge of the legal consequences thereof."

Article 4 of the Convention provides that sentenced persons "be informed by the sentencing State of the substance of [the] Convention." This furnishing of information is required in all cases, to ensure that the prisoner can take the initiative and express his/her wish to be transferred. In 1984, a procedure was established under the Convention[27] whereby the governments of Member States provide a brochure in their own language for prisoners, informing them about the Convention. These brochures are then forwarded to each of the contracting states for distribution by prison authorities to new prisoners of that country's nationality.

The convention, as do all others like it, also imposes the requirement of double criminality. This means that ". . . the acts or omissions on account of which the sentence has been imposed [must] constitute a criminal offence according to the law of the administering State or would constitute a criminal offence if committed on its territory. . . ." (Art. 3(1)(e)). This principle is always an indispensable requirement for the enforcement of foreign penal judgments. The basic idea of the double criminality requirement is that, regardless of differences in wording and legal classification, the essential constituent elements of the offense should be comparable under the law of both states.

The other main conditions for transfer are that the prisoner be a national of the administering state (Art. 3(1)(a)) and that the judgment be final (Art. 3(1)(b)). Each state may declare how it intends to define the term "national" for the purposes of the Convention (Art. 3(4)).

The Convention also regulates the period after the transfer has been performed. Article 8 provides that "[t]he sentencing State may no longer enforce the sentence if the administering State considers enforcement of the sentence to have been completed." Further,

---

[27] Committee of Ministers, Council of Europe, *Standard Text Providing Information About the Convention on the Transfer of Sentenced Persons* (Council of Eur. Doc. Mp/ R (84) 11, 21 June 1984).

Art. 9 provides that "[t]he enforcement of the sentence . . . be governed by the law of the administering State and that State alone shall be competent to take all appropriate decisions." Thus, it is the receiving State that makes all decisions concerning conditional release, parole, etc. Section 12, however, provides that both states ". . . may grant pardon, amnesty or commutation of the sentence. . . ." Only the sentencing state that has the right to review the judgment (Art. 13). In all circumstances the administering state is not permitted to increase the penalty imposed on the transferred person, either by its nature or duration (Art. 10(2), Art. 11(1)(d)).

Regarding the relationship of the Convention with the Euro. Conv. Int'l Val. Crim. Judg., Art. 22 provides that "[i]f a request for transfer falls within the scope of both the present Convention and the [Euro. Conv. Int'l Val. Crim. Judg.] . . . the requesting State shall . . . indicate on the basis of which instrument [the request] is made."

The European Convention on the International Validity of Criminal Judgements:[28] Under this Convention only a limited number of reservations are permitted, which creates a more uniform applicability. It differs from the Transfer Convention in two fundamental ways. It imposes an obligation on the requested state to enforce the sentence, and transfers are possible without the consent of the prisoner. It is also of wider application, being applicable even when the prisoner is not in the sentencing state and is also applicable to punishments not involving a deprivation of liberty. Transfers can also be made to the prisoner's country of residence, as well as the country of which he/she is a citizen.

Commonwealth Transfer Convention: There was a scheme[29] set up in 1986 which mirrors the Council of Europe's Convention on the Transfer of Sentenced Persons, but was designed for the Member States of the British Commonwealth.

American Convention: In June 1993, the Organization of American States voted in favor of a hemisphere-wide convention on prisoner transfers. Since then Canada, Costa Rica, the United States and Venezuela have signed the treaty. The treaty is expected to be very popular. Approximately 500 U.S. citizens will become eligible to return to the U.S., while about 7,500 prisoners will be eligible to transfer from the U.S. to their home countries.[30]

European Convention on the Supervision of Conditionally Sentenced or Conditionally Released Offenders:[31] This convention was opened for signature in 1964 and allows people on parole or probation in one country to be supervised in their home countries.

---

28 European Convention on the International Validity of Criminal Judgements of 1970, *opened for signature* May 28, 1970, Europ. T.S. No. 70 (*entered into force* July 26, 1974). As at Sept. 17, 1996 there were nine Member States to this Convention. They were: Austria, Cyprus, Denmark, Iceland, the Netherlands, Norway, Spain, Sweden and Turkey. In addition, at that date, seven states had signed, but not yet ratified the Convention. These were: Belgium, Germany, Greece, Italy, Lithuania, Luxembourg and Portugal.

29 *Scheme for the Transfer of Convicted Offenders within the Commonwealth*, 12 COMM. L. BULL. 1115-18 (1986), adopted at the meeting of Law Ministers in Harare in 1986.

30 Gary Hill, *International News-Update on International Prison Transfers*, CORRECTIONS COMPENDIUM, Mar., 1995, at 21.

31 European Convention on the Supervision of Conditionally Sentenced or Conditionally Released Offenders of 1964, *opened for signature* Nov. 30, 1964, Europ. T.S. No. 51 (*entered into force* Aug. 22, 1975). As at Oct. 4, 1996, there were 13 Member States to this convention. These were: Austria, Belgium, Bosnia and Herzegovina, Croatia, France, Italy, Luxembourg, the former Yugoslav Republic of Macedonia, Netherlands, Portugal, Slovenia, Sweden and the Ukraine. In addition, at that date, Denmark, Germany, Greece and Turkey had signed, but not yet ratified the Convention.

Transfer on the Basis of Reciprocity

Transfer of prisoners is also possible in the absence of any multilateral or bilateral treaties governing the question. One way in which states do this is by passing legislation which creates a mechanism for the transfer of prisoners on the basis of reciprocity. Such legislation exists in Turkey,[32] Austria,[33] Switzerland[34] and Germany.[35] Under the Austrian law a transfer of prisoners on the basis of reciprocity can be effected only with the prisoner's consent. A request for transfer submitted by the sentencing state will be acted on only if:

1. the sentenced person is an Austrian national with residence or domicile in Austria; and
2. the safeguards of Art. 6 of the European Convention for the Protection of Human Rights and Fundamental Freedoms[36] were observed in the proceedings in the sentencing state.[37]

Also, an Austrian request to transfer a prisoner from Austria to another country is precluded if there is reason to believe that the sentence would not be enforced in compliance with the requirements of Art. 3 of the Human Rights Convention or would be disadvantageous for the transferred person.[38]

Treatment of Foreign Prisoners

Research findings indicate that there is an increase in the number of foreign prisoners, causing growing problems in most countries, especially in European Countries. Statistics show that foreigners are over-represented in prison: their absolute and relative numbers are increasing, and detention rates are higher than those for citizens. In some countries foreigners may constitute more than a third of the prison population. In some prisons, particularly in major industrial centers, the majority of inmates may be foreign to the extent that publicity has therefore focused on linking foreigners with crime. It is important, however, to determine how national criminal justice systems react to the high prevalence of crime amongst foreigners. Their treatment is often influenced by language barriers, and special measures are necessary to redress difficulties which foreigners face, as they are not familiar with the (foreign) country or its prison system. Research findings indicate that discrimination is claimed to represent a feature in the treatment of foreigners in criminal justice in certain countries. The vulnerability of imprisoned foreigners to abuse has exposed the insufficient safeguards against racial discrimination within prison systems, and also the lack of human rights protection for foreigners. When a given society demonstrates an

---

32 Law No. 647 of July 16, 1965 on the Enforcement of Sentences, plus later regulation.

33 Austrian ARHG, Act on Extradition and Mutual Assistance, FEDERAL LAW GAZETTE No. 529/1979, enacted Jan. 1, 1980.

34 German IRG, Act on International Mutual Assistance in Criminal Matters, S.R. 353.1, enacted Jan. 1, 1983.

35 German IRG, Act on International Mutual Assistance in Criminal Matters, FEDERAL LAW GAZETTE 1982 I S. 2071, enacted July 1, 1983.

36 Europ. T.S. No. 5.

37 *See infra,* Chapter 16.

38 *Id.*

increasing hostility towards foreigners, the penitentiary system cannot remain immune to it. Prisons mirror societal problems in their extreme.

Prison administrations often point to difficulties in coping with large numbers of prisoners as an important and unresolved problem. Besides the obvious linguistic barriers, many problems related to foreigners cannot be solved in the same way as for citizens, such as contacts with the family or participation in educational programs. The traditional legal approach envisages transfer of foreigners to their home country. This is not widely applied in practice. One reason is the large number of foreign inmates. Another is their own unwillingness to be repatriated.[39]

The existing prison statistics provide initial guidance in determining the size of the foreign prison population. The basic criterion is citizenship; all those who are not citizens of the respective country are recorded as foreigners. This encompasses such diverse categories as short-term visitors, migrant workers, long-term residents, or second-generation migrants. Moreover, data may also include those foreigners who are detained under migration law. Prison statistics distinguish between citizens and foreigners (noncitizens). However this distinction does not necessarily reflect reality. In countries where access to citizenship is restricted, foreigners who have been living in the country for a long period, some even for generations, but who have not obtained citizenship remain classified as foreigners. The category of noncitizens encompasses a vast range of persons, from asylum seekers to tourists, from foreign students to undocumented aliens, from employees of foreign enterprises to families of migrant workers.[40] In Italy, for example, one of the changes that can be observed in the prisoners' composition concerns the growing presence of ethnic minorities. Between 1988 and 1992 their presence in Italian institutions almost doubled, from 3,150 to about 5,500, which constitutes more than 10 percent of the overall prison population.[41] In France, the most significant shift in the composition of prisoners regards the percentage of non-French-born: 31 percent of the total prison population in 1993 as compared to 18 percent in 1975. This phenomenal increase is due less to the prevalence of conventional offenders among foreigners than to the stricter regulations introduced in France as regards work permits to stay.[42]

Foreigners in many countries are often held in prison on migration rather than criminal grounds. Most often they are detained during the verification of their identity, investigation of their application to enter the country or remain in it. While such cases are subsumed under "detention" rather than "imprisonment," the differences between the two may not be apparent in practice. Governments have the power, recognized in international human rights law, to deprive foreigners of their liberty. The European Convention on Human Rights envisages detention of foreigners to prevent them from entering a country without authorization, and also their detention pending removal. Some countries apply detention during the procedure of determining whether the foreigner is permitted to enter or stay, as a sanction for a breach of migration law, and also detain foreigners pending their removal. Prison statistics in Europe for example, thus record large numbers of imprisoned foreigners

---

39 KATARINA TOMAŠEVSKI, FOREIGNERS IN PRISON 1-5 (1994) [hereinafter FOREIGNERS IN PRISON].

40 Katarina Tomaševski, *Data on foreigners*, *in* FOREIGNERS IN PRISON, *supra* note 39, at 5.

41 *See* WESTERN EUROPEAN PENAL SYSTEMS (Vincenzo Ruggiero ed., 1995).

42 *Id.* at 82g.

adding to migration flows from other regions, while at the time restrictive policies have been adopted to prevent immigration.[43]

In many countries foreigners may be detained while their admission to the country is being decided. Their admission into a country is a political decision. They are often detained because of unauthorized entry into the country, particularly, in cases when they are undocumented or their identity is suspected of being forged.

The most important reason for the vulnerability of foreigners in criminal justice is the fact that their legal protection is today in a state of flux. Paradoxically, international law had included protection of foreigners before human rights became part of it. The basis for the protection of foreigners was reciprocity: governments had to protect citizens of another state to be able to demand the same protection for their own citizens abroad. International human rights law does not contain a prohibition of discrimination against foreigners. On the contrary, many rights and freedoms are accorded only to citizens. However, noncitizens cannot be denied rights guaranteed to all human beings, and thus, paradoxically, may enjoy better protection in prison than at liberty. Moreover, foreigners are protected against discrimination on the universally prohibited grounds such as race, color, ethnic origin, language or religion.[44]

Prison administrations are just becoming aware at the necessity to cope with the increasing number of foreign prisoners. In some countries where the population of foreigners is particularly large in the prison population, imaginative responses have been developed. International co-operation in law enforcement has encompassed different forms of mutual assistance in criminal matters, and diverse methods in the transfer of criminal proceedings and in transferring foreign inmates.

The application of human rights to foreigners presents, paradoxically, fewer problems in prison than outside. Human Rights standards relating to the protection of people deprived of their liberty do not differentiate between citizens and foreigners. Nevertheless, even if these standards should apply in the same manner to citizens and foreigners, there often are procedural and other requirements applicable to foreigners which are not required in the case of citizens, or obstacles which foreigners commonly face but citizens do not. Therefore specific recommendations addressing particular problems which imprisoned foreigners commonly face have been adopted as part of international guidance for prison administration. Most of these do not constitute obligatory norms nor do they confer specific rights upon foreigners in prisons. The practice of adopting standard minimum rules, both at the regional and global levels, creates duties for prison administrations and individual officials, but not entitlement for individual inmates.[45]

Violations of the human rights of prisoners are more frequent than are violations of the human rights of persons at liberty, and therefore human rights litigation evolved first and foremost to protect persons deprived of their liberty. Since they are in the custody of the state, prisoners acquire a specific set of rights, deriving from their vulnerability and

---

43 Katarina Tomaševski, *Gaps in the legal protection of foreigners*, *in* FOREIGNERS IN PRISON, *supra* note 39, at 23.

44 For a comprehensive study on the issue of prisoner's transfer, *see* MICHAL PLACHTA, TRANSFER OF PRISONER, *supra* note 2.

45 Katarina Tomaševski, *Guidance for prison administrations*, *in* FOREIGNERS IN PRISON, *supra* note 39, at 49.

dependent status against the state which imprisons them.[46] The implementation of the United Nations Body of Principles for the Protection of all Persons under any Form of Detention or Imprisonment (General Assembly Resolution 43/173), the United Nations Standard Minimum Rules for the Treatment of Prisoners, the Basic Principles for the Treatment of Prisoners (General Assembly Resolution 45/11) and other relevant instruments, norms and guidelines of human rights, is of particular importance.

Conclusion

The model treaties developed by the United Nations and other bilateral, regional, and multilateral treaties on the transfer of foreign prisoners are complementary and mutually reinforcing. In the absence of comprehensive statistics on the seriousness and extent of the crimes committed by foreigners and the number of foreigners imprisoned, it becomes difficult to provide the reader with a global overview on their situation. However, available research findings indicate that penal systems in different parts of the world are handling increasing numbers of criminals, not only conventional ones but also members of ethnic minority groups and foreigners, including asylum seekers. The fact remains that the scope of the problem of foreign prisoners is sufficient to attract the attention of governments and relevant intergovernmental and nongovernmental organizations. There is a momentum for reform in this field. Developing effective mechanisms for crime prevention and fair and humane criminal justice systems are primary concerns of developed and developing nations alike. Foreign inmates should, *stricto sensu*, profit from the pronouncements of the various bilateral, regional and multilateral treaties. Testing new approaches in this field is of particular importance for the advancement of inter-state cooperation in this field. People over the globe continue to express the desire for a just state, capable of guaranteeing basic liberties, where there will not be room for injustice, tyranny and violence. How faithfully the pronouncements of such treaties and human rights standards will match practices depends on the commitment of governments and institutions to those principles.

---

46 Katarina Tomaševski, *Protection against ill-treatment*, *in* FOREIGNERS IN PRISON, *supra* note 39, at 50.

Policies and Practices of the United States[1]

M. Cherif Bassiouni and Grace M.W. Gallagher

Introduction

The U.S. has engaged in bilateral transfers of sentenced persons since 1976, after it ratified treaties with Mexico[2] and Canada[3] and enacted implementing legislation.[4] Since that time, the U.S. has entered into a number of bilateral[5] and multilateral[6] treaties involving the international transfer of sentenced persons. Initially the underlying reason that prompted the U.S. to become involved with international prisoner transfers was the number of U.S. citizens incarcerated in foreign prisons on drug charges and the reported intolerable conditions in which they were living.[7] The need for transfer of U.S. citizens sentenced in foreign states has, however, increased significantly since 1977 due to the ever-increasing number of persons involved in transnational and international crime.[8] Consequently, as more U.S. nationals become prisoners in foreign countries and more foreign nationals become incarcerated in the U.S., the need for the U.S. to become involved in transfer of prisoners becomes more significant.

The main policy reason behind this method of dealing with persons who have been convicted and sentenced to serve prison sentences in foreign prisons are: humanitarian

---

1 This article is based on M. Cherif Bassiouni, *Transfer Between the United States and Mexico and the United States and Canada, in* INTERNATIONAL CRIMINAL LAW: PROCEDURE, 239 (M. Cherif Bassiouni ed.) (1986), [hereinafter ICL Procedure] and updated to take into account recent developments in U.S. law and practices.

2 Treaty on the Execution of Penal Sentences, Nov. 25, 1976, U.S.- Mex., 28 U.S.T. 7399 [hereinafter U.S.-Mexican SentenceTreaty].

3 Treaty on the Execution of Penal Sentences, Mar. 2, 1977, U.S.-Can., 30 U.S.T. 6263 [hereinafter U.S.-Canada Sentence Treaty].

4 Transfer To or From Foreign Countries Act, 18 U.S.C. §§ 4100-4115 (1994); 18 U.S.C. § 3244 (1994); 10 U.S.C. § 955 (1994); 28 U.S.C. § 636(g) (1994).

5 The following bilateral U.S. treaties govern the transfer of sentenced prisoners: U.S.-Mexican Sentence Treaty; U.S.-Canada Sentence Treaty; Treaty on the Execution of Penal Sentences, Feb. 10, 1978, U.S.-Bol., 30 U.S.T. 796 [hereinafter U.S.-Bolivian Sentence Treaty]; Treaty on the Execution of Penal Sentences, Jan. 11, 1979, U.S.-Pan., 32 U.S.T. 1565 [hereinafter U.S.-Panama Sentence Treaty]; Treaty on the Enforcement of Penal Judgements, June 7, 1979, U.S.-Turk., 32 U.S.T. 3187 [hereinafter U.S.-Turkey Sentence Treaty]; Treaty on the Execution of Penal Sentences, July 6, 1979, U.S.-Peru, 32 U.S.T. 1471 [hereinafter U.S.-Peru Sentence Treaty]; Memorandum of Agreement on the Transfer of Prisoners of War/Civil Internees, Feb. 12, 1982, U.S.-Korea, 34 U.S.T. 1173 [hereinafter U.S.-Korea Transfer POW Treaty]; Treaty on Cooperation in the Execution of Penal Sentences, Oct. 29, 1982, U.S.-Thail., Hein's No. KAV 1942 [hereinafter U.S.-Thailand Sentence Treaty]; Convention on the Transfer of Sentenced Persons, Jan. 25, 1983, U.S.-Fr., 35 U.S.T. 2847 [hereinafter U.S.-France Sentence Treaty].

6 The following multilateral treaties govern the transfer of sentenced prisoners: Convention on the Transfer of Sentenced Persons, Mar. 21, 1983, 35 U.S.T. 2867 [hereinafter Euro. Conv. Trans. Sent. Per.]; Inter-American Convention on Serving Criminal Sentences Abroad, Jan. 10, 1995, S. TREATY DOC. No. 104-35, 104th Cong., 2d Sess. (1996) [hereinafter OAS Convention].

7 Abraham Abramovsky & Steven J. Eagle, *A Critical Evaluation of the Mexican-American Transfer of Penal Sanctions Treaty*, 64 IOWA L. REV. 275, 278 (1979).

8 Mark A. Sherman, *Book Review: Transfer of Prisoners Under International Instruments And Domestic Legislation: A Comparative Study, By Michael Plachts. Freiburg, Germany: Max-Planck-Institut, 1993. pp. 565. DM 58 (Softcover)*, 28 GEO. WASH. J. INT'L L. & ECON. 495 (1995).

concern and social rehabilitation or social reintegration of the sentenced person.[9] However, it is important to remember that legal or humanitarian goals are not the only driving force behind the increasing activity of the U.S. government's bilateral and multilateral treaties on the transfer of sentenced prisoners, these other motivations will be discussed throughout this article. Essentially these treaties require a transferred prisoner to serve the remainder of his foreign sentence in his country of origin (usually the country of his nationality or citizenship), subject to the receiving or administering state's laws concerning the execution of sentences including probation, parole and pardon.[10] The sentencing state retains exclusive jurisdiction of the conviction and sentence,[11] but the receiving state administers it. One of the practical goals of these treaties is to avoid the legal hurdles that face the recognition of foreign penal judgments between the individual countries, and to provide a simplified method of transfer which benefits all the parties concerned, i.e. the sentencing state, the administering state and, most importantly, the prisoner and his family.

This article will examine the treaties the U.S. has ratified the federal and state enabling legislation in this area, and the way U.S. courts have dealt with the constitutional and legal issues pertaining to this practice.

The Treaty Practice of the U.S.

Rationale of the Treaties

The purpose of the treaties and of the implementing legislation is to permit persons convicted of crimes in a foreign state to complete their sentences in their country of origin. The assumptions upon which the treaties are founded include: (1) that a state has an interest in the treatment of its citizens abroad;[12] (2) that a state has an interest in the future behavior

---

9 The following U.S. treaties governing the transfer of sentenced prisoners specifically state that the main goal of the treaty is that of social "rehabilitation" or social "reintegration" of the prisoner: U.S.-France Sentence Treaty, *supra* note 5; U.S.-Canada Sentence Treaty, *supra* note 3; U.S.-Bolivia Sentence Treaty, *supra* note 5; U.S.-Thailand Sentence Treaty, *supra* note 5; U.S.-Turkey Sentence Treaty, *supra* note 5; U.S.-Peru Sentence Treaty, *supra* note 5; U.S.-Mexican Sentence Treaty, *supra* note 2; U.S.-Panama Sentence Treaty, *supra* note 5; the Euro. Conv. Trans. Sent. Per., *supra* note 6; the OAS Convention, *supra* note 6.

The Model Agreement on the Transfer of Foreign Prisoners and recommendations on the treatment of foreign prisoners, at 53, SEVENTH UNITED NATIONS CONGRESS ON THE PREVENTION OF CRIME AND THE TREATMENT OF OFFENDERS, U.N. Doc. A/CONF.121/22/Rev.1 (1985), U.N. Sales No. E.86.IV.1 (1986) [hereinafter U.N. Model Agr. Tran. For. Pris.] states its goal is the social resettlement of offenders. The U.S. is not a party to the U.N. Model Agr. Tran. For. Pris..

The U.S.-Korea Transfer POW Treaty does not include these provisions.

10 Isaac Szpilzinger, *Examination of the United States Prisoner Transfer Treaties*, 6 N.Y.L. SCH. J. INT'L & COMP. L. 709, 713-714 (1986).

11 *Id.* at 717. This exclusive jurisdiction applies to any proceedings intended to challenge, modify or set aside the sentence imposed by the sentencing state.

12 Nationality of individuals has formed the basis of two theories of jurisdiction under international law: (1) the active personality (nationality) theory; and (2) the passive personality theory. *See* M. CHERIF BASSIOUNI, INTERNATIONAL EXTRADITION: UNITED STATES LAW AND PRACTICE, 346-353 (1996). On the protection of human rights and humanitarian doctrine, *see* American Convention on Human Rights, Nov. 22, 1969, O.A.S. Treaty S. No. 36, at 1-21; European Convention for the Protection of Human Rights and Fundamental Freedoms, Nov. 4, 1950, 213 U.N.T.S. 221 (1955); International Covenant on Civil and Political Rights, G.A. Res. 2200, U.N. GAOR, 21st Sess., Supp. No. 16, 52, U.N. Doc. A/6316 (1966); Universal Declaration of Human Rights, G.A. Res. 217A(111), U.N. GAOR, 3d Sess., U.N. Doc. A/810 (1948); COUNCIL OF EUROPE, EUROPEAN CONVENTION ON HUMAN RIGHTS: COLLECTED TEXTS, § 1, Doc. I (7th ed., 1971). *See* Gregory Gelfand, *International Penal Transfer Treaties: The Case For An Unrestricted Multilateral Treaty,* 64 B.U.L. REV. 563, 568-73 (1984), (discussing

of its citizens;[13] and (3) that states have a common interest in preventing and suppressing criminality.[14]

The first consideration emphasizes the humanitarian nature of the scheme in alleviating the hardships of serving sentences in a foreign jail and the accompanying personal hardship to the offender and his family. The second consideration recognizes that rehabilitation is largely a matter of resocialization, and therefore the social context in which it is attempted has a crucial bearing on the likelihood of its success. Moreover, this consideration recognizes that supervised custody in an alien environment can be rendered ineffective for

---

humanitarian treaties and arguing that the proposal for a multilateral treaty would be consistent with many nations' present practices).

Concern over treatment of nationals abroad, even when subject to jurisdiction of a foreign court, has been qualifiedly recognized in judicial decisions. In Gallina v. Fraser, 278 F.2d 77 (2d Cir. 1960), the court said:

> [W]e have discovered no case authorizing a federal court, in a habeas corpus proceeding challenging extradition from the United States to a foreign nation, to inquire into the procedures which await the relator upon extraditions. . . . Nevertheless, we confess to some disquiet at this result. We can imagine situations when the relator, upon extradition, would be subject to procedures or punishment so antipathetic to a federal court's sense of decency as to require reexamination of the principle set out above.

Id. 78-79.

Gallina had been tried and convicted *in absentia* by the Italian courts, and contended that if extradited, he would be imprisoned with no opportunity for retrial. *Accord* Peroff v. Hylton, 542 F.2d 1247,1249 (4th Cir. 1976), ("A denial of extradition by the Executive may be appropriate when strong humanitarian grounds are present . . . when it appears that, if extradited, the individual will be persecuted, not prosecuted, or subjected to grave injustice.") *See* BASSIOUNI, *supra* at 530-31. This same concern was expressed in Rosado v. Civiletti, 621 F.2d 1179 (2d Cir. 1980). The court in discussing the history of the U.S.-Mexican Sentence Treaty, indicates that the main impetus behind the Treaty was the outrageous conditions of confinement that U.S. citizens were subjected to in Mexican prisons. *Id.* at 1186-87.

[13] Rehabilitation is the principle of modern theories of criminal sanctions, recognized by all states in the U.S. and most countries of the world. *See e.g.*, M. CHERIF BASSIOUNI, SUBSTANTIVE CRIMINAL LAW 75-106 (1978); LEONARD ORLAND, JUDGEMENT, PUNISHMENT, TREATMENT: THE CORRECTIONAL PROCESS (1977); and Report to the Fifth U.N. Congress on Crime Prevention, *The Future of Imprisonment*, 1-12 (Geneva, Sept. 1975).

The importance of the rehabilitative process to the state whose nationality an offender holds arises from the general practice of returning foreign offenders to the state of their nationality once their sentences are completed. For an historical basis of rehabilitation, *see Jeremy Bentham, Principles of Penal Law, in* THE WORKS OF JEREMY BENTHAM pt. II, bk. I, ch. VI (Sir John Bowring ed. 1843). *See also*, Patrick J. Fitzgerald, *The Territorial Principle in Penal Law: An Attempted Justification*, 1 GA. J. INT'L & COMP. L. 29 (1970).

[14] For articles considering international cooperation in criminal matters, *see supra* Chapter IV. *See also* Heinrich Grutzner, *International Judicial Assistance and Cooperation in Criminal Matters, in* 2 A TREATISE ON INTERNATIONAL CRIMINAL LAW, 189 (M. Cherif Bassiouni & Ved P. Nanda eds., 1973) [hereinafter 2 TREATISE]; M. S. Harari, et. al., *Reciprocal Enforcement of Criminal Judgements*, 45 REVUE INTERNATIONALE DE DROIT PENAL 585 (1974); Ivan Shearer, *Recognition and Enforcement of Foreign Criminal Judgements*, 47 AUST. L. J. 585 (1973).

For the European Convention on the International Validity of Criminal Judgements, *see* Europ. T.S. No. 70, May 28, 1970. For a proposed convention on reciprocal enforcement, *see* EUROPEAN COMMITTEE ON CRIME PROBLEMS, COUNCIL OF EUROPE, EXPLANATORY REPORT OF THE EUROPEAN CONVENTION ON THE INTERNATIONAL VALIDITY OF CRIMINAL JUDGEMENTS (1970). *See also* EUROPEAN COMMITTEE ON CRIME PROBLEMS, COUNCIL OF EUROPE, ASPECTS OF THE INTERNATIONAL VALIDITY OF CRIMINAL JUDGEMENTS (1968).

For the Benelux Convention, *see* Convention concerning co-operation with regard to customs and excise, Sept. 5, 1952, Belgium-Luxembourg-Netherlands, 247 U.N.T.S. 329 (1956). *See also*, LE BENELUX COMMENTE, TEXTES OFFICIELS 147,209,306 (Jacques Karelle ed. 1961); Bert Swart, *The Benelux and Nordic Countries: European Subregional Agreements, in* 2 TREATISE *infra* this volume at p. 247. For a proposed Convention on reciprocal enforcement, *see* European Committee on Crime Problems.

The Scandinavian countries' arrangement for recognition and enforcement of penal judgements is reproduced in HEINRICH GRUTZNER, INTERNATIONALER RECHTSHILFEVERKEHR IN STRAFSACHEN, pt. IV (1967). The arrangement between France and certain African states is reproduced in 52 REV. CRITIQUE DE DROIT INTERNATIONAL PRIVÉ 863 (1963).

a variety of obvious reasons. Thus, permitting offenders to serve their sentences in their state of origin will enhance the chances for successful resocialization, a matter of particular importance to the states to which offenders will eventually return. The third consideration is no mere truism; the treatment of offenders, including extradition of offenders and mutual judicial assistance in obtaining witnesses and conducting investigations, is a significant factor in the development of close international cooperation in penal matters.

The underlying policies behind these stated ones relate to a number of considerations, i.e. the state has an interest in the welfare of the individual prisoner and in the broader state interests. The U.S. has an interest to see that its citizens receive a minimum standard of criminal justice, *e.g.* due process, when they are abroad. These determinations must be made on an *ad hoc* basis depending on the facts and circumstances of the particular case.[15] U.S. courts will probably consider whether the particular foreign conviction of an American citizen transferred under the terms of the treaty has been secured in a manner so patently offensive to U.S. minimum standards of criminal justice that the further detention of such a person by the U.S. would be contrary to its public policy.

Apart from the humanitarian aims of social rehabilitation and reintegration, the other equally important goals include: (1) mutual cooperation in law enforcement and combating crime;[16] (2) better administration of justice;[17] (3) achieving greater cooperation between treaty partners;[18] (4) the development of friendly relations between the contracting states.[19]

In many cases a foreign prisoner will be returned to his state of origin (the state in which he is a national or citizen) after the sentence has been completed. It is for this reason that the prisoner's state of origin desires to have its nationals returned to serve their sentences so that it may facilitate the social reintegration and rehabilitation of the individual prisoner. Foreign prisoners face a number of disadvantages not faced by other prisoners. They often face language, cultural, religious and social barriers because they are in a different country; this can extend to difficulties with climate and food. They do not have the opportunity to communicate with their own society, friends and family to the same degree as other

---

15 Rosado v. Civiletti, 621 F.2d 1179, 1189 (2nd Cir. 1980). In *Rosado* the Second Circuit adopted the approach taken by the *Schenckloth* court to the question of "voluntariness" stating: "[it is] a question of fact to be determined from all the circumstances." Schenckloth v. Bustamonte, 412 U.S. 218, 248-49 (1973). The *Rosado* court stated:

> [W]e believe these petitioners have a right to test the basis for their continued confinement in a United States court. In reaching this conclusion, we by no means imply that each element of due process as known to American criminal law must be present in a foreign criminal proceeding before Congress may give a conviction rendered by a foreign tribunal binding effect. . . . We simply hold that a petitioner incarcerated under federal authority pursuant to a foreign conviction cannot be denied all access to a United States court when he presents a persuasive showing that his conviction was obtained without the benefit of any process whatsoever.

Rosado, 621 F.2d at 1197-98.

In such a situation the court would be willing to consider the merits of the prisoners claim, unless some other consideration would require the court to withhold relief.

16 U.S.-Bolivia Sentence Treaty, *supra* note 5, at Preamble; U.S.-Thailand Sentence Treaty, *supra* note 5, at Preamble; U.S.-Panama Sentence Treaty, *supra* note 5, at Preamble; U.S.-Mexican Sentence Treaty, *supra* note 2, at Preamble; U.S.-Turkey Sentence Treaty, *supra* note 5, at Preamble; Euro. Conv. Trans. Sent. Per., *supra* note 6, at Preamble.

17 U.S.-Bolivia Sentence Treaty, *supra* note 5, at Preamble; U.S.-Thailand Sentence Treaty, *supra* note 5, at Preamble; U.S.-Panama Sentence Treaty, *supra* note 5, at Preamble; U.S.-Mexican Sentence Treaty, *supra* note 2, at Preamble; Euro. Conv. Trans. Sent. Per., *supra* note 6, at Preamble.

18 Euro. Conv. Trans. Sent. Per., *supra* note 6, at Preamble.

19 U.S.-Turkey Sentence Treaty, *supra* note 5, at Preamble.

prisoners. This is often not because of any barriers placed on them by the prison system, but rather the practical difficulties and expense involved for the individual prisoners and their families. Programs involving vocational training and information would not be of the same assistance to foreign prisoners who would not be able to benefit from them as they would if they were prisoners in their own country. There is also the problem of *de facto* discrimination faced by foreign prisoners, who are often denied the benefit of programs of furloughs and early release because they may be perceived as greater flight risks than other prisoners.[20]

In addition to the generally less favorable treatment that foreign prisoners may suffer, it must be recognized that prison authorities of the sentencing state face a number of difficulties with these prisoners, particularly where the foreign prisoner population is high.[21] It should also be realized that the foreign prisoner population is not a homogeneous group, it includes tourists, students, immigrants, businessmen and professional criminals.[22] The increased strain that foreign prisoners place on a prison system has led to the sentencing states having an incentive to transfer these prisoners in order to rid themselves of this substantial economic and administrative burden as well as the more humanitarian goal of the social reintegration of the offender.[23]

The Treaty Practice

The need to address the question of international transfer of prisoners initially arose because of the allegations of mistreatment which U.S. nationals were receiving at the hands of foreign police and prison authorities.[24] This caused a great deal of public and political concern and culminated with the U.S.-Mexican Treaty on Prisoner Exchange.[25] The reason that this issue was dealt with by treaty is that it seemed to be the most expedient manner to approach the question of U.S. nationals in foreign prisons and foreign nationals in U.S. prisons; although, at the time there did not appear to be a constitutional or statutory prohibition for dealing with this issue by some other manner.[26] The U.S. Congress enacted enabling legislation in the form of the Transfer To or From Foreign Countries Act, 18 U.S.C. §§ 4100-4115, which deals with transfer of prisoners to or from foreign countries.[27] The statute authorizes the Attorney General to make regulations[28] concerning such transfers.

---

20 Sherman, *supra* note 8, at 502.

21 Helmut Epp, *The European Convention, infra* Chapter 16.

22 Sherman, *supra* note 8, at 497.

23 Epp, *supra* note 21.

24 William V. Dunlap, *Dual Criminality in Penal Transfer Treaties*, 29 VA. J. INT'L L. 813, 821 (1989).

25 U.S.-Mexican Sentence Treaty, *supra* note 2.

26 Abraham Abramovsky, *A Critical Evaluation of the American Transfer of Penal Sanctions Policy*, WIS. L. REV. 25, 55-56 (1980). Prof. Abramovsky states that these treaties are unnecessary and unconstitutional. He suggests, among other things, the use of the Presidential power to demand the release of an American citizen wrongfully detained or the threat of withdrawal or reduction of foreign aid. *Id.* at 55.

27 18 U.S.C. §§ 4100-4115 (1994). Once these treaties were ratified it was necessary to pass implementing domestic legislation where a treaty is not deemed to be self-executing. *See* American Baptist Churches in the U.S.A. v. Meese, 712 F. Supp. 756, 769-770 (N.D. Cal. 1989).

28 18 U.S.C. § 4102(4) states the Attorney General is authorized "to make regulations for the proper implementation of such treaties in accordance with this chapter and to make regulations to implement this chapter." To date, no regulations have been issued although there has been litigation on this point. In Scalise v. Meese, 687 F. Supp. 1239, 1245 (N.D. Ill. 1988), *rev'd sub nom.* Scalise v. Thornburgh, 891 F.2d 640 (7th Cir. 1989), District Judge Duff held that the Attorney General had violated his duty under the Act because he failed to promulgate

The U.S. has entered into two types of treaties: (1) bilateral treaties, between the U.S. and other individual countries; and (2) multilateral treaties[29] with the Council of Europe[30] and Organization of American States[31] (hereinafter OAS). (There is also an United Nations Model Agreement on the Transfer of Foreign Prisoners and Recommendations on the Treatment of Foreign Prisoners,[32] but the U.S. is not a party to this Agreement.) The multilateral treaties generally recognize that the signatories can enter into bilateral agreements with individual countries and this will not affect the validity of the multilateral treaty.[33] There are advantages and disadvantages for the U.S. in signing both types of

---

regulations stating the guidelines and standards which would cover the international transfer of prisoner requests. The Seventh Circuit overturned this decision in Scalise v. Thornburgh, 891 F.2d at 649, where the court stated that the Attorney General was not obliged under 18 U.S.C. § 4102(4) to issue substantive regulations concerning his exercise of discretion in these matters.

29 The U.S. has ratified the Euro. Conv. Trans. Sent. Per., *supra* note 6. This Convention was drafted by the Council of Europe and opened for signature by non-member states. The following states are parties to the Convention: Austria, Bahamas, Belgium, Bulgaria, Canada, Croatia, Cyprus, Czech Republic, Denmark, Estonia, Finland, France, Germany, Greece, Hungary, Iceland, Ireland, Italy, Latvia, Liechtenstein, Lithuania, Luxembourg, Malta, Moldova, Netherlands, Norway, Poland, Portugal, Romania, Slovakia, Slovenia, Spain, Sweden, Switzerland, Trinidad & Tobago, Turkey, Ukraine, United Kingdom, United States (last modified June 12, 1997) (Council of Europe web page visited Sept. 11, 1996) <http://www.coe.fr/tablconv/112t.htm>. *See also supra*, Chapter 9.

Letter of Submittal, S. TREATY DOC. NO. 104-35, 104th Cong., 2d Sess. (1996). Canada and Venezuela ratified the OAS Convention and it came into force on April 13, 1996. The Convention is currently before the U.S. Senate for ratification. The U.S. has signed the OAS Convention. As of April 13, 1996, the following countries had signed this Convention: Costa Rica, Venezuela, Canada, Panama, Mexico, Ecuador and the United States. (last modified May 20, 1997) (Organization of American States web page visited Sept. 11, 1997 <gopher://oasunix1.oas.org:70/00/pub/english/treaties/series_a/a57e>).

30 The member states of the Council of Europe are: Belgium, France, Luxembourg, the Netherlands, the United Kingdom, Denmark, Ireland, Italy, Norway, Sweden, Greece, Turkey, Iceland, Federal Republic of Germany, Austria, Cyprus, Switzerland, Malta, Portugal, Spain, Liechtenstein, San Marino, Finland, Hungary, Poland, Bulgaria, Estonia, Lithuania, Slovenia, Czech Republic, Slovak Republic, Romania, Andorra, Latvia, Moldova, Albania, Ukraine, "former Yugoslav Republic of Macedonia," Russia, and Croatia. Countries with "*Special Guest Status*" are: Armenia, Azerbaijan, Bosnia and Herzegovina, and Georgia (Belarusia is currently suspended). Israel has "*Observer Status.*" (Council of Europe web page visited Sept. 11, 1997) <http:// www.coe.fr> <http:// stars.coe.fr/gen/aintro1b.htm>.

31 The member states of the OAS are: Antigua and Barbuda, Argentina, Bahamas, Barbados, Belize, Bolivia, Brazil, Canada, Chile, Columbia, Costa Rica, Cuba, Dominica, Dominican Republic, Ecuador, El Salvador, Grenada, Guatemala, Guyana, Haiti, Honduras, Jamaica, Mexico, Nicaragua, Panama, Paraguay, Peru, Saint Lucia, Saint Vincent and the Grenadines, Suriname, St. Kitts and Nevis, Trinidad and Tobago, the United States of America, Uruguay, and Venezuela. Countries which are "*Permanent Observers*" are: Algeria, Angola, Austria, Belgium, Bosnia and Herzegovina, Croatia, Cyprus, Czech Republic, Egypt, Equatorial Guinea, European Union, Finland, France, Germany, Greece, Holy See, Hungary, India, Israel, Italy, Japan, Kazakhstan, Republic of Korea, Latvia, Lebanon, Morocco, the Netherlands, Pakistan, Poland, Portugal, Romania, Russian Federation, Saudi Arabia, Spain, Sweden, Sri Lanka, Switzerland, Tunisia, Ukraine, and the United Kingdom. (Council of Europe web page visited Sept. 11, 1997) <http://www.oas.org>.

32 U.N. Model Agr. Tran. For. Pris., *supra* note 9.

33 Euro. Conv. Trans. Sent. Per., *supra* note 6, at art. 22, specifically refers to the "Relationship to other Conventions and Agreements" stating that the Euro. Conv. Trans. Sent. Per. does not affect other treaties and agreements entered into by the parties (signatory states), the parties are entitled to apply those other agreements in lieu of the Convention and the Convention does not affect the right of any state to enter into or conclude a bilateral or multilateral agreement.

The OAS Convention, *supra* note 6, at art. XII states: "None of the stipulations of this convention shall be construed to restrict other bilateral or multilateral treaties or other agreements between the parties."

The U.N. Model Agr. Tran. For. Pris., *supra* note 9, at annex II (9) states: "The conclusion of bilateral and multilateral agreements on supervision of and assistance to offenders given suspended sentences or granted parole could further contribute to the solution of the problems faced by foreign offenders."

treaties. In the case of bilateral treaties the U.S. can negotiate with the individual state in order to tailor an agreement to satisfy the specific needs of the states involved and to push to achieve its greatest interest.[34] This method is effective, but the negotiation process may be drawn-out and subject to unrelated political considerations and may not always be completed as soon as would be desirable. The great advantage of multilateral treaties is that a signatory can conclude treaties with many countries with one single document. However, it may take some time before there are sufficient signatory states to make it truly effective, and it suffers from a tendency to settle on the "least common denominator of cooperation."[35] This type of treaty is often drafted in broad terms and may not deal with the specific needs of a particular case, but it does enable the majority of cases to be covered easily. In any event, should the need arise the parties to a multilateral treaty can conclude bilateral treaties to deal with special situations.[36] It should be noted that the transfer of prisoners has been dealt with in other types of treaties to which the U.S. is a party, *e.g.* the various Status of Forces Agreements (SOFA),[37] and statutes which deal with military personnel.[38]

All three multilateral treaties on the international transfer of prisoners are not limited to the signature of member states alone, the Euro. Conv. Trans. Sent. Per., Art. 19 and the OAS Convention, Art. XV specifically state that they are open to signature by non-member states.

[34] Ethan A. Nadelmann, *The Role of the United States in the International Enforcement of Criminal Law*, 31 HARV. INT'L L.J. 37, 65-66 (1990).

[35] *Id.* at 65.

[36] It should be noted that both the U.S.-Korea Transfer POW Treaty and the U.S.-Panama Sentence Treaty were negotiated with the special needs of the U.S. military personnel in mind. These special considerations would not be present in negotiations with most other countries.

Art. II (4) of the U.S.-Panama Sentence Treaty, *supra* note 5, states:

> "Category I Offender" means a person who has been convicted and who is (a) a United States citizen employee or his dependent, or (b) a member of the United States Forces or his dependent, or (c) a member of the civilian component or his dependent. The terms "United States citizen employee," "dependent," "United States Forces," and "member of the civilian component" as used in this subparagraph have the meaning given to them in Article I of the Agreement in Implementation of Article III of the Panama Canal Treaty and Article I of the Agreement in Implementation of Article IV of the Panama Canal Treaty.

Art. II (5) of the U.S.-Panama Sentence Treaty states: "'Category II Offender' means all other offenders who are nationals of either the United States of America or the Republic of Panama."

[37] Status of Forces Agreements are treaties that the U.S. have entered into with other governments to govern the terms and conditions under which their military personnel will be present in that other country. The North Atlantic Treaty, Status of Forces, 4 U.S.T. 1792, June 19, 1951 (hereinafter "NATO SOFA") is one of the main agreements. Art. VII (3) of the NATO SOFA states:

> In cases where the right to exercise jurisdiction is concurrent the following rules shall apply:
>
> (a) The military authorities of the sending State shall have the primary right to exercise jurisdiction over a member of a force or of a civilian component in relation to
>
> (i) offences solely against the property or security of that State, or offences solely against the person or property of another member of the force of civilian component of that State or of a dependent;
>
> (ii) offences arising out of any act or omission done in the performance of official duty.
>
> (b) In the case of any other offence the authorities of the receiving state shall have the primary right to exercise jurisdiction.
>
> (c) If the State having the primary right decides not to exercise jurisdiction, it shall notify the authorities of the other State as soon as practicable. The authorities of the State having the primary right shall give sympathetic consideration to a request from the authorities of the other State for a waiver of its right in cases where that other State considers such waiver to be of particular importance.

Art. VII (8) of the Treaty goes on to provide protection against double jeopardy for the military prisoner but states that this does not include trying a member of its force for a violation of rules of discipline. Art. VII (9) of the treaty sets forth the list of procedural protections which must be observed by the receiving state.

Art. VII (7)(b) states: "The authorities of the receiving State shall give sympathetic consideration to a request from the authorities of the sending State for assistance in carrying out a sentence of imprisonment pronounced by

The U.S. treaties concerning international transfer of prisoners cover basically the same areas with some variations or modifications tailored to the specific needs of the parties to the bilateral treaties. This article addresses the broad points and refers to the specific provisions where relevant. Basically the structure of these treaties follows the same model and can be divided into common sections: statement of purpose and policy objectives; statements of bilateral prisoner transfer and recognition and enforcement by the parties; definition of terms; conditions of under which the treaty will apply; designation of authorities; formal procedures of transfer request; effects of transfer grant; prohibition of double jeopardy; retention of exclusive jurisdiction by sentencing country over the conviction and sentence; provision for youthful and mentally ill offenders; provision for passing of enabling legislation; and ratification, duration and termination provisions.[39]

Legal Requirements: Transfer Of Offenders Under Treaty And Implementing Legislation

The basic purpose of the treaties and the implementing legislation is to permit persons who are serving sentences in countries other than their own to complete their sentences in their respective country of origin.[40] In addition, the offense for which the offender has been convicted and sentenced must also constitute an offense under the laws of the receiving state. This provision embodies the "double criminality"[41] requirement which is well

---

the authorities of the sending State under the provisions of this Article within the territory of the receiving State."

There does not seem to be any prohibition against a prisoner seeking a transfer to the sending state under this treaty. Although the Transfer of Prisoners Treaties prohibit transfer in the case of military offenses this is not necessarily inconsistent with the provisions of the NATO SOFA because under this treaty the military authorities of the sending state would have primary authority to prosecute these types of offenses in other cases the ordinary criminal offences would be under the jurisdiction of the receiving state. *See,* Major James R. Coker, THE STATUS OF VISITING MILITARY FORCES IN EUROPE: NATO-SOFA, A COMPARISON, *in* 2 TREATISE, *supra* note 14, at 115. *See generally*, Major William K. Lietzau, *Using that Status of Forces Agreement to Incarcerate United States Service Members on Behalf of Japan*, 1996-Dec. Army Law 3.

38 10 U.S.C. § 955 (1994) states:

> (a) When a treaty is in effect between the United States and a foreign country providing for the transfer of convicted offenders, the Secretary concerned may, with the concurrence of the Attorney General, transfer to such foreign country any offender against chapter 47 of this title. Such transfer shall be effected subject to the terms of such treaty and [18 U.S.C. §§ 4100-4115].
>
> (b) Whenever the United States is party to an agreement on the status of forces under which the United States may request that it take custody of a prisoner belonging to its armed forces who is confined by order of a foreign court, the Secretary concerned may provide for the carrying out of the terms of such confinement in a military correctional facility of his department or in any penal or correctional institution under the control of the United States or which the United States may be allowed to use. Except as otherwise specified in such agreement, such person shall be treated as if he were an offender against chapter 47 of this title.

39 Szpilzinger, *supra* note 10, at 713.

40 *See* U.S.-Canada Sentence Treaty, *supra* note 3, at Preamble; S. REP. NO. 435. 95th Cong., 1st Sess. (1977).

41 Under the dual criminality requirement, the crimes need not be identical, rather they must be similar so as to be recognized as crimes in both jurisdictions in order for the prisoner to be eligible for transfer. This requirement has been criticized by Prof. Dunlap, who states:

> The dual criminality rule becomes an unnecessarily restrictive condition in the context of a penal transfer agreement, which is directed not at increasing a State's ability to enforce its own laws abroad, but at allowing convicted nationals to return home to serve prison terms in a more favorable environment. . . . [D]ual criminality constitutes a pointless restriction on a humane and socially valuable effort at international cooperation, and . . . this provision ought to be eliminated from existing treaties and avoided in future ones.

Dunlap, *supra* note 24, at 816.

established in extradition law and practice. The question of double, or dual, criminality is a threshold question which must be answered affirmatively before the prisoner can be considered for transfer.

United States Legislation

The treaties applying to the international transfer of prisoners are binding on and directly applicable to the federal government.[42] This means that foreign prisoners who are in the federal prison system have the benefit of the treaty provisions immediately. The treaties provide that each contracting state shall establish the necessary legislation or regulations to give the treaty effect within its territory. But these treaties are not self-executing,[43] and they therefore require implementing legislation, which was passed in 1977 as the Transfer of Offenders To Or From Foreign Countries Act, 18 U.S.C. §§ 4100-4115. With respect to persons sentenced under state law, the individual states need to have legislation permitting transfers.

Federal Regulations

To date there have been no federal regulations published which set forth the guidelines under which the Attorney General will exercise discretion pursuant to the statutory provisions of Transfer of Offenders To Or From Foreign Countries Act, 18 U.S.C. §§ 4100-4115.

This was the subject of litigation in *Scalise v. Meese*.[44] In that case, American prisoners serving prison sentences in England for stealing the Marlborough Diamond wished to be transferred to the U.S. but the Attorney General denied their request. The prisoners then sought a writ of *mandamus* requiring the Attorney General to set forth regulations[45]

An obvious effect of dual criminality is that some prisoners who would be eligible for transfer in all other respects may be disqualified from transfer and forced to serve the remainder of their sentences abroad because their home state, the one that would be administering the sentence, does not view their actions as criminal. *Id.* at 826-827. The result of this is that while dual criminality allows the transfer of prisoners who commit crimes which most countries view as wrong (*e.g.* murder, rape, theft), it would not permit the transfer of those prisoners convicted of conduct that is permitted in their own country. Prof. Dunlap further states:

> [I]t seems that dual criminality prevents the penal transfers to which a government should be most sympathetic—those of individuals imprisoned for conduct they may not have known to be criminal because of the differences between legal systems, for behavior considered trivial or protected by their own governments, of for crimes for which they cannot be punished at home because of their age or incapacity or a statute of limitations or, far worse, because they have already been punished at home for the very same offense.

Id. at 827.

42 Szpilzinger, *supra* note 10, at 718.

43 American Baptist Churches in the U.S.A. v. Meese, 712 F. Supp. 756, 769-770 (N.D. Cal. 1989).

44 687 F.Supp. 1239 (N.D. Ill. 1988).

45 The Attorney General is granted the authority to promulgate regulations for the implementation of transfer of prisoner treaties under 18 U.S.C. § 4102(4). The District Court looked to the legislative history and concluded that the Attorney General had violated his duty by not promulgating regulations. Scalise v. Meese, 687 F. Supp. at 1244, *citing* Flynn v. Schultz, 748 F.2d 1186 (7th Cir. 1984).

The *Scalise* court also cited Estate of Smith v. Heckler, 747 F.2d 583 (10th Cir. 1984), which held that the Secretary's failure to promulgate regulations under the Medicaid Act was an abdication of the Secretary's duty. It stated:

> [W]e find that jurisdiction exists and mandamus is an appropriate remedy. The Secretary has a duty to

concerning the exercise of his discretion in granting or denying transfer requests. District Judge Duff granted the writ and found that the Attorney General had violated his duty to promulgate regulations which would state the guidelines he would use regarding the transfer requests of American prisoners serving prison sentences abroad. He found that Congress clearly intended that the Attorney General should generally grant such requests and would promulgate regulations for those situations where a transfer request was denied.[46] Judge Duff stated that although the Attorney General did have discretion as to the content of the regulations, he had no discretion as to his duty to promulgate the regulations and therefore he issued the writ.[47]

The Seventh Circuit overturned this decision in *Scalise v. Thornburgh*;[48] the court found that the Transfer of Offenders To Or From Foreign Countries Act imposed no mandatory duty to issue regulations concerning the exercise of the Attorney General's discretion in international prisoner transfer requests.[49] The court further found that the Act did not raise a liberty interest for prisoners who sought an international prisoner transfer.[50]

More recently this matter was litigated in *Marquez-Ramos v. Reno*,[51] where the court held that the Attorney General's discretionary power to promulgate regulations was one which the judiciary could not control.[52] In this case the prisoner's transfer request was refused[53] and he sought a writ of *mandamus*; the court held that it was within Attorney General's discretion whether to grant or deny a prisoner's transfer request.[54]

There is some concern that the current international prisoner treaties have the potential for abuse by the government.[55] Some authors point out a number of areas which could be used by the government to convince a U.S. citizen in a foreign prison to cooperate with the government by forcing him to choose between being transferred back to the U.S. and forfeiting his appeal rights or remaining in a "substandard" foreign prison.[56] (Indeed, the Seventh Circuit seemed to have no difficulty accepting the Attorney General's argument that

---

> promulgate regulations which will enable her to be informed as to whether the nursing facilities receiving federal Medicaid funds are actually providing high quality medical care. This conclusion is fully supported by the statute and its legislative history. The statute vests broad discretion in the Secretary as to how that duty is best accomplished. The court is not a "super agency" and cannot control the specifics of how the Secretary satisfies the duty. This is not a question of controlling the Secretary's discretion because the Secretary has failed to discharge her statutory duty altogether. Thus, the court should "compel performance and thus effectuate the congressional purpose," behind the statutory scheme.

Id. at 591 (citation omitted).

46 687 F. Supp. at 1244.

47 *Id.*

48 891 F.2d 640 (7th Cir. 1989).

49 *Id.* at 647.

50 *Id.* at 649.

51 69 F.3d 477 (10th Cir. 1995).

52 *Id.* at 479.

53 "On February 15, 1994, 'after considering all appropriate factors,' the Attorney General denied the transfer on the basis of 'the seriousness of the offense and the prisoner's significant ties to the United States.'" *Id.* at 478. There is no elaboration in the case as to what "appropriate factors" the Attorney General considered.

54 The court looked at Art. IV (2) of the U.S.-Mexican Sentence Treaty which states: "[i]f the Authority of the Transferring State finds the transfer of an offender appropriate, and if the offender gives his express consent for his transfer, said Authority shall transmit a request for transfer, through diplomatic channels, to the Authority of the Receiving State." *Id.* at 480. The court also looked at Art. IV (4). *Id.*

The court stated: "Thus, by its own terms, the first clause of this section sets forth a necessary precondition to a prisoner transfer under the Treaty—whether the Attorney General finds a transfer 'appropriate.'" *Id.* at 480.

55 Abramovsky & Eagle, *supra* note 7, at 288-292.

56 *Id.* at 284.

the refusal to grant the transfer request in *Scalise v. Thornburgh* was because of the prisoners' "failure to cooperate in ongoing law-enforcement efforts to recover the stolen jewels."[57]) They illustrate how U.S. law enforcement officials could provide information (which was illegally obtained and therefore subject to the exclusionary rule in the U.S.) to foreign authorities in order to obtain a conviction,[58] or compel prisoners to cooperate through grants of immunity.[59] They also point out that law enforcement officials may indicate that the chances of the offender's release from prison or improvement of conditions would depend on the level of cooperation that the prisoner gave the authorities.[60]

The lack of regulations in the area of international transfer of prisoners and the subsequent decision by the Seventh Circuit in *Scalise v. Thornburgh* give credence to these stated concerns regarding potential abuse by government agents and prosecutors.

State Enabling Legislation

Foreign prisoners in state custody can only benefit from the provisions of prisoner transfer treaties if the individual state has enacted enabling legislation to approve and permit the transfer of foreign prisoners. This is specifically recognized by some of the bilateral treaties.[61] At present forty-one[62] have enacted the necessary legislation, which tends to be

---

57 Scalise v. Thornburgh, 891 F.2d 640, 643 (7th Cir. 1989).

58 Abramovsky & Eagle, *supra* note 7, at 289-290.

59 *Id.* at 291.

60 *Id.* at 289.

61 The U.S.-Mexican Sentence Treaty, *supra* note 2, at art. IV (5); U.S.-Bolivia Sentence Treaty, *supra* note 5, at art. X; U.S.-Turkey Sentence Treaty, *supra* note 5, at art. XXVIII; U.S.-Panama Sentence Treaty, *supra* note 5, at art XII; U.S.-Canada Sentence Treaty, *supra* note 3, at art. III (9).

Some treaties specifically provide that if the offender was sentenced by the courts of a state of one of the parties, the approval of the authorities of that state, as well as the federal authority, shall be required. The U.S.-Mexican Sentence Treaty, Art. IV (5) and the U.S.-Canada Sentence Treaty, Art. III (5) also provide that the federal authority of the receiving or administering state shall be responsible for the custody of the transferred offender.

62 The following states have enacted enabling legislation for the international transfer of prisoners: *Alabama*, ALA. CODE § 15-9-100. (1975)—Transfer of foreign nationals imprisoned in Alabama to country of citizenship; *Alaska*, ALASKA STAT. § 33.30.291. (Michie 1996)—Treaties; *Arizona*, ARIZ. REV. STAT. ANN. § 41-105. (West 1992)—Exchange of offenders under treaty; consent by governor; *Arkansas*, ARK. CODE ANN. § 16-94-102. (Michie 1987)—Transfer of convicted foreign citizens or nationals under treaty; *California*, CAL. [Government] CODE § 12012.1. (West 1992)—Transfer of offender to foreign country; approval; *Colorado*, COLO. REV. STAT. ANN. § 24-60-2301. (West 1990)—Transfer or exchange of foreign nationals convicted of a crime—authorization by governor; *Connecticut*, CONN. GEN. STAT. ANN. § 18-91a. (West Supp. 1997)—International transfer or exchange of prisoners; *Florida*, FLA. STAT. ANN. § 944.596. (West 1996)—Transfer of convicted foreign citizens or nationals under treaty; *Hawaii*, HAW. REV. STAT. § 353-16.5 (Supp. 1992)—Transfer of offenders under treaty; authority of governor; *Idaho*, IDAHO CODE § 20-104. (1997)—Transfer of convicted foreign citizens or nationals under treaty; *Illinois*, 730 ILL. COMP. STAT. ANN. 5/3-2-3.1. (West 1992)—Treaties; *Indiana*, IND. CODE ANN. § 11-8-4.5 (Michie Supp. 1996)—International prisoner transfer or exchange under treaty; *Iowa*, IOWA CODE ANN. § 7.22. (West 1995)—Exchange of offenders under treaty—consent by governor; *Kansas*, KAN. STAT. ANN. § 22-3723. (1995)—Transfer of offenders under treaties; *Kentucky*, KY. REV. STAT. ANN. § 196.073. (Michie 1995)—Governor's authority to authorize commissioner to consent to transfer of convicted offenders under federal treaty; *Louisiana*, LA. CODE CRIM. PROC. ANN. art. 892.3. (West 1997)—Transfer of foreign nationals or citizens; treaty; *Maine*, ME. REV. STAT. ANN. tit. 34-A, § 3072. (West 1988)—Treaty; transfer of noncitizens of the United States; *Maryland*, MD. CODE ANN. [Crimes and Punishments] § 690B (1996)—Transfer or exchange of convicted offenders under treaty ; *Massachusetts*, MASS. GEN. LAWS ANN. ch. 127 § 97B. (West 1991)—Treaties; transfer of prisoners to other countries; *Michigan*, MICH. COMP. LAWS ANN. § 791.265. (West Supp. 1997)—Transfer of prisoners; *Minnesota*, MINN. STAT. ANN. § 243.515. (West 1992)—transfer under treaty; extradition under treaty; *Missouri*, MO. ANN. STAT. § 217.137. (West

general in wording and basically authorize the states to consent to the transfer or exchange of prisoners where there is a treaty subject to the terms of the treaty, and if the prisoners consent to the transfer.

Operation of the Transfer of Offenders under the Treaties

To effect a transfer the sentencing state and administering state must be willing to transfer the offender (the precise treaty requirements will be examined later). Nothing in the treaties requires the contracting states to accept an offender.

A proposed transfer is always subject to the consent of the offender. The U.S., under the implementing legislation, will verify the consent of persons being transferred, either to or from it, through a U.S. judicial officer.[63] In the case of transfers to the U.S., a waiver must be secured from the offender of any rights he may have to challenge the validity of the foreign conviction and the sentence imposed by the foreign court in U.S. courts. The verification of the waiver and the offender's consent are subject to a right to counsel.[64]

The transfer is accomplished upon the receipt by the receiving state of whatever documents it may require in order for it to execute the completion of the offender's sentence. The offender is then delivered to the control of the receiving state for the completion of his sentence and is governed by the laws of the receiving state in all respects except for any matters pertaining to the conviction or sentence which are exclusively subject to the jurisdiction of the sentencing state. This jurisdictional dichotomy is in the treaties and the implementing legislation. Thus, the sentencing state retains jurisdiction over the conviction and sentence and the receiving state has jurisdiction over the execution of the sentence and

---

1996)—Prisoner transfers by United States treaty with foreign governments—governor's powers—director's duties; *Montana*, MONT. CODE ANN. § 53-1-106. (1995)—Exchange of offenders under treaty; *Nebraska*, NEB. REV. STAT. § 83-956. (1994)—Treaty; transfer of convicted offenders to foreign countries; Director of Correctional Services; duties; *Nevada*, NEV. REV. STAT. ANN. § 209.291. (Michie 1996)—Transfer of offenders: Within department; to other governmental agencies; between United States and foreign country; *New Hampshire*, N.H. REV. STAT. ANN. § 622-C:1 (Supp. 1996)—International Prisoner Transfer; *New Jersey,* N.J. STAT. ANN. § 30:7D-1. (West 1997)—Treaties providing for exchange or transfer of juvenile delinquent or criminals; authorization for commissioner to take actions necessary for participation; *New Mexico*, N.M. STAT. ANN. § 31-4-31. (Michie Supp. 1984)—Transfer under treaty; governor; *New York*, N.Y. [Correction Law] LAW § 71.1-a. (McKinney Supp. 1997)—Persons received into the custody of the department; *North Dakota*, N.D. CENT. CODE § 54-21-25. (1989)—Authority to contract with other governmental agencies for prisoners and juvenile delinquents, *repealed by* S.L. 1991, ch. 595, § 3, effective July 7, 1991; *Ohio*, OHIO REV. CODE ANN. § 5120.53 (West Supp. 1996)—Transfer or exchange of convicted offender to foreign country; *Oklahoma*, OKLA. STAT. ANN. tit. 57, § 96. (West 1991)—Foreign convicted offenders—Transfer or exchange; *Oregon*, OR. REV. STAT. § 421.229 (1993)—Transfer of foreign inmates; authority of Governor; written approval of inmate; *Rhode Island*, R.I. GEN. LAWS § 42-56-40. (Supp. 1996)—Transfer of foreign convicted offenders under treaty; *South Carolina*, S.C. CODE ANN. § 24-1-145. (Law. Co-op. Supp. 1996)—Transfer or exchange of foreign convicted offenders; *South Dakota*, S.D. CODIFIED LAWS § 1-15-32. (Michie Supp. 1997)—Participation in international prisoner transfer treaties; *Texas*, TEX. [Criminal Procedure] CODE ANN. § 42.17. (West 1979)—Transfer under treaty; *Utah*, UTAH CODE ANN. § 77-28b-3. (1995)—Eligibility criteria for international transfer; *Virginia*, VA. CODE ANN. § 53.1-220. (Michie 1994)—Transfer of prisoners pursuant to treaty; *Washington*, WASH. REV. CODE ANN. § 43.06.350. (West Supp. 1997) - Foreign nationals or citizens, convicted offenders—Transfers and sentences; *Wisconsin*, WIS. STAT. ANN. § 302.185. (West 1997)—Transfer to foreign countries under treaty; WIS. STAT. ANN. § 48.345(11) (West 1997)—Transfer to foreign countries under treaty; *Wyoming*, WYO. STAT. ANN. § 7-13-106. (Michie 1976)—Transfer of citizen or national of foreign country.

[63] 18 U.S.C. §§ 4107(a), 4108(a).

[64] 18 U.S.C. §§ 4107(c), 4108(c), 4109.

all related matters. There is no treaty or legislative provision for resolving possible jurisdictional conflicts, which will therefore be subject to the forum's interpretation.

Should an action be initiated in a U.S. court seeking to have the offender released, the court must first determine whether it has jurisdiction to hear the matter and then consider the jurisdictional division referred to above. This is immaterial, however, where the suit challenges the constitutionality of either the treaty or the implementing legislation in its application to the offender. In the latter case, the court would clearly have subject matter jurisdiction, even if the treaties and the legislation purport to preclude such actions based on the offender's consent to transfer and waiver to challenge the transfer. If a court orders the release of the transferred offender, there would be no valid basis for continued detention or supervision by U.S. authorities.

Although the treaties are silent on the point of releases prior to completion of sentence, section 4114 of the implementing statute provides for the return of such offenders to the sentencing state.[65] The statute creates a "return" mechanism separate from the process of extradition. The mechanism makes the return of such offenders virtually automatic upon a request by the sentencing state.

If the request for return is processed as prescribed, the offender may be able to challenge it in a U.S. court, and thereby obtain a ruling on the validity of the return procedure. A favorable decision would protect the offender from either detention by U.S. authorities or return to the sentencing state. An unfavorable decision would require return to be conditioned upon the receipt of proper credit for time spent in U.S. custody. The offender would then complete his sentence in the sentencing state. It should be noted that, under section 4102 of the Act, the Attorney General is empowered "to make regulations for the proper implementation of such treaties." Thus, any future procedural developments would have to be examined in light of administrative regulations pursuant to this legislative delegation of power.

Substantive Transfer Issues

Each treaty contains a definition section which sets forth the terms used in the treaty; for the sake of clarity the following terms are used throughout this paper, "Sentencing State"[66] means the state in which the offender has been sentenced and from which he is

---

[65] 18 U.S.C. § 4114.

[66] "*Sentencing State*" is used in the U.S.-France Sentence Treaty, *supra* note 5, at art. 1 (a); U.S.-Turkey Sentence Treaty, *supra* note 5, at art. I (a); Euro. Conv. Trans. Sent. Per., *supra* note 6, at art. 1 (c); OAS Convention, *supra* note 6, at art. 1 (1); U.N. Model Agreement, *supra* note 9. Other terms used in this context include: "*Requesting State*": U.S.-Turkey Sentence Treaty, *supra* note 5, at art. I (a); "*Transferring State*": U.S.-Mexican Sentence Treaty, *supra* note 2, at art IX (1); U.S.-Bolivia Sentence Treaty, *supra* note 5, at art. II (1); U.S.-Peru Sentence Treaty, *supra* note 5, at art. II (1); U.S.-Panama Sentence Treaty, *supra* note 5, at art. II (1); U.S.-Thailand Sentence Treaty, *supra* note 5, at art. I (1); "*Sending State*": U.S.-Canada Sentence Treaty, *supra* note 3, at art. I (a).

being transferred. "Administering State"[67] generally means the state to which the sentenced person is being transferred to serve his sentence.

Conditions and Eligibility for Transfer

There are a number of conditions that must be satisfied in order for a prisoner to be eligible for transfer under these treaties. These will be described in general terms and will briefly discuss any variations that exist in the individual treaties.

1. *Dual Criminality.*[68] This is a threshold requirement of these treaties and 18 U.S.C. § 4101(a) of the implementing legislation. This means that the offense the prisoner was convicted of must be generally punishable as a crime in both the Sentencing and Administering States. Dual criminality is not to be interpreted as meaning that the offenses are identical in both states, but they should be similar in character.[69] Certain offenses are excluded under the various treaties, *e.g.* under the Mexican Treaty violations of immigration or military laws[70] are not eligible for transfer. Similarly, political offenses[71] are not covered under the Mexican Treaty, although no definition of "political offense" is given in this treaty or the U.S.-Mexican extradition treaty.[72]

2. *Nationals of Administering State.* The treaties on the international transfer of prisoners generally only apply to the citizens or nationals of the Administering State[73] under 18 U.S.C. § 4100(b).[74] There are some slight variations on this general rule. Under the U.S.

67 *"Administering State"* is used in the U.S.-France Sentence Treaty, *supra* note 5, at art 1 (b); Euro. Conv. Trans. Sent. Per., *supra* note 6, at art. 1 (d); U.N. Model Agreement, *supra* note 9; *"Requested State"*: U.S.-Turkey Sentence Treaty, *supra* note 5, at art. I (b); "*Receiving State*": U.S.-Mexican Sentence Treaty, *supra* note 2, at art. IX (2); U.S.-Bolivia Sentence Treaty, *supra* note 5, at art. II (2); U.S.-Peru Sentence Treaty, *supra* note 5, at art. II (2); U.S.-Panama Sentence Treaty, *supra* note 5, at art. II (2); U.S.-Thailand Sentence Treaty, *supra* note 5, at art I (2); U.S.-Canada Sentence Treaty, *supra* note 3, at art. I (b); OAS Convention, *supra* note 6, at art. 1 (2).

68 18 U.S.C. § 4101(a) states:

"[D]ouble criminality" means that at the time of transfer of an offender the offense for which he has been sentenced is still an offense in the transferring country and is also an offense in the receiving country. With regard to a country which has a federal form of government, an act shall be deemed to be an offense in that country if it is an offense under the federal laws or the laws of any state or province thereof.

69 U.S.-Mexican Sentence Treaty, *supra* note 2, at art. II (1); U.S.-Bolivia Sentence Treaty, *supra* note 5, at art. III (1); U.S.-Peru Sentence Treaty, *supra* note 5, at art. III (1); U.S.-Panama Sentence Treaty, *supra* note 5, at art. III (1); U.S.-Turkey Sentence Treaty, *supra* note 5, at art. III (1); U.S.-Thailand Sentence Treaty, *supra* note 5, at art. II (1); U.S.-Canada Sentence Treaty, *supra* note 3, at art. II (a); Euro. Conv. Trans. Sent. Per., *supra* note 6, at art. 3 (1)(e); OAS Convention, *supra* note 6, at art III (3).

The U.N. Model Agr. Tran. For. Pris., *supra* note 9, at art I (3) also has a double criminality requirement.

70 U.S.-Mexican Sentence Treaty, supra note 2, at art. II (4).

71 U.S.-Mexican Sentence Treaty, supra note 2 art. II (4).

72 Treaty of Extradition, Feb. 22, 1899, U.S.-Mex., 31 Stat. 1818; Supplementary Extradition Convention, Aug. 16, 1939, 55 Stat. 1133.

73 U.S.-France Sentence Treaty, *supra* note 5, at art. 2 (b); U.S.-Mexican Sentence Treaty, *supra* note 2, at art. II (2); U.S.-Bolivia Sentence Treaty, *supra* note 5, at art. III (2); U.S.-Peru Sentence Treaty, *supra* note 5, at art. III (2); U.S.-Panama Sentence Treaty, *supra* note 5, at art. III (2); U.S.-Turkey Sentence Treaty, *supra* note 5, at art. IV (b); U.S.-Thailand Sentence Treaty, *supra* note 5, at art. II (2); European Convention, *supra* note 6, at art. 3 (1)(a); OAS Convention, *supra* note 6, at art. III (4).

74 18 U.S.C. § 4100(b) states:

An offender may be transferred from the United States pursuant to this chapter only to a country of which the offender is a citizen or national. Only an offender who is a citizen or national of the United States may be transferred to the United States. An offender may be transferred to or from the United States only with the offender's consent, and only if the offense for which the offender was sentenced satisfies the requirement of

treaties with Mexico and Turkey, domiciliaries of the Sentencing State are not eligible for transfer to the country of which they are nationals. This means that a citizen of the U.S. could be deprived of the right to avail of the benefits of the Transfer of Prisoner Treaty if he meets the criteria to be considered a "domiciliary" in the Sentencing State, even though the Administering State may be willing to accept the prisoner. The Mexican Treaty defines domiciliary as "a person who has been present in the territory of one of the parties for at least five years with an intent to remain permanently therein."[75] (One rationale for this is that the treaty has a humanitarian goal to alleviate the hardships felt by foreign prisoners in a foreign prison, but if the prisoner has spent sufficient time in the foreign country to be considered a domiciliary then he will not experience these hardships.) The result is that American citizens who are domiciliaries of Mexico are ineligible for transfer to the U.S., even though the Transfer To or From Foreign Countries Act makes no such distinctions. This exception could be deemed a violation of the Equal Protection Clause of the Fifth Amendment of the United States Constitution, since there is no rational basis for such discrimination within the same class of offenders.[76] By contrast, Art. II (b) of the Canadian Treaty provides that transfer of offenders between the two states shall apply to all their respective nationals and citizens and is therefore consistent with sections 4100(b) and 4102(6) of the implementing Act.

Both the Mexican and Canadian Treaties, by implication, exclude permanent residents of the U.S. who are not American citizens or nationals,[77] since such persons are not entitled to diplomatic protection abroad under traditional international law doctrine and practice. However, this does not address the issue of the applicability of U.S. law to permanent residents who are not nationals in light of United States Supreme Court decisions giving residents of the U.S. substantially the same rights as U.S. citizens.[78] Thus a permanent

---

> double criminality as defined in this chapter. Once an offender's consent to transfer has been verified by a verifying officer, that consent shall be irrevocable. If at the time of transfer the offender is under eighteen years of age, or is deemed by the verifying officer to be mentally incompetent or otherwise incapable of knowingly and voluntarily consenting to the transfer, the transfer shall not be accomplished unless consent to the transfer be given by a parent or guardian, guardian ad litem, or by an appropriate court of the sentencing country. The appointment of a guardian ad litem shall be independent of the appointment of counsel under section 4109 of this title.

[75] U.S.-Mexican Sentence Treaty, *supra* note 2, at art. IX (4).

[76] *See Implementation of Treaties for the Transfer of Offenders To or From Foreign Countries: Hearings on H.R. 7148 Before the House Subcomm. on Immigration, Citizenship and International Law of the House Comm. On the Judiciary*, 95th Cong., 1st Sess. 187-94 (1977) (statement of M. Cherif Bassiouni). *Transfer of Offenders and Administration of Foreign Penal Sentences: Hearings on S. 1682 Before the Subcomm. on Penitentiaries and Corrections of the Senate Comm. on the Judiciary*, 95th Cong., 1st Sess., 139-40 (1977) (statement of M. Cherif Bassiouni) [hereinafter *Judiciary Hearings*].

[77] "National" is defined in 8 U.S.C. § 1101(a)(21) (1994).

"The term 'national' means a person owing permanent allegiance to a state." *Id.*

"The term 'national of the United States' means (A) a citizen of the United States, or (B) a person who, though not a citizen of the United States, owes permanent allegiance to the United States." 8 U.S.C. § 1101(a)(22).

[78] A national is defined as a person owing permanent allegiance to the United States, which excludes permanent residents who have no such status. Aliens are as entitled to equal protection as "persons" even though they are not United States nationals.

> The Fourteenth Amendment provides, "[N]or shall any State deprive any person of life, liberty, or property, without due process of law; nor deny to any person within its jurisdiction the equal protection of the laws." It has long been settled, and it is not disputed here, that the term "person" in this context encompasses lawfully admitted resident aliens as well as citizens of the United States and entitles both citizens and aliens to the equal protection of the laws of the State in which they reside.

Graham v. Richardson, 403 U.S. 365, 371 (1971).

resident of the U.S. who has declared his intention to become a citizen, but has not yet been sworn as a citizen and who is convicted of an offense while vacationing in Canada or Mexico is ineligible for transfer to the U.S. This exclusion could also be the basis of a challenge to the constitutionality of the treaty and implementing statute under the Equal Protection Clause of the Fifth Amendment, since there is no rational basis for such discrimination within the same class of offenders. The exclusion would also be in contravention of the underlying purposes of the treaties and implementing statute as discussed above. The U.N. Model provides that it would facilitate the return of prisoners to the country of their nationality or residence.[79]

The question of the transfer of a prisoner whose native country is not a party to a treaty is one which should be seriously considered. "If the imposing country creates the mechanisms for transfer, any foreign prisoners in that country should be able to request transfer. This will satisfy humanitarian goals, and although the treaty contemplates transfer home, if countries agree to transfer to another country, there should be no obstacle."[80] This possibility would not seem to be feasible under 18 U.S.C. § 4100 (b), which confines the categories of eligible offenders to citizens or nationals.

3. *The Sentenced Person Must Give His Consent to the Transfer.*[81] This requirement is discussed in greater detail elsewhere in this article. It is important to realize that this is a three-way voluntary agreement between the Sentencing State, the Administering State and the prisoner. There is no obligation on any of these parties to agree to the proposed transfer. The U.S. implementing legislation is quite clear that the prisoner's consent must be made with full knowledge of the consequences of the transfer and this must be verified by a magistrate or judicial officer.[82] The consent to transfer and the waiver of the offender's right to challenge the sentence are subject to a right to counsel.[83]

4. *The Sentence Must be Final and Enforceable.* This means that the prisoner can have no further collateral attacks or appeals pending[84] to be eligible for transfer. The prescribed time for appeal must have expired at the time the transfer is requested. The U.S. implementing legislation clearly states that once the prisoner's consent to transfer has been given it is irrevocable.[85] The legislation only seems to require a consent to the transfer but

---

79 U.N. Model Agr. Tran. For. Pris., *supra* note 9, at art. I (1).

80 Gelfand, *supra* note 12, at 598.

81 U.S.-France Sentence Treaty, *supra* note 5, at art. 12 (2); U.S.-Mexican Sentence Treaty, *supra* note 2, at art. IV (2) and art. V; U.S.-Bolivia Sentence Treaty, *supra* note 5, at art. V (3); U.S.-Peru Sentence Treaty, *supra* note 5, at art. V (3); U.S.-Panama Sentence Treaty, *supra* note 5, at art. III (6); U.S.-Turkey Sentence Treaty, *supra* note 5, at art. IV (f); U.S.-Thailand Sentence Treaty, *supra* note 5, at art III (7); Euro. Conv. Trans. Sent. Per., *supra* note 6, at art. 3 (1)(d), 6 (2)(c), 7; OAS Convention, *supra* note 6, at art. V (5).

The requirement for the prisoner's consent is implied in the U.S.-Canada Sentence Treaty since he is the one who must initiate the process. U.S.-Canada Sentence Treaty, *supra* note 3, at art. III (10).

U.N. Model Agr. Tran. For. Pris., *supra* note 9, at art I (5) and (7).

82 18 U.S.C. §§ 4107(a), 4108(a).

83 18 U.S.C. §§ 4107(c), 4108(c), 4109.

84 U.S.-Mexican Sentence Treaty, *supra* note 2, at art. II (6); U.S.-Bolivia Sentence Treaty, *supra* note 5, at art. III (5); U.S.-Thailand Sentence Treaty, *supra* note 5, at art. II (5); U.S.-Canada Sentence Treaty, *supra* note 3, at art. II (e); U.S.-France Sentence Treaty, *supra* note 5, at art. 2 (d); Euro. Conv. Trans. Sent. Per., *supra* note 6, at art. 3 (1)(b); OAS Convention, *supra* note 6, at art. III (1); U.N. Model Agreement, *supra* note 9, at art. II (10).

85 18 U.S.C. §§ 4107(b)(4), 4108(b)(4).

implicit in that is a waiver[86] of the prisoner's rights to challenge the legality of the conviction because the Sentencing State retains jurisdiction in this matter.[87] There is concern in the U.S. that the waiver of these rights of appeal may be unconstitutional. The very fact that the prisoner may be faced with remaining in substandard prison conditions or being transferred to the U.S. but waiving his rights to appeal has not yet been found to constitute sufficient duress so as to nullify his waiver. In any event, there is always the danger for the prisoner that he may be returned to the Sentencing State for the remainder of his sentence if the transfer was found to be contrary to the provisions of the treaty of the laws of the Administering State.[88] The sentence must not only be final it must also be definite in order for the Administering State to be able to enforce it.[89]

5. *Minimum Sentence Remaining.* Generally the treaties require a minimum period of the sentence to be served at the time the request is made, usually six months[90] or one year.[91] The European Convention allows for a shorter period to exist on the sentence in exceptional cases.[92] This takes into consideration the expense involved in prisoner transfers. The Thai government planned to include a provision in its implementing legislation that would require the foreign prisoner to serve the lesser period of one-third of his sentence or four years in Thailand before he would be transferred to the Administering State.[93]

6. *Social Rehabilitation of the Prisoner.* In deciding whether to approve the transfer of the prisoner, some treaties provide that the state authorities shall bear in mind all factors bearing upon the probability that the transfer will contribute to the social rehabilitation of

---

86 "Although on its face [the] statutory language [of the Mexican and Canadian treaties] appears to foreclose any waiver of the right to appeal to secure eligibility at an earlier date, it is possible that a judicial determination would construe such a waiver as causing the time for appeal to elapse, and therefore allow the waiver." Bassiouni, *Transfer Between the United States and Mexico and the United States and Canada*, ICL PROCEDURE, *supra* note 1, at 243. The policy aspects that would influence this approach include: (1) humanitarian considerations where there is less than six months between the ending of the appeal period and the completion date of the sentence, especially in minor offenses; (2) where no purposes of the treaty would be adversely affected by such a construction principles of treaty interpretation would favor individual rights when the treaty is susceptible to more than one interpretation; (3) the legislative history of the implementing legislation is silent on the subject, indicating that the question is still open. *Id.*

87 18 U.S.C. § 4108(b)(1).

88 18 U.S.C. §§ 4107(b)(3), 4108(b)(3), 4114.

89 Hogan v. Koenig, 920 F.2d 6, 8 (9th Cir. 1990); here the prisoner was serving a sentence of 26 years to life. The Ninth Circuit stated that since California was not a party to the Treaty it had the power to deny the transfer. *Id.* The California Court of Appeal had decided Hogan was not eligible for transfer under the Treaty until the state had set a definite termination date for his sentence and he was under a life sentence within the terms of the Treaty. *In re* Hogan, 187 Cal. App.3d 819 (Cal. Ct. App. 1986).

90 U.S.-Mexican Sentence Treaty, *supra* note 2, at art. II (5); U.S.-Bolivia Sentence Treaty, *supra* note 5, at art. III (4); U.S.-Peru Sentence Treaty, *supra* note 5, at art. III (4); U.S.-Panama Sentence Treaty, *supra* note 5, at art. III (4); U.S.-Turkey Sentence Treaty, *supra* note 5, at art. IV (d); U.S.-Canada Sentence Treaty, *supra* note 3, at art. II (d); Euro. Conv. Trans. Sent. Per., *supra* note 6, at art. 3 (1)(c); OAS Convention, *supra* note 6, at art. III (6).

U.N. Model Agr. Tran. For. Pris., *supra* note 9, at art. II (11) also addresses the question of indeterminate sentences. It states: "At the time of the request for a transfer, the prisoner shall, as a general rule, still have to serve at least six months of the sentence; a transfer should, however, be granted also in cases of indeterminate sentences."

91 The U.S.-France Sentence Treaty, *supra* note 5, at art 2 (e), and the U.S.-Thailand Sentence Treaty, *supra* note 5, at art II (4) require a one year minimum of the sentence to be served at the time of the request.

92 Euro. Conv. Trans. Sent. Per., *supra* note 6, at art. 3 (2).

93 U.S.-Thailand Sentence Treaty, *supra* note 5, at Letter of Submittal, Hein's No. KAV 1942.

the prisoner,[94] including: the nature and severity of his offense;[95] the effects of the offense within the Sentencing and Administering States and any mitigating or aggravating circumstances;[96] his previous criminal record, if any;[97] his medical condition or status of his health;[98] the strength of his connections by residence, presence in the territory, family relations and otherwise to the social life of the Sentencing and Administering States;[99] that the transfer will be in the best interests of the offender.[100]

7. *Youthful*[101] *and Mentally Incompetent*[102] *Persons*. Many treaties make provision for the parties to deal with prisoners who are subject to the supervision of another person either because of the prisoner's youth or mental capacity. Consent to the transfer of these prisoners must be obtained from the legally authorized person.[103]

Persons under 18 years of age are eligible for transfer, provided that a parent, a guardian, or the court having jurisdiction over the offender consents to the transfer. The problem of waiver and consent to transfer by minors in this context is not unlike its counterpart in juvenile proceedings throughout the U.S. It is likely that some of the factors taken into account by juvenile courts throughout the U.S. will be relied upon. Among these factors, the most important is that the waiver and consent, both linked in the process of effectuating the transfer, may be deemed valid because of the benefits derived from the waiver. This factor would be particularly relevant where the parent, guardian, or court refuses to grant consent and thus deprives the minor of the benefit of transfer. Such a

---

94 In Hogan v. Koenig, 920 F.2d at 8, the court held that since California was not a party to the Treaty it was not bound to solely consider the best interests of the prisoner (U.S.-Canada Sentence Treaty, Art. III (6)) as a basis for its decision to transfer a prisoner. Here the prisoner was serving a sentence of 26 years-to-life, and the California authorities had initially denied the transfer stating Hogan was not eligible for transfer until a definite termination date for his sentence had been set. In any case, California had the power to decide where the sentence would be carried out. *Id.*

Walton v. Dep't of Corrections, 538 N.W.2d 66, 68 (Mich. App. 1995). The court held that the provision requiring the best interests of the prisoner to be considered under the U.S.-Canada Sentence Treaty applied to the original parties. Michigan's policy of denying a transfer to prisoners who did not satisfy certain criteria did not violate the treaty.

95 U.S.-Mexican Sentence Treaty, *supra* note 2, at art IV (4); U.S.-Bolivia Sentence Treaty, *supra* note 5, at art. V (6); U.S.-Peru Sentence Treaty, *supra* note 5, at art. V (5); U.S.-Panama Sentence Treaty, *supra* note 5, at art. V (6); U.S.-Thailand Sentence Treaty, *supra* note 5, at art III (3)(b); OAS Convention, *supra* note 6, at art. V (6).

96 U.S.-Thailand Sentence Treaty, *supra* note 5, at art. III (3)(b).

97 U.S.-Mexican Sentence Treaty, *supra* note 2, at art. IV (4); U.S.-Bolivia Sentence Treaty, *supra* note 5, at art. V (6); U.S.-Peru Sentence Treaty, *supra* note 5, at art. V (5); U.S.-Panama Sentence Treaty, *supra* note 5, at art. V (6); OAS Convention, *supra* note 6, at art. V (6).

98 U.S.-Mexican Sentence Treaty, *supra* note 2, at art. IV (4); U.S.-Bolivia Sentence Treaty, *supra* note 5, at art. V (6); U.S.-Peru Sentence Treaty, *supra* note 5, at art. V (5); U.S.-Panama Sentence Treaty, *supra* note 5, at art. V (6); OAS Convention, *supra* note 6, at art. V (6).

99 U.S.-Mexican Sentence Treaty, *supra* note 2, at art. IV (4); U.S.-Bolivia Sentence Treaty, *supra* note 5, at art. V (6); U.S.-Peru Sentence Treaty, *supra* note 5, at art. V (5); U.S.-Panama Sentence Treaty, *supra* note 5, at art. V (6); OAS Convention, *supra* note 6, at art. V (6).

100 U.S.-Canada Sentence Treaty, *supra* note 3, at art. III (6).

101 18 U.S.C. § 4110. *In re* Manuel P., 215 Cal. App.3d 48 (Cal. Ct. App. 1989).

102 18 U.S.C. § 4100(b).

103 U.S.-Mexican Sentence Treaty, *supra* note 2, at art. VIII (1); U.S.-Bolivia Sentence Treaty, *supra* note 5, at art. VIII (1); U.S.-Peru Sentence Treaty, *supra* note 5, at art. VIII (1); U.S.-Panama Sentence Treaty, *supra* note 5, at art. VIII (1); U.S.-Turkey Sentence Treaty, *supra* note 5, at art. IV (f); OAS Convention, *supra* note 6, at art. IX.

U.N. Model Agr. Tran. For. Pris., *supra* note 9, at art. I (9).

circumstance would fly in the face of the rationale for the process. Similar considerations would likely apply to mentally unsound persons.

8. *Double Jeopardy.*[104] The Administering State is prohibited from prosecuting, detaining or sentencing the prisoner after transfer for the same offense that he was convicted of and sentenced for in the Sentencing State.[105] This is a requirement of the Fifth Amendment to the United States Constitution. Some treaties require that the Administering State will not prosecute for any offense if it has become statute barred under the law of that state if the sentence had been imposed by one of its federal or state courts.[106]

9. *Miscellaneous*. A number of countries have set forth exclusions to their respective Transfer of Prisoners treaties. These include: (1) purely military offenses;[107] (2) political offenses, within the meaning of the relevant extradition treaties;[108] (3) offenses for which the prisoner would be eligible for the death penalty;[109] (4) offenses contrary to immigration laws.[110] The Thai Treaty states that the prisoner will not be eligible for transfer if he committed an offense against the internal or external security of the state, or against the Head of State of the Sentencing State, or against legislation protecting national art treasures.[111]

---

[104] U.S. v. Fontanez, 869 F.2d. 180 (2nd Cir. 1989). Following the defendant's transfer to the U.S. following a Canadian conviction for a drug charge he was convicted of travel in interstate commerce in order to carry on an unlawful business involving narcotics, contrary to 18 U.S.C. § 1952(a) (1982), arising out of the same transaction. While the U.S. sentence ran concurrently with the foreign sentence and added no extra time, it apparently delayed Fontanez's eligibility for parole. *Id.* at 182. The defendant appealed on the ground that it violated the Double Jeopardy Clause of the Constitution and the U.S.-Canada Sentence Treaty. The court held that there was no double jeopardy violation because the elements of the Canadian offence and the U.S. offence were not the same. *Id.* at 183. Here a number of charges had been dropped and the court held that "jeopardy had not attached unless the defendant was first 'put to trial.'" *Id.* (citations omitted). The court also found that "the foreign conviction bars a prosecution in the receiving jurisdiction where such a prosecution would have been barred if the foreign conviction had instead been a conviction entered in a court of the Receiving State or a sister state or in a federal court." *Id.*

U.S. v. Patterson, 812 F.2d 1188 (9th Cir. 1987). In *Patterson* the court held that the defendant's prior Mexican counterfeiting conviction did not bar federal counterfeit and conspiracy charges following his transfer to the U.S. The federal charges required proof of different facts, therefore double jeopardy did not bar the prosecution. *Id.* at 1191-1192. The court also permitted the use of a voluntary statement to a Secret Service Agent. This statement occurred after the defendant was severely beaten by Mexican officials, but the U.S. agent did not know about the beating. *Id.* at 1193. A voluntary statement made to the U.S. agent prior to a Miranda warning was permitted to establish probable cause for a search warrant. *Id.* at 1193-1194.

[105] U.S.-Mexican Sentence Treaty, *supra* note 2, at art. VII; U.S.-Bolivia Sentence Treaty, *supra* note 5, at art. VI (1); U.S.-Peru Sentence Treaty, *supra* note 5, at art. VI (1); U.S.-Panama Sentence Treaty, *supra* note 5, at art. VI (1); U.S.-Canada Sentence Treaty, *supra* note 3, at art. VI; OAS Convention, *supra* note 6, at art. VII (1); U.N. Model Agr. Tran. For. Pris., Art. II (13).

[106] 18 U.S.C. § 4111. U.S.-Mexican Sentence Treaty, *supra* note 2, at art. VII; U.S.-Turkey Sentence Treaty, *supra* note 5, at art. V (h); U.S.-Canada Sentence Treaty, *supra* note 3, at art. VI.

[107] U.S.-France Sentence Treaty, *supra* note 5, at art. 3; U.S.-Mexican Sentence Treaty, *supra* note 2, at art II (4); U.S.-Bolivia Sentence Treaty, *supra* note 5, at art. III (3); U.S.-Peru Sentence Treaty, *supra* note 5, at art. III (3); U.S.-Panama Sentence Treaty, *supra* note 5, at art. III (3); U.S.-Turkey Sentence Treaty, *supra* note 5, at art. V (b); U.S.-Canada Sentence Treaty, *supra* note 3, at art. II (c).

[108] U.S.-Mexican Sentence Treaty, *supra* note 2, at art. II (4); U.S.-Turkey Sentence Treaty, *supra* note 5, at art. V (b).

[109] U.S.-Bolivia Sentence Treaty, *supra* note 5, at art. III (3); U.S.-Peru Sentence Treaty, *supra* note 5, at art. III (3); U.S.-Panama Sentence Treaty, *supra* note 5, at art. III (3); OAS Convention, *supra* note 6, at art. III (5).

[110] U.S.-Mexican Sentence Treaty, *supra* note 2, at art. II (4); U.S.-Canada Sentence Treaty, *supra* note 3, at art. II (c).

[111] U.S.-Thailand Sentence Treaty, *supra* note 5, at art. II (3).

It should be noted that the doctrine of double jeopardy is not the same thing as the "rule of specialty." While the treaties prevent prosecution for the same offense under the concept of double jeopardy, they do not prevent a prosecution for other offenses.[112] This rule of specialty means that a country that received a criminal defendant by means of an extradition treaty may only try the defendant for the offense for which he was extradited[113] (which is of the utmost importance in an extradition case where the person is merely accused of a crime). With the exception of the Turkish Treaty,[114] none of the other bilateral or multilateral treaties include this provision.

The lack of reference to the rule of specialty could be important in the case of a prisoner who has already been convicted and is serving his foreign sentence, because once the prisoner is sent back to his country of origin, he can then be tried for any pending cases and possibly serve his sentence concurrently with the foreign sentence rather than waiting to complete the foreign sentence and then be deported to his country of origin where he would still have to face any pending charges.

There has been concern that there was no treaty provision in the Mexican Treaty that required the offender be informed of his susceptibility to other prosecutions in his state of origin.[115] This issue was dealt with in the Transfer To Or From Foreign Countries Act, which clearly states that the offenders consent to be transferred to or from the U.S. must be verified by a magistrate and that consent must be given with the full knowledge of the consequences of the transfer[116] and with the right to counsel pursuant to the statute.[117] This is very important because the courts will not allow a prisoner to waive his constitutional due process rights without being fully aware of the consequences of such a waiver. In both of these transfer situations once the consent to transfer is made it is irrevocable.[118] The statute specifically states that if a court determines in a proceeding initiated by the prisoner that the transfer was not accomplished according to the terms of the treaty or the laws of the Administering State, he may be returned upon the request of the Sentencing State to complete his sentence.[119]

Initiating the Transfer Process

Under the International Transfer of Prisoner Treaties a transfer request (petition or application) can be made by three different methods or a combination of these: (1) the sentenced person may submit his request to one of the states;[120] (2) the Sentencing State may

---

112 Abramovsky & Eagle, *supra* note 7, at 286.

113 INTERNATIONAL CRIMINAL LAW, CASES AND MATERIALS, 282 (Jordan J. Paust *et al.* eds., 1996).

114 U.S.-Turkey Sentence Treaty, *supra* note 5, at art. VI.

115 Abramovsky & Eagle, *supra* note 7, at 295.

116 18 U.S.C. § 4107(a) deals with the verification of consent by an offender for a transfer from the United States. 18 U.S.C. § 4108 (a) deals with the verification of consent by an offender for a transfer to the United States.

117 18 U.S.C. § 4109.

118 18 U.S.C. §§ 4107(b)(4), 4108(b)(4).

119 18 U.S.C. §§ 4107(b)(3), 4108(b)(3), 4114.

120 U.S.-France Sentence Treaty, *supra* note 5, at art. 11 (a); U.S.-Mexican Sentence Treaty, *supra* note 2, at art IV (1); U.S.-Canada Sentence Treaty, *supra* note 3, at art. III (3); OAS Convention, *supra* note 6, at art. V (1).

The U.N. Model Agr. Tran. For. Pris., *supra* note 9, at art. I (4) allows a prisoner or one of his close relatives to express an interest in the transfer procedure to either the Sentencing or Administering State.

make the request;[121] (3) the Administering State may make a transfer request.[122] The requests should be in writing, indicating the identity of the sentenced person and sent through diplomatic channels.[123] Some treaties require that the consul of the Administering State acknowledge that the prisoner is giving his consent voluntarily and with full knowledge of the consequences of the transfer.[124] The Administering State should promptly inform the Sentencing State of its decision on the request.

The treaties operate on the presumption that the foreign prisoner would wish to return to the state of his nationality, but nothing compels the prisoner to accept the transfer,[125] in fact the treaties are quite clear that the prisoner's consent is required for any transfer under the treaties.[126] Regardless of the method by which the transfer request is initiated, it is necessary that all three of the parties agree to the transfer. There is nothing in the treaties which compels the states to agree to the transfer. Administrative intercession in the respective states may be sought by the petitioning offender's counsel, family or friends. The U.S. Attorney General has indicated that all petitions and applications shall be entertained, provided that they comply with the applicable treaties and legislation in force. (Close relatives are also permitted to request a prisoner transfer under the U.N. Model Agreement.[127]) While the Attorney General may be willing to entertain all requests for transfer, the lack of regulations means a prisoner does not know the criteria which will be considered and it will be very difficult to successfully challenge the refusal of the transfer request.[128]

The French Treaty contains provisions on the mandatory and discretionary refusals of requests for transfer. Art. 4 states that a transfer of a sentenced person shall be refused: "(a) if the sentence leading to the request is based on facts that have formed the object of a final judgement in the Administering State; (b) if enforcement of the sentence is barred by

---

[121] U.S.-France Sentence Treaty, *supra* note 5, at art. 11 (b); U.S.-Mexican Sentence Treaty, *supra* note 2, at art. IV (1); U.S.-Canada Sentence Treaty, *supra* note 3, at art. III (3); Euro. Conv. Trans. Sent. Per., *supra* note 6, at art. 2 (3); OAS Convention, *supra* note 6, at art. V (1).

U.N. Model Agr. Tran. For. Pris., *supra* note 9, at art. I (4).

[122] U.S.-France Sentence Treaty, *supra* note 5, at art. 11 (c); U.S.-Bolivia Sentence Treaty, *supra* note 5, at art. V (1) and (2); U.S.-Peru Sentence Treaty, *supra* note 5, at art. V (1) and (2); U.S.-Panama Sentence Treaty, *supra* note 5, at art. V (1) and (2); U.S.-Thailand Sentence Treaty, *supra* note 5, at art. III (2); Euro. Conv. Trans. Sent. Per., *supra* note 6, at art. 2 (3); OAS Convention, *supra* note 6, at art. V (1); U.N. Model Agr. Tran. For. Pris., Art. I (4).

[123] U.S.-France Sentence Treaty, *supra* note 5, at art. 12; U.S.-Bolivia Sentence Treaty, *supra* note 5, at art. V (3); U.S.-Panama Sentence Treaty, *supra* note 5, at art. V (1) and (2); U.S.-Thailand Sentence Treaty, *supra* note 5, at art. III (2); Euro. Conv. Trans. Sent. Per., *supra* note 6, at art. 5; OAS Convention, *supra* note 6, at art. V (2).

[124] U.S.-France Sentence Treaty, *supra* note 5, at art 12 (2); U.S.-Bolivia Sentence Treaty, *supra* note 5, at art. V (10); U.S.-Peru Sentence Treaty, *supra* note 5, at art. V (3) and (9); U.S.-Panama Sentence Treaty, *supra* note 5, at art. III (6).

[125] Reynolds v. Ralston, No. 79-3232-CV-S-WRC (W.D.Mo. filed June 1980) concerned a U.S. citizen sentenced in Mexico, when Reynolds appeared before a U.S. magistrate in Mexico authorized under 18 U.S.C. § 4108 to conduct verification proceedings, Reynolds refused to execute the consent. At a later hearing, without Reynolds being present, the magistrate appointed a guardian who signed the petition for Reynolds' transfer. At this time there was no finding by either the psychiatrist or verifying officer that Reynolds was incompetent to execute a knowing or voluntary consent. On this basis the District Judge directed that Reynolds be released. *Cited in* Robert E. Dalton, *Protecting United States Citizens Abroad Through Treaties: United States Treaties on the Execution of Penal Sentences, in* INTERNATIONAL ASPECTS OF CRIMINAL LAW, 195-196 (1981).

[126] 18 U.S.C. §§ 4107(a), 4108(a).

[127] U.N. Model Agr. Tran. For. Pris., *supra* note 9, at art. I (4).

[128] Scalise v. Thornburgh, 891 F.2d 640 (7th Cir. 1989).

limitation under the law of either State."[129] The states have discretion to refuse the transfer under Art. 5: (1) where either state considers the transfer will jeopardize its sovereignty, its security, its public policy, the basic principles relating to the organization of criminal jurisdiction under its legal system or any other of its essential interests; (2) where the competent authorities of the Administering State have decided to abandon, or to initiate proceedings based on the same facts; (3) where the facts upon which the conviction is based are also the object of proceedings in the Administering State; (4) where the sentenced person has not paid any sums, fines, court costs, damages or any other pecuniary penalties imposed upon him by the judgement.[130]

The Thai Treaty specifies that the parties have discretion to refuse a transfer where the Sentencing State considers that the transfer would jeopardize its sovereignty, security or public order, or where the prisoner is also a national of the Sentencing State.[131] This would seem to make dual nationals ineligible for transfer under this treaty.

The Turkish Treaty has a similar provision allowing for the refusal of transfer requests. Art. V of the Turkish Treaty seems to envision that transfers will not be refused, in whole or in part, except in the following situations:

> (a) Where enforcement would run counter to the fundamental principles of the legal system of the [Administering] state; or (b) Where the [Administering] state considers the offense for which the sentence was passed to be of a political nature or connected with such an offense or a purely military one; or (c) Where the enforcement would be contrary to the international undertakings of the [Administering] state; or (d) Where the act is already the subject of proceedings in the [Administering] state or where the [Administering] state decides to institute proceedings in respect of the act; or (e) Where the competent authorities in the [Administering] state have decided not to take proceedings or to drop proceedings already begun, in respect of the same act; or (f) Where the act was committed outside the territory of the [Sentencing] State; or (g) Where the [Administering] state is precluded from satisfying the requirements of its law relating to implementation of this Treaty or is otherwise unable to enforce the judgement; or (h) Where under the law of the [Administering] state the sanction imposed can no longer be enforced because of the lapse of time; or (i) Where at the time of the offense, that age of the sentenced person was such that he could not have been proceeded against in the [Administering] state; (j) Where the enforcement is contrary to the rule 'Ne Bis in Idem'.[132]

Some of these grounds for refusal of transfer are covered in other treaties as conditions necessary before a prisoner is eligible for transfer.

Waiver Consent

---

129 U.S.-France Sentence Treaty, *supra* note 5, at art. 4.

130 U.S.-France Sentence Treaty, *supra* note 5, at art. 5 (d).

131 U.S.-Thailand Sentence Treaty, *supra* note 5, at art. II (7).

132 "The character of *ne bis in idem* prevents the retrial or punishment of a person already subject to a final judgement on the merits for the same offense. . . ." INTERNATIONAL CRIMINAL LAW, CASES AND MATERIALS, *supra* note 113, at 577.

Consent by the offender is a precondition to transfer. The obligation of the Sentencing State to inform the prisoner of his rights under an International Transfer of Prisoners Treaty depends on the provisions of the individual treaty. The multilateral treaties, Canadian and French treaties require the Sentencing State to provide the prisoner with this information.[133] The Thai Treaty states that each party may inform an offender who is within the scope of the present treaty of the substance of the treaty.[134] As stated previously, the consent of the prisoner must be obtained before the transfer can take place. The enabling legislation requires that this consent be made voluntarily and with full knowledge of the consequences of the transfer.[135] In order to ensure this, the statute provides a right to counsel and requires verification by a U.S. magistrate or judge;[136] a federal public defender will be appointed for indigent prisoners. If a prisoner initiates the transfer request these safeguards would still apply.

The prisoner's consent involves two things: (1) he must consent to the transfer to the Administering State; and (2) he must waive his right to judicial review and collateral attacks of his sentence or conviction in the Administering State.[137] It is this waiver that has led to constitutional questions about the validity of these treaties. The main questions are: (a) whether it is legitimate for the U.S. to imprison U.S. citizens under foreign convictions which may have been obtained in violation of that citizen's constitutional rights; and (b) whether limitations placed upon the transferred prisoner's access to U.S. courts to challenge the validity of their confinement is constitutional.[138]

As to the first question of whether the U.S. may legitimately imprison U.S. citizens for foreign convictions which were obtained in violation of his constitutional rights, the government concluded that the voluntariness of a prisoner's waiver would not be vitiated by the conditions in foreign jails[139] based on judicial authority.[140] In certain circumstances where the actions of the foreign authorities fell significantly below the acceptable minimum U.S. standards that a waiver may not withstand scrutiny. A more favorable solution would be to separate the waiver of judicial review of the sentence from the consent to transfer,

---

[133] U.S.-Canada Sentence Treaty, *supra* note 3, at art. III (2); Euro. Conv. Trans. Sent. Per., *supra* note 6, at art. 4 (1); OAS Convention, *supra* note 6, at art. IV (1); U.N. Model Agr. Tran. For. Pris., *supra* note 9, at art I (4).

[134] U.S.-Thailand Sentence Treaty, *supra* note 5, at art. III (1).

[135] U.S. v. Fleishman, 684 F.2d 1339, 1346 (9th Cir. 1982). The Ninth Circuit permitted the prior "uncounseled" Mexican convictions of the defendants to be considered in sentencing because the defendants had been involved in similar drug-related offences and had not learned from their experiences. There was no need for a sentencing rehearing since the district judge was not under the belief that the foreign conviction would have been valid under the U.S. Constitution.

Boyden v. Bell, 631 F.2d 120, 123 (9th Cir. 1980). The Ninth Circuit stated that the prisoner's reclassification as a "recidivist offender" was not a modification of his sentence since it did not extend the sentence of the foreign court. (However, this may have grave consequences for the prisoner in the future if he is convicted again and may be liable for an enhancement of sentence.)

[136] 18 U.S.C. §§ 4107, 4108; 28 U.S.C. § 636(g).

[137] 18 U.S.C. §§ 4107(b)(1), 4108(b)(1).

[138] Szpilzinger, *supra* note 10, at 720.

[139] *Id.* at 722-723.

[140] *Id.* at 723 n. 106, *citing* United States *ex rel.* Delman v. Butler, 390 F. Supp. 606 (E.D.N.Y. 1975), *citing* Brady v. United States, 397 U.S. 742 (1970). The *Delman* Court stated that "the coercive impact of the Hobson's choice of compromising valuable constitutional rights out of fear of greater punishment should they be asserted in full, does not of itself constitute impermissible coercion." *Delman*, 309 F. Supp. at 609.

although both should be pre-conditions to transfer.[141] The implementing legislation only calls for a consent to transfer which impliedly includes the waiver.[142]

This issue was addressed in *Rosado v. Civiletti*,[143] where the petitioners sought a writ of *habeas corpus* claiming that their due process rights were violated by their continued detention following their transfer from a Mexican jail. In this case the petitioners were arrested while on vacation. They were never informed of the charges against them and repeatedly tortured. They were convicted without being given the opportunity to answer the charges against them, confront the witnesses against them or seek the assistance of counsel. They were sentenced to nine years imprisonment and were routinely beaten and in constant fear of their lives. The Second Circuit found the petitioners showed their convictions "manifested a shocking insensitivity to their dignity as human beings and were obtained under a criminal process devoid of even a scintilla of rudimentary fairness and decency."[144] The court held that federal courts did have the authority to hear due process claims raised by citizens imprisoned within the territorial jurisdiction of the U.S.[145] The court looked at the actions the petitioners complained of and found that the rationale which would justify the grant of the *habeas corpus* writ would be one which would deter government action. In this case the court was in no position to deter any actions because they were committed by Mexican officials acting within the Mexican jurisdiction and without any American involvement. The court stated that "[a]lthough the Bill of Rights does apply extraterritorially to protect American citizens against the illegal conduct of United States agents . . . it does not and cannot protect our citizens from the acts of a foreign sovereign committed within its territory."[146] The court further stated that while the "Constitution cannot limit the power of a foreign sovereign to prescribe procedures for the trial and punishment of crimes committed within its territory, it does govern the manner in which the United States may join the effort."[147] (This is the same rationale which would dictate whether the courts should apply the exclusionary rule when a foreign conviction is based upon evidence which would have been excluded in an American court.[148]) The court found that the petitioners were estopped from arguing that their continued imprisonment, based on their foreign convictions, violated their rights to due process of law when they had voluntarily[149] and intelligently agreed to

---

141 Szpilzinger, *supra* note 10, at 723, *citing* the Senate, *Transfer of Offenders and Administration of Foreign Penal Sentences: Hearings on S-1682 Before the Subcomm. on Penitentiaries and Corrections of the Senate Comm. on the Judiciary,* 95th Cong., 1st Sess. (1977) at 144 (statement of M. Cherif Bassiouni).

142 18 U.S.C. §§ 4107(b)(1), 4108(b)(1).

143 Rosado v. Civiletti, 621 F.2d 1179 (2nd Cir. 1980).

144 *Id.* at 1182.

145 *Id.*

146 *Id.* at 1189.

147 *Id.* at 1195-1196.

148 U.S. v. Patterson, 812 F.2d 1188 (9th Cir. 1987). The court also permitted the use of a voluntary statement made, without Miranda warnings, to a Secret Service Agent. (The defendant had stipulated as to the voluntariness of the statement. *Id.* at 1192.) This statement occurred after the defendant was severely beaten by Mexican officials, but the U.S. agent did not know about the beating. *Id.* at 1193. The statement made to the U.S. agent prior to a Miranda warning was permitted to establish probable cause for a search warrant. *Id.* at 1193-1194. The court expressed no view as to other uses of the statement.

149 The court analogized the voluntariness of the petitioners' waiver with the voluntariness of guilty pleas stating:

> In our view the choice that faces an American imprisoned in Mexico in deciding whether to transfer more closely resembles a decision confronted by nearly every criminal defendant today: whether to plead guilty and accept a set of specified sanctions ranging from probation to a possibly long prison sentence, or to stand trial and face unknown dispositions ranging from possible acquittal to a severe maximum sentence or even death.

forego their rights to challenge the validity of their foreign conviction viewed in the light of their available alternatives.[150] The court gave consideration to the other U.S. citizens imprisoned abroad and the effect that allowing the petitioners to rescind their waiver, it stated: "In holding these petitioners to their bargain, we by no means condone the shockingly brutal treatment to which they fell prey. Rather, we hold open the door for others similarly victimized to escape their torment."[151] It would seem that political considerations still play a role with the Mexican Transfer of Prisoners Treaty.[152]

The same issue arose in the cases of *Mitchell v. United States*[153] and *Pfeifer v. United States Bureau of Prisons*.[154] In *Mitchell* the prisoner claimed that his consent was involuntary because he would have agreed to anything in order to leave the Mexican prison. The court accepted the prisoner's claims but denied the writ because the Mexican judgment was immune from constitutional attack and it found that Mitchell had knowingly and voluntarily waived his rights to challenge the Mexican conviction.[155] The court in *Pfeifer* similarly denied the prisoner relief stating "[t]he Treaty does not create new rights which enable a foreign convict to have a review of an otherwise final foreign judgement."[156] The Ninth Circuit concentrated on the prisoner's agreement not to challenge the conviction. The court stated that the waiver of rights must be voluntarily and knowingly made, with the benefit of competent counsel and that "[a]n offender's consent to be transferred pursuant to the Treaty is a constitutionally valid waiver of any constitutional rights he might have regarding his conviction."[157]

Rosado also addressed the second question of whether limitations placed upon the transferred prisoner's access to U.S. courts to challenge the validity of their confinement is constitutional. The court stated that the petitioners had a right to test their continued confinement in a U.S. court.[158] It held that "a petitioner incarcerated under federal authority pursuant to a foreign conviction cannot be denied all access to a United States court when he presents a persuasive showing that his conviction was obtained without the benefit of any process whatsoever."[159]

> In the plea bargaining context, as in the case at bar, the choice involves liberty and incarceration on both sides of the equation.

Rosado, 621 F.2d at 1190.

It further stated: "the voluntariness of a given plea is to be judged by whether it was a knowing, intelligent act 'done with sufficient awareness of the relevant circumstances and likely consequences.'" *Id.* at 1191, *citing* Brady v. United States, 397 U.S. 742, 748 (1970).

150 *Rosado*, 621 F.2d at 1199.

151 *Id.* at 1200-1201.

152 After the decision in Velez v. Nelson, 475 F. Supp. 865 (D.Conn. 1979), *rev'd sub nom.* Rosado v. Civiletti, 621 F.2d 1179 (2nd Cir. 1980), where the court granted *habeas corpus* relief because of the abuse the petitioners had suffered while incarcerated in Mexico, the Mexican Government threatened to suspend all future transfers under the treaty. Szpilzinger, *supra* note 10, at 726-727.

153 Mitchell v. U.S., 483 F. Supp. 291 (E.D. Wis. 1980).

154 615 F.2d 873 (9th Cir. 1980).

155 The court stated: ". . . the petitioner argues that this consent was not voluntarily given since he would have agreed to nearly anything to secure his release from the Mexican prison. This fact alone, however, does not vitiate the voluntariness of the consent, since the Constitution does not forbid 'the making of difficult judgements.' McMann v. Richardson, 397 U.S. 759, 769 (1970)." *Mitchell*, 483 F. Supp. at 294.

156 *Pfeifer*, 615 F.2d at 876.

157 *Id.*

158 *Rosado*, 621 F.2d at 1197.

159 *Id.* at 1198.

Review of Sentence or Conviction

One of the main reasons that the consent of the prisoner is such an important prerequisite to the transfer of prisoners is that he is waiving his right to challenge the foreign conviction when he gives his consent. The Sentencing State retains the exclusive jurisdiction over any proceedings which are intended to challenge, modify, or set aside the sentences handed down by the courts of the Sentencing State. This is clearly set forth in the enabling legislation in 18 U.S.C. §§ 4107(b)(1)[160] and 4108(b)(1).[161] Since there is no requirement that the offences be identical, the Administering State does have the option to either continue the enforcement of the sentence or convert the sentence, where it will substitute the penalty imposed by the Sentencing State for one that is provided by its own legislation.[162] In both of these cases the prisoner would be entitled to any credit he has earned towards his sentence.[163] There was also uncertainty as to whether it is the U.S. Parole Commission or the Bureau of Prisons who was responsible for calculating and applying the foreign credits,[164] this will soon be a moot point since the U.S. Parole Commission will be abolished on Nov. 1, 1997.[165] Because the Administering State is entitled to convert the transferred prisoner's sentence, there has been speculation as to whether this would modify the transferred prisoner's sentence contrary to treaty provisions.[166]

The U.S. has adopted the U.S. Sentencing Guidelines,[167] which effectively replaces the role of the Parole Commission, and as a result it converts the sentence of a transferred prisoner under its guidance. The Parole Commission treated the foreign conviction as if it were a conviction handed down by a U.S. District Court.[168] This had an effect on how

---

160 18 U.S.C. § 4107(b)(1) states: "only the appropriate courts in the United States may modify or set aside the conviction or sentence, and any proceedings seeking such action may only be brought in such courts."

161 18 U.S.C. § 4108(b)(1) states: "only the country in which he was convicted and sentenced can modify or set aside the conviction or sentence, and any proceedings seeking such action may only be brought in that country."

162 Sherman, *supra* note 8, at 523.

163 18 U.S.C. § 4105. Powell v. U.S. Bureau of Prisons, 695 F.2d 868, 871 (5th Cir. 1983) dealt with the application of work credit towards the sentence of a transferred prisoner and held that grant or revocation of credits will be carried out according to the laws of the Administering State.

164 *See,* Asare v. U.S. Parole Comm'n, 2 F.3d 540 (4th Cir. 1993); Ajala v. U.S. Parole Comm'n, 997 F.2d 651 (9th Cir. 1993). *But see* Cannon v. U.S. Parole Comm'n, 973 F.2d 1190 (5th Cir. 1992) (hereinafter *Cannon II*), where the Fifth Circuit held that the Parole Commission, rather than the Bureau of Prisons, was required to make the release date determination.

This will become a moot point as of Nov. 1, 1997, this is the date the Parole Commission is abolished pursuant to Pub.L. 98-473, 98 Stat. 2027.

165 The U.S. Parole Commission will be abolished 10 years after the implementation of the U.S. Sentencing Guidelines. 18 U.S.C. §§ 4201-4218 (1994 & Supp. 1997) *repealed by* Pub.L. 98-473, 98 Stat. 2027.

166 Sherman, *supra* note 8, at 545-547. *Cannon II*, 973 F.2d 1190 (5th Cir. 1992); Trevino-Casares v. U.S. Parole Comm'n, 992 F.2d 1068, 1070 (10th Cir. 1993), where the Bureau of Prisons makes the determination.

167 U.S. Sentencing Comm'n, Federal Sentencing Guidelines Manual (1994-95 ed) [hereinafter Federal Sentencing Guidelines], *cited in* Sherman, *supra* note 8, at 532 n. 246.

168 28 C.F.R. § 2.62(a)(1). Trevino-Casares v. U.S. Parole Comm'n, 992 F.2d 1068 (10th Cir. 1993). In this case, the Tenth Circuit found that the Parole Commission had incorrectly translated the prisoner's foreign sentence so as to foreclose the application of service credits. The manner in which the sentence was translated was tantamount to the imposition of a federal sentence and therefore appealable to the Court of Appeals. *Id.* at 1069-1070. Generally, the matter of a prisoner's service credits is a matter for *habeas corpus* review, not direct appeal, although the Tenth Circuit did address the issue of credits in this case. *Id.* at 1070.

sentences were converted.[169] 18 U.S.C. § 4105 requires that an offender serving a prison sentence in a foreign country who is transferred to the U.S. shall remain in custody under the same conditions and for the same period of time as an offender who had been sentenced by a court in the U.S. He will also be eligible for credits for time served and good time. Under the various treaties, the Administering State is not permitted to extend the sentence imposed by the Sentencing State. There have been a number of cases litigating the manner in which sentences are converted and how credits are awarded and applied.[170] In *Cannon II* the court held that the combined period of imprisonment and supervised release had to equal the term imposed by the Sentencing State, any lesser period would amount to a modification of sentence, which was prohibited by the treaty.[171] The Fifth Circuit held that where the Parole Commission used the Federal Sentencing Guidelines to convert the foreign sentence into a period less than the foreign sentence, the foreign sentence must serve as the statutory minimum[172] (but this sentence shall include the total period of incarceration plus the period of supervised release[173]). A different panel of the Fifth Circuit found in *Paura v. United States Parole Commission*[174] that a foreign sentence will not necessarily be considered a minimum mandatory sentence if the Federal Guidelines allow for a computation less than the foreign sentence. As a result of the conflicting authority the question of what amounts to a modification of sentence is unclear. The mandatory application of the Federal Sentencing Guidelines to prisoners' sentences will be a consideration in future transfers which must be clearly explained to the prisoner in order for his consent to be valid.

The treaties envision that each party shall regulate by legislation the extent, if any, to which it will entertain collateral attacks[175] upon the convictions or sentences handed down by it in the cases of offenders who have been transferred by it. Upon being informed by the Sentencing State that the conviction or sentence has been set aside or otherwise modified, the Administering State shall take appropriate action in accordance with such information.[176] The Sentencing State shall inform the Administering State without delay of any decision or action taken in its territory which terminates the right of enforcement. The competent authorities of the Administering State shall terminate administration upon being informed of any decision or action as a result of which the sentence ceases to be enforceable.[177]

---

169 Herrmann v. Meese, 849 F.2d 101 (3rd Cir. 1988). Here the prisoner was convicted in the United Kingdom of possessing counterfeit currency. The Third Circuit held that although the treaty provided that the foreign sentence could be adapted by the Administering State this was a permissive provision and the treaty was not violated if the sentence was not adapted.

170 Powell v. U.S. Bureau of Prisons, 695 F.2d 868 (5th Cir. 1983); Paura v. U.S. Parole Comm'n, 18 F.3d 1188 (5th Cir. 1994); Cannon v. U.S. Parole Comm'n, 961 F.2d 82 (5th Cir. 1992) [hereinafter *Cannon I*], *reh'g denied*, *Cannon II*, 973 F.2d 1190 (5th Cir. 1992); Herrmann v. Meese, 849 F.2d 101; Asare v. U.S. Parole Comm'n, 2 F.3d 540 (4th Cir. 1993); Trevino-Casares v. U.S. Parole, Comm'n, 992 F.2d 1068; Boyden v. Bell, 631 F.2d 120 (9th Cir. 1980); Hamilton v. U.S., 464 F. Supp. 210 (M.D. Fla. 1979).

171 *Cannon II*, 973 F.2d at 1192. In making this finding the court found that it had erred in the case of Thorpe v. U.S. Parole Comm'n, 902 F.2d 291 (5th Cir. 1990). *See Cannon II*, at 973 F.2d at 1195.

172 *Cannon II*, 973 F.2d at 1196.

173 *Id.* at 1192.

174 18 F.3d 1188 (5th Cir. 1994).

175 *Cannon II*, 973 F.2d at 1193. The Fifth Circuit stated that "[t]he prohibition against direct or collateral attacks upon the sentence in any court except the foreign sentencing court, however, does not otherwise preclude or suspend the transferee's right to seek a writ of habeas corpus on other matters related to the manner of execution of the sentence." (footnote omitted).

176 U.S.-Canada Sentence Treaty, *supra* note 3, at art. V.

177 U.S.-France Sentence Treaty, *supra* note 5, at art. 6 (2).

Generally the Sentencing State shall retain the power to pardon or grant amnesty to the offender, and the Administering State shall release the offender when advised by the Sentencing State.[178] Both the European Convention[179] and the U.N. Model Agreement[180] have a provision which would enable both the Sentencing State and the Administering State to grant pardon or amnesty, this provision is not found in any of the other treaties.

Transfer of Documents and Records

The Sentencing State must provide the Administering State with the necessary documents to enable it to supervise the remainder of the prisoner's sentence. These documents vary under each treaty.[181] If the Administering State considers that it has received insufficient information, it may request additional information; some treaties also address the question of translation of documents. Due to the discretionary nature of the transfer process, a failure by the Sentencing State to provide the necessary documents may prevent the Administering State from accepting the transfer. Although some of the information in such documents and records may be damaging to the offender, there will be an opportunity to attack its reliability or admissibility in any U.S. judicial proceeding. These materials may also contain other information beneficial to the offender.

Transferred Prisoner's Civil Rights

The Transfer To or From Foreign Countries Act addresses the question of loss of rights and disqualification. It provides that a person may suffer only such losses and

---

178 U.S.-Mexican Sentence Treaty, *supra* note 2, at art. V (2); U.S.-Peru Sentence Treaty, *supra* note 5, at art. VII; U.S.-Panama Sentence Treaty, *supra* note 5, at art. VII; U.S.-Thailand Sentence Treaty, *supra* note 5, at art. IV; U.S.-Canada Sentence Treaty, *supra* note 3, at art. IV (1).

179 Euro. Conv. Trans. Sent. Per., *supra* note 6, at art. 12 states: "Each Party may grant pardon, amnesty or commutation of the sentence in accordance with its Constitution or other laws."

180 U.N. Model Agr. Tran. For. Pris., *supra* note 9, at art. IV (22) states: "Both the sentencing and the administering State shall be competent to grant pardon and amnesty."

181 Examples of the documents provided by the Sentencing State to the Administering State include: (1) the original or certified copy of the judgment (trial record) convicting the offender. [U.S.-Bolivia Sentence Treaty, *supra* note 5, at art. V (8); U.S.-Peru Sentence Treaty, *supra* note 5, at art. V (7); U.S.-Panama Sentence Treaty, *supra* note 5, at art. V (8)] The judgment shall certify the enforceability of the judgment, and it shall make as clear as possible the circumstances of the offense, the time and place it was committed and its designation in law, (termination date). [U.S.-France Sentence Treaty, *supra* note 5, at art. 13 (1); U.S.-Mexican Sentence Treaty, *supra* note 2, at art. IV (7); U.S.-Thailand Sentence Treaty, *supra* note 5, at art. III (5) and (6); U.S.-Canada Sentence Treaty, *supra* note 3, at art. III (8); Euro. Conv. Trans. Sent. Per., *supra* note 6, at art. 4 and 6; OAS Convention, *supra* note 6, at art. V (7)]. When the Administering State considers such information insufficient, it may request at its expense, principal portions of the trial record or such additional information as it deems necessary. [U.S.-Peru Sentence Treaty, *supra* note 5, at art. V (7); U.S.-Panama Sentence Treaty, *supra* note 5, at art. V (8)] (2). The Sentencing State shall provide full information about the length of the sentence remaining to be served, about the periods spent in pre-trial and post-trial custody, as well as remissions of sentence granted or earned. [U.S.-France Sentence Treaty, *supra* note 5, at art. 13 (2); U.S.-Mexican Sentence Treaty, *supra* note 2, at art. IV (7); U.S.-Bolivia Sentence Treaty, *supra* note 5, at art. V (8); U.S.-Thailand Sentence Treaty, *supra* note 5, at art. III (5); U.S.-Canada Sentence Treaty, *supra* note 3, at art. III (8); Euro. Conv. Trans. Sent. Per., *supra* note 6, at art. 6 (2)(b); OAS Convention, *supra* note 6, at art. V (7)]. Whenever appropriate the Sentencing State will send any medical or social reports on the sentenced person, information about the treatment he has received in the Sentencing State and recommendations for his further treatment [Euro. Conv. Trans. Sent. Per., *supra* note 6, at art. 6 (2)(d)].

disqualification as "would result from the fact of the conviction in the foreign country."[182] The purpose of this provision is to eliminate disabilities, but neither the treaties nor the statute provides for expungement of records of transferred offenders. This is a serious problem in the U.S. because such persons would have a U.S. detention record based on a foreign conviction without the right of expungement, which might have been available had the conviction been rendered by a U.S. court. The possible judicial outcome is uncertain for an action for expungement of records brought under the Act as presently written. The court could apply all relevant provisions on expungement to such records by analogy without the need for specific legislation.

There are positive and negative effects the Administering State's recognition of a foreign penal judgment may have on a prisoner. The positive effect is that it allows the enforcement of the judgment in the Administering State and the prisoner can transfer back to his country of origin.[183] A further indirect benefit is that if a sentencing court knows the administering court will enforce and supervise its judgments, it may be willing to grant the offender probation or suspend his sentence.[184]

A negative effect of the recognition of a foreign judgment in the Administering State is the impact it may have on a prosecution or sentence in the offender's home state, *e.g.*, it may impact on the severity of a sentence if the offender's prior criminal record is a factor.[185] Foreign convictions can be used to enhance the sentence for a subsequent criminal conviction of a crime committed in the Administering State.[186] Foreign convictions may also subject the person to a less favorable classification in light of their criminal record in the Administering State, *e.g.*, he could be classified as a first offender in the Sentencing State and a recidivist offender in the Administering State, and this could have grave consequences if he is convicted again[187] or affect his classification upon transfer[188] and eligibility for parole. However, this negative effect of recognition of a foreign judgment may actually be to the offender's benefit by prohibiting a new prosecution under the doctrines of double jeopardy and *ne bis in idem.*[189] Some treaties specifically refer to the fact that the transferred prisoner should not suffer any additional disabilities under the law of the Administering State other than those created by the fact of his conviction.[190]

Miscellaneous Provisions

The cost of the transfer and detention subsequent transfer is generally the responsibility of the Administering State. The Administering State shall not be entitled to be reimbursed

---

182 18 U.S.C. § 4112 deals with "Loss of rights, disqualification," it states:
An offender transferred to the United States to serve a sentence imposed by a foreign court shall not incur any loss of civil, political, or civic rights nor incur any disqualification other than those which under the laws of the United States or of the State in which the issue arises would result from the fact of the conviction in the foreign country.

183 Dunlap, *supra* note 24, at 842-843.

184 *Id.* at 843.

185 *Id.*

186 U.S. v. Fleishman, 684 F.2d 1339, 1346 (9th Cir. 1982).

187 *Id.*

188 Boyden v. Bell, 631 F.2d 120 (9th Cir. 1980).

189 Dunlap, *supra* note 24, at 843.

190 U.S.-Mexican Sentence Treaty, *supra* note 2, at art. V (6); U.S.-Canada Sentence Treaty, *supra* note 3, at art. IV (6); U.S.-Thailand Sentence Treaty, *supra* note 5, at art. V (3).

for its costs. If either state does not approve the transfer it should communicate that decision without delay and without the necessity of explaining its reasons. There is usually provision made between the states, especially in the multilateral conventions, concerning the translation of documents and related costs. The governments will usually address the question of the authenticity and admissibility of documents in order to facilitate the transfer process. The place of transfer will be decided by the governments in question; the Administering State will be responsible for custody and transport of the prisoner once he is delivered by the Sentencing State. It is also the responsibility of the Administering State to secure the necessary cooperation of third states when the prisoner is being transferred either from the third state or through that state. Some treaties have requirements, either mandatory or upon request, for status reports to be provided concerning those prisoners who have been transferred.[191]

Each treaty provides a mechanism by which the treaty will be ratified and come into force. Depending on the terms of the treaty, it will either be renewed automatically every two-to-five years or it will remain in force for the state until that state wishes to terminate their participation in the treaty.

Enforcement of Sentence

A distinction must be made between recognition, enforcement, and execution of foreign judgments[192] because historically the U.S. has held the position that it does not enforce foreign penal judgments.[193] The Full Faith and Credit Clause of Article IV of the U.S. Constitution does not even require the enforcement of sister-state penal judgments. The U.S. has been giving effect to foreign penal judgments, and one of the rationales behind this is that prisoner transfers can be viewed as a form of cooperation rather than a traditional form of assistance.[194] "In a typical prisoner transfer case . . . the sentencing state does not *need* the assistance of another in enforcing the judgement, as the former is capable of accommodating the foreign prisoner in some fashion if necessary. Rather, the sentencing state (or a foreign prisoner with the help of either the sentencing state or his home country) merely *wants* the assistance of the other in enforcing the sentence."[195]

---

191 U.S.-Turkey Sentence Treaty, *supra* note 5, at art. XVII (3); U.S.-France Sentence Treaty, *supra* note 5, at art. 16; U.S.-Canada Sentence Treaty, *supra* note 3, at art. IV (5); U.S.-Thailand Sentence Treaty, *supra* note 5, at art. V (5); U.S.-Panama Sentence Treaty, *supra* note 5, at art. VI (3); U.S.-Mexican Sentence Treaty, *supra* note 2, at art. V (5); U.S.-Bolivia Sentence Treaty, *supra* note 5, at art. VI (3), U.S.-Peru Sentence Treaty, *supra* note 5, at art. VI (3).

192 *See* U.S.-Mexican Sentence Treaty, *supra* note 2, at art. V; U.S.-Canada Sentence Treaty, *supra* note 3, at art. IV (1); *Hearings on Ex. D and Ex. H Before the Senate Comm. on Foreign Relations,* 95th Cong., 1st Sess. 262-65 (1977) (statement of M. Cherif Bassiouni).

193 In *The Antelope*, 23 U.S. (10 Wheat.) 66, 123 (1825), Chief Justice Marshall declared: "The Courts of no country execute the penal laws of another." It may be noted that the penal sentences involved in the Mexican and Canadian treaties do not include fines or criminal sanctions other than restraints on liberty, confinement, probation, parole, and some forms of supervision. *But see* Cooley v. Weinberger, 518 F.2d 1151 (10th Cir. 1975) (Iranian conviction for the murder of a woman's spouse was given legal effect in the context of determining her eligibility to receive social security benefits). *See also* Mary Anne Foran-Rogers, *Recognition of Foreign Countries' Penal Judgements—Cooley v. Weinberger*, GLOBE, vol. 14, no. 6, at 1-7 (Illinois State Bar Association Newsletter 1977).

194 Sherman, *supra* note 8, at 511.

195 *Id.* (footnotes omitted).

The sentence imposed by the Sentencing State shall be directly enforceable[196] in the Administering State and shall be in accordance with the law (and procedures) of that state,[197] including those governing conditions for service of imprisonment, confinement or other deprivation of liberty, probation and parole, and those providing for the reduction of the term of imprisonment, confinement or other deprivation of liberty by parole, conditional release or otherwise.[198] As stated earlier, the Administering State can substitute its own penalty for a similar offense, but the nature of this penalty or measure shall correspond insofar as possible to the sentence imposed.[199] The Administering State may not impose a sentence which would aggravate, by its nature or duration, the penalty imposed by the Sentencing State nor exceed the maximum prescribed by the law of the Administering State.[200] Only the Administering State is competent to make decisions on the manner of the execution of the transferred prisoner's sentence, including decisions on the length of the period of incarceration. The Administering State shall take account of the information provided to it by the Sentencing State (i.e., length of time to be served, pre-trial and post-trial custody, remissions of sentence granted or earned).[201]

Post-transfer Issues

Most of the litigation involving American citizens will occur after their transfer to the U.S., because the U.S. courts will not have any jurisdiction to consider the individual case before that time.

Parole, Probation and Supervision

The Transfer To Or From Foreign Countries Act states that except as otherwise provided, "an offender serving a sentence of imprisonment in a foreign country transferred to the custody of the Attorney General shall remain in the custody of the Attorney General under the same conditions and for the same period of time as an offender who had been committed to the custody of the Attorney General by a court of the U.S. for the period of time imposed by the sentencing court."[202] The transferred prisoners are to be given credit for all the time served in the Sentencing State,[203] including credit for good time, labor or any other credit.[204] The implementing statute makes all matters relating to probation and parole

---

196 Boyden v. Reno, 106 F.3d 267, 269 (9th Cir. 1997). The Ninth Circuit denied *habeas corpus* relief to a prisoner arrested for a parole violation. The court found that although the prisoner's sentence could not be extended beyond the foreign sentence, U.S. law governed the effect of a parole violation on the computation of the sentence. Here the parole violation had the effect of tolling the parolee's sentence after the warrant had issued. *Id.*

197 U.S.-Thailand Sentence Treaty, *supra* note 5, at art. V (1).

198 The Third Circuit held that a defendant was required to serve a sentence of home detention in the United States, so that the probation authorities could adequately monitor his compliance, and address any violations. U.S. v. Porat, 17 F.3d 660, 670 (3rd Cir. 1994).

199 U.S.-France Sentence Treaty, *supra* note 5, at art. 9 (3).

200 U.S.-France Sentence Treaty, *supra* note 5, at art. 9 (3); U.S.-Canada Sentence Treaty, *supra* note 3, at art. IV (3).

201 U.S.-France Sentence Treaty, *supra* note 5, at art. 9 (4).

202 18 U.S.C. § 4105(a).

203 18 U.S.C. § 4105(b).

204 18 U.S.C. § 4105(c)(1).

subject to U.S. jurisdiction in accordance with 18 U.S.C. § 4203.[205] Accordingly, whereas an offender may have been ineligible for parole in the foreign country, upon his arrival in the U.S., immediate eligibility for parole is possible under section 4106(c). This grants transferees greater benefits than persons convicted under U.S. law. Under 18 U.S.C. §§ 4104(c) and 4106(b), transferred probationers and parolees shall be treated as if their conviction had been rendered by a U.S. court, but presumably without the benefit of collateral attacks upon the conviction.

Procedural Challenges

If the transfer was not accomplished in accordance with the terms of the treaty or laws of the Administering State, this may provide a basis to attack the validity of the transfer and detention in a proceeding initiated by the prisoner or on his behalf.[206] This does not necessarily mean that the prisoner would be released, instead it would bring into play the "return" provision of the statute.[207] Whether the prisoner would be returned to the Sentencing State to complete his sentence after he successfully challenged the validity of the transfer and detention would depend on the validity of the return procedures. If the prisoner successfully attacked the validity of the transfer prior to his transfer, he would remain in the Sentencing State.

Waiver as a Bar to Judicial Challenges and Sentence

The waiver of the prisoner's rights to challenge his conviction at the time of transfer is a cause for concern as already stated. This waiver acts not only to protect the conviction itself but also bars collateral attacks[208] including the writ of *habeas corpus*.[209] The three most

---

205 18 U.S.C. § 4106. 18 U.S.C. § 4203 gives power to the Parole Commission to establish guidelines. This statute will be repealed on Nov. 1, 1997, pursuant to Pub. L. 98-473, 98 Stat. 2027.

206 18 U.S.C. §§ 4107(b)(3), 4108(b)(3).

207 18 U.S.C. §§ 4107(b)(3), 4108(b)(3).

208 Kass v. Reno, 83 F.3d 1186, 1189-90 (10th Cir. 1996). The court found that the U.S.-Mexican Sentence Treaty barred U.S. courts from exercising jurisdiction over collateral attacks on Mexican convictions after prisoners were transferred to the U.S. This limitation was viewed as a proper exercise of the treaty power and the authority of Congress to limit federal court jurisdiction. The court found there was a valid waiver and since U.S. prisoners have no right of relief available to them from U.S. courts while they are in foreign prisons, they lose nothing by agreeing not the challenge the Mexican conviction in U.S. courts. *Id.* at 1190. The court further held that the prisoner forfeited his potential benefits of early-release good-time credits when he agreed to transfer to the U.S. since U.S. law governed conditions for early release. *Id.* at 1192.

The Sixth Circuit rejected the prisoner's *habeas corpus* petition finding that he had voluntarily waived his right to collaterally attack the foreign conviction. The court stated: "[T]he scope of the Suspension Clause of the Constitution with respect to habeas corpus relief, should be limited to what was recognized at the time the Constitution was adopted when habeas corpus relief was granted only where the criminal court lacked jurisdiction. Habeas corpus relief to collaterally attack a judgement was not heard of." Kanasola v. Civiletti, 630 F.2d 472 (6th Cir. 1980), *citing* Swain v. Pressley, 430 U.S. 372, 384 (1976) (Burger, C.J., concurring).

209 The concept of *habeas corpus* lies so close to the roots of constitutional notions of due process that its elimination, other than as provided under the President's emergency powers by the Constitution, is unlikely to withstand judicial scrutiny.

The problems relating to rendering *habeas corpus* relief unavailable by jurisdictional allocation or otherwise are discussed in authorities collected in Note, *Constitutional Problems in the Execution of Foreign Penal Sentences: The Mexican-American Prisoner Transfer Treaty*, 90 HARV. L. REV. 1500,1510-1517 nn. 53-90 (1977). *See also* discussion of this problem in Abramovsky & Eagle, *supra* note 7, at 300-02 (discussing that preclusion of *habeas corpus* relief is unnecessary). *See also* Rosado v. Civiletti, 621 F.2d 1179, 1197-98 (2d Cir. 1980) (the

likely attacks on the validity of the prisoner's waiver are: (1) where the prisoner may have been imprisoned in such dire or inhumane conditions that this alone may be considered coercive and would invalidate the waiver; (2) where the prisoner was not adequately informed that he was waiving his appeal rights when he consented to the transfer to the Administering State; and (3) where the provisions of the treaty and implementing legislation are not followed. The courts are very reluctant to allow these challenges, even where the facts clearly demonstrate that the prison conditions were far below what would be considered acceptable,[210] although the prisoner will be allowed some access to the courts despite the waiver.[211] The implementing legislation attempts to deal with the second and third basis for attack, 18 U.S.C. §§ 4107 and 4108 require that the prisoner's consent is voluntary and with full knowledge of the consequences. The same sections require that the waiver and consent to transfer must be given in the presence of a judicial officer and with the advice of counsel, if this is not done the prisoner may be sent back to the Sentencing State. These provisions ensure that there is no valid basis for attack in most transfer situations.

Collateral Attack of Sentence or Conviction.

The treaties expressly reserve jurisdiction over collateral attacks on convictions and sentences to the Sentencing State which imposed them.[212] The transfer of custody of detainees is premised on two assumptions: (1) that a foreign penal judgment can be enforced in the U.S.; and (2) the United States Constitution and criminal justice standards do not apply extraterritorially. Both assumptions are, however, only partially justified in light of U.S. law and practice. It is relevant in this context to note that the treaties with Mexico and Canada are based upon these two premises and presume to preclude their judicial testing in the respective domestic courts by prohibiting collateral attack on the conviction and sentence rendered abroad. The same limitations appear in the implementing statutes of the three states.

1. *Recognition, Enforcement, and Execution of Foreign Judgment.* A distinction has been made between recognition, enforcement, and execution of foreign judgments.[213] Foreign penal judgments have nonetheless been given effect in the U.S., *e.g.*, the U.S. gives effect to a foreign penal judgment under extradition procedures by relying on it to execute the return of a person accused or convicted in a foreign state.[214] Should the treaties on transfer of prisoners be merely an administrative consequence of recognizing a foreign penal judgment, then the scheme finds strong support in the long-established practice of extradition. It must also be noted, however, that if such an interpretation is not given to the scheme, and U.S. courts should consider the treaties to be a form of enforcement of foreign penal judgments, some precedent exists for that approach. These precedents include the

---

court holds that transferred prisoners do have a right to challenge convictions of foreign courts rendered without any process whatsoever). *See also* Jordan J. Paust, *The Unconstitutional Detention of Mexican and Canadian Prisoners by the United States Government*, 12 VAND. J. TRANSNAT'L L. 67 (1979).

[210] Rosado v. Civiletti, 621 F.2d at 1182.

[211] *Id.* at 1197-1198.

[212] U.S.-Canada Sentence Treaty, art. V; U.S.-Mexican Sentence Treaty, art. VI.

[213] *See supra* text accompanying note 193. *See* U.S.-Mexican Sentence Treaty, *supra* note 2 and U.S.-Canada Sentence Treaty; *supra* note 3; *Hearings on Ex. D and Ex. H Before the Senate Comm. on Foreign Relations*, 95th Cong., 1st Sess. 262-65 (1977) (statement of M. Cherif Bassiouni).

[214] M. CHERIF BASSIOUNI, INTERNATIONAL EXTRADITION IN U.S. LAW AND PRACTICE (1996). *See also* United States v. Rauscher, 119 U.S. 407 (1886).

enforcement in the U.S. of penal sanctions imposed by foreign consular officers,[215] the enforcement of status of forces agreements,[216] and case law in giving judicial effect to foreign penal judgment.[217]

2. *U.S. Public Policy in Minimum Standards of Criminal Justice, the Recognition and Enforcement of Foreign Penal Judgements and the Execution of Foreign Penal Sentences.* It is a well-settled principle of private international law that no state shall recognize or enforce the judgments of other states if they are contrary to the public policy of the recognizing or enforcing state.[218] The question therefore arises whether certain minimum standards of criminal justice, as embodied in the meaning of the Due Process Clauses of the Fifth and Fourteenth Amendments to the Constitution and those specific rights enunciated in the Bill of Rights which have been incorporated in the Due Process Clause, must be observed in the process leading to the recognition, enforcement or execution of a foreign penal judgment which the U.S. will recognize, enforce, or execute. Nothing in the Constitution requires that only systems of criminal justice which are similar to that of the U.S. be given recognition. In fact, the position of the United States Supreme Court on extradition[219] and on the constitutionality of status of forces agreements[220] has been to respect other criminal justice systems even though they may be very different from that of the U.S. Nevertheless, contrary to established jurisprudence, there are some indications that certain constitutional protections may be held applicable extraterritorially whenever U.S. agents abroad engage in behavior which is violative of certain constitutional principles.[221]

---

[215] *See* Gordon B. Baldwin, Department of State, *Report on Prisoner Exchange Agreements* (July 20, 1976) (unpublished), who refers to various U.S. precedents on the enforcement of foreign criminal penalties such as § 5 of the Service Courts of Friendly Foreign Forces Act. Act of June 30, 1944, c. 326, § 5, 58 Stat. 644, (codified at 22 U.S.C. § 705 (1994)), which authorizes confinement in federal facilities of persons serving sentences imposed by foreign courts-martial. Baldwin also refers to the enforcement in the U.S. of criminal sanctions imposed by the foreign consular officers under 22 U.S.C. §§ 256-258a (1994). Sections 256-258a were upheld in Dallemagne v. Moisan, 197 U.S. 169 (1905), thus providing a precedent for enforcement of foreign final judgments.

[216] Facilities and Areas and the Status of United States Armed Forces in Korea, July 9, 1966, U.S.-Kor. 17 U.S.T. 1677.

[217] *See* Cooley v. Weinberger, 518 F.2d 1151 (10th Cir. 1975).

[218] *See* ALBERT A. EHRENZWEIG & ERIK JAYME, 2 PRIVATE INTERNATIONAL LAW, 81-83 (1973); HERBERT F. GOODRICH & EUGENE F. SCOLES, CONFLICT OF LAWS, 14-15 (4th ed. 1964); EDWARD S. STIMSON, CONFLICT OF CRIMINAL LAWS, 20-26 (1936); Monrad G. Paulsen & Michael I. Sovern "*Public Policy" in the Conflict of Laws*, 56 COLUM. L. REV. 969 (1956). *Cf.* Huntington v. Attrill, 146 U.S. 657 (1892) (enforcement between domestic states); Intercontinental Hotels Corp. (Puerto Rico) v. Golden, 203 N.E.2d 210 (N.Y. 1964) (enforcement of gambling debt incurred in Puerto Rico).

[219] *See* Factor v. Laubenheimer, 290 U.S. 276 (1933).

[220] *See e.g.*, Wilson v. Girard, 354 U.S. 524 (1957); Reid v. Covert, 351 U.S. 487 (1956), *rev'd on rehearing*, 354 U.S. 1 (1957); Holmes v. Laird, 459 F.2d 1211 (D.C. Cir. 1972); Major James R. Coker, THE STATUS OF VISITING MILITARY FORCES IN EUROPE: NATO-SOFA, A COMPARISON, *in* 2 TREATISE, *supra* note 14, at 115.

[221] Traditionally the U.S. has accepted the fact that *in personam* jurisdiction secured by fraud or force is recognizable by the courts. Frisbie v. Collins, 342 U.S. 519 (1952); Ker v. Illinois, 119 U.S. 436 (1886). Recently, however, there are indications that if illegal conduct is performed by a U.S. agent abroad, it could be the basis of the application of the exclusionary rule if the conduct is patently offensive to due process. *See* United States v. Toscanino, 500 F.2d 267 (2d Cir. 1974). The holdings in *Toscanino* was subsequently limited in U.S. *ex rel.* Lujan v. Gengler, 510 F.2d 62 (2d. Cir. 1975); and United States v. Lira, 515 F.2d 68 (2d Cir. 1975). *See generally* M. Cherif Bassiouni, *Unlawful Seizures and Irregular Rendition Devices as Alternatives to Extradition,* 7 VAND. J. TRANSNAT'L L. 25 (1973), *reprinted in* BASSIOUNI, INTERNATIONAL EXTRADITION AND WORLD PUBLIC ORDER, 121-201 (1974). On the question of territorial application of U.S. law, *see* The Exchange, 11 U.S. (7 Cranch) 116 (1812); 6 MARJORIE WHITEMAN, DIGEST OF INTERNATIONAL LAW 889-904 (1968); M. Cherif Bassiouni, *Theories of Jurisdiction and Their Application in Extradition Law and Practice*, 5 CAL. W. INT'L L. J. 1 (1974); S. Z. Feller,

Therefore, inquiry should be made into the facts upon which the conviction was based to find out to what extent a U.S. agent may have been involved in practices which are patently offensive to due process standards.[222]

On its face, there is nothing in the criminal justice system of Canada (or other common law countries) which would warrant a finding that it is incompatible with the public policy of minimum criminal justice standards of the U.S.[223] However, civil law and non-common law countries' criminal justice systems represent a greater variation from that of the U.S. Nevertheless, the non-common law systems of criminal justice theoretically offer certain minimum guarantees which make them somewhat compatible with the criminal justice standards of the U.S. These systems often afford an accused the right to be adequately informed of the charges, the right to counsel, the right to open and public hearings conducted by an impartial judge, the right to competent testimony in determining guilt and the right to appeal.[224] For example, at least on its face, the criminal justice system of Mexico does not patently violate the public policy of the U.S.

There is, however, a public policy in the U.S. with respect to minimum standards of criminal justice as applied. The execution of a foreign penal sentence rendered on the basis of violations of such standards would warrant the denial of execution of such judgments. Such issues can only be determined on an *ad hoc* basis, however, since the denial of such minimum standards to a given individual would depend upon the facts and circumstances of each case. It is very unlikely that the United States Supreme Court would hold the treaties to be unconstitutional on the grounds that they purport to execute the penal sentences of a

---

Jurisdiction over Offenses with a Foreign Element, in 2 TREATISE, *supra* note 14, at 5; B. J. George Jr., *Extraterritorial Application of Penal Legislation*, 64 MICH. L. REV. 609 (1966).

[222] In this regard *see* Abramovsky & Eagle, *supra* note 7, at 302-305, where they argue that the U.S. becomes a joint venturer just by carrying out a foreign sentence. Accordingly, they would seem to argue that any transfer would require that the foreign conviction must meet full U.S. constitutional safeguards.

[223] MICHAEL P. BOLTON, PROCEDURE AND PRACTICE IN CANADIAN CRIMINAL TRIALS (1974); CASES AND MATERIAL ON CANADIAN CRIMINAL PROCEDURE (Anthony Hooper ed., 1974); ARTHUR E. POPPLE, CRIMINAL PROCEDURE MANUAL (1956); ROGER E. SALHANY, CANADIAN CRIMINAL PROCEDURE (2d ed. 1972).

[224] Robert L. Miller, *Mexican Jails and American Prisoners*, 51 LOS ANGELES B.J. 439, 442-43 (1976); and WALTER G. SANCHEZ, DERECHO MEXICANO DE PROCEDIMENTOS PENALES (4th ed. 1977). All constitutional guarantees of the Constitution Politica de los Estados Unidos Mexicanos are expressly made applicable to foreigners by article 33 of the document. The guarantees relevant here include:

Art. 14—Prosecution must occur before previously established tribunals in which the essential formalities of procedure shall be complied with in conformance with laws then in effect.

Art. 16—Arrest orders will be issued only by competent judicial authority upon a complaint supported by an affidavit of a reliable person, except when the crime occurs in the presence of a detaining officer.

Art. 19—No detention may exceed three days unless there is a formal judicial order stating the crime alleged and its elements, and establishing a *prima facie* showing of responsibility.

Art. 20(II)—The accused may not be compelled to testify against himself nor held incommunicado for the purpose of coercion.

Art. 20(III)—The accused shall be told in a public hearing within 48 hours of formal detention the name of his accuser and the nature of the charges.

Art. 20(IV)—The accused has a right to confront and cross examine witnesses against him.

Art. 20(V)—An accused may call his own witnesses and is entitled to court assistance in procuring them.

Art. 20(VI)—The accused is entitled to a public trial by a judge or a jury of his peers if the sentence faced is more than one year in prison.

Art. 20(IX)—The accused has the right to be represented by counsel of his choice or by public defender.

Art. 20(X)—Time served prior to sentencing is subtracted from the sentence.

Art. 22—Excessive and unusual penalties are forbidden.

ICL PROCEDURE, *supra* note 1, at 249-250 n.36.

foreign state whose minimum criminal justice standards are not patently offensive *per se* to U.S. standards. What the U.S. courts are more likely to consider is whether on an *ad hoc* basis the foreign conviction of an American citizen transferred to the U.S. under the terms of the treaties for execution of a sentence has been secured in a manner so patently offensive to U.S. minimum standards of criminal justice that the further detention of such a person by the U.S. would be contrary to its public policy. Thus, the concern should not be over the constitutionality of the treaties, but over the criteria of minimum standards of criminal justice which the United States Supreme Court would hold to be applicable to American citizens abroad as a condition to the use of the power processes of this country to execute the sentence of a foreign penal judgment. U.S. courts would have to inquire into the facts supporting the foreign conviction, which would entail recognition of a right to make a collateral attack on the conviction in *habeas corpus* proceedings. Such collateral attack is ostensibly barred by the treaties and the implementing act as discussed above. This preclusion as set forth in provisions of both the treaties and the implementing statute is likely to be held unconstitutional, unless the courts interpret the provisions in such a broad manner that collateral attacks fall within the scope of the provisions.

The waiver of the rights to collaterally attack the conviction which is specified in the treaties[225] will of course be raised[226] by the government of the Sending State whenever a transferred offender would seek to attack the validity of his foreign conviction in a U.S. court. There is some authority to the effect that such a waiver, if made knowingly and intelligently in the presence of a U.S. magistrate, is constitutionally valid when made with the assistance of counsel and in order to gain certain benefits otherwise not available.[227] A court may hold that such a waiver was not freely given because an offender was in detention at the time of making the waiver. However, the existence of such conditions, as well as the coercive effect on the waiver of the transferred offender, will have to be proven and therefore will necessarily be determined on an *ad hoc* basis, and to date these challenges have not been successful.

In the U.S. *habeas corpus* proceedings would require, at a minimum, that the U.S. detaining authority demonstrate the applicability of the treaty and implementing statute to the offender, and that the scope of inquiry could by some rational extrapolation be extended to the basis for the offender's conviction and sentence. Success at this stage would result in the release of the offender, but it would also result in the government's attempt to return the released offender to the Sending State.

---

[225] Faretta v. California, 422 U.S. 806 (1975) (for the waiver of right to assistance of counsel); Boykin v. Alabama, 395 U.S. 238, 243 (1969) (where guilty plea operates as waiver of rights against self-incrimination, to trial by jury and to confrontation of witnesses); Bumper v. North Carolina, 391 U.S. 543 (1968). *But see* Rosado, 621 F. 2d at 1199-1201 (2d Cir. 1980) (the court upheld the waiver given by the petitioners, reasoning that petitioners gained certain benefits by the transfer, and that invalidating the waiver would prejudice those persons still incarcerated in Mexican prisons). *See also* Pfeifer v. United States Bureau of Prisons, 615 F.2d 873, 877 (9th Cir. 1980) (court upheld petitioner's waiver as valid).

[226] This seems to be what the court held in Rosado v. Civiletti, 621 F.2d 1179 (2d Cir. 1980), while recognizing a right to collateral attack the court found that this right had been validly waived by the petitioners.

[227] *See* Tollett v. Henderson, 411 U.S. 258 (1973).

Return of Released Offenders

The implementing statute purports to create a mechanism that would operate speedily and smoothly to return to the state that convicted and sentenced the transferred offenders released by U.S. courts before their sentences are completed.[228] On its face, this provision would appear to render attacks on the validity of transfer of collateral attacks on conviction and sentence useless, since success in such attack would merely result in the return of the offender to the state from whence he came. In *Tavarez v. Attorney General*[229] the prisoner had been convicted in the U.S. of voluntary manslaughter and sentenced to eight years. He was later transferred to Mexico under the treaty and escaped from a Mexican prison and returned to the U.S. The Fifth Circuit found that the Attorney General could apprehend a transferred prisoner who had committed a crime in the U.S. and returned to the U.S. The state did not lose its power to hold a convicted prisoner[230] by transferring him to another country pursuant to treaty.[231] The return of Tavarez did not necessitate extradition proceedings if he was given an opportunity to consult with a lawyer and petition for *habeas corpus* relief concerning the legality of his return.[232]

The validity of section 4114 is questionable, however. To examine its validity the provision should be considered in relation to extradition, as that practice is followed in the various signatory states.

Extradition under the United States-Mexico and the United States-Canada extradition treaties requires not only that the offense for which the relator is sought be criminal in both states (double criminality), but also that it be among those offenses expressly listed in the extradition treaty.[233] The treaties on transfer of prisoners, however, permit transfer whenever the offense in question is criminal in both states, regardless of whether it is listed in any treaty as an extraditable offense. Thus, the possibility exists under 18 U.S.C. § 4114 of the Act that an offender could be returned for an offense which is not among those listed in the extradition treaty between the parties. While a state may make a request for extradition at any time, under section 4114, the request for return must be made within six months of the offender's release. Finally, as a precondition to extradition, federal law requires that probable cause be shown in a hearing.[234] That is, it must be shown that there is sufficient evidence of the offender's guilt of the crime in question as would justify holding him for trial under U.S. law.[235] Under section 4114, it is sufficient to produce a certified copy of the conviction rendered by the court of the state seeking the offender's return. Should a U.S.

---

[228] 18 U.S.C. § 4114.

[229] 668 F.2d 805 (5th Cir. 1982).

[230] "The statute also makes clear that while the laws of the receiving nation shall govern the manner in which the sentence is served, the laws of the sentencing nation shall continue to govern both the validity of the conviction and the term of the sentence." *Id.* at 808.

[231] *Id.* at 809.

[232] *Id.* at 810-811.

[233] Treaty of Extradition, Feb. 22, 1899, U.S.-Mexico, Art. II, 31 Stat. 1818; Treaty on Boundaries, Slave Trade, Extradition (Webster-Ashburton Treaty), Aug. 9, 1842, U.S.-Great Britain, Art. X, 8 Stat. 572; Treaty of Extradition (Supplementary Convention), July 12, 1889, U.S.-Great Britain, Art. I, 26 Stat. 1508; *see* 18 U.S.C. § 3184 (1994).

[234] 18 U.S.C. § 3184.

[235] *See* 18 U.S.C. § 3184. *See also* Beck v. Ohio, 379 U.S. 89 (1964) (reasonableness of probable cause); Brinegar v. United States, 338 U.S. 160, 172-173 (1949) (distinction between probable cause and proof of guilt); Carroll v. United States, 267 U.S. 132, 161-162 (1925) (definition of probable cause).

court find that such "return" procedures are merely a form of extradition under another label, it may consider that section 4114 discriminates against returnees as opposed to extraditees who are governed by 18 U.S.C. § 3181 *et seq.*, without any rational basis and consider that provision a denial of equal protection.[236]

Probable cause as required by 18 U.S.C. § 3184 for extradition may be deemed inapplicable to "return" procedures under section 4114 because, in this case, the return is predicated on a conviction rather than an accusation. If, however, the release was due to a finding by the releasing U.S. court that the conviction was in violation of minimum criminal justice standards, the question remains how another U.S. court could rely on the validity of that judgment to order the offender's return. Should the Sending State request extradition of the transferred offender rather than requesting his return under section 4114, the Requesting State would have to meet a variety of requirements not included in the simple return mechanism of section 4114. Therefore, release without return is a possibility.

Other Policy Considerations

The initial policy consideration behind the transfer of prisoner treaties was a humanitarian one which would help alleviate the additional hardships suffered by a prisoner serving his sentence in a foreign prison. More recently, additional considerations have come to the fore. One of the practical results of transferring a prisoner back to his home country was that it frees up tax dollars and prison facilities that would otherwise be spent accommodating the needs of the foreign prisoner, which could then be used to reduce the strain on overcrowded prison facilities or for benefit other prisoners who were citizens.[237] However, there has been a shift in the U.S. domestic attitude towards crime and punishment and this may affect the issue of prisoner transfer treaties and how they are used and the motivations behind subsequent negotiations. It should also be realized that U.S. Sentencing Guidelines may have an effect on these treaties.

The humanitarian concerns that prompted the adoption of prisoner transfer treaties still exist. Prison systems, particularly in developing countries, may be unwilling or unable to improve the conditions in which foreign prisoners are held. Indeed, if they were able to do so they may prefer to pass these benefits on to their own nationals instead of the foreign prisoner. The main problems facing a foreign prisoner are the cultural and language barriers, the lack of rehabilitation programs and refusal of conditional release programs (due to the perceived flight risk), and the general prejudice faced by the foreign prisoner, other prisoners, and prison staff. Prisoner transfer treaties were seen as a way to alleviate these additional burdens on the foreign prisoner. However, it would appear that these treaties are now also seen as a method by which the sentencing country can expel foreign prisoners[238] and relieve itself of a considerable financial strain, which is a motive which runs contrary to the humanitarian goals of these treaties.

---

236 On denial of equal protection for an unjustified discriminatory reason, *see* United States Dept. of Agriculture v. Moreno, 413 U.S. 528 (1973) (interference with rights to food stamps); Shapiro v. Thompson, 394 U.S. 618 (1969) (right to travel interstate); Skinner v. Oklahoma *ex rel* United States, 316 U.S. 535 (1942) (statute propounding the sterilization of "habitual criminals" who had been convicted two or more times of "felonies involving moral turpitude"). The compelling state interest standard is characterized in Printing Indus. of the Gulf Coast v. Hill, 382 F. Supp. 801, 808-09 (S.D. Tex. 1974); Coleman v. Coleman, 291 N.E.2d 530, 534 (Ohio 1972).

237 Sherman, *supra* note 8, at 495, 541.

238 *Id.* at 537.

Conclusion

On the whole, the Transfer of Prisoners Treaties have been an important step in the international community's attempt to both combat crime and ensure that the individual prisoners do not suffer a double penalty for their crimes. Although other motivations may have entered into the equation, the overriding one still seems to be humanitarian. It has been recognized by the courts that the U.S. cannot impose its own standards of criminal procedure on other states. This has led to claims that these treaties are open to abuse by the U.S. and its officials. However, it must be realized that when a U.S. national commits a crime in a foreign country he runs the very substantial risk of becoming subject to that country's criminal laws. There is no obligation on the foreign country to return any prisoner to his country of origin, and this is recognized by the waiver provisions that have been incorporated into the enabling legislation. A prisoner must give a voluntary and knowing waiver of his rights to challenge the conviction. This has been strictly imposed by the courts and while it appears to be unfair to those prisoners who have suffered torture and abuse in foreign prisons, it has also been the mechanism by which they have returned to their home country. It would appear that these treaties have not been used as a means to "spring" U.S. citizens, and this has meant they have become an effective tool in the international approach to criminal law and procedure. These treaties are not a perfect solution to this problem, but they are the best solution for this time. The challenge is to try to eliminate the causes of the injustices resulting when innocent persons are tortured and convicted and subsequently transferred to their home country to serve a sentence for crimes they did not commit.

Appendix 12

Convention Between the United States and France on the Transfer of Sentenced Persons

Transmitting:
The Convention Between the United States of America and the Republic of France on the Transfer of Sentenced Persons, Signed at Washington on January 25, 1983

MARCH 1, 1984—Convention was read the first time, and together with the accompanying papers, referred to the Committee on Foreign Relations and ordered to be printed for the use of the Senate.

LETTER OF TRANSMITTAL

THE WHITE HOUSE, March 1, 1984.

To the Senate of the United States:

With a view to receiving the advice and consent of the Senate to ratification, I transmit herewith the Convention Between the United States of America and France on the Transfer of Sentenced Persons, which was signed at Washington on January 25, 1983.

I transmit also, for the information of the Senate, the report of the Department of State with respect to the treaty.

The Convention would permit citizens of either nation who had been convicted in the courts of the other country to serve their sentences in their home country; in each case the consent of the offender as well as the approval of the authorities of the two Governments would be required.

This Convention is significant because it represents an attempt to resolve a situation which has inflicted substantial hardships on a number of citizens of each country and has caused concern to both Governments. The treaty is similar to those currently in force with Bolivia, Canada, Mexico, Panama, Peru and Turkey. I recommend that the Senate give favorable consideration to this Convention at an early date.

RONALD REAGAN.

LETTER OF SUBMITTAL

DEPARTMENT OF STATE,
Washington, February 15, 1984.

The PRESIDENT,
The White House.

THE PRESIDENT: I have the honor to submit a Convention Between the United States of America and the Republic of France on the Transfer of Sentenced Persons which was signed at Washington on January 25, 1983. I recommend that the Convention be transmitted to the Senate for its advice and consent to ratification.

The Convention is similar to those currently in force with Bolivia, Canada, Mexico, Panama. Peru and Turkey and consistent with a treaty with Thailand which you recently transmitted to the Senate. It would permit citizens of either nation who had been convicted in the courts of the other country to serve their sentences in their home country; in each case the consent of the offender as well as the approval of the authorities of the two Governments would be required.

The treaty is intended to relieve the special hardships on prisoners incarcerated far from home, to improve the prospects for rehabilitation of offenders, and also to relieve the strains that can arise in diplomatic and law enforcement relations between the two countries because of the imprisonment of a number of each country's nationals in the institutions of the other. It constitutes part of an ongoing effort to improve relations between the two countries.

The basic terms of the Convention are as follows: The treaty generally applies to a prisoner who has been convicted and sentenced for an offense punishable as a crime in both the Sentencing State and the Administering State (the country to which the offender is to be transferred) provided that the prisoner is a national of the latter, the sentence is final, no appeal is pending, the sentenced person has at least one year left to serve at the time of the request, and the provisions of the sentence, other than the period of detention, have been complied with. The Convention does not apply to purely military offenses. Requests for transfer must be refused if the sentence leading to the request is based on facts that have formed the object of a final judgment in the Administering State or if enforcement of the sentence is barred by limitation under the law of either State.

Each transfer requires the consent of the prisoner. Article 5 lists the circumstances under which the country which imposed the sentence or the country to which the prisoner is to be transferred may refuse a transfer. The reference in paragraph (a) of that Article to "the basic principles relating to the organization of criminal jurisdiction under its legal system" is designed to permit the United States to continue the policy it has developed under existing treaties of affording to the authorities of a state of the United States which has sentenced a foreign national to incarceration an opportunity to refuse transfer of that national. (*See, e.g.*, Article IV para 5 of the Mexican Treaty, TIAS 8718.)

When a prisoner has been transferred the following procedures govern his treatment: The original sentence is directly enforceable in the Administering States. Deductions for good behavior in prison and during pre-trial confinement are preserved. The Sentencing State retains the power to grant pardon or amnesty. With these exceptions, the execution of the sentence is to be carried out according to the rules and practices prevailing in the Administering State (Article 9). Any collateral attack on the sentence must proceed through the courts of the country which imposed the sentence (Article 7).

The Treaty may be implemented under Public Law 94-144; no new legislation will be proposed.

Respectfully submitted.

GEORGE P. SCHULTZ.

CONVENTION BETWEEN THE UNITED STATES OF AMERICA AND THE REPUBLIC OF FRANCE ON THE TRANSFER OF SENTENCED PERSONS

The Government of the United States of America and the Government of the Republic of France,

Desiring to enable persons under sentence, with their consent, to serve their sentences of deprivation of liberty in the country of which they are nationals in such a way as to facilitate their reintegration into society,

Have resolved to conclude the present Convention.

CHAPTER I
Basic Principles

Article 1

For the purposes of this Convention:

(a) the expression "Sentencing State" means the State in which the offender has been sentenced and from which he is being transferred;

(b) the expression "Administering State" means the State to which the sentenced person is being transferred to serve his sentence;

(c) the term "sentenced person" means any person who has been sentenced by a court of law in the territory of either State and required to serve, in confinement, a sentence involving deprivation of liberty.

Article 2

The application of this Convention is subject to the following conditions:

(a) the offense which leads to a request for transfer would be punishable as a crime under the law of both States;

(b) the sentenced person is a national of the country to which he is to be transferred;

(c) the sentenced person gives his consent;

(d) the sentence referred to in Article 1 is a final and enforceable one; and

(e) at the time of the request for transfer the sentenced person has left to serve a period of at least one year.

Article 3

This Convention shall not apply when the offense for which the offender has been sentenced is a purely military offense.

Article 4

The transfer of a sentenced person shall be refused:

(a) if the sentence leading to the request is based on facts that have formed the object of a final judgement in the Administering State;

(b) if enforcement of the sentence is barred by limitation under the law of either State.

Article 5

The transfer may be refused:

(a) if the transfer is considered by the Sentencing State or the Administering State to be such as to jeopardize its sovereignty, its security, its public police, the basic principles relating to the organization of criminal jurisdiction under its legal system or any other of its essential interest;

(b) if the competent authorities of the Administering State have decided to abandon, or not to initiate, proceedings based on the same facts;

(c) if the facts upon which the conviction is based are also the object of proceedings in the Administering State;

(d) if the sentenced person has not paid any sums, fines, court costs, damages or any other pecuniary penalties imposed upon him by the judgment.

Article 6

1. The Sentencing State shall inform the Administering State without delay of any decision or action taken in its territory which terminates the right of enforcement.

2. The competent authorities of the Administering State shall terminate administration upon being informed of any decision or action as a result of which the sentence ceases to be enforceable.

Article 7

The Sentencing State has the sole right to decide on any action for review of the conviction or sentence.

Article 8

The Sentencing State shall inform sentenced persons of the possibilities open to them under this Convention.

CHAPTER II

Administration of Sentences Involving Deprivation of Liberty

Article 9

1. The sentence imposed by the Sentencing State shall be directly enforceable in the Administering State.

2. The enforcement of the sentence in the Administering State shall be in accordance with the law of that state.
3. If need be under the law, the Administering State may substitute for the penalty imposed by the Sentencing State the penalty or measure provided by its own law for a similar offense. The nature of this penalty or measure shall correspond insofar as possible to that imposed in the sentence to be enforced. The sentence may not aggravate by its nature or duration the penalty imposed by the Sentencing State nor exceed the maximum prescribed by the law of the Administering State.
4. The Administering State alone is competent to take with respect to the sentenced person decisions on the manner of the execution of the sentence, including decisions on the length of the period of incarceration. However, it shall take account of any information furnished by the Sentencing State pursuant to Article 13 of this Convention.

Article 10

The costs of transfer and detention subsequent to transfer are the responsibility of the Administering State.

CHAPTER III
Procedure

Article 11

A transfer request may be submitted by:
(a) the person under sentence himself, who submits a request to this effect to one of the States;
(b) the Sentencing State; or
(c) the Administering State.

Article 12

1. Every request shall be in writing. It shall indicate the identity of the sentenced person and his address in both the Sentencing State and the Administering State.
2. The request shall be completed prior to transfer by a statement taken by a consul of the Administering State acknowledging that the sentenced person's consent was given voluntarily and with full knowledge of the consequences of the transfer.

Article 13

1. The Sentencing State shall send the Administering State the original or a certified copy of the judgment convicting the offender. It shall certify the enforceability of the judgment, and it shall make as clear as possible the circumstances of the offense, the time and place it was committed and its designation in law.
2. The Sentencing State shall provide full information about the length of the sentence remaining to be served, about the periods spent in pre-trial and post-trial custody, as well as remissions of sentence granted or earned.

Article 14

The request shall be addressed to the French Ministry of Justice, if the requesting State is the United States of America, and to the Department of Justice of the United States of America if the requesting State is France.

Article 15

If one of the States deems the information provided by the other to be insufficient to allow it to implement this Convention. it shall request the supplementary information required for this purpose.

Article 16

Either State shall furnish to the other State upon request at any time a complete report on the status of the execution of the penalty of the sentenced person transferred under this Convention

Article 17

All documents produced by either State in accordance with this Convention maybe in English or in French.

Article 18

Documents transmitted by one Contracting State to the other in connection with the application of this Convention shall require no further certification authentication or other legalization to be admissible in any proceeding relating to the application of the Convention in the State receiving such documents.

Article 19

Costs of administration incurred in the Administering State shall not be reimbursed.

Article 20

1. Both States shall cooperate in facilitating the transit through their territory of sentenced persons transferred from a third State.

2. The transit shall be subject to the conditions established for transfer by Articles 2(a), (b), (d) and (e), 3 and 4 of this Convention. Its duration shall not exceed 24 hours. The State which intends to carry out such a transit shall give advance notice to the other State together with all necessary information. No notice shall be required if transport is by air over the territory of the other State and no landing there is scheduled.

CHAPTER IV
Final Provisions

Article 21

1. Each of the Contracting Parties shall notify the other upon the completion of the constitutional procedures required to allow this Convention to come into force. Notification of the completion of these procedures shall be exchanged as soon as possible at Paris.

2. This Convention shall come into force on the first day of the second month after the day such exchange is effected.

3. Each of the Contracting Parties may terminate this Convention at any time by sending the other, through diplomatic channels, written notice of termination. In this case, termination shall take effect one year after the date the said notice is received.

IN WITNESS WHEREOF the undersigned, being duly authorized thereto by their respective Governments, have signed this Convention and hereunto affixed their seals.

DONE in duplicate at Washington in the English and French languages, both equally authentic. this twenty-fifth day of January 1983.

FOR THE GOVERNMENT OF THE
UNITED STATES OF AMERICA
FOR THE GOVERNMENT OF
THE REPUBLIC OF FRANCE

RATIFICATION OF CONVENTION WITH FRANCE ON THE TRANSFER OF SENTENCED PERSONS

June 20,1984—Ordered to be printed
Mr. PERCY, from the Committee on Foreign Relations,
submitted the following

REPORT

[To accompany Treaty Doc. 98-15]

The Committee on Foreign Relations, to which was referred the Convention Between the United States of America and the Republic of France on the Transfer of Sentenced Persons, signed at Washington on January 25,1983, having considered the same, reports favorably thereon without amendment and recommends that the Senate give its advice and consent to ratification thereof.

PURPOSE

The Convention would permit citizens of either Contracting State who had been convicted in the courts of the other country to serve their sentences in their home countries. The consent of the offender to transfer as well as the approval of the authorities of the two Governments would be required in each case.

The Convention is intended to relieve the special hardships on prisoners incarcerated far from home, to improve the prospects for rehabilitation of offenders, and also to relieve the strains that can arise in diplomatic and law enforcement relations between the two countries because of the imprisonment of a number of each country's nationals in the institutions of the other. It constitutes part of an ongoing effort to improve relations between the two countries.

BACKGROUND

The problem of Americans imprisoned abroad for a variety of offenses, especially drug-related ones, has mushroomed during the past fifteen years. In 1983, over 3,000 United States citizens were arrested abroad and over 1,800 remained in jail at the end of that year. This is not just an American problem but involves citizens of many other countries, particularly those of Western Europe.

The solution that developed to cope with this growing problem was the implementation of treaties on the transferability of penal sanctions, otherwise known as prisoner transfer treaties. The underlying purposes of such treaties are to assist in law enforcement. relieve the country in which a foreigner may be imprisoned of an unwanted economic and administrative burden, and promote the social rehabilitation of the offender in his home country where he may be placed in more favorable environment and where he may receive the support of family and friends.

The United States has previously entered into bilateral prisoner transfer treaties with Mexico, Canada, Panama, Peru, Bolivia, and Turkey. In general, these treaties allow the return of prisoners to their home country to serve out their foreign sentence, provided that a set of conditions are met. In 1977, the United States enacted implementing legislation to authorize the transfer of offenders to and from foreign countries (18 U.S.C. 4100-4115).

COMMITTEE ACTION AND RECOMMENDATIONS

The Committee on Foreign Relations held a public hearing on the Convention with France on the Transfer of Sentenced Persons on June 14, 1984 at which time Mr. Daniel McGovern, Deputy Legal Advisor, Department of State and Mr. Mark Richard, Deputy Assistant Attorney General, Department of Justice, testified in its support. Two public witnesses testified, Mr. Nick Navarro of Dade County. Florida, and Mr. Richard Atkins of Philadelphia, Pennsylvania. Both witnesses testified, that if carefully implemented and enforced, the Convention can serve significant law enforcement and humanitarian objectives.

MAJOR PROVISIONS

The Department of State has provided the Committee with the following summary of the Conventions major provisions:

The basic terms of the Convention are as follows: The Treaty generally applies to a prisoner who has been convicted and sentenced for an offense punishable as a crime in both the Sentencing State and the Administering State (the Country to which the offender is to be transferred) provided that the prisoner is a national of the latter, the sentence is final, no appeal is pending, the sentenced person has at least one year left to serve at the time of the request, and the provisions of the sentence, other than the period of detention, have been complied with. The Convention does not apply to purely military offenses. Requests for transfer must be refused if the graph (a) of that Article to "the basic principles relating to the organization of criminal jurisdiction under its legal system" is designed to permit the United States to continue the policy it has developed under existing treaties of affording to the authorities of a state of the United States which has sentenced a foreign national to incarceration an opportunity to refuse transfer of that national. (See, e.g.. Article IV para 5 of the Mexican Treaty, TIAS 8718.)

When a prisoner has been transferred. the following procedures govern his treatment: The original sentence is directly enforceable in the Administering States. Deductions for good behavior in prison and during pre-trial confinement are preserved. The Sentencing State retains the power to grant pardon or amnesty. With these exceptions, the execution of the sentence is to be carried out according to the rules and practices prevailing in the Administering State (Article 9). Any collateral attack on the sentence must proceed through the courts of the country which imposed the sentence (Article 7).

The Treaty may be implemented under Public Law 94-144; no new legislation will be proposed.

ENTRY INTO FORCE

The Convention shall come into force on the first day of the second month after the day such exchange is effected.

RESOLUTION OF RATIFICATION

Resolved, (two-thirds of the Senators present concurring therein). That the Senate advise and consent to the ratification of the Convention Between the United States of America and the Republic of France on the Transfer of Sentenced Persons, signed at Washington on January 25, 1983.

Appendix 13

United States Legislation on Transfer of Prisoners - Title 18 U.S.C.

CHAPTER 306—TRANSFER TO OR FROM FOREIGN COUNTRIES

CHAPTER REFERRED TO IN OTHER SECTIONS

This chapter is referred to in title 10 section 955.

§ 4100. Scope and limitation of chapter

(a) The provisions of this chapter relating to the transfer of offenders shall be applicable only when a treaty providing for such a transfer is in force, and shall only be applicable to transfers of offenders to and from a foreign country pursuant to such a treaty. A sentence imposed by a foreign country upon an offender who is subsequently transferred to the United States pursuant to a treaty shall be subject to being fully executed in the United States even though the treaty under which the offender was transferred is no longer in force.

(b) An offender may be transferred from the United States pursuant to this chapter only to a country of which the offender is a citizen or national. Only an offender who is a citizen or national of the United States may be transferred to the United States. An offender may be transferred to or from the United States only with the offender's consent, and only if the offense for which the offender was sentenced satisfies the requirement of double criminality as defined in this chapter. Once an offender's consent to transfer has been verified by a verifying officer, that consent shall be irrevocable. If at the time of transfer the offender is under eighteen years of age the transfer shall not be accomplished unless consent to the transfer be given by a parent or guardian or by an appropriate court of the sentencing country.

(c) An offender shall not be transferred to or from the United States if a proceeding by way of appeal or of collateral attack upon the conviction or sentence be pending.

(d) The United States upon receiving notice from the country which imposed the sentence that the offender has been granted a pardon, commutation, or amnesty, or that there has been an ameliorating modification or a revocation of the sentence shall give the offender the benefit of the action taken by the sentencing country.

[Added Pub. L. 95-144, § 1, Oct. 28, 1977, 91 Stat. 1212.)

AUTHORIZATION OF APPROPRIATIONS

Section 5(a) of Pub. L. 95-144 provided that: "There is authorized to be appropriated such funds as may be required to carry out the purposes of this Act [which enacted this chapter and sections 955 of Title 10, Armed Forces, and 2256 of Title 28, Judiciary and Judicial Procedure, amended section 636 of Title 28, and enacted provisions set out as notes under sections 3006A, 4100, and 4102 of this titled]."

§ 4101. Definitions

As used in this chapter the term—

(a) "double criminality" means that at the time of transfer of an offender the offense for which he has been sentenced is still an offense in the transferring country and is also an offense in the receiving country. With regard to a country which has a federal form of government, an act shall be deemed to be an offense in that country if it is an offense under the federal laws or the laws of any state or province thereof;

(b) "imprisonment" means a penalty imposed by a court under which the individual is confined to an institution;

(c) "juvenile" means—

(1) a person who is under eighteen years of age; or

(2) for the purpose of proceedings and disposition under chapter 403 of this title because of an act of juvenile delinquency, a person who is under twenty-one years of age:

(d) "juvenile delinquency" means—

(1) a violation of the laws of the United States or a State thereof or of a foreign country committed by a juvenile which would have been a crime if committed by an adult; or

(2) noncriminal acts committed by a juvenile for which supervision or treatment by juvenile authorities of the United States, a State thereof, or of the foreign country concerned is authorized;

(e) "offender" means a person who has been convicted of an offense or who has been adjudged to have committed an act of juvenile delinquency;

(f) "parole" means any form of release of an offender from imprisonment to the community by a releasing authority prior to the expiration of his sentence, subject to conditions imposed by the releasing authority and to its supervision;

(g) "probation" means any form of a sentence to a penalty of imprisonment the execution of which is suspended and the offender is permitted to remain at liberty under supervision and subject to conditions for the breach of which the suspended penalty of imprisonment may be ordered executed;

(h) "sentence" means not only the penalty imposed but also the judgment of conviction in a criminal case or a judgment of acquittal in the same proceeding, or the adjudication of delinquency in a juvenile delinquency proceeding or dismissal of allegations of delinquency in the same proceedings;

(i) "State" means any State of the United States, the District of Columbia, the Commonwealth of Puerto Rico, and any territory or possession of the United States;

(j) "transfer" means a transfer of an individual for the purpose of the execution in one country of a sentence imposed by the courts of another country; and

(k) "treaty" means a treaty under which an offender sentenced in the courts of one country may be transferred to the country of which he is a citizen or national for the purpose of serving the sentence. (Added Pub. L. 95-144, § 1, Oct. 28, 1977, 91 Stat. 1213.)

§ 4102. Authority of the Attorney General

The Attorney General is authorized—

(1) to act on behalf of the United States as the authority referred to in a treaty;

(2) to receive custody of offenders under a sentence of imprisonment, on parole, or on probation who are citizens or nationals of the United States transferred from foreign countries and as appropriate confine them in penal or correctional institutions, or assign them to the parole or probation authorities for supervision;

(3) to transfer offenders under a sentence of imprisonment, on parole, or on probation to the foreign countries of which they are citizens or nationals;

(4) to make regulations for the proper implementation of such treaties in accordance with this chapter and to make regulations to implement this chapter;

(5) to render to foreign countries and to receive from them the certifications and reports required to be made under such treaties;

(6) to make arrangements by agreement with the States for the transfer of offenders in their custody who are citizens or nationals of foreign countries to the foreign countries of which they are citizens or nationals and for the confinement, where appropriate, in State institutions of offenders transferred to the United States;

(7) to make agreements and establish regulations for the transportation through the territory of the United States of offenders convicted in a foreign country who are being transported to a third country for the execution of their sentences, the expenses of which shall be paid by the country requesting the transportation;

(8) to make agreements with the appropriate authorities of a foreign country and to issue regulations for the transfer and treatment of juveniles who are transferred pursuant to treaty, the expenses of which shall be paid by the country of which the juvenile is a citizen or national;

(9) in concert with the Secretary of Health, Education, and Welfare, to make arrangements with the appropriate authorities of a foreign country and to issue regulations for the transfer and treatment of individuals who are accused of an offense but who have been determined to be mentally ill; the expenses of which shall be paid by the country of which such person is a citizen or national;

(10) to designate agents to receive, on behalf of the United States, the delivery by a foreign government of any citizen or national of the United States being transferred to the United States for the purpose of serving a sentence imposed by the courts of the foreign country, and to convey him to the place designated by the Attorney General. Such agent shall have all the powers of a marshal of the United States in the several districts through which it may be necessary for him to pass with the offender, so far as such power is requisite for the offender's transfer and safekeeping; within the territory of a foreign country such agent shall have such powers as the authorities of the foreign country may accord him;

(11) to delegate the authority conferred by this chapter to officers of the Department of Justice. (Added Pub. L. 95-114, § 1, Oct. 28, 1977, 91 Stat. 1214.)

Change of Name

The Secretary and Department of Health, Education, and Welfare was redesignated the Secretary and Department of Health and Human Services by Pub. L. 96-88, title V, § 509(b), Oct. 17, 1979, 93 Stat. 695, which is classified to section 3508(b) of Title 20, Education.

Certification by Attorney General to Secretary of State for Reimbursement of Expenses Incurred under Transfer Treaty

Section 5(b) of Pub. L. 95-144 provided that: "The Attorney General shall certify to the Secretary of State the expenses of the United States related to the return of an offender to the foreign country of which the offender is a citizen or national for which the United States is entitled to seek reimbursement from that country under a treaty providing for transfer and reimbursement."

§ 4103. Applicability of United States laws

All laws of the United States, as appropriate, pertaining to prisoners, probationers parolees, and juvenile offenders shall be applicable to offenders transferred to the United States, unless a treaty or this chapter provides otherwise. (Added Pub. L. 95-144, §1, Oct. 28,1977, 91 Stat. 1215.)

§ 4104. Transfer of offenders on probation

(a) Prior to consenting to the transfer to the United States of an offender who is on probation, the Attorney General shall determine that the appropriate United States district court is willing to undertake the supervision of the offender.

(b) Upon the receipt of an offender on probation from the authorities of a foreign country, the Attorney General shall cause the offender to be brought before the United States district court which is to exercise supervision over the offender.

(c) The court shall place the offender under supervision of the probation officer of the court. The offender shall be supervised by a probation officer, under such conditions as are deemed appropriate by the court as though probation had been imposed by the United States district court.

(d) The probation may be revoked in accordance with section 3653 of this title and rule 32(f) of the Federal Rules of Criminal Procedure. A violation of the conditions of probation shall constitute grounds for revocation. If probation is revoked the suspended sentence imposed by the sentencing court shall be executed.

(e) The provisions of sections 4105 and 4106 of this title shall be applicable following a revocation of probation.

(f) Prior to consenting to the transfer from the United States of an offender who is on probation, the Attorney General shall obtain the assent of the court exercising jurisdiction over the probationer.
(Added Pub. L. 95-144, § 1, Oct. 28, 1977, 91 Stat. 1215.)

§ 4105. Transfer of offenders serving sentence of imprisonment

(a) Except as provided elsewhere in this section, an offender serving a sentence of imprisonment in a foreign country transferred to the custody of the Attorney General shall remain in the custody of the Attorney General under the same conditions and for the same period of time as an offender who had been committed to the custody of the Attorney General by a court of the United States for the period of time imposed by the sentencing court.

(b) The transferred offender shall be given credit toward service of the sentence for any days prior to the date of commencement of the sentence, spent in custody in connection with the offense or acts for which the sentence was imposed.

(c) (1) The transferred offender shall be entitled to all credits for good time, for labor, or any other credit toward the service of the sentence which had been given by the transferring country for time served as of the time of the transfer. Subsequent to the transfer, the offender shall in addition be entitled to credits for good time, computed on the basis of the time remaining to be served at the time of the transfer and at the rate provided in section 4161 of this title for a sentence of the length of the total sentence imposed and certified by the foreign authorities. These credits shall be combined to provide a release date for the offender pursuant to section 4164 of this title.

(2) If the country from which the offender is transferred does not give credit for good time, the basis of computing the deduction from the sentence shall be the sentence imposed by the sentencing court and certified to be served upon transfer, at the rate provided in section 4161 of this title.

(3) A transferred offender may earn extra good time deductions, as authorized in section 4162 of this title, from the time of transfer.

(4) All credits toward service of the sentence, other than the credit for time in custody before sentencing, may be forfeited as provided in section 4165 of this title and may be restored by the Attorney General as provided in section 4166 of this title.

(5) Any sentence for an offense against the United States, imposed while the transferred offender is serving the sentence of imprisonment imposed in a foreign country, shall be aggregated with the foreign sentence, in the same manner as if the foreign sentence was one imposed by a United States district court for an offense against the United States.
(Added Pub. L. 95-144, § 1, Oct. 28, 1977, 91 Stat. 1215.)

SECTION REFERRED TO IN OTHER SECTIONS

This section is referred to in section 4104 of this title.

§ 4106. Transfer of offenders on parole; parole of offenders transferred

(a) Upon the receipt of an offender who is on parole from the authorities of a foreign country, the Attorney General shall assign the offender to the United States Parole Commission for supervision.

(b) The United States Parole Commission and the Chairman of the Commission shall have the same powers and duties with reference to an offender transferred to the United States to serve a sentence of imprisonment or who at the time of transfer is on parole as they have with reference to an offender convicted in a court of the United States except as otherwise provided in this chapter or in the pertinent treaty. Sections 4201 through 4204; 4205(d), (e), and (h); 4206 through 4216; and 4218 of this title shall be applicable.

(c) An offender transferred to the United States to serve a sentence of imprisonment may be released on parole at such time as the Parole Commission may determine

(Added Pub. L. 95-144, § 1, Oct. 28, 1977, 91 Stat. 1216.)

SECTION REFERRED TO IN OTHER SECTIONS

This section is referred to in section 4104 of this title.

§ 4107. Verification of consent of offender to transfer from the United States

(a) Prior to the transfer of an offender from the United States. the fact that the offender consents to such transfer and that such consent is voluntary and with full knowledge of the consequences thereof shall be verified by a United States magistrate or a judge as defined in section 451 of title 28, United States Code.

(b) The verifying officer shall inquire of the offender whether he understands and agrees that the transfer will be subject to the following conditions:

(1) only the appropriate courts in the United States may modify or set aside the conviction or sentence, and any proceedings seeking such action may only be brought in such courts;

(2) the sentence shall be carried out according to the laws of the country to which he is to be transferred and that those laws are subject to change;

(3) if a court in the country to which he is transferred should determine upon a proceeding initiated by him or on his behalf that his transfer was not accomplished in accordance with the treaty or laws of that country, he may be returned to the United States for the purpose of completing the sentence if the United States requests his return; and

(4) his consent to transfer, once verified by the verifying officer, is irrevocable.

(c) The verifying officer, before determining that an offender's consent is voluntary and given with full knowledge of the consequences, shall advise the offender of his right to consult with counsel as provided by this chapter. If the offender wishes to consult with counsel before giving his consent, he shall be advised that the proceedings will be continued until he has had an opportunity to consult with counsel.

(d) The verifying officer shall make the necessary inquiries to determine that the offender's consent is voluntary and not the result of any promises, threats, or other improper inducements, and that the offender accepts the transfer subject to the conditions set forth in subsection (b). The consent and acceptance shall be on an appropriate form prescribed by the Attorney General.

(e) The proceedings shall be taken down by a reporter or recorded by suitable sound recording equipment. The Attorney General shall maintain custody of the records.

(Added Pub. L. 95-144, § 1, Oct. 28, 1977, 91 Stat. 1216.)

SECTION REFERRED TO IN OTHER SECTIONS

This section is referred to in section 4109 of this title; title 28 section 636.

§ 4108. Verification of consent of offender to transfer to the United States

(a) Prior to the transfer of an offender to the United States, the fact that the offender consents to such transfer and that such consent is voluntary and with full knowledge of the consequences thereof shall be verified in the country in which the sentence was imposed by a United States magistrate, or by a citizen specifically designated by a judge of the United States as defined in section 451 of title 28, United States Code. The designation of a citizen who is an employee or officer of a department or agency of the United States shall be with the approval of the head of that department or agency.

(b) The verifying officer shall inquire of the offender whether he understands and agrees that the transfer will be subject to the following conditions:

(1) only the country in which he was convicted and sentenced can modify or set aside the conviction or sentence, and any proceedings seeking such action may only be brought in that country;

(2) the sentence shall be carried out according to the laws of the United States and that those laws are subject to change;

(3) if a United States court should determine upon a proceeding initiated by him or on his behalf that his transfer was not accomplished in accordance with the treaty or laws of the United States, he may be returned to the country which imposed the sentence for the purpose of completing the sentence if that country requests his return; and

(4) his consent to transfer, once verified by the verifying officer, is irrevocable.

(c) The verifying officer, before determining that an offender's consent is voluntary and given with full knowledge of the consequences, shall advise the offender of his right to consult with counsel as provided by this chapter. If the offender wishes to consult with counsel before giving his consent, he shall be advised that the proceedings will be continued until he has had an opportunity to consult with counsel.

(d) The verifying officer shall make the necessary inquiries to determine that the offender's consent is voluntary and not the result of any promises, threats, or other improper inducements, and that the offender accepts the transfer subject to the conditions set forth in subsection (b). The consent and acceptance shall be on an appropriate form prescribed by the Attorney General.

(e) The proceedings shall be taken down by a reporter or recorded by suitable sound recording equipment. The Attorney General shall maintain custody of the records.

(Added Pub. L. 95-144, § 1, Oct. 28, 1977, 91 Stat. 1217.)

SECTION REFERRED TO IN OTHER SECTIONS

This section is referred to in title 28 section 636.

§ 4109. Right to counsel, appointment of counsel

In proceedings to verify consent of an offender for transfer, the offender shall have the right to advice of counsel. If the offender is financially unable to obtain counsel—

(1) counsel for proceedings conducted under section 4107 shall be appointed in accordance with the Criminal Justice Act (18 U.S.C. 3006A). Such appointment shall be considered an appointment in a misdemeanor case for purposes of compensation under the Act;

(2) counsel for proceedings conducted under section 4108 shall be appointed by the verifying officer pursuant to such regulations as may be prescribed by the Director of the Administrative Office of the United States Courts. The Secretary of State shall make payments of fees and expenses of the appointed counsel, in amounts approved by the verifying officer, which shall not exceed the amounts authorized under the Criminal Justice Act (18 U.S.C. 3006(a))[1] for representation in a misdemeanor case. Payment in excess of the maximum amount authorized may be made for extended or complex representation whenever the verifying officer certifies that the amount of the excess payment is

---

1 SO IN ORIGINAL. PROBABLY SHOULD BE '(18 U.S.C. 3006A)'.

necessary to provide fair compensation, and the payment is approved by the chief judge of the United States court of appeals for the appropriate circuit. Counsel from other agencies in any branch of the Government may be appointed: *Provided*, that in such cases the Secretary of State shall pay counsel directly, or reimburse the employing agency for travel and transportation expenses. Notwithstanding section 3324(a) and (b) of title 31, the Secretary may make advance payments of travel and transportation expenses to counsel appointed under this subsection.[2]

(Added Pub. L. 95-144, § 1, Oct. 28, 1977, 91 Stat. 1218, and amended Pub. L. 97-258, § 3(e)(2), Sept. 13, 1982, 96 Stat. 1964.)

REFERENCES IN TEXT

The Criminal Justice Act, referred to in text, probably means Pub. L. 88-455, Aug. 20, 1964, 78 Stat. 552, as amended, known as the Criminal Justice Act of 1964, which enacted section 3006A of this title, and provisions set out as notes under section 3006A of this title. For complete classification of this Act to the Code, see Short Title note set out under section 3006A of this title and Tables.

AMENDMENTS

1982—Par. (2), Pub. L. 97-258 substituted "section 3324(a) and (b) of title 31" for "section 3648 of the Revised Statutes as amended (31 U.S.C. 529)."

SECTION REFERRED TO IN OTHER SECTIONS

This section is referred to in title 28 section 636.

§ 4110. Transfer of juveniles

An offender transferred to the United States because of an act which would have been an act of juvenile delinquency had it been committed in the United States or any State thereof shall be subject to the provisions of chapter 403 of this title except as otherwise provided in the relevant treaty or in an agreement pursuant to such treaty between the Attorney General and the authority of the foreign country.

(Added Pub. L. 95-144, § 1, Oct. 28,1977, 91 Stat. 1218.)

§ 4111. Prosecution barred by foreign conviction

An offender transferred to the United States shall not be detained, prosecuted, tried, or sentenced by the United States, or any State thereof for any offense the prosecution of which would have been barred if the sentence upon which the transfer was based had been by a court of the jurisdiction seeking to prosecute the transferred offender, or if prosecution would have been barred by the laws of the jurisdiction seeking to prosecute the transferred offender if the sentence on which the transfer was based had been issued by a court of the United States or by a court of another State.

(Added Pub. L. 95-144, § 1, Oct. 28, 1977, 91 Stat. 1218.)

§ 4112. Loss of rights, disqualification

An offender transferred to the United States to serve a sentence imposed by a foreign court shall not incur any loss of civil, political, or civic rights nor incur any disquaiification other than those which under the laws of the United States or of the State in which the issue arises would result from the fact of the conviction in the foreign country.

(Added Pub. L. 95-144, § 1, Oct. 28, 1977, 91 Stat 1218.)

§ 4113. Status of alien offender transferred to a foreign country

(a) An alien who is deportable from the United States but who has been granted voluntary departure pursuant to section 1252(b) or section 1254(e) of title 8, United States Code, and who is

---

[2] SO IN ORIGINAL.

transferred to a foreign country pursuant to this chapter shall be deemed for all purposes to have voluntarily departed from this country.

(b) An alien who is the subject of an order of deportation from the United States pursuant to section 1252 of title 8, United States Code, who is transferred to a foreign country pursuant to this chapter shall be deemed for all purposes to have been deported from this country.

(c) An alien who is the subject of an order of exclusion and deportation from the United States pursuant to section 1226 of title 8, United States Code, who is transferred to a foreign country pursuant to this chapter shall be deemed for all purposes to have been excluded from admission and deported from the United States.

(Added Pub. L. 95-144, § 1, Oct. 28, 1977, 91 Stat. 1219.)

§ 4114. Return of transferred offenders

(a) Upon a final decision by the Courts of the United States that the transfer of the offender to the United States was not in accordance with the treaty or the laws of the United States and ordering the offender released from serving the sentence in the United States the offender may be returned to the country from which he was transferred to complete the sentence if the country in which the sentence was imposed requests his return. The Attorney General shall notify the appropriate authority of the country which imposed the sentence, within ten days, of a final decision of a court of the United States ordering the offender released. The notification shall specify the time within which the sentencing country must request the return of the offender which shall be no longer than thirty days.

(b) Upon receiving a request from the sentencing country that the offender ordered released be returned for the completion of his sentence the Attorney General may file a complaint for the return of the offender with any justice or judge of the United States or any authorized magistrate within whose jurisdiction the offender is found. The complaint shall be upon oath and supported by affidavits establishing that the offender was convicted and sentenced by the courts of the country to which his return is requested; the offender was transferred to the United States for the execution of his sentence; the offender was ordered released by a court of the United States before he had completed his sentence because the transfer of the offender was not in accordance with the treaty or the laws of the United States; and that the sentencing country has requested that he be returned for the completion of the sentence. There shall be attached to the complaint a copy of the sentence of the sentencing court and of the decision of the court which ordered the offender released.

A summons or a warrant shall be issued by the justice, judge or magistrate ordering the offender to appear or to be brought before the issuing authority. If the justice, judge, or magistrate finds that the person before him is the offender described in the complaint and that the facts alleged in the complaint are true, he shall issue a warrant for commitment of the offender to the custody of the Attorney General until surrender shall be made. The findings and a copy of all the testimony taken before him and of all documents introduced before him shall be transmitted to the Secretary of State, that a return warrant may issue upon the requisition of the proper authorities of the sentencing country, for the surrender of offender.

(c) A complaint referred to in subsection (b) must be filed within sixty days from the date on which the decision ordering the release of the offender becomes final.

(d) An offender returned under this section shall be subject to the jurisdiction of the country to which he is returned for all purposes.

(e) The return of an offender shall be conditioned upon the offender being given credit toward service of the sentence for the time spent in the custody of or under the supervision of the United States.

(f) Sections 3186, 3188 through 3191, and 3195 of this title shall be applicable to the return of an offender under this section. However, an offender returned under this section shall not be deemed to have been extradited for any purpose.

(g) An offender whose return is sought pursuant to this section may be admitted to bail or be released on his own recognizance at any stage of the proceedings.

(Added Pub. L. 95-144, § 1, Oct. 28,1977, 91 Stat. 1219.)

§ 4115. Execution of sentences imposing an obligation to make restitution or reparations if in a sentence issued in a penal proceeding of a transferring country an offender transferred to the United States has been ordered to pay a sum of money to the victim of the offense for damage caused by the offense, that penalty or award of damages may be enforced as though it were a civil judgment rendered by a United States district court. Proceedings to collect the moneys ordered to be paid may be instituted by the Attorney General in any United States district court. Moneys recovered pursuant to such proceedings shall be transmitted through diplomatic channels to the treaty authority of the transferring country for distribution to the victim. (Added Pub. L. 95-144, § 1, Oct. 28, 1977, 91 Stat. 1220.)

List of States which Enacted Legislation Authorizing Transfer of Prisoners from State Custody. As of June 30, 1985

Arizona	Maryland	Nevada	South Carolina
California	Michigan	New Mexico	Texas
Colorado	Minnesota	New York	Virginia
Florida	Missouri	North Dakota	Washington
Illinois	Montana	Oklahoma	Wisconsin
Kansas	Nebraska	Oregon	Wyoming

The European Convention

Helmut Epp

Introduction

The problem of the recognition of foreign penal judgments has often been discussed in detail, stressing in most cases the question of what value should be given to a foreign judgment in the national judiciary system.[1] In this respect, it is of particular interest in what way a foreign judgment could bar the initiation of new criminal proceedings for the same offense[2] and whether a foreign conviction could be recognized for the assumption of recidivism. Apart from this, there is also the question of recognition of foreign judgments in a wider sense, for example by enforcement and execution.[3] This article will deal only with the latter aspect, which has become of increasing importance in the last decade.

Apart from medieval transfer arrangements like those in Upper Italy, which were aimed not at the offender's resocialization but rather at the exploitation of the condemned person's working capacities,[4] most of the contemporary penal codes explicitly precluded the enforcement of foreign penal judgments.[5] Because of the increasing mobility resulting from improved travel facilities, a certain internationalization of criminality and humanitarian reasons caused a revision of this strict position in the late 1960s. It was realized that one of the main goals of the sanctioning system, the social reintegration of the offender, was jeopardized by various situations which were faced by foreign prisoners: language barriers, different social and cultural background, lack of communication with the outside world, and lack of information and vocational training. There were even instances of *de facto* discrimination against foreigners who were less eligible for more favorable forms of treatment such as furloughs.[6] Moreover, the prison authorities were confronted with increasing difficulties caused by foreign prisoners, in particular in countries where the proportion of foreigners within the prison population was high (20 percent in Sweden and Belgium, 25 percent in Switzerland, and 14 percent in the Netherlands).[7]

---

[1] *See* Dietrich Oehler, *Recognition of Foreign Penal Judgements and Their Enforcement*, *in* 2 A TREATISE ON INTERNATIONAL CRIMINAL LAW 261 (M. Cherif Bassiouni & Ved P. Nanda eds., 1973) [hereinafter TREATISE], *infra* this volume.

[2] The principle of double jeopardy (*non bis in idem*) is generally recognized in national legislations but its application is restricted internationally. *See* U.S. v. Ryan, 360 F. Supp. 270 (E.D.N.Y.1973), and U.S. v. Martinez, 616 F.2d 185 (5th Cir. 1980) (it was stated that the prohibition of double jeopardy which applied territorially within the U.S. to all persons does not apply extraterritorially except for U.S. citizens). *See also* A. Kenneth Pye, *Recognition of Foreign Criminal Judgements*, *in* INTERNATIONAL CRIMINAL LAW, 479 (Gerhard O.W. Mueller & Edward M. Wise eds., 1965).

[3] *See* M. Cherif Bassiouni and Grace M.W. Gallagher, Policies and Practices of the United States, *infra* this volume.

[4] *See* Oehler, *supra* note 1, at 262.

[5] *See e.g.*, Austrian Penal Code (1945) which was applicable until 1974: "In no case shall a sentence by a foreign penal authority be executed in Austria."

[6] *See* Helmut Epp, *Der Auslander im Strafvollzug unter besonderer Berücksichtigung der Übertragung der Strafvollstreckung*, 37 OSTERREICHISCHE JURISTEN-ZEITUNG 119 (1982) [hereinafter OEJZ].

[7] *See* Theodore Simon & Robert L. Pisani, *Prisoner Transfer Treaties in the Americas: An Overview*, contribution to the XXIII Conference of the Inter-American Bar Association, 1982.

The political and the human rights situation in many countries as well as the enormous migration in the 1990s have even increased this problem,[8] which had already been recognized in the 1980s and which had led to the negotiation of international instruments providing for the repatriation of prisoners to their home countries to serve their sentences.

However, it should not be assumed that all problems in this field could be solved by repatriation: foreigners still have to stay in the country of the commission of the crime for the period of trial and until the procedural conditions for their repatriation are met unless transfer of criminal proceedings instruments can be applied.[9] [10] In addition, there will remain some cases in which transfer instruments cannot be applied because some of their conditions cannot be fulfilled.[11] Thus, the consideration of foreign prisoners' treatment is still important.[12]

Existing Transfer Instruments

Because of the advantages of repatriation of foreign prisoners to ensure their better resocialization and to alleviate the problems faced by prison authorities, several multilateral and bilateral agreements were concluded. The increasing importance of these new instruments of international cooperation led to the conviction that a certain unification of such agreements would be desirable. In evaluating existing treaties and recognizing their similarity, it was realized that unification would be achievable. Thus, on the level of the United Nations, efforts were undertaken to elaborate a model agreement on the transfer of prisoners.[13]

Multilateral Agreements

Uniform Legislation. At the multilateral level, the uniform legislation of the Scandinavian countries should be mentioned first. Efforts for unification were already undertaken in 1948 when the Scandinavian countries concluded an agreement on the recognition and enforcement of criminal judgments, being restricted, however, only to the enforcement of fines.[14] This was followed by uniform legislation in 1963 covering the enforcement of custodial sentences.[15] This uniform legislation is not restricted only to the enforcement of sentences of imprisonment and fines, but in addition covers the enforcement

---

8 By Sept. 1995 the proportion of foreign prison inmates in Austrian prisons was almost 27 percent.

9 *Cf.* European Convention on Mutual Assistance in Criminal Matters, Europ. T.S. 30, Art. 21; European Convention on the Transfer of Proceedings in Criminal Matters, Europ. T.S. 73.

10 *Cf.* moreover the *U.N. Model Treaty on the Transfer of Proceedings in Criminal Matters*, as adopted by the 8th U.N. Congress on the Prevention of Crime and the Treatment of Offenders, Havana, 1990, A/CONF.144/28.Rev.1, at 89.

11 *See* Council of Europe, Recommendation No. R (84) 12 (relating to the treatment of foreign prisoners).

12 *Cf. also Recommendations on the Treatment of Foreign Prisoners*, as adopted by the 7th U.N. Congress on the Prevention of Crime and the Treatment of Offenders, Milan, 1985, A/CONF.121/22/Rev.1, at 57.

13 *Cf. Model Agreement on the Transfer of Foreign Prisoners*, as adopted by the 7th U.N. Congress on the Prevention of Crime and the Treatment of Offenders, Milan, 1985, A/CONF.121/22/Rev.1, at 53.

14 *See* Peter Wilkitzki, *Rechtshilfe durch Vollstreckung*, 37 (N.S.) JR 227 (1983).

15 Act on Cooperation between Finland and Other Scandinavian Countries in the Enforcement of Sentences given in Criminal Cases, June 20, 1963.

of judgments regarding conditionally sentenced or conditionally released persons.[16] Of particular interest is that enforcement based on this uniform legislation is not restricted to nationals of the requested state, but is also provided in cases where the sentenced person is a domiciliary of the requested state.[17]

Similar efforts were also undertaken by the Benelux states by an agreement of September 26, 1968,[18] which is, however, not yet ratified.[19]

European Convention on the International Validity of Criminal Judgements.[20] Apart from the European Convention on the Punishment of Road Traffic Offences of 1964,[21] regulating transfer of proceedings and the enforcement of foreign judgments regarding road traffic offenses, and the Extradition Convention of the Arabic League,[22] which in Article 17 regulates the transfer of prisoners on the condition of the prisoner's consent without, however, regulating procedural questions in more detail, the European Convention on the International Validity of Criminal Judgements is the first comprehensive multilateral instrument for a transfer of enforcement of penal sanctions. It is comprehensive in two aspects: it regulates the procedure for a transfer of enforcement, taking into particular account the question of double jeopardy,[23] and it covers custodial sentences, fines, judgements rendered *in absentia*, *ordonnances penales*, and confiscations and disqualifications. Taking into account the rather difficult procedures of this convention, it has been ratified by only a few countries.

Berlin Convention. The former Socialist countries had regulated their relations regarding the repatriation of prisoners by the Convention on the Transfer of Persons Sentenced to Imprisonment for Enforcement of the Sanction in the State of their Nationality of 1978.[24] According to Article 22, this convention is open to accession by other states on invitation of all states party to it.

As indicated by the title of the convention, it was guided by the principle of nationality, thereby excluding a transfer to the country of ordinary residence or domicile; it was, however, similar to the U.S.-Mexican Treaty, not applicable when the offender was a resident of the sentencing state. The authority to request enforcement fell primarily within the competence of the sentencing state but did not exclude initiatives by the prisoner's country of nationality, the prisoner, or his close relatives from making a request. Similar to the European Convention on the International Validity of Criminal Judgements, the consent of the prisoner was not required.

---

16 *See also* The European Convention on the Supervision of Conditionally Sentenced or Conditionally Released Offenders of 1964, Europ. T. S. No. 51.

17 The notion of domicile is also contained in the Treaty on the Execution of Penal Sentences, Nov. 25, 1976, U.S.-Mexico, T.I.A.S. No. 8718 Art. 11(2) (3) [hereinafter U.S.-Mexico Sentence Treaty] (excluding a transfer of persons to their country of nationality if they are 'domiciliaries' of the sending state). *See also* Bassiouni, *supra* note 3, at 225.

18 *See* 4 HEINRICH GRUTZNER, INTERNATIONALER RECHTSHILFEVERKEHR IN STRAFSACHEN pt. B1, 27. (1967).

19 *See* Wilkitzki, *supra* note 14, at 233.

20 *See* European Convention on the International Validity of Criminal Judgements of 1970, Europ. T.S. No. 70 [hereinafter Eur. Conv. Int'l Val. Crim. Judg.].

21 Europ. T. S. No. 52.

22 Ratified by the Council on Sept. 14, 1952.

23 Eur. Conv. Int'l Val. Crim. Judg., *supra* note 20, at Art. 53.

24 Ratifications by Bulgaria, C.S.S.R., Cuba, German Democratic Republic, Hungary, Mongolia, Poland, U.S.S.R. (May 19, 1978).

Convention on the Transfer of Sentenced Persons. Although the European Convention on the International Validity of Criminal Judgements represents a comprehensive regulation of the transfer of enforcement, it has to date been ratified by only nine member states of the Council of Europe.[25] This situation seems to indicate that the transformation of the convention into national law, particularly the procedural provisions concerning the enforcement of special sanctions such as confiscations, disqualifications, judgments rendered *in absentia* and *ordonnances penales*, was deemed to be too complicated.[26] With such complex regulations, the convention did not satisfy the requirements necessary for this type of instrument, that is, a simple and quick transfer of prisoners to their home countries.[27] Realizing these obstacles to ratification, the European Ministers of Justice, at their 11th Conference,[28] adopted a resolution by which the Committee of Ministers of the Council of Europe was invited to ask the European committee on Crime Problems (CDPC) "to consider the possibility of drawing up a model agreement providing for a simple procedure for the transfer of prisoners which could be used between member states or by member states in their relations with non-member states."[29] Following this resolution, an expert committee was established which, when discussing its terms of reference, expressed the opinion that it wished to elaborate a binding transfer instrument rather than only a model agreement. This opinion was approved by the Committee of Ministers under the condition that such new convention not conflict with the dispositions of already existing European conventions.[30] This committee, composed of experts of member states and representatives of Canada, the U.S., and Commonwealth Secretariat, adopted the convention which was finally opened for signature on March 21, 1983;[31] after ratification by France, Spain, Sweden and the U.S., it entered into force July 1, 1985.[32]

Bilateral Agreements

At the bilateral level, negotiations were held between Denmark and Spain resulting in a treaty of February 3, 1972, that became effective on June 1, 1973. The majority of agreements were, however, concluded between American states, starting with a transfer

---

25 Austria, Cyprus, Denmark, Iceland, Netherlands, Norway, Sweden, Spain, and Turkey.

26 *See e.g.*, the Austrian reservations declared when ratifying the convention whereby the application of the sections on judgments rendered *in absentia, ordonnances penales*, confiscation, and disqualifications were excluded.

27 *See* Hans-Jürgen Bartsch, *Strafvollstreckung im Heimatstaat*, NJW 513 (1984).

28 Copenhagen, June 21-22, 1978.

29 *See* European Committee on Crime Problems, Council of Europe, *Explanatory Report on the Convention on the Transfer of Sentenced Persons*, ¶ 1 (1983) [hereinafter *Explanatory Note*].

30 Erik Harremoes, *Une nouvelle Convention du Conseil de l'Europe: le transferement des personnes condamnees*, 1983 Revue de Science Criminelle et Droit Pénal Comparé 235.

31 Convention on the Transfer of Sentenced Persons of 1983, Europ. T. S. No. 112 [hereinafter Euro. Conv. Trans. Sent. Per.]. The convention was signed by Canada and the U.S. on Mar. 21, 1983: in addition as of March 1985 it has been signed by all of the Council of Europe member states except Iceland, the Republic of Ireland, Malta, and Turkey.

32 The participation of common law countries was of particular importance, taking into account the experiences of those countries with transfer of prisoners, as most of the bilateral transfer treaties were negotiated and are applicable between those countries. The participation of Canada and the U.S. resulted in the adoption of special final clauses, giving these states the option to sign the convention from the outset, without formal invitation to accede to it.

treaty between the U.S. and Mexico.[33] This agreement was the model for further treaties within the Americas, which were initially negotiated by the U.S. and Canada with other countries of that area.[34] After this period, the necessity to regulate relations with the European countries concerning the transfer of prisoners also arose. The first treaties between the U.S. and Turkey and between Canada and France are of particular interest because of the differences in these countries' legal systems.[35] These differences required special regulations regarding procedural conditions and the competence to handle repatriation[36] as well as the different sanctioning systems. In the latter respect, reference should be made to the Canada-France agreement,[37] which influenced the provisions of the Convention on the Transfer of Sentenced Persons concerning the option of "continued enforcement."[38] A similar regulation is also contained in the U.S.-France Convention of 1983.[39]

In Europe, France is, apart from its conventions with the U.S. and Canada, in a particular situation. The presence in France of a large number of nationals of former French colonies necessitated the conclusion of transfer agreements with those countries.[40] Similar patterns of migration also led to the conclusion of a transfer treaty between Austria and the former Yugoslavia of 1982,[41] which regulated the mutual enforcement of prison sentences and also the supervision of conditionally sentenced or conditionally released offenders.

Considering the increasing drug criminality, particularly in the Far East countries, transfer agreements have been negotiated between Thailand and the U.S., France, Italy, Canada, Spain, and Austria.[42] While the other agreements have evidenced a certain similarity,

---

[33] *See* U.S.-Mexico Sentence Treaty, *supra* note 17; *see also* Simon & Pisani, *supra* note 7.

[34] U.S.-Canada, Mar. 2, 1977, becoming effective on July 19, 1978, T.I.A.S. No. 9552; U.S.-Bolivia, becoming effective on Aug. 17, 1978, T.I.A.S. No. 9219; Canada-Mexico, Nov. 22, 1977, becoming effective on Mar. 29, 1979; Canada-Panama, signed on Mar. 6, 1980; Canada-Peru, becoming effective on July 1, 1980; U.S.-Panama of Jan. 11, 1979, becoming effective on June 17, 1980, T.I.A.S. No. 9787; U.S.-Peru, becoming effective on July 21, 1980, T.I.A.S. No. 9784.

[35] U.S.-Turkey of June 7, 1979, becoming effective on June 17, 1981, T.I.A.S. No. 9892; Canada—France of Feb. 9, 1979.

[36] *See* U.S.-Turkey Treaty, *supra* note 35, at Art. 24, which says: "A sanction imposed in the requesting state shall be enforced in the requested state only after recognition of the validity of the judgement imposing the sanction by the competent authority empowered to do so under the law of the requested state."

[37] Canada-France Treaty, *supra* note 35, at Art. VI: "When a penalty imposed in Canada is unknown in French law, or when it is imposed under different conditions, France shall substitute for this penalty whenever appropriate, that penalty or measure provided in its own law for a similar violation. France shall inform Canada of this before the transfer request is accepted. This penalty or measure shall correspond in nature, as far as possible, to that imposed by the judgement that is to be executed, and it shall not exceed the maximum provided in French law or increase in nature or in duration the penalty imposed in Canada."

[38] *Id.* at Art. 10, ¶ 2.

[39] Convention between the U.S. and the Republic of France on the Transfer of Sentenced Persons, signed Jan. 25, 1983.

[40] *See e.g.*, the treaty between France and Morocco of Aug. 10, 1981.

[41] Entering into force on Jan. 1, 1984, 1984 AUSTRIAN LAW GAZETTE 547.

[42] Treaty on cooperation in the Execution of Penal Sentences between the Government of the U.S. and the Government of the Kingdom of Thailand: Convention entre le Gouvernement du Royaume de Thailande et le Gouvernement de la Republique Francaise sur la Cooperation en Matiere d'Execution des Condamnations Penales; Treaty On the Cooperation in the Execution of Penal Sentences between the Government of the Kingdom of Thailand and the Government of the Republic of Italy; Treaty on the Cooperation in the Execution of Penal Sentences between the Government of the Kingdom of Thailand and the Government of Canada: Treaty on Cooperation in the Execution of Penal Sentences between the Government of the Kingdom of Spain and the Government of the Kingdom of Thailand, May 6, 1983. Treaty between the Republic of Austria and the Kingdom of Thailand on the Transfer of Offenders and on the Cooperation in the Enforcement of Penal Sentences, which

some of the regulations in these treaties are new and to a certain extent extraordinary, as they do not provide for an early repatriation. On the contrary, the person is eligible for transfer only after serving a considerable part of the sentence in the transferring (sentencing) state. According to the original version of the treaty between Thailand and France, a person would serve four years or one-third of the sentence, whichever was shorter, before transfer.[43] Although this condition was later amended in this treaty, as well as in the following treaties,[44] there is no substantial change in the position of Thailand. The national legislation of Thailand was amended at the same time, providing for even less favorable conditions than were included in the treaty with France.[45]

U.N. Model Agreement on the Transfer of Prisoners

Considering the disadvantages to offenders serving their prison sentences abroad, as well as realizing the problems of prison administrations in this respect, the Fifth United Nations Congress on the Prevention of Crime and the Treatment of Offenders in 1975 discussed the problem of foreign prisoners and their repatriation. These discussions were continued at the Sixth Congress in Caracas in 1980, and in Resolution 13[46] member states were urged to "consider the establishment of procedures whereby such transfers of offenders may be effected, recognizing that any such procedures can only be undertaken with the consent of both the sending and receiving countries and either with the consent of the prisoners or in his interest."

By operative paragraph 3 of this resolution, the Committee on Crime Prevention and Control was requested "to give priority to the development of a model agreement for the transfer of offenders with a view to presenting it to the General Assembly as soon as possible." Thus, after evaluating existing transfer instruments and recognizing the similarity of these transfer instruments, a draft model agreement on the transfer of prisoners was elaborated. This model was considerably influenced by the regulations contained in the Council of Europe draft convention on the transfer of sentenced persons. In this respect, it was of particular importance that in addition to civil law countries and apart from the U.K., representatives of Canada, the U.S. and the Commonwealth Secretariat also contributed to its elaboration. This ensured that the convention would be acceptable for common law

---

entered into force Aug. 1, 1994.

43 Art. II "L'application de la present Convention est soumise aux conditions suivantes" ¶ 6: "que dans le cas d'un emprisonnement ou d'une autre peine privative de liberte, le delinquant ait, au moment du transférement, purge dans l'Etat transférant au moins un tiers de la durée de la peine d'emprisonnement ou d'une autre peine privative de liberté ou quatre ans, en prenant la moins longue des deux durées."

44 U.S.-Thailand Treaty, *supra* note 42, at Art. II, ¶ b: "That in the case of imprisonment, confinement or other form of deprivation of liberty, the offender shall, at the time of transfer, have served in the Transferring State any minimum period of the sentence stipulated by the law of the Transferring State."

45 § 25 of the Statute of July 11, 1984: "The transfer of foreign prisoners shall not take place under any one of the following circumstances: (2) Foreign prisoners who have served a prison sentence in the Kingdom less than one third of the total sentence imposed or ordered or less than four years, whichever period is less, but this period of less than four years shall be changed to eight years in the case of a sentence imposed on a foreign prisoner, whether wholly or partially, for charges of production distribution import for distribution or possession for distribution of narcotics, as proscribed by the Narcotics Act, specifically for offenses for which the law prescribes a sentence of life imprisonment."

46 Resolution 13, Sixth U.N. Congress on the Prevention of Crime and the Treatment of Offenders, U.N. Doc. A/CONF. (87)14/Rev. 1.

countries in their relations between themselves, as well as in their relations to civil law countries. The elaboration of the U.N. model proved also the importance of a close cooperation of the United Nations with nongovernmental organizations. After elaboration, the draft model was first discussed in February 1983 at an international seminar organized by the Alliance of Non-Governmental Organizations on Crime Prevention and Criminal Justice (Vienna) in cooperation with the United Nations Crime Prevention and Criminal Justice Branch of the Centre for Social Development and Humanitarian Affairs in Vienna.[47] These discussions were continued on the occasion of a conference organized by the Centro Nazionale di Difesa Sociale in Milan in June 1983, and finally at a seminar held at the International Institute for Higher Studies in Criminal Sciences in Siracusa, Italy in January 1984. The results of these meetings were, on the U.N. level, discussed at all regional preparatory meetings and by the Committee on Crime Prevention and Control at its Eighth Session, which gave favorable comments. It was eventually submitted to ECOSOC, which, at its Spring Session 1984 took note of the model and transmitted it to the Seventh Congress on the Prevention of Crime and the Treatment of Offenders for adoption.

This model which was intended to serve as a basis for bilateral as well as multilateral agreements providing for a repatriation of convicted offenders, was finally endorsed by the Seventh United Nations Congress on the Prevention of Crime and the Treatment of Offenders.[48]

The tradition of elaborating model treaties for the international cooperation in criminal matters was continued at the Eighth United Nations Congress on the Prevention of Crime and the Treatment of Offenders,[49] where such models on extradition, mutual assistance in criminal matters, the transfer of proceedings in criminal matters and on the supervision of offenders conditionally sentenced or conditionally released were adopted.

With a view to the enforcement of penal sanctions, the Eighth U.N. Congress requested the Committee on Crime Prevention and Control to consider the question of the transfer of enforcement of penal sanctions and the possibility of the formulation of a model agreement thereon with a view to submitting it to the Ninth United Nations Congress on the Prevention of Crime and the Treatment of Offenders for further deliberations.[50] With a view to the already adopted model agreement on the transfer of prisoners, this request was aimed at the elaboration of a comprehensive model including also the enforcement of other sanctions than those consisting in the deprivation of liberty.

According to the decision taken at the Eighth U.N. Congress, the Ninth United Nations Congress on the Prevention of Crime and the Treatment of Offenders,[51] noting the United Nations model treaties on international cooperation as an important tool for the development of international cooperation, urged the examination of practical recommendations for the further development and promotion of mechanisms of international cooperation, including the United Nations model treaties on international cooperation.[52]

---

47 Vienna, March 21-30, 1984.

48 Milan, Aug. 26-Sept. 6, 1985.

49 Havana, Aug. 27-Sept. 7, 1990.

50 *See* A/CONF.144/28/rev.1, at 196.

51 Cairo, 1995.

52 *See* A/CONF.169.16, at 15.

Legal Problems

The enforcement of foreign penal judgments is an act of international legal cooperation, thus certain general prerequisite and guarantees as to the proceedings[53] must be provided. Probably the most important consideration in this connection is the existence of similar political, social and legal structures in the country which assumes the duty of enforcement and in the country which pronounces penal judgment.[54] Humanitarian considerations might also require an action toward repatriation between countries without such similarities and even when the standards of the administering state's legal safeguards have not been observed in the sentencing state, particularly when the prison conditions in the sentencing state impose special hardship on the prisoner. The application of any repatriation instrument between countries of different regions, of different political, social or cultural backgrounds, or of different climatic conditions, could cause a dilemma, particularly for the authorities of the administering state: Should they refuse a request of the sentencing state or the prisoner himself when he has a formal right to apply for his transfer[55] when there are doubts as to the conduct of the criminal proceedings in the sentencing state, or should the humanitarian considerations be given priority? In this respect, the consent of the prisoner as well as regulations concerning the possibility to withdraw the consent after surrender are of great importance.[56] However, even if the prisoner consents to his transfer, thereby agreeing to disregard shortcomings in the criminal proceedings leading to his conviction, the enforcement of a foreign judgment must not infringe the national *ordre public* of the administering state. Such national interests would be damaged if the foreign penal judgments to be executed violated essential constitutional principles or were incompatible with a protected fundamental human right.[57]

The dilemma between the legal and humanitarian considerations was discussed in the U.S. in connection with the first transfer treaty with Mexico, the issue being whether it was constitutional for the U.S. to enforce a foreign penal judgment which lacked the constitutional safeguards applied in the U.S.[58] In this connection, the U.S. authorities, stressing the importance of the prisoner's consent, elaborated a system of safeguards involving consular authorities, verifying that this consent was voluntarily given with full knowledge of the legal consequences thereof.[59] Notwithstanding these safeguards, this treaty

---

53 In particular double criminality and the observation of minimal human rights concerning the defense.

54 *See* Oehler, *supra* note 1, at 276.

55 *See e.g.*, U.S.–Canada Sentence Treaty, *supra* note 34, at Art. III, ¶ 3. "Every transfer under this Treaty shall be commenced by a written application submitted by the Offender to the authority of the Sending State. . . ."

56 *Volenti non fit iniuria*. The prisoner might also wish to prove his innocence by reviewing proceedings in the sentencing state; moreover, the country of nationality might have jurisdiction based on the principle of active personality. In the latter case, the prisoner could be acquitted in the country of nationality, thereby avoiding negative effects arising from the recognition of foreign penal judgments in his home country. However, a new examination of the case by the courts of the prisoner's home country would be excluded when the prisoner was surrendered in application of a transfer treaty.

57 *See* Oehler, *supra* note 1, at 277.

58 *See* Bassiouni, *supra* note 3.

59 This U.S. experience also influenced the Euro. Conv. Trans. Sent. Per., *supra* note 31: *see* Art. 4. ¶¶ 1 & 5 and in particular Art. 7 of the convention.

has been challenged in two U.S. cases, *Pfeifer v. United States Bureau of Prisoners*[60] and *Rosado v. Civiletti*.[61] In both cases, however, the appellate courts refused to grant a writ of *habeas corpus* to the petitioners and upheld the validity of the treaty. In *Pfeifer*, the petitioner charged that his convictions in the Mexican trial was invalid because the trial did not comport with U.S. notions of due process. The court held, however, that procedures in foreign courts, while not in compliance with the U.S. procedures, did not render the treaty unconstitutional.[62] In *Pfeifer* and *Rosado*, the petitioners claimed that the consent for transfer given was invalid. In *Pfeifer*, the court disposed of this argument by finding that the petitioner's consent was voluntarily and knowingly given.[63] In *Rosado,* the court, while noting the influence that conditions in the Mexican prison may have on the prisoner's consent, also found the consent to be voluntary. The court based this decision in part on the need for the U.S. to uphold its treaty obligations, and also because of concerns for other U.S. citizens held in Mexican prisons.[64]

The Convention on the Transfer of Sentenced Persons

General Considerations

As previously noted, this convention is not intended to supersede the European Convention on the International Validity of Criminal Judgements:[65] On the contrary, when the expert committee was established, the terms of reference expressed that this new convention should not conflict with the dispositions of already existing European conventions.[66] In compliance with this condition, the Convention can be distinguished from the European Convention on the International Validity of Criminal Judgements in four major respects: (a) it provides for a simplified procedure which, in its practical application, is likely to be less cumbersome; (b) a transfer may be requested not only by the state in which the sentence was imposed, but also by the state of which the sentenced person is a national; (c) the transfer is subject to the sentenced person's consent; and (d) the convention does not contain an obligation on contracting states to comply with a request for transfer, and for this reason it was not necessary to list any grounds for refusal.[67] Moreover, the convention is applicable only for sanctions involving deprivations of liberty,[68] while the Convention on International Validity of Criminal Judgements covered a full range of sanctions; the Transfer Convention provides only for a transfer to the country of nationality while the International

---

[60] Pfeifer v. U.S. Bureau of Prisoners, 448 F. Supp. 920 (S.D. Cal. 1979), 615 F.2d 873 (9th Cir. 1980), *cert. denied*, 447 U.S. 908 (1980). *Cf.* Simon & Pisani, *supra* note 7; *supra* note 32.

[61] Rosado v. Civiletti, 621 F.2d 1179 (2d Cir. 1980), *cert. denied,* No. 79-6990 (U.S. Oct.6, 1980). *Cf.* Simon & Pisani, *supra* note 7; *supra* note 32.

[62] 6l5 F.2d at 876.

[63] *Id.* at 877.

[64] 621 F.2d at 1198-1200.

[65] As to the International Validity Convention, *see* Heinrich Grutzner, *Die zwischenstaatliche Anerkennung europaischer Strafurteile*, 22 NJW 345 (1969); Robert Linke, *Wechselseitige Anerkennung und Vollstreckung europascher Strafurteile*, 26 OEJZ 29 (1971).

[66] *See supra* Chapter 2, § 1(d).

[67] *See Explanatory Note*, *supra* note 29, ¶ 11.

[68] Prison sentences as well as other measures such as commitment to a mental institution.

Validity Convention is applicable if any of the conditions of its Article 5 are met.[69] Finally, the Transfer Convention is applicable only for "transfers", thus excluding its application in cases where the prisoner is already in his country of nationality, for example, after having absconded to his home country or after the suspension of a sentence has been revoked.[70]

It should be noted that the title of the convention does not, unlike the other conventions on international cooperation in criminal matters prepared under the auspices of the Council of Europe,[71] contain the word "European" in its title. The reason for this is that the convention was designed to be applicable outside of Europe, allowing accession of like-minded non-European democratic states.[72] The foundation for such broad applicability was laid by the representation and active association of Canada and the U.S. in the elaboration of the text, which is reflected in the final clauses of the convention.[73] In addition, other countries have already expressed an interest in acceding to the convention after its entry into force.[74]

The practicability of this convention is clearly demonstrated by the number of ratifications going far beyond the members of the Council of Europe.[75] Also the practice has changed in recent years. While in the initial stage of this kind of cooperation, transfers were often hindered by the transferring state's refusal to have the sentence reviewed by judicial authorities of the receiving state, the enforcement in the offender's home country has gained priority over other more theoretical considerations.

In order to improve cooperation in this field, the European Union has drafted a convention by which the Convention on Transfer of Sentenced Persons should be applied among the members of the Union without any reservations made at the time of ratification. However, this convention has not yet come into force.

The Role of the States Concerned. As previously mentioned, the convention does not impose any obligation on either state to request a transfer or to enforce the sanction. International cooperation in the field of criminal law should further the ends of justice and the social rehabilitation of the sentenced person. Encompassed within this goal is the belief that foreigners, who are deprived of their liberty as a result of a criminal conviction should be given the opportunity to serve their sentences within their own society.[76] Under this convention, however, the parties agree only to undertake to afford one another the widest measure of cooperation regarding the transfer of sentenced persons.[77] Thus, compliance with

---

69 This list has, however, to be read in conjunction with Art. 6 as well as with possible reservations made by individual states.

70 *See* Euro. Conv. Trans. Sent. Per., *supra* note 31, at Art. 2, ¶ 1. "The Parties undertake to afford each other the widest measure of cooperation in respect of the *transfer of sentenced persons. . . .*" *See also id.* at Art. 1, ¶ (c),(d).

71 *See e.g.*, European Convention on Extradition of 1957, Europ. T.S. No. 24, and European Convention on Mutual Assistance in Criminal Matters of 1959, Europ. T.S. No. 30.

72 *See Explanatory Note*, *supra* note 29.

73 *See* Euro. Conv. Trans. Sent. Per., *supra* note 31, at Art. 18, ¶ 1: "This Convention shall be open for signature by the member States of the Council of Europe and non-member States which have participated in its elaboration."

74 *See id.* at Art. 19.

75 Austria, Bahamas, Belgium, Bulgaria, Canada, Croatia, Cyprus, Denmark, Finland, France, Germany, Greece, Hungary, Iceland, Italy, Luxemburg, Malta, Netherlands, Norway, Poland, Portugal, Slovakia, Slovenia, Spain, Sweden, Switzerland, Trinidad and Tobago, Czech Republic, Turkey, Ukraine, U.K., U.S.

76 *See id.* at pmbl., ¶¶ 3-5.

77 *Id.* at Art. 2, ¶ 1.

a request depends on the national legislation of the requested state.[78] Thus, it was not necessary to list any grounds for refusal, nor to require the requested state to give reasons for a refusal.

Regardless of the conditions that have to be fulfilled according to the national transfer regulations of the states concerned, their agreement to effect the transfer is the legal basis of public international law.[79] If the prisoner refuses to consent, action toward a transfer cannot be taken, but the prisoner's consent is still of minor significance compared to the sovereign state's agreement. Thus, it might be misleading to refer to individual transfer agreements as "tripartite" agreements, as the prisoner himself cannot, even when he has the right to apply for his transfer, be a party on the international level. The convention does not give the prisoner the right to apply for a transfer, thus requiring the state addressed to take action upon the application, but it does grant the prisoner the right to express his interest in being transferred under this convention to the sentencing state[80] or to the administering state.[81] The formal request can be made by the sentencing state or the administering state.[82]

Applicability. The convention is applicable for "any punishment or measure involving deprivation of liberty ordered by a court for a limited or unlimited period of time on account of a criminal offense."[83] Thus, administrative decisions fall outside the scope of application of the convention. If the judicial decision involves deprivation of liberty, it makes no difference whether the person concerned is already serving the sentence or not.[84] The convention is also applicable for measures that involve a deprivation of liberty, other than imprisonment, such as in the case of a mentally disabled offender. The convention is applicable even if the latter offenders cannot be convicted because of their lack of criminal liability.[85] The convention contains special regulations to be followed when a person, because of his mental condition, is unable to understand the facilities offered by the convention, thus being unable to consent to the transfer.[86]

In addition to these conditions, the convention is generally applicable only when the sentenced person has at least six months to serve at the time of the request for transfer, or if the sentence is indeterminate.[87] States are not bound by this limit if they agree to a transfer in an exceptional case where a shorter period remains to be served.[88] In all cases a transfer

---

78 In this respect, *see infra* ch. V.

79 *See* Euro. Conv. Trans. Sent. Per., *supra* note 31, at Art. 3, ¶ 1(f).

80 *Id.* at Art 1, ¶ 1 (c): ". . . means the State in which the sentence was imposed on the person who may be, or has been, transferred."

81 *Id.* at Art. 1, ¶ 1(d): ". . . means the State at which the sentenced person may be or has been transferred in order to serve his sentence."

82 *See id.* at Art. 2, ¶ 3. Additionally, the position that a formal request for international cooperation can arise only from a sovereign state is taken in treaties granting the prisoner an even more influential position, such as the U.S.-Canada Sentence Treaty, *supra* note 34: "If the authority of the Sending State approves, it will transmit the application, together with its approval, through diplomatic channels to the authority of the Receiving State." Concerning the obligation to transfer a sentenced person, the Austria-Yugoslavia Transfer Treaty, *supra* note 41, takes a unique position: The administering state is obliged to enforce the sanction imposed in the sentencing state on the latter state's request; if, however, the administering state requests for the transfer of his national who has been sentenced in the sentencing state, this state has no obligation to comply with the request.

83 Euro. Conv. Trans. Sent. Per., *supra* note 31, at Art. 1, ¶ (a).

84 *See Explanatory Note*, *supra* note 29, ¶ 13.

85 Euro. Conv. Trans. Sent. Per., *supra* note 31, at Art. 9, ¶ 4.

86 *Id.* at Art. 3, ¶ 1(d).

87 *Id.* at Art. 3, ¶ 1(c).

88 *Id.* at Art. 3, ¶ 2.

can be effected only after the judgment is final, that is, after all ordinary legal remedies have been exhausted or after the time limit for requesting such remedy has expired.[89]

The convention not only specifies what sanctions can be the basis for a transfer, but also delineates certain conditions that must be met in regard to the offense underlying the conviction. In this respect, the convention follows the regulations of other existing agreements on international cooperation in criminal matters by requiring the double criminality of the offense.[90] The principle of double criminality is an indispensable condition for the enforcement of foreign penal judgments. Otherwise the detention of the transferred person in the administering state, if the behavior was not considered to be an offense, would be in contradiction to the fundamental right of personal freedom. Thus even the consent of the prisoner to serve a sentence imposed on him is a behavior not constituting a criminal offense in his country of nationality, could not outweigh constitutional considerations.[91]

When examining the condition of double criminality, the last phrase of Article 3, paragraph l(e)[92] is of particular interest: The offense should, for this examination, be considered as if it had been in the territory of the administering state. This "transformation of facts" is also applied in extradition cases. It is of less importance if universally recognized and protected interests, such as the right to life or personal property, have been damaged or jeopardized by the offense. No state would hesitate to extradite a murderer. If, however, the offender committed an offense against state interests such as perjury, the transformation of facts is necessary to grant extradition or to grant a request for transfer of enforcement.[93] National penal codes protect, apart from the universally recognized individual interests, only interests of the state itself: its own public order, its own judiciary, its own public documents. Thus an offense committed against the interests of a foreign country, such as perjury before a foreign judge, could only be considered as an offense against a foreign individual and would thus not be punishable. For this reason extradition, as well as transfer of prisoners, would not be possible without the transformation of facts, whereby the offense has to be considered as committed against the requested state's public interests.[94] For the condition of double criminality[95] to be fulfilled, it is however, not necessary that the criminal offense be precisely the same under the law of both the sentencing state and the administering state. The basic idea is that, regardless of differences in wording and legal classification, the essential constituent elements of the offense should be comparable under the law of both states.[96]

Regarding the applicability of the convention, one further regulation has to be mentioned: a sentenced person may be transferred under this convention only if that person

---

89 *Id.* at Art. 3, ¶ 1(b).

90 *Id.* at Art. 3, ¶ 1(e): "if the acts or omissions on account of which the sentence has been imposed constitute a criminal offense according to the law of the administering State or would constitute a criminal offense if committed on its territory."

91 *See* Oehler, *supra* note 1.

92 *See supra* note 90.

93 The same problems would arise in cases of falsification of public documents, also reporting to police authorities or any offenses against public officials in connection with their duties.

94 As to the transformation of facts, *see* Helmut Epp, *Der Frundsatz der identen Normen und die beiderseitige Strafbarkeit*, 36 OEJZ 197 (1981).

95 Also called dual criminal liability.

96 *See Explanatory Note*, *supra* note 29, ¶ 54.

is a national of the administering state.[97] Thus, this convention is narrower in scope of applicability than the European Convention on the International Validity of Criminal Judgements.[98] In an effort to render application of the convention as simple as possible, and considering that no obligation is imposed on the parties to comply with a request, the reference to the sentenced person's nationality was preferred to other classifications. The terms "ordinarily resident in the other State" and the "State of origin" as used in the International Validity Convention in practical application might give rise to problems of interpretation.[99] In addition, the convention gives the parties to it the authority to define the term "national" for the purposes of the convention.[100]

The Role of the Prisoner. Following the basic ideology of most of the existing transfer agreements, the prisoner's consent constitutes one of the basic elements of the transfer mechanism.[101] This condition was agreed upon not only to facilitate the convention's applicability but also with a view to the main goal of a transfer: the prisoner's social resettlement. It would be almost impossible to contribute to the prisoner's resocialization when, against his expressed will he is transferred to another country to serve his sentence. He could not be expected to cooperate with the educational program designed to fulfill the goal of the sanctioning system; the reintegration of offenders into society. The consent is also of utmost importance because the convention does not provide for a rule of speciality.[102] Under this system, the administering state could prosecute the offender for offenses other than those for which the sanction was already imposed in the sentencing state. By requiring consent and not applying the rule of speciality, the convention follows the already existing system of simplified extradition procedures.[103] The basic idea for requiring consent is that the prisoner will know if further proceedings are pending against him in the administering state, and whether, in such a case, he is willing to submit to the proceedings.

In the application of this principle, states were facing difficulties when a sentenced person escaped from the sentencing state and returned to the territory of his nationality in order to avoid execution of the sentence. This situation often cannot be dealt with by way of existing instruments, as the consent required by the European Convention on the Transfer of Sentenced Persons cannot be achieved, and extradition would not be granted, taking into consideration that many states refuse extradition of their own nationals. Thus the only solution would be to try the person again in his home country.

Facing this situation, the Council of Europe drafted an Additional Protocol to the Convention on the Transfer of Sentenced Persons which is based on the implicit assumption

---

[97] *See* Euro. Conv. Trans. Sent. Per., *supra* note 31, at Art. 3, ¶ 1(a).

[98] *See supra* Chapter 4, § 1.

[99] *See* Hans-Jürgen Bartsch, *Council of Europe-Legal Cooperation in 1982, Repatriation of Foreign Prisoners*, Y.B. EUR. L. 306 (1982).

[100] *See* Euro. Conv. Trans. Sent. Per., *supra* note 31, at Art. 3, ¶ 4.

[101] *See* Bartsch, *supra* note 99, at 307. Note also that only the European Convention on the International Validity of Criminal Judgements and the Berlin Convention do not require the prisoner's consent.

[102] This is provided for in the European Convention on the International Validity of Criminal Judgements of 1970 in Art. 9.

[103] *See e.g.*, § 32 of the Austrian Act on Extradition and Mutual Assistance (Austrian ARHG), FEDERAL LAW GAZETTE No. 529/1979; according to similar provisions of the Act on International Mutual Assistance in Criminal Matters of the Federal Republic of Germany (German IRG), FEDERAL LAW GAZETTE, 1982 IS 2071, § 41 an option is given to the person consenting to be extradited, either to relinquish the protection of speciality or to require its observation.

that the sentenced person's voluntary departure amounts to a consent, if not to be transferred, at least to serve the sentence in his home country. Taking that understanding of the person's consent, the drafters did not consider it necessary to provide for the application of the principle of speciality.

Considering that the convention is applicable not only for prison sentences but also for measures involving deprivation of liberty imposed on mentally disabled offenders who could not be held criminally liable for their acts, serious doubts are raised regarding the validity of such persons' consent. Moreover, the sentenced person's mental or physical condition might raise doubts as to the person's comprehension of the legal consequences of his consent. Thus, in cases where one of the two states considers it necessary, in view of the age or the physical or mental condition of the sentenced person, consent is to be given by the sentenced person's legal representative.[104] The reference to the sentenced person's legal representative is not meant to imply that the representative must be legally qualified; it includes any person duly authorized by law to represent the sentenced person, such as a parent or someone specially authorized by the competent authority.[105]

The provision regarding consent must be read in conjunction with Article 2, paragraph 2 of the convention, granting the sentenced person the right to express his interest in being transferred to either the sentencing state or the administering state. Any such initiative of the prisoner must be considered under the addressed state's domestic legislation and not at the international level; there is no international obligation of the addressed state based on international public law to react to such an initiative, as there is no obligation on a state to request a transfer under this convention.[106]

The trend to base any transfer on the consent of the sentenced person can be demonstrated by the development of the U.N. Model Agreement on the Transfer of Sentenced Persons.[107] While Resolution No. 13 of the Sixth Congress[108] mentioned the possibility of effecting a transfer in the prisoner's interest even without consent, the model, as noted by ECOSOC, requires the indispensable consent of the prisoner for any transfer. Thus, it embodies the considerations of the regional preparatory meetings, where

> it was emphasized that the model should be based on the principle of mutual respect for national sovereignty and jurisdiction and on the principle of voluntary transfer, that is the transfer should be dependent on the consent of both the sentencing and the administering State, as well as on that of the prisoner.[109]

But, the opinion expressed by the European Preparatory Meeting did not distinguish between the agreement of the states concerned and the consent of the prisoner. The different level of

---

104 Euro. Conv. Trans. Sent. Per., *supra* note 31, at Art. 8, ¶ 1(d).

105 *Explanatory Note*, *supra* note 29, ¶ 23.

106 *See infra* Chapter 4, § 2 for the arguments concerning the notion of "agreement" to transfer.

107 *See Report on the Eighth Session of the Committee on Crime Prevention and Control*, ECOSOC Records, Supp. No. 6, E/AC.57/1984/18, Dec. 8/2 (1984).

108 *See supra* note 46.

109 *See Report of the European Regional Preparatory Meeting on the Prevention of Crime and the Treatment of Offenders*, Sofia, June 6-10, 1983, A.CONF 121/RPM/1, ¶ 100.

importance to be accorded to the state's agreement as compared to the prisoner's consent was stressed by the Asia and Pacific Regional Preparatory Meeting[110] where it was expressed

> that it was of vital importance that the request be made by the State whose national was the offender (and not the prisoner directly), because of the necessity of ensuring that the sentence would be properly executed. Therefore, even if the agreement needed, and was based on, tripartite consent (the receiving State, the administering State and the prisoner), it was indispensable to have the request from the receiving State, go through the official channels.

The consent of the prisoner was also emphasized at the Interregional Preparatory Meeting on topic 5 of the 7th U.N. Congress on the Prevention of Crime and the Treatment of Offenders[111] as well as by the XIIIth International Congress on Penal Law[112] where, by Resolution 12 of Section 4[113] it was emphasized that if the offender was imprisoned in the sentencing state, the transfer should be effected only with the offender's consent.

The questions of voluntariness of the prisoner's consent had already been discussed when dealing with legal problems in connection with the humanitarian considerations of the transfer.[114] To ensure voluntariness of the consent, the sentencing state has to afford an opportunity to the administering state to verify, through a consul or other official agreed upon with the administering state, that the consent is given voluntarily and with full knowledge of the legal consequences thereof.[115] The form of consent, however, is left to the sentencing state's legal regulations.

To ensure that the prisoner is aware of the possibility of being transferred and the legal consequences of transfer, the convention contains an obligation to furnish information to the prisoner, and only when a state concerned has already made request for the prisoner's transfer, but in all cases, to ensure that the prisoner himself can take an initiative by expressing his wish to be transferred.[116] To this provision, the Committee of Ministers of the Council of Europe adopted Recommendation No. R (84) 11 Concerning Information about the Convention on the Transfer of Sentenced Persons, together with an annex.[117] By this Recommendation, the governments of member states were invited to provide an authoritative translation of the standard text annexed to it into their official language or languages, taking into account any reservations or declarations to the convention which the potential transferees would need to be aware of and to deposit the translation with the Secretary-General of the Council of Europe. The Secretary-General was instructed to forward copies of the translations so received to each of the contracting states for use by

---

110 *Id.* ¶ 93.

111 Varenna, Italy, Oct. 24-28, 1984.

112 Cairo, Oct. 1-7, 1984.

113 INTERNATIONAL CONGRESS OF PENAL LAW, STRUCTURES AND METHODS OF INTERNATIONAL COOPERATION, Cairo (Nov. 1984).

114 *See supra* ch. III; *see also* the U.S. reasoning in Rosado v. Civiletti, 621 F.2d 1179 (2d Cir. 1980), *cert. denied*, No. 79-6990 (U.S. Oct. 6, 1980), and Pfeiffer v. U.S. Bureau, 448 F. Supp. 920 (S.D. Cal. 1979), 615 F.2d 873 (9th Cir. 1980), *cert. denied*, 447 U.S. 908 (1980).

115 Euro. Conv. Trans. Sent. Per., *supra* note 31, at Art. 7, ¶ 1.

116 *Id.* at Art. 4, ¶ 1.

117 Committee of Ministers, Council of Europe, *Standard Text Providing Information About the Convention on the Transfer of Sentenced Persons*, Council of Europe Doc. Mp/ R(84) 11 (June 21, 1984).

their prison authorities. This is intended to ensure early notice to foreign prisoners in a language they understand without the necessity of interpretation services. The standard text takes into consideration the form of *exequatur* procedure as used by the administering state[118] as well as the absence of a rule of speciality.[119]

Effects of a Transfer. Taking custody of the sentenced person by the authorities of the administering state has effects on both states concerned. For the sentencing state, Article 8 safeguards the principle *non ibis in idem* in respect to the enforcement of the sentence after a transfer has been effected. In particular, the sentencing state is prevented from enforcing the sentence if the administering state considers enforcement of the sentence to have been completed.[120] This regulation is based on the principle that the enforcement of the sentence is "governed by the law of the administering State and that State alone shall be competent to take all appropriate decisions,"[121] not only in the field of prison regime but also including conditional release, parole, etc. In regard to pardons, amnesty and commutation both states concerned are competent to grant such benefits.[122] Because the sentencing state retains competence regarding pardon, amnesty and commutation, the sentencing state must inform the administering state of any decision or measure by which the sentence ceases to be enforceable.[123] The same applies if the judgment is reviewed, as the sentencing state alone is competent to make such review;[124] this regulation is based on the understanding that the administering state is bound by the facts as they appear explicitly or implicitly from the judgment imposed in the sentencing state.[125]

As to the effects of a transfer in the administering state, it has to be re-emphasized that this state is bound by the facts established by the sentencing state.[126] This principle is, however, expressed only in connection with the "conversion procedure" which is based on the understanding that the administering state when adopting a sentence would not re-examine the conviction, but would continue the enforcement being, in general, bound by the legal nature and duration of the sentence.[127]

Regardless of which procedure the administering state applies, it is prevented from aggravating the prisoner's penal situation.[128] This refers not only to the length of sentence, which must not exceed that imposed in the sentencing state, but also the kind of sanction to be enforced, which must not be harsher than that imposed in the sentencing state. If, for example, under the law of the administering state, the offense carries a more severe form of punishment than that which the judgment imposed (*e.g.*, penal servitude or forced labor

---

118 "Continued Enforcement" (Art. 9, ¶ 1(a), Art. 10) or "conversion of sentence" (Art. 9, ¶ 1(b), Art.11); *see also infra* Chapter 4, § 2(d).

119 "Please note that in the event of your transfer the authorities at the administering State are entitled to prosecute, sentence, or detain you for any offense other than that for which your current sentence was imposed."

120 Euro. Conv. Trans. Sent. Per., *supra* note 31, at Art. 8, ¶ 2.

121 *Id.* at Art. 9, ¶ 3.

122 *See id.* at Art. 12. Comparing Art 12 with the regulations of other transfer treaties, the convention follows the majority of such instruments: some of them distinguish however between acts of grace (individual pardon) and amnesty (collective pardon). For example, the Berlin Convention restricts the right to grant grace to the administering state.

123 *See* Euro. Conv. Trans. Sent. Per., *supra* note 31, at Art 14.

124 *Id.* at Art. 13.

125 *Id.* at Art. 11, ¶ 1(a).

126 *Id.* at Art. 11, ¶ 1(e).

127 *Id.* at Art. 10.

128 *See id.* at Art. 10, ¶ 2, and Art. 11, ¶ 1(d).

instead of imprisonment), the administering state is precluded from enforcing this harsher sanction.[129] Moreover, the prohibition of aggravation rule implies that the administering state is not bound by any minimum penalties as prescribed by its laws for the offense or offenses committed.[130] In any case, differences in prison regime should not be taken into consideration.

The rule of nonaggravation raises a further question which is not regulated by the convention: Should regulations concerning conditional release or parole of the sentencing state, which are more favorable for the transferred prisoner than the administering state's regulations, be taken into consideration? Does the application of harsher conditions for parole or for a conditional release in the administering state[131] violate the prohibition of aggravation? None of the existing treaties contains any indication regarding this question. Austrian courts, in applying the European Convention on the International Validity of Criminal Judgements[132] have reasoned that more favorable conditions for a conditional release have to be taken into consideration in the course of the *exequatur* proceedings. Based on these considerations, an Austrian delegation, when negotiating a transfer treaty with Hungary, has proposed the following formulation:

> By the enforcement of the sentence in the administering State the prisoner's penal situation in its entirety must not be aggravated compared to the situation as given in case of the further enforcement in the sentencing State. The enforcement of the sentence shall be governed by the law of the administering State. Regulations of the sentencing State concerning the conditional release and being more favorable for the convicted person shall, according to the administering State's law, be applied.[133]

It must be realized that this formulation is not a final solution to the problem, as it requires national implementation measures taking into account foreign legislation. However, it is a first step toward interpretation of the rule of nonaggravation.

The basic provisions of the convention are those concerning the enforcement of the sanction in the administering state. In this respect, the convention deviates from the regulations of the European Convention on the International Validity of Criminal Judgements which, in the case of sanctions involving deprivation of liberty, explicitly requires *exequatur* proceedings.[134] The mandatory character of this provision is, however, in contradiction to the existing legislation of some countries[135] and has thus been an obstacle for the ratification of this convention. For this reason, the new convention is based on a compromise formula.[136] The administering State has the option to choose between two procedures: It may either continue the enforcement immediately, or through a court or administrative order,[137] or it may convert the sentence through a judicial or administrative

---

129 *See Explanatory Note*, *supra* note 29, ¶ 57.

130 *See* Euro. Conv. Trans. Sent. Per., *supra* note 31, at Art. 11, ¶ 1(d).

131 As already indicated, only the administering state's law is applicable for the enforcement of the sentence and for the necessary decisions in this connection. *Id.* at Art. 9, ¶ 3.

132 Art. 44, ¶ 2. *See* Eur. Conv. Int'l Val. Crim. Judg., *supra* note 20, at Art. 44, ¶ 2.

133 This provision was accepted at the negotiations; the treaty was signed on May 6, 1985.

134 *See* Eur. Conv. Int'l Val. Crim. Judg., *supra* note 20, at Arts. 37 & 44.

135 *E.g.*, the legislation of France.

136 *See* Bartsch, *supra* note 27, at 516.

137 *See* Euro. Conv. Trans. Sent. Per., *supra* note 31, at Art. 9, ¶ 1(a).

procedure into a decision of that state, thereby substituting for the sanction imposed in the sentencing state a sanction prescribed by the law of the administering state for the same offense.[138] If requested, the administering state must inform the sentencing state which of these procedures it will follow before the transfer of the sentenced person.[139]

There is one basic difference between "continued enforcement" and the "conversion of sentence" procedure. In the case of continued enforcement, the administering state continues to enforce the sanction imposed in the sentencing state. In the latter case, the sanction is converted into a sanction of the administering state, with the result that the sentence enforced is no longer directly based on the sanction imposed in the sentencing state.[140]

When applying the continued enforcement procedure,[141] the administering state is, in principle, bound by the legal nature and duration of the sentence as determined by the sentencing state. The notion of "legal nature" refers to the kind of penalty imposed in the sentencing state where the law of this state provides for a diversity of penalties involving deprivation of liberty;[142] for example, different forms of imprisonment or the imposition of other measures. The notion of "duration" means that the sentence to be served in the administering state, subject to any later decision of that state on conditional release or remission, corresponds to the period of the original sentence, taking into account the time served and any remission earned in the sentencing state up to the date of transfer.[143]

Having in mind the divergences of the sanctioning systems and considering the prohibition against aggravating the prisoner's penal situation, a restricted adaptation may also be necessary when applying the continued enforcement procedure. Such adaptation may be necessary if the sanction imposed in the sentencing state exceeds the maximum penalty as provided by the administering state's law; moreover, different forms of sanctions involving deprivation of liberty may give rise to adaptation. But any such adaptation is restricted: Apart from preventing an aggravation of the prisoner's situation, the adapted punishment or measure has to correspond as nearly as possible with that imposed in the sentencing state.[144] Notwithstanding such adaptations this procedure is still to be considered as continued enforcement, as the adaptation is restricted to such degree as may be necessitated by the administering state's penal system.[145]

In contrast to the continued enforcement procedure, the conversion procedure[146] follows the ideology of the European Convention on the International Validity of Criminal Judgements: When applying this procedure, the administering state substitutes a sanction prescribed by its own law for the sanction imposed in the sentencing state. In doing so, the competent authorities are guided by the principles of award of punishment as applied by the

---

138 *Id.* at Art. 9, ¶ 1(b).

139 *Id.* at Art. 9, ¶ 2.

140 *See* Bartsch, *supra* note 99, at 307.

141 Euro. Conv. Trans. Sent. Per., *supra* note 31, at Art. 10.

142 *See Explanatory Note*, *supra* note 29, ¶ 49.

143 *Id.*

144 If, for example, the sentence imposes incarceration for a period of six years, the maximum penalty in the administering state being five years of imprisonment, the latter state has, notwithstanding later decisions on conditional release, to adapt the sanction to the nearest equivalent available under its law, that is, five years of imprisonment.

145 This regulation was influenced in particular by Art. VI of the French-Canadian transfer treaty, *supra* note 35.

146 Euro. Conv. Trans. Sent. Per., *supra* note 31, at Art. 11 (this is also called *exequatur* procedure).

judiciary when fixing the individual sanction between the upper and lower limits of punishment according to that state's law. The conversion is, however, restricted to the substitution of sanctions and does not allow a review of the findings as to the facts.[147] The conversion procedure merely serves to impose an enforceable sanction in the administering state.[148] Moreover, the competence of the administering state to substitute for the penalty imposed in the sentencing state is restricted in three further respects: According to the principle of nonaggravation, the administering state is not bound by any minimum penalty as provided in its law for similar offenses;[149] the period of deprivation of liberty already served by the sentenced person has to be fully deducted;[150] and finally, a sanction involving deprivation of liberty may not be converted into a pecuniary sanction.[151]

Relationship to Other Conventions. Article 22 considers the relationship of this convention to other conventions on extradition and mutual assistance in criminal matters, as well as to existing agreements, including uniform legislation on the transfer of sentenced persons. In this convention, only the relationship to the European Convention on the International Validity of Criminal Judgements will be considered.

The convention follows the principle that the requesting state must determine on which instrument it will base its request if both states concerned are parties to both conventions.[152] This decision of the requesting state will be guided with a view to the different regulations of the conventions. Although the new convention provides for a simplified procedure, the advantages of the International Validity Convention should not be disregarded. The influence of national legislations when implementing this convention is restricted, as only a limited number of reservations is admitted, thereby creating a more uniform applicability of this instrument. In addition, the International Validity Convention imposes an obligation on the requested state to enforce the sentence: it is applicable whether or not the prisoner is still in the sentencing state and whether or not the sentences involve a deprivation of liberty. Moreover, according to the International Validity Convention, a transfer is possible without the consent of the prisoner, and a transfer can be made to his country of residence.[153] On the other hand, the Transfer Convention has, apart from its procedure and possible implementation according to national law, the advantage of being applicable also for sentences passed before the entry into force of that convention.[154] Thus a reasonable co-existence of these instruments can be expected.

National Legislation

Examining the Convention on the Transfer of Sentenced Persons, it must be realized that in order to make possible the ratification by many countries, most of the provisions are

---

147 This applies to both "objective" facts relating to the commission of the act and its results, as well as to "subjective" facts relating, for instance, to premeditation and intent on the part of the convicted person; *see Explanatory Note*, *supra* note 29, ¶ 54; *see also* arguments in ¶ 2 of this subsection.

148 *See* Bartsch, *supra* note 99, at 308.

149 Euro. Conv. Trans. Sent. Per., *supra* note 31, at Art. 11, ¶ 1(d).

150 *Id.* at Art. 11, ¶ 1(c).

151 *Id.* at Art. 11, ¶ 1(b).

152 *Id.* at Art. 22, ¶ 4.

153 *See* Bartsch, *supra* note 27, at 517; Epp, *supra* note 6, at 120.

154 *Compare* Euro. Conv. Trans. Sent. Per., *supra* note 31, *with* Eur. Conv. Int'l Val. Crim. Judg., *supra* note 20, at Art. 68.

not self-executing and have to be implemented into national law. To achieve this goal, two different methods are conceivable: to pass legislation only for the implementation of the convention, or to create, at the same time, a mechanism for the transfer of prisoners without treaty on the basis of reciprocity.

Transfer on the Basis of Reciprocity. Legislation implementing international transfer instruments which also provides for a repatriation of prisoners on the basis of reciprocity has been passed in Europe, first by Austria,[155] and followed by Switzerland,[156] and the Federal Republic of Germany.[157] These statutes do not, however, regulate only the transfer of prisoners: they are instead comprehensive instruments of international cooperation[158] regulating extradition, mutual assistance, transfer of proceedings and transfer of the enforcement of sentences.[159] Turkey has also enacted legislation providing for a repatriation of prisoners on the basis of reciprocity. The former Turkish position was that a transfer could be granted only under the condition that the entire sanction as imposed in the sentencing state was enforced in the administering state.[160] This position has recently been amended and now allows adaptation procedures to be conducted in the administering state.[161]

When considering the Austrian, Swiss and German acts on international cooperation, particularly the provisions concerning the transfer of prisoners, one must mention that, in general, international agreements, being self-executing, have priority over the provisions of these acts.[162] Thus, different and additional provisions contained in international agreements but not contained in national laws will still be effective for directing states' actions. If, however, the provisions are not self-executing, national law must be applied to interpret such provisions, or additional implementation legislation has to be adopted.[163]

Although the Austrian ARHG[164] was adopted together with the ratification of the International Validity Convention by Austria, establishing the internal implementation procedures for application of the convention, a transfer of prisoners on the basis of reciprocity can be effected only on the basis of the prisoner's consent. When enforcing a foreign sentence, the Austrian regulations[165] are governed by the adaptation procedure and the rule of speciality is not applied. A request for enforcement submitted by the sentencing

---

155 Austrian ARHG, Act on Extradition and Mutual Assistance, FEDERAL LAW GAZETTE No. 529/1979, enacted Jan. 1, 1980.

156 Swiss IRSG, Act on International Mutual Assistance in Criminal Matters, S.R. 353.1, enacted Jan. 1, 1983.

157 German IRG, Act on International Mutual Assistance in Criminal Matters, FEDERAL LAW GAZETTE 1982 I.S. 2071, enacted July 1, 1983.

158 *See* Robert Linke, *Leitende Grundsatze der Reform des Auslieferungs und Rechtshilferechts*, 52 OEJZ 365 (1980).

159 The Austrian ARHG also contains regulations concerning the supervision of conditionally sentenced or conditionally released offenders.

160 Law No. 647 of July 16, 1965 on the Enforcement of Sentences, at Art. 18.

161 The regulation of Law No. 647, *supra* note 160, was, however, of a subsidiary nature, thus allowing for an adaptation if so provided for by an international agreement, such as the Eur. Conv. Int'l Val. Crim. Judg., *supra* note 20.

162 *See* Austrian ARHG, *supra* note 155, § 1; Swiss IRSG, *supra* note 156, at Art. 1, ¶ 1 ; German IRG, *supra* note 157, § 1, ¶ 3.

163 Such implementation provisions can also be established by reservations or declarations to the international instrument when adopted by the legislative body in proceedings as provided for by constitutional law.

164 *Cf.* EDITH PALMER, THE AUSTRIAN LAW ON EXTRADITION AND MUTUAL ASSISTANCE IN CRIMINAL MATTERS (Library of Congress trans., 1983).

165 *See* Austrian ARHG, *supra* note 155, § 64.

state will be acted on only if the sentenced person is an Austrian national with residence or domicile in Austria, and when the safeguards of Article 6 of the Convention for the Protection of Human Rights and Fundamental Freedoms[166] have been observed in the proceedings of the sentencing state.[167] On the other hand, an Austrian request to enforce a judgment passed by Austrian courts is precluded if there is reason to believe that the sentence would not be enforced in compliance with the requirements of Article 3 of the Human Rights Convention, or would be disadvantageous for the transferred person "on account of his descent, race, religion, association with a particular ethnic group, his nationality, or on account of his political view," of "if the person would have to expect other serious disadvantages from any one of these reasons."[168]

The Swiss IRSG[169] provides, with regard to the execution of foreign criminal judgments,[170] only for a restricted adaptation of the sanction imposed in the sentencing state; that is, if the maximum penalty provided by Swiss law for a corresponding offense is exceeded.[171] The Swiss IRSG does, in contrast to the Austrian ARHG, extend the applicability of the transfer instrument, as it is not limited to nationals but extends to convicted persons with habitual residence in Switzerland.[172] However, an important restriction on the enforcement of foreign penal sanctions on the basis of reciprocity is contained in the Swiss IRSG.[173] The rules concerning the execution of foreign penal judgments are not applicable if the Swiss Penal Code explicitly excludes (Article 6 Penal Code) or explicitly prescribes (Article 5 Penal Code) the execution of the penalty imposed abroad. But these provisions of the Swiss Penal Code apply only to Swiss nationals and preclude the enforcement of a foreign judgment unless the offense would be extraditable according to Swiss law. Thus, a foreigner with habitual residence in Switzerland could more easily benefit from the transfer provisions unless he has committed an offense against a Swiss national abroad, in which case the enforcement of a foreign judgment is precluded by Article 5 of the Swiss Penal Code.[174] These provisions do restrict a repatriation on the basis of reciprocity, as both the Austrian ARHG and the Swiss IRSG are applicable only for the enforcement of sentences passed against the nationals of the administering state. As to Swiss requests for enforcement, the Swiss IRSG also requires the prisoner's consent.[175]

---

166 Europ. T.S. No. 5.

167 Considering that the Human Rights Convention is on a constitutional level in the Austrian legislation, this condition complies with the demands of Oehler, *supra* note 1, at 277, that enforcement should be refused if the foreign penal judgment to be executed violated essential constitutional principles or were compatible with a protected fundamental right.

168 *Compare* Austrian ARHG, *supra* note 155, § 76 *with* Austrian ARHG § 19, ¶ 3. *See also* in this respect Resolution No. 16 of § 4 of the Cairo Congress, *see supra* notes 103, 104: "Calls on States not to use these international instruments of transfer of proceedings and of prisoners in cases, where the offender might face capital punishment or be confronted with any form of cruel, inhumane or degrading treatment. States should, moreover, abstain from using these instruments as a means of disguised extradition."

169 *See* Lionel Frei, *Das neue Bundesgesetz uber Internationale Rechtshilfe in Strafsachen—Neue Losungen und neue Probleme*, 96 SCHW ZSTRR 57 (1983); Jean J. Gauthier, *La nouvelle legislation suisse sur l'entraide internationale in matiere penale*, 97 SCHW ZSTRR 51 (1984).

170 Swiss IRSG, *supra* note 156, at pt. 5, ch. 1.

171 *Id.* at Art. 94, ¶ 2.

172 *Id.* at Art. 94, ¶ 1(a).

173 *Id.* at Art. 94, ¶ 3.

174 *See* Dominique Schouwey, *Nouvelles perspectives pur les ressortissants suisses condamnes a Petranger*, 3 REVUE INTERNATIONALE DE CRIMINOLOGIE ET DE POLICE TECHNIQUE 342 (1985).

175 Swiss IRSG, *supra* note 156, at Arts. 100 and 101.

Similar to the provisions of the other acts on mutual assistance in criminal matters, the IRG of the Federal Republic of Germany,[176] relating to enforcement of foreign penal judgments, requires the prisoner's consent; however, the application of these provisions is, based on reciprocity, restricted to German nationals.[177] Apart from the condition of double criminality, which is contained in all acts, an adaptation procedure is provided only in cases where the maximum penalty as provided by German law is exceeded. The enforcement of penalties not used in the sanctioning system of the Federal Republic of Germany, such as corporal punishment, is precluded. Moreover, the enforcement of a foreign judgment is permitted only if minimal procedural safeguards have been observed in the criminal proceedings of the sentencing state. In this regard, it is recognized[178] that this condition could prevent a transfer of a German national where particularly severe circumstances would make it highly desirable.[179]

Implementation Legislation. Apart from the legislation just discussed, which serves as both implementing machinery for international agreements and a basis for repatriation of prisoners, some countries, granting a transfer only on the basis of international agreements have passed legislation for the implementation of such treaties.[180] The most recent legislation in this respect, the Repatriation of Prisoners Act of 1984,[181] has been adopted in the U.K. This act is intended to "make provision for facilitating the transfer between the U.K. and places outside the British Islands of persons for the time being detained in prisons, hospitals or other institutions by virtue of orders made in the course of the exercise by courts and tribunals of their criminal jurisdiction." Thus, it could also serve as a national basis for the ratification of the Convention on the Transfer of Sentenced Persons, which was signed by the U.K. on August 25, 1983. The regulations of this act are based on the recommendations of a working group set up by the British Home Secretary in April 1978.[182] Noting the crucial conditions of any transfer regulations, this act requires the prisoner's consent; the enforcement of a foreign judgment is not, however, restricted to British nationals but can also be granted where the person has close ties with the U.K.

Future Aspects

The unification of transfer of prisoners principles, as evidenced particularly by the Convention on the Transfer of Sentenced Persons as well as by the U.N. Model Agreement on the Transfer of Prisoners, demonstrates the increasing awareness that the social resettlement of offenders who have committed criminal offenses abroad can best be achieved

---

[176] *Cf.* Theo Vogler et al., *Kommentar zum IRG*, *in* HEINRICH GRUTZNER & PAUL G. POTZ, 1 INTERNATIONALER RECHTSHILFEVERKEHR IN STRAFSACHEN pt. A2 (1980); Theo Vogler, *Das neue Gesetz uber dieinternationale Rechtshilfe in Strafsachen*, 36 NJW 2114 (1983); Peter Wilkitzki, *Rechtshilfe durch Vollstreckung—Zur praktischen Anwendung des neuen Rechtsinstituts*, *supra* note 14.

[177] *See* German IRG, *supra* note 157, §§ 48, 49.

[178] *Cf.* Wilkitzki, *supra* note 14, at 229.

[179] *See also* Chapter 3.

[180] *See e.g.*, the U.S. legislation implementing the U.S.-Mexico Treaty, Act of Oct. 28, 1977, Pub. L. No. 95-144, 91 Stat. 1212; or the Canadian Transfer of Offenders Act, Bill C-21 of Mar. 17, 1978 ("an Act to implement treaties on the transfer of persons found guilty of criminal offences").

[181] 1984, ch. 47.

[182] CRIMINAL POLICY DEP'T., THE REPATRIATION OF PRISONERS, REPORT OF THE INTERDEPARTMENTAL WORKING PARTY (Feb. 1980).

by an early repatriation to the offender's home country. However, the proceedings and the conviction in the sentencing state cause some delay in the repatriation of offenders. For this reason, the possibility of transferring the criminal proceedings together with the alleged offender being held in pre-trial custody has been discussed.[183] Such regulations are already in force among Council of Europe member states,[184] and an extension to common law states would be desirable.[185] Of course, some obstacles for the implementation of a transfer of proceedings instrument in the latter states, particularly regarding the competence of the court and what evidentiary requirements to impose, must be overcome. However, such initiatives would, as already discussed at the XIIIth International Congress on Penal Law,[186] have positive prospects if, similar to transfer of prisoner's arrangements, the alleged offender have some influence on the decision of whether he should be transferred to his home country for prosecution.[187]

---

183 *See Report of the European Regional Preparatory Meeting*, *supra* note 109, ¶ 102.

184 *See* Art. 21 of the European Convention on Mutual Assistance in Criminal Matters of 1959, Europ. T.S. No. 30; and in particular the European Convention on the Transfer of Criminal Proceedings of 1970, Europ. T.S. No. 70, by which a request to prosecute establishes a jurisdiction of the requested state.

185 *Cf.* in this respect the U.N. Model Treaty on the Transfer of Proceedings in Criminal Matters, adopted at the Eighth United Nations Congress on the Prevention of Crime and the Treatment of Offenders, Havana Aug. 27-Sept. 7, 1990, A/CONF.144/28/Rev.1, at 89.

186 *Supra* note 112.

187 *See id.* at Res. 11, § 4 of the XIIIth International Penal Law Congress of the International Association of Penal Law held in Cairo, Oct. 1-7, 1984: "Invites States to conclude agreements on the transfer of criminal proceedings to the country of nationality or residence of the offender. If the offender is detained in the country where the proceedings were initiated, the transfer should be effected only with his consent." 56 REVUE INTERNATIONALE DE DROIT PENAL 473 (1986).

Appendix 14

European Convention on the Transfer of Sentenced Prisoners*

The member States of the Council of Europe and the other States, signatory hereto,

Considering that the aim of the Council of Europe is to achieve a greater unity between its members;

Desirous of further developing international co-operation in the field of criminal law;

Considering that such co-operations should further the ends of justice and the social rehabilitation of sentenced persons;

Considering that these objectives require that foreigners who are deprived of their liberty as a result of their commission of a criminal offence should be given the opportunity to serve their sentences within their own society; and

Considering that this aim can best be achieved by having them transferred to their own countries;

Have agreed as follows:

ARTICLE I
Definitions

For the purposes of this Convention:

(a) "sentence" means any punishment or measure involving deprivation of liberty ordered by a court for a limited or unlimited period of time on account of a criminal offence;

(b) "judgement" means a decision on order of a court imposing a sentence;

(c) "sentencing State" means the State to which the sentenced person may be, or has been, transferred in order to serve his sentence.

ARTICLE 2
General principles

1. The Parties undertake to afford each other the widest measure of co-operation in respect of the transfer of sentenced persons in accordance with the provisions of this Convention.
2. A person sentenced in the territory of a Party may be transferred to the territory of another Party, in accordance with the provisions of this Convention, in order to serve the sentence imposed on him. To that end, he may express his interest to the sentencing State or to the administering State in being transferred under this Convention.
3. Transfer may be requested by either the sentencing State or the administering State.

ARTICLE 3
Conditions for transfer

1. A sentenced person may be transferred under this Convention only on the following conditions:

(a) if that person is a national or the administrating State;

(b) if the judgement is final;

(c) if, at the time of receipt of the request for transfer, the sentenced person still has at least six months of the sentence to serve or if the sentence is indeterminate;

(d) if the transfer is consented to by the sentenced person or, where in view of his age or his physical or mental condition one of the two States considers it necessary, by the sentenced person's legal representative;

---

* This Convention is open to states that are non-members in the Council of Europe. The United States has acceded to that Convention and has ratified it.

(e) if the acts or omissions on account of which the sentence has been imposed constitute a criminal offence according to the law of the administering State or would constitute a criminal offence if committed on its territory; and

(f) if the sentencing and administering States agree to the transfer.

2. In exceptional cases, Parties may agree to a transfer even if the time to be served by the sentenced person is less than that specified in paragraph 1.c.

3. Any State may, at the time of signature or when depositing its instrument of ratification, acceptance, approval or accession, by a declaration addressed to the Secretary General of the Council of Europe, indicate that it intends to exclude the application of one of the procedures provided in Article 9.1.a and b in its relations with other Parties.

4. Any State, may at any time, by a declaration addressed to the Secretary General of the Council of Europe, define, as far as it is concerned, the term "national" for the purposes of this Convention.

ARTICLE 4
Obligation to furnish information

1. Any sentenced person to whom this Convention may apply shall be informed by the sentencing State of the substance of this Convention.

2. If the sentenced person has expressed an interest in the sentencing State in being transferred under this Convention, that State shall so inform the administering State as soon as practicable after the judgement becomes final.

3. The information shall include

(a) the name, date and place of birth of the sentenced person;

(b) his address, if any, in the administering State;

(c) a statement of the facts upon which the sentence was based;

(d) the nature, duration and date of commencement of the sentence.

4. If the sentenced person has expressed his interest to the administering State, the sentencing State shall, on request, communicate to that State the information referred to in paragraph 3 above.

5. The sentenced person shall be informed, in writing, of any action taken by the sentencing State or the administering State under the preceding paragraphs, as well as of any decision taken by either State on a request for transfer.

ARTICLE 5
Requests and replies

1. Request for transfer and replies shall be made in writing.

2. Requests shall be addressed by the Ministry of Justice of the requesting State to the Ministry of Justice of the requested State. Replies shall be communicated through the same channels.

3. Any Party may, by a declaration addressed to the Secretary General of the Council of Europe indicate that it will use other channels of communication.

4. The requested State shall promptly inform the requesting State of its decision whether or not to agree to the requested transfer.

ARTICLE 6
Supporting documents

1. The administering State, if requested by the sentencing State, shall furnish it with:

(a) a document or statement indicating that the sentenced person is a national of that State;

(b) a copy of the relevant law of the administering State which provides that the acts or omissions on account of which the sentence has been imposed in the sentencing State constitute a criminal offense according to the law of the administering State, or would constitute a criminal offence if committed on its territory;

(c) a statement containing the information mentioned in Article 9.2.

2. If a transfer is requested, the sentencing State shall provide the following documents to the administering State, unless either State has already indicated that it will not agree to the transfer:

(a) a certified copy of the judgement and the law on which it is based;

(b) a statement indicating how much of the sentence has already been serve including information on any pre-trial detention, remission, and any other factor relevant to the enforcement of the sentence;

(c) a declaration containing the consent to the transfer as referred to in Article 3.1.d; and

(d) whenever appropriate, any medical or social reports on the sentenced person, information about his treatment in the sentencing State, and any recommendation for his further treatment in the administering State.

3. Either State may ask to be provided with any of the documents or statements referred to in paragraphs 1 or 2 above before making a request for transfer or taking a decision on whether or not to agree to the transfer.

ARTICLE 7

Consent and its verification

1. The sentencing State shall ensure that the person required to give consent to the transfer in accordance with Article 3.1.d does so voluntarily and with full knowledge of the legal consequences thereof. The procedure for giving such consent shall be governed by the law of the sentencing State.

2. The sentencing State shall afford an opportunity to the administering State to verify, through a consul or other official agreed upon with the administering State, that the consent is given in accordance with the conditions set out in paragraph 1 above.

ARTICLE 8

Effect of transfer for sentencing State

1. The taking into charge of the sentenced person by the authorities of the administering State shall have the effect of suspending the enforcement of the sentence in the sentencing State.

2. The sentencing State may no longer enforce the sentence if the administering State considers enforcement of the sentence to have been completed.

ARTICLE 9

Effect of transfer for administering State

1. The competent authorities of the administering State shall:

(a) continue the enforcement of the sentence immediately or through a court or administrative order, under the conditions set out in Article 10, or

(b) convert the sentence, through a judicial or administrative procedure, into a decision of that State, thereby substituting for the sanction imposed in the sentencing State a sanction prescribed by the law of the administering State for the same offense, under the conditions set out in Article 11.

2. The administering State, if requested, shall inform the sentencing State before the transfer of the sentenced person as to which of these procedures it will follow.

3. The enforcement of the sentence shall be governed by the law of the administering State and that State alone shall be competent to take all appropriate decisions.

4. Any State which, according to its national law, cannot avail itself of one of the procedures referred to in paragraph 1 to enforce measures imposed in the territory of another Party on persons who for reasons of mental condition have been held not criminally responsible for the commission of the offence, and which is prepared to receive such persons for further treatment may, by way of a declaration addressed to the Secretary General of the Council of Europe, indicate the procedures it will follow in such cases.

ARTICLE 10

Continued enforcement

1. In the case of continued enforcement, the administering State shall be bound by the legal nature and duration of the sentence as determined by the sentencing State.

2. If, however, this sentence is by its nature or duration incompatible with the law of the administering State, or its laws so requires, that State may, by a court or administrative order, adapt the sanction to the punishment or measure prescribed by its own law for a similar offense. As to its nature, the punishment or measure shall, as far as possible, correspond with that imposed by the sentence to be enforced. It shall not aggravate, by its nature or duration, the sanction imposed in the sentencing State, nor exceed the maximum prescribed by the law of the administering State.

ARTICLE 11

Conversion of sentence

1. In the case of conversion of sentence, the procedures provided for by the law of the administering State apply. When converting the sentence, the competent authority:

(a) shall be bound by the findings as to the facts insofar as they appear explicitly by or implicitly from the judgement imposed in the sentencing State;

(b) may not convert a sanction involving deprivation of liberty to a pecuniary sanction;

(c) shall deduct the full period of deprivation of liberty served by the sentenced person; and

(d) shall not aggravate the penal position of the sentenced person, and shall not be bound by any minimum which the law of the administering State may provide for the offence or offences committed.

2. If the conversion procedure takes place after the transfer of the sentenced person the administering State shall keep that person in custody or otherwise ensure his presence in the administering State pending the outcome of that procedure.

ARTICLE 12

Pardon, amnesty, commutation

Each Party may grant pardon, amnesty or commutation of the sentence in accordance with its Constitution or other laws.

ARTICLE 13

Review of judgement

The sentencing State alone shall have the right to decide on any application for review of the judgement.

ARTICLE 14

Termination of enforcement

The administering State shall terminate enforcement of the sentence as soon as it is informed by the sentencing State of any decision or measure as a result of which the sentence ceases to be enforceable.

ARTICLE 15

Information on enforcement

The administering State shall provide information to the sentencing State concerning the enforcement of the sentence:

(a) when it considers enforcement of the sentence to have been completed;

(b) if the sentenced person has escaped from custody before enforcement of the sentence has been completed; or

(c) if the sentencing State requests a special report.

ARTICLE I 6

Transit

1. A Party shall, in accordance with its law, grant a request for transit of a sentenced person through its territory if such a request is made by another Party and that State has agreed with another Party or with a third State to the transfer of that person to or from its territory.

2. A Party may refuse to grant transit:

(a) if the sentenced person is one of its nationals, or

(b) if the offense for which the sentence was imposed is not an offense under its own law.

3. Requests for transit and replies shall be communicated through the channels referred to in the provisions of Article 5.2 and 3.

4. A Party may grant a request for transit of a sentenced person through its territory made by a third State if that State has agreed with another Party to the transfer to or from its territory.

5. The Party requested to grant transit may hold the sentenced person in custody only for such time as transit through its territory requires.

6. The Party requested to grant transit may be asked to give an assurance that the sentenced person will not be prosecuted, or, except as provided in the preceding paragraph, detained, or otherwise subjected to any restriction on his liberty in the territory of the transit State for any offence committed or sentence imposed prior to his departure from the territory of the sentencing State.

7. No request for transit shall be required if transport is by air over the territory of a Party and no landing there is scheduled. However, each State may, by a declaration addressed to the Secretary General of the Council of Europe at the time of signature or of deposit of its instrument of ratification, acceptance, approval or accession, require that it be notified of any such transit over its territory.

8. In respect of any acceding State, the Convention shall enter into force on the first day of the month following the expiration of a period of three months after the date of deposit of the instrument of accession with the Secretary General of the Council of Europe.

ARTICLE 20

Territorial application

1. Any State may at the time of signature or when depositing its instrument of ratification. acceptance, approval or accession, specify the territory or territories to which this Convention shall apply.

2. Any State may at any later date, by a declaration addressed to the Secretary General of the Council of Europe, extend the application of this Convention to any other territory specified in the declaration. In respect of such territory the Convention shall enter into force on the first day of the month following the expiration of a period of three months after the date of receipt of such declaration by the Secretary General.

3. Any declaration made under the two preceding paragraphs may, in respect of any territory specified in such declaration, be withdrawn by a notification addressed to the Secretary General. The withdrawal shall become effective on the first day of the month following the expiration of a period of three months after the date of receipt of such notification by the Secretary General.

ARTICLE 21

Temporal application

This Convention shall be applicable to the enforcement of sentences imposed either before or after its entry into force.

ARTICLE 22

Relationship to other Conventions and Agreements

1. This Convention does not affect the rights and undertakings derived from extradition treaties and other treaties on international cooperation in criminal matters providing for the transfer of detained persons for purposes of confrontation or testimony.

2. If two or more Parties have already concluded an agreement or treaty on the transfer of sentenced persons or otherwise have established their relations in this matter, or should they in future do so, they shall be entitled to apply that agreement or treaty or to regulate those relations accordingly, in lieu of the present Convention.
3. The present Convention does not affect the right of States party to the European Convention on the International Validity of Criminal judgements to conclude bilateral or multilateral agreements with one another on matters dealt with in that Convention in order to supplement its provisions or facilitate the application of the principles embodied in it.
4. If a request for transfer falls within the scope of both the present Convention and the European Convention on the International Validity of Criminal judgements or another agreement or treaty on the transfer of sentenced persons, the requesting State shall, when making the request, indicate on the basis of which instrument it is made.

ARTICLE 23
Friendly settlement

The European Committee on Crime Problems of the Council of Europe shall be kept informed regarding the application of this Convention and shall do whatever is necessary to facilitate a friendly settlement of any difficulty which may arise out of its application.

ARTICLE 24
Denunciation

1. Any Party may at any time denounce this Convention by means of a notification addressed to the Secretary General of the Council of Europe.
2. Such denunciation shall become effective on the first day of the month following the expiration of a period of three months after the date of receipt of the notification by the Secretary General.
3. The present Convention shall, however, continue to apply to the enforcement of sentences of persons who have been transferred in conformity with the provisions of the Convention before the date on which such a denunciation takes effect.

ARTICLE 25
Notifications

The Secretary General of the Council of Europe shall notify the member States of the Council of Europe, the non-member States which have participated in the elaboration of this Convention and any State which has acceded to this Convention of:

(a) any signature;

(b) the deposit of any instrument of ratification, acceptance, approval or accession;

(c) any date of entry into force of this Convention in accordance with Articles 18.2 and 3, 19.2 and 20.2 and 3;

(d) any other act, declaration, notification or communication relating to this Convention.

In witness whereof the undersigned, being duly authorized thereto, have signed this Convention.

Done at Strasbourg, this 21st day of March 1983, in English and French, both texts being equally authentic, in a single copy which shall be deposited in the archives of the Council of Europe. The Secretary General of the Council of Europe shall transmit certified copies to each member State of the Council of Europe, to the non-member States which have participated in the elaboration of this Convention, and to any State invited to accede to it.

For the Government of the Republic of Austria:

D. BUKOWNKI

(Council of Europe)

EXPLANATORY REPORT ON THE CONVENTION ON THE TRANSFER OF SENTENCED PERSONS

Strasbourg 1983

INTRODUCTION

1. At their 11th Conference (Copenhagen, 21 and 22 June 1978), the European Ministers of Justice discussed the problems posed by prisoners of foreign nationality, including the question of providing procedures for their transfer so that they may serve their sentence in their home country. The discussion resulted in the adoption of Resolution No. 1, by which the Committee of Ministers of the Council of Europe is invited to ask the European Committee on Crime Problems (CDPC), *inter alia*, "to consider the possibility of drawing up a model agreement providing for a simple procedure for the transfer of prisoners which could be used between member states or by member states in their relations with non-member states."

2. Following this initiative, the creation of a Select Committee of Experts on Foreign Nationals in Prison was proposed by the CDPC at its 28th Plenary Session in March 1979 and authorised by the Committee of Ministers at the 306th meeting of their Deputies in June 1979.

3. The committee's principal tasks were to study the problems relating to the treatment of foreigners in prison and to consider the possibility of drawing up a model agreement providing for a simple procedure for the transfer of foreign prisoners. With regard to the latter aspect. the CDPC (at its 29th Plenary Session in March 1980) authorised the Select Committee, at its own request, to prepare a multilateral convention rather than a model agreement, provided it would not conflict with the provisions of existing European conventions.

4. The Select Committee was composed of experts from fifteen Council of Europe member states (Austria, Belgium, Denmark, France, Federal Republic of Germany, Greece, Italy, Luxembourg, Netherlands, Portugal, Spain, Sweden, Switzerland, Turkey, United Kingdom). Canada and the United States of America as well as the Commonwealth Secretariat and the International Penal and Penitentiary Foundation were represented by observers. Mr. J. J. Tulkens (the Netherlands) was elected Chairman of the Select Committee. The secretariat was provided by the Directorate of Legal Affairs of the Council of Europe.

5. The draft for a Convention on the Transfer of Sentenced Persons was prepared during the Select Committee's first five meetings, held from 3 to 5 October 1979, 4 to 6 March 1980, 7 to 10 October 1980,1 to 4 June 1981 and 1 to 4 December 1981 (enlarged meeting to which experts from all member states were invited). In addition, a drafting group met from 7 to 9 October 1980 (during the Select Committee's 3rd meeting) and from 24 to 26 November 1980.

6. The draft convention was finalised by the CDPC at its 31st Plenary Session in May 1982 and forwarded to the Committee of Ministers.

7. At the 350th meeting of their Deputies in September 1982, the Committee of Ministers approved the text of the convention. At their 354th meeting in December 1982, the Ministers' Deputies decided to open it for signature on 21 March 1983.

GENERAL CONSIDERATIONS

8. The purpose of the Convention is to facilitate the transfer of foreign prisoners to their home countries by providing a procedure which is simple as well as expeditious. In that respect it is intended to complement the European Convention on the International Validity of Criminal Judgements of 28 May 1970 which, although allowing for the transfer of prisoners, presents two major shortcomings: it has, so far, been ratified by only a small number of member states, and the procedure it provides is not conducive to being applied in such a way as to ensure the rapid transfer of foreign prisoners.

With a view to overcoming the last-mentioned difficulty, due to the inevitable administrative complexities of an instrument as comprehensive and detailed as the European Convention on the International Validity of Criminal Judgements, the Convention on the Transfer of Sentenced Persons seeks to provide a simple, speedy and flexible mechanism for the repatriation of prisoners.

9. In facilitating the transfer of foreign prisoners, the convention takes account of modern trends in crime and penal policy. In Europe, improved means of transport and communication have led to a greater mobility of persons and, in consequence, to increased internationalisation of crime. As penal policy has come to lay greater emphasis upon the social rehabilitation of offenders, it may be of paramount importance that the sanction imposed on the offender is enforced in his home country rather than in the state where the offense was committed and the judgement rendered. This policy is also rooted in humanitarian considerations: difficulties in communication by reason of language barriers, alienation from local culture and customs, and the absence of contacts with relatives may have detrimental effects on the foreign prisoner. The repatriation of sentenced persons may therefore be in the best interests of the prisoners as well as of the governments concerned.
10. The convention distinguishes itself from the European Convention on the International Validity of Criminal Judgements in four respects:

> With a view to facilitating the rapid transfer of foreign prisoners, it provides for a simplified procedure which, in its practical application, is likely to be less cumbersome than that laid down in the European Convention on the International Validity of Criminal judgements.
>
> A transfer may be requested not only by the state in which the sentence was imposed ("sentencing state"), but also by the state of which the sentenced person is a national ("administering state"), thus enabling the latter to seek the repatriation of its own nationals.
>
> The transfer is subject to the sentenced person's consent.
>
> The Convention confines itself to providing the procedural framework for transfers. It does not contain an obligation on Contracting States to comply with a request for transfer, for that reason, it was not necessary to list any grounds for refusal, nor to require the requested state to give reasons for its refusal to agree to a requested transfer.

11. Unlike the other conventions on international co-operation in criminal matters prepared within the framework of the Council of Europe, the Convention on the Transfer of Sentenced Persons does not carry the word "European" in its title. This reflects the draftsmen's opinion that the instrument should be open also to like-minded democratic states outside Europe. Two such states Canada and the United States of America—were in fact, represented on the Select Committee by observers and actively associated with the elaboration of the text.

Commentaries on the Articles of the Convention

Article 1—Definitions
12. Article 1 defines four terms which are basic to the transfer mechanism which the convention provides.
13. The definition of "sentence" a makes clear that the convention applies only to a punishment or measure which involves deprivation of liberty, and only to the extent that it does so, regardless of whether the person concerned is already serving his sentence or not.
14. It follows from the definition of " judgement" b that the convention applies only to sentences imposed by a court of law.
15. The two states involved in the transfer of a sentenced person are defined as "sentencing state" and "administering state" c and d.

Article 2—General principles
16. Paragraph 1 contains the general principle which governs the application of the convention. Its wording is inspired by Article 1.1 of the European Convention on Mutual Assistance in Criminal Matters. The reference to "the widest measure of cooperation in respect of the transfer of sentenced persons" is intended to emphasize the convention's underlying philosophy: that it is desirable to enforce sentences in the home country of the person concerned.

17. Paragraph 2 refers the sentencing state to the possibility, afforded by the convention, of having the sentenced person transferred to another Contracting State for the purpose of enforcing the sentence. That other state, that is the "administering state" is—by virtue of Article 3.1.a—the state of which the sentenced person is a national.

Although the sentenced person may not formally apply for his transfer (see paragraph 3), he may express his interest in being transferred under the Convention, and he may do so by addressing himself to either the sentencing state or the administering state.

18. According to paragraph 3, transfers may be requested by either the sentencing state or the administering state. This provision signifies an important departure from the rule of the European Convention on the international Validity of Criminal judgements that only the sentencing state is entitled to make the request. It acknowledges the interest which the prisoner's home country may have in his repatriation for reasons of cultural, religious, family and other social ties.

Article 3—Conditions for transfer

19. The first paragraph of Article 3 enumerates six conditions which must be fulfilled if a transfer is to be effected under the terms of the convention.

20. The first condition a is that the person to be transferred is a national of the administering state. In an effort to render the application of the convention as easy as possible, the reference to the sentenced person's nationality was preferred to including in the convention other notions which, in their practical application, might give rise to problems of interpretation as, for instance, the terms "ordinarily resident in the other state" and "the state of origin" used in Article 5 of the European Convention on the International Validity of Criminal Judgements.

It is not necessary for the person concerned to be a national of only the administering state. Contracting States may decide to apply the convention, when appropriate, in cases of double or multiple nationality even when the other nationality (or one of the other nationalities) is that of the sentencing state. It is to be noted, however, that even where all the conditions for transfer are satisfied, the requested state remains free to agree or not to agree to a requested transfer. A sentencing state is therefore free to refuse a requested transfer if it concerns one of its own nationals.

Paragraph 1.a is to be read in conjunction with paragraph 4 which grants Contracting States the possibility to define, by means of a declaration, the term "national."

This possibility, corresponding with that provided in Article 61 b of the European Convention on Extradition, is to be interpreted in a wide sense: the provision is intended to enable Contracting States to extend the application of the convention to persons other than "nationals" within the strict meaning of their nationality legislation as, for instance, stateless persons or citizens of other states who have established roots in the country through permanent residence.

21. The second condition b is that the judgement must be final and enforceable, for instance because all available remedies have been exhausted, or because the time-limit for lodging a remedy has expired without the parties having availed themselves of it. This does not preclude the possibility of a later review of the judgement in the light of fresh evidence, as provided for under Article 13.

22. The third condition c concerns the length of the sentence Stir to be served. For the convention to be applicable, the sentence must be of a duration of at least six months at the time of receipt of the request for transfer, or be indeterminate.

Two considerations have led to the inclusion of this condition: the first is that the convention is conceived as an instrument to further the offender's social rehabilitation, an objective which can usefully be pursued only where the length of the sentence still to be served is sufficiently long. The second reason is that of the system's cost-effectiveness; the transfer of a prisoner is costly, and the considerable expenses incurred by the states concerned must therefore be proportionate to the purpose to be achieved, which excludes recourse to a transfer where the person concerned has only a short sentence to serve.

In exceptional cases, however, Contracting States may—in application of paragraph 2—agree to a transfer even though the time to be served is less than that specified, as the general rule, in paragraph

1.c. The introduction of this element of flexibility was deemed useful to cover cases where the aforementioned two considerations do not fully apply, for instance where the prospects of rehabilitation are favourable despite a sentence of less than six months or where the transfer can be effected expeditiously and at low cost, for example between neighbouring states.

23. The fourth condition d is that the transfer must be consented to by the person concerned. This requirement which is not Contained in the European Convention on the International Validity of Criminal Judgements constitutes one of the basic elements of the transfer mechanism set up by the convention. It is rooted in the convention's primary purpose to facilitate the rehabilitation of offenders: transferring a prisoner without his consent would be counter-productive in terms of rehabilitation.

This provision is to be read in conjunction with Article 7 which contains rules on the way in which consent is to be given and on the possibility for the administering state to verify that consent has been given in accordance with the conditions laid down in that article.

Consent is to be given by the sentenced person's legal representative in cases where one of the two states considers it necessary in view of the age or of the physical or mental condition of the sentenced person. The reference to the sentenced person's "legal representative" is not meant to imply that the representative must be legally qualified; it includes any person duly authorised by law to represent the sentenced person, for example a parent or someone specially authorised by the competent authority.

24. The fifth condition e is intended to ensure compliance with the principle of dual criminal liability.

The condition is fulfilled if the act which gave rise to the judgement in the sentencing state would have been punishable if committed in the administering state and if the person who performed the act could, under the law of the administering state, have had a sanction imposed on him.

For the condition of dual criminal liability to be fulfilled it is not necessary that the criminal offense be precisely the same under both the law of the administering state and the law of the sentencing state. There may be differences in the wording and legal classification. The basic idea is that the essential constituent elements of the offense should be comparable under the law of both states.

25. The sixth condition f confirms the convention's basic principle that a transfer requires the agreement of the two states concerned.

26. Paragraph 3 is to be seen in connection with Article 9 which grants the administering state a choice between two enforcement procedures: it may either continue enforcement or convert the sentence. If requested, it must inform the sentencing state as to which of these two procedures it will follow (Article 9, paragraph 2). The general rule is, therefore, that the administering state may choose between the two enforcement procedures in each individual case.

If, however, a Contracting State wishes to exclude, in a general way, the application of one of the two procedures, it can do so under the provisions of paragraph 3: by way of a declaration, it may indicate that it intends to exclude the application of either the "continued enforcement procedure" or the "conversion procedure" in its relations with other Contracting States. As the declaration made under paragraph 3 applies to the relations with other parties it enables the state making such a declaration to exclude one of the two enforcement procedures not only where it is in the position of the administering state but also where it is the sentencing state; in the latter case the declaration would have the effect of making that state's agreement to a requested transfer dependent on the administering state not applying the excluded procedure.

Article 4—Obligation to furnish information

27. Article 4 concerns the transmission of various elements of information to be furnished during the course of the transfer proceedings to the sentenced person, the administering state, and the sentencing state. The provision applies to three different phases of the procedure: paragraph 1 concerns information by the sentencing state to the sentenced person on the substance of the convention; paragraphs 2 to 4 refer to information between the two states concerned after the sentenced person has

expressed an interest in being transferred; paragraph 5 concerns information to be given to the sentenced person on the action or decision taken with regard to a possible transfer.

28. Affording to paragraph 1, any sentenced person who may be eligible for transfer under the convention shall be informed by the sentencing state, of the convention's substance. This is to make the sentenced person aware of the possibilities for transfer offered by the convention and the legal consequences which a transfer to his home country would have. The information will enable him to decide whether he wishes to express an interest in being transferred. It is to be noted, however, that the sentenced person cannot himself make the formal request for transfer; it follows from Article 2.3 that transfer may be requested only by the sentencing or the administering state.

The information to be given to the sentenced person must be in a language he understands.

29. Paragraphs 2 and 3 apply where the sentenced person has expressed an interest to the sentencing state in being transferred under the convention. In that event, the sentencing state informs the state of which the sentenced person is a national that he has expressed an interest in being transferred. This information has to be provided as soon as practicable after the judgement becomes final and enforceable, and it must include the elements enumerated in paragraph 3.

30. The principal purpose of conveying this information to the authorities (including the consular authorities) of the person's home country is to enable that state to decide whether it wants to request a transfer, the assumption being that normally the sentenced person's home country will take the initiative to have its own national repatriated.

31. If the sentenced person has expressed his interest in a transfer not to the sentencing state, but to the state of which he is a national, paragraph 4 applies: in that case, the sentencing state provides the information referred to in paragraph 3 only upon the express request of the state of which the person is a national.

32. By virtue of paragraph 5, the sentenced person who has expressed an interest in being transferred must be kept informed, in writing, of the follow-up action taken in his case. He must, for instance, be told whether the information referred to in paragraph 3 has been sent to his home country, whether a request for transfer has been made and by which state, and whether a decision has been taken on the request.

Article 5—Requests and replies

33. This article specifies the form and the channels of transmission to be used for requests for transfer and replies thereto.

34. Requests and replies must be made in writing (paragraph 1). They must, in principle, be transmitted between the respective Ministries of Justice (paragraph 2), but Contracting States may declare that they will use other ways of transmission as, for instance, the diplomatic channel (paragraph 3).

35. In line with the convention's aim to provide a procedure for the speedy transfer of sentenced persons, paragraph 4 requires the requested state promptly to inform the requesting state whether it agrees to the requested transfer.

Article 6—Supporting documents

36. Article 6 states which supporting documents must be provided, on request, by the administering state to the sentencing state (paragraph 1), and by the sentencing state to the administering state (paragraph 2). These documents must be provided before the transfer is effected. As regards the documents to be provided by the sentencing state, they may be sent to the administering state either together with the request for transfer or afterwards; they need not be sent if either state has already indicated that it will not agree to the transfer.

37. In addition, paragraph 3 provides that either of the two states may request any of the documents or statements referred to in paragraph 1 or 2 before making a request for transfer or taking a decision on whether or not to agree to the requested transfer. This provision is intended to avoid setting the transfer procedure in motion when there are doubts as to whether all the conditions for transfer are

satisfied. The sentencing state may, for instance, wish to ascertain beforehand—that is before making a request for transfer or before agreeing to a requested transfer—whether the sentenced person is a national of the administering state, or the administering state may wish to ascertain beforehand that the sentenced person consented to his transfer.

Article 7—Consent and its verification

38. The sentenced person's consent to his transfer is one of the basic elements of the transfer mechanism established by the convention. It was therefore deemed necessary to impose an obligation on the sentencing state to ensure that the consent is given voluntarily and with full knowledge of the legal consequences which the transfer would entail for the person concerned, and to give the administering state an opportunity to verify that consent has been given in accordance with these conditions.

39. Under paragraph 2, the administering state is entitled to that verification either through a Consul or through another official on which the two states agree.

40. As the convention is based on the principle that enforcement in the administering state requires the sentenced person's prior consent, it was not considered necessary to lay down a rule of speciality to the effect that the person transferred under the convention with a view to the enforcement of a sentence may not be proceeded against or sentenced or detained for an offense other than that relating to the enforcement for which the transfer has been effected. Other conventions which provide for this rule of speciality, as, for instance, the European Convention on Extradition in its Article 14 or the European Convention on the International Validity of Criminal Judgements in its Article 9, do not require the consent of the person concerned, so that in those cases the rule of speciality is a necessary safeguard for him.

The absence of a speciality rule should be included in the information on the substance of the convention which is to be given to sentenced persons under Article 4.1 .

Article 8—Effects of transfer for sentencing state

41. This article safeguards the application of the principle of ne bis in idem in respect of the enforcement of the sentence after a transfer has been effected.

42. To avoid the sentenced person's serving a sentence for the same acts or omissions more than once, Article 8 provides that enforcement in the sentencing state is suspended at the moment when the authorities of the administering state take the sentenced person into charge (paragraph 1), and that the sentencing state may no longer enforce the sentence once the administering state considers enforcement to have been completed (paragraph 2).

Article 9—Effect of transfer for administering state

43. This article concerns the enforcement of the sentence in the administering state. It states the general principles which govern enforcement; the details of the different enforcement procedures are regulated in Articles 10 and 11.

44. According to paragraph 1, the administering state may choose between two ways of enforcing the sentence: it may either continue the enforcement immediately or through a court or administrative order (Article 10), or convert the sentence, through a judicial or administrative procedure, into a decision which substitutes a sanction prescribed by its own law for the sanction imposed in the sentencing state (Article 11). It is to be noted, however, that in accordance with Article 3.3, Contracting States have the possibility to exclude, in a general way, the application of one of these two procedures.

45. If requested, the administering state must inform the sentencing state as to which of these two procedures it intends to apply (paragraph z). This obligation has been imposed on the administering state because the information may have a bearing on the sentencing state's decision on whether or not to agree to a requested transfer.

46. The basic difference between the "continued enforcement" procedure under Article 10 and the "conversion of sentence" procedure under Article 11 commonly called "exequatur"—is that, in the first Case, the administering state continues to enforce the sanction imposed in the sentencing state (possibly adapted by virtue of Article 10 paragraph 2), whereas, in the second case, the sanction is converted into a sanction of the administering state, with the result that the sentence enforced is no longer directly based on the sanction imposed in the sentencing state.
47. In both cases, enforcement is governed by the law of the administering state (paragraph 3). The reference to the law of the administering state is to be interpreted in a wide sense; it includes, for instance, the rules relating to eligibility for conditional release. To make this clear, paragraph 3 states that the administering state alone shall be competent to take all appropriate decisions.
48. Paragraph 4 refers to cases where neither of the two procedures can be applied in the administering state because the enforcement concerns measures imposed on a person who for reasons of mental condition has been held not criminally responsible for the commission of the offense. The provision allows the administering state, if it is prepared to receive such a person for further treatment, to indicate, by way of a declaration addressed to the Secretary General of the Council of Europe, the procedures which it will follow in such cases.

Article 10—Continued enforcement
49. Where the administering state opts for the "continued enforcement" procedure, it is bound by the legal nature as well as the duration of the sentence as determined by the sentencing state (paragraph 1): the first condition ("legal nature") refers to the kind of penalty imposed where the law of the sentencing state provides for a diversity of penalties involving deprivation of liberty, such as penal servitude, imprisonment or detention. The second condition ("duration") means that the sentence to be served in the administering state, subject to any later decision of that state on, for example, conditional release or remission, corresponds to the amount of the original sentence, taking into account the time served and any remission earned in the sentencing state up to the date of transfer.
50. If the two states concerned have different penal systems with regard to the division of penalties or the minimum and maximum lengths of sentence, it might be necessary for the administering state to adapt the sanction to the punishment or measure prescribed by its own law for a similar offence. Paragraph 2 allows that adaptation within certain limits: the adapted punishment or measure must, as far as possible, correspond with that imposed by the sentence to be enforced; it must not aggravate, by its nature or duration, the sanction imposed in the sentencing state; and it must not exceed the maximum prescribed by the law of the administering state. In other words: the administering state may adapt the sanction to the nearest equivalent available under its own law, provided that this does not result in more severe punishment or longer detention. As opposed to the conversion procedure under Article 11, under which the administering state substitutes a sanction for that imposed in the sentencing state, the procedure under Article 10.2 enables the administering state merely to adapt the sanction to an equivalent sanction prescribed by its own law in order to make the sentence enforceable. The administering state thus continues to enforce the sentence imposed in the sentencing state, but it does so in accordance with the requirements of its own penal system.

Article 11—Conversion of sentence
51. Article 11 concerns the conversion of the sentence to be enforced, that is the judicial or administrative procedure by which a sanction prescribed by the law of the administering state is substituted for the sanction imposed in the sentencing state, a procedure which is commonly called "exequatur." The provision should be read in conjunction with Article 9.1.b. It is essential for the smooth and efficient functioning of the convention in cases where, with regard to the classification of penalties or the length of the custodial sentence applicable for similar offense, the penal system of the administering state differs from that of the sentencing state.
52. Tile article does not regulate the procedure to be followed. According to paragraph 1, the conversion of the sentence is governed by the law of the administering state.

53. However, as regards the extent of the Conversion and the criteria applicable to it, paragraph I states four conditions to be observed by the competent authority of the administering state.
54. Firstly, the authority is bound by the findings as to the facts insofar as they appear explicitly or implicitly—from the judgement pronounced in the sentencing state a. It has, therefore, no freedom to evaluate differently the facts on which the judgement is based, this applies to "objective" facts relating to the commission of the act and its results, as well as to "subjective" facts relating, for instance, to premeditation and intent on the part of the convicted person. The reason for this condition is that the substitution by a sanction of a different nature or duration does not imply any modification of the judgement, it merely serves to obtain an enforceable sentence in the administering state.
55. Secondly a sanction involving deprivation of liberty may not be converted into a pecuniary sanction b. This provision reflects the fact that the Convention applies only to the transfer of sentenced persons, "sentence" being defined in Article l.a as a punishment or measure involving deprivation of liberty. However, it does not prevent conversion to a non-custodial sanction other than a pecuniary one.
56. Thirdly, any period of deprivation of liberty already served by the sentenced person must be deducted from the sentence as converted by the administering state c. This provision applies to any part of the sentence already served in the sentencing state as well as any provisional detention served during remand in custody prior to conviction, or any detention served during transit.
57. Fourthly, the penal position of the sentenced person must not be aggravated d. This prohibition refers not only to the length of the sentence, which must not exceed that imposed in the sentencing state, but also to the kind of sanction to be enforced. it must not be harsher than that imposed in the sentencing state. If, for instance, under the law of the administering state the offence carries a more severe form of deprivation of liberty than that which the judgement imposed (e.g. penal servitude or forced labour instead of imprisonment), the administering state is precluded from enforcing this harsher hind of sanction. In addition. paragraph 1 d provides in respect of the length of the sentence to be enforced, that the authority which converts that sentence is not bound by any minimum which its own law may provide for the same offence, that is that it is allowed not to respect that minimum with the result that it can enforce the sanction imposed in the sentencing state even if it is less than the minimum laid down in its own law.
58. As the conversion procedure may take some time, paragraph 2 requires the administering state, if the procedure takes place after the transfer of the sentenced person, to keep that person in custody or otherwise ensure his presence in the administering state, pending the outcome of that procedure.

Article 12—Pardon. amnesty, commutation
59. Whereas Article 9.3 makes the administering state solely responsible for the enforcement of the sentence, including any decisions related to it (e.g. the decision to suspend the sentence), pardon, amnesty or commutation of the sentence may be granted by either the sentencing or the administering state, in accordance with its Constitution or other laws.

Article 13—Review of judgement
60. This article provides that the sentencing state alone has the right to take decisions on applications for review of the judgement. The exclusive competence of the sentencing state to review the judgement is justified by the fact that, technically speaking review proceedings are not part of enforcement so that Article 9.3 does not apply. The object of an application for review is to obtain the re-examination of the final sentence in the light of any new elements of fact. As the sentencing state alone is competent to re-examine the materiality of facts, it follows necessarily that only that state has jurisdiction to examine such an application, especially as it is better placed to obtain new evidence on the point at issue.
61. The term "review" within the meaning of Article 13 covers also proceedings which in some states may result in a new examination of the legal aspects of the case after the judgement has become final.

62. The sentencing state's competence to decide on any application for review should not be interpreted as discharging the administering state from the duty to enable the sentenced person to seek a review of the judgement. Both states must, in fact, take all appropriate steps to guarantee the effective exercise of the sentenced person's right to apply for a review

Article 14—Termination of enforcement

63. Article 14 concerns the termination of enforcement by the administering state in cases where the sentence ceases to be enforceable as a result of any decision or measure taken by the sentencing state (e.g., the decisions referred to in Articles 12 and 13). In such cases, the administering state must terminate enforcement as soon as it is informed by the sentencing state of any such decision or measure.

Article 15—Information on enforcement

64. This article provides for the administering state to inform the sentencing state on the state of enforcement: a when it considers enforcement of the sentence to have been completed (e.g., sentence served, remission, conditional release, pardon, amnesty, commutation); b if the sentenced person has escaped from custody before completion of the sentence, and c whenever the sentencing state requests a special report.

65. It is to be noted that the information to be supplied by virtue of Article 15.a may be provided either for each individual case or by means of periodical—for example annual—reports covering, for a given period, all cases in which completion of sentence has occurred.

Article 16—Transit

66. This article has been drafted on the lines of Article 21 of the European Convention on Extradition and Article 13 of the European Convention on the International Validity of Criminal Judgements. It lays down rules governing the transit of persons passing from the sentencing state to the administering state through the territory of another Contracting State.

67. Paragraph 1 imposes an obligation on Contracting States to grant requests for transit, in accordance with their national law, but this obligation is subject to a double condition: the request for transit must be made by another Contracting State, and that state must have agreed with another Contracting State or with a third state to the transfer of the sentenced person. The latter condition means that the obligation to grant transit becomes effective only when the sentencing and the administering state have agreed on the transfer of the sentenced person.

68. It is to be noted that the obligation to grant transit applies only where the request emanates from a Contracting State. If it is made by a third state, paragraph 4 applies. It contains an option, not an obligation: a request for transit may be granted if the requesting third state has agreed with another Contracting State to the transfer of the sentenced person.

69. Paragraph 1 does not exclude the transit of a national of the state of transit, but paragraph 2.n entitles a Contracting State to refuse transit if the person concerned is one of its own nationals. This applies also where transit is to be effected by air and the state concerned has made the declaration under paragraph 7.

Paragraph 2.b entitles a Contracting State to refuse to grant transit if the offense for which the sentence was imposed is not an offense under its own law.

70. As regards the channels of communication for requests for transit and replies, paragraph 3 makes the provisions of Article 5, paragraphs 2 and 3, applicable: in principle. requests and replies must pass through the Ministries of justice of the two states concerned, but Contracting States may declare that they will use other ways of transmission.

71. Paragraph 5 provides for the state of transit to hold the sentenced person in custody only for such time as transit through its territory requires.

72. Paragraph 6 concerns the sentenced person's immunity from arrest and prosecution in the state of transit. It provides that the state requested to grant transit may be asked to give an assurance to the

effect that the sentenced person will enjoy immunity in respect of any offense committed or sentence imposed prior to his departure from the territory of the sentencing state, with the exception of custody which the transit state may impose in application of paragraph 5. There is, however, no obligation on the state of transit to give such an assurance.

73. Paragraph 7 deals with transit by air where no landing in the territory of the state of transit is scheduled. In such cases, no request for transit is required. Contrary to the provisions of Article 21.4.a of the European Convention on Extradition which require notification of the transit state in such cases, paragraph 6 of Article 16 leaves it to each Contracting State to decide, by means of a declaration, whether it wishes to require such notification.

Article 17—Languages and costs

74. This article deals with the questions of language (paragraphs 1 to 3), certification (paragraph 4), and costs (paragraph 5).

75. With regard to the languages to be used for the purposes of applying the Convention, Article 17 distinguishes between the information exchanged between the two states concerned in accordance with Article 4, paragraphs 2 to 4, which must be furnished in the language of the recipient state or in one of the official languages of the Council of European (paragraph 1), and requests for transfer and supporting documents for which it is stated that no translation is required (paragraph 2), unless the state concerned has declared that it requires requests for transfer and supporting documents to be accompanied by a translation (paragraph 3).

76. Paragraph 4 provides that with the exception of the copy of the judgement imposing the sentence—referred to in Article 6.2.o—supporting documents transmitted in application of the convention need not be certified.

77. As concerns costs, paragraph 5 provides that they shall be borne by the administering state, with the exception of those costs which are incurred exclusively in the territory of the sentencing state. By precluding Contracting States from claiming refund from each other of any expenses incurred during the transfer procedures, the provision intends to facilitate the practical application of the Convention.

The administering state, however, is not prevented from seeking to recover all or part of the cost of transfer from the sentenced person.

Articles 18 to 25—Final clauses

78. With the exception of Articles 18 and 19, the provisions contained in Articles 18 to 25 are, for the most part, based on the "'Model final clauses for conventions and agreements concluded within the Council of Europe" which were approved by the Committee on Ministers of the Council of Europe at the 315th meeting of their Deputies in February 1980. Most of these articles do not therefore call for specific comments, but the following points, relating to Articles 18,19, 21, 22 and 23, require some explanation.

79. Articles 18 and 19 have been drafted on the precedent established in Articles 19 and 20 of the Convention on the Conservation of European Wildlife and Natural habitats of Sty September 1979 which allow for signature, before the convention's entry into force, not only by the member states of the Council of Europe, but also by nonmember states which have participated in the elaboration of the convention. These provisions are intended to enable the maximum number of interested states, not necessarily members of the Council of Europe, to become Contracting Parties as soon as possible. As similar considerations apply in the case of the convention on the Transfer of Sentenced Persons, Article 18 provides that it is open for signature by the member states of the Council of Europe as well as by non-member states which have participated in its elaboration. The provision is intended to apply to two non-member states, Canada and the United States of America, which were represented on the Select Committee by observers and actively associated with the elaboration of the convention. They may sign the convention, just as the member states of the Council of Europe, before its entry into force. According to Article 18.2, the convention enters into force when three member states have expressed their consent to be bound by it. Non-member states other than those referred to in Article

18.1 may, by virtue of Article 19, be invited by the Committee of Ministers to accede to the convention, but only after his entry into force and after consultation of the Contracting States.
80. Article 21 ensures the convention's full temporal application. It enables Contracting States to avail themselves of the transfer mechanism with regard to any enforcement which falls within the convention's scope of application and which is to be effected after its entry into force, regardless of whether the sentence to be enforced has been imposed before or after that date.
81. Article 22 intends to ensure the smooth co-existence of the convention with other treaties—multilateral or bilateral—providing for the transfer of detained persons.

Paragraph 1 concerns extradition treaties and other treaties providing for the transfer of detained persons for purposes of confrontation or testimony. Paragraph 2 safeguards the continued application of agreements, treaties or relations relating to the transfer of sentenced persons, including uniform legislation as it exists, for instance, within the Nordic co-operation. Paragraph 3 concerns complementary agreements concluded in application of Article 64.2 of the European Convention on the International Validity of Criminal Judgements. Paragraph 4 applies where a request for transfer fails within the scope of both the present convention and the European Convention on the International Validity of Criminal judgements or any other instrument on the transfer of sentenced persons. In such a case, the requesting state must indicate on the basis of which instrument it makes the request. Such indication is binding on the requested state.
82. Article 23 which makes the European Committee on Crime Problems of the Council of Europe the guardian over the application of the convention follows the precedents established in other European conventions in the penal field, namely in Article 28 of the European Convention on the Punishment of Road Traffic Offences, in Article 65 of the European Convention on the International Validity of Criminal Judgements, in Article 44 of the European Convention on the Transfer of Proceedings in Criminal Matters, in Article 7 of the Additional Protocol to the European Convention on Extradition, in Article 10 of the Second Additional Protocol to the European Convention on Extradition, in Article 10 of the Additional Protocol to the European Convention on Mutual Assistance in Criminal Matters, and in Article 9 of the European Convention on the Suppression of Terrorism. The reporting requirement which Article 23 lays down is intended to keep the European Committee on Crime Problems informed about possible difficulties in interpreting and applying the convention so that it may contribute to facilitating friendly settlements and proposing amendments to the convention which might prove necessary.

Section VI

Recognition of Foreign Penal Judgments

The European System

Dietrich Oehler

Introduction

Many countries are developing notions restricting strict nationalistic adherence to the application of foreign legal doctrines. A parallel development appears in increased cooperation among nations in the economic, cultural, political, and legal spheres. Both of these give rise to the question of whether, and to what extent, acts of states, especially measures relating to criminal justice, are capable of having effects in another country. The courts and other authorities of one country are confronted with the problem of whether to take into account the legal acts of a foreign country if they are compelled to or want to proceed against a punishable offense upon which judgment has already been passed abroad. For example, subject *A* of country *D*, already having been punished many times for theft in his home country, drives to country *S*, commits another theft there and, while in flight, slightly injures a person through his careless driving. He is arrested in country *S* and is prosecuted there. The sentence is suspended confinement or probation and the prohibition to drive a car for a certain period of time. Thereafter, *A* returns to his home country *D* and again carelessly causes an accident.

This example raises many legal questions:

1. Can *A* be prosecuted in his country of origin again for the offense he committed abroad?

2. Could *A*'s country of origin have prosecuted *A* if he had served the sentence in the foreign country and then returned to his country of origin?

3. Can the sentence of the country of origin for the theft be considered a prior conviction for purposes of punishment abroad (recidivism)?

4. May the foreign judgment be enforced by the country of origin?

5. May the probation sentence abroad be revoked by the country of origin?

These questions constitute only a segment of the problems which arise from the handling of foreign penal judgments. The answers to such questions depend upon the extraterritorial effects, positive or negative, which a foreign judgment may have; that is, upon the extent to which it is recognized by the authorities of another country.

The Treatment of Foreign Penal Judgments in the Past

The problem of whether to recognize foreign judgments did not arise while the countries had clearly national views of their positions. The recognition of legal acts of a foreign state would have been contrary to the deeply ingrained concept of sovereignty. In the independent countries of medieval Middle Europe, the authorities made certain that their sovereignty was not violated in any way. Even the impression that their sovereignty had been encroached upon was to be avoided. In the Middle Ages, indeed, treaties were concluded among particular countries, especially in Upper Italy, which provided for the enforcement of judgments passed abroad. But the reasons for these conventions were not of a legal character; on the contrary, some countries saw fit to assume the enforcement of foreign judgments because they desired to exploit the condemned person's working capacities. Venice, for example, took over criminals sentenced abroad in order to maintain the number of galley slaves who were needed for the Venetian fleet.[1]

Some treaties containing provisions for the treatment of penal judgments passed by a foreign court were to be found in the nineteenth century. One of these old conventions, the Revised Act of the Shipment on the Rhine (*Revidierte Rheinschiffahrtsakte*) of October 17, 1868, is still valid today. By virtue of this Act, the border states of the Rhine—Belgium, Germany, France, the Netherlands, and Switzerland—on the basis of reciprocity, enforce judgments of the courts of the Rhine border states (*Rheinufergerichte*). This is true even in cases where the court is situated outside the borders of the country in which the judgment is to be enforced.[2] The enforcement of such foreign judgments, however, relates only to fines. Article 30 of the Swiss Federal Act of January 22, 1892 (Extradition Act) provides that the Federal Council, in conjunction with all the interested parties, may authorize a prison sentence imposed abroad to be served in a Swiss penitentiary.

Not until the last decades of this century did the problem of recognition of foreign penal judgments gain pressing importance.[3] This was mainly due to the development of international extradition treaties and national criminal statutes as an effective means of control of criminality on the international level. This had not always been possible, and the continued lack of cooperation among states in criminal matters did not benefit the interests of the affected countries nor those of the accused. For example, there is an advantage to the convicted who is sentenced abroad to permit him to serve that sentence in his country of origin because he would be better acquainted with the common mores of his own country which will facilitate the execution of the sentence unimpeded by communications problems. This is the better approach to resocialization. Also, for reasons of justice, it is advisable to recognize foreign judgments, as experience reveals that a judge usually will not suspend a punishment or grant probation, unless he is sure that the delinquent will be supervised, and that there is the possibility of revoking the suspension of the sentence or probation. This can take place only if the supervision of the probation can be effectuated abroad and full effect given to the judge's revocation of the probation in case of violation of its terms.[4]

The recognition and enforcement of foreign penal judgments gained further importance through the various alliances made between European countries. The problem of the effects of foreign penal judgments was the subject of a meeting of the Institut de Droit International

---

1 *Cf.* H. LAMMASH, AUSLIEFERUNGSPFLICHT UND ASYLRECHT 824 n.1 (1887).

2 Revised Act of Navigation on the Rhine of 1868, Art. 40 ¶ 1, BGBl. I, 645 (1952) quoted *infra* note 54.

3 This is shown by several international conventions, *e.g.*, the Scandinavian Act of Enforcement of 1963, a parallel legislation in the five Scandinavian countries, partly altered by the Act of June 19, 1964, *reproduced in* HEINR GRUTZNER, INTERNATIONALER RECHTSHILFEVERKEHR IN STRAFSACHEN pt. IV (1970) and the Convention Among Belgium, Luxembourg, and the Netherlands on the Cooperation in the Field of Customs and Excises of 1952 (JACQUE KARELLE, LE BENELUX COMMENTE, TEXTES OFFICIELS 147, 209, 306 (1961).

4 On this theme *see* Heinr Grutzner, *Die zwischenstaatliche Anerkennung europaischer Strafurteile*, 1964 NEUE JURISTICHE WOCHENSCHRIFT (NJW) 347.

at Bath in 1950, and became the subject of the research of many international conferences and conventions,[5] which tried to achieve a basic solution.

The Effects of Foreign Penal Judgments

The effects of a foreign penal judgment may either be negative or positive. A negative effect concerns the question of whether the home authorities are prevented by a foreign judgment from starting a prosecution at home in the same case. A positive effect refers to the question as to which measures the home courts and authorities can or must legally take if a foreign court has already passed judgment in the same case.[6]

Negative Effects of Foreign Penal Judgments

The occurrence of the effect of blocking of the inadmissability of a renewed prosecution, because of the existence of a foreign judgment, depends upon the way the home country treats the foreign judgment under its own criminal law. In the first instance, the range of application of the criminal law must be considered as it is provided for by each particular country. The more a state confines the scope of its own criminal law, the more readily it will be to recognize a foreign penal judgment. Secondly, there is the question of whether internationally valid principles, mainly the maxim *ne bis in idem*, prevents the home country from a renewed prosecution after the foreign judgment has already been passed.

The Local Range of Application of the National Criminal Law

The diversity of theories of jurisdiction used as national standards demonstrates the variety in patterns of application. Among them, are the principle of territoriality; the principle of active personality, accompanied totally or partially by the principle of application of foreign law,[7] sometimes combined with the principle of disposition;[8] the principle of passive personality;[9] the principle of protected interest, and the principle of universality. Their application is not uniform and the combination of some of them is also very diverse. The increase in international movement of persons and the growing number of foreign residents and immigrant workers increase the number of offenses committed by or against foreigners in a domestic jurisdiction. This situation therefore creates many

---

[5] Above all we mention European Convention on the Punishment of Road Traffic Offenders of 1964, Europ. T.S. No 52; European Convention on the International Validity of Criminal Judgments of 1970, Europ. T.S. No. 70 [hereinafter Eur. Conv. Int'l Val. Crim. Judg.], *reprinted in* Appendix 15; European Convention on the Transfer of Proceedings in Criminal Matters of 1972, Europ. T.S. No. 73; European Convention on the International Effects of Deprivation of the Right to Drive a Motor Vehicle of 1976, Europ. T.S. No. 88; European Convention on the Suppression of Terrorism of 1977, Europ. T.S. No. 90; Convention on the Transfer of Sentenced Persons of 1983, Europ. T.S. No. 112 (this convention, not yet in force, is not named European because it is open to all states), *reprinted in* Appendix 14.

[6] Hans Buhler, Die Bedeutung ausländischer Strafurteile nach deutschem, französischem und schweizerischem Recht, Diss. Koln 1 (1966).

[7] By this is understood the principle that the national judge has to apply foreign law while judging an offense.

[8] This principle means that a foreign judgment disposes of the national claim to prosecute.

[9] This principle means that a foreigner is allowed to be prosecuted by another country for an offense committed abroad if the offense damages interests of a subject of this other country.

overlapping jurisdictional problems in the concerned countries. A multiplying factor of such overlapping is brought about by the concurrence of principles of personality and territoriality[10] and by the extensive definition given to the concept of the "place of commission" (*locus delicti*) by different laws.[11] This mixture of international and municipal law principles reveals that the drafters of most national criminal codes have hardy taken into account the difficulties and possibilities of conflict at the international level between their respective penal statutes. The most important purpose of national legislation is to safeguard national interests. In an attempt to secure those interests, the scope of the national criminal law is widened even at the risk of conflicting with the jurisdiction of other countries. The frequent jurisdictional conflicts which result from the same offense demonstrate that national criminal codes do not contribute to a rational determination of whether or not to recognize foreign judgments. On the contrary, criminal codes aggravate the situation by not distinguishing between the exclusive jurisdiction of one country or another.[12]

The Recognition of Foreign Judgments by Some Countries and Reservations Thereto

The legislative authorities of many countries deliberately avoided treating the problem of the recognition of foreign penal judgments and its effect with regard to precluding renewed prosecution. The criminal codes of some countries, however, contain rules which exclude to some extent a renewed prosecution after a valid foreign judgment,[13] whenever the punishment was fully served abroad or the delinquent was pardoned by that jurisdiction, or whenever the prosecution is authorized only by order of the highest domestic authority of the administration of the justice.[14] But these statutes do not provide for the general recognition of all foreign judgments; on the contrary, they often permit renewed prosecution. For example, a country is frequently allowed to commence a renewed prosecution if the offense concerned was against its own safety.[15]

Three reasons account principally for the difficulties in achieving broad recognition of the international effectiveness of penal judgments: (1) A restriction on national sovereignty, since the recognizing country is precluded from exercising its own jurisdiction provided for by its national law; (2) The limited confidence in the foreign country's administration of justice coupled with doubts about the way the prosecution is executed by the foreign court (these doubts need not be of a constitutional character);[16] (3) Grave practical difficulties arising from the recognition of foreign judgments and their transformation into the

---

[10] *Compare* Pietr Nuvolone, *Die Kollisionsnormen auf dem Gebiet des Strafrechts in Europa*, 66 ZEITSCHRIFT FÜR DIE GESAMTE STRAFRECHTSWISSENSCHAFT 567 (1954) *with* DIETRICH OEHLER, INTERNATIONALES STRAFRECHT 111 *et seq*. (2d ed. 1983).

[11] *E.g.*, German Criminal Code § 9; Swiss Criminal Code Art. 7; and Code de procedure penale (French) Art. 693 (Supp. Art. 690).

[12] The Harvard Study Draft Convention on Jurisdiction with Respect to Crime, 29 AM. J. INT'L L. 439 (Supp. 1935), does not try to find a solution, either.

[13] *E.g.*, Danish Criminal Code § 10 ¶ 3; Code de procedure penale Art. 692; Greek Criminal Code Art. 9; Dutch Criminal Code Art. 68 ¶ 2; Swiss Criminal Code Art. 6 No. 2; and 11 HALSBURY'S LAWS OF ENGLAND ¶ 88 (4th ed. 1983).

[14] *E.g.*, Belgian introductory act to the Code de procedure penale Art. 13 ¶ 1; Turkish Criminal Code Art. 8; Swedish Criminal Code ch. 2, § 5 ¶ 2; and Italian Criminal Code Art. 11.

[15] *E.g.*, Code de procedure penale Art. 694.

[16] These doubts may arise if a judgment is passed in the absence of the offender or if the offender does not defend himself though sufficiently being presented with the opportunity to do so.

respective national law.[17] Up to now, these reasons have made it impossible to establish mandatory standards toward securing the international effectiveness of penal judgments. The various problems arising out of nonrecognition of foreign penal judgments have received several treatments.

The Elimination of Double Jeopardy by Means Other Than Recognition of Foreign Judgments

Extradition Laws

There are many reciprocal conventions by virtue of which offenders are extradited to a foreign country if they committed a crime on its territory or against its possessions. The extradition of a foreigner will probably be granted, unless the request for extradition shows that the offense in question is a political one or unless there are doubts that the relator will not receive a fair trial in the requesting state. The situation differs when the relator is a citizen of the state of refuge. Most European countries will not extradite their own subjects who also cannot always be prosecuted in their national jurisdiction for offenses committed abroad. This is a great weakness in criminal justice. Countries which will extradite their own subjects, such as Great Britain and the U.S., on the basis of reciprocal treaty obligations, will, however, refuse to extradite their own subjects in the absence of reciprocity by the requesting state. These latter states do not usually prosecute for offenses committed abroad; therefore, the danger that such offenses will go unprosecuted is increased.[18] The possibility of double prosecution and double jeopardy arises where the delinquent is prosecuted and sentenced at home as well as abroad for an offense committed outside the territorial jurisdiction of his national jurisdiction. This will occur because of the special circumstances of the offense or because the jurisdictional theory of active personality has been applied. In this type of problem, however, the classical methods of international cooperation are ineffective in closing gaps between theories of criminal jurisdiction and fail to prevent double jeopardy.[19]

The Resolution of Jurisdictional Conflicts in Treaties

The treaties dealing with this matter lost much of their importance as a result of numerous reservations of the respective countries and because of the rarity of their use. Furthermore, the few countries involved in most such treaties are geographically distant from one another. Among arrangements are the Treaty on International Penal Law, signed at Montevideo, January 23, 1889 (in force among some South American countries); Article 296 *et seq.* of the Bustamante Code, adopted at Havana, February 20, 1928 (in force among fifteen Central and South American countries); Treaty on International Penal Law, signed

---

[17] Questions such as the following must be answered. What shall be the method of procedure along with recognition of the judgment? To what extent is a foreign judgment to be examined along with the recognition? How are the punishments to be adopted?

[18] OEHLER, *supra* note 10, at 137 *et seq.*.

[19] *Cf.* the Resolution of the 10th International Congress on Criminal Law at Rome in 1969, on theme IV; the German contributions to the theme are to be found in 81 ZEITSCHRIFTY FÜR DIE GESAMTE STRAFRECHTSWISSENSCHAFT (1969); OEHLER, *supra* note 10, at 955.

at Montevideo, March 19, 1940 (ratified to date by only Uruguay and Paraguay). These treaties have, however, very imperfectly settled the conflict in the realm of national criminal laws.

The Council of Europe attempted to fix jurisdiction limits in order to exclude the danger of a renewed prosecution for the same offense. The main aim of Recommendation 420 (1965) of the Council of Europe on the settlement of conflicts in criminal matters[20] was to grant supreme importance to the principle of territoriality; all other principles, especially the one of the active personality, were to be held insignificant in comparison with this principle. This Recommendation, which contains the draft of a European Convention, explicitly points out, however, that not only the country in which the offense is committed will have jurisdiction (principle of territoriality) but also the home country of the offender (principle of personality). Furthermore, the country where the delinquent has had his domicile, and the country where the criminal was arrested[21] will also have jurisdiction. While acknowledging the principles which govern most national criminal laws with respect to the range of application, the Recommendation assigns to each of these principles a certain grade of importance. It provides that jurisdiction arising from the principle of active personality is subsidiary to the one based on the principle of territoriality.[22] This gradation of principles[23] derives from the assumption that the concept of territoriality is recognized as the dominating principle in criminal law.[24] This is certainly true for some countries, above all for those adhering to the Anglo-Saxon accusatorial system of criminal justice. In many countries, however, the principle of territoriality is supplemented by the principles of active personality, passive personality and other theories as well. In these countries adhering to multiple jurisdictional theories, criminal laws had to be altered considerably before the Recommendation could be ratified as a convention.

Grave offenses committed in a country other than the national jurisdiction increase the motivation of that national jurisdiction to prosecute the offender. In that case, the national jurisdiction wherein prosecution may be about to take place will not easily yield to the country where the offense was committed and which has jurisdiction resulting from the principle of territoriality. In the event the state in which the offense was committed is not on very friendly terms with the state of refuge, the offender may not only not be surrendered, but even not prosecuted. Furthermore, the Recommendation does not take into account the widespread European practice of not extraditing nationals, which also inhibits its impact and reduces the special importance given the principle of territoriality in the Recommendation. The application of the principles of the Recommendation causes difficulties also in cases of offences committed extraterritorially or offenses which can be committed in one state, punishable there, but having an effect in one or more foreign countries where the result is also punishable. At present, the principles settled by Recommendation 420 have achieved no common acceptance. Despite its deficiencies, it is certain that the Recommendation would have helped to solve the problems resulting from the recognition of foreign judgments

---

20 Recommendation 420 (1965) on the settlement of conflicts in criminal matters in Consultative Assembly of the Council of Europe—Sixteenth Ordinary Session.

21 *Id.* at Art. 2 ¶ 1 and Art. 4 ¶ 1.

22 *Id.* at Art. 4 ¶ 2.

23 As for the principle of protection, *see id.* at Art. 2 ¶ 2.

24 Report by M. deGrailly on the Settlement of Conflict of Jurisdiction in Criminal Matters (No. 62), European Consultative Assembly, Doc. No. 1873 (Feb. 27, 1965).

by partially eliminating conflicts of jurisdiction, but the Recommendation with its attached draft convention containing these jurisdictional theories was not ratified. The convention that was ratified does not contain all the provisions of the Recommendation discussed above.[25]

Recognition of a Foreign Judgment by Applying the Principle Ne Bis in Idem *on the International Level*

The most significant opportunity to reach a recognition of foreign judgments, by virtue of which a renewed prosecution at home would be inadmisible, is to be found in the application of the principle *ne bis in idem* on the international level. The legal systems reveal that every state founded on constitutional principles acknowledges the principle of *ne bis idem* as a national maxim. This maxim declares that nobody should be punished more than once for the same offense.[26] This not only means that double jeopardy is precluded, but also that renewed prosecution is inadmissible after a national court has once passed judgment against an individual for an offense. But, according to nearly unanimous opinion in the literature concerning jurisdiction, a renewed prosecution is not excluded if a foreign court has acted before,[27] so that the borders of the country and the scope of the maxim *ne bis idem* coincide.

As mentioned above, numerous penal systems prohibit criminal proceedings against certain categories of offenders; for example, where a foreign court has already rendered a criminal judgment of conviction or aquittal or whenever a sentence was executed or remitted by the foreign jurisdiction.[28] The actual question thus becomes whether the recognition of negative effects of foreign judgments is to be acheived by awarding common international validity to the maxim *ne bis in idem.* For the last century this theme has been the subject of scientific research and the topic of several international congresses. The recurring question is whether and to what extent the recognition of the maxim *ne bis in idem* is a principle of international criminal law.[29] Contemporary tendency is that this maxim ought to prohibit not only a renewed punishment for the same offense, but also renewed prosecution for the same criminal conduct. The European Convention on the International Validity of Criminal Judgments of 1970, Art. 53, expresses itself accordingly.[30] The maxim, however, is applied differently by particular countries and this gives rise to some reservations concerning the uniform international application of the maxim.

---

25 The efforts for unification of European criminal law are no longer pursued in the Council of Europe. This kind of law is too dependent on national tradition.

26 *See, e.g.*, Art. 103 ¶ 3 Grundgesetz (GG).

27 Buhler, *supra* note 6, at 45.

28 *Supra* note 13.

29 *Cf.* the Harvard Study, *supra* note 12; the Resolutions of the Institut de Droit International at Bath, in 1950; the Resolutions of the Franko-Belgian colloquium of the International Union of Judges of Apr. 6-7, 1962 at Strasbourg; the Resolutions of the 2nd International Congress of Judges at The Hague of June 14, 1963; the Resolution of the 9th International Congress on Criminal Law at The Hague in 1964, 77 ZEITSCHRIFT FÜR DIE GESAMTE STRAFRECHTSWISSENSCHAFT 685 (1965); general report by Hans Schultz to the 7th Congres de l'Academie de Droit Compari at Uppsala (*reprinted in* 22 (2) REVUE DE SCIENCE CRIMINEL ET DROIT COMPARE 330 (1968)).

30 Eur. Conv. Int'l Val. Crim. Judg., *supra* note 5.

The Application of the Maxim Ne Bis in Idem *According to the Place of Commission*

The prohibition against renewed prosecution after a foreign penal judgment has been rendered is an application of the maxim by a municipal system in recognition of an international rule. The recognition of the foreign penal decree to the extent that it will preclude renewed local prosecution, embodies the maxim but will depend on whether the criminal conduct was commited in the national jurisdiction or in another one. Thus, the real significance of the court rendering the judgment[31] remains in the *situs* of the criminal conduct. For example, a judgment passed by Country *B* for an offense commited in Country *A* does not, according to most penal systems which acknowledge in any way the recognition of foreign judgments, make a renewed prosecution in Country *A* inadmissible. On the other hand, in cases where an offense is committed beyond the borders of Country *A*, a renewed prosecution will usually be, with few exceptions, inadmissible.

The reasons given for this solution are: (1) practical considerations[32] (availability of witnesses, evidence, etc); and (2) consideration of public order in the country wherein the offense was committed. These reasons are said to give to the territorially competent jurisdiction authority to prosecute the offender once again on its own territory.[33] For the present, it is not likely that a country will allow itself to be deprived of the authority to pass judgments for offenses which have been committed on its own territory, even though it appears to be at the cost of individual justice. The solution could be to give the offender credit for any sentence he may have incurred in a foreign jurisdiction.

The Application of the Maxim Ne Bis in Idem *Subject to the Enforcement of the Punishment*

The maxim *ne bis in idem* meets another restriction at the international level. At home, a renewed judgment for the same offense is inadmissible as soon as the judgment becomes enforceable. A foreign judgment will only have this effect when the sentence passed is served.[34] Otherwise, there would be unjustified results, since the punishment not yet served or still partly to be served would, unless the offender returns to the country where the judgment had been passed, become meaningless. This consequence is a result of the common practice of not executing foreign judgments at home,[35] and the widespread custom not to extradite one's own citizens. The proscription of the execution or the later exemption from execution by judicial or pardoning decision, either totally or partly, should not, however, obstruct the effect of the maxim *ne bis in idem*.

---

31 *I.e.*, whether the court of the place of commission, of arrest, or of the place of domicile.

32 *Cf.* HENRI DONNEDIEU DE VABRES, 43 (2) ANNUAIRE DE L'INSTITUT DE DROIT INTERNATIONAL 260 (1950).

33 *See supra* note 5, at Art. 53.

34 *Compare supra* note 5, at Art. 53 ¶ 1 (the maxim is also applicable when the offender has been acquitted, has been given amnesty or pardon, and when the offender was convicted but no sentence was imposed).

35 Up to now there were only some exceptions. *See e.g.*, the Scandinavian Act of Enforcement; Swiss Criminal Code Art. 5 ¶ 3; Swiss Extradition Act (to a limited extent); and in Turkey, Act of July 13, 1965, Art. 18. *Cf. supra* note 5 and *infra* notes 55-58.

The Application of the Maxim Ne Bis in Idem *Subject to the Contents of the Judgment*

A different way of applying the maxim *ne bis in idem* at the national and international level can result from the contents of the foreign judgment of the foreign country or from the special character of the offense upon which the foreign judgment is based. There is a prevailing understanding that if the recognition of foreign penal judgments is provided for at all, it does not matter whether the judgment is for conviction or acquittal.[36] Some legal systems allow a renewed prosecution notwithstanding a prior acquittal in order to grant their own subjects the utmost protection by virtue of their own criminal laws[37] or in order to ascertain whether the acquittal was justified.

The Application of the Maxim Ne Bis in Idem *Subject to the Character of the Offense*

The character of an offense which is the subject of foreign proceedings can bring about a limitation in the application of the maxim at the international level. Political offenses are particularly affected, since they appear to leave, though judgment has been passed abroad, vital interests of the "offended" country unpunished. Thus a renewed prosecution at home seems justified. This situation is why many legal systems exclude offenses against the safety or other interests of the state from the application of an obligation to give recognition to foreign penal judgments.[38] This concept of safety has been taken into account at the international level, with respect to foreign judgments regarding conduct of a political character. This situation has always been granted a special position in international consultations concerning recognition of foreign judgments. State jurisdiction for offenses against the safety of a state enjoys a preferred status. Consequently, the home country may proceed against a person already adjudged abroad without being obliged to take into account the foreign judgment.[39] Consider the effects of political offenses in matters of extradition wherein an offense of a political character will give the state of refuge the right to refuse extradition.[40]

In consequence of the political and military associations of certain Western countries, the maxim *ne bis in idem* is now recognized, to a limited extent, in the European Convention on the International Validity of Criminal Judgements. It will be the beginning of further international development.

---

36 *E.g.*, Greek Criminal Code Art. 9; Turkish Criminal Code § 7 and *supra* note 34.

37 Hans Schultz, *Bemerkungen zum Verhältnis von Völkerrecht und Landesrecht im Strafrecht*, 19 ANNUAIRE SUISSE DE DROIT INT'L 9, 30 (1962).

38 The recognition of foreign judgments which concern crimes against the safety of the state as denied by Code de procedure penale Art. 689 ¶ 2, sentence 2, and Greek Criminal Code Art. 9.

39 The 9th International Congress on Criminal Law at The Hague, *supra* note 29, adopted this view in Resolution II(1)(c) on Theme IV. The Eur. Conv. Int'l Val. Crim. Judg., *supra* note 5, at Art. 6(b) is more progressive. It takes into consideration that judgments for political crimes might be enforced at home, although there is no obligation to do so. *See also supra* note 5, at Art. 53 ¶ 2 and *infra* note 67.

40 M. Cherif Bassiouni, *Ideologically Motivated Offenses and the Political Offense Exception in Extradition: A Proposed Juridical Standard for an Unruly Problem*, 19 DEPAUL L.REV. 217 (1970).

The Significance of Identity of Parties to the Application of the Maxim Ne Bis in Idem

The international validity of the maxim *ne bis in idem* also depends on the extent to which the principle of "identity of parties participating in the prosecution" is applied. Within the borders of a country, it does not matter who appears as public accuser against the delinquent. Every person authorized do so may act accordingly, and each valid judgment will thus exclude renewed prosecution. It is doubtful, though, whether this principle, which functions so well on the national level, will retain its ease of application within an international framework.

Unless the foreign proceedings make a renewed prosecution at home inadmissible, the maxim will be of no significance.[41] The essential problem posed here revolves around the questions of what functions the prosecuting authorities of a country will perform and what interests they will represent. Should they be concerned with the maintenance of the public safety and order of their respective country alone? In that case, there will probably be an interest in renewed prosecution and, accordingly, a disregard for the previous activities of the foreign prosecuting authority which led to the judgment abroad. Should the prosecuting authorities of a given country, in addition to the above, also represent the common interest of civilized nations in effectively repressing criminality, a renewed prosecution would not be permitted.[42]

A recent decision of the Italian Constitutional Court dealing with the question of the validity of *ne bis in idem* affirms that a foreign judgment will bar a renewed prosecution only when the social and legal-political valuation of human acts in the different countries is equal.[43] Obviously, because of differences in tradition and legal conscience, the ideas among the various nations concerning the extent to which their legal order has been disturbed will always differ. Consequently, the Italian Court's decision will find every accuser promoting the policy of his own country and commencing a renewed prosecution for an offense upon which judgment has already been passed abroad.[44] The posture of this Court is, in itself, representative of the situation internationally.

Significance of Identity of Offense to the Application of the Principle Ne Bis in Idem

Conduct encompassed with the concept of "identity of the offense" may not be prosecuted twice by the respective countries which claim that they have been affected by the said conduct. As the definition of the concept varies in each country, it is difficult to determine how it is to be defined on the international level. The Anglo-Saxon law stresses identity of legal characterization, so that another country will be permitted to undertake a

---

[41] Exceptions may follow from the principle of opportunity (*Opportunitätsprinzip*) according to the law of criminal procedure only.

[42] *See* DE VABRES, *supra* note 32, at 257; LES PRINCIPES MODERNES DE DROIT INTERNATIONAL 312 (1928); and M. Cherif Bassiouni, *World Public Order and Extradition, in* AKTUELLE PROBLEME DES INTERNATIONALEN STRAFRECHT (Oehler & Potz eds., 1970).

[43] Corte Costituzionale of Apr. 18, 1967, No. 48, 3 RIVISTA DI DIRITTO INTERNAZIONALE PRIVATO E PROCESSUALE 580 (1967).

[44] The countries then deduct the punishment served abroad from the sentence of the national judgment, *e.g.*, German Criminal Code § 51 ¶ 3.

renewed prosecution based on different legal categorizations.[45] On the other hand, the IXth International Congress of Criminal law meeting at the Hague in 1964 concerned itself with the basic facts which underlie the offense without confining "identity" to legal definition.[46] This understanding corresponds to the German and many other continental legal orders. But it is difficult to conceive that the offense (*idem*) at the international level will acquire its significance through underlying basic facts, because the criminal statutes of the particular countries vary. Yet a special legal position can arise in the law of extradition whenever a country requests extradition because the acts committed and deemed an offense fulfill the legal requirements of its statute as well as those of the requesting country. This satisfies the requirement of "double criminality," and the request for extradition will be granted. Accordingly, the maxim *ne bis in idem* will apply to prohibit the prosecution of the offender who was extradited to the requesting state.[47] The scope of the maxim at the international level would thus depend upon the fortuitous order of prosecution among countries; whereas at the national level, according to many continental laws, a renewed prosecution based on the same event is not permitted, and recognition of foreign judgments, leading to the inadmissibility of a renewed prosecution, is restricted to the extent to which the valuation of the basic event by the foreign court is possible.[48]

Some Solutions to the Problems of Ne Bis in Idem

As indicated above, the range of application of the maxim *ne bis in idem* within the scope of recognition of foreign penal judgments is a very restricted one, whereas, at the national level this maxim has unlimited validity. The basis for restriction of the maxim on the international level is the diversity of national legislation and of opinions as to what acts should be punished.

There are, however, several suggested possibilities by virtue of which the effective scope of the maxim could be enlarged within the international sphere. A unification of national criminal codes is one manner of expansion, but it appears unlikely to take place in the near future. A change to the pure principle of territoriality has been suggested,[49] but it would not totally satisfy the interests of each country, especially in the area of political offenses. Presently, Great Britain has numerous exceptions from the principle of territoriality, which has been the prevailing common law theory. The U.S. maintains nearly absolute application of the principle of territoriality, even though there are some exceptions.[50] One of the reasons for this is historical. Before the war of independence, the King of England had American political prisoners transported to Great Britain to sentence them there, and the U.S. became gravely suspicious of all other principles.

---

[45] U.S. v. Lanza, 260 U.S. 377 (1922); a critical view of this position is found in M. CHERIF BASSIOUNI, CRIMINAL LAW AND ITS PROCESSES 129 (1969); for a general discussion of double jeopardy, *see* BASSIOUNI, *id.* at 126-36.

[46] On this theme, *cf.* Hans-Heinrich Jescheck, *Rapport general provisoire*, 34 REVUE INTERNATIONAL DE DROIT PÉNAL 209 (1963); OEHLER, *supra* note 10, at 972 *et seq.*.

[47] *See Symposium on Extradition and National Reports in Preparation of X International Penal Law Congress of Rome 1969*, 39 REVUE INTERNATIONALE DE DROIT PÉNAL 375-867 (1968).

[48] Buhler, *supra* note 6, at 92.

[49] Such as that of Luther, *Zum Verbrauch der Strafklage im Internationalen Recht*, 1969 NJW 1027.

[50] *See* BASSIOUNI, *supra* note 45, at 329-30.

Certainly, the goal that nobody should be punished twice for the same offense could be reached to a great extent by unifying the rules of conflicts of criminal laws, and by extensively undertaking the execution of foreign penal judgments. There has already been some settlement of jurisdiction conflicts in the European Convention on the International Validity of Criminal Judgements.[51]

Today, generally only in those cases where national legal mandates provide for it or where international conventions provide for the recognition of foreign judgment is a renewed prosecution precluded. The maxim *ne bis in idem* can not be regarded as a basic rule of international criminal law and will never become such as long as there is not a greater similarity of approach among the various countries, or at least among particular groups of nations, to the problem of inadmissibility of a renewed prosecution by virtue of previous foreign judgment. So long as reservations against the foreign jurisdiction (*Rechtspruchung*) are presented as practical difficulties, affecting the national interest, the only remedies that will remain are pardon, the principle of opportunity (*Opportunitäts prinzip*), the quashing of proceedings (when it is legaly admissible), and the deduction of foreign punishment from the renewed sentence at home.[52]

The Enforcement of Foreign Criminal Judgments

National and International Settlements

Until recently, the criminal codes of all countries, with few exceptions, contained the principle that foreign penal judgments could not be enforced at home.[53] The reasons given are that such enforcement would constitute a restriction on sovereignity and that practical execution would be too difficult and therefore justify the consistent practice of nonrecognition. The argument that sovereignity, by the enforcement of a foreign judgment, would be impinged upon has become weak as it has gradually become understood that although the country enforcing the foreign judgment does indeed take over the execution of acts of a foreign sovereignity, there is at the same time a widening of the potential range of its own sovereignity by the enforcement of the judgments of its own courts abroad. Although there had already existed a few multilateral conventions, restricted with respect to the contents, concerning the enforcement of foreign judgments,[54] the first comprehensive

---

51 *See* Eur. Conv. Int'l Val. Crim. Judg., *supra* note 5, at Art. 6. (A country is obligated to enforce penal judgments passed in another country, with some exceptions, if it is requested to do so.)

52 The principle of deduction is to be applied according to the law of most of the countries of the European-Continental sphere of law, and consequently also in Central and South America, anyway.

53 *Compare* OEHLER, *supra* note 10, at 20 *et seq. with* 980 *et seq.*

54 *Cf.* Revised Rhine Navigation Convention of 1868 Art. 40 ¶ 1 and Art. 34 (revised). The Rhine Navigation tribunals are competent 1) in criminal matters for the investigation and punishing of all contraventions of the shipping and river police regulations; 2). . . . Art. 40 ¶ 1. The decisions of Rhine Navigation tribunals in each of the riparian states shall be enforceable in all other states, according to the procedure laid down by the law of a country in which such decisions are executed. *See also* Benelux Convention on Customs and Excises of 1952, Art. 13. If the judgment against an author of an offense concerning customs and excise be enforceable in the country where it was pronounced, the recovery of the fines and costs and the execution of confiscations also may be extended to the property which the condemned person possesses in another country, according to the laws of this country, after an *exequatur* has been obtained there. The enforcing authority of the first country for this purpose addresses a request, which is accompanied by an execution of the judgment, directly to the competent authority of the second country. There is a new Benelux Convention on the Transfer of Criminal Proceedings of 1974,

treatment of enforcement of foreign judgments was formulated by the Scandinavian Act of Enforcement. The IXth International Penal Law Congress meeting at the Hague in 1963 initiated steps toward a basic international settlement of this problem. The European conventions and other special North American conventions represent the latest developments.[55] A convention on the Transfer of Prisoners among the Communist Countries should also be mentioned.[56] In 1981 Austria promulgated a law on extradition and assistance in criminal matters, in the same year Switzerland promulgated a law on international assistance in criminal matters, and in 1982 West Germany promulgated a law on international assistance in criminal matters. These three laws[57] provide that a sentence imposed by the state on a foreigner will be served in the state where the sentenced person is a national, by transferring the person to such state. The laws also provide that a state can request the transfer of a national, under certain conditions, so the national can serve a sentence imposed by a foreign state in the home state. The International Law Association has proposed the Convention on Expatriation of Accused Persons for Trial and Sentence and Repatriation for Enforcement of Sentences.[58] Under this proposal the national, on the request of the sentencing state and the sentenced person, will be delivered up to his own state for enforcement of the sentence, or will be expatriated for sentencing, to the state where the act occurred and then repatriated for enforcement of the sentence.

General Prerequisites for the Assumption of the Enforcement of Foreign Criminal Judgments

If the enforcement of foreign penal judgments is to be accomplished by virtue of a somewhat restricted international convention, at least certain general prerequisites and guarantees as to all proceedings must be provided. Probably, the most important consideration in this connection is the existence of similar cultural, political, social, and legal structures in the country which assumes the duty of enforcement and in the country which pronounces penal judgment. International enforcement would prove easiest in those countries which have had similar cultural development and in which, therefore, a judgment would be similarly interpreted. Among such countries, it is probable that the crime for which foreign judgment is passed is also punishable in the country which is requested to enforce

---

Tractaatenblad (Dutch), No. 184 (1974).

55 *See supra* note 5 (listing the relevant European conventions). *See also* Treaty on Prisoner Transfer, Nov. 25, 1976, U.S.-Mexico, T.I.A.S. No. 8718; Treaty on the Execution of Penal Sentences, Mar. 2, 1977, U.S.-Canada, T.I.A.S. No. 9552; and Treaty between Canada and Mexico, Nov. 22, 1977, 1979 Can. T.S. No. 3 (these treaties all regarding the mutual execution of penal sentences). For a discussion of the U.S. Treaties, *see* M. Cherif Bassiouni, *Perspectives on the Transfer of Prisoners Between the United States and Mexico and the United States and Canada*, 11 VAND. J. TRANSNAT'L L. 249 (1978). For a discussion of the treaty between Canada and Mexico, *see* Kos-Rabcewicz, *Translado de las Personas y la Validez Internacional de las Sanciones Penales*, 1981 BOLETIN MEXICANO DE DERECHO COMPARDO 595.

56 *See* Lech Gardocki, *The Socialist System*, in 2 INTERNATIONAL CRIMINAL LAW 133 (M. Cherif Bassiouni ed., 1986).

57 These laws were discussed at the Conference of the Association of Comparative Law, 96 ZEITSCHRIFT FÜR DIE GESAMTE STRAFRECHTSWISSENSCHAFT 555 (1984) (Reports by Linke (Austria), Oehler (Germany), Schultz (Switzerland)).

58 International Law Association 377 (1982) (Report of the 60th Conference at Montreal) (International Criminal Law Committee, chairman Kos-Rabcewicz-Zubkowski). This draft convention will be submitted to the United Nations for consideration.

the judgment.[59] Thus, by enforcing a foreign judgment, a country would be protecting its own legal and social order. From this analysis it would seem that mutual punishability must be a general prerequisite to international enforcement of penal judgments.

The assumption is that the enforcement of a foreign judgment must not infringe on the national *ordre public*. Important national interests would be damaged if the foreign penal judgment to be executed violated essential constitutional principles or was incompatible with a protected fundamental human right.[60] The execution of foreign penal judgments should therefore be accomplished only where the proceedings on which a foreign judgment is based accords with the fundamental principles of just prosecution as set forth in many national constitutions and by the European Convention for the Protection of Human Rights and Fundamental Liberties, November 4, 1950 (with amendments). Pertinent protections include the following: (1) The accused has sufficient facilities of defense; (2) He has the opportunity to be heard by the court in person; 3) His confession is not forced; and (4) His guilt must be proved. Not until such basic conditions have been secured by reciprocal declarations among the various countries will the execution of foreign judgments be possible.

The Execution of Foreign Judgments Passed in Absentia

The problem of the enforcement of foreign judgments which have been passed in the absence of the condemned person is closely connected with the question of the maintenance of constitutional safeguards in foreign proceedings. Generally, a judgment passed in the absence of the accused is not founded on as broad a knowledge of the facts of the case as a judgment which has been passed after the accused was permitted to be heard and actually took part in the proceedings.[61] The judge of a trial which is proceeding in the absence of the accused has to rely totally upon the inquiries of prosecuting authorities; he cannot form an objectively balanced picture of the criminality of the accused, and consequently will pass sentence based upon the nature and scope of the offense alone.[62]

Because such proceedings are prone to mistakes as to the proof of facts and unable to properly determine punishment, one must act very cautiously when assuming to enforce a foreign judgment passed in the absence of the accused. Enforcement should be in such cases only for offenses of minor importance.[63]

It seems equitable that if a person has been accused and convicted before a foreign court, and up to the time judgment was passed did not have the opportunity to be heard, he should be permitted to choose to defend himself either before the court which has passed sentence abroad, or before the court of his home country or country of domicile where the foreign judgment is to be enforced. Of course, if the accused applies to the national court, the decision of that court must be accorded the same validity as though the accused had

---

59 *See* Eur. Conv. Int'l Val. Crim. Judg., *supra* note 5, at Art. 4 ¶ 1.

60 *See id.*, at Art. 6(a), (c).

61 For a discussion of the accused's right to confrontation and cross-examination, *see* BASSIOUNI, *supra* note 45, at 502-04.

62 *Cf.* Hulsman, *The Role of Sentences Passed in the Absence of the Accused, in Arrangements for the Enforcement of Foreign Criminal Sentences, in Aspects of the International Validity of Criminal Judgements*, European Committee on Crime Problems 29 (1968).

63 The German Act of Criminal Procedure Art. 21 *et seq.*, no longer recognizes any judgment *in absentia*; the Eur. Conv. Int'l Val. Crim. Judg., *supra* note 5, does not distinguish between major and minor offenses.

applied to the foreign court in making his appeal.[64] Finally, no country should be obliged to enforce a foreign judgment passed against an absent person,[65] if it exceeds the scope of legal consequences which the requested country has provided relating to judgments against absent persons in general; *ultra vires* actions must not be given validity.[66]

The Principle of Deduction

One positive effect of foreign penal judgments which has already been recognized to some extent is the principle of deduction. Most countries founded on constitutional rules recognize this principle by providing in their laws that the punishment, totally or partially served abroad, must be deducted from the time involved in subsequent sentencing for the same offense.

Proceedings Relating to Undertaking Enforcement of Foreign Penal Judgments

The country requested to enforce the punishments and measures pronounced by a foreign penal judgment must classify that foreign judgment according to its own system of law. Because of the diversity of possible sentences for a single crime, and above all because one country assumes to enforce foreign acts of sovereignity, there are many uncertainties with regard to the procedure to be followed in such cases.

Enforcement Proceedings and the Examining Authority of the Judge Undertaking Enforcement of a Foreign Penal Judgment

A foreign judgment, in order to effectively assume validity and enforcement at home, should be recognized through a procedure of *exequatur*. Such a procedure is provided for in the European Convention of the International Validity of Criminal Judgements and has already proven its success for several years of application under the terms of the Scandinavian Act of Enforcement. By this procedure, a foreign judgment after judical examination may be declared nationally enforceable. Opinions concerning the extent to which the foreign judgment ought to be examined differ considerably. According to some opinions, the foreign judgment can be enforced—with limited examination of its original rendering. Others believe that the judgment must be harmonized with the national interests of the enforcing country. A full examination of the judgment with reference to facts and legal aspects should not, however, be undertaken by the judical authorities of the enforcing state, as it would tend to reopen the original trial in its entirety.

The penal judgment which is the object of a request for enforcement is still a foreign one, and is not transformed into a national judgment of the enforcing country by the procedure of *exequatur*. The judge of the enforcing state must respect the foreign judgment and is bound by the statements of the requesting foreign judge. Thus, a thorough

64 *Cf.* Eur. Conv. Int'l Val. Crim. Judg., *supra* note 5, at Art. 24 *et seq.*

65 *See id.*, at app. I(d).

66 On the enforcement of foreign judgments passed in the absence of the accused, *supra* notes 63 and 64, and Benelux Draft Convention Concerning the Enforcement of Criminal Sentences and Draft Explanatory Memorandum, both drafts quoted and are partly reproduced in Hulsman, *supra* note 61, at 38.

examination of the foreign judgment is not admissible. The procedure of *exequatur* is a filter through which it is ascertained whether the foreign judgment harmonizes with the most fundamental legal principles of the requested country. Only if that is so will the requested country usually agree to assume enforcement of the judgment. Consequently, the procedure of *exequatur* will not excessively refer to the contents of judgment, but to the way in which the judgment came to pass. Above all, the observance of constitutional principles within the foreign state's proceedings will be considered.

The judge of the requested country is authorized by the *exequatur* procedure to examine to a certain extent the contents of the judgment with regard to proof of the facts and to legal evaluation. There are a number of cases where special offenses are the object of foreign judgments, and the enforcement of them will principally serve only the interests of the requesting country. The requested country, therefore, will treat these judgments reservedly and examine them with scrutiny if it does not refuse the enforcement a *priori*.[67] Apart from the special offenses of a political, military, and fiscal nature, a thorough examination of the foreign judgment and additional inquiries and legal valuations will be made, if from the request for enforcement the requested judge draws conjectures which hint at the existence of justifications, excuses, and other grounds recognized by the laws of the requested country which preclude punishment there but which were not taken into consideration by the foreign court.[68] For example, should it be obvious according to the facts stated by the foreign judgment that the convicted person killed someone in self-defense, he cannot be punished for murder according to the criminal law of the Federal Republic of Germany (§ 53 of its criminal code). Thus, if the Federal Republic of Germany is requested by a foreign country to enforce a penal judgment and self-defense has not been taken into consideration by the verdict of the foreign judgment, the requested judge must determine whether the actual prerequisites of self-defense have been fulfilled and, accordingly, recognize the results of that determination by accepting the foreign judgment or rejecting it.

The Transformation of Punishment Pronounced by the Foreign Judgment

General Conception

Penalties pronounced by foreign judgment may differ from those of the enforcing state. The sentence may involve a fine, confinement, or both. It may provide for safety and rehabilitative measures or derivative penalties such as the prohibition to exercise a profession or to drive a car. Along with the enforcement of the foreign judgment, the measure of punishment pronounced by the foreign judgment must be translated into the terminology of the national penal system, and its derivative effects must also be assessed.

A basic principle in the transformation of the punishment pronounced by a foreign judgment is that the convicted person must not suffer any greater disadvantages than under

---

[67] This facility is provided for by the Eur. Conv. Int'l Val. Crim. Judg., *supra* note 5, at Art. 6(a), (b), (c), and app. I(a), (b).

[68] This may be due to an error of the court passing the judgment, but also to the fact that the criminal law of the foreign country does not know the national justifications, excuses, etc.. *Cf.* Eur. Conv. Int'l Val. Crim. Judg., *supra* note 5, at Art. 40 ¶ 1(b).

the punishment decided by the foreign state. The enforcing state must not be more severe than the requesting state.

The Transformation of a Fine

The transformation of a fine is accomplished by levying the fine in the currency of the requested country, taking into consideration the rate of exchange at the time of the assumption of enforcement. If the fine passed by the foreign judgment is beyond the limits which exist for the same offense in the requested country, the judge of the requested country is not bound to enforcement beyond the limits of the fine stipulated by his national criminal law. In those countries which translate nonpayment of fines with imprisonment, it will depend on the public policy of the enforcing state.

As to other forms of levy of fines such as confiscation of property, some multilateral conventions provide for that instance as well.[69]

The Transformation of a Confinement

The national criminal laws, within the scope of which a foreign judgment is to be enforced, often designate several kinds of confinements, the names and gradations of which are not handled in a uniform way among the various countries. A confinement, called arrest by a foreign judgment, can be interpreted quite differently in the requested country. The transformation of punishment, pronounced by a foreign judgment by application of name alone, might not be adequate to the offense nor to the offender. The confinement, therefore, is to be transformed by taking into consideration the offense and the offender, and the corresponding in-country counterpart of the punishment pronounced abroad.[70] The limits of the national criminal law must not be exceeded in so doing.

The Transformation of Additional Punishments

As there is great variation in secondary effects and additional punishments in the particular national laws, the obstacles to their transformation are very great. For example, if the law of the requested country does not have the institution of protective custody, what

---

[69] The Swedish (Nordic) Act of Enforcement of May 22, 1963 (partly altered by the act of June 29, 1964). The Act has 36 sections.

The Enforcement of Fines, etc.

§ 1 — A judgement, which has been passed in Denmark, Finland, Iceland, or Norway, and by virtue of which a person has been fined or subjected to confiscation or sentenced to pay the law costs in criminal matters, will on request be enforced in Sweden.

That applies to decrees (decisions), too, which have been passed in one of the mentioned countries in order to secure claims for fines, confiscation, compensation, or the payment of law costs and which concern a seizure, a restraint of alienation, or the sequestration of the property of a person having been charged with a punishable offense.

§ 2 — The enforcement will be executed according to Swedish law, but there will be no decisions concerning the transformation of a fine.

§ 3 — The enforcement of a judgement, passed in Sweden, or one of the decrees (decisions) mentioned in § 1 may be left to the authorities of Denmark, Finland, Iceland, or Norway.

[70] Eur. Conv. Int'l Val. Crim. Judg., *supra* note 5, at Arts. 43-48. (These articles make transformation difficult but it could be overcome if there were a universal uniform confinement.).

shall the requested judge do? His national law does not permit him to pronounce it. Should he not consider the protective custody order of the foreign judgment at all? In case the requested country which has assumed enforcement does not have adequate legal facilities to accomplish the additional punishment or the secondary effect contained in the foreign judgment, the requested judge must decide which measure he will pronounce to replace them.[71]

The problem of recognition of foreign penal judgments gives rise to many unanswered questions, particularly as to the recognition of its negative or positive effects. The international supervision of conditionally sentenced or conditionally released offenders[72] is only one of the derivative issues among many others. It is certain that one should strive as intensively as possible at the international level for the simultaneous consideration of the relationship between foreign judgments and recidivism as has already been done by some national criminal laws. It is possible that foreign judgments might in the future influence the prescription (statute of limitations) of offenses on the national level and might even have consequences on civil or public law.

Not all of the questions which pose themselves in this area will be conclusively settled in the near future, but every progress in this field will be a step toward a more intensive international control of crime and, concurrently, a more equitable valuation and treatment of criminals.

---

71 *See id.*, at Arts. 49-52.

72 See on this matter the provisions of the Scandinavian Act of Enforcement and the European Convention on the Supervision of Conditionally Sentenced or Conditionally Released Offenders of 1964.

Appendix 15

European Convention on the International Validity of Criminal Judgements

European Treaty Series.
No. 70

PREAMBLE

The member States of the Council of Europe, signatory hereto,

Considering that the fight against crime, which is becoming increasingly an international problem, calls for the use of modern and effective methods on an international scale;

Convinced of the need to pursue a common criminal policy aimed at the protection of society

Conscious of the need to respect human dignity and to promote the rehabilitation of offenders;

Considering that the aim of the Council of Europe is to achieve greater unity between its Members,

Have agreed as follows:

PART I

Definitions

Article 1

For the purposes of this Convention:

(a) "European criminal judgement" means any final decision delivered by a criminal court of a Contracting State as a result of criminal proceedings;

(b) "Offence" comprises, apart from acts dealt with under the criminal law, those dealt with under the legal provisions listed in Appendix II to the present Convention on condition that where these provisions give competence to an administrative authority there must be opportunity for the person concerned to have the case tried by a court;

(c) "Sentence" means the imposition of a sanction;

(d) "Sanction" means any punishment or other measure expressly imposed on a person, in respect of an offense, in a European criminal judgement, or in an "ordonannce pénale";

(e) "Disqualification" means any loss or suspension of a right or any prohibition or loss of legal capacity;

(f) "Judgement rendered in absentia" means any decision considered as such under Article 21, paragraph 2;

(g) "Ordonnance pénale" means any of the decisions delivered in another Contracting State and listed in Appendix III to this Convention.

PART II

Enforcement of European Criminal Judgements

Section 1

General Provision

(a) *General conditions of enforcement*

ARTICLE 2

This Part is applicable to:
(a) sanctions involving deprivation of liberty;
(b) fines or confiscation;
(c) disqualifications.

ARTICLE 3

1. A Contracting State shall be competent in the cases and under the conditions provided for in this Convention to enforce a sanction imposed in another Contracting State which is enforceable in the latter State.
2. This competence can only be exercised following a request by the other Contracting State.

ARTICLE 4

1. The sanction shall not be enforced by another Contracting State unless under its law the act for which the sanction was imposed would be an offence of committed on its territory and the person on whom the sanction was imposed liable to punishment if he had committed the act there.
2. If the sentence relates to two or offences, not all of which fulfil the requirements of paragraph 1, the sentencing State shall specify which part of the sanction applies to the offences that satisfy those requirements.

ARTICLE 5

The sentencing State may request another Contracting State to enforce the sanction only if one or more of the following conditions are fulfilled:

(a) if the person sentenced is ordinarily resident in the other State;

(b) if the enforcement of the sanction in the other State is likely to improve the prospects for the social rehabilitation of the person sentenced;

(c) if, in the case of a sanction involving deprivation of liberty, the sanction could be enforced following the enforcement of another sanction involving deprivation of liberty which the person sentenced is undergoing or is to to undergo in the other State;

(d) if the other State is the State of origin of the person sentenced and has declared itself willing to accept responsibility for the enforcement of that sanction;

(e) if it considers that it cannot itself enforce the sanction, even by having recourse to extradition, and that the other State can.

ARTICLE 6

Enforcement requested in accordance with the foregoing provisions may not be refused, in whole or in part, save:

(a) where enforcement would run counter to the fundamental principles of the legal system of the requested State;

(b) where the requested State considers the offence for which the sentence was passed to be of a political nature or a purely military one;

(c) where the requested State considers that there are substantial grounds for believing that the sentence was brought about or aggravated by considerations of race, religion, nationality or political opinion;

(d) where enforcement would be contrary to the international undertakings of the requested State;

(e) where the act is already the subject of proceedings in the requested State or where the requested State decides to institute proceedings in respect of the act;

(f) where the competent authorities in the requested State have decided not to take proceedings or to drop proceedings already begun, in respect of the same act;

(g) where the act was committed outside the territory of the requesting State;

(h) where the requested State is unable to enforce the sanction;

(i) where the request is grounded on Article 5(e) and none of the other conditions mentioned in that Article is fulfilled;

(j) where the requested State considers that the requesting State is itself able to enforce the sanction;

(k) where the age of the person sentenced at the time of the offence was such that he could not have been prosecuted in the requested State;

(l) where under the law of the requested State the sanction imposed can no longer be enforced because of the lapse of time;

(m) where and to the extent that the sentence imposes a disqualification.

ARTICLE 7

A request for enforcement shall not be complied with if enforcement would run counter to the principles recognised in the provisions of Section 1 of Part III of this Convention.

(b) Effects of the transfer of enforcement

ARTICLE 8

For the purpose of Article 6, paragraph 1 and the reservation mentioned under (c) of Appendix I of the present Convention any act which interrupts or suspends a time limitation validly performed by the authorities of the sentencing State shall be considered as having the same effect for the purpose of reckoning time limitation in the requested State in accordance with the law of that State.

ARTICLE 9

1. A sentenced person detained in the requesting State who has been surrendered to the requested State for the purpose of enforcement shall not be proceeded against, sentenced or detained with a view to the carrying out of a sentence or detention order for any offence committed prior to its surrender other that that for which the sentence to be enforced was imposed, nor shall he for any other reason be restricted in his personal freedom, except in the following cases:

(a) when the State which surrendered him consents, a request for consent shall be submitted, accompanied by all relevant documents and a legal record of any statement made by the convicted person in respect of the offence concerned. Consent shall be given when the offence for which it is requested would itself be subject to extradition under the law of the State requesting enforcement or when extradition would be excluded only by reason of the amount of the punishment;

(b) when the sentenced person, having had an opportunity to leave the territory of the State to which he has been surrendered, has not done so within 45 days of his final discharge, or if he has returned to that territory after leaving it.

2. The State requested to enforce the sentence may, however, take any measure necessary to remove the person from its territory, or any measures necessary under its law, including proceedings by default, to prevent any legal effects of lapse of time.

ARTICLE 10

1. The enforcement shall be governed by the law of the requested State and that State alone shall be competent to take all appropriate decisions, such as those concerning conditional release.

2. The requesting State alone shall have the right to decide on any application for review of sentence.

3. Either State may exercise the right of amnesty or pardon.

ARTICLE 11

1. When the sentencing State has requested enforcement it may no longer itself begin the enforcement of a sanction which is the subject of that request. The sentencing State may, however,

begin enforcement of a sanction involving deprivation of liberty when the sentenced person is already detained on the territory of that State at the moment of the presentation of the request.

2. The right of enforcement shall revert to the requesting State:

(a) if it withdraws its request before the requested State has informed it of an intention to take action on the request;

(b) if the requested State notifies a refusal to take action on the request;

(c) if the requested State expressly relinquishes its right of enforcement. Such relinquishment shall only be possible if both the States concerned agree or if enforcement is no longer possible in the requested State. In the latter case, a relinquishment demanded by the requesting State shall be compulsory.

ARTICLE 12

1. The competent authorities of the requested State shall discontinue enforcement as soon as they have knowledge of any pardon, amnesty or application for review of sentence or any other decision by reason of which the sanction ceases to be enforceable. The same shall apply to the enforcement of a fine when the person sentenced has paid it to the competent authority in the requesting State.

2. The requesting State shall without delay inform the requested State of any decision or procedural measure taken on its territory that causes the right of enforcement to lapse in accordance with the preceding paragraph.

(c) Miscellaneous provisions

ARTICLE 13

1. The transit through the territory of a Contracting State of a detained person, who is to be transferred to a third Contracting State in application of this Convention, shall be granted at the request of the State in which the person is detained. The State of transit may require to be supplied with any appropriate document before taking a decision on the request. The person being transferred shall remain in custody in the territory of the State of transit, unless the State from which he is being transferred requests his release.

2. Except in cases where the transfer is requested under Article 34 any Contracting State may refuse transit:

(a) on one of the grounds mentioned in Article 6(b) and (c);

(b) on the ground that the person concerned is one of its own nationals.

3. If air transport is used, the following provisions shall apply:

(a) when it is not intended to land, the State from which the person is to be transferred may notify the State over whose territory the flight is to be made that the person concerned is being transferred in application to this Convention. In the case of an unscheduled landing such notification shall have the effect of a request for provisional arrest as provided for in Article 32, paragraph 2, and a formal request for transit shall be made;

(b) where it is intended to land, a formal request for transit shall be made.

ARTICLE 14

Contracting States shall not claim from each other the refund of any expenses resulting from the application of this Convention.

Section 2
Requests for enforcement

ARTICLE 15

1. All requests specified in this Convention shall be made in writing. They, and all communications necessary for the application of this Convention, shall be sent either by the Ministry of Justice of the

requesting State to the Ministry of Justice of the requested State or, if the Contracting States so agree, direct by the authorities of the requesting State to those of the requested State; they shall be returned by the same channel.

2. In urgent cases, requests and communications may be sent through the International Criminal Police Organisation (INTERPOL).

3. Any Contracting State may, by declaration addressed to the Secretary General of the Council of Europe, give notice of its intention to adopt other rules in regard to the communications referred to in paragraph 1 of this Article.

ARTICLE 16

The request for enforcement shall be accompanied by the original, or a certified copy, of the decision whose enforcement is requested and all other necessary documents. The original, or a certified copy, of all or part of the criminal file shall be sent to the requested State, if it so requires. The competent authority of the requesting State shall certify the sanction enforceable.

ARTICLE 17

If the requested State considers that the information supplied by the requesting State is not adequate to enable it to apply this Convention, it shall ask for the necessary additional information. It may prescribe a date for the receipt of such information.

ARTICLE 18

1. The authorities of the requested State shall promptly inform those of the requesting State of the action taken on the request for enforcement.

2. The authorities of the requested State shall, where appropriate, transmit to those of the requesting State a document certifying that the sanction has been enforced.

ARTICLE 19

1. Subject to paragraph 2 of this Article, no translation of requests or of supporting documents shall be required.

2. Any Contracting State may, at the time of signature or when depositing its instrument of ratification, acceptance or accession, by a declaration addressed to the Secretary General of the Council of Europe, reserve the right to require that requests and supporting documents be accompanied by a translation into its own language or into one of the official languages of the Council of Europe or into such one of those languages as it shall indicate. The other Contracting States may claim reciprocity.

3. This Article shall be without prejudice to any provisions concerning translation of requests and supporting documents that may be contained in agreements or arrangements now in force or that may be concluded between two or more Contracting States.

ARTICLE 20

Evidence and documents transmitted in application of this Convention need not be authenticated.

Section 3
Judgements rendered in absentia and "ordonnances pénales"

ARTICLE 21

1. Unless otherwise provided in this Convention, enforcement of judgements rendered in absentia and of "ordonnances pénales" shall be subject to the same rules as enforcement of other judgements.

2. Except as provided in paragraph 3, a judgement in absentia for the purposes of this Convention means any judgement rendered by a court in a Contracting State after criminal proceedings at the hearing of which the sentenced person was not personally present.

3. Without prejudice to Articles 25, paragraph 2, 26, paragraph 2 and 29, the following shall be considered as judgements rendered after a hearing of the accused:

(a) any judgement in absentia and any "ordonnance pénale" which have been confirmed or pronounced in the sentencing State after opposition by the person sentenced:

(b) any judgement rendered in absentia on appeal, provided that the appeal from the judgement of the court of first instance was lodged by the person sentenced.

ARTICLE 22

Any judgements rendered in absentia and any "ordonnances penales" which have not yet been the subject of appeal or opposition may, as soon as they have been rendered, be transmitted to the requested State for the purpose of notification and with a view to enforcement.

ARTICLE 23

1. If the requested State sees fit to take action on the request to enforce a judgement rendered in absentia or an ordonnance penale," it shall cause the person sentenced to be personally notified of the decision rendered in the requesting State.

2. In the notification to the person sentenced information shall also be given:

(a) that a request for enforcement has been presented in accordance with this Convention;

(b) that the only remedy available is an opposition as provided for in Article 24 of this Convention;

(c) that the opposition must be lodged with such authority as may be specified; that for the purposes of its admissibility the opposition is subject to the provisions of Article 24 of this Convention; and that the person sentenced may ask to be heard by the authorities of the sentencing State;

(d) that, if no opposition is lodged within the prescribed period, the judgement will, for the entire purposes of this Convention, be considered as having been rendered after a hearing of the accused.

3. A copy of the notification shall be sent promptly to the authority which requested enforcement.

ARTICLE 24

1. After notice of the decision has been served in accordance with Article 23, the only remedy available to the person sentenced shall be an opposition. Such opposition shall be examined, as the person sentenced chooses, either by the competent court in the requesting State or by that in the requested State. If the person sentenced expresses no choice, the opposition shall be examined by the competent court in the requested State.

2. In the cases specified in the preceding paragraph, the opposition shall be admissible if it is lodged with the competent authority of the requested State within a period of 30 days from the date on which the notice was served. This period shall be reckoned in accordance with the relevant rules of the law of the requested State. The competent authority of that State shall promptly notify the authority which made the request for enforcement.

ARTICLE 25

1. If the opposition is examined in the requesting State, the person sentenced shall be summoned to appear in that State at the new hearing of the case. Notice to appear shall be personally served not less than 21 days before the new hearing. This period may be reduced with the consent of the person sentenced. The new hearing shall be held before the court which is competent in the requesting State and in accordance with the procedure of that State.

2. If the person sentenced fails to appear personally or is not represented in accordance with the law of the requesting State, the court shall declare the opposition null and void and its decision shall be communicated to the competent authority of the requested State. The same procedure shall be followed if the court declares the opposition inadmissible. In both cases, the judgement rendered in absentia or

the "ordonnance penale" shall, for the entire purposes of this Convention, be considered as having been rendered after a hearing of the accused.

3. If the person sentenced appears personally or is represented in accordance with the law of the requesting State and if the opposition is declared admissible, the request for enforcement shall be considered as null and void.

ARTICLE 26

1. If the opposition is examined in the requested State the person sentenced shall be summoned to appear in that State at the new hearing of the case. Notice to appear shall be personally served not less than 21 days before the new hearing. This period may be reduced with the consent of the person sentenced. The new hearing shall be held before the court which is competent in the requested State and in accordance with the procedure of that State.

2. If the person sentenced fails to appear personally or is not represented in accordance with the law of the requested State, the court shall declare the opposition null and void. In that event, and if the court declares the opposition inadmissible, the judgement rendered in absentia or the "ordonnance pénale" shall, for the entire purposes of this Convention, be considered as having been rendered after a hearing of the accused.

3. If the person sentenced appears personally or is represented in accordance with the law of the requested State, and if the opposition is admissible, the act shall be tried as if it had been committed in that State. Preclusion of proceedings by reason of lapse of time shall, however, in no circumstances be examined. The judgement rendered in the requesting State shall be considered null and void.

4. Any step with a view to proceedings or a preliminary enquiry, taken in the sentencing State in accordance with its law and regulations, shall have the same validity in the requested State as if it had been taken by the authorities of that State, provided that assimilation does not give such steps a greater evidential weight than they have in the requesting State.

ARTICLE 27

For the purpose of lodging an opposition and for the purpose of the subsequent proceedings, the person sentenced in absentia or by an "ordonnance penale" shall be entitled to legal assistance in the cases and on the conditions prescribed by the law of the requested State and, where appropriate, of the requesting State.

ARTICLE 28

Any judicial decisions given in pursuance of Article 26, paragraph 3, and enforcement thereof, shall be governed solely by the law of the requested State.

ARTICLE 29

If the person sentenced in absentia or by an "ordonnance pénale" lodges no opposition, the decision shall, for the entire purposes of this Convention, be considered as having been rendered after the hearing of the accused.

ARTICLE 30

National legislations shall be applicable in the matter of reinstatement if the sentenced person, for reasons beyond his control, failed to observe the time-limits laid down in Articles 24, 25 and 26 or to appear personally at the hearing fixed for the new examination of the case.

Section 4
Provisional measures

ARTICLE 31

If the sentenced person is present in the requesting State after notification of the acceptance of its request for enforcement of a sentence involving deprivation of liberty is received, that State may, if it deems it necessary in order to ensure enforcement arrest him with a view to his transfer under the provisions of Article 43.

ARTICLE 32

1. When the requesting State has requested enforcement, the requested State may arrest the person sentenced:

(a) if, under the law of the requested State, the offense is one which justifies remand in custody, and

(b) if there is a danger of abscondence or, in case of a judgement rendered in absentia a danger of secretion of evidence.

2. When the requesting State announces its intention to request enforcement, the requested State may, on application by the requesting State, arrest the person sentenced, provided that requirements under (a) and (b) of the preceding paragraph are satisfied. The said application shall state the offence which led to the judgement and the time and place of its perpetration, and contain as accurate a description as possible of the person sentenced. It shall also contain a brief statement of the facts on which the judgement is based.

ARTICLE 33

1. The person sentenced shall be held in custody in accordance with the law of the requested State; the law of that State shall also determine the conditions on which he may be released.

2. The person in custody shall in any event be released:

(a) after a period equal to the period of deprivation of liberty imposed in the judgement;

(b) if he was arrested in pursuance of Article 32, paragraph 2, and the requested State did not receive, within 18 days from the date of the arrest, the request together with the documents specified in Article 16.

ARTICLE 34

1. A person held in custody in the requested State in pursuance of Article 32 who is summoned to appear before the competent court in the requesting State in accordance with Article 25 as a result of the opposition he has lodged, shall be transferred for that purpose to the territory of the requesting State.

2. After transfer, the said person shall not be kept in custody by the requesting State if the condition set out in Article 33, paragraph 2(*a*), is met or if the requesting State does not request enforcement of a further sentence. The person shall be promptly returned to the requested State unless he has been released.

ARTICLE 35

1. A person summoned before the competent court of the requesting State as a result of the opposition he has lodged shall not be proceeded against, sentenced or detained with a view to the carrying out of a sentence or detention order nor shall he for any other reason be restricted in his personal freedom for any act or offense which took place prior to his departure from the territory of the requested State and which is not specified in the summons unless he expressly consents in writing. In the case referred to in Article 34, paragraph 1, a copy of the statement of consent shall be sent to the State from which he has been transferred.

2. The effects provided for in the preceding paragraph shall cease when the person summoned, having had the opportunity to do so, has not left the territory of the requesting State during 15 days after the date of the decision following the hearing for which he was summoned to appear or if he returns to that territory after leaving it without being summoned anew.

ARTICLE 36

1. If the requesting State has requested enforcement of a confiscation of property, the requested State may provisionally seize the property in question, on condition that its own law provides for seizure in respect of similar facts.

2. Seizure shall be carried out in accordance with the law of the requested State which shall also determine the conditions on which the seizure may be lifted.

Section 5
Enforcement of sanctions
(a) *General clauses*

ARTICLE 37

A sanction imposed in the requesting State shall not be enforced in the requested State except by a decision of the court of the requested State. Each Contracting State may, however, empower other authorities to take such decisions if the sanction to be enforced is only a fine or a confiscation and if these decisions are susceptible of appeal to a court.

ARTICLE 38

The case shall be brought before the court or the authority empowered under Article 37 if the requested State sees fit to take action on the request for enforcement.

ARTICLE 39

1. Before a court takes a decision upon a request for enforcement the sentenced person shall be given the opportunity to state his views. Upon application he shall be heard by the court either by letters rogatory or in person. A hearing in person must be granted following his express request to that effect.

2. The court may, however, decide on the acceptance of the request for enforcement in the absence of a sentenced person requesting a personal hearing if he is in custody in the requesting State. In these circumstances any decision as to the substitution of the sanction under Article 44 shall be adjourned until, following his transfer to the requested State, the sentenced person has been given the opportunity to appear before the court.

ARTICLE 40

1. The court, or in the cases referred to in Article 37, the authority empowered under the same Article, which is dealing with the case shall satisfy itself:

(a) that the sanction whose enforcement is requested was imposed in a European criminal judgement;

(b) that the requirements of Article 4 are met;

(c) that the condition laid down in Article 6(a) is not fulfilled or should not preclude enforcement;

(d) that enforcement is not precluded by Article 7;

(e) that, in case of a judgement rendered in absentia or an "ordonnance pénale" the requirements of Section 3 of this Part are met.

2. Each Contracting State may entrust to the court or the authority empowered under Article 37 the examination of other conditions of enforcement provided for in this Convention.

ARTICLE 41

The judicial decisions taken in pursuance of the present section with respect to the requested enforcement and those taken on appeal from decisions by the administrative authority referred to in Article 37, shall be appealable.

ARTICLE 42

The requested State shall be bound by the findings as to the facts insofar as they are stated in the decision or insofar as it is impliedly based on them.

(b) *Clauses relating specifically to enforcement of sanctions involving deprivation of liberty*

ARTICLE 43

When the sentenced person is detained in the requesting State he shall, unless the law of that State otherwise provides, be transferred to the requested State as soon as the requesting State has been notified of the acceptance of the request for enforcement.

ARTICLE 44

1. If the request for enforcement is accepted, the court shall substitute for the sanction involving deprivation of liberty imposed in the requesting State a sanction prescribed by its own law for the same offense. This sanction may, subject to the limitations laid down in paragraph 2, be of a nature or duration other than that imposed in the requesting State. If this latter sanction is less than the minimum which may be pronounced under the law of the requested State, the court shall not be bound by that minimum and shall impose a sanction corresponding to the sanction imposed in the requesting State.
2. In determining the sanction, the court shall not aggravate the penal situation of the person sentenced as it results from the decision delivered in the requesting State.
3. Any part of the sanction imposed in the requesting State and any term of provisional custody, served by the person sentenced subsequent to the sentence shall be deducted in full. The same shall apply in respect of any period during which the person sentenced was remanded in custody in the requesting State before being sentenced insofar as the law of that State so requires.
4. Any Contracting State may, at any time, deposit with the Secretary General of the Council of Europe a declaration which confers on it in pursuance of the present Convention the right to enforce a sanction involving deprivation of liberty of the same nature as that imposed in the requesting State even if the duration of that sanction exceeds the maximum provided for by its national law for a sanction of the same nature. Nevertheless, this rule shall only be applied in cases where the national law of this State allows, in respect of the same offense, for the imposition of a sanction of at least the same duration as that imposed in the requesting State but which is of a more severe nature. The sanction imposed under this paragraph may, if its duration and purpose so require, be enforced in a penal establishment intended for the enforcement of sanctions of another nature.

(c) *Clauses relating specifically to enforcement opines and confiscations*

ARTICLE 45

1. If the request for enforcement of a fine or confiscation of a sum of money is accepted, the court or the authority empowered under Article 37 shall convert the amount thereof into the currency of the requested State at the rate of exchange ruling at the time when the decision is taken it shall thus fix the amount of the fine, or the sum to be confiscated, which shall nevertheless not exceed the maximum sum fixed by its own law for the same offense, or failing such a maximum, shall not exceed the maximum amount customarily imposed in the requested State in respect of a like offense.
2. However, the court or the authority empowered under Article 37 may maintain up to the amount imposed in the requesting State the sentence of a fine or of a confiscation when such a sanction is not provided for by the law of the requested State for the same offense, but this law allows for the

imposition of more severe sanctions. The same shall apply if the sanction imposed in the requesting State exceeds the maximum laid down in the law of the requested State for the same offense, but this law allows for the imposition of more severe sanctions.

3. Any facility as to time of payment or payment by instalments, granted in the requesting State, shall be respected in the requested State.

ARTICLE 46

1. When the request for enforcement concerns the confiscation of a specific object, the court or the authority empowered under Article 37 may order the confiscation of that object only insofar as such confiscation is authorised by the law of the requested State for the same offense.

2. However, the court or the authority empowered under Article 37 may maintain the confiscation ordered in the requesting State when this sanction is not provided for in the law of the requested State for the same offense but this law allows for the imposition of more severe sanctions.

ARTICLE 47

1. The proceeds of fines and confiscations shall be paid into the public funds of the requested State without prejudice to any rights of third parties.

2. Property confiscated which is of special interest may be remitted to the requesting State if it so requires.

ARTICLE 48

If a fine cannot be exacted, a court of the requested State may impose an alternative sanction involving deprivation of liberty insofar as the laws of both States so provide in such cases unless the requesting State expressly limited its request to exacting of the fine alone. If the court decides to impose an alternative sanction involving deprivation of liberty, the following rules shall apply:

(a) if conversion of a fine into a sanction involving deprivation of liberty is already prescribed either in the sentence pronounced in the requesting State or directly in the law of that State, the court of the requested State shall determine the nature and length of such sanction in accordance with the rules laid down by its own law. If the sanction involving deprivation of liberty already prescribed in the requesting State is less than the minimum which may be imposed under the law of the requested State, the court shall not be bound by that minimum and shall impose a sanction corresponding to the sanction prescribed in the requesting State. In determining the sanction the court shall not aggravate the penal situation of the person sentenced as it results from the decision delivered in the requesting State.

(b) In all other cases the court of the requested State shall convert the fine in accordance with its own law, observing the limits prescribed by the law of the requesting State.

(d) *Clauses relating specifically to enforcement of disqualification*

ARTICLE 49

1. Where a request for enforcement of a disqualification is made such disqualification imposed in the requesting State may be given effect in the requested State only if the law of the latter State allows for disqualification for the offense in question.

2. The court dealing with the case shall appraise the expediency of enforcing the disqualification in the territory of its own State.

ARTICLE 50

1. If the court orders enforcement of the disqualification it shall determine the duration thereof within the limits prescribed by its own law, but may not exceed the limits laid down in the sentence imposed in the requesting State.

2. The court may order the disqualification to be enforced in respect of some only of the rights whose loss or suspension has been pronounced.

ARTICLE 51

Article 11 shall not apply to disqualifications.

ARTICLE 52

The requested State shall have the right to restore to the person sentenced the rights of which he has been deprived in accordance with a decision taken in application of this section.

PART III
International Effects of European Criminal Judgements

Section 1
Ne bis in idem

ARTICLE 53

A person in respect of whom a European criminal judgement has been rendered may for the same act neither be prosecuted nor sentenced nor subjected to enforcement of a sanction in another Contracting State:

(a) if he was acquitted;

(b) if the sanction imposed:

(i) has been completely enforced or is being enforced or

(ii) has been wholly or with respect to the part not enforced, the subject of a pardon or an amnesty, or

(iii) can no longer be enforced because of lapse of time;

(c) if the court convicted the offender without imposing a sanction.

2. Nevertheless, a Contracting State shall not, unless it has itself requested the proceedings, be obliged to recognise the effect of ne bis in idem if the act which gave rise to the judgement was directed against either a person or an institution or any thing having public status in that State, or if the subject of the judgement had himself a public status in that State.

3. Furthermore, any Contracting State where the act was committed or considered as such according to the law of that State shall not be obliged to recognise the effect of ne bis in idem unless that State has itself requested the proceedings.

ARTICLE 54

If new proceedings are instituted against a person who in another Contracting State has been sentenced for the same act, then any period of deprivation of liberty arising from the sentence enforced shall be deducted from the sanction which may be imposed.

ARTICLE 55

This Section shall not prevent the application of wider domestic provisions relating to the effect of ne bis in idem attached to foreign criminal judgements.

Section 2
Taking into consideration

ARTICLE 56

Each Contracting State shall legislate as it deems appropriate to enable its courts when rendering a judgement to take into consideration any previous European criminal judgement rendered for another offense after a hearing of the accused with a view to attaching to this judgement all or some of the effects which its law attaches to judgements rendered in its territory. It shall determine the conditions in which this judgement is taken into consideration.

ARTICLE 57

Each Contracting State shall legislate as it deems appropriate to allow the taking into consideration of any European criminal judgement rendered after a hearing of the accused so as to enable application of all or part of a disqualification attached by its law to judgements rendered in its territory. It shall determine the conditions in which this judgement is taken into consideration.

PART IV
Final provisions

ARTICLE 58

1. This Convention shall be open to signature by the member States represented on the Committee of Ministers of the Council of Europe. It shall be subject to ratification or acceptance. Instruments of ratification or acceptance shall be deposited with the Secretary General of the Council of Europe.
2. The Convention shall enter into force three months after the date of the deposit of the third instrument of ratification or acceptance.
3. In respect of a signatory State ratifying or accepting subsequently, the Convention shall Come into force three months after the date of the deposit of its instrument of ratification or acceptance.

ARTICLE 59

1. After the entry into force of this Convention, the Committee of Ministers of the Council of Europe may invite any non-member State to accede thereto, provided that the resolution containing such invitation receives the unanimous agreement of the members of the Council who have ratified the Convention.
2. Such accession shall be effected by depositing with the Secretary General of the Council of Europe an instrument of accession which shall take effect three months after the date of its deposit.

ARTICLE 60

1. Any Contracting State may, at the time of signature or when depositing its instrument of ratification, acceptance or accession, specify the territory or territories to which this Convention shall apply.
2. Any Contracting State may, when depositing its instrument of ratification, acceptance or accession or at any later date by declaration addressed to the Secretary General of the Council of Europe, extend this Convention to any other territory or territories specified in the declaration and for whose international relations it is responsible or on whose behalf it is authorised to give undertakings.
3. Any declaration made in pursuance of the preceding paragraph may, in respect of any territory mentioned in such declaration, be withdrawn according to the procedure laid down in Article 66 of this Convention.

ARTICLE 61

1. Any Contracting State may, at the time of signature or when depositing its instrument of ratification, acceptance or accession, declare that it avails itself of one or more of the reservations provided for in Appendix I to this Convention.
2. Any Contracting State may wholly or partly withdraw a reservation it has made in accordance with the foregoing paragraph by means of a declaration addressed to the Secretary General of the Council of Europe which shall become effective as from the date of its receipt.
3. A Contracting State which has made a reservation in respect of any provision of this Convention may not claim the application of that provision by any other State; it may, however, if its reservation is partial or conditional, claim the application of that provision in so far as it has itself accepted it.

ARTICLE 62

1. Any Contracting State may at any time, by declaration addressed to the Secretary General of the Council of Europe, set out the legal provisions to be included in Appendices 11 or III to this Convention.
2. Any change of the national provisions listed in Appendices II or Ill shall be notified to the Secretary General of the Council of Europe if such a change renders the information in these Appendices incorrect.
3. Any changes made in Appendices II or III in application of the preceding paragraphs shall take effect in each Contracting State one month after the date of their notification by the Secretary General of the Council of Europe.

ARTICLE 63

1. Each Contracting State shall, at the time of depositing its instrument of ratification. acceptance or accession supply the Secretary General of the Council of Europe with relevant information on the sanctions applicable in that State and their enforcements for the purposes of the application of this Convention.
2. Any subsequent change which renders the information supplied in accordance with the previous paragraph incorrect, shall also be notified to the Secretary General of the Council of Europe.

ARTICLE 64

1. This Convention affects neither the rights and the undertakings derived from extradition treaties and international multilateral Conventions concerning special matters, nor provisions concerning matters which are dealt with in the present Convention and which are contained in other existing Conventions between Contracting States.
2. The Contracting States may not conclude bilateral or multilateral agreements with one another on the matters dealt with in this Convention, except in order to supplement its provisions or facilitate application of the principles embodied in it.
3. Should two or more Contracting States, however, have already established their relations in this matter on the basis of uniform legislation. or instituted a special system of their own, or should they in future do so, they shall be entitled to regulate those relations accordingly notwithstanding the terms of this Convention.
4. Contracting States ceasing to apply the terms of this Convention to their mutual relations in this matter shall notify the Secretary General of the Council of Europe to that effect.

ARTICLE 65

The European Committee on Crime Problems of the Council of Europe shall be kept informed regarding the application of this Convention and shall do whatever is needful to facilitate a friendly settlement of any difficulty which may arise out of its execution.

ARTICLE 66

1. This Convention shall remain in force indefinitely.
2. Any Contracting State may, insofar as it is concerned, denounce this Convention by means of a notification addressed to the Secretary General of the Council of Europe.
3. Such denunciation shall take effect six months after the date of receipt by the Secretary General of such notification.

ARTICLE 67

The Secretary General of the Council of Europe shall notify the member States represented on the Committee of Ministers of the Council, and any State that has acceded to this Convention, of:

(a) any signature;
(b) any deposit of an instrument of ratification, acceptance or accession;

(c) any date of entry into force of this Convention in accordance with Article 58 thereof;
(d) any declaration received in pursuance of Article 19, paragraph 2;
(e) any declaration received in pursuance of Article 44, paragraph 4;
(f) any declaration received in pursuance of Article 60;
(g) any reservation made in pursuance of the provisions of Article 61, paragraph 1, and the withdrawal of such reservation;
(h) any declaration received in pursuance of Article 62, paragraph 1, and any subsequent notification received in pursuance of that Article, paragraph 2;
(i) any information received in pursuance of Article 63, paragraph 1, and any subsequent notification received in pursuance of that Article, paragraph 2;
(j) any notification concerning the bilateral or multilateral agreements concluded in pursuance of Article 64, paragraph 2, or concerning uniform legislation introduced in pursuance of Article 64, paragraph 3;
(k) any notification received in pursuance of Article 66, and the date on which denunciation takes effect.

ARTICLE 68

This Convention and the declarations and notifications authorised thereunder shall apply only to the enforcement of decisions rendered after the entry into force of the Convention between the Contracting States concerned.

In witness whereof the undersigned, being duly authorised thereto, have signed this Convention.

Done at The Hague, this 28th day of May 1970 in English and French, both texts being equally authoritative in a single copy which shall remain deposited in the archives of the Council of Europe. The Secretary General of the Council of Europe shall transmit certified copies to each of the signatory and acceding States.

Section VII

Transfer of Criminal Proceedings

The European System

Julian Schutte

Introduction

The transfer of proceedings in criminal matters is a form of international legal assistance. A transfer of criminal proceedings takes place when a state waives its claims to prosecute and try a particular case in order to enable another state to do so instead.

This form of international legal assistance and the international transfer of the execution of decisions in criminal matter together form what is known as primary legal assistance. Such assistance involves one state taking over responsibility from another state for trying particular criminal cases or for executing judicial decisions. International cooperation consisting merely in the performance of actions in connection with criminal proceedings which are already under way in another state or in the enforcement of a sentence imposed there is described as secondary or minor legal assistance.[1] The main instruments of secondary international legal assistance are letters rogatory and extradition.

In its most customary form, the transfer of proceedings in criminal matters is based on the existence of concurrent or competing claims to exercise jurisdiction by two (or more) states in respect to the same criminal offense. Concurrent or competing claims arise when differing principles of jurisdiction entitle more than one state to take cognizance of the same offense. Subjects of states whose legislation provides for the "active" nationality principle (i.e. the jurisdictional rule that entitle a national court to take cognizance of certain punishable offenses committed by nationals of the state in question outside its territory) may be tried in respect to offenses committed abroad, either in the country of the *locus delicti,* on the ground of the territoriality principle applicable there, or in their own country. In such cases, the country of the *locus delicti* can benefit from this knowledge by refraining from instituting criminal proceedings itself and leaving it to the suspect's country of origin to do so. Sometimes it may even actively encourage the country of origin to institute proceedings.

The reasons why a country might wish to waive proceedings are obvious. There may be advantages in a number of respects to having a foreigner tried in his own country. First of all, it may be preferable from the point of view of the suspect himself if he is tried in his own surroundings, in his own language and according to the law of his own country. If the proceedings are likely to result in a conviction, it may be better for him, certainly in cases where a custodial punishment is imposed, that he serve the sentence in his own country, where measures can be taken to prepare him for his reintegration to his own social environment. Another major advantage of a transfer may be a saving in court time and costs. If the suspect is already in his own country, there will often be good grounds for not trying him in his absence in the country of the *locus delicti.* For one thing, it will be impossible to have him extradited, since his return will be precluded on the ground of his nationality. The

---

[1] The distinction between the categories of primary and secondary legal assistance in criminal cases was made the first time by L.H.C. Hulsman in his article, *Transmission des poursuites pénales à l'Etat de séjour et exécution des décisions pénales étrangères, in* LE DROIT PÉNAL INTERNATIONAL, RECUEIL D'ÉTUDES EN HOMMAGE À J.M. VAN BEMMELEN, 108 (1965).

value of a trial conducted in the absence of the defendant is even more dubious if there is no real prospect that the sentence will be carried out.

The knowledge that foreign suspects may be tried in their own country may also have a moderating influence on the readiness of the judicial authorities to remand them in custody.[2] Finally, it may be preferable to transfer criminal proceedings if it is known that the suspect will stand trial in his country of origin for other offenses as well, and whether this can be tried by the same court for a number of offenses at the same time. When sentence is passed, it will then be possible for the court to take account of the fact that the suspect has committed offenses in different countries and of any possible connection between them.

Transfer of Criminal Proceedings and Deportation

The transfer of criminal proceedings is an important instrument for achieving the aim of international legal assistance in criminal matters, which is to promote the proper and rational administration of justice. Nevertheless, the applicability of this instrument is subject to various limitations. The most important is that all that is to be transferred in such cases is the file on a particular suspect; in other words, information, and not the person of the suspect, as is the case in extradition proceedings. If a suspect is arrested by the state of the *locus delicti* at its own initiative and then transferred in custody to the country of his origin for trial by the authorities of that country, this would merely be a form of disguised extradition which is universally considered to be unlawful, failing justification in international law.[3] This is why a request for a transfer of criminal proceedings should not in principle be made by the state of the *locus delicti* to another state until the suspect has left its territory or has been given the opportunity to leave it.

Various situations can arise. The alien may simply have been passing through the country of the *locus delicti* or have been there for a short visit (for instance as a tourist or on business) and then allowed to return to his own country. The suspicion that an alien has committed a punishable offense may be a ground for deporting him from the territory of the country of the *locus delicti*. It should be noted, of course, that deportation is an unilateral

---

[2] Aliens are remanded in custody for indictable offenses in the Netherlands on average about twice as frequently in relative terms as Dutch nationals (27 percent as opposed to 13 percent of all cases). If offenses are split up into categories of gravity, measured in terms of the possible sentence, it can be seen that the lighter the maximum sentence, the greater the disparity in the use made of remand in custody between aliens and Dutch nationals. It should be noted, however, that under Dutch law suspects who have a fixed abode or place of residence in the Netherlands cannot be remanded in custody unless the offense of which they are suspected carries a sentence of at least four years imprisonment. Since aliens do not usually possess a fixed abode in the Netherlands they cannot benefit from this provision. *See* V. *v.d. Werf & A.Av.d. Zee-Nefkens, Strafrechtelijke vervolgingen bestraffing van Nederlanders en buitenlanders*, WODC (1979); A.C. BERGHUUS & C.C.M. TIGGES, VOORLOPIGE HECHTENIS BU BUITENLANDERS DELIKT & DELINKWENT (1981).

[3] The literature on the subject of disguised extradition is copious. *See e.g.* M. CHERIF BASSIOUNI, INTERNATIONAL EXTRADITION: UNITED STATES LAW AND PRACTICE (3d rev ed. 1996); K. Bushbeck, Verschleierte Auslieferung Durch Ausweisung (1973); Andre Decocq, *Law Livraision des Delinquants en Dehors du Droit Commun de l'Extradition*, 53 REVUE CRITIQUE DE DROIT INTERNATIONAL PRIVE 411 (1964); P.B. Heymann & I.H. Gershengorn, *A Missed Opportunity (US v. Alvarez Machain)*, 4 CRIM. L.F. 155-75 (1993); J.A. Lonner, *Official Government Abductions in the Presence of Extradition Treaties*, 83 CRIM. L. & CRIMINOLOGY 998-1023 (1993); Paul O'Higgings, *Unlawful Seizure and Irregular Extradition*, 279 BRIT. Y.B. INTL'L L. (1960).

administrative measure and is not an instrument of mutual international cooperation.[4] Its object is simply to expel the person concerned from the country; the destination is immaterial.

An alien who is to be deported is in theory free to choose the country to which he is to be taken. In practice, however, countries, other than the country of origin are often not prepared to grant him entry, either on the grounds of public order or because he is not in possession of valid travel documents or adequate funds. In such cases the alien is deported to this country of origin, where he may then be tried for the offenses which he committed there or in the country that has deported him. If the criminal justice authorities of the country of origin have indicated before a deportation takes place that they are willing to grant a request to institute criminal proceedings, and are notified beforehand of the time and place of the deportation, the deportation is clearly instrumental in the transfer of criminal proceedings and amounts in this author's view to a disguised form of extradition. This is not the case, however, if the primary aim of the deporting state is to secure the removal from its territory of an undesirable alien and the person concerned is unable to designate any country other than his country of origin which would be prepared to grant him entry. To put it another way, if a country decides to deport an alien who it suspects has committed an offense to his country of origin, it should not request the authorities of the latter country to institute criminal proceedings in respect to such an offense until after the deportation has taken place.

If the country of the *locus delicti* decides not to deport the alien but instead to simply let him go, expecting that he will sooner or later return to his country of origin voluntarily, it cannot reasonably be expected to ensure that he has left its territory before it lodges a request for the transfer of criminal proceedings. The essential point is that he is at liberty, and is therefore free to go to another country.

There is, however, a legitimate way in which the transfer of criminal proceedings can be combined with the forcible removal of the suspect. This is where use is made of another form of international legal assistance involving the forcible transfer of the person of the suspect, such as extradition or transfer after conviction. If, for instance, the extradition of an alien is requested by his country of origin for offenses committed there, the requested state may decide to discontinue its own proceedings against him for other offenses and give priority to extraditing him to his country of origin. In such a case, the country of origin may be requested to take over the prosecution commenced by the requested state for other offenses. A procedure of this nature, which amounts to a mutual agreement by the two states concerned to waive the rule of speciality, means that the extradition is used partly for the purpose of the transfer of criminal proceedings. There is, of course, no question of a disguised form of extradition in such cases.

The discussion above is based on the assumption that there is no justification in international law for a transfer of criminal proceedings combined with the physical removal of an accused, unless he is being extradited or is transferred as a convicted prisoner. This

---

[4] This is not altered by the fact that some states have concluded bilateral agreements regarding the handing over of deportees at the border. In such cases the contracting parties have given mutual undertakings, subject to certain conditions, that persons who have been deported by the one state will not be turned back at the border but will be granted entry. Such agreements are designed not to ensure that deportees are passed over to the judicial authorities of the neighboring state but to prevent decisions on deportation by the states in question from being frustrated by a refusal of other states to accept the deportees.

is not to say, however, that what would otherwise constitute a disguised and unlawful form of extradition may not be legitimated by a special rule of international law. If it is permissible under international law for the country of the *locus delicti* to induce the country of origin to request the extradition of an alien for offenses committed in the former country, and for the suspect to be held in custody pending a decision on the request, there would appear to be no reason why states would not be able to agree, subject to certain conditions, to transfer custody of aliens who have been remanded pending prosecution and trial. I do not, however, know of any such agreements.[5]

International Conventions Governing the Transfer of Criminal Proceedings

As I have said, the principle underlying the transfer of criminal proceedings is based on the existence of concurrent or competing jurisdictional claims by two or more states regarding the same criminal offense. This means that application of this instrument of international cooperation in criminal matters does not need to be based on a convention for which both the states involved in the transfer are able to derive certain powers or rights. The applicability of the instrument is determined by the scope of application of the criminal law of the states concerned. It will not, therefore, be possible to transfer proceedings to states whose law does not provide for extraterritorial jurisdiction in criminal matters. Such jurisdiction is unusual, for instance, in most common law countries. This need not, of course, prevent these countries from transferring criminal proceedings to other countries.

For various reasons, however, the need has arisen in recent years to draw up international rules governing the transfer of criminal proceedings. One matter which it was felt needed regulating was the manner in which requests should or could be transmitted from one state to another. Article 21 of the European Convention on Mutual Assistance in Criminal Matters of 1959[6] and article 42 of the Benelux Convention on Extradition and Mutual Legal Assistance in Criminal Matters of 1962[7] both provide, for instance, that information laid by one contracting party with a view to proceedings in the courts of another party must be transmitted between the Ministries of Justice concerned. In this way a middle path has been chosen between transmitting information through diplomatic channels and transmitting it directly between the criminal justice authorities. Both the treaty provisions in question also stipulate that the requested party must notify the requesting party of any action taken on such information.

---

5 In recommendation No R(79)12 (June 14, 1979), the Committee of Ministers of the Council of Europe recommended to the governments of the member states that in applying the European Convention on the Transfer of Proceedings in Criminal Matters of 1972, they should be "guided" in cases where the suspected person is present in the territory of the requesting state, by the rules laid down either in their national law or in the European Convention of Extradition of 1957, 597 U.N.T.S. 338, Europ.T.S. No.24 and the European Convention on the International Validity of Criminal Judgements of 1970, Europ.T.S. No.70 in respect of the suspected person's provisional arrest, his transfer to the requested state, his transit through the territory of another state and in respect of the "principle of speciality." In making this Recommendation, the Committee of Ministers evidently assumed, wrongly as it happens, that the European Convention permits the transfer of a suspect in connection with a transfer of criminal proceedings. For this to have been possible, the Convention would have had to have been amended or supplemented by a Protocol. A mere Recommendation by the Committee of Ministers would seem to provide an insufficient basis in international law.

6 472 U.N.T.S. 185, Europ. T.S. No.30.

7 616 U.N.T.S. 79, Benelux Basic Texts, pt. 4, III (supp.20 t.23).

It was not very long, however, before it was realized that a procedural provision of this kind was not sufficient and that more detailed international agreements would have to be made regarding the transfer of criminal proceedings, in order to provide uniform replies to a number of questions connected with the practical application of this instrument of international cooperation. Various examples can be given of these questions. On what grounds, for instance, can a request for the transfer of criminal proceedings be based or refused? What formal requirements can be imposed in respect to a request for transfer and the accompanying documents? What are the legal consequences of a request and the granting thereof both in the requesting state and the requested state? May the requested state resort, in urgent cases, to the use of coercive measures of a provisional nature even before the formal request has been handed over? Under what circumstances may the requesting state recover its right to take criminal proceedings? These and other questions have been answered in the conventions drawn up by the Council of Europe and by Benelux, which have given shape and substance to the instrument of the transfer of criminal proceedings.

Both the Council of Europe and Benelux first introduced the new rules in a special and limited field of law and extended their application in a general convention only later. The European Convention on the Punishment of Road Traffic Offences was concluded on 30 November 1964.[8] Section II of the Convention, which was ratified by only four countries, provides a rudimentary procedure for the transfer of criminal proceedings in respect of traffic offenses. The most important provision is that a contracting party which is requested by another party to take over the prosecution of a traffic offense committed by a resident of the requested state is stated to be competent to take cognizance of the offense.[9] In addition, the convention lays down regulations concerning the legal consequences of a request for the transfer of criminal proceedings in the requesting state,[10] the effect of such a request on the time limit for criminal proceedings in the requesting and requested state,[11] the position of the injured party and the value in the requested state of evidence supplied by the requesting state.[12] The general provisions of the convention also contain regulations governing the formal requirements which such a request must satisfy.[13]

The convention has largely been superseded by the European Convention on the Transfer of Proceedings in Criminal Matters of 1972,[14] which regulates this form of international legal assistance at a general level. Ten states are now parties to the convention, which has been signed by six other states as well. The most important provisions of the conventions are as follows.

1. There is a list of a large number of cases in which a request for the transfer of criminal proceedings can be made.[15] In such cases the competent prosecuting authorities must "take that possibility into consideration."[16] If a request for transfer is made, the requested state is in principle bound to grant the request, unless it can invoke one of the

---

8 865 U.N.T.S. 99, Europ. T.S. No. 52.
9 European Convention on the Punishment of Road Traffic Offenses. Art. 3.
10 *Id.* at Art. 5.
11 *Id.* at Art. 6,¶ I & 2.
12 *Id.* at Art. 7.
13 *Id.* at Art. 14-23.
14 Europ. T.S. No. 73.
15 European Convention on the Transfer of Proceedings in Criminal matters, Art. 8.
16 *Id.* at Art. 6, ¶ 2.

numerous grounds for refusal.[17] No action may be taken on a request for transfer if the requirement that the offense and the offender are punishable under the law of both requesting and the requested state is not met,[18] if the institution of proceedings would constitute a violation of the *ne bis in idem* rule,[19] or if the time limit for criminal proceedings has already expired in the requested state.[20] A request may be refused at the discretion of the requested state if the suspected person is not a national of the requested state[21] or ordinarily resident in it,[22] if the offense of which he is suspected is of a political, military or fiscal nature,[23] if the offense was committed outside the territory of the requesting state,[24] if the request does not comply with the formal requirements laid down by the convention,[25] if there are insufficient grounds for believing that acceptance of the request is in the interests of justice[26] or if proceedings would be contrary to the fundamental principles of the legal system of the requested state.[27] If a request for transfer is refused, the reasons for the refusal must be communicated to the requesting state.[28]

2. Like the Convention on the Punishment of Road Traffic Offences referred to above, the 1972 convention provides, in article 2, that the courts of the requested state derive their competence to prosecute the offense by virtue of the request of the requesting state, insofar as they do not already possess under their own municipal law. Article 2 provides:

> 1. For the purposes of applying this Convention, any Contracting State shall have competence to prosecute under its own criminal law any offence to which the law of another Contracting State is applicable.
>
> 2. The competence conferred on a Contracting State exclusively by virtue of paragraph I of this Article may be exercised only pursuant to a request for proceedings presented by another Contracting State.

In this way the convention confers directly upon the contracting states the extraterritorial competence necessary in order to prosecute and try offenses which their own judicial authorities could not take cognizance of under their municipal law. This power is, however, subject to a special condition, namely that a charge may only be brought by the prosecuting authorities in such cases upon an express request from another state for the institution of proceedings. In view of the form in which this type of extraterritorial competence is cast, it can be said to be based on a principle of "secondary" jurisdiction, which can perhaps best be described as the "deputization" principle. The idea behind it is that in exercising jurisdiction on the basis of this principle, the requested state is deputizing for, or representing the interests of, the requesting state. In order to exercise this jurisdiction,

---

17 *Id.* at Art. 10 (provisions for mandatory refusal) and Art. 11 (provision for refusal at the option of the requested state).

18 *Id.* at Art. 7, ¶ 1.

19 *Id.* at Art. 10 (a).

20 *Id.* at Art. 10 (c).

21 *Id.* at Art. 11 (c).

22 *Id.* at Art. 11 (b).

23 *Id.* at Art. 11 (d).

24 *Id.* at Art. 11 (h).

25 *Id.* at Art. 11 (k).

26 *Id.* at Art. 8 (e).

27 *Id.* at Art. 11 (j).

28 *Id.* at Art. 16.

the requested state requires an express mandate from the state on whose behalf competence is being exercised. The convention therefore obliges the contracting states to make clear distinction between the establishment of competence in theory and the right to exercise it in specific cases. Since, as we have seen, the convention enables the requested state to accept only requests relating to suspects who are nationals of such state or who are ordinarily resident there, the contracting states can therefore stipulate that the competence conferred upon them by Article 2 of the convention is to be exercised in accordance with the domicile principle, i.e. by stipulating as a condition of acceptance that the suspect must be ordinarily resident in the state where proceedings are to be brought.

3. The deputization principle created by article 2 of the convention is closely connected with the requirement of "double punishability." This requirement is formulated in the following way:

> Proceedings may not be taken in the requested State unless the offence in respect of which the proceedings are requested would be an offence if committed in its territory and when, under these circumstances, the offender would be liable to sanction under its own law also.[29]

Since the requested state is merely representing the interests of the requesting state, the former is not obliged and indeed not competent to do more than the requesting state. This means not only that acts of the type which the suspect is thought to have committed must be punishable under the law of both the states concerned,[30] but also that the offender must be deemed to be criminally liable in the specific case in question under the law of both states that there are no impediments to prosecution. In addition to checking that the act in question is in principle punishable under the criminal law of the requesting state, the requested state must therefore also ensure that there are no grounds under the law of that state which the suspect could have invoked to bar punishment. It would not be right, for instance, if a suspect against whom proceedings were dropped in the requesting state because the authorities there considered that he could not be held accountable for his actions owing to mental disability were to be prosecuted and tried in the requesting state.

In one respect, the first paragraph of article 7 permits a fiction in the assessment of the requirement of double punishability, since the requested state may treat the offense as though it were concluded in its territory. A similar fiction is incorporated in the second paragraph of article 7 regarding persons or institutions of public status. The object of these provisions is to ensure that the statutory description of the offense in respect of which the charge is brought contains elements of territoriality or nationality. In this way a provision such as without the authorization of the government of (requesting state) can be read and incorporated in the charge as "without the authorization of the government of (requested state)" and an offense such as "bribery of an official of (requesting state)," can be embodied in the charge as "bribery of an official of (requesting state).

---

29 *Id.* at Art. 7,¶ 1.

30 Or quasi-criminal law: Article I of the Convention treats as offenses *inter alia* unlawful behavior designated as such by the contracting party concerned in its national administrative legislation, provided that the person in question has the right to have the case tried by the court (*e.g.*, "Ordungswirdrigkeiten" under German law and minor administrative offences under Italian law).

4. The convention contains detailed provisions governing the procedural arrangements: the channels along which requests and documents must be exchanged (usually the Ministries of Justice),[31] the language in which the document should be drawn up,[32] the status of the documents to be handed over[33] and the costs incurred in connection with the transfer.[34] The appropriate method of making a request is apparent from the regulations governing the legal consequences of requests and the acceptance thereof.

5. The convention also regulates the legal consequences of a request for the transfer of proceedings in the requesting and requested states.[35] The most important legal consequence for the requesting state is that after it has made the request it may no longer prosecute the suspect for the offense in question,[36] i.e. it may not institute criminal proceedings before its own courts, even if the suspect should be found in its territory again. The convention does, however, permit the requesting state to perform certain acts in connection with the detection and prosecution of the suspect even after the request for transfer been made.[37] Further, evidence may, for instance, be collected and sent to the requested state. It may take such steps on its initiative, however, only "until the requested state's decision on the request for proceedings has been received."[38] The right of prosecution does not revert to the requesting state unless it withdraws its request before the requested state's decision has been communicated to it or the requested state has been given notification of a decision "not to institute proceedings or to discontinue them."[39]

In view of all these provisions, the formal procedure is therefore as follows. The Ministry of Justice of the requesting state submits a request for transfer to the Ministry of Justice of the requested state. The latter notifies the former that the request has been accepted (provisionally). After receipt of this message, the judicial authorities of the requesting state can no longer take any action on their own initiative with a view to investigate or prosecute the case. The Ministry of Justice of the requested state then notifies its counterpart in the requesting state of the final decision upon the request. This may be a prosecution leading to acquittal or conviction, a decision that the matter should be settled out of court (for instance by payment of a fine), a decision to exercise the discretionary power not to prosecute (for instance because of lack of evidence or because prosecution would be against the public interest), or a decision that the request should on reflection be refused. Except in cases where the requested state institutes criminal proceedings, the right of prosecution reverts to the requesting state after its receipt of the decision on the request.[40]

This arrangement is not entirely satisfactory. It is regrettable, for instance, that for the purposes of the *ne bis in idem* rule other accepted means of disposing of criminal cases such as settlement out of court, a conditional decision not to prosecute, and even an unconditional decision not to prosecute on the grounds of public interest, have not been fully equated with

---

31 *Supra note* 15, Art. 13,¶ 1.
32 *Id.* at Art. 18.
33 *Id.* at Art. 15.
34 *Id.* at Art. 20.
35 *Id.* at Arts. 21-2 (referring to the requesting state) and Arts. 23-6 (referring to the requested state).
36 *Id.* at Art. 21, ¶ 1.
37 *Id.*
38 *Id.*
39 *Id.* at Art. 21, ¶ 2.
40 *Id.* at Art. 21, ¶ 2.

prosecution and trial.[41] This is perhaps explicable by reference to the fact that these methods of disposal were not used so widely when the convention was drawn up as they are now. Another effect of the request for the transfer of criminal proceedings is that the time limit for proceedings in the requesting state is extended by six months.[42] The purpose of this provision is to ensure that if and when it is finally established that a request for transfer will not be accepted, the requesting state will not be barred by lapse of time from exercising the right of prosecution that has reverted to it.

A request for transfer of proceedings has legal consequences of a different nature in the case of the requested state. We have already seen that the main effect is that the requested state obtains the competence to deal with the case.[43] Other effects are connected with the conditions for prosecution. The time limit for proceedings is extended in the requested state too;[44] normally time would begin to run at the moment the offense is committed, but the requested state is usually totally unaware of the commission of the offense. If the submission of a complaint by the injured party is a condition of prosecution, it can be deemed to have been brought in the requested state.[45] Finally, it is provided that acts carried out in the requesting state in connection with the detection and prosecution of the suspect have the same validity in the requested state as if they had been taken by the authorities of that state.[46] The evidential weight of such acts is no greater in the requested state, however, than in the requesting state. Any such act which interrupts the time limitation in the one state has the same effect in the other state.[47]

These rules equating the legal effects of acts carried out in different states could present difficulties of a practical and legal nature. The courts of the requested state, in particular, may be required to answer questions relating to the admissibility of methods of detection employed in the requesting state and to the value of official reports drawn up under oath of office by law enforcement officers in another country. The rules will be of little practical value in countries where the procedure of the criminal courts is largely governed by the principle that the evidence should be adduced as far as possible during the trial in the presence of the court (and the jury) and not during a preliminary judicial investigation.[48]

6. Before transmitting a formal request or the transfer of criminal proceedings, with the accompanying documents, the requesting state may ask the requested state to take various provisional measures such as remanding the suspect in custody or seizing property or claims.[49] A remand in custody is in such cases comparable to provisional arrest under extradition law, prior to the submission of a formal request for extradition, and is likewise

---

41 *Id.* at Art. 35 (For the purposes of the *ne bis in diem* rule the listed provisions must be seen as an exclusive listing).

42 *Id.* at Art. 22.

43 *Id.* at Art. 2.

44 *Id.* at Art. 23.

45 *Id.* at Art. 24, ¶ 1.

46 *Id.* at Art. 26, ¶ 1.

47 *Id.* at Art. 26, ¶ 2.

48 The existing limitations upon the extraterritorial applicability of the criminal law are not the only factor which makes it difficult for the common law countries to agree to the transfer of criminal proceedings. Another major stumbling block is that owing to the interrogatory nature of criminal proceedings under the common law system and the specific rules of evidence which the system necessitates, evidence collected abroad does not in principle have any value for the purposes of proceedings in such countries.

49 *Supra* note 15, Art. 25, ¶ 1.

subject to certain time limits.[50] The requested state is therefore empowered to remand a suspect in custody even if it derives its competence solely from the request for the transfer of proceedings.[51]

7. Finally the convention contains detailed rules regarding the *ne bis in idem* principle in international relations.[52] Some of the main points are that they create international obligations only in relations between contracting parties,[53] that they are applicable generally and not just in the case of the transfer of criminal proceedings, and that in principle only final judgements of a court of a contracting state constitute a bar to proceedings for the same offense in other contracting states.[54] To constitute a bar, such a judgment must contain:

- either an acquittal, i.e. a decision that the charge against the suspect has not been proved;[55]
- or a conviction and a sanction (punishment or other measure), provided that the sanction has been or is being completely enforced, or is the subject of a pardon or amnesty, or can no longer be enforced because of lapse of time;[56]
- or a conviction, without a sanction being imposed.[57]

If a suspect has been convicted and sentenced, but the sanction has not been enforced or not completely enforced because the suspect has not been apprehended or has absconded, the *ne bis in them* protection afforded by the convention does not apply. Other exceptions are where the offense was committed in the territory of the state which wishes to take new proceedings or where the offense was committed by or against a person having public status in that state.[58] Where new proceedings are instituted, however, any period during which the person concerned has already been deprived of his liberty must be deducted from the sanction imposed by the second state bringing the proceedings.[59] The convention is silent on the question of the deduction of fines already imposed.

Finally, it is provided that the regulations do not prevent the application of wider domestic provisions relating to the effect of *ne bis in idem* attached to foreign criminal judgments.[60] Some countries, for instance, apply the *ne bis in idem* rule in full even in cases where the offense was committed on their territory, while others regard the existence of a final conviction of a foreign court as in itself sufficient to bring the rule into operation, irrespective of whether or not the sentence was executed. It should be noted that here too the application of wider provisions is restricted to foreign judicial decisions and that extra-judicial methods of disposal are overlooked. Since out-of-court settlements, conditional discontinuation of proceedings and other forms of extra-judicial disposal are now being used to an increasing extent, this omission no longer seems justified.

---

50 *Id.* at Art. 29.
51 *Id.* at Art. 27.
52 *Id.* at Arts. 35-37.
53 *Id.* at Art. 35, ¶ 1.
54 *Id.*
55 *Id.* at Art. 35, ¶ 1 (a).
56 *Id.* at Art. 35, ¶ 1 (b).
57 *Id.* at Art. 35, ¶ 1 (c).
58 *Id.* at Art. 35, ¶ 2.
59 *Id.* at Art. 36.
60 *Id.* at Art. 37.

The developments relating to the transfer of criminal proceedings that have taken place between the Benelux countries are to some extent similar to those that have occurred in the context of the Council of Europe. The Benelux Agreement of 29 April 1969 on cooperation in the field of administrative and criminal law,[61] which was the first instrument to be introduced in this respect by the three countries concerned, relates to a specific and relatively narrow field, not the punishment of traffic offenses, as in the case of the Council of Europe, but the enforcement of rules designed to achieve the object of the Benelux economic union, namely rules governing the import, export and transit of goods, customs, excise duties and turnover tax and regulations governing rates for the carriage of goods by road.

Articles 10 to 15 of the Agreement of 29 April 1969 and the three Protocols[62] contain a number of rules governing the transfer of criminal proceedings. The agreement provides first of all that the statutory provisions in force in each of the three Benelux countries in the fields covered by the agreement also apply to offenses committed in the territory of either of the other countries.[63] This therefore provides the requisite extraterritorial competence.

The agreement goes on to establish a system whereby the three states decide between them where a person who infringes one of the rules of regulations referred to above must be tried.[64] This will usually be the country where the suspect is resident. In addition, it provides that criminal proceedings may be transferred pursuant to article 42 of the Benelux Convention On Extradition and Mutual Legal Assistance in Criminal Matters;[65] the requested state thus derives its competence to prosecute the offense in question from the request for transfer. The 1969 agreement was followed by the Benelux Convention on the Transfer of Criminal Proceedings of 11 May 1974,[66] which regulates international legal assistance of this kind at a general level between the three states. Its provisions are very similar to and indeed served largely as a model for those of the Council of Europe Convention, even though the latter in fact predated it. The Benelux Convention does not contain a general *ne bis in idem* rule because the municipal legislation of the three states is already very similar in this respect. It does, however, go somewhat further than the European Convention in elaborating various procedural regulations. Unlike the European Convention, it has not yet come into force, and the transfer of criminal proceedings between the Benelux countries has until now been practiced for the most part without reference to any treaty provisions. On 6 November 1990 the then-12 Member States of the European Communities concluded an agreement on the transfer of proceedings in criminal matters. This agreement was signed by only eight of the members (it was not signed by Germany, Ireland, the Netherlands and the United Kingdom), and has been ratified by March 1996 by just one member state (France).

This agreement was negotiated because it was felt by a number of EC Member States that the Council of Europe Convention of 1972 was too complex in structure, would be too difficult to apply in practice and would, despite its many safeguards, not offer sufficient flexibility to the states parties.

---

61 779 U.N.T.S. 111, Benelux Basic Texts, pt. 5 (supps. 31 and 47).

62 *Id.*

63 *Id.* at Art. 9, ¶ 1.

64 *Id.* at Art. 10.

65 *Id.* at Art. 11. *See also supra* note 7.

66 Benelux Basic Texts, pt. 4, III (supp. 75).

Although clearly inspired by the 1972 Convention, the agreement[67] accordingly introduces a series of simplifications, the most important one being that the agreement does not impose any international obligation on the parties to cooperate in the field of the transfer of proceedings. Consequently, the agreement does not contain a list of grounds of refusal nor a list of cases in which requests for proceedings should be taken into consideration.

The agreement does contain, however, provisions similar to Article 2 of the Council of Europe Convention on the taking of jurisdiction as a consequence of a request to that purpose[68] and article 7 of the Council of Europe Convention on the interpretation of the rule on double criminality.[69] As far as the legal consequences of a request for proceedings are concerned, both in the requesting and in the requested Member State, the agreement is much more summary than the Council of Europe Convention. It is noted, in particular, that no specific provisions have been included with a view to cases where the jurisdiction of the requested Member State would be based solely on the request for proceedings from the requesting Member State. On the legal relationship between the agreement and the conventions of the Council of Europe and the Benelux, the agreement clearly confirms its complementary character. According to article 15, the agreement is to be applied in relations between Member States of the EC which are parties to the Council of Europe and Benelux Conventions, only where it supplements the provisions of those Conventions or facilitates the application of the principles enshrined therein. This is in accordance with article 43 paragraph 2 of the Council of Europe Convention, which stipulates that the contracting parties may not conclude bilateral or multilateral agreements with one another on matters dealt with in that Convention, except in order to supplement its provisions or facilitate application of the principles embodied in it.

Object and Function of the Transfer of Criminal Proceedings

The transfer of criminal proceedings is one of the instruments which can be used by states in mutual cooperation in order to combat crime involving an international dimension. It should therefore be used to further the object of this international cooperation; i.e. to promote a rational policy on criminal law. Such a policy involves ensuring that the disposal of cases involving an international component does not necessarily lead to the application of measures that are more vexatious and restrictive from the suspect's point of view than would be usual in cases of a purely domestic nature. At the same time, it involves making effective use of the institutions and authorities instrumental to and responsible for the maintenance and application of the criminal law.

If these aims are to be achieved, the states cooperating together must hold very much the same views and opinions on the organization and functioning of the criminal law system and must put them into practice in similar ways. This explains why the instruments for international cooperation in the field of criminal law can best be designed at regional level. Only at this level is it possible to achieve the harmonization of criminal law systems which is needed if there is to be intensive cooperation between states. This applies not only to basic principles and objects, but also to their practical implementation.

---

[67] The text is reproduced in Appendix 16.

[68] Article 4 of the agreement.

[69] Article 3 of the agreement.

It is difficult to define in theory what function the transfer of criminal proceedings has in relation to other forms of international legal assistance (letters rogatory, extradition, transfer of the enforcement of sentences). The explanatory report to the European Convention of 1972 cites two examples of cases in which the procedure can usefully be employed: first, when the suspect is no longer in the territory of the state of the *locus delicti* and has returned to his own state, as a result of which he can no longer be extradited, and the institution of proceedings in his absence is pointless;[70] and second, when the chances of successfully rehabilitating the offender would be greater, in view of the likely sentence, if the proceedings were to be transferred to his country of residence.[71] The same effect could of course be achieved in the latter case by a transfer of the execution of the sanction.

If the transfer of criminal proceedings is to be an instrument of an active policy on criminal law, the state of the *locus delicti* must not only resort to it in cases in which the suspect has evaded apprehension there, but also consider its advantages in the initial stages of the detection and prosecution of all offenses committed by aliens, in particular when a decision has to be taken on whether or not to remand the suspect in custody. Various factors are of importance in this connection:

> (a) *The gravity of the offense and the likely sentence.* Depending on the personal circumstances of the suspect, proceedings can generally be transferred if the offense falls within the category between grave and petty and will probably result in the imposition of a custodial penalty. Unless the suspect has not been apprehended before his trial, a more obvious course of action in the case of grave offenses is to transfer execution of the sentence.
>
> (b) *The position of the suspect.* (Where is he? Can he be extradited? Is he likely to abscond? Does he need psychiatric help? etc.)
>
> (c) *The nature of the case.* Are there accomplices of a different nationality? Are there difficulties in producing evidence? Is there a link with offenses committed abroad?

Responsibility for weighing these various factors rests primarily with the prosecuting authorities of the state of the *locus delicti,* since it is they who must take the initiative to submit a request for the transfer of criminal proceedings. Thereafter it is up to the requesting and the requested state to reach agreement on the division of competence between them, and thereby to prevent any chance of a jurisdictional conflict, this being the aim of transferring of criminal proceedings.

The question arises in this connection of the position of the suspect. A transfer of criminal proceedings should, after all, be in the interests of the proper administration of justice and therefore in the interests of suspects as well. Does or should the suspect himself have any say in the matter, for instance by being able to compel or oppose a transfer of proceedings? The existing conventions do not deal with this point. The European Convention merely provides that if the competence of the requested state is exclusively grounded on the request for the transfer of proceedings, that state must inform the suspect of the request for proceedings "with a view to allowing him to present his views" on the

---

[70] See Explanatory Report on the European Convention on the Transfer of Proceedings in Criminal Matters, Particular Observations, pt. 3, Art. 8, ¶ 1 (h).

[71] *Id.* pt. 3, art. 8, ¶ 1 (a)(b).

matter before that state has taken a decision of the request.[72] This provision is evidently based on the assumption that the suspect is already in the territory of the requested state. The question whether the suspect should have means at his disposal of contesting the decision or intention of the requesting state to transfer the criminal proceedings against him is left to the municipal law of the contracting parties.

It is quite conceivable that a suspect may have objections to a transfer of proceedings. While he does not of course have the right to choose the legal forum in which he will be called to account for his actions, he may well have grounds in a particular case for disputing that a transfer of criminal proceedings would be in the interests of the proper administration of justice, for instance if it was the intention of the requesting state to ensure that the suspect was tried under a significantly stricter system of criminal law than its own, or if the requesting state has manifestly indicated that it intends to prosecute and try the suspect itself but changes its mind at the last moment and transfers proceedings.

The laws of some countries provide that a suspect has the right to be tried by his "natural" judge or in the jurisdiction where he committed the offense.[73] In some other countries, however, there is the principle that offenses committed in the territory of that country must be prosecuted and that the prosecuting authorities do not in principle have a discretionary power not to prosecute.[74]

Factors of this kind militate against the transfer of criminal proceedings since they can make it impossible for a country to choose freely whether or not to try the offense itself. In so doing, they also prevent the transfer of proceedings from being used as an instrument for achieving a more active international policy on criminal law.

Factors such as those to which I have just referred can of course be relegated to the background if a state enters into obligations under an international convention. It is doubtful, however, whether the infringement of such principles by a treaty would be acceptable to the state in question without the introduction of procedural provisions in its municipal legislation whereby the suspect, for example, is granted the right to refer to the courts a decision to transfer criminal proceedings against him to another state. Questions as to when such an appeal should lie and what procedure should be followed would have to be answered by the legislation of the state concerned. In any event, a balance would have to be found between, on the one hand, protecting the rights and interests of the suspect, and on the other ensuring and promoting effective international cooperation in criminal matters. Excessive emphasis on the former could frustrate the whole object of international cooperation, namely to make the best possible use of the authorities and institutions involved, to combat crime effectively and to have the damage done repaired.

A suspect could conceivably be granted a right of appeal in the following cases: (a) if he is remanded in custody in the requesting state and has not absconded; (b) if he has been summoned in the requesting state to stand trial; (c) if he is still in the territory of the requesting state; (d) if he is suspected of certain grave offenses; (e) if administrative proceedings on the question of whether he should have been deported are still pending.

---

72 *Supra* note 15, at Art. 17.

73 *See e.g.*, Constituzione (Constitution Art. 25 (Italy)): (Nul ne peut etre soustrait *au juge naturel designé par la loi)*, and U.S. Constitution, Amend. VI (In all criminal prosecutions the accused shall enjoy the right to a speedy and public trial by an impartial jury of the state and district *wherein the crime shall have been committed*).

74 The legality principle, as it is known, applies for example in countries such as Austria, Germany, Sweden and Italy.

A right of appeal could be refused in the following cases: (a) if the offenses in question are of a minor nature; (b) if the suspect has evaded the jurisdiction of the requesting state by absconding; (c) if the suspect is identified as such for the first time when he is abroad.

Injured parties (i.e. victims of offenses) may also have valid reasons for objecting to a transfer of criminal proceedings, since their chances of obtaining some form of compensation as an incidental consequence of the criminal proceedings may well be diminished as a result. The European Convention is silent on this point, but the Benelux Convention contains a provision dealing with it expressly:

> If a civil party has already joined action, the institution of criminal proceedings may be requested of another Contracting State only with the consent of such party pursuant to a decision of the court to the effect that it is in the interests of the proper administration of justice that the criminal proceedings be brought in that state.[75]

The interests of injured parties should be protected in this way not only in cases in which they join action before proceedings are instituted, but also in cases where criminal proceedings are initiated by the injured party itself, as is possible in some countries.[76]

The Transfer of Criminal Proceedings in Practice

To my knowledge no empirical comparative research has been carried out into the legal practice of the transfer of criminal proceedings by states. It is difficult, therefore, to indicate what role the transfer of criminal proceedings plays in relation to the other instruments of international cooperation in criminal matters. What is abundantly clear, however, is that there is every chance of using it to the full in Western Europe, where the proximity of twenty states in a limited geographical area, each with its own legal system, and the mobility and freedom of movement of the population have combined to ensure that there is a great willingness and need to cooperate in this field. Nevertheless, I have the impression that in relative terms this particular instrument of legal assistance is used only very sparingly in practice. There has, for instance, been little rush to ratify the existing conventions in this field. The 1972 European Convention by March 1996 had been ratified by only ten countries (Austria, Czech Republic, Denmark, Netherlands, Norway, Slovakia, Spain, Sweden, Turkey and the Ukraine) and been signed by six others (Belgium, Greece, Iceland, Liechtenstein, Luxembourg, the Netherlands, Portugal and Spain). No fewer than 24 member states of the Council of Europe have not yet signed it. They include such major countries as France, Germany, Italy, Poland, Switzerland and the United Kingdom. The 1974 Benelux Convention too has still not come into force and has been ratified by the Netherlands only. The agreement of the EC Member States of 1990, despite its intended simplified schemes, does not attract rapid ratifications either: five years after its adoption it has been ratified by one Member State only (France).

The absence of special provisions relating to the transfer and taking over of criminal proceedings in the municipal legislation of the various countries may, however, be indicative of a general lack of awareness of the possibilities presented by this form of legal assistance.

---

75 *Supra* note 66, at Art. 1, ¶ 2.

76 *See e.g.*, Code of Criminal Procedure, Art. 2 (France); Code of Criminal Procedure, Arts. 3, 4, and 182 of the preliminary title (Belgium).

An exception must be made here for the Scandinavian countries, which have introduced uniform legislation in this field[77] and for countries such as Austria and Switzerland, which have recently introduced new legislation governing international legal assistance in criminal matters.[78] Special statutory regulations on the transfer and taking over of criminal proceedings have also been introduced in the Netherlands, and have taken effect when the Netherlands ratified the European and Benelux Conventions on the subject.[79]

For some years now, in fact, efforts have been made in the Netherlands to make the prosecuting authorities actively aware of the advantages of this form of legal assistance. In 1982, for instance, the procurators-general at the Courts of Appeal sent a circular to all the members of the Public Prosecutions Department urging that even then, before the entry into force of treaty provisions, criminal proceedings against aliens should as a rule be transferred to the offender's country of origin in cases where the person concerned had already returned there of his own volition or would in any event be deported or extradited to that country in due course. They added that proceedings should not be transferred in cases:

- which would be dropped in the Netherlands under the discretionary powers vested in the prosecuting authorities;
- which would probably result only in the imposition of a small fine (less than Fl. 250);
- where the alien had a valid permit for residence in the Netherlands.

It was stated in the circular that the proposals related mainly to the other Member States of the Council of Europe, with the exception of the common law countries and others where it was virtually impossible to bring a prosecution for an offense committed abroad.

In practice there has been a steady increase in recent years in the number of criminal cases transferred by the Dutch criminal justice authorities to other countries, while the number of cases transferred to the Netherlands from abroad has remained fairly constant at a low level. This is illustrated by the following figures:

Transfer of criminal proceedings from the Netherlands to abroad[80]

1984	1985	1986	1987	1988	1989	1990	1991	1992	1993	1994	1995
685	728	644	733	731	728	801	960	1141	1123	1025	1472

Transfer of criminal proceedings from abroad to the Netherlands[81]

1984	1985	1986	1987	1988	1989	1990	1991	1992	1993	1994	1995
72	76	88	100	91	90	105	124	123	169	152	297

---

77 Agreement on Cooperation in Criminal Prosecutions in another Nordic country than the one in which the offense has been committed, as revised on 12 Oct. 1979.

78 Loi Fédèrale sur l'entraide en matierè penale (Switzerland) (1995). Bundesgesetz fiber die Auslieferung und die Rechtshilfe in Strafsachen (Austria)(Dec. 4, 1979).

79 Act of Mar. 1985 *(entered into force on 19 July 1985)* amending the Criminal Code and the Code of Criminal Procedure with a view to the transfer of proceedings to and from the Netherlands, and implementation of the relevant European and Benelux Conventions.

80 Unpublished Statistics, Ministry of Justice (Netherlands).

81 *Id.*

Only a very small percentage of the criminal proceedings brought in respect of crimes committed in the Netherlands are transferred abroad. Every year many hundreds of summonses issued for infringements of the legislation on driving time and stopping periods are transferred abroad, but even if these are included in the above figures, the percentage remains small. Approximately half of the cases transferred to the Netherlands from abroad result in a conviction.[82] In the remainder of the cases, either the defendants are acquitted or proceedings are dropped for lack of evidence or because of prosecution policy.[83] On the other hand, far more than 50 percent of the cases transferred by the Netherlands to other countries result in a conviction.[84] This would seem to indicate that the effectiveness of transfers of proceedings as a legal instrument increases with use, and in particular when the persons administering the criminal justice system in practice become more conversant with the advantages and procedures.

It would seem logical, therefore, to take active steps to encourage the acquisition of the necessary knowledge and skills. This should be done not only nationally, by organizing special seminars for the members of the Public Prosecutions Department, the judiciary and the bar, but also internationally, by creating conditions for the exchange of information between the prosecuting authorities of various countries (preferably those with common borders).

As L.C.H. Hulsman once wrote: "In themselves International Conventions on mutual cooperation in criminal matters change nothing in the lives of men. They create opportunities which can be used or neglected. They are merely instruments of criminal policy."[85] It is time that the use of these instruments became common practice.

---

[82] *Id.*

[83] *Id.*

[84] *Id.*

[85] L.H.C. Hutsman, *The European Conventions on Mutual Assistance in Criminal Matters seen as anInstrument of Common Criminal Policy* (Paper for a meeting to discuss the European Conventions on criminal law), Council of Europe Doc. DPC/CEPC/71/8 (Sept. 1971).

Appendix 16

European Convention on the Transfer of Proceedings in Criminal Matters

European Treaty Series
No. 73

The member States of the Council of Europe, signatory hereto,

Considering that the aim of the Council of Europe is the achievement of greater unity between its Members

Desiring to supplement the work which they have already accomplished in the field of criminal law with a view to arriving at more just and efficient sanctions

Considering it useful to this end to ensure, in a spirit of mutual confidence, the organisation of criminal proceedings on the international level, in particular, by avoiding the disadvantages resulting from conflicts of competence

Have agreed as follows:

PART I
Definitions

ARTICLE 1

For the purposes of this Convention:

(a) "offence" comprises acts dealt with under the criminal law and those dealt with under the legal provisions listed in Appendix III to this Convention on condition that where an administrative authority is competent to deal with the Offense it must be possible for the person concerned to have the case tried by a court;

(b) "sanction" means any punishment or other measure incurred or pronounced in respect of an Offense or in respect of a violation of the legal provisions listed in Appendix III.

PART II
Competence

ARTICLE 2

1. For the purposes of applying this Convention, any Contracting State shall have competence to prosecute under its own criminal law any offence to which the law of another Contracting State is applicable.
2. The competence conferred on a Contracting State exclusively by virtue of paragraph 1 of this Article may be exercised only pursuant to a request for proceedings presented by another Contracting State.

ARTICLE 3

Any Contracting State having competence under its own law to prosecute an Offense may, for the purposes of applying this Convention, waive or desist from proceedings against a suspected person who is being or will be prosecuted for the same offense by another Contracting State. Having regard to Article 21, paragraph 2, any such decision to waive or to desist from proceedings shall be provisional pending a final decision in the other Contracting State.

ARTICLE 4

The requested State shall discontinue proceedings exclusively grounded on Article 2 when to its knowledge the right of punishment is extinguished under the law of the requesting State for a reason other than time-limitation, to which Articles 10(c), 11(f) and (g), 22, 23 and 26 in particular apply.

ARTICLE 5

The provisions of Part III of this Convention do not limit the competence given to a requested State by its municipal law in regard to prosecutions.

PART III

Transfer of Proceedings

Section 1: Request for Proceedings

ARTICLE 6

1. When a person is suspected of having committed an offense under the law of a Contracting State, that State may request another Contracting State to take proceedings in the cases and under the conditions provided for in this Convention.

2. If under the provisions of this Convention a Contracting State may request another Contracting State to take proceedings, the competent authorities of the first State shall take that possibility into consideration.

ARTICLE 7

1. Proceedings may not be taken in the requested State unless the Offense in respect of which the proceedings are requested would be an offense if committed in its territory and when, under these circumstances, the offender would be liable to sanction under its own law also.

2. If the offence was committed by a person of public status or against a person, an institution or any thing of public status in the requesting State, it shall be considered in the requested State as having been committed by a person of public status or against such a person, an institution or any thing corresponding, in the latter State, to that against which it was actually committed.

ARTICLE 8

1. A Contracting State may request another Contracting State to take proceedings in any one or more of the following cases:

(a) if the suspected person is ordinarily resident in the requested State;

(b) if the suspected person is a national of the requested State or if that State is his State of origin;

(c) if the suspected person is undergoing or is to undergo a sentence involving deprivation of liberty in the requested State;

(d) if proceedings for the same or other offenses are being taken against the suspected person in the requested State;

(e) if it considers that transfer of the proceedings is warranted in the interests of arriving at the truth and in particular that the most important items of evidence are located in the requested State;

(f) if it considers that the enforcement in the requested State of a sentence if one were passed is likely to improve the prospects for the social rehabilitation of the person sentenced;

(g) if it considers that the presence of the suspected person cannot be ensured at the hearing of proceedings in the requesting State and that his presence in person at the hearing of proceedings in the requested State can be ensured;

(h) if it considers that it could not itself enforce a sentence if one were passed, even by having recourse to extradition, and that the requested State could do so,

2. Where the suspected person has been finally sentenced in a Contracting State, that State may request the transfer of proceedings in one or more of the cases referred to in paragraph 1 of this Article

only if it cannot itself enforce the sentence, even by having recourse to extradition, and if the other Contracting State does not accept enforcement of a foreign judgement as a matter of principle or refuses to enforce such sentence.

ARTICLE 9

1. The competent authorities in the requested State shall examine the request for proceedings made in pursuance of the preceding Articles. They shall decide, in accordance with their own law, what action to take thereon.

2. Where the law of the requested State provides for the punishment of the offense by an administrative authority, that State shall, as soon as possible, so inform the requesting State unless the requested State has made a declaration under paragraph 3 of this Article.

3. Any Contracting State may at the time of signature, or when depositing its instrument of ratification, acceptance or accession, or at any later date indicate, by declaration addressed to the Secretary General of the Council of Europe, the conditions under which its domestic law permits the punishment of certain offenses by an administrative authority. Such a declaration shall replace the notification envisaged in paragraph 2 of this Article.

ARTICLE 10

The requested State shall not take action on the request:

(a) if the request does not comply with the provisions of Articles 6, paragraph 1, and 7, paragraph 1;

(b) if the institution of proceedings is contrary to the provisions of Article 35:

(c) if, at the date of the request, the time-limit for criminal proceedings has already expired in the requesting State under the legislation of that State.

ARTICLE 11

Save as provided for in Article 10 the requested State may not refuse acceptance of the request in whole or in part, except in any one or more of the following Cases:

(a) if it considers that the grounds on which the request is based under Article 8 are not justified;

(b) if the suspected person is not ordinarily resident in the requested State;

(c) if the suspected person is not a national of the requested State and was not ordinarily resident in the territory of that State at the time of the offence;

(d) if it considers that the offence for which proceedings are requested is an offense of a political nature or a purely military or fiscal one;

(e) if it considers that there are substantial grounds for believing that the request for proceedings was motivated by considerations or race, religion, nationality or political opinion;

(f) if its own law is already applicable to the offense and if at the time of the receipt of the request proceedings were precluded by lapse of time according to the law; Article 26, paragraph 2, shall not apply in such a case;

(g) if its competence is exclusively grounded on Article 2 and if at the time of the receipt of the request proceedings would be precluded by lapse of time according to its law, the prolongation of the time-limit by six months under the terms of Article 23 being taken into consideration;

(h) if the offence was committed outside the territory of the requesting State;

(i) if proceedings would be contrary to the international undertakings of the requested State;

(j) if the proceedings would be contrary to the fundamental principles of the legal system of the requested State;

(k) if the requesting State had violated a rule of procedure laid down in this Convention.

ARTICLE 12

1. The requested States shall withdraw its acceptance of the request if, subsequent to this acceptance, a ground mentioned in Article 10 of this Convention for not taking action on the request becomes apparent.

2. The requested State may withdraw its acceptance of the request;

(a) if it becomes apparent that the presence in person of the suspected person cannot be ensured at the hearing of proceedings in that State of that any sentence, which might be passed, could not be enforced in that State;

(b) if one of the grounds for refusal mentioned in Article 11 becomes apparent before the case is brought before a court; or

(c) in other cases, if the requesting State agrees.

Section 2: Transfer Procedure

ARTICLE 13

1. All requests specified in this Convention shall be made in writing. They, and all communications necessary for the application of this Convention, shall be sent either by the Ministry of Justice of the requesting State to the Ministry of Justice of the requested State or, by virtue of special mutual agreement, direct by authorities of the requesting State to those of the requested State; they shall be returned by the same channel.

2. In urgent cases requests and communications may be sent through the International Criminal Police Organisation (INTERPOL).

3. Any Contracting State may, by declaration addressed to the Secretary General of the Council of Europe, give notice of its intention to adopt insofar as it itself is concerned rules of transmission other that those laid down in paragraph 1 of this Article.

ARTICLE 14

If a Contracting State considers that the information supplied by another Contracting State is not adequate to enable it to apply this Convention, it shall ask for the necessary additional information. It may prescribe a date for the receipt of such information.

ARTICLE 15

1. A request for proceedings shall be accompanied by the original, or a certified copy, of the criminal file and all other necessary documents. However, if the suspected person is remanded in custody in accordance with the provisions of Section 5 and if the requesting State is unable to transmit these documents at the same time as the request for proceedings, the documents may be sent subsequently.

2. The requesting State shall also inform the requested State in writing of any procedural acts performed or measures taken in the requesting State after the transmission of the request which have a bearing on the proceedings. This communication shall be accompanied by any relevant documents.

ARTICLE 16

1. The requested State shall promptly communicate its decision on the request for proceedings to the requesting State.

2. The requested State shall also inform the requesting State of a waiver of proceedings or of the decision taken as a result of proceedings. A certified copy of any written decision shall be transmitted to the requesting State.

ARTICLE 17

If the competence of the requested State is exclusively grounded on Article 2 that State shall inform the suspected person of the request for proceedings with a view to allowing him to present his views on the matter before that State has taken a decision on the request.

ARTICLE 18

1. Subject to paragraph 2 of this Article, no translation of the documents relating to the application of this Convention shall be required.

2. Any Contracting State may, at the time of signature or when depositing its instrument of ratification, acceptance or accession, by declaration addressed to the Secretary General of the Council of Europe, reserve the right to require that, with the exception of the copy of the written decision referred to in Article 16, paragraph 2, the said documents be accompanied by a translation. The other Contracting States shall send the translations in either that national language of the receiving State or such one of the official languages of the Council of Europe as the receiving State shall indicate. However, such an indication is not obligatory. The other Contracting States may claim reciprocity.

3. This Article shall be without prejudice to any provisions concerning translation of requests and supporting documents that may be contained in agreements or arrangements now in force or that may be concluded between two or more Contracting States.

ARTICLE 19

Documents transmitted in application of this Convention need not be authenticated.

ARTICLE 20

Contracting Parties shall not claim from each other the refund of any expenses resulting from the application of this Convention.

Section 3: Effects in the requesting State of a request for proceedings

ARTICLE 21

1. When the requesting State has requested proceedings, it can no longer prosecute the suspected person for the offence in respect of which the proceedings have been requested or enforce a judgement which has been pronounced previously in that State against him for that offence. Until the requested State's decision on the request for proceedings has been received, the requesting State shall, however, retain its right to take all steps in respect of prosecution, short of bringing the case to trial, or, as the case may be, allowing the competent administrative authority to decide on the case.

2. The right of prosecution and of enforcement shall revert to the requesting State:

(a) if the requested State informs it of a decision in accordance with Article 10 not to take action on the request;

(b) if the requested State informs it of a decision in accordance with Article 11 to refuse acceptance of the request;

(c) if the requested State informs it of a decision in accordance with Article 12 to withdraw acceptance of the request;

(d) if the requested State informs it of a decision not to institute proceedings or discontinue them;

(e) if it withdraws its request before the requested State has informed it of a decision to take action on the request.

ARTICLE 22

A request for proceedings, made in accordance with the provisions of this Part, shall have the effect in the requesting States of prolonging the time-limit for proceedings by six months.

Section 4: Effects in the requested State of a request for proceedings

ARTICLE 23

If the competence of the requested State is exclusively grounded on Article 2 the time-limit for proceedings in that State shall be prolonged by six months.

ARTICLE 24

1. If proceedings are dependent on a complaint in both States, the complaint brought in the requesting State shall have equal validity with that brought in the requested State.
2. If a complaint is necessary only in the requested State, that State may take proceedings even in the absence of a complaint if the person who is empowered to bring the complaint has not objected within a period of one month from the date of receipt by him of notice from the competent authority informing him of his right to object.

ARTICLE 25

In the requested State the sanction applicable to the offence shall be that prescribed by its own law unless that law provides otherwise. Where the competence of the requested State is exclusively grounded on Article 2, the sanction pronounced on that State shall not be more severe than that provided for in the law of the requesting State.

ARTICLE 26

1. Any act with a view to proceedings, taken in the requesting State in accordance with its law and regulations, shall have the same validity in the requested State as if it had been taken by the authorities of that State, provided that assimilation does not give such act a greater evidential weight than it has n the requesting State.
2. Any act which interrupts time-limitation and which has been validly performed in the requesting State shall have the same effects in the requested State and vice versa.

Section 5: Provisional measures in the requested State

ARTICLE 27

1. When the requesting State announces its intention to transmit a request for proceedings, and if the competence of the requested State would be exclusively grounded on Article 2, the requested State may, on application by the requesting State and by virtue of this Convention, provisionally arrest the suspected person:

(a) if the law of the requested State authorises remand in custody for the offence, and

(b) if there are reasons to fear that the suspected person will abscond or that he will cause evidence to be suppressed.

2. The application for provisional arrest shall state that there exists a warrant of arrest or other order having the same effect, issued in accordance with the procedure laid down in the law of the requesting State; it shall also state for what offence proceedings will be requested and when and where such offence was committed and it shall contain as accurate a description of the suspected person as possible. It shall also contain a brief statement of the circumstances of the case.
3. An application for provisional arrest shall be sent direct by the authorities in the requesting State mentioned in Article 13 to the corresponding authorities in the requested State, by post or telegram or by any other means affording evidence in writing or accepted by the requested State. The requesting State shall be informed without delay of the result of its application.

ARTICLE 28

Upon receipt of a request for proceedings accompanied by the documents referred to in Article 15, paragraph 1, the requested State shall have jurisdiction to apply all such provisional measures, including remand in custody of the suspected person and seizure of property, as could be applied under its own law if the offence in respect of which proceedings are requested had been committed in its territory.

ARTICLE 29

1. The provisional measures provided in Articles 27 and 28 shall be governed by the provisions of this Convention and the law of the requested State. The law of that State, or the Convention shall also determine the conditions in which the measures may lapse.
2. These measures shall lapse in the cases referred to in Article 21, paragraph 2.
3. A person in custody shall in any event be released if he is arrested in pursuance of Article 27 and the requested State does not receive the request for proceedings within 18 days from the date of the arrest.
4. A person in custody shall in any event be released if he is arrested in pursuance of Article 27 and the documents which should accompany the request for proceedings have not been received by the requested State within 15 days from the receipt of the request for proceedings.
5. The period of custody applied exclusively by virtue of Article 27 shall not in any event exceed 40 days.

PART IV

Plurality of Criminal Proceedings

ARTICLE 30

1. Any Contracting State which, before the institution or in the course of proceedings for a offence which it considers to be neither of a political nature nor a purely military one, is aware of proceedings pending in another Contracting State against the same person in respect of the same offence shall consider whether it can either waive or suspend its own proceedings, or transfer them to the other State.
2. If it deems it advisable in the circumstances not to waive or suspend its own proceedings it shall so notify the other State in good time and in any event before judgement is given on the merits.

ARTICLE 31

1. In the eventuality referred to in Article 30, paragraph 2, the States concerned shall endeavour as far as possible to determine, after evaluation on each case of the circumstances mentioned in Article 8, which of them alone shall continue to conduct proceedings. During this consultative procedure the States concerned shall postpone judgement on the merits without however being obliged to prolong such postponement beyond a period of 30 days as from the despatch of the notification provided for in Article 30, paragraph 2.
2. The provisions of paragraph 1 shall not be binding:

(a) on the State despatching the notification provided for in Article 30, paragraph 2, if the main trial has been declared open there in the presence of the accused before despatch of the notification;

(b) on the State to which the notification is addressed, if the main trial has been declared open there in the presence of the accused before the receipt of the notification.

ARTICLE 32

In the interests of arriving at the truth and with a view to the application of an appropriate sanction, the States concerned shall examine whether it is expedient that one of them alone shall conduct proceedings and, if so, endeavour to determine which one, when:

(a) several offences which are materially distinct and which fall under the criminal law of each of those States are ascribed either to a single person or several persons having acted in unison;

(b) a single offence which falls under the criminal law of each of those States is ascribed to several persons having acted in unison.

ARTICLE 33

All decisions reached in accordance with Articles 31, paragraph 1, and 32 shall entail, as between the States concerned, all the consequences of a transfer of proceedings as provided for in this Convention. The State which waives its own proceedings shall be deemed to have transferred them to the other State.

ARTICLE 34

The transfer procedure provided for in Section 2 of Part III shall apply in so far as its provisions are compatible with those contained in the present Part.

PART V
Ne bis in idem

ARTICLE 35

1. A person in respect of whom a final and enforcable criminal judgement has been rendered may for the same act neither be prosecuted nor sentenced nor subjected to enforcement of a sanction in another Contracting State:
   (a) if he was aquitted;
   (b) if the sanction imposed:
      (i) has been completely enforce or is being enforced, or
      (ii) has been wholly, or with respect to the part not enforced, the subject of a pardon or an amnesty, or
      (iii) can no longer be enforced because of lapse of time;
   (c) if the court convicted the offender without imposing a sanction.
2. Nevertheless, a Contracting State shall not, unless it has itself requested the proceedings, be obliged to recognise the effects of *ne bis in idem* if the act which gave rise to the judgement was directed against either a person or an institution or any thing having public status in that State, or if the subject of the judgement had himself a public status in that State.
3. Furthermore, a Contracting State where the act was committed or considered as such according to the law of that State shall not be obliged to recognise the effect of *ne bis in idem* unless that State has itself requested the proceedings.

ARTICLE 36

If new proceedings are instituted against a person who in another Contracting State has been sentenced for the same act, then any period of deprivation of liberty arising from the sentence enforced shall be deduced from the sanction which may be imposed.

ARTICLE 37

This Part shall not prevent the application of wider domestic provisions relating to the effect of *ne bis in idem* attached to foreign criminal judgements.

PART V
Final Clauses

ARTICLE 38

1. This Convention shall be open to signature by the member States of the Council of Europe. It shall be subject to ratification or acceptance. Instruments of ratification or acceptance shall be deposited with the Secretary General of the Council of Europe.
2. This Convention shall enter into force three months after the date of the deposit of the third instrument of ratification or acceptance.

3. In respect of a signatory State ratifying or accepting subsequently, the Convention shall come into force three months after the date of the deposit of its instrument of ratification or acceptance.

ARTICLE 39

1. After the entry into force of this Convention, the Committee of Ministers of the Council of Europe may invite any non-member State to accede thereto provided that the resolution containing such invitation receives the unanimous agreement of the Members of the Council who have ratified the Convention.
2. Such accession shall be effected by depositing with the Secretary General of the Council of Europe an instrument of accession which shall take effect three months after the date of its deposit.

ARTICLE 40

1. Any Contracting State may, at the time of signature or when depositing its instrument of ratification, acceptance or accession, specify the territory or territories to which this Convention shall apply.
2. Any Contracting State may, when depositing its instrument of ratification, acceptance or accession or at any later date, by declaration addressed to the Secretary General of the Council of Europe, extend this Convention to any other territory or territories specified in the declaration and for whose international relations it is responsible or on whose behalf it is authorised to give undertakings.
3. Any declaration made in pursuance of the preceeding paragraph may, in respect of any territory mentioned in such declaration, be withdrawn according to the procedure laid down in Article 45 of this Convention.

ARTICLE 41

1. Any Contracting State may, at the time of signature or when depositing its instrument of ratification, acceptance or accession, declare that it avails itself of one or more of the reservations provided for in Appendix I or make a declaration provided for in Appendix II to this Convention.
2. Any Contracting State may wholly or partly withdraw a reservation or declaration it has made in accordance with the foregoing paragraph by means of a declaration addressed to the Secretary General of the Council of Europe which shall become effective as from the date of its receipt.
3. A Contracting State which has made a reservation in respect of any provision of this Convention may not claim the application of that provision by any other Contracting State; it may, however, if its reservation is partial or conditional, claim the application of that provision insofar as it has itself accepted it.

ARTICLE 42

1. Any Contracting State may at any time, by declaration addressed to the Secretary General of the Council of Europe, set out the legal provisions to be included in Appendix II to this Convention.
2. Any change of the national provisions listed in Appendix III shall be notified to the Secretary General of the Council of Europe if such a change renders the information in this Appendix incorrect.
3. Any changes made in Appendix III in application of the preceding paragraphs shall take effect in each Contracting State one month after the date of their notification by the Secretary General of the Council of Europe.

ARTICLE 43

1. This Convention affects neither the rights and the undertakings derived from extradition treaties and international multilateral conventions concerning special matters, nor provisions concerning matters which are dealt with in the present Convention and which are contained in other existing conventions between the Contracting States.

2. The Contracting States may not conclude bilateral or multilateral agreements with one another on the matters which are dealt with in the present Convention and which are contained in other existing conventions between Contracting States.
3. Should two or more Contracting States, however, have already established their relations in this matter on the basis of uniform legislation, or instituted a special system of their own, or should they in the future do so, they shall be entitled to regulate those relations accordingly, notwithstanding the terms of this Convention.
4. Contracting States ceasing to apply the terms of this Convention to their mutual relations in this matter in accordance with the provisions of the preceding paragraph shall notify the Secretary General of the Council of Europe to that effect.

ARTICLE 44

The European Committee on Crime Problems of the Council of Europe shall be kept informed regarding the application of this Convention and shall do whatever is needful to facilitate a friendly settlement of any difficulty which may arise out of its execution.

ARTICLE 45

1. This Convention shall remain in force indefinitely.
2. Any Contracting State may, insofar as it is concerned, denounce this Convention by means of a notification addressed to the Secretary General of the Council of Europe.
3. Such denunciation shall take effect six months after the date of receipt by the Secretary General of such notification.

ARTICLE 46

The Secretary General of the Council of Europe shall notify the member States of the Council and any State which has acceded to this Convention of:

(a) any signature;
(b) any deposit of an instrument of ratification, acceptance or accession;
(c) any date of entry into force of this Convention in accordance with Article 38 thereof;
(d) any declaration received in pursuance of the provisions of Article 9, paragraph 3;
(e) any declaration received in pursuance of the provisions of Article 13, paragraph 3;
(f) any declaration received in pursuance of the provisions of Article 18, paragraph 2;
(g) any declaration received in pursuance of the provisions of Article 40, paragraphs 2 and 3;
(h) any reservation or declaration made in pursuance of the provisions of Article 41, paragraph 1;
(i) the withdrawal of any reservation or declaration carried out in pursuance of the provisions of Article 41, paragraph 2;
(j) any declaration received in pursuance of Article 42, paragraph 1, and any subsequent notification received in pursuance of paragraph 2 of that Article;
(k) any notification received in pursuance of the provisions of Article 43, paragraph 4;
(l) any notification received in pursuance of the provisions of Article 45 and the date on which denunciation takes effect.

ARTICLE 47

This Convention and the notifications and declarations authorised thereunder shall apply only to offences committed after the Convention comes into effect for the Contracting States involved.

In witness whereof, the undersigned, being duly authorised thereto, have signed this Convention.

Done at Strasbourg, this 15th day of May 1972, in English and in French, both texts being equally authoritative, in a single copy, which shall remain deposited in the archives of the Council of Europe.

The Secretary General shall transmit certified copies to each of the signatory and acceding Governments.

Section VIII

Assets Freeze and Seizure

International and National Responses to the Globalization of Money Laundering*

M. Cherif Bassiouni and David S. Gualtieri

Introduction

Drug trafficking, organized crime, corruption and other economic crimes that generate large financial gains have made the suppression of money laundering[1] one of the primary law enforcement issues of the past several years.[2] The international response to this situation has resulted in an unprecedented level of international cooperation in criminal matters as the nations of the world seek to combat serious crime and the money laundering that inevitably follows.[3] The initiatives that have resulted from these international efforts are the focus of this chapter.

Discussions of efforts to curb money laundering often focus on drug trafficking and its enormous proceeds.[4] The cultivation, distribution and use of drugs have increased and

* This article is an expanded version of *International and National Responses to the Globalization of Money Laundering,* which appeared in RESPONDING TO MONEY LAUNDERING: AN INTERNATIONAL PERSPECTIVE (Ernesto U. Savona ed., 1997)

1 Money laundering is generally defined as the "process by which one conceals the existence, illegal source or illegal application of income, and then disguises that income to make it appear legitimate." PRESIDENT'S COMMISSION ON ORGANIZED CRIME, INTERIM REPORT TO THE PRESIDENT AND THE ATTORNEY GENERAL, THE CASH CONNECTION: ORGANIZED CRIME, FINANCIAL INSTITUTIONS AND MONEY LAUNDERING 7 (1984). In recent years, the international community has recognized that criminal activity generates tremendous profits and that, as a result, organizations seek to hide the actual source of these profits. Money laundering often involves the use of foreign banks, usually located in countries with strict bank secrecy laws and lax financial regulations, which transfer the laundered cash back to its country of origin as seemingly clean, legitimate funds.

2 The pressing nature of the money laundering situation is indicated by the degree to which national governments have responded to the issue. By the end of 1993, it was estimated that 47 nations had adopted laws or other measures to combat money laundering. Many states have gone so far as to create anti-money-laundering units as part of of their national law enforcement initiatives. *United Nations General Assembly to Hold Special Meetings on International Cooperation Against Illicit Drugs*, PR Newswire, Oct. 25, 1993, *available in* LEXIS, NEXIS Library, Wires File. *See also More Countries Enact, Strengthen Laundering Laws*, Money Laundering Alert, Sept. 1993, at 7. For a detailed description and analysis of national laws in this area, *see generally* Ernesto Savona & Michael D. DeFeo, *Money Trails: International Money Laundering Trends and Prevention/Control Policies* (1994) (draft report presented at the International Conference on Preventing and Controlling Money Laundering and the Use of Proceeds of Crime: A Global Approach, Courmayeur Mont Blanc, Italy, June 18-20, 1994).

3 *See* Felix Soh, *Cleaning Up Dirty Money,* THE STRAITS TIMES (Singapore), Jan. 8, 1995; *U.N. Gathers 49 Nations to Prompt Action Against Money Laundering*, Money Laundering Alert, Sept. 1994, at 7 (summarizing the conclusions of conference on money laundering held in Courmayeur Mont Blanc, Italy in June 1994).

4 Despite this almost inevitable focus on drug trafficking and organized crime, it must be remembered that many of the initiatives discussed in this paper are critical to the suppression of all serious offenses that generate large profits. All too frequently, however, governments ignore large-scale corruption and other forms of abuse of power by government officials that lead to enormous financial losses to their countries. The selective approach of most governments, particularly those of major developed countries, ignores the use of money laundering techniques to conceal drug transactions and other financial transactions carried out by intelligence agencies. Lastly, there are a whole host of economic crimes, whether in developed or developing countries, that use the same techniques of money laundering that are used by drug traffickers and other offenders. To understand that the same channels and techniques are used by money launderers is indispensable to understanding why efforts to control and curb money laundering are so far only partially and selectively successful. For example, it is estimated that as much as US$300

engulfed the world in a tidal wave that seems impossible to stem. With an estimated US$500 billion annual business,[5] it should be no surprise that 13 international instruments have been created in response to the illicit drug traffic.[6] For the most part, however, efforts to control production and consumption have failed, as evidenced by the increase in supply and demand.[7] Irrespective of what the exact figures are, there is no doubt that the markets for drugs are expanding, the utilization is increasing, the supply base is growing, and the proceeds are multiplying. These facts are recorded in the consistently increased seizures of drugs and assets by law enforcement agencies all over the world, without any apparent reason to believe that the supply is in shortage, or that the proceeds and profits are diminished. The only visible result is the increased income to law enforcement agencies from the seizure of such proceeds. Another obvious consequence of the increased profits available to those engaged in such criminal activities is their utilization of these funds for investment in so-called legitimate business and financial enterprises and activities. But these funds are also used to corrupt legitimate business and public officials, and to buy political favors. This is where the real dangers lie to organized societies.

It is axiomatic that money has no color or smell, and that all money, whether derived from legal or illegal sources, uses the same financial channels. As a result, once money from drug traffic, corruption or other offenses is in the world's financial pipelines, it is very difficult to detect it.[8] The points of entry and exit are the ones that offer the greatest opportunities for control and eventual seizure.[9] But because of international financial interests in keeping the entry and exit channels of the world's financial pipelines open, it is difficult to have effective control at these most crucial points. For reasons stated above, governments too have an interest in keeping the world's financial pipelines relatively free, open, and confidential. Thus these competing interests make the task of controlling money laundering, only for some activities and not for others, more arduous to achieve positive

---

billion is "laundered" through the world's banking system each year. REPORT SUBMITTED BY THE SUBCOMM. OF NARCOTICS, TERRORISM, AND INTERNATIONAL OPERATIONS TO THE SENATE FOREIGN RELATIONS COMM., 101st Cong., 2d Sess. Other estimates claim that US$85 billion enters the international financial stream from the sale of drugs in the United States and Europe alone. European Committee on Crime Problems, Recommendations by the Financial Action Task Force on Money Laundering (done at Strasbourg, 7 Feb. 1990), at 6. For other economic crimes potentially involving money laundering, *see* INTERNATIONAL CRIMINAL LAW: A GUIDE TO U.S. PRACTICE AND PROCEDURE (Ved P. Nanda & M. Cherif Bassiouni eds., 1987).

[5] *See* M. Cherif Bassiouni, *Critical Reflections on International and National Control of Drugs*, 18 DENV. J. INT'L L. & POL'Y 311, 321 (1990) (*citing* DRUG TRAFFICKING AND THE WORLD ECONOMY, U.N. Dept. of Public Information, U.N. Doc. DPI/1040b-40076 (Jan. 1990)).

[6] M. Cherif Bassiouni, *The International Narcotics Control Scheme, in* 1 INTERNATIONAL CRIMINAL LAW 505 (M. Cherif Bassiouni ed. 1986). *See also* UNITED NATIONS, DIVISION OF NARCOTIC DRUGS, EXTRADITION FOR DRUG-RELATED OFFENSES: A STUDY OF EXISTING EXTRADITION PRACTICES AND SUGGESTED GUIDELINES FOR USE IN CONCLUDING EXTRADITION TREATIES, ST/Nar/5 (1985).

[7] Illegal drug sales in the United States alone may be as high as US$200 billion. *See* Dr. Irving V. Tragen, *Drugs in America—A World View*, Address to the Drug/Alcohol Education Training Seminar (July 5-9, 1989), *reprinted in* 135 Cong. Rec. 20,219 (1989).

[8] One such technological breakthrough, electronic wire transfers, has benefitted drug traffickers, organized criminals and money launderers. International financial institutions electronically transfer approximately US$500 billion daily, and it is estimated that each year, US$100 billion to US$300 billion of those transfer involve illicit proceeds. *See generally* Gerard Wyrsch, *Treasury Regulation of International Wire Transfer and Money Laundering: A Case for a Permanent Moratorium*, 20 DENV. J. INT'L L. & POL'Y 515 (1992).

[9] *See* M. Cherif Bassiouni, *Effective National and International Action Against Organized Crime and Terrorist Criminal Activities,* 4 EMORY INT'L L. REV. 9, 21 (1990). *See also* David P. Stewart, *Internationalizing the War on Drugs: The U.N. Convention Against Illicit Traffic in Narcotic Drugs and Psychotropic Substances*, 18 DENV. J. INT'L L. & POL'Y 387, 389-91 (1990).

results. As a consequence, the detection of illegal proceeds is selective and sporadic, and thus of little impact on the drug business.

Recent asset control efforts consist of two fundamental parts: (1) the immobilization and forfeiture of assets[10] and (2) efforts to criminalize, discover and curb money laundering under both international and domestic law. The immobilization and seizure of assets and the criminalization of money laundering have been employed throughout the world as powerful new weapons against many forms of criminal activity.[11] Undergirding this entire approach is a primary need for effective inter-state cooperation in penal matters to guarantee the proper implementation of these innovative international law enforcement measures.[12] The requirement to freeze and seize assets, contained in mutual legal assistance treaties (MLATs) or mutual legal assistance provisions in multilateral agreements, has become central to the prevention, investigation, and ultimate prosecution of money laundering.

This chapter focuses on the many international initiatives designed to control the flow of proceeds generated by criminal activity. Initiatives will be discussed at levels ranging from the global approach of the 1988 United Nations Drug Convention to the strictly regional activities of the Organization of American States.[13]

This chapter begins by considering the context within which money laundering has been addressed. Through a web of bilateral, regional, and nearly global initiatives, the principles of international criminal law have been applied to solve this ever-expanding threat of corruption in the international financial sector. To implement the most recent initiatives, those who would tackle this dilemma must fully comprehend the rubric of international criminal law—particularly international criminal law's tendency to operate at many levels or tiers.

In this connection, it must be understood that a global approach to money laundering will hinge on effective inter-state cooperation in penal matters. The mechanisms of mutual legal assistance must be implemented effectively and fairly. Because criminal organizations practice in an international sphere, so too must law enforcement authorities. The second section of this chapter presents an overview of the principles of inter-state cooperation in penal matters. The effectiveness of these principles can be seen, at least on a bilateral level,

---

[10] Each of the instruments to be discussed provides two types of procedures. First, assets are either seized, frozen or restrained in anticipation of eventual forfeiture or confiscation. Then, following an adjudication of guilt by a court, assets that are deemed to be the instrumentalities or proceeds of illicit activity are ordered forfeited to or confiscated by the government and are appropriately disposed of by the government. The terms forfeiture and confiscation are commonly used interchangeably, although, in fact, their meanings are not identical.

The fundamental distinction between the two procedures is clear: immobilization of assets is based on suspicion while forfeiture or confiscation is based on an adjudication of guilt and represents a criminal penalty. Criminal suspects often transfer or harbor their assets from the reach of government authorities, and the immobilization of assets by freezing bank accounts or seizing houses, cars and businesses ensures that these assets will be available for forfeiture.

[11] *See generally* Scott Carlson & Bruce Zagaris, *International Cooperation in Criminal Matters: Western Europe's International Approach to International Crime*, 15 NOVA L. REV. 551 (1991) (discussing the approaches of various nations in implementing asset seizure and forfeiture by means of inter-state cooperation in penal matters).

[12] *See generally* Bruce Zagaris, *Developments in International Judicial Assistance and Related Matters*, 18 DENV. J. INT'L L. & POL'Y 339 (1990). *See also* Bruce Zagaris, *Protecting the Rule of Law from Assault in the War Against Drugs and Narco-Terrorism*, 15 NOVA L. REV. 703, 712 (1991) (arguing that the absence of effective extradition and mutual assistance allow organized criminal organizations to circumvent international law).

[13] Domestic initiatives will also be considered to the extent that they reflect the progress achieved by international efforts to thwart money laundering and to control the flow of ill-gotten gains.

by analyzing the experience of the United States government in using mutual legal assistance treaties (MLATs) to control the flow of illicit assets into and from many money laundering havens.

Two major multilateral instruments, the 1988 United Nations Convention and the 1990 Council of Europe Laundering Convention, employ the freezing and seizing of illicit proceeds to suppress drug trafficking, organized crime, and other offenses which generate large sums of money. These two agreements provide a framework which is implemented through other regional, subregional, and regional initiatives on inter-state cooperation. The discussion of these instruments focuses on three topics: (1) provisions relating to the freezing and seizing of assets; (2) the manner in which inter-state cooperation is handled; and (3) obligations to make money laundering a crime under national law.

The paramount example of this international approach, and the first initiative discussed, is the 1988 United Nations Convention Against Illicit Traffic in Narcotic Drugs and Psychotropic Substances ("U.N. Drug Convention").[14] Its strong provisions requiring states to cooperate with each other to accomplish the freezing and forfeiture of illicit proceeds and the requirement to criminalize money laundering indicate a commitment on the part of the United Nations to strike at the economic foundations of the illicit drug trade.[15] The cooperation contemplated by this treaty will require both bilateral participation and domestic legislation to effectuate any bilateral agreements. Any discussion of international efforts to control the economic gains from illicit activity must begin with this major development in international law enforcement. Significantly, however, the U.N. Drug Convention is limited to proceeds from drug offenses.

The second major initiative considered is the 1990 Council of Europe Convention on Laundering, Search, Seizure and Confiscation of the Proceeds from Crime ("European Money Laundering Convention").[16] This multilateral instrument, which is open to accession by like-minded states which are not members of the Council of Europe, is an excellent example of the integrated approach to inter-state penal cooperation. The European Money Laundering Convention also makes significant achievements in recognizing the need to harmonize domestic legislation with international norms. The Convention was formulated with reference, in principle, to all kinds of offenses and is not directed particularly at drug trafficking or organized crime.[17] In fact, the broad scope of this treaty is a reminder that

---

[14] United Nations Convention Against Illicit Traffic in Narcotic Drugs and Psychotropic Substances, *opened for signature* Dec. 20, 1988, U.N. Doc. E/Conf.82/15 Corr. 1 and Corr. 2, 28 I.L.M. 493 (1989) (*entered into force* Nov. 1990) [hereinafter U.N. Drug Convention]. *See also* PAOLO BERNASCONI, NEW JUDICIAL INSTRUMENTS AGAINST INTERNATIONAL BUSINESS CRIMES (1995); WILLIAM C. GILMORE, DIRTY MONEY: THE EVOLUTION OF MONEY LAUNDERING COUNTER-MEASURES (1995).

[15] For a summary of the recent efforts of the United Nations in the area of inter-state cooperation in penal matters, including reproductions of relevant documents and United Nations model agreements in the field, see Eduardo Vetere, *The Role of the United Nations: Working for More Effective International Co-operation, in* PRINCIPLES AND PROCEDURES FOR A NEW TRANSNATIONAL CRIMINAL LAW 713 (Albin Eser & Otto Lagodny eds., 1992).

[16] Council of Europe Convention on Laundering, Search, Seizure and Confiscation of the Proceeds from Crime, Nov. 8, 1990, Europ. T.S. No. 141, 30 I.L.M. 148 (*entered into force* Mar. 1, 1991) [hereinafter Euro. Conv. Money Laundering], *reprinted in* 2 EUROPEAN INTER-STATE CO-OPERATION IN CRIMINAL MATTERS: THE COUNCIL OF EUROPE'S LEGAL INSTRUMENTS 1405 (Ekkehart Müller-Rappard & M. Cherif Bassiouni eds., rev'd 2d ed. 1993). *See also* BERNASCONI, *supra* note 14; GILMORE, *supra* note 14.

[17] The Euro. Conv. Money Laundering, unlike the U.N. Drug Convention, is not limited to drug-related offenses. Rather, Article 1(e) of the Euro. Conv. Money Laundering defines a "predicate offense" as "any criminal offense as a result which proceeds were generated that may become the subject of an offense as defined in Article

organized crime and narco-trafficking are not the only criminal enterprises that launder and recycle funds. Indeed, a multitude of criminal endeavors generate huge amounts of currency that must be made to appear legitimate.

Four other international initiatives are significant and worthy of discussion. First, the European Community has issued a directive on the role of financial institutions in combating money laundering.[18] Another example of a large scale undertaking to thwart international money laundering is the work of the Financial Action Task Force (FATF), a group begun by the Group of Seven industrialized nations (G-7), which has since expanded to include a number of other nations.[19] Many of the 40 recommendations made by this body have been implemented, in one manner or another, in many national legal systems.[20] Third, the Organization of American States (OAS) has adopted model regulations related to laundering offenses and illicit drug trafficking.[21] Finally, the Basle Committee on Banking Regulations and Supervisory Practices ("Basle Committee") has developed a set of principles urging banks to take measures to curb money laundering.[22]

The international initiatives to curb money laundering create potent new law enforcement mechanisms. The final section of this chapter discusses how these new mechanisms, while important to effective international law enforcement, will inevitably affect the individual rights of criminal suspects as well as innocent third parties whose assets have become intermingled with laundered proceeds.

The Structure of International Criminal Law and the Role of Inter-State Cooperation in Penal Matters

Initiatives designed to curb money laundering are a product of the current status of international criminal law. As such, they will have to operate within the context of enforcement mechanisms employed in inter-state cooperation in penal matters. This context is important to understanding domestic and international implications of efforts to combat money laundering.

---

6 of this Convention." The Euro. Conv. Money Laundering is intended to combat all forms of serious crimes, especially drug offenses, arms dealing, terrorism or other offenses which generate large profits. *See* Council of Europe, Explanatory Report on the Convention on Laundering, Search, Seizure and Confiscation of the Proceeds From Crime (1991) ¶ 8, *reprinted in* 2 EUROPEAN INTER-STATE CO-OPERATION IN CRIMINAL MATTERS: THE COUNCIL OF EUROPE'S LEGAL INSTRUMENTS 1419 (Ekkehart Müller-Rappard & M. Cherif Bassiouni eds., rev'd 2d ed. 1993).

18 Council Directive No. 91/308, 1991 O.J. (L 166) 77.

19 *See* European Committee on Crime Problems, Recommendations by the Financial Action Task Force on Money Laundering (done at Strasbourg, Feb. 7, 1990). *See also* BERNASCONI, *supra* note 14; GILMORE, *supra* note 14.

20 *See* Hans G. Nilsson, *The Council of Europe Laundering Convention: A Recent Example of a Developing International Criminal Law*, 2 CRIM. L.F. 419, 420, n.4 (1991). *See* Note, *The International Attack on Money Laundering: European Initiatives*, 1991 DUKE J. COMP. & INT'L L. 213.

21 OEA/Ser. L/XIV.2, CICAD/INF.58/92 (July 9, 1992). *See also* GILMORE, *supra* note 14.

22 Basle Committee on Banking Regulations and Supervisory Practices, December 1988 Statement on Prevention of Criminal Use of the Banking System for the Purpose of Money-Laundering [hereinafter Basle Committee Statement], *reprinted in* INTERNATIONAL EFFORTS TO COMBAT MONEY LAUNDERING 273-77 (W.C. Gilmore ed. 1992) (nearly every major anti-money-laundering initiative of the past several years is reproduced in this reference text). *See generally* Hogarth, Beyond the Vienna Convention: International Efforts to Suppress Money Laundering (1994) (presented at the International Conference on Preventing and Controlling Money Laundering and the Use of Proceeds of Crime: A Global Approach, Courmayeur Mont Blanc, Italy, June 18-20, 1994). *See also* BERNASCONI, *supra* note 14; GILMORE, *supra* note 14.

International criminal law has always been a challenging subject, if for no other reason than its pluri-disciplinary nature. It is the convergence of the penal aspects of international law and regional law, and national criminal laws and procedures, with the addition of their respective related legal subjects. Perhaps the most important peculiarities of international criminal law are the different international, regional and domestic legal processes through which these multiple areas of the law interact.

International criminal law, and, by implication, international efforts to control illicit proceeds, are based on a three-tiered system. The first tier consists of substantive multilateral treaties that proscribe certain types of activities or conduct. These treaties may also contain provisions pertaining to inter-state cooperation in penal matters.

So far, the 24 categories of international and transnational crimes identified below are essentially the product of conventional international law; only piracy and the laws and customs of war are the product of customary international law. But few of these conventions contain any more than general provisions for enforcement. Furthermore, all of them rely on the "indirect enforcement system," namely, reliance on national criminal justice systems for substantive and procedural enforcement. In addition, multilateral and bilateral conventions provide the framework and specifics of certain mechanisms for inter-state cooperation in penal matters. Thus, substantive and procedural international criminal law are not integrated, but juxtaposed. Lastly, national legislation makes applicable and enforceable both the substantive and procedural aspects of international criminal law.

There are 315 international instruments, elaborated mostly on an *ad hoc* basis between 1815-1988, which cover 24 categories of offenses.[23] Typically, any one of ten penal provisions characterize substantive international criminal law instruments:

1. Explicit recognition of proscribed conduct as constituting an international crime, or a crime under international law.
2. Implicit recognition of the penal nature of the act by establishing a duty to prohibit, prevent, prosecute, punish, or the like.
3. Criminalization of the proscribed conduct.
4. Duty or right to prosecute.
5. Duty or right to punish the proscribed conduct.
6. Duty or right to extradite.

---

[23] The categories of offenses are: aggression; war crimes; crimes against humanity; unlawful use of weapons; genocide; apartheid; slavery and slave-related practices; torture; unlawful human experimentation; piracy; aircraft hijacking; offenses against international maritime navigation; threat and use of force against diplomats and other international protected persons; taking of civilian hostages; drug offenses; international traffic in obscene materials; destruction or theft of national treasures; environmental violations; theft of nuclear materials; unlawful use of the mails; interference with sub-marine cables; falsification and counterfeiting; bribery of foreign public officials; and mercanerism. *See* M. Cherif Bassiouni, DRAFT STATUTE INTERNATIONAL CRIMINAL TRIBUNAL, 9 *bis* NOUVELLES ÉTUDES PÉNALES Annex 1 (1993). *See also* INTERNATIONAL CRIMES: DIGEST/INDEX OF INTERNATIONAL INSTRUMENTS 1815-1985 (M. Cherif Bassiouni ed. 1986), which digests 312 international instruments up to 1985. The three post-1985 instruments are Protocol for the Suppression of Unlawful Acts of Violence at Airports Servicing Civil Aviation, adopted by the International Civil Aviation Organization, at Montreal, Feb. 24, 1988, 27 I.L.M. 627 (1988); Convention and Protocol From the International Conference on the Suppression of Unlawful Acts Against the Safety of Maritime Navigation, adopted by the International Maritime Organization (IMO), at Rome, Mar. 10, 1988, I.M.O. Doc. SVA/CON/15; U.N. Drug Convention, *supra* note 14. *See also* UNITED NATIONS, DIVISION OF NARCOTIC DRUGS, EXTRADITION FOR DRUG-RELATED OFFENSES: A STUDY OF EXISTING EXTRADITION PRACTICES AND SUGGESTED GUIDELINES FOR USE IN CONCLUDING EXTRADITION TREATIES, ST/Nar/5 (1985).

7. Duty or right to cooperate in prosecution and punishment (including a duty to provide mutual legal assistance).

8. Establishment of a criminal jurisdictional basis.

9. Reference to the establishment of an international criminal court or international tribunal with penal characteristics.

10. No defense of obedience to superior orders.[24]

Of the above, several arise from recognition of the fact that states must cooperate with each other to enforce the substantive norms contained in a particular instrument.

The second tier of the system is made up of regional and bilateral treaties on inter-state cooperation in penal matters that facilitate the exchange of information and other enforcement functions between states. These treaties sometimes complement, or work in conjunction with, inter-state cooperation obligations contained in substantive multilateral treaties.

The third tier required to enforce international criminal law is national implementing legislation. This legislation also provides the domestic legal basis for the provision of inter-state cooperation.

Inter-state Cooperation in Penal Matters

The manner in which states cooperate with one another in the enforcement of both domestic and international criminal law is called inter-state cooperation in penal matters.[25] Inter-state cooperation in penal matters consists of six modalities or techniques: recognition of foreign penal judgments, extradition, mutual legal assistance in penal matters, transfer of penal proceedings, transfer of prisoners and, most recently, the seizure and forfeiture of the illicit proceeds of crime. The law enforcement objectives of this final modality are of special importance in controlling all forms of money laundering. The tracing, seizing and confiscation of illicit proceeds are expressly provided for in the U.N. Drug Convention and the European Money Laundering Convention, and also play a prominent role in "soft law" proposals such as the recommendations of the Financial Action Task Force.

---

[24] M. Cherif Bassiouni, *Characteristics of International Criminal Law Conventions, in* 1 INTERNATIONAL CRIMINAL LAW: CRIMES 7 (M. Cherif Bassiouni ed.,1986). Some of these penal characteristics are based on the duty to prosecute or extradite. *See* M. CHERIF BASSIOUNI & EDWARD H. WISE, AUT DEDERE AUT JUDICARE: THE DUTY TO PROSECUTE OR EXTRADITE IN INTERNATIONAL LAW (1995).

[25] This is a broad term that typically involves an obligation of the judicial, law enforcement and administrative arms of a national government to provide assistance in both criminal and administrative penal matters. The forms of cooperation that states can provide to one another are defined by both domestic and international law. Typically, the various forms of inter-state cooperation are provided through bilateral and multilateral agreements, although inter-state cooperation can be provided as a matter of comity.

Most countries require that cooperation can only be provided pursuant to national implementing legislation. In real terms, treaty obligations can only be fulfilled to the extent permitted by a state's national criminal justice system and to the extent that that system is capable of executing a request. Therefore, the effectiveness of the modalities of inter-state cooperation varies among countries. This diversity of implementation allows launderers to seek out jurisdictions where they can exploit loopholes and weaknesses of national implementation measures in order to evade the controls prescribed by international criminal law treaties and other initiatives.

The essence of international criminal law enforcement is the "indirect enforcement scheme,"[26] whereby substantive provisions contained in international criminal law conventions are enforced through national legal systems and by the cooperation of member-states. Consequently, the specificity of these modalities of international cooperation is critical to their effectiveness. These modalities are, to a great extent, accomplished in the U.N. Drug Convention and the European Money Laundering Convention (discussed *infra*), both of which contain detailed provisions delineating a state's enforcement obligations and the role of inter-state cooperation in penal matters.

Mutual Legal Assistance

Law enforcement officials in the United States and many other nations have long recognized that organized crime and drug trafficking are international endeavors and that a key to the success of these organizations is their ability to keep their illicit proceeds beyond the reach of law enforcement agencies. In the United States, for example, law enforcement officials have struggled in their efforts to investigate money laundering activities in foreign jurisdictions, even though United States courts have subpoena authority to demand the production of evidence located abroad.[27] That technique can be effective only if there exist mutual legal assistance treaties with the country where the subpoena is to have effect. Otherwise, subpoena powers in the U.S. can be enforced only through the court's civil contempt powers, and that can apply only when the court in question has *in personam* jurisdiction. Moreover, obtaining legal assistance through letters rogatory,[28] whereby a court in one jurisdiction formally seeks the assistance of a court in another jurisdiction, lacked the force of law and was inefficient, costly, and time-consuming.[29] To counter these obstacles in carrying out investigations and obtaining evidence admissible in court, the United States and many other countries have entered into mutual legal assistance treaties (MLATs) aimed at discovering, freezing and eventually forfeiting assets in other countries, including many of the world's most notorious laundering havens.[30]

---

[26] The "indirect enforcement scheme" derives from the notion that states obligate themselves, through various regional and international instruments, to enforce international criminal law. The "direct enforcement scheme," on the other hand, presupposes the existence of an international criminal code, an international criminal court, and the existence of international enforcement machinery. For a thorough discussion of both schemes and the Draft International Criminal Code and the Draft Statute for an International Criminal Tribunal, *see generally* M. Cherif Bassiouni, DRAFT STATUTE INTERNATIONAL CRIMINAL TRIBUNAL, *supra* note 23; M. Cherif Bassiouni, A DRAFT INTERNATIONAL CRIMINAL CODE AND DRAFT STATUTE FOR AN INTERNATIONAL CRIMINAL TRIBUNAL (1987).

[27] *See* 28 U.S.C. § 1783. *See also* RESTATEMENT (THIRD) OF THE FOREIGN RELATIONS LAW OF THE UNITED STATES § 473.

[28] *See* 28 U.S.C. § 1782.

[29] According to one commentator, letters rogatory "have proven ill-suited to the increasingly complex and voluminous needs of modern international law enforcement methods." *Most Effective Forms of International Cooperation for the Prevention and Control of Organized Transnational Crime at the Investigative, Prosecutorial and Judicial Levels*, U.N. Doc. E/CONF.88/4 (Sept. 1, 1994) (background document to the World Ministerial Conference on Organized Transnational Crime), ¶ 66 (citing ETHAN A. NADELMANN, COPS ACROSS BORDERS 319 (1993)).

[30] *See supra*, Chapter 12. *See also* Zagaris, *Protecting the Rule of Law from Assault in the War Against Drugs and Narco-Terrorism, supra* note 12, at 728-30 (discussing the benefits of ongoing cooperation in judicial assistance, such as the use of memoranda of understanding while MLATs are being negotiated; specifically, the author points out the value of model extradition and mutual legal assistance treaties, such as those prepared by the United Nations Crime Prevention Committee, in helping states to adopt a comprehensive treaty negotiation

Most bilateral MLATs contain 15 to 20 articles. While the precise terms may differ, MLATs (and mutual legal assistance provisions in multilateral treaties) generally provide for the following forms of assistance: (1) executing requests related to criminal matters; (2) taking of testimony or statements; (3) production of documents, records, or articles of evidence; (4) serving of judicial documents such as writs, summonses and records of judgments; (5) effecting the appearance of witnesses before the court of the requesting state; (6) locating persons; and (7) providing judicial records, evidence and information.[31] In addition to these provisions, many recent MLATs provide for the immobilization and forfeiture of assets (discussed in detail *infra*).[32] The law of the requested state will apply to the execution of all forms of assistance.

MLATs have several advantages over letters rogatory. First, MLATs represent obligations between states, while letters rogatory function merely as a matter of comity. Second, MLATs are more effective in securing evidence in a form that is admissible in United States courts. Third, MLATs are more efficient because requests travel through "central authorities;" letters rogatory must pass through courts in both countries, their respective foreign and justice ministries, and embassies.[33] Fourth, MLATs avoid the costs of employing foreign attorneys to pursue the assistance sought by a letter rogatory.[34] Fifth, letters rogatory create a situation whereby evidence may be taken in civil law jurisdictions in a manner that is not admissible in the common law country requesting the assistance.[35] Finally, MLATs are substantially more effective in overcoming bank secrecy laws that have impeded efforts to thwart organized crime and money laundering. (However, a MLAT will only supersede domestic bank secrecy laws where this is a term of the MLAT; otherwise a requesting party is as restricted as the law enforcement authorities of the requested state).

Based on the foregoing, an effective MLAT must contain these provisions that do the following: (1) expressly permit the use of the requested party's government process to obtain evidence for the entire investigation and prosecution process, including grand jury proceedings; (2) to avoid conflicts with the doctrine of "dual criminality,"[36] expressly permit the use of the requested party's process to obtain evidence for nonfamiliar or nonuniversal forms of crime (*e.g.*, money laundering, racketeering, continuing criminal enterprise, structuring, or mail fraud) in addition to traditional crimes; (3) expressly permit the waiver of the requested state's bank secrecy laws under specified conditions; and (4) expressly provide for an expedited means of securing evidence which will be admissible in the courts of the requesting state.[37] The requirements of a mutual legal assistance agreement are

---

program).

31 *See* Ellis & Pisani, *supra* note 30, at 158-59.

32 *See* Morocco (Art. 12), Italy (Art. 18), Bahamas (Art. 14), Cayman Islands (Art. 16), Canada (Art. 17), Thailand (Art. 15).

33 *See* Zagaris, *Developments in International Judicial Assistance and Related Matters*, *supra* note 12, at 351-52.

34 *See id.* at 352-53.

35 Evans, The Proceeds of Crime: Problems of Investigation and Prosecution (1994) (paper presented at the International Conference on Preventing and Controlling Money Laundering and the Use of Proceeds of Crime: A Global Approach, Courmayeur Mont Blanc, Italy, June 18-20, 1994).

36 Under this doctrine, the offenses in question must be punishable under the laws of both parties in order for assistance to be provided.

37 *See* James I.K. Knapp, *Mutual Legal Assistance Treaties as a Way to Pierce Bank Secrecy*, 20 CASE W. RES. J. INT'L L. 405, 410 (1988). Moreover, many states must enact legislation to implement these treaties because many MLATs are non-self-executing. *See id.* at 410, n.15.

considered in greater detail with respect to the U.N. Drug Convention and the European Money Laundering Convention.

The Newest Modality: The Obligation to Trace, Immobilize and Confiscate Criminal Proceeds

The requirement to trace, immobilize, and confiscate criminal proceeds has emerged as a powerful new modality of inter-state cooperation. Interestingly, this new modality is most often executed within the context of mutual legal assistance treaties. This arrangement is illustrated by the adoption by the Eighth United Nations Congress on the Prevention of Crime and the Treatment of Offenders of a U.N. Model MLAT on Mutual Assistance in Criminal Matters that includes an Optional Protocol related to "proceeds of crime."[38] Although not concerned explicitly with money laundering, the Optional Protocol deals with assistance related to the enforcement of orders authorizing the tracing, seizing and confiscating of proceeds of crime.[39] Forms of assistance to be provided by a requested state include location of proceeds of crime within its jurisdiction, tracing of assets, investigations of financial dealings, and the securing of evidence which will assist in the recovery of the proceeds of crime.[40]

Where suspected proceeds of crime are located, the requested state must take measures to prevent the dealing in, transfer, or disposal of the assets pending a final, judicial determination in relation to those proceeds.[41] These procedures will be conducted in accordance with the law of the requested state.[42] Similarly, a requested state must, to the extent allowed by its law, give effect to a final order of confiscation made by a court of the requesting state.[43] Any measure taken under the Protocol must protect the rights of *bona fide* third parties.[44]

The drafters of the Protocol recognized that, although related in many ways, immobilizing proceeds of crime is conceptually different than confiscating assets.[45] Confiscation of proceeds, as discussed *infra*, is a matter that falls under the rubric of the enforcement of penal judgments. The immobilization of assets, on the other hand, is generally accepted as a matter that falls within the modality of mutual legal assistance.[46] However, in the context of this model treaty, "proceeds of crime" and immobilization measures conducted thereon were included only as an Optional Protocol. This result reflects

---

38 G.A. Res. 45/117 (1990), *reprinted in* Eighth United Nations Congress on Crime Prevention and the Treatment of Offenders (Havana, Cuba, Aug.-Sept. 1990), A/Conf.144/28/Rev. 1, at 77-89 [hereinafter Model Treaty]. "Proceeds of crime" is defined as "any property suspected, or found by a court, to be property directly or indirectly derived or realized as a result of the commission of an offense or to represent the value of property and other benefits derived from the commission of an offense." *Id.* at Optional Protocol, ¶ 1.

39 *See* Commission on Crime Prevention and Criminal Justice, *Money Laundering and Associated Issues: The Need for International Cooperation*, U.N. Doc. No. E/CN.15/1992/4/Add.5 [hereinafter *U.N. Money Laundering Report*], ¶ 72, for a discussion of how this initiative is related to other international efforts to control the proceeds of crime.

40 Model Treaty, *supra* note 38, at Optional Protocol, ¶¶ 2-3.

41 *Id.* ¶ 4.

42 *Id.*

43 *Id.* ¶ 5.

44 *Id.* ¶ 6.

45 *Id.* at n.91.

46 *Id.*

the notion that immobilization and legal assistance, the subject of the model treaty, are conceptually and substantively different.

The Optional Protocol, the U.N. Drug Convention, and the European Money Laundering Convention contemplate that a requested state will enforce the forfeiture portion of a penal sentence handed down by a court of the requesting state. In bridging the gap between different legal systems, both Conventions allow the direct execution of an order made by a foreign court or, alternatively, the institution of confiscation proceedings in the state where the proceeds are located if so requested.[47]

For example, when confiscation is sought under the European Money Laundering Convention, a requested state is obligated to "enforce a confiscation order made by a court of a requesting Party."[48] To effect cooperation, the requesting party must submit a certified copy of the confiscation order and a statement of the grounds which served as the basis for the order. The requesting party must also certify that the confiscation order is enforceable and not subject to appeal.[49]

The Recognition of Foreign Penal Judgments

When included in a MLAT or in a multilateral agreement, the requirement to freeze and eventually forfeit proceeds derived from illicit activities will require a state, at some point, to recognize the penal judgment of another state.[50] This process is quite similar to the enforcement of a confiscation order under a treaty governing the recognition of foreign penal judgments—a modality distinct from mutual legal assistance which engenders both similar and distinct difficulties. As the European Money Laundering Convention illustrates, under legal assistance treaties and other instruments which contemplate the enforcement of confiscation orders, the modality of mutual legal assistance overlaps with the modality of the recognition of foreign penal judgments.

A treaty governing the recognition of foreign penal judgments rests on several guiding principles.[51] Under such a treaty, a state may be asked to enforce any of several types of penal sanctions, including prison sentences, fines, confiscations or disqualifications (*e.g.*, the suspension of a right, such as to practice law or medicine). The principles of dual criminality and *ne bis in idem* (double jeopardy) will be applied to and act as a restriction upon any request to enforce a penal judgment. In order for a requested state to enforce the sentencing state's penal sanction, the sentenced person must have had the opportunity to present a sufficient defense in a proceeding which recognizes basic principles of justice and human rights. Any decision must be final and enforceable. A further limitation is that the offense which resulted in a sanction or confiscation must not be of a political, military or fiscal nature.

---

[47] *See U.N. Money Laundering Report, supra* note 39, ¶ 79. For a full discussion of these seizure and confiscation procedures, *see* the textual discussion of the U.N. Drug Convention and the Euro. Conv. Money Laundering *infra* pt. III.A-B.

[48] Euro. Conv. Money Laundering, *supra* note 16, at Art. 13(1)(a).

[49] *Id.* at Art. 27(3).

[50] Confiscation may be treated as a penal measure at the administrative level in some states and at the criminal level in other states. In either case, these measures will be considered to the extent that they are penal or punitive in nature.

[51] *See* European Convention on the International Validity of Criminal Judgements, May 28, 1970, Europ. T.S. No. 70. For a more thorough discussion of the transfer or recognition of foreign penal judgments, *see supra*, Chapters 9 and 17.

Generally, in making a request, a state must submit the following: (1) a certified copy of the decision or order; (2) a description of the offense which gave rise to the sanction; (3) a copy of the provision under which the act or omission is considered an offense; (4) a description of the sanction (*e.g.*, confiscation of assets); (5) an indication of any portion of the sanction which has already been enforced; (6) a statement of the identity and location of the person sought; and, (7) in the case of confiscation, information relating to the property sought.[52]

Many of these provisions and general requirements parallel those of the U.N. Drug Convention and the European Money Laundering Convention, evidencing an overlap of these modalities in the various instruments. This overlap is problematic and suggests that in the area of the seizure and forfeiture of assets a separate convention should be concluded which governs the recognition of that particular form of penal judgment.

Approaches to Inter-state Cooperation in Penal Matters

The "Bilateral Approach"

While inter-state cooperation in penal matters can surely be a subject of multilateral arrangements, it has most often been the subject of bilateral efforts covering only one of the six modalities of inter-state cooperation. The "bilateral approach" to inter-state cooperation in penal matters, which forces states to rely on a web of agreements, has been criticized for its piecemeal results and the quirks of historical, political and diplomatic factors which eventually influence and undermine these agreements.[53] In addition, these enforcement modalities arise under diverse international, regional, and national law-making processes,[54] and their application differs in scope and legal technique.

States are generally more comfortable with the "bilateral approach," despite its inadequacies. Governments prefer to deal bilaterally with their closest allies, partners, friends, and those they can pressure into accepting bilateral terms, as opposed to dealing with the complex and competing interests of many governments in the context of multilateral

---

52 These provisions and requirements are primarily derived from the Draft U.N. Model MLAT on the Transfer of Enforcement of Penal Sanctions prepared by a Committee of Experts which convened December 3-8, 1991, at the International Institute of Higher Studies in Criminal Sciences in Siracusa, Italy. The conference was sponsored by the Institute, the United Nations Crime Prevention and Criminal Justice Branch and the International Association of Penal Law. The document is contemplated as a United Nations U.N. Model MLAT to be added to the package of United Nations Model Treaties in the area of international criminal cooperation, which presently includes the Model Agreement on the Transfer of Foreign Prisoners, U.N. Model MLAT on Extradition, U.N. Model MLAT on Mutual Assistance in Criminal Matters, U.N. Model MLAT on the Transfer of Proceedings in Criminal Matters, U.N. Model MLAT on the Transfer of Supervision of Offenders Conditionally Sentenced or Conditionally Released and U.N. Model MLAT for the Prevention of Crimes that Infringe on the Cultural Heritage of Peoples in the Form of Movable Property. For a discussion of these model agreements, *see generally* Roger S. Clark, *Crime: The U.N. Agenda on International Cooperation in the Criminal Process*, 15 NOVA L. REV. 475 (1991).

53 *See generally* M. Cherif Bassiouni, *Policy Considerations on Inter-State Cooperation in Criminal Matters, in* PRINCIPLES AND PROCEDURES FOR A NEW TRANSNATIONAL CRIMINAL LAW 807 (Albin Eser & Otto Lagodny eds., 1992).

54 *See generally supra*, Chapters 8, 9, 10, 12, 16, 17 and 18. *See also* G.O.W. Mueller, *Enforcement Models of International Criminal Law, in* NEW HORIZONS IN INTERNATIONAL CRIMINAL LAW 85 (1985); Julian Schutte, *Expanding the Scope of Extradition and Judicial Assistance and Cooperation in Penal Matters, in* NEW HORIZONS IN INTERNATIONAL CRIMINAL LAW 79 (1985).

treaty negotiations. But their reliance on bilateralism (and regionalism to a lesser extent) has resulted in agreements which generally contain only one or a few of the methods of international penal cooperation, thereby failing to integrate several modalities into a single, enforceable instrument. The result of this approach is that a state must rely on one of several instruments depending on the type of cooperation required, and this fragmentation creates a number of gaps and loopholes which often make these bilateral agreements ineffective.[55]

The "Bilateral Approach" in Practice: U.S. Experience with Mutual Legal Assistance Treaties

The United States has consistently adhered to the principles of the bilateral approach, erecting a comprehensive framework of MLATs in the war on drugs and money laundering. The United States concluded the first of these treaties with Switzerland in 1973.[56] Since then, the United States has concluded and ratified MLATs with the following countries: Argentina,[57] the Bahamas,[58] Belgium,[59] Canada,[60] the Cayman Islands,[61] Colombia,[62] Italy,[63] Jamaica,[64] Mexico,[65] Morocco,[66] the Netherlands,[67] Spain,[68] Thailand,[69] Turkey[70] and

---

[55] *See* Bassiouni, *supra* note 9, at 37-40. *See also* Zagaris, *Developments in International Judicial Assistance and Related Matters, supra* note 12, at 355-57.

[56] Treaty on Mutual Assistance in Criminal Matters, May 25, 1973, U.S.-Switzerland, 27 U.S.T. 2019, 12 I.L.M. 916 (*entered into force* Jan. 23, 1977) [hereinafter Swiss Treaty].

[57] Treaty on Mutual Legal Assistance in Criminal Matters, Dec. 4, 1990, U.S.-Argentina, S. TREATY DOC. NO. 18, 102d Cong., 1st Sess (1991) (*entered into force* Feb. 9, 1993).

[58] Treaty on Mutual Legal Assistance in Criminal Matters, Aug. 18, 1987, U.S.-Bahamas, S. TREATY DOC. NO. 16, 100th Cong., 2d Sess. (1988) (*entered into force* July 18, 1990).

[59] Treaty on Mutual Legal Assistance in Criminal Matters, Jan. 28, 1988, U.S.-Belgium, S. TREATY DOC. NO. 16, 100th Cong., 2d Sess. (1988) (advice and consent of the U.S. Senate Oct. 24, 1989).

[60] Treaty on Mutual Legal Assistance, Dec. 9, 1987, U.S.-Canada, S. TREATY DOC. NO. 13, 100th Cong., 2d Sess (1988), 24 I.L.M. 109 (*entered into force* Jan. 24, 1990).

[61] Treaty Between the United States and the United Kingdom of Great Britain and Northern Ireland Concerning the Cayman Islands Relating to Mutual Legal Assistance in Criminal Matters, July 3, 1986, S. TREATY DOC. NO. 8, 100th Cong., 2d Sess. (1987), 26 I.L.M. 536 (*entered into force* Mar. 19, 1990) [hereinafter Cayman Islands Treaty].

[62] Treaty on Mutual Legal Assistance, Aug. 20, 1980, U.S.-Colombia, S. TREATY DOC. NO. 11, 97th Cong., 1st Sess. (1981) (advice and consent of the U.S. Senate Dec. 2, 1981). This treaty is not likely to come into force due to Columbia's failure to ratify the instrument based on that nation's political climate. *See* Knapp, *supra* note 37, at 413, n.31.

[63] Treaty on Mutual Assistance in Criminal Matters, Nov. 9, 1982, U.S.-Italy, S. TREATY DOC. NO. 25, 98th Cong., 2d Sess. (1984), 24 I.L.M. 1536 (*entered into force* Nov. 13, 1985) [hereinafter Italian Treaty].

[64] Treaty on Mutual Legal Assistance in Criminal Matters, July 7, 1989, U.S.-Jamaica, S. TREATY DOC. NO. 16, 102d Cong., 1st Sess. (1991) (advice and consent of the U.S. Senate July 2, 1992).

[65] Treaty on Mutual Legal Assistance in Criminal Matters, Dec. 9, 1987, U.S.-Mexico, S. TREATY DOC. NO. 13, 100th Cong., 2d Sess. (1988) (*entered into force* May 3, 1991).

[66] Convention on Mutual Assistance in Criminal Matters, Oct. 17, 1983, U.S.-Morocco, S. TREATY DOC. NO. 24, 98th Cong., 2d Sess. (1984) (advice and consent of the U.S. Senate June 29, 1984).

[67] Treaty on Mutual Legal Assistance in Criminal Matters, June 12, 1981, U.S.-Netherlands, T.I.A.S. No. 10734, 21 I.L.M. 48 (*entered into force* Sept. 15, 1983) [hereinafter Netherlands Treaty].

[68] Treaty on Mutual Legal Assistance, Nov. 20, 1990, U.S.-Spain, S. TREATY DOC. NO. 21, 102d Cong., 2d Sess. (1992) (*entered into force* June 30, 1993).

[69] Treaty on Mutual Assistance in Criminal Matters, Mar. 19, 1987, U.S.-Thailand, S. TREATY DOC. NO. 18, 100th Cong., 2d Sess. (1988) (*entered into force* June 10, 1993).

[70] Treaty on Extradition and Mutual Assistance in Criminal Matters, June 7, 1979, U.S.-Turkey, 32 U.S.T. 3111 (*entered into force* June 1, 1981).

Uruguay.[71] MLATs with Nigeria,[72] Panama,[73] the Republic of Korea,[74] and the United Kingdom and Northern Ireland[75] have been signed but not ratified.

The United States has also entered into several interim executive agreements which cover only drug offenses with the Turks and Caicos Islands,[76] Montserrat,[77] Anguilla[78] and the British Virgin Islands.[79] In addition, the United States has entered into interim executive agreements providing formal liaison procedures for exchange of evidence (while also calling for the negotiation of a complete MLAT) with Haiti,[80] Great Britain,[81] and Nigeria.[82] Finally, the United States has entered into negotiations with West Germany, Australia, Sweden, and Israel in the hopes of concluding MLATs.

In concluding MLATs, the United States has focused its efforts on nations that have traditionally been havens for laundered funds or sources of narcotics and illicit drugs.[83] With this purpose in mind, one of the primary forms of assistance is the procurement of financial bank or corporate records.[84] Therefore, it is crucial that any MLAT concluded by the United States contain a provision which allows the United States to pierce the other nation's bank secrecy laws.[85]

---

71 Treaty on Mutual Legal Assistance in Criminal Matters, May 6, 1991, U.S.-Uruguay, S. TREATY DOC. NO. 19, 102d Cong., 1st Sess. (1991) (advice and consent of the U.S. Senate July 2, 1992).

72 Treaty on Mutual Assistance in Criminal Matters, Sept. 13, 1989, U.S.-Nigeria, S. TREATY DOC. NO. 26, 102d Cong., 2d Sess (1992).

73 Treaty on Mutual Assistance in Criminal Matters, Apr. 11, 1991, U.S.-Panama, S. TREATY DOC. NO. 15, 102d Cong., 1st Sess (1991).

74 Treaty on Mutual Legal Assistance on Criminal Matters, U.S.-Korea, S. TREATY DOC. NO. 104-1 (transmitted to the Senate Jan. 12, 1995).

75 July 6, 1994.

76 *See* Exchange of Letters concerning the Turks and Caicos Islands and any Matter Related to any Activity Referred to in the Single Convention on Narcotic Drugs (1961), as amended Sept. 6, 1986, U.S.-U.K., *cited in* DEP'T ST. BULL., June 1987.

77 *See* Exchange of Letters concerning Montserrat and Matters Related to any Activity Referred to in the Single Convention on Narcotic Drugs (1961), as amended May 14, 1987, U.S.-U.K., *cited in* DEP'T ST. BULL., Aug. 1987.

78 *See* Exchange of Letters concerning Anguilla and Matters Related to any Activity Referred to in the Single Convention on Narcotic Drugs (1961), as amended Mar. 11, 1987, U.S.-U.K., *cited in* DEP'T ST. BULL., June 1987.

79 *See* Exchange of Letters concerning the British Virgin Islands and any Matter Related to any Activity Referred to in the Single Convention on Narcotic Drugs (1961), as amended Apr. 14, 1987, U.S.-U.K., *cited in* DEP'T ST. BULL., Sept. 1987.

80 *See* Agreement on Procedures for Mutual Assistance in Law Enforcement Matters, Aug. 15, 1987, U.S.-Haiti, T.I.A.S. No. 11389.

81 *See* Interim Executive Agreement Concerning the Investigation of Drug Trafficking Offenses and the Seizure and Forfeiture of Proceeds and Instrumentalities of Drug Trafficking, Feb. 9, 1988, U.S.-Great Britain.

82 *See* Agreement on Procedures for Mutual Assistance in Law Enforcement Matters, Nov. 2, 1987, U.S.-Nigeria.

83 *See* S. Rep. on Bahamas MLAT, S. TREATY DOC. NO. 16, Exec. Rept. 100-27, 100th Cong., 2d Sess. 1988:

> The committee believes that [MLATs] are a key element in the U.S. strategy to improve international cooperation against crime, particularly narcotics-related offenses such as RICO, CCE and money laundering. The Bahamas are a major transit point for narcotics trafficking and an important international banking center. The MLAT with the Bahamas will assist U.S. efforts to obtain bank records and other evidence of narcotics related money laundering.

Id. at 3-4.

84 *See generally* James D. Harmon, *United States Money Laundering Laws: International Implications*, 9 N.Y.L. SCH. J. INT'L & COMP. L. 1, 25 (1988).

85 *Id.*

To a great extent, the terms of an MLAT must be tailored to the specific needs of the two states. For instance, the MLAT with Canada provides for wide assistance and cooperation due to the shared border and the large volume of cases.[86] Briefly, other examples include: (1) the focus on bank secrecy in the Swiss MLAT; (2) the conclusion of an MLAT with Belgium based on that nation's financial status and legal system; and 3) the focus on inbound investment found in MLATs concluded with offshore banking centers (the Bahamas, the Cayman Islands, the Dutch Antilles, etc.).[87]

MLATs are not only beneficial to the United States, and the treaties are not merely efforts to protect United States interests at the expense of a smaller state's banking industry.[88] First, all nations have an interest in suppressing the effects of drug trafficking (*e.g.*, related crime and local drug addiction). Second, a state may need to obtain evidence from the United States in order to effectuate local law enforcement. Third, states generally prefer to maintain friendly relations with the United States and seek to avoid United States legislation which is adverse to their interests. Fourth, states seek to discourage unilateral law enforcement measures (*e.g.*, subpoenas *duces tecum* and other "self-help" methods) which infringe on foreign sovereignty and foreign interests.[89]

The Swiss Treaty

An appropriate starting point in analyzing United States experience with bilateral MLATs is the U.S.-Swiss MLAT(signed in 1973 and in force since 1977).[90] Since the treaty has been in force, the United States has made approximately three times more requests for judicial assistance than the Swiss have made.[91] The use of the treaty has generally been very successful and has led to scores of federal and state convictions.[92] A recent use of the treaty

---

86 *See* Bruce Zagaris, *Dollar Diplomacy: International Enforcement of Money Movement and Related Matters—A United States Perspective*, 22 GEO. WASH. J. INT'L. L. & ECON. 465, 498 (1989), and sources cited therein.

87 *Id.* at 498-99 and sources cited therein.

88 *See* Knapp, *supra* note 37, at 411.

89 *Id.* Consider this statement by Swiss Justice Minister Elisabeth Kopp:

> Increased economic interdependence has led to increased numbers of requests regarding new forms of criminality. International mutual assistance is, contrary to the popular perception in Switzerland, not a one side process. Although U.S. authorities have made three times as many requests as the Swiss, our authorities have been able to obtain search and seizure or freeze orders in the U.S. too.

WALL ST. J., Oct. 28, 1987, at 33 (emphasis added). *See also* HANS SCHULTZ, BANKING SECRECY AND MUTUAL ASSISTANCE IN CRIMINAL MATTERS (Swiss Bank Corp., 1983).

90 Swiss Treaty, *supra* note 56. The discussion of the U.S.-Swiss MLAT will be the most thorough for several reasons: (1) being the first treaty, the lessons learned from use of the U.S.-Swiss MLAT often apply to the other MLATs; and (2) the purpose of the U.S.-Swiss MLAT was to pierce bank secrecy and there is extensive documentation of the way the Swiss MLAT has helped to pierce Swiss bank secrecy laws.

91 This figure applies to the first eight years that the treaty has been in force (1977-85). *See* Exec. Rep. 100-30, 100th Cong., 2d Sess., Sept. 26, 1988, Bahamas MLAT Report, *supra* note 83, at 1. *See also* Knapp, *supra* note 37, at 414 (for the first six years the U.S. made 202 requests to Switzerland's 65 requests).

92 During the first six years that the treaty was in force, the evidence obtained contributed to over 145 convictions. Notably, mutual assistance from Switzerland contributed to the fraudulent transactions and money-laundering convictions of Michele Sindona (United States v. Sindona, 636 F.2d 792 (2d Cir. 1980), *cert. denied*, 451 U.S. 912 (1981)) and mobster Anthony Giacalone (United States v. Giacalone, No. S 80 Cr. 123 S.D.N.Y., indictment filed Feb. 6, 1980). These convictions were facilitated by access to Swiss bank and business records. *See* Knapp, *supra* note 37, at 415.

resulted in the seizure from Zurich bank accounts of US$150 million in drug money sought by United States officials.[93]

However, the U.S.-Swiss MLAT has been plagued by one basic problem. Swiss law allows requests to be challenged and litigated, with objections considered seriatim rather than jointly.[94] The obvious result is that delays in obtaining evidence may be particularly severe when the legitimacy of the request is challenged.[95] Another result of Article 36(a)[96] of the treaty has been to warn suspects of government investigations earlier than required by the Federal Rules of Criminal Procedure.[97]

Another provision also operates to slow United States investigations and provides suspects with an opportunity to cover their tracks. Article 29(1)(a) requires that all requests include "the subject matter of the nature of the investigation or proceeding" and a description of the "essential acts alleged or sought to be ascertained."[98] This provision can tip off suspects to the government's case and affords them an opportunity to prepare their defense much earlier than they would be able to in the United States.[99] Moreover, this early disclosure may result in "sticking" the prosecution with a theory of the case which is not yet certain and which, under Article 36(a), will be open to challenge in the Swiss courts.[100]

One of the primary United States objectives in negotiating the U.S.-Swiss MLAT was to pierce the Swiss bank secrecy laws.[101] Article 47 of the Swiss Banking Code[102] and Article 273 of the Swiss Penal Code[103] had, for years, blocked United States efforts to obtain bank and business records. In the MLAT, the Swiss sought to protect the identities of innocent third parties whose names appear on requested documents and to prevent the United States from using the information obtained for the prosecution of fiscal (*e.g.*, tax) offenses.[104]

In respect to the first concern, the United States sought to eradicate the Swiss practice of excising the names of third parties from requested documents (a practice which made the documents inadmissible in United States courts and disrupted the "paper trail"). Article 10

---

93 *Most Effective Forms of International Cooperation for the Prevention and Control of Organized Transnational Crime at the Investigative, Prosecutorial and Judicial Levels*, U.N. Doc. E/CONF.88/4 (Sept. 1, 1994) ¶ 68 (background document to the World Ministerial Conference on Organized Transnational Crime), (citing *U.S.-Swiss MLAT Yields $150 Million Seizure in Swiss Bank*, Money Laundering Alert, May 1994, at 3).

94 *See* Swiss Treaty, *supra* note 56, at Art. 37, § 2 which provides that Swiss law and procedure will govern the validity of a treaty request to Switzerland.

95 *See* Knapp, *supra* note 37, at 415-16.

96 Art. 36(a) provides in pertinent part that "upon receipt of a request for assistance, the requested state shall notify . . . any person from whom a statement or testimony or documents, records, or articles of evidence are sought." Swiss Treaty, *supra* note 56, at Art. 36(a).

97 This early warning also gives suspects an opportunity to move the assets before they can be detected and thus destroy the paper trail. *See* Ethan A. Nadelmann, *Negotiations in Criminal Law Assistance Treaties*, 33 AM. J. COMP. L. 467, 479 (1985).

98 *See* Swiss Treaty, *supra* note 56, at Art. 29(1)(a).

99 *See* Nadelmann, *supra* note 97, at 479. In United States courts, defendants usually do not learn of the theory of the government's case until the indictment is returned.

100 *Id.*

101 *See* Nadelmann, *supra* note 97, at 472-74. Much of Nadelmann's research included interviews with the United States negotiators of the Swiss Treaty.

102 Swiss Banking Code Article 47 provides that any officer or employee of a bank who violates his duty of secrecy or anyone who induces or attempts to so induce a person to violate that duty may face six months imprisonment or a fine of 50,000 francs.

103 Swiss Penal Code Article 273 makes it a crime to "elicit a manufacturing or business secret in order to make it available to any foreign official agency or to a foreign organization or private enterprise" either directly or through an agent, and to make such secrets available to such foreign authorities or organizations.

104 *See* Nadelmann, *supra* note 97, at 476-77.

of the treaty respects this Swiss concern by allowing the requested party to balance the interest of an innocent party with the importance of the criminal proceeding in the requesting state.[105] This provision may be construed to mean that the Swiss will allow the piercing of bank secrecy only if the United States demonstrates a compelling interest.[106]

This article generally sets forth conditions where testimony or production of documents will not be compelled (*e.g.*, attorney/client privilege). However, Article 10 does not comprehend bank secrecy laws as providing any source of a right to remain silent.[107] Moreover, execution of a request which would mean the disclosure of information normally protected by bank secrecy does not implicate Article 3(1)(a) as a request "likely to prejudice its sovereignty, security or similar essential interest."[108]

A primary motivation for the conclusion of this treaty was the mutual concern that organized crime had, for years, used Swiss bank secrecy laws to secrete illicit proceeds. The result of this concern was a special section, Articles 6-8, governing organized crime. Generally, when an investigation concerns organized crime, the Swiss must render assistance even when the alleged offenses do not meet the dual criminality test or do not appear on the Schedule.[109]

However, if the request concerns an investigation for income tax violations, requests will be honored only when the suspect is an "upper echelon" figure.[110] Even if the suspect is such a figure, the United States must demonstrate that assistance: (1) is essential to the case; (2) will facilitate the successful prosecution; (3) will result in imprisonment for a significant period of time; and (4) that such imprisonment will have a significant adverse effect on the criminal organization.[111] This Article also overrides Article 5's requirement of "specialty of use," a provision designed to prevent the use of requested information for the purpose of prosecuting tax offenses.

While the U.S.-Swiss MLAT has generally been effective in the prosecution of organized crime (through the use of other provisions), the organized crime provisions have rarely been utilized.[112] The treaty has been seen as successful, in part, because publicity surrounding it and the possibility of piercing bank secrecy laws have encouraged organized crime to seek out alternative tax and banking havens, primarily Caribbean, offshore banks.[113]

---

105 *See id.* at 477. *See also* Swiss Treaty, *supra* note 56, at Art. 10(2). However, even if an innocent third party is implicated, Switzerland is required to furnish the information if these conditions are met:

(1) the request concerns the investigation or prosecution of a serious offense;

(2) the disclosure is of importance for obtaining or proving facts which are of substantial significance for the investigation of proceeding;

(3) reasonable but unsuccessful efforts have been made in the United States to obtain the information in other ways.

Id. See Technical Analysis of the Treaty Between the United States and Switzerland on Mutual Assistance in Criminal Matters [hereinafter Technical Analysis], at 48.

106 Technical Analysis, *supra* note 105.

107 *Id.* This provision is not substantially different from Swiss jurisprudence which allows the piercing of bank secrecy where the government interest is compelling. *See* Exec. Rept. 94-29, 94th Cong., 2d Session, at 5.

108 *Id.*

109 *See* Nadelmann, *supra* note 97, at 478.

110 *Id.*

111 *Id. See also* Swiss Treaty, *supra* note 56, at Art. 7(a-c).

112 This lack of use can probably be attributed to a lack of Swiss cooperation and a paucity of United States requests due to the stringent criteria. *See* Nadelmann, *supra* note 97, at 478-79.

113 *Id.* at 479.

This result has been viewed as generally beneficial because depositors (criminals) have less confidence in the banking systems of Caribbean nations with bank secrecy laws.[114]

Because the U.S.-Swiss MLAT was the first MLAT negotiated by the United States, subsequent treaties have been negotiated with the benefit of the protracted negotiations that produced the Swiss Treaty. Several lessons were learned from the conclusion of that MLAT: (1) the avoidance of drawn-out and complex negotiations; (2) avoidance of long and complex clauses; and (3) limitation of the number of clauses.[115] These objectives, as shall be seen, have largely been met, considering the brevity (15-20 articles) and relative simplicity of the subsequent MLATs negotiated by the United States.

The Netherlands Treaty

The U.S.-Netherlands MLAT has been functioning well and is used to obtain evidence and information approximately 25 times per year (the Dutch make about half as many requests per year).[116] About half of these requests concern the Dutch Antilles—an offshore banking and tax haven.[117] The United States was particularly interested in concluding this agreement because it would provide a model for MLATs with other European states; moreover, the Dutch have a liberal view on international cooperation in penal matters and are interested in innovative methods of assistance.[118] The treaty calls for double criminality (offenses punishable in both states for more than one year) in order to execute searches and seizures or to compel the production of documents. An annex requires assistance for various tax offenses which carry a maximum of one year imprisonment.[119]

Tax matters are a significant part of the U.S.-Netherlands MLAT because the United States was renegotiating its tax treaty with the Dutch at the same time as the MLAT negotiations.[120] Desiring (to some extent) to protect their tax haven status, the Dutch reserved the right to refuse assistance for fiscal offenses until the Tax Treaty had been renegotiated.[121]

The Turkish and Italian Treaties

The Turkish Treaty has been used 98 times by the Turks while the United States has made only one request.[122] Similarly, the U.S.-Italian MLAT has been used approximately twice as often by Italy as by the United States during the first two years that the treaty has

114 *Id.* at 478-79.

115 *Id.* at 482-83.

116 *See* Knapp, *supra* note 37, at 416.

117 *Id.*

118 *See* Nadelmann, *supra* note 97, at 488.

119 *Id.* at 489. *See also* 26 U.S.C. § 7203.

120 Nadelmann, *supra* note 97, at 489-91. As a result the IRS played a key role in the negotiation of the Netherlands MLAT. The IRS sought to repeal the Dutch Antilles status as a tax haven (as granted by the 1963 U.S.-Netherlands Tax Treaty) as the Antilles had become "one of the four countries having the most 'iron clad secrecy.'" Statement of Asst. Sec'y of the Treasury in Charge of Enforcement, Hearings Before the Commerce, Consumer and Monetary Affairs Committee, 98th Cong., 1st Sess., at 569.

121 Nadelmann, *supra* note 97, at 491. *See also* Netherlands Treaty, *supra* note 67, at Art. 20.

122 *See* Knapp, *supra* note 37, at 416 (as of 1988). *See also* Nadelmann, *supra* note 97, at 483-84, for an interesting discussion of the impact of the film *Midnight Express* on the MLAT negotiation process (a package which resulted in prisoner transfer, extradition and legal assistance provisions).

been in force.[123] These statistics are likely attributable to two factors: (1) neither Turkey nor Italy is a bank secrecy jurisdiction; and (2) many Turks and Italians (and their relatives) reside in and travel to the United States.[124]

Two particular points of interest in the U.S.-Italian MLAT are the forfeiture provisions of Article 18 and the international subpoena provision of Article 15. Article 18 provides for the immobilization and forfeiture of assets.[125] The forfeiture provisions are contingent on implementing legislation; however, it was agreed that ratification would not be delayed by the enactment of legislation. The United States inactivity in this regard had been a point of contention.[126] Similar provisions appear in most of the MLATs concluded after the Italian Treaty. Article 15's provisions for the taking of testimony in the requesting state represents the first instance where the barrier of witness consent was removed.[127]

The Cayman Islands Treaty

Of the MLATs most recently concluded, the U.S.-Cayman Islands MLAT has been especially effective.[128] Since it entered into force in 1987, nearly one hundred requests have

---

123 *Id.*

124 The U.S.-Italian MLAT was used extensively in the "Pizza Connection" prosecution, allowing several Italian police officers to travel to New York in order to testify. *See* United States v. Badalamenti, 626 F.Supp. 658 (S.D.N.Y. 1986). The Italians also made extensive use of the MLAT during the "Maxi-Trial" in Sicily where over 400 defendants were prosecuted (including two money launderers). *See* Giovani Abate and 467 People, No. 2289-92 (Palermo).

125 Article 18 of the U.S. - Italian MLAT provides as follows:

Immobilization and Forfeiture of Assets

1. In emergency situations, the Requested State shall have authority to immobilize assets found in that state which are subject to forfeiture.
2. Following such judicial proceedings as would be required under the laws of the Requested State, that State shall have the authority to order the forfeiture to the Requesting State of assets immobilized pursuant to paragraph 1 of this Article.

Italian Treaty, *supra* note 63. The effect of paragraph 2 is that the proceeds forfeited profit the requesting state. This arrangement provides incentive for a requested party to provide assistance. *Id.*

126 *See* Nadelmann, *supra* note 97, at 494. A provision in the Anti-Drug Abuse Act of 1986 has eradicated this problem. 18 U.S.C. § 981 provides statutory authority 1) to forfeit the proceeds of a foreign drug trafficking offense and 2) when authorized by a treaty, to sell the property and transfer the proceeds to a foreign country (at least where there has been joint participation in the investigation leading to the proceeds). *See* Knapp, *supra* note 37, at 423 for a discussion of how proceeds should be disposed of once confiscated by the requested state.

127 Article 15 of the U.S.-Italian MLAT provides as follows:

Taking Testimony in the Requesting State

1. The Requested State upon request that a person in that State appear and testify in connection with a criminal investigation or proceeding in the Requesting State, shall compel that person to appear and testify in the Requesting State by means of the procedures for compelling the appearance and testimony of witnesses in the Requested State if:

a. the Requested State has no reasonable basis to deny the request

b. the person could be compelled to appear and testify similar circumstances in the Requested State; and

c. the Central Authority of the Requesting State certifies that the person's testimony is relevant and material.

2. A person who fails to appear as directed shall be subject to sanctions under the laws of the Requested State as if that person had failed to appear in similar circumstances in that State. Such sanctions shall not include removal of the person to the Requesting State.

Italian Treaty, *supra* note 63. Article 17(1)(b) provides protection for a witness compelled to testify by granting immunity from prosecution based on truthful testimony. *Id.*

128 These figures refer to the Cayman Islands Agreement (*see* Exchange of Letters Concerning the Cayman Islands and Matters Connected with any Narcotics Activity Referred to In the Single Convention Narcotic Drugs 1961, *as amended* July 26, 1984, U.S.-U.K., 14 I.L.M. 1110), which was utilized since 1984 and until the

been made to the Cayman Islands and the evidence thus obtained has contributed to the conviction of 95 drug traffickers.[129] This assistance has been particularly helpful in asset forfeiture proceedings pursuant to Article 16.[130]

The "Integrated Approach"

The clearest way to overcome the problems inherent in the "bilateral approach" is to conclude, instead, multilateral or regional agreements which are more comprehensive and integrate several modalities of international cooperation.[131] The various modalities of inter-state cooperation should be integrated in a comprehensive codification that would permit the cumulative and alternative use of these modalities, enhance their effectiveness, and streamline cooperation efforts.[132] The integration of several modalities of cooperation could be adopted at the domestic level (in national legislation) and the bilateral, sub-regional, regional, and multilateral levels (in treaties on inter-state cooperation and substantive international criminal law). With a comprehensive instrument at their disposal, law enforcement authorities will be able to easily shift from one modality to another and utilize a uniform set of procedures, no longer having to resort to a separate instrument with a separate set of procedures for each type of cooperation sought.

The Council of Europe has been considering this type of integrated approach since 1987 on the basis of a project developed by an *ad hoc* Committee of Experts, which convened twice at the International Institute of Higher Studies in Criminal Sciences in Siracusa, Italy. There, the Committee of Experts determined that the Council of Europe should integrate all of the European Conventions into a single, integrated code of inter-state penal cooperation.

---

ratification of the Cayman Islands Treaty.

[129] *See* Knapp, *supra* note 37, at 417, and sources cited therein. Of those 95 convictions, one-third were convicted of CCE (18 U.S.C. § 848) violations. This is a much higher percentage than the total number of defendants charged in the overall enforcement task force program. *Id.*

[130] This provision is important because it is similar to the provisions in the five other treaties concluded at the same time. Article 16 of the U.S.-Cayman Islands MLAT provides as follows:

Proceeds of Crime

1. The Central Authority of one Party may notify the Central Authority of the Other Party when it has reason to believe that proceeds of a criminal offense are located in the territory of the other Party.
2. The Parties shall assist each other to the extent permitted by their respective laws in proceedings related to:

(a) the forfeiture of the proceeds of criminal offenses;
(b) restitution to the victims of criminal offenses; and
(c) the collection of fines imposed as a sentence for a criminal offense.

Cayman Islands Treaty, *supra* note 61.

[131] *See generally* M. Cherif Bassiouni, *Critical Reflections on International and National Control of Drugs*, 18 DENV. J. INT'L. L. & POL'Y 311, 331-34 (1990). This recommendation must not be seen, however, as a suggestion that bilateral treaties are *per se* limited to a single modality while multilateral treaties necessarily represent the integration of a number of modalities. Certainly, bilateral legal assistance treaties may contain a number of modalities while multilateral treaties may, in some instances, concern only a single modality.

[132] An important issue to consider in adopting an integrated approach is which modalities of inter-state penal cooperation are sufficiently accepted as to be included in a comprehensive instrument. Legal assistance provisions contained in broadly-negotiated multilateral conventions provide excellent examples of widely accepted norms. Also, model treaties on various forms of inter-state cooperation provide excellent examples of widely applicable provisions for each modality because they reflect differences in legal systems and contain only widely agreed-upon provisions.

This conclusion was supported by a Resolution of the Council of Ministers of Justice in 1987 and the development of a Draft Comprehensive Convention.[133]

Whether on the global, regional, bilateral or domestic level, an integrated approach to inter-state cooperation is an eminently desirable course of conduct. Regrettably, however, it has not gained much governmental support on the international, regional and domestic levels. This result is somewhat surprising in light of the fact that Austria, Germany and Switzerland have successfully implemented legislation that integrates several forms of inter-state cooperation in a single act.[134] In addition, both the U.N. Drug Convention and the European Money Laundering Convention, discussed *infra*, employ an integrated approach to inter-state cooperation, albeit in a limited fashion.

Much of the work of the United Nations has acknowledged the need to harmonize and make consistent inter-state cooperation efforts. The United Nations General Assembly has adopted a series of model treaties on inter-state penal cooperation approved by the Eighth United Nations Congress on the Prevention of Crime and the Treatment of Offenders (Havana, August-September 1990). The United Nations has developed the following model treaties on legal assistance: *U.N. Model MLAT on Extradition,*[135] *U.N. Model MLAT on Mutual Assistance in Criminal Matters* and its Optional Protocol on the freezing and seizing of illicit proceeds,[136] and *U.N. Model MLAT on the Transfer of Proceedings in Criminal Matters.*[137] The General Assembly also adopted measures for international cooperation for crime prevention and criminal justice.

These model treaties are expected to provide a useful framework for states interested in negotiating bilateral arrangements in these areas. They provide excellent examples of widely applicable provisions for each modality because they reflect differences in legal

---

133 *See* Council of Europe, Rec. No. R/87/1 of the Committee of Ministers of Justice to the Member States on Inter-State Cooperation in Penal Matters among Member States (adopted Jan. 19, 1987). The *Draft (European) Comprehensive Convention on Inter-State Cooperation in the Penal Field* contains provisions applicable to most forms of legal assistance and individual sections relating to the individual types of inter-state cooperation. That instrument suggests four types of cooperation: extradition, mutual legal assistance, prosecution (*e.g.*, transfer of proceedings), and enforcement and supervision (*e.g.*, recognition of foreign penal judgements and transfer of proceedings). The original text of this instrument is contained in 2 EUROPEAN INTER-STATE CO-OPERATION IN CRIMINAL MATTERS: THE COUNCIL OF EUROPE'S LEGAL INSTRUMENTS 1661 (Ekkehart Müller-Rappard & M. Cherif Bassiouni eds., rev'd 2d ed. 1993). The revised version of that text is contained in *Draft European Comprehensive Convention on International Co-òperation in Criminal Matters, reprinted in,* Council of Europe, European Committee in Crime Problems, *Committee of Experts on the Operation of European Conventions in the Penal Field: Interim Activity Report*, PC-OC (94) 5 (Strasbourg, Apr. 21, 1994).

134 National laws in Austria, Germany, and Switzerland utilize more than one modality in a single law. *See* Austrian Law on Mutual Assistance in Criminal Matters, Bundesgesetz vom 4, December 1979, über die Auslieferung und die Rechtshilfe in Strafsachen (AHRG), BGBI. Nr. 529/1979; (Germany) Act Concerning International Mutual Assistance in Criminal Matters, "Gesetz über die Internationale Rechtshilfe in Strafsachen" (Dec. 31, 1982, *entered into force* Jan. 7, 1983), BGBI, Teil I, S. 2071 (Federal Official Gazette); and Swiss Federal Law on International Mutual Assistance in Criminal Matters, S.R. 353.1 (Jan. 1, 1983), Entraide Internationale in Materie Penale of 20 March 1981. *See also* Theo Vogler, *The Expanding Scope of International Judicial Assistance and Cooperation in Legal Matters*, 66 DIE FRIEDENS-WARTE 287 (1986).

135 G.A. Res. 45/116 (Dec. 14, 1990).

136 G.A. Res. 45/117 (Dec. 14, 1990).

137 G.A. Res. 45/118 (Dec. 14, 1990). Other model agreements include: Model Agreement on the Transfer of Foreign Prisoners, U.N. Model MLAT on the Transfer of Supervision of Offenders Conditionally Sentenced or Conditionally Released and U.N. Model MLAT for the Prevention of Crimes that Infringe on the Cultural Heritage of Peoples in the Form of Movable Property. For a discussion of all of the above model agreements, *see generally* Roger S. Clark, *Crime: The U.N. Agenda on International Cooperation in the Criminal Process*, 15 NOVA L. REV. 475 (1991).

systems and contain only widely agreed-upon provisions. Because the legal and administrative systems of states vary widely, these model treaties contain few mandatory rules. Instead, they contain optional rules that states can adopt in bilateral and multilateral conventions. These treaties are also expected to enhance the ability of states to harmonize their national legal schemes with international obligations to provide cooperation in penal matters. To enhance the usefulness of these model agreements, the Crime Prevention and Criminal Justice Branch of the United Nations is preparing two manuals to assist states in the implementation of the model treaties on mutual assistance and extradition.

A shortcoming of these model treaties, however, is that each treaty concerns only a single modality of inter-state cooperation and, thus, does not represent an integrated approach.[138] By following the lead of the Council of Europe's Draft Comprehensive Convention, the United Nations could significantly contribute to the adoption of the integrated approach by elaborating a U.N. Model MLAT that effectively integrates the modalities of inter-state penal cooperation.

Multilateral Conventions Aimed at Money Laundering

The 1988 United Nations Drug Convention

Perhaps the most telling indication of the perceived threat of illegal drug trafficking on a global level is the 1988 United Nations Convention Against Illicit Traffic in Narcotic Drugs and Psychotropic Substances ("U.N. Drug Convention").[139] This Convention reflects the desire of states to utilize the immobilization and forfeiture of assets as a means to combat drug trafficking and the accompanying money laundering. The Convention's provision for legal assistance also indicates a recognition of the importance of inter-state cooperation in fighting drug trafficking on an international level.

Before analyzing the provisions of the U.N. Drug Convention, bear in mind that any infirmities which are indicated are likely necessary in an agreement of such scope (106 states took part in drafting this convention[140]), considering the compromises necessary to maximize the number of signatures and take account of disparate legal systems. Second, this Convention is the first step towards recognizing and codifying an international commitment to the suppression of the illegal drug trade.[141] Finally, this Convention contemplated

[138] Despite these institutional differences, and in recognition of the fact that the United Nations has not adopted an integrated approach, one of the writers has propounded such an approach in a report submitted to a Committee of Experts Meeting at ISISC (Siracusa) June 1990 and presented to the Eighth United Nations Congress on Crime Prevention and the Treatment of Offenders (Havana, Cuba, Aug.-Sept. 1990), A/Conf.144/NGO (July 31, 1990), *reprinted in* M. Cherif Bassiouni, *A Comprehensive Strategic Approach on International Cooperation for the Prevention, Control and Suppression of International and Transnational Criminality*, 15 NOVA L. REV. 354 (1991).

[139] U.N. Drug Convention, *supra* note 14. As of February 1994, 99 states have become parties to the Convention. Another 26 states have signed the Convention but have not yet become parties. For the history of the U.N. Drug Convention, *see* United Nations Economic and Social Counsel, Final Act of the United Nations Conference for the Adoption of a Convention against Illicit Traffic in Narcotic Drugs and Psychotropic Substances, Vienna, Austria, Nov. 25-Dec. 20, 1988. *See* BERNASCONI, *supra* note 14; GILMORE, *supra* note 14.

[140] *See* Zagaris, *Developments in International Judicial Assistance and Related Matters, supra* note 12, at 340.

[141] The U.N. Drug Convention improves upon two previous multilateral agreements (the 1961 Single Convention on Narcotic Drugs and the 1971 Convention on Psychotropic Substances) that sought to limit the trade in illicit drugs. However, these treaties focused on the supply of narcotic drugs and tried to limit their supply in a

subsequent bilateral and regional agreements. While the Convention empowers states to cooperate based on the convention alone, the drafters likely contemplated subsequent agreements as the true enforcement mechanism and not the convention itself.[142]

The U.N. Drug Convention is also noteworthy in that it makes great use of the integrated approach to inter-state cooperation. In a single text, the treaty utilizes four of the six modalities of inter-state cooperation: recognition of foreign penal judgments (*e.g.*, the recognition of orders of forfeiture); the freezing and seizing of assets; extradition; and mutual legal assistance.

The U.N. Drug Convention requires the parties to enact implementing legislation consistent with their domestic legislative systems.[143] States must carry out their obligations consistent with the principles of sovereign equality and territorial integrity.[144] The parties also agree not to exercise jurisdiction or perform functions that are reserved for the authorities of the other state.[145] These provisions seem intended to prevent larger, consuming nations from interfering with the internal affairs of smaller, producing nations.[146]

Article 3 defines the offenses and sanctions covered by the U.N. Drug Convention.[147] First, as the title indicates, the U.N. Drug Convention applies only to the various crimes associated with drug trafficking and, tangentially, money laundering. More specifically, the convention obligates states to criminalize nearly every conceivable facet of the production, cultivation, distribution, sale or possession of illicit drugs. While the convention thoroughly exhausts the possible offenses associated with illicit drug traffic, it falls short of other initiatives that cover violent crimes, terrorist acts, organized crime and other non-drug-related offenses that generate large profits.[148]

Seizure and Forfeiture

Consistent with the increased use of criminal forfeiture in bilateral agreements and domestic legislation, the U.N. Drug Convention contains a powerful confiscation provision that requires signing parties to implement legislation enabling them to confiscate the

---

way that hindered diversion to illicit traffic. These treaties did not provide for the prosecution of drug traffickers and approached the issue from a regulatory, and not criminal law enforcement, standpoint. *See* Single Convention on Narcotic Drugs, Mar. 30, 1961, 18 U.S.T. 1409, 520 U.N.T.S. 204 (amended Mar. 25, 1972, 26 U.S.T. 1441, 976 U.N.T.S. 3); Convention on Psychotropic Substances of 1971, Feb. 21, 1971, 32 U.S.T. 543, 1019 U.N.T.S. 175.

[142] Provisions for immobilization and forfeiture of assets become more vague and less effective as the community for which they are intended expands. Because of the number of states involved in its negotiation, the U.N. Drug Convention may lack sufficient specificity to make its use effective absent some sort of bilateral or regional agreement.

[143] U.N. Drug Convention, *supra* note 14, at Art. 2(1). For a discussion of the implementation tasks posed by the treaty, as well as models for implementing legislation, *see generally* UNITED STATES DEPT. OF JUSTICE, CRIMINAL DIVISION, NARCOTICS AND DANGEROUS DRUGS SECTION, MANUAL FOR COMPLIANCE WITH THE UNITED NATIONS CONVENTION AGAINST ILLICIT TRAFFIC IN NARCOTIC DRUGS AND PSYCHOTROPIC SUBSTANCES (Oct. 1992).

[144] U.N. Drug Convention, *supra* note 14, at Art. 2(2).

[145] *Id.* at Art. 2(3).

[146] *See* Zagaris, *Developments in International Judicial Assistance and Related Matters, supra* note 12, at 342.

[147] *See* U.N. Drug Convention, *supra* note 14, at Art. 3.

[148] One such initiative is the Euro. Conv. Money Laundering, *supra* note 16. In addition, many bilateral mutual legal assistance agreements, such as those concluded between the United States and a number of laundering havens, apply to all serious offenses and not just drug-related offenses. *See* Bassiouni, *supra* note 9, at 37.

proceeds or instrumentalities used in or intended for use in drug offenses.[149] Furthermore, parties are required to adopt measures to enable their competent authorities to identify, trace and freeze or seize proceeds, property or instrumentalities for eventual confiscation.[150] In order to effectuate these procedures and reach more assets, each state must empower its judicial or other authorities to order the seizure of bank, financial or commercial records; no state can deny compliance based on bank secrecy laws.[151]

Bank secrecy laws shield the tremendous profits of drug trafficking from law enforcement efforts and facilitate the techniques of money laundering.[152] The U.N. Drug Convention may provide the tool to obviate bank secrecy laws and, as a result, amend existing bilateral treaties to aid in the discovery of substantial assets.[153]

States are obligated, upon the request of another state, to submit any request to their competent authorities in order to gain an order of confiscation or to give effect to an order of confiscation issued by the requesting party.[154] Similarly, states agree to take measures to identify, trace, freeze or seize proceeds, property and instrumentalities for the purpose of eventual confiscation ordered by the requesting or requested party.[155] Pursuant to paragraphs 6-19 of Article 7 on mutual legal assistance, the requesting state must provide a description of the property to be confiscated and sufficient facts to enable the requested state to seek confiscation under domestic law or, in the event the confiscation is sought pursuant to an order issued by the requesting state, a legally admissible copy of the order and a statement of the facts upon which the order was secured.[156] If freezing of the assets is sought, a statement of facts must accompany the request.[157] Forfeiture, on the other hand, will require an order of forfeiture issued, after conviction, by an appropriate court.

Article 5 also requires parties to try to conclude bilateral and multilateral treaties to enhance the effectiveness of confiscation, tracing and freezing of assets.[158] Where a state's domestic law requires such treaties to give effect to the provisions of Article 5, a state must consider this Convention as the necessary and sufficient treaty basis.[159] This provision may be seen as amending existing treaties on mutual assistance in penal matters to provide for confiscation if those treaties lack confiscation procedures. As a result, the Convention may extend the reach of restraint and forfeiture orders to nations that have not included such provisions in their mutual assistance agreements but who are party to the U.N. Drug

---

149 U.N. Drug Convention, *supra* note 14, at Art. 5(1)(a)-(b).

150 *Id.* at Art. 5(2).

151 *Id.* at Art. 5(3).

152 Governments have a legitimate interest in maintaining the secrecy of transactions. On a macro level, for instance, the confidentiality of transactions is important in the shoring up of a nation's currency. But the public sector and legitimate industries seek the same type of financial secrecy as money launderers. This is particularly true of the arms industry, whose financial dealings have recently been shown to utilize the same channels as drug dealers and money launderers. For a complete discussion of the manner in which bank secrecy can be abused to facilitate money laundering, *see* Commission on Crime Prevention and Criminal Justice, *Money Laundering and Associated Issues: The Need for International Co-operation*, U.N. Doc. No. E/CN.15/1992/4/Add.5 (21-30 Apr. 1992) ¶¶ 25-60.

153 *See* Stewart, *supra* note 9, at 399. However, with this increased access, privacy violations are more likely as officials go fishing through private bank records for potentially forfeitable assets.

154 U.N. Drug Convention, *supra* note 14, at Art. 5(4)(a)(i)-(ii).

155 *Id.* at Art. 5(4)(b).

156 *Id.* at Art. 5(4)(d)(i)-(ii). *See also id.* at Art. 7(6)-(19).

157 *Id.* at Art. 5(4)(d)(iii).

158 *Id.* at Art. 5(6)(g).

159 *Id.* at Art. 5(6)(f).

Convention. Whether this will prove true, in practice, remains to be seen as states may be reluctant to take such steps in the absence of a specific agreement.

Once assets are confiscated, they will be disposed of according to the domestic law of the requested state, but states may conclude agreements with other states to (1) contribute the proceeds of confiscation to intergovernmental law enforcement bodies, or (2) share the proceeds with other parties on a case-by-case basis.[160] If assets have been converted or transformed into other property, any converted property will be subject to restraint or confiscation.[161] If the proceeds have been intermingled with legitimate assets, only an amount equal to the intermingled assets may be confiscated.[162] Also, states may reverse the burden of proof regarding the lawful origin of the assets, subject to a party's principles of domestic law—a clear indication of the prosecutorial perspective of this instrument.[163] Finally, Article 5 provides that the provisions of this article shall not interfere with the rights of *bona fide* third parties.[164]

Mutual Legal Assistance

Article 7 of the Convention requires parties to provide the "widest measure of mutual legal assistance" in investigations, prosecutions and judicial proceedings related to Article 3(1) violations, including money laundering. The Drug Convention provides a non-exhaustive list of the types of mutual legal assistance to be provided: taking evidence or statements from persons; effecting service of judicial documents; executing searches and seizures; examining objects and sites; providing information and evidentiary items; providing records and documents, including bank, financial, corporate or business records; and identifying or tracing proceeds, instrumentalities or other things for evidentiary purposes.[165] Moreover, parties may provide any other type of assistance allowed by the domestic law of the requested party.[166] This article does not encompass mutual legal

---

160 *Id.* at Art. 5(5). An interesting consequence of this provision, and similar provisions in other treaties regarding the allocation of confiscated assets, is that law enforcement activities may become driven by the profit motive. The purpose of this type of provision is to give incentive to the agencies responsible for seizing and freezing assets. However, such a profit motive may create a *de facto* policy of giving priority in international cooperation and enforcement to those crimes involving the greatest sums of money susceptible to seizure. Consequently, serious crimes that do not involve the potential for confiscation of assets (*e.g.*, hijacking, taking of hostages, and terrorism) may become secondary in certain international cooperation and enforcement efforts.

161 *Id.* at Art. 5(6)(a).

162 *Id.* at Art. 5(6)(b).

163 *Id.* at Art. 5(7).

164 *Id.* at Art. 5(8). This provision could possibly be used to allow the exemption of attorney fees from restraint or confiscation. *See* Zagaris, *Developments in International Judicial Assistance and Related Matters*, *supra* note 12, at 345.

165 U.N. Drug Convention, *supra* note 14, at Art. 7(2)(a)-(g).

166 *Id.* at Art. 7(3). The obligations under Article 7, and some of the confiscation provisions of Article 5, create a "miniature mutual legal assistance treaty." Because methods of acquiring admissible evidence vary from country to country, it was impossible to negotiate legal assistance provisions as detailed and comprehensive as those in bilateral or regional agreements. Thus, while the U.N. Drug Convention contains many of the "key elements of mutual legal assistance relations," it does not, and could not, contain more detailed procedures. *See Report of the United States Delegation to the United Nations Conference for the adoption of a Convention Against Illicit Traffic in Narcotic Drugs and Psychotropic Substances*, S. EXEC. REP. NO. 15, 101st Cong., 1st Sess., *reprinted in* INTERNATIONAL EFFORTS TO COMBAT MONEY LAUNDERING 98, 127 (W.C. Gilmore ed. 1992). This lack of specificity, however, will inevitably result in countries interpreting their legal assistance obligations differently according to national law. This limitation in the U.N. Drug Convention contrasts with the greater

assistance in regard to restraint and confiscation of assets because Article 5 contains its own provisions.

Article 7 reiterates the mandate that parties may not decline assistance based on bank secrecy laws.[167] As stated with respect to confiscation, this provision will help to overcome the hindrance of business and bank confidentiality which has undermined mutual legal assistance and efforts to suppress money laundering.[168] This provision may bolster existing and future legal assistance treaties, especially in light of paragraphs 6 and 7, which provide that the obligations of states under existing treaties are not affected by this Convention.[169] Also, if states are not party to a bilateral or multilateral legal assistance treaty, the mutual legal assistance provisions (as detailed in paragraphs 8-19) will apply; even if the states are party to such a treaty, they may agree to apply the provisions of the Convention.[170]

The confiscation and mutual legal assistance provisions, especially the bank secrecy provisions, of the U.N. Drug Convention will enable authorities to gain access to more assets either for the purpose of pre-trial seizure or to give effect to adjudicated orders of forfeiture. In either event, instruments such as these will significantly deprive drug traffickers and organized criminal organizations engaged in drug trafficking or money laundering of the use of their ill-gotten assets.

Money Laundering

In addition to criminalizing nearly every violation associated with drug trafficking, the U.N. Drug Convention also contains several provisions specifically designed to thwart the effects of money laundering associated with illicit drug trafficking. As previously discussed, the Convention requires the signatory states to adopt legislation to facilitate the freezing, seizing and forfeiture of assets.[171]

Article 3 of the Convention defines the offenses and sanctions. Signatory parties are obligated to take the appropriate measures necessary to criminalize these offenses.[172] Several provisions of Article 3(1) govern drug-related money laundering.[173] The knowing conversion or transfer of property derived from a predicate offense with the purpose of concealing its

---

comprehensiveness and detail of regionally motivated multilateral instruments like the Euro. Conv. Money Laundering and the Draft Inter-American Convention on Mutual Assistance in Criminal Matters discussed *infra.* Issues of interpretation will be diminished under these instruments.

An interesting example of a legal assistance obligation in a widely negotiated multilateral instrument is Article VII, paragraph 2 of the 1993 Chemical Weapons Convention (CWC) which provides as follows:

> Each State Party shall cooperate with other States Parties and afford the appropriate form of legal assistance to facilitate the implementation of obligations. . .

While the CWC's application of principles of inter-state penal cooperation to arms control is historic, the treaty gives no further indication of the types of assistance to be provided under the treaty. As a result, the legal assistance obligation will be defined, in great part, by the domestic legislation adopted to implement the CWC. For a discussion of how this broad, undefined obligation to provide legal assistance could be interpreted by states-parties, *see* BARRY KELLMAN ET AL., MANUAL FOR NATIONAL IMPLEMENTATION OF THE CHEMICAL WEAPONS CONVENTION 106-28 (1993).

[167] U.N. Drug Convention, *supra* note 14, at Art. 7(5).

[168] *See* Zagaris, *Developments in International Judicial Assistance and Related Matters, supra* note 12, at 346.

[169] U.N. Drug Convention, *supra* note 14, at Art. 7(6).

[170] *Id.* at Art. 7(7).

[171] *Id.* at Art. 5(2),(4)(g).

[172] *Id.* at Art. 3(1).

[173] *See id.* at Art. 3(1)(b)(i)-(ii), -(c)(i), -(c)(iv).

illegal origin is an offense under the Convention.[174] Moreover, assisting any person committing such an offense to evade the legal consequences of his acts is also an offense.[175]

Signatory parties must criminalize the concealment or disguise of the true source of property knowing that such property is derived from one of the offenses of Article 3(1)(a).[176] The Convention also requires a signatory state to criminalize, subject to its constitutional principles and the basic concepts of its legal system, the knowing acquisition, possession or use of property derived from a predicate offense.[177] Finally, the convention also criminalizes the participation in or conspiracy to commit, and any aiding, abetting and counseling the commission of any of the above offenses.[178]

The Convention also obliges each party to make all of the above offenses punishable by sanctions which take into account the gravity of drug-related offenses.[179] Such sanctions may include imprisonment, other deprivations of liberty, pecuniary sanctions and confiscation.[180] In a significant step, the Convention provides that the listed offenses shall not be considered fiscal offenses or political offenses or regarded as politically motivated for the purposes of mutual legal assistance as provided by the Convention.[181]

A few critical points about the U.N. Drug Convention's mutual legal assistance provisions and money laundering provisions merit reiteration. First, recall that Article 5 generally provides for the freezing, seizing and eventual confiscation of assets derived from predicate offenses.[182] Pursuant to this goal, the Convention also provides that each party must adopt measures to identify, trace and freeze or seize illicit proceeds, property or

---

174 *Id.* at Art. 3(1)(b)(i).

175 Art. 3(1)(b)(i) provides that each Party shall establish as an offense:

> The conversion or transfer of property, knowing that such property is derived from any offense or offenses established in accordance with subparagraph (a) of this paragraph, or from an act of participation in such offense or offenses, for the purpose of concealing or disguising the illicit origin of the property or of assisting any person who is involved in the commission of such an offense or offenses to evade the legal consequences of his actions.

Id.

176 Art. 3(1)(b)(ii) provides that each Party shall establish as an offense:

> The concealment or disguise of the true nature, source, location, disposition, movement, rights with respect to, or ownership of property knowing that such property is derived from an offense or offenses established in accordance with subparagraph (a) of this paragraph or from an act of participation in such an offense or offenses.

Id.

177 Art. 3(1)(c)(i) provides that each Party shall establish as an offense:

> (c) Subject to its constitutional principles and the basic concepts of its legal system:
>
> (i) The acquisition, possession or use of property, knowing, at the time of receipt, that such property was derived from an offense or offenses established in accordance with subparagraph (a) of this paragraph or from an act of participation in such offense or offenses.

Id.

178 Art. 3(1)(c)(iv) provides that each Party shall establish as an offense:

> Participation in, association or conspiracy to commit, attempts to commit and aiding, abetting, facilitating and counselling the commission of any of the offenses established in accordance with this Article.

Id. Article 7 of the Convention amends existing mutual legal assistance treaties to include the offenses listed in Article 3. Therefore, via the Convention, money laundering will fall within the reach of existing mutual legal assistance treaties. *See* Stewart, *supra* note 9, at 398. *See* Zagaris, *Developments in International Judicial Assistance and Related Matters, supra* note 12, at 346-47.

179 *See* U.N. Drug Convention, *supra* note 14, at Art. 3(4)(a).

180 *Id.*

181 *See id.* at Art. 3(10). This provision will be a significant aid for the purposes of mutual legal assistance and extradition. *See* Stewart, *supra* note 9, at 394 n.23.

182 *See* U.N. Drug Convention, *supra* note 14, at Art. 5(1), (4).

instrumentalities.[183] However, the most important and innovative provision of Article 5 will be of tremendous assistance in detecting and thwarting drug-related money laundering. Article 5(3) requires that signatory states empower their courts and competent authorities to order that bank, financial or commercial records be made available or be seized.[184] Parties cannot invoke domestic bank secrecy laws as a grounds for refusing a request under this article.[185]

Second, a similar provision appears in Article 7 of the Convention. In addition to its general requirements that parties shall provide each other with the widest measure of mutual legal assistance,[186] Article 7 also prohibits a party from declining to render mutual legal assistance on the basis of domestic bank secrecy laws. This prohibition also extends to other bilateral conventions affected by the Convention.[187]

The Council of Europe's 1990 Laundering Convention

As discussed above, the U.N. Drug Convention represents a significant step towards an integration of several forms of inter-state cooperation in penal matters by incorporating provisions for the following: extradition (Article 6); transfer of proceedings (Article 8); mutual legal assistance (taking of statements, service of process, provision of evidentiary items, executing searches and seizures, etc.) (Article 7); and the newest modality of assistance in penal matters—the seizure and confiscation of assets (Article 5). The U.N. Drug Convention is also significant from a norm-building standpoint in that, due to its global scope, its prohibitions and mechanisms are more likely to become integral parts of international penal law. However, as discussed above, that instrument is also limited by its global scope. Thus, additional bilateral and multilateral agreements like the 1990 Council of Europe Convention on Laundering, Search, Seizure and Confiscation of the Proceeds from Crime are necessary to make the international control scheme more effective.

The European Money Laundering Convention offers a partially integrated approach to mutual legal assistance. It incorporates the mechanisms of mutual legal assistance, provisional measures, and confiscation of assets, and is also intended to work in concert with

---

183 *See id.* at Art. 5(2). Thus, national legislation must provide for eventual confiscation and all other measures necessary to confiscate proceeds—including provisional measures.

184 Article 5(3) provides as follows:

> In order to carry out the measures referred to in this article, each Party shall empower its courts or other competent authorities to order that bank, financial or commercial records be made available or be seized. A Party shall not decline to act under the provisions of this paragraph or on the ground of bank secrecy.

Id.

185 *Id.* Bank secrecy is a common barrier to discovery in forfeiture proceedings. *See generally* Newcomb, *United States Litigation and Foreign Bank Secrecy: The Origins of Conflict*, 9 N.Y.L. SCH. J. INT'L. & COMP. L. 47 (1988). *See also* Knapp, *supra* note 37. This provision, however imposes an affirmative obligation on signatory parties to not shield from discovery bank and financial records for the purposes of seizure, freezing and forfeiture proceedings. *See* Stewart, *supra* note 9, at 395.

186 Article 7(1) provides as follows:

> The parties shall afford one another, pursuant to this article, the widest measure of mutual legal assistance in investigations, prosecutions and judicial proceedings in relation to criminal offenses established in accordance with Article 3, paragraph 1.

U.N. Drug Convention, *supra* note 14.

187 Article 7(5) provides that "A Party shall not decline to render mutual legal assistance under this article on the ground of bank secrecy." *Id. See also* Stewart, *supra* note 9, at 399.

other Council of Europe conventions on judicial assistance.[188] Therefore, while the European Money Laundering Convention is not exactly a paradigm of the integrated approach to inter-state cooperation in penal matters, it represents a significant step toward this aim by at least integrating a few modalities of international cooperation to work in connection with existing instruments covering other modalities.[189] In so doing, the Convention accomplished its goal of establishing a complete set of rules that cover all stages of criminal procedure from the initial investigation to the final imposition and recognition of the confiscation sentence.[190] This approach provides an effective but flexible means of international cooperation.[191]

Two other objectives motivated the negotiation of the European Money Laundering Convention. A primary purpose of the Convention was to complement existing Council of Europe instruments related to inter-state cooperation, such as the European Convention on Mutual Assistance in Criminal Matters,[192] the European Convention on the International Validity of Criminal Judgements,[193] and the European Convention on the Transfer of Proceedings in Criminal Matters.[194] However, the European Money Laundering Convention does not use the word *European* in its title, indicating that it is open for signature by non-member, like-minded states.[195] The treaty is also noteworthy because, rather than reflecting the commonality of the many civil law systems in Europe (as has been the case with many

---

[188] Nilsson, *supra* note 20, at 419. *See also, e.g.*, Ekkehart Müller-Rappard, *The European Response to International Terrorism, in* LEGAL RESPONSES TO INTERNATIONAL TERRORISM 388-91 (M. Cherif Bassiouni ed. 1987); *supra*, Chapter 9. *See also* MARIO PISANI & FRANCO MOSCONI, CODICE DELLE CONVENZIONI DI ESTRADIZIONE E DI ASSISTENZA GIUDIZIARIA IN MATERIA PENALE (2d ed. 1993). *See also* BERNASCONI, *supra* note 14; GILMORE, *supra* note 14.

[189] The Euro. Conv. Money Laundering focuses on the recognition of foreign confiscation or forfeiture judgments and contains the provisional and investigative measures of freezing and seizing of assets along with the necessary judicial assistance. Thus, although it utilizes several modalities of inter-state cooperation, it does so only in order to facilitate the freezing and seizing of assets. This focus on one modality arises because the Council of Europe has concluded 18 other conventions relating to inter-state penal cooperation and the Euro. Conv. Money Laundering is expected to operate in concert with those agreements.

These instruments are of a better technical legal quality than many other international instruments, including the 1988 U.N. Drug Convention, for three primary reasons. First, the 23 nations that comprise the Council of Europe are more cohesive than the 100-plus nations that participated in the elaboration of the U.N. Drug Convention. As a result, the Council of Europe is not as concerned with maximizing the number of signatures as is the United Nations. Second, the Council of Europe, as with most regional law-making bodies, does not face as great a problem of conflicting legal and criminal justice systems as does the United Nations. The legal systems of the 24 nations that made up the Council of Europe until 1990 contain many similarities. With the admission of Eastern and Central European countries, this situation differs. But the Council of Europe has the ability to spend more time, exert more effort and expend greater resources in the conclusion of a treaty than does a body like the United Nations. The Council of Europe is also consulted by more governments than the United Nations and has the benefit of additional expertise and input. *See* M. Cherif Bassiouni, *Policy Considerations on Inter-State Cooperation in Criminal Matters, in* PRINCIPLES AND PROCEDURES FOR A NEW TRANSNATIONAL CRIMINAL LAW 807, 810-11 (Albin Eser & Otto Lagodny eds., 1992). *See also* LA CONVENZIONE EUROPA DI ASSISTENZA GIUDIZIARIA IN MATERIA PENALE (P. Laszloczky ed. 1984); THEO VOGLER & PETER WILKITZKI, GESETZ ÜBER DIE INTERNATIONALE RECHTSHILFE IN STRAFSACHEN, (IRG) Kommentar (1992); Carlson & Zagaris, *supra* note 11; Christine Van den Wyngaert, *Criminal Law and the European Communities: Defining Issues, in* TRANSNATIONAL ASPECTS OF CRIMINAL PROCEDURE (1983).

[190] Nilsson, *supra* note 20, at 425.

[191] *Id.*

[192] Apr. 20, 1959, Europ. T.S. No. 30.

[193] May 28, 1979, Europ. T.S. No. 70.

[194] May 15, 1972, Europ. T.S. No. 73. See Nilsson, *supra* note 20, at 424, for a more complete discussion of how the relevant instruments are intended to interact.

[195] *Id.* at 5.

other Council of Europe instruments), the European Money Laundering Convention was elaborated with differing legal systems in mind. For example, Australia, Canada and the United States were represented on the expert committee that drafted the Convention.[196] The treaty "emphasizes the objectives to be achieved," but leaves the methodology for implementation to respective laws of the member states.[197]

Another important objective of the European Money Laundering Convention was to obligate states to adopt efficient measures in their domestic laws to combat serious offenses and deprive criminals of their profits.[198] Specifically, the European Money Laundering Convention will require states to align their legislation and adopt efficient legislation to investigate offenses, implement provisional measures and confiscate instrumentalities and profits of illegal activities.[199] This is not a requirement to harmonize legislation, but rather a means to enable states to cooperate effectively.[200] In pursuit of these objectives, the European Money Laundering Convention seeks to demonstrate how the integrated approach

---

196 Nilsson, *supra* note 20, at 424. As of December 1995, eight states have ratified the Convention (Bulgaria, the United Kingdom, the Netherlands, Switzerland, Italy, Lithuania, Finland, and Norway). France, Spain, Sweden, and Germany are expected to ratify soon. Ratifications may number as many as 20 within the next two years. *See Bulgarian Says Embezzled Money from East Flowing Into Western Banks*, BNA's Banking Report, Dec. 5, 1994, at 851. States that have signed but not ratified include Austria, Belgium, Cyprus, Denmark, France, Germany, Greece, Iceland, Liechtenstein, Luxembourg, Portugal, San Marino, Slovenia, Spain, Sweden, and Australia. *See Czech Republic Becomes 25th Nation to Sign Convention on Money Laundering*, BNA Banking Daily, Dec. 19, 1995; Maria Riccarda Marchetti, *Commento L. 9/8/1993 n. 328 - Ratifica e esecuzione delle convenzione sul riciclaggio, la ricerca, il sequestro e la confisca dei proventi di reato, fatta a strasburgo l'8 novembre 1990*, LA LEGISLAZIONE PENALE 4 (No. 3/94, 1994). *See also* LUIGI MAGISTRO, RICICLAGGIO DEI CAPITALI ILLECITI (1991).

The United States has yet to ratify this agreement, but United States involvement in an instrument such as this is almost certain. Agreements of this nature highlight the differences between hard power (the unilateral action of seizing criminals abroad and bringing them to the United States) and soft power (the use of international agreements and judicial assistance). Advocates of both sides represent the powers that be in the United States Department of Justice. Carlson & Zagaris, *supra* note 11, at 557, and sources cited therein (arguing that the hard power approach is untenable in Western Europe and that United States policy makers must conform to the European regime).

197 Herman Woltring, *Money Laundering: Impediments to Effective International Cooperation*, UNICRI 199, at 5 (conference paper presented to the International Conference on Preventing and Controlling Money Laundering and the Use of the Proceeds of Crime: A Global Approach, Courmayeur Mont Blanc, Italy, June 18-20, 1994).

198 *See* Nilsson, *supra* note 20, at 424.

199 There can be no doubt that implementing a number of these elements of international co-operation, and particularly the immobilizing and confiscation of assets, will require the enactment of innovative legislation. Recognizing the differences in legal systems and the likelihood of disputes, the Committee of Experts provided the equally innovative solution of an arbitral tribunal as an option for the settlement of disputes. Euro. Conv. Money Laundering, *supra* note 16, at Art. 42. *See also* Arbitral Tribunals Under the Laundering Convention, Recommendation No. R (91) 12, ¶ 11.

200 *Id.* at 425. Nevertheless, states desiring to become bound by the Convention may find it necessary to substantially amend existing legislation. *Id.* Particular attention was paid to the fact that, in relation to measures to be taken at the national level, the national law of states differs significantly. As a result, the harmonization of national implementation measures was not sought—except in regard to the criminalizing of money laundering. This flexibility recognizes the varied characteristics of national law and will, hopefully, ensure "a minimum common degree of effectively (sic)." Polimeni, *The Council of Europe Convention on Laundering Search, Seizure and Confiscation of the Proceeds of Crime,* Conference Paper: The Money Laundering Conference, M.L 92(15) (Strasbourg, Sept. 28-30, 1992).

An important actor in this area has been the Pompidou Group. Formed in 1971 and operating under the auspices of the Council of Europe (since 1980), the Pompidou Group has endeavored to coordinate international responses to drug trafficking. The Group encourages the development of international agreements and was an active advocate in the conclusion of the Euro. Conv. Money Laundering. *See* Carlson & Zagaris, *supra* note 11, at 565-67.

can bolster the effectiveness of the immobilization and seizure of assets in combating serious offenses and the concomitant money laundering.

Seizure and Forfeiture and Mutual Legal Assistance

In regard to the seizure and eventual forfeiture of assets, the European Money Laundering Convention is perhaps the most forceful international instrument yet contemplated. Owing to its intention to undercut the effectiveness of money laundering in sustaining the economic bases of criminal organizations, the Convention's focus is naturally twofold: 1) requiring states to criminalize the offense of money laundering and 2) providing states the means to confiscate illicit proceeds, including provisional measures to immobilize those assets for eventual forfeiture. The preamble to the Convention notes the Council's belief that the fight against serious crime is an international concern requiring modern and effective methods of an international character and that depriving criminals of proceeds from crime is one of those methods. In light of this concern, the Council intended that this Convention combat all forms of serious crimes, especially drug offenses, arms dealing, terrorist offenses or any offenses which generate large profits.[201] The European Money Laundering Convention draws much of its strength from its broad scope and its adoption of the trend to extend the definition of money laundering beyond drug-related offenses.[202] Therefore, the Convention overcomes the U.N. Drug Convention's biggest infirmity: its restriction to drug-related offenses.

Chapter II (dealing with measures to be taken at the national level) and Chapter III (concerning international cooperation) require parties to enact legislation and other measures necessary to accomplish the following: (1) confiscate instrumentalities and proceeds of crime;[203] (2) identify and trace property liable to confiscation (investigative measures);[204] (3) prevent the transfer or disposal of such property (provisional measures);[205] (4) empower its courts or authorities to order the availability of bank, commercial or financial records and require that no party may deny a request on grounds of bank secrecy;[206] and (5) ensure that interested parties affected by confiscation or provisional measures have effective legal remedies in order to preserve their rights.[207] The Convention then enumerates each party's duties as to international cooperation.

The Convention's strength emanates from the format of these provisions. Each section concerns a form of assistance (investigative assistance, provisional measures, or

---

[201] Euro. Conv. Money Laundering, *supra* note 16, at Art. 1(e) (defining a "predicate offense" as "any criminal offense as a result of which proceeds were generated that may become the subject of an offense as defined in Article 6 of this Convention"). *See also* Council of Europe, Explanatory Report on the Convention on Laundering, Search, Seizure and Confiscation of the Proceeds From Crime (1991) ¶ 8, [hereinafter Explanatory Report], *reprinted in* 2 EUROPEAN INTER-STATE CO-OPERATION IN CRIMINAL MATTERS: THE COUNCIL OF EUROPE'S LEGAL INSTRUMENTS 1419 (Ekkehart Müller-Rappard & M. Cherif Bassiouni eds., rev'd 2d ed. 1993)

[202] *See* William C. Gilmore, *International Responses to Money Laundering: A General Overview*, Conference Paper: The Money Laundering Conference, M.L 92(10) (Strasbourg, Sept. 28-30, 1992). *See also* GILMORE, *supra* note 14.

[203] Euro. Conv. Money Laundering, *supra* note 16, at Art. 2(1).

[204] *Id.* at Art. 3.

[205] *Id.*

[206] *Id.* at Art. 4(1).

[207] *Id.* at Art. 5.

confiscation) and each section begins with an obligation to assist, followed by the method of execution (as governed by the law of the requested state). With this format, the Convention integrates the mutual legal assistance requirements with the procedure itself so that there can be no confusion as to what type of assistance a party is to render once it receives a confiscation request. Article 7 embodies these general goals of international cooperation by requiring that parties provide the widest extent of cooperation in investigations and proceedings aimed at confiscation.[208] Furthermore, each party is required to adopt legislation to enable it to comply with requests for investigation, preliminary measures and confiscation.[209]

Upon request, parties must afford each other the widest possible measure of assistance in identifying and tracing proceeds and instrumentalities liable to confiscation, and any assistance must be carried out in accordance with the domestic law of the requested state.[210] Parties are also allowed, without a prior request, to transmit information about instrumentalities and proceeds when a party believes that information might assist another party in carrying out its own investigations or proceedings.[211]

Parties are also obligated, upon request of a party which has instituted criminal proceedings or proceedings aimed at confiscation, to take necessary provisional measures such as freezing or seizing property which may be subject to confiscation.[212] Provisional measures must also be conducted in accordance with domestic law and, before any measures may be lifted, the requesting party must be given an opportunity to give its reasons for continuing the measures.[213]

The Convention adopts the two types of confiscation commonly used in Council of Europe States: property confiscation and value confiscation. All states have systems of property confiscation whereby the ownership rights in the property are transferred to the state. Under this method, specific property can be confiscated, and such property may include items or substances whose possession is itself illegal, instrumentalities used in the offense, indirect or direct proceeds from the offense, and substituted property.[214] When presented with a request for confiscation of property located within its territory a party must; (1) enforce a confiscation order made by a court of a requesting party; or (2) submit a request for confiscation to its competent authorities for the purpose of securing an order for confiscation and, if such an order is granted, the party must enforce it.[215]

A second method of confiscation adopted by the Convention, and already used by some Council of Europe member states, is value confiscation. Under this method, the state can exert a requirement to pay a sum of money corresponding to the value of the proceeds. If payment is not obtained, the requested party may realize the claim on any property available (whether legally or illegally obtained) for that purpose.[216]

---

208 *Id.* at Art. 7(1).

209 *Id.* at Art. 7(2).

210 *Id.* at Arts. 8 and 9.

211 *Id.* at Art. 10. No such discretion is granted by the U.N. Drug Convention. *See U.N. Money Laundering Report, supra* note 39, ¶ 82.

212 *Id.* Euro. Conv. Money Laundering, *supra* note 16, at Art. 11(1).

213 *Id.* at Art. 12.

214 Nilsson, *supra* note 20, at 426.

215 Euro. Conv. Money Laundering, *supra* note 16, at Art. 13.

216 *Id.* at Art. 13(3). *See also* Nilsson, *supra* note 20, at 427.

Execution of a confiscation request must be carried out pursuant to the domestic law of the requested state.[217] Moreover, the requested party is bound by the findings of fact stated in a conviction or judicial decision of the requesting party or any facts implicit in such decisions.[218] Any confiscated property will be disposed of in accordance with the domestic law of the requested state.[219]

The Convention provides some grounds for refusal to fulfill a request: requests based on political or fiscal offenses; lack of dual criminality; or any request which is contrary to the *ordre public* of the requested state or is otherwise contrary to the fundamental principles of the requested state's principles of justice.[220] A party may not invoke bank secrecy as a grounds for refusal; however, where a request would require the lifting of bank secrecy, the requested party may require that the request be authorized by a judge or another judicial authority.[221]

Money Laundering

While the U.N. Drug Convention treated money laundering as tangential to illicit drug trafficking, the European Money Laundering Convention tackles money laundering as a major offense in and of itself. Moreover, the European Money Laundering Convention will reach laundered proceeds from a wider array of offenses than the U.N. Drug Convention.[222] A major aim of the European Money Laundering Convention is to undercut the effectiveness of money laundering in sustaining the economic bases of criminal organizations.[223] Hence, the Convention's focus is naturally on the discovery, immobilization and eventual forfeiture of proceeds of criminal activity. In support of this objective, the preamble to the Convention states the Council's belief that the fight against serious crime is an international concern requiring modern and effective methods of an international character and that depriving criminals of proceeds from crime is one of those methods.[224]

Article 6 of the European Money Laundering Convention governs laundering offenses and, like many other provisions of the Convention, Article 6 is largely based on the U.N. Drug Convention.[225] First, signatory parties are required to criminalize money laundering under their domestic laws.[226] This requirement is nearly identical to Article 3 (b)(i), (b)(ii), (c)(i), and (c)(iv) of the U.N. Drug Convention. The knowing conversion or transfer of illicit proceeds for the purpose of disguising or concealing the illicit origin of the property is an offense under the European Money Laundering Convention.[227] Like the U.N. Drug Convention, the European Money Laundering Convention also criminalizes assisting any

---

217 Euro. Conv. Money Laundering, *supra* note 16, at Art. 14(1).

218 *Id.* at Art. 14(2).

219 *Id.* at Art. 15.

220 *See id.* at Art. 18.

221 *Id.* at Art. 18(7).

222 *See* Euro. Conv. Money Laundering, *supra* note 16, at Art. 1(e) (defining a "predicate offense" as "any criminal offense as a result of which proceeds were generated that may become the subject of an offense as defined in Article 6 of this Convention"). *See also* Explanatory Report, *supra* note 201, ¶ 8.

223 *See* Euro. Conv. Money Laundering, *supra* note 16, at Pmbl.. *See also* Explanatory Report, *supra* note 201, ¶ 8.

224 *See* Euro. Conv. Money Laundering, *supra* note 16, at Pmbl.

225 *See* Explanatory Report, *supra* note 201, ¶ 32.

226 Euro. Conv. Money Laundering, *supra* note 16, at Art. 6(1).

227 *Id.* at Art. 6(1)(a).

person who has committed a predicate offense to evade the legal consequences of his actions.[228] The knowing concealment or disguise of the true nature or source of illicit proceeds is also an offense under the act.[229]

Subject to a party's constitutional principles and the basic concepts of its legal system, a signatory party must criminalize: (1) the acquisition, use or possession of property known, at the time of receipt to be illicit proceeds;[230] and (2) participation in, association or conspiracy to commit, attempts to commit and aiding and abetting and counseling the commission of any of the above offenses.[231]

The most significant difference between the U.N. Drug Convention and the European Money Laundering Convention, regarding offenses which a party must criminalize, is that the European Money Laundering Convention is not limited to drug-related offenses.[232] The European Money Laundering Convention is not limited to drug offenses because the drafters believed that it was not necessary to prevent states from limiting the scope of application vis-a-vis the U.N. Drug Convention.[233] Consequently, Article 6(4) echoes Article 2(2) and provides that states may, by declaration at the time of signature or ratification, enumerate the predicate offenses to which Article 6 (and likewise the confiscation measures of Article 2) will apply.[234] A similar result is that the Convention does not include "participation" as an element of Article 6(1)(a)-(b) and (c).[235]

Paragraphs 2 and 3 of Article 6 are, for the most part, not contained in the U.N. Drug Convention and are intended to assist states in implementing the provisions of paragraph 1. First, it is immaterial whether the predicate offense was subject to the criminal jurisdiction of the Party.[236] The Committee wanted to make clear that the Convention was intended to cover extraterritorial offenses. As a result, the universality principle of jurisdiction will apply to predicate offenses.[237]

Second, states may provide that the laundering offenses do not apply to the person who committed the predicate offense.[238] This provision recognizes that the penal systems of some states provide that if a person has committed a predicate offense he may not be tried for an

---

228 *Id.*

229 *See id.* at Art. 6(1)(b).

230 *See id.* at Art. 6(1)(c).

231 *See id.* at Art. 6(1)(d). To the extent that criminalization does not conflict with these principles, the state is obligated to criminalize the above acts. *See also* Explanatory Report, *supra* note 201, ¶ 32.

232 *See* Euro. Conv. Money Laundering, *supra* note 16, at Art. 1(e). *Cf.* U.N. Drug Convention, *supra* note 14, at Art. 3(1)(a)(i)-(iv) (generally defining predicate offenses as any activity related to the manufacture, possession and trafficking of illicit drugs).

233 *See* Explanatory Report, *supra* note 201, ¶ 32.

234 *See* Euro. Conv. Money Laundering, *supra* note 16, at Arts. 2(2), 6(4). As a result, the offenses referred to in respect to confiscation are not necessarily the same offenses referred to with respect to a predicate offense for the purposes of the laundering provisions. *See* Explanatory Report, *supra* note 201, ¶ 34.

235 The U.N. Drug Convention includes participation as an element of every laundering offense under Art. 3(1)(b)(i)-(ii), -(c)(i), -(c)(iv). The committee did not feel that it was necessary to include participation due to the approach taken (i.e., because the Convention is not limited to drug offenses). *See* Explanatory Report, *supra* note 201, ¶ 32.

236 *See* Euro. Conv. Money Laundering, *supra* note 16, at Art. 6(2)(a).

237 Nilsson, *supra* note 20, at 431. The author explains, by way of illustration, that under this principle if the offense of trading in endangered species was committed in Country A and the proceeds were laundered in Country B, it would not matter if trade in endangered species was illegal in Country B. *Id.*

238 Euro. Conv. Money Laundering, *supra* note 16, at Art. 6(2)(b).

additional offense of laundering the proceeds of that offense.[239] Finally, knowledge, intent or purpose as an element of the laundering offense may be inferred from the facts.[240]

Paragraph 3 provides for additional offenses which are not covered by the U.N. Drug Convention. States are not obligated to adopt such offenses, but they may adopt these measures if they consider such adoption necessary.[241] Briefly, this article imposes a negligence standard for those who *should have* assumed that the property was proceeds.[242] In addition, the European Money Laundering Convention seeks to reach those who transact business with criminals knowing that payment is being made with the proceeds from crime.[243] This paragraph also seeks to criminalize the promotion of further criminal activity.[244]

Other International Efforts Related to Money Laundering

In addition to the broadly negotiated international conventions already discussed, an array of other initiatives have been propounded by intergovernmental organizations, international task forces and committees, and national governments. While some of these efforts have a global scope, many of them have focused on how money laundering concerns can be addressed in a regional context or what measures can be taken domestically to prevent money laundering. Taken as a whole, however, these initiatives suggest a consistent approach to the money laundering problem that could, eventually, be integrated into a global regime designed to suppress money laundering.

The EC Directive

On June 10, 1991, the Council Directive on Prevention of the Use of the Financial System for the Purpose of Money Laundering ("Directive"),[245] was passed by the European Community Council of Economic Finance Ministers (ECOFIN). With the Directive, EC

---

239 The committee also recognized that several states have laws providing the contrary. *See* Explanatory Report, *supra* note 201, ¶ 32.

240 Euro. Conv. Money Laundering, *supra* note 16, at Art. 6(2)(c). This provision mirrors Art. 3(4) of the U.N. Drug Convention, *supra* note 14.

241 *See* Euro. Conv. Money Laundering, *supra* note 16, at Art. 6(3), which provides as follows:

> Each Party may adopt such measures as it considers necessary to establish also as offenses under its domestic law all or some of the acts referred to in paragraph 1 of this Article, in any or all of the following cases where the offender:
>
> a. ought to have assumed that the property was proceeds;
>
> b. acted for the purposes of making a profit;
>
> c. acted for the purpose of promoting the carrying on of further criminal activity.

242 *See id.* at Art. 6(3)(a).

243 *See id.* at Art. 6(3)(b). *See also* Explanatory Report, *supra* note 201, ¶ 32.

244 Euro. Conv. Money Laundering, *supra* note 16, at Art. 6(3)(c).

245 Council Directive No. 91/308, 1991 O.J. (L 166) 77 (June 10, 1991) [hereinafter EC Directive]. For a discussion of how the EC Directive may influence the Euro. Conv. Money Laundering and a comparison of their provisions see Nilsson, *supra* note 20, at 429-31. Under the terms of the Treaty of Rome, the EC can only "prohibit" an offense as it is not within its competence to "criminalize" activity. *See* Treaty Establishing the European Economic Community, Mar. 25, 1957, 298 U.N.T.S. 11. *See also* BERNASCONI, *supra* note 14; GILMORE, *supra* note 14.

member states took a common stance in efforts to thwart money laundering.[246] The Directive's two primary aims are (1) to require member states to introduce laws prohibiting money laundering by January 1, 1993,[247] and (2) to increase cooperation among member states in investigating and prosecuting money laundering. The Directive imposes significant obligations and duties upon a wide range of financial institutions, including the insurance industry. It also applies sanctions to credit and financial institutions which refuse to comply with the Directive's reporting requirements.[248]

Credit and financial institutions will be required to demand the identity of customers and must confirm the identity of the client[249] if the amount of the transaction exceeds 15,000 European Credit Units (ECU's) (equivalent to approximately US$18,500).[250] The Directive also requires the lifting of bank secrecy laws in the applicable jurisdictions.[251] Many states have implemented the Directive's requirements with new or amended national legislation.[252]

The Member States of the European Community are also planning a supranational European police force to regulate anticipated problems with currency movement once Europe is integrated in 1992,[253] while many Caribbean nations are discussing the benefits of a regional criminal court and a multi-national narcotics strike force.[254]

---

246 *EC Ministers to Adopt Formally Money Laundering Law*, Reuter Library Report, June 7, 1991, *available in* LEXIS, NEXIS Library, Wires File. *See also* Carlson & Zagaris, *supra* note 11, at 572. The EC Directive adopted the definition of money laundering in the U.N. Drug Convention. EC Directive, *supra* note 245, at Art. 1. However, the Directive does not limit its scope to drug-related offenses ("since money laundering occurs not only in relation to the proceeds of drug-related offenses but also in relation to the proceeds of other criminal offenses . . . the Member States should, within the meaning of their legislation, extend the effects of the Directive to include the proceeds of such activities.. . ."). *Id.* at Pmbl.

247 EC Directive, *supra* note 245, at Art. 16(1). The requirements extend to the branches of foreign-owned subsidiaries. *Id.* at Art. 1.

248 Carlson & Zagaris, *supra* note 11, at 573. Sanctions are to be developed by the member states. EC Directive, *supra* note 245, at Art. 14.

249 EC Directive, *supra* note 245, at Art. 3.

250 *Id.* at Art. 3. For transactions below the threshold amount, financial institutions must obtain identification information if there is a suspicion of money laundering. *Id.* These records must be maintained for a minimum of five years after the relationship with the customer ends. *Id.* at Art. 4. *See also* Reuter Library Report, June 7, 1991, *supra* note 246.

251 EC Directive, *supra* note 245, at Art. 9. For a more detailed discussion of the Directive, *see* INTERNATIONAL EFFORTS TO COMBAT MONEY LAUNDERING xvi-xviii (W.C. Gilmore ed. 1992). *See also* Duncan E. Alford, *Anti-Money Laundering Regulations: A Burden on Financial Institutions*, 19 N.C.J. INT'L L. & COM. REG. 437 (1994).

252 For example, on December 30, 1993, Spain's law implementing the Directive (Law 19/1993) went into effect. *Implementation of Money Laundering Directive*, Financial Regulation Report, Jan. 1994 *available in* LEXIS, NEXIS Library, Curnws File. As of April 1, 1994, financial institutions in the U.K. will face additional requirements as a result of the new law implementing the EC Directive (as part of the 1993 Criminal Justice Act). *U.K. Gears Up to Enforce Tough New Anti-Laundering Law*, Money Laundering Alert, Mar. 1994, *available in* LEXIS, NEXIS Library, Curnws File.

253 For a discussion of other EC initiatives directed at drug trafficking and money laundering, *see Address by Mr. Padraig Flynn to the United Nations General Assembly—Special Session on Drugs—New York, 26 October 1993*, RAPID, Oct. 27, 1993, *available in* LEXIS, NEXIS Library, Wires File.

254 *See* Fred Strasser, *Crime Has No Borders So Countries Close Ranks: Drugs Spur Efforts*, NAT'L L.J., Oct. 30, 1989, at 1 (summarizing current international efforts to thwart drug trafficking and money laundering).

The Financial Action Task Force and the Caribbean Financial Action Task Force

The Financial Action Task Force (FATF), initiated in July 1989 by the G-7 nations and presently consisting of 28 members,[255] prepared a report on money laundering ("Task Force Report"[256]) which has been called "the single most comprehensive, significant and forceful international declaration on money laundering to date."[257] These nations represent 80 percent of the world's 500 largest banks. At the time of the Task Force Report, only a few of these nations had criminalized money laundering.[258]

While the FATF's smaller membership eases implementation and is conducive to developing consistent policies, there are some drawbacks to its Eurocentric composition. FATF members are mainly states with sophisticated, highly developed economies where financial regulation is commonplace. These states also have a high number of drug users and are major importers, rather than producers, of illicit substances. Though the FATF conducts international outreach programs, its current makeup does not adequately represent states that are traditional laundering havens, drug-producing states, and states with uneven or emerging economies.[259]

The Task Force Report consists of 40 recommendations and, while it has no legal effect, it is a useful tool in formulating a unified policy to combat money laundering.[260] This section discusses that ground-breaking report and digests the progress of the FATF in its first five years of operation. In its most recent report, FATF-V decided to continue its work for an additional five years (until 1998-99).

The topics covered by the Task Force Report are comprehensive and include definition of the offense of money laundering,[261] provisional measures and confiscation,[262] customer

---

[255] *See* Gilmore, *supra* note 202, at 9. As of December 1992, the FATF consisted of 26 member countries as well as the Commission of the European Communities and the Gulf Corporation Council. The member states include: Australia, Austria, Belgium, Luxembourg, the Netherlands, Spain, Sweden, Switzerland, Denmark, Norway, Greece, Ireland, Portugal, Turkey, Finland, New Zealand, the United States, the United Kingdom, Hong Kong, Singapore, Italy, Germany, Canada, Japan, and France. *See* Polimeni, *Presentation on Behalf of the Presidency, Financial Action Task Force*, Conference Paper: The Mafia Challenge: What to Do Now?, International Conference, Palermo Italy (Dec. 10-12, 1992).

[256] European Committee on Crime Problems, Recommendations by the Financial Action Task Force on Money Laundering (done at Strasbourg Feb. 7, 1990) [hereinafter Task Force Report]. It must be noted that the FATF is not a G-7 structure, although it was created, at first, under the aegis of the G-7.

[257] Statement of Deputy Treasury Secretary John E. Robson, *Group of 7 Asks Money-Laundering Curbs*, N.Y. TIMES, Apr. 20, 1990, § D, at 1, *cited in* Note, *The International Attack On Money Laundering: European Initiatives*, 1991 DUKE J. COMP. & INT'L L. 213, 218. For additional, detailed discussion of the measures contained in the FATF report, *see U.N. Money Laundering Report, supra* note 39, ¶¶ 43-55.

[258] *See G-7 Nations Launch Global Laundering Assault*, Money Laundering Alert, May 1990, at 1, *available in* LEXIS, NEXIS Library, Arcnws File. At the time of the FATF's inception, money laundering was an offense in Australia, Canada, France, Italy, Luxembourg, the United Kingdom and the United States. As of February 1990, legislation creating an offense was pending in four Task Force countries: Belgium, Germany, Sweden, and Switzerland. There is no money laundering offense in the remaining four countries: Netherlands, Spain, Austria, and Japan. Task Force Report, *supra* note 256, at 11.

[259] *See* Hogarth, *supra* note 22.

[260] These recommendations have been referred to as the "action steps." *See* Gilmore, *supra* note 202, at 9.

[261] Task Force Report, *supra* note 256. Recs. 4-7 encourage the implementation of legislation criminalizing drug money laundering. Liability could be based on laundering funds derived from any serious offense and criminal liability should extend to corporations. *Id.*

[262] Measures similar to those of the U.N. Drug Convention should be adopted to facilitate investigation, seizure and confiscation of laundered funds, proceeds from crime or instrumentalities used in crime. *Id.* at Rec. 8.

identification and record-keeping requirements,[263] the increased diligence of financial institutions,[264] measures to cope with nations that have insufficient or no anti-money-laundering measures,[265] administrative cooperation,[266] and mutual legal assistance in extradition and confiscation.[267] The overarching recommendations of the Task Force Report strongly encourage implementation of the U.N. Drug Convention, the limitation of bank secrecy so as not to impede the detection and suppression of money laundering, and increased mutual legal assistance in money laundering investigations.[268]

The delegations to the FATF agreed to continue its work for a period of five years. This five-year period will be marked by continuous review of the FATF's effectiveness and the need to continue its mission. In a report prepared after its first full year of implementation,[269] the Task Force identified several areas where the 1990 recommendations had been effective and other areas which needed further attention. The FATF's observations and commentary upon review can be divided into three categories: (1) an assessment of the implementation of the 40 1990 recommendations; (2) a need to extend the geographical reach of the FATF recommendations; and (3) a projection of the FATF's role in the future of combatting money laundering. Only the first of these categories merits detailed discussion here.

As of May 1991, most FATF countries and participating countries had substantially implemented the legal measures recommended by the 1990 FATF.[270] Very few nations indicated that implementation of a particular measure was not foreseeable.[271] However, of the nations participating in the follow-up survey, several indicated obstacles to improving domestic legislation (recommendations 4-8) that is designed to facilitate mutual legal

---

263 Anonymous accounts or accounts in fictitious names should be prohibited and institutions should be required to take reasonable steps to ascertain the "true identity of clients." *Id.* at Recs. 12-13. Records of transactions or customer identification should be maintained for five years and should be sufficient to reconstruct individual transactions. *Id.* at Rec. 14. Institutions should pay special attention to suspicious transactions and should be permitted to report suspicious transactions without fear of civil or criminal liability for breach of any bank secrecy regulation or contract. This is essentially a good faith, "safe harbor" provision. *Id.* at Rec. 15.

264 Institutions should develop internal procedures against money laundering and should not warn customers of reported suspicions. *Id.* at Recs. 17-20.

265 Special attention should be paid to transactions originating from institutions or companies located in countries with insufficient or no anti-money laundering measures. *Id.* at Rec. 21. These recommendations should apply to offshore subsidiaries—especially when located in countries with insufficient money laundering controls. *Id.* at Rec. 22. A reporting requirement for all transactions over a certain fixed amount should be considered and alternatives to cash (*e.g.*, checks, direct deposit, payment cards) should be encouraged. *Id.* at Recs. 23 & 24. Regulatory authorities should guard against the control or acquisition of financial institution by criminals or their confederates (case in point, BCCI). *Id.* at Rec. 29.

266 A record of international currency flows should be maintained and disseminated as should a compilation of the latest developments in money laundering and money laundering techniques. *Id.* at Recs. 30-31. Information regarding suspicious transactions should be available "upon request" and should be disseminated in a manner that protects privacy and data. *Id.* at Rec. 32.

267 *Id.* at Recs. 33-40. Bilateral and multilateral agreements should be concluded to give the broadest possible mutual legal assistance (such as the Euro. Conv. Money Laundering). The seizure of persons and evidence should be aided by mutual assistance as should the identification, freezing, seizing and confiscation of assets. Procedures should be developed to provide for the sharing of confiscated assets.

There should be a mechanism for selecting the best venue for criminal prosecutions and money laundering should be recognized as an extraditable offense. Finally, extradition should be expedited by inter-ministry communications, extradition based solely on arrest warrants, extradition of nationals and a simplified procedure where the relator has consented to extradition.

268 Task Force Report, *supra* note 256, at Recs. 1-3.

269 Financial Action Task Force on Money Laundering, *Report* (May 13, 1991).

270 *Id.* at 6.

271 *Id.*

assistance and other forms of cooperation (recommendations 32-40).[272] Particular obstacles included defining predicate offenses and the apparent inability of some states to establish corporate criminal liability.[273] These difficulties, in turn, impede or preclude effective mutual legal assistance because many states will be unable to fulfill the requirement of dual criminality.[274] The FATF believes that these obstacles may be overcome by flexible relations and the harmonization of domestic legislation.[275]

Several other obstacles were identified through the survey process, including the increasingly large role played by non-traditional financial institutions and businesses and professions which deal in large sums of currency.[276] To cope with this growing dilemma, the FATF classified these professions under four broad headings in order to facilitate the implementation of recommendation 11 relating to such organizations.[277] Another enforcement problem identified by the survey related to a lack of cooperation between law enforcement authorities. Often, technical and legal difficulties, such as rights of privacy and confidentiality, hinder effective legal assistance. These difficulties may be attributed to the inability to satisfy dual criminality, which leads to a refusal to provide information.[278]

In its third year, FATF-III began to look more closely at the level of compliance with FATF recommendations of its members. It is expected that all of the member countries will be evaluated by the end of 1994. Another task of the FATF is to keep abreast of "evolving money laundering techniques." This function is made easier by the fact that the FATF is the world's only body which is concerned solely with the dilemma of money laundering. Efforts have also been made, in the third year, to coordinate efforts with nonmember countries and relevant international bodies. Particular attention has been paid to nations in the Caribbean region, the Asia-Pacific region, Central Europe, Eastern Europe and Africa.[279]

The FATF's fourth annual report, released in June 1993, indicated that nearly all of the twenty-six member countries had made further progress in implementing the FATF's 40 recommendations. For example, ten members had enacted measures to criminalize money laundering and an additional eight members were in the process of doing the same. In its fourth year, the FATF focused on three primary areas: (1) evaluating the progress of its members in implementing the FATF's recommendations; (2) monitoring developments in money laundering techniques and considering their implications on possible counter

---

272 *Id.*

273 *Id.* at 7.

274 *Id.* at 8.

275 *Id.*

276 *Id.* at 11-12.

277 *Id.* at 12. These categories are (1) organizations whose main function is to provide a financial service; (2) gambling organizations (*e.g.*, lotteries, casinos, etc.); (3) organizations which buy and sell high value items; and (4) professionals who offer clients account facilities.

278 *Id.* at 14.

279 For a comprehensive review of the activities of FATF-III, see European Committee on Crime Problems, Financial Action Task Force on Money Laundering: Annual Report 1991-1992, M.L 92(8) (Strasbourg, Sept. 28-30, 1992). *See also* European Committee on Crime Problems, Annexes to the Annual Report - Financial Action Task Force, M.L 92(9) (Strasbourg, Sept. 28-30, 1992). These reports were prepared as a result of the Money Laundering Conference of the European Committee on Crime Problems at Strasbourg, France Sept. 28-30, 1992 under the auspices of the Council of Europe. For a commentary on the work of FATF-III and its relation to the current state of money laundering *see generally* Polimeni, *Presentation on Behalf of the Presidency, Financial Action Task Force*, Conference Paper: The Mafia Challenge: What to Do Now?, International Conference, Palermo Italy (Dec. 10-12, 1992).

measures; and (3) implementing an external relations program to promote efforts to combat money laundering.[280]

The report indicated that the FATF continued its task of conducting in-depth evaluations of the money laundering efforts of its members. Evaluations consisted of on-site visits by money laundering and financial experts and an analytical report of the findings. The report contained summaries of evaluations for eight member countries: Austria, Belgium, Canada, Denmark, Italy, Luxembourg, Switzerland, and the United States.[281]

The FATF did not discern any genuinely new laundering techniques. But one of the gravest concerns identified by the FATF during 1992-93 was that non-financial institutions (such as currency exchanges, check cashers and casinos) continued to be significant centers of money-laundering activities.

Though no new recommendations were adopted during FATF-V (1993-1994), the FATF's report on its fifth year of operation revealed significant developments in the implementation of the original 40 recommendations and suggested new possibilities for bringing money laundering under control.[282] Nearly all FATF members have criminalized money laundering, and all members either permit or require their banks to report "suspicious" transactions. Many members have also had some success in amending their bank secrecy laws, which will assist those members that have constructed a legal framework for mutual assistance in criminal matters. Providing assistance in the freezing, seizing and confiscation of assets is a priority for many FATF members; many members have ratified the European Money Laundering Convention.

Several trends continue to emerge in money laundering. As nations move toward closer regulation of the traditional financial sector, FATF-V revealed that money launderers continue to identify alternative routes such as shell companies, electronic funds transfers, non-bank financial institutions (*e.g.*, currency exchanges), and non-financial institutions (*e.g.*, travel agents and auto dealers). Areas of the globe identified as particularly conducive to laundering include Central and Eastern Europe, Asia, and South America.

Perhaps the most significant development of FATF-V is the decision to continue the FATF for an additional five years, during which time the FATF will: (1) continue to monitor the progress of members in implementing recommendations;[283] (2) review money laundering techniques and countermeasures; and (3) carry out external relations to promote worldwide action against money laundering.

Some members have encountered difficulties in implementing the FATF recommendations. For instance, some members have constitutional or other legal impediments to establishing corporate criminal liability for laundering offenses. In addition, only about half of the FATF members have ratified the U.N. Drug Convention.

---

[280] Council of Europe, European Committee on Crime Problems, *Information on the Activities of the Financial Action Task Force on Money Laundering in 1992-93*, CDPC (93) 6 (Strasbourg, Apr. 16, 1993).

[281] FATF's fourth report and the evaluations of the eight member countries are summarized in *FATF Pinpoints Non-Bank Entities as Laundering Meccas*, Money Laundering Alert, July 1993; *Annual FATF Report Puts Eight Countries Under Microscope*, Money Laundering Alert, Aug. 1993.

[282] OECD, Financial Action Task Force on Money Laundering: 1993-1994 (June 1994).

[283] FATF-V evaluated nine members in 1993-1994 (Netherlands, Germany, Norway, Japan, Greece, Spain, Finland, Hong Kong and Ireland). In all, 21 members have been evaluated; the remainder will be evaluated in FATF-VI.

A significant development closely related to the FATF is the formation of the Caribbean Financial Action Task Force (CFATF) in June of 1990.[284] In November 1992 at a Ministerial meeting in Kingston, Jamaica, the CFATF agreed to follow the 40 recommendations of the FATF, as well as 21 additional recommendations.[285] The CFATF also agreed to establish procedures to monitor the implementation of the recommendations. In December 1994, implementing the CFATF recommendations was one of many action items relating to money laundering in the "Plan of Action" that emerged from the Summit of the Americas in Miami, Florida.[286]

OAS Initiatives to Combat Money Laundering

In recent years, the Organization of American States (OAS) has taken steps to suppress the flow of narcotics and illicit proceeds throughout its territory. Two instruments in particular deserve mention: the Draft Inter-American Convention on Mutual Assistance in Criminal Matters ("Draft Convention")[287] and the *Model Regulations Concerning Laundering Offenses Connected to Illicit Drug Trafficking and Related Offenses* ("Regulations").[288]

Although it appears to be a typical mutual legal assistance treaty in many regards, the Draft Convention utilizes several procedures related to the freezing and seizing of assets that have characterized the mutual legal assistance treaties recently concluded between the United States and several laundering hubs. First, a requested state must execute requests for the search, seizure, attachment and surrender of any items, documents, records or effects.[289] The law of the requested state will apply to any such procedure.[290] Second, the central authority of any party may convey, to the central authority of any other party, any information related to the existence of any proceeds, fruits or instrumentalities of a crime within its territory.[291] Finally, if proceeds are found, the parties must assist each other in taking precautionary measures to secure the proceeds, fruits and instrumentalities of the crime.[292] The extent of assistance permitted will be determined by the laws of each state.[293]

---

[284] The CFATF was formed during the June 1990 Caribbean Drug Money Laundering Conference. *See* Berta Esperanza Hernandez, *RIP to IRP—Money Laundering and Drug Trafficking Controls Score a Knockout Victory Over Bank Secrecy*, 18 N.C.J. INT'L L. & COM. REG. 235, 289 (1993). For a description of developments in the Caribbean leading up to the adoption of the FATF's recommendations *see* William C. Gilmore, *International Responses to Money Laundering: A General Overview*, Conference Paper: The Money Laundering Conference, M.L 92(10) 13-14 (Strasbourg, Sept. 28-30, 1992).

[285] *Money Launderers Turning to New Institutions, Task Force Reports*, BNA's Banking Report, July 5, 1993, at 34.

[286] *Summit of the Americas, "Plan of Action,"* Notisur—Latin American Political Affairs, Dec. 16, 1994, *available in* LEXIS, NEXIS Library, Curnws File. Other items included ratifying the U.N. Drug Convention; enacting legislation for the freezing, seizing and confiscation of assets; and encouraging better reporting by financial institutions.

[287] *Report of the Chairman of the Working Group to Study the Draft Inter-American Convention on Mutual Assistance in Criminal Matters*, OEA/Ser.G/CP/CAJP.860/92 [hereinafter *Working Group Report*] at 17-35.

[288] OEA/Ser.L/XIV.2/CICAD/INF.58/92 (July 9, 1992) [hereinafter Regulations].

[289] *Working Group Report*, *supra* note 287, at Art. 13, at 23.

[290] *Id.*

[291] *Id.* at Art. 14.

[292] *Id.* at Art. 15, at 24. Articles 14 and 15 were patterned after Article 11 of the mutual legal assistance treaty between the United States and Mexico. *Id.* at 10.

[293] *Id.*

These provisions represent recognition on the part of the OAS member states of the importance of inter-state cooperation in controlling the proceeds of crime and presaged more detailed efforts like the Regulations discussed *infra.*

In 1990 the OAS adopted the mandates of the *Declaration and Program of Action of Ixtapa* and embarked upon a course dedicated to halting money laundering and controlling the proceeds from crime.[294] Several of the measures recommended by the declaration related to money laundering and judicial assistance, including *inter alia*: emphasizing the need for legislation that criminalizes money laundering and makes it possible to trace, seize and confiscate illicit proceeds; recommending to member states that they develop mechanisms of bilateral and multilateral cooperation to prevent the laundering of proceeds and facilitate the tracing, seizing and forfeiture of assets; and, finally, proposing to the OAS General Assembly that it direct the Inter-American Drug Abuse Control Commission (CICAD) to draft model regulations in conformity with the 1988 U.N. Drug Convention.[295]

In response to this command, CICAD drafted, and the General Assembly adopted, *Model Regulations Concerning Laundering Offenses Connected to Illicit Drug Trafficking and Related Offenses* ("Regulations").[296] The General Assembly of the OAS recommends that these measures be adopted by the member states, pursuant to their respective legal systems; the regulations have no independent legal force.[297] The Regulations are extensive—comprising 19 lengthy and detailed articles that broadly define laundering offenses.[298] They include, *inter alia*, the freezing[299] and eventual confiscation of proceeds of crime;[300] the freezing of proceeds connected to illicit traffic committed against the laws of another country;[301] various measures related to inter-state cooperation[302] (traditional mutual legal

---

[294] The Declaration was adopted at the 20th regular session of the General Assembly of the Organization of American States, June 4-9, 1990. *See* Inter-American Drug Abuse Control Commission, *Final Report of the Group of Experts to Prepare Model Regulations Concerning Laundering Offenses Connected to Illicit Drug Trafficking and Related Offenses* [hereinafter *OAS money laundering report*], OEA/Ser.L/XIV.2.11/CICAD/doc.391/92 (Mar. 9, 1992) at 1.

[295] *Id.* at 2. The measures thought necessary under the U.N. Drug Convention were: (1) criminalizing money laundering; (2) preventing the use of financial institutions for the purposes of money laundering; (3) enabling authorities to trace, freeze and confiscate proceeds; (4) changing regulatory regimes to ensure that bank secrecy laws do not impede law enforcement efforts related to illicit proceeds; and (5) studying the feasibility of reporting large currency transactions and permitting the interstate communication of such information.

[296] Regulations, *supra* note 288. The General Assembly of the OAS adopted these regulations at its twenty second regular session, held in the Bahamas, from May 18-23, 1992. *Id.* at iii.

[297] *Id.* at Introduction.

[298] *Id.* at Art. 2. Laundering is committed by anyone who converts, transfers, acquires, possesses, uses, conceals, disguises or impedes the establishment of the true nature of property which he knows, should have known or is intentionally ignorant that such property is proceeds from illicit traffic or related proceeds. The definition also includes traditional conspiracy and aiding and abetting criminal liability. The knowledge required as an element of the offense can be inferred from objective factual circumstances.

[299] *Id.* at Art. 4. In accordance with law, and without prior notice or a hearing, the court may order any provisional or preventive measure necessary to preserve the availability of proceeds of crime. Such measures may include a freezing or seizure order.

[300] *Id.* at Art. 5. Once convicted of an illicit traffic or related offense, the court must order that any property or proceeds related to the offense be forfeited. The Regulations also impose the theory of value confiscation found in the Euro. Conv. Money Laundering such that, where the proceeds cannot be forfeited, the court must order the forfeiture of any other property of the person of an equivalent value to the forfeiture order. In the alternative, the court may order the person to pay a fine in the amount of the forfeiture order.

[301] *Id.* at Art. 8. The doctrine of dual criminality will apply to this provision.

[302] *Id.* at Art. 18.

assistance and provisional measures[303] and the recognition of foreign orders of forfeiture[304]); and a prohibition against the use of bank secrecy as an impediment to enforcement.[305] In addition, significant protections are accorded to the property rights of *bona fide* third parties.[306] Special note should be taken that, like the U.N. Drug Convention, the Regulations suffer from the limitation that offenses criminalized under them only include drug-related money laundering.[307]

The bulk of the Regulations, however, pertain to significant requirements and restraints which will apply to a broad array of financial institutions.[308] Under the Regulations, financial institutions may not keep anonymous accounts or accounts under fictitious names and they are further required to record and verify the identity of clients.[309] Any records must be turned over promptly to the competent authorities, who may then share that information with other domestic and foreign competent authorities in cases concerning drug-related violations.[310]

The Regulations employ a system of currency transaction reporting similar to that mandated by many domestic statutes (most notably CTR's that must be filed in the United States) whereby financial institutions will be subject to extensive reporting requirements for transactions which exceed a specified amount.[311] Records must be kept for five years and must be made available to the courts or competent authorities for use in civil, criminal, and administrative proceedings related to illicit traffic or illicit offenses.[312] Special provisions apply to suspicious transactions; any such transaction must be promptly reported to the competent authorities.[313] Any such report, if made in good faith, will not subject the institution or any individual to civil or criminal liability related to the making of an unauthorized disclosure.[314] One shortcoming of the Regulations is that no provision is made for the regulation of electronic wire transfers, although to the extent that any such transactions are "suspicious," they must be reported.

Stiff penalties apply to financial institutions or employees thereof found to be in violation of the regulations. The institution itself will be held criminally liable for the actions of its employees, staff, directors, owners, or authorized representatives and may be subjected to fines and suspension of an operating license or operating charter.[315] Liability must be

---

303 *Id.* at (1)-(2), (4).

304 *Id.* at (3).

305 *Id.* at Art. 19.

306 *Id.* at Art. 6. Notice must be given to all those claiming a legitimate interest in the property. Upon a showing of good faith and lack of culpability, property will be returned to a *bona fide* third party.

307 *Id.* at Art. 2.

308 *Id.* at Arts. 9-16. The category of financial institutions includes traditional financial institutions (*e.g.*, banks, trust companies, savings and loan associations, credit unions, etc.), securities brokers, currency exchanges, and any institution performing any of a number of financial activities (cashing of checks, sale of traveler's checks and money orders, substantial transmitting of funds, and any other activity subject to supervision by government banking authorities). *Id.* at Art. 9. Special provision has also been made whereby the Regulations will apply to establishments which carry out transactions in excess of the specified amounts, such as real estate, weapons sales, jewelry, automobiles, travel services, casinos and professional services (*e.g.*, accountants and lawyers). *Id.* at Art. 16.

309 *Id.* at Art. 10. Records must be kept for at least five years.

310 *Id.* at Art. 11. Financial institutions cannot warn customers of investigations as they are barred from notifying any person, other than those authorized by law, that a request for information has been made.

311 *Id.* at Art. 12(1).

312 *Id.* at (3), (6).

313 *Id.* at Art. 13(1)-(2).

314 *Id.* at (4).

315 *Id.* at Art. 14(1)-(2).

premised on a willful failure to comply with the Regulations or the willful filing of a false report.[316] These Regulations, drafted in such detail, will likely prove indispensable to the development of the type of domestic legislation necessary to the effective implementation of multilateral instruments related to narco-trafficking and money laundering.

Basle Committee's Statement of Principles on Money Laundering

In a statement issued in December 1988, the Basle Committee on Banking Regulations and Supervisory Practices ("Basle Committee") declared that it would direct its attention toward halting international money laundering. The Committee, comprised of representatives of the Group of 10 industrialized nations (G-10),[317] issued a statement of principles urging banks to take several measures to curb money laundering.[318] The statement is not legally binding, but is, instead, an example of the "soft law" approach that recommends measures to be adopted. Banks were urged to take these measures: obtaining identification information about customers; taking steps to ascertain the true ownership of accounts and assets; refusing to conduct business with customers that refuse to provide identification information; refusing to carry out suspicious transactions; and taking appropriate legal actions in response to suspicious transactions.[319] To implement these measures, banks were requested to adopt formal procedures and develop specific policies for the identification of customers and the maintenance of financial records.

National Strategies to Control Money Laundering

Though money laundering is a complex problem with global dimensions and potentially very damaging effects on national societies, the substantive elements of a domestic strategy to control it are not difficult. But they require political will by governments, administration, resources, and technical personnel to make them effective. Several of the initiatives discussed above contain the same basic elements and they are all somewhat consistent in their approach to better regulation of financial institutions and establishment of money laundering as a serious criminal offense. The actions taken at the domestic level are encompassed in the following strategies:[320]

Criminalize Money Laundering

Countries may create the substantive offense of money laundering as a matter of domestic policy or they may do so under the auspices of an international treaty. For instance,

---

316 *Id.* at (3).

317 The G-10 consists of Belgium, Canada, France, Germany, Great Britain, Italy, Japan, Luxembourg, The Netherlands, Sweden, and the United States. The European Community also participates in the G-10.

318 Basle Committee Statement, *supra* note 22.

319 *See* Hernandez, *supra* note 284, at 286.

320 For a more thorough description of national strategies to control money laundering, including the analysis of many examples of national legislation, *see generally* Zagaris & Castilla, *Constructing an International Financial Enforcement Subregime: The Implementation of Anti-Money-Laundering Policy*, 19 BROOK. J. INT'L L. 872 (1993); Savona & DeFeo, *supra* note 2; Note, *Putting Starch in European Efforts to Combat Money Laundering*, 60 FORDHAM L. REV. 429, 441-57 (1992) (summary of domestic initiatives in many European states); *The Cash Connection: Organized Crime, Financial Institutions, and Money Laundering* (President's Commission on Organized Crime, 1984).

Recommendation 4 of the FATF suggests that countries take measures to criminalize the offense of money laundering in accord with the U.N. Drug Convention, which requires member states to criminalize drug-related money laundering. In addition, the European Money Laundering Convention requires member states to make all money laundering a criminal offense.

National strategies to criminalize money laundering differ in two primary ways. First, the predicate offenses that generate the illicit proceeds vary from country to country. Some states have criminalized money laundering only with respect to drug-related offenses, but FATF Recommendation 5 urges states to consider criminalizing money laundering based on all serious offenses. This approach has been adopted by many countries and is illustrated by the European Money Laundering Convention. National strategies also vary with respect to the scienter or *mens rea* required before a charge of money laundering can be made. Most countries require that the defendant know that the funds were derived from criminal activity; other countries allow intent to be inferred from the circumstances or even criminalize conduct that is reckless or negligent.

Enable Authorities to Trace, Freeze and Confiscate Illicit Proceeds

As has been discussed with regard to the U.N. Drug Convention and the European Money Laundering Convention, enabling national authorities to trace, freeze, and confiscate the proceeds of crime has emerged as a significant weapon in the war on money laundering. Countries should be able to take these measures as a matter of domestic law enforcement and in response to an appropriate request from another country. A request will most likely be appropriate if both the requesting and requested states are parties to the U.N. Drug Convention, the European Money Laundering Convention, or one of the growing number of mutual legal assistance treaties that contain such a provision. The importance of implementing these procedures at the national level is embodied by FATF Recommendation 8.

Of course, national schemes to implement these measures will vary. Some states will compel forfeiture of assets only as part of a criminal conviction; other states allow assets to be frozen and confiscated during civil and administrative actions as well. Similarly, some states will provide assistance in the freezing and confiscating of assets only under the principle of dual criminality (*i.e.*, the offense giving rise to the proceeds and the charge of money laundering itself must be a criminal offense in both the requesting and requested states). Finally, some countries limit the application of these measures to drug-related offenses, including money laundering.

Require Financial Institutions to Obtain Customer Identification Information and Prohibit Anonymous Accounts

One of the primary techniques employed by national regulations is the requirement that financial institutions gather additional information about their customers and keep other types of records that could eventually aid law enforcement activities. Governments have taken steps to obtain more information about financial transactions by creating regulations for banks and financial institutions that require them to: (1) obtain information about the true identity of customers; (2) abolish anonymous accounts and accounts handled through intermediaries like attorneys and accountants; (3) keep more extensive records and retain those records for a period of at least five years; and (4) establish internal procedures designed to detect money laundering. The importance of customer identification and achievement of some level of transparency in banking is reflected by the prominence of such initiatives in the FATF Recommendations, the EC Directive, and the Basle Committee Statement. Implementing these record-keeping requirements, combined with the reporting requirements discussed below, necessarily involves a limitation on the application of bank secrecy laws and the right to financial privacy.

Require Financial Institutions to Report Large Cash Transactions and All "Suspicious" Transactions

By using an instrument known as the currency transaction report (CTR), many countries require both traditional and non-traditional financial institutions to report large or "suspicious" cash transactions to the government. In countries that have enacted such requirements, all cash transactions that exceed a threshold amount must be reported to the government.[321] This requirement does not apply only to banks; businesses such as casinos, securities dealers, automobile dealerships, currency exchange houses and other cash intensive businesses are also required to report large cash transactions. Some national laws also require banks to report all "suspicious transactions."[322] This requirement raises some thorny legal issues. For instance, some countries impose criminal liability on bank officials that fail to report such transactions. Additional penalties apply to bank officials that warn customers of current or pending investigations. Another complication concerns the possibility of an erroneous report of illegal activity, subjecting banks to potential civil liability from lawsuits filed by customers erroneously accused of wrongdoing. Customers may also sue banks for disclosure of private financial information that violates a contractual obligation or national bank secrecy laws. Many countries resolve this dilemma by granting banks immunity for reports of suspicious transactions made in "good faith."

Place More Forceful Controls on Professionals

National mechanisms to control money laundering are beginning to focus on the role that professionals such as lawyers, accountants, and securities dealers play in the process of money laundering. Some national laws place strict record-keeping and reporting requirements on all professionals involved in the financial sector. This is the least effective area of national control. The difficulties associated with means of professional self-controls, and other means of prevention and control of independently regulated professions, are discussed below.

---

321 FATF Recommendation 24 urges countries to develop a system "where banks and other financial institutions and intermediaries would report all domestic and international currency transactions above a fixed amount, to a national central agency with a computerized database. . . ."

322 *See* FATF Recommendation 16.

Provide for Inter-state Cooperation in Criminal Matters

In order to implement the requirements of international conventions, states will invariably be required to enact legislation permitting them to provide a variety of inter-state cooperation in penal matters, including recognition of foreign penal judgments (*e.g.*, the recognition of orders of forfeiture); extradition; mutual legal assistance; the freezing and seizing of assets; and transfer of proceedings. Accordingly, many countries already have legislation covering these topics, and that legislation may simply need to be amended to include these anti-money laundering conventions. Issues of note in this area include: (1) resolution of questions of *mens rea*; (2) creation of mechanisms to deal with dual criminality; (3) harmonization of domestic implementation with international requirements; and (4) establishment of efficient means of gathering and transmitting information.

The various initiatives designed to fight money laundering, including the "hard law" of treaties and the "soft law" of international directives, will require states to implement novel law enforcement techniques. States will need assistance in developing these domestic initiatives. Even though the obligation to provide legal assistance stems from treaties—either bilateral, regional or multilateral—any such request must be executed according to domestic law.[323] Therefore, as states formulate and implement domestic measures in order to comply with multilateral agreements which require a degree of inter-state cooperation, such as the U.N. Drug Convention and the European Money Laundering Convention, they will require guidance as to how domestic measures can be drafted in a manner that complies with the multilateral instrument.[324]

Toward this end, it has been suggested that the United Nations should assist member states in developing laws which are sufficiently compatible and harmonious to render international cooperation effective.[325] A model of such a law has already been propounded in the Model Regulations developed by the OAS and discussed fully *infra*. In addition, as noted above, Austria, Germany and Switzerland have each adopted the integrated approach in their domestic legislation.

---

[323] That national law will govern a state's capacity and mode of executing a request is usually a provision of the agreement on inter-state cooperation. Commission on Crime Prevention and Criminal Justice, *Money Laundering and Associated Issues: The Need for International Cooperation*, U.N. Doc. No. E/CN.15/1992/4/Add.5 [hereinafter *U.N. Money Laundering Report*], ¶ 63.

[324] Many countries have made tremendous progress in enacting domestic measures to thwart money laundering. *See Putting Starch in European Efforts to Combat Money Laundering*, *supra* note 320, at 441-57; Ernesto Savona, *Mafia Money Laundering Versus Italian Legislation*, EUR. J. CRIM. POL'Y & RES. (June 1993) (discussion of Italian response to money laundering). For a description of United States legislation related to money laundering and the regulation of financial institutions, arguably the most complex set of controls in the world, *see* Joseph J. Duffy & John A. Hedges, *United States Money Laundering Statutes: The Business Executive's Conundrum*, *in* INTERNATIONAL TRADE: AVOIDING CRIMINAL RISKS 14-1 (1991); Charles M. Carberry & Stuart E. Abrams, *The Money Laundering Laws—Civil and Criminal Ramifications*, CORPORATE COUNSEL'S QUARTERLY, Apr. 1990, at 88 (1990); John K. Villa, *A Critical View of Bank Secrecy Act Enforcement and the Money Laundering Statutes*, 37 CATH. U. L. REV. 489, 492 (1988); James D. Harmon, *United States Money Laundering Laws: International Implications*, 9 N.Y.L. SCH. J. INT'L & COMP. L. 1, 25 (1988); Note, *Recordkeeping and Reporting in an Attempt to Stop the Money Laundering Cycle: Why Blanket Recording and Reporting of Wire and Electronic Funds Transfers is Not the Answer*, 66 NOTRE DAME L. REV. 863 (1990).

[325] *UN Money Laundering Report*, *supra* note 39, ¶ 63.

Individual Rights Issues Raised by Efforts to Combat Money Laundering

Recent international developments demonstrate a commitment on the part of the world's nations to devise and apply powerful new weapons in the fight against money laundering. They also demonstrate the modern trend to include direct and intrusive enforcement measures in international instruments.[326] The measures contemplated by the international initiatives discussed above may come into conflict with the domestic and international obligations of many states to respect the rights of their citizens. In exercising these potentially powerful new law enforcement tools, both requesting and requested states will be subject to two major limitations: (1) those contained in the treaties themselves (which incorporate the limits of domestic law); and (2) those imposed by international human rights norms and standards.

Both of the initiatives of primary concern here, the U.N. Drug Convention and the European Money Laundering Convention, contain important safeguards to protect the rights of suspects and defendants. Both treaties also strive to protect the property interests of *bona fide* third parties. States must comply with these procedures when making and granting requests. However, despite these built-in protections, several potential problems inhere whenever law enforcement measures are drafted from a purely prosecutorial perspective and, unfortunately, neither treaty makes significant advances in solving these problems.

Both treaties employ a similar approach to protect the rights of interested persons. First, both treaties require that in providing legal assistance or other forms of cooperation, including the enforcement of confiscation orders, the law of the requested state will apply.[327] Therefore, suspects and defendants will be entitled to any procedural protections afforded by the constitutions, domestic statutory or judge-made law of the requested state. Second, both treaties require a requesting party to supply at least some explanation and documentation to support the request for cooperation; insufficient requests can justifiably be refused by the requested party.[328] For instance, under the European Money Laundering Convention, requests for any form of cooperation must specify the authority making the request, the object and reason for the request, relevant facts and circumstances related to the investigations or proceedings, and texts of relevant statutes and laws (including an indication that the measure or cooperation sought could be taken in the requesting party under its own law).[329]

Third, both the United Nations and the Council of Europe treaties provide states the discretion to refuse to grant a request if it violates certain well-established principles of

---

[326] An excellent example of this trend is the intrusive and elaborate verification regime of the Convention on the Prohibition of the Development, Production, Stockpiling and Use of Chemical Weapons, signed in Paris on January 13, 1993. The verification provisions of this treaty will require the inspection of private property, possibly even private homes. In addition, states are required to enact "penal" legislation to enforce the treaty's prohibitions. As a result, this arms control instrument will directly impact the lives of private citizens.

[327] *See* U.N. Drug Convention, *supra* note 14, at Art. 5(4)(c) (execution of confiscation); *Id.* at Art. 7(3) (execution of legal assistance); Euro. Conv. Money Laundering, *supra* note 16, art. 9 (execution of investigative assistance); *Id.* at Art. 12 (execution of provisional measures); *Id.* at Art. 14(1) (execution of confiscation).

[328] *See* U.N. Drug Convention, *supra* note 14, at Arts. 5(4)(d), 7(10); Euro. Conv. Money Laundering, *supra* note 16, at Arts. 27-28.

[329] Euro. Conv. Money Laundering, *supra* note 16, at Art. 27. Additional, specific requirements apply to requests for provisional measures (such as the freezing of assets) and the confiscation of assets.

legality.[330] Article 18 of the European Money Laundering Convention provides states with several grounds for legitimately refusing to grant a request—most of which are concerned with protecting the rights of the accused and defending important principles of national legal systems.[331] A request can be refused if the action sought would be contrary to the fundamental principles of the legal system of the requested state, the request is based on a political or fiscal offense, it violates the principles of dual criminality or *ne bis in idem*, or it is contrary to the *ordre public* or other essential interests of the requested state.[332] Bank secrecy in not an accepted ground for refusal, but the requested party may require that the request be authorized by a judge or another judicial authority.[333] It is essential to note that all grounds for refusal are discretionary or optional. A state is not obligated to refuse a request for assistance, even if a violation of legal protections is imminent.[334]

In effectuating these new modalities, states and their law enforcement bodies are also governed by human rights norms and standards which arise from treaty obligations, regional obligations, customary international law, and general principles of international law. National governments are bound to respect human rights under a framework of international human rights instruments consisting of, *inter alia*, the European Convention for the Protection of Human Rights and Fundamental Freedoms[335] the American Convention of Human Rights,[336] the American Declaration of the Rights and Duties of Man,[337] and the African Charter on Human and Peoples' Rights.[338] There also exist United Nations instruments, such as the Universal Declaration on Human Rights[339] and the International Covenant on Civil and Political Rights.[340]

Parties to these human rights instruments have evinced their intent to recognize the rights of individuals. Criminal suspects and defendants will have the clear right to invoke the provisions of these treaties to the extent that a party seeking or providing legal assistance is a signatory to a relevant human rights instrument. For example, requests for inter-state cooperation or confiscation under the European Money Laundering Convention will, in the case of most states, be subject to the requirements of the European Convention for the Protection of Human Rights and Fundamental Freedoms. However, the European Money

---

330 *See* Christine Van den Wyngaert, *Rethinking the Law of International Cooperation: The Restrictive Function of International Human Rights Through Individual-Oriented Bars, in* PRINCIPLES AND PROCEDURES FOR A NEW TRANSNATIONAL CRIMINAL LAW 489 (Albin Eser & Otto Lagodny eds., 1992) (discussing the distinction, and differences in effectiveness, between bars to assistance contained in inter-state cooperation agreements and reliance on fundamental human rights as codified in international agreements).

331 *See* Polimeni, *supra* note 200, at 7.

332 *See* Euro. Conv. Money Laundering, *supra* note 16, at Art. 18. Additional, specific grounds for refusal can be applied to certain forms of cooperation under the treaty. For example, investigative cooperation can be refused if the requested action would not be permitted under the law of the requested party or the requesting party.

333 *Id.* at Art. 18(7).

334 "It goes without saying that the requested state is not obliged to invoke a ground for refusal even if it has the power to do so." Explanatory Report, *supra* note 201, ¶ 58. States may, however, make some grounds for refusal mandatory in their domestic implementing measures. *Id.*

335 Nov. 4, 1950, 218 U.N.T.S. 221, Europ. T.S. No. 5 and its Eight Protocols.

336 O.A.S. Off. Rec. OEA/Ser. L/V/II. 23 Doc. 21 Rev. 6, *opened for signature* Nov. 20, 1969, *entered into force* July 18, 1978.

337 Adopted by the Ninth International Conference of American States (Mar. 30-May 2, 1948), O.A.S. Off. Rec. OEA/Ser.L/V/I.4 Rev. (1965).

338 Done at Banjul, June 26, 1981, *entered into force* Oct. 21, 1986, O.A.U. Doc. CAB/LEG/67/3 Rev. 5, *reproduced in* 21 I.L.M. 59 (1982).

339 Dec. 10, 1948, U.N.G.A. Res. 217A (III), 3 U.N. GAOR 71, U.N. Doc., A/810.

340 Dec. 16, 1966, U.N.G.A. Res. 2200 (XXI), 21 U.N. GAOR, Supp. (No. 16) 52, U.N. Doc. A/6316.

Laundering Convention is also open to signature by like-minded non-European states that are not necessarily party to the European Convention for Human Rights; thus, these states will not be subject to the limitations of the EHRC. Defendants may, however, be entitled to protections to the extent that such treaties and the subsequent practice of states have brought the protection of human rights into the ambit of customary international law.

The protection of human rights is enormously important to a discussion of international law enforcement and the control of illicit assets. Although a complete discussion of these issues is beyond the scope of this paper, a brief discussion of several potential individual rights issues is warranted. The following issues are of primary concern:

- *Right to Privacy Considerations*, to wit, increased access to financial information during the tracing of assets and requirements for searches and seizures in order to freeze assets;
- *Due Process Considerations*, to wit, the possibility that assets can be seized in the absence of a hearing, inadequate procedural protections for *bona fide* third parties and a lack of procedures to challenge seizures and forfeitures;
- *Presumption of Innocence Considerations*, to wit, shifting of the burden of proof during confiscation proceedings based on "indicia" of wrongdoing;
- *Fair Trial and Equality of Arms Considerations*, to wit, the unavailability of these mechanisms to criminal defendants for the purposes of putting on a defense; and
- *Right to Counsel Considerations*, to wit, the inability of attorneys to accept *bona fide* fees and the possibility of criminal liability for attorneys and other professionals.

Differences in national legal traditions and the ambiguities of international human rights law mean that the possible rights issues raised herein will be dealt with in a manner that is appropriate for each country attempting to implement these anti-money-laundering measures. Therefore, this section does not presume the application of any particular legal standard, apart from acknowledging universally accepted human rights, nor does it seek to undermine international efforts to control illicit proceeds by erecting legal barriers to their effective implementation.

Right to Privacy Considerations

As states implement many of these recent initiatives, they will be required to take investigative measures in order to identify and trace assets for the purpose of eventual confiscation. States will also be required to provide certain forms of mutual legal assistance, including executing searches and seizures. These law enforcement activities will, necessarily, entail additional infringement on individual privacy rights,[341] particularly in light

[341] The right to privacy is an international human right. Most countries recognize this right under constitutional, statutory or judge-made law. The right to privacy is also enshrined in many international human rights agreements. *See, e.g.*, The Universal Declaration of Human Rights, Art. 12 ("no one shall be subject to arbitrary interference in his privacy, family, home, or correspondence. . . ."); International Covenant on Civil and Political Rights, Art. 17 ("no one shall be subjected to arbitrary or unlawful interference with his privacy. . . ."); European Convention for the Protection of Human Rights and Fundamental Freedoms, Art. 8 ("Everyone has the right to respect for his private and family life, his home and correspondence.").

of the ability of government agencies to search massive databases and financial records by means of computers.[342]

Apart from the procedures discussed above (such as the limitations of domestic law), these initiatives do little to preserve privacy rights or restrict the activities of law enforcement officers. For instance, neither the U.N. Drug Convention nor the European Money Laundering Convention requires a showing that a warrant, writ, or other indication of reasonable suspicion has been obtained by authorities in the requesting state before a search or asset tracing can be conducted. The information required for a valid request for assistance will not necessarily enable the authorities of the requested state to establish reasonable suspicion or to assess whether the assistance sought would be permissible if it were carried out in the requesting state. The lack of some type of reasonable suspicion standard in the treaties themselves creates the possibility that law enforcement officials in states with strict prohibitions against unreasonable searches and seizures might be tempted to try to execute searches in other states based on less than the probable cause or reasonable suspicion that would be required for a domestic search.[343]

Another possible rights issue concerns the infringement of these initiatives upon financial privacy rights. When providing legal assistance or executing provisional measures under the U.N. Drug Convention and the European Money Laundering Convention, states must lift their bank secrecy requirements and provide access to financial information. The FATF, the EC Directive and other initiatives also emphasize the need to lift bank secrecy laws. Financial privacy concerns are also heightened by requirements that financial institutions "get to know" their customers, report large transactions, and make inquiries into suspicious transactions. Although sound in a law enforcement sense, the proliferation of new requirements suggests a tendency to place the interests of law enforcement above the legitimate and once undisputed right to financial privacy.[344]

Due Process Considerations

Due process of law is protected by domestic law in most countries and must be provided under international human rights instruments.[345] Several aspects of these initiatives could threaten the due process rights of criminal defendants and innocent third parties. Each of

---

342 *See generally* Comment, *The Right to Financial Privacy Versus Computerized Law Enforcement: A New Fight in an Old Battle*, 86 NW. U.L.REV. 1169 (1992).

343 For a discussion of how searches executed on less than probable cause pursuant to a legal assistance treaty could violate a defendant's privacy rights, *see supra*, Chapter 12.

344 Indeed, no one would advocate that drug traffickers and money launderers have the right to conduct their illicit dealings in utter privacy. But legitimate rationales support the traditions of bank secrecy and financial privacy, and these interests must be weighed fairly against the government's crime fighting objectives. According to one commentator: "Secrecy laws have served to shield persons from financial loss in countries plagued by instability, weak currency and run-away inflation rates. Secrecy laws have also served to protect wealthy individuals or those who promote unpopular political causes by allowing them to hide their assets to avoid the threat of kidnapping or persecution." Hernandez, *supra* note 284, at 235. *See also* Peter W. Schroth, *Bank Confidentiality and the War on Money Laundering in the United States*, 42 (Supp.) AM. J. COMP. L. 369, 369 (1994) (arguing that the war on drugs and money laundering has eroded universally accepted rights to financial privacy and bank confidentiality: "Since 1970, the steadily escalating indirect war on drug traffickers has been conducted almost without regard to privacy, property rights, the costs to financial institutions and government. . . .").

345 *See e.g.*, European Convention for the Protection of Human Rights and Fundamental Freedoms, Arts. 5 and 6; American Declaration of the Rights and Duties of Man, Art. XXVI ("every person accused of an offense has the right to be given an impartial and public hearing. . . .").

these issues falls under the broad heading of due process: (1) insufficient procedural protections before assets can be frozen, including an insufficient burden of proof and a lack of procedures allowing defendants to challenge a seizure or forfeiture; and (2) vague descriptions of the assets to be frozen.

Insufficient Procedural Protections

Although both the U.N. Drug Convention and the European Money Laundering Convention require that the law of the requested state applies to requests and both grant states the discretion to refuse insufficient or improper requests, neither treaty specifies a minimum burden of proof before assets can be restrained; requires proof of a restraining order issued by a court of the requested country; nor specifies a minimum of procedural protections that must be accorded to the accused or *bona fide* third parties.

For instance, the execution of provisional measures under the European Money Laundering Convention requires very little from a requesting state before assets can be frozen or seized. The requirement of a criminal proceeding or investigation is easily met and is quite vague. As a result, assets may be frozen and placed beyond the defendant's reach without the benefit of a hearing (either before or after the seizure) in the requested state if the law of the requested state does not require a hearing or other procedural safeguards. Under these terms, a state party could probably request seizure of assets based solely upon the investigation of a suspect.

Under the European Money Laundering Convention, as with many bilateral mutual assistance agreements and the U.N. Drug Convention, a suspect or defendant's only protection will be the law of the requested state. Law enforcement officers may be tempted to take advantage of a requested state's standards and try to freeze assets they would not be able to freeze under their own law. While the legislative history indicates that seizure or freezing may be most appropriate where the offense concerned is serious or where the defendant or suspect has substantial property located in the requested state, there is no guarantee that requests for seizure or freezing of assets will not be granted based on sparse facts or the mere existence of a criminal investigation.[346]

The confiscation provisions are less objectionable because any confiscation requires some form of adjudication of guilt in the requesting state, including a record of the conviction and an order of confiscation issued by a court in the requesting state. More importantly, not allowing criminals or their organizations to prosper from their illegal activities is logical and easily reconciled. Confiscation is only objectionable when it interferes with a defendant's right to secure legal counsel or if his assets are confiscated without due process. Society's interest in depriving criminals of their ill-gotten gains is not so great as to deprive defendants of the ability to defend themselves.

In contrast to the U.N. Drug Convention, the European Money Laundering Convention more explicitly recognizes the property rights of *bona fide* third parties by requiring the requested party to recognize any judicial decision with respect to property rights claimed by third parties; moreover, a requested state party can refuse to grant a request for confiscation if third parties were not given adequate opportunity to assert their interests in the property to be confiscated.[347] In addition, parties must offer mutual assistance in serving judicial

---

[346] *See* Explanatory Report, *supra* note 201, ¶ 41.

[347] Euro. Conv. Money Laundering, *supra* note 16, at Art. 22.

documents to persons affected by provisional measures and confiscation, including the accused.[348] Parties to the Convention must adopt legislation to provide effective legal remedies in order to protect the rights of interested parties, including the accused.[349] The accused is entitled to such remedies only as long as an order of confiscation has not been made against him, while *bona fide* third parties can defend their interests at any time.[350]

That neither Convention provides (or even mandates) a system whereby a defendant may challenge a seizure or forfeiture proceeding against him suggests a final procedural inadequacy. The defendant will be entitled only to the procedural protections afforded by the law of the requested state, which frequently amount to less than trial rights where the proceeding concerns inter-state cooperation, such as procedures for the freezing of the accused's assets.

Vague Definition of Assets Subject to Seizure

Neither Convention limits the amount of assets that are subject to restraint or seizure, while both require that confiscation be limited to the amount of the confiscation order. Both instruments merely require that the assets may, at some time in the future, be subject to forfeiture.[351] Obviously, this minimal requirement can be applied quite broadly where states are not required to meet a strict burden of proof when asserting what assets may eventually be subject to forfeiture; the absence of a burden of proof (such as probable cause or reasonable suspicion) creates the possibility that all of the defendant's assets may be frozen or seized. As a result, the defendant may be left without means to hire an attorney.

Presumption of Innocence Considerations

A closely held tenet of international human rights law and the domestic law of most nations is that a defendant is presumed innocent until proved guilty in criminal proceedings.[352] However, the sometimes quasi-criminal nature of confiscation proceedings, and the focus on the *res* rather than the defendant, creates an ambiguity that undermines the

---

[348] *See id.* at Art. 21(1).

[349] *See* Euro. Conv. Money Laundering, *supra* note 16, at Art. 5 ("Each Party shall adopt such legislative and other measures as may be necessary to ensure that interested parties affected by measures under Articles 2 and 3 shall have effective legal remedies in order to preserve their rights").

[350] This provision implies that there should be a system whereby interested parties are informed of their right to challenge an action against them, that (in the case of third parties) a challenge can be raised even if a confiscation order has become enforceable, that interested parties have a right to a court hearing, and that the party has a right to legal representation. *See* Explanatory Report, *supra* note 201, ¶ 31. Compare this provision with Art. 5(8) of the U.N. Drug Convention, *supra* note 14, protecting only the rights of *bona fide* third parties.

[351] *See e.g.*, Euro. Conv. Money Laundering, *supra* note 16, at Art. 11(1) ("a Party shall take the necessary provisional measures, such as freezing or seizing, to prevent any dealing in, transfer or disposal or property which, at a later stage, may be the subject of a request for confiscation. . . ."); *Id.* at Art. 27(2) ("A request for provisional measures . . . in relation to seizure of property on which a confiscation order consisting in the requirement to pay a sum of money may be realized shall also indicate a maximum amount for which recovery is sought in that property").

[352] *See e.g.*, American Convention on Human Rights, Art. 8(2) ("Every person accused of a criminal offense has the right to be presumed innocent so long as his guilt has not been proven according to law."); African Charter on Human and Peoples' Rights, Art. 7(1)(b) ("Every individual shall have the right to have his cause heard. This comprises . . . b) the right to be presumed innocent until proved guilty by a competent court or tribunal"); Universal Declaration of Human Rights, Art. 11(1) ("Everyone charged with a penal offense has the right to be presumed innocent until proved guilty according to law. . . .").

presumption of innocence. Under civil forfeiture laws, the property is presumed guilty; but under criminal forfeiture, as is contemplated by the initiatives herein, the property ought to be presumed innocent. This has not proven to be the case.[353]

Most of the seizure and confiscation proceedings pursuant to these initiatives require the defendant and persons claiming to be innocent owners to establish that there is no nexus between the property concerned and the criminal acts alleged. Thus, once the government proves that there is reason to believe that property could be subject to forfeiture, the burden of proof is shifted from the government to the criminal defendant to prove that the assets are not tied to wrongdoing. Indeed, Article 5, paragraph 7 of the U.N. Drug Convention explicitly permits states, consistent with domestic law, to "ensur[e] that the onus of proof be reversed regarding the lawful origin of alleged proceeds."

This shifted burden is complicated by the fact that the owner is required to prove a negative (i.e., the lack of a nexus). Once currency enters the stream of commerce and is commingled with other proceeds, it is exceedingly difficult, if not impossible, to prove that a specific portion of the proceeds has not been tainted by illegality. The initiatives considered above do not provide defendants with a sufficient opportunity to show that proceeds are not tainted. While the rights of *bona fide* third parties are recognized, these innocent owners may also be placed at the disadvantage of having to prove a negative.

Fair Trial and Equality of Arms Considerations

Neither the U.N. Drug Convention nor the European Money Laundering Convention makes its powerful information-gathering capabilities available to the accused for the purposes of gathering exculpatory evidence. Instead, defendants must rely on the inefficient process of letters rogatory. As a result, other state parties will not be required to provide legal assistance, and they will only do so on a voluntary basis. This hindrance in the preparation of a defense may diminish a defendant's right to a fair trial[354] and, at the very least, create an imbalance in the equality of arms. Akin to bilateral and regional mutual assistance treaties, it is obvious that these two new Conventions are drafted entirely for the benefit of law enforcement officials, possibly to the point of derogating the individual rights of the accused if these information-gathering powers remain unavailable to them.

---

[353] One commentator has noted that an international standard is emerging whereby assets can be subjected to forfeiture based on "indicia" of wrongdoing: "This notion of indicia—that which is or might be wrong, not under fact-finding standards, but under skewed presumptions—is paramount in dealing with international drug trafficking and money laundering problems. In this context, the scienter standard of the United States forfeiture laws, now being incorporated in the international arena, will not protect any legitimate business person from persecution." Hernandez, *supra* note 284, at 302.

[354] *See e.g.,* Universal Declaration of Human Rights, Art. 10 ("Everyone is entitled in full equality to a fair and public hearing by an independent and impartial tribunal, in the determination of his rights and obligations and of any criminal charge against him."); *Id.* at Art. 11 ("Everyone charged with a penal offense has the right to be presumed innocent until proved guilty according to law in a public trial at which he has all the guarantees necessary for his defence."); European Convention for the Protection of Human Rights and Fundamental Freedoms, Art. 6(1) ("everyone is entitled to a fair and public hearing within a reasonable time by an independent and impartial tribunal established by law."); American Convention on Human Rights, Art. 8.

Right to Counsel Considerations and Criminal Liability of Defense Attorneys

Concern over the application of immobilization and confiscation provisions to attorneys' fees has raised a significant degree of controversy. The greater controversy has surrounded the U.N. Drug Convention. While the U.N. Drug Convention protects *bona fide* third parties,[355] the Convention's confiscation provisions could possibly be interpreted to reach legitimate attorneys' fees.[356]

The money laundering provisions of Article 3 are particularly troublesome where attorney fees and advice are considered. A broad construction of Article 3(b)(i) could make it a crime for an attorney to accept laundered funds in order to prepare a legal defense or, by giving advice, to assist his client to "evade the legal consequences of his actions."[357] In light of the difficulties observed regarding attorney fees and attorneys as *bona fide* purchasers for value, the Convention heightens attorneys' worries about accepting fees from clients charged with drug-related offenses.

The provision could also be construed to mean that a third party who transfers assets to an attorney for the means of a criminal defense would be converting funds to help the defendant/money launderer evade the legal consequences of his acts.[358] Combined with the criminal forfeiture provisions, and the forfeiture of substitute assets should tainted assets be unavailable, these money-laundering provisions, strictly construed, could make it difficult for drug offenders to secure counsel.[359]

Article 3(c)(i) and (iv) of the U.N. Drug Convention also pose a potential threat to criminal defense attorneys. Under these provisions, a criminal defense attorney would be subject to prosecution if he knowingly accepted tainted assets.[360] Fear of accepting fees from defendants in drug-related cases could chill the defense bar in many state parties. Moreover, under Article 3(c)(iv), an attorney may be subject to prosecution to the extent national implementing measures consider the advice or actions of an attorney as "aiding, abetting, facilitating, and counseling" the commission of a drug or money-laundering offense. It is unlikely, however, that national legal systems will construe this provision so broadly as to criminalize the legitimate counseling of drug offenders.[361]

Because the European Money Laundering Convention is so similar to the U.N. Drug Convention, the same concerns over attorney fees exist. However, the commentary to the Convention acknowledges the challenges made to the U.N. Drug Convention on these grounds and declares that the European Money Laundering Convention cannot be

---

355 *See* U.N. Drug Convention, *supra* note 14, at Art. 5(8).

356 *But see* Zagaris, *supra* note 12 (arguing that Art. 5(8) may protect attorney fees).

357 *See id.* at Art. 3(b)(i); *see also U.N. Treaty on Drugs Worries the Defense Bar*, NAT'L L. J., Sept. 25, 1990, at 5.

358 *See* Zagaris, *Developments in International Judicial Assistance and Related Matters, supra* note 12, at 342.

359 *See* NAT'L L. J., *supra* note 357. It should be noted that this perceived fear is based, to some degree, on the effects of the U.N. Drug Convention in light of United States jurisprudence. Different legal systems with different definitions of "conspiracy" or "association" and varying levels of prosecutorial discretion may encounter significantly different obstacles. *See* Stewart, *supra* note 9, at 393.

360 Under the forfeiture provisions of some domestic statutes, attorneys are uniquely unable to qualify as *bona fide* purchasers for value. Any attorney who exercises due diligence (as ethically required) will likely be aware of the tainted/laundered source of the funds.

361 Of course, in most legal systems, legal advice given for the purpose of furthering a criminal scheme will not be entitled to legal professional privilege and, provided all elements are proved, an attorney giving advice of this nature would rightfully be subject to prosecution.

misinterpreted to mean that it is illegal to hire a lawyer or for a lawyer to accept a fee.[362] Possible objections over right to counsel considerations may be complicated by the European Money Laundering Convention's broad, although optional, provisions regarding *mens rea.* Under Article 6, parties can criminalize situations where the offender "ought to have assumed that the property was proceeds." This equivalent of a "negligence standard" could expose attorneys to potential liability for accepting fees that have been laundered.

However they may be interpreted by parties implementing them, the initiatives considered herein include broad provisions that grant, or at least contemplate, powerful enforcement authority. The development and inclusion of these mechanisms indicate the prosecutorial perspective that motivates the conclusion of these initiatives. These initiatives will undoubtedly be forceful tools in the war on serious crime and money laundering and should be models for future instruments. The combination of forceful obligations and effective methods of enforcement will make future agreements less ambiguous, more binding and, overall, more effective. However, drafters of future instruments must carry out their mandate in a manner that recognizes fundamental human rights in a way that incorporates procedural protections for criminal suspects and defendants. Confiscation is a rational and logical means of undermining organized criminals and narcotics traffickers, yet criminal sanctions must not be imposed on defendants in the absence of fair enforcement techniques and before a finding of guilt. These instruments are incomplete until they provide, within the instruments themselves, minimal procedural protection for suspects and defendants.

Conclusion

The international legal community has responded to money laundering with action at various levels—internationally, regionally, and domestically—though with differing commitments and widely different means. The various mechanisms outlined above have, at least in the area of drug money laundering, wrought profound changes in international penal law enforcement. According to William Gilmore, "it is no exaggeration to say that in the area of drug-related money laundering the landscape of international cooperation has been radically and positively transformed."[363] It can only be presumed that, in due time, these efforts to seriously hamper money laundering will be applied to other crimes that generate significant profits, as can be seen in the 1990 European Money Laundering Convention, the EC Directive, and the work of the FATF. The extension of these modalities to all forms of criminality, in some way, repudiates the narrow approach that seeks to regulate only drug-related money laundering.

The policies and modalities of enforcement which have been instituted so far, as discussed above, are broad-based and far-reaching, though they still hardly scratch the surface of the problem. Domestic and international law enforcement authorities now recognize that the financial aspects of criminal activity should be a primary focus of law enforcement strategies, though governments must yet provide the resources to render such efforts effective. Either through the implementation of international agreements or measures taken on their own initiative, national governments are starting to use powerful new tools to battle money laundering and the criminal activities that give rise to money laundering. In the main, these new tools have two basic purposes: (1) they seek to make money laundering

---

[362] *See* Explanatory Report, *supra* note 201, ¶ 33.

[363] INTERNATIONAL EFFORTS TO COMBAT MONEY LAUNDERING xix (W.C. Gilmore ed. 1992).

a crime and provide penalties for activities in support of money laundering; and (2) they seek to apply the traditional modalities of inter-state cooperation in penal matters to the detection, suppression and punishment of money laundering, including the implementation of a new modality to trace, freeze and seize the proceeds of crime. Aside from this two-part strategy, the initiatives discussed above, which range in scope from global to domestic, all rely upon the same basic national mechanisms which are still inadequately supported by governments.

The current international strategy to address the problem of money laundering, and especially drug-related money laundering, is powerful and well reasoned. The components of this strategy to detect, suppress and punish money laundering are well defined, but the likelihood of their successful implementation among the world's nations is, so far, unclear. It will be difficult to assess whether these initiatives are likely to succeed until states enact and implement domestic legislation and, in turn, attempt to cooperate with each other in their implementation. Suffice it to say that, at this stage, recently adopted theories of enforcement depend on a number of assumptions, some of which may eventually prove erroneous. Thus, the basic premises of these new regimes should be scrutinized in order to: (1) avoid the development of unrealistic expectations; (2) identify potential pitfalls; and (3) make the first step toward devising workable solutions.

Assumption #1: Because money laundering is a global concern, multilateralism is the most effective means of controlling it.

This rapidly developing regime assumes that new principles of multilateralism in international criminal law will operate successfully. Because crime is a global concern, inter-state cooperation in penal matters has moved well beyond the bilateral and regional scope; instruments like the U.N. Drug Convention and the European Money Laundering Convention demonstrate an assumption that the suppression of serious offenses such as money laundering should proceed in a nearly global context. Nevertheless, many of the international instruments required for a truly effective global enforcement strategy are non-existent.

International controls against money laundering and the illicit proceeds of crime require that states provide each other with an unprecedented level of mutual assistance. States will be expected to share information, execute searches, and seize assets at the investigatory or pre-trial stage; exchange information and documentation at the adjudicatory stage; and, finally, recognize and give effect to foreign judgments at the enforcement stage. While it is relatively simple for states to enact domestic measures as required by these treaties, it remains to be seen whether they can live up to the sweeping and loosely defined obligations in regard to inter-state cooperation.

In addition, while the conclusion of international treaties suggests that states have accepted a more multilateral approach to international criminal law by agreeing to provide each other the various forms of inter-state cooperation, the traditional barrier of national sovereignty still exists and may interfere with efforts to implement international controls. Several realities of the current status of international criminal law will also present obstacles for a global strategy to control money laundering. There is, for example, no single international treaty covering the range of activities that need to be controlled; no international enforcement mechanisms to which all (or substantially all) countries adhere; no legal obligations binding all (or substantially all) countries to enact the same or similar measures in their national legislation; and, finally, there are no arrangements for inter-state cooperation in penal matters binding on all (or substantially all) countries. Thus, states are forced to rely upon a flawed, limited, and inconsistent system of enforcement and inter-state cooperation.

Assumption #2: National controls on financial institutions are (or can be) sufficient to support international efforts to combat money laundering.

Criminal organizations are attracted to laundering hubs—those countries with few or no domestic regulations on their financial industry. Thus, in this new era of multilateral regulation, the most crucial component is domestic legislation which supports international efforts to curb money laundering. While most states can enact the necessary legislation with relative ease, effectively mobilizing the administrative structures and resources required by domestic banking and financial controls is a different issue altogether. Potential difficulties associated with domestic implementation could include overburdened systems of criminal justice, lack of administrative resources, lack of skilled personnel, inexperience in the area of financial controls, and, perhaps most importantly, an ineffective national apparatus for providing or seeking inter-state cooperation.

Problems can plague even those governments that have developed ostensibly comprehensive financial controls designed to operate in an integrated international financial system. Because money is fungible, it is impossible to identify the source of funds once they enter the international financial pipeline. Therefore, practice has demonstrated that the most effective point of control is when funds enter the financial stream. In most cases, that point will be a domestic financial institution that is subject to domestic, but not international, financial regulations.

The most widely used national control scheme is what some national legislations refer to as the "currency transaction report" or CTR. These regulations, which can serve both banking and tax purposes, require financial institutions to report all cash transactions over a threshold amount to government authorities and to keep records of all financial transactions for a period of years. These controls are clearly contemplated by the EC Directive, the FATF, the Basle Committee, and the OAS initiatives.

These schemes typically require a governmental authority to oversee all CTR requirements.[364] Three problems exist with this framework. First, in many countries, the administrative bodies required to exercise control are frequently nonexistent, inadequately funded and staffed, overburdened or insufficiently prepared technically to carry out effective internal controls. The costs and difficulties associated with exercising or implementing international controls can be even greater. Even in countries with seemingly sufficient resources, the financial and bureaucratic costs of contending with thousands of daily transactions are overwhelming.[365]

Second, to obviate the enormous burdens on the private banking industry (which is reluctant to assume the cost burdens of such control) and the burdens on public institutions

---

364 This role may be assumed by a central or national bank in many countries.

365 For example, forced to deal with millions of CTRs annually, reporting requirements have placed a tremendous burden on the United States Department of the Treasury. *See generally* Note, *Recordkeeping and Reporting in an Attempt to Stop the Money Laundering Cycle: Why Blanket Recording and Reporting of Wire and Electronic Funds Transfers is Not the Answer*, *supra* note 324, at 863.

like central banks, national regulations authorize financial institutions to grant exceptions from CTR requirements to "legitimate" cash-intensive businesses. In the future, industry resistance to additional regulations is likely to be placated by the creation of broad exemptions from reporting requirements—allowing businesses such as restaurants, casinos, currency exchanges, etc., to slip through the regulatory cracks. Money launderers and criminal organizations will naturally gravitate to industries with nonexistent or less intrusive reporting requirements for the purposes of recycling.

This shortcoming in the CTR scheme also highlights the indispensability of developing an international regime that does not focus solely on banking and other traditional financial industries. In its 1993 report, the FATF indicated that non-financial institutions (such as currency exchanges, check cashers and casinos) continued to be significant centers of money-laundering activities.

Third, by their very nature, and owing greatly to administrative difficulties in handling so many of them, CTRs necessarily lag behind the criminal conduct they are meant to expose. The large volume of CTR reports are such that even the central banks or control agencies with the most resources are unable to catch-up with the backlog, creating long delays between the time of reporting and the time when control can be effectuated. The result is that many transactions are discovered long after the fact, reducing the effectiveness of control strategies. Thus, the assumption that national controls on financial institutions are effective is questionable, even in those countries with advanced control strategies. Inefficiencies at the domestic level could weaken international controls that may subsequently apply.

Assumption # 3: The international financial industry will cooperate with national and international controls, including restrictions on wire transfers.

A third major assumption is that the international financial industry can and will cooperate with efforts to secure more information about financial transactions. Due to domestic efforts to comply with treaties and initiatives like the EC Directive and Basle Committee statement, institutions will be faced with a battery of new regulations and commensurate burdens. They will be required to gather more information about customers, inquire into the source of funds, and report thousands of transactions to the government—costly requirements that will diminish profitability. While greater accountability for large cash transactions from the banking community is a long overdue virtue of these initiatives, the idea is likely to face resistance from the industry in the implementation phase. For instance, the banking community might argue that these additional requirements are not banking functions at all but are, instead, enforcement methods that are more appropriately the responsibility of the central bank or law enforcement authorities. It is one thing to develop a set of recommendations, but it is quite another to convince a powerful industry to endorse additional regulations.

Co-opting the international financial industry—both traditional and nontraditional—will be critical to the effectiveness of the controls contained in multilateral instruments like the U.N. Drug Convention. One means of co-opting the financial sector is to stress how important it is that a bank, or even an entire national banking system, be perceived as a "clean place to do business."[366] If the financial integrity of a bank is impugned, legitimate business will be driven out and profits ultimately lost. The work of the EC, the FATF, the Basle Committee, and others has stressed the importance of financial integrity and has deftly moved toward greater accountability for financial institutions. However, financial institutions are the focus of money laundering, and more can and should be done.

For instance, though this paper has chronicled several control mechanisms to be applied to financial institutions, woefully little is being done in regard to the international regulation of electronic wire transfers. These electronic transactions, nearly untraceable because customers are only required to provide minimal amounts of identification information, facilitate the international movement of huge sums of money in just seconds. A single such transfer is routinely in the range of millions of dollars and it is estimated that trillions of dollars in funds and securities are exchanged in this manner daily.[367]

The volume of these transactions, both in daily numbers and with respect to the value of each transaction, make electronic transfers very difficult to control. Any additional controls will result in significant additional regulations for the financial institutions and clearinghouses involved in these transactions—many of whom contend that the vast majority of their transactions are made with longtime, respected clients. At present, there are no effective international controls on electronic transfers, particularly international ones.

Among the reasons why the international controls of electronic transfers are lacking is that governments have an interest in preserving the confidentiality of a variety of types of financial transactions and greater transparency in financial dealings would be inimical to many government interests. For example, governments insist on confidentiality when the central bank intervenes to control the fluctuation of their national currencies. Should these transactions become known they would defeat the purposes of intervention and become a prime source of information for currency speculators who could then play havoc with the stability of national currencies and financial markets. A variety of other governmental commercial transactions rely on confidentiality, including arms transactions, major oil transactions, and other transactions that may be marginally legal (*e.g.*, complicated transactions designed to circumvent an embargo).

A system to regulate international electronic transfers would tend to make these transactions discoverable and could prejudice the governments engaging in them. As a result, controls have not been put in place and confidentiality is maintained — allowing criminal organizations to benefit from the same confidentiality that governments enjoy with respect to their monetary transactions. A method must be devised, at the national, regional and international levels, whereby legitimate government claims to confidentiality can be respected while, at the same time, control is exerted over other transactions involving criminally-derived funds. Despite the difficulties inherent in a such a discriminatory system, including opportunities for corruption and abuses of power, devising such a method will be an important step in solidifying the political will of governments to implement financial controls.

---

366 Statement of Dilwyn Griffiths, Secretary of the FATF, *in* Rupert Bruce, *Offshore Financial Centers Move to Shake the Stigma of Shadiness*, INT'L HERALD TRIB., Feb. 11, 1995.

367 *See* Bruce Zagaris & Scott B. MacDonald, *Money Laundering, Financial Fraud, and Technology: The Perils of an Instantaneous Economy*, 26 GEO.WASH. J. INT'L L. & ECON. 62, 72 (1992). There may be as many as one trillion electronic financial transactions a day. *See* O'Brien, *Moving Money by Stealth: Electronic Transactions Give Fugitives an Edge*, CLEV. PLAIN DEALER, Oct. 30, 1994, at 1H.

Assumption #4: Professionals (such as lawyers, accountants, and brokers) can be relied upon to act ethically and can be effectively regulated by ethical standards and self-policing.

Because money-laundering activities are often shaped by the advice of professionals (such as lawyers, accountants, and tax specialists), international financial controls and resultant government initiatives rely on the ethical integrity of several professions that handle large sums of cash. The trade in tainted assets has been quick to recognize the benefit of employing a category of professionals who enjoy the privilege of confidentiality. These "commercialists"—lawyers, accountants, tax advisers, securities dealers, etc.—have used their legal privileges to erect another wall of confidentiality between their laundering clients and the inquiries of law enforcement bodies.[368] In many countries, the primary means of control applied to these professionals are self-imposed ethical standards and ethics boards that review the conduct of practicing professionals and discipline violators of established standards.

Unfortunately, codes of conduct are often inadequately enforced or are nonexistent. Moreover, without anything but the strictest of reporting requirements and more forceful controls on "commercialists," national enforcement efforts will be premised on the hope that these professionals adhere to general standards of ethical conduct.

Assumption #5: The international protection of human rights can be subjugated to meet compelling law enforcement objectives.

A fifth, and final, consideration is that the drafters of these instruments have assumed that applying intrusive investigative measures and freezing and confiscating "suspicious" assets can be done in a manner consonant with the fundamental human rights of defendants, suspects, and innocent property owners. While this assumption will probably prove true at some time in the future, significant legal questions already surround the authority of governments to implement these strong new measures. Even in the United States, whose system of asset tracing, freezing and forfeiture has been a paradigm for many years, recent judicial decisions have undercut the government's authority to control allegedly illicit proceeds. The possible impact of these initiatives on individual rights warrants further study.

Money laundering is a global problem that can be addressed only by the use of global measures. This means that a new system for the international control of financial transactions must be established. But the effectiveness of such a system depends essentially on global participation by governments and national financial institutions. So far, the political will of states is lacking, and no such global system yet exists. To a large extent, this may be due to the economic interest that some states have in keeping their financial institution free from the controls that are indispensible if international money laundering is to be controlled. But governments also have an interest in preserving the secrecy of their financial transactions. These transactions use the same channels and methods employed by individuals who launder their illegal gains. Thus, the dilemma of having some controls over some transactions and not over others is apparent. But because the world's financial

---

[368] In many instances, however, claims to confidentiality may be well founded. Law enforcement efforts to obtain more information about financial dealings will inevitably intrude upon the professional/client relationship and come into conflict with legitimate claims of professional privilege.

pipelines are the same for all money, it is very difficult to see how effective controls of illicit money laundering in certain categories of criminal activities can be controlled while others are not.

Appendix 17

United Nations Convention Against Illicit Traffic in Narcotic Drugs and Psychotropic Substances

ARTICLE 5

Confiscation

1. Each Party shall adopt such measures as may be necessary to enable confiscation of:

(a) Proceeds derived from offences established in accordance with article 3, paragraph 1, or property the value of which corresponds to that of such proceeds;

(b) Narcotic drugs and psychotropic substances, materials and equipment or other instrumentalities used in or intended for use in any manner in offences established in accordance with article 3, paragraph 1.

2. Each Party shall also adopt such measures as may be necessary to enable its competent authorities to identify, trace, and freeze or seize proceeds, property, instrumentalities or any other things referred to in paragraph 1 of this article, for the purpose of eventual confiscation.

3. In order to carry out the measures referred to in this article, each Party shall empower its courts or other competent authorities to order that bank, financial or commercial records be made available or be seized. A Party shall not decline to act under the provisions of this paragraph on the ground of bank secrecy.

4. (a) Following a request made pursuant to this article by another Party having jurisdiction over an offence established in accordance with article 3, paragraph 1, the Party in whose territory proceeds, property, instrumentalities or any other things referred to in paragraph 1 of this article are situated shall:

(i) Submit the request to its competent authorities for the purpose of obtaining an order of confiscation and, if such order is granted, give effect to it; or

(ii) Submit to its competent authorities, with a view to giving effect to it to the extent requested, an order of confiscation issued by the requesting Party in accordance with paragraph 1 of this article, in so far as it relates to proceeds, property, instrumentalities or any other things referred to in paragraph 1 situated in the territory of the requested Party.

(b) Following a request made pursuant to this article by another Party having jurisdiction over an offence established in accordance with article 3, paragraph 1, the requested Party shall take measures to identify, trace, and freeze or seize proceeds, property, instrumentalities or any other things referred to in paragraph 1 of this article for the purpose of eventual confiscation to be ordered either by the requesting Party or, pursuant to a request under subparagraph (a) of this paragraph, by the requested Party.

(c) The decisions or actions provided for in subparagraphs (a) and (b) of this paragraph shall be taken by the requested Party, in accordance with and subject to the provisions of its domestic law and its procedural rules or any bilateral or multilateral treaty, agreement or arrangement to which it may be bound in relation to the requesting Party.

(d) The provisions of article 7, paragraphs 6 to 19 are applicable mutatis mutandis. In addition to the information specified in article 7, paragraph 10, requests made pursuant to this article shall contain the following:

(i) In the case of a request pertaining to subparagraph (a)(I) of this paragraph, a description of the property to be confiscated and a statement of the facts relied upon by the requesting Party sufficient to enable the requested Party to seek the order under its domestic law;

(ii) In the case of a request pertaining to subparagraph (a)(ii), a legally admissible copy of an order of confiscation issued by the requesting Party upon which the request is based, a statement of the facts and Information as to the extent to which the execution of the order is requested.

(iii) In the case of a request pertaining to subparagraph (b), a statement of the facts relied upon by the requesting Party and a description of the actions requested.

(e) Each Party shall furnish to the Secretary-General the text of any of its laws and regulations which give effect to this paragraph and the text of any subsequent changes to such laws and regulations.

(f) If a Party elects to make the taking of the measures referred to in subparagraphs (a) and (b) of this paragraph conditional on the existence of a relevant treaty, that Party shall consider this Convention as the necessary and sufficient treaty basis.

(g) The Parties shall seek to conclude bilateral and multilateral treaties, agreements or arrangements to enhance the effectiveness of international cooperation pursuant to this article.

5. (a) Proceeds or property confiscated by a Party pursuant to paragraph 1 or paragraph 4 of this article shall be disposed of by that Party according to its domestic law and administrative procedures.

(b) When acting on the request of another Party in accordance with this article, a Party may give special consideration to concluding agreements on:

(i) Contributing the value of such proceeds and property, or funds derived from the sale of such proceeds or property, or a substantial part thereof, to intergovernmental bodies specializing in the fight against illicit traffic in and abuse of narcotic drugs and psychotropic substances;

(ii) Sharing with other Parties, on a regular or case-by-case basis, such proceeds or property, or funds derived from the sale of such proceeds or property, in accordance with its domestic law, administrative procedures or bilateral or multilateral agreements entered into for this purpose.

6. (a) If proceeds have been transformed or converted into other property, such property shall be liable to the measures referred to in this article instead of the proceeds.

(b) If proceeds have been intermingled with property acquired from legitimate sources, such property shall, without prejudice to any powers relating to seizure or freezing, be liable to confiscation up to the assessed value of the intermingled proceeds.

(c) Income or other benefits derived from:

(i) Proceeds;

(ii) Property into which proceeds have been transformed or converted; or

(iii) Property with which proceeds have been intermingled shall also be liable to the measures referred to in this article, in the same manner and to the same extent as proceeds.

7. Each Party may consider ensuring that the onus of proof be reversed regarding the lawful origin of alleged proceeds or other property liable to confiscation, to the extent that such action is consistent with the principles of its domestic law and with the nature of the judicial and other proceedings.

8. The provisions of this article shall not be construed as prejudicing the rights of bona fide third parties.

9. Nothing contained in this article shall affect the principle that the measures to which it refers shall be defined and implemented in accordance with and subject to the provisions of the domestic law of a Party.

Appendix 18

Council of Europe
Convention on Laundering, Search, Seizure and Confiscation of the Proceeds from Crime

Preamble

The member States of the Council of Europe and the other States signatory hereto,

Considering that the aim of the Council of Europe is to achieve a greater unity between its members;

Convinced of the need to pursue a common criminal policy aimed at the protection of society;

Considering that the fight against serious crime, which has become an increasingly international problem, calls for the use of modern and effective methods on an international scale;

Believing that one of these methods consists in depriving criminals of the proceeds from crime;

Considering that for the attainment of this aim a well-functioning system of international cooperation also must be established,

Have agreed as follows:

CHAPTER 1
Use of Terms

Article 1
Use of terms

For the purposes of this Convention:

a. "proceeds" means any economic advantage from criminal offences. It may consist of any property as defined in sub-paragraph b of this article;

b. "property" includes property of any description, whether corporeal or incorporeal, movable or immovable,and legal documents of instruments evidencing title to, or interest in such property;

c. "instrumentalities" means any property used or intended to be used, in any manner, wholly or in part, to commit a criminal offence or criminal offences;

d. "confiscation" means a penalty or a measure, ordered by a court following proceedings in relation to a criminal offence or criminal offences resulting in the final deprivation of property;

e. "predicate offence" means any criminal offence as a result of which proceeds were generated that may become the subject of an offence as defined in Article 6 of this Convention.

CHAPTER II
Measures to Be Taken at National Level

Article 2
Confiscation measures

1. Each Party shall adopt such legislative and other measures as may be necessary to enable it to confiscate instrumentalities and proceeds or property the value of which corresponds to such proceeds.

2. Each Party, at the time of signature or when depositing its instrument of ratification, acceptance, approval or accession, by a declaration addressed to the Secretary General of the Council of Europe, declare that paragraph 1 of this article applies only to offences or categories of offences specified in such declaration.

ARTICLE 3

Investigative and provisional measures

Each Party shall adopt such legislative and other measures as may be necessary to enable it to identify and trace property which is liable to confiscation pursuant to Article 2, paragraph 1, and to prevent any dealing in, transfer or disposal of such property.

ARTICLE 4

Special investigative powers and techniques

1. Each Party shall adopt such legislative and other measure as may be necessary to empower its courts or other competent authorities to order that bank, financial or commercial records be made available or be seized in order to carry out the actions referred to in Articles 2 and 3. A Party shall not decline to act under the provisions of this article on grounds of bank secrecy.
2. Each Party shall consider adopting such legislative and other measures as may be necessary to enable it to use special investigative techniques facilitating the identification and tracing of proceeds and the gathering of evidence related thereto. Such techniques may include monitoring orders, observation, interception of telecommunications, access to computer systems and orders to produce specific documents.

ARTICLE 5

Legal remedies

Each Party shall adopt such legislative and other measures as may be necessary to ensure that interested parties affected by measures under Articles 2 and 3 shall have effective legal remedies in order to preserve their rights.

ARTICLE 6

Laundering offences

1. Each Party shall adopt such legislative and other measures as may be necessary to establish as offences under its domestic law, when committed intentionally:

a. the conversion or transfer of property, knowing that such property is proceeds, for the purpose of concealing or disguising the illicit origin of the property or of assisting any person who is involved in the commission of the predicate offence to evade the legal consequences of his actions;

b. the concealment or disguise of the true nature, source, location, disposition, movement, rights with respect to, or ownership of, property, knowing that such property is proceeds;

and subject to its constitutional principles and the basic concepts of its legal system:

c. the acquisition, possession or use of property, knowing, at the time of receipt, that such property was proceeds;

d. participation in, association or conspiracy to commit, attempts to commit and aiding, abetting, facilitating and counselling the commission of any of the offences established in accordance with this article.

2. For the purposes of implementing or applying paragraph 1 of this article:

a. it shall not matter whether the predicate offence was subject to the criminal jurisdiction of the Party;

b. it may be provided that the offences set forth in that paragraph do not apply to the persons who committed the predicate offence;

c. knowledge, intent or purpose required as an element of an offence set forth in that paragraph may be inferred from objective, factual circumstances.

3. Each Party may adopt such measures as it considers necessary to establish also as offences under its domestic law all or some of the acts referred to in paragraph 1 of this article, in any or all of the following cases where the offender:

a. ought to have assumed that the property was proceeds;

b. acted for the purpose of making profit;

c. acted for the purpose of promoting the carrying on of further criminal activity.

4. Each Party may, at the time of signature or when depositing its instrument of ratification, acceptance, approval or accession, by declaration addressed to the Secretary-General of the Council of Europe declare that paragraph 1 of this article applies only to predicate offences or categories of such offences specified in such declaration.

CHAPTER III
INTERNATIONAL CO-OPERATION

Section 1
Principles of international co-operation

ARTICLE 7
General principles and measures for international co-operation

1. The Parties shall co-operate with each other to the widest extent possible for the purposes of investigations and proceedings aiming at the confiscation of instrumentalities and proceeds.

2. Each Party shall adopt such legislative or other measures as may be necessary to enable it to comply, under the conditions provided for in this chapter, with requests:

a. for confiscation of specific items of property representing proceeds or instrumentalities, as well as for confiscation of proceeds consisting in a requirement to pay a sum of money corresponding to the value of proceeds;

b. for investigative assistance and provisional measures with a view to either form of confiscation referred to under a above.

Section 2
Investigative assistance

ARTICLE 8
Obligation to assist

The Parties shall afford each other, upon request, the widest possible measure of assistance in the identification and tracing of instrumentalities, proceeds and other property liable to confiscation. Such assistance shall include any measure providing and securing evidence as to the existence, location or movement, nature, legal status or value of the aforementioned property.

ARTICLE 9
Execution of assistance

The assistance pursuant to Article 8 shall be carried out as permitted by and in accordance with the domestic law of the requested Party and, to the extent not incompatible with such law, in accordance with the procedures specified in the request.

ARTICLE 10
Spontaneous information

Without prejudice to its own investigations or proceedings, a Party may without prior request forward to another Party information on instrumentalities and proceeds, when it considers that the disclosure of such information might assist the receiving Party in initiating or carrying out investigations or proceedings or might lead to a request by that Party under this chapter.

Section 3
Provisional measures

ARTICLE 11
Obligation to take provisional measures

1. At the request of another Party which has instituted criminal proceedings or proceedings for the purpose of confiscation, a Party shall take the necessary provisional measures, such as freezing or seizing, to prevent any dealing in, transfer or disposal of property which, at a later stage, may be the subject of a request for confiscation or which might be such as to satisfy the request.
2. A Party which as received a request for confiscation pursuant to Article 13 shall, if so requested, take the measure mentioned in paragraph 1 of this article in respect of any property which is the subject of the request or which might be such as to satisfy the request.

ARTICLE 12
Execution of provisional measures

1. The provisional measures mentioned in Article 11 shall be carried out as permitted by and in accordance with the domestic law of the requested Party and, to the extent not compatible with such law, in accordance with the procedures specified in the request.
2. Before lifting any provisional measure taken pursuant to this article, the requested Party shall, wherever possible, give the requesting Party an opportunity to present its reason in favour of continuing the measure.

Section 4
Confiscation

ARTICLE 13
Obligation to confiscate

1. A Party, which has received a request made by another Party for confiscation concerning instrumentalities or proceeds, situate in its territory, shall:

a. enforce a confiscation order made by a court of a requesting Party in relation to such instrumentalities or proceeds; or

b. submit the request to its competent authorities for the purpose of obtaining an order of confiscation and, if such order is granted, enforce it.

2. For the purposes of applying paragraph 1.b of this article, any Party shall whenever necessary have competence to institute confiscation proceedings under its own law.
3. The provisions of paragraph 1 of this article shall also apply to confiscation consisting in a requirement to pay a sum of money corresponding to the value of proceeds, if property on which the confiscation can be enforced is located in the requested Party. In such cases, when enforcing confiscation pursuant to paragraph 1, the requested Party shall, if payment is not obtained, realise the claim on any property available for that purpose.
4. If a request for confiscation concerns a specific item of property, the Parties may agree that the requested Party may enforce the confiscation in the form of a requirement to pay a sum of money corresponding to the value of the property.

ARTICLE 14
Execution of confiscation

1. The procedures for obtaining and enforcing the confiscation under Article 13 shall be governed by the law of the requested Party.
2. The requested Party shall be bound by the findings as to the facts in so far as they are stated in a conviction or judicial decision of the requesting Party or in so far as such conviction or judicial decision is implicitly based on them.

3. Each Party may, at the time of signature or when depositing its instrument of ratification, acceptance, approval or accession, by a declaration addressed to the Secretary General of the Council of Europe, declare that paragraph 2 of this article applies only subject to its constitutional principles and the basic concepts of its legal system.
4. If the confiscation consists in the requirement to pay a sum of money, the competent authority of the requested Party shall convert the amount thereof into the currency of that Party at the rate of exchange ruling at the time when the decision to enforce the confiscation is taken.
5. In the case of Article 13, paragraph 1.a, the requesting Party alone shall have the rights to decide on any application for review of the confiscation order.

ARTICLE 15

Confiscated property

Any property confiscated by the requested Party shall be disposed of by that Party in accordance with its domestic law, unless otherwise agreed by the Parties concerned.

ARTICLE 16

Right of enforcement and maximum amount of confiscation

1. A request for confiscation made under Article 13 does not affect the right of the requesting Party to enforce itself the confiscation order.
2. Nothing in this Convention shall be so interpreted as to permit the total value of the confiscation to exceed the amount of the sum of money specified in the confiscation order. If a Party finds that this might occur, the Parties concerned shall enter into consultations to avoid such an effect.

ARTICLE 17

Imprisonment in default

The requested Party shall not impose imprisonment in default or any other measure restricting the liberty of a person as a result of a request under Article 13, if the requesting Party has so specified in the request.

Section 5

Refusal and postponement of co-operation

ARTICLE 18

Grounds for refusal

1. Co-operation under this chapter may be refused if:

a. the action sought would be contrary to the fundamental principles of the legal system of the requested Party; or

b. the execution of the request is likely to prejudice the sovereignty, security, *ordre public* or other essential interests of the requested Party; or

c. in the opinion of the requested Party, the importance of the case to which the request relates does not justify the taking of the action sought; or

d. the offense to which the request relates is a political or fiscal offence; or

e. the requested Party considers that compliance with the action sought would be contrary to the principle of *ne bis in idem*; or

f. the offence to which the request relates would not be an offence under the law of the requested Party if committed within its jurisdiction. However, this ground for refusal applies to co-operation under Section 2 only in so far as the assistance sought involves coercive action.

2. Co-operation under Section 2, in so far as the assistance sought involves coercive action, and under Section 3 of this chapter, may also be refused if the measures sought could not be taken under the domestic law of the requested Party for the purposes of investigations or proceedings, had it been a similar domestic case.

3. Where the law of the requested Party so requires, co-operation under Section 2, in so far as the assistance sought involves coercive action, and under Section 3 of this chapter may also be refused if the measures sought or any other measures having similar effects would not be permitted under the law of the requesting Party, or, as regards the competent authorities of the requesting Party, if the request is not authorised by either a judge or another judicial authority, including prosecutors, any of these authorities acting in relation to criminal offences.

4. Co-operation under Section 4 of this chapter may also be refused if:

a. under the law of the requested Party confiscation is not provided for in respect of the type of offence to which the request relates; of

b. without prejudice to the obligation pursuant to Article 13, paragraph 3, it would be contrary to the principles of the domestic laws of the requested Party concerning the limits of confiscation in respect of the relationship between an offence and:

i. an economic advantage that might be qualified as its proceeds; or

ii. property that might be qualified as its instrumentalities; or

c. under the law of the requested Party confiscation may no longer be imposed or enforced because of the lapse of time; or

d. the request does not relate to a previous conviction, or a decision of a judicial nature or a statement in such a decision that an offence or several offences have been committed, on the basis of which the confiscation has been ordered or is sought; or

e. confiscation is either not enforceable in the requesting Party, or it is still subject to ordinary means of appeal; or

f. the request relates to a confiscation order resulting from a decision rendered *in absentia* of the person against whom the order was issued and, in the opinion of the requested Party, the proceedings conducted by the requesting Party leading to such decision did not satisfy the minimum rights of defence recognised as due to everyone against whom a criminal charge is made.

5. For the purposes of paragraph 4.f of this article a decision is not considered to have been rendered *in absentia* if:

a. it has been confirmed or pronounced after opposition by the person concerned; or

b. it has been rendered on appeal, provided that the appeal was lodged by the person concerned.

6. When considering, for the purposes of paragraph 4.f of this article, if the minimum rights of defence have been satisfied, the requested Party shall take into account the fact that the person concerned has deliberately sought to evade justice or the fact that the person, having had the possibility of lodging a legal remedy against the decision made *in absentia*, elected not to do so. The same will apply when the person concerned, having been duly served with the summons to appear, elected not to do so nor to ask for adjournment.

7. A Party shall not invoke bank secrecy as a ground to refuse any co-operation under this chapter. Where its domestic law so requires, a Party may require that a request for co-operation which would involve the lifting of bank secrecy be authorised by either a judge or another judicial authority, including public prosecutors, any of these authorities acting in relation to criminal offences.

8. Without prejudice to the ground for refusal provided for in paragraph 1.a of this article:

a. the fact that the person under investigation of subjected to a confiscation order by the authorities of the requesting Party is a legal person shall not be invoked by the requested Party as an obstacle to affording any co-operation under this chapter;

b. the fact that the natural person against whom an order of confiscation of proceeds has been issued has subsequently died or the fact that a legal person against whom an order of confiscation of proceeds has been issued has subsequently been dissolved shall not be invoked as an obstacle to render assistance in accordance with Article 13, paragraph 1.a.

ARTICLE 19

Postponement

The requested Party may postpone action on a request if such action would prejudice investigations or proceedings by its authorities.

ARTICLE 20

Partial or conditional granting of a request

Before refusing or postponing co-operation under this chapter, the requested Party shall, where appropriate after having consulted the requesting Party, consider whether the request may be granted partially or subject to such conditions as it deems necessary.

Section 6

Notification and protection of third parties' rights

ARTICLE 21

Notification of documents

1. The Parties shall afford each other the widest measure of mutual assistance in the serving of judicial documents to persons affected by provisional measures and confiscation.

2. Nothing in this article is intended to interfere with:

a. the possibility of sending judicial documents, by postal channels, directly to persons abroad;

b. the possibility for judicial officers, officials or other competent authorities of the Party of origin to effect service of judicial documents directly through the consular authorities of that Party or through judicial officers, officials or other competent authorities of the Party of destination, unless the Party of destination makes a declaration to the contrary to the Secretary General of the Council of Europe at the time of signature or when depositing its instrument of ratification, acceptance, approval or accession.

3. When serving judicial documents to persons abroad affected by provisional measures or confiscation orders issued in the sending Party, this Party shall indicate what legal remedies are available under its law to such persons.

ARTICLE 22

Recognition of foreign decisions

1. When dealing with a request for co-operation under Section 3 and 4, the requested Party shall recognise any judicial decision taken in the requesting Party regarding rights claimed by third parties.

2. Recognition may be refused if:

a. third parties did not have adequate opportunity to assert their rights; or

b. the decision is incompatible with a decision already taken in the requested Party on the same matter; or

c. it is incompatible with the *ordre public* of the requested Party; or

d. the decision was taken contrary to provisions on exclusive jurisdiction provided for by the law of the requested Party.

Section 7

Procedural and other general rules

ARTICLE 23

Central authority

1. The Parties shall designate a central authority or, if necessary, authorities, which shall be responsible for sending and answering requests made under this chapter, the execution of such requests or the transmission of them to the authorities competent for their execution.

2. Each Party shall, at the time of signature or when depositing its instrument of ratification, acceptance, approval or accession, communicate to the Secretary General of the Council of Europe the names and addresses of the authorities designated in pursuance of paragraph 1 of this article.

ARTICLE 24
Direct communication

1. The central authorities shall communicate directly with one another.
2. In the event of urgency, requests or communications under this chapter may be sent directly by the judicial authorities, including public prosecutors, of the requesting Party to such authorities of the requested Party. In such cases a copy shall be sent at the same time to the central authority of the requested Party through the central authority of the requesting Party.
3. Any request or communication under paragraphs 1 and 2 of this article may be made through the International Criminal Police Organisation (Interpol).
4. Where a request is made pursuant to paragraph 2 of this article and the authority is no competent to deal with the request, it shall refer the request to the competent national authority and inform directly the requesting Party that it has done so.
5. Requests or communications under Section 2 of this chapter, which do not involve coercive action, may be directly transmitted by the competent authorities of the requesting Party to the competent authorities of the requested Party.

ARTICLE 25
Form of request an languages

1. All requests under this chapter shall be made in writing. Modern means of telecommunications, such as telefax, may be used.
2. Subject to the provisions of paragraph 3 of this article, translations of the requests of supporting documents shall not be required.
3. At the time of signature or when depositing its instruments of ratification, acceptance, approval or accession, any Party may communicate to the Secretary General of the Council of Europe a declaration that it reserves the right to require that requests made to it and documents supporting such requests made to it and documents supporting such requests be accompanied by a translation into its own languages as it shall indicate. It may on that occasion declare its readiness to accept translations in any other language as it may specify. The other Parties ma apply the reciprocity rule.

ARTICLE 26
Legislation

Documents transmitted in application of this chapter shall be exempt from all legalisation formalities.

ARTICLE 27
Content of request

1. Any request for co-operation under this chapter shall specify:

   a. the authority making the request and the authority carrying out the investigations or proceedings;

   b. the object of and the reason for the request;

   c. the matters, including the relevant facts (such as date, place and circumstances of the offence) to which the investigations or proceedings relate, except in the case of a request for notification;

   d. in so far as the co-operation involves coercive action:

i. the text of the statutory provisions or, where this is not possible, a statement of the relevant law applicable; and

ii. An indication that the measure sought or any other measures having similar effects could be taken in the territory of the requesting Party under its own law;

e. where necessary and in so far as possible:

i. details of the person or persons concerned, including name, date and place of birth, nationality and location, and, in the case of a legal person, its seat; and

ii. the property in relation to which co-operation is sought, its location, its connection with the person or persons concerned, any connection with the offence, as well as any available information about other persons' interests in the property; and

f. any particular procedure the requesting Party wishes to be followed.

2. A request for provisional measures under Section 3 in relation to seizure of property on which a confiscation order consisting in the requirement to pay a sum of money may be realised shall also indicate a maximum amount for which recovery is sought in that property.

3. In addition to the indications mentioned in paragraph 1, any request under Section 4 shall contain:

a. in the case of Article 13, paragraph 1.a:

i. a certified true copy of the confiscation order made by the court in the requesting Party and a statement of the grounds on the basis of which the order was made, if they are not indicated in the order itself;

ii. an attestation by the competent authority of the requesting Party that the confiscation order is enforceable and not subject to ordinary means of appeal;

iii. information as to the extent to which the enforcement of the order is requested; and

iv. information as to the necessity of taking any provisional measures;

b. in the case of Article 13, paragraph 1.b, a statement of the facts relied upon by the requesting Party sufficient to enable the requesting Party to seek the order under its domestic law;

c. when third parties have had the opportunity to claim rights, documents demonstrating that this has been the case.

ARTICLE 28

Defective requests

1. If a request does not comply with the provisions of this chapter or the information supplied is not sufficient to enable the requested Party to deal with the request, the Party may ask the requesting Party to amend the request or to complete it with additional information.

2. The requested Party may set a time-limit for the receipt of such amendments or information.

3. Pending receipt of the requested amendments or information in relation to a request under Section 4 of this chapter, the requested Party may take any of the measures referred to in Sections 2 or 3 of this chapter.

ARTICLE 29

Plurality of requests

1. Where the requested Party receives more than one request under Sections 3 or 4 of this chapter in respect of the same person or property, the plurality or requests shall not prevent that Party from dealing with the requests involving the taking of provisional measures.

2. In the case of plurality of requests under Section 4 of this chapter, the requested Party shall consider consulting the requesting Parties.

ARTICLE 30

Obligation to give reasons

The requested party shall give reasons for any decision to refuse, postpone or make conditional any co-operation under this chapter.

ARTICLE 31

Information

1. The requested Party shall promptly inform the requesting Party of :

a. the action initiated on a request under this chapter;

b. the final result of the action carried out on the basis of the request;

c. a decision to refuse, postpone or make conditional, in whole or in part, any co-operation under this chapter;

d. any circumstances which render impossible the carrying out of the action sought or are likely to delay it significantly; and

e. in the event of provisional measures than pursuant to a request under Sections 2 or 3 of this chapter, such provisions of its domestic law as would automatically lead to the lifting of the provisional measure.

2. The requesting Party shall promptly inform the requested Party of:

a. any review, decision or any other fact by reason of which the confiscation order ceases to be wholly or partially enforceable; and

b. any development, factual or legal, by reason of which any action under this chapter is no longer justified.

3. Where a Party, on the basis of the same confiscation order, requests confiscation in more than one Party, it shall inform all Parties which are affected by an enforcement of the order about the request.

ARTICLE 32

Restriction of use

1. The requested party may make the execution of a request dependent on the condition that the information or evidence obtained will not, without its prior consent, be used or transmitted by the authorities of the requesting Party for investigations or proceedings other than those specified in the request.

2. Each Party may, at the time of signature or when depositing its instrument of ratification, acceptance, approval or accession, by declaration addressed to the Secretary General of the Council of Europe, declare that, without its prior consent, information or evidence provided by it under this chapter may not be used or transmitted by the authorities of the requesting Party in investigations or proceedings other than those specified in the request.

ARTICLE 33

Confidentiality

1. The requesting Party may require that the requested Party keep confidential the facts and substance of the request, except to the extent necessary to execute the request. If the requested Party cannot comply with the requirement of confidentiality, it shall promptly inform the requesting Party.

2. The requesting Party shall, if not contrary to basic principles of its national law and if so requested, keep confidential any evidence and information provided by the requested Party, except to the extent that its disclosure is necessary for the investigations or proceedings described in the request.

3. Subject to the provisions of its domestic law, a Party which has received spontaneous information under Article 10 shall comply with any requirement of confidentiality as required by the Party which supplies the information. If the other Party cannot comply with such requirement, it shall promptly inform the transmitting Party.

ARTICLE 34

Costs

The ordinary costs of complying with a request shall be borne by the requested Party. Where costs of a substantial or extraordinary nature are necessary to comply with a request, the Parties shall consult in order to agree the conditions on which the request is to be executed and how the costs shall be borne.

ARTICLE 35

Damages

1. When legal action on liability for damages resulting from an act or omission in relation to co-operation under this chapter has been initiated by a person, the Parties concerned shall consider consulting each other, where appropriate, to determine how to apportion any sum of damages due.

2. A Party which has become subject of a litigation for damages shall endeavour to inform the other Party of such litigation if that Party might have an interest in the case.

CHAPTER IV
FINAL PROVISIONS

ARTICLE 36

Signature and entry into force

1. This Convention shall be open for signature by the member States of the Council of Europe and non-member States which have participated in its elaboration. Such States may express their consent to be bound by:

a. signature without reservation as to ratification, acceptance or approval; or

b. signature subject to ratification, acceptance or approval, followed by ratification, acceptance or approval.

2. Instruments of ratification, acceptance or approval shall be deposited with the Secretary General of the Council of Europe.

3. This Convention shall enter into force on the first day of the month following the expiration of a period of three months after the date on which three States, of which at least two are member States of the Council of Europe, have expressed their consent to be bound by the Convention in accordance with the provisions of paragraph 1.

4. In respect of any signatory State which subsequently expresses its consent to be bound by it, the Convention shall enter into force on the first day of the month following the expiration of a period of three months after the date of the expression of its consent to be bound by the Convention in accordance with the provisions of paragraph 1.

ARTICLE 37

Accession to the Convention

1. After the entry into force of this Convention, the Committee of Ministers of the Council of Europe, after consulting the Contracting States to the Convention, may invite any State not a member of the Council and not having participated in its elaboration to accede to this Convention, by a decision taken by the majority provided for in Article 20.d of the Statute of the Council of Europe and by the unanimous vote of the representatives of the Contracting States entitled to sit on the Committee.

2. In respect of any acceding State the Convention shall enter into force on the first day of the month following the expiration of a period of three months after the date of deposit of the instrument of accession with the Secretary General of the Council of Europe.

ARTICLE 38

Territorial application

1. Any State may, at the time of signature or when depositing its instrument of ratification, acceptance, approval or accession, specify the territory or territories to which this Convention shall apply.

2. Any State may, at any later date, by a declaration addressed to the Secretary General of the Council of Europe, extend the application of this Convention to any other territory specified in the declaration. In respect of such territory the Convention shall enter into force on the first day of the month following the expiration of a period of three months after the date of receipt of such declaration by the Secretary General.

3. Any declaration made under the two preceding paragraphs may, in respect of any territory specified in such declaration, be withdrawn by a notification addressed to the Secretary General. The withdrawal shall become effective on the first day of the month following the expiration of a period of three months after the date of receipt of such notification by the Secretary General.

ARTICLE 39

Relationship to other conventions and agreements

1. This Convention does not affect the rights and undertakings derived from international multilateral conventions concerning special matters.
2. The Parties to the Convention may conclude bilateral or multilateral agreements with one another on the matters dealt with in this Convention, for purposes of supplementing or strengthening its provisions or facilitating the application of the principles embodied in it.
3. If two or more Parties have already concluded an agreement or treaty in respect of a subject which is dealt with in this Convention or otherwise have established their relations in respect of that subject, they shall be entitled to apply that agreement or treaty or to regulate those relations accordingly, in lieu of the present Convention, if it facilitates international co-operation.

ARTICLE 40

Reservations

1. Any State may, at the time of signature or when depositing its instrument of ratification, acceptance, approval or accession, declare that it avails itself of one or more of the reservations provided for in Article 2, paragraph 2, Article 6, paragraph 14, paragraph 3, Article 21, paragraph 25, paragraph 3 and Article 32, paragraph 2. No other reservation may be made.
2. Any State which has made a reservation under the preceding paragraph may wholly or partly withdraw it by means of a notification addressed to the Secretary General of the Council of Europe. The withdrawal shall take effect on the date of receipt of such notification by the Secretary General.
3. A Party which has made a reservation in respect of a provision of this Convention may not claim the application of that provision by any other Party; it may, however, if its reservation is partial or conditional, claim the application of that provision in so far as it has itself accepted it.

ARTICLE 41

Amendments

1. Amendments to this Convention may be proposed by any Party, and shall be communicated by the Secretary General of the Council of Europe to the member States of the Council of Europe and to every non-member State which has acceded to or has been invited to accede to this Convention in accordance with the provisions of Article 37.
2. Any amendment proposed by a Party shall be communicated to the European Committee on Crime Problems which shall submit to the Committee of Ministers its opinion on that proposed amendment.
3. The Committee of Ministers shall consider the proposed amendment and the opinion submitted by the European Committee on Crime Problems and may adopt the amendment.
4. The text of any amendment adopted by the Committee of Ministers in accordance with paragraph 3 of this article shall be forwarded to the Parties for acceptance.
5. Any amendment adopted in accordance with paragraph 3 of this article shall come into force on the thirtieth day after all Parties have informed the Secretary General of their acceptance thereof.

ARTICLE 42

Settlement of disputes

1. The European Committee on Crime Problems of the Council of Europe shall be kept informed regarding the interpretation and application of this Convention.

2. In case of a dispute between Parties as to the interpretation or application of this Convention, they shall seek a settlement of the dispute through negotiation or any other peaceful means of their choice, including submission of the dispute to the European Committee on Crime Problems, to an arbitral tribunal whose decisions shall be binding upon the Parties, or to the International Court of Justice, as agreed upon by the Parties concerned.

ARTICLE 43

Denunciation

1. Any Party may, at any time, denounce this Convention by means of a notification addressed to the Secretary General of the Council of Europe.
2. Such denunciation shall become effective on the first day of the month following the expiration of a period of three months after the date of receipt of the notification by the Secretary General.
3. The present Convention shall, however, continue to apply to the enforcement under Article 14 of confiscation for which a request has been made in conformity with the provisions of this Convention before the date on which such a denunciation takes effect.

ARTICLE 44

Notifications

The Secretary General of the Council of Europe shall notify the member States of the Council and any State which has acceded to this Convention of:

a. any signature;
b. the deposit of any instrument of ratification, acceptance, approval or accession;
c. any date of entry into force of this Convention in accordance with Articles 36 and 37;
d. any reservation made under Article 40, paragraph 1;
e. any other act, notification or communication relating to this Convention.

In witness whereof this undersigned, being duly authorised thereto, have signed this Convention.

Done at Strasbourg, this 8th day of November 1990, in English and French, both texts being equally authentic, in a single copy which shall be deposited in the archives of the Council of Europe. The Secretary General of the Council of Europe shall transmit certified copies to each member State of the Council of Europe, to the non-member States which have participated in the elaboration of this Convention, and to any State invited to accede to it.

Section IX

International and Regional Developments in the Field of Inter-State Cooperation in Penal Matters

The Council of Europe

Peter Wilkitzki*

Introduction

The institutional framework, the methods, the contents and the instruments of co-operation in penal matters within the Council of Europe have been extensively dealt with in the article by Müller-Rappard.[1] This article is, therefore, restricted to a depiction of the efforts of the Council of Europe, of its European Committee on Crime Problems (CDPC), and its permanent Committee on the Operation of European Conventions in the Penal Field (PC-OC), with regard to the preparation of new criminal law conventions and/or of a "second generation" Comprehensive (Merger) Convention once the complete network of criminal law conventions, the like of which is unknown the world over, has been completed, and which the Council of Europe has been putting together since the 1950s.[2]

The chequered history of the "Merger Convention" project has also been depicted in concrete terms by Müller-Rappard,[3] who may rightly be described as the father of this idea. It begins with two meetings of experts at the International Institute of Higher Studies in Criminal Sciences, Siracusa, Italy, between 1984 and 1986, which led to the preparation of the first complete Preliminary Draft of a comprehensive (European) Convention on Inter-State Co-operation in the penal field.[4]

Under a resolution made by the Ministers of Justice of the Council of Europe at their meeting held in Oslo in 1986,[5] this draft, which was already extraordinarily advanced even in comparison with the revised draft which appeared eight years later and was the subject of intensive discussions over the ensuing eight years, on the CDPC, in particular on the PC-OC permanent committee (as well as in a working group of the PC-OC which was created specifically for this purpose). In March 1994, the latter then submitted a revised second version of the draft,[6] which is appendixed to this article.

The CDPC was to decide the fate of the consolidated draft at its 43rd Plenary Session in June 1994. As had already been hinted at in the CDPC's discussions in previous years with regard to the progress of the work, it was not possible to achieve a consensus with regard to holding a final session of the PC-OC at which a final text would have been decided on for

* The views presented herein do not represent those of the German Federal Ministry of Justice.

1 *See supra*, Chapter 9.

2 Listed in: Conventions and Agreements, Chart showing signatures and ratifications of Conventions and Agreements concluded within the Council of Europe; Loose-leaf publication by the Directorate of Legal Affairs, Treaty Section, Council of Europe, Strasbourg (last updating as at Mar. 5, 1996); II: Simplified tables by subject-matter, pp. 38 *et seq*. Criminal law Compilation of all relevant texts (including Recommendations) *in* 2 EKKEHART MÜLLER-RAPPARD & M. CHERIF BASSIOUNI, EUROPEAN INTER-STATE CO-OPERATION IN CRIMINAL MATTERS 1725 (rev. 2d. ed., 1991).

3 *Supra* note 1.

4 The 1986 draft, as well as the relevant Resolutions, adopted by the Conferences of European Ministers of Justice 1986 and 1988, have been published *in* MÜLLER-RAPPARD & BASSIOUNI, *supra* note 2, at 1661-1688.

5 *Id.*

6 Council of Europe document PC-OC/INF (96) 13; published for the first time as Appendix 19, *infra*, following declassification of the text by the Committee of Ministers (577th meeting, Nov. 14-15 1996).

submission to the Committee of Ministers. What was achieved at least was to prevent the draft as a whole being definitively laid to rest. The compromise which was reached consisted of the decision to merely suspend work on the draft and to review this decision not later than in 1998 in the light of developments in international legal co-operation.[7] This meant that the door was left open to "defrosting" the "frozen" draft. In addition, the CDPC decided that the considerable work accomplished up to June 1994 should not be lost and that ways should be found in which the PC-OC could use that work positively in the future.

Thus, it could contribute to understanding and improving the operation of the existing Conventions. Furthermore, the CDPC instructed the PC-OC that when examining the operation of existing Conventions they were to be guided by the text of the draft and the thinking underlying it. Where appropriate, they could submit proposals, including proposals which would incorporate elements of the draft into new instruments (Additional Protocols or Recommendations).[8]

The author of this article—who himself has been actively involved with the project since 1984, and who was for several years Chairman of both the PC-OC and the CDPC—shares Müller-Rappard's heart-felt regret at the provisional end of work on the draft. He does, however, believe that it may be of service in future attempts to arrive at a satisfactory conclusion. If the reasons for the freezing decision, which was taken in 1994 (they were not merely excuses), can be made transparent and analyzed by means of this article, and with the aim of avoiding mistakes and overcoming problems which were the cause of its provisional demise the project may be subsequently reinstated. By publishing the text of the latest version of the draft, and thus opening it up to academic debate and the fact of the progress being depicted below which was made in this text as against previous instruments, it might also be possible to prevent the progress which has been made from being lost forever. The course of the sessions held by the PC-OC since June 1994, and their results, allow one to believe that this hope is more than just calculated optimism. In this respect, this article will report on the further problems and areas for regulation which the Committee has identified since 1994.

Reasons for the freezing of the Draft of the Comprehensive Convention in 1994

The ambitious aim of the project was two-fold:

1. to structure and simplify what had already been achieved at international level, i.e., to amalgamate the existing 20 Council of Europe Conventions in the penal field into one single treaty and thus to facilitate and simplify their application;

2. at the same time, however, to update the provisions of the existing Conventions (some of them concluded in the 1950s), i.e., to adapt them to the requirements of present-day international co-operation, to modern developments in criminal policy and to modern treaty language.

---

7 *Id.*

8 Summary report of the 43rd plenary session of the CDPC, Council of Europe document CDPC (94) 23 (Restricted).

In an ideal world, these two aims would not be mutually exclusive but would complement one another in a sensible way. In the real world of treaty policy pursued by states and governments, however, it was quickly revealed that these elements were in conflict with each other. In the reality of state practice, the overall picture of the application of conventions depends not only on the wording of the Conventions, Protocols and Additional Protocols which have been ratified in each case, but also on the restrictions and exceptions emerging from the reservations submitted by the contracting parties on ratification of the instruments.[9] In this respect, each state has paid careful attention to adherence to its "acquis."

It is a part of the basic philosophy of the Merger Convention that each of its parts replaces for each acceding state the convention or conventions which it supersedes. In that respect, each state may submit the same reservations as it had submitted under the previous Conventions, but not more. If, however, the Merger Convention is intended to go further on an individual point, to be more modern than the respective preceding provision, this obligation to the status quo *ante* is abolished. Each state is then free to demand that new and more extensive reservations be accepted, and if these are not allowed, to threaten not to ratify the "subsequent chapter."

This is an experience the draftsmen of the Merger Convention repeatedly faced. Almost every advance with regard to the range or modernity of an individual regulation had to be bought by accepting more reservations, with the consequence that gains in modernity were at risk of being canceled out by shortcomings in application in practice.

A further fundamental conceptual problem of the Merger Convention has thus already been hinted at: it can only succeed if the complex network existing between the contracting parties to the 20 Council of Europe conventions in the area of criminal law is transferred as quickly as possible, with the minimum of friction, and without losing substance, to a new, well-functioning system on the basis of the Merger Convention.

At the end of this process, we should not be in a situation which either quantitatively or qualitatively lags behind the present state of affairs, be it only in areas of cooperation, or in a "no-man's-land," from a treaty policy point of view, appearing between the present state of the Conventions and achieving the aim in which during a transitional period an unclear, contradictory patchwork characterized by coincidences exists in the relationships between the contracting parties. As early as the Conference of Ministers of Justice held in Oslo in 1986, the Dutch delegation pointed out that "it would be counterproductive if the comprehensibility of the applicable law were to be reduced rather than enhanced by the addition of a new Convention covering the same ground as the Conventions already in existence" and therefore drafted a scenario consisting of seven steps which was said to be essential for the success of the project. It could only function and "the seeds of new and higher quality plants could only germinate in the fertile soil of mutual respect, understanding and confidence."[10]

---

[9] For reservations and declarations made by states when acceding to criminal law conventions, *see* compilation by MÜLLER-RAPPARD & BASSIOUNI, *supra* note 2.

[10] International Co-operation in criminal matters between the member States of the Council of Europe; Report submitted by the Netherlands delegation to the 15th Conference of European Ministers of Justice, Oslo 1986; Council of Europe Doc. MJU-15 (86) 3.

The final chapter of the draft which was completed in 1994 constituted an attempt to take account of this requirement and of these warnings. However, in 1986 the architects of the draft saw themselves confronted by a new development which with the best will in the world could not have been foreseen. In 1986 the number of member states of the Council of Europe was 21, ten years later it had almost doubled (to 39). Fifteen of the 18 new arrivals are states of the former Eastern Bloc or successor states of the former Yugoslavia.[11] These are, therefore, states whose legal and contractual policy traditions are fundamentally different from those of the states of Western Europe. All of these states were now afforded the opportunity, as well as the challenge, of ratifying and implementing the criminal law Conventions of the Council of Europe, with which they had no connection until the beginning of the 1990s. This need to be done as quickly and as comprehensively as possible in order to become a part of the enlarged network of co-operation in Europe. This challenge on its own was gigantic, and many new member states tackled it with admirable energy. Their efforts should not be placed in doubt by their being burdened with uncertainty as to whether the contractual relationships which have been newly established will not soon be superseded by a second generation Convention, especially however by a muddled weave of parts of the old instruments and parts of the new Convention. This author is of the opinion that, in the very serious discussions held by the CDPC in June 1994, it was this concern, and not the critical financial situation of the Council of Europe (which was of course also a consideration) which was the final reason for the decision that the first half of this decade was not a suitable time for this "reform of the century" to work.

A further argument which played a role in the discussions was connected both with the admission of the states of Central and Eastern Europe and the zero growth of the budget of the Council of Europe. The PC-OC, which had previously had a two-fold mandate—review of the operation of the existing treaties and elaboration of a Merger Convention—was able to commit all its efforts (as of 1995 once more with two sessions per year with the participation of all member states) to the task of discussing in the enlarged circle all the real problems which occur in the day-to-day application of the existing Conventions, in particular for those member states which do not have decades of experience with these instruments. The Draft of the Comprehensive Convention, which had been put on ice, offered the additional opportunity to at least use it as a reservoir of ideas, i.e. wherever possible to use the fruits of eight years of work as an aid in interpretation for the application of the existing Conventions or as material for the preparation of new "piecemeal" instruments (additional protocols, recommendations).

Finally, two further reasons as regards content should be pointed out for the partial failure of the project which were not discussed in detail on the CDPC, but which however played a role in forming the opinions of the delegations.

The aim of creating a compact Convention, existing as a unified whole, is of a necessity conditional on the parts of the Convention which are concerned with the individual fundamental forms of co-operation. Each case governs the particularities which refer

---

[11] Hungary (1990), Poland (1991), Bulgaria (1992), Estonia (1993), Lithuania (1993), Slovenia (1993), Czech Republic (1993), Slovakia (1993), Romania (1993), Latvia (1995), Albania (1995), Moldova (1995), Ukraine (1995), The Former Yugoslav Republic of Macedonia (1995), Russia (1996). Next arrivals could be: Croatia, Bosnia-Herzegovina, Belarus. *See* Peter Wilkitzki, *On Judicial Mutual Assistance in Criminal Matters Between the States of Western and Eastern Europe*, 1995 EUR. J. ON CRIM. POL'Y & RES. 91.

specifically to these part areas, but every overall element applicable to all or several areas being transferred to a provision in the General Chapter, renders it applicable to each of these areas. In Chapter I—General Provisions—the architects of the draft faced up to this task. They discovered, however, that this is connected with problems which cast doubts on the consistency and readability of the Convention as a whole. Should "common" provisions already be agreed upon if they concern only two of the four main areas, or only if they cover three or all of the Chapters? What if with regard to such a general clause the common ground is less substantial than the modifications required for all or some chapters—will the Convention not then be less clear instead of clearer?

This problem can be illustrated in light of the example of "provisional measures." The general rule is in Article I.15; special regulations with a varying range are made in Article II.8 bis, Provisional arrest (extradition), in Article IV.6; Provisional measures (transfer of proceedings), in Article V.16; and Provisional arrest (Enforcement of sanctions), without the relationship between the general and the specific regulation becoming convincingly clear for each of these chapters. Another example is the ground for refusal, "Fiscal offence," which does not appear in the grounds for refusal contained in the general part. It does appear as a potential reservation in Article II.11 (b) ii and Article III.14 (a) for extradition and mutual assistance. On the other hand, the similar ground for refusal of "Political offence" in Article I.9 para. 1 (d) and para. 2 is worded in general terms, whilst also being made a potential reservation in Article II.11 (b) i. The situation is similarly confusing as regards possibilities of refusing to cooperate from the point of view "*ne bis in idem*" (*cf.* Article I.9 para. 1 (g) and (h), Article II.3 para. 1 and Article III.14 (e)). The technique of standardizing extensive "grounds for refusal" in Chapter I becomes entirely doubtful in light of its application to those Chapters which do not create strict duties incumbent on the acceding States to execute the request, i.e. Chapters IV and V.

Even if an ideal solution were to be found with regard to the relationship between the four specific chapters and their relationship to the general chapter, a fundamental problem of international co-operation would nevertheless remain. To date, this has not been solved. In a time when the commission of cross-border crime has become a lot easier than cross-border prosecution, it is unavoidable, and sometimes even indispensable, for several national jurisdictions to exist for one and the same criminal offence. If a second generation Convention wishes to be completely justified in calling itself comprehensive, one should actually be able to expect it to offer not only all instruments of co-operation which are necessary the final analysis to nurture one of these jurisdictions to success. Moreover, by means of the optimum selection and combination of the instruments which are the most suitable in individual cases, the offence should always be prosecuted and the sanction enforced by the state or states which taking all legitimate interests into account (interests of the administration of justice, of the offenders and of the victims) are best suited for this.

In order to ensure that this aim can be fulfilled, the draft—as all international instruments of co-operation previously prepared—contains only a minimum approach (*cf.* for instance Article I.7-Concurrent requests). Those who are concerned on a day-to-day basis with solving these problems cannot deny their deep-seated skepticism as to whether more could be achieved at present. The framework conditions for the work of the judiciary are too varied in the states in the world. The sacred principle of national sovereignty is still over-emphasized by national legal systems and governments for it to be possible to expect a satisfactory solution of this fundamental problem. The fact that the problem has been recognized is nevertheless demonstrated by the circumstance that the "need for reasonable planning where different jurisdictions are involved" is an integral element of the "checklist" of the future work of the PC-OC.[12]

Progress made by the provisions contained in the draft in comparison to the existing Conventions

In order to make the wording and the meaning of the provisions contained in the draft as comprehensively useful as possible for the work of the PC-OC, as was decided by the CDPC in 1994, the Secretariat of the Committee in July 1995 prepared a list of the main differences between the Draft Comprehensive Convention and the existing Conventions.[13] This overview, which has proved highly useful in the further work of the Committee, formed the basis of the subsequent report. Only deviations which the author considers to be of fundamental significance for a revision of the way in which cooperation is regulated are mentioned.

Extradition (in comparison to the 1957 European Convention on Extradition and its Additional Protocols dated 1975 and 1978).[14]

Grounds for refusal

For all types of co-operation, Articles I.9 para. 1 (a), (b), (c) and (i) specify as general grounds for refusal cases where "the execution of the request would be contrary to the fundamental principles" of the requested party, where "the execution of the request is likely to prejudice its sovereignty, security, ordre public or other of its essential interests," where "the procedure is manifestly disproportionate to the seriousness of the offence or to the penalty likely to be enforced," or where "compliance with such a request is likely to have particularly serious consequences for the person concerned on account of his age, state of health or other personal reasons." (An additional ground for refusal "Incompatibility with the European Convention on Human Rights" was originally considered but in the end was not included in the text of the draft for reasons of principle.)

Such broad grounds for refusal, based on superior general principles of *ordre public*, reason of state, or for humanitarian reasons, are not contained in the wording of the Convention on Extradition. In its practical application, however, they are based, by many states, either on corresponding reservations submitted on ratification or on *jus cogens*, which in accordance with the general principles of international law is superior to the written provisions.

The fact that they have now been expressly included in the draft may be regarded both as progress and as a step backwards. It is progress because in this way a circumstance which previously was based on various legal sources, some of which were unclear, is governed in a treaty, which contributes to more uniform and clearer operation. However, it is a step

12 *See supra* note 35.
13 Council of Europe document PC-OC (95) 2 (Restricted).
14 Europ. T. S. No. 24 (1957), 86 (1975) and 98 (1978).

backwards in the sense that this might create the impression that the contractual obligations arising from the Convention were placed at the disposition of the contracting parties to a greater degree than has hitherto been the case, and that these states could call upon such an "escape clause" almost whenever they wished to do so if it became too burdensome for them to fulfill the obligations. (That said, experience gathered in practice has shown that a state which is determined not to fulfill one of these duties will in any case always find a way of circumventing it.)[15]

The circumstance that all grounds for refusal—the general ones contained in Chapter I as well as the special ones in Chapter II, with the exception of the ground for refusal of "threat of the death penalty"—are uniformly worded as optional and not compulsory, a consequence of the phenomenon, already mentioned, that broad sections of the Comprehensive Convention anyway do not give rise to binding duties for the contracting parties, is more serious. At first sight, the freedom of the acceding states to refuse or, indeed, not to refuse to extradite where grounds exist for refusal leads to an extension of cooperation. Nevertheless, from a dogmatic point of view, it is difficult to justify why states should be free to grant extradition even where the ground for refusal exists of a "threat of prosecution in violation of human rights" (Article I.9 para. 1 (e)).

The differences which are made by the Convention on Extradition (Articles 8 and 9) and the First Additional Protocol (Article 2) with regard to the principle of *ne bis in idem* have been leveled out in the draft. In this respect, for all cases of pending or concluded proceedings in respect of the same offence, provision is made for two broad optional grounds for refusal (Article I.9 para. 1 (g) and (h)).

With regard to the ground for refusal of a "political offence," the draft is closely linked to the existing treaties. The fundamental decision of the PC-OC not to integrate the European Convention on the Suppression of Terrorism[16] into the Comprehensive Convention should be emphasized here. Because of its special character, it should exist in addition to the latter.

The only regulation on refusal which is worded more stringently than in the existing Conventions concerns the threat of imposition or enforcement of the death penalty. Whilst Article 11 of the Convention on Extradition merely grants to the requested party the possibility of refusing to extradite, if the requesting party does not give sufficient assurance that the death penalty will not be carried out, the draft (Article II.3 para. 4) provides for an absolute ground for refusal ("shall be refused") if there is an actual threat of the death penalty being carried out, and opens up the possibility of granting extradition if sufficient assurance is given that it will not be carried out only in the second sentence of the provision.

The duty to carry out own proceedings if extradition is refused (*aut dedere aut judicare*), which according to the Convention on Extradition (Article 6 para. 2) only applies to the ground for refusal of "extradition of nationals" (as has been stated, the special case applying under Article 7 of the Terrorism Convention is not covered by the draft), was extended to the ground for refusal "threat of the death penalty" but not to further grounds for refusal, and weakened for both cases by the addition of "if they (own proceedings) are considered appropriate."

---

15 Peter Wilkitzki, *Defences, Exceptions and Exemptions in the Extradition Law and Practice and the Criminal Policy of the F.R.G. . . . in Extradition, Acts of the International Seminar held at the I.S.I.S.C., Siracusa (Italy), 4-9 December 1989,* 62 INT'L REV. OF PENAL L. 281, 288 (1991).

16 Europ. T. S. No. 90 (1977).

Principle of speciality

The draft governs the problem of speciality in a way which is simpler and clearer than the Convention on Extradition, in particular by merging the cases of further prosecution in the original requesting party and re-extradition to a third state (Articles 14 and 15) in a uniform provision (Article II.7), and thus does away with doubts which had previously arisen with regard to the applicability of all rules on speciality to cases of re-extradition. Furthermore, Article II.7 para. 5 takes account of the inclusion of a provision on simplified extradition by creating the possibility for cases where the person extradited consents to waive the consent of the requested party to further prosecution.

Simplified extradition

A possibility which is one of the most significant achievements, in practical terms, since the creation of the Convention on Extradition is one which is now anchored in the national law of many states of Europe, namely that of waiving formalities of the extradition proceedings, and in particular the requirement to submit certain documents and to carry out court proceedings should the person concerned declare his or her consent to extradition after being provided with comprehensive information by a judicial instance and being advised by legal counsel. This simplified procedure serves not only the interests of the administration of justice of both of the states concerned, but also those of the person to be extradited, who does not need to remain in detention in the requested party any longer than absolutely necessary, and who is afforded the opportunity of all accusations which are being leveled against him or her being dealt with in one proceeding—where appropriate with the possibility of a "discount." In Germany, Austria and Switzerland, which have included suitable regulations in their national laws over the past few decades, almost two-thirds of all cases of extradition are now carried out in this kind of simplified procedure.

Since the procedure for deciding on an extradition request on principle falls within the discretion of the requested party, it is possible for simplifications to be effected even without the existence of a corresponding regulation in a treaty. Nevertheless, it is useful for this to be regulated in a treaty because of the motivating effect which this has on the states, as well as because such regulations specify uniform procedural principles and guarantees which are necessary for this kind of procedure. The "Schengen Agreement" (Article 66)[17] quite successfully created this kind of regulation; the member states of the European Union have elaborated a corresponding EU Convention.[18]

---

[17] "Schengen Agreement": Convention of 19 June 1990, applying the Schengen Agreement of 14 June 1985 between the Governments of the States of the Benelux Economic Union, the Federal Republic of Germany and the French Republic, of the Gradual Abolition of Checks at their Common Borders. *See also*, *supra*, Chapter 6.

[18] Convention (of Mar. 9, 1995), drawn up on the basis of Art. K.3 of the Treaty on European Union, on Simplified Extradition Procedure (not yet in force).

Mutual assistance (in comparison to the European Convention on Mutual Assistance on Criminal Matters dated 1959 and its Additional Protocol dated 1978).[19]

Scope of application

In the light of the developments which have taken place over the past decades, the architects of the draft were faced with the question of whether the entire Convention or at least the chapter on mutual assistance could be extended to cover proceedings in respect of sanctions which, whilst not being of a genuinely criminal law nature, may however be brought before a court with jurisdiction for criminal cases (for instance proceedings in respect of "administrative offences" *Ordnungs- widrigkeiten* under German law).[20] In the end, they opted for cautious extension of the area of application: the General Chapter (Article I.1) remains restricted to "criminal matters," whilst, however, an opening clause was included in Article III.1, paragraph 2 which allows the parties to include other proceedings in the area of application of Chapter III.

The existing Convention contains a few special provisions with regard to different types of mutual assistance falling under Chapter III, but has neither an exhaustive or an exemplary list of measures which may be requested and granted on the basis of the Convention. Article III.1, paragraph 3 closes this gap in accordance with the pattern of bilateral treaties and multilateral (U.N.) Conventions[21] by inserting a list, which, however, is not exhaustive ("in particular"). It is not constitutive in nature, but will in particular make it easier for the newly-acceding states to "get into" the Chapter.

Coercive measures

The existing Convention contains only one regulation on this category of requests for mutual assistance which is of practical significance (Article 5), according to which "letters rogatory for search or seizure of property" may by means of a declaration to be made dependent on one or more special condition or conditions, in particular dual criminality and consistency with the law of the requested party. Nothing is said either with regard to the further substantive restrictions, or about other types of coercive measures. This no longer corresponds to the present-day situation in criminal proceedings and in mutual assistance, in particular the multifarious coercive measures which are nowadays part and parcel of criminal proceedings, such as surveillance of telecommunications, physical examinations, gene analysis and the like. The instruments provided by the convention on mutual Assistance in Criminal Matters are not geared to this, and the contracting parties are not even certain as to whether and to what extent such measures fall within its area of application.[22]

---

19 Europ. T. S. Nos. 30 (1959) and 99 (1978).

20 *Cf.* the "opening clause" in Art. 1 (b) of the European Convention on the International Validity of Criminal Judgements: " 'Offence' comprises, apart from acts dealt with under the criminal law, those dealt with under the legal provisions listed in Appendix II to the present Convention on condition that where these provisions give competence to an administrative authority there must be the opportunity for the person concerned to have the case tried by a court," *infra* note 29.

21 *Cf.* Art. 7, ¶ 2, of the U.N. Convention Against Illicit Traffic in Narcotic Drugs and Psychotropic Substances of Dec. 20, 1988.

22 *Cf.* Council of Europe Recommendation No. R (85) 10 concerning letters rogatory for the interception of telecommunications.

The architects of the draft were not able to create detailed new regulations with regard to all this material. Nevertheless, Article III.5 quater contains the general principle, which is wrapped up in a formal provision, that the affording of mutual assistance may be made dependent on it not being possible to adequately achieve the purpose of the request by other means of investigation (principle of deploying the least encroaching means) or on it not being possible for the coercive measure to be taken on the territory of the requesting party under its law. The intention here is for the requesting party not to be placed in a better position from a legal point of view than if it executed the act itself on its own territory (for instance, a request for surveillance of telecommunications in respect of a criminal offence which is one of the listed offenses in respect of which such measures may be ordered in accordance with the law of the requested party, but not under that of the requesting party). Furthermore, Article III. 14 (c) offers the acceding states the possibility to make the execution of requests for coercive measures dependent on special conditions.

With regard to seizure in response to a mutual assistance request, Article III.5 bis closes a loophole with regard to the existing Convention by determining that this measure may not only serve the purpose of procuring evidence but also the purpose of restitution to the rightful owner; a variation which previously had only been expressly regulated in some additional treaties to the Convention. The third alternative of seizure and transmission of property for the purpose of preparing a decision imposing forfeiture in the requesting party will be subsumed under the measures which are possible under either Chapter III or Chapter V, depending on the domestic law on mutual assistance of the requested party. The draft contains no express provisions on this.

"Speciality" principle in connection with mutual assistance

The existing Convention says nothing about the duty incumbent on both states concerned to confidentially treat personal information transmitted in connection with the making and execution of requests, nor about the duty incumbent on the requesting party not to use the information transmitted in the execution of a request for other purposes than for that (of specific criminal proceedings) for which they were transmitted, unless the requested party consents. Restrictions of this nature arise under the Convention only from general reservations or those related, to specific cases imposed by the requested party, whilst newer Conventions (*cf.* for instance Article 50 para. 3 of the 1990 Council of Europe Money Laundering Convention[23] or newer U.N. instruments[24] which contain express regulations on this).

The draft (Article III.6 bis) follows these examples. However, it did not opt for a general prohibition of such use of data, but only for the granting of the possibility to the requested party to link execution of the request to the condition that the items of evidence which have been transmitted are not to be used for proceedings with regard to which the requested party could refuse to afford mutual assistance.

---

23 *Cf. infra* note 31.

24 *Cf.* Art. 7, ¶ 13 and 14 of the U.N. Drug Convention of Dec. 20, 1988, *supra* note 21.

Temporary transfer of detained persons

Article 11 of the Convention governs the transfer to the requesting party, for evidentiary purposes, of persons who are in custody in the requested party, but not the converse case where the requesting party requests that persons who are in custody on its territory be transferred to the requested party for purposes of confrontation or for other evidentiary purposes, held there for the duration of the transfer and then transferred back to the requesting party. A need for this kind of regulation has arisen in practice, and to date has only been taken account of in some additional treaties to the Convention. Article III.9 bis closes this loophole.

Right to decline evidence

Article III.11 bis is also concerned with a practically relevant question which as yet is not covered by the Convention. Since the national codes of criminal procedure, even when the legal systems are closely related, demonstrate differences with regard to the right to decline evidence (for instance on the part of in-laws), giving evidence before a court may entail risks for foreign witnesses which are difficult to assess. Are they only able to call on rights to refuse to give evidence which they have brought with them, only on those of the state in which they give evidence, or on both cumulatively? The draft solves the problem in the latter sense, along the lines of the Commonwealth Scheme relating to mutual assistance in criminal matters.

Information on foreign law

A special form of "mutual assistance" of a nontechnical nature is constituted by executing requests where judicial authorities ask for information on provisions contained in foreign legal orders in order to be able to carry out their functions. This material is governed in the Additional Protocol dated 15 March 1978 to the European Convention on Information on Foreign Law,[25] an instrument which—in the same way as its "Mother Convention"—is used astonishingly infrequently even by newly acceding states. Its provisions are to be included in the Comprehensive Convention. They are, however, not to be taken into Chapter II, but since this kind of request can refer to all areas of co-operation, into Chapter I (Article I.1 bis).

Transfer of proceedings (in comparison to the European Convention on the Transfer of Proceedings in Criminal Matters dated 1972,[26] and corresponding provisions contained in other Conventions).

In contrast to the Conventions on Extradition and on Mutual Assistance, the 1972 Convention has a poor record in the "success statistics" of the best-accepted criminal law Conventions of the Council of Europe. As of the beginning of 1996 it has only been ratified by ten states, although one must take into consideration that a few states which have not

---

25 Europ. T. S. No. 97 (1978).

26 Europ. T. S. No. 73 (1972).

acceded, including the Federal Republic of Germany, achieve similar legal effects by using additional treaties to the Convention on Mutual Assistance in order to make the regulations concerning Article 21 of this Convention (laying of information with a view to proceedings) into "mini-transfer Conventions." It is, therefore, logically consistent for Article 21 of the Convention on Mutual Assistance to be included by means of Article VI.4, paragraph 1 (c) of the draft in the provisions which are to be superseded by Chapter IV, and not by Chapter III.

Similarly to the "Validity Convention," one of the main causes of the relatively poor acceptance of the 1972 Convention lies in its very detailed, complex regulations which pose difficulties in operation. As was the case with the Agreement which was worked out between the EU Member States,[27] upon which Chapter IV was molded, the architects of the Comprehensive Convention also attempted to draw up a "more open," more flexible, clearer and thus "more ratification-friendly" model. The consequence of this was that some questions which in the 1972 Convention were resolved down to the slightest detail, are left in Chapter IV up to the interpretation of national governments and courts. Comparing the dimensions of the two instruments makes the difference clear. Whilst the 1972 Convention (without its final clauses) contains 37 Articles and three Appendices, Chapter IV of the Draft Comprehensive Convention only has six Articles.

This "leanification" is also made easier by the fact that Chapter IV refrains from establishing strict legal duties not only for the potentially requesting party—which goes without saying—but also for the party receiving a request for a transfer. Rather, its obligation is restricted (Article IV.3, paragraph 1) to after examination deciding, in accordance with its own law, whether to accept the request. Since, aside from the general duty contained in Article IV.1, paragraph 1 (to ". . . undertake to afford each other the widest possible measure of assistance"), parties are free in their decision, there was also no need to include any special grounds for refusal (*cf.* Articles 10-12 of the 1972 Convention).

Another existing Convention which contains regulations (in anticipation of the provisions of the 1972 Convention) on the transfer of proceedings in connection with a specific category of crime is the 1964 Convention on the Punishment of Road Traffic Offences.[28] The relevant provisions contained here are also to be superseded by Chapter IV (Article VI.4, paragraph 1 (c).

Enforcement of sanctions (in comparison to the European Convention on the International Validity of Criminal Judgements dated 1970,[29] the Convention on the Transfer of Sentenced Persons dated 1983,[30] the European Convention on the Supervision of Conditionally Sentenced or Conditionally Released Offenders dated 1964,[31] as well as other Conventions).

The task which the architects of the draft were set to achieve, at the same time a synthesis, a simplification and a modernization of the existing instruments, proved to be particularly difficult in Chapter V, as is shown already by the list of "reference Conventions"

---

27 Agreement between the EU Member States on the Transfer of Proceedings in Criminal Matters, Nov. 6, 1990 (not yet in force).

28 Europ. T. S. No. 52 (1964).

29 Europ. T. S. No. 70 (1970).

30 Europ. T. S. No. 112 (1983).

31 Europ. T. S. No. 51 (1964).

in the title, i.e. Conventions which not only govern varying material, but which come from different "generations" and some of which, therefore, even follow different fundamental concepts. Thus, for instance, the *raison d'etre* of the 1983 Transfer Convention is largely defined in the light of the relative failure of the 1970 Validity Convention, and attempts hence to eliminate all unclear detailed provisions on the procedure. At the same time, however, it is restricted to parts of the area of application of the latter (only sanctions involving deprivation of liberty, no application to cases where the convict is already in the potential administering state) and places resocialisation concepts, i.e. the interests of the convict, on the same footing as the proper administration of justice, i.e. the interests of the two states concerned. This in turn entails a series of conceptual deviations from the 1970 Convention, for instance with regard to the stringency of the provisions (no strict duties under international law for the acceding states), the legal position of the convict (transfer only with his or her consent) or the provisos required for his or her protection (no principle of speciality).

The work of those who prepared Chapter V was complicated even further by virtue of the fact that two further Conventions were also to be included, whose acceptance has been poor, and which concern part areas, namely the 1964 Supervision Convention and the 1964 Road Traffic Offences Convention.[32] Conversely, the "enforcement part" of the Convention of 8 November 1990 on Laundering, Search and Seizure of the Proceeds from Crime,[33] one of the most modern criminal law Conventions of the Council of Europe, the content and philosophy of which cannot be amalgamated with the "old" Conventions, has been dropped.

Thus, we have a situation where most of the provisions of Chapter V correspond to some but certainly not all of the corresponding provisions of the existing Conventions which have been mentioned. Even if the synthesis of these very heterogeneous elements contained in Chapter V appears to have been a success in principle, the fact remains, which poses a hindrance to the Contracting Parties to the old Conventions having a smooth transition into the new Chapter, that a something has been created which is a new whole, but which in comparison with the earlier instruments is still a "newcomer."

This could reduce the acceptance of this Chapter for those states which would be willing to accede.

Final clauses

The final chapter (Chapter VI) corresponds to the standardized clauses as they are common in Council of Europe Conventions. Since these clauses have been the subject of repeated modifications in the life of the Council of Europe, deviations from details of the final clauses of the existing Conventions would be unavoidable.

Article VI.4 reflects the philosophy according to which all existing criminal law Conventions are to be taken up into the relevant Chapters of the Comprehensive Convention, and therefore names the Conventions or parts of Conventions on each of the Chapters of the special part which are to be superseded by the respective Chapter. The fact that this cannot

---

32 *Supra* note 28.

33 Europ. T. S. No. 141 (1990). The most recent criminal law convention of the Council of Europe—also not to be amalgamated—is the Agreement on Illicit Traffic by Sea, Jan. 31, 1995, Implementing Art. 17 of the U.N. Convention against Illicit Traffic in Narcotic Drugs and Psychotropic Substances (not yet in force).

be achieved in all cases without a residue has been explained above by means of examples (especially Chapter V).

Progress, which is of significance from both an academic and a practical point of view, in comparison with the first generation Conventions has been made by Article VI.8 bis which, in accordance with the model of the second generation Conventions, such as the 1990 Money Laundering Convention and the Recommendation issued to it,[34] contains a detailed system for the settlement of disputes. Finally, Article VI.3 bis—Federal Clause—is worth mentioning, as it determines that the duties arising from the Convention apply in the same manner to federal states and to parties which are not federal or non-unitary states.

Further work of the PC-OC since 1994; identification of new material which could or should be included in the draft.

As has been explained, the work of the PC-OC since 1994 has been aimed at fruitfully utilizing the immense amount of work which has been invested in the draft and assessing it as a reservoir of ideas for applying and extending the existing Conventions. Since the discussions on this matter were first of all concerned with the Chapters "Mutual assistance" and "Transfer of sentenced persons," the following comments are limited to these areas, i.e. Chapters III and V of the draft.

Mutual assistance

The Committee is presently examining with regard to all the provisions of Chapter III whether they should be included in a binding instrument under international law—perhaps a "Second Additional Protocol" to the 1959 Convention—or merely in (nonbinding) recommendations. There has also been some brainstorming on the question of which further regulation materials need to be included in a new instrument in the light of developments in practice or in academic circles.[35]

A Preliminary Draft of a Second Additional Protocol to the Convention on Mutual Assistance has now been prepared by the PC-OC,[36] and it contains Articles on the following matters:

Material taken over from the Draft Comprehensive Convention:

1. Duty incumbent on the requested party, where requests specify any given procedure, or any procedural requirement which is necessary under the law of the requesting party, even if unfamiliar to the requested party, to comply with such requests to the extent that the action sought is not contrary to fundamental principles of its law (*cf.* Article III.1 bis of the draft);

---

[34] *Supra* note 33; Council of Europe Recommendation No. R (91) 12 on setting up and functioning of arbitral tribunals under Art. 42, ¶ 2, of Convention Europ. T. S. No. 141.

[35] Summary Report of the 30th meeting of the PC-OC, Council of Europe document PC-OC (95) 1 (Restricted), No. 49: "Open-ended list of issues concerning mutual assistance that require further discussion."

[36] Council of Europe document PC-OC (96) 8/Appendix IV (Restricted).

2. Extension of the possibility of surrender of property beyond evidentiary purposes through to the purpose of its restitution to the rightful owner (*cf.* Article III.5 bis of the draft);

3. Facilitating the temporary transfer of detained persons, for the purposes of evidence, also to the requested Party (*cf.* Article III.9 bis of the draft);

4. Inclusion of a differentiated provision on exceptions from the principle that refund of any costs resulting from the application of the Convention must not be claimed from the other Party; in particular, it must be possible to require the requesting party to meet costs of a substantial or extraordinary nature (*cf.* Article I.6, paragraph 2 of the draft);

5. Restriction of the use by the requesting party of information obtained by mutual assistance—possibility for the requested party to make the execution of a request dependent on the condition that the evidence obtained will not be used by the authorities of the requesting party for other purposes than those specified in the request (*cf.* Article III.6 bis of the draft).

Newly included materials and issues which could also be included:

1. (In connection with the above mentioned fundamental duty to respect the wishes of the requesting party with regard to the procedure to be adhered to) permission of the presence of defense counsel at the execution of the request and at the hearing in the form of examining and cross-examining the person, either directly or through the examining authority, by defense counsel and the prosecution; a procedure which makes mutual assistance considerably easier, especially between common law and civil law states;

2. (Also in connection with the principle which has been mentioned of largely fulfilling special wishes as regards procedure) use of audio and video means in connection with hearing accused persons, witnesses or experts, or carrying out confrontations, in two alternatives, either for the purpose of transmitting to the requesting party the electronic records thus obtained, or by simultaneously organizing an audio-link or video-link between the place of the hearing and court chambers in the requesting party, whereby it is possible conversely to distinguish between whether the judicial authorities of the requesting Party and/or defense counsel or other interested persons are only allowed to follow the hearing, or also to intervene in the procedure. Here too it is a question of a method which is already in practice in the common law legal area, but for which the legal requirements are largely yet to be created in continental Europe;

3. Standards under the law on mutual assistance for tapping and tracing of telecommunications, including mobile telephones, going beyond the minimum solution to be found in Article III.5 quater for all coercive measures, including interception of direct communications other than telecommunications;

4. Solution of the difficult question connected with the inclusion of electronic evidence in mutual assistance (access, including on-line access to computer data bases in another state, searches in networks, including international networks). In that respect, a specially constituted Council of Europe Committee, which brought together the expertise of both lawyers and computer experts, has been doing sterling preparatory work.[37]

---

[37] Committee (PC-PC) which drafted Recommendation No. R (95) 13 on problems of criminal procedural law connected with information technology.

5. Creation of the possibility of the judicial authorities of the requesting party being able to directly address, by post, a summons to appear on its territory to witnesses or experts who are on the territory of the potential requested party. This possibility has been introduced in continental Europe by Article 52 of the Schengen Agreement.[38] It is suited to relieve the mutual assistance system of a considerable part of the burden arising from routine requests, but gives rise not only to problems of national sovereignty, but also of a human rights nature (can it be guaranteed that it will be translated into a language which is understandable to the recipient?). Related to this, but to date not governed in mutual assistance instruments, is making possible examination or service—at least with regard to the own nationals of the requesting party—on consular premises of the host country;

6. Creation of the legal basis for cross-border observations and hot pursuit. Here too, it is a question of material for which the Schengen Agreement (Articles 40 and 41) has done pioneer work in Europe in order to counter the considerable legal as well as psychological problems which remain associated with the concept of law enforcement officials of one state crossing national frontiers, even in a Europe with open borders. The extraordinarily stringent restrictions contained in the declarations which have been submitted on this matter by most of the Schengen states bear particular witness to this. The facilitation of controlled delivery of goods and money over state borders, which has shown itself to be indispensable, is also related to this, especially in the area of narcotics- related crime and organized crime, as well as the facilitation of crossborder use of technical devices, such as using direction finders on suspicious vehicles (not yet discussed);

7. Facilitating the granting, in response to a mutual assistance request, of authorization for undercover investigators or agents to continue their investigative activities on the territory of the requested party. It is particularly a question here of making the stringent but frequently varying requirements, compatible which the national laws of criminal procedure have set up for the deployment of such UCA's in order to arrive at a definition of these tasks, as well as of the legal situation of such investigators, which is as uniform as possible. This task would be made all the more difficult if an attempt were to be made to regulate the deployment of informers in mutual assistance and other provocative methods (reverting operations). Europe would be treading new ground here;

- facilitating the establishment of joint investigation teams (not yet discussed);
- extension of the restrictions which are to apply to the utilization of the sensitive, personal data which are transmitted via mutual assistance channels not only in the requesting party, but also in the requested party (confidential treatment of the fact that a request has been made and of its content). Here lies a challenge for the future of mutual assistance, which on the one hand will not be able to do without sufficient protection of data according to the particularities of certain areas, but which also may not be subjected to too tight restrictions in pursuing serious and the most serious cross-border crime. This applies for instance, to the question of compensation if data are not treated with all due care, as well as to that of the harmonizing provisions applying in the states concerned for the erasure of such data.

---

[38] *Supra* note 17.

Transfer of sentenced persons

In this respect, in 1995/96 the PC-OC prepared a draft of an Additional Protocol to the 1983 Convention[39] which is to regulate the following two sets of problems:

1. Application of the Convention also to cases in which the convict has already traveled to the potential administering state;

2. Waiver of the requirement of the consent of the convict if the relevant judgment is handed down concurrently with an order under criminal or administrative law determining the person's expulsion after conclusion of enforcement in the state in which the judgement was given. Both cases concern material in respect of which it would be possible to find a solution with regard to application of the Validity Convention, but as yet not with regard to application of the 1983 Convention, and hence real examples of the amalgamation of Conventions intended to be achieved by Chapter V of the draft.

Outlook

The list of unknown territories in respect of which the PC-OC has made initial further attempts to achieve progress after the "freezing decision" was taken in 1994 is impressive. The second list of areas in which detailed discussions are yet to take place, however, appears more so. The Committee is faced with a remarkable challenge, and if it is able to overcome these there is every chance that the ten years of work on the draft not only will not have been in vain, but that the "Comprehensive Convention" phoenix will rise from the ashes in the next millennium, shining in a manifestation which is even more advanced, more comprehensive and further developed both from a dogmatic and a practical point of view. This article is intended to be both a small contribution and an incentive towards this vision.

---

[39] Council of Europe Doc. PC-OC (96) 8/Appendix III (Restricted).

Appendix 19

Draft European Comprehensive Convention on International Co-operation in Criminal Matters

Text approved by the Committee PC-OC
at its meeting from 21 to 25 March 1994

Chapter I
General Provisions

Article I.1
Scope

This Convention applies to co-operation in criminal matters concerning extradition (Chapter II), mutual assistance (Chapter III), transfer of proceedings (Chapter IV) and enforcement of sanctions (Chapter V).

Article I.1 bis
Information on foreign law

1. The Parties undertake to supply one another with information on their substantive and procedural law and judicial organization in the criminal field, including prosecuting authorities, as well as on the law concerning the enforcement of penal measures.
2. A request for information may:

   a. emanate from a court or from any judicial authority having jurisdiction to prosecute offences or execute sentences that have been imposed with a final and binding effect; and

   b. be made not only where proceedings have actually been instituted, but also when the institution of proceedings is envisaged.

Article I.2
Applicable law

The law of the requested Party shall be applicable when it acts upon a request made under this Convention, unless otherwise provided for in this Convention.

Article I.3
Channels of communication

1. Each Contracting Party shall designate a central authority, or if its constitutional system so requires, central authorities, that shall be competent to send, receive and answer requests specified in the Chapters of this Convention. However, any Contracting Party may specify that requests or certain categories of requests and replies thereto may also be transmitted directly to or by its judicial authorities.
2. In cases of urgency, requests and communications may be exchanged directly between the judicial authorities of the Contracting Parties. Where appropriate, the International Criminal Police Organization (INTERPOL) channels may be used.
3. Where an authority which receives a request has no competence to comply therewith, it shall, ex officio, transmit the request to the competent authority of its country and shall so inform the requesting authority.
4. Each Contracting Party shall, when depositing its instrument of ratification, acceptance, approval or accession, by a declaration addressed to the Secretary General of the Council of Europe define its central authority or authorities and what authorities it will for the purposes of this Convention deem judicial authorities. That declaration may be changed at any time.

5. A Contracting Party may, at any time, declare the competence of its judicial authorities to communicate requests directly.

Article I.4
Form and contents of requests

1. All requests specified in this Convention shall be made in writing. Requests may be deemed to be in writing when they have been sent by any method leaving a written record.
2. All requests shall indicate:
   a. the authority making the request and the authority from which the request originated;
   b. the object of and the reason for the request;
   c. details of the person or persons concerned, including the name, nationality, address and, where appropriate, any other information which may help to establish his identity and location, and, in the case of a legal person, its seat;
   d. a brief statement of the basic facts, except in the case of a request relating to notification;
   e. the text of the statutory provisions or, where this is not possible, a statement of the relevant law, except in the case of a request for mutual assistance under Chapter III which does not involve the use of coercive measures;
   f. the legal qualification of the facts;
   g. any specific information, such as required under Chapters II to V below;
3. Unless otherwise provided for, documents transmitted pursuant to this Convention shall not require any form of authentication.

Article I.4 bis
Supplementary information

1. If the information communicated by the requesting Party is found to be insufficient to allow the requested Party to make a decision in pursuance of this Convention, the latter Party may request supplementary information and fix a time-limit for its provision.
2. If the requested Party does not receive the desired information within the fixed time-limit, it may refuse to comply with the request.

Article I.5
Languages

1. The requests, communications and documents referred to in Articles 3, 4 and 4 bis above shall be in the language of the requested Party or in one of the official languages of the Council of Europe.
2. Subject to paragraph 3 below, no translation of communications and documents shall be required.
3. Any Contracting Party may, at the time of signature or when depositing its instrument of ratification, acceptance, approval or accession, by a declaration addressed to the Secretary General of the Council of Europe, require that requests and supporting documents be accompanied by a translation into its own language or into either one or both, as specified, of the official languages of the Council of Europe. It may on that occasion also declare that it accepts translations in any language other than the official languages of the Council of Europe.

Article I.6
Costs

1. Parties shall not claim from each other the refund of any costs resulting from the application of this Convention, unless otherwise provided in this Convention.
2. If it appears that compliance with a request for assistance will entail costs of a substantial or extraordinary nature, the Parties shall consult with each other, with a view to determining the conditions under which the request may be executed as well as making arrangements for the payment of the costs.

Article I.7
Concurrent requests

If co-operation is requested concurrently by more than one State for the same offence or for different offences, the requested Party shall make its decision having regard to all the circumstances of the specific case in the interests of proper administration of justice and of the resocialisation of the offender.

Article I.9
Grounds for refusal

1. The requested Party may refuse a request for co-operation if:

a. the execution of the request would be contrary to the fundamental principles of its legal system;

b. the execution of the request is likely to prejudice its sovereignty, security, ordre public or other of its essential interests;

c. the procedure is manifestly disproportionate to the seriousness of the offence or to the penalty likely to be enforced;

d. it regards the offence in respect of which co-operation is requested as a political offence or as an offence connected with a political offence;

e. it has substantial grounds for believing that the request for co-operation for an ordinary criminal offence has been made for the purpose of prosecuting or punishing a person on account of his race, religion, nationality, or political opinion, or that the person's position may be or has been prejudiced for any one of these reasons;

f. the offence in respect of which co-operation is requested is an offence under military law which is not an offence under ordinary criminal law;

g. its competent authorities are taking proceedings in respect of the offence or offences for which co-operation is requested, or have decided either not to institute or to terminate proceedings in respect of those offences;

h. it considers that compliance with the request would be contrary to the principle of *ne bis in idem*;

i. compliance with such a request is likely to have particularly serious consequences for the person concerned on account of his age, state of health or other personal reasons;

j. according to the law of either the requesting or the requested Party there is immunity from prosecution or execution of punishment by reason of lapse of time.

2. For the application of this Convention, none of the following shall be regarded as a political offence or as an offence connected with a political offence:

a. the taking or attempted taking of the life of a Head of State or a member of his family;

b. the crimes against humanity specified in the Convention on the Prevention and Punishment of the Crime of Genocide adopted on 9 December 1948 by the General Assembly of the United Nations;

c. the violations specified in Article 50 of the 1949 Geneva Convention for the Amelioration of the Condition of the Wounded and Sick in Armed Forces in the Field, Article 51 of the 1949 Geneva Convention for the Amelioration of the Condition of Wounded, Sick and Shipwrecked Members of Armed Forces at Sea, Article 130 of the 1949 Geneva Convention relative to the treatment of Prisoners of War and Article 147 of the 1949 Geneva Convention relative to the Protection of Civilian Persons in Time of War;

d. any comparable violations of the laws of war having effect when this Convention enters into force and of customs of war existing at that time, which are not already provided for in the above-mentioned provisions of the Geneva Conventions.

Article I. 11

Communication of decisions

The requested Party shall without delay inform the requesting Party of its decision on the request for cooperation. Reasons shall be given for any refusal or postponement of cooperation under Chapters II and III.

Article I.13

Transit

1. Requests for transit through the territory of a Party shall be accompanied by the documents provided for in Article I.4, unless that Party has declared that it requires additional documents.
2. Upon the submission of a request in conformity with paragraph 1, transit shall be granted.
3. The requested Party may refuse transit where it would not, under similar circumstances, grant the co-operation that constitutes the purpose of the transit.
4. However, a request for transit shall not be required where air transport is used and no stopover is scheduled in transit through the territory of a Party.

Article I.15

Provisional measures

1. If a Party expressly asks to do so, and if the forms of co-operation provided for in this Convention are not manifestly inadmissible or inappropriate, the requested Party may take provisional measures for the purpose of maintaining an existing situation, protecting endangered legal interests or preserving evidence.
2. The requested Party may state any conditions it requires to be met in applying such measures, and it may indicate the time-limit within which the request for co-operation must be submitted.

CHAPTER II

Extradition

Article II.1

Principle

The Parties undertake to surrender to each other all persons wanted by the requesting Party for the purpose of prosecution or enforcement of a sanction involving deprivation of liberty.

Article II.2

Extraditable offences

1. Extradition shall be granted in respect of offences punishable under the laws of the requesting Party and the requested Party by a sanction involving at least a deprivation of liberty for a maximum period of one year. Furthermore, where extradition is requested for the purpose of enforcing a sanction involving deprivation of liberty, the period remaining to be served must he at least six months.
2. In exceptional cases, Parties may agree to grant extradition in respect of offences punishable by a sanction involving deprivation of liberty for a maximum period of less than one year. Again in exceptional cases, Parties may also agree to grant extradition for the purpose of enforcing a sanction involving deprivation of liberty even if the period remaining to be served is less than six months.
3. For offences in connection with taxes, duties, customs and exchange, extradition may not be refused on the ground that the law of the requested Party does not impose the same kind of tax or duty or does not contain a tax, duty, customs or exchange regulation of the same kind as the law of the requesting Party, if the offence under the law of the requested Party corresponds to an offence of the same nature.
4. If the request concerns more than one offence each of which is punishable under the laws of the requesting Party and the requested Party by a sanction involving deprivation of liberty, but of which one or more does or do not fulfil the conditions with regard to the nature or the amount of the sanction,

referred to in paragraph 1, the requested Party shall also have the right to grant extradition for the latter offences.

Article II.3
Grounds for refusal

1. The requested Party may refuse to extradite a person claimed for an offence which is regarded by its law as having been committed, in whole or in part, in its territory or in a place treated as its territory. When the offence for which extradition is requested has been committed outside the territory of the requesting Party, extradition may be refused if the law of the requested Party does not allow prosecution for the same category of offence when committed outside the latter Party's territory.

2. a. The requested Party may refuse to extradite its nationals.

b. Any State may, by a declaration addressed to the Secretary General of the Council of Europe, define, as far as it is concerned, the term "national" within the meaning of this Chapter.

c. Nationality shall be determined as at the time of the decision concerning extradition.

3. a. When extradition is requested for the purpose of enforcing a sanction imposed by a decision rendered in absentia, the requested Party may refuse to extradite for this purpose if, in its opinion, the proceedings leading to the judgment did not satisfy the minimum rights of defense recognized as due to everyone charged with a criminal offence.

b. Extradition shall be granted, however, if the requesting Party gives an assurance, considered sufficient by the requested Party, to guarantee to the person claimed the right to new proceedings which safeguard the rights of defense. This decision will authorize the requesting Party either to enforce the judgment in question if the convicted person does not object or, if he does, to take proceedings against the person extradited.

c. When the requested Party informs the person claimed of the judgment rendered against him in absentia, the requesting Party shall not regard this communication as a formal notification for the purposes of the criminal procedure in that State.

4. If the offence for which extradition is requested is punishable by death under the law of the requesting Party, and if the death penalty is not provided for by the law of the requested Party, or is not provided for in respect of such an offence, or is not usually carried out, extradition shall be refused. However, the requested Party may grant extradition if the requesting Party gives an assurance, considered sufficient by the requested Party, that the death penalty will not be carried out.

Article II.5
Aut dedere aut judicare

1. If the requested Party refuses extradition on any of the grounds mentioned in Article II.3, paragraphs 2 and 4, it shall, at the request of the requesting Party, submit the case to its competent authorities, in order that proceedings may be taken if they are considered appropriate.

2. The Parties shall take the necessary measures for establishing jurisdiction in order to comply with the provisions of paragraph 1.

3. The requesting Party shall, without charge, provide the files, information and exhibits relating to the offence.

4. The requested Party shall without delay inform the requesting Party of its decision concerning prosecution. Where proceedings are taken, the provisions of Article IV.3, paragraphs 2 to 5, and Article IV.4 shall apply.

Article II.5 bis
Supporting documents

In addition to the documents provided for in Article I.4, the request shall be accompanied by the original or a certified copy of:

a. an arrest warrant or of any other order having the same effect and issued in accordance with the law of the requesting Party; or

b. an enforceable decision.

Article II.6
Surrender of the Person

1. If the request is agreed to, the requesting Party shall be informed of the place and date of surrender and of the length of time for which the person claimed was detained with a view to surrender.
2. Subject to the provisions of paragraph 3 of this Article, if the person claimed has not been taken over on the appointed date, he may be released after the expiry of 15 days and shall in any case be released after the expiry of 30 days. The requested Party may refuse a subsequent extradition request for the same offence.
3. If circumstances beyond its control prevent a Party from surrendering or taking over the person to be extradited, it shall notify the other Party. The two Parties shall agree on a new date for surrender and the provisions of paragraph 2 of this Article shall apply.

Article II.6 bis
Postponed or temporary surrender

1. The requested Party may, after making its decision on the request for extradition, postpone the surrender of the person claimed in order to bring proceedings or to enforce a sanction involving deprivation of liberty for an offence other than that for which extradition is requested.
2. The requested Party may, instead of postponing surrender, temporarily surrender the person claimed to the requesting Party in accordance with conditions to be determined by agreement between the Parties.

Article II.7
Rule of speciality

1. A person who has been extradited shall not be proceeded against, sentenced, detained with a view to enforcing a sanction involving deprivation of liberty, restricted in his personal freedom for any other reason, or re-extradited to any other State for any offence committed prior to his surrender to the requested State other than that for which he was extradited, except in the following cases:
   a. when the Party which surrendered that person consents;
   b. when that person, after having had the opportunity to leave the territory of the requesting Party, does not do so within 45 days of his final discharge or has returned to that territory after leaving it.
2. The requesting Party may, however, take any measures necessary under its law, including proceedings in absentia, to prevent any legal effects of lapse of time.
3. When the description of the offence charged is altered in the course of proceedings, the extradited person shall only be proceeded against or sentenced in so far as the offence under its new description is shown by its constituent elements to be an offence which would allow extradition.
4. To obtain the consent referred to in paragraph l.a, the requesting Party shall submit a request, accompanied by the documents mentioned in Article II.5 bis and a legal record of any statement made by the extradited person in respect of such request. Consent shall be given when the offence for which it is requested is itself subject to extradition in accordance with the provisions of this Chapter.
5. Any State may, by a declaration addressed to the Secretary General of the Council of Europe, indicate the conditions under which its consent under Paragraph l.a is not required in cases where the surrendered person consents to being proceeded against or sentenced in respect of any other offence committed prior to his surrender.

Article II.8 bis
Provisional arrest

1. In case of urgency, the requesting Party may ask for the provisional arrest of the person sought. The requested Party shall decide the matter in accordance with its law and inform the requesting Party of its decision without delay.

2. Such a request shall state which of the documents referred to in Article II.5 bis exists, including the date on which and the authority by which such a document has been issued, and that it is intended to send a request for extradition. It shall also contain:

a. the name of the offence as well as a brief indication of the facts constituting it, including the time and place of its commission;

b. information on the maximum sanction for such an offence and, where applicable, an indication that in respect of a sanction actually imposed a period of at least six months remains to be served;

c. particulars concerning the identity of the person sought.

3. Provisional arrest may be terminated if, within a period of 18 days after arrest, the requested Party has not received the request for extradition and the documents referred to in Article II.5 bis. It shall not, in any event, exceed 40 days from the date of such arrest. The possibility of provisional release at any time is not excluded, but the requested Party shall take any measures which it considers necessary to prevent the escape of the person sought.

4. Release shall not prejudice re-arrest and extradition if a request for extradition is received subsequently.

Article II.8 ter

Simplified extradition

1. The requested Party may decide to surrender the person sought to the requesting Party by applying a procedure of simplified extradition, provided the person sought consents to his surrender before a judicial authority, having been fully informed of the legal consequences of his consent, in particular whether, according to the law of the requested Party, his consent has the effect that the rule of speciality mentioned in Article II.7 does not apply. He shall have the right to be assisted, under the conditions laid down by the law of the requested Party, by a lawyer or by another person qualified to provide that legal assistance.

2. Any State which applies the simplified extradition procedure referred to in paragraph 1 shall indicate, when granting extradition, whether the rule of speciality applies.

Article II.10

Handing-over of property

1. The requested Party shall, in so far as its law permits and at the request of the requesting Party, seize and hand over property:

a. which may be required as evidence;

b. which has been acquired as a result of the offence and which, at the time of the arrest, is found in the possession of the person claimed or is discovered subsequently.

2. The property mentioned in paragraph 1 shall be handed over even if extradition, having been agreed to, cannot be carried out owing to the death or the escape of the person claimed.

3. When the said property is liable to seizure or confiscation in the territory of the requested Party, the latter may, in connection with pending criminal proceedings, temporarily retain it or hand it over on the condition that it is returned.

4. Any rights which the requested Party or third Parties may have acquired in the said property shall be preserved. Where these rights exist, the property shall be returned without charge to the requested Party as soon as possible after the trial.

5. When handing over property without demanding that it be sent back, the requested Party shall not enforce any demand for customs, duty or any other claim under its customs or fiscal legislation unless the owner of the property who was the victim of the offence is himself liable for payment.

Article II.ll

Reservations

Any State may reserve the right:

a. to grant extradition only for offences which under the laws of the requesting Party and the requested Party are punishable by a sanction involving deprivation of liberty of a longer duration than that laid down in paragraph 1 of Article II.2;

b. to refuse extradition for:

i. any offence referred to in Article I.9.2 relating to offences regarded as political;

ii. fiscal offences or any categories thereof;

c. to grant transit of a person only on some or all of the conditions on which extradition is granted.

CHAPTER III
Mutual Assistance

Article III.1
Principle

1. The Parties shall afford each other the widest possible measure of mutual assistance in proceedings in respect of offences the punishment of which falls within the jurisdiction of the judicial authorities of the requesting Party.
2. The Parties may afford each other mutual assistance in respect of administrative offences or offences against regulations provided the person concerned has the opportunity to bring the matter before a court.
3. Mutual assistance shall include in particular:
   a. providing information;
   b. furnishing documents;
   c. providing statements of witnesses or experts;
   d. searching persons and property;
   e. seizing property;
   f. serving procedural documents and court decisions;
   g. providing information relating to the enforcement of sanctions and serving procedural documents and court decisions concerned with enforcement of sanctions or recovery of costs of proceedings.

Article III.1 bis
Execution of requests

If the requesting Party wishes a specific procedure to be applied in the execution of the request for assistance, it shall expressly so request, and the requested Party shall comply with the request in so far as this is not incompatible with its law or practice.

Article III.5
Execution of letters of request

1. The requested Party shall execute requests addressed to it for the purpose of procuring evidence or transmitting articles to be produced in evidence, records or documents.
2. At the express request of the requesting Party, the requested Party shall state the date and place of the execution.
3. Officials of the requesting Party and other persons concerned shall be allowed to be present at the execution of the request in so far as this is not incompatible with the law or practice of the requested Party.
4. Subject to the provisions of Article III.1 bis, the requested Party shall require witnesses or experts to give evidence on oath.

Article III.5 bis

Transmission of property for the purpose of restitution

Apart from the articles to be produced in evidence, mentioned in Article III.5.1, property obtained through an offence may also be transmitted for the purpose of its restitution, having due regard to any claim concerning that property raised by a third person.

Article III.5 ter

Contents of requests for service

In addition to the documents provided for in Article I.4, requests for service shall indicate the name and address of the person to be served, his status in the case and the nature of the document to be served.

Article III.5 quater

Coercive measures

In addition to the indications mentioned in Article I.4, requests for assistance involving coercive measures shall contain the following information:

a. an indication of why the purpose of the request cannot be adequately achieved by other means of investigation, and

b. an indication that in like circumstances the coercive measure could be taken in the territory of the requesting Party under its law.

Article III.6

Postponement of the handing over and return of articles. records or documents

1. The requested Party may delay the handing over of articles, records or documents requested if it requires these in connection with an investigation or pending criminal proceedings.

2. Any articles, as well as original records and documents, handed over in execution of letters of request shall be returned by the requesting Party to the requested Party as soon as possible.

3. The requested Party may decide to waive the return provided for in the preceding paragraph, in particular if this is likely to facilitate rapid restitution of the property.

Article III.6 bis

Use of information

The requested Party may make the execution of a request dependent on the condition that the evidence obtained will not be used by the authorities of the requesting Party for investigations or proceedings as specified by the requested Party in respect of which that Party could refuse assistance under this Convention.

Article III.7

Service of procedural documents and court decisions

1. The requested Party shall serve procedural documents and court decisions, including those concerned with enforcement of sanctions or recovery of costs of proceedings, transmitted to it for this purpose by the requesting Party.

2. Service may be effected by simple transmission of the document or decision to the person to be served. Subject to the provisions of Article III.1 bis service shall be effected by the requested Party in the manner provided for the service of similar documents in its own law, or in a special manner.

3. Proof of service shall be given in the form of a receipt dated and signed by the person served, or a declaration by the requested Party, confirming the fact, form and date of service. One or other of these documents shall immediately be sent to the requesting Party.

4. If service cannot be effected as requested, the requested Party shall immediately inform the requesting Party of the reasons.

5. A summons addressed to an accused person in the territory of the requested Party must be received by that Party at least 30 days before the date of the hearing. In individual cases, the requested Party may waive this requirement.

Article III.7 bis
Failure to appear

A witness or expert who has failed to answer a summons to appear, service of which has been requested, shall not, even if the summons contains a notice of penalty, be subjected to any punishment or measure of constraint, unless he later voluntarily enters the territory of the requesting Party and is there again duly summoned.

Article III.8
Special measures for securing the appearance of witnesses and experts

If the requesting Party attaches particular importance to the personal appearance of a witness or expert before its judicial authorities, it shall so indicate in its request for service of the summons. The requested Party shall inform the witness or expert accordingly and enquire whether he is willing to attend. It shall inform the requesting Party of the reply of the witness or expert.

Article III.8 bis
Expenses and allowances

1. The allowances to be paid and the travel and subsistence expenses to be refunded to a witness or expert by the requesting Party shall cover expenses incurred in the territories of both the requesting and the requested Party and shall be calculated from his place of residence. They shall be at rates at least equal to those provided for in the scales and the regulations applying in the country where the hearing is to take place.
2. If asked to do so by the requesting Party, in particular in cases where that Party attaches particular importance to the personal appearance of a witness or expert, the requested Party may grant the witness or expert an advance. The advance shall be refunded by the requesting Party.

Article III.9
Temporary transfer of detained persons to the requesting Party

1. A person in detention whose personal appearance for evidentiary purposes other than for standing trial is applied for by the requesting Party shall be temporarily transferred to its territory, provided that he shall be returned into the custody of the requested Party within the period indicated by it, and subject to the provisions of Article III.11 in so far as these are applicable.
2. The transfer shall be refused if:
    a. the person in detention does not consent, or
    b. transfer would prolong his detention.
3. The transfer may be refused if:
    a. the presence of the person in detention is necessary in criminal proceedings pending in the territory of the requested Party, or
    b. there are other overriding grounds for not transferring him to the territory of the requesting Party.
4. The transferred person shall remain in detention in the territory of the requesting Party unless the requested Party advises that his detention is no longer required.

Article III..9 bis
Temporary transfer of detained persons to the requested Party

Where, pursuant to an agreement between the Parties, a person detained in the territory of the requesting Party is temporarily transferred, for evidentiary purposes, to the territory of the requested Party, he shall remain in detention in the territory of that Party unless the requesting Party advises that his detention is no longer required, and he shall be returned into the custody of the requesting Party within the period indicated by it. The provisions of Article III.ll shall apply by analogy.

Article III.ll
Safe conduct

1. A witness or expert, whatever his nationality, appearing on a summons before the judicial authorities of the requesting Party, shall not be prosecuted or detained or subjected to any other restriction of his personal liberty in the territory of that Party in respect of acts or convictions anterior to his departure from the territory of the requested Party.
2. A person, whatever his nationality, summoned before the judicial authorities of the requesting Party to answer for acts forming the subject of proceedings against him, shall not be prosecuted or detained or subjected to any other restriction of his personal liberty for acts or convictions anterior to his departure from the territory of the requested Party and not indicated by the summons.
3. The immunity provided for in this Article shall cease when the witness or expert or prosecuted person, having had for a period of fifteen consecutive days from the date when his presence is no longer required by the judicial authorities an opportunity of leaving, has nevertheless remained in the territory, or having left it, has returned.

Article III.11 bis
Right to decline evidence

1. A person, whatever his nationality, appearing on a summons before the judicial authorities of the requesting Party, may claim a right to decline evidence on the basis of:
   a. any provision of the law of the requesting Party which has application to his evidence, and
   b. any provision of the law of the requested Party which has application to his evidence and which would apply were the witness giving evidence in the territory of the requested Party.
2. Where a person claims a right to decline evidence under the law of the requested Party and there is doubt about the existence of such a right, the requesting Party may ask the requested Party for a declaration. If the requested Party declares that its law does not confer such right, the judicial authority of the requesting Party is no longer bound to take the claimed right into consideration.
3. The provisions of paragraphs 1 and 2 of this Article shall apply by analogy where a person, whatever his nationality, appears on a summons before the judicial authorities of the requested Party.

Article III.11 ter
Information from criminal records

1. A requested Party shall communicate extracts from and information relating to criminal records, requested from it by the judicial authorities of a Party and needed in a criminal matter, to the same extent that these may be made available to its own judicial authorities in a similar case.
2. In any case other than that provided for in paragraph 1 of this Article the request shall be complied with in accordance with the conditions provided for by the law, regulations or practice of the requested Party.
3. Each Party shall inform, at least once a year, any other Party of all criminal convictions and, insofar as national law and practice permit, of subsequent measures in respect of nationals of the latter Party, entered in the criminal records. Where the person concerned is considered a national of two or more other Parties, the information shall be given to each of these Parties, unless the person is a national of the Party in the territory of which he was convicted.
4. Furthermore, any Party which has supplied the above-mentioned information shall communicate to the Party concerned, on the latter's request in individual cases, a copy of the convictions and measures in question as well as any other information relevant thereto, in order to enable it to consider whether they necessitate any measures at the national level.

Article III.14
Reservations

Any State may declare that it reserves the right:

a. to refuse mutual assistance or certain forms thereof in respect of offences in connection with taxes, duties, customs and exchange or any categories thereof;

b. to refuse mutual assistance in the form described in Article III.1.3.g;

c. to make the execution of letters of request involving coercive measures dependent on particular conditions;

d. not to apply Article III.5 bis.

e. not to afford mutual assistance save in proceedings in respect of offences the punishment of which, at the time of the request for assistance, falls within the jurisdiction of the judicial authorities of the requesting Party.

CHAPTER IV
TRANSFER OF PROCEEDINGS

Article IV.1
Principle

1. The Parties undertake to afford each other the widest possible measure of assistance in the transfer of proceedings.
2. Any Party having competence under its law to prosecute an offence may request another Party to take proceedings, in accordance with the provisions of this Chapter.
3. For the purposes of applying this Chapter, the requested Party shall have competence to prosecute under its own law any offence to which the law of the requesting Party is applicable.

Article IV.1 bis
Criteria for transfer

For the purpose of making or complying with a request for transfer of proceedings, the Party concerned shall take into consideration in particular:

a. whether the alleged offender is ordinarily resident in the territory of the requested Party;

b. whether the alleged offender is a national of the requested Party;

c. whether the alleged offender is undergoing or is to undergo a sentence involving deprivation of liberty in the territory of the requested Party;

d. whether the proceedings for the same or other offences are being taken against the alleged offender by the requested Party;

e. whether the most important evidence is located in the territory of the requested Party or the evidence available may better be produced in that territory.

Article IV.2
Dual criminality

1. Proceedings may only be taken by the requested Party if, under its law, the offence in respect of which the proceedings are requested would be an offence and the offender would be liable to sanction had the facts constituting the offence occurred within the jurisdiction of that Party.
2. Where the competence of the requested Party to prosecute is exclusively grounded on the provisions of this Chapter, that Party cannot take or continue proceedings with respect to an offence if prosecution with respect to the same offence is no longer possible under the law of the requesting Party.
3. If the offence was committed by a person of public status in the requesting Party or against a person of public status, an institution or property of a public nature in that Party, it shall be treated by the requested Party as if it had been committed by a corresponding person or against a corresponding person, institution or property in that Party.

Article IV.3
Effects in the requested Party

1. The competent authorities of the requested Party shall after examination decide, in accordance with their own law, whether to accept the request. The requested Party shall without delay communicate its decision to the requesting Party.
2. Any act occurring in the territory of the requesting Party which is relevant to proceedings shall be treated in the requested Party as if it had occurred in that Party. Assimilation shall not give any act greater evidential weight than it has in the requesting Party.
3. If a complaint is necessary only in the requested Party, that Party may take proceedings even in the absence of a complaint if the person who is empowered to bring the complaint has not objected within a period of one month from the date of receipt by him of notice from the competent authority informing him of his right to object.
4. The sanction applicable to the offence in the requested Party shall be that prescribed by its own law unless that law provides otherwise. Where the competence of the requested Party is exclusively grounded on a request from the requesting Party, the sanction pronounced in that Party shall not be more severe than that provided for in the law of the requesting Party.
5. The requested Party shall without delay inform the requesting Party of a waiver of proceedings or of the decision taken as a result of the proceedings, including whether that waiver or decision presents an obstacle to further proceedings according to the law of the requested Party, and it shall transmit a copy of any written decision.

Article IV.4
Effects in the requesting Party

Where the requested Party has communicated its acceptance of the request to proceed against the alleged offender, the requesting Party shall no longer prosecute him for the same offence. The requesting Party may, however, resume proceedings upon notification by the requested Party that it has decided to terminate the proceedings, either on its own motion or at the request of the requesting Party, and that there is no obstacle to further proceedings according to its law.

Article IV.6
Provisional measures

Where a Party announces its intention to transmit a request for proceedings and the competence of the requested Party would be exclusively grounded on the provisions of this Chapter, that Party may, if asked to do so, apply all such provisional measures as could be applied under its own law if the offence in respect of which proceedings are to be requested had been committed in its territory.

CHAPTER V
Enforcement of Sanctions

Article V.1
Principle

1. Parties undertake to afford each other the widest possible co-operation with regard to the transfer of enforcement of sanctions imposed by another Party, including the supervision of the offender, and disqualifications in accordance with the provisions of this Chapter.
2. The transfer of enforcement may be requested either by the sentencing State or by the administering State.
3. For the purposes of this Chapter:
   a. "sanction" shall mean:
      i. any punishment or measure involving deprivation of liberty ordered by a court for a limited or unlimited period of time on account of a criminal offence,

ii. any pecuniary sanction imposed, either by a court, or by an administrative authority for an administrative offence or an offence against regulations provided the person concerned has had the opportunity to bring the matter before a court;

b. "sentencing State" shall mean the Party in which the sanction in respect of which transfer of enforcement has been or may be requested, was imposed;

c. "administering State" shall mean the Party to which enforcement of the sanction has been or may be transferred;

d. "enforcement of a sanction" shall mean the enforcement of a sanction including the enforcement of a supervision order.

Article V.2
General conditions

The transfer of the enforcement of a sanction needs the agreement of the sentencing State and the administering State. It shall be subject to the following conditions:

a. the judgment is final and enforceable;

b. the act for which the sanction was imposed would be an offence under the law of the administering State if committed on its territory and the person on whom the sanction was imposed would be liable to punishment if he had committed the act there;

c. if the sanction relates to two or more offences, not all of which fulfil the requirements of sub-paragraph (b), the sentencing State shall specify which part of the sanction applies to offences that satisfy those requirements;

d. the sanction was not imposed in respect of an offence or offences for which a final judgment against the person concerned has been passed and enforced upon him by the competent authorities either of the administering State or of a third Party.

Article V.3
Judgments in absentia

The implementation of this Chapter shall not be affected by the fact that the judgment was rendered in absentia of the person concerned if the proceedings leading to such a judgment satisfy the minimum rights of the defense recognised as due to everyone against whom a criminal charge is made. If the judgment has been confirmed or pronounced after opposition by the person concerned or it has been rendered on appeal lodged by the person concerned, it is not considered to have been rendered in absentia.

Article V.4
Findings as to the facts

When deciding on the enforcement of a sanction, the administering State shall be bound by the findings as to the facts insofar as they appear explicitly or implicitly from the judgment imposed in the sentencing State.

Article V.5
Applicable law

The enforcement of the sanction shall be governed by the law of the administering State and that State alone shall be competent to take all appropriate decisions.

Article V.6
Review, Pardon, Amnesty and Commutation

1. The sentencing State alone shall have the right to decide on any application for review of sentence.

2. Each Party may grant pardon, amnesty or commutation of the sentence in accordance with its Constitution or other laws. If however, only supervision is carried out, these rights may be exercised only by the sentencing State.

Article V.7

Discontinuance of Enforcement

1. The sentencing State shall without delay inform the administering State of any decision or measure taken on its territory as a result of which the sentence ceases to be enforceable.

2. The administering State shall discontinue enforcement of the sanction or supervision as soon as it has knowledge of any decision or measure as a result of which the sentence ceases to be enforceable.

Article V.8

Completion of enforcement

The authorities of the administering State shall inform the sentencing State that the sanction has been enforced.

Article V.9

Effects in the Sentencing State

1. The sentencing State may not proceed with the enforcement of the sanction once the administering State has agreed to the request to enforce that sanction. However, the sentencing State may continue the enforcement of a sanction involving deprivation of liberty until surrender of the sentenced person to the administering State.

2. The right of enforcement shall revert to the sentencing State upon notification by the administering State that it has withdrawn its acceptance, or that it is unable to enforce or to complete the enforcement of the sanction; the Parties, however, may agree otherwise. Should the administering State no longer he able to ensure enforcement, it shall promptly notify the sentencing State.

Article V.10

Enforcement of Sanctions Involving Deprivation of Liberty

1. The transfer of enforcement of a sanction involving deprivation of liberty may be requested where:

   a. the person concerned is in the territory of the sentencing State, or
   b. the person concerned is in the territory of the administering State and:
      i. he is a national of or is ordinarily resident in the territory of that State, or
      ii. his extradition has been refused would be refused if requested, or is not possible, or
      iii. he is serving or is to serve a custodial penalty there.

2. The person concerned may express an interest to either the sentencing State or the administering State in the transfer of the enforcement under this Convention of the sanction imposed upon him.

3. The transfer of enforcement as provided for in paragraph l(a) will only be effected subject to the following conditions:

   a. that the person concerned consents to the transfer to the administering State;
   b. that the sentence still to be served at the time of the receipt of the request is at least six months;
   c. that the sentenced person is either a national of or has his ordinary residence in the territory of the administering State, unless otherwise agreed upon between the Parties concerned.

4. Subject to the agreement of the sentencing and the administering States, paragraph 3(a) above shall not apply where a final decision of expulsion has been rendered with respect to the person concerned.

5. Where the person concerned is in the territory of the administering State the transfer of enforcement is not subject to that person's consent.

6. In exceptional cases, Parties may agree to transfer even if the duration of the sanction to be served by the sentenced person is less than that specified in paragraph 3(b).

7. The person concerned shall be informed, in writing, of any action taken by the sentencing State or the administering State under paragraph l(a), as well as of any decision taken by either State subsequently to that person having expressed an interest in being transferred.

Article V.11

Requirements with respect to consent

1. The sentencing State shall ensure that the person required to give consent to his transfer does so voluntarily and after having been fully informed of both the enforcement procedure the administering State will follow and of the legal consequences of his consent, in particular whether the rule of speciality applies or not.

2. Where in view of his age or his physical or mental condition the sentenced person is unable to consent to his transfer, such consent may only be given by his legal representative.

3. The sentencing State shall afford an opportunity to the administering State to verify, through a consul or other official agreed upon with the administering State, that the consent is given in accordance with the conditions set out in paragraphs 1 and 2 above.

Article V.12

Rule of Speciality

1. A person transferred shall not be proceeded against, sentenced or detained with a view to the carrying out of a sentence or detention order, for any offence committed prior to his surrender other than that for which the sentence to be enforced was imposed, nor shall he for any other reason be restricted in his personal freedom, except in the following cases:

a. when the sentencing State authorizes a request for authorization shall be submitted, accompanied by all relevant documents and a legal record of any statement made by the convicted person in respect of the offence concerned. Authorisation shall be given when the offence for which it is requested would itself be subject to extradition under the law of the sentencing State or when extradition would be excluded only by reason of the amount of punishment;

b. when the sentenced person, having had an opportunity to leave the territory of the administering State, has not done so within 45 days of his final discharge, or if he has returned to that territory after leaving it.

2. Paragraph 1 does not apply where a person is transferred upon his consent, provided that:

a. the consent has been given in conformity with the provisions of Article V.11, and

b. the sentencing State does not object to it.

Article V.13

Options as to the Enforcement

1. The competent authorities of the administering State shall:

a. continue to enforce the sanction by a court or administrative order, under the conditions set out in Article V.14, or

b. convert the sanction, through a judicial or an administrative procedure, into a decision of that State, thereby substituting for the sanction imposed in the sentencing State a sanction prescribed by the law of the administering State for the same offence, under the conditions set out in Article V.15.

2. Any State may, by way of a declaration, indicate that it intends to exclude the application of one of the procedures mentioned in paragraph 1.

3. Any State which, according to its national law, cannot avail itself of one of the procedures referred to in paragraph 1 to enforce measures imposed in the territory of another Party on persons who for reasons of mental conditions have been held not criminally responsible for the commission of the offence, and which is prepared to receive such persons for further treatment may, by way of a declaration, indicate the procedures it will follow in such cases.

Article V.13 bis

Deduction of Custody

In both the cases of continued enforcement and conversion of the sentence any part of the sanction imposed in the sentencing State and any term of provisional custody, served by the person concerned sentenced subsequent to the sentence, shall be deduced in full. The same shall apply in respect of any period during which the person concerned was remanded in custody in the sentencing State before being sentenced insofar as the law of that State so requires.

Article V.14
Continued Enforcement

1. In the case of continued enforcement, the administering State shall be bound by the legal nature and duration of the sanction as determined by the sentencing State.
2. If, however, this sanction is by its nature or duration incompatible with the law of the administering State, or its law so requires, that State may, by a court or administrative order, adapt the sanction to the punishment or measure prescribed by its own law for a similar offence. As to its nature, the punishment or measure shall, as far as possible, correspond with that imposed by the sentence to be enforced. It shall not aggravate, by its nature or duration, the sanction imposed in the sentencing State, nor exceed the maximum prescribed by the law of the administering State.

Article V.15
Conversion of Sentence

1. In the case of conversion of sentence, the procedures provided for by the law of the administering State apply. When converting the sentence, the competent authority:
   a. may not convert a sanction involving deprivation of liberty of more than six months to a pecuniary sanction;
   b. shall deduct the full period of deprivation of liberty served by the sentenced person; and
   c. shall not aggravate the penal position of the sentenced person, and shall not be bound by any minimum which the law of the administering State may provide for the offence or offences committed.
2. If the conversion procedure takes place after the transfer of the sentenced person, the administering State shall keep that person in custody or otherwise ensure his presence in the administering State pending the outcome of that procedure.

Article V.16
Provisional Arrest

The administering State may, as soon as the sentencing State has requested or accepted the transfer of enforcement of a sanction involving deprivation of liberty imposed on a person who is in its territory, arrest the person concerned or apply other provisional measures in accordance with its law.

Article V.17
Enforcement of Pecuniary Sanctions

1. The transfer of enforcement of a pecuniary sanction may be requested when:
   a. the person concerned is a natural person who is permanently resident in the territory of the administering State or has realizable property or income in the territory of that State, or
   b. the person concerned is a legal person having its seat in the territory of the administering State or having realizable property or funds in the territory of that State.
2. Where the request for enforcement of a pecuniary sanction is granted, the competent authorities of the administering State shall convert the amount thereof not yet recovered into the currency of that State according to the exchange rate applicable at the time when the decision to grant enforcement is taken.
3. The converted amount may be recovered only up to the maximum prescribed by the law of the administering State in respect of the same offence. However, where the law of the administering State permits the imposition of sanctions of a different and more severe nature in respect of the same offence, its competent authorities shall leave the amount of the pecuniary sanction imposed in the sentencing State unchanged.
4. Where enforcement of the pecuniary sanction proves wholly or partially impossible, an alternative custodial sanction may be applied by the administering State if the law of both States so provides, unless this has been explicitly excluded by way of a declaration by the sentencing State. If the

competent authorities of the administering State decide to impose an alternative custodial sanction, they shall determine its duration in accordance with the rules prescribed by their own law but may not aggravate the penal situation of the person concerned, as established by the decision given in the sentencing State.

5. The proceeds of fines shall accrue to the administering State unless otherwise agreed upon between that State and the sentencing State.

Article V.18
Supervision Requests

1. Where, according to a final judgment, a person has:

a. been found guilty by a court and placed on probation without sentence having been pronounced; or

b. been given a suspended sentence involving deprivation of liberty, in whole or in part, either at the time of the sentence or subsequently; or

c. has been given a sentence involving deprivation of liberty of which the enforcement has been conditionally suspended, in whole or in part, either at the time of the sentence or subsequently, the sentencing State may request the State in whose territory the offender establishes his ordinary residence, to assume responsibility for supervising the compliance with the conditions imposed by the person concerned.

2. The administering State shall, to the extent necessary, adapt to its own law the condition or measure prescribed, provided that such condition or measure is not more severe than that pronounced in the sentencing State.

3. In respect of a request made under this Article, the sentencing State may also request the administering State to take responsibility for applying the sentence, including the eventual revocation and enforcement of the sentence.

4. The sentencing and administering States shall keep each other informed of all circumstances likely to affect measures of supervision or enforcement in the territory of the administering State.

Article V.19
Contents of requests

1. In addition to the documents provided for in Article I.4, when the enforcement or supervision is requested by the sentencing State the request shall be accompanied by:

a. a certified copy of the judgement and, where appropriate, of any subsequent decision envisaged in Article V.18.1;

b. a statement certifying any period of provisional detention already served or any part of the sentence which. where appropriate, has been enforced and any other matter of relevance for the enforcement of the sentence or for the supervision.

2. The request shall in every case be accompanied by documents enabling the requested State to decide whether or not to agree to the transfer of the enforcement of the sanction or the supervision.

3. The administering State may, for the purpose of lodging a request for enforcement or supervision, request any one or more of the documents mentioned in paragraphs 1 or 2.

Article V.20
Disqualifications

1. Where, upon criminal proceedings, a disqualification is imposed in a Party, that Party shall, spontaneously or upon request, inform another Party or Parties of the disqualification whenever it deems that the disqualification should also have effects on their territory.

2. Any Party that receives information according to paragraph 1 shall consider the advisability of extending to its own territory the effects of the disqualification imposed and communicate its decision to the Party where the disqualification was imposed.

3. Where the extension of the disqualification is examined by a criminal court, that court shall be bound by the findings as to the facts insofar as they appear explicitly or implicitly from the judgment imposing the disqualification.

Article V.21
Limited application

Parties may declare that they will refuse requests other than requests for the transfer of enforcement of a sanction involving deprivation of liberty with respect of a person who is in the territory of the sentencing State.

CHAPTER VI
Final Clauses

Article VI.1
Signature and entry into force

1. This Convention shall be open for signature by the member States of the Council of Europe. It is subject to ratification, acceptance or approval. Instruments of ratification, acceptance or approval shall be deposited with the Secretary General of the Council of Europe.
2. This Convention shall enter into force on the first day of the month following the expiration of a period of three months after the date in which fifteen member States of the Council of Europe have expressed their consent to be bound by the Convention in accordance with the provisions of paragraph 1.
3. In respect of any member State which subsequently expresses its consent to be bound by it, the Convention shall enter into force on the first day of the month following the expiration of a period of three months after the date of the deposit of the instrument of ratification, acceptance or approval.

Article VI.2
Accession

1. After the entry into force of this Convention, the Committee of Ministers of the Council of Europe may invite any State not a member of the Council to accede to this Convention, by a decision taken by the majority provided for in Article 20(d) of the Statute of the Council of Europe and by the unanimous vote of the representatives of the Contracting states entitled to sit on the Committee.
2. In respect of any acceding State, the Convention shall enter into force on the first day of the month following the expiration of a period of three months after the date of deposit of the instrument of accession with the Secretary General of the Council of Europe.

Article VI.3
Territorial application

1. Any State may at the time of signature or when depositing its instrument of ratification, acceptance, approval or accession. specify the territory or territories to which this Convention shall apply.
2. Any State may at any later date, by a declaration addressed to the Secretary General of the Council of Europe, extend the application of this Convention to any other territory specified in the declaration. In respect of such territory, the Convention shall enter into force on the first day of the month following the expiration of a period of three months after the date of receipt of such declaration by the Secretary General.
3. Any declaration made under the two preceding paragraphs may, in respect of any territory specified in such declaration, be withdrawn by a notification addressed to the Secretary General. The withdrawal shall become effective on the first day of the month following the expiration of a period of three months after the date or receipt of such notification by the Secretary General.

Article VI.3 bis
Federal clause

The obligations of the federal or central government of those Parties which have a federal or non-unitary constitutional system shall be the same as for those Parties which are not federal or non-unitary States.

Article VI.4
Relationship to other Treaties

1. In conjunction with Chapter I:

a. Chapter II of this Convention shall, in respect of those States to which it applies, supersede the provisions of any extradition treaties between two or more Parties, as well as the European Convention on Extradition and its two additional Protocols;

b. Chapter III of this Convention shall, in respect of those States to which it applies, supersede the provisions of any treaties on mutual assistance in criminal matters between two or more Parties, as well as the European Convention on Mutual Assistance in Criminal Matters, its additional Protocol and the Protocol to the European Convention on Information on Foreign Law;

c. Chapter IV of this Convention shall, in respect of those States to which it applies, supersede the provisions of any treaties on the transfer of criminal proceedings between two or more Parties, as well as the European Convention on the Transfer of Proceedings in Criminal Matters, Article 21 of the European Convention on Mutual Assistance in Criminal Matters and the European Convention on the Punishment of Road Traffic Offences;

d. Chapter V of this Convention shall, in respect of those States to which it applies, supersede the provisions of any treaties between two or more Parties on the transfer or prisoners as well as the Convention on International Validity of Criminal Judgments, the Convention on the Transfer or Sentenced Persons, the European Convention on the Supervision of Conditionally Sentenced or Conditionally Released Offenders and the European Convention on the Punishment of Road Traffic Offences.

2. However, if two or more Parties have already concluded a treaty in respect of a subject which is dealt with in this Convention, as far as the latter applies to them, or have otherwise established their relations in respect of that subject, they shall only be entitled to apply that treaty or to regulate those relations accordingly, to the extent that it facilitates international co-operation in criminal matters.

3. Parties may conclude bilateral or multilateral treaties with one another on the matters dealt with in this Convention, as far as it applies to them, for purposes of supplementing or strengthening its provisions or facilitating international co-operation in criminal matters.

Article VI.5
Temporal Application

1. Chapter II of this Convention shall be applicable to extradition for offences committed either before or after its entry into force.

2. Chapter III of this Convention shall be applicable to mutual assistance in relation to offences committed either before or after its entry into force.

3. Chapter IV of this Convention shall be applicable to the transfer of proceedings in relation to offences committed either before or after its entry into force, unless the competence of the requested State to take proceedings is exclusively grounded on a request made to that effect.

4. Chapter V of this Convention shall be applicable to the enforcement of sanctions imposed either before or after its entry into force.

Article VI.6
Partial acceptance

1. Any State may declare that it does not consent to be bound by the provisions of:

a. Chapter II, unless it is a Party to the European Convention on Extradition;

b. Chapter III, unless it is a Party to the European Convention on Mutual Assistance in Criminal Matters;

c. Chapter IV, unless it is a Party to the European Convention on the Transfer of Proceedings in Criminal Matters;

d. Chapter V, unless it is a Party to the Convention on the International Validity of Criminal Judgements, or to the Convention on the Transfer of Sentenced Persons.

2. Reservations as contemplated in the previous paragraph may be made only where the application of the rules contained in the Chapter or Chapters concerned would run counter to the fundamental principles of the legal system of the State concerned.

3. When extending the application of the Convention to one or more territories in conformity with Article VI.3, Parties may specify which Chapter or Chapters of the Convention they consent to be bound by with respect to each territory.

Article VI.7
Reservations

1. Any Contracting State may, at the time of depositing its instrument of ratification, acceptance, approval or accession, declare that it avails itself of one or more of the reservations provided for in Chapters II (Article 11), III (Article 14) and VI (Articles 6 and 8 bis). No other reservations may be made to the provisions of the Convention.

2. Without prejudice to the provisions of paragraph 4, reservations shall be valid for a maximum period of ten years from the entry into force of this Convention for the Party concerned. They may however be renewed for successive periods of five years by means of a declaration addressed. before the expiration of each period, to the Secretary General of the Council of Europe.

3. Two years before the date of expiry of reservations, the Secretary General shall give notice of that to the Parties that made the reservations.

4. Any Contracting State may at any time wholly or partially withdraw a reservation it has made or renewed in accordance with the foregoing paragraphs, by means of a declaration addressed to the Secretary General of the Council of Europe, which shall become effective as from the date of its receipt.

5. A Contracting State which has made a reservation in respect of any provision of this Convention may not claim the application of that provision by another Contracting State. It may, however, if its reservation is partial or conditional, claim the application of that provision insofar as it has itself accepted it.

Article VI.8
Amendments

1. Amendments to this Convention may be proposed by any Party, and shall be communicated by the Secretary General of the Council of Europe to the member States of the Council of Europe and to any State not a member of the Council which has acceded to, or has been invited to accede to the Convention in accordance with the provisions of Article VI.2.

2. Any amendment proposed by a Party shall be communicated to the European Committee on Crime Problems, which shall submit to the Committee of Ministers its opinion on the proposed amendment.

3. The Committee of Ministers shall consider the proposed amendment and the opinion submitted by the European Committee on Crime Problems, and may adopt the amendment.

4. The text of any amendment adopted by the Committee of Ministers in accordance with paragraph 3 of this Article shall be forwarded to the Parties for acceptance.

5. Any amendment adopted in accordance with paragraph 3 of this Article shall come into force on the first day of the month following the expiration of a period of one month after the date in which all the Parties will have notified the Secretary General of their acceptance thereof.

Article VI.8.bis
Settlement of disputes

1. The European Committee on Crime Problems of the Council of Europe shall be kept informed of the interpretation and application of this Convention.
2. In case of a dispute between Parties as to the interpretation or application of this Convention, the Parties involved shall seek a settlement of the dispute through negotiation or any other peaceful means of their choice, including submission of the dispute to the European Committee on Crime Problems or to an arbitral tribunal whose decisions shall be binding upon the Parties, mediation, conciliation or judicial process, as agreed upon by the Parties concerned.
3. Any State may, at the time of signature or when depositing its instrument of ratification, acceptance, approval or accession, or on any later date, by a declaration addressed to the Secretary General of the Council of Europe, declare that, in respect of any dispute concerning the interpretation or application of this Convention, it recognizes as compulsory, without prior agreement, and subject to reciprocity, the submission of the dispute to arbitration.
4. Each of the Parties that has submitted the dispute to arbitration in conformity with paragraph 3, shall nominate an arbitrator and the two arbitrators shall nominate a presiding arbitrator. If any Party has not nominated its arbitrator within the three months following the request for arbitration, he shall be nominated at the request of the other Party by the Secretary General of the Permanent Court of Arbitration. The same procedure shall be observed if the arbitrators cannot agree on the choice of a presiding arbitrator. The arbitration tribunal shall lay down its own rules of procedure. Its decisions shall be taken by majority vote and shall be final and binding upon the Parties concerned.
5. Any dispute which has not been settled in accordance with paragraphs 2 or 3 of this Article shall be referred, at the request of any one of the parties to the dispute, to the International Court of Justice for decision.
6. Any State may, at the time of signature or when depositing its instrument of ratification, acceptance, approval or accession, or on any later date, by a declaration addressed to the Secretary General of the Council of Europe, declare that it does not consider itself bound by paragraph 5 of this Article.

Article VI.9
Denunciation

1. This Convention shall remain in force indefinitely.
2. Any Contracting State may, insofar as it is concerned, denounce the Convention by means of a notification addressed to the Secretary General of the Council of Europe.
3. Such denunciation shall take effect three months after the date of receipt by the Secretary General of such notification.
4. The Convention shall, however, continue to apply to proceedings or the enforcement of sanctions which have been transferred in conformity with the provisions of the Convention before the date on which such denunciation takes effect.

Article VI.10
Notification

The Secretary General of the Council of Europe shall notify the member States of the Council of Europe and any State which has acceded to this Convention of:

a. any signature;
b. the deposit of any instrument of ratification, acceptance, approval or accession;
c. any date of entry into force of this Convention in accordance with Article 1, 2 and 3 of this Chapter;
d. any other act, declaration, notification or communication relating to this Convention.

In witness whereof the undersigned, being duly authorized thereto, have signed this Convention.

The United Nations

Herman F. Woltring

Introduction

Both the United Nations, and its predecessor, the League of Nations, have and had an interest in criminal justice matters. This interest was further advanced as a result of the development in the nineteenth century of the "multilateral" treaty or convention, and the recognition in the twentieth century that there were some forms of conduct which were of legitimate concern to the international community and could only be dealt with on an international basis.[1] Early conventions elaborated under the auspices of the League of Nations dealt with issues such as slavery,[2] the trade in women and children,[3] offenses relating to the counterfeiting of currency[4] and the trade in illicit drugs.[5] Until recently, such conventions identified the type of conduct to be prohibited, but failed adequately to address international co-operation in the investigation, prosecution and punishment of such conduct.

The United Nations interest in criminal justice issues dates back to 1946, when the Economic and Social Council (ECOSOC), a principal organ created by the U.N. Charter, established a Temporary Social Commission which was, *inter alia*, to "report to the Council on the advisability of bringing Under the Council the activities in the social field hitherto carried on by the League of Nations and such other activities as the work on the treatment of offenders now carried on by the International Penal and Penitentiary Commission."[6] In 1948 a Secretariat Unit, then known as the Social Defense Section, was created by ECOSOC. This body later became the Crime Prevention and Criminal Justice Branch, which continues to be the Secretariat body responsible for crime prevention and criminal justice policies within the United Nations. It served as the secretariat to an Ad Hoc Advisory Committee of Experts which advised both ECOSOC and the Secretary-General. This Committee, established in 1950 and comprising seven members, became in 1965 a ten-person Advisory Committee of Experts on the Prevention of Crime and the Treatment of Offenders. In 1971 its membership was increased to 15, it was renamed the U.N. Committee on Crime Prevention and Control and it became a subsidiary organ of ECOSOC. In 1979 the Committee was increased to 27 members elected on the principle of equitable geographic distribution. The members continued to serve in their individual capacities as experts. This

---

1 *See* M. CHERIF BASSIOUNI, A DRAFT INTERNATIONAL CRIMINAL CODE AND DRAFT STATUTE FOR AN INTERNATIONAL CRIMINAL TRIBUNAL (1987) which, at pages 355-475, provides a comprehensive list of multilateral conventions on criminal law subject matters.

2 *E.g.*, the Slavery Convention, Sept. 25, 1926, 60 L.N.T.S. 253.

3 *E.g.*, the International Convention for the Suppression of the Traffic in Women and Children, Sept. 30, 1921, 9 L.N.T.S. 415.

4 The International Convention for the Suppression of Counterfeiting Currency, Apr. 20, 1929, 112 L.N.T.S. 37.

5 *E.g.*, the International Opium Convention, Jan. 23, 1912, 8 L.N.T.S. 187.

6 E.S.C. Res 7(1), 1 U.N. ESCOR, 1st Sess., Resolutions, at 127 (1946). For a complete history of the development of the United Nations Crime Prevention and Criminal Justice Programme and its achievements *see* ROGER S. CLARK, THE UNITED NATIONS CRIME PREVENTION AND CRIMINAL JUSTICE PROGRAM: FORMULATION OF STANDARDS AND EFFORTS AT THEIR IMPLEMENTATION (1994).

Committee was finally dissolved in 1992 when it was abolished by ECOSOC and replaced by the intergovernmental Commission on Crime Prevention and Criminal Justice, comprised of 40 member states elected by ECOSOC.[7] Thus, in 1992 control of the U.N. crime program passed from individual experts to governments.

Supporting the Crime Prevention and Criminal Justice Branch, which is the central organ, is a network of Institutes and other Centres collectively referred to as the United Nations Crime Prevention and Criminal Justice Programme Network.[8]

The bodies which make up this Network are:

- the Crime Prevention and Criminal Justice Branch of the U.N. Office at Vienna, which is the Secretariat of the Commission on Crime Prevention and Criminal Justice and answerable to it for the carrying out of the program and hence for co-ordination;
- the United Nations Interregional Crime and Justice Research Institute (UNICRI), formerly UNSDRI, which was the first interregional institute, founded in 1968 and located in Rome, Italy;
- the Asia and Far East Institute for the Prevention of Crime and the Treatment of Offenders (UNAFEI), founded in 1962 pursuant to an agreement between the United Nations and Government of Japan, and based in Tokyo. It is the oldest institute in the Programme Network and serves the region suggested by its name;
- the Latin American Institute for the Prevention of Crime and the Treatment of Offenders (ILANUD), founded on June 11, 1975, pursuant to an agreement between the United Nations and the Government of Costa Rica. This institute serves the Latin American and Caribbean countries;
- the European Institute for Crime Prevention and Control, (HEUNI), founded on December 23, 1981, pursuant to an agreement between the United Nations and the Government of Finland. It serves Europe, with an increasing workload in the countries in transition in Central and Eastern Europe;
- the African Institute for the Prevention of Crime and the Treatment of Offenders (UNAFRI), located at Kampala, Uganda;
- the Arab Security Studies and Training Centre (ASSTC) based in Riyadh, Saudi Arabia, founded in 1980 and an associated Centre since then, serving the League of Arab States;
- the Australian Institute of Criminology (AIC), a subregional Institute founded in 1971 which entered into association with the U.N. crime program in 1989;
- the International Institute of Higher Studies in Criminal Sciences (ISISC) based in Siracusa, Sicily, which held consultative status with ECOSOC since 1972 and became formally associated with the U.N. crime program in 1992;
- the International Centre for Criminal Law Reform and Criminal Justice Policy (ICCLRCPJ), founded in 1991 and based in Vancouver, Canada, which became formally associated in 1995; and whose activities, like UNICRI's, are of an interregional nature;
- the International Centre for the Prevention of Crime, based in Montreal, which is also of an interregional nature but specializing in urban safety and crime prevention, founded in 1994; and

---

[7] E.S.C. Res. 1992/1, U.N. ESCOR, Supp. No.1, at 11.

[8] *See* THE CONTRIBUTIONS OF SPECIALIZED INSTITUTES AND NON-GOVERNMENTAL ORGANIZATIONS TO THE UNITED NATIONS CRIMINAL JUSTICE PROGRAM (M. Cherif Bassiouni ed., 1995).

- the National Institute of Justice, based in Washington, USA, which became associated in 1995 in the light of increasing interest in crime statistics and criminal justice management. It is also hoped that it will assist in the development of enhanced information and communication technologies of the Programme Network;
- the International Scientific and Professional Advisory Council (ISPAC) based in Milan, Italy, which serves as a forum to harness the support and contributions of Non-Governmental Organizations and the academic community.

Each of the Institutes carries out research, training, field activities, technical co-operation and other projects, as well as providing facilities for the exchange and dissemination of information of relevance to crime prevention and criminal justice policy makers and administrators at the international, regional and national level. Frequently, the services of these bodies are also solicited by local and city governments in areas such as urban criminality.

Recent developments have increased the needs for these bodies. The globalization and increased sophistication of organized crime, and the Commission's interest in them, has widened the scope of the programme dramatically. However, this may create some tensions as the global priorities of the Commission may not always reflect the immediate needs or self-perceived priorities of all countries in all regions. The institutes can close this gap and fulfill these needs, whilst also ensuring that truly international concerns are addressed in a uniform manner.

Aside from the United Nations itself, U.N. Specialized Agencies and other bodies were also active in criminal justice matters relevant to their mandates, particularly in the development of multilateral conventions requiring the criminalization of conduct regarded as requiring multilateral action. Examples include the International Civil Aviation Organization (ICAO),[9] the International Maritime Organization (IMO)[10] and the United Nations International Drug Control Program (UNDCP).[11]

The "offense specific" conventions, with one exception, suffer from the same defects as the earlier League of Nations Conventions. Whilst they identify the conduct which signatory states are required to criminalize, they do not provide the necessary mechanisms to provide for assistance, including extradition, in the investigation, prosecution and punishment of perpetrators. Rather, they presupposed the existence of such mechanisms, incorporating bilateral relationships by reference regardless of the fact that these relationships may not exist. For example, a number of them attempt to facilitate extradition by adding the relevant offense to the list of extradition offenses contained in existing extradition treaties or by providing that the convention itself may be regarded as a sufficient basis for extradition even in the absence of an extradition treaty. The former postulates the

---

9 Responsible for the Montreal Convention for the Suppression of Unlawful Acts against the Safety of Civil Aviation of Sept. 23, 1971, 974 U.N.T.S. 177, and the Hague Convention for the Suppression of Unlawful Seizure of Aircraft of Dec. 16, 1970, 860 U.N.T.S. 105.

10 Responsible for the Convention for the Suppression of Unlawful Acts against the Safety of Maritime Navigation, and the Protocol for the Suppression of Unlawful Acts against the Safety of Fixed Platforms Located on the Continental Shelf.

11 Responsible for the Single Convention on Narcotic Drugs 1961, as amended by the 1972 Protocol Amending the Single Convention on Narcotic Drugs 1961, 976 U.N.T.S. 1, and the 1988 Convention against Illicit Traffic in Narcotic Drugs and Psychotropic Substances, U.N. document E/CONF. 82/15.

existence of extradition treaties and the latter the existence of laws permitting extradition in the absence of treaties. Frequently neither existed.

Notwithstanding the weaknesses of these offense-specific conventions, they did achieve a degree of "harmonization" or "complementarity" of national laws insofar as the signatories agreed to define certain conduct as offenses. This ensured that the principle of "dual criminality" could not thwart extradition or other forms of mutual assistance in criminal matters in relation to them. However, to date no such obligations exist in relation to the broad spectrum of criminal conduct. Furthermore, the offense-specific conventions did not address differences in legal systems which acted as impediments to effective international co-operation.

International Co-operation

The crime prevention and criminal justice mandate conferred on the United Nations in 1950 was based on the then-prevailing attitudes of the "nationality" of crime. Traditionally, states asserted criminal jurisdiction only over crimes committed within their borders—territorial jurisdiction—and, in some cases, over crimes committed outside their borders by or against their nationals. Crime was, in nature as well as in legal theory, a local matter and fugitive offenders could be subjected to the competent jurisdiction as a result of extradition.

Accordingly, the program in its early years devoted most of its resources to what today would be perceived as domestic issues rather than issues of an international or multilateral nature.

At the Fifth United Nations Congress on the Prevention of Crime and the Treatment of Offenders held in 1975 at Geneva, Switzerland, this attitude changed.[12] The Congress, attended by representatives of 101 governments, had as its theme "Crime Prevention and Control: the Challenge of the Last Quarter of the Century." It considered changes in the form and dimensions of criminality at both national and transnational levels, the concept of "crime as business" (organized crime) and, *inter alia*, the economic and social consequences of crime. This Congress, more than any of its predecessors, broadened the agenda of the United Nations criminal justice program, emphasizing the need to deal with prevention and control of criminal activity at both a transnational and national level. It set in motion the process of the development of practically oriented model treaties, subsequently adopted by the Eighth and Ninth Congresses, designed to foster international co-operation in the fight against organized crime. It turned the activities of the programme away from the development of nonbinding norms, standards and guidelines on issues perceived by some as being primarily domestic. These had been its principal focus.

The model treaties were designed to represent the state of the art in their respective areas, to identify areas of difficulty, particularly those due to differences in legal systems, and to suggest possible solutions.

---

[12] Quinquiennial Congresses were held by the International Penal and Penitentiary Commission since the latter half of the nineteenth century. The practice was continued when the work of the IPPC was taken over by the United Nations in 1950.

The United Nations Model Treaties

As noted earlier, the offense-specific conventions, whilst assisting in harmonizing substantive criminal laws, failed to adequately address the problems of international co-operation in the investigation, prosecution and punishment of the offenses with which they dealt. Frequently they incorporated by reference pre-existing—and in many cases nonexistent—bilateral and other relationships. Consideration was given to the possibility of developing a multilateral extradition and mutual assistance convention, but the difficulties were seen as almost insurmountable given the differences in legal systems which needed to be accommodated.[13] Accordingly, the programme embarked on a process designed to modernize existing areas traditionally dealt with at the bilateral, and sometimes at the regional, level, by the provision of model treaties to which countries could have access in negotiating such relationships. The model treaties are designed both to enhance international co-operation and to secure the rehabilitation of offenders. They were also designed to recognize areas of difficulty and to suggest "bridges" between legal systems. The model treaties, in order of their adoption, are discussed below:

Model Agreement on the Transfer of Foreign Prisoners[14]

This model treaty was developed for human rights, sociological and practical reasons. It recognizes the language, culture, customs and religious difficulties faced by prisoners in foreign prisons, and that the goals of re-integration of offenders would be enhanced by giving such prisoners the opportunity to serve their sentences in either their country of nationality or residence. Another relevant, although unstated, consideration is the difficulties faced by prison administrators in dealing with a large number of foreign prisoners within their respective settings.

The model draws on present bilateral treaties and seeks to identify "best practice" methods where there is a deviance.

Thus, transfers can be effected only on the basis of:

- mutual respect for national sovereignty and jurisdiction;
- double criminality, i.e. the offence for which the custodial sentence was imposed must also be known to the law of the state to which the transfer is to be effected;
- the consent of both the sending and receiving state **and** the informed consent of the prisoner who must be advised of any consequences of the transfer, including the possibility of prosecution for other offenses; and
- a guarantee against double jeopardy.

---

[13] *See* Albin Eser, *Common Goals and Different Ways in International Criminal Law: Reflections from a European Perspective*, 31 HARV. INT'L L.J. 117 (1990)(identifying difficulties in reaching agreements between, in particular, civil and common law jurisdictions).

[14] Seventh United Nations Congress on the Prevention of Crime and the Treatment of Offenders, Milan, Aug. 26-Sept. 6, 1985, Report prepared by the Secretariat, U.N. Doc. A/CONF./121/22/Rev.1, 53 (1986), and Compendium of United Nations Standards and Norms in Crime Prevention and Criminal Justice, U.N. Sales No. E.92.IV. at 105 [hereinafter Compendium]. This Model Treaty was developed by a committee of experts meeting at ISISC.

Where the transfer occurs, the authorities of the state to which the prisoner is transferred must either enforce the sentence as passed in the state where the sentence was imposed or, where this is not possible, convert the sanction imposed into one known to its law. However, a sanction of imprisonment may not be converted into a pecuniary penalty. Finally, the state to which the prisoner is transferred must give full faith and credit to the findings of fact in the sentencing state, and the latter state is the only one competent to review the sentence, with time spent in custody in both states to be fully deducted from the final sentence determined.

Model Treaty on Extradition[15]

Whilst extradition is one of the oldest known forms of international co-operation in criminal matters, it is still a process fraught with technical difficulties. The text contains a number of brackets and footnotes relating to areas where jurisdictions may wish, or need as a result of domestic legal requirements, to vary provisions or insert additional provisions. The model treaty was based on existing bilateral treaties, the European Convention on Extradition and on a model bilateral treaty drawn up by Australia, a country which was then engaged in a large-scale bilateral treaty negotiating program and which had amended its domestic extradition legislation so as to overcome some traditional extradition impediments, particularly as between common law and civil law jurisdictions.

The Model Treaty on Extradition has as its basis the agreement by the parties to extradite to each other persons wanted in the requesting state for an "extraditable offense" or for the imposition or enforcement of a sentence already imposed for such offense. An extraditable offense is defined as an offence punishable under the laws of both parties by imprisonment or other deprivation of liberty for an agreed minimum period or a more severe penalty. Where the person is sought for the enforcement of a sentence already imposed, extradition would only be granted if an agreed minimum of the penalty remains to be served. This definition thus embodies the traditional "dual criminality" requirement and obviates the now dated "list of offenses" approach.

The model also contains, with some suggested variations, the traditional mandatory and discretionary grounds of refusal.

It retains the mandatory "political offense" ground of refusal whereby extradition must be refused if the offense for which extradition is requested is regarded by the state in which the fugitive offender is found as an offense of a political nature. A bracketed alternative is provided, given the fact that "political nature" is not defined and that different tests have been applied in different jurisdictions. The alternative is as follows:

> Reference to an offence of a political nature shall not include any offence in respect of which the Parties have assumed an obligation, pursuant to any multilateral convention, to take prosecutorial action where they do not extradite, nor any other offence agreed by the Parties not to be an offence of a political character for the purposes of extradition.[16]

---

15 G.A. Res. 45/116, U.N. GAOR, 45th Sess., Supp No. 49A, and Compendium, *supra* note 14, at 48.

16 *Id.* at Art. 3(a).

Where adopted, this would amount to an agreement not to regard as an offence of a political character:

1. offenses in respect of which the parties have assumed an *aut dedere aut judicare* obligation in one of the offense-specific conventions;
2. the offenses of genocide or apartheid in cases where the parties are signatories to those conventions; and
3. such other offenses as may be agreed upon by the parties on a bilateral or regional basis.

The related ground of refusal, namely that the requested state has substantial grounds for believing that the request for extradition has been made for the purpose of prosecuting or punishing a person on account of his or her race, religion, nationality, ethnic origin, political opinions, sex or status, or that the person's position may be prejudiced on account of those reasons has, quite properly, also been retained. Similarly, extradition must be refused in cases where the fugitive offender has been or would be subjected to torture or cruel, inhuman or degrading treatment or punishment or has not or will not receive the minimum guarantees in criminal proceedings as provided for in the International Covenant on Civil and Political Rights. The traditional *ne bis in idem* and military offense exceptions have also been retained.

What is not provided for as a mandatory exception, other than in a footnote, is the *prima facie* case requirement sought by common law countries in the past. Indeed, until 1990, it was a mandatory ground of refusal in the 1996 Commonwealth Scheme for the Rendition of Fugitive Offenders.

The suggested deletion of this requirements will be referred to later in this chapter.

Turning to the discretionary grounds of refusal, these are fairly traditional, but again with some variations. The first ground is that the fugitive offender is a national of the requested state. This ground is of importance to non-common-law states which frequently have a constitutional prohibition against the surrender of nationals but which can usually try their nationals for offenses committed by them overseas—the active personality jurisdiction. Common law states, which normally exercise only territorial jurisdiction, although exceptions to this are increasing, have tended to surrender their own nationals. In a provision based on the *aut dedere aut judicare* principle contained in offense-specific multilateral conventions, the model treaty imposes an obligation on the requested state to submit the case to its own authorities for prosecution if so requested by the state seeking extradition in cases where extradition is declined solely on grounds of nationality. It is probably the first bilateral type treaty to contain this requirement.

Similarly, extradition may be refused if the offense is also triable in the requested state and the authorities there have either decided not to institute, or to terminate proceedings or if proceedings are pending for that offense.

The death penalty exception is also contained in the discretionary grounds of refusal, although it is recognized that in the case of many countries this "discretion" will always be exercised in one way unless the necessary assurances are given. In short it allows a country which does not impose the death sentence, or does not impose it for the relevant offense, to decline to extradite unless the requesting state gives acceptable assurances that the death penalty will not be imposed or, if imposed, will not be carried out. The provision thus binds the prerogative powers of the executive authorities. In a footnote it is noted that some countries may wish to add a similar provision to the imposition of a life or indeterminate sentence, reflecting in particular the views expressed by a number of Latin American countries, the laws of which preclude the passing of such sentences.

Given the growth in assertions of extraterritorial jurisdiction, the model treaty also permits the refusal of extradition in cases where the relevant offense was committed outside the territory of either the requested or requesting state in cases where the requested state would not have the jurisdiction to try such an offense committed in comparable circumstances outside its territory.

Similarly, if the requested country regards the offense as having been committed either in whole or in part within its territorial jurisdiction, it may decline to extradite but, on request by the other state, must submit the case to its own authorities for consideration of prosecution.

Given the increasing importance of human rights law in relation to extradition, one traditional and one new ground of discretionary refusal are contained. The first applies to case where the fugitive would, in the requesting state, be tried or sentenced by an extra-ordinary or ad hoc tribunal or has been sentenced by such a tribunal. This is a traditional ground which precludes a trial in a court other than a court responsible for enforcing the ordinary criminal law of the requesting state. The final, and exceptional ground, permits a state to decline to surrender in cases where extradition would be incompatible with humanitarian considerations in view of the age, health or other personal circumstances of the person. Whilst this appears to be a broad exception, the requested state must take into account the nature of the offense and the interests of the requesting state.

The model treaty then provides for normal procedural requirements relating to channels of communication, the form and content of requests, additional information, provisional arrest, surrender and transit. Undoubtedly, some of these provisions will need to be revisited in the light of improved methods of communication and transport.

In a departure from traditional treaties, the model permits, subject to the law of the requested state and the consent of the fugitive, a simplified form of extradition. This would permit surrender after the receipt of a request for provisional arrest but before the formal request for surrender. The fugitive thus agrees, where permitted by law, to forego the formal extradition hearing.[17]

Finally, the model expressly preserves the "rule of speciality," precluding trial in the requesting state, or surrender to a third state, in respect of an offense committed before surrender other than an offense for which extradition was granted or in respect of which the requested state consents. A footnote reflects the view of some states which would, in the latter case, also require the consent of the accused person.

Model Treaty on Mutual Assistance in Criminal Matters[18]

Mutual assistance, sometimes referred to as mutual legal assistance or mutual judicial assistance, is a rapidly evolving area of international co-operation which excludes extradition, enforcement of penal sanctions imposed in other states, transfer of proceedings or transfer of prisoners to serve sentences imposed elsewhere. Thus, mutual assistance is

---

17 Art. 6.

18 G.A. Res. 45/117, U.N. GAOR, 45th Sess., Supp. No. 49A, at 215; Compendium, *supra* note 14, at 61.

only one aspect, albeit an important one, in the growing arsenal of international co-operation against crime.

In short, mutual assistance is designed to assist countries in enforcing their own criminal laws in cases where the necessary evidence or witnesses are located outside their own jurisdiction. Its underlying philosophy is that, subject to the limitations laid down, law enforcement and curial bodies may exercise the same powers—including compulsory powers—on behalf of other states as they could exercise in relation to offenses triable within their own jurisdictions. Again, given the procedural and substantive differences in legal systems and the wider range of permitted activities, the model treaty contains a number of "bridges" to ensure that material obtained in one jurisdiction is admissible in proceeding in the requesting state.

The first of these bridges is the name itself. The model treaty is on mutual assistance, not mutual legal or mutual judicial assistance, or MLAT, the normal American or Canadian "jargon." The reason is that "legal" in some languages is translated as "judicial," thereby excluding assistance in the non-judicially supervised investigative process of the common law world. If assistance is limited to judicial assistance, then the request is usually made by a "letter rogatory,"[19] a process not normally available in common law jurisdictions until investigations are concluded and proceedings are on foot. This is a "chicken and egg" situation, because the evidence being sought may be that which permits proceedings to be brought.

The model treaty provides that the assistance to be afforded may include:

> (a) Taking of evidence or statements from persons;
> (b) Assisting in making available of detained persons or others to give evidence or assist in investigations;
> (c) Effecting service of judicial documents;
> (d) Executing searches and seizures;
> (e) Examining objects and sites;
> (f) Providing information and evidentiary items; and
> (g) Providing originals or certified copies of relevant documents and records, including bank, financial, corporate or business records."[20]

The references to "statements" in subparagraph (a), "assist in investigations" in subparagraph (b), and "information" in subparagraph (f) were also included to reflect the non-judicial nature of the common law investigating process. For example, material provided by a witness in a civil law judicially supervised investigation would amount to evidence in that it becomes part of the judicial file. In the common law investigative phase such material would only amount to information until such time as the material is presented to the court and admitted into evidence by it after the institution of proceedings.

The model treaty sets out a number of discretionary grounds for refusal which, in the main, are similar to those under the model extradition treaty. One additional ground is where the requested state is of the opinion that compliance with the request would prejudice its sovereignty, security, public order (*ordre public*) or other essential interests. This provision reflected, *inter alia*, the concern of some countries which, in response to what they had

---

[19] *See, e.g.*, the European Convention on Mutual Assistance in Criminal Matters, Europ. T. S. No. 30.

[20] Art. VI (2).

perceived as unwarranted claims to extraterritorial jurisdiction particularly in corporate matters, had enacted laws precluding the provision of certain evidentiary material to other countries without the prior consent of the Attorney-General, Minister of Justice or other designated Minister or official.

Another novel provision is a positive statement that co-operation may not be refused solely on grounds of bank secrecy or secrecy relating to other financial institutions.

The fact that the principles in relation to mutual assistance are not yet as well-settled as those in relation to extradition can be seen from the footnote to the refusal article. That footnote raises a plethora of other issues which countries may wish to raise as grounds for refusal including, *inter alia*, fiscal offenses, capital punishment, forms of emerging possible methods of assistance including telephone communication and DNA tests and dual criminality. Some of these issues will need to be revisited once mutual assistance gains greater acceptance as a form of international co-operation.

Some regard it as unfortunate that most of the "extradition"-type exceptions are finding their way into mutual assistance arrangements. In extradition the fugitive is in the hands of the requested state and precedents from time immemorial have recognized the rights of that state to place some limitations on the activities of the requesting state *vis à vis* the accused. In the case of mutual assistance the requested state is assisting the requesting state to enforce its own criminal laws usually against a person within that latter state's jurisdiction. Arguably, some of the envisaged or suggested grounds for refusal will be seen as an unwarranted interference in the internal affairs of the requesting state. Others argue that, given the increasing importance of human rights issues, such exceptions are merely balancing human rights and law enforcement interests.

The model treaty, in Article 5, sets out the requirements as to the contents of any request for assistance and, again in an endeavor to maximize the utility of the material provided, goes on in Article 6 to provide, *inter alia*, that a request should be carried out in the manner specified by the request unless this is inconsistent with the law and practice of the requested state.

Various other articles deal in greater detail with specific heads of assistance or substantive requirements relating thereto, including issues such as the rights or obligations to decline to give evidence, the availability of witnesses and the safe conduct to be afforded them as well as search and seizure. Suffice it to say that the number of footnotes, as well as the frequent use of the qualifying "in so far as its law permits" in substantive articles, again highlight the developing nature of this type of assistance.

One matter which would appear to be a significant omission from the model treaty is dealt with in an "Optional Protocol." This relates to the tracing, freezing of dealings in, and ultimate confiscation or seizure of proceeds of crime. The provisions are in broad and general terms indicating the embryonic nature of this form of assistance at the time of development of the model treaty.

Model Treaty on the Transfer of Proceedings in Criminal Matters[21]

This model treaty serves both human rights and law enforcement objectives.

---

[21] G.A. Res. 45/118, U.N. GAOR, 45th Sess., Supp. 49A, at 219, Compendium, *supra* note 14, at 76. This Model Treaty was developed by a Committee of Experts Meeting at ISISC.

It permits a party to the treaty, if requested by another party, to take proceedings in respect of an offense over which the second party would have jurisdiction. The model imposes an obligation on parties to enact legislation to give jurisdiction to their relevant administrative and curial bodies to exercise such jurisdiction if requested. This concept of "vicarious jurisdiction" is better known to the civil law system—which already has in many cases jurisdiction to try a national for offenses committed outside the jurisdiction—but is alien to most common law "territorial" jurisdictions.

The model goes on to provide substantive and procedural requirements, and, like the other model treaties, provides a number of grounds for refusal of a request, albeit more limited than those contained in both the model treaties on extradition and mutual assistance in criminal matters. A principal ground of refusal is that the suspect is neither a national or ordinary resident of the requested state, again re-enforcing the human rights aspects of the model treaty.

The model also precludes double jeopardy by providing that where proceedings against the person are pending in the requested state, the requesting state shall provisionally discontinue its own proceedings. Once the requested state notifies the requesting state that the case has been finally disposed of, the latter state is obliged to refrain from any further prosecution action.[22]

Model Treaty on the Transfer of Supervision of Offenders Conditionally Sentenced or Conditionally Released[23]

This model treaty is included merely for the sake of completeness. It is, in effect, an extension on the model agreement on the transfer of foreign prisoners, dealing with noncustodial or deferred custodial sentences, whereas the former dealt solely with custodial sanctions.

Other U.N. Bodies

At the same time that the United Nations crime prevention and criminal justice programme was developing the model bilateral treaties referred to above, a multilateral convention, albeit still an "offense-specific" one, was being developed under the auspices of the United Nations Commission on Narcotic Drugs. It was to become a milestone in the development of international co-operation efforts at the global level.

On December 20, 1988, a plenipotentiaries conference adopted the United Nations Convention against Illicit Traffic in Narcotic Drugs and Psychotropic Substances.[24] That convention came into force on November 11, 1990, namely on the ninetieth day after the date of deposit with the U.N. Secretary-General of the twentieth instrument of ratification, approval or acceptance by states.

This Convention, albeit "offense"-or "conduct"-specific, in that it is directed at narcotic and narcotic-related activity, breaks new ground in a number of respects.

First, it creates an obligation on the part of all signatories to criminalize conduct constituting what may be loosely referred to as "money laundering" in relation to narcotics

---

22 Arts. 10, 11 and 13.

23 G.A. Res. 45/119, U.N. GAOR, 45th Sess., Supp. 49A, at 221; Compendium, *supra* note 14, at 126.

24 U.N. Doc. E/CONF. 82/15.

activity, thereby facilitating international co-operation which, due to the application of the dual criminality principle, is presently hampered by the fact that many countries do not criminalize such conduct.[25]

Secondly, rather than presupposing the existence of workable mutual assistance and extradition arrangements, the Convention makes specific provisions relating to them. Article 6, dealing with extradition, imposes obligations on countries, *inter alia*, to conclude bilateral and multilateral agreements to carry out or to enhance the effectiveness of extradition[26] and, in relation to the conduct proscribed by the Convention, to expedite extradition procedures and to simplify the attendant evidentiary requirements.[27] Article 7, whilst preserving the operation of other mutual assistance in criminal matters treaties—both existing and future—provides in paragraphs 8-19 a virtual mini-treaty binding on such signatory states as are not bound in a given situation by any other mutual legal assistance treaty. The Article also exhorts countries to conclude multilateral or bilateral agreements or arrangements that would serve the purposes of, give practical effect to, or enhance the operation of the Convention.[28]

Thirdly, Article 5 deals comprehensively with the identifying, tracing, freezing and confiscating of proceeds, or instrumentalities, of conduct proscribed by the Convention and obliges countries to adopt such measures as are necessary to enable them to fulfill those obligations, both nationally and on behalf of other signatory states. It also adopts the mutual assistance provisions contained in Article 7 and applies them *mutatis mutandis* to requests for action in relation to proceeds. It also obliges countries to seek to conclude bilateral and multilateral treaties, agreements or arrangements to enhance the effectiveness of international co-operation in relation to the tracing, freezing and confiscating of proceeds of crime, including "indirect" or converted proceeds as well as profits or income earned on such proceeds.[29]

The Convention also expressly prohibits a refusal of assistance based on bank secrecy.[30]

This is the first multilateral United Nations Convention which imposes international co-operative mechanisms on its signatories, whilst at the same time exhorting those signatory states to conclude bilateral or other arrangements that would enhance the operation of the obligations contained in the drug convention.

Given the treaty negotiation obligations contained in the 1988 Drug Convention, it was both timely and appropriate that the Eighth United Nations Congress on the Prevention of Crime and the Treatment of Offenders adopted by consensus the model treaties on Extradition and Mutual Assistance in Criminal Matters. It is also unfortunate that the proceeds provisions were only adopted as an Optional Protocol to the latter model treaty.

Conclusions

It is evident that modalities and objectives of international co-operation have continually evolved. That process is ongoing and new modalities will continue to develop to meet emergent criminality and other factors. Developments are taking place, for example, in areas

25 *See* sub-paras. (b)(i) and (ii) and (c)(i) of Art. 3.
26 Art. 6 ¶ 11.
27 Art. 6 ¶ 7.
28 Art. 7 ¶ 20.
29 Art. 5 ¶¶ 4(9) and 6.
30 Art. 7 ¶ 5 and Art. 5 ¶ 3.

of corporate and securities regulation and customs in addition to the traditional law enforcement areas. Exchanges of police intelligence, and of cash transaction reporting information are two areas currently being mooted.

Notwithstanding these developments, significant impediments still exist. There still cannot be said to exist a universally effective mutual assistance scheme in relation to criminal conduct generally, nor is one likely to develop in the near future.

Impediments, some of which have already been adverted to, include:

1. Differences in legal systems, stages of economic development, cultural and social values;

2. Differences in approaches, particularly by emphasizing methodology as opposed to the objective sought to be achieved—*e.g.*, the "letter rogatory" basis of the European Convention on Mutual Assistance in Criminal Matters or the *prima facie* case requirement under the laws of a number of common law jurisdictions;

3. Earlier multilateral conventions are both conduct-specific and erroneously assumed the existence of workable modalities and networks;

4. Even the recent 1988 convention containing the potentially most effective mechanisms—including obligations to negotiate bilateral treaties—is conduct-specific in that it is limited to drug-related activities.

A potent reason for failure of a universally effective scheme to develop to date has as its genesis the differences in both political and legal systems. Many countries have not been prepared to enter into a broad-based universal mutual assistance scheme of general application. They would, with one exception, wish to retain some degree of control over the other jurisdictions *vis-à-vis* which they would be prepared, even on a reciprocal basis, to enter into such obligations. The exception has proven to be in relation to such conduct regarded as sufficiently reprehensible by the bulk of the international community. In such cases nations have proved themselves willing, at least in principle, to assume such obligations in relation to all other nations prepared to assume reciprocal obligations. Hence the offense or conduct-specific conventions. Even here, nations have not been prepared to go as far as providing that offenses covered by those Conventions are not to be regarded —with two exceptions—as offenses of a political nature for the purpose of extradition.

Given this apparent reluctance of nations, the only manner in which a truly effective scheme of international co-operation is likely to develop in the foreseeable future is by means of an extensive array of either bilateral or regional arrangements (including commonality of systems-based arrangements such as the European and Commonwealth arrangements). The adoption by the Eighth United Nations Congress on the Prevention of Crime and the Treatment of Offenders of, in particular, the model bilateral treaties on Extradition and Mutual Assistance in Criminal Matters is therefore of great significance.

By reference to those model treaties, and the footnotes contained therein, it is possible to see how some of the impediments to effective co-operation stemming from differences in legal systems have been, or can be, addressed. As the relevant refusal grounds, with one exception, are common to the two model treaties, it is convenient to deal with them together.

The exception is the "*prima facie* case" requirement in extradition, which is probably the greatest impediment to the successful outcome of extradition requests made by non-common law countries of common law countries. A number of common law countries,

Australia included, either have addressed or are addressing, this problem, although the solutions are not always uniform.

The *prima facie* case requirement contains two concepts, namely sufficiency and admissibility of evidence under the law of the requested state. Not only does the requesting country have to produce a sufficient case to warrant committal for trial of the person had the conduct for which extradition is sought occurred in the requested (common law) state, it is also required to establish that case by evidence admissible in the requested state. Accordingly, foreign countries, particularly, but not only, civil law countries could only succeed in securing extradition from a common law country by producing a case acceptable to a legal system, and subject to evidentiary laws, alien to them. This often resulted in affluent and well-advised fugitives escaping justice on purely technical, and unmeritorious, grounds. A 1985 British Government Green Paper put the problem succinctly:

> Something like a third of applications made to the United Kingdom . . . fail, often because of the inability of the requesting state to satisfy the prima facie case requirement. Furthermore there are occasions on which some states are deterred from making a request at all because they believe it will be too difficult to meet the requirement.[31]

It is also relevant to note that in 1978 Spain unilaterally abrogated its extradition treaty with the United Kingdom on the basis that it had never succeeded in securing the surrender of a fugitive from that country, due to the technicalities inherent in the *prima facie* case requirement.

Australia removed the *prima facie* case requirement from its legislation dealing with extradition to and from non-common law countries in 1985,[32] requiring in lieu, where a person is sought for prosecution, a statement in writing setting out a description of each offense for which extradition is requested, including a statement of the acts or omissions constituting those offenses. Australia's extradition laws are now more analogous to those of civil law countries and, as a result, in the past ten years Australia has negotiated or is in the process of negotiating, in excess of 50 extradition treaties or arrangements—all bar one with non-common law countries. By contrast, between 1966 and 1985 it had negotiated only five such treaties or arrangements with non-common law countries.

Australia unsuccessfully sought the removal of the *prima facie* case requirement from the Commonwealth Scheme for the Rendition of Fugitive Offenders at the Commonwealth Law Ministers Meeting held in Harare, Zimbabwe, in 1986. However, at the same meeting held in Auckland, New Zealand in 1990, the Scheme was amended permitting Commonwealth countries to opt to abrogate it. A number of countries have now done so.

The United Kingdom has recently enacted laws which would allow it to abolish the *prima facie* case requirement, but only in relation to non-Commonwealth countries.[33] A motivating factor in passing this law was said to be the wish of the Government of the United Kingdom to accede to the European Extradition Convention. Canada, due to requirements in its Charter of Rights, is believed to be considering the retention of the *prima*

---

31 Cmnd. 9241, H.M.S.O., London at 4 (1985).

32 Sub-sec. 17(6) Extradition (Foreign States) Act, now sub-secs. 19(2) and (3) of the Extradition Act 1988.

33 Extradition Act 1989 (UK), sub-secs. 9(4) and (8).

facie case but abolishing the hearsay rule and other technical evidentiary rules, a major component of the second concept referred to above. This would achieve the same objective, albeit by a different means.

Before leaving the *prima facie* case requirement, it should be noted that the second part of it, namely the requirement that evidence be admissible under the laws of the requested state, would also constitute a serious impediment in relation to the *aut dedere aut judicare* principle in a number of the offense-specific conventions. Where a fugitive is not surrendered by a common law country to a non-common law one and the common law country exercises its obligation to try in lieu of surrender, then the non-common law country must present its evidence in accordance with common law requirements. This would, in many cases, result in acquittal so that, at least in those cases, the principle of *aut dedere aut judicare* could not be said to be an effective means of international co-operation.

Turning now to other principal aspects of the two model treaties adopted by the Eighth Congress, and the grounds for refusal contained therein, the following observations and suggestions might be born in mind during the negotiating process to ensure that the treaties arrived at serve both the interests of the bilateral parties and the interests of the international community at large.

The first common ground for refusal of both extradition and mutual assistance relates to what is generally adverted to as the "political offense" exception. This exception dates back to the evolution of modern concepts of extradition—in the nineteenth[34] century and, as we have seen before, even in multilateral U.N. Conventions on only two occasions have offenses been expressly excluded from the political offense exception, (the crimes of genocide and apartheid).

The difficulty raised by the political offense exception is that in no convention, nor, as far as the author is aware, in any legislation is the concept of political offense positively defined. Rather, it is left for the various judicial and administrative authorities to decide whether particular conduct in respect of which a request for assistance is made constitutes a political offense. This has led to differing criteria being applied throughout the world.

For example, in Australia and the United Kingdom the idea behind the concept of the political offense has been narrowly defined by the judiciary. In a leading case it was said:

> In my opinion the idea that lies behind the phrase 'offence of a political character' is that the fugitive is at odds with the State that applies for his extradition on some issue connected with the political control or government of the country. The analogy of "political" in this context is with "political" in such phrases as "political refugee" "political asylum" or "political prisoner." It does indicate, I think that the requesting state is after him for reasons other than the enforcement of the criminal law in its ordinary, what I might call its common or international aspect.[35]

So seen, British and Australian courts have reduced the political offense exception to its basic *raison d'etre*, namely the protection of the individual against a retaliatory trial by political adversaries.

---

[34] LASSA OPPENHEIM, 1 INTERNATIONAL LAW 512 (3d ed. 1920).

[35] Per Viscount Radcliffe in Regina v. Governor of Brixton Prison, *ex parte* Schtraks, 1964 AC 556 at 591-92 (Austl.), adopted by the High Court of Australia in R v. Wilson *ex parte* Witness T, 135 C.L.R 179 (1976) (Australia).

Swiss and Austrian courts, on the other hand, have developed a "relation of means and purpose" test, in which the court assesses whether the means employed by the fugitive are excessive in relation to the political end sought.[36] Applying this concept, it has been held in Switzerland that "where murder is concerned, such a relationship (proportion of means and purpose) exists only if homicide is the sole means of safeguarding more important interests and attaining the political aim."[37] United States courts have held, without reference to a proportion of means and purpose test, that murders committed in Northern Ireland by members of the Provisional Irish Republican Army are political offenses and that therefore the offenders were not subject to extradition.[38] An Irish court has held that a bank robbery, the proceeds of which were to fund the Irish Republican Army, constituted a political offense,[39] although that decision was subsequently overturned.

The impossibility of defining the phrase "offense of a political character" has been recognized for a long time and, indeed, it has at times been regarded as an advantage that there is no definition.[40] The model treaty on extradition, albeit only in a footnote, attempts to deal with this problem by providing a negative definition as follows:

> Reference to an offence of a political nature shall not include any offence in respect of which the Parties have assumed an obligation, pursuant to any multilateral convention, to take prosecutorial action where they do not extradite, nor any other offence agreed by the Parties not to be an offence of a political character for the purpose of extradition.

This half-way solution would exclude offenses constituted by conduct proscribed in the offense or conduct-specific conventions containing an *aut dedere aut judicare* obligation, plus give some scope to countries to introduce, for example, a proportion of means and purpose concept. It is not dissimilar to the solution in the European Convention on the Suppression of Terrorism[41] and in the laws of some countries, including Australia.[42]

The related exception, namely the "persecution" or "discrimination" exception earlier adverted to, is contained in both model treaties and justifiably so.

Another well-entrenched exception to extradition is the "double criminality" rule, whereby a fugitive in the requested state will not be surrendered in respect of conduct which, although criminal in the requesting state, is not considered criminal in the former state. It is probably too late to change this rule, although it does apply regardless of the different states of development of countries. For example, a developing country which for reasons of its own economic well-being imposes currency export laws subject to criminal sanctions might regard it as amiss if a developed country in which the fugitive is found, and which does not have such laws, declines either to extradite or to render other assistance due to a lack of dual criminality (or because of a fiscal offense exception which is contained in some extradition

---

36 Re Kavic, 19 I.L.R. 371 (Swiss Federal Tribunal 1952); *Hungarian Deserter* case, 28 I.L.R. 343 (Austrian Supreme Court 1959).

37 Ktir v. Ministere Public Federal, 34 I.L.R. 143 (Swiss Federal Tribunal 1961).

38 *See* Note, *Political Legitimacy in the Law of Political Asylum*, 99 HARV. L. REV. 450, 452 (1985); and John F. Murphy, *Legal Controls and the Deterrence of Terrorism: Performance and Prospects*, 13 RUTGERS L. J. 465, 479 (1982).

39 McGuire v. Keane, 1986 I.L.R.M. 235.

40 OPPENHEIM, *supra* note 34, at 515; *see* the *Schtraks* case, *supra* note 35, at 589.

41 Art. 1.

42 Extradition Act 1988, § 5.

and mutual assistance treaties).[43] On the other hand, social, cultural, and religious differences can lead to difficulties in abrogating the dual criminality rule. Laws in some countries criminalize "immoral" conduct, whereas other countries do not regard the criminal law as the appropriate mechanism for dealing with such conduct. Some authors have suggested that the dual criminality ground should be abolished and replaced with a ground of refusal based on public policy,[44] although some would regard such a ground to be more open-ended than dual criminality.

Other impediments to effective mutual assistance arise from the inherent differences in legal systems. As mentioned earlier, the "letter rogatory" basis of mutual assistance in the European Convention on Mutual Assistance precludes most common law countries from acceding to that Convention—it precludes assistance for investigations which, unlike in civil law countries, are conducted independently of the judiciary. It was a principal reason for the decision by the Australian government not to seek accession to it but to seek the conclusion of bilateral treaties. It is interesting to note that letters rogatory do not feature in the subsequent European Convention on Laundering, Search, Seizure and Confiscation of the Proceeds from Crime, in the elaboration of which common law jurisdictions participated.

Even basic differences can, given goodwill, be overcome. For example, Australia has negotiated some 20 mutual assistance treaties with non-common law countries in the past four years, and a number of devices have been used to overcome them. In some cases, the letter rogatory concept has been eliminated. In cases where this was not possible, the Australian Attorney-General or his or her delegate, the only persons authorized to make formal mutual assistance requests on behalf of Australia under Australian law, are in effect recognized as judicial authorities by the other negotiating party even though under Australian law they clearly are not such authorities.[45] By these stratagems a broad similarity of both obligations and benefits are achieved.

An obverse example could also be given. Australian law has for many years allowed evidence to be taken on behalf of a foreign country where "proceedings" are on foot. "Proceedings" in this sense meant curial or judicial proceedings in the common law sense, namely post-investigation and decision to prosecute. Recognizing the limited utility of this to non-common law countries, "proceedings" are now defined so as to include the civil law judicially supervised investigative process[46] which is normally not known to Australian law.

It is noteworthy that the U.N. Congress adopted model treaty on Mutual Assistance in Criminal Matters has avoided these pitfalls by referring to both investigations or court proceedings in the principal articles defining the obligations—see for example, Article 1 (Scope of application) and Article 5 (contents of request)—and by providing in Article 3 for designating of appropriate authorities.

Some final points should be made under this heading.

First, negotiators frequently reach an impasse as a result of attitudinal or systemic differences, focusing not on the objectives to be achieved but rather on the methods for achieving them. Both the model treaties in their terms largely adopt the former attitude, leaving methodology to the respective laws of the negotiating parties. A prime example is afforded by the Optional Protocol to the Model Treaty on Mutual Assistance in Criminal

---

43 *See, e.g.*, ¶ 2(a) of the European MLAT Convention.

44 *See, e.g.*, Albin Eser, *supra note* 13, at 123.

45 *See, e.g.*, Art. 3 of the Australia/Spain Mutual Assistance Treaty.

46 Mutual Assistance in Criminal Matters Act 1987, § 3.

Matters concerning the Proceeds Crime, which has as its clear objective the dispossession of criminals of their ill-gotten gains but leaves the means of achieving this to individual laws. For example, some countries are prepared to give full faith and credit to orders of foreign courts whilst others would wish to institute confiscation proceedings in their own courts based on material made available by the requesting state. As earlier noted, a similar approach was adopted in the recently opened-for-signature European Convention on the same subject matter,[47] and, for that matter, in the 1988 Drug Convention.[48]

Secondly, and related to the above, is the principle of reciprocity. It may not be necessary that every obligation owed by one state to another have a precise mirror counterpart. It could be possible, as in the case of the proceeds of crime articles referred to above, to negotiate treaties with obligations which do not precisely mirror each other. In this way states would gain the flexibility needed to include extradition and mutual assistance treaties in spite of attitudinal and systemic differences based on differences in procedure and principle, yet fully respecting their respective national laws.

Finally, given the dual criminality requirement in relation to various forms of mutual assistance, an effective universal scheme can evolve only if all countries ensure that—at least in relation to conduct proscribed by the bulk of international community—their laws criminalize such conduct. Money laundering provides an excellent example. Well-advised criminals will soon identify countries which do not criminalize such conduct and hence cannot give mutual assistance in respect of it. Whilst such countries might enjoy a short-term benefit in attracting off-shore funds, they may well find that the long-term price is too high to pay. There are recent examples of cases where criminal organizations have become so strong that they can threaten or destabilize governments. Another important example is dealt with by the common law concept of "conspiracy." Conspiracy was an early attempt to deal with the phenomenon of persons combining for purposes that are illegal, a main characteristic of organized crime. Many countries do not criminalize the agreement to commit crime, notwithstanding the requirement of Article 36 (2)(a)(ii) of the Single Convention on Narcotic Drugs 1961 to penalize, *inter alia*, conspiracy to commit any of the Convention offences. Accordingly, extradition and mutual assistance may, on the basis of dual criminality, not be available on other than the antiquated individual-responsibility-for-individual-acts basis. This would leave untouched organizers and financiers whose conduct is as, if not more, reprehensible. In some cases, where certain associative conduct is criminalized but not in terms of conspiracy, a clause could be drafted referring to the conduct as known to the laws of both the negotiating parties thereby extending the scope of the treaty.

---

[47] Art. 13.

[48] Art. 5 ¶ 4.